# THE COMPLETE
# ENCYCLOPAEDIA
## OF
# ASTON VILLA

## FOOTBALL CLUB

OFFICIALLY ENDORSED BY

ASTON VILLA
PREPARED

*Compiled by Tony Matthews*

A
**britespot**
PUBLICATION

# ACKNOWLEDGEMENTS

So many people have contributed in some small way to making this Encyclopaedia what it is - a terrific publication. But I must award a special 'thank you' to the following who have certainly assisted far more than they perhaps realise, namely David Goodyear, John Russell, my good friend Reg Thacker (the Aston Villa archivist), Dave and Pam Bridgewater, Paul Yeomans, supporter Paul Delaney and fellow statistician Jim Creasey (Surrey).

Also, I say thank you to John Smith, Ruby Elias, John Tibble, Michael Jeans, Robert Dore (from Stratford-upon-Avon) and BS Dhingsa (from Moseley), and also to Norman Edwards, cartoonist extraordinaire, for allowing me to reproduce some of his superb drawings of the older Villa players which he sketched whilst working for the Birmingham Gazette many years ago.

I also acknowledge the assistance afforded to me by Abdul Rashid, Commercial Manager of Aston Villa Football Club who kindly gave me access to the vast picture library at Villa Park and, indeed, for agreeing to endorse the book itself and publicise it through the various channels within the club.

Thank you, too - and 'sorry' for the inconvenience caused - to my wife Margaret. For hours on end she's been left alone as I've sat at the computer, tip-tapping away on the keyboard and ploughing through scores of reference books, matchday programmes and soccer magazines, checking and re-checking thousands of statistics and facts as well as travelling to and from the Midlands from sunny Devon.

Last but by no means least I must give a sincere thank you to everyone who has worked on the book at Britespot Publishing, especially to Roger Marshall, Paul Burns, Darren Cartwright and Chris Sweet.

• Most of the pictures used in this book have come direct from the Aston Villa archives department. Some are from old scrapbooks, photograph albums and programmes owned by supporters and collectors of footballing memorabilia. However we have been unable to establish clear copyright on a few others and therefore the publishers would be pleased to hear from anyone whose copyright has been unintentionally infringed so that we may include the appropriate acknowledgement in any subsequent edition.

Author Tony Matthews with Aston Villa's 1957 F.A. Cup winning goalkeeper Nigel Sims

First published in Great Britain by Britespot Publishing Solutions Limited,
Chester Road, Cradley Heath, West Midlands B64 6AB.

November 2001

© Copyright: Tony Matthews 2001

Dedicated to all Aston Villa supporters wherever you are!

ISBN 0 9539 2883 7

Cover Design and Artwork © Britespot Publishing Solutions Limited.
Printed and bound in Great Britain by Cradley Print Limited, Chester Road, Cradley Heath, West Midlands B64 6AB.

# INTRODUCTION

I have attempted to make this Encyclopaedia of Aston Villa Football Club as comprehensive as possible, utilising statistical information which I have obtained from various sources over the past 15 years.

I first started compiling this book, in a manner of speaking, at the same time I began putting together 'The Complete Record of Aston Villa Football Club' with David Goodyear in 1986. Following that publication, which was released in 1988, I have continued to add to my collection of Villa facts and figures, producing an up-dated 'Complete Record' in 1992 and compiling an Aston Villa 'Who's Who' 1874-1989.

As a result I have finally brought out this bumper 275,000-word encyclopaedia covering, in detail, the history of one of the biggest clubs in world football.

- There is an-updated and complete 'Who's Who'... a write-up on every player who has represented the club down the years.
- Villa's complete playing record at senior level is covered in depth with details of their Premiership/Football League, FA Cup and League Cup records given against each club they have opposed. Villa's European record is also featured fully.
- There is an international section listing the honours won by Villa players past and present, along with details of the club's top appearance-makers and champion goalscorers, attendance figures (home and away) and sendings-off.
- There are biographies of all Villa's managers, some chairmen and secretaries.
- There is a mini-history of Villa Park, the club's headquarters since April 1897.
- We have a section on substitutes, all the big-money and record-breaking transfers, players' nicknames and much, much more....
  You can see that I have tried to cover everything there is to cover on Aston Villa.

Over the past year or so, I have chatted with soccer statisticians and archivists, supporters and ex-players about Aston Villa. I have gathered in sheet after sheet of information regarding the team and the club itself.
As a result literally hundreds of facts and figures (some interesting, some not so interesting) have been driven into the computer, along with scores of fond memories, many points of view, some sobering thoughts and a great deal of general news appertaining to Aston Villa.

Whether supplied verbally, by letter, by fax or E-mail, it has all been fed into the system and as a result I feel I have put together a bumper book, perhaps one of the best ever produced (statistically) on a major football club, certainly in the U.K.

As you can see, I have tried to cram as much into the book as I possibly could.. I just hope I haven't missed too much, but if I have, I would dearly love to hear from you, so that my records can be updated and/or amended in readiness for the next 'big book' on Aston Villa which hopefully will be an up-dated version of The Complete Record.

With so many facts and figures, statistics, listings and features condensed in this publication, I feel sure there will be a discrepancy, a small error, a spelling mistake, even a missing player or a word somewhere down the line. I am only human, like every one else, and even the great writers of the past made the odd mistake here and there, or missed out something which should have been included, got a year or a date wrong. Please accept my apologies if something is amiss. I have, with the assistance of several willing helpers, tried to ensure that everything in this book is factual, up-to-date and precise in every detail.

Aston Villa is a big, big club...but the team has not yet won the Premiership. That will surely come later.
The diehard supporters last cheered on a League Championship winning side 20 years ago and quickly followed up by celebrating victory in the European Cup Final in Rotterdam and then in the 1990s there were those two League Cup triumphs at Wembley.

Villa Park is now one of the country's finest all-seater stadiums and when Villa are winning, the support they can generate is tremendous with an average turnout of 35,000 plus guaranteed at every home game.

Slowly but surely the ground capacity is being increased and who knows, one day Villa Park may once again be able to accommodate 50,000 or more spectators - most of them cheering on their favourites in claret and blue.

There is plenty in this book to keep you occupied during the winter months and certainly enough information contained within the pages to enable you to get your friends and colleagues talking continuously about Aston Villa down the pubs and clubs, in the stands, on the streets, anywhere in fact, where football - and Villa - is the major subject!

Best wishes
Tony Matthews

## ABANDONED MATCHES

Aston Villa, holders of the FA Cup, were disqualified from the competition in January 1888 after several disruptions had caused an 85th minute abandonment of their 5th round tie against Preston North End, who were leading 3-1 at the time. In fact, owing to the unruly behaviour of several hundred spectators in a record crowd of almost 27,000 at Villa's Wellington Road ground in Perry Barr, both teams wanted to class the game as a friendly and play the cup-tie at a later date. But the FA would have none of it. They insisted that the score should stand, eliminated Villa and severely censured the club for failing to maintain order and control the spectators.

On 5 December 1892, a friendly match against West Bromwich Albion was abandoned in the 35th minute through bad weather with the scores level at 1-1.

Villa were leading Burnley 2-1 in a home League game on 12 December 1896 when the referee abandoned proceedings at half-time. The re-arranged game saw Burnley win 3-0!

Villa were leading Blues 4-0 in another friendly match at Wellington Road in January 1898 when the weather again caused the referee to call off the contest in the second-half. Poor weather conditions caused the abandonment of Villa's League game at Bolton on 2 January 1899. At the time the Wanderers were 1-0 ahead. The re-arranged fixture ended goalless.

On 6 September 1901, Woolwich Arsenal were leading Villa 3-1 at home when bad light caused the League game to be abandoned in the 80th minute. The Gunners won the 'replay' 1-0.

Villa's home First Division game with Notts County on 30 March 1903 was abandoned at half-time through heavy rain. Villa were 1-0 ahead - and they won the April 'replay' 2-1.

In February 1904, Villa were leading Tottenham Hotspur 1-0 in a Second Round FA Cup-tie at White Hart Lane when hundreds of 'home' supporters behind one of the goals spilled onto the pitch. The game was abandoned with the FA ordering the replay to take place at Villa Park, but on this occasion Spurs won 1-0! The Lord Mayor of Birmingham Charity Cup Final between Blues and Aston Villa in 1905 was abandoned early in the second-half because of the atrocious weather conditions. Villa were 1-0 ahead at the time but the game was declared a draw and each side held the trophy for six months.

A Football Festival game between Aston Villa and Blues at Villa Park in March 1909 was abandoned due to weather after 65 minutes play. Blues were 2-1 up at the time.

Six months later (6 September 1909) Villa's away game with Woolwich Arsenal was called off through bad light with the Gunners 3-1 ahead. Arsenal won the 'replay' 1-0.

Another Woolwich Arsenal-Villa League game on 21 January 1911 was abandoned in the 81st minute through fading light with the Londoners 2-1 in front at the time. The re-arranged game ended in a 1-1 draw.

Snow caused the half-time abandonment of the Villa-Derby County 1st round FA Cup-tie at Villa Park in January 1913. The scores were level at 1-1. The game, 'replayed' the following Wednesday afternoon, ended in a 3-1 win for Villa.

On 16 January 1926 with Villa 1-0 ahead, thick fog caused the abandonment of the home League match with Leeds United in the 82nd minute. The 'replay' three weeks later resulted in a 3-1 win for Villa.

There have been two West Bromwich Albion v Aston Villa League encounters at The Hawthorns abandoned due to the weather. Heavy snow called a halt to proceedings in the 26th minute of the match on 22 February 1936 with Albion 1-0 ahead whilst torrential rain stopped play in the 51st minute of the game on 14 December 1965 which at the time was goalless. Villa went back to The Hawthorns to win the 'replay' in 1936 by 3-0 and the re-run of the 1965 tussle finished 2-2.

Another Villa v Albion match - the Wartime League North fixture at Villa Park on Boxing Day 1944 - was abandoned through fog in the 81st minute with Albion winning 4-3. The result was allowed to stand.

Villa's Christmas Day League game with Bradford in 1937 was abandoned early on through fog with the score goalless. Four months later Villa won the 'replay' 2-0.

On 15 March 1947 the weather (snow and ice) caused the 57th minute abandonment of the Villa v Stoke City League game at Villa Park. There scores were level at 2-2 and almost 50,000 fans were present. The re-arranged fixture was played on 26 May when Stoke won 1-0.

A third League game between Arsenal and Villa was called off on 2 January 1954, this time in the 23rd minute when fog swept down on Highbury. There were 30,000 fans present when the referee took the players off with Arsenal 3-0 ahead. Lucky Villa, as the 'replay' finished level at 1-1.

The weather ruined the Portsmouth v Aston Villa League game at Fratton Park on 15 January 1955. Over 14,500 fans saw the abandonment after 79 minutes with Villa ahead at 2-1. The 'replay' ended in a 2-2 draw.

A month after that Pompey match, Villa's 4th round FA Cup 3rd replay against Doncaster Rovers at Hillsborough was abandoned at the end of 90 minutes. It was 0-0 at the time and the game remained in the records. Rovers won 3-1 when the teams met in the next 'replay' at The Hawthorns.

In December 1960, a League Cup 4th round replay between Plymouth Argyle and Aston Villa at Home Park was abandoned after 90 minutes with the scoresheet blank. This game was also retained in the record books and Villa won the 'replay' 5-3.

On 22 December 1962, in front of 21,264 fans, snow, ice, sleet, frost, wind (everything an arctic winter could conjure up) prevented the Villa-Manchester City League game progressing beyond the 48th minute at Villa Park. City were 1-0 in front at the time, yet Villa won the re-arranged game 3-1!

On 27 December 1965, only 30 minutes of the Villa v West Ham League match could be played before the weather caused the referee to call a halt to proceedings with the scoresheet blank. There were

*A muddy pitch - soon to cause an abandonment*

On a dark, wet and windy afternoon, the Sheffield Wednesday v Aston Villa League Division One game at Olive Grove on 26 November 1898 was abandoned through bad light with a little over ten minutes left to play. The match itself had kicked off late after referee Aaron Scragg from Crewe had failed to arrive on time. Local official Fred Bye stepped in and started proceedings at 2.30pm instead of the scheduled 2 o'clock. Scragg got to the ground in time for the second half, but it was far too dark to complete the full 90 minutes and he called it a day with a just over 10 minutes remaining. At the time Wednesday were leading 3-1. However, a request from the home side and, indeed, from Villa, for the result to stand was rejected by the Football League committee and Villa had to travel back to Sheffield on 13 March 1899 to play out the remaining 630 seconds. In that time Wednesday scored a fourth goal. Villa's goalscorer Frank Bedingfield did not play in the 'second' match, his place went to Billy Garraty. Wednesday made five changes.

THE COMPLETE ENCYCLOPAEDIA OF ASTON VILLA F.C.  THE COMPLETE ENCYCLOPAEDIA OF ASTON VILLA F.C.

2

30,382 fans inside Villa Park. The Hammers returned in February to win the 'replay' 2-1.

The reigning Scottish League champions and League Cup winners Glasgow Rangers played a friendly at Villa Park on 9 October 1976 in front of a crowd of 18,000 (10,000 of them Scots). But it turned out to be far more than a 'friendly' as scores of visiting supporters invaded the pitch, throwing bottles, cans, coins and other dangerous items around indiscriminately. They fought a fierce battle with the police and generally caused havoc, so much so that the game had to be abandoned in the 51st minute with Villa 2-0 ahead. More than a hundred spectators were injured and fifty arrested. Dennis Howell, MP, who was at the match, later discussed the events with the home secretary. Rangers' manager Willie Waddell said: "This is the worst thing that has happened to us since Barcelona 1972. After this, no club will ever invite us for friendlies." On 14 October an FA inquiry cleared Aston Villa of any blame for the riot. One Rangers' fan was later jailed for six months by Birmingham magistrates.

A friendly between Sheffield United and Villa at Bramall Lane was abandoned at half-time on 30 January 1987.

The last Villa game to be abandoned was a friendly against Nettleham (away) in season 1989-90 which was cut short owing to a floodlight failiure. Villa were leading 5-1 at the time.

## Wintry Notes

Villa had 20 games postponed during the harsh winter of 1947. They played their last Central League fixture that season on 14 June - having started on 31 August.

During the arctic winter of 1962-63 Villa did not complete a single League game between 16 December and 18 January. They finally met Blackburn Rovers (home) on 19 January, but then had to wait until 13 February before playing again. Over a period of eight weeks (mid-December to mid-February) Villa fulfilled just three first team matches, two League games, one FA Cup-tie.

All 22 players were out on the pitch prior to Villa's home game with Northampton Town on Christmas Day 1944. But before play could begin a thick fog descended on the ground and the match was postponed.

Villa's home Birmingham Combination match against Darlaston at the Alexander Sports Stadium, Perry Barr in season 1938-39 was abandoned after spectators invaded the pitch following a refereeing decision. The re-arranged fixture was played behind closed doors with only the respective club's officials present.

## ACCRINGTON

Villa's playing record against Accrington:

Football League

| Venue | P | W | D | L | F | A |
|---|---|---|---|---|---|---|
| Home | 5 | 4 | 0 | 1 | 26 | 12 |
| Away | 5 | 1 | 2 | 2 | 9 | 10 |
| Totals | 10 | 5 | 2 | 3 | 35 | 22 |

As founder members of the Football League Aston Villa and Accrington first met in season 1888-89. A crowd of just 600 (the lowest crowd ever to watch a Villa home League game) saw a seven-goal thriller go Villa's way by 4-3 at Perry Barr. In contrast 5,000 spectators witnessed the 1-1 draw at Accrington.

On 12 March 1892 Villa recorded their biggest-ever League victory, beating Accrington 12-2 at Perry Barr. Around 8,000 fans saw the action and applauded four-timers from Jack Devey and Louis Campbell. The unlucky Accrington 'keeper was Tommy Hay.

Twelve months later Villa beat Accrington 6-4 at home with Devey scoring twice on this occasion.

There are no instances of players serving with both clubs.

## ACCRINGTON STANLEY

Aston Villa never played against Accrington Stanley - a League club from 1921 to 1962.

Players with both clubs include: F Farrell (Stanley reserve), MK Ferguson, S Lynn, J Walters (Stanley reserve), T Waring.

Also: RE Blackburn (Villa player, Stanley trainer & manager).

## ADAM, JAMES

Born in Glasgow on 13 May 1931.

Career: Blantyre Celtic (amateur), Aldershot (amateur 1948, professional August 1951), Spennymoor United (August 1952), Luton Town (July 1953), Aston Villa (August 1959), Stoke City (July 1961), Falkirk (July 1963), Spennymoor United (coach 1967-69). A fast-raiding winger, Jimmy Adam was able to occupy both flanks. He spent two seasons at Villa Park during which time he scored three goals in 25 appearances, gaining a Second Division championship medal in 1960. He had previously made over 150 appearances for The Hatters.

## ADMISSION PRICES

Before the commencement of League Football in 1888, the charge for admission to the 'ground' (terraces) for a Villa home game (depending on the context of the fixture) varied from 1d to 6d (2 1/2p).

Once League football had arrived, the 6d charge remained as a minimum entrance fee until after World War One (1919) when it was increased to one shilling (5p). For the next 23 years that ('bob') shilling admission price remained in force, but for the 1942-43 Wartime season it went up to 1s 3d (7p). And it 1946 it was up to 1s 6d (7 1/2p). Thereafter it rose steadily: 1952-53 to 1s 9d (9p); 1955-56 to 2s (10p); 1959-60 to 2s 6d (12 1/2p); 1960-61 to 3s (15p); 1962-63 to 4s (20p); 1966-67 to 5s (25); 1969-70 to 6s (30p); 1970-71 to 7s 6d (38p) and then upwards from 40p to 50p and on to a £1 by 1978-79, rising after that to £1.30, £1.50, £2.00, £3.00, £5.00 and then £6.00 before the all-seater stadium came into force.

The general admission charge to the Witton Lane stand in 1939-40 (paying on the day of the match) was 3s (15p).

In 1947-48 it was 3s (15p) to stand at the Holte End. However, increases thereafter to the minimum entrance fee and the highest admittance charge have both been gradual......4s (20p) in the early 1950s, rising to 4s.6d (22 1/2p) and the up to 5s (25p) by 1960-61.

It was 6s (30p) in the mid '60s, then 10s (50p) in the late 1960s and twenty-five years ago the entrance fee had risen to £1.00. It then rose steadily after that: £1.50, £2.00 and up to £2.50 by 1980.

Guide to the dearest admission prices to Villa Park since 1991:

| Season | Terraces | Seats |
|---|---|---|
| 1991-92 | £5.00 | £10.00 |
| 1992-93 | £6.00 | £12.00 |
| 1993-94 | - | £13.00 |
| 1994-95 | - | £14.00 |
| 1995-96 | - | £15.00 |
| 1996-97 | - | £17.00 |
| 1997-98 | - | £18.00 |
| 1998-99 | - | £22.00 |
| 1999-00 | - | £25.00 |
| 2000-01 | - | £25.00 |
| 2001-02 | - | £25.00 |

THE COMPLETE ENCYCLOPAEDIA OF ASTON VILLA F.C.    THE COMPLETE ENCYCLOPAEDIA OF ASTON VILLA F.C.

3

VILLA V DYNAMO KIEV (2ND LEG)
EURO CUP RD 3    K.O. 7.30PM
DOOR W    NORTH STD BLOCK 72
ROW  SEAT
H   64    GUEST    250211342

aston villa

ASTON VILLA FOOT...
Villa Park, Birmingham...

ASTON VILLA FOOTBALL CLUB LTD.    No. 993
Monday, October 19th, 1959.    Kick-off 7-15 p.m.
AT VILLA PARK, BIRMINGHAM

Aston Villa v. Rapid Vienna
RESERVED SEAT 7/-
Row A
Entrance Door:
Seat No. 64
TRINITY ROAD
KEEP THIS TICKET
This Ticket is issued subject to the By-laws and Regulations of the Football Association

## Complimentary Tickets

For Football League matches, the visiting club can normally claim in the region of 40 complimentary tickets - 25 for use by the players, manager and coach - and 12 for the Directors. However, there is no set limit on how many complimentary tickets the home club can issue.

## AGE

### Oldest

The oldest player ever appear for Aston Villa in a League or major Cup game is Ernie Callaghan, who was 39 years, 257 days old when he lined up for the last time for Villa, at home to Grimsby Town in a First Division match on 12 April 1947. A crowd of 34,000 saw Callaghan have a hand in one of Villa's goals in the 3-3 draw.

### Youngest

Jimmy Brown (left), at the age of 15 years, 349 days, became the youngest player ever to appear in a senior game for the club when he made his debut against Bolton Wanderers at Burnden Park in a Second Division match on 17 September 1969. Bolton won 2-1. The previous youngest had been Ken O. Roberts, aged 17 years, ten months, versus Blackpool (away) on 23 January 1954.

### Age Concern

Billy Hampson, aged 41 years, 8 months, is the oldest player ever to appear in an FA Cup Final - for Newcastle United against Villa in 1924.

Nigel Spink is the oldest goalkeeper and the second oldest player to appear in a major competition for West Bromwich Albion. He was aged 39 years and 19 days when he lined up for the Baggies against Cambridge United in a Coca-Cola Cup-tie in August 1997. Earlier Spink became the oldest Albion debutant at 37 years, 179 days v Ipswich Town (away) in February 1996, following his transfer from Aston Villa. Leslie Smith, soon to join Villa, was the youngest player to appear in an FA Amateur Cup Final - for Wimbledon against Bishop Auckland in 1935, aged 15.

The club's former centre-half Frank Barson was aged 49 when he guested for Villa against Sutton Town in October 1940.

Alick Jeffrey (Doncaster Rovers) was only 16 when he played and scored against Aston Villa in the FA Cup in 1955, making him the youngest player ever to appear in this competition.

Villa goalkeepers John Burridge (left), Mervyn Day, Les Sealey and Nigel Spink and all played League football when over the age of 35.

Burridge was aged 41 years, 338 days when he became Scarborough's oldest-ever League player v Doncaster Rovers in November 1993. A little over two years later, in December 1995, he played for Scarborough in an Auto-Windscreen Shield game against Notts County just a week after his 44th birthday. 'Budgie' also holds the record of being Darlington's oldest League player, aged 44 years, six days on 9 December 1995 (v Scarborough) - and he is the oldest player ever to star in the Premiership, aged 43 years, five months, 11 days when lining up for Manchester City on 14 May 1995 against QPR at Maine Road. Burridge played in his last FA Cup-tie for

## Season Tickets

An 1880s ground season ticket to watch Aston Villa cost the supporter 3s (15p); in those days a club used to play between 15 and 20 home matches per season. When League Football arrived in 1888-89, the average price for a season ticket was 5s (25p). At the turn of the century (1900-01) the price had risen to 10s (50p) and in the first season after the Great War (1919-20) a season ticket at Villa Park was priced at 15s (75p).

Over the next 20 years or so the overall price rose slowly - in 1930 supporters paid 30s a time (£1.50); in 1934 it had risen to £2 per season ticket and just before League Football was suspended in 1939 a season ticket (reserved seat) in the Trinity Road stand cost £4 guineas (£4.20); similar ones, in different areas in the Witton Lane stand were priced at three guineas (£1.5) and £2.4s.6d (£2.23).

Immediately after World War Two, the admission charge had reached £4 a time; it was £5 ten years later (in 1956) and in 1960 the average price of a season ticket was £8.

Between 1961 and 1974 season ticket prices went up slowly - from £9 to £10 to £12 to £15 to £18 and for the 1974-75 campaign fans at Villa Park were paying up £20, plus an extra £6 for five cup matches and £17 (plus £5) in the main stand. In 1979-80, the price for an adult of a Villa season ticket (in the main stand) was around the £60 mark (this was the norm up and down the country for the majority of First Division clubs). Since then the general cost of a season ticket has risen steadily, from £50 (terraces) and £100 (seats) in 1984-85, from £55/£120 within four years, quickly rising to round the £85/£150 mark in 1990. Once Premiership football arrived, the season tickets rose rapidly - £150/£200. Then upwards of £250 and in season 2000-01 the dearest season tickets at Villa Park were priced at £300 plus. There was a lengthy waiting list for season tickets at Villa Park as long ago as 1949-50.

THE COMPLETE ENCYCLOPAEDIA OF ASTON VILLA F.C.  THE COMPLETE ENCYCLOPAEDIA OF ASTON VILLA F.C.

4

Darlington v. Rochdale on 12 December 1995 (aged 44 years, nine days). He played his last competitive game (in the FA Cup) for Blyth Spartans v Blackpool in November 1997, a month or so before his 46th birthday.

Future Aston Villa player Steve Watson was the youngest League debutant for Newcastle United - aged 16 years, 223 days v Wolverhampton Wanderers (Division 1) on 10 November 1990.

Paul Rideout became Swindon Town's youngest-ever player when he made his League debut against Hull City on 29 November 1980. He joined Villa in June 1983.

Kevin Gage, aged 17 years, 15 days, became Wimbledon's youngest first-team player when he made his Football League debut against Bury on 2 May 1981. He signed for Villa in 1987.

Winger Ken O. Roberts was only 15 years, 158 days old when he made his League debut for Wrexham against Bradford Park Avenue on 1 September 1951. He shares the record with Albert Geldard of Everton for being the youngest player ever to appear in a Football League game in this country. Roberts signed for Villa in 1953.

Ronnie Dix became Bristol Rovers' youngest-ever League player when, at the age of 15 years, 180 days, he made his debut versus Norwich City on 3 March 1928 (Division 3 South).

Ian 'Chico' Hamilton made his Football League debut for Chelsea against Tottenham Hotspur on 18 March 1967 at the age of 16 years, 138 days, making him the Stamford Bridge club's youngest-ever footballer.

Ex-Villa goalkeeper Billy George was trainer at St Andrew's when in an emergency he replaced Horace Bailey for the League game against Barnsley in September 1911 at the age of 37....the oldest player to make his debut for Blues!

## AGGREGATE SCORE

A record number of goals (16 in total) were scored in the Villa's two-legged fourth round FA Cup-tie with Millwall in January 1946. Villa won 4-2 at The Den and then went goal crazy in the return leg by beating the Lions 9-1 with Frank Broome netting a smart hat-trick to register a 13-3 aggregate victory.

Fifteen goals were netted in the two-legged Wartime League Cup encounter between Villa and Wolves in March 1943. The first game at Villa Park ended in a 5-2 win for Villa (a hat-trick here for Eric Houghton) and at Molineux a week later Villa again came out on top, winning by 5-3 with guest star Dicky Davis a hat-trick hero this time. In season 1985-86 Aston Villa played Exeter City in a two-legged Football League Cup tie when a total of 14 goals were scored over the two matches. At St James' Park on 25 September Simon Stainrod netted all Villa's goals on his debut in a 4-1 win and a fortnight later he found the net again when the Grecians were hammered 8-1.

Villa beat arch rivals Birmingham City 7-0 on aggregate (2-0 away, 5-0 at home) in a 2nd round League cup-tie in 1988-89.

## AITKEN, CHARLES ALEXANDER

Born: Edinburgh, 1 May 1942

Career: Gorsebridge Juniors, Edinburgh Thistle, Aston Villa (August 1959), New York Cosmos (May 1976), Worcester City (1977-78), Aston Villa Old Stars, Talbot Tankards FC.

Charlie Aitken spent 17 years at Villa Park and holds the club's all-time appearance record of 660 (including three as a substitute). He also netted 16 goals. A total of 561 of those appearances came in the Football League and he missed only 18 out of a possible 252 First Division matches between April 1961 and May 1967. Playing his first and last League games for Villa against the same club - Sheffield Wednesday, he won a League Cup winners tankard in 1975, having earlier collected two runners-up medals in the same competition (1963 and 1971). He was in Villa's Third Division championship winning side of 1972 and was voted 'Midland Footballer of the Year' three years later. Capped once by Scotland at Under-23 level, Aitken had a well-

deserved Testimonial match v Coventry City in 1970. One of the club's all-time greats, he was hardly ever spoken to by the match referee. He skippered Villa on several occasions and above all was a terrific clubman, admired by the fans and, indeed, by his fellow professionals.

After retiring he ran a successful antiques shop in Acocks Green, Birmingham for a number of years.

Aitken became an Aston Villa vice-President in the 1990s.

## ALDERSHOT

Villa's playing record against the Shots:

FA Cup

| Venue | P | W | D | L | F | A |
|-------|---|---|---|---|---|---|
| Home  | 1 | 0 | 1 | 0 | 0 | 0 |
| Away  | 1 | 0 | 0 | 1 | 1 | 2 |
| Totals | 2 | 0 | 1 | 1 | 1 | 2 |

The Shots caused a major upset when they knocked Villa out of the FA Cup in 1963-64. Almost 22,000 saw them battle to earn a replay at Villa Park and then despite a Tony Hateley goal, they came through the replay 2-1 in front of 13,566 fans at The Recreation Ground. Villa boss Joe Mercer left the club after this defeat.

Players with both clubs include: J Adam, RD Davis (WW2 guest for both clubs), JR Martin (Shots WW2 guest), C Wilson (Villa reserve, Shots WW2 guest).

Also: J Mercer (Shots WW2 guest, Villa manager), HC Slade (Villa player, 'Shots coach).

## ALDIS, BASIL PETER

Born: Kings Heath, Birmingham, 11 April 1927.

Career: Pineapple School (Stirchley), Cadbury Works FC, Hay Green (1947), Aston Villa (amateur, November 1948, professional January 1949), Hinckley Athletic (July 1960), then in Australia for five years (1963-68) with Slavia FC (as player-manager), FC Wilhelmina and The Lions Club, Alvechurch (player-manager July 1968-May 1970).

Peter Aldis, like Charlie Aitken, also occupied the left-back position and he, too, gave Aston Villa tremendous service. An ex-Cadbury chocolate maker, Aldis was the player with a sunshine smile and during his time at Villa Park he made 295 appearances and scored one goal - a spectacular 35 yard header in the League game v Sunderland in 1952. He also helped Villa win the FA Cup in 1957 and whilst 'down under' was voted Australia's 'Footballer of the Year' in 1966. After retiring from football in 1970 Aldis worked for a firm in Earlswood prior to

becoming an Education and Welfare Officer in Redditch, also acting as groundsman at a School in Solihull. When he was with Hinckley, Aldis became one of only two players ever to appear in 13 rounds of the FA Cup in one season!

## ALDRIDGE, ALBERT A. JAMES
Born: Walsall, April 1864. Died: Birmingham, May 1891.
Career: Walsall Council and Pleck Schools, Walsall Swifts (August 1881), West Bromwich Albion (March 1886, professional July 1886), Walsall Town Swifts (July 1888), Aston Villa (August 1889-April 1891).
An England international full-back (two caps gained) Albert Aldridge presented a formidable barrier, being hardy, resolute and unyielding...the harder the tussle, the better he played.
He won an FA Cup winners medal with West Bromwich Albion in 1888 (v PNE), having collected a runners up medal the previous year (v Aston Villa). But after making only 14 senior appearances for Villa, he was forced to retire through ill-health (April 1891) and sadly died a month later in Birmingham, aged 27.

## ALEXANDER STADIUM
Aston Villa used the Alexander Sports Stadium in Perry Barr regularly during the 1930s for third team matches.

## ALLEN, ALBERT ARTHUR
Born: Aston, Birmingham, 7 April 1867.
Died: October 1899.
Career: St Phillips FC (Aston), Aston Villa (August 1884-May 1891).
Died: Birmingham, 13 October 1899.
Albert Allen was a prolific goalscorer as well as being a hard-working utility forward, able to play on the wing or inside, who drew up a wonderful understanding with Denny Hodgetts. One pen-portrait of Allen revealed: 'Lack of height and size did not affect his pluck; he dribbled like an artist and shot with force and good aim. A modest, unassuming player.'
He notched a hat-trick in his only international game for England v Ireland in March 1888 and he also grabbed Villa's first ever Football League hat-trick v Notts County six months later. Unfortunately Allen was forced to retire through injury at the end of the 1890-91 season after scoring 33 goals in just 56 senior appearances for Villa. He was only 32 when he died.

## ALLEN, BARNEY WILLIAM
Born: Hockley, Birmingham, 1882. Deceased.
Career: Hockley Hill School, Icknield Street Old Boys, Aston Villa (April-December 1905), Westbourne Celtic, Winson Green All Saints.
Barney Allen was an efficient outside-right, who scored once in three outings for Villa when deputising for Billy Brawn. He served the club for a period of eight months in 1905.

## ALLEN, JAMES PHILLIPS
Born: Poole, Dorset, 16 October 1909. Died: Southsea, 8 February 1995.
Career: Longfleet St Mary's School, Poole Central, Poole Town (August 1927), Portsmouth (£1,200, July 1932), Aston Villa (£10,775, June 1934-May 1944), Colchester United (manager July 1948-April 1953). Later a licensee in Southsea.
Jimmy Allen was a solid defender who had the ideal frame for the 'stopper' centre-half. He played for Portsmouth in the 1934 FA Cup Final and was a record signing by Aston Villa in June of that same year. He helped Villa win the Second Division title in 1938 and was capped twice by England. Allen also represented the Football League and guested for several teams during the Second World War, including Birmingham, Fulham and his former club, Portsmouth. For three years

*Jimmy Allen*

from 1944, he was the Sports & Welfare Officer at a prominent Birmingham company before returning to soccer as boss of Colchester, leading the 'U's' into the Football League in 1950.
Allen retired in 1944 through injury after scoring three goals in 160 senior appearances for Villa.

## ALLEN, MALCOLM
Born: Caernarfon, 27 March 1967
Career: Watford (apprentice 1983, professional March 1985), Aston Villa (on loan September/October 1987), Norwich City (August 1988), Millwall (March 1989), Newcastle United (August 1993).
Allen had just four outings on loan with Villa from Watford as a replacement forward in 1987. He amassed over 160 League appearances and scored 42 goals during his career. He also won 14 full caps for Wales and represented his country at both Youth and 'B' team levels.

## AMATEURS
Over the years several amateurs have played for Villa at senior level.
Among them we have: centre-half Dr William Ewart Barnie-Adshead, full-back Walter 'Watty' Corbett, inside-forward Billy Dinsdale, wing-half Dr Vic Milne, four goalkeepers Mike Pinner, Len Richards, Leigh Richmond Roose and Ken Tewksbury and inside-forwards Dick Sloley and Oliver Whateley.
Corbett represented Great Britain in the 1908 Olympic Games and won a Gold Medal at soccer.
Dinsdale played for Crook Town in the 1920s.
The first amateur to appear in an FA Cup Final at Wembley was Vic Milne - for Aston Villa against Newcastle United in 1924.
Mike Pinner was capped 51 times by England at Amateur level and he made four League appearances for Villa in the mid-1950s.
LR Roose (below) played for several League clubs. He won 24 senior caps for Wales (1900-11) and also appeared once for his country at amateur level (1911).
Barnie-Adshead (2 caps), Corbett (1) Sloley (2) and Tewksbury (6) all represented England in Amateur internationals. Sloley also assisted the famous Corinthians.
Winger Les (LGF) Smith played in the 1935 FA Amateur Cup Final for Wimbledon and represented England at both amateur and senior levels before joining Villa in 1945.
Oliver Whateley was an FA Cup winner with Aston Villa in 1887 and gained two full England caps in 1883.
Before turning professional, inside-forward Phil Woosnam was voted 'Amateur Footballer of the Year' with Sutton United in 1955.
Ex-Villa FA Cup Final winner Bob Chatt added an FA Amateur Cup winners' medal to his collection with Stockton in 1899.
Villa played the famous Amateur sides Corinthians and Queen's Park (Glasgow) in the FA Cup competition and they also encountered the latter club twice in the Sheriff of London Charity Shield.

## ANDERLECHT (RSC)

Villa's playing record against Anderlecht:
European Cup

| Venue | P | W | D | L | F | A |
|---|---|---|---|---|---|---|
| Home | 1 | 1 | 0 | 0 | 1 | 0 |
| Away | 1 | 0 | 1 | 0 | 0 | 0 |
| Totals | 2 | 1 | 1 | 0 | 1 | 0 |

Aston Villa met the Belgium champions Anderlecht over two legs in the semi-final of the European Cup in 1981-82. A crowd of 38,539 saw Villa gain a 1-0 advantage from their home leg thanks to Tony Morley's goal and then, in front of 38,050 fans, held out for a goalless draw in Anderlecht to enter the Rotterdam final with Bayern Munich.
Players with both clubs: G De Bilde, N Lamptey,

## ANDERSON, DAVID

Born: Hockley, Birmingham, 1861.
Career: Hockley Belmont (1878), Aston Villa (August 1881), Abbey (June 1883).
Dave Anderson was a well-built wing-half who played in five FA Cup games for Aston Villa in season 1882-83. A spate of niggling injuries led to him leaving the club.

## ANDERSON, WILLIAM JOHN

Born: Liverpool, 24 January 1947.
Career: Liverpool & Merseyside Boys, Manchester United (junior April 1962, professional February 1964), Aston Villa (£20,000, January 1967), Cardiff City (£60,000, February 1973), Portland Timbers, NASL (July 1977), retiring in 1979.
Willie Anderson was a fast raiding left-winger and first reserve to George Best at Old Trafford before joining Villa in 1967. With his film star looks, Anderson was a huge favourite with the female supporters everywhere he went. He won an FA Youth Cup winners medal with the Reds and also gained England Youth international honours. He lined up for Villa in the 1971 League Cup Final v Tottenham Hotspur and helped them win the Third Division championship the following season. The club's top marksman with six goals in 1968-69, he scored in all five games against Wrexham in 1971-72 and found the net 45 times in his 267 appearances for Villa before joining Cardiff. Quitting football in 1979, Anderson later became an Executive with a commercial radio station in Oregon, U.S.A.

## ANGEL, JUAN PABLO

Born: Colombia, 24 October 1975
Career: Colombian football, River Plate of Argentina (summer, 1995), Aston Villa (£9.5 million, January 2001).
Colombian international striker Juan Pablo Angel became Aston Villa's record signing when he joined the club in January 2001 after tedious on-off negotiations finally ended in Villa's favour.
Angel had already drawn up an excellent goalscoring record prior to moving to England from League football in Argentina. In fact, he had scored 17 goals in 17 club games during the season that had just ended when Villa moved in to secure his signature.

Boss John Gregory had flown some 6,000 miles from England to Buenos Aires in Argentina to watch Angel play and he had no qualms about signing him, saying: "He has all the qualities to become a real star in the Premiership."
Capped almost 30 times by his country, Angel has pace, power, accuracy, ability and commitment - and he can score goals! He made his Villa debut against Manchester United and claimed his first goal in English football in the 3-2 Premiership home win over Coventry City on 5 May 2001 - a result that sent the Sky Blues down...and hopefully there are some more to come from this talented Colombian.
Angel's Villa record at the end of the 2000-01 season was 10 Premiership appearances and one goal.

## ANSELL, BARRY

Born: Small Heath, Birmingham, 29 September 1947
Career: Waverley Grammar School, Aston Villa (junior, June 1965, professional October 1967-May 1969), non-League football.
Reserve left-back Barry Ansell made just one League appearance for Villa, against Cardiff City (away) in December 1967 when he replaced Charlie Aitken.

## ANSTEY, BRENDEL

Born: Bristol 1887. Died: Wednesbury, December 1933.
Career: Hanham Juniors, Bristol Rovers (August 1910), Aston Villa (March 1911), Leicester City (September 1919), Mid-Rhondda (August 1920-May 21).
Brendel Anstey was a competent goalkeeper who was signed by Villa, initially as a replacement for Billy George, but thereafter acted as understudy to England No.1 Sam Hardy. He played in 45 competitive games for Villa before leaving the club for Leicester City in 1919.

## ANTWERP (FC ROYAL)

Villa's playing record against the Belgians:

| Venue | P | W | D | L | F | A |
|---|---|---|---|---|---|---|
| Home | 1 | 0 | 0 | 1 | 0 | 1 |
| Away | 1 | 0 | 0 | 1 | 1 | 4 |
| Totals | 2 | 0 | 0 | 2 | 1 | 5 |

Antwerp were Villa's first ever European opponents, meeting over two legs in the opening round of the 1975-76 UEFA Cup tournament.
A crowd of 20,000 witnessed the first leg in Belgium which Villa lost 4-1, Ray Graydon their goalscorer, while Kodat netted a hat-trick for the home side. After that it was always going to be an uphill battle and in front of 31,513 fans at Villa Park Antwerp again took the honours with a 1-0 second leg victory to go through comfortably 5-1 on aggregate. Not the greatest of starts in Europe for Aston Villa!
This was the first Villa line-up on the European circuit: Jim Cumbes; John Gidman, Charlie Aitken; Ian Ross, Chris Nicholl, Leighton Phillips; Ray Graydon, Bobby McDonald, Sammy Morgan, Ian Hamilton, Frank Carrodus. Subs: John Robson, Steve Hunt (both used).

## APPEARANCES

Here are the top appearance-makers for Villa in all major competitions:

### Football League
| 561* | Charlie Aitken |
|---|---|
| 478 | Billy Walker |
| 431 | Joe Bache |
| 414* | Gordon Cowans |

THE COMPLETE ENCYCLOPAEDIA OF ASTON VILLA F.C.    THE COMPLETE ENCYCLOPAEDIA OF ASTON VILLA F.C.

7

| | | |
|---|---|---|
| 405 | Tommy Smart | |
| 392 | Johnny Dixon | |
| 380 | Allan Evans | |
| 361 | Eric Houghton | |
| 361* | Nigel Spink | |
| 358 | Billy George | |
| 356 | Dicky York | |
| 355 | Arthur Dorrell | |
| 339 | Harry Hampton | |
| 337 | Tommy Mort | |
| 320 | Harry Parkes | |
| 317* | Dennis Mortimer | |
| 316 | James Cowan | |
| 314 | Charlie Wallace | |

| | | |
|---|---|---|
| 20* | Tony Morley |
| 18 | Gary Williams |
| 17 | Gary Shaw |
| 14* | Colin Gibson |
| 13* | Nigel Spink |

**All major competitions**

| | |
|---|---|
| 660* | Charlie Aitken |
| 531 | Billy Walker |
| 528* | Gordon Cowans |
| 474 | Joe Bache |
| 469* | Allan Evans |
| 460 | Nigel Spink |
| 452 | Tommy Smart |
| 430 | Johnny Dixon |
| 406 | Dennis Mortimer |
| 402 | Billy George |
| 392 | Eric Houghton |
| 390 | Arthur Dorrell |
| 390 | Dicky York |
| 373 | Harry Hampton |
| 368 | Tommy Mort |
| 356 | James Cowan |
| 351 | Vic Crowe |
| 350 | Charlie Wallace |
| 345 | Harry Parkes |
| * Total includes | |
| | substitute appearances |

**FA Cup**

| | |
|---|---|
| 53 | Billy Walker |
| 47 | Tommy Smart |
| 42 | Joe Bache |
| 41 | Archie Hunter |
| 40 | Billy George |
| 38 | Charlie Athersmith |
| 38 | James Cowan |
| 38 | John Devey |
| 37 | Dennis Hodgetts |
| 36 | Stan Lynn |
| 36 | Peter McParland |
| 35* | Charlie Aitken |
| 35 | Arthur Dorrell |
| 35 | Howard Spencer |
| 35 | Charlie Wallace |
| 34 | Vic Crowe |
| 34 | Harry Hampton |
| 34 | Dicky York |
| 32 | Peter Aldis |
| 32 | Billy Kirton |
| 31 | Eric Houghton |

**World War II appearances**

| | |
|---|---|
| 195 | Vic Potts |
| 183 | Alan Wakeman |
| 177 | George Cummings |
| 173 | Bob Iverson |
| 157 | Eric Houghton |
| 151 | Ernie Callaghan |
| 142 | Ronnie Starling |
| 135 | Frank Broome |
| 134 | Harry Parkes |
| 131 | Alex Massie |
| 125 | George Edwards |
| 83 | Freddie Haycock |

**Football League Cup**

| | |
|---|---|
| 61 | Charlie Aitken |
| 45 | Nigel Spink |
| 44* | Gordon Cowans |
| 43* | Allan Evans |
| 38 | Dennis Mortimer |
| 31 | Ian Hamilton |
| 30* | Brian Little |
| 30* | Paul McGrath |
| 29 | Gary Williams |
| 27* | Paul Birch |
| 27 | Frank Carrodus |
| 27 | Chris Nicholl |
| 26 | Colin Gibson |
| 26* | Ray Graydon |
| 25 | John Gidman |
| 25 | Andy Gray |
| 24 | Ron Wylie |
| 23 | Willie Anderson |
| 23 | Vic Crowe |
| 23 | Jimmy Rimmer |

**Picture Key:**

1. Vic Crowe
2. Harry Parkes
3. Allan Evans
4. Dennis Mortimer
5. Charlie Aitken
6. Nigel Spink
7. Joe Bache
8. Gordon Cowans
9. Des Bremner

**Appearance Fact File**

Eric Houghton appeared in more than 700 games for Aston Villa at first team, reserve and intermediate levels. He starred in 549 major first team matches (361 Football League, 31 FA Cup and 157 Wartime).

Goalkeeper John Burridge appeared in 915 first-class matches during his 29-year career....771 in the Football League alone.

In his playing career - in England, Italy and at international level - midfielder Gordon Cowans amassed in excess of 750 club appearances. Cowans also holds the record for most consecutive appearances for Villa - 216 between August 1979 and May 1983. This tally included 168 in the Football League

Dennis Mortimer, too, appeared in more than 700 competitive games as a professional, including almost 600 in the Football League.

Danny Blanchflower also made over 700 appearances as a 'pro'.

Striker Andy Gray amassed over 600 appearances at club level during his career that also saw him assist two Scottish clubs.

Ex-Villa players John Burridge (771), Chris Nicholl (647), Gordon Cowans (594), Dennis Mortimer (590), Bruce Rioch (564) and Charlie Aitken (561)....plus manager Graham Turner (650)....all figure in the top 50 all-time Football League appearance-makers.

Dwight Yorke made most substitute appearances for Villa at competitive level - total 40 (36 League, 2 FAC and 2 League Cup).

Charlie Aitken and Gordon Cowans both appeared in five full seasons of League football with Villa (see Ever-Presents).

**European Competitions**

| | |
|---|---|
| 30 | Gordon Cowans |
| 28 | Dennis Mortimer |
| 22 | Ken McNaught |
| 22 | Jimmy Rimmer |
| 22 | Peter Withe |
| 20 | Des Bremner |
| 20* | Allan Evans |

THE COMPLETE ENCYCLOPAEDIA OF ASTON VILLA F.C.  THE COMPLETE ENCYCLOPAEDIA OF ASTON VILLA F.C.

8

## Consecutive Appearances

Detailed list of players who drew up excellent runs of consecutive appearances in League football for Aston Villa:

| Games | Player | Dates |
|---|---|---|
| 168 | GS Cowans | 18.8.1979 to 14.5.1983 |
| 136 | AD Talbot | 9.9.1929 to 5.11.1932 |
| 127 | I Ross | 7.4.1973 to 3.4.1976 |
| 126 | CA Aitken | 5.10.1963 to 1.10.1966 |
| 125 | JJ Rimmer | 29.12.1979 to 27.12.1982 |
| 107 | LGF Smith | 31.8.1946 to 25.12.1948 |
| 104 | JJ Rimmer | 20.8.1977 to 19.12.1979 |
| 102 | CW Wallace | 27.3.1909 to 23.12.1911 |
| 98 | H Morton | 22.4.1933 to 12.10.1935 |

Alan Wright's total of 79, starting on 30.8.1997 and ending on 11.9.1999, gives him the record of most consecutive appearances for Aston Villa in the Premiership.

*Ian Ross*

## Consistency

Charlie Aitken appeared in 561 League games for Villa out of a possible 624 between April 1960 and January 1976.

Goalkeeper Jimmy Rimmer made 229 League appearances out of 230 between August 1977 and December 1982.

Another goalkeeper, Billy George, played in 358 out of 480 League games for Villa over a ten-year period (1898-99 to 1908-09).

Gordon Cowans starred in 237 of the 252 Football League games played by Villa between August 1977 and May 1983.

Winger Charlie Athersmith was absent from 38 of Villa's 308 League games the club filled over a decade from March 1891 to April 1901.

Before leaving for Spurs, wing-half Danny Blanchflower made 148 out of a possible 155 League appearances for Villa (1951-55).

Jas Cowan played in 316 out of 357 League games for Aston Villa between 7 September 1889 and 21 September 1901.

Arthur Dorrell's tally of 355 League appearances for Villa were made out of a possble 440 between September 1919 and December 1929.

Eric Houghton appeared in 361 out of a possible 404 League games for Villa during his senior playing days at the club (from his debut in January 1939 until his last outing in Septmber 1947). In that time he missed only 12 games in seven years (1930-36 inclusive).

Irish international Peter McParland missed only three League games in three seasons: 1957-60.

Goalkeeper Harry Morton was missing from five League matches (out of 179) between November 1931 and January 1936. He missed only one League game out of 126 between 1932 and 1935.

Centre-half Chris Nicholl was out of the Villa team just eight times

during a run of 199 League fixtures between March 1972 and November 1977. He was absent on 16 occasions out of a possible 225 games during his stay at Villa Park.

Full-back Harry Parkes missed 12 League games in seven seasons with Villa: 1947-54. In all, he was sidelined from 28 out of a possible 348 League encounters between making his First Division debut and playing in his last game.

Left wing-back Alan Wright was missing from just nine of Villa's 235 or so Premiership games played between March 1995 and May 2001.

Other consistent performers include: Nigel Sims (nine games missed in four seasons; 1956-60); Kenny Swain (four missed in three seasons: 1979-82); Alec Talbot (three missed in three seasons: 1929-32); Charlie Wallace (nine missed in four seasons: 1908-12), Fred Wheldon (four games missed out of 128 in four seasons: 1896-1900) and Dicky York (324 League appearances in nine seasons: 1921-30).

## One Match Wonders

Listed here are players who made just one senior appearance for Villa: B Ansell, WW Ashmore, F Bedingfield, L Benwell, F Brookes, R Brown, RW Chandler, GB Clarke, NF Clarke, S Cooke, WA Dickie, TB Dodds, D Duffy, TT Dutton, EE Elson, AJ Fisher, JH Garfield, A Gittings, H Goddard, H Griffin, CC Harley, EJ Harris, T Harrison, AJ Hickton, T Hitzlsperger, T Horton, AJ Jaszczun, AR Jones, WH Leigh, AA Lescott, AE Lindon, CR McElney, WH Maiden, FD Mann, JJ Martin, TD Moore, F Mwila, JR Nicholson, W Podmore, A Proudler, T Purslow, A Rachel, A Ralphs, WW Randle, SA Ritchie, B Rowan, DF Skea, LF Skiller, HH Smart, W Tainton, MS Taylor, KC Tewkesbury, R Thomas, OE Tidman, AE Watkins, WH Williams & JJ Willis.

## APPERLEY, CHARLES WILLIAM

Born: Birmingham, 1861. Died: South Africa, 1926.
Career: Birmingham St George, Aston Villa (August 1882), emigrated to South Africa 1884.
A well-built reserve defender, Charlie Apperley made only eight appearances for Villa during his two seasons with the club.

## ARMFIELD, WILLIAM CHARLES WASSELL

Born: Handsworth, Birmingham 7 July 1904. Deceased.
Career: Ellisons FC (1920), Aston Villa (August 1921), Exeter City (June 1929), Gillingham (August 1932), Brierley Hill Alliance (August 1933).
A tall, skilful winger, Billy Armfield scored twice in 12 senior outings for Villa whom he served (mainly as a reserve to Dicky York) for eight seasons until 1929. He scored 17 goals in 80 first team appearances for Exeter, figuring in the Grecians' FA Cup giant-killing side of 1930-31, but two weeks after joining Brierley Hill he broke his right leg in a pre-season friendly. A couple of months later he had the limb amputated.

## ARSENAL (ROYAL, WOOLWICH,)

Villa's playing record against the Gunners:
Football League/Premiership

| Venue | P | W | D | L | F | A |
|---|---|---|---|---|---|---|
| Home | 72 | 38 | 17 | 17 | 141 | 99 |
| Away | 72 | 20 | 15 | 37 | 81 | 118 |
| Totals | 144 | 58 | 32 | 54 | 222 | 217 |

FA Cup

| Venue | P | W | D | L | F | A |
|---|---|---|---|---|---|---|
| Home | 4 | 2 | 1 | 1 | 5 | 4 |
| Away | 8 | 1 | 2 | 5 | 8 | 21 |
| Totals | 12 | 3 | 3 | 6 | 13 | 25 |

League Cup

| Venue | P | W | D | L | F | A |
|---|---|---|---|---|---|---|
| Home | 2 | 0 | 2 | 0 | 1 | 1 |
| Away | 3 | 2 | 1 | 0 | 5 | 3 |
| Totals | 5 | 2 | 3 | 0 | 6 | 4 |

THE COMPLETE ENCYCLOPAEDIA OF ASTON VILLA F.C.   THE COMPLETE ENCYCLOPAEDIA OF ASTON VILLA F.C.

9

| Wartime | | | | | | |
|---|---|---|---|---|---|---|
| Home | 1 | 1 | 0 | 0 | 5 | 1 |
| Away | 1 | 1 | 0 | 0 | 4 | 2 |
| Totals | 2 | 2 | 0 | 0 | 9 | 3 |

On the opening day of the 1909-10 season Villa beat the Gunners 5-1 at home, and in September 1911, Villa registered a 4-1 victory on the same ground. Joey Walters scored in both matches for Villa while Harry Hampton scored twice in the latter game.

Villa completed the double over the Gunners in 1912-13, winning 4-1 at home and 3-0 at Plumstead.

Billy Walker's hat-trick set Villa up for a comprehensive opening day 5-0 home win over the Gunners in August 1920 in front of 47,000 fans. Villa netted 21 goals when recording five League wins on the trot over Arsenal between January 1928 and May 1930. The scores were in order: 3-0 (a), 5-2 (a), 4-2 (h), 5-2 (h) and 4-2 (a). 'Pongo' Waring hit a hat-trick in the first five-goal romp and George Brown netted three times in the second nap-hand victory.

Arsenal quickly bounced back by beating Villa 5-2 at Highbury in November 1930 only to lose 5-1 at Villa Park four months later!

There were more goals to cheer in 1932-33 as Villa won 5-3 at home but lost 5-0 at Highbury. A combined total of close on 129,000 fans saw these two matches.

And there were more goals to report soon afterwards as Ted Drake scored the lot for Arsenal as they beat Villa 7-1 at Villa Park in a First Division game in December 1935. Drake only had eight shots at goal that afternoon! This is the most goals ever scored by any one player in a competitive game against Villa.

On 24 September 1938, a crowd of 66,456 - the biggest anywhere in the First Division throughout that season - witnessed the goalless draw between Arsenal and Villa at Highbury.

After some very tight and even exchanges over a period of ten years, in October 1957 Arsenal suddenly whipped Villa 4-0 at Highbury but two months later over 40,000 fans saw Villa gain revenge with a 3-0 home victory.

Tommy Ewing scored a dramatic last minute goal to earn Villa a terrific 5-4 victory over the Gunners at Highbury in March 1962.

This completed the double following a 3-1 home win earlier in the season.

Andy Gray scored twice in Villa's excellent 5-1 home victory over Arsenal in October 1976 and the following season Villa achieved two 1-0 victories to complete another League double over the Gunners. There was another 5-1 Villa home victory in April 1979. This time midfielder Gary Shelton netted a hat-trick (including a penalty).

A seven-goal thriller ended in Arsenal favour by 4-3 at Highbury in March 1982 and then Tony Woodcock hit a fivetimer when the Gunners won 6-2 at Villa Park in October 1983.

A miserable crowd of just 10,584 saw Arsenal win 4-1 at Villa Park in March 1986 - one of the lowest attendances on record for a game between the two clubs.

Seven months later the Gunners returned to Villa Park and won 4-0 in front of a crowd of 21,658.

Then, in April 1991, 20,000 more than that - 41,868 - saw Arsenal race to a 5-0 League win at Highbury.

Arsenal won 4-0 at Villa Park in April 1995 to inflict upon Villa their heaviest home defeat for four years, Dean Saunders missed a penalty as John Hartson and Ian Wright both netted twice for the Londoners.

The first time Villa met Arsenal in the FA Cup, a crowd of 71,446 packed into Villa Park to witness the 1-1 draw in the opening round in 1925-26. The replay attracted 55,400 fans as Arsenal won 2-0.

Three years later, in 1928-29, a record crowd of 73,686 saw 'Pongo' Waring's goal beat Arsenal in a quarter-final tie at Villa Park. Then in 1930-31, another massive Villa Park audience of 73,632 (the biggest ever recorded on the ground for a mid-week game) watched Villa lose a 3rd round replay 3-1 after earning a 2-2 draw at Highbury.

Arsenal again knocked Villa out of the FA Cup in 1933-34, winning a 6th round tie at Highbury by 2-1 before a 67,556 crowd whilst the Gunners ran up 5-1 and 4-1 home victories in the 3rd and 4th rounds in 1953-54 and 1955-56 respectively.

In 1973-74, Villa played superbly well when beating Arsenal 2-0 in a 4th round replay in front of almost 48,000 fans, having gained a hard-fought 1-1 draw in London. Sammy Morgan netted in both of these matches.

Villa defeated the Gunners in the 1996 League Cup semi-final on the away goal rule. They drew 0-0 at Villa Park after a 2-2 draw at Highbury.

George Edwards scored four times when Villa defeated the Gunners 5-1 in a League South game in September 1945.

Players with both clubs include: R Bloomfield, CS Buckley, G Charles (Gunners trialist), AJ Cropley, JM Deehan (Arsenal trialist), A Ducat, R Gordon, G Graham (also Gunners manager), CB Hare, S Howarth (Arsenal trialist), F Lloyd, MR Keown, P Kyle, F Lloyd, JM MacLeod, PC Merson, MJ Pinner (Arsenal Amateur), DB Platt, K Richardson, J Rimmer, LR Roose, D Simmons, N Sims (Gunners' guest, 1959), TC Southren (Arsenal Amateur), RB Templeton, A Young.

Also: T Docherty & J Mercer (Arsenal players, Villa managers), BD Rioch (Villa player, Arsenal manager), D Sexton (Arsenal assistant-manager, Villa coach), C Clarke (Arsenal reserve, Villa coach), P Barron (Arsenal player, Villa coach), AE Lindon (Villa goalkeeper, Arsenal scout), B Whitehouse (scout/trainer at both clubs).

*League action from the Arsenal v Villa game at Highbury in 1938*

### ASHE, NORMAN JAMES
Born: Bloxwich, 16 November 1943.
Career: Brierley Hill Schoolboys, Aston Villa (Amateur July 1958, professional November 1960), Rotherham United (March 1963).
Right-winger Norman Ashe made his Football League debut for Aston Villa at the age of 16 years, 48 days in January 1960 against Swansea Town (Division Two). He had just four more appearances after that before leaving for Rotherham on the transfer deadline in 1963. Ashe - who joined Villa with Alan Baker - won England Schoolboy and Youth international honours as a teenager.

### ASHFIELD, GEORGE OWEN
Born: Manchester, 7 April 1934.
Career: Stockport County, Aston Villa (March 1954), Chester (February 1959). Retired through injury, 1961.

THE COMPLETE ENCYCLOPAEDIA OF ASTON VILLA F.C.

THE COMPLETE ENCYCLOPAEDIA OF ASTON VILLA F.C.

10

Reserve full-back or centre-half George Ashfield made only 10 first team appearances for Aston Villa during his five years with the club.

## ASHINGTON

Villa's playing record against Ashington:

FA Cup

| Venue | P | W | D | L | F | A |
|-------|---|---|---|---|---|---|
| Away  | 1 | 1 | 0 | 0 | 5 | 1 |

Aston Villa visited Third Division (North) Ashington in the first round of the FA Cup in January 1924 and in front of a near 12,000 crowd came away with a 5-1 victory, Billy Walker scoring two of the goals.

## ASHMORE, WALTER WILLIAM

Born: Smethwick, 1867.
Career: West Bromwich Standard (1886), Aston Villa (August 1888), Aston Unity (April 1889).
Reserve goalkeeper Wally Ashmore made just one League appearance for Villa, deputising for Jimmy Warner against Everton (home) in September 1888.

## ASHTON, DEREK

Born: Worksop, 4 July 1922.
Career: Wolverhampton Wanderers (professional September 1941), Aston Villa (May 1946), Wellington Town (August 1951).
Able to play at full-back or centre-half, Derek Ashton - nicknamed 'Paleface' - spent five 'War' years at Molineux. He made his first appearance in the claret and blue strip against Blackpool in September 1946 - his second came two years later. He was given six more outings after that before quitting League football in 1951.

## ASKEW, LESLIE W.

Born: London, 1887. Died: 1955.
Career: Xylonite FC, Tottenham Gothic Works FC, Chadwell Heath, Southend United, Norwich City, Aston Villa (August 1910), West Ham United (May 1912-May 1915)
Half-back Leslie Askew spent two years at Villa Park during which time he was given just two first team outings. He went on to make well over 100 appearances for the Hammers (up to 1915). He did not figure after the Great War.

## ASPINALL, WARREN

Born: Wigan 13 September 1967.
Career: Wigan Athletic (junior 1983, professional August 1985),
Everton (£150,000, February 1986), Wigan Athletic (on loan, February 1986), Aston Villa (£300,000, February 1987) Portsmouth (£315,000, August 1988), Bournemouth (on loan, August 1993), Swansea City (on loan, October 1993), Bournemouth again (£20,000, December 1993), Carlisle United (free transfer, March 1995), Brentford (£50,000 November 1997), Colchester United (free transfer, February 1999), Brighton & Hove Albion (free, September 1999). Forced to retire through injury in November 2000 he later became Brighton's scout (early 2001).
The only player recruited by Villa manager Billy McNeill, Aspinall was a goalscoring forward who developed into an efficient midfielder. He won

England Youth honours as a teenager and over the years has done very well at competitive level, scoring plenty of goals. He helped Wigan win the Freight Rover Trophy in 1985, collected a winners' medal when Carlisle lifted the Auto Windscreen Shield in 1997 and gained promotion from Division Three with Colchester in 1999. Having made his senior debut in 1985, Aspinall went on to amass in excess of 575 club appearances, scoring 110 goals. His record with Villa was 50 first team outings and 16 goals scored.

*Warren Aspinall*

## ASTLEY, DAVID JOHN

Born: Dowlais, near Merthyr, Glamorgan, 11 October 1909.
Died: Birchington, Kent, 7 November 1989.
Career: New Road Amateurs, Dowlais Welfare (1926), Merthyr Town (July 1927, professional August 1927), Charlton Athletic (£100, December 1927), Aston Villa (£1,500 in June 1931), Derby County (£5,250, November 1936), Blackpool (January 1939), guested for Charlton and Leyton Orient during the War. After the hostilities he coached in Italy (Inter Milan), France and Sweden (with Djurgardens IF) up to 1956 before becoming mine host of the White Horse in Ramsgate, Kent.
One of the best marksmen ever to come out of Wales, Dai Astley, an ex-miner, had a fine playing career which spanned some fifteen years during which time he netted 200 goals for his five major clubs (172 coming in 376 League games). He gained 13 full caps for Wales (12 goals scored) and added four more to his tally during the War (all versus England). He drew up a terrific set of statistics with Aston Villa (100 goals in 173 appearances) and in 1933-34 - his best season with the club - he netted 33 times in 44 outings. In fact, Astley finished up as Villa's leading scorer in three successive seasons, 1933 to 1936.

## ASTON BROOK ST MARY'S RUGBY CLUB

It is now on record that Aston Villa's second game was a 15-a-side friendly against Aston Brook St Mary's Rugby Club on 13 March 1875. The first-half was played with an oval ball under rugby union rules while the second half saw a normal football used, hired by Villa for 1s 6d (7¹/₂p) and was played under Sheffield Association rules. Villa won the game 1-0, Jack Hughes scoring the only goal halfway through the second period in front of 200 spectators.
The Villa team for this match was: W Scattergood (goal); WH Price (captain), WW Weiss, FJ Knight (full-backs); EB Lee, G Matthews, H Matthews, CH Midgley (half-backs) and J Hughes, W Such, H Whateley, G Page, A Robbins, WB Mason and WG Sothers (Forwards).

## ASTON, CHARLES LOUIS

Born: Wolverhampton, 1870. Died: Birmingham, 1941.
Career: Willenhall White Star, Walsall (August 1891), Aston Villa (April 1898), Queen's Park Rangers (August

*Dai Astley*

THE COMPLETE ENCYCLOPAEDIA OF ASTON VILLA F.C.    THE COMPLETE ENCYCLOPAEDIA OF ASTON VILLA F.C.

11

1901), Burton United (1903), Watford (July 1906), Leyton (1909) retiring 1910.

An efficient right-back who enjoyed floating long passes down the wing or across the field, Charlie Aston moved on without ever establishing himself at Villa Park yet later he took his career appearance record to around the 300 mark, with 106 outings in the Southern League with Watford. He played in 24 games for Villa and later returned to the club as a trainer.

## ASTON LOWER GROUNDS MEADOW (1875-78)

The Aston Lower Grounds Meadow stood within kicking distance of the land upon which Villa Park was to be built. The Meadow was, in fact, situated on the 'lower' grounds of Aston Hall. A variety of sporting events were staged there including athletics meetings, cycle racing, lacrosse and even cricket matches. The famous Gloucestershire batsman W.G. Grace twice starred on the Lower Grounds Meadow, for the South of England XI against Birmingham in July 1878 (when he captured 21 wickets) and for an England XI against the Australian tourists in May 1884. The Aussies won this contest inside four-and-a-half hours! Warwickshire also played a number of county matches at the Lower Grounds Meadow prior to moving to Edgbaston.

**The Meadow was the venue for three FA Cup semi-finals:**

| | | | |
|---|---|---|---|
| 1882-83 | Blackburn Olympic 4 Old Carthusians 0 | Att. | 2,500 |
| 1883-84 | Blackburn Rovers 1 Notts County 0 | Att. | 15,000 |
| 1885-86 | Small Heath 0 West Bromwich Albion 4 | Att. | 4,100 |

In 1897, Buffalo Bill (Wild Bill Hickok) brought his star-studded Wild West Road Show to the Aston Lower Grounds Meadow which was attended by 5,000 spectators.

However, it is believed that the record turn out for football match at the Lower Grounds Meadow was that of 15,000 for the FA Cup semi-final of 1884 between Blackburn Rovers and Notts County.

In October 1888, Villa played their first game against overseas opposition when they entertained the Canadian touring side in a friendly at the Lower Grounds Meadow, instead of staging it at their Wellington Road ground in Perry Barr.

A game played under electric lights between Birmingham and Nottingham took place at the Lower Grounds on 28 October 1878. Birmingham won 2-1.

## ASTON PARK

It is now understood that Aston Villa played quite a few matches on a measured strip of land on the old deer park surrounding Aston Hall. At the time it was called the Aston Upper Grounds (notably Aston Park today) and the average attendance here was said to be between 1,500 and 2,000, bearing in mind that the pitch itself was fenced off!

It is probably true that the first game Villa played at Aston Park took place in January 1875 when they met neighbours Aston Park Unity.

However, it is unsure as to what playing formation the clubs agreed to use, as both had 14 players on the pitch.

Villa's 'side' (under Sheffield Association rules) was: W Scattergood (goalkeeper), G Matthews (captain), WH Price, S McBenn, WB Mason, A Walters, EB Lee, J Hughes, A Robbins, WW Wiess, H Matthews, TF Smith, C Midgley and FA Lewis.

It was reported in a newspaper that Villa lost 'a well-contested game'. Without confirmation, this may well have been Aston Villa Football Club's first match!

## ASTON (PARK) UNITY

Villa's playing record against Unity:
FA Cup

| Venue | P | W | D | L | F | A |
|---|---|---|---|---|---|---|
| Home | 1 | 1 | 0 | 0 | 3 | 1 |

Aston Unity - also a very useful cricket club in the Birmingham League - met Aston Villa in the third round of the FA Cup in January 1883. A crowd of 4,000 at Perry Barr saw Villa win 3-1 with goals from Eli Davis, Howard Vaughton and Archie Hunter.

Formerly known as Aston Park Unity, they were Villa's first-ever opponents, playing a friendly game at Aston Hall in January 1875, which they won 'narrowly'.

Players with both clubs include: WW Ashmore, JH Burton, FHH Dawson, JHG Devey, W Devey, TW Green, SR Law, WW Randle.

## ATHERSMITH, WILLIAM CHARLES

Born: Bloxwich, Staffs, 10 May 1872. Died: Shifnal, 18 September 1910.
Career: Walsall Road Council School, Bloxwich Wanderers, Bloxwich Strollers, Unity Gas Depot, Aston Villa (February 1891). Birmingham (June 1901), Grimsby Town (trainer June 1907 to May 1909).

One of the fastest and fleetest right-wingers of his time, Charlie Athersmith reigned supreme on his day with only Billy Bassett (West Bromwich Albion) comparable to him for speed and ability. A great touchline player, he centred with unerring precision but at times was a trifle wayward ...and he was penalised several times for straying offside, so eager was he to get forward!

He spent ten excellent years at Villa Park during which time he won five League championship medals (1894, '95,'97,'99 and 1900) and two FA Cup winners' medals (1895 and '97). He also won 12 England caps and in 1896-97 won every honour in the game as Villa captured the coveted League and Cup double. It is reported that during one game (v Sheffield United) the rain was so severe that Athersmith borrowed an umbrella from one of the spectators to shield himself as he ran up and down the wing. After scoring 86 goals in 311 senior appearances for Villa he went on to play over 100 times for rivals Birmingham.

## ATHLETIC BILBAO

Villa's playing record against Bilbao:
UEFA Cup

| Venue | P | W | D | L | F | A |
|---|---|---|---|---|---|---|
| Home | 2 | 2 | 0 | 0 | 4 | 1 |
| Away | 2 | 0 | 2 | 0 | 1 | 1 |
| Totals | 4 | 2 | 2 | 0 | 5 | 2 |

Aston Villa first played the Spanish club Athletic Bilbao in a two-legged third round UEFA Cup-tie in season 1977-78. After winning their home match 2-0 in front of almost 33,000 fans (visiting 'keeper Iribar with an own-goal and John Deehan the scorers), Villa travelled to the Basque region of Spain and before a 39,000 crowd forced a 1-1 draw in the return leg to go through 3-1 on aggregate. Dennis Mortimer scored a fine goal for Villa in Bilbao.

The third and fourth meetings were also in the UEFA Cup in season 1997-98 and again Villa went through, beating the Spaniards 2-1 at home (after a 0-0 away draw) in a tightly contested second round tie. There were 46,000 fans inside Bilbao's 'Cathedral' ground in Spain and almost 36,000 at Villa Park where Ian Taylor (28 minutes) and Dwight Yorke (50) scored important goals before substitute Ziggy Gonzales replied on 70 minutes with his first touch!

## ATLETICO MADRID

Villa's playing record against Atletico:

UEFA Cup

| Venue | P | W | D | L | F | A |
|---|---|---|---|---|---|---|
| Home | 1 | 1 | 0 | 0 | 2 | 1 |
| Away | 1 | 0 | 0 | 1 | 0 | 1 |
| Totals | 2 | 1 | 0 | 1 | 2 | 2 |

Aston Villa and Atletico met each other in the quarter-finals of the UEFA Cup in March 1998. Around 47,000 fans saw Villa lose by a goal to nil - scored from the penalty spot in the 42nd minute by Italian Christian Viera - inside the impressive Vicente Calderon Stadium in Madrid, and there were 39,163 spectators present for the return fixture fortnight later which Villa won 2-1.....but to no avail as they went out of the competition on the away goal rule!

Caminero put Atletico ahead at Villa Park on 33 minutes; Ian Taylor equalised on 72 and Stan Collymore made it 2-1 soon afterwards (via the crossbar) but Villa couldn't score again and went out gallantly. As for Atletico, they were eliminated in the semi-final by Lazio.

Ron Atkinson managed both Atletico Madrid (1988-89) and Aston Villa (1991-94).

## ATKINSON, DALIAN ROBERT

Born: Shrewsbury, 21 March 1968.

Career: Ipswich Town (apprentice, June 1984, professional, June 1987), Sheffield Wednesday (£450,000, June 1989), Real Sociedad (£1.7 million, August 1990), Aston Villa (£1.6 million, July 1991), Fenerbahce (June 1996).

A stocky, well-built striker, Dalian Atkinson had mixed fortunes during time at Villa Park. On his day he was terrific, but he did have his moments! Capped by England 'B', he battled against injury for long periods but nevertheless was a fine player who gained a League Cup winners medal with Villa in 1994 and went on to score 36 goals in 114 appearances for the club before leaving for Turkey in 1996.

## ATKINSON, RONALD FREDERICK

Born: Liverpool, 18 March 1939

Career: Lea Village School (Stechford), BSA Tools (worker and footballer), Aston Villa (professional, May 1956), Wolverhampton Wanderers (trialist), Headington United, now Oxford United (July 1959), Witney Town (May 1971), Kettering Town (player-manager, October 1971), Cambridge United (manager, November 1974), West Bromwich Albion (manager January 1978), Manchester United (manager, June 1981), West Bromwich Albion (manager, again, September 1987), Atletico Madrid (manager, October 1988-January 1989), Sheffield Wednesday (manager, February 1989-May 1991), Aston Villa (manager, June 1991-November 1994), Coventry City (manager, February 1995- November 1996), Sheffield Wednesday (briefly in 1998), Nottingham Forest (manager, second half of 1998-99 season).

A man who loves jewellery, 'Big Ron' had a fine footballing life - some 43 years to be precise from 1956 to 1999 - and in that time he certainly had his ups and downs.

As a player Ron Atkinson, who never made the first XI at Villa Park, amassed over 500 League and Cup appearances during a twelve-year association at The Manor Ground, being part of the Oxford United team that gained entry into the Football League in 1962 and which won the Fourth Division title in 1968.

As boss of Kettering, he guided them to the championships of both the Southern League North and Premier Divisions and came within one vote of getting the non-League team into the Football League! He then assembled a side at Cambridge which was good enough to win promotion from the Fourth Division in 1977. Indeed, they were well on their way to winning promotion to the Second Division when he took over at The Hawthorns in 1978. He quickly guided the Baggies into the semi-finals of the FA Cup and to the quarter-finals of the UEFA Cup. He twice won the FA Cup during his spell at Old Trafford (1983 and 1985) and in 1990-91 led Sheffield Wednesday into the top flight. He also guided Wednesday to victory over his former club Manchester United in the Rumbelows-sponsored League Cup Final and then saw the Owls finish second in the same competition two

years later. As the manager of Aston Villa, he built a fine young side which at one time looked as if it might win a few top honours, including the Premier League title, but the team ran out of steam near the end of the 1992-93 campaign and Manchester United took control after that. However, he did see the League Cup come back to Villa Park the following season before he left for pastures new. While he was team manager, Villa played a total of 140 League matches. They won 55, drew 36 and lost 49.

Ron Atkinson once said: "Women should be in the kitchen, the discotheque and the boutique - but not in football!"

Another quote from Ron: "It's bloody tough being a legend."

In October 1978 Atkinson was offered £1,000-a-week to manage the NASL club Philadelphia Fury. He turned it down saying: "There's a lot happening at West Brom and I don't want to miss it!"

## ATTENDANCES

The all-time record crowd at Villa Park is that of 76,588 for the sixth round FA Cup-tie against Derby County on 2 March 1946.

The biggest League crowd ever to assemble on the ground is 69,472 for the Midlands derby with Wolverhampton Wanderers on Boxing Day 1949 (Trevor Ford scored four goals in Villa's 5-1 victory over the FA Cup holders). This beat the previous record of 68,099, set two years earlier, also against Wolves.

The biggest mid-week crowd at Villa Park - 73,632 - assembled there in January 1931 for the visit of Arsenal in a third round FA Cup replay. In the Football League Cup, the best crowd at Villa Park to date has been that of 58,667 for the visit of Manchester United in the semi-final second leg clash on 23 December 1970.

In European Cup football, the biggest single attendance for a Villa home game is 49,619 v Barcelona (UEFA Cup) on 1 March 1978. (90,000 fans saw the return leg in the Nou Camp Stadium).

When Santos of Brazil (including Pele) visited Villa Park for a friendly match in 1972 the attendance that night was 54,437 (with £35,000 taken in gate receipts).

A crowd of 68,029 - the second biggest ever recorded for a Second Division match (Newcastle United had one higher) - saw Villa entertain Coventry City on 30 October 1937. Almost 45,000 saw the return fixture at Highfield Road in March.

A record crowd for a Third Division match - 48,110 - attended the Aston Villa v Bournemouth encounter at Villa Park in February 1972.

THE COMPLETE ENCYCLOPAEDIA OF ASTON VILLA F.C.  THE COMPLETE ENCYCLOPAEDIA OF ASTON VILLA F.C.

13

The record attendance at Villa's Wellington Road ground was 26,849 for their FA Cup-tie with Preston North End on 7 January 1888.

A crowd of 99,225 saw the 1957 FA Cup Final between Villa and Manchester United. Nine games prior to that, just 8,252 fans had witnessed the Villa-Sunderland League game at Villa Park!

Villa's lowest League attendance has been 600 - for the visit of Accrington to Perry Barr on 27 October 1888.

The lowest League crowd ever recorded at Villa Park is 2,900 for the visit of Brentford on 13 February 1915.

And the smallest turn out for an FA Cup-tie on the same ground the ground has been 12,205 v Millwall in January 1986.

Villa were forced to play their 1st round 1st leg European Cup-tie against Besiktas (Turkey) behind closed doors at Villa Park and the official attendance was given as just 167.

The last game at Villa Park before the outbreak of the Second World War was a Central League game against Derby County. It was attended by 5,000 spectators (2 September 1939).

**This is how the Villa Park attendance record has been broken:**

| | | |
|---|---|---|
| 17 Apr 1897 | Villa v Blackburn Rovers (League) | 15,000 |
| 19 Apr 1897 | Villa v Wolves (League) | 35,000 |
| 15 Jan 1898 | Villa v Sheffield United (League) | 41,200 |
| 29 Apr 1899 | Villa v Liverpool (League) | 41,357 |
| 7 Mar 1900 | Villa v Sheffield United (League) | 50,000 |
| 22 Apr 1911 | Villa v Manchester United (League) | 50,885 |
| 21 Sept 1913 | Villa v West Brom. Albion (League) | 55,064 |
| 23 Apr 1913 | Villa v Sunderland (League) | 59,740 |
| 6 Nov 1920 | Villa v West Brom. Albion (League) | 66,094 |
| 5 Feb 1926 | Villa v Arsenal (FA Cup) | 71,446 |
| 2 Mar 1929 | Villa v Arsenal (FA Cup) | 73,686 |
| 25 Jan 1930 | Villa v Walsall (FA Cup) | 74.626 |
| 5 Mar 1938 | Villa v Manchester City (FA Cup) | 75,540 |
| 2 Mar 1946 | Villa v Derby County (FA Cup) | 76,588 |

**Villa's average home League attendances: 1888 to 2001:**

| | | | |
|---|---|---|---|
| 1888-89 | 4,781 | 1952-53 | 33.440 |
| 1889-90 | 5,727 | 1953-54 | 30,401 |

| | | | |
|---|---|---|---|
| 1901-02 | 19,647 | 1965-66 | 20,702 |
| 1902-03 | 20,272 | 1966-67 | 21,576 |
| 1903-04 | 19,818 | 1967-68 | 19,745 |
| 1904-05 | 16,235 | 1968-69 | 24,547 |
| 1904-06 | 18,842 | 1969-70 | 27,534 |
| 1906-07 | 24,631 | 1970-71 | 26,123 |
| 1907-08 | 20,236 | 1971-72 | 31,952 |
| 1908-09 | 19,078 | 1972-73 | 27,689 |
| 1909-10 | 22,157 | 1973-74 | 23,413 |
| 1910-11 | 23,104 | 1974-75 | 27,654 |
| 1911-12 | 20,270 | 1975-76 | 38,874 |
| 1912-13 | 26,771 | 1976-77 | 34,759 |
| 1913-14 | 24,450 | 1977-78 | 35,463 |
| 1914-15 | 13,842 | 1978-79 | 32,838 |
| 1919-20 | 32,155 | 1979-80 | 27,995 |
| 1920-21 | 35,052 | 1980-81 | 33,641 |
| 1921-22 | 32,690 | 1981-82 | 26,875 |
| 1922-23 | 28,237 | 1982-83 | 23,752 |
| 1923-24 | 29,732 | 1983-84 | 21,245 |
| 1924-25 | 27,410 | 1984-85 | 18,318 |
| 1925-26 | 28,117 | 1985-86 | 15,270 |
| 1926-27 | 28,917 | 1986-87 | 18,171 |
| 1927-28 | 33,649 | 1987-88 | 18,342 |
| 1928-29 | 31,883 | 1988-89 | 23,310 |
| 1929-30 | 28,671 | 1989-90 | 25,544 |
| 1930-31 | 30,042 | 1990-91 | 25,663 |
| 1931-32 | 32,285 | 1991-92 | 24,814 |
| 1932-33 | 31,294 | 1992-93 | 29,594 |
| 1933-34 | 28,983 | 1993-94 | 29,015 |
| 1934-35 | 32,365 | 1994-95 | 29,756 |
| 1935-36 | 39,106 | 1995-96 | 32,616 |
| 1936-37 | 36,797 | 1996-97 | 36,027 |
| 1937-38 | 41,856 | 1997-98 | 36,137 |
| 1938-39 | 34,638 | 1998-99 | 36,937 |
| 1946-47 | 41,436 | 1999-2000 | 31,696 |
| 1947-48 | 36,843 | 2000-01 | 31,596 |
| 1948-49 | 47,168 | | |
| 1949-50 | 40,080 | | |
| 1950-51 | 38,780 | * Premiership football since 1992-93 |
| 1951-52 | 38,940 | | |

*A full house at Villa Park in 1930.*

| | | | |
|---|---|---|---|
| 1890-91 | 5,818 | 1954-55 | 29,066 |
| 1891-92 | 6,546 | 1955-56 | 29,856 |
| 1892-93 | 7,540 | 1956-57 | 30,547 |
| 1893-94 | 10,626 | 1957-58 | 28,719 |
| 1894-95 | 8,700 | 1958-59 | 32,837 |
| 1895-96 | 13,143 | 1959-60 | 34,711 |
| 1896-97 | 13,200 | 1960-61 | 33,720 |
| 1897-98 | 16,323 | 1961-62 | 32,323 |
| 1898-99 | 20,618 | 1962-63 | 32,074 |
| 1899-00 | 17,734 | 1963-64 | 22.322 |
| 1900-01 | 16,882 | 1964-65 | 21,845 |

**Attendances of over 63,000 recorded at Villa Park:**

| | | |
|---|---|---|
| 22 Mar 1969 | Everton v Man City (FA Cup s/f) | 63,025 |
| 16 Feb 1957 | Villa v Bristol City (FA Cup) | 63,099 |
| 27 Dec 1948 | Villa v Wolves (League) | 63,572 |
| 3 Oct 1936 | Villa v Coventry City (League) | 63,686 |
| 12 Jan 1946 | Villa v Birmingham City (FL South) | 63,820 |
| 22 Jan 1949 | Villa v Arsenal (League) | 64,190 |
| 1 Feb 1961 | Villa v Peterborough Utd (FA Cup) | 64,531 |
| 20 Aug 1962 | Villa v Tottenham Hotspur (League) | 64,751 |
| 27 Apr 1963 | Man Utd v Southampton (FA Cup s/f) | 64,767 |
| 19 Aug 1950 | Villa v West Brom Albion (League) | 65,036 |
| 30 Mar 1937 | Villa v Newcastle Utd (League) | 65,437 |
| 3 Feb 1945 | England v Scotland (Victory Int.) | 65,780 |
| 28 Feb 1948 | Villa v Arsenal (League) | 66,045 |
| 6 Nov 1920 | Villa v West Brom Albion (League) | 66,694 |
| 27 Mar 1965 | Chelsea v Liverpool (FA Cup s/f) | 67,686 |
| 10 Nov 1948 | England v Wales (International) | 67,770 |
| 30 Oct 1937 | Villa v Coventry City (League) | 68,029 |
| 26 Dec 1947 | Villa v Wolves (League) | 68,099 |
| 21 Mar 1953 | Blackpool v Tottenham (FA Cup s/f) | 68,221 |
| 27 Mar 1954 | Port Vale v W.B.A (FA Cup s/f) | 68,221 |
| 19 Feb 1949 | Villa v Manchester Utd (League) | 68,354 |
| 22 Jan 1938 | Villa v Blackpool (FA Cup) | 69,208 |
| 27 Dec 1949 | Villa v Wolves (League) | 69,462 |
| 23 Mar 1946 | Bolton v Charlton Ath. (FA Cup s/f) | 70,819 |
| 18 Feb 1961 | Villa v Tottenham Hot. (FA Cup) | 69,672 |

THE COMPLETE ENCYCLOPAEDIA OF ASTON VILLA F.C.  THE COMPLETE ENCYCLOPAEDIA OF ASTON VILLA F.C.

14

*Villa Park for the visit of Arsenal in 1951.*

| 12 Mar 1960 | Villa v Preston North End (FA Cup) | 69,732 |
| 22 Mar 1958 | Fulham v Manch Utd. (FA Cup s/f) | 69,745 |
| 17 Mar 1956 | Man City v Tottenham (FA Cup s/f) | 69,788 |
| 18 Mar 1961 | Burnley v Tottenham H (FA Cup s/f) | 69,968 |
| 13 Mar 1948 | Blackpool v Tottenham (FA Cup s/f) | 70,687 |
| 4 Jan 1949 | Villa v Cardiff City (FA Cup) | 70,718 |
| 5 Feb 1926 | Villa v Arsenal (FA Cup) | 71,446 |
| 14 Jan 1931 | Villa v Arsenal (FA Cup) | 73,632 |
| 2 Mar 1929 | Villa v Arsenal (FA Cup) | 73,686 |
| 28 Feb 1948 | Man Utd v PNE (FA Cup replay) | 74,213 |
| 25 Jan 1930 | Villa v Walsall (FA Cup) | 74,626 |
| 5 Mar 1938 | Villa v Manchester City (FA Cup) | 75,540 |
| 2 Mar 1946 | Villa v Derby County (FA Cup) | 76,588 |

## Attendance Facts & Figures

A crowd of 101,117 saw the 1905 FA Final between Aston Villa and Newcastle United at The Crystal Palace.

Eight years later, on the same ground, there were 121,919 spectators present for the 1913 FA Cup Final between Villa and Sunderland - the biggest audience any Villa team has played in front of.

Four days after that 1913 Final, almost 60,000 spectators packed into Roker Park to see the vital League game between the two clubs.

The third six-figure attendance to watch Aston Villa in action - 110,000 - assembled inside the huge Reichsportfield in Berlin to watch a friendly game against a German Select XI in May 1938.

A record crowd of 64,612 (beaten in March 1937) saw the West Bromwich Albion v Aston Villa FA Cup-tie at The Hawthorns in February 1925.

On 30 October 1937, a Second Division crowd record of 68,029 saw Villa held to a 1-1 draw at home by Coventry City.

Villa's first home League game after the Second World (v Middlesbrough on 31 August 1946) attracted a crowd of 50,572.

The fourth round FA Cup replay between Aston Villa and non-League Peterborough United at Villa Park on 1 February 1961 attracted an evening attendance of 64,531.

A record crowd of 75,031 packed into The Valley to see the Charlton Athletic v Aston Villa 5th round FA Cup-tie in February 1938.

The biggest League attendance for a game at Old Trafford is 70,504, Manchester United v Aston Villa on 27 December 1920. In contrast there were only 7,953 spectators present at the same venue when Villa played Burnley in a League Cup semi-final replay in 1961.

A crowd of 70,000 saw the Manchester City- Villa League game at Maine Road in December 1929. And there were 66,456 fans present at Highbury for the Arsenal-Villa First Division clash in September 1938 - the biggest attendance anywhere in the country during this last full season before WW2.

The average League attendance of 34,711 at Villa Park in 1959-60 was the best in the Second Division that season..... better than 14 in the First Division and topped all in the two other Divisions (3 & 4).

The top attendance at Home Park, Plymouth has been 43,596 - when Villa were the visitors for a Second Division game in October 1936.

On 12 March 1938, a crowd of 44,930 packed into Highfield Road to watch the Coventry City-Villa Second Division game. This was to remain a ground record for the Sky Blues until surpassed in 1967 when over 51,000 fans saw a promotion game against Wolves.

The biggest crowd ever to assemble at Vale Park did so in February 1960, when 48,749 spectators witnessed the 5th round FA Cup-tie between Port Vale and Villa.

The three FA Cup games between Villa and Charlton in February 1938 attracted a total of 201,344 spectators and the three League Cup Final matches between Villa and Everton was seen by an aggregate of 205,812 fans.

The biggest attendance ever to watch a second XI game at Villa Park has been 23,667 - for the Villa v Birmingham Central League fixture in February 1928. 'Pongo' Waring made his Villa debut in the fixture.

The first time the one million spectator barrier was broken in attendance figures for a single season at Villa Park was in 1937-38 when the average League crowd was almost 42,000 (aggregate 878,976) and three cup-ties pulled in 206,278) giving an overall figure of 1,085,254. The nearest Villa's League crowds have come to topping the one million mark was in 1947-48 - the 21 home matches realising an aggregate of 990,528 (average 47,168 - a club record).

## AWAY FROM HOME

Aston Villa's best away win in the Football League (goals scored) has been 8-3 at Leicester City on 2 January 1932.

They also won 7-3 at Nottingham Forest in a First Division match in December 1903; triumphed 6-0 at Old Trafford in March 1914; won by the same scoreline at Oldham in November 1971; beat Burnley 6-2 at Turf Moor in October 1889; whipped Darwen 5-1 in October 1891; succeeded handsomely by 6-3 at West Bromwich Albion in October 1893 and won well at Burnley again by 6-3 in April 1894.

Villa's best Cup victory on the road (in any major competition) has been that of 9-0 at Shankhouse in a 4th round FA Cup-tie in December 1887. Villa also defeated Clapton Orient (now Leyton Orient) 8-0 in a 4th round FA Cup replay in January 1929, Wednesbury Old Athletic 7-4 in a 3rd round tie in December 1883 and Notts County 6-0 as recently as January 1982, also in the 3rd round of the FA Cup.

The greatest number of away victories in a League season has been 13 - in 1987-88 when promotion was gained from the Second Division.

Villa went 13 away games without defeat in the League between 5 September 1987 and 23 January 1988.

Villa won six away League games in succession between 6 February and 11 September 1897.

Villa lost 10 successive away League games between 12 December 1924 and 13 April 1925.

In the Premiership so far, Villa's best win tally for a season has been 21 out of 42 - in the initial campaign of 1992-93.

Villa failed to record a single away win in the Football League in season 1975-76.

THE COMPLETE ENCYCLOPAEDIA OF ASTON VILLA F.C.          THE COMPLETE ENCYCLOPAEDIA OF ASTON VILLA F.C.

15

Villa's only away League win in season 1969-70 was just across the city - 2-0 over Blues at St Andrew's.

Aston Villa have gained more away victories in the League against Everton (22) than they have against any other club. They have won 20 times at Arsenal.

Villa did not lose a pre-semi-final FA Cup game away from home between the 5th round in 1928 and the 4th round in 1939. In that period they played 14 matches (won 9 and drew 5). However, they did lose seven home games on the trot as well as three semi-finals on neutral grounds.

## BACHE, JOSEPH WILLIAM

Born: Stourbridge, 8 February 1880. Died: 10 November 1960.
Career: Stourbridge (July 1897), Aston Villa (professional, December 1900), Mid Rhondda (player-manager, August 1919), Grimsby Town (player/coach, August 1920), Rot Weiss FC Frankfurt (coach-trainer, May 1921), Mannheim FC (player, October 1924). He returned to Villa

Park as reserve team coach in 1926-27. A cultured inside-forward Joe Bache had few equals in the art of dribbling, although at times he could be somewhat selfish! A good-tempered, brainy footballer he displayed a masterly technique out on the pitch and gave Villa great service as a player, accumulating a terrific record - 184 goals in 474 first-team appearances. He won seven England caps between 1903 and 1911 and succeeded Howard Spencer as the Villa captain. He formed a wonderful left-wing partnership with Albert Hall and gained two FA Cup winners' medals (1905 and 1913) and a First Division championship medal in 1910. In later years he became a licensee in Aston and attended most of Villa's home matches.

## BAIRD, JOHN

Born: Dumbartonshire, Scotland, 1871. Died: Scotland c 1937.
Career: Vale of Leven (1886), Vale Wanderers (1887), Kidderminster Olympic (1888), Kidderminster Harriers (1889), Aston Villa (October 1891), Leicester Fosse (August 1895-April 1896). Retired and returned to Scotland.
Strength, skill and stamina were the attributes of John Baird, a real teak-tough defender who could play as a full-back or left-half. He appeared for Aston Villa in their 1892 FA Cup Final defeat at the hands of neighbours West Bromwich Albion and made 69 first team appearances in the claret and blue strip.

## BAKER, ALAN REEVES

Born: Tipton, 22 June 1944,
Career: Brierley Hill Schoolboys, Aston Villa (junior, June 1958, professional, July 1961), Walsall (£10,000, July 1966). Retired in 1971 to become a leather cutter in Walsall
Highly-rated as a youngster, inside-forward Alan Baker - who played alongside Norman Ashe as a Schoolboy - went on to have a very useful footballing career. He gained a League Cup runners-up prize with Aston Villa in 1963 and scored 17 goals in 109 senior outings during his stay at Villa Park. After leaving the club he netted 36 times in 164 appearances for the Saddlers.

## BALABAN, BOSKO

Born: Rijeka, Croatia, 15 October 1978.
Career: Dinamo Zagreb, Aston Villa (£6 million August 2001).
A Croatian International striker, Balaban chose Villa ahead of Fiorentina and Marseille saying "I want to grace the English Premiership."

## BALL, JOHN HENRY

Born: Birmingham, 1857.
Career: Arcadians (1877), Aston Villa (August 1879), Walsall Town Swifts (July 1880-May 1884).
Goalkeeper John Ball was only 5ft. 6ins tall, the first of his two senior appearances for Aston Villa being in the club's initial FA Cup-tie against Stafford Road in December 1879. He did not play competitive football after 1884.

## BALL, THOMAS EDGAR

Born: Unsworth, County Durham, 11 February 1899. Died: Brick Kiln Lane, Perry Barr, 11 November 1923.
Career: Felling Colliery FC (1915), Newcastle United (July 1919), Aston Villa (January 1920-November 1923).
Tommy Ball was only 24 years of age when he was tragically shot dead in November 1923 by his policeman neighbour, George Stagg who was later found guilty and sentenced to death (subsequently commuted to life imprisonment).
Ball was a strapping centre-half, who was being groomed to replace Frank Barson at the heart of the Villa defence. He was a gentleman off the field and a real lion on it! His death came as a bitter blow to the club, for Ball was destined for international honours without a shadow of doubt. He had appeared in 77 games for Villa.

## BANIK OSTRAVA

Villa's playing record against the Czechs:
UEFA Cup

| Venue | P | W | D | L | F | A |
|-------|---|---|---|---|---|---|
| Home | 1 | 1 | 0 | 0 | 3 | 1 |
| Away | 1 | 1 | 0 | 0 | 2 | 1 |
| Totals | 2 | 2 | 0 | 0 | 5 | 2 |

Aston Villa beat Banik Ostrava 5-2 on aggregate over two legs in a 1st round UEFA Cup-tie in 1990-91. The opening game at Villa Park on 19 September resulted in a 3-1 win in front of 27,317 fans and a fortnight later Villa made progress by taking the return leg 2-1 in Czechoslovakia where the turnout was 24,164. Villa's centre-back Derek Mountfield scored in both games.

## BANKS, HERBERT EDWARD

Born: Coventry, 1874. Died: Smethwick, 1947.
Career: Everton (1896-97), Third Lanark (August 1897), Millwall Athletic (June 1898), Aston Villa (April 1901), Bristol City (November 1901), Watford (May 1903). Retired 1904 and later worked for a Birmingham-based engineering firm.
Inside-forward Herbie Banks was signed a month after playing for England against Ireland. He made five appearances for Villa and after leaving the club scored 18 goals in 40 in League games for Bristol City and 21 in only 19 outings for Watford.

## BARBER, THOMAS

Born: West Stanley, 12 July 1886. Died: Birmingham, September 1925 (of tuberculosis).
Career: Todd's Nook Boarding School, Hamotley FC (1905), Bolton Wanderers (junior, August 1907, professional, July 1908) Aston Villa (December 1912), Stalybridge Celtic (March 1919), Crystal Palace (1919-20 season), Merthyr Town (September 1920), Pontypridd (January 1921), Walsall (August 1921-May 1922).

THE COMPLETE ENCYCLOPAEDIA OF ASTON VILLA F.C.    THE COMPLETE ENCYCLOPAEDIA OF ASTON VILLA F.C.

16

Wing-half Tommy Barber scored 10 goals in 68 appearances for Aston Villa and also played for the Footballers' Battalion during the Great War when he was unfortunately wounded in combat, the injury eventually forcing him to quit football in 1922.

A clever, enterprising half-back, Barber won a Second Division championship medal with Bolton in 1910 and then scored the winning goal (a smartly taken header) for Villa in the 1913 FA Cup Final versus Sunderland in front of almost 122,000 spectators at The Crystal Palace.

## BARCELONA (CF)

Villa's playing record against the Spanish club:

| Venue | P | W | D | L | F | A |
|---|---|---|---|---|---|---|
| Home | 2 | 1 | 1 | 0 | 5 | 2 |
| Away | 2 | 0 | 0 | 2 | 1 | 3 |
| Totals | 4 | 1 | 1 | 2 | 6 | 5 |

Aston Villa first encountered the Spanish giants on 1 March 1978, in the first leg of a 4th round UEFA Cup-tie at Villa Park. In front of a 49,619 crowd, Barcelona took a 2-0 lead through Johan Cruyff and Rafael Zuvira. Then in the 82nd minute, the impressive Cruyff was taken off and Villa capitalised, scoring twice, first through Ken McNaught and secondly, late on, through John Deehan to earn a creditable 2-2 draw - against the odds! A fortnight later Villa went to the Nou Camp Stadium and with 90,000 fans present, they lost narrowly by two goals to one to bow out of the competition 3-4 on aggregate. It may well have been a different story had John Gidman not been sent-off as early as the 23rd minute, but even then Villa took the lead through Brian Little but couldn't hold on as Migueli and the Italian Aseni delivered killer blows for the Spaniards. (Barcelona lost in the semi-final to PSV Eindhoven).

Villa returned to the Nou Camp to play Barcelona in the first leg of the European Super Cup on 19 January 1983. This time there were 40,000 inside the stadium to see the Spanish club take a one goal lead, Marcos scoring on 57 minutes. In the return fixture at Villa Park a week later, a crowd of 31,570 saw Villa storm back to win 3-0 (after extra time) and so take the trophy in style. Gary Shaw, Gordon Cowans (snapping in a penalty rebound) and McNaught were the scorers in a match that was littered with cynical fouls, off-the-ball incidents, spitting, elbowing and the faking of injury as well as diving! Three players were sent-off - Alberto of Barcelona (57 minutes for a second yellow card), his colleague Marcos (for spitting at Hughes) and Villa's Allan Evans, late on. Besides the three sendings-off, there were five more yellow cards handed out (four in just 55 seconds), fouls galore with over 40 free-kicks being awarded (27 against the Spaniards). It was obvious that Barcelona had one main aim - not to lose! They came unstuck - and rightly so!

*Deehan (left) in sight of goal in the Nou Camp, 1978.*

*Leighton Phillips and Johann Cruff exchange pennants prior to the UEFA Cup game at Villa Park in 1978.*

## BARI

The Italian club paid £850,000 to Aston Villa for the services of Gordon Cowans and Paul Rideout on 1 July 1988. A shade over three years later, in August 1991, David Platt left Villa Park for the same club in a £5.5 million deal.

## BARKER, JEFFREY

Born: Scunthorpe, 16 October 1915. Died: 1985.
Career: Goole Town, Scunthorpe United (Aston Villa, November 1936), Huddersfield Town (November 1945), Scunthorpe United (August 1948). Retired June 1952.

Left-half Jeff Barker made only three appearances for Aston Villa, stepping into Bob Iverson's boots for First Division League games against Burnley, Sheffield United and Tottenham Hotspur in November/December 1937. He left the club for Huddersfield Town and later returned to his first love, Scunthorpe United in August 1948 and starred for the 'Iron' in their first season of League Football in 1950-51. He retired in 1952 having amassed over 150 senior appearances during his career.

## BARNET

Aston Villa have yet to meet Barnet in League or Cup football.
Player with both clubs: IV Powell.

## BARNIE-ADSHEAD, DR. WILLIAM EWART

Born: Dudley, 9 April 1901. Died: Birmingham, January 1951.
Career: Birmingham University, Corinthians (1919), Aston Villa (August 1920), Corinthians (June 1923).

An amateur centre-half, Barnie-Adshead appeared in only two first team games for Villa (owing to his University studies) before returning to non-League action 1923. Also a very useful county cricketer with Worcestershire (12 games played, averaging 11.61 from 22 innings) he won England Amateur international honours at soccer whilst at University where he duly qualified as a surgeon.

## BARNSLEY

Villa's playing record against the Tykes:
Football League/Premiership

| Venue | P | W | D | L | F | A |
|---|---|---|---|---|---|---|
| Home | 6 | 3 | 2 | 1 | 9 | 3 |
| Away | 6 | 5 | 1 | 0 | 16 | 2 |
| Totals | 12 | 8 | 3 | 1 | 25 | 5 |

THE COMPLETE ENCYCLOPAEDIA OF ASTON VILLA F.C.  THE COMPLETE ENCYCLOPAEDIA OF ASTON VILLA F.C.

17

FA Cup

| | | | | | | |
|---|---|---|---|---|---|---|
| Home | 1 | 1 | 0 | 0 | 4 | 1 |
| Away | 1 | 1 | 0 | 0 | 2 | 0 |
| Totals | 2 | 2 | 0 | 0 | 6 | 1 |

League Cup

| | | | | | | |
|---|---|---|---|---|---|---|
| Home | 2 | 2 | 0 | 0 | 4 | 1 |
| Away | 1 | 1 | 0 | 0 | 1 | 0 |
| Totals | 3 | 3 | 0 | 0 | 5 | 1 |

Aston Villa first met Barnsley in 1936-37 doubling up over the Tykes, winning both Second Division matches, 4-2 at home and 4-0 away. They won the two League games the following season as well - 3-0 at home and 1-0 at Oakwell either side of Christmas. Some 34 years later - in 1971-72 - Villa recorded their third double over the Tykes by winning 4-0 at Barnsley (in September) and 2-0 at home (in January). Over 30,500 fans saw the latter game.

When they met and subsequently beat Barnsley 3-0 at Oakwell in a Premiership game in September 1997, it was the first time the teams had played against each other in a League match since January 1988 when Villa won 3-1 on the same ground.

Jasper McLuckie scored a hat-trick when Villa beat Barnsley 4-1 at home in a 2nd round FA Cup-tie in 1902-03.

Villa dumped Barnsley out of the FA Cup in the 3rd round in January 1995, winning 2-0 at Oakwell.

In 1990-91 Villa won both League Cup games 1-0 against the Tykes.

Players with both clubs include: F Barson, A Blair, RD Blanchflower, C Boden, L Butler, F Cornan, JM Deehan, J Findlay, D Geddis, S Gray, HV Henshall (Tykes WW1 guest), B Jones, AE Lindon (Tykes reserve), A Little, H Leigh, G Reeves, AF Phoenix, JW Smith (Villa reserve), C Tiler, JE Travers, T Waring, C Wigmore (Villa reserve), GJ Williams, NJ Young.
Also: R Downes (Barnsley player, Villa coach).

*Carl Tiler played for both clubs.*

### BARRETT, EARL DELLISER

Born: Rochdale, 28 April 1967
Career: Manchester City (juniors 1983, professional April 1985), Chester City (loan, March 1986), Oldham Athletic (November 1987), Aston Villa (£1.7 million, February 1992), Everton (£1.7 million, January 1995), Sheffield United (on loan, January 1998), Sheffield Wednesday (February 1998-July 1999, retired).

Stylish defender, able to play at right-back or as a centre-back, Earl Barrett appeared in exactly 150 first-class games for Aston Villa (two goals scored) before transferring to Everton for precisely the same amount of money he had cost when leaving Boundary Park some three years earlier. Capped three times by England, Barrett also represented his country at 'B' and Under-21 levels and played for the Football League side. He gained a Second Division championship in 1991 with Oldham and a League Cup winners' medal in 1994 with Villa, picking up a Charity Shield prize with Everton in 1995. Barrett made over 400 League appearances in all.

### BARRETT, KENNETH BRIAN

Born: Bromsgrove, 5 May 1938.
Career: Stoke Works FC (Bromsgrove), Aston Villa (amateur, January 1957, professional February 1957), Lincoln City (July 1959).

Winger Ken Barrett was spotted by former Aston Villa inside-forward Frank Shell playing in the local Bromsgrove League. Acting as cover for Les Smith and Peter McParland, he scored three goals in five games for Villa before transferring to Sincil Bank in 1959.

### BARROW

Aston Villa have never met Barrow in League or Cup competition. Players with both clubs include: J Burridge, JJ Hindle, HB Parkes, HJ Reece, and D Reid, (Villa reserves), T Thompson, P Withe.

### BARRY, GARETH

Born: Hastings, 23 February 1981.
Career: Brighton & Hove Albion (associate Schoolboy forms), Aston Villa (apprentice, June 1997, professional 27 February 1998).

Gareth Barry made rapid strides to reach the top of the professional football ladder after just two years at Villa Park. Born just before Aston Villa clinched the League championship in 1981, he joined the club's apprentice staff on leaving School (despite being urged on by Brighton & Hove Albion to join them) and was upgraded to professional after just eight months of intermediate and reserve team football, playing mainly in midfield. He made his senior debut as a substitute in the penultimate Premiership game of the 1997-98 season away to Sheffield Wednesday and then his full debut followed in the final encounter against Arsenal, which resulted in a 1-0 victory. Since then Barry has got better and better. Now an established defender, he passed the milestone of 100 first-class outings for Villa  during the first half of the 2000-01 campaign. He has already represented England at senior, Under-21 and Youth team levels, gaining his first two full caps as a 'sub' against Ukraine and Malta in the run-up to the Euro 2000 championships.

Barry ended the 2000-01 season with a Villa record of 121 appearances with one goal scored.

### BARSON, FRANK

Born: Grimethorpe, Sheffield, 10 April 1891. Died: Winson Green, Birmingham, 13 September 1968.
Career: Albion FC (Sheffield), Cammell Laird FC (Sheffield), Barnsley (August 1911), Aston Villa (£2,850, October 1919), Manchester United  (August 1922), Watford (May 1928), Hartlepool United (player/coach, May 1929), Wigan Borough (October 1929, initially registering as an Amateur, taking professional status again in July 1930), Rhyl Athletic (player-manager, June 1931), Stourbridge (manager, briefly, July-August 1935), Aston Villa (Youth team coach, August 1935, senior coach and head trainer, October 1935), Swansea Town (trainer, July 1947 to February 1954), Lye Town (trainer July 1954 to April 1956). He retired from football on his 65th birthday.

Frank Barson was a bastion in defence, a captain and centre-half who was a great inspiration to the rest of the team. A hard, tough, rugged Yorkshireman, he played non-League soccer in the Sheffield area for three years before becoming a professional with Barnsley in 1911. Eight years later he was transferred to Aston Villa for a then club

THE COMPLETE ENCYCLOPAEDIA OF ASTON VILLA F.C.   THE COMPLETE ENCYCLOPAEDIA OF ASTON VILLA F.C.

18

record fee and seven months later was clutching an FA Cup winners medal after Villa had defeated Huddersfield Town 1-0 in the Final. Barson also won his solitary England cap that same season, against Wales at Highbury in March 1920. He went on to appear in 108 first-class matches for Villa, scoring 10 goals before moving to Manchester United in 1922 ....after refusing to move from his Yorkshire home and live in Birmingham! He was adamant that he would never move to 'Brummagem' and often had heated words with the Aston Villa Directors. On Boxing Day 1920, so determined was he to play for Villa, and due to a train derailment, he trudged seven miles through heavy snow to make sure he arrived in time for an away game at Old Trafford. He played out of his skin and helped Villa win 3-1 in front of a record crowd of 70,504.

With United, he perhaps performed even better than he did with Villa, going on to star in 152 games for the Reds (four goals scored) in six years, up to 1928 when he switched to Watford. A very controversial player, Barson was often in trouble with referees and during his career was sent-off twelve times (twice with Villa). Indeed, he was suspended in total, for twelve months, having one lengthy ban of six months during his Watford days. He also received an eight-week suspension following an incident in the Manchester United v Manchester City FA Cup semi-final at Sheffield in March 1926 when it was alleged he had fouled Sam Cowan, City's centre-half, who was   knocked out!

Barson was promised a pub if he skippered Manchester United back to the First Division. This happened and Barson was handed a hotel in Ardwick Green. Scores of punters, full of flattery, turned up for the official opening but after 15 minutes Barson was so fed up that he handed the keys over to the head-waiter, walked out and never returned. He then quickly telegraphed his wife asking her to cancel the delivery of the furniture!

## BARTON, ANTHONY EDWARD

Born: Sutton (Surrey), 8 April 1937. Died: 20 August 1993, after a second heart attack.

Career: Surrey County FA, London Schools, Sutton United, Fulham (junior, June 1953, professional May 1954), Nottingham Forest (December 1959), Portsmouth (December 1961, later becoming player/coach and then assistant-manager/coach at Fratton Park), Aston Villa (assistant-manager June 1974, manager February 1982), Northampton Town (manager July 1984-April 1985), Southampton (assistant-manager September 1985-May 1988), Portsmouth (assistant-manager, then caretaker-manager February-June 1991). Thereafter scouted for several southern-based clubs.

A forceful England Schoolboy and Youth international right-winger, Tony

Barton retired as a player in May 1967, after making 130 League appearances at club level. He continued to serve Pompey until June 1974 when he became Ron Saunders' assistant at Villa Park (the pair had been playing colleagues in the same forward-line during their time together at Fratton Park). When Saunders quit as Villa's boss in February 1982, Barton was upgraded to team manager and within three months was celebrating European Cup success in Rotterdam! In May 1984, Barton left the club to take over as boss of Northampton Town, a position he held until September 1985 when he was forced to leave following a heart attack. At that point he accepted the post of assistant-manager to former Villa defender Chris Nicholl at Southampton. He remained at The Dell until May 1988 when he left to returned to Portsmouth as assistant-manager, taking over briefly as caretaker manager in February 1991 following the sacking of Alan Ball. Over the next two years Barton scouted for a number of clubs.

While Barton was manager of Aston Villa, the team played 103 League games, winning 47, drawing 19 and losing 37.

## BASEL (FC)

Villa's playing record against the Swiss:

| Venue | P | W | D | L | F | A |
|---|---|---|---|---|---|---|
| Home | 1 | 1 | 0 | 0 | 4 | 1 |
| Away | 1 | 0 | 1 | 0 | 1 | 1 |
| Totals | 2 | 1 | 1 | 0 | 5 | 3 |

Villa met the Swiss side in the Final of the InterToto Cup in August 2001. After a 1-1 draw in Switzerland, Villa won the return leg 4-1, to qualify for the UEFA Cup.

## BATH CITY

Villa's playing record against Bath:
Wartime

| Venue | P | W | D | L | F | A |
|---|---|---|---|---|---|---|
| Home | 1 | 1 | 0 | 0 | 1 | 0 |
| Away | 1 | 0 | 1 | 0 | 3 | 3 |
| Totals | 2 | 1 | 1 | 0 | 4 | 3 |

Aston Villa met the Southern League side in the quarter-final of the Wartime League North Cup competition in April 1944. After gaining a single goal advantage from the first leg at home (courtesy of Frank O'Donnell's 38th minute strike), Villa had to fight every inch of the way before edging through by the narrowest of margins following a 3-3 draw at Bath.

Harry Parkes scored Villa's first goal after eight minutes in the second encounter. Bob Iverson made it 2-0 five minutes later. Bath then hit back to draw level through Rosenthal and Johnson before Ronnie Starling made it 3-2 only for Gregory to snatch a late equaliser for the non-League side.

The game at Bath attracted 15,597 spectators, whilst there were 29,488 fans at Villa Park for the first leg.

Players with both clubs include: RT Edwards (also manager of Bath), WH Harris, P Maggs, AF Phoenix, CH Slade, T Waring.

Also: BC Godfrey, IV Powell (Villa players, Bath managers)

## BAXTER, WILLIAM

Born: Leven, near Methil, Fife, 21 September 1924.

Career: Vale of Leven Schools, Wolverhampton Wanderers (junior,

THE COMPLETE ENCYCLOPAEDIA OF ASTON VILLA F.C.     THE COMPLETE ENCYCLOPAEDIA OF ASTON VILLA F.C.

19

1959, professional September 1945), Aston Villa (November 1953, retiring as a player in 1956 to become the club's reserve team coach, later appointed assistant-trainer and then senior trainer at Villa Park, July 1964), St Mirren (manager, 1968-70).

Bill Baxter's footballing career spanned 31 years (1939-70) first as an aggressive, workmanlike wing-half, then coach, trainer and finally manager. He made a record 213 Central League appearances for Wolves but was unable to gain a regular first team place at Molineux due to the quality of the half-backs within the club during the time he was a professional there. After leaving in 1953 he went on to make 108 appearances for Villa (six goals scored).

## BAYERN MUNICH

Villa's playing record against the Bavarian side:
European Cup

| Venue | P | W | D | L | F | A |
|-------|---|---|---|---|---|---|
| Neutral | 1 | 1 | 0 | 0 | 1 | 0 |

Aston Villa, under manager Tony Barton, who had been in office for just seven weeks, defeated the German champions Bayern Munich 1-0 in the Final of the European Champions Cup in Rotterdam in May 1982. Peter Withe scored the all-important goal in the 67th minute with a mis-hit, close-range tap-in after some splendid work down the left by Tony Morley. After Nigel Spink had been called off the bench as early as the tenth minute to replace the injured Jimmy Rimmer in goal, Villa were second best overall, but some dogged determination, total commitment and will-power saw them through. There were upwards of 15,000 Villa supporters in a crowd of 39,776 and they celebrated in style into the early hours of the next morning. And by lifting the coveted European Cup £2 million went into Villa's bank account!

Villa's winning team in Rotterdam was: Rimmer (Spink); Swain, Williams;

*Peter Withe's winning goal in Rotterdam.*

Evans, McNaught, Mortimer; Bremner, Shaw, Withe, Cowans, Morley.
Players with both clubs: T Hitzlsperger, A McInally

## BEARD, MALCOLM

Born: Cannock, 3 May 1942.
Career: Birmingham City (junior, June 1957, professional May 1959), Aston Villa (July 1971), Atherstone United (in season 1972-73), Saudi Arabia (coach), Birmingham City (scout mid-1970s), Aston Villa (Chief Scout from 1982), Middlesbrough (coach, 1987), Portsmouth (coach, 1990), Aston Villa (reserve team coach/manager, 1997).

After scoring 32 goals in 405 senior appearances for Blues, the ever-reliable Malcolm Beard played in just six more games for Aston Villa before quitting top-class football in 1972. A tremendous wing-half, Beard won England Youth international honours, helped Blues reach the final of the Inter-Cities Fairs Cup in 1961 and was also in their League Cup winning side of 1963 - at Villa's expense!

## BEATON, WILLIAM

Born: Kincardine-on-Forth, 30 September 1935.
Career: Dunfermline Athletic, Aston Villa (£30,000, October 1958), Airdrieonians (February 1960).

As a lad Billy Beaton preferred rugby but quickly took up soccer, and made his senior debut as a goalkeeper for Dunfermline at the age of 15 against Leith. He became a competent custodian north of the border and was signed by Aston Villa manager Eric Houghton as cover for Nigel Sims. Beaton was handed just one first team outing by the club (away at Leicester soon after signing). It wasn't the greatest of baptisms as Villa crashed to a 6-3 defeat. That was his only senior outing for the club and after Houghton had been sacked and Joe Mercer moved in, Beaton became surplus to requirements and duly returned to Scotland to sign for Airdrie.

## BEDINGFIELD, FRANK

Born: Sunderland, March 1877. Died: South Africa, November 1902.
Career: South Shields Schools football, Rushden (1896), Aston Villa (June 1898), Queen's Park Rangers (August 1899), Portsmouth (September 1900). Collapsed after playing in an FA Cup-tie for Pompey in 1902. Went over to South Africa where he died of consumption, aged 25.

A useful centre-forward at reserve team level, Frank Bedingford didn't play a complete first team game for Villa! He was one of the 11 players who lined up in that unfinished League game against Sheffield Wednesday at Hillsborough in November 1898 when he scored his side's only goal. The game ended early and when Villa travelled back to play out the remaining few minutes against the Owls in March 1899 - his place was taken by Billy Garraty.

After leaving Villa Park he had brief associations with QPR (he scored 21 goals in 32 games for the London club) and Portsmouth.

## BEESON, GEORGE WILLIAM

Born: Clay Cross, Chesterfield, 31 August 1908. Died: Wythall (near Kings Heath, Birmingham), January 1999, from Alzheimer's Disease.
Career: Clay Cross FC, Chesterfield (August 1927), Sheffield Wednesday (March 1929), Aston Villa (August 1934 - in exchange for Joe Nibloe), Walsall (July 1938). Retired in 1940.

A fine figure of a man, George Beeson was a strong-tackling, hard kicking full-back who never shirked a tackle. He made 75 appearances for Sheffield Wednesday, was an England reserve and represented the Football League before joining Aston Villa in 1934 in exchange for Joe Nibloe. Beeson, who often ate two pre-match dinners (to give him strength) made 71 first team appearances in the claret and blue strip. He quit football soon after the outbreak of the Second World War and later ran a highly-successful business in Birmingham.

## BEINLICH, STEFAN

Born: Germany, 13 January 1972.
Career: PFV Bergman Bosnig (German Second Division), Aston Villa (October 1991-May 1993). Returned to Germany.

A defender, who could man midfield (if required) Beinlich was signed along with his fellow countryman Matthius Breit-kruetz. He was only 19 when he arrived at Villa Park and went on to score one goal in his 16 League appearances (nine as a substitute) before leaving the club in 1993.

THE COMPLETE ENCYCLOPAEDIA OF ASTON VILLA F.C.    THE COMPLETE ENCYCLOPAEDIA OF ASTON VILLA F.C.

20

## BENEFIT, CHARITY & TESTIMONIAL MATCHES

Here is an unofficial list of benefit, charity, testimonial and fund-raising matches which Aston Villa have taken part in over the years.

**1879-80**
Walsall Swifts 2 Villa 1                    (re Birchills Hall Iron Works)
**1883-84**
Villa 4 Walsall Swifts 0                    (S Law)
**1884-85**
Villa 5 Blackburn Rovers 2                  (Andy Hunter)
Villa 3 West Brom Albion 2                  (Archie Hunter)
**1885-86**
Villa 2 Blackburn Rovers 0                  (A Brown)
Villa 2 Derby County 0                      (E Davis)
Villa 3 West Brom Albion 1                  (ex-players)
**1886-87**
West Brom Albion 5 Villa 1                  (S Richardson)
Villa 6 West Brom Albion 3                  (S Richardson)
Villa 3 Midlands Select XI 0                (Ar. Hunter, H Vaughton)
**1887-88**
Villa 4 Crewe Alexandra 2                   (F Dawson)
**1888-89**
B'ham St George's 3 Villa 2                 (BSG players)
Villa 1 Renton 3                            (A Brown)
**1889-90**
Villa 7 Kilbirnie 3                         (Archie Hunter)
Small Heath 2 Villa 2                       (C Charsley)
Shropshire XI 1 Villa 7                     (Salop Charities)
Villa 1 West Brom Albion 0                  (J Burton, A Allen)
**1893-94**
Villa 1 Preston North End 3                 (D Hodgetts)
Villa 6 Notts County 2                      (Warwickshire CCC)
**1893-94**
Villa 4 Sheffield United 0                  (H Devey)
Small Heath 3 Villa 3                       (Small Heath club)
**1894-95**
Villa 1 Football League XI 3                (W McGregor)
Wolverhampton Wds 3 Villa 0                 (Club benefit)
**1895-96**
Villa 2 West Brom Albion 1                  (Archie Hunter's family)
Small Heath 1 Villa 3                       (E Devey)
West Brom Albion 1 Villa 1                  (R McLeod)
**1896-97**
Villa 2 Derby County 1                      (J Devey)
Stoke 3 Villa 0                             (W Dickson)
Woolwich Arsenal 1 Villa 3                  (Arsenal players)
Villa 1 Small Heath 1                       (J Elliott)
Small Heath 2 Villa 1                       (W Walton)
Villa 3 West Brom Albion 1                  (Villa players)
Notts County 1 Villa 2                      (W Bramley)
**1897-98**
West Brom Albion 2 Villa 0                  (J Reader)
Villa 2 Burlsem Port Vale 3                 (R Chatt)
**1898-99**
Villa 6 West Brom Albion 1                  (F Burton)
West Brom Albion 4 Villa 0                  (T Perry)
**1899-1900**
Villa 2 Wolverhampton Wds 2                 (S Smith)
West Brom Albion 3 Villa 2                  (J Banks)
**1900-01**
Villa 5 Sheffield United 1                  (H Spencer)
Villa 3 Celtic 1                            (AJ Evans)
**1901-02**
Villa 3 Celtic 1                            (A Evans)
Villa 1 Small Heath 1                       (Ibrox Disaster Fund)
**1902-03**
West Brom Albion 1 Villa 5                  (H Hadley)
Villa 2 West Brom Albion 1                  (W George)

**1903-04**
Villa 4 Wolverhampton Wds 0                 (W Garraty)
West Brom Albion 3 Villa 3                  (J Simmonds)
Southampton 1 Villa 1                       (H Wood)
Villa 3 West Brom Albion 0                  (J Johnson)
**1904-05**
Villa 3 Wolverhampton Wds 0                 (J Grierson, A Hall)
**1906-07**
Villa 3 Bristol City 2                      (J Bache))
**1907-08**
Villa 2 Manchester City 2                   (Colliery Disaster Fund)
**1909-10**
Villa 0 West Brom Albion 1                  (Theatrical Sports Benefit)
Villa 3 George Robey's XI 1                 (Charity benefit)
Villa 4 Newcastle United 0                  (In Aid of H Hampton)
**1912-13**
Stoke 1 Villa 2                             (T Wilkes)
**1913-14**
Combined Bristol XI 0 Villa 3               (Local Bnefit Fund)
**1918-19**
Villa 1 Birmingham 2                        (Birmingham Association)

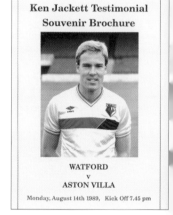

**1920-21**
Villa 1 Birmingham 1                        (Mayor's Unemployment Fund)
**1924-25**
Villa 5 West Brom Albion 5                  (Ambulance Fund)
**1925-26**
Villa 6 Birmingham 3                        (EW Strange)
**1937-38**
Cardiff City 3 Villa 0                      (At Yeovil, Charity Fund)
**1938-39**
Villa 1 West Brom Albion 1                  (League Jubilee Fund)
**1939-40**
Villa 1 West Brom Albion 1                  (League Jubilee Fund)
ICI Metals FC 1 Villa 5                     (At Perry Barr, Charity Match)
Birmingham 2 Villa 1                        (H Hibbs)
**1941-42**
Villa 1 RAF XI 2                            (Wartime Charity Match)
**1942-43**
Villa 1 Portsmouth 1                        (Wartime Charity Match)
**1943-44**
Villa 3 Portsmouth 3                        (Wartime Charity Match)
**1944-45**
Portsmouth 3 Villa 4                        (VE Day+1 Charity Match)
**1948-49**
Reading 1 Villa 1                           (M McPhee)
**1959-60**
Swindon Town v Villa                        (Swindon Town player)
**1962-63**

THE COMPLETE ENCYCLOPAEDIA OF ASTON VILLA F.C.     THE COMPLETE ENCYCLOPAEDIA OF ASTON VILLA F.C.

21

| | |
|---|---|
| Hereford United 3 Villa 2 | (G Morris) |
| 1963-64 | |
| Birmingham/Villa XI 1 London XI 6 | (V Crowe) |
| 1967-68 | |
| Wellington Town v Villa | (J Bentley) |
| Kidderminster Harriers v Villa | (D Gilbert) |
| Yeovil Town v Villa | (W Muir & W Herritty) |
| 1968-69 | |
| Bedford Town v Villa | (J Campbell) |
| 1969-70 | |
| Southend United 3 Villa res 2 | (P Robinson) |
| Villa 3 Coventry City 3 | (C Aitken) |
| 1971-72 | |
| Kidderminster Harriers v Villa | (R Cockcroft) |
| Villa '57 XI v Midlands XI (Villa Park) | (E 'Mush' Callaghan) |
| 1972-73 | |
| Hereford United 2 Villa 2 | (Benefit match) |
| Coventry City 1 Villa 1 | (E Machin) |
| Exeter City 2 Aston Villa 2 | (B Sharples) |
| 1973-74 | |
| Villa/WBA XI 2 Blues/Wolves XI 1 | (T Brown) |

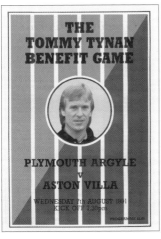

| | |
|---|---|
| 1974-75 | |
| Villa 3 Stoke City 1 | (M Wright) |
| WBA 2 Villa 2 | (R Wilson) |
| 1975-76 | |
| Villa 0 West Brom Albion 1 | (F Turnbull) |
| 1976-77 | |
| Tamworth 0 Villa XI 3 | (DJ Seedhouse) |
| Wellingborough 1 Villa 4 | (G Knibbs) |
| Villa 1 Midland All Stars 6 | (C Aitken) |
| 1977-78 | |
| Walsall 0 Villa 3 | (B Davies) |
| Select XI 2 Midlands XI 1 (Villa Park) | (J Taylor, referee) |
| | |
| 1978-79 | |
| Villa 1 Villa LC '75 XI 2 | (K Leonard) |
| Villa 6 International XI 6 | (J Robson) |
| Coventry 2nd XI 2 Villa 2nd XI 2 | (C Thompson) |
| 1979-80 | |
| Villa 2 Birmingham City 3 | (R Saunders) |
| 1980-81 | |
| Birmingham City 3 Villa 6 | (J Gallagher) |
| Walsall 1 Villa 1 | (I Paul) |
| 1981-82 | |
| Villa 3 England XI 2 | (B Little) |
| J Cumbes XI v D Waterman's XI | (Charity/Moor Green FC) |
| 1982-83 | |
| Portsmouth 3 Villa 4 | (A Cropley) |

| | |
|---|---|
| Hereford United 1 Villa 2 | (T Hughes) |
| Rotherham United 1 Villa 3 | (R Finney) |
| Mansfield Town v Villa | (K Bird) |
| 1983-84 | |
| Torquay United 2 Villa 1 | (I Twitchen) |
| West Brom Albion 1 Villa 2 | (B Batson) |
| Worcester City v Villa | (MP) |
| 1984-85 | |
| Bristol Rovers v Villa | (M Barrett) |
| Aldershot 4 Villa 1 | (J Jopling) |
| Villa 1 England XI 4 | (D Mortimer |
| Birmingham City 3 Villa 6 | (J Gallagher) |
| Villa 3 West Brom Albion 3 | (Bradford Fire Disaster) |
| Leeds United 3 Villa 1 | (Ethiopia Appeal) |
| Cardiff City 3 Villa 0 | (J Hemmerman) |
| Kidderminster Harriers v Villa XI | (M Mullen) |
| 1985-86 | |
| Birmingham City 2 Villa 2 | (K Broadhurst) |
| Atherstone Town v Villa XI | (Club benefit) |
| Hednesford Town v Villa XI | (B Morris) |
| Villa v J Powell XI | (Charity/benefit) |
| 1987-88 | |
| Villa 2 Wolverhampton Wds 1 | (NP Spink) |
| Derby County v Villa | (J Guthrie) |
| 1988-89 | |
| Walsall 2 Villa 4 | (W Evans) |
| Harworth FC v Villa res | (Club benefit) |
| Bromsgrove Rovers v Villa XI | (O'Grady) |
| 1989-90 | |
| Halesowen 1 Villa 6 | (Joinson bros & M Penn) |
| Watford 1 Villa 6 | (K Jackett) |
| 1989-90 | |
| Bromsgrove Rovers 0 Villa 4 | (M O'Connell) |
| 1990-91 | |
| Bristol City 2 Villa 0 | (Rob Newman) |
| 1991-92 | |
| West Midlands Police 1 Villa res 6 | (M Fogarty) |
| Cheltenham Town 4 Villa 3 | (Cheltenham player) |
| Worcester City 1 Villa res 4 | (WC player Benefit) |
| Evesham United XI v Villa res | (K Mullen) |
| Plymouth Argyle 1 Villa 2 | (T Tynan) |
| Hibernian 4 Villa 2 | (A Sneddon) |
| Villa 2 Wolverhampton Wds 3 | (P Birch) |
| 1992-93 | |
| Wolverhampton Wds 2 Villa 2 | (S Cullis) |
| Villa 2 Birmingham City 2 | (J Dugdale) |
| Villa 1 Manchester United 1 | (M Brown, in Belfast) |
| Peterborough United 1 Villa 1 | (C Turner) |
| Villa 4 Stoke City 1 | (G Cowans) |
| 1993-94 | |
| Port Vale 2 Villa 3 | (J Rudge) |
| Kidderminster Harriers 2 Villa 3 | (P Davis) |
| West Bromwich Albion 1 Villa 2 | (G Robson) |
| Kings Lynn v Villa res | (Kings Lynn funds) |
| Bilston Select 1 Villa res 8 | (M Richards) |
| Forest Green Rovers 0 Villa res 4 | (FGR) |
| 1994-95 | |
| Villa 2 Birmingham City 0 | (P McGrath) |
| Gloucester City v Villa | (G Willetts) |
| Coventry City 1 Villa 2 | (S Ogrizovic) |
| Oxford United 3 Villa 3 | (K Fish) |
| Birmingham City 1 Villa 1 | (Commemorative Match)* |
| Villa XI v All Stars XI | (A Barton) |
| 1995-96 | |
| Birmingham City 0 Villa 6 | (J Frain) |
| 1996-97 | |
| Oldham Athletic 0 Villa 3 | (I Olney) |

| West Brom Albion 0 Villa I | (R Allen) |
| 1997-98 | |
| Fraserburgh 3 Villa 5 | (J Young) |
| Kidderminster Harriers I Villa 5 | (G Allner) |
| Port Vale 3 Villa 5 | (Vale player) |
| 1998-99 | |
| Cardiff City 0 Villa 3 | (C Dale) |
| Hednesford Town 0 Villa 4 | (K Collins) |
| Hereford United 0 Villa 2 | (C Price) |
| Seville I Villa 2 | (Testimonial in Spain) |
| 1999-2000 | |
| Cheltenham Town v Villa | (Banks) |
| Kidderminster Harriers v Villa | (M Weir) |
| Swansea City v Villa | (Walker) |
| Tamworth 3 Villa XI 4 | (Tamworth FC) |

*This game, played on 15 November 1994, was to celebrate the official opening of the new Tilton Road and Kop stands at St Andrew's. The attendance was 19,766.

## Benefit Countdown

On 23 May 1880, Villa lost 2-1 to Walsall Swifts in a special match arranged for the sufferers of the explosion at Birchills Hall Iron Works in Staffordshire when several people were killed and dozens injured.

Jack Devey's testimonial match v. Derby County in October 1896 raised almost £90. Ten years later, Joe Bache received £400 from his benefit match v Bristol City in December 1906.

Archie Hunter was awarded three benefit matches by Aston Villa - plus one for his family!

A crowd of 9,200 (recs. £5,012) attended Vic Crowe's testimonial match at Villa Park in 1963-64.

The Alan Sneddon testimonial match at Easter Road in October 1991 between Hibs and Villa was also for the Abercromby Cup.

A crowd of 10,000 saw the Wolves-Villa clash in aid of Stan Cullis' benefit in August 1992. Matt Breitkreutz scored both Villa goals and Steve Bull likewise for Wolves.

A crowd of 22,000 saw the Villa-Manchester United game at Windsor Park, Belfast in May 1993, which was arranged in honour of the late Irish League Secretary, Mervyn Brown. The gate receipts amounted to almost £100,000. Yorke equalised for Villa after Michael Phelan had scored for United.

Mark Bosnich, wearing number 7, played up front for Villa late on during Gary Robson's testimonial match at West Bromwich Albion in 1994. Almost 16,300 fans saw this game.

And for Ronnie Allen's testimonial game at The Hawthorns in 1997 the turnout was almost 17,000.

Ex-Aston Villa player Ernie Callaghan was also granted a testimonial - after announcing his retirement in 1971-72.

## BENWELL, LEONARD ARTHUR

Born: Berwick-on-Tweed, 1870.

Career: Berwick Rangers (1890), Aston Villa (June 1893), Walsall Town Swifts (August 1894), Berwick Rangers (May 1895).

Deputy to goalkeeper Bill Dunning, Len Benwell was 23 years of age when he played in his only Football League game for Villa against Bolton Wanderers (away) in November 1893. He had been recruited six months earlier but after a season with neighbours Walsall Town Swifts, he returned to Scotland in May 1895 after becoming 'homesick.'

## BERESFORD, JOSEPH

Born: Chesterfield, 26 February 1906. Died: Birmingham, 26 February 1978.

Career: Mansfield Town (May 1926), Aston Villa (May 1927), Preston North End (September 1935), Swansea Town (December 1937), Stourbridge (August 1938 to 1942 when he retired). After a spell as a fish shop manager in Kingstanding, Birmingham, Beresford was employed for 11 years at ICI (Witton) and attended most of Villa's home matches.

Inside or centre-forward Joe Beresford was Aston Villa's 'human dynamo' for eight years (1927-35) during which time he scored 73 goals in 251 first-class matches. After bedding himself in at Villa Park, Beresford became a fitting partner to Tom 'Pongo' Waring and Billy Walker in Villa's attack. Capped once by England against Czechoslovakia in Prague in 1934, his career with Villa ended when manager Jimmy McMullan moved in. He was immediately transferred to Preston and in 1937 appeared in the FA Cup Final at Wembley, collecting a loser's medal against Sunderland. Later that year Beresford moved to Swansea and in 1938 was re-united with his former Villa Park team-mate Alex Talbot at Stourbridge before hanging up his boots during the Second World War (after guesting for Hartlepools United).

## BESIKTAS

Villa's playing record against the Turkish side:

European Cup

| Venue | P | W | D | L | F | A |
| --- | --- | --- | --- | --- | --- | --- |
| Home | I | I | 0 | 0 | 3 | I |
| Away | I | 0 | I | 0 | 0 | 0 |
| Totals | 2 | I | I | 0 | 3 | I |

As holders of the trophy, Aston Villa met the Turkish side over two legs in the first round of the European Cup in September 1982. The game at Villa Park was played behind closed doors (following crowd trouble at Villa Park during the previous season) and, in fact, only 167 witnesses (press, club officials, guests etc) saw the Turks beaten 3-1. Peter Withe, Tony Morley and Dennis Mortimer were the Villa scorers.

There were 45,000 spectators present for the return leg a fortnight later which ended goalless to see Villa ease through comfortably on aggregate by 3-1.

## BETTS, ANTHONY THOMAS

Born: Sandiacre, Nottinghamshire, 31 October 1953.

Career: Aston Villa (junior, May 1969, professional March 1972), Southport (loan, December 1974), Port Vale (on trial, September 1975), Boldmere St Michael's (November 1975), then in NASL with Portland Timbers & Minnesota Kicks (late 1970s). Inside-forward Tony Betts won both Amateur and Youth international caps for England as a teenager. He made only five first team appearances for Villa before transferring to Port Vale in 1975. Betts, who did well for three years in the NASL, gained an FA Youth Cup winners' medal with Villa in 1972.

## BEWERS, JONATHAN

Born: Kettering, 10 September 1982.

Career: Schoolboy football, Aston Villa (trainee, June 1998, professional, 16 September 1999).

Jonathan Bewers, who can play as a full-back, central-defender or in midfield, made his Premiership debut for Aston Villa at Tottenham Hotspur in April 2000, coming on as a late substitute. He had already been capped by England at Schoolboy and both under 16 and under 17 levels

THE COMPLETE ENCYCLOPAEDIA OF ASTON VILLA F.C.     THE COMPLETE ENCYCLOPAEDIA OF ASTON VILLA F.C.

23

## BIDDLESTONE, THOMAS FREDERICK

Born: Pensnett near Dudley, 26 November 1906. Died: Great Barr, Birmingham, 7 April 1977.

Career: Hickman's Park Rangers (1921), Moxley Wesleyans (1922), Wednesbury Town, Bilston Boys Club, Sunbeam Motors, Bloxwich Strollers, Walsall (professional, April 1929), Aston Villa (£1,750, April 1930), Mansfield Town (August 1939). Retired cs 1944.

Fred Biddlestone was a centre-half before becoming a goalkeeper in 1922. He continued to do well at non-League level, especially with Wednesbury Town and Bloxwich Strollers, and in 1929 was signed as a professional by Walsall, switching to Aston Villa in 1930 after playing brilliantly in an FA Cup-tie for the Saddlers at Villa Park! He went on to appear in 160 first team games for Villa, up to August 1939, when he

moved to Field Mill, retiring in 1944. Nicknamed 'The Councillor' he was sound rather than spectacular and helped Villa win the Second Division championship in 1938 producing a series of excellent displays.

## BIRCH, JAMES

Born: Blackwell, Derbyshire, 1888. Died: London, 1940.

Career: Buxton Lime Firms, Stourbridge, Aston Villa (May 1910), Queen's Park Rangers (June 1912), Brentford (1926). Retired 1927.

An aggressive centre-forward, Jimmy Birch scored twice in his three senior outings for Aston Villa while deputising for Harry Hampton. He did exceedingly well with QPR, netting 144 goals in 363 first team matches before moving across London to Griffin Park where he spent a season in the Bees' second team.

## BIRCH, PAUL

Born: West Bromwich, 20 November 1962.

Career: West Bromwich Boys, Aston Villa (apprentice in June 1978, professional, July 1980), Wolverhampton Wanderers (£400,000, February 1991), Preston North End (loan, March 1996), Doncaster Rovers (July 1996), Exeter City (March 1997-May 1998), Hednesford Town.

In his 13 years at Villa Park, Paul Birch was a totally committed footballer, a player who enjoyed his game, often preferring a role wide on the right side of midfield. He scored 25 goals in 219 senior appearances whilst at Villa Park. He gained a European Super Cup winners medal in 1982, helped Villa win promotion from Division Two in 1988 and won an FA Youth Cup winners medal in 1980. He was awarded a well-deserved Testimonial Match in August 1991 when Villa met Wolves. When he finally pulled out of top-class League and Cup football in the summer of 1998, Birch had amassed a fine record of 465 appearances and 53 goals.

## BIRCH, TREVOR

Born: West Bromwich, 20 November 1933.

Career: Accles & Pollock FC, Aston Villa (amateur, July 1949, professional 1952), Stockport County (November 1960-May 1962).

Right-half Trevor Birch was spotted by Aston Villa playing for in the Birmingham Works League. He became a professional within three years of joining the club and then acted, in the main, as reserve to Danny Blanchflower, Vic Crowe and Bill Baxter, making 22 senior appearances before leaving Villa Park for Edgeley Park in 1960. He moved into non-League football in Cheshire in 1962 and retired from the game in 1965.

## BIRMINGHAM CITY

Villa's playing record against Blues:

Football League

| Venue | P | W | D | L | F | A |
|---|---|---|---|---|---|---|
| Home | 48 | 23 | 13 | 12 | 82 | 60 |
| Away | 48 | 16 | 12 | 20 | 68 | 74 |
| Totals | 96 | 39 | 25 | 32 | 150 | 134 |

FA Cup

| Venue | P | W | D | L | F | A |
|---|---|---|---|---|---|---|
| Home | 1 | 1 | 0 | 0 | 1 | 0 |
| Away | 2 | 1 | 1 | 0 | 4 | 0 |
| Totals | 3 | 2 | 1 | 0 | 5 | 0 |

League Cup

| Venue | P | W | D | L | F | A |
|---|---|---|---|---|---|---|
| Home | 3 | 2 | 1 | 0 | 6 | 0 |
| Away | 3 | 2 | 0 | 1 | 4 | 3 |
| Totals | 6 | 4 | 1 | 1 | 10 | 3 |

Simod Cup

| Venue | P | W | D | L | F | A |
|---|---|---|---|---|---|---|
| Home | 1 | 1 | 0 | 0 | 6 | 0 |

Wartime

| Venue | P | W | D | L | F | A |
|---|---|---|---|---|---|---|
| Home | 8 | 5 | 2 | 1 | 18 | 7 |
| Away | 7 | 2 | 1 | 4 | 10 | 11 |
| Totals | 15 | 7 | 3 | 5 | 28 | 18 |

Aston Villa first met Blues then known as 'Small Heath Alliance' on 27 September 1879 in what was billed as a 'local friendly' at Muntz Street. Blues registered a 1-0 victory but after the game the Villa players claimed that the pitch was only suitable for pot holing!

The first League tussle between the clubs took place on 1 October 1894 and in front of a sun-drenched 20,000 crowd at Villa's Wellington Road ground, Blues, now 'Small Heath' were defeated 2-1. The return game on 20 October, finished all square at 2-2, Dennis Hodgetts equalising for Villa from the penalty spot after Fred Wheldon, with Blues' first ever penalty kick, and Jack Hallam had given the visitors a 2-1 lead.

In September 1895, Villa walloped Blues 7-3 at Perry Barr. John Campbell scored four of his side's goals that day and had a helping hand in the two registered by Jack Devey. The attendance was 13,000. Later that season Villa doubled up with a 4-1 win at Muntz Street, Devey again scoring twice.

Blues, by now known as 'Birmingham' finally registered their first League victory over Villa on 16 September 1905 at the eleventh attempt - winning 2-0 at Muntz Street before a crowd of 30,000.

Four months later around 40,000 fans saw Villa defeated 3-1 at home as Blues completed the double over their arch-rivals.

The first 'second City' local derby at St Andrew's was played on 19 January 1907 and a 50,000 crowd saw Villa take the honours with a 3-2 victory.

England international Billy Walker scored two penalties in Villa's 3-0 home win over Blues in March 1923.

The League game between Villa and Blues in October 1925 produced six goals. Villa were leading 3-0 with time fast running out as hundreds of fans in the 55,000 crowd were already making their way home. Then Blues produced a devastating finish, scoring three times late on to earn a point.

Villa had blitzed the Blues defence in the first-half. Walker scored twice before the break with Len Capewell adding a third halfway through the second half. But then Joe Bradford made it 3-1 on 79 minutes and two minutes later he scored again. With the referee ready to blow the final whistle, Villa's goalkeeper Cyril Spiers went for a high cross but slipped, and in trying to recover his ground he knocked the ball into the net to concede an own-goal for the equaliser. Villa's right-half Vic Milne fractured a bone in his right foot during the first-half of this game and was a virtual passenger for almost an hour.

*Blues v Villa at St. Andrews in 1950. Ivor Powell (Villa) is in the centre.*

The last pre-Second World War League encounter between Villa and Blues took place in March 1939. A crowd of almost 41,000 saw Jackie Martin score a hat-trick as Blues were crushed 5-1 at Villa Park.

In December 1948, a crowd of 61,632 saw Jackie 'Jack-in-the-box' Stewart run rings round Villa's defence to score twice in Blues' 3-0 win at Villa Park.

Villa succumbed to their first League defeat at St Andrew's for 19 years in August 1957 when over 50,800 spectators saw Blues defeat the FA Cup holders 3-1. After going a goal down, Blues stormed back to beat relegation-threatened Villa 4-1 on the same ground in December 1958.

England international Gerry Hitchens became the first player to score a hat-trick in post-War second city derbies when he achieved the feat in Villa's 6-2 home win in October 1960. Alan O'Neill made a scoring debut for Villa in this game and 'keeper Nigel Sims saved a penalty from Blues' winger Gordon Astall.

In March 1963 - two months before the League Cup Final - Villa beat Blues 4-0 at home in front of 46,680 fans, Harry Burrows cracking in a penalty.

The first Second Division meeting between the clubs took place on 7 October 1967...and Blues won it by 4-2 at Villa Park in front of 49,984 fans. A year or so later, in September 1968, Villa crashed 4-0 at St Andrew's, all the goals coming in a rather one-sided second-half!

When Villa won 2-0 at St Andrew's in March 1970, it ended a run of 22 away League games without a victory!

After Villa had spent some time in the Second and Third Divisions they got back to serious League action with Blues in season 1975-76. They won 2-1 at Villa Park but crashed to a 3-1 defeat at St Andrew's.

Two goals by Wayne Clarke and another by Steve Whitton gave Blues a handsome 3-0 win at Villa Park in March 1986 - the last time the teams met in the top flight of English football! The crowd was 26,294.

The last League meeting between the two clubs took place in

December 1987 when a brace by Garry Thompson gave Villa a 2-1 victory at St Andrew's in a Division Two contest.

Thousands of supporters boycotted Villa's away FA Cup clash with Blues in March 1901 because of increased admission prices. Instead an expected 25,000 crowd, only 18,000 fans turned up. The game ended goalless and Villa won the replay 1-0.

The other FA Cup meeting between Villa and Blues was played at Muntz Street on 5 November 1887 - the same day that Buffalo Bill Cody took his famous Wild West Show to the Aston Lower Grounds Meadow. A crowd of 12,000 saw Villa hammer Blues 4-0 while 5,000 spectators cheered on the Indians and cowboys three miles away!

Villa's only League Cup defeat against Blues came in the first leg of the 1962-63 Final at St Andrew's (3-1). A crowd of 31,580 saw Blues get one hand on the trophy with a fine performance and they duly took the prize after holding Villa to a 0-0 draw in the return leg in front of almost 38,000 fans.

In this same competition Villa beat Blues 5-0 at home in October 1988, taking the tie 7-0 on aggregate after their     2-0 victory at St. Andrew's.

Goalkeeper Mark Bosnich saved John Frain's first-half penalty when Villa beat Blues 1-0 at St Andrew's in a League Cup encounter in September 1993.

Blues were also hammered 6-0 at Villa Park in a Simod Cup-tie in November 1988 when the attendance was under 8,400. Villa were 5-0 up at the interval.

On 12 January 1946 Villa were held to a 2-2 draw by Blues in a Football League (South) game at Villa Park before 63,280 fans.

Neil Dougall equalised for Blues five minutes from time after Villa's Harry Parkes had missed a penalty.

In the return game a week later, Blues won 3-1 in front of 40,000 spectators - and they went on to pip Villa by just 0.036 of a goal to win the League (South) championship that season.

Villa played Blues at St Andrew's in April 1940 in a 'farewell' (benefit) game for legendary goalkeeper Harry Hibbs. Blues won 2-1 in front of 15,000 fans (recs. £650).

Villa crashed 5-2 to Blues in the Lord Mayor of Birmingham Charity Cup at St Andrew's in September 1908. During the second-half Villa were awarded a penalty which Harry Hampton took only to shoot straight at the Blues' 'keeper Jack Dorrington. The ball rebounded to Joe Bache, but as he was about to shoot he was felled inside the area by Frank Womack, the Blues full-back, resulting in a second spot-kick. Again Hampton fired directly at Dorrington, who this time held the ball before clearing his lines.

*Johnny Vincent (left) and Mike Tind (right) clash at Villa Park in August 19*

In a pre-season friendly at Perry Barr in August 1889, Football Alliance side Small Heath beat Football League runners-up Aston Villa 4-0!

An audience of 23,667 saw Villa beat Blues 6-2 in a Central League game at Villa Park in February 1928. The big crowd turned out to see the debut of the home club's new signing, Tom 'Pongo' Waring, who

*Captains Ron Wyle (Blues) and Brian Tiler (Villa) toss up at Villa Park in September 1968.*

Phoenix, K Poole, A Rees, BD Rioch, PJ Robinson, K Rogers, L Sealey (Blues N/C), FH Shell (Blues reserve), J Slueewenhoek, B Small, EW Strange (Blues reserve), KC Tewkesbury, MR Thomas (on loan to Villa), RGM Thomson, C Tiler, JE Travers, AS Turner, A Vale, GA Vowden, C Wallace Blues WW1 guest), S Webb (Villa reserve), T Weston (Blues WW1 guest), G F Wheldon, JM Wilcox, P Withe, C Withers and RM Wylie (also coach at Villa Park).

Also: RE Brocklebank (Villa player, Blues manager), R Saunders (manager of both clubs), KM Bradley, I Ross & NP Spink (Villa players, Blues coaches), D Dorman (Blues player and scout, Villa scout), HA Parkes (Villa player and Director of both clubs), D Ellis (Director with both clubs - appointed by Blues in 1967 - also Villa Chairman), PD Doherty (Blues WW2 guest, Villa chief scout), G Leggatt (Blues player, assistant-trainer/coach with Villa), K Leonard (Villa player, Blues coach), R Shaw (Blues player & coach, Villa trainer & physio), J Barron & W Shorthouse (coach/trainer at both clubs), K Smith (lottery staff both clubs).

celebrated by scoring a hat-trick!

Blues visited Villa Park to contest a 'Football League Founders Day' centenary match on 13 April 1988. Villa won 5-2.

Billy Walker made most appearances (22) and scored most goals (11) in derby matches for Villa against Blues. Tommy Mort made 19 appearances, Dicky York 18 and Arthur Dorrell 17.

Villa's best sequence of results against Blues came during the 1920s, early '30s when they lost only twice in 16 League matches.

Twelve players - Des Bremner, Alan Curbishley, Cammie Fraser, David Geddis, Tony Hateley, Mark Jones, Stan Lynn, Charlie Phillips, John Sleeuwenhoek, Peter Withe, Colin Withers and Ron Wylie - all played in second city derby matches for both clubs.

Brian Little signed for Blues from Aston Villa on 3 July 1979 subject to a medical report...72 hours later the deal was called off!

On 20 September 1946 four players all left Villa Park to join Birmingham City. They were Reg Beresford, Les Godfrey, George Lunn and Frank Shell.

Among the players who made their debuts for Villa against Blues we have Keith Bradley, Wilson Briggs, John Burridge, Gerry Hitchens and Alan O'Neill.

Players with both clubs include: JP Allen (Blues WW2 guest), B Anstey, WC Athersmith, M Beard, R Beresford, N Blake, J Bradford (Villa trialist), D Bremner, FC Buckley, FH Broome (Blues WW2 guest), F Carrodus, F Chapple, GA Charles, C Charsley (guest), WS Corbett, F Cornan, A Coton (Villa trialist), GW Cummings (Blues WW2 guest), LC Curbishley, W Devey, HA Dobson, H Edgley (Blues WW1 guest), GR Edwards (Blues WW2 guest), E Eyre, S Fox (on associate Schoolboy forms with Villa), F Foxall, JC Fraser, W Freeman, D Geddis, W George, L Godfrey, H Hampton, CB Hare, R Harper, H Harvey (Blues reserve), A Hateley, J Herriot (Villa loan), JB Higgins (Villa reserve), T Hockey, D Hodgetts, R Hopkins, GC Hunter (Blues WW1 guest), RTJ Iverson (Blues WW2 guest), RJ Jeffries (Blues trialist), LR Jenkins, MAW Jones, JM Kearns, MI Kendall, F Kerns, A Leake, AE Lindon, I Linton, G Lunn, S Lynex (Villa trialist), S Lynn, A McClure (also Blues assistant-manager), R Martin, A Massie (Blues WW2 guest), CJH Millington, TJ Mooney (Villa Reserve), AW Morley, D Mortimer, F Moss jnr (Blues WW2 guest), A Mulraney, JA Murray, C Phillips, AF

## BIRMINGHAM COMBINATION

Prior to the Second World War, Aston Villa entered a junior team in this local competition ....and they carried off the championship twice: in 1935-36 and 1938-39. Many future stars graduated through the 'Combination' side and former Villa winger Charlie Wallace was given the responsibility of coaching and organising the youngsters in the late 1930s.

Wallace - along with other prominent coaches/trainers - also looked after the Villa team that participated in the J.O.C. and the Midland Midweek League around the same time. In season 1938-39, when Villa won the J.O.C. championship, centre-forward Jack Ward scored 89 goals - 50 in the League and 39 in two Cup tournaments.

## BIRMINGHAM & DISTRICT LEAGUE

The Birmingham & District League was formed in 1889 with Aston Villa one its first and keenest members. It being primarily for the reserve teams of major League clubs.

In season 1894-95 Villa claimed their first of twelve B&D League championships, dropping only five points in 30 games while rattling in a total of 133 goals. A year later they successfully defended their title with ease.

They won the prize again in 1895-96, but on this occasion they managed only 84 goals!

Their third title success arrived in 1899-1900 and then in 1902-03 Villa began a tremendous run of success, winning the first of eight successive B&D League championships. In this period of sheer supremacy, Villa's second string whipped Coventry City's first team 14-1 at home and Dudley Town 11-2 away. They scored 449 goals in four seasons (1903-07 inclusive).

In January 1910 - on the way to their 11th championship - Villa completed a tremendous record of 17 consecutive B&D League victories. They attracted some excellent attendances, especially at Villa Park, with 12,000 fans turning out for the local derby against Birmingham, while 15,000 went to The Victoria Ground for the game against Stoke.

Centre-forward Bert Goode (later to do very well with Wrexham) scored 46 goals (out of 91) in his only season at Villa Park (1910-11) but the reserve side failed to take the Birmingham & District League championship finishing second to Stoke.

Villa's last B&D League triumph arrived in season 1911-12 when they rattled in 111 goals in 34

*John Slueewenhoek, player with both Villa and Blues.*

THE COMPLETE ENCYCLOPAEDIA OF ASTON VILLA F.C.   THE COMPLETE ENCYCLOPAEDIA OF ASTON VILLA F.C.

26

matches to canter home nine points clear (53-44) of the second-place team Darlaston.

Aston Villa's second XI was a very strong, purposeful unit during the period from 1900 to 1912 and Haydn Price (a reserve/third team player) was actually capped by Wales against Scotland in 1907 without ever making Villa's first team!

The Central League came into being shortly before the Great War, and after the hostilities were over Aston Villa entered this competition for the first time in 1919-20, placing their third and sometimes fourth team in the B&D League.

During the first part of the Second World War, Aston Villa's first team played in the Birmingham & District League, and in season 1941-42 they won the title with a terrific record of 15 wins from 18 games.

(See also under Reserves and Wartime Football)

## BIRMINGHAM LEAGUE CUP

Fielding their first team, Aston Villa won the Birmingham League Cup in season 1941-42, beating Worcester City 4-2 in the Final.

In the opening round, Villa defeated Wellington Town 6-2 on aggregate (5-0 & 1-2) before eliminating RAF (Hednesford) 14-1 in round 2, Alex Massie showing his goal-flare with a fivetimer while Frank Broome netted four. In the semi-final Hednesford were eclipsed 3-2 at home (Broome scoring twice) and then in front of 1,000 fans at Solihull's ground, Billy Goffin (2), Dicky Davis and Eric Houghton scored the goals that saw off Worcester in the Final.

## BIRMINGHAM SENIOR CUP

In December 1875, the Birmingham County FA was formed at a meeting in Edgbaston, convened by the Calthorpe and Aston Unity clubs and as a result the Senior Cup was quickly introduced by the new body. In those early days of the competition there were as many as 40 teams eligible to enter with all the major clubs including Aston Villa, Shrewsbury Town, Stafford Road FC (Wolverhampton) and Wednesbury Old Athletic, participating annually.

From the outset in 1875 until 1912, Villa's first team competed earnestly and professionally for the then prestigious Birmingham Senior Cup and during that period of time (37 years) they won the trophy a record 17 times.

**Villa's appearances in the Senior Cup Final (1st team only):**

1875-76   lost to Tipton 1-0
1879-80   beat Saltley College 3-2
1880-81   lost to Walsall Town Swifts 1-0
1881-82   beat Wednesbury Old Athletic 2-1
1882-83   beat Wednesbury Old Athletic 3-2
1883-84   beat Walsall Swifts 4-0
1884-85   beat Walsall Swifts 2-0
1887-88   beat West Bromwich Albion 3-2
1888-89   beat Wolverhampton Wanderers 3-0
1889-90   beat West Bromwich Albion 2-0
1890-91   beat Wednesbury Old Athletic 3-0
1892-93   lost to Wolverhampton Wanderers 3-0
1894-95   lost to West Bromwich Albion 1-0 (after 0-0)
1895-96   beat Sheffield United 2-0
1898-99   beat Burslem Port Vale 4-0
1900-01   lost to Stoke 4-3 (after 1-1)
1901-02   lost to Wolverhampton Wanderers 1-0
1902-03   beat West Bromwich Albion 3-2
1903-04   beat Wolverhampton Wanderers 3-1

1905-06   beat Birmingham 3-1
1907-08   beat Walsall 6-0
1919-10   beat Stoke 2-1
1911-12   beat Willenhall Pickwick 2-1
1923-24   lost to Wolverhampton Wanderers 2-1
1925-26   Final postponed due to National Strike
1982-83   lost to Birmingham City 1-0
1984-85   beat Wednesfield Social 3-1*
1995-96   lost to Birmingham City 2-0

*Villa's team comprised mainly second and third team players.

## BSC News

A year after losing to Tipton in the 1876 Final, Villa withdrew from the competition, having gained revenge over Tipton (1-0) in the opening round of the 1876-77 tournament..

When Villa won the Senior Cup in 1880, it was their first trophy success. En-route to the Final, after receiving a bye in the first round when Harborne Unity scratched, they ousted Excelsior (8-1), Newport (7-0), Aston Unity (1-0) and Walsall Swifts (2-1) before accounting for Saltley College 3-2 at the Lower Grounds Meadow on 3 April to take the star prize. A crowd of 6,000 saw Eli Davis, William Mason and George Ramsay score Villa's goals that day.

In reaching the 1881 Final Villa beat Newport (Salop) 6-0, Sutton 10-1 and Wednesbury Old Athletic 6-0 in the first three rounds.

Villa's 1882 success was achieved at the Aston Lower Grounds Meadow and on their way to the Final they ousted Sutton Coldfield 9-0, Stoke 8-0 (after a 0-0 draw), Wednesbury Strollers 3-1 and Walsall Swifts 1-0.

When winning the Cup the following season (1882-83) Villa scored 53 goals in just six matches, putting out, in turn, Sutton Coldfield (a) 5-0, Derby Midland 4-0, Small Heath Swifts 21-0, Aston Unity 16-0 and Birmingham St George's 4-0 before accounting for Old Athletic in the Final. In the 21-0 romp over the hapless Swifts (Villa's biggest-ever first team victory incidentally) Arthur Brown scored 10 times; out of the team's tally of 53 goals Brown claimed 21.

In the 1883-84 competition, Villa's overall goal-ratio was 23-2 and included a 12-0 home win over Halesowen.

In 1884-85, Villa started off by beating Burton Strollers 7-0 and

*Villa, Birmingham Senior Cup Winners 1880.*
Back row (l-r): J Hughes (umpire), William McGregor (vice-president), WB Mas
E B Lee, H Simmonds, T Pank, E Davis, F Johnstone (vice-president), J Jeffrie
(honorary secretary).
Front row (l-r): Andy Hunter, G B Ramsay, W A Ellis (President), Archie Hunte
C S Johnstone.
On ground: S Law and W F Ball.

THE COMPLETE ENCYCLOPAEDIA OF ASTON VILLA F.C.    THE COMPLETE ENCYCLOPAEDIA OF ASTON VILLA F.C.

27

Wednesbury Town 4-0 (both away). Then after taking out Staveley 5-0 in a replay, they whipped Wednesbury Old Athletic by the same score in the semi-final before defeating Walsall Swifts 2-0 in the Final to claim their fourth successive victory.

Villa beat the FA Cup winners West Bromwich Albion in the 1888 Final and in 1889 they defeated the FA Cup runners-up of that year Wolves in the Final at the Warwickshire County Cricket Ground (Edgbaston), after slamming Ironbridge 9-1 in the semis.

Wolves were defeated again in the 1890 semi-final before Villa nudged out Albion in the Final.

On their way to victory in 1891, Villa thrashed Kidderminster Harriers 10-0, Wolves 6-0 and Albion 3-2 in the semis, the latter after two replays.

The following year (1892) Albion gained revenge by dumping Villa out at the semi-final stage and then Wolves also took revenge with a victory in the 1893 Final.

Albion were again victors over Villa in the 1895 Final at the Lower Grounds Meadow, following a stalemate at Small Heath's Muntz Street ground.

Villa accounted for Albion 3-0, Sheffield Wednesday 4-3 (after extra-time) and Burton Swifts before defeating another Sheffield side, United, in the Final of 1896.

In 1898 Villa suffered a humiliating 5-0 home drubbing at the hands of Wolves in the semi-final, but in 1899 they were back to winning ways, with a comfortable four-goal victory in the Final over Burlsem Port Vale.

After going out to Wolves in the semi-final of 1900, Villa then lost a seven-goal thriller against Stoke in the 1901 Final.

Villa went down narrowly by 1-0 to Wolves at The Hawthorns in the 1902 Final before notching their twelfth Birmingham Cup triumph in 1903, adding number 13 a year later with another three-goal victory over Albion.

Six months before Small Heath became Birmingham and moved to St Andrew's, Villa beat them 3-1 in the 1906 Senior Cup Final.

Two years later (1908) Walsall were crushed 6-0 as Villa took their record-breaking 15th Senior Cup Final victory. This brought to an end a brilliant run of success by the first XI before the second string (the reserves) took over the fixtures - although from time to time the seniors did participate....i.e. contesting the Finals of 1983 and 1996 after the stiffs and juniors had done all the spadework to get there! Villa's second string won the trophy three times off their own bat after the seniors had ended their run before the First World War.

When Wednesfield Social were defeated in the 1984-85 Final, Villa fielded a mixture of reserve and youth team players.

The 1996 Final at St Andrew's was a heated affair which resulted in four players being sent-off late on, three from Blues and Ben Petty of Villa.

The 'old' Birmingham Senior Cup is now called the Aston Villa Cup.

## BLACKBURN, GEORGE FREDERICK

Born: Willesden Green, London, 18 March 1899.    Died: Cheltenham, 3 July 1957.

Career: Hampstead Town, Army football, Aston Villa (amateur December 1920, professional, January 1921), Cardiff City (July 1926), Mansfield Town (June 1931), Cheltenham Town (player-manager, May 1932), Moor Green (coach, August 1934), Birmingham (trainer, 1937, later taking over as coach). He retired from football in May 1948.

George Blackburn became a professional at Villa Park just four weeks after joining the club. A sound footballer, preferring the left-half berth, he quickly established himself in the first XI at Villa Park and during his six years with the club made 145 senior appearances, scored two goals and lined up in the 1924 FA Cup Final defeat by Newcastle United.

A month after that Wembley encounter he was capped by England against France in Paris. Blackburn left Villa for Cardiff in 1926 but missed out on the Bluebirds splendid FA Cup Final win over mighty Arsenal the following year even though he was a regular in the side. He netted once in 116 games for the Welsh side before joining Mansfield

(with Harry Wake). At the end of the 1931-32 season he became player-manager of Cheltenham and two years later took over as coach of Moor Green prior to his appointment as Birmingham's trainer in 1937, retaining that position for seven years prior to acting as coach until the late 1940s.

## BLACKBURN, ROBERT ERNEST

Born: Crawshaw Booth near Rawtenshall (Manchester), 23 April 1892. Died: Birkenhead, 13 July 1964.

Career: Loveclough FC (1907), Manchester Youth Club (1911), The Army (from 1915), Aston Villa (April 1919), Bradford City (May 1922), Accrington Stanley (trainer, August 1923, then manager at Peel Park, October 1924-January 1932), Wrexham (manager, January 1932-January 1936), Hull City (manager December 1936-January 1946), Tranmere Rovers (manager, September 1946-May 1955, taking over as club secretary in June 1955 until May 1959 when he retired from football).

Ernie Blackburn was an effective right or left-back who joined Aston Villa straight after serving with the Royal Medical Corps.

*Ernie Blackburn*

Blackburn remained at Villa Park for three seasons, making just 33 first team appearances. Unfortunately his career was cut short through injury in the summer of 1923 and a year later he became trainer with Accrington Stanley, later moving up the ladder into soccer management, first at Peel Park and then with Wrexham, Hull City and Tranmere. He worked under considerable pressure at Accrington (no money at all) and was the first manager to lose his job after the Second World War. Blackburn earned a reputation as a hard worker, a fine judge of player and financial economist.

## BLACKBURN ROVERS

Villa's playing record against the Rovers:
Football League/Premiership

| Venue | P | W | D | L | F | A |
|---|---|---|---|---|---|---|
| Home | 67 | 35 | 17 | 15 | 139 | 70 |
| Away | 67 | 18 | 12 | 37 | 90 | 144 |
| Totals | 134 | 53 | 29 | 52 | 229 | 214 |

FA Cup

| Venue | P | W | D | L | F | A |
|---|---|---|---|---|---|---|
| Home | 4 | 3 | 0 | 1 | 8 | 3 |
| Away | 3 | 0 | 2 | 1 | 4 | 11 |
| Totals | 7 | 3 | 2 | 2 | 12 | 14 |

In the first season of League football - 1888-89 - the two games between Aston Villa and Rovers produced 13 goals. Villa won 6-1 at home but lost 1-5 at Blackburn's Leamington Road ground.

Villa crashed 7-0 at Blackburn in October 1889 (their joint heaviest defeat in League football) and a year later they lost 5-1 on their first visit to Ewood Park.

When Villa lost 4-3 at Blackburn on 25 September 1897 it ended their record-breaking run of 15 League games without defeat and also brought to an end a run of nine successive League victories.

Villa made up for that defeat by winning the return fixture 5-1.

Villa completed the League double over Rovers in 1902-03, winning 5-0 at home and 2-0 away.

When Villa lost 3-2 to Blackburn in December 1903, their 14-match unbeaten home run of League games came to an end.

Ten goals were registered in 1928-29 as Villa beat Rovers 2-1 at home and 5-2 away.

Villa completed a terrific double over Rovers in 1932-33, winning 4-0 at home and 5-0 at Ewood Park. George Brown scored six goals in total, four in the latter game.

Villa ended the 1934-35 season by crashing to a 5-0 defeat at Ewood Park.

Villa and Rovers, both founder members of the Football League in 1888, were relegated together for the first time at the end of the 1935-36 season....after Rovers, who finished bottom of the table, had achieved the double, winning 5-1 (h) and 4-2 (a).

*Graham Fenton, player with both clubs.*

Villa themselves claimed a double in 1958-59 (3-2 away and 1-0 at home) before Rovers raced to another convincing double in 1964-65 - winning 5-1 at Ewood Park and 4-0 at Villa Park.

When Villa beat Rovers 4-1 at home in October 1971, all five goals were scored in a thrilling first-half of Third Division football.

Well over 30 years later, in season 1997-98, Rovers again whipped Villa in both matches, gaining a 4-0 win at Villa Park and a 5-0 victory at Ewood Park in the Premiership.

In a 3rd round FA Cup-tie at Blackburn in March 1889, Villa crashed to a humiliating 8-1 defeat - their worst ever in the competition.

Villa's only FA Cup home lapse against Rovers came in the opening round of the 1922-23 tournament, beaten 1-0 in front of 47,000 spectators

Seven years later, a bumper crowd of almost 70,000 packed into Villa Park to see George Brown net a hat-trick in Villa's excellent 4-1 defeat of Rovers in a 5th round tie in 1930.

The last time Villa and Rovers met in the FA Cup was in 1989-90 when Villa won a 3rd round replay 3-1, after a 2-2 draw at Ewood Park.

Players with both clubs include: F Carr, A Comyn (Rovers 'A' team), GS Cowans, A Cunliffe, RW Dix, AD Dougan, G Fenton, M Ferguson, B Gallacher, S Grayson, G Hardy, BG Hole, N Mackay (Rovers reserve), D Mail (Villa reserve), G Moseley, C Price, J Reynolds, T Riley, G Smith, JJ Willis, TC Wilson, AG Wright.
Also: GF Lee (Villa full-back, Rovers' manager), A Proudler (Villa player, Rovers coach), J Walker (Rovers player, Villa physio).

## BLACKPOOL (SOUTH SHORE)

Villa's playing record against the Seasiders:
Football League

| Venue | P | W | D | L | F | A |
|---|---|---|---|---|---|---|
| Home | 31 | 16 | 9 | 6 | 65 | 39 |
| Away | 31 | 10 | 7 | 14 | 44 | 51 |
| Totals | 62 | 26 | 16 | 20 | 109 | 90 |
| FA Cup | | | | | | |
| Home | 1 | 1 | 0 | 0 | 4 | 0 |
| Away | 1 | 1 | 0 | 0 | 4 | 2 |
| Totals | 2 | 2 | 0 | 0 | 8 | 2 |
| League Cup | | | | | | |
| Away | 1 | 0 | 0 | 1 | 1 | 4 |
| Wartime | | | | | | |
| Home | 2 | 2 | 0 | 0 | 6 | 3 |
| Away | 2 | 0 | 0 | 2 | 2 | 5 |
| Totals | 4 | 2 | 0 | 2 | 8 | 8 |

Tom 'Pongo' Waring rapped in a hat-trick as Villa beat Blackpool 5-1 at home in November 1931 and he was a two-goal hero the following March as Villa doubled up with a 3-1 victory at Bloomfield Road.

Sixteen goals were scored in the two League games between Villa and Blackpool in 1932-33 and by coincidence each side won 6-2 on their home ground. There were 30,000 at Villa Park to see Eric Houghton lead the goal-rush on 5 November and then Phil Watson scored a hat-trick for Blackpool in the first-half of the return game at Bloomfield Road on 18 March. In fact, the Seasiders were 5-0 up at the break, but didn't claim their last goal until the 90th minute!

Frank Broome scored three goals in Villa's 4-0 home win over Blackpool in a Second Division game in March 1937. Villa had won 3-2 at Bloomfield Road earlier in the season.

Blackpool gained a League double over Villa in 1948-49, winning 1-0 at Bloomfield Road and 5-2 at Villa Park.

Both League games favoured Villa in 1951-52 who won 4-0 at home and 3-0 at Bloomfield Road, but Blackpool took the honours in 1955-56, winning 6-0 at home and drawing 1-1 at Villa Park.

Blackpool beat Villa 5-3 at Bloomfield Road in August 1960 but Villa gained revenge in September 1961 with a 5-0 home victory as Peter McParland scored a hat-trick.

Harry Burrows then followed in the footsteps of 'Super Mac' with a hat-trick himself in Villa's emphatic 4-0 win at Blackpool in September 1963

Over 69,000 fans saw Villa beat Blackpool 4-0 at home in a 4th round FA Cup-tie in 1937-38.

Villa's only League Cup defeat was suffered at Bloomfield Road in the 1971-72 campaign. Villa had reached the Final the season before

Villa lost over two legs to Blackpool in the Wartime League Cup in 1942-43. The following season they met the Seasiders again in the League North Cup competition and this time lifted the trophy by winning 4-2 at home after going down 2-1 at Bloomfield Road. Almost 55,000 fans saw Villa fight back to win that second leg.

Players with both clubs include: DJ Astley, D Blair, T Bowman, AF Brown, J Burridge, D Byfield, RW Dix ('Pool WW2 guest), TC Donovan, AS Dyke, G Fenton, T Gardtner ('Pool WW2 guest), CJ Gibson, AJ Jaszczun, P King, P Maggs, A Mulraney ('Pool trialist), FJ O'Donnell, IV Powell ('Pool WW2 guest), A Rachel, HJ Reece (Villa reserve), G Reeves, K Richardson, L Sealey, GR Shaw, R Walker, AG Wright.
Also: FC Buckley & S McMahon (Villa players, 'Pool managers), A Cox (Villa coach/assistant & caretaker-manager, 'Pool assistant-manager), PD Doherty (scout for both clubs), R Downes ('Pool player, Villa coach).

## BLAIR, ANDREW
Born: Kirkcaldy, Fife, 18 December 1959
Career: Warwickshire Schoolboys, Coventry City (trainee, July 1975, professional October 1977), Aston Villa (£300,000, August 1981), Wolverhampton Wanderers (on loan, October 1983), Sheffield Wednesday (£60,000, August 1984), Aston Villa (March 1986), Barnsley (on loan, March 1988), Northampton Town (October 1988), Kidderminster Harriers (August 1989).
Capped five times by Scotland at Under-21 level, midfielder Andy Blair appeared in over 100 games for the Sky Blues before moving to Villa Park. He made his debut in the claret and blue strip as a substitute in the FA Charity Shield game against Tottenham Hotspur at Wembley in August 1981. Later he

THE COMPLETE ENCYCLOPAEDIA OF ASTON VILLA F.C.    THE COMPLETE ENCYCLOPAEDIA OF ASTON VILLA F.C.

29

helped Villa win the European Super Cup and starred in more than 30 League games, as well as having a loan spell at Molineux, before moving to Hillsborough. There he had the distinction of scoring a hat-trick of penalties in a Milk Cup-tie for the Owls against Luton Town prior to his return to Villa Park for a second spell in 1986. He pushed his appearance record with Villa up to the 60 mark (two goals scored) before switching to Northampton (after a loan spell at Oakwell). When he pulled out of League football in 1989, Blair had chalked up a useful record in the competition of 224 appearances and 10 goals.

## BLAIR, DANIEL

Born: Glasgow, 2 February 1906. Died: Blackpool, 1976.
Career: Whitehall Higher Grade School (Glasgow), junior football in Ireland, then Devonport Albion, Toronto Scottish FC, Rhode Island, Willy's Overland Motor Works' side and Providence FC in Canada & USA, Parkhead Juniors, Glasgow (1924), Clyde (1925), Aston Villa (£7,000 plus another player, November 1931), Blackpool (June 1936). Retired during the War and was later appointed coach at Bloomfield Road (1946-50).

Despite being on the small side, left-back Danny Blair was a competitive footballer, honest and efficient. After studying agriculture in Ireland, he travelled over to North America to do the same sort of thing. Over there he played for a handful of different clubs before returning 'home' in 1924. After a spell with Clyde he joined Villa in 1931 for what was the second highest fee splashed out by the club at that time. Capped eight times by Scotland (1929-33), Blair also represented the Scottish League on three occasions having earlier played for his country at Schoolboy level. He went on to amass 138 appearances for Villa, up to June 1936 when he transferred to Blackpool (having lost his place to George Cummings). He retired as a player during the Second World War and after four years as a coach at Bloomfield Road, he quit football to become a successful Market Gardener in Blackpool.

## BLAKE, NOEL LLOYD GEORGE

Born: Jamaica, 12 January 1962.
Career: Sutton Coldfield (August 1977), Aston Villa (professional, August 1979), Shrewsbury Town (on loan, March 1982), Birmingham City (£55,000, September 1982), Portsmouth (£150,000, August 1984), Leeds United (July 1988), Stoke City (February 1990), Bradford City (on loan, February 1992, signing permanently, July 1992), Dundee (December 1993), Exeter City (as a player/assistant-manager, August 1995, then coach/caretaker-boss January 1999 and manager, May 2000). Rugged, no-nonsense centre-half, Noel Blake had a fine playing career that spanned 20 years before he hung up his boots to become manager of the Grecians. After starting out in non-League soccer Blake became a professional at Villa Park in 1979 but made only four appearances in the claret and blue before transferring to neighbouring Blues in 1982 to rejoin his former manager Ron Saunders. All told, Blake played in 694 first-class matches and scored 40 goals.

## BLANCHFLOWER, ROBERT DENNIS

Born: Belfast, 10 February 1926. Died: Surrey, 9 December 1993.
Career: Belfast Technical College, Blossomfield United (East Belfast, 1939-44), Connsbrook (Gaelic football, 1940), RAF (in Scotland), Glentoran (Amateur, December 1945, professional January 1946), Swindon Town (Wartime guest), Barnsley (£6,000, April 1949), Aston

Villa (£15,000, March 1951), Tottenham Hotspur (£30,000, October 1954-June 1964 when he retired as a player), Showbiz XI, Northern Ireland manager (June 1976-November 1978), Chelsea (manager, December 1978-September 1979), Sports journalist for Sunday Express: 1964-88.

Danny Blanchflower played Gaelic football as a youngster as well as assisting the Belfast-based junior side, Blossomfield United and after serving in the RAF he signed for Glentoran halfway through the 1945-46 transitional season. In April 1949, Barnsley brought him into the Football League and the talented wing-half developed fast, bringing the scouts flooding into Yorkshire! On the transfer deadline of March 1951, Aston Villa boss George Martin swooped to bring him to the Midlands to fill the right-half berth vacated earlier in the season by Ivor Powell. Blanchflower, cool and composed, a thinker and tremendous passer of the ball, spent three-and-a-half years at Villa Park, appearing in 155 senior games and scoring 10 goals while also skippering the side. Then, three months into the 1954-55 season, Bill Nicholson, manager of Spurs, who was in the process of strengthening his side, moved in and enticed Blanchflower to White Hart Lane for £30,000. The Irishman, a master tactician with the ability to spot weaknesses in the opposition defence and exploit them visibly, became a member of one of the greatest midfield units in post-War football, linking up with two Scots, Jimmy White and Dave Mackay. Blanchflower was twice voted 'Footballer of the Year' in 1958 and 1961, the latter after Spurs had won the coveted League and FA Cup double. The first club to do so since Villa in 1897. He then lifted the European Cup winners Cup in 1963 and went on to gain 50 full caps for Northern Ireland. He toured Canada with the Irish FA in 1953 (8 games played out of 10) and in 1955 represented Great Britain against the Rest of Europe. He also played for the Football League v the Irish League in October 1960 and captained London v Basle and Barcelona in the semi-final and Final of the Inter Cities Fairs Cup in 1958. Blanchflower, troubled by a knee injury, retired in the summer of 1964 after appearing in 720 matches as a professional. He was out of the game for quite a while, but continued his love for football by becoming a journalist with the Sunday Express, displaying in his writing the same innovative, forceful and at times controversial attributes that had marked his career as a player. For two-and-a-half years from June 1976, he managed the Northern Ireland national team before taking charge of Chelsea in December 1978, a position he held until September 1979. In May 1990, Blanchflower received an honour never open to him in his playing days when Spurs met a Northern Ireland XI in a benefit Match for one of their all-time greats in the club's history.

Danny Blanchflower was the first player to skipper two successive FA Cup winning teams, leading Spurs in the 1961 and 1962 Finals against Leicester and Burnley respectively.

During the War he played rugby union, Gaelic football, soccer, hockey, cricket, golf, squash, table tennis and badminton.

* Danny's brother, Jackie Blanchflower, centre-half of Manchester United, was seriously injured in the Munich air disaster in 1958.

THE COMPLETE ENCYCLOPAEDIA OF ASTON VILLA F.C.     THE COMPLETE ENCYCLOPAEDIA OF ASTON VILLA F.C.

30

## BLOOMFIELD, RAYMOND GEORGE

Born: Kensington, London, 15 October 1944.

Career: Kensington Boys, Arsenal (Amateur, May 1960, professional, November 1961), Aston Villa (August 1964-August 1966).

Nephew of Jimmy Bloomfield (ex-Birmingham City), Ray was also a midfielder who made three appearances for Villa during his two years with the club. He represented England at both Schoolboy and Youth team levels and quit League soccer after leaving Villa Park.

## BOATENG, GEORGE

Born: Nkawkaw, Ghana, 5 September 1975.

Career: Excelsior FC, Feyenoord, Coventry City (£250,000, December 1997), Aston Villa (£4.5 million, July 1999).

Midfielder George Boateng captained Holland at under-18 level before going on to gain eighteen Under-21 caps while playing in Dutch League football with Feyenoord. He skippered his country several times, more so in the former internationals. A strong-running player with good distribution and an appetite for hard-work, Boateng joined Coventry after starring against the Sky Blues in a pre-season friendly with Feyenoord. He was in Villa's 2000 FA Cup Final side against Chelsea. He has now made almost 80 appearances for the club (four goal scored).

## BODEN, CHRISTOPHER DESMOND

Born: Wolverhampton, 13 October 1973.

Career: Aston Villa (trainee, 1989, professional, December 1991), Barnsley (loan, October 1993), Derby County (£150,000, March 1995-May 1996), Shrewsbury Town (loan January/February 1996).

Full-back or left-sided midfielder Chris Boden made just one substitute appearance for Aston Villa in the Premiership away at Leicester City on 3 December 1995, before moving to Derby County as cover for Shane Nicholson. He dropped out of League football at the end of the 1995-96 season.

## BODEN, JOHN ARTHUR

Born: Northwich, Cheshire, 1881. Died: c 1942.

Career: Glossop North End (1902), Clapton Orient (August 1904), Aston Villa (March 1906), Reading (August 1907), Croydon Common (1909-10), Plymouth Argyle (1910-12), Gillingham (1912-13), Northwich Victoria (1913-14).

Centre-half Jack Boden (deputy to Alec Leake) scored twice in 18 games for Aston Villa. He later occupied the left-half and centre-forward positions with Plymouth scoring 31 goals in 65 outings for the Pilgrims. He was forced to retire through injury in the summer of 1914.

## BODYMOOR HEATH

Aston Villa's training ground at Bodymoor Heath near Kingsbury, Warwickshire spans 20 acres of land and was officially opened in 1971 by Bert Bond, who had been Villa's head groundsman for 30 years.

With financial support from the Aston Villa Development Association, the whole complex cost £65,000 and was built by Ellmanton Construction Ltd.

*Villa in action at Bodymoor Heath, 1978.*

## BOLTON WANDERERS

Villa's playing record against the Trotters:

Football League/Premiership

| Venue | P | W | D | L | F | A |
|---|---|---|---|---|---|---|
| Home | 65 | 35 | 15 | 15 | 139 | 84 |
| Away | 65 | 17 | 13 | 35 | 67 | 126 |
| Totals | 130 | 52 | 28 | 50 | 206 | 210 |

FA Cup

| | | | | | | |
|---|---|---|---|---|---|---|
| Home | 2 | 1 | 1 | 0 | 3 | 2 |
| Away | 3 | 0 | 1 | 2 | 0 | 3 |
| Neutral | 1 | 0 | 1* | 0 | 0 | 0 |
| Totals | 6 | 1 | 3 | 2 | 3 | 5 |

* Villa won on penalties.

As founder members of the Football League, Villa first met Bolton at this level on 20 October 1888 when they won 3-2 at Pyke's Lane. The return fixture ended: Villa 6 Bolton 2, Tommy Green scoring twice.

Only 700 spectators - the lowest in Bolton's history - witnessed the League game against Aston Villa on 18 November 1893. Villa won 1-0, Charlie Hare the scorer.

On Boxing Day 1914, Villa crashed 7-1 to Bolton - their heaviest home League defeat up to that time. Six days later the return clash at Burnden Park ended all square at 2-2.

Frank Barson and Clem Stephenson failed to show up for Villa's League game at Bolton on 15 September 1920. The Wanderers won 5-0!

Villa conceded 11 League goals against Bolton in 1920 - losing 6-3 at home in April and 5-0 at Burnden Park in September.

George Brown rattled in four goals when Villa whipped Bolton 6-1 at home in September 1932.

*Alan Thompson, player with both clubs.*

Villa commenced their 1951-52 League season with a crushing 5-2 defeat at Burnden Park, Bolton scoring three times in the second-half after Villa had battled to make it 2-2 by half-time.

In April 1958 Villa lost 4-0 at Bolton but four days later reversed that scoreline to a goal with an identical victory at Villa Park.

Ten goals were scored in the two Villa v Bolton League games in 1962-63. Villa won 5-0 at home but lost 4-1 at Burnden Park.

A total of 141,874 spectators saw the three 3rd round FA Cup encounters between Villa and Bolton in 1948-49. Villa eventually won 3-1 at home after 1-1 and 0-0 draws.

Villa beat the Wanderers in an FA Cup semi-final penalty shoot-out in 2000 after the game had initially finished goalless after extra-time.

Players with both clubs include: T Barber, G Bergsson (Villa junior trialist), W Brown, F Carr, NJ Cox, S Curcic, G Farrelly, A Gittins, S Gray, S Greenhalgh, JC Gregory (also Villa manager), TP Griffiths, H Morton (Wanderers' trialist), D Richards (Villa trialist/reserve), CL Roberts (Villa reserve), H Shutt (Wanderers' reserve), B Small, D Stokes (Villa reserve), A Thompson, R Westwood (Villa trialist), TC Wilson.

Also: J Hogan (Wanderers' player, Villa manager & coach), BD Rioch (Villa player, Wanderers' manager).

## BOOKS

Listed here are some of the many football books that have a direct reference to Aston Villa FC. Some have been written by men (players etc) who have been associated with the club....

● Andy Gray - Shades Of Gray (McDonald, 1986).

THE COMPLETE ENCYCLOPAEDIA OF ASTON VILLA F.C.    THE COMPLETE ENCYCLOPAEDIA OF ASTON VILLA F.C.

31

- Aston Villa (Newservice, 1948)...brief history by Fred Ward.
- Aston Villa - A Complete Record: 1874-1988 (Breedon Books, 1988)...statistical history of club by Tony Matthews & David Goodyear.
- Aston Villa - A Complete Record: 1874-1992 (Breedon Books, 1992)...up-dated version of previous book by Tony Matthews & David Goodyear.
- Aston Villa: A Portrait In Old Picture Postcards (SB Publications, 1991)...compiled by Derrick Spinks with 88 postcards.
- Aston Villa Cup Record: 1880-1924 (General, 1924)
- Aston Villa - Double Winners 1896-97 (Sports Projects, 1996)...100th anniversary of Villa winning the double.
- Aston Villa Greats (Donald/Sportsprint, 1990)...10 Villa Greats, the choice of Leon Hickman.
- Aston Villa On Cigarette & Trade Cards (Brewin Books, 1993)...compiled by Derrick Spinks.
- Aston Villa: The First 100 Years, 1874-1974 (Aston Villa FC, 1974)...history of club by Peter Morris.
- Aston Villa: The History of a Great Football Club, 1874-1960 (Naldrett Press, 1960)...history by Peter Morris.
- Aston Villa: The History of a Great Football Club, 1874-1961 (The Sportsmans Book Club)...history by Peter Morris.
- Aston Villa - The 25-year Record: 1970-71 to 1994-95 (Soccer Book Publishing, 1995).
- Aston Villa - Total Guide (Soccer Publishing, 1979)...match details 1946-79.
- Aston Villa 2000 - The Official Graphic History (Sports Days).
- Deadly...autobiography of Aston Villa Chairman, Doug Ellis (Sports Projects, 1998).
- Forty Years of Aston Villa, volumes 1 & 2, (by Keith Dickinson)
- Going For Goal - Peter McParland (Souvenir Press, 1960).
- Hamlyn Illustrated History of Aston Villa (Hamlyn, 1998).
- Let's Talk About Aston Villa (Sentinel, 1946)...part of a series by Tom Morgan.
- Paul McGrath: Ooh, Aah, Paul McGrath - The Black Pearl of Inchicore (mainstream Publishing, 1994)...McGrath's story.
- Pinnacle of the Perry Barr Pets (Juma Printing & Publishing, 1997)...story of Villa's double-winning season of 1896-97.
- Play Up Villa - The Story of a Unique FA Cup Tie (Rob Wolley, 1977)...written in conjunction with Johnny Dixon.
- Return of the Little Villan (Sports Projects, 1996)...Brian Little's story of his first 20 months as Villa's manager.
- Ron Saunders' Aston Villa Scrapbook (Pictorial Publications, 1981).
- Soccer In The Blood - Billy Walker (Stanley Paul, 1960)...the playing and managerial career of an all-time Villa Great.
- Stride Inside The Villa (Sports Projects, 1997)...Steve Stride's story of 25 years at Villa Park.
- Super Clubs (Aston Villa) 1998-99 (DP/Dempsey Parr).
- The Aston Villa Story (Arthur Baker, 1981)...by Ian Johnson
- The Aston Villa Story (Breedon Books, 1993)...by Anton Rippon.
- The Aston Villa Who's Who (Paper Plane, 1990)...pen picture biographies of all Villa players: 1874-1990 by Tony Matthews.
- The Aston Villa Quiz Book (Mainstream Publishing, 1989)... 1110 questions & answers on the Villa, compiled by Derrick Spinks.
- The Boss (John Gregory: 2000)
- The Great Years of Aston Villa: 1886-1992 (David Goodyear, 1992).
- The History of Aston Villa (Richard Digance Card Co. Ltd, 1995)...cartoon history of Aston Villa FC.
- The Murder of Tommy Ball - An Aston Villa Tragedy (Protean, 1996)...Paul Lester's story of the death of a great player.

- The Story of Aston Villa (Moreland, 1981)...by Anton Rippon.
- The Story of Aston Villa: A Cartoon History (Birmingham Evening Despatch, 1947)...by Norman Edwards.
- The Villans - Day-to-Day Life at Villa Park (Mainstream Publishing, 1998)...diary compiled by Graham Betts.
- Tommy Docherty Speaks, by the 'Doc' (Pelham Books, 1967)
- Triumphs of the Football Field (Sports Projects, 1997)...story of Archie Hunter, narrated by himself and first serialised in 1890 in the Birmingham Weekly Mercury.
- Villa at the Millennium (Birmingham Post & Mail, 1999)...76-page lightweight publication with reports from the archives of the Evening Mail & Sports Argus.
- Villa Park Encyclopaedia (Mainstream Publishing, 1997).
- Villa in the Blood (Breedon Books, 1998)...memories of Villa.
- Villa Park 100 Years (Sports Projects, 1997)...history of Villa Park by Simon Inglis.

### Book Leaves
The Aston Villa Annual (issued at the start of each season) ran from 1930-1 until 1950-51 inclusive. It was then replaced by the Aston Villa Official handbook and after that the Aston Villa Yearbook and then the Aston Villa Annual.

Another publication was 'My Villa Years'....Charlie Aitken's 1969-70 testimonial brochure. Then in November 1999 the Evening Mail published a paperback (76 pages @ £1.25) entitled 'Villa At The Millennium' whilst various Aston Villa diaries (both official and some unofficial) have been produced over the years.

**Books written/co-compiled by persons with a Villa connection!**
Danny Blanchflower (The Double and Before - autobiography, 1961); (Biography of a Visionary, 1997); Trevor Ford (I Lead The Attack, Stanley Paul, 1957); Ron Atkinson (Big Ron - A Different Ball Game, 1998), Tony Cascarino (Autobiography, 2000), Derek Dougan (Attack, 1969; The Sash He Never Wore, 1972; Doog, 1980; How Not To Run Football, 1981); David Ginola (St. Tropez to St. James' Park & El Magnifique, 2000); Peter Doherty (Spotlight on Football, 1946), Tommy Docherty (Soccer from The Shoulder, 1960), Peter Schmeichel (The Autobiography), Graham Taylor (The Only Way Is Up, 1989) David Platt (Achieving the Goal), Paul Merson (Hero & Villain), Shades of Gray (Andy Gray) and Dwight Yorke (Official Biography by Hunter Davies).

### BOOTLE
Villa never met the former Football League club at competition level, and only one player - WG Evans - served both clubs.

### BORDEAUX
Villa's playing record against the French side:
UEFA Cup

| Venue | P | W | D | L | F | A |
|-------|---|---|---|---|---|---|
| Home | 1 | 1 | 0 | 0 | 1 | 0 |
| Away | 1 | 0 | 1 | 0 | 0 | 0 |
| Totals | 2 | 1 | 1 | 0 | 1 | 0 |

The French side were beaten 1-0 on aggregate by Villa in a two-legged UEFA Cup-tie in September 1997. Some 16,000 fans saw the first game in Bordeaux end goalless and then at Villa Park, before a 33,072 crowd, a Savo Milosevic goal 21 minutes into extra-time took Villa through to round two.

THE COMPLETE ENCYCLOPAEDIA OF ASTON VILLA F.C.    THE COMPLETE ENCYCLOPAEDIA OF ASTON VILLA F.C.

32

## BOSNICH, MARK JOHN

Born: Sydney, Australia, 13 January 1972.

Career: Sydney Croatia, Liverpool (trialist), Manchester United (non-contract, June 1989), Croatia Sydney (June 1991), Aston Villa (February 1992), Manchester United (July 1999), Chelsea (2000).

Goalkeeper Mark Bosnich was brought up in the Croatian community of Sydney and played for the local team before getting the urge to move to Britain! After unsuccessful trials at Anfield he joined Manchester United on a non-contract basis (as an Amateur) in the summer of 1989. He stayed at Old Trafford for two years during which time he also attended Manchester Polytechnic as a student. He made just three first team appearances for the Reds before returning to the Sydney-based club in Australia. Then, in February 1992, Bosnich moved back to England to join Aston Villa (as a replacement for Nigel Spink). He went on to play in 228 matches before, ironically, going back to his former club, Manchester United on a free transfer in July 1999.

Capped by his country at Youth and

*Mark Bosnich.*

Under-23 levels, Bosnich has also played in 18 full internationals and starred for Australia in the semi-final of the Olympic Games in Barcelona in 1992, but did not play for his 'host' country in the 2000 Games. 'Bozzie' - who has drawn up a remarkable record for saving penalty kicks - gained two League Cup winners' medals with Aston Villa in 1994 and 1996. After helping United win the Premiership title in 2000, he suddenly found himself third choice at Old Trafford, following the arrival of French World Cup star Fabien Barthez. In 2000 he turned down the chance to join the Scottish club, Celtic - preferring to fight for his place at United! He never got it - and subsequently he joined Chelsea as third choice 'keeper!

Bosnich was fined £1,000 as well as receiving a stern warning from the FA for his 'Hitler-style' impression ('Sieg Heil') at White Hart Lane in October 1996.

## BOTANICAL GARDENS

Aston Villa's AGM in April 1968 was held at The Botanical Gardens, Edgbaston, Birmingham.

## BOURNE, HUBERT E.

Born: Bromsgrove, 1895. Died: Birmingham, 1965.

Career: Manchester United (1914), Aston Villa (July 1919-April 1922). Hubert Bourne was an inside-forward who scored twice in just seven outings for Aston Villa during his three seasons with the club. He was forced to retire with a serious knee injury in 1922.

He had been at Old Trafford before the Great War, but did not receive a first team call. After calling it a day (as a player) Bourne remained at Villa Park and looked after the third team for a while, before taking over as trainer of the second XI before becoming the first team trainer in August 1934, a position he held until July 1953. He was trainer to the full England team on four occasions (1948-51) and was eventually succeeded at Villa Park by the former Portsmouth and Scottish footballer Jimmy Easson.

## BOURNEMOUTH (AFC)

Villa's playing record against the Cherries:
Football League

| Venue | P | W | D | L | F | A |
|---|---|---|---|---|---|---|
| Home | 2 | 1 | 1 | 0 | 3 | 2 |
| Away | 2 | 1 | 0 | 1 | 2 | 4 |
| Totals | 4 | 2 | 1 | 1 | 5 | 6 |

A record Third Division crowd of 48,110 saw Villa beat Bournemouth 2-1 at home in a vital promotion game in February 1972.

On 17 October 1987, Aston Villa became the first club to score 6,000 goals in the Football League and the player who was responsible for that achievement was Mark Walters who found the net in the 1-1 home draw with AFC Bournemouth (Division 2).

Players with both clubs include: W Aspinall, T Berry (Bournemouth juniors, Villa reserve), BA Greenhalgh, TW Mitchinson, TB Moore, A O'Neill, CL Roberts (Villa reserve), AJ Scott, D Simmonds, TC Southren, S Teale, JJ Tyrrell, GJ Williams, A Young.

Also: A Cunliffe (Villa player, Bournemouth trainer/physio), B Tiler (Villa player, Cherries' administration officer etc.),

## BOWEN, SAMUEL EDWARD

Born: Hednesford, 17 November 1903. Died: Stafford, 4 March 1981.

Career: West Hill School (Hednesford), Hednesford Town (August 1918), Hednesford Primitives, Hednesford Town (1921), Aston Villa (August 1923), Norwich City (October 1934-May 1938).

Though heavily built, Teddy Bowen was a very consistent full-back who was described in 1933 as being 'dainty, gentle, efficient and canny'. He came from a footballing family and after his school days were over he joined his hometown club (the Pitmen). After a brief spell with rivals, the Primitives, he returned to Cross Keys for a second term prior to signing as professional with Aston Villa for the start of the 1923-24 season. Bowen stayed at Villa Park for over eleven years during which time he made 199 first team appearances (it would have been decidedly more if Messrs Mort and Smart hadn't been around at the same time). In 1934 Bowen joined Norwich and added a further 139 outings to his tally with the Canaries before retiring in May 1938. After the War he worked for the Hednesford and District Social Services Department, a job he did until his death in 1981.

## BOWMAN, THOMAS

Born: Tarbolton, Strathclyde, 26 October 1873. Died: Southampton, 27 August 1958.

Career: Annbank, Blackpool (June 1896), Aston Villa (October 1897), Southampton (May 1901), Portsmouth (May 1904-June 1909), Endsleigh Athletic (August 1909-May 1912).

Tommy Bowman played initially as a right-back for Annbank before joining Blackpool. He was then transferred to Villa Park in October 1897 and developed into a 'hard to beat' reliable, purposeful clean-tackling full-back or centre-half who went on to appear in 116 first-class matches for Villa, scoring two goals. He also gained League championship-winning medals in 1899 and 1900, and a year after leaving Villa Park for Southampton (with Albert Brown) he collected an FA Cup runners-up medal. Bowman later spent five years with and in all he made well over 170 Southern League appearances for both Saints and Pompey. After announcing his retirement in 1912, Boyman - a boiler scaler by trade - worked in the Southampton dockyards for many years.

He died in a Southampton hospital shortly before his 85th birthday.

THE COMPLETE ENCYCLOPAEDIA OF ASTON VILLA F.C.  THE COMPLETE ENCYCLOPAEDIA OF ASTON VILLA F.C.

33

## BOXING
British boxers Randolph Turpin, Danny McAlinden and Jack Bodell have all fought in major championship bouts at Villa Park! (See Villa Park)

## BOYMAN, WILLIAM RICHARD
Born: Richmond, Surrey, 10 August 1891. Died: 1966.
Career: Kent County FA, Cradley Heath (1915), Aston Villa (August 1919), Nottingham Forest (October 1921), Stourbridge (January 1923).
Inside-forward Dick Boyman scored a hat-trick in his second game for Aston Villa at Middlesbrough in October 1919. He went on to net 11 times in his 22 outings for the club whom he served for just over two years. Having played representative football for the adjoining county of his birth (Kent) as a teenager, he surprisingly moved to the Black Country to sign for Cradley Heath just before the Great War. He had the misfortune to miss the 1920 FA Cup Final because he was cup-tied. Boyman broke his leg on the last day of the 1920-21 season and never really recovered his composure, eventually retiring from the game in 1924 after a short spell with Stourbridge.

## BOYNE, REGINALD
Born: Leeds, 10 October 1891. Died: Yorkshire, 1939.
Career: New Zealand football, Aston Villa (trialist September 1913, professional December 1913), Leicester Fosse (WW1), Brentford (August 1920-May 1921).
Inside-forward Reg Boyne emigrated to New Zealand (with his family) as a teenager and played soccer on Long Island before returning to England in 1912. After starring in local football for a year or so, he was spotted by an enthusiastic Aston Villa scout who invited him along for trials. They were successful, Boyne signing as a professional shortly before Christmas in 1913. He appeared in eight competitive and five Wartime games for Villa before leaving the club soon after the hostilities to spend a season with Brentford, for whom he scored 10 goals in 21 League games in 1920-21.

## BRADFORD CITY
Villa's playing record against the Bantams:
Football League/Premiership

| Venue | P | W | D | L | F | A |
| --- | --- | --- | --- | --- | --- | --- |
| Home | 16 | 11 | 2 | 3 | 35 | 12 |
| Away | 16 | 5 | 5 | 6 | 21 | 24 |
| Totals | 32 | 16 | 7 | 9 | 56 | 36 |
| FA Cup | | | | | | |
| Home | 2 | 1 | 0 | 1 | 3 | 4 |
| Away | 1 | 0 | 1 | 0 | 2 | 2 |
| Totals | 3 | 1 | 1 | 1 | 5 | 6 |
| League Cup | | | | | | |
| Home | 1 | 1 | 0 | 0 | 7 | 1 |
| Away | 1 | 1 | 0 | 0 | 4 | 3 |
| Totals | 2 | 2 | 0 | 0 | 11 | 4 |
| Simod Cup | | | | | | |
| Home | 1 | 0 | 0 | 1 | 0 | 5 |

Aston Villa and City first met at League level in season 1908-09 (Division One). After a 1-1 draw in Yorkshire, Villa crashed 3-1 at home in the rturn fixture.
Villa doubled up over the Bantams the following season, winning 3-1 at home and 2-1 away and did likewise in 1910-11 with victories of 2-1 away and 4-1 at home (Harry Hampton netting twice in the latter contest).
Billy Walker scored a hat-trick of penalties when Villa beat the Bantams 7-1 at home in a First Division match on 12 November 1921. A week earlier Villa had lost 3-2 at Valley Parade.
South African-born inside-forward Gordon Hodgson scored Villa's first Second Division hat-trick when the Bantams were beaten 5-1 at Villa Park in September 1936.

Villa's 1-0 victory over City at Valley Parade on 22 April 1972 guaranteed their promotion from the Third Division. It was satisfying that Charlie Aitken should score the all-important goal in front of 9,289 spectators (4,500 of them being Villa supporters).
Over 36,400 fans saw David Platt score the goal that gave Villa a 1-0 home win over the Bantams in May 1988 and virtually guarantee them promotion to the First Division.
In 2000-01, Villa beat Bradford 2-0 at home, with goals by Gareth Southgate and a Dion Dublin penalty, and 3-0 away - these defeats helped send the Bantams back to the Nationwide League Division One after just two seasons in the Premiership. The game at The Pulse Stadium on 3 February was in fact, Villa's 4,000th in League and Premiership football.

*Platt's goal against City at Villa Park in May 1988.*

All three FA Cup encounters took place over a two-year period. Villa drew 2-2 at Bradford in the 3rd round in January 1933 before winning the replay 2-1, Joe Tate scoring the deciding goal in front of 35,000 spectators. City gained revenge with a 3-1 victory at Villa Park, also in the 3rd round, in January 1935.
Only 7,882 fans saw Tony Hateley score four goals when Villa beat the Bantams 7-1 in a League Cup-tie in 1964-65. It was 4-0 and game over at half-time.

*Dean Saunders, player with both clubs.*

Just 4,217 fans turned up to see Villa hammered 5-0 at home by Bradford City in a Simod Cup-tie in 1987-88.

Players with both clubs include: RE Blackburn, NLG Blake, FC Buckley MS Burke, RM Campbell, B Carbone, WG Clarke, S Collymore, GS Cowans, G Crudgington, DG Evans, J Graham, T Hockey, I Ormondroyd, IV Powell (also City manager), D Saunders, B Small, S Staunton, G Williams.
Also: RE Brocklebank (Villa player, Bantams manager).

THE COMPLETE ENCYCLOPAEDIA OF ASTON VILLA F.C.

THE COMPLETE ENCYCLOPAEDIA OF ASTON VILLA F.C.

34

## BRADFORD PARK AVENUE

Villa's playing record against Park Avenue:
Football League

| Venue | P | W | D | L | F | A |
|---|---|---|---|---|---|---|
| Home | 5 | 4 | 0 | 1 | 12 | 4 |
| Away | 5 | 1 | 2 | 2 | 8 | 16 |
| Totals | 10 | 5 | 2 | 3 | 20 | 20 |
| FA Cup | | | | | | |
| Away | 1 | 1 | 0 | 0 | 5 | 0 |

On 27 September 1919 Villa crashed 6-1 at Park Avenue, but a week later they turned things round (just) by winning 1-0 at Villa Park. Both Villa goals came from Clem Stephenson.
On 20 November 1920 Villa beat Park Avenue 4-1 at home. A week later they lost the return fixture 4-0!
Villa's excellent FA Cup win over Park Avenue was achieved in the 4th round in 1912-13, Harry Hampton scoring a hat-trick in front of 24,000 spectators.

Players with both clubs include: WA Dinsdale, RW Dix (BPA WW2 guest), AJ Fisher, W Hanson (Villa reserve), JH Harvey (Villa trialist), G Reeves, A Talbot, KC Tewkesbury, AE Wood.
Also: KO Roberts (Villa player, Park Avenue assistant-manager).

## BRADLEY, DARREN MICHAEL

Born: Kings Norton, Birmingham, 24 November 1965.
Career: St Thomas Aquinas School, Kings Norton Boys, West Midlands County Schools, South Birmingham Schools, Broadmeadow All Stars, Aston Villa (trainee June 1982, professional December 1983), West Bromwich Albion (March 1986 in a £90,000 deal involving Steve Hunt), Walsall (August 1995), Hibernians (Malta - on loan), Solihull Borough (July 1997), Hednesford Town (2000).
After leaving Aston Villa, the versatile Darren Bradley amassed almost 300 appearances for West Bromwich Albion, skippering the Baggies to victory in the 1993 Division Two play-off Final at Wembley. He joined Villa as a youngster, turned professional a month after his 18th birthday, and moved to The Hawthorns after 23 outings in the claret and blue strip. He remained an Albion player until 1995 when he transferred to nearby Walsall. Able to play as a full-back, central defender or in midfield, Bradley left the Saddlers to enter non-League football with Solihull Borough in 1997.

## BRADLEY, KEITH

Born: Ellesmere Port, Cheshire, 31 January 1946
Career: Everton (junior June 1961), Aston Villa (trainee July 1962, professional June 1963), Peterborough United (November 1972). He retired in the summer of 1976 and became Youth coach with Birmingham City, later coaching in Cyprus and also the Middle East, under the guidance of the former Bristol City manager Alan Dicks.
A full-back, Keith Bradley failed to make the grade at Goodison Park and moved from Merseyside to Villa Park, initially as an apprentice before being taken on the professional staff. At the time he had Charlie Aitken, Gordon Lee and Mick Wright to contest a first team place with but after making steady progress he eventually gained a place in the side and went on to appear in 144 first-class matches, scoring two goals. After ten excellent years at Villa Park, during which time he played at Wembley in the 1971 League Cup Final and helped Villa win the Third Division championship, Bradley moved to Peterborough in 1972. After several coaching positions he quit football and purchased a bar/restaurant in Mojacar, Spain.

## BRAWN, WILLIAM FREDERICK

Born: Wellingborough, 1 August 1878. Died: London, 18 August 1932.
Career: Wellingborough White Star, Wellingborough Principals, Northampton Town (July 1895), Sheffield United (professional, January 1900), Aston Villa (December 1901), Middlesbrough (March 1906),

Chelsea (November 1907), Brentford (August 1911). Retired May 1919 (after guesting for Spurs in War). Later advisory-manager at Griffin Park.
Billy Brawn was said to be one of 'the most dangerous outside-rights

in the kingdom' during the early 1900s. Renowned for his speed and shooting ability, he was unusually tall for a winger (6ft 2ins) and was also weighty, tipping the scales at 13st 5lbs. He could use both feet scoring and making many goals. Brawn, who gained two England caps and collected an FA Cup winners' medal with Aston Villa in 1905, netted a total of 20 goals in 107 first-class appearances during his time at Villa Park before transferring to Middlesbrough in 1906. He later assisted Chelsea, starring in the London club's first-ever season in Division One, and their neighbours Brentford, finally retiring in 1913 with over 350 League and Cup appearances to his name. He later ran a pub (the King's Arms) in Boston Road, Brentford while also acting as advisory-manager at Griffin Park, a position he held until his death in 1932.

## BREITKREUTZ, MATTHIAS

Born: Germany 12 May 1971.
Career: PFV Bergmann Bosnig (1987), Aston Villa (October 1991), PFV Bergman Bosnig (August 1993).
Matt Breitkreutz joined Aston Villa along with his fellow countryman Stefan Beinlich three months into the 1991-92 season A midfielder, he just made 13 League appearances for the club before returning to his homeland at the end of the 1992-93 campaign.

## BREMNER, DESMOND GEORGE

Born: Aberchider, Kirkcaldy, 7 September 1962.
Career: Kirkcaldy Schoolboy football, Banks O' Dee 'A'. Deverondale FC (Highland League), Hibernian (July 1971, professional November 1972), Aston Villa (£250,000, September 1979 in a deal involving Joe Ward), Birmingham City (October 1984-May 1989), Fulham (August 1989), Walsall (March-May 1990), Stafford Rangers (1990-92), Aston Villa (coach, 1999).

For a period of five years, the hard-working and forceful midfield play of Des Bremner was always evident in the Aston Villa side. He made 227 League and Cup appearances for the club, scored 10 goals and created several more chances for his colleagues. After leaving Villa Park in 1984, he went on to give Blues excellent service, making almost 200 appearances for the St Andrew's club prior to teaming up with Fulham on a free transfer. Later, for three months at the end of the 1989-90 season he returned to the Midlands to assist Walsall. With Villa he won a League Championship medal in 1981 and European Cup and Super

THE COMPLETE ENCYCLOPAEDIA OF ASTON VILLA F.C.   THE COMPLETE ENCYCLOPAEDIA OF ASTON VILLA F.C.

35

Cup prizes soon afterwards. He was capped just once by Scotland at senior level and nine times by the Under-23s, becoming the oldest player ever to appear in a League game for the Saddlers: aged 37 years 240 days v Bristol City, May 1990. In 1999 he returned to Villa as coach at the club's Football Academy Centre at Bodymoor Heath.

## BRENTFORD

Villa's playing record against the Bees:
Football League

| Venue | P | W | D | L | F | A |
|---|---|---|---|---|---|---|
| Home | 3 | 2 | 1 | 0 | 12 | 4 |
| Away | 3 | 3 | 0 | 0 | 8 | 3 |
| Totals | 6 | 5 | 1 | 0 | 20 | 7 |

FA Cup

| Home | 1 | 0 | 1 | 0 | 0 | 0 |
|---|---|---|---|---|---|---|
| Away | 1 | 1 | 0 | 0 | 2 | 1 |
| Totals | 2 | 1 | 1 | 0 | 2 | 1 |

Wartime

| Home | 1 | 0 | 1 | 0 | 1 | 1 |
|---|---|---|---|---|---|---|
| Away | 1 | 1 | 0 | 0 | 1 | 0 |
| Totals | 2 | 1 | 1 | 0 | 2 | 1 |

Aston Villa first met Brentford in League action on 21 September 1935 when goals by Tom 'Pongo' Waring and Dai Astley gave them a 2-1 victory at Griffin Park in front of 20,000 fans. Double that amount of spectators saw the return game at Villa Park end all square at 2-2 (January 25), Astley again on target.
Aston Villa scored nine goals against the Bees in season 1938-39 - winning 5-0 at home before a near 50,000 crowd and 4-2 at Griffin Park. Albert Kerr and Jackie Martin both scored twice in the first game while Frank Broome did likewise in the second.
In the first season after the War, Villa again did the business, beating the Bees 5-0 (h) and 2-0 (a).

Villa progressed into the 5th round of the FA Cup with a 2-1 replay victory over the Bees in 1952-53.

Players with both clubs include: W Aspinall, J Birch, WF Brawn (also Bees' advisory-manager), PF Broadbent, FH Broome, T Bullivant, F Chapple, GW Cook, RD Davis (WW2 guest for both clubs), S Dearn (Villa reserve), R Dorsett (Bees' WW2 guest), CJ Drinkwater, D Geddis, TA Gibson, JS Hisbent, GC Hunter (Bees' WWI guest), C McEleny, PC Merson, AP Mitchell (Villa reserve, Bees' player-manager), PH Mortimer, T Riley, CL Roberts (Villa reserve), R Sloley (Bees reserve), LGF Smith, B Small (Bees trialist), E Wright.
Also: J Hogan (Villa manager/coach, Bees coach).

## BRETT, FRANK BERNARD
Born: Kings Norton, 10 March 1899. Died: Chichester, 21 July 1988
Career: Redditch (1916), Aston Villa (amateur July 1919), Manchester United (signed as a professional for £300, February 1921), Aston Villa (August 1922), Northampton Town (May 1923), Brighton & Hove Albion (May 1930), Tunbridge Wells Rangers (September 1935), Hove FC (as an Amateur, September 1936-May 1937). Retired to go into business in Sussex.
Full-back Frank Brett was released by Aston Villa without getting a first team outing - signed by Manchester United for just £300, a transaction that clearly upset the supporters. The matter was subsequently placed before the FA Committee and as a result United were fined ten guineas (£10.50p) for having registered Brett as one of their players before his transfer from Villa Park had actually been sanctioned. Brett returned to Villa Park at the start of the 1922-23 season but failed to impress and was released to join Northampton for whom he made

over 250 League appearances. He later did just as well with Brighton (131 League games in five seasons) before drifting out of top-class soccer in 1935. During his competitive footballing career Brett amassed well over 400 League and Cup appearances.

## BRIBERY
During a League match at Villa Park on 29 April 1905 Billy Meredith, the Manchester City and Welsh international right-winger, was alleged to have bribed an Aston Villa player with £10.
Thirteen weeks later, on 4 August, after the matter had been looked into by an FA Commission, it was announced that Meredith had been suspended for nine months (until the end of that 1905-06 season).

## BRIERLEY HILL ALLIANCE
No competitive match action between Villa and Brierley Hill but plenty of other links!

Players with both clubs include: WCW Armfield, J Corbett, G Garratt, JS Gillan, J Graham, AW Green, JB Higgins (Villa reserve), CJH Millington, AF Phoenix, T Smart, D Stokes (Villa reserve), GH Tranter, R Westwood (Villa trialist), JE Worrell, RE York.
Also: A Mulraney & JT Tate (Villa players, Alliance player-managers)

## BRIGGS, WILSON WAITE
Born: Gorebridge, near Edinburgh, Scotland, 15 May 1942.
Career: Armiston Rangers, Gorebridge Youths, Musselburgh Welfare, Aston Villa (August 1959-May 1964), Falkirk (August 1965-68), East Fife (1968-70).
Full-back Wilson Briggs, who was an apprentice butcher, played Amateur football north of the border for three useful sides before joining Aston Villa on the same day as Charlie Aitken in 1959. Aitken made the grade, Briggs didn't. In fact, Briggs took part in only two senior games for the club during his five year stay at Villa Park, his League debut coming at right-back against rivals Birmingham City at St Andrew's in March 1962. He remained a permanent reserve at the club until returning to Scotland in the summer of 1964. Later he did much better with Falkirk and East Fife (1968-70). He retired from the game in 1975 after spending five year in non-League soccer in Scotland.

## BRIGHTON & HOVE ALBION
Villa's playing record against the Seagulls:
Football League

| Venue | P | W | D | L | F | A |
|---|---|---|---|---|---|---|
| Home | 8 | 6 | 2 | 0 | 16 | 4 |
| Away | 8 | 3 | 2 | 3 | 8 | 7 |
| Totals | 16 | 9 | 4 | 3 | 24 | 11 |

FA Cup

| Home | 1 | 1 | 0 | 0 | 4 | 2 |
|---|---|---|---|---|---|---|
| Away | 1 | 0 | 1 | 0 | 2 | 2 |
| Totals | 2 | 1 | 1 | 0 | 6 | 4 |

FA Charity Shield

| Neutral | 1 | 0 | 0 | 1 | 0 | 1 |
|---|---|---|---|---|---|---|

Aston Villa and Albion first met at League level on 22 August 1959. The Second Division encounter took place at The Goldstone Ground and in front of almost 32,000 fans Villa won 2-1, Jimmy MacEwan and Jackie Sewell their scorers. Villa won the return fixture 3-1.

Villa had to fight every inch of the way before knocking Albion out of the FA Cup in a 3rd round replay in 1954-55, winning a 4-2 after a 2-2 draw at The Goldstone Ground. Tommy Thompson scored in both matches while Irishman Norman Lockhart netted twice in the replay.

THE COMPLETE ENCYCLOPAEDIA OF ASTON VILLA F.C.        THE COMPLETE ENCYCLOPAEDIA OF ASTON VILLA F.C.

36

***Goal for Thompson at Brighton in 1955.***

Albion defeated Villa 1-0 in the annual FA Charity Shield encounter at neutral Stamford Bridge in 1910-11.

Players with both clubs include: W Aspinall, G Barry (Albion junior), FB Brett (Villa reserve), CS Buckley, FC Buckley, S Crowther, LC Curbishley, AJ Fisher, SB Foster, B Gallacher, JC Gregory, R Guttridge, T Hughes, MAW Jones, MR Keown, P King, SJ Morgan, DG Mortimer, G Moseley, JTS Phillips, D Saunders, G Sidebottom, JG Thompson, H Vallance (Villa reserve), PS Varco, W Yates (Villa reserve).
Also: P Saward (Villa player, Albion manager), C Dobson & DJ Sexton (Albion players, Villa coaches).

## BRISTOL CITY
Villa's playing record against the Robins:
Football League

| Venue | P | W | D | L | F | A |
|---|---|---|---|---|---|---|
| Home | 16 | 10 | 3 | 3 | 27 | 19 |
| Away | 16 | 5 | 6 | 5 | 18 | 14 |
| Totals | 32 | 15 | 9 | 8 | 45 | 33 |
| FA Cup | | | | | | |
| Home | 3 | 3 | 0 | 0 | 7 | 3 |
| Away | 3 | 2 | 1 | 0 | 7 | 1 |
| Totals | 6 | 5 | 1 | 0 | 14 | 4 |
| Wartime | | | | | | |
| Home | 1 | 1 | 0 | 0 | 2 | 1 |
| Away | 1 | 0 | 1 | 0 | 0 | 0 |
| Totals | 2 | 1 | 1 | 0 | 2 | 1 |

Aston Villa and City first met in the League in 1906-07 - and it was Villa who took the honours, winning both matches, 3-2 at home and 4-2 away. Harry Hampton scored a hat-trick at Bristol.
The first 4-4 League draw at Villa Park was between Villa and City in October 1907.
On 21 November 1959 - Gerry Hitchens grabbed a hat-trick as Villa won 5-0 at Ashton Gate in a Second Division match.
Later that season Stan Lynn blasted in two penalties as Villa doubled up with a 2-1 home win.
Gary Shaw scored his first hat-trick for Villa in a 3-1 away win at Bristol City on 29 December 1979.

Jack Devey scored four times when Villa beat City 4-0 in an away FA Cup-tie in 1899-1900 and a record attendance of 49,734 saw Villa beat City 2-0 in a first round tie on 8 January 1921. Clem Stephenson burst the ball with his penalty kick in this game. Then in 1956-57, over 63,000 turned up to see Villa enter the quarter-finals of the FA Cup with a 2-1 home win over the Robins.
Gary Shaw netted the tie's only goal when Villa last met City in the FA Cup, at Ashton Gate in the 4th round in 1981-82.

Players with both clubs include: HE Banks, F Chapple, RW Dix (City WW2 guest), AJ Fisher, WH Harris, JH Harvey (Villa trialist), S Howarth

(City trialist), JH Kearns, GH Lawrence (Villa trialist), W Leigh, WW Marriott (City reserve), R Milne (Villa trialist), PH Mortimer, AJ Moss, S Murray, G Shelton, RJ Wilson,
Also: A Proudler (Villa player, City coach), PD Doherty (Villa chief scout, City manager).

## BRISTOL ROVERS
Villa's playing record against the Pirates:

Football League

| Venue | P | W | D | L | F | A |
|---|---|---|---|---|---|---|
| Home | 4 | 3 | 1 | 0 | 8 | 3 |
| Away | 4 | 2 | 1 | 1 | 4 | 4 |
| Totals | 8 | 5 | 2 | 1 | 12 | 7 |
| FA Cup | | | | | | |
| Home | 2 | 1 | 1 | 0 | 5 | 1 |
| Away | 3 | 2 | 1 | 0 | 6 | 2 |
| Totals | 5 | 3 | 2 | 0 | 11 | 3 |
| League Cup | | | | | | |
| Home | 1 | 1 | 0 | 0 | 1 | 0 |
| Away | 1 | 0 | 1 | 0 | 1 | 1 |
| Totals | 2 | 1 | 1 | 0 | 2 | 1 |

Aston Villa first met Bristol Rovers in the Football League in season 1959-60 (Division 2). More than 26,000 supporters saw the 1-1 draw at Eastville on 5 September and then, with Villa sitting on top of the table, a crowd of 29,726 assembled for the return clash in the Midlands to see Rovers humbled 4-1. Bobby Thomson (2), Vic Crowe and Jimmy Adam were on target for Villa while England international Geoff Bradford netted a consolation goal for plucky Rovers.

A little over 10 years later (in 1970-71) a Third Division match between the clubs ended in a 1-1 draw in front of 32,082 spectators at Villa Park on 30 September (Andy Lochhead the Villa scorer, Ray Graydon, later to sign for Villa on target for the Pirates). And then almost 26,000 fans packed into Eastville to see Rovers beaten 2-1 in the return fixture on 9 January.
The following season Willie Anderson's goal gave Villa a 1-0 win at Bristol and then Lochhead netted twice as Villa completed the double with another 2-1 victory later in the campaign - on their way to the Third Division championship.
Rovers joined Villa in the Second Division for season 1974-75 and they won the game in Bristol by 2-0 before Villa gained revenge with a hard-earned 1-0 home victory on Boxing Day, Graydon scoring the vital goal, this time against his former club!

Gerry Hitchens and Bobby Thomson shared the goals in Villa's 4-0 win over Rovers in a 3rd round FA Cup replay in January 1961.
Dean Saunders missed a penalty in Villa's 1-1 home FA Cup draw with Rovers in January 1993 and then the Welsh international missed again from the spot in the replay at Twerton Park. But he made amends with two goals in Villa's 3-0 win as Rovers had defender Billy Clark was sent-off.

On their way to reaching the 1971 League Cup Final, Villa ousted a resilient Rovers side 1-0 at home in a 5th round replay, Pat McMahon the hero with an 88th minute winner. In the 1-1 draw at Eastville, McMahon had scored one of the fastest goals for Villa in competitive Cup action - after just 52 seconds.

***Ray Graydon - player with both clubs.***

THE COMPLETE ENCYCLOPAEDIA OF ASTON VILLA F.C.  THE COMPLETE ENCYCLOPAEDIA OF ASTON VILLA F.C.

37

Villa were the first team to play Rovers at their old Eastville Stadium, doing so on 3 April 1897 in a friendly.

Players with both clubs include: B Anstey, A Cartlidge, WG Clarke, RD davis (WW2 guest for both clubs), RW Dix, W Gerrish, BC Godfrey, JA Gray, R Graydon, JWE Jones, F Kerns, G Kinsey, JW McKenzie, W Marriott, GK Penrice, CL Roberts (Villa reserve), MR Thomas (Villa loanee), OE Tidman, ME Walters, GH Webb (Villa reserve).
Also: JP Ward (Villa coach/assistant-manager, Rovers manager), G Thompson (Villa player, Rovers coach), C Dobson (Rovers player, Villa coach).

## BRITTLETON, JOHN THOMAS
Born: Winsford, Cheshire, 5 May 1906. Died: Cheshire, 1970.
Career: Winsford Celtic (1922-26), Chester (1926), Aston Villa (February 1928), Winsford United (June 1930). Retired 1930.
A resilient defender, full-back Tom Brittleton started playing football in earnest with his local side Winsford Celtic before establishing himself with Chester in 1926. After leaving Sealand Road he made just ten first team appearances for Villa before returning 'home' to sign for Winsford United in 1930, retiring three years later with a knee problem. He was the son of the former England international James Thomas Brittleton who played League football for Stockport County, Sheffield Wednesday and Stoke between 1902 and 1925, Tom Brittleton died in 1955, aged 72.

## BROADBENT, PETER FRANK
Born: Elvington, Kent, 15 May 1933
Career: Dover (1949), Brentford (professional, May 1950), Wolverhampton Wanderers (£10,000, February 1951), Shrewsbury Town (January 1965), Aston Villa (October 1966), Stockport County (October 1969), Bromsgrove Rovers (October 1970). Retired May 1971.
Peter Broadbent was a brilliant inside-forward, who spent 17 years playing League football in the West Midlands - 14 with Wolverhampton Wanderers and three with Aston Villa. He was the workhorse in Wolves' centre-field, linking up with England international wingers Johnny Hancocks and Jimmy Mullen and then Norman Deeley and the South African import Des Horne. He grafted hard, driving forward, spraying passes wide and long. He created goalscoring

opportunities galore for his colleagues and netted some fine goals himself in his tally of 145 in 497 games for the Wanderers, whom he helped Wolves win three League titles in the 1950s and the FA Cup in 1960. He gained seven England caps and also represented his country at 'B' and Under-23 levels as well as playing for the Football League XI and Young England (v England) in 1958. Broadbent had the pleasure of netting Wolves' first-ever European goal versus the German side FC Schalke 04 in 1958. He left Wolves early in 1965 for Shrewsbury (soon after his friend and manager Stan Cullis had departed) and in October 1966 he moved to Villa Park. Unfortunately his experience failed to prevent Villa from being relegated to the Second Division and he quit the club three months into the 1969-70 season after netting four times in 68 outings. Broadbent's wonderful career in top-class football ended in 1970 with him having amassed 631 League appearances.
He eventually hung up his boots at the age of 38 and later opened a

baby-wear shop in Halesowen.
● Broadbent is also a very fine golfer and in 1967-68 won the professional footballers' golf title, having finished runners-up in 1965 and 1966.

## BROCKLEBANK, ROBERT EDWARD
Born: Finchley, 23 May 1908. Died: Brixham, September 1981.
Career: Finchley Boys, Finchley AFC, Aston Villa (May 1929), Burnley (March 1935), Chesterfield (manager, September 1945-January 1949), Birmingham City (manager, January 1949-October 1954), West Bromwich Albion (scout/trainer/scout: October 1954-March 1955), Hull City (manager, March 1955-May 1961), Bradford City (manager, May 1961 to October 1964 when he resigned). He chose to retire from football, immediately and moved to the Devon fishing resort of Brixham.
Inside-forward Bob Brocklebank was one of eight brothers. After leaving school in 1925 he became one of Finchley's most illustrious players before leaving the amateur scene to join Aston Villa in the Football League. Nicknamed 'The Toff' he had limited opportunities during his six-year stay at Villa Park (scoring twice in 20 appearances). But after that he did exceptionally well with Burnley, netting 38 goals in 128 senior games for the Clarets, playing alongside Tommy Lawton on many occasions. On leaving Turf Moor, Brocklebank took over as manager of Chesterfield, later holding similar positions with Birmingham City, Hull City and Bradford City as well as being scout/trainer/coach under manager Vic Buckingham at West Bromwich Albion for almost a season. He guided Hull to the runners-up spot in Division Three (North) in 1959. On retiring from football in 1964 he moved to the Devon fishing town of Brixham.
Unfortunately Brocklebank gained only one honour in football, steering Hull to the runners-up spot in Division Three in 1958-59.
He was also a very accomplished cricketer and handy golfer.

## BROOKES, FRANKLIN
Born: Aston, February 1859. Died: Birmingham.
Career: Wesleyan Chapel FC, Aston Villa (August 1880), Centaurs FC of Smethwick (May 1882).
Utility forward Frank Brookes made only one first team appearance for Aston Villa, lining up against Notts County in an away FA Cup-tie in January 1882. He joined Villa after doing well in church football but never fulfilled his promise and left after just one season with the club.

## BROOME, FRANK HENRY
Born: Berkhamstead, Herts, 11 June 1915. Died: Bournemouth, 10 September, 1994.
Career: Berkhamstead Victoria Church of England School, Boxmoor United juniors & seniors (September 1929-May 1932), Berkhamstead Town (August 1932), Aston Villa (November 1934), WW2 guest for Birmingham, Chelmsford City & Wolverhampton Wanderers, Derby County (September 1946), Notts County (October 1949), Brentford (July 1953), Crewe Alexandra (October 1953), Shelbourne (February 1955), Notts County (assistant-trainer June 1955, caretaker-manager at Meadow Lane, January-May 1957, assistant-manager to Tommy Lawton, June-December 1957), Exeter City (manager, January 1958-May 1960), Southend United (manager, May-December 1960), Bankstown, NSW, Australia (manager/coach, July 1961-October 1962), Corinthians, Sydney (manager/coach, late 1962), Exeter City (manager, May 1967-February 1969), thereafter coaching appointments in the Middle East until 1976.
Frank Broome was Aston Villa's top-scorer three seasons running: 1936-39. A small, thrustful winger who could also play as either centre or inside-forward, he was adept at switching positions during a game defenders all sorts of trouble. A terrific marksman, speedy and extremely dangerous inside the penalty area, he went on to score 90 goals in 151 senior games for Villa, and added another 90 goals in 136

THE COMPLETE ENCYCLOPAEDIA OF ASTON VILLA F.C.    THE COMPLETE ENCYCLOPAEDIA OF ASTON VILLA F.C.

38

Wartime appearances in the claret and blue strip. With Villa he gained a Second Division championship medal in 1938 and a Wartime League Cup North winners medal in 1944 while in between times he helped Wolves win the Wartime League Cup in 1942. After leaving Villa Park in 1946 Broome continued his intriguing career with useful spells at Derby, Notts County (Division Three South champions 1950), Brentford, Crewe Alexandra and Shelbourne in Ireland.

He occupied four different forward-line positions while representing England on eight occasions (seven at full international level, once in the War). He also toured Australia with the FA party in 1951. During his playing days he amassed some 600 first-class appearances and scored well over 250 goals.

After hanging up his boots in 1955 Broome became assistant-trainer at Meadow Lane before gradually edging himself into management.

## BROWN, ALBERT ARTHUR

Born: Aston, Birmingham, 7 January 1862. Died: Birmingham.
Career: Mitchells St George (1881), Aston Villa (August 1884). Retired through injury, July 1894.

The younger brother of Arthur, Albert Brown could play as a right-half, outside-right or inside-right. He joined Villa at the start of the 1884-85 season and remained at the club for ten years, scoring 54 goals in 106 senior appearances. He played in the 1887 FA Cup Final victory over West Bromwich Albion and lined up for Villa in their first-ever League game, away to Wolves on 8 September 1888. He then had the pleasure of scoring in Villa's first League win, 5-1 at home over Stoke a week later. He was injured during the away game at Preston in January 1891 and although he struggled on for a year after that (mainly in the reserves) he was forced to retire in the summer of 1894.

## BROWN, ALBERT FREDERICK

Born: Tamworth, April 1879. Died: Birmingham, late 1940s.
Career: Atherstone County School, Atherstone Star (1894), Tamworth

(August 1899), Aston Villa (July 1900), Southampton (May 1901), Queen's Park Rangers (October 1902), Preston North End (May 1904), Blackpool (March 1906). Retired through injury in 1908.

Albert Brown was a decidedly speedy outside-right or centre-forward, who was aptly nicknamed the 'Tamworth Sprinter' and said to be the fastest footballer in the kingdom! He did well for his School team and at junior and non-League levels before entering the bigtime with Aston Villa in 1898. Unfortunately he was never able to establish himself in the first XI and was handed just two senior outings, scoring twice on his League debut away to Sheffield United in November 1900, when he replaced George Johnson. In the summer of 1901 he was transferred (with Tommy Bowman) to Southampton. He quickly made his mark as a quality marksman at The Dell and in December 1901 entered the Saints record books by scoring seven goals out of a total of 11 against Northampton Town in a Southern League game (a record that still stands today). Brown went on to net 29 times in 34 competitive matches that season, when he also played in the FA

Cup Final. Unfortunately he sustained a bad injury in the summer of 1902 and struggled to regain his place in the side after that. He was subsequently transferred to QPR and later assisted Blackpool.

## BROWN, ARTHUR ALFRED

Born: Aston, 15 March 1859. Died: Aston, July 1909.
Career: Aston Park School, Florence FC (1874), Aston Unity (1876), Aston Villa (August 1878), Mitchell St George's (August 1879), Birchfield Trinity, Excelsior FC, Aston Villa (February 1880-May 1886). Retired due to his health but still remained on the club's staff until 1908.

Arthur Brown (sometimes referred to as 'AA') was a splendid, all-action utility forward who gave Aston Villa grand service during his second spell at the club. He first joined Villa in 1878 but left after just twelve months, returning to the fold for a second spell in 1880, playing until 1886 when he retired through ill-health. He still kept his ties with the club, acting as a coach, working with the groundstaff and as a matchday steward right up until 1908. Despite his height (5ft 8ins) Brown was a strong, sturdy player, determined and goal-happy who scored 15 goals in 22 FA Cup appearances for Villa. He was then replaced in the side by his brother Albert Brown, who, in fact, had starred in the same forward-line as Arthur during the 1884-85 & 1885-86 seasons. 'AA' linked up supremely well with Archie Hunter and in 1882 appeared in three internationals for England, scoring four times on his debut against Ireland in Belfast when his Villa colleague, Howard Vaughton scored a five-timer in an emphatic 13-0 victory. A real opportunist, Brown had the knack of keeping his shorts clean even in the muddiest of conditions!

## BROWN, GEORGE

Born: Mickley, Northumberland, 22 June 1903. Died: Birmingham, 10 June 1948, after a short illness.
Career: Mickley Colliery, Huddersfield Town (trialist, March 1921, professional April 1921), Aston Villa (£5,000, August 1929), Burnley (£1,400, October 1934), Leeds United (£3,100, September 1935), Darlington (£1,000, player-manager, October 1936-October 1938 when retired from football).

George Brown was one of the most prolific marksmen in the history of the game, netting a total of 276 goals in 444 League matches between 1921 and 1938 (his record in all competitions was 298 goals in 473 appearances). A clever dribbler, his eye for snapping up the half-chance, allied to his power and accuracy with his shooting (especially his right foot rockets) earned him the nicknamed of 'Bomber'. That was particularly revelant during his Villa days when he notched 89 goals in only 126 senior outings, including a five-timer against Leicester City in

January 1932. He was, of course, part of a terrific forward-line that also included Tom 'Pongo' Waring, Billy Walker and Eric Houghton. Brown worked at the local colliery and played for the pit team as a youngster. In late May 1921, when on strike, he asked Huddersfield Town for a trial. Manager Herbert Chapman liked what he saw and signed Brown on professional forms within a fortnight! 'Bomber' went on to

THE COMPLETE ENCYCLOPAEDIA OF ASTON VILLA F.C.  THE COMPLETE ENCYCLOPAEDIA OF ASTON VILLA F.C.

39

score 159 goals in 229 games for the Terriers, being a key member of their attack when they completed a treble of League championship triumphs in the mid-1920s. In the last of those successes (1925-26) he equalled the club's scoring record of 35 goals in a season.

After missing Huddersfield's 1922 FA Cup Final victory over Preston, Brown played in the 1928 Final, but on this occasion Blackburn beat Huddersfield 3-1 to ruin his big day! Capped eight times by England, he also represented the Football League XI whilst at Leeds Road and after transferring to Villa Park at the start of the 1929-30 season, he added one more full cap to his collection. After Villa, Brown served with Burnley and Leeds United before taking over as player-manager of Third Division North side Darlington, who paid £1,000 for his services - their highest outlay for 10 years. After helping the Quakers avoid re-election, he retired from football in October 1938, taking over a pub (the Star Vaults) in Aston, later 'mine host' of The Plume and Feathers, Stratford Road, Shirley.

● George Brown's uncle, Joe Spence, also a dynamic forward, had a distinguished playing career with Manchester United and England.

## BROWN, JAMES KEITH

Born: Wallyford, Midlothian, 3 October 1953
Career: Edinburgh & District Schools, Midlothian Boys, Aston Villa (associated Schoolboy, May 1969, professional October 1970), Preston North End (October 1975), Ethnikos, Greece (August 1978-December 1979), Portsmouth (February 1980), Hibernian (November 1980), Worcester City (July 1981), Heart of Midlothian (1982), Worcester (again, 1982-83), Sutton Coldfield Town, Aston Villa Old Stars, footballing coach in local community.

Jimmy Brown became the youngest player ever to appear in a first-class game for Aston Villa when, at the age of 15 years, 349 days, he made his debut against Bolton Wanderers at Burnden Park in a Second Division match on 17 September 1969. After that, Brown, strong and competitive in midfield, steadily added to his appearance-tally and when he left Villa Park for Deepdale in 1975, he had amassed 88 appearances and scored one goal, away at Brighton (won 3-1) in January 1973.

Brown was capped by his country at Youth team level, gained a League Cup runners-up medal tankard in 1971, helped Villa win the Third Division championship in 1972 and also received the annual Aston Villa supporters' annual 'Terrace Trophy' award in 1973.

## BROWN, JAMES

Born: Renton, Scotland, June 1868. Died: Scotland, 1923.
Career: Renton Union, Renton Thistle, Renton (1888), Aston Villa (June 1890), Leicester Fosse (October 1893), Loughborough (September 1899-May 1901, when he retired).
A moustachio'd Scottish 'professor', Jimmy Brown was a useful footballer, awkward at times owing to his round-shouldered gait, but totally reliable who could occupy a variety of positions from right-half to centre-half to centre-forward. A junior international north of the border, he joined Aston Villa in the summer of 1890, having previously done well with three Renton-based clubs. An excellent prompter, he scored four goals in 56 first-team appearances for Villa before leaving the club in 1893. He did well with Leicester Fosse, netting 21 goals in 153 senior appearances in a total of six years. He retired in 1901 and twelve months later became a Football League referee.

## BROWN, RALPH

Born: Nottingham, 26 February 1944.
Career: Ilkeston Boys, Derby County, Aston Villa (junior, March 1959, professional, February 1961), Notts County (May 1962).
Ralph Brown played just once for Aston Villa's senior side, lining up as a raw-boned 17 year-old in the first leg of the 1960-61 League Cup Final against Rotherham United...thus entitling him to a winners' tankard!

An inside or centre-forward, he was on Schoolboy forms at The Baseball Ground before moving to Villa Park. An England Youth team trialist, he became surplus to requirements at the end of the 1961-62 season and left for Notts County. He later entered non-League football (commencing August 1963) and continued to play at this level until May 1979, when he retired at the age of 35. He then became a Nottinghamshire coalminer.

## BROWN, ROBERT ALBERT JOHN

Born: Great Yarmouth, 7 November 1915.
Career: Gorleston Town (1932-34), Charlton Athletic (August 1934), guested for Newcastle United, West Ham United, Millwall, York City, Leicester City, Manchester City, Wolverhampton Wanderers and East Fife during the hostilities; Nottingham Forest (£6,750, May 1946), Aston Villa (£10,000, October 1947), Gorleston Town (player/coach, June 1949). Retired 1954.

Inside or centre-forward Albert 'Sailor' Brown scored plenty of goals during his two seasons with Gorleston Town. His efforts were rewarded and he was immediately snapped up by Charlton. He remained at The Valley for twelve years, although the conflict and disruption of World War Two severely dented his progress despite him guesting for several clubs up and down the country. With his balding head and ambling action, he went on to score 23 goals in 50 League and FA Cup games for the Addicks up to the outbreak of the hostilities in 1939 and then he served in the Greenwich Auxiliary Police from September 1939 to January 1940 before joining the RAF.

After one full season back at The Valley (1945-46) when he scored once in ten FA Cup outings including an appearance in the Final against Derby County, he moved to Nottingham Forest. In 1947 he was recruited by Aston Villa (to accompany Trevor Ford) and in his two seasons with the club scored nine goals in 31 appearances before announcing his retirement from competitive football in June 1949, after suffering a badly fractured jaw in a game against Portsmouth.

Just before the War (in May-June 1939) Brown had toured South Africa with the FA party, playing in one Test match. He skippered the RAF team in Norway, Denmark and Sweden during the hostilities, gained two League South Cup runners-up medals (with Charlton v Chelsea in 1944 and with Millwall v Chelsea in 1945) and he also played for England in seven Wartime/Victory internationals in 1945 and 1946.

In August 1949, he was appointed player-manager of Gorleston, a position he held until May 1956, although during the last two years he was also part of Villa's scouting unit. Brown also indulged in a sports shop business (1954 to 1959) and later, in partnership with Joe Jobling (a former Charlton team-mate) he took over a betting shop in Gorleston. Brown then organised sporting events at a Gorleston holiday centre for five years and his last job was that of a timber merchant which involved driving a 10-ton truck. He finally retired (from work) in 1982.

## BROWN, WILLIAM GEORGE

Born: Cheadle, 1880. Died: Birmingham.
Career: Heywood Boys Club, Bolton Wanderers (1898), Aston Villa (July 1904), Dudley Town (August 1906), Westbourne Celtic (Handsworth), Handsworth Victoria, Farcroft Rangers. Retired 1916.
Full-back Bill Brown made over 100 appearances for Bolton Wanderers before joining Aston Villa. He had 13 outings during his two seasons at Villa Park (covering for Albert Evans and Howard Spencer)

THE COMPLETE ENCYCLOPAEDIA OF ASTON VILLA F.C.    THE COMPLETE ENCYCLOPAEDIA OF ASTON VILLA F.C.

40

although he did make his debut for the club as an emergency outside-right in the home League against Preston North End on the opening day of the 1904-05 season. He was eventually released in August 1906.

## BROWNE, PAUL
Born: Glasgow, 17 February 1975.
Career: Aston Villa (YTS, June 1991, professional July 1993). A central defender, highly-rated at one stage, he appeared in just two League games before leaving the club in May 1996.

## BRYAN, THOMAS
Born: Walsall, 1859. Died: May, 1913.
Career: Saltley College, Wednesbury Strollers (August 1879), Aston Villa (August 1881), Bilston (April 1883), Darlaston (1887-89).
Thrustful and strong, left-back Tom Bryan played in two FA Cup-ties for Villa in 1882 - against Walsall Swifts and Wednesbury Old Athletic. He also represented the Birmingham Association in local representative matches.

## BUCKLEY, CHRISTOPHER SEBASTIAN
Born: Urmston, Manchester, 9 November 1886. Died: January 1973.
Career: Manchester Catholic Collegiate Institute, Manchester Ship Canal FC, Manchester City (amateur, 1903), West Bromwich Albion (trialist), Xaverian Brothers' College, Brighton & Hove Albion (1905), Aston Villa (August 1906), Arsenal (July 1914), then non-League football (1919-23 when he retired. He later returned to Aston Villa as a Director (1936-67), holding office as Chairman for 11 years (1955-66).

A relatively small man (he stood 5ft. 9ins. tall and weighed barely 11 stones) Chris Buckley had played in Manchester City's second team and made 17 appearances for Brighton in the Southern League before establishing himself in the first XI at Villa Park as a wing-half in 1907. He was then sidelined for twelve months after breaking an ankle but returned to action in a determined fashion and helped Villa win the League title in 1910. Nicknamed 'Ticker' he scored three goals in 144 appearances during his seven years at Villa Park.
After the Great War, having made 60 appearances for Arsenal, he entered non-League football, only to fracture his leg again in 1922, an injury which effectively ended his career. He then took up farming in Redditch and became co-owner of a large Manchester Warehouse. In 1936 Buckley joined the board of Directors at Aston Villa, later taking over as club Chairman (from 1955). He resigned his seat in 1966, handing over the duties to Norman Smith. He stayed on the board for a further 12 years, taking his overall service as a Director to 31 years. A typical English sportsman, he participated in athletics, cricket, cycling, golf and of course soccer.
On 2 September 1912, Buckley, one of five brothers including Major Frank (below) was suspended by Aston Villa over the payment of a benefit cheque. The matter was quickly resolved and Buckley eventually received a cheque for £450.

## BUCKLEY, MAJOR FRANKLIN CHARLES
Born: Urmston, Manchester, 9 November 1883. Died: Walsall, 22 December 1964.

Career: Schoolboy football, Army (1898, serving in the Boer War), Aston Villa (April 1903), Brighton & Hove Albion (May 1905), Manchester United (June 1906), Manchester City (September 1907), Birmingham (July 1909), Derby County (May 1911), Bradford City (May 1914), CO of the Footballers' Battalion, the Middlesex Wanderers, in World War I, Norwich City (player-manager, March 1919-July 1920), Commercial Traveller (1920-23), Blackpool (manager, July 1923-May 1927), Wolverhampton Wanderers (manager, May 1927-March 1944), Notts County (manager, March 1944-May 1946), Hull City (manager, May 1946-March 1948), Leeds United (manager, March 1948-April 1953), Walsall (manager, April 1953-September 1955).
Major Frank Buckley was associated with football for 53 years. On leaving School he enlisted in the Army before joining Aston Villa as a defender in 1903. Unfortunately he failed to make the grade at Villa Park and in 1905 moved to Brighton (with his brother Chris). He then had spells with both Manchester clubs and made 50 appearances for Blues (1909-11). He then played for Derby and Bradford City prior to the First World War, when he joined the Army, attaining the rank of Major in 1918.
Whilst with Derby, Buckley gained his only England cap (v Ireland in 1914) ....having helped County win promotion to the First Division two years earlier. He stepped into management with Norwich City in 1919 and except for a three-year spell in the early 1920s, he continued to manage football clubs right up until 1955. He transformed Wolves from a mediocre Second Division side into positive First Division outfit, leading them to the Second Division championship in 1932, the FA Cup Final in 1939 and Wartime League Cup success in 1942. He introduced many great players, to Molineux, including Stan Cullis, Bryn Jones, Jimmy Mullen, Dennis Westcott and Billy Wright. He then brought the legendary John Charles into the game at Leeds United. He quit football at the age of 72. As a player he was an attack-minded centre-half who tackled hard but fair. Known as the 'Iron Major' Buckley was unequivocal, progressive, ambitious and voluble. His ideas were freely communicated to the local and national press. He was totally against the use of the white football and it was he who advocated the numbering of players' jerseys for the benefit of supporters. He died still enjoying his football.
● For the record, Chris and Frank Buckley between them amassed in excess of 400 League and Cup appearances.

## BULLIVANT, TERENCE PAUL
Born, Lambeth, South East London, 23 September 1956.
Career: Fulham (Schoolboy forms 1969, apprentice 1972, professional May 1974), Aston Villa (£220,000, November 1979), Charlton Athletic (£90,000, June 1982), Brentford (July 1983), Reading (on loan, March-April 1984). Retired 1986, Fulham (part-time Youth coach, later first team coach).

Midfielder Terry Bullivant represented the local school team as a youngster and actually joined Fulham at the age of 13. After leaving Craven Cottage he was unable to command a regular first team place, scoring four goals in just 11 appearances for Villa. He subsequently returned to the capital to sign for Charlton Athletic and later assisted Brentford and Reading. He began to struggle with injuries in the mid-1980s and was forced to quit the professional game at the age of 30. At that juncture he rejoined the Cottagers' as a part-time Youth coach. Later he was called into action for a reserve team game in 1988-89. All told, Bullivant netted seven goals in 181 League games for his five clubs. He gained England Youth caps as a teenager and collected a runners-up medal with Brentford (v Wigan Athletic) in the Freight Rover Trophy Final at Wembley in 1985.

## BURKE, MARK STEPHEN
Born: Solihull, 12 February 1969.
Career: Aston Villa (June 1985, professional February 1987),

THE COMPLETE ENCYCLOPAEDIA OF ASTON VILLA F.C.  THE COMPLETE ENCYCLOPAEDIA OF ASTON VILLA F.C.

41

Middlesbrough (December 1987), Darlington (on loan, October 1990), Wolverhampton Wanderers (March 1991), Luton Town (March 1994), Tottenham Hotspur (trialist), Sporting Lisbon (trialist), Port Vale (August 1994), Fortuna Sittard (August 1995), Bradford City, Rapid Bucharest (loan, March-May 2000).

Winger Mark Burke played for England Youths before turning professional at Villa Park. He scored three times in five first team outings for Villa before departing to join Middlesbrough whom he helped win promotion from the Second Division in 1988. After 60 League outings for the Teesiders, and a loan spell at Darlington, Burke switched to Molineux. He then had a further loan spell with Luton plus trials with both Spurs and the Portuguese club Sporting Lisbon before teaming up with John Rudge's Port Vale. Given a 'free transfer' by the Valiants in the summer of 1995, Burke then tried his luck in Holland with Fortuna Sittard before returning to England to assist Bradford City. He later had a spell in Romania.

## BURNLEY

Villa's playing record against the Clarets is:
Football League

| Venue | P | W | D | L | F | A |
|---|---|---|---|---|---|---|
| Home | 47 | 28 | 12 | 7 | 109 | 47 |
| Away | 47 | 11 | 8 | 28 | 71 | 113 |
| Totals | 94 | 39 | 20 | 35 | 180 | 160 |

FA Cup

| | P | W | D | L | F | A |
|---|---|---|---|---|---|---|
| Home | 4 | 2 | 1 | 1 | 6 | 3 |
| Away | 6 | 3 | 1 | 2 | 9 | 8 |
| Neutral | 1 | 1 | 0 | 0 | 3 | 0 |
| Totals | 11 | 6 | 2 | 3 | 18 | 11 |

League Cup

| | P | W | D | L | F | A |
|---|---|---|---|---|---|---|
| Home | 2 | 1 | 1 | 0 | 4 | 2 |
| Away | 1 | 0 | 1 | 0 | 1 | 1 |
| Neutral | 1 | 1 | 0 | 0 | 2 | 0 |
| Totals | 4 | 2 | 2 | 0 | 7 | 3 |

As founder members of the Football League, Aston Villa first met the Clarets on 22 December 1888 and beat them 4-2 at Perry Barr in front of 2,000 spectators.
Villa played with only ten men in the return game at Burnley in January 1889. Archie Hunter was the man missing ....and as a result the Clarets won 4-0!
Villa's first 4-4 draw in League football was against Burnley (at home) in November 1890.
Villa defeated Burnley 6-1 at home but lost 4-1 away in 1891-92 then

two seasons later Villa scored 10 goals against Burnley, winning 4-0 at home and 6-3 away.
A 5-0 Villa win in April 1895 was followed seven months later by a 5-1 victory at home and a 4-3 triumph at Burnley. Charlie Athersmith scored five of those nine goals including a hat-trick in the Perry Barr contest.
Villa then doubled up over Burnley in 1898-99, winning 4-0 (home) and 4-1 (away), Athersmith again scoring in both matches.
Villa lost 7-1 at Burnley in February 1921 and then drew 0-0 at Villa Park four days later!
Dicky York bagged all Villa's goals when Burnley were beaten 1-0 at Turf Moor and 3-1 at Villa Park in December 1922.
On 29 August 1925 (when the new offside rule law was first introduced) Villa hammered Burnley 10-0 at home with Len Capewell (5), Billy Walker (3), Dicky York and Clem Stephenson finding the net in front of 43,000 spectators. The opposing goalkeeper was Jerry Dawson. This is the Clarets' joint heaviest defeat and later in the season Villa won 3-1 at Turf Moor to complete the double.
In January 1927 Villa returned to Turf Moor but this time they got thumped 6-3!
Between March 1951 and March 1958, Villa won eight consecutive home League games against Burnley. Their best victories were 4-1 in March 1952 and 5-1 in April 1954.
In 1972-73 Burnley doubled up over Villa, winning 4-0 at Turf Moor and 3-0 at Villa Park.

*Andy Lochhead, player with both clubs.*

Burnley Directors declined an offer of £500 from Aston Villa to play their 1st round FA Cup-tie at Villa Park instead of Turf Moor in January 1907. Villa still won 3-1.
Villa reached the 1924 FA Cup Final by beating Burnley 3-0 in the semis at Bramall Lane, Billy Kirton and Dicky York (2) the scorers in front of 54,531 fans.
Villa crashed 5-1 at Turf Moor in a 3rd round tie in 1947. Burnley went on to reach the Final that year (losing to Charlton).

In 1957 Burnley were defeated in a 6th round replay 2-0 at Villa Park and in another quarter-final contest in 1959 over 60,000 fans saw the 0-0 draw at Villa Park before Eric Houghton's side made progress with a 2-0 win at Turf Moor (Peter McParland scoring twice).

Villa played Burnley in the 1960-61 League Cup semi-final. After two drawn games (2-2 at Villa Park and 1-1 at Turf Moor) they went through to the Final with a 2-1 replay victory at neutral Old Trafford, where Stan Lynn almost tore a hole in the net with his penalty kick!
Villa then knocked the Clarets out of the League Cup on their way to the 1971 Final.

*Action from the 6th Round F.A. Cup tie between Burnley and Villa in 1959.*

THE COMPLETE ENCYCLOPAEDIA OF ASTON VILLA F.C.     THE COMPLETE ENCYCLOPAEDIA OF ASTON VILLA F.C.

42

Players with both clubs include: RE Brocklebank, G Brown, JGT Clayton, GS Cowans, JW Crabtree (captain of both clubs), P Crichton (Villa on loan), A Cunliffe, TC Donovan, T Gardner, AP Heath, TW Jones (Burnley reserve), AE Leake, A Lee, B Little (Burnley trialist), A Lochhead, C McElney, AW Morley, H Morton (Burnley reserve), C Nicholl, DJ Winton.
Also: T Cummings & J Hogan (Burnley players, Villa managers), GW Cummings (Villa player, Burnley scout)

## BURRIDGE, JOHN
Born: Workington, 3 December 1951.
Career: Workington (apprentice, June 1968, professional December 1969), Blackpool (£10,000, April 1971), Aston Villa (£100,000, September 1975), Southend United (on loan, January 1978), Crystal Palace (£65,000, March 1978), Queen's Park Rangers (£200,000, December 1980), Wolverhampton Wanderers (£75,000, August 1982), Derby County (on loan, September 1984), Sheffield United (£10,000, October 1984), Southampton ((£30,000, August 1987 - signed to replace Peter Shilton!), Newcastle United (£25,000, October 1989), Hibernian (July 1991), Newcastle again (free transfer, August 1993), Scarborough (non-contract, October 1993), Lincoln City (non-contract, December 1993), Enfield (on loan, February 1994), Aberdeen (non-contract, March 1994), Barrow (non-contract, September 1994), Dumbarton (October 1994), Falkirk (November 1994), Manchester City (free transfer, December 1994), Notts County (free transfer, August 1995), Witton Albion (October 1995), Darlington (free transfer, November 1995), Grimsby Town (free transfer, December 1995), Northampton Town (non-contract/reserve, January 1996), Gateshead (March 1996), Queen of the South (March-April 1996), Blyth Spartans (player July 1996),

*John Burridge.*

Scarborough (on loan, December 1996), Blyth Spartans (player-manager, March 1997), China (goalkeeping coach, May 1997), Blyth Spartans (November-December 1997). Burridge also acted as coach at Leeds United.
A fitness fanatic, goalkeeper John Burridge, whose career spanned four decades (commencing 1968-69), had a superb career. When he quit the professional game during the 1997-98 season (having joined his first club, Workington, 29 years earlier) he had accumulated an appearance record bettered by only one other 'keeper - Peter Shilton. Burridge, in fact, played in a total of 915 competitive matches at club level (it was well over 1,000 if one was to include friendlies, tour games, charity matches etc).
He made his Football League debut (his first senior game) for Workington against Newport County on 8 May 1969 and was on the winning side (3-2).
Then, 28 years and six months later - a month short of his 46th birthday - he played his last competitive game....for Blyth Spartans in the first round of the FA Cup versus Blackpool in November 1997. He had earlier appeared in his last League game on 14 May 1995 - 26 years and six days after appearing in his first!
He was aged 45 when he turned out for Scarborough in the Auto-Windscreen Shield game against Notts County in December 1996....giving him the honour of being the oldest player ever to appear

for the Seaside club. He is also Scarbrough's oldest League player (41 years, 388 days, in 1993) and likewise he became the oldest-ever Darlington player, when at the age of 44 years, six days in December 1995, he lined up against Scarborough at The McCain Stadium. Besides these landmarks, the effervescent 'Budgie' Burridge is the oldest player so far to appear in the Premiership - he was aged 43 years, five months and 11 days old when he kept goal for Manchester City against QPR at Maine Road on 14 May 1995. At the time he was also listed as goalkeeping coach at Newcastle. Burridge won an Anglo-Italian Cup winners medal with Blackpool in 1970, a League Cup winners medal with Villa in 1977, a Division Two championship medal with Crystal Palace in 1979 and a Scottish Premier League Cup winners' medal with Hibs in 1991. He also helped Wolves win promotion from Division Two in 1983 and the following season was voted the Molineux club's 'Player of the Year'. He made 80 appearances for Villa and 81 for Wolves.
He either served with and/or was associated with 23 different League clubs (18 English, five Scottish), playing for 22 of them! He lined up against 89 other Football League clubs (out of a possible 101 whilst he was playing) and played against 22 of the 40 Scottish League clubs north of the border.
Burridge conceded 1,080 goals in his 915 senior games, keeping 298 clean sheets. He was beaten 899 times in his 771 League games (255 clean sheets).
Some time ago, while John was still deeply involved in football, his wife said: "We've been married for 17 years. John's had 14 clubs, we've lived in six different houses and seven rented places. He's so wrapped up in football, I've heard him giving commentator Gerald Sinstadt, a TV interview in his sleep."
See also under AGE.

## BURROWS, HENRY
Born: Haydock, 17 March 1941
Career: Aston Villa (amateur, April 1956, professional March 1958), Stoke City (£30,000, March 1965), Plymouth Argyle (August 1973-May 1977). Non-League football until 1979.
Harry Burrows bided his time at Villa Park before making the outside-left position his own in 1961-62, having acted as reserve to the Irish international Peter McParland. Fast and direct, with a fair amount of skill and a cracking left-foot shot, Burrows was an old-fashioned winger with an eye for goal. He attended the same school as Walter Hazelden before moving to Birmingham to sign for Villa, spotted by scout Peter Downes. Nicknamed 'The Blast', Burrows gained one England Under-23 cap and helped Villa win the Second Division championship and the Football League Cup in successive years (1960 and 1961). He also played in the

1963 losing League Cup Final against Blues. He scored 73 goals in 181 appearances for Villa (top-scoring in 1961-62 and 1962-63) before transferring to Stoke in 1965. He did a shade better at The Victoria Ground than he'd done at Villa Park, netting 75 goals in almost 270 outings for the Potters. He then assisted Plymouth before having a couple of seasons in non-League football when he also assisted the Villa Old Stars in various charity matches. Burrows later became a publican in Stoke and in the early 1990s, ran a post office in Abbots Bromley.

## BURTON (SWIFTS, TOWN, UNITED, WANDERERS)

Aston Villa have never met any of the Burton-upon-Trent based football teams at competitive level, but several players have been associated with both the Villans and one or more of the non-League clubs, as follows:

**Swifts:** L Campbell, JH Dawson, JS Gillan, G Kinsey, T McKnight, M Noon, AW Stokes.

**Town:** J Humphreys (Villa reserve)

**United:** CL Aston, TA Gibson, JS Gillan, G Harper, H Harvey, CJ Mann, W Podmore, IH Price, JG Tooth & S Webb (Villa reserves).

**Wanderers:** W Devey.

* Burton Albion did not play in the Football League but three players - RW McDonald, F Potter and S Sims - all served with Villa and Albion.

## BURTON, GEORGE FRANK

Born: Aston, June 1868. Died: Birmingham, c 1936.

Career: Aston Park School, Birmingham St Luke's, Walsall Town, Aston Villa (August 1892-June 1898). Retired through injury.

Hard-tackling wing-half Frank Burton scored three goals in 53 appearances for Villa during his six years with the club. Unfortunately he seemed to be on the treatment table quite regularly during his Villa days and in the end was forced to retire with a knee problem.

## BURTON, JOHN HENRY

Born: Handsworth, Birmingham, September 1863 Died: Hockley, Birmingham, April 1914.

Career: Grove Lane School, Handsworth, Hamstead Hall, Handsworth Victoria, Aston Park Unity, Aston Villa (April 1885-August 1893). Retired through injury.

An FA Cup winner with Aston Villa in 1887, half-back Jack Burton was as strong as an ox and could kick a ball as hard as any player. He was forced to retire with a knee injury at the age of 29.

## BURY

Villa's playing record against the Shakers is:

Football League

| Venue | P | W | D | L | F | A |
|-------|---|---|---|---|---|---|
| Home | 26 | 17 | 6 | 3 | 59 | 31 |
| Away | 26 | 10 | 6 | 10 | 39 | 39 |
| Totals | 52 | 27 | 12 | 13 | 98 | 70 |

| FA Cup | | | | | | |
|--------|---|---|---|---|---|---|
| Home | 1 | 1 | 0 | 0 | 3 | 2 |
| Neutral | 1 | 0 | 0 | 1 | 0 | 3 |
| Totals | 2 | 1 | 0 | 1 | 3 | 5 |

Aston Villa and Bury first met at League level in season 1895-96 and after beating the Shakers 2-0 at home, the return trip ended in disappointment as Villa slipped to a 5-3 defeat before 10,000 fans.

Villa completed their first double over Bury in 1897-98 but had to wait until 1904-05 until registering their second.

George Travers hit a hat-trick in Villa's 3-0 home win on Boxing Day 1908. Harry Hampton weighed in with a treble when Villa won 4-1, also at home in March 1910 and the same player struck four more goals when Villa crushed the Shakers 5-2 again at home in March 1912.

Another hat-trick hero was Dicky York in a 3-2 win at Gigg Lane in October 1925.

Bury were certainly 'shaken' as they crashed 7-1 at Villa Park in October 1928. Dicky York scored a hat-trick and assisted in two more goals.

The Shakers rumbled Villa out of the FA Cup in the 1902-03 semi-final at Liverpool, winning 3-0.

Two years later Villa gained some revenge with a 3-2 home win in round 2.

Players with both clubs include: WJ Carey (Bury reserve), F Carrodus, AA Gray, D Hickson, S Howarth (Bury Amateur), J McLuckie, A Massie, T Mort & H Morton (Bury trialists), N Lockhart, DF Skea, B Small, DP Spink (Villa reserve).

## BUTCHER, FREDERICK WILLIAM

Born: Hemmingfield near Barnsley, April 1910. Died: Bournemouth, May 1996.

Career: Wombwell FC (1929), Aston Villa (April 1931), Blackpool (August 1936), Swindon Town (August 1938). Retired during the War.

Left-back Fred Butcher made just two first team appearances for Villa before fracturing his leg during the 1934-35 season which effectively ended his Villa Park career, although he did play in four League games for Blackpool and 36 for Swindon in the last full campaign before World War Two.

## BUTLER, LEE SIMON

Born: Sheffield, 30 May 1966.

Career: Harworth Colliery FC, Lincoln City (professional, June 1986), Aston Villa (£100,000, August 1987), Hull City (on loan March 1991), Barnsley (July 1991), Scunthorpe United (on loan February 1996), Wigan Athletic (July 1996), Dunfermline Athletic (July 1998), Halifax Town (September 1999).

Goalkeeper Lee Butler made ten appearances between the posts for Villa when deputising for Nigel Spink. He had worked and played for Harworth Colliery before becoming a professional at Sincil Bank. He was recruited by Villa boss Graham Taylor in 1987, but couldn't resist the offer of regular first team football with Barnsley. He appeared in 120 League games for the Tykes before leaving Oakwell in 1996. He then spent a season in Scotland with Dunfermline Athletic, returning to the Nationwide League with Halifax soon after the start of the 1999-2000 campaign. Butler - who was vioted Halifax's 'Player of the Year' in 2000 - has now amassed more than 370 senior appearances at club level.

## BUTTRESS, MICHAEL DAVID

Born: Whittlesey near Peterborough, 23 March 1958.

Career: Aston Villa (junior, June 1975, professional February 1976), Gillingham (March 1978), West Midlands Police Force (1979 to date).

Mike Buttress (six feet tall) was a reserve full-back with Aston Villa, making three appearances in the first team. He surprisingly quit League football in 1979 to become an officer in the West Midlands Police Force, playing for the constabulary's soccer team in the Midland Combination.

## BYFIELD, DARREN

Born: Sutton Coldfield, 29 September 1976.

Career: Aston Villa (YTS, 1992, professional February 1994), Preston North End (on loan, November 1998), Northampton Town (on loan, August 1999), Cambridge United (on loan, September 1999), Blackpool (on loan, March 2000), Walsall (July 2000).

Striker Darren Byfield joined Villa as a trainee on leaving school and made good progress at intermediate and reserve team levels. His first team outings were limited to just 10 and after loan spells with four League clubs, he left to sign for nearby Walsall in the summer of 2000 - bought by former Villa player Ray Graydon to replace Michael Ricketts who was sold to First Division Bolton Wanderers. He helped the Saddlers win the 2001 PlayOoff Final v. Reading.

## CALDERWOOD, COLIN

Born: Glasgow, 20 January 1965.

Career: Mansfield Town (juniors, June 1980, professional March 1982), Swindon Town (£30,000, June 1985), Tottenham Hotspur (£1.25 million,

THE COMPLETE ENCYCLOPAEDIA OF ASTON VILLA F.C.  THE COMPLETE ENCYCLOPAEDIA OF ASTON VILLA F.C.

44

July 1995), Aston Villa (£225,000, March 1999), Nottingham Forest (£70,000, March 2000), Notts County (loan, March-May 2001). Retired.

Despite being a Scotsman and representing his country in Schoolboy internationals, centre-back Colin Calderwood surprisingly started his professional career with Mansfield Town. Three years and 117 appearances later he left Field Mill for Swindon. He did well at The County Ground and went on to accumulate a splendid record of over 400 games for the Robins. His performances didn't go unnoticed and he was duly signed by Gerry Francis, manager of Premiership side Tottenham Hotspur. With 36 full caps for Scotland he went on to play almost 200 games for the London club before his transfer to Villa Park in March 1999. After a bright start, when he formed part of a three-man defence along with Ugo Ehiogu and Gareth Southgate, Calderwood then lost his place to young Gareth Barry. He became unsettled and after 30 appearances for the club was eventually sold to Nottingham Forest - signed by ex-Villa star David Platt! Calderwood retired in May 2001.

## CALLAGHAN, ERNEST

Born: Newtown, Birmingham, 29 July 1907. Died: Aston, Birmingham, March 1972.

Career: Walmer Athletic (1925), Hinckley Athletic (August 1928), Atherstone Town (July 1929), Aston Villa (September 1930-May 1947). Retired to become the 'odd-job man' at Villa Park.

Ernie 'Mush' Callaghan is the oldest player ever to appear for Aston Villa in a Football League or major Cup game. He was 39 years, 257

days old when he lined up against Grimsby Town in a First Division match at Villa Park on 12 April 1947.

He played non-League football for five years before signing (without hesitation) a professional contract at Villa Park. His defensive displays were admired by players and supporters alike and went on to become a household name, amassing a fine record of 125 League and 17 FA Cup appearances for the club (six goals scored), plus another 151 outings in Wartime football.

He was a magnificent partner to full-back George Cummings and later on became a resolute centre-half. He helped Villa win the Second Division championship in 1937-38 and the Wartime League Cup in 1944. During the hostilities (when he also guested for a handful of teams) he was awarded the B.E.M. for 'conspicuous bravery' during the Birmingham Blitz of September 1942 when he was serving with the Police Reserve. On announcing his retirement in May 1947 he became the 'odd-job' man at Villa Park, a position he held for many years. 'Mush' was awarded a testimonial by Villa for his service and dedication to the club.

## CALLAGHAN, NIGEL IAN

Born: Singapore, 12 September 1962.

Career: Watford & District Schools, Hertfordshire County Schools, (apprentice, June 1978, professional July 1980), Derby County (February 1987), Aston Villa (February 1989), Derby County (on loan, September 1990), Watford (on loan, March 1991), Huddersfield Town (on loan, January 1992), non-League football 1993-97,

Left-sided midfielder who loved to hug the touchline, Nigel Callaghan gained nine England Under-21 caps before joining Aston Villa at the age of 26. He had already scored 60 goals in some 375 competitive matches for the Hornets and Rams, helping the latter club win the Second Division title in 1987. He managed just one strike in 16 outings for Villa before quitting League soccer in 1992.

## CAMBRIDGE UNITED

Villa's playing record against United:

FA Cup

| Venue | P | W | D | L | F | A |
|---|---|---|---|---|---|---|
| Home | 1 | 1 | 0 | 0 | 4 | 1 |
| Away | 1 | 0 | 1 | 0 | 1 | 1 |
| Totals | 2 | 1 | 1 | 0 | 5 | 2 |
| League Cup | | | | | | |
| Away | 1 | 0 | 0 | 1 | 1 | 2 |

Cambridge United, the League's newcomers, put on a plucky display at London Road before losing 4-1 at Villa Park in an FA Cup 4th round replay in January 1980, Terry Donovan scoring twice in front of 36,835 fans. However Villa were embarrassingly beaten 2-1 by United in a 3rd round League Cup-tie at The Abbey Stadium in eight months later.

Players with both clubs: D Byfield, D Dublin, J Fashanu (United junior), MK Ferguson, BA Greenhalgh, SJ Morton, D Simmonds, R Walker, RM Walker.
Also: R Atkinson (manager of both clubs).

## CAMPBELL, ARCHIBALD

Born: Crook, August 1904. Deceased.

Career: Spennymoor United (1921), Aston Villa (December 1922), Lincoln City (August 1925).

Nicknamed 'Aussie', Archie Campbell was a rough and ready defender. Nephew of John Campbell, he was fringe player at Villa Park and consequently was given only four first team outings before transferring to Sincil Bank in 1935. For the Imps he netted eight goals in 59 League appearances up to May 1928 when he was released.

## CAMPBELL, GEORGE

Born: Ayr, Scotland, February 1871. Died: Dundee, 1 August 1940.

Career: Renton, Aston Villa (October 1890), Dundee (August 1893-96).

Nicknamed 'Monkey Brand' by his colleagues, George Campbell was an amazing character who could play anywhere and often did - just to get a game! He occupied both full-back berths, all three half-back positions, inside-forward and even in goal! He took over between the posts against Sunderland in a League game at Roker Park in March 1892 when he replaced Jimmy Warner who had refused to play after performing so badly against West Bromwich Albion in the FA Cup Final the previous week. Exceptionally good on the ball, Campbell was badly injured while playing for Dundee and his career was cut short at the very early age of 25.

## CAMPBELL, JOHN JAMES

Born: Glasgow, 1871. Died: Scotland, December 1947.

Career: St Alexandra's, Glasgow Benburb (August 1888), Celtic (professional, May 1890), Aston Villa (May 1895), Celtic (August 1897),

THE COMPLETE ENCYCLOPAEDIA OF ASTON VILLA F.C.

THE COMPLETE ENCYCLOPAEDIA OF ASTON VILLA F.C.

45

Third Lanark (August 1903-April 1906 when he retired).

Johnny Campbell scored over 50 goals in two seasons for Glasgow Benburb before joining Celtic in 1890. He became an instant hit at Parkhead, continuing to score plenty of goals, including two in the 1892 Scottish Cup Final win and 12 in a reserve team game in 1891. His

transfer to Aston Villa in 1895 allowed Bob Chatt to move into the half-back line. Campbell made an immediate impact, finishing up as top-scorer in the country at the end of his first season in English football with a total of 26 goals while also helping Villa win the League title. The following season he was again instrumental as Villa captured the League and Cup double, netting once in the Cup Final against Everton and having the pleasure of scoring the first ever goal at Villa Park in a 3-0 win over Blackburn Rovers in April 1897. An excellent dribbler, Campbell spent just two years on the English circuit, returning to Celtic after notching 43 goals in only 63 outings for Villa. Back in Scotland he continued to find the net and went on to claim over 100 goals for the Bhoys (including a League record of 90 in 169 appearances). He won 12 full caps for Scotland (1893-1903 inclusive); represented the Scottish League on four occasions and also played three times for the Glasgow Select XI. Besides his three English medals with Villa and his initial Cup success with Celtic, Campbell went on to win two more League titles in Scotland (1899 and 1900). He also collected a total of three Scottish League runners-up medals and after leaving Celtic for Third Lanark in 1903, he quickly added yet another League title to his tally. He retired in the summer of 1906 and lived a further 41 years before his death in 1947, aged 76.

In his League career (north and south of the border) Campbell scored 141 goals in 264 appearances.


## CAMPBELL, LOUIS (LEWIS)

Born: Edinburgh, April 1864. Died: Scotland.

Career: Dumbarton (1883-86), Helensburgh FC (1887), Glasgow United (1888), Hibernian (1889), Aston Villa (January 1890), Burslem Port Vale (August 1893), Walsall Town Swifts (May 1894), Burton Swifts (1895), Dumbarton (1896-97).

A fast and tricky winger, Louis Campbell had done well north of the border before joining Villa for whom he appeared in 48 senior games and scored 23 goals before going on to net 15 times in more than 30 outings for Port Vale.


## CAMPBELL, ROBERT McFAUL

Born: Belfast, 13 September 1956.

Career: Aston Villa (apprentice, June 1972, professional January 1974), Halifax Town (on loan, February 1975), Huddersfield Town (£5,000, April 1975), Sheffield United (£10,000, July 1977 - after a loan spell), Vancouver Whitecaps, NASL (June 1978), Huddersfield Town (September 1978), Halifax Town (October 1978), Brisbane City, Australia (May, 1979), Bradford City (December 1979), Derby County (£70,000, August 1983), Bradford City (on loan, September 1983, signed for £35,000, November 1983), Wigan Athletic (£25,000, October 1986-88). Capped by Northern Ireland at Youth and senior levels (he was in his country's squad for the 1982 World Cup Finals), Bobby Campbell had an interesting career - and overall he did exceedingly well as a striker, scoring more than 200 goals in some 600 club and international matches, in England and abroad. His League record was very impressive: 179 goals in 476 appearances including 121 in 274 outings in his two spells at Valley Parade.


## CANNING, LAWRENCE

Born: Cowdenbeath, 1 November 1925.

Career: Paget Rangers (March 1940), Aston Villa (December 1943, professional October 1947), Kettering Town (August 1954), Northampton Town (June 1956), Nuneaton Borough (season 1957-58). Retired and later became an Aston Villa Director and also a very successful BBC radio sports reporter and journalist.

Reserve right-winger Larry Canning, who also occupied the right and left-half, centre-forward and outside-left berths, played in a handful of games for Villa during the War, but overall he amassed only 41 appearances at competitive level (three goals scored) before leaving the club in 1954.

● Canning is the cousin of the former Scottish international Alex Venters who also played for Blackburn Rovers and Glasgow Rangers.


## CANTRELL, JAMES

Born: Sheepbridge, Chesterfield, 7 May 1882. Died: Basford, 31 July 1960.

Career: Chesterfield Schools, Bulwell Red Rose, Bulwell Whitestar, Hucknall Constitutionals, Aston Villa (July 1904), Notts County (March 1908), Tottenham Hotspur (October 1912), Sutton Town (August 1923). Retired 1925.

Inside-right or centre-forward Jimmy Cantrell played for a number of junior teams in Derbyshire before joining Aston Villa in readiness for the 1904-05 season. He made a scoring debut in a 4-0 home win over his future club Notts County on 12 November 1904 and eventually gained a regular place in the forward-line halfway through the 1906-07 campaign when he partnered Charlie Millington on the right-wing, having Harry Hampton to his left. Far removed from the battering-ram type of forward, Cantrell was in fact, an unusually subtle, dainty player, smart and alert with an excellent right-foot who remained at Villa Park for almost four seasons, scoring 23 goals in 52 appearances before transferring to Notts County in 1908. He moved next to Tottenham in 1912 after netting 63 times in 131 League games for the Magpies, top-scoring at Meadow Lane in three of his four seasons there. At White Hart Lane he continued to rattle in the goals - amassing 95 in almost 200 competitive matches, 19 coming in 29 outings when Spurs won the Second Division title in 1920. a year later he helped Spurs win the F.A. Cup. Surprisingly Cantrell never gained an England cap, but one has to remember that there were several high-class marksmen in the game at the same time as himself. During the First World War he guested for his former club Notts County and, with his best years behind him, he still continued to League soccer right up until 1923 when he joined Sutton Town, finally retiring in 1925. He is the oldest player ever to don a Spurs jersey (40 years, 349 days v Birmingham in April 1923). After leaving football Cantrell became a golf professional.


## CAPEWELL, LEONARD KING

Born: Bordesley Green, Birmingham, 8 June 1895. Died: Evesham, November 1978.

Career: Washwood Heath Council School, Saltley Baptists, Wolseley Athletic Works FC, Wellington Town, served with Royal Engineers (Belgium) for almost four years during Great War, Aston Villa (£700 as a professional, August 1920), Walsall (February 1930), Wellington Town (August 1932-May 1935 when he retired).

Known as the 'King' at Villa Park, inside or centre-forward Len Capewell was a tremendous

THE COMPLETE ENCYCLOPAEDIA OF ASTON VILLA F.C.      THE COMPLETE ENCYCLOPAEDIA OF ASTON VILLA F.C.

46

goalscorer, a player who it was said 'sliced his way through some of the tightest defences in the game with all the defiance of a pint-sized battleship.' He was an early version of Bolton's 'Lion of Vienna' Nat Lofthouse!

Aston Villa actually pipped neighbours Birmingham for his signature in 1920. The club's assistant secretary, Wally Strange, had got wind of Blues' keenness to sign Beresford and was waiting, with a cheque, at Wellington's home ground when Beresford returned from an away game at Wrexham. Beresford spent almost two seasons in Villa's reserve team before scoring three times in five League games at the end of the 1921-22 campaign, including a goal on his debut against Blackburn Rovers.

He eventually established himself in the first XI in 1923-24 (netting 26 goals in 45 League and Cup games) lining up in a dashing forward-line with Dicky York, Billy Kirton, Billy Walker and Arthur Dorrell. Unfortunately that campaign ended with defeat in the FA Cup Final at Wembley.

Capewell scored exactly 100 goals in 156 appearances for Villa including a fivetimer in a 10-0 win over Burnley in August 1925 - the first day of the new offside law - four in an FA Cup win over Port Vale in January of that same year and a hat-trick, with a dislocated shoulder, in a 5-3 League win over Everton in December 1926. He eventually left Villa Park to join Walsall in 1930 (following the arrival of George Brown from Huddersfield Town) and later returned to his former club Wellington Town. After retiring Capewell worked at BSA for 22 years before spending the rest of his life living in Droitwich.

## CAPTAINS

Here are some of the many players (listed in A-Z order) who have captained Aston Villa at first team level, some much longer than others: Charlie Aitken, Frank Barson, Danny Blair, Danny Blanchflower, Jimmy Brown, Lew Chatterley, Gordon Cowans, Jimmy Crabtree, Vic Crowe, George Cummings, Jack Devey, Johnny Dixon, Dicky Dorsett, Andy Ducat, Ugo Ehiogu, Albert Evans, Tom Gardner, Jimmy Gibson, Brian Godfrey, 'Harry' Gregory, Denny Hodgetts, Barrie Hole, Eric Houghton, Archie Hunter, Bob Iverson, Stan Lynn, Paul McGrath, Con Martin, Alex Massie, George Matthews, Paul Merson, Alf Miles, Dr Vic Milne, Dennis Mortimer, Frank Moss senior, Frank Moss junior, Chris Nicholl, Harry Parkes, Leighton Phillips, David Platt, Vic Potts, Ivor Powell, Walter Price, George Ramsay, John Reynolds, Kevin Richardson, Bruce Rioch, Ian Ross, John Slueewenhoek, Peter Schmeichel, Gareth Southgate, Howard Spencer, Alec Talbot, Joe Tate, Brian Tiler, Andy Townsend, Billy Walker, Fred Wheldon and Ron Wylie.

Many more skippered the side on the odd occasion.

*George Cummings (Villa) and Fred Harris (Blues) before the local derby at St. Andrews in 1945.*

## Captain's Log

George Matthews is named (in the newspaper) as Aston Villa's first captain for the friendly game against Aston Park Unity in January 1875. Walter Price was the next skipper and he was on duty in that capacity for the friendly against Aston Brook St Mary's rugby club on 13 March 1875.

George Ramsay followed him in 1876 and then it was Archie Hunter (1878).

Archie Hunter was Villa's captain when they won the FA Cup for the first time in 1887.

Jack Devey skippered Villa to FA Cup glory over West Bromwich Albion in 1895 and he was again 'leader of the pack' when Villa completed the League and FA Cup double in 1896-97.

Howard Spencer captained Aston Villa for many years and he duly went up to receive the FA Cup in 1905. Joe Bache was team captain when the FA Cup was won in 1913 and in 1920 it was Andy Ducat; Frank Moss skippered Villa against Newcastle United in the losing final of 1924 and a beaming Johnny Dixon gleefully lifted the Cup in 1957, becoming the first Villa player to hold aloft a silver trophy at Wembley. Jimmy Crabtree (in the 1890s) was the first Villa player to skipper England ....leading his country against Scotland, Ireland and Wales.

Other Aston Villa skippers who have led their country in full international matches include: Howard Spencer, Frank Moss (England v Scotland in 1924 - the first to do so at Wembley), inside-left Billy Walker (England, three times), Danny Blanchflower (Northern Ireland), David Platt (England), Vic Crowe and Leighton Phillips (Wales), Con Martin, Paul McGrath, Steve Staunton & Andy Townsend (Republic of Ireland) and Jimmy McMullan and Alex Massie (both of Scotland). Future Villa manager Billy McNeill also skippered Scotland.

*Gareth Southgate on duty as Villa skipper.*

THE COMPLETE ENCYCLOPAEDIA OF ASTON VILLA F.C.    THE COMPLETE ENCYCLOPAEDIA OF ASTON VILLA F.C.

47

Platt captained his country 16 times in all (seven wins, five draws, four defeats). He was also skipper for the abandoned international v Eire.

Dicky Dorsett skippered Villa on his 200th appearance for the club v Burnley in April 1951.

Vic Crowe was Villa's captain when the Second Division title was won in 1960 and he also skippered the side that won the League Cup the following year,

Bruce Rioch skippered Villa to the Third Division title in 1971-72.

Ian Ross went up to collect the Football League Cup in 1975, Northern Ireland centre-half Chris Nicholl did likewise in 1977, England midfielder Kevin Richardson followed suit in 1994 and then Republic of Ireland international Andy Townsend walked up the 39 steps to collect the trophy in 1996.

Dennis Mortimer had the honour of lifting the Football League championship trophy in 1981, the European Champions Cup in 1982 as well as the European Super Cup. He also skippered England 'B' v Australia.

Jimmy Brown has been Villa's youngest first team captain.

Full-back Cammie Fraser skippered Villa to the Central League championship in 1963-64 - his last season with the club before moving to Birmingham City.

Ugo Ehiogu, who skippered Villa's reserve side to their respective championship in season 1992-93, also captained the first XI and the England Under-21 side.


## CARBONE, BENITO

Born: Begnana, Italy, 14 August 1971.

Career: Calabra Asanti, Torino (August 1989), Reggiana (1990), Casertana (July 1991), Ascoli (August 1992), Torino (June 1993), Napoli (September 1994), Inter Milan (July 1995), Sheffield Wednesday (£3 million, October 1996), Aston Villa (undisclosed fee, believed to be £100,000, October 1999), Bradford City (Bosman free, July 2000), Derby County (October 2001).

The Italian striker spent just seven months with Aston Villa whom he joined on 21 October 1999 from Sheffield Wednesday. In his 30 outings for the club, he netted eight goals, including a stunning hat-trick in a 5th round FA Cup-tie against Leeds United. After scoring at Goodison Park in the 6th Round. Carbone was dismissed in the second half. Very talented with tremendous on-the-ball skills, he played initially for a junior team in Calabara before establishing himself in Italy's Serie 'A' with Torino for whom he made his senior debut at the age of 17 in a 0-0 draw v. Pisa in January 1989.

Thereafter he had seasonal spells with Reggiana, Casertana, Ascoli, Torino (again) for the 1993-94 season, Napoli and Inter Milan. He appeared in over 200 games in Serie 'A' and 'B' (24 goals scored) playing with and against some of the finest footballers in Europe. He gained a UEFA Under-21 championship medal in 1994 before quitting Italian soccer in mid-October 1996 to enter the English Premiership, with Sheffield Wednesday at a cost of £3 million. He did very well at Hillsborough, scoring 26 goals in 107 first-class appearances for the Owls. Then, after a much-publicised dispute with the Yorkshire club he opted to team up with John Gregory's Aston Villa for a fee agreed on the number of appearances he made. The fans took to him immediately and his presence on the field certainly commanded respect. His three-goal salvo in the Cup against Leeds included one majestic effort that won him the 'Goal of the Season' award. He also netted a cracker against Darlington in the third round. But alas, he blotted his copybook by getting himself sent-off in the dying minutes of Villa's 6th round tie at Everton - and then he failed to perform in either of Villa's two games at Wembley in April/May 2000 (v. Bolton in the semi-final and Chelsea in the Final). Soon afterwards 'Benny' departed for Bradford City on a Bosman free, signing a contract at The Pulse Stadium worth £30,000-a-week! Unfortunately his presence in the Bantams line-up couldn't prevent the Yorkshire club from being relegated to the Nationwide League Division One at the end of the season.


## CARDIFF CITY

Villa's playing record against the Bluebirds:

Football League

| Venue | P | W | D | L | F | A |
|---|---|---|---|---|---|---|
| Home | 22 | 14 | 3 | 5 | 39 | 20 |
| Away | 22 | 8 | 2 | 12 | 23 | 30 |
| Totals | 44 | 22 | 5 | 17 | 62 | 50 |

FA Cup

| | | | | | | |
|---|---|---|---|---|---|---|
| Home | 2 | 1 | 0 | 1 | 7 | 3 |
| Away | 1 | 0 | 0 | 1 | 1 | 2 |
| Totals | 3 | 1 | 0 | 2 | 8 | 5 |

The first season of League football between the two clubs was in 1921-22 when Aston Villa completed the double over Cardiff City - winning 2-1 at home and 4-0 away right at the start of the campaign. Frank Barson scored twice at Ninian Park.

The following season the Bluebirds gained revenge by doing the double over Villa, winning 3-0 at home and 3-1 away.

When Villa registered a 1-0 win at Ninian Park on 23 February 1974 they ended a club record sequence of 12 League games without a victory. Earlier that season Villa had beaten the Bluebirds 5-0 at home!

When Villa beat Cardiff 6-1 at home in the 3rd round of the FA Cup in January 1929 the crowd topped 51,000. Twenty years later over 70,700 spectators saw the Welsh side return to Villa Park and win 2-1 in a 4th round tie.

Villa were the first team to play at Cardiff's Ninian Park ground - competing in a friendly there on 1 September 1910 which they won 2-1.

Players with both clubs include: W Anderson, GF Blackburn, M Devaney, T Ford, CH Gibson, TP Heard, GA Hitchens, BG Hole, RD Hughes, AE Layton, G Moseley, F Moss snr, HE Nash, JR Nicholson, L Phillips, D Saunders, MR Thomas (Villa on loan), GL Thompson, RJ Wilson.

Also: CH Spiers (Villa player, City manager), J Reynolds (Villa player, City coach), KD Macdonald (City player, Villa coach), AE Lindon (Villa player, City assistant-manager).


## CAREY, WILLIAM JAMES

Born: Manchester, June 1913. Died: Colchester, September 1998.

Career: Sedgley Park, Hereford United, Aston Villa (May 1936), Bury (July 1939), Hereford United (WW2 guest). Retired 1945.

Reserve to Fred Biddlestone, goalkeeper Bill Carey made just four senior appearances for Aston Villa during his three years with the club. They all came in the 1937-38 season, three of them in the League: against Newcastle United (home), Chesterfield (away) and Plymouth Argyle (home) and one in the FA Cup v Charlton Athletic at Highbury. He did not concede a League goal, Villa winning all three matches on their way to taking the Second Division championship.


## CARLISLE UNITED

Villa's playing record against the Cumbrians:

Football League

| Venue | P | W | D | L | F | A |
|---|---|---|---|---|---|---|
| Home | 5 | 4 | 1 | 0 | 5 | 1 |
| Away | 5 | 2 | 2 | 1 | 6 | 6 |
| Totals | 10 | 6 | 3 | 1 | 11 | 7 |
| League Cup | | | | | | |
| Home | 1 | 1 | 0 | 0 | 1 | 0 |

Aston Villa first met the Cumbrians at League level on 19 August 1969, in a Third Division game at Brunton Park. The result was a 1-1 draw,

THE COMPLETE ENCYCLOPAEDIA OF ASTON VILLA F.C.    THE COMPLETE ENCYCLOPAEDIA OF ASTON VILLA F.C.

48

Chico Hamilton on target for Villa in front of 12,504 fans.

The return fixture that season saw Villa win 1-0 with a Dave Rudge goal before 24,447 spectators.

United virtually clinched promotion to the First Division with a 2-0 home win over Villa on 27 April 1974.

A goal by Brian Tiler gave Villa a hard-earned 1-0 home win over United in a 4th round League Cup-tie in October 1970.

Players with both clubs include: W Aspinall, TB Craig, MR Day, RD Hughes, D Kubicki, D Mountfield, J Sewell (United WW2 guest), B Small (United trialist), B Tiler.

Also: IV Powell (Villa player, United manager), A Ashman (Carlisle player and manager, Villa scout).

### CARR, FRANZ ALEXANDER

Born: Preston, 24 September 1966.

Career: Blackburn Rovers (apprentice, July 1982, professional, July 1984), Nottingham Forest (£100,000, August 1984), Sheffield Wednesday (on loan, December 1989), West Ham United (on loan, March 1991), Newcastle United (£250,000, June 1991), Sheffield United (£120,000, January 1993), Leicester City (£100,000, September 1994), Aston Villa (£250,000, February 1995), Reggiana, Italy (Bolton Wanderers (October 1997), West Bromwich Albion (February 1998), Grimsby Town (trials, August 1998), Runcorn (1999-2000).

Mercurial winger Franz Carr was never given a chance at Ewood Park, but after moving to Nottingham Forest he developed into a fine player, winning nine England Under-21 caps to go with those he gained for his country at Youth team level. He appeared in over 150 games under Brian Clough's management, but then lost his way and after loan spells at Hillsborough and Upton Park he left The City Ground for St James' Park in the summer of 1991. Long periods in the wilderness disrupted Carr's progress at Bramall Lane and in 1994 he moved again, this time to Filbert Street. Five months later he arrived at Villa Park, but again he struggled with his form and after just four outings he left for a spell in Italy with Reggiana. He eventually wound down his League career with Bolton Wanderers and West Bromwich Albion and was also given trials with Grimsby by manager Alan Buckley.

### CARRODUS, FRANK

Born: Manchester, 31 May 1949.

Career: Manchester & District Schools, Altrincham (July 1964), Manchester City (£5,000, professional, November 1969), Aston Villa (£95,000, August 1974), Wrexham (£70,000, December 1979), Rebel Tour to South Africa (summer of 1982), Birmingham City (August 1982), Bury (October 1983-May 1984), Witton Albion, Runcorn and Altrincham. Retired in 1990.

Frank Carrodus worked as a civil servant before entering League football. A hard-working midfielder who attended regular PE classes, he spent five years at Villa Park, making 196 appearances and scoring 10 goals. He helped Villa win promotion from the Second Division and gained two League Cup winners' medals in 1975 & 1977 - having collecting a losers' prize in the same competition with Manchester City in 1974. After three years with Wrexham he chose to go on the 'Rebel Tour' to South Africa, returning unscathed and none the wiser to join Birmingham City. He only had a handful of outings during his short stay at St. Andrew's but

amassed a grand total of 331 in League football during his career. Carrodus is a pigeon fancier and a keen hiker, who established his own promotions business in Altrincham after hanging up his boots in 1990.

### CARRUTHERS, MARTIN GEORGE

Born: Nottingham, 7 August 1972.

Career: Aston Villa (YTS July 1988, professional July 1990), Hull City (on loan, October 1992), Stoke City (£100,000, July 1993), Peterborough United (November 1996), York City (on loan, January 1999), Darlington (March 1999), Southend United (on loan, August 1999, signed for £50,000, September 1999), Scunthorpe United (March 2001).

Looked to have a promising career ahead of him when he started out with Aston Villa but he failed to make an impact under managers Josef Venglos or Ron Atkinson and was eventually transferred to Stoke for £100,000 after just six first team outings for Villa (four as a substitute). Since leaving Villa Park Carruthers has done well, and he ended the 2000-01 season with some 75 goals to his credit in more than 300 competitive games.

### CARTLIDGE, ARTHUR

Born: Hanley, Stoke-on-Trent, 1880.

Died: Stoke-on-Trent, August 1940

Career: Penkhull Victoria, Market Drayton (1898), Stoke (September 1899), Bristol Rovers (April 1901), Aston Villa (April 1909), Stoke (August 1911), South Shields (September 1913). Retired 1915.

Arthur Cartlidge was regarded as one of the best goalkeepers in the Southern League during his eight years with Bristol Rovers. A six-footer, weighing 14 stones, he won a Southern League championship medal in 1905 and made almost 300 senior appearances for the Pirates before transferring to Aston Villa toward the end of the 1908-09 campaign. He gained a Football League championship medal at the end of his first full season at Villa Park and went on to have 55 outings between the posts during his two years at Villa Park.

### CASCARINO, ANTHONY GUY

Born: St Paul's Cray, 1 September 1962.

Career: Orpington Schools, Crockenhill FC, Gillingham (professional, January 1982), Millwall (June 1987), Aston Villa (record £1.5 million, March 1990), Glasgow Celtic, Chelsea (£1.1 million, February 1992), Olympique Marseille (July 1993), FC Nancy, Red Star in France (1999).

Centre-forward Tony Cascarino was educated in Kent and did exceptionally well at The Priestfield Stadium, scoring 78 goals in 219 League appearances for the Gills before transferring to Millwall in 1987. He continued to find the net for the Lions, claiming almost 50 goals in 128 senior outings up to the time he joined Aston Villa. He netted twelve times in 54 outings in almost two years at Villa Park and then, on 19 July 1991, he moved to Celtic, returning to the Football League with Chelsea seven months later. On leaving Stamford Bridge in the summer of 1993, Cascarino then began a seven-year stint in France during which time he served with Olympique Marseille, Nancy and unknown Red Star. Cascarino scored

THE COMPLETE ENCYCLOPAEDIA OF ASTON VILLA F.C.    THE COMPLETE ENCYCLOPAEDIA OF ASTON VILLA F.C.

49

19 goals in a then record 88 appearances for the Republic of Ireland at full international level....a record he wrestled from another former Villa player, Paul McGrath, who won 83 caps.

## CASUALS (LONDON)

Villa's record against the Casuals:
FA Cup

| Venue | P | W | D | L | F | A |
|---|---|---|---|---|---|---|
| Home | 1 | 1 | 0 | 0 | 13 | 1 |

Aston Villa completely overwhelmed the London Casuals 13-1 in front of 5,000 fans at Perry Barr in a 1st round FA Cup-tie in January 1891. Denny Hodgetts led the goal-rush with a fourtimer. Louis Campbell also grabbed a hat-trick (3) while Tom McKnight, Albert Brown and Graham each scored twice.
This is Villa's second biggest win in the competition (goal-difference).

Player with both clubs: R Sloley.

## CELTA VIGO

Villa's record against the Spanish club:
UEFA Cup

| Venue | P | W | D | L | F | A |
|---|---|---|---|---|---|---|
| Home | 1 | 0 | 0 | 1 | 1 | 3 |
| Away | 1 | 1 | 0 | 0 | 1 | 0 |
| Totals | 2 | 1 | 0 | 1 | 2 | 3 |
| InterToto Cup | | | | | | |
| Home | 1 | 0 | 0 | 1 | 1 | 2 |
| Away | 1 | 0 | 0 | 1 | 0 | 1 |
| Totals | 2 | 0 | 0 | 2 | 1 | 3 |

A crowd of 25,000 saw Villa - fielding an all-English XI - beat Vigo 1-0 in Spain in the first leg of a 1st round UEFA Cup-tie in September 1998. But things went all wrong in the return fixture as Villa succumbed to a 3-1 defeat in front of almost 30,000 fans to lose the contest 3-2 on aggregate.
Vigo then knocked Villa out of the InterToto Cup at the start of the 2000-01 season. After winning 1-0 in Spain in front of 12,164 spectators, they defeated Villa in the return fixture at The Hawthorns 2-1 before an 11,909 crowd to claim a 3-1 aggregate victory. Three players were sent-off in the second leg - Ian Taylor and Alan Thompson of Villa along with Velasco of Vigo. Merson missed a first-half penalty for Villa while Gareth Barry scored one. In a game that saw red and yellow cards waved in the air willy-nilly by a fussy referee, Villa's Steve Stone had to leave the field to have 17 stitches inserted in a head wound when he was struck by a flying boot as he went in for a cross. A penalty was awarded for dangerous play but Merson missed it. South African-born striker Bennie McCarthy scored both Vigo's goals.
Neither manager was satisfied with Swiss referee Dieter Schoch - or his assistants! Villa boss John Gregory said: "He was incredible. I had heard reports that he was tetchy but he took it completely beyond the realms of commonsense. At half-time, having already sent-off Velasco, he warned that other players would follow....and they did."

## CENTENARY MATCH

On 7 August 1974, Aston Villa football club celebrated its centenary with a home friendly match against Leeds United. Ray Graydon missed two penalties in this fixture as the Elland Road club recorded a 2-1 victory in front of 29,481 spectators.

## CENTURIANS

Aston Villa and Sunderland became the first English clubs to play against each other in 100 Football League matches, achieving that

milestone in January 1953 at Roker Park. The 100th game ended in a 2-2 draw.
The first player to appear in 100 League games for Villa was Denny Hodgetts who reached that milestone on 7 January 1893 when he scored twice in a 5-1 home win over Sheffield United.
The first Villa player to score 100 League goals for the club was Jack Devey - on 21 March 1895, in a 5-3 defeat at Bury.

## CHAIRMEN

Here is a list of Aston Villa's Chairmen in order of holding office:

| | |
|---|---|
| Josuah Margoschis | 1885-1897 |
| William McGregor | 1897-1898 |
| Frederick W. Rinder | 1898-1925 |
| Jack Jones | 1926-1936 |
| Frederick Normansell | 1936-1955 |
| Chris Buckley | 1955-1966 |
| Norman Smith | 1966-1968 |
| H Douglas Ellis | 1968-1976 |
| Sir William Dugdale | 1976-1979 |
| Harry Kartz | 1979-1981 |
| Ronald Bendall | 1981-1982 |
| H Douglas Ellis | 1982 to date |

*Sir William Dugdale.*

### Chairman's Minutes

A selected committee ran Aston Villa Football Club in the early days and after the bedding in period, Josuah Margoschis was elected chairman of the committee, holding office from 1885 to 1896 with William McGregor also taking office during this period.
McGregor was Chairman of the Football Association when the English Schools Football Association was formed in 1904 having also been Chairman of the Football League from 1888 to 1894.
During his time as Chairman Fred Rinder tried nine times without success to gain election to the FA Management Committee. He was finally accepted in 1917.
Rinder resigned as Villa's Chairman in July 1925 in opposition to the building of the Trinity Road stand. He returned to the board in 1936 after 11 years in the wilderness.
Chairman Fred Normansell had a wholesale fish business in Birmingham. He died in March 1955, aged 68.
Former Aston Villa half-back Chris Buckley was a member of the board of Directors for 31 years: 1936-67 inclusive. He was Chairman of the club for eleven years, up to October 1966.
Buckley was replaced as Chairman by 66 year-old Norman Smith who held the office until December 1968.
Birmingham-born Ron Bendall, a former pupil at Camp Hill Grammar School, joined the Board of Directors at Villa Park on 25 February 1975, and at the time was largest shareholder in Aston Villa Football Club. As a youngster he played soccer and cricket and represented Pickwick CC. He later took up golf and played out of the Gay Hill & Olton GC before joining the Ramsey club on the Isle of Man where he lived after retiring. His son, Donald, joined the Board of Directors in 1978-79.
Doug Ellis returned for a second spell as Villa Chairman in December 1982, taking over from Ron Bendall.
* Directors Mr J Ansell and Mr J Hartley both held the position of club Chairman, albeit on a temporary basis.

## CHAMBERS, JOHN FREDERICK

Born: Birmingham 7 October 1949
Career: Birmingham Boys, Aston Villa (apprentice, June 1965, professional October 1966), Southend United (July 1969), Hereford United (1970), Stourbridge (June, 1972), Kidderminster Harriers (player-manager 1980), Stourbridge (player-manager, August 1988), Halesowen Town (manager).

THE COMPLETE ENCYCLOPAEDIA OF ASTON VILLA F.C.    THE COMPLETE ENCYCLOPAEDIA OF ASTON VILLA F.C.

50

*Villa - League Champions 1893-94.*

John Chambers was a useful Youth and Central League players for Villa for whom he made just two senior appearances, his League debut coming at the age of 19 against Blackburn Rovers (away) in August 1968. He later did well as a non-League club manager,

## CHAMPIONSHIPS (FOOTBALL LEAGUE)
Aston Villa won the Football League championship seven times, the Second Division twice and the Third Division once.
This is their complete playing record in each winning seasons:
Division 1

| Season | P | W | D | L | F | A | Pts |
|---|---|---|---|---|---|---|---|
| 1893-94 | 30 | 19 | 6 | 5 | 84 | 42 | 44 |
| 1895-96 | 30 | 20 | 5 | 5 | 78 | 45 | 45 |
| 1896-97* | 30 | 21 | 5 | 4 | 73 | 38 | 47 |
| 1898-99 | 34 | 19 | 7 | 8 | 76 | 40 | 45 |
| 1899-00 | 34 | 22 | 6 | 6 | 77 | 35 | 50 |
| 1909-10 | 38 | 23 | 7 | 8 | 84 | 42 | 53 |
| 1980-81 | 42 | 26 | 8 | 8 | 72 | 40 | 60 |

* Aston Villa won the League and FA Cup double this season.
Division 2

| 1937-38 | 42 | 25 | 7 | 10 | 73 | 35 | 57 |
|---|---|---|---|---|---|---|---|
| 1959-60 | 42 | 25 | 9 | 8 | 89 | 43 | 59 |

Division 3

| 1971-72 | 46 | 32 | 6 | 8 | 85 | 32 | 70 |
|---|---|---|---|---|---|---|---|

## CHANDLER, ROBERT W.
Born: Calcutta, India, September 1894.
Career: Aston Town, Upper Thomas Street Boys, Glossop (1911), Aston Villa (August 1913), Walsall (September 1914). Retired during War.
A competent goalkeeper who understudied Sam Hardy during his only season at Villa Park when he made one League appearance, in a 3-0 home win against Sheffield United on Boxing Day 1913. He was injured before he could make his first team debut for Walsall.

## CHAPMAN, HAROLD
Born: Liverpool, 4 March 1921.
Career: Ellesmere Port (1938), Kidderminster Harriers (1945), Aston Villa (February 1947), Notts County (March 1949), non-League football in Cheshire League: 1951-56 when he retired.
Harry Chapman was a neat little player who occupied either the right-half or inside-right berths. He was a reserve at Villa Park for two years during which time he appeared in six first team matches, making debut against Charlton Athletic at the Valley in March 1948. He went on to score once in 53 League games for Notts County.

## CHAPMAN, ROY CLIFFORD
Born: Kingstanding, Birmingham, 18 March 1934. Died: Stoke-on-Trent, 21 March 1983.
Career: Kingstanding Youth Club, Kynochs Works FC, Birmingham County FA, Aston Villa (amateur November 1951, professional February 1952), RAF (1955-57), Lincoln City (November 1957), Mansfield Town (£7,000, August 1961), Lincoln City (player-manager, January 1965), Port Vale (August 1967), Chester (June 1969), Nuneaton Borough (August 1969), Stafford Rangers (manager, October 1969), Stockport County (manager, September 1975-May 1976), Port Vale (coach, August 1976-May 1977), Stafford Rangers (manager, August 1977-February 1980), later Walsall SportsCo (manager, 1980-82).
Roy Chapman scored well over 200 goals in a fine career, netting for each of his five League clubs. His record with Villa was eight goals in 19 first team outing, acting in the main as reserve to Johnny Dixon and Derek Pace. During his time as a player with Port Vale he developed sciatica (October 1968) and was never the same again. As a manger he struggled to keep Lincoln out of the re-election danger-zone and with Stockport he fared little better. He enjoyed his best managerial days with Stafford Rangers, guiding them to the Northern Premier League title and FA Vase double in 1971-72, a year after finishing runners-up in the NPL. He was also a Staffordshire Cup winner three times and played for the FA XI v South Africa. He was only 49 when he died.
* Roy's son is striker Lee Chapman, formerly of Stoke City, Arsenal, Sunderland, Sheffield Wednesday, West Ham United, Leeds United, etc.

## CHAPPLE, FREDERICK J.
Born: Treharris, South Wales, 1880. Died: c 1945.
Career: Treharris Boys' Club, Bristol Schools, Aston Villa (August 1906), Birmingham (December 1908), Crewe Alexandra (June 1910), Brentford (September 1912), Bristol City (June 1913), Blyth Spartans (August 1918). Retired June 1920.

A nippy footballer, elusive at times, Fred Chapple was utilised in an inside-forward position, but found it tough at Villa Park, making only eight first team appearances and scoring three goals before switching across the city to St Andrew's. He flattered to deceive with Blues, yet still netted 16 times in 53 appearances before moving to Crewe in 1910. He later had a good spell with Brentford (12 goals in 29 League outings).

## CHARLES, GARY ANDREW
Born: Newham, 13 April 1970.
Career: Newham & District Schools, trialist with Arsenal and Leyton Orient (1985), Nottingham Forest (YTS June 1986, professional November 1987), Leicester City (on loan, March 1989), Derby County (£750,000, July 1993), Aston Villa (£1.45 million, January 1995), Benfica (£1.5 million, January 1999), West Ham United (£1.2 million, October 1999), Birmingham City (on loan, September 2000).

THE COMPLETE ENCYCLOPAEDIA OF ASTON VILLA F.C.     THE COMPLETE ENCYCLOPAEDIA OF ASTON VILLA F.C.

51

Capped twice by England at senior level and four times by the Under-21s, right wing-back Gary 'Fluff' Charles gained a Simod Cup winners medal with Nottingham Forest in 1992 and a League Cup winners medal with Aston Villa in 1996. In fact, before joining Villa he had already amassed in excess of 160 appearances at club level. He added 105 more to his tally (four goals scored) before leaving Villa Park for Portugal early in 1999 - three years after suffering a badly fractured ankle in the end-of-season League game with West Ham. A player with great pace and balance, Charles loves to join his attack whenever possible. He was the unfortunate victim of a reckless challenge by Spurs' midfielder Paul Gascoigne in that 1991 FA Cup Final at Wembley.

## CHARLTON ATHLETIC

Villa's playing record against the Addicks:

Football League/Premiership

| Venue | P | W | D | L | F | A |
|---|---|---|---|---|---|---|
| Home | 21 | 11 | 6 | 4 | 46 | 23 |
| Away | 21 | 6 | 7 | 8 | 26 | 36 |
| Totals | 42 | 17 | 13 | 12 | 72 | 59 |

FA Cup

| | | | | | | |
|---|---|---|---|---|---|---|
| Home | 3 | 1 | 2 | 0 | 5 | 4 |
| Away | 2 | 0 | 1 | 1 | 1 | 2 |
| Neutral | 1 | 1 | 0 | 0 | 4 | 1 |
| Totals | 6 | 2 | 3 | 1 | 10 | 7 |

Wartime

| | | | | | | |
|---|---|---|---|---|---|---|
| Home | 1 | 0 | 0 | 1 | 0 | 2 |
| Away | 1 | 0 | 1 | 0 | 0 | 0 |
| Neutral | 1 | 0 | 1 | 0 | 1 | 1 |
| Totals | 3 | 0 | 2 | 1 | 1 | 3 |

The first time Aston Villa met Charlton Athletic in a League game was on 3 December 1938 in front of 24,146 fans at Villa Park. Hundreds of supporters never saw Villa's opening goal - scored after just 9.3 seconds by Bob Iverson - the fastest on record for the club. The return fixture at The Valley attracted 17,000 spectators and this time Villa lost 1-0.

Villa scored twice in the last three minutes when they beat the Addicks 4-0 at home in a First Division match in October 1946.

But there was no joy for Villa at The Valley in March 1953 as they slumped to a 5-1 defeat.

Charlton doubled up over Villa in 1954-55, winning 6-1 at The Valley and 2-1 at Villa Park.

Gerry Hitchens scored five goals (in the 2nd, 29th, 40th, 46th and 60th minutes) when Villa beat Charlton 11-1 in front of their lowest League crowd of the season, under 22,000, in a Second Division match in November 1959. Bobby Thomson (2), Peter McParland (2), Ron Wylie and Jimmy MacEwan also found the net as Villa recorded the second-biggest League win in the club's history whilst inflicting upon the Addicks their heaviest reverse in the competition. The scores were level at 1-1 before Hitchens netted his second goal and thereafter the Addicks' defence collapsed - although they did use three goalkeepers! Willie Duff dislocated his finger after conceding the first six goals; his replacement Don Townsend let in three and then striker Stuart Leary conceded the last two. There have only ever been two 11-1 scorelines in Division Two football - this was the second.

Later in the season Charlton gained revenge by winning 2-0 at The Valley.

In May 1999 Charlton, battling to retain their Premiership status, won 4-3 at Villa Park, scoring the winning goal in the last minute.

When the Addicks returned to the top flight for the 2000-01 campaign, they were defeated 2-1 at Villa Park. The return fixture at The Valley ended all square at 3-3.

Over 201,000 spectators attended the three 5th round FA Cup games between Villa and Charlton in February 1938. A record turnout of 75,031 witnessed the first clash at The Valley that ended 1-1. A crowd of 61,530 then saw the replay finish 2-2 at Villa Park before Frank Broome's hat-trick in front of 64,783 fans at Highbury helped Villa win through to the quarter-finals with a comprehensive 4-1 victory.

After Villa (lying next to bottom of the Second Division) had lost to Charlton in an FA Cup 3rd round replay in January 1970 they also lost their manager, Tommy Docherty. Vic Crowe taking over as boss.

Villa and Charlton drew 1-1 at neutral Stamford Bridge in a challenge match between the winners of the respective Football League North and League South Wartime Cup competitions in May 1944. A crowd of 38,540 saw Eric Houghton score Villa's goal.

Players with both clubs include: DJ Astley, RAJ Brown, T Bullivant, CJ Drinkwater, JA Dunn, PM Elliott, G (H) Gregory, HJ Halse, WWF Johnson, AW Kerr (Charlton WW2 guest), AE Lindon (also Athletic assistant-manager & manager), R milne (Villa trialist), PH Mortimer, JTS Phillips, L Phillips, GT Stephenson, C Tiler, H Vallance (reserve with both clubs), C Wilson (Villa reserve, Addicks WW2 guest). Also: R Saunders (Charlton player, Villa manager), LC Curbishley (Villa player, Athletic player & manager), MR Day (Villa player, Charlton coach), S Harrison (Charlton player, Villa coach), M Musgrove (coach at both clubs), B Whitehouse (Charlton player, Villa scout).

**Ron Saunders - player with Charlton, manager of Villa.**

## CHATT, ROBERT S.

Born: Barnard Castle, August 1870. Died: c 1935.

Career: Cleator Moor, Middlesbrough Ironopolis (1889), Aston Villa (August 1893), Stockton (June 1898), South Shields, Willington Athletic, Manchester City (trainer, August 1906).

A very useful footballer, Bob Chatt began his career as an out-and-out centre-forward but as time went by he also occupied both the inside-right and inside-left berths as well as the two wing-half positions, giving manly performances in all five! He is credited with having scored Villa's winning goal against West Bromwich Albion in the 1895 FA Cup Final - after just 39 seconds play. That was one of 26 he netted in 94 senior appearances for the club. He also gained two League championship medals with Villa (1896 and 1897). After leaving Villa Park, Chatt went on to collect an FA Amateur Cup winners' medal with Stockton. He played twice for an England XI and also represented the Football League whilst with Villa.

## CHATTERLEY, LAWSON COLIN

Born: Birmingham, 15 February 1945.

Career: Birmingham Schools, Birmingham Boys, Aston Villa (apprentice June 1960, professional February 1962), Doncaster Rovers (on loan, March 1971), Northampton Town (September 1971), Grimsby Town (February 1972), Southampton (March 1974), Torquay United

THE COMPLETE ENCYCLOPAEDIA OF ASTON VILLA F.C.        THE COMPLETE ENCYCLOPAEDIA OF ASTON VILLA F.C.

52

*Lew Chatterley*

(player/coach, February 1975), Chicago Sting, USA (player/coach 1978), Southampton (coach 1979), Sunderland (coach July 1985), manager of the Chump Inn in Southampton, then Poole Town (manager, June 1987), Reading (coach, June 1988), Southampton (Youth Development Officer, January 1990, coach at The Dell, July 1991-92),

Lew Chatterley had the distinction of being the first substitute to score for Aston Villa - finding the Blackpool net in a 3-2 home win in January 1967.

A solid defender who could also man midfield with efficiency, he won England Youth honours as a teenager (1962-63) and went on to appear in 164 senior games for Villa, scoring 27 goals. He was leading marksmen in 1966-67 with 13 goals and skippered the team in Division Two the following season. Chatterley was a regular for three years before leaving for Northampton Town after 11 years at Villa Park. He went on to amass more than 350 appearances at club level (324 in the Football League) and later did very well as a coach, serving with Lawrie McMenemy at Southampton and Sunderland, having played under 'Mac' at Grimsby. He later became Ian Branfoot's right hand man at both The Dell and Reading.

## CHELMSFORD CITY

No competitive action as yet between Villa and non-League Chelmsford City but over the years several personnel have been associated with both clubs.

Players: FH Broome & GR Edwards (City WW2 guests), JT Palethorpe, C Phillips, OE Tidman, NP Spink.
Also: WH Walker (Villa player, City manager), D Sexton (City player, Villa coach).

## CHELSEA

Villa's playing record against the London club:
Football League/Premiership

| Venue | P | W | D | L | F | A |
|---|---|---|---|---|---|---|
| Home | 54 | 27 | 14 | 13 | 105 | 76 |
| Away | 54 | 17 | 10 | 27 | 64 | 79 |
| Totals | 108 | 44 | 24 | 40 | 169 | 155 |
| FA Cup | | | | | | |
| Home | 2 | 1 | 1 | 0 | 3 | 2 |
| Away | 4 | 3 | 0 | 1 | 6 | 4 |
| Neutral | 2 | 1 | 0 | 1 | 3 | 2 |
| Totals | 8 | 5 | 1 | 2 | 12 | 8 |
| League Cup | | | | | | |
| Home | 1 | 0 | 0 | 1 | 2 | 3 |
| Away | 2 | 0 | 1 | 1 | 2 | 5 |
| Totals | 3 | 0 | 1 | 2 | 4 | 8 |
| Wartime | | | | | | |
| Home | 1 | 0 | 0 | 1 | 0 | 3 |
| Away | 1 | 0 | 1 | 0 | 2 | 2 |
| Totals | 2 | 0 | 1 | 1 | 2 | 5 |

Aston Villa first met Chelsea in a League game on 28 December 1907 (Division 1). The venue was Villa Park; the score 0-0 and the crowd 25,000. On the last day of that season (25 April) Villa won 3-1 at Stamford Bridge, Albert Hall scoring twice in front of 22,000 spectators.

Villa celebrated Christmas Day in style in 1919, beating Chelsea 5-2 at home. In this game Frank Barson scored with a booming 35-yard header!

When Villa beat Chelsea 3-0 on 28 March 1921, it ended a record eight-match no win sequence of home games in League football. Twenty four hours later Chelsea won the return fixture 5-1 at Stamford Bridge!

'Pongo' Waring weighed in with four goals as Villa - fielding an 8-man attack at times - caned Chelsea 6-3 at Stamford Bridge in September 1931, but surprisingly, later that season, the Blues came to Villa Park and won 3-1.

In the last season before World War Two Villa beat Chelsea 6-2 at home with Freddie Haycock and Frank O'Donnell both scoring twice. O'Donnell was making his home debut.

Trevor Ford and Johnny Dixon scored in both matches as Villa beat Chelsea 4-0 (h) and 3-1 (a) in 1949-50.

On 14 April 1952, just three days after drawing 2-2 at Stamford Bridge, Villa walloped Chelsea 7-1 at home (their biggest win, home or away, over the Londoners). Billy Goffin scored a hat-trick. Five months later it was 4-0 to Villa on the same ground!

Almost 44,000 fans welcomed Villa back to the First Division in August 1960 when Chelsea were defeated 3-2 at Villa Park. Later in the season

*Action from the Chelsea v. Aston Villa League game at Stamford Bridge, 1951.*

Villa completed the double with a 4-2 victory at Stamford Bridge.

After winning 6-2 at Villa Park in September 1966 (it was 4-0 at half-time) Chelsea had to wait until September 1992 before registering another League victory at Villa Park (3-1). England international Bobby Tambling scored five goals in that Chelsea win in 1966.

In between times - in December 1986 - Villa lost 4-1 at Stamford Bridge.

Villa suffered their first home defeat in the Premiership on 2 September 1992, losing 3-1 to Chelsea. The scoreline was reversed when the teams met at Villa Park on 20 April 1993 as Garry Parker scored his first goal in the claret and blue strip.

Villa failed to score a goal in five successive home Premiership games against Chelsea: 1995-2000. They lost 0-1, 0-2, 0-2 and 0-3 and drew 0-0 in that order.

Villa 'keeper David James presented Jimmy Floyd Hasselbaink with the game's only goal of a Premiership clash at Stamford Bridge on New Year's Day 2001, hitting his clearance (from Steve Staunton's routine back-pass) straight at the Dutch striker, who chipped the ball back over James' head!

Villa beat Chelsea 3-1 in the 1920 FA Cup semi-final at Bramall Lane. If Chelsea had won, it would have been the first time that a team had

THE COMPLETE ENCYCLOPAEDIA OF ASTON VILLA F.C.          THE COMPLETE ENCYCLOPAEDIA OF ASTON VILLA F.C.

53

played in the Final on its home ground, for that season saw Villa beat Huddersfield Town 1-0 at Stamford Bridge to win the trophy.

Villa won both legs of a 5th round FA Cup-tie against Chelsea in the transitional season of 1945-46.

A crowd of 55,994 saw Villa win a 4th round tie at Stamford Bridge in 1958-59 and the following season 66,671 fans attended the same ground to see Villa triumph by the same score in the same round.

A late goal by the Italian Roberto Di Matteo gave Chelsea a 1-0 victory over Villa in the 2000 FA Cup Final at Wembley.

Chelsea defeated Villa 4-3 on aggregate in the semi-final of the 1964-65 League Cup competition.

One of Villa's heaviest League Cup defeats came at Stamford Bridge in season 1998-99, when Chelsea won 4-1.

Players with both clubs include: JP Allen (Chelsea WW2 guest), MJ Bosnich, WF Brawn, AG Cascarino, LM Craddock (Chelsea Amateur), S Crowther, AR Dorigo, PM Elliott, G Graham, HJ Halse, IM Hamilton, A Hateley, T Hughes, GH Hunter, (reserve), P McMahon (Chelsea trialist), JTS Phillips, MJ Pinner, LGF Smith (Chelsea WW2 guest), K Swain, AD Townsend, J Whitley (also trainer at Stamford Bridge), RE York (Chelsea WW1 guest).

Also: T Docherty (manager of both clubs), RD Blanchflower and J Neal (Villa players, Chelsea managers), J Barron & F Upton (Chelsea players, Villa coaches), DJ Sexton (Chelsea assistant-coach & manager, Villa coach), A McAndrew (Chelsea player, Villa coach), A Bennett was assistant-secretary at Chelsea and secretary at Villa Park.

## CHELTENHAM TOWN

No competitive match action between Villa and Cheltenham as yet.

Players with both clubs include: GF Blackburn (also Town manager), AM Gray, DW Norton.
Also: J Barron (Town manager, Villa coach).

## CHESTER CITY

Villa's playing record against Chester:

FA Cup
| Venue | P | W | D | L | F | A |
|---|---|---|---|---|---|---|
| Home | 1 | 1 | 0 | 0 | 3 | 1 |

League Cup
| | P | W | D | L | F | A |
|---|---|---|---|---|---|---|
| Home | 2 | 2 | 0 | 0 | 8 | 2 |
| Away | 3 | 2 | 1 | 0 | 5 | 3 |
| Totals | 5 | 4 | 1 | 0 | 13 | 5 |

Sammy Morgan scored twice when Villa beat Chester 3-1 in a 3rd round FA Cup-tie in January 1974 in front of 16,545 spectators.

When Villa defeated Chester 5-4 on aggregate in the League Cup semi-final the following season (3-2 at home, 2-2 away) there were 19,000 fans at Sealand Road and 47,732 at Villa Park. In 1999-2000, a two-legged second round League Cup encounter finished 6-0 on aggregate in Villa's favour (5-0 at home, 1-0 at the Deva Stadium).

Players with both clubs: GO Ashfield, E Barrett, M Blackwood (Villa reserve), JT Brittleton, R Butcher (Villa reserve), RC Chapman, N Cutler, RW Dix (Chester WW2 guest), RE Evans (Chester trialist), BC Godfrey (Chester trialist), HJ Goode, WA Harvey, SF Horne, W Myerscough, D Pountney, A Ralphs, C Regis, CL Roberts (Villa reserve), G Shelton.
Also: G Turner (Villa manager, Chester player), KO Roberts (Villa player, Chester assistant-manager & manager), T Gardner (Villa player, Chester trainer & club steward).

## CHESTER, REGINALD ALFRED

Born: Long Eaton, 21 November 1904. Died: Long Eaton, 24 April 1977.
Career: Long Eaton Rangers, Notts County (trialist), Mansfield Town (trialist), Peterborough & Fletton United (August 1920), Stamford Town (1921), Long Eaton Rangers, Aston Villa (Amateur December 1924, professional April 1925), Manchester United (May 1935), Huddersfield Town (player-exchange involving Tommy Long, December 1935), Darlington (July 1937-May 1938), Arnold Town (1938), Woodborough United (1938-40, retired).

A utility forward, Reg Chester was a loyal and dedicated club man who spent eleven-and-a-half years at Villa Park during which time he scored 34 goals in 96 senior appearances. Never able to command a regular place in the side, his best season was in 1929-30 (nine goals in 20 outings). He started out as a centre-forward but one suspects he did not have the necessary physique nor aggression to fulfil that role, choosing to play on the wing most of the time. He made his debut for Villa in September 1925 against the team he was later to join - Manchester United. Chester top-scored for Darlington in the Third Division (N) in season 1937-38 with nine goals in 28 appearances.

## CHESTERFIELD

Villa's playing record against the Spire-ites:
Football League
| Venue | P | W | D | L | F | A |
|---|---|---|---|---|---|---|
| Home | 4 | 2 | 1 | 1 | 7 | 4 |
| Away | 4 | 3 | 0 | 1 | 8 | 3 |
| Totals | 8 | 5 | 1 | 2 | 15 | 7 |

FA Cup
| | P | W | D | L | F | A |
|---|---|---|---|---|---|---|
| Home | 1 | 1 | 0 | 0 | 2 | 0 |
| Away | 1 | 0 | 1 | 0 | 1 | 1 |
| Totals | 2 | 1 | 1 | 0 | 3 | 1 |

League Cup
| | P | W | D | L | F | A |
|---|---|---|---|---|---|---|
| Away | 1 | 1 | 0 | 0 | 3 | 2 |

The first time Aston Villa met the Spire-ites at League level was in in season 1936-37 (Division Two). Villa won 6-2 at home but lost 1-0 at The Recreation Ground.

Villa's first-ever game in the Third Division was played on 15 August 1970 away at Chesterfield, and in front of 16,760 spectators victory went to Villa by 3-2, Bruce Rioch (2) and Pat McMahon the goalscorers.

On Friday night 5 May 1972 - just sixteen days after winning 4-0 at Chesterfield - Villa beat the Spire-ites 1-0 in front of 45,586 fans at Villa Park (Ian Ross the scorer) to clinch the Third Division championship with a record 70 points. Therefore - by good planning or sheer accident Chesterfield had the distinction of being Villa's first and last opponents in Third Division soccer! And Villa won both matches.

Villa knocked Chesterfield out of the FA Cup after a 3rd round replay in 1933-34.

Players with both clubs: GW Beeson, WW Gerrish, S Hardy, HV Henshall, W Morris, W Pointon & CL Roberts (Villa reserves), PJ Robinson, A Wilkes, C Wilson (Villa reserve, Chesterfield trialist), J Yates (Chesterfield reserve).

Also: R Brocklebank & H Hadley (Villa players, Chesterfield managers), A Cox (Chesterfield manager, Villa coach/assistant & caretaker-manager).

## CHRISTMAS DAY

Aston Villa have played a total of 33 League and Wartime games on Christmas Day. Here is the full list.

Football League

| 1889 | v Preston North End (a) 2-3 |
|---|---|
| 1895 | v Liverpool (a) 3-3 |
| 1896 | v Everton (a) 1-2 |
| 1901 | v Everton (a) 3-2 |
| 1907 | v Nottingham Forest (h) 4-0 |
| 1908 | v Liverpool (h) 1-1 |
| 1909 | v Sheffield United (a) 1-2 |
| 1913 | v Derby County (a) 2-0 |
| 1914 | v Blackburn Rovers (a) 2-1 |
| 1919 | v Chelsea (h) 5-2 |
| 1920 | v Manchester United (h) 3-4 |
| 1922 | v Burnley (a) 1-0 |
| 1923 | v West Ham United (h) 1-1 |
| 1924 | v Leeds United (a) 0-6 |
| 1925 | v West Ham United (a) 2-5 |
| 1926 | v Sheffield United (h) 4-0 |
| 1928 | v Portsmouth (a) 3-2 |
| 1929 | v Manchester City (h) 0-2 |
| 1930 | v Chelsea (a) 2-0 |
| 1931 | v Middlesbrough (h) 7-1 |
| 1933 | v Wolverhampton Wds (h) 6-2 |
| 1934 | v Chelsea (a) 0-2 |
| 1935 | v Huddersfield Town (h) 4-1 |
| 1936 | v Chesterfield (a) 0-1 |
| 1946 | v Huddersfield Town (h) 2-2 |
| 1948 | v Wolverhampton Wds (a) 0-4 |
| 1950 | v Charlton Athletic (a) 2-2 |
| 1951 | v Wolverhampton Wds (h) 3-3 |
| 1956 | v Sunderland (a) 0-1 |

Wartime

| 1941 | v West Bromwich Albion (?) 2-0 |
|---|---|
| 1942 | v Leicester City (a) 5-2 |
| 1943 | v Leicester City (h) 3-1 |
| 1945 | v Wolverhampton Wds (a) 2-1 |

Summary

| P | W | D | L | F | A |
|---|---|---|---|---|---|
| 33 | 16 | 6 | 11 | 75 | 58 |

### Festive Facts

Aston Villa's last-ever competitive match on Christmas Day was a First Division clash at Roker Park in 1956 when they lost 1-0 to Sunderland in front of 18,223 spectators.

Villa's final home League game on Christmas Day was in 1951 when they drew 3-3 with Wolverhampton Wanderers, again in the First Division, in front of 49,525 fans.

Joe Bache scored all Villa's goals in their 4-0 festive season win over Nottingham Forest in 1907.

There was a hat-trick apiece for Eric Houghton and Joe Beresford when Villa whipped Middlesbrough 7-1 on 25 December 1931.

Four years later, Welshman Dai Astley was a three-goal hero in an emphatic 4-0 victory over Huddersfield.

Villa's best-ever Christmas was in season 1968-69 when they won three successive League games and followed up with a 3rd round FA Cup victory.

Their worst Christmas was in season 1958-59. They suffered three successive defeats between the 20th and 27th of December and were then beaten for a fourth time on 3rd January.

## CHURCH

It is highly likely that most of the founder members of Aston Villa Football Club were churchgoers, attending the local Villa Cross Wesleyan Chapel, Heathfield Road, Lozells. They were certainly connected to the Wesleyan Chapel cricket team and several played both sports (cricket and football, with a few also participating in rugby)

## CLARKE, ALBERT WILLIAM

Born: Walsall, 7 July 1860. Died: Birmingham.
Career: Wednesbury Old Athletic, Aston Villa (August 1880), Bilston Town (May 1884).

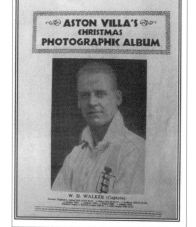

ASTON VILLA'S CHRISTMAS PHOTOGRAPHIC ALBUM

W. H. WALKER (Captain).

Goalkeeper Billy Clarke was all set to make a big name for himself in the Aston Villa side when unfortunately he broke his right leg in a friendly game against Wednesbury Strollers in December 1882. Although he regained full-fitness he was only second choice after that and eventually left the club for at the end of the 1883-84 season after making seven first-team appearances. He later worked as a printer.

## CLARKE, GEORGE BADEN

Born: Bolsover, 24 July 1900. Died: London, 11 February 1977.
Career: Bolsover Main County School, Welbeck Colliery (1918), Mansfield Town (July 1921), Aston Villa (December 1922), Crystal Palace (July 1925), Queen's Park Rangers (August 1933), Folkestone (season 1934-35).

Reserve to Arthur Dorrell, outside-left George Clarke spent three years at Villa Park, during which time he was given just seven first team outings. He was then transferred to Crystal Palace for whom he amassed a fine record of 105 goals in 299 League and FA Cup appearances. He ended his senior career in London with QPR.

## CLARKE, NORMAN FREDERICK

Born: Birmingham, 31 October 1934.
Career: Aston Boys (1947-50), Aston Villa (juniors, 1950, professional July 1953), Torquay United (July 1956).

Wing-half 'Nobby' Clarke set a new record by representing Birmingham Boys in each of four successive seasons from 1947. He later won an England Youth cap but failed to make the grade at Villa Park, appearing in just one League game, in place of Bill Baxter against Charlton Athletic in February 1955, before leaving for Plainmoor in 1953. He had 55 games in the Third Division (South) for Torquay.

## CLARKE, WILLIAM GIBB

Born: Mauchline, Ayr, c 1880. Died: c 1940.
Career: Third Lanark (1897), Bristol Rovers (1900), Aston Villa (September 1901), Bradford City (£2000, August 1905), Lincoln City (December 1909), Croydon Common (season 1911-12).

When he joined Aston Villa in 1901, Billy Clarke was described in the local press as a 'flying winger with great ball skills.' Later reporters saw him play 'pretty and brilliant football, his retention giving much satisfaction.' Signed to replace Charlie Athersmith, unfortunately he was plagued by injuries to both knees and his right ankle, and was consequently sidelined for long periods, his best season coming in

THE COMPLETE ENCYCLOPAEDIA OF ASTON VILLA F.C.    ASTON VILLA    THE COMPLETE ENCYCLOPAEDIA OF ASTON VILLA F.C.

55

1902-03 (20 appearances). After scoring six times in 43 first-class games for Villa he moved to Bradford City with whom he won a second Division championship medal in 1908. He made 98 League and Cup appearances during his four years at Valley Parade and followed up with 35 for the Imps.

## CLARKSON, THOMAS
Born: Stourbridge, April 1865. Died: West Bromwich, July 1915.
Career: Stourbridge Invicta, Halesowen Town, Aston Villa (August 1889), Oldbury Town (June 1893).
A strong-tackling, forceful wing-half, Tom Clarkson spent four seasons with Aston Villa, being a permanent reserve for the last two. He made just 17 first-team appearances.

## CLAYTON, JAMES GORDON THOMAS
Born: Sunderland, July 1910. Deceased.
Career: Shotton Colliery, Wolverhampton Wanderers (October 1932), Aston Villa (October 1937), Burnley (October 1938). Retired during the War.
Jim Clayton was a tall, strapping centre-forward who was recruited from Wolves in 1937 to bolster up Aston Villa's attack during their Second Division championship winning campaign. He was a temperamental player who lost his place in the Villa side to Frank Shell. Clayton scored 39 goals in only 54 games for Wolves; he netted once (the winner v Sheffield United in November 1937) in 11 outings for Villa and grabbed 10 goals in 16 games for Burnley.

## CLEAN SHEETS
Aston Villa goalkeeper Jimmy Rimmer kept a total of 23 clean sheets during the course of the 1981-82 season (12 League, two FA Cup, two League Cup and seven European Cup).

Jim Cumbes amassed 22 shut-outs during the 1974-75 season (18 in the League, three in the League Cup and one in the FA Cup).
John Dunn had 21 clean sheets to his credit in 1970-71 (16 League, five League Cup); Jimmy Rimmer was 'clean' in 19 games in 1977-78 (14 League, one League Cup & four UEFA Cup); Nigel Spink also had 19 'blanks' behind him in 1989-90 (15 League, three League Cup, one ZDSC) while both Tommy Jackson (1923-24 with 14 League and four FA Cup) and Fred Biddlestone (1937-38....17 League & one FA Cup) both kept their goal in tact on 18 occasions.
Other impressive clean-sheet seasons for Villa

*Jim Cumbes, 15 clean sheets in 1972-73.*

'keepers include: Cumbes 15 in 1972-73 (14 League, one Cup); Nigel Sims 15 in 1959-60 (14 League, one Cup); Rimmer 16 in 1980-81 (15 League, one Cup); Harry Morton 14 in 1932-33 (all League) & Cyril Spiers 13 in 1922-23.
Tommy Jackson kept a total of seven blank score sheets in successive matches between 27 October and 1 December 1923 inclusive.
Former Villa 'keeper John Burridge kept a clean sheet 298 occasions during the 915 competitive matches he appeared in 1969-97.
Burridge remained 'unbeaten' 255 times in 771 League outings and was 'goal-free' in 42 out of 179 Cup games. He also had one blank sheet in his two play-off fixtures.
Up to the end of the 2000-01 season Aston Villa goalkeepers, between them, had managed to keep 1,057 clean-sheets during the club's total of 4,014 Football League and Premiership matches.

## COACHES
Over the years there have been scores of men (some ex-players) who have been employed as a coach (at various levels) by Aston Villa. Prior to the Second World a 'coach' was, in fact, classified (in the main) as a trainer, and since 1960, a coach, besides being referred to as a trainer, has also been listed as the club's physiotherapist.

### Coaching Clipboard
Former manager Jimmy Hogan returned to Villa Park as coach under Eric Houghton in 1953.
Ex-Villa players Joe Bache, Frank Barson, Bill Baxter, Malcolm Beard, Hubert Bourne, Harry Cooch, James Cowan, Gordon Cowans, Vic Crowe, George Cummings, John Deehan, Johnny Dixon, Dicky Dorsett, Andy Gray, Bob Iverson, Keith Leonard, Brian Little, Alf Miles, Frank Moss jnr and Ron Wylie have all held coaching positions at Villa Park.
Bobby Downes, who won Third Division championship medals with Barnsley and Brighton, has been a coach at Aston Villa.
Alan Hodgkisson (ex-Sheffield United and England) and Paul Barron (once of Arsenal, Crystal Palace, QPR and WBA) have both been employed as goalkeeping coaches by Aston Villa, with Barron later assuming the role of Fitness Consultant.
The former Wolverhampton Wanderers defender Bill Shorthouse and the ex-Chelsea centre-half Frank Upton were together as reserve and Youth team coaches at Villa Park.
The Aston Villa coaching staff in the mid-1990s comprised: Dave Richardson (Director of Youth), Dave Sexton, Jim Barron, Richard Money and Colin Clarke, with Roger Spry as fitness expert and Jim Walker as physiotherapist.
In the late 1990s Kevin MacDonald and Tony McAndrew both worked together as coaches at Villa Park, while ex-Villa midfielder Des Bremner was a part-time coach at the club's School of Excellence at Bodymoor Heath.
Former Villa caretaker-manager Arthur Cox was coach to the England national team under Kevin Keegan for two years. He resigned on 8 October 2000.
Scottish international James F. Easson, who made 314 appearances for Portsmouth between 1928 and 1938, was Aston Villa's trainer/coach immediately after the Second World War.
Ex-Aston Villa inside-forward Hubert Bourne was England's trainer/coach from 1948 to 1951.
Other coaches at the club down the years include Leo Crowther (under manager Eric Houghton in the 1950s) and Steve Burns (1990s).

## COBLEY, WILLIAM ARTHUR
Born: Leicester, 31 December 1913.
Career: Leicester Schoolboy football, Leicester Ivanhoe, Aston Villa (semi-professional 1932, full-time professional, September 1933). Retired through injury in 1945.
Left-back Bill Cobley spent 13 years at Villa Park, acting mainly as reserve to George Cummings. He was ever-reliable and appeared in 47 first team matches, his best season coming in 1936-37 when he starred in 34 Second Division encounters and one FA Cup-tie. He made his debut in the goalless draw with Coventry City in front of 63,868 fans at Villa Park on 3 October 1936.

*Bill Cobley.*

THE COMPLETE ENCYCLOPAEDIA OF ASTON VILLA F.C.    THE COMPLETE ENCYCLOPAEDIA OF ASTON VILLA F.C.

56

## CODLING, ROLAND J.

Born: Durham, October 1879. Died: c 1960.
Career: Durham Youth Club, Stockton (1898), Swindon Town (August 1901), Stockport County (October 1903) Clapton Orient (1905), Aston Villa (March 1906), Northampton Town (July 1909), Croydon Common (October 1909), Manchester City (August 1910), Denton (July 1911). Retired 1914.

Sturdy left-half whose playing career spanned 16 years during which time he appeared in over 200 first-class matches. He was stern tackler with a strong shot and was a regular in the Villa side for two full seasons (1906-08) helping the team claim runners-up spot in the First Division in the latter. In all he made 82 appearances for the club before becoming surplus to requirements following the arrival of Frank Cornan and the form of Jimmy Logan.

## COLCHESTER UNITED

Villa's playing record against United:
League Cup

| Venue | P | W | D | L | F | A |
|---|---|---|---|---|---|---|
| Home | 1 | 0 | 0 | 1 | 0 | 2 |
| Away | 2 | 2 | 0 | 0 | 4 | 1 |
| Totals | 3 | 2 | 0 | 1 | 4 | 3 |

A dramatic League Cup-tie between Villa and United in 1979-80 was decided on penalties. Villa won the first leg 2-0 at Layer Road but were then pegged back by United who won the return fixture by the same score at Villa Park. A tension-packed penalty shoot-out followed which Villa won 9-8.
On their way to the 1975 League Cup Final Villa had ousted United 2-1 at Layer Road in round 5.

Players with both clubs include: W Aspinall, R Hopkins, J Martin and D Simmonds, who scored for United in their historic FA Cup victory over Leeds in 1971.
Also: JP Allen (Villa player, United manager).

## COLLYMORE, STANLEY VICTOR

Born: Groundslow Hospital, Swynnerton, Stafford, 22 January 1971.
Career: Broomhill Primary & Sherbrook Comprehensive Schools Cannock, Longmoor Boys, Walsall (YTS, June 1989), Wolverhampton Wanderers (non-contract, July 1989), Stafford Rangers (July 1990), Crystal Palace (£100,000, December 1990), Southend United (£100,000, November 1992), Nottingham Forest (£2.25 million, July 1993), Liverpool (£8.5 million, June 1995), Aston Villa (£7 million, May 1997), Fulham (on loan, July 1999), Leicester City (£250,000, rising to £500,000, February 2000), Bradford City (free transfer, October 2000), Real Oviedo, Spain (free transfer, January-March 2001). Quit football at this point, hinting that he might enter politics!
The son of a Barbadian tax officer, also called Stanley, Collymore Junior did not stay long with the Saddlers, leaving to sign for Wolves (his boyhood heroes). He failed to fit in at Molineux and switched to non-League soccer before returning to the Football League in December 1990. After two years and 20 games for the Eagles he moved to Southend and eight months later Nottingham Forest boss Frank Clark splashed out £2.25 million to bring him to The City Ground. He netted over 40 goals in two seasons

for Forest, helping them gain promotion to the Premiership and a place in Europe. In the summer of 1995 he was snapped up by Liverpool and whilst at Anfield made his England debut and played in the 1996 FA Cup Final defeat by Manchester United. In May 1997 he joined Aston Villa. That was a staggering £17.75 million splashed out on Collymore in three moves in four years! In July 1999 he was loaned out to Fulham before re-entering the Premiership with Leicester City under manager Martin O'Neill in February 2000. Eight months later, Collymore moved again, this time on a 'free' to the Pulse Stadium and scored with a terrific overhead kick on his debut for the Bantams against Leeds United (1-1). He left English football for sunny Spain in 2001....but he played over there for barely six weeks!
Holding three full England caps, Collymore made 61 appearances for Villa and netted 15 goals. He had his problems with manager John Gregory at Villa Park and indeed, he's hit the headlines for various reasons, with most of the clubs he's served. He's a character, 'Stan The Man' who could well have been a world-beater if he'd put his mind to playing football!
Injuries and suspensions interrupted his career, but nevertheless, during his prime he was an exciting, powerful striker whose great talent has not always been fully exploited. He's partnered some of the finest marksman around - Ian Wright at Crystal Palace, Ian Rush and Robbie Fowler at Liverpool and Emile Heskey and Tony Cottee at Leicester - and has scored some spectacular goals. When the curtain came down of the 2000-01 season Collymore's overall record at senior club level was impressive: 125 goals scored in 317 appearances (all clubs).

## COLOURS

Aston Villa's colours at the outset were (like most of the other teams in the area) comprised generally plain shirts, either white or a shade of blue, with either black or white shorts.
For a few years after that (1877-79) the team wore a variety of kits from all white, blue and black, red and blue to plain green.
Then, for the 1879-80 season, black jerseys with a lion embroidered on the chest were introduced by William McGregor.
This remained the first choice strip for over six years.
On Monday, 8 November 1886, an entry in the club's official minute books states: Proposed and seconded that the colours be chocolate and sky blue shirts and that we order two dozen. Proposed and seconded that Mr McGregor be requested to supply them at the lowest quotation. The chocolate colour later became claret.
Villa wore claret and blue stripes for the 1887 FA Cup Final clash with West Bromwich Albion and they repeated that style 70 years later when they beat Manchester United 2-1 in the 1957 Final while in 1995 (when they lifted the League Cup) stripes were again prominent, with blue sectioning off the claret.
The traditional claret body and blue-sleeved shirt remained in force for quite a long time, although the design itself has been altered slightly, certainly over the last twenty years or so.
The neck-line, too, has seen its changes - from a hoop-type/lace-up to a button-up style, a 'V' neck to a crew-neck to a round-neck and also one featuring a collar.
The away kit has been changed regularly and over the years supporters have seen Villa wear all white, sky blue, all yellow, green and black, red (occasionally), black and white, navy blue, grey etc.
• A set of replica Villa home shirts in 1910 cost 26s (£1.30) a dozen (or 11p each). Footballs cost between 7s 6d (38p) and 9s 6d (48p) each.
• At the start of the 1992-93 season Villa went back to wearing an 1890s style jersey.

## COMMERCIAL DEPARTMENT

Eric Woodward, former sports reporter with the Birmingham Post, Evening Mail and Sports Argus, became Aston Villa's first Commercial Manager, appointed in the 1968-69 season.

THE COMPLETE ENCYCLOPAEDIA OF ASTON VILLA F.C.　　THE COMPLETE ENCYCLOPAEDIA OF ASTON VILLA F.C.

57

Tony Stephens has also acted as Commercial Manager at Villa Park, so too has Tom Cardall, while Sue Walker was Villa's first lady Commercial Manager.

Abdul Rashid has been the club's Commercial Manager since 1 July 1988. Formerly the club's Pools Office assistant (under Keith Smith), he joined Villa's full-time staff on leaving the Holte Comprehensive School, Wheeler Street, Lozells in 1977 - having supported the club since he was 13. Born in Birmingham, Abdul is now one of the longest-serving employees at Villa Park.

## COMYN, ANDREW JOHN
Born: Wakefield, 2 August 1968.
Career: Wakefield Schools, Blackburn Rovers 'A', Manchester United 'A' & 'B' teams, Alvechurch (season 1987-88), Aston Villa (£34,000, August 1989), Derby County (£200,000, August 1991), Plymouth Argyle (£200,000, August 1993), West Bromwich Albion (non-contract, March 1996), Hednesford Town.
Andy Comyn was given a surprise Football League debut at right-back by Aston Villa manager Graham Taylor against Liverpool just a few days after setting foot inside Villa Park as a University Graduate. He wasn't overawed and in front of almost 36,000 fans helped his side to a 1-1 draw. He went on to make 20 appearances for the club (deputising for various defenders) before transferring to Derby County at the start of the 1991-92 season. In September 1992, Comyn came off the bench for the Rams against Bristol City and with the first touch of the ball headed an own-goal....nine seconds after entering the action!
When with Hednesford, Comyn skippered the FA XI v Combined Services at Worcester (January 1999) and he also won four semi-professional caps for England.

## CONNOR, JAMES
Born: Birmingham, April 1867. Died: Birmingham, 1929.
Career: Warwick County, Aston Villa (August 1889), Burslem Port Vale (trialist, August 1891), Kings Heath (September 1891).
Reserve wing-half for two seasons, Jim Connor made his League debut in a 2-1 home defeat by Bolton Wanderers in January 1890 when he deputised for Harry Devey.

*Harry Cooch.*

## COOCH, HAROLD
Born: Birmingham, 1877. Died: Birmingham, 1935.
Career: Local Schoolboy football, Aston Villa (professional, August 1901). Retired in May 1908 after losing a finger. He later acted as coach/trainer at Villa Park.
Deputy to goalkeeper Billy George, Harry Cooch spent seven years at Villa Park, making 25 first team appearances, with at least one coming in every campaign. His League debut was at Newcastle in April 1902 (lost 2-1) and his last outing was against Manchester United at Villa Park in September 1907 (lost 4-1). He also occupied a defensive position in the second XI.

## COOK, GEORGE WILLIAM
Born: Evenwood, County Durham, 27 February 1895. Died: Colwyn Bay, 31 December 1980.
Career: Royal Artillery, Bishop Auckland (1919), Rotherham County (May 1922), Huddersfield Town (May 1923), Aston Villa (February 1927), Tottenham Hotspur (June 1929-April 1931), Brentford (August 1931), Colwyn Bay (August 1932). Retired 1934.
An accomplished footballer, Billy Cook won many honours during the game. He made his mark after the Great War with Bishop Auckland, whom he helped win the FA Amateur Cup in 1921 and 1922. His performances around this time attracted the attention of League clubs and it was Rotherham who enticed him to turn professional. A year later he signed for Herbert Chapman's forceful Huddersfield Town side and gained three League championship medals with the Terriers in successive seasons before joining Aston Villa. Having scored 35 goals in 91 games for Huddersfield (as partner to George Brown, later to join Villa), he added 40 more goals in just 61 outings for Villa when he played between Joe Beresford and Billy Walker in the forward-line. Cook struggled to get into the side during his second season at Villa Park (following the arrival of 'Pongo' Waring) and this led to his departure to White Hart Lane. Although over 34 when he joined Spurs, he still gave the London club excellent service, notching another 30 goals in 73 appearances before winding down his career with Brentford and finally Colwyn Bay.

## COOKE, STEPHEN
Born: Walsall 15 February 1983,
Career: Schoolboy football, Aston Villa (junior June 1999, professional February 2001).
Strong-running midfielder who made his senior debut for Villa in the second leg of the InterToto Cup encounter with Celta Vigo at The Hawthorns at the start of the 2000-01 season.....Cooke's only appearance to date.

*Neale Cooper*

## COOPER, NEALE JAMES
Born: Darjeeling, India, 24 November 1963.
Career: Hazelhead Academy, Aberdeen (amateur 1979, professional November 1981), Aston Villa (£300,000, July 1986), Glasgow Rangers, Reading (July 1991). Later manager of Ross County (from July 1999).
Neale Cooper played as a sweeper for Scotland's Youth and Under-21 sides while with Aberdeen. He was a key midfield anchorman in the Dons' trophy winning sides of the 1980s, when they won three Premier Division titles, lifted the Scottish Cup on four occasions, clinched the League Cup once and were victorious in both the European Cup Winners Cup and European Super Cup. He netted 10 goals in 245 outings for the Scottish club. Then, following his transfer to Villa Park, he was injured and out of the game for the first half of the 1986-87 campaign and also missed most of the following season. He made just 22 appearances for Villa (one goal scored - against Chelsea at home in a 3rd round FA Cup-tie) before returning to Scotland, going on to win another Premiership medal with Rangers.

## COPLEY, GEORGE H.
Born: Birmingham, February 1861. Died: Birmingham.
Career: Saltley College, Aston Villa (August 1879), Birmingham St George's (July 1881).
Goalkeeper George Copley was a commanding figure between the posts for Aston Villa during his two seasons with the club, making over 50 appearances in total (four in the FA Cup). On one game he 'took out' three opposing forwards in one fiercesome challenge during a home friendly.

THE COMPLETE ENCYCLOPAEDIA OF ASTON VILLA F.C.  THE COMPLETE ENCYCLOPAEDIA OF ASTON VILLA F.C.

58

## CORBETT, JOSEPH
Born: Brierley Hill, 19 June 1902. Deceased.
Career: Brierley Hill Schools, Cradley Heath Victoria, Aston Villa (trialist (1919), Brierley Hill Alliance, Aston Villa (August 1921), Stourbridge (July 1929-May 1931).
Joe Corbett spent most of his first three years with Villa playing as a wing-half in the Central League side, making only one senior appearance during that time - against Nottingham Forest, away, on 12 April 1924 when he deputised for George Blackburn. He was reserve for that year's FA Cup Final. Corbett added six more first team games to his tally before leaving the club for Stourbridge in 1929.

## CORBETT, WALTER SAMUEL
Born: Wellington, 26 November 1886. Died: Birmingham, 1955.
Career: Vicarage Road & King Edward Grammar Schools Birmingham, Thornhill FC, Astbury Richmond, Headingly FC, Soho Villa (all based in

*Wally Corbett*

Handsworth, Birmingham), Bournbrook, Aston Villa (June 1904), Birmingham (July 1907), Queen's Park Rangers (on loan, September 1907), Birmingham (October 1907), Wellington Town (on loan, April 1909), Birmingham August 1909-May 1911), Wolverhampton Old Church (August 1911). Retired 1913.
'Watty' Corbett was a grand full-back who played in 18 Amateur and three full internationals for England before the First World War. He also gained a soccer Gold Medal for Great Britain at the 1908 Olympic Games. One of the best Amateur footballers in the game during the six-year period from 1905-11, Corbett showed infinite resource, possessed a fine turn of speed, tackled well and was such a consistent performer. He helped Villa's reserve side win the Birmingham & District League three seasons running; he skippered Birmingham & District Juniors v. Scotland in 1903-04-05 and was selected to represent a mixed Amateur & Professional XI on tour to the continent in 1906, as partner to the great Bob Crompton of Blackburn Rovers and England. Corbett always carried a handkerchief in his withered left hand and whilst a student at Grammar School (where he also played rugby and cricket) he became an expert linguist. After retiring from football he was appointed manager of a Birmingham Export House (1922) and in 1945 became head of the wages department of the Birmingham City Transport. He made just 13 League appearances for Villa, 46 for Blues and one for QPR.

## CORDELL, JOHN GRAHAM
Born: Bloxwich, 6 December 1928.
Career: Hillary Street School Walsall, Walsall Schoolboys, Walsall Star, Aston Villa (amateur June 1949, professional September 1949), Rochdale (May 1953), Hednesford Town (August 1955-May 1957).
Nicknamed 'lemon squash' John Cordell was fifth, sometimes sixth choice goalkeeper during his time at Villa Park. He made his five League appearances, his debut for the club coming against Tottenham Hotspur (away) on 20 October 1951 in front of more than 49,000 spectators. He later made 15 senior appearances for Rochdale.

## CORINTHIANS (CORINTHIAN CASUALS)
Villa's playing record against the Amateur side:
Sheriff of London Charity Shield

| Venue | P | W | D | L | F | A |
|---|---|---|---|---|---|---|
| Neutral | 2 | 1 | 0 | 1 | 2 | 2 |

Aston Villa met the Amateur club twice in successive seasons in the annual 'Charity Shield' game at The Crystal Palace - losing 2-1 on 8 November 1899 and winning 1-0 on 2 March 1901. Bill Garraty scored in the first encounter in front of 8,000 spectators and then Charlie Athersmith notched the winner in the second contest before a crowd of 10,000.
During the early part of the 20th century, Villa met the Corinthians several times in friendly matches when goals were plentiful. Indeed, in 10 encounters between the two clubs a total of 81 were scored, Villa winning eight and drawing one against the Corinthians lone success. Villa's biggest win was 8-2. (See under friendlies).

Players with both clubs: Dr WE Barnie-Adshead, A Ducat, AA Gray, R Sloley.

On the left are The Corinthians, posing with Aston Villa in 1901. Nine years before, this legendary club had filled all eleven positions for England in an international against Wales.

## CORNAN, FRANK
Born: Sunderland, 5 May 1880. Died: Halifax 3 May 1971.
Career: Sunderland Black Watch, Willington, Barnsley (1903), Birmingham (April 1905), Aston Villa (September 1908), Spennymoor United (August 1909), Barnsley (September 1909), Nelson (1910-11), Exeter City (October 1911), Barnsley (July 1912), non-League football from August 1913. Retired 1914-15.
A hard-tackling, steely, wing-half, Frank Cornan tackled with venom. He made 89 League appearances for Barnsley (in three spells at Oakwell), 26 for Blues and 16 Villa (all during the second half of the 1908-09 season), plus 27 for Exeter in the Southern League. He had a fine life, passing away just before his 91st birthday.

## COULTON, FRANK
Born: Walsall, February 1860. Died: Birmingham, March 1929.
Career: Walsall Swifts (August 1884), Aston Villa (August 1886). Retired through injury, April 1895.
A stylish full-back, Frank Coulton won an FA Cup winners' medal with Villa in 1887 and he also played in the club's first-ever League game in game, against Wolves. A damaged knee ended his career after he had made 60 senior appearances for the club.

## COURT CASES
● In 1912, a legal test case was heard in the King's Bench Division: Aston Villa Football Club v player, H.C.L.J. Kingaby.
Kingaby argued that he clearly thought that he was entitled to a percentage of a transfer fee that had been negotiated six years earlier. In the end the judgement and costs went in Villa's favour.
● On 23 May 1994, a court case began in the High Court involving former Aston Villa defender Paul Elliott (then of Chelsea) and striker Dean Saunders, then a striker with Aston Villa. The case referred to an

THE COMPLETE ENCYCLOPAEDIA OF ASTON VILLA F.C.

THE COMPLETE ENCYCLOPAEDIA OF ASTON VILLA F.C.

59

incident in which Saunders, playing for Liverpool, allegedly put in a dangerous tackle which effectively ended the playing career of Elliott, who was then a Chelsea player. The hearing lasted until 19 June when Saunders was cleared of making a 'reckless challenge'. Elliott, however, faced a legal bill of around £500,000. Summing up, Lord Justice Drake admitted that players should have the right to seek compensation from the courts for career-wrecking injuries as a result of foul play. However, he was satisfied in this case that Saunders made an honest attempt to play the ball.

● In 1995 foreign-born goalkeepers Bruce Grobbelaar and Hans Segers along with Aston Villa striker John Fashanu were charged by police with match-fixing. All appeared before the courts and all three were found not guilty after a long drawn-out trial, but Grobbelaar was later found guilty of irregularities.

## COVENTRY CITY (SINGERS FC)

Villa's playing record against the Sky Blues:

Football League/Premiership

| Venue | P | W | D | L | F | A |
|---|---|---|---|---|---|---|
| Home | 27 | 16 | 10 | 1 | 44 | 18 |
| Away | 27 | 13 | 7 | 7 | 39 | 32 |
| Totals | 54 | 29 | 17 | 8 | 83 | 50 |

FA Cup

| | P | W | D | L | F | A |
|---|---|---|---|---|---|---|
| Home | 3 | 2 | 0 | 1 | 5 | 1 |
| Away | 1 | 0 | 0 | 1 | 1 | 2 |
| Totals | 4 | 2 | 0 | 2 | 6 | 3 |

Zenith Data Systems Cup

| | P | W | D | L | F | A |
|---|---|---|---|---|---|---|
| Away | 1 | 1 | 0 | 0 | 2 | 0 |

Wartime

| | P | W | D | L | F | A |
|---|---|---|---|---|---|---|
| Home | 8 | 5 | 3 | 0 | 25 | 6 |
| Away | 8 | 4 | 1 | 3 | 16 | 12 |
| Totals | 16 | 9 | 4 | 3 | 41 | 18 |

Aston Villa first met Coventry in a League match on 3 October 1936. That day a crowd of 63,686 witnessed the 0-0 draw in Division 2. Later that season 40,000 fans saw Villa beaten 1-0 at Highfield Road. Then, on 30 October 1937, in front of a then record crowd for a Second Division game of 68,029, the teams fought out another draw (this time 1-1). But Ronnie Starling, at the fourth attempt, finally gave Villa their first win over Coventry with the game's only goal in the fixture at Highfield Road in mid-March 1938 in front of 44,930 fans.

Villa's first encounter with the Sky Blues in Division One was in August 1975 when Ray Graydon's goal earned a 1-0 home win in front of more than 41,000 spectators.

In March 1978, Garry Thompson (later to serve with Villa) made his League debut for Coventry in the First Division encounter against Villa at Highfield Road. Villa won 3-2.

In March 1983 Peter Withe netted twice in Villa's comprehensive 4-0 home win over City and the following season six goals were shared in a 3-3 draw at Highfield Road before Villa won 2-0 on home soil, Brendan Ormsby and Paul Birch the scorers.

There was another 3-3 draw between the teams in January 1986. Future Villa star Cyrille Regis scored for City as did Brian Kilcline with a penalty but Allan Evans missed from the spot for Villa.

Villa ended a club record run of 12 League matches without a win when they defeated the Sky Blues 1-0 at home on 28 March 1987.

In November 1989, in front of a disappointing crowd of 22,803, City's Trevor Peake conceded an own-goal to help Villa on their way to a 4-1 win. Ian Ormondroyd also netted twice and David Platt whipped in a penalty.

The first Premiership game took place on Boxing Day 1992, when City registered a 3-0 victory at Highfield Road. All the goals came in a frantic ten-minute spell early in the second-half.

Dwight Yorke opened the scoring for Villa after just 13 seconds in the League game against the Sky Blues at Highfield Road in September 1995. This was to be the fastest Premiership goal of the season. Savo Milosevic netted the other two in the 84th and 87th minutes.

Three months later in-form Milosevic bagged a hat-trick as Villa completed the double over City with a 4-1 home win in front of 28,476 spectators.

Coventry recorded their first ever League win at Villa Park in February 1999 when they won a Premiership game 4-1. This was their 25th attempt! Gary McSheffery made his debut for the Sky Blues in this game at the age of 16 years and 198 days, becoming the club's youngest-ever player at competitive level.

The Colombian striker Juan Pablo Angel scored his first goal for Villa in a 3-2 home Premiership win over Coventry on 5 May 2001 - a result that sent the Sky Blues down after 34 years in the top flight of English football. A full-house of almost 40,000 saw the action as Villa came back from 2-0 down to claim a dramatic victory with a late Paul Merson goal

Villa came back from a first leg deficit of 2-1 to beat Coventry 2-0 (3-2 on aggregate) in the 3rd round of the 1945-46 FA Cup competition.

In another third round FA Cup-tie, in January 1965, two goals by Tony Hateley helped Villa to a 3-0 home win in front of 47,656 spectators.

The Sky Blues recorded their first ever win at Villa Park in February 1998, winning a 5th round FA Cup-tie 1-0.

The Zenith Data Systems Cup clash took place at Highfield Road in October 1991 when Villa beat the 10 men of Coventry 2-0 in front of just 6,447 fans.

George Edwards scored four times when Villa beat Coventry 9-2 at home in a Wartime game in May 1945. Earlier that season Villa had won 6-0 at Highfield Road.

*Deehan in action against the Sky blues in 1978-79.*

Coventry City have had more players sent-off whilst playing against Aston Villa than any other club - total eight, starting with goalkeeper Bob Ward in the 1945 FA Cup encounter, Alan Dugdale, John Beck, Garry Thompson, Terry Butcher (in the ZDSC game), Kevin Richardson, Paul Williams and Gary Breen. Villa have only had one player dismissed against the Sky Blues - defender Allan Evans in 1979.

Players with both clubs include: A Blair, G Boateng, J Cumbes (City non-contract), G Curtis (also City manager), W Dorrell, D Dublin, AS Dyke,

J Eccles, GR Edwards (City WW2 guest), J Findlay, S Froggatt, R Graydon, M Hadji, W Hanson (Villa reserve), GA Harris, JC Harrison, A Hateley, WE Houghton (City WW2 guest), SK Hunt, J Joachim, JH Kearns, W Kimberley, WJ Kirton, N Lamptey, J Lawrence, AE Lindon, N Lockhart, A McClure, RW McDonald, DG Mortimer, A Moult (City & Villa reserve), W Myerscough, HE Nash, A Pember (Villa reserve), C Regis, K Richardson, P Saward, L Sealey, GL Thompson, JG Tooth (Villa reserve), GF Wheldon, C Wilson (Villa reserve), J Yates (City trialist), W Yates (Villa reserve).

Also: AJ Evans (Villa player, City manager), Ron Atkinson & J Mercer (managers of both clubs), DJ Sexton (City manager, Villa coach), R Wylie (Villa player & coach, City coach), K Macdonald (City player, Villa coach), A Cox (City player & coach, Villa coach/assistant & caretaker-manager), D Dorman (City player, Villa chief scout), EJ Vinall & RA Ryan (City players, Villa scouts).

## COWAN, JAMES S

Born: Bonhill, near Renton, Dunbartonshire, 17 October 1868. Died: Scotland, December 1915.
Career: Bonhill Council School, Jamestown, Vale of Leven (1887), Aston

*James Cowan.*

Villa (August 1889). Retired June 1902. Stayed on at Villa Park for a short time, coaching the juniors. He was then licensee of The Grand Turk, High Street, Aston, 1904 until December 1906. Six months later he became Queen's Park Rangers' first-ever manager, holding office until 1913 when he left the London club to return to Scotland.
James Cowan, with his untiring energy and skilful, timely tackling, was the mainstay of the Aston Villa defence throughout the 1890s. As a centre-half he was of immense value to the team, being undismayed and uncomplaining after the hardest of games. Known as the 'Prince of half-backs' Cowan was a shrewd tactician, surprisingly quick and certainly a fine footballer, one of Villa's all-time greats. He was only 5ft. 7ins tall and weighed less than 11 stone, but he was as solid as a rock at the heart of the Villa defence. He won three full caps for Scotland, gained two FA Cup winners' medals (1895 and 1897) and collected five League championship medals during his 13 years with Villa, appearing in 356 senior games.
In December 1895, Cowan missed five of Villa's League games, choosing instead to train away from the ground and then travel north to Scotland to enter the famous Powderhall Sprint - which he won and duly collected £80 in prize money! He was later fined four weeks wages and suspended by the furious Villa committee who, in fact, knew nothing about his venture north of the border. Whilst he was away Villa lost two games, at Preston and Everton. He returned to the team in early January and was at his best thereafter as Villa surged on to win the championship.

## COWAN, JOHN

Born: Bonhill, near Renton, Dunbartonshire, December 1870. Died: Scotland, May 1937.
Career: Vale of Leven, Preston North End (briefly in 1893), Glasgow Rangers, Aston Villa (August 1895), Dundee Harp (June 1899-1901).
A fast and direct winger with a strong shot, Jack Cowan, brother of James (above) scored 28 goals in 74 League and FA Cup appearances for Aston Villa during his four years with the club. He was a valuable member of two First Division championship winning sides (1896 and 1897) and starred in Villa's FA Cup Final victory in the latter year when they completed the double. Cowan lost his place in the Villa side to Steve Smith.

## COWANS, GORDON SIDNEY

Born: Cornworth, County Durham, 27 October 1958.
Career: County Durham & District Schools, Aston Villa (apprentice July 1974, professional August 1976), Bari, Italy (£450,000, with Paul Rideout valued at £400,000, June 1985), Aston Villa (£250,000, July 1988), Blackburn Rovers (£200,000, November 1991), Aston Villa (free transfer, July 1993), Derby County (£80,000, February 1994), Wolverhampton Wanderers (£20,000, December 1994), Sheffield United (free transfer, December 1995), Bradford City (free transfer, July 1996), Stockport County (free transfer March 1997), Burnley (free transfer, as reserve-team player/coach, August 1997-May 1998), Aston Villa (assistant-manager/coach, August 1998).
Midfielder 'Sid' Cowans spent 15 years in three separate spells as a player at Villa Park. He amassed a fine record: 528 appearances at first team level and 59 goals scored. He is currently lying third in Villa's all-time list of appearance-makers.

*Gordon Cowans.*

He helped Villa win the Football League Cup in 1977, the First Division title in 1981, the European Cup and the European Super Cup, both in 1982 and in all was capped 10 times by England, making his first full international appearance against Wales in February 1983 and his last against the Republic of Ireland in Dublin, in November 1990 (World Cup qualifier). He also represented his country in two 'B' and five Under-21 internationals, having earlier played at Youth team level. He later helped Stockport win promotion to the First Division before leaving Edgeley Park in 1997. The much-travelled Cowans was player/coach under Chris Waddle at Turf Moor and when Waddle left the Clarets so did Cowans, who went back to Villa Park for a fourth time as assistant-manager/coach to John Gregory (May 1998).
When he quit top-class football, Cowans had accumulated a personal statistical record in club and international competitions of 825 appearances (75 goals scored).
One of the finest left-sided midfielders in the country during the late 1970s/early '80s, Cowans could deliver a 30-40 yard defence-splitting pass with pin-point accuracy. He was an expert with in-swinging corner-kicks and free-kicks and he packed a fair shot himself. He was part of two exceptionally brilliant engine-room units at Villa Park - the first with John Gregory and Dennis Mortimer and then with Des Bremner and Mortimer. Cowans was a ball-artist who was voted the Barclay 'Young Player of the Year' in 1979-80 when he was an ever-present in the ranks as Villa, under manager Ron Saunders, prepared themselves to take on the rest of the top Division teams and go on to win their first Football League title for 71 years in 1980-81.

## COX, ARTHUR

Born: Southall, Warwickshire, 14 December 1939.
Career: Coventry City (player 1955-58, retired with a badly shattered leg to become coach at Highfield Road, looking after the Youth team, Walsall (coach), Aston Villa (coach, July 1968-January 1970, acting as caretaker-manager briefly from mid-November to mid-December 1968), Preston North End (coach, 1970), Halifax Town (coach 1971-72), Blackpool (assistant-manager), Sunderland (assistant-manager, 1973-76]), Galatasaray, Turkey (coach, July-September 1976), Chesterfield (manager, October 1976-September 1980), Newcastle United (manager, September 1980-May 1984), Derby County (manager, May 1984-93), scouted for various clubs, Fulham (Director of Football, 1998-2000), also England coach (under Kevin Keegan: 1998-2000).

THE COMPLETE ENCYCLOPAEDIA OF ASTON VILLA F.C.   THE COMPLETE ENCYCLOPAEDIA OF ASTON VILLA F.C.

61

Appointed Chief Scout by Manchester City in May 2001.

A tough, dour man, Cox made a name for himself by keeping a relatively low profile, working with some difficult Directors and chairmen! He was fairly successful as manager at three clubs: Chesterfield, Newcastle United and Derby County. He guided the Magpies to promotion from Division Two in 1984 and led the Rams to promotion from Division Three in 1986 and then into the top flight as Second Division champions twelve months.

He held the fort as caretaker-boss at Villa Park for five matches in November/December 1968 (one win, one draw and three defeats) prior to the arrival of Tommy Docherty. He was on the coaching staff at Deepdale when PNE won the Third Division title in 1969-70. He was Bob Stokoe's assistant at Roker Park when they beat Leeds United 1-0 to win the FA Cup in 1973 and he was also on Wearside when Sunderland clinched the Second Division championship three years later. He was a surprise choice to take the manager's seat at St James' Park, his appointment being criticised by Brian Clough! He helped Chris Waddle on the road to stardom and also introduced Kevin Keegan, Terry McDermott and Peter Beardsley to Gallowgate. Beardsley was signed for just £120,000 and later United sold him to Liverpool for £1.8 million! Cox stunned supporters when he resigned from Newcastle over the duration of his contract....shortly after promotion was achieved in 1984.

He took over at Derby on a reduced wage - just as the Baseball Ground club had survived a winding-up order! The Rams were in a mess at the time but Cox turned things round, bringing in some exceptionally fine players including Mark Wright and Peter Shilton, these two signings being made possible by Robert Maxwell. He later added future Aston Villa star Dean Saunders to his squad for £1 million. Reports indicated that Villa wanted Cox as their new manager in 1990 but the Rams refused to let him go. Cox stayed put (after a few ups and downs) and added several more players to his side, among them Marco Gabbiadini, Paul Kitson, Paul Simpson, Tommy Johnson, Martin Kuhl, Mark Pembridge, Darren Wassall and Craig Short. But despite spending millions Cox was unable to steer Derby into the play-offs for a possible Premiership challenge and eventually he was held responsible for lack of success. During the 1990s he acted as a scout for a number of clubs before joining Kevin Keegan's coaching staff and having a spell at Craven Cottage.

## COX, GERSOM

Born: Birmingham, March 1863. Died: Birmingham, September 1940.
Career: Excelsior FC, Walsall Town (trialist), Aston Villa (August 1887), Willenhall Pickwick (June 1893), Walsall Brunswick (1895), Bloxwich Strollers (1898). Retired 1900 after breaking his right leg. Became a successful market trader and at the age of 40 joined the Birmingham City Police Force as a special constable, attending most of Villa's home games in his blue uniform instead of a claret and blue strip! He also held a brief appointment as coach of Gravesend.

Gersom Cox, a well built, versatile full-back, had the misfortune to score the first own goal in the Football League, giving Wolverhampton Wanderers the lead at Dudley Road on the opening day of the competition - 8 September 1888. He spent six years with Villa, appearing in 97 League and FA Cup matches, gaining an FA Cup winners medal in 1892.

## COX, NEIL JAMES

Born: Scunthorpe, 8 October 1971.
Career: Scunthorpe United (YTS, June 1988, professional March 1990), Aston Villa (£400,000, February 1991), Middlesbrough (£1 million, July 1994), Bolton Wanderers (£1.2 million, May 1997), Watford (£500,000, November 1999).

Capped six times by England at Under-21 level during the early part of his career, right-back Neil Cox appeared in 57 first-class games for Villa (4 goals scored) before dropping out of the top flight to sign for

Middlesbrough .....a few months after gaining a League Cup winners' medal. He quickly helped 'Boro climb into the Premiership, however, making 40 League appearances in 1994-95. A tough-tackling, uncompromising defender, sound and committed, Cox, who enjoys getting forward at every opportunity, was a very popular player at both Middlesbrough and Bolton and was signed by ex-Villa boss Graham Taylor for Watford in 1999.

## CRABTREE, JAMES WILLIAM

Born: Burnley, 23 December 1871. Died: Birmingham, 18 June 1908.
Career: Burnley Royal Swifts (1885), Burnley (August 1889) Rossendale (August 1890), Heywood Central (July 1891), Burnley (professional, August 1892), Aston Villa (£250, August 1895), Plymouth Argyle (January-April 1904). Retired as a player in May 1904 and for two years coached several non-League clubs before becoming the licensee of the Royal Victoria Cross, William Street, Lozells, Birmingham, 1906 until his death in 1908.

One of England's greatest players during the period 1894-1902, Jimmy

Crabtree preferred a half-back position from where he kicked cleanly and with rare precision. Described in reference books as being 'a keen, skilful tackler, clever at close quarters and equally reliable in open play, he was cool and resourceful and brainy. He excelled in the finer points of the game and was one of the most versatile players in the country, being unrivalled in his position (left-half) on for many years.' He was very sensitive to cricticism and often stormed off in a temper.

One of the best-paid footballers in the land, he quickly bedded himself in the first team at Villa Park following his record £250 move from Burnley. He went on to appear in 202 first-class matches for the club (seven goals scored) after a brief spell with Plymouth Argyle he quit playing soccer with an apparent drink problem. Capped 14 times by England (between 1894-1902), Crabtree gained four League championship-winning medals (1896, 1897, 1899 & 1900) and also helped Villa win the FA Cup in 1897, when they achieved the double. He skippered Burnley, Aston Villa and his country. After a number of fits (some serious) Crabtree died at the age of 36.

## CRADDOCK, LEONARD MILLER

Born: Newent, Herefordshire, 21 September 1926. Died: Ledbury, 30 April 1960.
Career: Broomesberrow School, Chelsea (Amateur, 1945), Newport County (May 1946), Hereford United (August 1947), Aston Villa (September 1948).

A sprightly forward, able to occupy several positions, Miller Craddock's promising career came to an abrupt end in May 1951 when doctors ordered him to give up the game due to a heart problem. After a nightmare debut when Villa lost 6-0 at Middlesbrough on 11 December 1948 he went on to score 10 goals in 34 games for the club before his enforced retirement. Craddock, who was awarded a benefit match in October 1955, sadly died at the age of 33.

THE COMPLETE ENCYCLOPAEDIA OF ASTON VILLA F.C.  THE COMPLETE ENCYCLOPAEDIA OF ASTON VILLA F.C.

62

## CRAIG, THOMAS BROOKS
Born: Penilee, Glasgow, 21 November 1950.
Career: Avon Villa Juveniles, Drumchapel Amateurs (1965), Aberdeen (groundstaff, June 1966, professional November 1968), Sheffield Wednesday (£100,000, May 1969), Newcastle United (£110,000, December 1974), Aston Villa (£270,000, January 1978), Swansea City (£150,000, July 1979), Carlisle United (player/coach, March 1982), Hibernian (player/coach, October 1984), Celtic (assistant-manager/coach 1987), Newcastle United (coach).
Midfielder Tommy Craig was the first Scotsman to join an English League club for a six-figure fee when he moved from Pittodrie Park to Hillsborough in 1969. He made 210 appearances for Sheffield Wednesday and 122 for Newcastle United before joining Villa halfway through the 1977-78 season.
A left sided player, direct and skilful with excellent shot, he netted twice in 32 outings for Villa. Capped by Scotland against Switzerland in 1976, Craig also represented his country at Schoolboy, Youth, Under-21 and Under-23 levels. He played for Newcastle in the 1976 League Cup Final defeat by Manchester City and left St James' Park after being involved in a heated argument with the club's Board of Directors over the 'Nillis Affair'.

## CREWE ALEXANDRA
Villa's playing record against the Alex:
FA Cup

| Venue | P | W | D | L | F | A |
|---|---|---|---|---|---|---|
| Home | 1 | 1 | 0 | 0 | 3 | 0 |
| Away | 1 | 1 | 0 | 0 | 3 | 2 |
| Totals | 2 | 2 | 0 | 0 | 6 | 2 |

League Cup

| | P | W | D | L | F | A |
|---|---|---|---|---|---|---|
| Home | 1 | 1 | 0 | 0 | 1 | 0 |
| Away | 1 | 0 | 1 | 0 | 2 | 2 |
| Totals | 2 | 1 | 1 | 0 | 3 | 2 |

A crowd of 41,000 saw Billy Cook score a hat-trick when Aston Villa beat the Alex 4-0 at home in a 4th round FA Cup-tie in 1927-28.
The other meeting in this competition was staged at Gresty Road in January 1989 when Villa scraped through 3-2.

Villa knocked Crewe out of the League Cup in a 3rd round replay on their way to the 1975 Final with Norwich City.

Players with both clubs include: FH Broome, F Chapple, G Crudgington, N Cutler, HH Edgley, G Garratt, T Haywood, JF Inglis, K Jones, AH Lockett, AJ Moss, JTS Phillips, DA Platt, S Ritchie, K Swain (also Alex coach), J Walters (died before making his Alex debut), AM Watkins.

## CRICKETING-FOOTBALLERS
Jack Sharp played for England at both football and cricket, starring for Lancashire in the County Championship. He appeared in three Test Matches and scored 105 runs in one innings against Australia at The Oval in 1909. He spent 26 years as Lancashire's all-rounder (1899-1925), the last three as skipper. He amassed 22,715 runs, including 38 centuries, in 518 matches (average 31.11) and took 441 wickets (average 27.41), his best return coming against Worcestershire: 9-77. He also snapped up 226 catches - mainly in the cover point/gully area.
Jack Sharp's brother, Bert, was also a useful cricketer and in 1900 averaged 40 with the bat for Herefordshire.
Jack Devey, when playing for Warwickshire, scored 246 runs against Derbyshire in the

County Championship in the summer of 1900. He accumulated over 6,500 runs during his time at Edgbaston (1888-1907). Devey also scored 14 centuries for Aston Unity CC in the Birmingham League.
Fred Wheldon played for Worcestershire in the County Championship for 27 years (1899-1926). He scored 4,938 runs in 138 matches for an average of 22.54. He secured three centuries and took 95 catches (some as a wicket-keeper). He also played for Carmarthenshire CC.
Andy Ducat, appearing in one Test Match for England and was dismissed unluckily when, after playing a shot, saw a piece of wood fly

*Eric Houghton (centre of front row) ready to take the field for Warwickshire, 1949.*

off his bat and dislodge a bail. Ducat scored over 23,000 runs for his county, Surrey, between 1906 and 1931. Ducat also played football for England.
Villa's Amateur footballer Dr William Ewart Barnie-Adshead played 12 matches for Worcestershire CCC, returning an average of 11.61 with the bat from 22 innings.
South African-born forward Gordon Hodgson played cricket for Transvaal against several touring countries and then in England he joined Lancashire CCC, spending four years with the County in the 1930s during which time he appeared in 56 matches, taking 148 wickets at an average of 27.75. He also played for the Forfarshire CC in Scotland.
Villa's reserve goalkeeper in the 1890s, Ted Diver, played in 75 matches for Surrey CCC (1883-88) and 118 for Warwickshire (1894-1901). He averaged over 23 with the bat during an excellent career. Diver also assisted Cambridgeshire CC and Monmouthshire CC.
Fast bowler Jim Cumbes played for Surrey (29 first-class matches), Lancashire (9), Worcestershire (109) and Warwickshire (14) as well as assisting West Bromwich Dartmouth (Birmingham League). He averaged 7.56 runs per innings with the bat and notched 379 wickets at an average of 30.20. He later acted as Commercial Manager of both Warwickshire CCC (Edgbaston) and Lancashire CCC (Old Trafford) before becoming Commercial Executive at the latter club.
Eric Houghton played for Warwickshire's club and ground during the 1930s and early '40s and in 1946 made his County debut.
Jim Welford, Villa's full-back in the 1890s, played regularly for the Warwickshire Club & Ground while George Jakeman was a competent cricketer with the Worcestershire second XI.
Trevor Ford, known generally as a dynamic Welsh international centre forward, was 12th man for Glamorgan - and on the field of play - when West Indian all-rounder Gary Sobers, batting for Nottinghamshire, struck six sixes in one over from spinner Malcolm Nash at swansea in the summer of 1968.

*Tommy Craig.*

Other Villa footballers who also enjoyed playing cricket include: Charlie Athersmith, Joe Bache, Bob Brocklebank, goalkeeper Billy George (an all-rounder who played for Shropshire and Wiltshire), Albert Hall (Stourbridge CC), Brian Handley (captain of Paignton CC: 1961-66), Sammy Law (Warwickshire club & ground), Alec Leake, Charlie Millington (Lincolnshire CC), Nigel Spink, Billy Walker, Howard Vaughton (Warwickshire second XI & Staffordshire).

Alan Smith kept wicket for Warwickshire and England. He became an Aston Villa Director and later was the Chief Executive of the Test and County Cricket Board.

Villa Chairman Ron Bendall was a useful cricketer with Pickwick CC. 'Stumps', an indoor cricket centre adjoining Villa Park, was opened by England fast bowler Graham Dilley.

For over 70 years, commencing as far back as 1912, Aston Villa met neighbours West Bromwich Albion in an annual cricket match.

### CROPLEY, ALEXANDER JAMES
Born: Aldershot, 16 January 1951.
Career: Edina Hearts (1966-67), Hibernian (July 1968), Arsenal (£150,000, December 1974), Aston Villa (£125,000, September 1976), Newcastle United (on loan, February-March 1980), Toronto Blizzard (briefly, summer 1981), Portsmouth (September 1981), Hibernian (September 1982). Retired 1985 and soon afterwards became a licensee in Edinburgh. Later he became a taxi driver in that city.

Raised in Edinburgh despite being born in deepest England, Alex Cropley was a lovely left-sided midfielder who could also be used as an out-and-out winger.

He twice broke his leg in League action - the first playing for Arsenal against Birmingham City in November 1975 and then in a tackle with West Brom's Ally Brown at Villa Park in October 1977. He won two full caps for Scotland to add to the three he gained at Under-23 level before joining the Gunners. He also starred in two League Cup winning sides: Hibernian in 1973 and Aston Villa in 1977.
● Cropley's father, John Thomas, played in over 160 League games for Aldershot from 1947-63.

*Alex Cropley.*

### CROSSLAND, WILLIAM SAMUEL
Born: West Bromwich, February 1856. Died: Birmingham, February 1923.
Career: West Bromwich Baptist, Hockley Heart of Oak, Oldbury Town, Aston Villa (August 1879). Retired through injury, May 1882.
Bill Crossland was a powerful footballer who played in Villa's first-ever FA Cup-tie against Stafford Road on 13 December 1897. He went on to have four more outings in the same competition before injury forced him into an early retirement. He later worked in the Birmingham jewellery quarter.

### CROWD DISTURBANCES
In January 1888, Aston Villa's home 5th round FA Cup-tie against Preston North End, was abandoned in the 85th minute due to crowd disturbances, with the visitors 3-1 ahead.
The result was allowed to stand and Villa, the holders of the trophy, were disqualified from the competition. The FA also severely censured the club for failing to maintain order and control the spectators.

(See Abandoned Matches).
Scottish giants Glasgow Rangers came south to play a friendly at Villa Park on 9 October 1976. A 18,000-strong crowd (10,000 supporting the 'Gers) turned out but as the game progressed hundreds of visiting supporters invaded the pitch, throwing bottles, cans, coins and other dangerous items around indiscriminately. They fought with the police and caused havoc. The game was subsequently abandoned in the 51st minute. Over 100 spectators were injured (some women and children) and 50 more arrested. Five days later an FA inquiry cleared Aston Villa of any blame for the riot.
(See Abandoned Matches).

The Leicester City v Aston Villa League game at Filbert Street in October 1977, was held up for 10 minutes due to crowd disturbances. As a result of crowd trouble the previous season, the Aston Villa versus Besiktas European Cup encounter at Villa Park, on 15 September 1982, was played behind closed doors. The attendance was officially recorded as NIL but with club officials, photographers, press and other guests allowed in to the ground, the actual crowd was recorded as 167.
There was also some crowd trouble at the RSC Anderlecht v Villa European Cup semi-final clash in Belgium in 1981-82.

### CROWE, VICTOR HERBERT
Born: Abercynon, Glamorgan, 31 January 1932.
Career: Handsworth Wood School, Erdington Albion, West Bromwich Albion (amateur, 1950), Aston Villa (amateur trialist, March 1951), Stirling Albion (amateur player while on national service in Scotland), Aston Villa (professional, June 1952), Peterborough United (July 1964), Atlanta Chiefs NASL (assistant-manager, 1967-69), Aston Villa (assistant-coach, August 1969, manager January 1970-May 1974), Portland Timbers NASL (coach/manager 1975-76). Later a scout in Midlaands non-League football and also advisory manager of Bilston Town (1988-89).

Vic Crowe left Wales at the age of two and was brought up in the Handsworth area of Birmingham. He joined West Bromwich Albion as an amateur but was not retained and subsequently tried his luck at Villa Park. He did well and after his national service he was handed a professional contract. He went on to give Villa, and Wales, excellent service as a wing-half before joining Peterborough. Known as 'Spike' his red hair stood out like a beacon in centre-field where he performed manfully, never shirking a tackle, always totally committed and producing some sterling work for both club and country. He replaced Danny Blanchflower at right-half in the Villa side in 1954 and went on to score 12 goals in 351 senior games for the club, skippering the side to the 1960 Second Division championship and victory in the 1961 League Cup Final over Rotherham United. He missed the 1957 FA Cup win due to injury. Later Crowe played in two FA Cup semi-finals defeats (in 1959 and 1960), won the supporters' Terrace Trophy' award in the latter year and was capped 16 times by Wales. He was a member of the national squad for the 1958 World Cup Finals in Sweden before eventually captaining the Red Dragons for the first time in 1960. With Posh he helped them reach the 1966 League Cup semi-final before returning to Villa Park where he subsequently became manager. Villa played 192 League games under Crowe's guidance. They were unbeaten in 140 of them, winning 86 and drawing 54. Crowe now lives in Sutton Coldfield.

THE COMPLETE ENCYCLOPAEDIA OF ASTON VILLA F.C.    THE COMPLETE ENCYCLOPAEDIA OF ASTON VILLA F.C.

64

## CROWTHER, STANLEY

Born: Bilston, Staffs. 3 September 1935.

Career: Stonefield Secondary Modern School, West Bromwich Albion (Amateur, 1950, also assisting Erdington Albion at the same time), Bilston Town (August 1952), Aston Villa (£750, August 1955), Manchester United (£18,000, February 1958), Chelsea (£10,000, December 1958), Brighton & Hove Albion (March 1961), Rugby Town (August 1965), Hednesford Town (July 1967-69).

Wing-half Stan Crowther left Villa Park to join Manchester United in one of the most dramatic transfers in the game's history! One hour and 16 minutes after signing for the Reds he stepped out in front of almost 60,000 fans inside the Old Trafford cauldron for a nervous FA Cup encounter against Sheffield Wednesday in the immediate aftermath of the Munich air disaster. At the time it was reported that he was the first player ever to appear for two different teams in the same FA Cup competition, having earlier assisted Aston Villa against Stoke City. It was, however, overlooked that Jimmy Scoular, a future Scottish international, had played for Gosport against Salisbury and for Portsmouth against Birmingham City in the 1945-46 tournament.

Prior to him leaving for Old Trafford, Crowther had scored four goals in 62 first team matches during his two-and-a-half years with Villa. Indeed, he had also helped Villa beat Manchester United 2-1 in the 1957 FA Cup Final. He was only acquired as a stop-gap by United stand-in boss Jimmy Murphy and after 20 outings for the Lancashire club, moved south to Chelsea for whom he made over 50 League appearances before ending his career with Brighton. Orphaned at the age of 15, Crowther won three England Under-23 caps and represented the Football League whilst at Villa Park. He was on the losing side for Manchester United (v. Bolton) in the 1958 FA Cup Final. After quitting football Crowther became a senior foreman for Armitage Shanks in Wolverhampton.

## CRUDGINGTON, GEOFFREY

Born: Wolverhampton, 14 February 1952.

Career: Wolverhampton & District Schools, Wolverhampton Wanderers (junior), Aston Villa (professional, September 1969), Bradford City (on loan, March-April 1971), Preston North End (on loan), Toronto Blizzard (summer, 1971), Crewe Alexandra (£5,000, March 1972), Swansea City (£20,000, July 1978), Plymouth Argyle (£40,000, October 1979). Later appointed coach and then Football in the Community Officer at Home Park.

Six-foot goalkeeper Geoff Crudgington played for England Schoolboys as a teenager before making five senior appearances for Aston Villa as stand-in for John Dunn and Tommy Hughes. He went on to appear in over 275 games for Crewe and 374 for Argyle, playing for the latter in the 1984 FA Cup semi-final against Watford at Villa Park.

## CRYSTAL PALACE

Villa's playing record against the Eagles:

Football League/Premiership

| Venue | P | W | D | L | F | A |
|---|---|---|---|---|---|---|
| Home | 12 | 8 | 2 | 2 | 22 | 9 |
| Away | 12 | 2 | 6 | 4 | 6 | 10 |
| Totals | 24 | 10 | 8 | 6 | 28 | 19 |

FA Cup

| | P | W | D | L | F | A |
|---|---|---|---|---|---|---|
| Home | 2 | 2 | 0 | 0 | 9 | 3 |

League Cup

| | P | W | D | L | F | A |
|---|---|---|---|---|---|---|
| Home | 2 | 1 | 1 | 0 | 3 | 1 |
| Away | 3 | 0 | 2 | 1 | 3 | 6 |
| Neutral | 1 | 1 | 0 | 0 | 3 | 0 |
| Totals | 6 | 2 | 3 | 1 | 9 | 7 |

Aston Villa and Crystal Palace first met at League level in season 1967-68 (Division 2). The Eagles won 1-0 at Villa Park whilst Villa claimed an identical result at Selhurst Park. Villa lost 4-2 in London the following season (when all six goals came after the interval) before they registered their first victory over the Eagles in October 1973, winning 2-1 at home.

Villa's biggest win to date over the Eagles has been 4-1, at home, in October 1987. Mark Walters scored a hat-trick in this game - the only Villa player to achieve this feat against the Eagles.

Villa went on to record their first Premiership victory over Palace, 3-0 at home on 5 September 1992, Dwight Yorke, Steve Froggatt and Steve Staunton the scorers in front of 17,120 fans.

Harold Halse and Clem Stephenson both scored twice when Villa beat Palace 5-0 in a 3rd round FA Cup-tie in front of 44,500 fans in 1912-134 and Harry Burrows netted twice in an exciting 4-3 victory at the same stage of the 1961-62 competition when the crowd topped 45,000.

Villa defeated Palace 3-0 at neutral Coventry in the 1978-79 League Cup competition after 1-1 and 0-0 draws.

Palace dumped Villa out of the League Cup to the tune of 4-1 at Selhurst Park in November 1994, scoring all their goals in the second-half, including two from future Villa star Gareth Southgate.

Keith Smith, who worked for the Villa Development Association after retiring from football, scored a League goal just six seconds after kick-off for Palace against Derby County in November 1964. It is believed to be the third fastest goal of all-time.

Players with both clubs include: JP Allen (Palace WW2 guest), T Barber, S Beaton (Villa reserve, Palace WW1 guest), VP Blore (Villa reserve), W Brown, J Burridge, GB Clarke, SV Collymore, S Curcic, J Fashanu, G Garratt, G Graham, AA Gray, R Houghton, PH Mortimer, FH Norris, FJ O'Donnell (Palace WW2 guest), JT Palethorpe, JTS Phillips, A Proudler, CL Roberts (Villa reserve), P Saward (Palace Amateur), G Southgate, CH Spiers, S Staunton, GL Thompson, CW Wallace, WM Watkins. Also: A Leake (Villa player, Palace trainer/coach, reserve player), P Barron (Palace 'keeper, Villa coach), EF Goodman (Villa reserve & assistant-secretary, Palace secretary & manager), B Whitehouse (Palace player, Villa chief scout) and K Smith (see above).

## CUMBES, JAMES

Born: Didsbury near Manchester, 4 May 1944

Career: Didsbury County School, Manchester Boys (trialist), Whalley Grange FC (Manchester Amateur League), Runcorn, Southport, Tranmere Rovers, West Bromwich Albion (£33,350, August 1969) Aston Villa (£36,000, November 1971), Portland Timbers NASL (March 1976), Coventry City (non-contract, September 1976), Runcorn (semi-professional, August 1977), Southport (non-contract, January 1978), Worcester City (1978-81), Kidderminster Harriers (1982-84), WBA All Stars (1980s). He played cricket for Lancashire (1963-67 and 1971), Surrey (1968 & 1969), Worcestershire (1972-81) and

*Jim Cumbes.*

Warwickshire (1982) as well as West Bromwich Dartmouth in the Birmingham League (1982-84). He retired in 1984 to become Commercial Manager of Warwickshire CCC, a position he held until

THE COMPLETE ENCYCLOPAEDIA OF ASTON VILLA F.C.    THE COMPLETE ENCYCLOPAEDIA OF ASTON VILLA F.C.

65

August 1987, when he switched to Lancashire CCC, where he's now employed as Commercial Executive, based at Old Trafford.

Tall, agile and competent goalkeeper with good technique who was also a very fine fast bowler on the county cricket scene, Jim Cumbes won a Cheshire Bowl Final medal with Runcorn, he played in 137 League games for Tranmere and then contested the number one position with John Osborne at The Hawthorns before transferring to Aston Villa in 1971, after 79 outings for the Baggies. He stayed five years at Villa Park, making 183 senior appearances and gaining a Third Division championship medal and a League Cup winners' prize in the process. Replaced by John Burridge between the posts at Villa Park, Cumbes amassed over 400 League and Cup appearances during his career. As a cricketer, he won both County championship and knockout Cup medals with Worcestershire. In all he played in 161 first-class cricket matches, averaging 7.56 with the bat and taking 379 wickets at 30.20 each, with a best return of 6-24. He also took 38 catches.

## CUMMINGS, GEORGE WILFRED

Born: Thornbridge, near Falkirk, Scotland, 5 June 1913. Died: Birmingham, April 1987.
Career: Laurieston School, Stirlingshire, Thornbridge Waverley (1928), Thornbridge Welfare (1930), Grange Rovers (1931), Partick Thistle (August 1932), Aston Villa (£9,350, November 1935). Guested for Birmingham, Falkirk, Nottingham Forest, Northampton Town during World War Two. Retired May 1949 to become Villa's third team coach. Later appointed Hednesford Town (manager) and scout for both Burnley and Wolves.
George Cummings made 232 first-class appearances for Aston Villa and another 177 during WW2.
Nicknamed 'Icicle' for his coolness and composure, he was a masterful full-back, as hard as a block of granite with a superb physique. His kicks were strong and long, his bone-

*Cummings leads out Villa.*

shaking tackles were thorough and positive, his attitude determined and resourceful while his brain never stopped working. A great footballer who served Villa superbly well for 14 years, Cummings helped the team win the Second Division title in 1938 and lift the Wartime League (North) Cup in 1944. He won nine full caps for Scotland between 1935-39, six as a Villa player. He toured the USA and Canada with the Scottish FA in 1935 and also represented the Scottish League XI on two occasions, appeared in one Wartime international and lined up for an All-British team and the Football League side in 1939-40. As a youngster he had played for Scottish Junior FA (1929-30). Cummings skippered Villa for four years (1945-49), taking over the mantle from Alex Massie. He scouted for Burnley and Wolves whilst in full employment at the Dunlop Rubber Company.

## CUMMINGS, THOMAS SMITH

Born: Sunderland, 12 September 1928.
Career: Stanley United, Hylton Colliery Welfare, Burnley (October 1947), Mansfield Town (March 1963, player/manager July 1963-July 1967), Aston Villa (manager, July 1967-November 1968). Later scout for Burnley and Sunderland. Was the Chairman of the PFA for two years before taking over as manager at Field Mill.
As a centre-half Tommy Cummings gained three England 'B' caps and represented the Football League. He helped Burnley win the First Division title in 1960 and reach the 1962 FA Cup Final before assisting Mansfield in gaining promotion from the Fourth Division in 1963. He made 434 appearances during his 16 years at Turf Moor.
Cummings appointed the former West Ham United player Malcolm Musgrove as his right-hand man and senior coach when he took charge of Aston Villa who were already a struggling Second Division team with very little money to spend on players. His first two signings were both from his former club Mansfield, Tommy Mitchinson (£18,000) and Dick Edwards (£30,000). They couldn't perform miracles, neither could Cummings who was sacked in November 1968 with Villa heading for the Third Division! As manager at Villa Park, Cummings had a poor record in the Football League. Of the 60 games played under his guidance, only 17 were won, 14 drawn and 29 lost.

## CUNLIFFE, ARTHUR

Born: Blackrod, near Wigan, 5 February 1909. Died: Bournemouth, 28 August 1986.
Career: Adlington FC (aged 14), Chorley (August 1927), Blackburn Rovers (professional, January 1928), Aston Villa (May 1933, joint deal involving Ronnie Dix), Middlesbrough (December 1935), Burnley (April 1937), Hull City (June 1938), Rochdale (August 1946, trainer at Spotland July 1947), Bournemouth (trainer, July 1950, Cherries' physiotherapist 1971-74).
Early in his career Arthur Cunliffe was an aggressive right-winger but in later years he developed into an international outside-left, winning two full England caps in that position. Very quick, he had good ball skills and whipped in a positive centre, given the chance. He was a regular marksman throughout his career, scoring 47 goals in 129 League games for Blackburn, five in 27 for Middlesbrough, 19 in 42 for Hull and five in 23 for Rochdale. His record with Villa (League and Cup) was 13 goals in 75 appearances. He spent nearly 25 years with Bournemouth.

## CURBISHLEY, LLEWELLYN CHARLES (ALAN)

Born: Forest Gate, London, 8 November 1957.
Career: West Ham United (apprentice 1973, professional July 1975), Birmingham City (£225,000, July 1979), Aston Villa (£100,000 plus Robert Hopkins, March 1983), Charlton (£40,000, December 1984), Brighton & Hove Albion (£32,000, August 1987). He returned to Charlton as player/coach in July 1990, became assistant-manager three months later and was upgraded to first team boss in June 1995 after four years as joint-manager with Steve Gritt. In May 1998, Curbishley celebrated when Premiership football came to The Valley for the first time. He took the Addicks up again in 2000 and later that same year was named as a possible choice as an additional coach to the England national squad under new coach Sven Goran Eriksson.
As a midfield player himself Curbishley never reached the heights he

THE COMPLETE ENCYCLOPAEDIA OF ASTON VILLA F.C.

THE COMPLETE ENCYCLOPAEDIA OF ASTON VILLA F.C.

66

had hoped for, although he did represent England at Schoolboy, Youth and Under-23 levels and made well over 600 senior appearances while serving with five different League clubs. He gained an FA Youth Cup runners-up medal with the Hammers in 1975, helped Blues win promotion from Division Two in 1980. After 155 appearances for the St Andrew's club he then went on to have 43 outings for Villa (one goal scored).

## CURCIC, SASA
Born: Belgrade, Yugoslavia, 14 February 1972.
Career: Partizan Belgrade, Bolton Wanderers, (£1.5 million, October 1995), Aston Villa (£4 million, August 1996), Crystal Palace (£1 million, March 1998), New Jersey Metros (July 1999), Tranmere Rovers (trialist, August 2000).

Capped 10 times by Yugoslavia before joining Bolton for a club record fee, attacking midfielder Sasa Curcic settled in quickly at Burnden Park and was voted Wanderers' 'Player of the Year' in his only season with the club. He then moved to Villa Park for a another club record fee, but after an encouraging start he found himself out of favour for long spells, prompting calls from the player that he should never have left Bolton! Failing to get on with manager Brian Little, Curcic submitted a transfer request in February 1997 but did not leave Villa Park until thirteen months later - after he had got married and had his work permit renewed. A moody player at times, he made 34 appearances for Villa and scored one goal, while taking his tally of international caps up to 13. He played with a lot more purpose and heart under Terry Venables at Selhurst Park, but when he left the Eagles' nest Curcic again became unsettled, as well as being devastated to learn about the NATO bombings on his homeland.

## CURTIS, GEORGE WILLIAM
Born: Dover, 5 May 1939.
Career: Snowdown Colliery, Coventry City (amateur, May 1954, professional, May 1956), Aston Villa (£25,000, December 1969-May 1972). Retired and later returned to Coventry City to join the club's Commercial staff (1974). Became Managing-Director at Highfield Road in September 1983, taking over as team manager (jointly with John Sillett) in April 1986 and holding office until May 1987, after the Sky Blues had won the FA Cup. He is still at Highfield Road.
As a solid, uncompromising centre-half, George Curtis made 538 senior appearances for the Sky Blues - a club record that was eventually broken by Steve Ogrizovic in 1996. He was voted 'Midland Footballer of the Year' in 1963-64 and three years later helped the Sky Blues gain promotion to Division One for the first time in the club's history. Curtis, in fact, played in four different Divisions of the Football League with City. Bought as a stop-gap, he made just 57 appearances and netted four goals for Aston Villa before retiring at the end of the 1971-72 season - after he had added a Third Division championship medal to his collection.

## CUTLER, NEIL ANTHONY
Born: Birmingham, 3 September 1976
Career: West Bromwich Albion (YTS, June 1992, professional September 1993), Chester City (on loan, March 1996), Crewe Alexandra (July 1996), Chester City (on loan, August 1996 - signed permanently July 1998), Aston Villa (November, 1999), Oxford United (on loan, December 2000), Stoke City (July 2001).
Former England Youth international goalkeeper who played in one Premiership game for Aston Villa, as a substitute for the injured David James in a 4-0 win at Middlesbrough in February 2000.

## DALEY, ANTHONY MARK
Born: Birmingham, 18 October 1967.
Career: Aston Manor School, Holte Comprehensive School, Birmingham Boys, Aston Villa (YTS, June 1983, professional May 1985), Wolverhampton Wanderers (£1.25 million, June 1994), Watford (July 1998), FC Madeira (Portugal), Hapoel Haifa (Cyprus), Walsall (June 1999), Nailsworth FC, Forest Green Rovers (October 1999).
After playing for his country at Youth team level, dashing right or left-winger Tony Daley bided his time at Villa Park before gaining a place in the first XI. Once in, he stayed and did very well, gaining one 'B' and seven full England caps as well as helping Villa win the League Cup in 1994. Direct, skilful with an eye for goal, Daley went on to make 290 appearances for the Villans (40 goals scored) before being sold to Wolves in the summer of 1994. But sadly injuries ruined his career at Molineux, hence his departure in 1998 to Watford where he linked up again with his former Wolves boss Graham Taylor. Later on he played briefly overseas, had a brief association with Walsall and was then engaged by the Nationwide Conference side Forest Green Rovers in 1999.

## DALY, PATRICK
Born: Dublin, 4 December 1927.
Career: Dublin City Boys, Shamrock Rovers, Aston Villa (November 1949), Shamrock Rovers (May 1951),
Chatty Irishman Pat Daly was signed as a replacement for Dicky Dorsett but unfortunately he failed to settle in at Villa Park and returned to his homeland after making just four senior appearances in the claret and blue strip. His League debut was away at Blackpool in January 1950 when he did well against Stan Matthews. He represented the Republic of Ireland against Finland in 1951 and also played for the League of Ireland when with Shamrock Rovers.

## DARLINGTON
Villa's playing record against the Quakers:

FA Cup
| Venue | P | W | D | L | F | A |
| --- | --- | --- | --- | --- | --- | --- |
| Home | 1 | 1 | 0 | 0 | 2 | 1 |

Darlington, knocked out in an earlier round of the 1999-2000 FA Cup, became the first club ever to be given a wild card re-entry into the competition, rejoining the competition in the third round after Manchester United had withdrawn. The Quakers were paired away to Aston Villa and after a plucky performance, eventually lost 2-1 in front of 22,101 spectators. Benito Carbone and Dion Dublin scored for Villa.

*Martin Carruthers, played for both clubs.*

Players with both clubs include: M Armstrong (Villa reserve), G Brown (Quakers player-manager), MS Burke, J Burridge, M Carruthers, RA Chester, P Crichton (Villa on loan), RD Davis (Villa WW2 guest), WA

THE COMPLETE ENCYCLOPAEDIA OF ASTON VILLA F.C.     THE COMPLETE ENCYCLOPAEDIA OF ASTON VILLA F.C.

67

Dinsdale, A Evans, D Geddis, J Gidman (also Quakers' assistant-manager), D Kubicki, C Liddle (Villa reserve), CH Slade, N Tarrant (Villa reserve). Also: B Little (Villa player & manager, Quakers' manager), A McAndrew (Darlington player, Villa coach).

## DARWEN

Villa's playing record against Darwen:

Football League

| Venue | P | W | D | L | F | A |
|---|---|---|---|---|---|---|
| Home | 2 | 2 | 0 | 0 | 16 | 0 |
| Away | 2 | 1 | 1 | 0 | 6 | 2 |
| Totals | 4 | 3 | 1 | 0 | 22 | 2 |
| FA Cup | | | | | | |
| Home | 2 | 2 | 0 | 0 | 5 | 2 |
| Away | 1 | 0 | 0 | 1 | 4 | 5 |
| Totals | 3 | 2 | 0 | 1 | 9 | 7 |

Aston Villa beat Darwen 5-1 in Lancashire in October and then doubled up with an emphatic 7-0 home victory on Boxing Day in the first two League games between the two clubs in season 1891-92.
When they met again in 1893-94, it was 1-1 at Darwen before Villa cruised to an easy 9-0 win at home, 12,500 fans seeing six players share the goals with Jack Devey, Albert Brown and Denny Hodgetts all scoring twice.
On their way to the 1887 and 1892 FA Cup Finals, Villa ousted Darwen 3-2 and 2-0 at home in rounds six and two respectively. Darwen, though, gained revenge when they beat Villa 5-4 in a nine-goal thriller in a 1st round tie in front of 6,000 spectators at Barley Bank in January 1893.

Players with both clubs include: J McLuckie, DF Skea, J Whitley.

## DAVIS, ARTHUR GEORGE

Born: Birmingham, July 1892. Died: Birmingham, c 1955.
Career: Birmingham St George's, Evesham, Aston Villa (July 1919), Queen's Park Rangers (August 1922), Notts County (August 1923), Crystal Palace (July 1928), Kidderminster Harriers (August 1929).
Arthur Davis was a reserve inside or outside-left who was given few opportunities at Villa Park, scoring once in his five senior games. He later amassed more than 200 League appearances while playing for QPR, Notts County and Palace.

## DAVIS, ELISHA

Born: Dudley, December 1855. Died: Birmingham, December 1897.
Career: Hockley Hill Council School, Florence FC (Birmingham), Wednesbury Strollers, Aston Villa (August 1879). Retired through injury, May 1886. Later became landlord of the Golden Lion, Aston, Birmingham.
Eli Davis played in Aston Villa's first ever FA Cup-tie in 1879, a 1-1 draw away at Stafford Road (Wolverhampton). A wholehearted performer, he was quite unflagging and especially good at dribbling, although a little imprudent at times. Davis scored two goals in his 21 senior appearances for Villa before being forced out of the game with a serious knee injury.

## DAVIS, GEORGE

Born: Birmingham, 1868.
Career: St Phillips FC, Aston Villa (August 1889), Witton White Star (season 1891-92).
Relatively unknown goalkeeper who made just one League appearance for Aston Villa - deputising for Jimmy Warner in a 6-2 away win at Burnley on 5 October 1889.

## DAVIS, GEORGE ARCHIBALD

Born: Handsworth, Birmingham, 1870. Died: Birmingham.
Career: Victoria FC, Aston Manor, Aston Villa (July 1892), Smethwick Centaur (August 1893), Wesleyans FC.
Reserve centre-forward who spent only one season with Aston Villa, appearing once in the League side as striking partner to Jack Devey and Denny Hodgetts in a 3-2 defeat at West Bromwich Albion on 19 September 1892. Davis scored Villa's second and equalising goal.

## DAVIS, NEIL

Born: Bloxwich, 15 August 1973.
Career: Redditch United, Aston Villa (£25,000, professional, May 1991), Wycombe Wanderers (on loan, October 1996), Walsall (August 1998), Hednesford Town (September 1998).
Hard-working striker Neil Davis made three substitute appearances for Aston Villa (two in the Premiership). He also had 14 games for Wycombe but only one for Walsall before entering non-League soccer in 1998.

## DAVIS, RICHARD DANIEL

Born: Birmingham, 22 January 1922. Died: Bishops Stortford, August 1999.
Career: Morris & James FC (Birmingham), Sunderland (February 1939), Aston Villa (WW2 guest: September 1940-October 1943), also guested for Aldershot, Brentford, Bristol Rovers, Notts County & Rochdale: 1943-45), Darlington (May 1954). Retired through injury in 1957.
Dicky Davis - an England Schoolboy international - was a guest player for Aston Villa during the Second World - and what an impact he had! He was only 18 years of age when he came to the club in September 1940 and then as an out-and-out goalscorer, occupying the centre-forward position, he gave defenders a torrid term with his precise, all-action commitment and devastating marksmanship. He netted 67 goals in only 53 Wartime games for Villa. His haul contained 10 hat-tricks (two in one game - a sixtimer) and in season 1941-42 he was simply unstoppable inside the penalty-area, cracking home no fewer than 30 goals in just 18 outings. After the War, Davis returned to Roker Park and went on to score 79 goals in 154 League and FA Cup games for Sunderland before ending his career with Darlington for whom he claimed 32 goals in 93 Third Division (North) matches. One of the game's greatest strikers, Davis notched more than 200 goals (at various levels) during a fine career.

## DAVIS, RICHMOND

Born: Walsall, April 1861. Died: Birmingham, 1934.
Career: Broadway Council School (Walsall), Walsall Swifts (1881), Aston Villa (August 1884). Retired through injury, May 1888.
Rich Davis was a player who enjoyed to run with the ball, but was somewhat greedy at times and lost possession in dangerous situations. Nevertheless, a very competitive footballer who could play in all of the five forward-line positions. He gained an FA Cup winners medal in 1887 when he helped set up his side's second goal in their 2-0 victory over West Bromwich Albion. A knee injury ended his career.

## DAWSON, FREDERICK HENRY HERBERT

Born: Birmingham, December 1858. Died: Birmingham, 19 November 1938.
Career: Handsworth New Road Council School, Aston Unity, Aston Villa (August 1880). Retired through injury, September 1889.
A key member of Villa's 1887 FA Cup winning side, wing-half Fred Dawson played the game with evident enjoyment, tenacity and constructiveness, always putting himself about! He lined-up at left-half in Villa's first-ever League game in September 1888 against Wolverhampton Wanderers - one of 20 senior appearances he made for the club (two goals scored).

## DAWSON, JAMES HUBERT

Born: Stoke-on-Trent, August 1859. Died: Burton-on-Trent, February 1927.

Career: Forest Courtiers FC (Stoke), Aston Villa (August 1880), Burton Swifts (May 1882).

Right-half Jim Dawson was adept with both feet and possessed a fearsome tackle. He burst the ball when clearing his line during an FA Cup-tie between Villa and Notts County in January 1882 - one of five senior appearances he made for the club.

## DAY, MERVYN RICHARD

Born: Chelmsford, 16 June 1955.

Career: Chelmsford & Essex Schools, West Ham United (apprentice June 1971, professional March 1973), Leyton Orient (£100,000, July 1979), Aston Villa (£15,000, August 1983), Leeds United (£30,000, January 1985), Luton Town (on loan, March 19932), Sheffield United (on loan, April 1992), Carlisle United (July 1993-May 1994). Later coach at Brunton Park, then Carlisle's Director of Coaching (from January 1995) and team manager 1996-97; Charlton Athletic first team coach, 1999-2001.

A goalkeeper with good technique, cool and composed with exceptional positional sense, Mervyn Day made his Football League debut for the Hammers as an 18 year-old in 1973. Whilst at Upton Park, he won both England Youth and Under-23 honours, was named 'Young Footballer of the Year' and gained an FA Cup winners medal in 1975 when the Hammers beat Fulham 2-0 in the Final. He also played in the European Cup Winners Cup Final of 1976 In the Heysel Stadium) and made 231 appearances for West Ham before going on to star in 138 games for Orient. He played in 33 games for Villa, when he briefly displaced Nigel Spink between the posts. In 1987 Day kept goal for Leeds United in the FA Cup semi-final defeat by Coventry City and also in the end-of-season play-off Final against Charlton Athletic.

## DEACY, EAMONN STEPHEN

Born: Galway (Ireland) 1 October 1958.

Career: Galway Rovers, Aston Villa (March 1979), Derby County (on loan, October 1983), Galway United (July 1984). Later worked in the family fruit and vegetable business in Ireland.

During the 1978-79 season full-back Eamonn Deacy - one of nine brothers - wrote at least 20 letters in eight months to Aston Villa asking for a trial. He finally got one and spent five years at the club, making 40 senior appearances and scoring one goal - in a 3-2 home win over Norwich City in March 1983. He won four caps for the Republic of Ireland in season 1981-82.

*Alan Deakin.*

## DEAKIN, ALAN ROY

Born: Balsall Heath, Birmingham, 27 November 1941.

Career: Dennis Road Junior School Balsall Heath, South Birmingham Boys, Cannon Hill Rovers, Aston Villa (juniors, 1956, professional December 1958), Walsall (October 1969), Metropolitan Cammell FC, Aston Villa Old Stars (1979-88).

Alan Deakin was an outstanding wing-half in the early 1960s, rated as one of the most talented of the 'Mercer Minnows'. He successfully took over the number 6 shirt from Irishman Pat Saward but his career took a nosedive in 1965 following a series of injuries which included a broken leg, fractured ankle, damaged toe and twisted knee. He returned, however, to skipper the

side in 1966-67, fulfilling a lifetime's ambition to lead his favourite team at League level, having skippered the Youth team some ten years earlier. Deakin helped Villa win the League Cup in 1961 and collected a losers' medal two years later when Birmingham won the Final 3-1 on aggregate. He also gained six England Under-23 caps and made 270 senior appearances for Villa (nine goals scored) before transferring to Walsall in 1969. On leaving the soccer scene, Deakin became a welder for the Gamwell Engineering Co. (Witton).

● Deakin's brother, Mike, played for Crystal Palace, Aldershot and Northampton Town.

## DEATHS

Aston Villa's reserve goalkeeper Arthur Sabin died at the age of 19 in March 1958, four months after chipping a bone in his neck.

Villa's brilliant goalscoring forward Archie Hunter suffered a heart attack while playing against Everton on 4 January 1890. He was rushed to hospital in Liverpool but never recovered full health and died four years later, aged 35.

Andy Hunter, brother of Archie (above) died in Australia in June 1888 at the age of 23. His registration papers were still with Aston Villa at the time, the player having been forced to retire through injury.

Former Villa 1890s striker Jimmy Logan died at the age of 25 following a short illness.

Albert Woolley (a Villa player from 1892-95) died aged 25 in 1896.

Three Aston Villa players sadly lost their lives during the First World War. Billy Gerrish, serving with the Footballers' Battalion, the Middlesex Regiment, died in the attack on Guillemont at the Battle of the Somme in France in 1916; Arthur Dobson, on duty with the North Staffs Regiment in Germany, was killed in 1918 and Walter Kimberley died of T.B. in France in May 1918. Gerrish, in fact, died after losing both his legs.

Aston Villa defender Tommy Ball was shot dead by his policeman neighbour George Stagg in November 1923.

Aston Villa's former Scottish international Peter Dowds died in 1895 at the age of 27 following a chest complaint. He was a heavy drinker.

Villa's England international full-back Albert Aldridge also died at the age of 27 in 1891.

Some eight years later (in October 1899) another England star, and ex-Villa goal-ace Albert Allen died, aged 32.

Former Villa wing-half Andy Ducat died whilst playing cricket for the Surrey Home Guard against the Sussex Home Guard at Lords in July 1942.

George Abner Harris, a former Villa defender, was tragically killed in a shipyard accident in June 1923. He was 45.

Villa's 1960s centre-half John Slueewenhoek was only 45 when he died of a heart attack in 1989. Les Sealey likewise in 2001, aged 41.

Former Villa skipper Brian Tiler was tragically killed in a car accident in Italy on 30 June 1990. He was Chief Executive of Bournemouth AFC at the time and the passenger in the car - Harry Redknapp was seriously injured.

Tommy Barber, whose headed goal won Villa the FA Cup Final in 1913, died of tuberculosis in 1925, aged 39.

Ex-Villa star Joey Walters died of pneumonia in 1923. He was only 37.

Welsh midfielder Trevor Hockey collapsed and died of a heart-attack in April 1987, aged 43.

In May 1897, Villa's former Welsh international full-back Gwynne Evans died at his home after catching a chill while attending a funeral. He was only 30 years of age.

## DE BILDE, GILLES ROGER GERARD

Born: Zellick, Belgium, 9 June 1971.

Career: FC Aalst, RSC Anderlecht, PSV Eindhoven, Sheffield Wednesday (£3 million, July 1999), Aston Villa (on loan from October 2000 to January 2001), RSC Anderlecht (June 2001).

Capped over 25 times by his country, Gilles De Bilde, who can play as

THE COMPLETE ENCYCLOPAEDIA OF ASTON VILLA F.C. 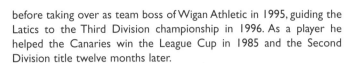 THE COMPLETE ENCYCLOPAEDIA OF ASTON VILLA F.C.

69

an attacking midfielder or out-and-out striker, did exceedingly well in Belgian and Dutch League soccer before his £3 million transfer to Hillsborough in the summer of 1999. But with the Owls his overall form suffered as he played in a struggling Premiership side that was eventually relegated, although De Bilde top-scored with 11 goals in 45 senior appearances. He played for Belgium in Euro 2000, yet found it hard to fit in with Villa's style of play and returned to Wednesday after his three-month loan period had expired in late December 2000. He was given just four first-team outings by manager John Gregory.

## DEBUTS

When Aston Villa performed in the first-ever League season of 1888-89 they used a total of 19 players during the course of the campaign, all of whom, of course, made their League debuts for the club.
Simon Stainrod, making his debut for the club, netted all Aston Villa's goals in their 4-1 League Cup victory at Exeter in September 1985.
Harold Nash scored a hat-trick when making his Football League debut for Villa against Liverpool in the First Division in April 1915, and Frank Shell weighed in with three goals on his home League debut against Stockport County in December 1937 (Division 2).
Left-back Norman Young joined Villa in June 1926. A little over nine years later, in September 1935, he finally made his League debut.
Eric Houghton made his debut for Aston Villa in a Central League game against Sheffield United at Bramall Lane in 1928 and then received his first England cap on the same ground in October 1930.
Recognised full-back Stan Lynn made his home League debut for Villa at centre-forward against Derby County (at home) on 23 December 1950 - and he scored in the 1-1 draw!
Ten players made their senior debuts for Villa in 1994-95, among them Gary Charles, John Fashanu, Tommy Johnson, Ian Taylor and Alan Wright.

## DEEHAN, JOHN MATTHEW

Born: Solihull, 6 August 1957
Career: St Peter's School ·Solihull, Olton British Legion FC, Arsenal (trialist, 1972), Aston Villa (apprentice, July 1973, professional April 1975), West Bromwich Albion (£424,000, September 1979), Norwich City (£175,000, November 1981), Ipswich Town (June 1986), Manchester City (player/coach, July 1988), Barnsley (player/coach, January 1990), Norwich City (assistant-manager/coach 1991, then manager January 1994-June 1995), Wigan Athletic (manager, November 1995-July 1998), Sheffield United (chief scout), Aston Villa (coach, July 2001). Served on the PFA Management Committee in the 1980s.
John Deehan had an Irish father, but chose to play for England and he won three Youth and seven Under-21 caps for his country, while also being a non-playing substitute for the senior side v Brazil in 1981.
A very competent striker, Deehan scored 51 goals for Villa in 139 appearances before transferring to West Bromwich Albion a month or so into the 1979-80 season. In just over two years at The Hawthorns, he made 50 appearances and hit five goals. He then did exceedingly well with Norwich City (70 goals in 199 League and Cup games), played over 50 times for Ipswich and was positive during his coaching appointments at Maine Road and Oakwell. He then returned to Carrow Road as assistant-manager/coach and was given the manager's job at Norwich in place of Mike Walker

before taking over as team boss of Wigan Athletic in 1995, guiding the Latics to the Third Division championship in 1996. As a player he helped the Canaries win the League Cup in 1985 and the Second Division title twelve months later.
In July 2001 Deehan returned to Villa Park as a coach.

## DEFEATS

Aston Villa's heaviest League defeat has been 7-0, suffered on five occasions: versus Blackburn Rovers (a) on 19 October 1889, Everton (a) on 4 January 1890, West Bromwich Albion (h) 19 October 1935, and twice against Manchester United (a) on 8 March 1950 and 24 October 1964 (also away). Villa also lost 7-1 at Notts County in November 1890, 7-1 at home to Arsenal and 7-2 at home to Middlesborough both in 1935-36. Villa also went down 6-0 at Sunderland in January 1893, crashed 6-0 at Leeds in December 1924 and succumbed to a 6-0 defeat at Middlesbrough in December 1948. Their worst reverse in the FA Cup came on 16 February 1889 when they lost 8-1 at Ewood Park against Blackburn Rovers.
In the League Cup, Villa crashed 6-1 at The Hawthorns against West Bromwich Albion in September 1966.
In Europe their heaviest defeat so far has been 4-1, suffered in Belgium against Antwerp in September 1975.
Aston Villa went down 6-0 at Derby in a Wartime game in May 1945. And Villa suffered a club record 11 straight League defeats between 23 March and 4 May 1963.

## DEFENSIVE RECORDS

A mere 32 goals were conceded by Aston Villa's mean and miserly defence in their 46 Third Division matches in 1971-72 (10 at home, 22 away). This defensive record was repeated in 1974-75 when Villa played 42 Second Division matches.
Only 35 goals were conceded in the club's 42 Second Division matches in 1937-38 (12 at home, 23 away).
In 42 First Division matches in season 1923-24, Villa's defence gave away 37 goals (11 at home, 26 away).
Villa's best defensive season in the Premiership so far was in 1996-97 when the let in only 34 goals in 38 matches.
Villa's efficient defence conceded only six goals in 21 home League games in season 1974-75 ....a club record.
In 1971-72, Villa played 23 home Third Division matches and conceded only 10 goals in total.
Villa conceded 11 goals in their 21 home League games in seasons 1922-23, 1923-24 and 1968-69. The most goals conceded by Villa at home in one single League season is 56 in 1935-36; they gave away 36 in 1919-20, 1934-35 and 1948-49.
The most goals conceded in away League games in one season has been 60 - in 21 First Division encounters in 1957-58. Villa's defence conceded 58 in 1964-65 and 54 in 1935-36, 1958-59 and 1986-87.
When Villa were relegated for the first time at the end of the 1935-36 season, they went down having conceded 110 goals in their 42 League Division One matches. The previous season Villa gave away 88 goals (in 42 matches) making it 198 conceded in a total of 84 League games.
In terms of a goals-per-games ratio, Villa's worst season defensively before the Great War came in

*John Deehan.*

1890-91 when they let in 58 goals in only 22 matches (40 in their 11 away games). In 1892-93, Villa's defence conceded 62 goals in 30 League games with 38 coming in 15 away matches and 72 were struck into Villa's net in 38 fixtures in 1914-15.

Twenty-six goals were fired through a leaky Villa defence in five successive League games halfway through the 1890-91 season.

Villa succumbed to three seven-goal drubbings at home in 1935-36.

### DELANEY, MARK ANTHONY

Born: Haverfordwest, 13 May 1976.

Career: Carmarthen FC, Cardiff City (free transfer, July 1998), Aston Villa (£250,000+, March 1999).

Full-back (or wing-back) Mark Delaney established himself as a first-team regular at Villa Park halfway through the 1999-200 season, having earlier contested a place in the side with Steve Watson. Initially capped by Wales at 'B' team level, he went on to appear in four full interntionals (with more honours to come) he is a busy player with good pace, who had the misfortune to be sent-off three times in the space of ten matches - twice while playing for his club and once for his country. He received a red card during Villa's FA Cup semi-final with Bolton Wanderers at Wembley in April 2000 and then took early baths in an international match against Portugal soon afterwards and in Villa's Inter-Toto Cup clash in Prague against FC Marila Pribram. He has now made close on 60 senior appearances for Villa (one goal scored).

### DENNINGTON, LESLIE ARTHUR

Born: West Bromwich, June 1902. Deceased.

Career: Dartmouth Council School, West Bromwich Sandwell, Wolseley Motors FC, Aston Villa (December 1924), Reading (July 1925), Exeter City (November 1928). Retired May 1931.

Strongly built reserve centre-half or left-half who made just one first team appearance for Villa, against Huddersfield Town in February 1925. He made 65 appearances for Exeter before suffering a nasty ankle injury.

### DEPORTIVO LA CORUNA

Villa's playing record against the Spanish side:

UEFA Cup

| Venue | P | W | D | L | F | A |
|---|---|---|---|---|---|---|
| Home | 1 | 0 | 0 | 1 | 0 | 1 |
| Away | 1 | 0 | 1 | 0 | 1 | 1 |
| Totals | 2 | 0 | 1 | 1 | 1 | 2 |

Aston Villa went out of the 1993-94 UEFA Cup in the 2nd round, beaten by a forceful La Coruna side, playing in their first European competition. Villa seemed to have done the hard work when drawing 1-1 in front of 27,500 fans in the Riazor Stadium in Spain, although Villa were somewhat disappointed not to have won that encounter, allowing Pedro Riesco to equalise Dean Saunders' 78th minute goal with time fast running out. As early as the third minute 'keeper Mark Bosnich (making his European debut with Bryan Small) had saved a penalty taken by the Brazilian Bebeto.

Javier Manjarin scored the all-important goal at Villa Park nine minutes before half-time (from Fernando Nando's cross) to stun the home support in the 26,737 crowd and send La Coruna through 2-1 on aggregate. They lost in the next round to Eintracht Frankfurt.

### DERBY COUNTY

Villa's playing record against the Rams:

Football League/Premiership

| Venue | P | W | D | L | F | A |
|---|---|---|---|---|---|---|
| Home | 57 | 38 | 10 | 9 | 141 | 60 |
| Away | 57 | 19 | 11 | 27 | 76 | 95 |
| Totals | 114 | 57 | 21 | 36 | 217 | 155 |

FA Cup

| | | | | | | |
|---|---|---|---|---|---|---|
| Home | 5 | 4 | 0 | 1 | 22 | 10 |
| Away | 7 | 2 | 1 | 4 | 11 | 15 |
| Totals | 12 | 6 | 1 | 5 | 33 | 25 |

League Cup

| | | | | | | |
|---|---|---|---|---|---|---|
| Home | 1 | 1 | 0 | 0 | 2 | 1 |
| Away | 1 | 0 | 1 | 0 | 1 | 1 |
| Totals | 2 | 1 | 1 | 0 | 3 | 2 |

Full Members Cup

| | | | | | | |
|---|---|---|---|---|---|---|
| Home | 1 | 1 | 0 | 0 | 4 | 1 |

Simod Cup

| | | | | | | |
|---|---|---|---|---|---|---|
| Away | 1 | 0 | 0 | 1 | 1 | 2 |

Wartime

| | | | | | | |
|---|---|---|---|---|---|---|
| Home | 5 | 2 | 1 | 2 | 7 | 6 |
| Away | 6 | 1 | 1 | 4 | 8 | 17 |
| Totals | 11 | 3 | 2 | 6 | 15 | 23 |

*Brian Godfrey (left) waits for a slip v. Derby County in March 1969.*

As founder members of the Football League, Villa first met County at home on 29 December 1888 and registered a 4-2 victory, Tommy Green scoring twice in front of 4,000 fans at Perry Barr.

On the last day of that initial season, however, the Rams gained revenge with a 5-2 win at their old Racecourse Ground, four of their goals coming from Sandy Higgins. Nine months later, this very same player slammed in all his side's goals when Villa crashed 5-1 in Derby - Villa having won 7-1 earlier in the season at Perry Barr!

In October 1890 Villa went down 5-4 at Derby, but a week later they won the return fixture 4-0 at home - such is football.

Twelve goals came in the two League clashes of 1891-92 - Villa won 6-0 at home but lost 4-2 at Derby.

When Villa defeated the Rams 6-2 at home in October 1892, Charlie Athersmith scored twice and laid on three more goals for his colleagues.

In November 1898, Villa overpowered Derby when handing them another 7-1 beating, this time at Villa Park. Some 20,000 fans saw Fred Wheldon score twice and have a hand in four of the other five goals.

Harold Halse scored all Villa's goals in their emphatic 5-1 home win over the Rams on 19 October 1912. This equalled Harry Hampton's feat set a fortnight earlier against Sheffield Wednesday.

On Boxing Day 1927 Villa crashed 5-0 at Derby and then lost 1-0 at home 24 hours later.

THE COMPLETE ENCYCLOPAEDIA OF ASTON VILLA F.C.        THE COMPLETE ENCYCLOPAEDIA OF ASTON VILLA F.C.

71

Two former Aston Villa players - Dai Astley and Ronnie Dix - scored County's goals in their 2-1 win over Villa in December 1938.

Villa's first League win after the Second World War was against the Rams, 2-1 at The Baseball Ground on 7 September 1946. Johnny Dixon and Billy Goffin were the goalscorers in front of 28,454 spectators.

Villa's record equalling 15-match unbeaten League run came to an end when they lost 3-2 at Derby on 31 August 1949.

On 25 August 1951 Villa - with Con Martin in goal for the first time in a League game - beat the Rams 4-1 at Villa Park in front of 37,548 fans. Villa ran up a sequence of five successive home Premiership victories over the Rams from 1995-96, winning 2-0, 2-1, 1-0, 2-0 and 4-1 in that order. In the latter victory (achieved on 30 September 2000) Julian Joachim scored twice.

Villa defeated the Rams 5-3 in a 2nd round FA Cup-tie in February 1889 and on their way to the 1895 Final they ousted County in the opening round. But it was Derby who took the honours in the 1895-96 and 1897-98 competitions, knocking Villa out each time in the first round.

Harry Hampton thrilled the 45,000 crowd at Villa Park with a hat-trick when Derby were defeated 6-1 in the 2nd round in 1910, but a 1st round clash between the two teams in January 1913 was abandoned at half-time due to snow with scores level at 1-1. Villa won the 'replay' 3-1 on a frozen pitch.

Billy Walker grabbed a hat-trick in another 6-1 home FA Cup win for Villa in January 1922 and on 2 March 1946, a never-to-be-beaten record crowd of 76,588 squeezed into Villa Park to see Derby win a thrilling 1st leg quarter-final encounter by 4-3. A week later Villa drew 1-1 at The Baseball Ground but went out 5-4 on aggregate.

There was another 4-3 scoreline in the 4th round of the FA Cup in 1992 - this time Villa took the honours at Derby when Dwight Yorke netted a hat-trick in front of 22,452 spectators.

Some-one in the crowd blew a whistle, the Derby players stopped, Tony Daley didn't and the Villa man went to score and so earn his side a 1-1 draw against The Rams in a League Cup-tie at the Baseball Ground in October 1986.

Just over 5,000 fans saw Villa beat the Rams 4-1 in a Full Members Cup encounter in 1986-87. Double that number saw the Rams gain revenge with a 2-1 Simod Cup Win at The Baseball Ground in 1988-89.

Players with both clubs include: DJ Astley, VP Blore (Villa reserve), C Boden, F Broome, R Brown (County junior), FC Buckley, J Burridge, NI Callaghan, RM Campbell, B Carbone, GA Charles, A Comyn, GS Cowans, W Crooks (Villa WW2 guest), ES Deacy, RW Dix, AR Dorigo, D Duncan (Villa WW2 guest), J Findlay, AL Goodall, JC Gregory, JH Hampton (Rams WW1 guest), A Hateley (on Schoolboy forms with Derby), SB Hodge, D Hunt, T Johnson, VA Jones (Villa reserve), G Kinsey, GH Lawrence (Villa trialist), MA Lillis, P McGrath, W Matthews, W Morris, G Moseley, BA Olney, I Ormondroyd, BD Rioch, JD Robson, D Saunders, GT Stephenson, GH Webb (Villa reserve), AE Wood, A Woolley.

Also: T Docherty & Arthur Cox (managers of both clubs, Cox also Villa coach & assistant-manager), R Money & F Upton (County players, Villa coaches), RA Ryan (County player, Villa scout), A Ashman (scout for both clubs), PD Doherty (Derby player, Villa chief scout).

## DERBY MIDLAND

Villa's playing record against the Derby club:
FA Cup

| Venue | P | W | D | L | F | A |
|-------|---|---|---|---|---|---|
| Home  | 1 | 1 | 0 | 0 | 6 | 0 |

This effortless 6-0 F.A. Cup win over Derby Midland came in the 2nd round in November 1886. Arthur Loach and Arthur Brown both scored twice in front of 6,000 spectators.
Players with both clubs: A Dixon, WA Harvey, W Podmore.

## DEVEY, HARRY PERCIVAL

Born: Newtown, Birmingham, March 1860. Died: Birmingham, c 1924.
Career: Aston Hall School, Aston Clarendon FC (1881), Montrose YC, Aston (1884), Excelsior (June 1888), Aston Villa (August 1887). Retired through injury, May 1893.

One of identical twins (the other was Arthur, a Villa trialist), Harry Devey came from a family of eight (being the eldest of seven brothers and one sister). He was a keen, hard-tackling wing-half, typically of many players of his era. He enjoyed 'carrying' the ball forward and often tried long range shots at goal, albeit not too successful, as he claimed only one goal in 84 first team appearances for the club. He lined up in Villa's first-ever League game in September 1888 against Wolverhampton Wanderers x and collected an FA Cup runners-up medal in 1892.

## DEVEY, JOHN HENRY GEORGE

Born: Newtown, Birmingham on 26 December 1866, Died: Birmingham, 13 October 1940.
Career: Aston Brook School, Montrose YC (Aston), Wellington Road FC, Birmingham Excelsior, Aston Unity, Aston Manor, Mitchell's St George (1890), Aston Villa (professional, March 1891). He remained a player with the club for 11 years, retiring in April 1902 to become a club Director.

For a player so skilful, thorough and effective, Jack Devey's merits, when in his prime, were inexplicably overlooked by the England selectors. He could play in any forward position and there is no doubt that he was one of the finest goalscorers in the country in the 1890s. A close dribbler with good pace (when required) Devey was alive to every movement on the field and possessed the rare gift of 'intelligent anticipation'. He knew the game inside out. He never lacked initiative, but was a strong believer in combination, bringing his fellow forwards (and half-backs) into the game as often as possible. He was exceptionally clever with his head as he was with both feet and often scored goals from distance when he caught the opposing goalkeeper off guard.

Capped just twice by England, Devey helped Villa win the Football League championship five times (1894-96-97-99-1900) and the FA Cup twice (1895 & 1897). He also collected a Cup runners-up medal in 1892 and was a key figure in the double-winning side of 1896-97, appearing in 29 of the 30 League games and in all seven Cup matches. He went on to score 186 goals in 308 senior appearances for the club and after retiring he joined the Board of Directors at Villa Park, retaining office until September 1934. During his time on the Board, Devey ran a successful sports-outfitters shop in Lozells. Between 1888 and 1907 he played county cricket for Warwickshire, scoring well over 6,500 first-class runs, including eight centuries. It is on record that Devey actually made his sporting 'debut' for Villa in March 1890 - at baseball!

## DEVEY, WILLIAM

Born: Newtown, Birmingham, 12 April 1865. Died: Perry Barr, 10 June 1935.
Career: Aston Brook School, Wellington, Aston Unity, Small Heath (August 1885), Wolverhampton Wanderers (August 1891), Aston Villa (July 1892), Walsall Town Swifts (May 1894), Burton Wanderers (1895), Notts County (1896), Walsall (1897), Burton Wanderers, Small Heath (July 1898). Retired May 1900.
A skilful player, occupying mainly the inside-right berth, Will Devey scored twice in 10 first team games for Villa. He did far better things with his other clubs,

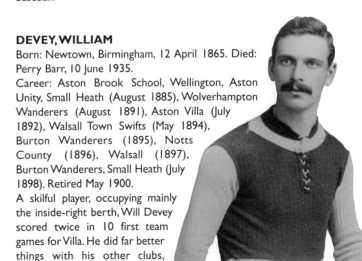
*Jack Devey*

THE COMPLETE ENCYCLOPAEDIA OF ASTON VILLA F.C.  THE COMPLETE ENCYCLOPAEDIA OF ASTON VILLA F.C.

72

securing 18 goals in only 13 first-class games for Blues and netting 18 times in 42 League outings for Wolves. He made a total of 121 League appearances in all and notched 42 goals.

## DICKIE, WILLIAM (WALTER) ARTHUR
Born: Wednesbury, September 1867. Died: Birmingham, March 1931.
Career: Wednesbury White Star, Walsall Swifts, Aston Villa (August 1889), Darlaston (September 1890), Bilston Town (1891-93).
Small, industrious wing-half, second reserve to Jack Burton and Tom Clarkson, Bill Dickie had just one FA Cup-tie for Villa, lining up against Notts County at Meadow Lane in February 1990 (lost 4-1).

## DICKSON, IAN WILLIAM
Born: Maxwell, Dumfries, Scotland, September 1902. Deceased.
Career: Queen of the South (1919), Aston Villa (January 1921), Middlesbrough (December 1923), Westbrough FC. Retired 1928 through injury.
A robust centre-forward who used his weight to good effect, Ian Dickson was marvellously adept at stealing in unnoticed behind a defence, during a useful career averaging a goal every 130 minutes of football. He scored 39 times in 83 appearances for Villa and netted 12 goals in 38 games for Middlesbrough.

## DICKSON, WILLIAM ALEXANDER
Born: Crail, Fife, 27 August 1866. Died: Stoke-on-Trent, 1 June 1910.
Career: Dumfries Schools, Dundee Strathmore (1885), Sunderland (July 1888), Aston Villa (August 1889), Stoke (July 1892). Retiring through injury in May 1897, he remained at The Victoria Ground as a coach for a number of years, his knowledge of the game proving invaluable to the younger members of the club. He then became a licensee in the Potteries and later joined the Board of Directors at Stoke (1907).
Billy Dickson was a centre-forward of the highest quality who grabbed four goals in his only international appearance for Scotland against Ireland in 1888. He skippered Villa on several occasions and played in the 1892 FA Cup Final defeat by West Bromwich Albion. He netted 34 goals in 64 appearances for Villa and followed up with a record of 48 in 134 League and Cup games for the Potters.

## DINAMO BUCHAREST
Villa's playing record against Dinamo:
European Cup

| Venue | P | W | D | L | F | A |
|---|---|---|---|---|---|---|
| Home | 1 | 1 | 0 | 0 | 4 | 2 |
| Away | 1 | 1 | 0 | 0 | 2 | 0 |
| Totals | 2 | 2 | 0 | 0 | 6 | 2 |

Gary Shaw scored five goals against Dinamo as Villa eased through their second round European Cup-tie in October/November 1982. He netted twice in front of 70,000 fans in Romania in the first leg and then claimed a hat-trick when Dinamo were beaten 4-2 in the return contest at Villa Park when the crowd was 22,244.

## DINSDALE, WILLIAM ARTHUR
Born: Darlington, 12 July 1903. Died: Darlington, 21 February 1984.
Career: St Phillip's School, Rise Carr Juniors, Darlington (amateur, August 1921), Darlington Railway Athletic, Crook Town (1922), Aston Villa (March 1925), Lincoln City (May 1926), Bradford Park Avenue (£1,200, February 1929), Lincoln City (May 1930), Darlington (August 1931-May 1932). Retired.
Understudied Len Capewell and Billy Walker at Villa Park, making just eight first team appearances before moving to Lincoln City where he developed into one of the Imps' all-time greats, going on to net 89 goals in 125 first team games during his two spells at Sincil Bank. A contemporary described a Dinsdale as "...a big, bustling type of player with no great ball control...he could give or take hard knocks with equanimity and was as happy as a sandboy when his side scored a goal."

## DIRECTORS
Aston Villa FC has had a Board of Directors since 1885 when the club became a professional organisation.
When the team entered the Football League as founder members in 1888, the Board comprised: Messrs F Doughty, J Warrilow, J Margoschis (Chairman), I Whitehouse, Dr V Jones, JA Hinks, A Albut, P Clamp (also honorary secretary for four years) and J Gorman.
In season 1906-07 Fred Rinder (Chairman), H Toney (Vice-Chairman), J Devey, PWM Bate and Cllr. JE Jones formed the Board of Directors at Villa Park.
The Board of Directors for season 1924-25 comprised: FW Rinder (Chairman), JE Jones (vice-Chairman), Capt. PWM Bate, ex-players J Devey and H Spencer with the secretary GB Ramsay.
In 1939, just before the Second World War broke out, the Villa board comprised: FH Normansell, JP (Chairman), J Broughton (vice-Chairman), CS Buckley, J Riley, NL Smith.

### Service
Directors who have served the club since World War Two include (listed in A-Z order): Messrs JA Alderson, MJ Ansell (Executive/Financial Director), R Bendall, D Bendall, J Broughton, CS Buckley, H Cressman, Sir W Dugdale, PD Ellis, HD Ellis, AT Gill, R Greenhalgh, J Hartley, AJ Hales, J Heath, WE Houghton, H Kartz, WE Lovesy, R Mackay, FB Normansell, FH Normansell JP, J Normansell, DM Owen, HA Parkes, GB Robinson, AC Smith, E Smith, NL Smith, SM Stride, Dr D Targett & G Taylor (non-Executive Member).

*The Villa Board of directors in December 1968 with manager Tommy Docherty next to Doug Ellis in the centre.*

THE COMPLETE ENCYCLOPAEDIA OF ASTON VILLA F.C.

THE COMPLETE ENCYCLOPAEDIA OF ASTON VILLA F.C.

73

## Director's Minutes

Ex-player John (Jack) Devey was an Aston Villa Director for 32 years: from July 1902 until September 1934. He was replaced on the Board at Villa Park by Albert Wilkes (see below).

Another former player and team skipper Howard Spencer was a Director of the club for 29 years (1907-36).

Howard was followed on to the board by ex-Villa player Chris Buckley, who later became the club's Chairman.

Prior to that, Albert Wilkes, himself an ex-Villa footballer, had joined the Board of Directors (September 1934-August 1936). He took the place of Devey.

Other ex-players who joined the Board of Directors at Villa Park include: Larry Canning, Eric Houghton, Harry Parkes and Howard Vaughton. Houghton was also a Director of Walsall FC.

Doug Ellis has been a Director of Aston Villa, Birmingham City and Wolverhampton Wanderers.

## DIVER, EDWIN JOHN

Born: Cambridge, 20 March 1861. Died: Portardawe, Swansea, 27 December 1924.

Career: Perse School (Cambridge), Surrey AFC, Aston Villa (August 1891). Retired from playing football in April 1894 to concentrate on his cricket.

Reserve goalkeeper to Albert Hinchley and Jimmy Warner, Ted Diver played in just three League games for Villa before deciding to quit soccer. He played in 75 matches for Surrey CCC during the 1883-86 seasons and then served with Warwickshire from May 1894 until September 1901. During his seven years at Edgbaston he participated in 118 matches. An opener or middle order right-hand batsman, during his cricketing career he averaged 23 runs per innings (from a total of 7,245 runs). His best year was in 1899 when he scored 1,096 runs for an average of almost 30 (184 being his highest single score). He was also as an occasional medium pace bowler and captured a handful of wickets with a best return of 6-58 as well as keeping wicket on occasions. Diver also assisted both Monmouthshire and Cambridgeshire cricket clubs, acting as joint secretary/treasurer of the latter club in 1889.

## DIX, RONALD WILLIAM

Born: Bristol, 5 September 1912. Died: 2 April 1998.

Career: South Central School, Bristol Schools, Gloucestershire Schools, England Schools, aged 13), Bristol Rovers (amateur, July 1927, professional September 1929), Blackburn Rovers (May 1932), Aston Villa (with Arthur Cunliffe, March 1933), Derby County (February 1937), Tottenham Hotspur (June 1939), guested for Blackpool, Bradford PA, Bristol City, Chester, Liverpool, Wrexham and York City during the War, Reading (November 1947). Retired June 1949.

The youngest player ever to score a League goal, Ronnie Dix was just 15 years, 180 days old when he found the net for Bristol Rovers against Norwich City in a Third Division (South) game in March 1928.

Dix, who joined Villa after a proposed move to Everton had fallen through, was a fine footballer, a clever constructive inside-forward of high consistency who made the ball do the work! He scored 30 goals in 104 games during his four years at Villa Park and in his career as a whole he bagged almost 140 goals in 442 League and FA Cup matches. Capped by England against Norway in 1939, he had earlier represented the Football League (1926) and in 1943 won a League North Cup winners medal with Blackpool, following on with a runners-up medal twelve months later when the Seasiders lost to his old club Aston Villa in the two-legged Final.

## DIXON, ARTHUR ALBERT

Born: Matlock, July 1867.

Career: Derby Midland (1886), Aston Villa (August 1888), Stoke

(August 1889), Leek Alexandra (September 1891).

Wiry, aggressive wing-half, Archie Dixon was knocked out when making his Villa debut against his future club Stoke on 15 September 1888 - Villa's first home game in the Football League. He had only two more games before transferring to The Victoria Ground.

## DIXON, JOHN THOMAS

Born: Hebburn, County Durham, 10 December 1923.

Career: Hebburn Boys Club, Durham County Boys, Spennymoor United (1940), Newcastle United (amateur trialist), guested for Hull City, Middlesbrough, Newcastle United and Sunderland during the War, Aston Villa (August 1944, professional January 1946). Retired May 1961 and remained at Villa Park coaching the youngsters for three years before taking over as second team trainer: July 1964 to May 1967. He also played regularly in charity matches for Villa Old Stars (until 1990) and was a qualified FA Coach.

Johnny Dixon enjoyed 17 wonderful years as a player with Aston Villa. One of the stars of the 1950s, he skippered the team to FA Cup glory at Wembley in 1957 and amassed a fine record of 430 senior appearances and 144 goals, top-scoring three seasons running: 1950-53. Named as reserve for England against Wales in 1953, he established himself in the side during the 1948-49 campaign and went on to occupy all five forward-line positions and that of left-half for Villa, with inside-left undoubtedly his favourite berth. Voted the supporters' 'Terrace Trophy' winner in 1959, Dixon broke his nose playing his last game for the club against Sheffield Wednesday in April 1961 - the day Charlie Aitken made his League debut! A tee-totaller and non-smoker, Dixon ran a very successful ironmonger's shop in Wylde Green for many years before selling up in September 1985. He still attends the occasional match at Villa Park as he heads proudly toward his 80th birthday.

*Johnny Dixon kisses the F.A. Cup in 1957.*

## DOBSON, HENRY ARTHUR

Born: Chesterton, Staffs, April 1893. Died: 1918 (killed in action while serving with the North Staffordshire Regiment in Germany).

Career: Chesterton Forresters, Audley (1911), Aston Villa (August 1912-18).

A very promising half-back, Arthur Dobson was fatally wounded during World War One. He made seven first team appearances for Villa.

## DOCHERTY, THOMAS HENDERSON

Born: Pershaw, Glasgow, 24 August 1928.

Career: School in the Gorbals district of Glasgow, Shettleston juniors, Highland Light Infantry (playing for his regiment in Palestine), Celtic (July 1948), Preston North End (£4,000, November 1949), Arsenal (£28,000, August 1958), Chelsea player/coach, February 1961, retired as player June 1961, then manager - after Ted Drake's departure -

THE COMPLETE ENCYCLOPAEDIA OF ASTON VILLA F.C.  THE COMPLETE ENCYCLOPAEDIA OF ASTON VILLA F.C.

74

*Tommy Docherty, centre, with his newspaper and players.*

goalkeeper) and fielded one of the youngest sides in the club's history for the next game! He eventually transferred 14 players from Millmoor for a total of £70,000.

His second spell in charge of QPR lasted for just 29 days - quitting after being refused permission to sign Brian Tiler (from Rotherham).

The first player Docherty signed, as Villa's manager, was - yes, Brian Tiler. Unfortunately, having arrived in a blaze of publicity, the 'Doc' failed to bring success to Villa Park, bringing in a defensive policy, which kept them in the Second Division just. He became a huge favourite as the attendances at Villa Park doubled but he was soon courting controversy when he was accused of poaching the backroom staff at Rotherham and criticising Carlisle United boss Bob Stokoe over his team's negative tactics. He was sacked by Chairman Doug Ellis after 13 months in office. When in charge of Porto, he narrowly missed out on winning the Portuguese League title; he was Terry Neill's assistant at Hull; he restored Scotland's pride on the international front; did well enough at Old Trafford before losing his job following his affair with the wife of United physio Laurie Brown; succeeded to keep Derby in the top Division; had mixed fortunes at QPR when he was arrested and brought back to The Baseball Ground to be questioned over the transfer of certain Rams' players to clubs in the NASL; he didn't always enjoy his sojourn in Australia and when at Molineux he saw Wolves go down into the Third Division.

The 'Doc' once said: "The ideal Board of Directors should be made up of three men, two dead and one dying." He also passed these comments about Ray Wilkins when he was at Old Trafford: "He can't run, he can't tackle and he can't head a ball. The only time he goes forward is to toss the coin."

Under Docherty's leadership, Villa played 45 League games....13 were won, 15 drawn and 17 lost.

September 1961-October 1967), Rotherham United (manager, November 1967-November 1968), Queen's Park Rangers (manager, November 1968), Aston Villa (manager, December 1968-January 1970), FC Porto (manager, February 1970-June 1971), Hull City (assistant-manager July-September 1971), Scotland national team manager (September 1971-December 1972), Manchester United (manager December 1972-July 1977), Derby County (manager September 1977-May 1979), Queen's Park Rangers (May 1979-October 1980), Preston North End (manager June-December 1981), Sydney Olympic (manager to June 1982), South Melbourne (manager, July-December 1982), Sydney Olympic (manager to July 1983), Wolverhampton Wanderers (manager, June 1984-July 1985), Altrincham (manager, October 1987-February 1988). He quit football to concentrate on after-dinner speaking, travelling all over the world in the process.

Tommy Docherty had a long and very interesting career in association football as a player and manager. One could quite easily write a book entirely about the 'Doc.' He was capped 25 times by Scotland, he also represented his country in one 'B' international and played in more than 450 League and Cup games north and south of the border. He played in the shadow of Bobby Evans at Celtic and then gained a Second Division championship medal with Preston when he lined up behind the great Tom Finney. He also played for the Lillywhites in the 1954 FA Cup Final when they lost 3-2 to WBA. As a manager he guided Manchester United to the Second Division title in 1975 and FA Cup glory two years later after finishing runners-up in 1976 (beaten by Southampton). He led Chelsea into the First Division in 1963, to League Cup success in 1965 and to the FA Cup Final in 1967 when they lost 2-1 to Spurs. He broke Chelsea's transfer record four times during his time in charge at Stamford Bridge, including the signing of ex Villa star Tony Hateley and the WBA striker Derek Kevan. He also sold several quality players including Terry Venables and George Graham, another ex-Villa man. He resigned from his position at Chelsea after several incidents at home and abroad (he was fined £100 for making ungentlemanly remarks to a referee and was also suspended for 28 days after threatening to call off a tour to Bermuda). When he was in charge of Rotherham he dropped ten first team players (all except the

## DOCTORS

Aston Villa have had two doctors who have represented the club as players at senior level: Dr William Ewart Barnie-Adshead and Dr Victor Milne.

Goalkeeper Leigh Richmond Roose was hoping to become a doctor at King's College Hospital in London, but despite his keen interest in bacteriology, he never qualified and remained a perpetual student.

Dr H. J. Jessop was the official Doctor of Aston Villa from 1903 to 1928. The late Dr David Targett was doctor to Aston Villa for over 25 years.

## DODDS, THOMAS BLACK

Born: South Shields, 20 December 1918. Deceased.
Career: Hebburn YMCA, North Shields (1937), Aston Villa (January 1939), Swansea Town (January 1947).

A strong, virile inside or centre-forward, Tommy Dodds made just one senior appearance for Villa, in the first League game after World War Two at home to Middlesbrough in August 1946. He went to The Vetch Field as part of the deal that brought Trevor Ford to Villa Park. Dodds scored twice in 11 League games for the Swans.

## DOHERTY, PETER DERWENT

Although only employed by Aston Villa as chief scout in the late 1960s, a book of this nature cannot ignore the soccer career of such a great footballer like Peter Doherty.

Doherty was a marvellous inside-forward. He was born in Magherafelt (Ireland) on 5 June 1913 and died at Fleetwood, Lancashire on 6 April 1990.

He played, in turn, for Station United (in Northern Ireland), Coleraine,

THE COMPLETE ENCYCLOPAEDIA OF ASTON VILLA F.C.  THE COMPLETE ENCYCLOPAEDIA OF ASTON VILLA F.C.

75

Glentoran, Blackpool (1933-36), Manchester City (1936-45), Derby County (1945-46), Huddersfield Town (1946-49) and finally Doncaster Rovers (as player-manager 1949-53, then manager until 1958). He made well over 400 League appearances and scored 197 goals and was capped 16 times by Northern Ireland. He gained a League championship medal with Manchester City in 1937 and a Third Division (North) championship medal with Doncaster in 1950.

With Derby County in 1946, he won an FA Cup winners' medal, 14 years after collecting a similar prize when Glentoran won the Irish Cup in 1932.

After retiring as a player Doherty remained at Belle Vue (Doncaster) for a further five years. Thereafter he continued to manage the Irish national team (which he had been doing since 1951) and guided them into the quarter-finals of the World Cup in Sweden in 1958 (with Danny Blanchflower, ex-Villa as the Irish skipper). He was in charge of Bristol City (1958-60), became joint advisor at Notts County (with Andy Beattie) in December 1965 and was chief scout at Villa Park from July 1968 until October 1970. Doherty then became assistant-manager of Preston North End, later taking an identical position with Sunderland (1973-74) before ending his soccer days as a scout with Blackpool (late 1970s).

### DONCASTER, STUART

Born: Gainsborough, September 1890. Died: Derbyshire, 1955.
Career: Gainsborough County School, Buxton, Stourbridge, Aston Villa (August 1912), Glossop (December 1913), Matlock (1915).
Tall, hard-working reserve centre-forward who scored once (at home to Liverpool in April 1913) in his two League outings for Villa.

### DONCASTER ROVERS

Villa's playing record against Rovers:
Football League

| Venue | P | W | D | L | F | A |
|---|---|---|---|---|---|---|
| Home | 2 | 1 | 1 | 0 | 4 | 3 |
| Away | 2 | 0 | 0 | 2 | 1 | 3 |
| Totals | 4 | 1 | 1 | 2 | 5 | 6 |

FA Cup

| | | | | | | |
|---|---|---|---|---|---|---|
| Home | 1 | 0 | 1 | 0 | 2 | 2 |
| Away | 1 | 0 | 1 | 0 | 0 | 0 |
| Neutral | 3 | 0 | 2* | 1 | 2 | 4 |
| Totals | 5 | 0 | 4 | 1 | 4 | 6 |

*One game abandoned after 90 minutes.

Aston Villa's first League Division Three victory at home was against Rovers on 5 September 1970, Andy Lochhead (2) and Pat McMahon the scorers in a 3-2 success in front of 23,602 fans.

All five FA Cup games took place in the 4th round of the 1954-55 competition. After a goalless draw at Belle Vue, Villa were then held 2-2 at home in the replay before the teams travelled to Maine Road for a third clash which also finished level at 1-1. The fourth meeting at Hillsborough stood at 0-0 before bad light caused the referee to abandon proceedings after 90 minutes. And so to a fifth clash, this time at The Hawthorns, where Alick Jeffery starred for Rovers who won the tie 3-1.

Players with both clubs include: P Birch, LC Chatterley, P Crichton (Villa on loan), B Gallacher, JT Gavin, A Hale, A Little, LJ Martin, M Moralee (Rovers WW2 guest), B Ormsby, LC Pember (Villa reserve), F Potter, VE Potts, A Wakeman.
Also: PD Docherty (Rovers player/manager, Villa WW2 guest & chief scout).

### DONOVAN, TERENCE CHRISTOPHER

Born: Liverpool, 27 February 1958.
Career: Clee Grammar School, Louth United, Grimsby Town (professional August 1976), Aston Villa (£75,000, September 1979), Portland Timbers (on loan, June-August 1982), Oxford United (on loan, February 1983), Burnley (£25,000, February 1983), Rotherham United (£15,000, September 1983), Blackpool (on loan, October 1984). Moved into non-League football in 1985.

Honoured by the Republic of Ireland at Schoolboy level, utility forward Terry Donovan later added Under-21 and senior caps to his collection. Son of Donal, the former Everton and Grimsby full-back, he drew up an impressive strike record with Villa's Central League side (over 70 goals scored in 120 matches) but failed to establish himself in the first XI and netted 11 times in 24 appearances before moving to Burnley. He was Grimsby's record transfer 'out' when he left the Mariners for Villa Park in 1979. His hobbies include squash and golf.

*Terry Donovan (right) v. Arsenal.*

### DORIGO, ANTHONY ROBERT

Born: Melbourne, Australia, 31 December 1965.
Career: Birmingham Schoolboy football, Aston Villa (apprentice 1981, professional January 1982), Chelsea (£475,000, July 1987), Leeds United (£300,000, May 1991), Torino (free transfer, June 1997), Derby County (free transfer, October 1998), Stoke City (free transfer, July 2000).

Left-back Tony Dorigo, who holds three different passports: Australian, Italian and British, was a very efficient and steady defender who

enjoyed his forays upfield. He won seven England Under-21 caps whilst with Villa who gave him a trial after he had pestered the office staff to answer his letters! He scored one goal in 135 appearances for Villa before moving to Stamford Bridge in 1987. He skippered the England Under-21 side when he was with Chelsea, adding four more intermediate caps to his tally as well as playing seven times for England 'B' and making the first of 15 full international appearances for his adopted country! He

*Tony Dorigo.*

THE COMPLETE ENCYCLOPAEDIA OF ASTON VILLA F.C.   THE COMPLETE ENCYCLOPAEDIA OF ASTON VILLA F.C.

76

helped the London club win the Second Division title in 1989 and the FMC (at Wembley) in 1990, while adding a further 180 first-class appearances to his tally before switching his allegiance to Elland Road. He sent six years with Leeds, gaining both a First Division championship medal and a Charity Shield prize in 1992, accumulating another 209 senior appearances in the process. After fifteen months in Italy's Serie 'A' he returned to Premiership football with Derby County in 1998 and continued in the Nationwide League with Stoke City in 2000. Dorigo amassed in excess of 650 League and Cup appearances at club and international level before announcing his retirement from the first-class game in May 2001.

## DORRELL, ARTHUR REGINALD

Born: Small Heath, Birmingham 30 March 1896. Died: Alum Rock, Birmingham 14 September 1942.

Career: Belper Road School (Leicester), Carey Hall FC (Leicester), Army Service/RASC (from 1916), Aston Villa (May 1919), Port Vale (June 1931). Retired, August 1932 and became 'mine host' at the Pelham Arms, Alum Rock.

Arthur Dorrell was a fast-raiding orthodox left-winger who was capped four times by England over a period of two years: 1925-26. Nothing ruffled or disturbed Dorrell - even the most exciting game left him ice-cool! He joined Villa on his demob from the Army in 1919 and went on to score 65 goals in 390 first-class games for the club over the next 12 years, frequently combining in style and brilliance with Billy Walker. Besides his full international honours he also represented the Football League in 1923 and played in two FA Cup Finals for Villa - 1920 and 1924, collecting a winners' medal in the first (v Huddersfield).

During the Great War, Dorrell made quite a name for himself on the athletics track, sprinting to victory in the Army championships in France.

Arthur Dorrell's father Billy (below) prompted his son to become a professional footballer!

## DORRELL, WILLIAM

Born: Coventry, 1873. Died: c 1939.

Career: Leicester Fosse (1892), Aston Villa (August 1894), Burslem Port Vale (trialist, August 1897), Belper (September 1897). Retired 1905.

Billy Dorrell, like his son Arthur (above) was also an outside-left who could play at inside-right. He had to contest a first team place with such fine players as Steve Smith and Albert Woolley and made only 12 senior appearances for the club (4 goals scored) before being released at the end of the 1896-97 campaign.

## DORSETT, RICHARD

Born: Brownhills, Staffs, 3 December 1919. Died: Brownhills, 1998.

Career: Walsall Boys, Birmingham County FA, Wolverhampton Wanderers (groundstaff, April 1935, professional December 1936), guested for Liverpool, Grimsby Town, Southampton, Brentford and Queen's Park Rangers during the War, Aston Villa (£3,000, September 1946). Retired in May 1953, but remained at Villa Park as Youth team coach, later becoming assistant-trainer at Liverpool (July 1957) before

returning to the Midlands to take over a local side in Brownhills in 1962. He was also employed by BRD & BIP (Strelly Works).

Known as the 'Iron Man', 'Brick Wall' and the 'Brownhills Bomber' Dicky Dorsett was as tough as they come, a player who never shirked a tackle, was totally committed and as rugged and as strong as an elephant! In 1946, whilst on tour with Wolves in Copenhagen, he was sent-off after an incident involving a Danish player.

Recalled Dorsett: 'He kicked me in the back as I was shielding the ball. With no 'Clean Air' act in operation I told him precisely what I thought. He retorted by spitting at me, so I smacked him one'.

This upset the club. Dorsett didn't play for Wolves again - and he immediately joined Villa. He slammed in 13 goals in his first season at Villa Park but early in the 1947-48 campaign was moved into the right-half berth vacated by Bob Iverson. Then, as time progressed, Dorsett was switched to the left-back slot and did well (as usual) until Peter Aldis and Harry Parkes came onto the scene.

In January 1950 his playing days almost came to an abrupt end when he was involved in a nhorrific car crash, but he survived and went on to give Aston Villa grand service, ending with a record of 36 goals in 271 senior appearances. He had netted 35 times in only 52 outings for Wolves including their goal in the 1939 FA Cup Final when, as favourites, the Wanderers were beaten 4-1 by Portsmouth. He also helped Wolves win the 1942 Wartime League Cup.

Dicky Dorsett was the nephew of the former West Bromwich Albion and Manchester City brothers, George and Joe Dorsett.

## DOUBLE WINNERS

In season 1896-97 Villa became the second team to complete the League and FA Cup double, following Preston's achievement in 1888-89. This is Villa's record for that season.

### Football League Division One

| Opponents | H | A |
|---|---|---|
| Blackburn R. | 3-0 | 5-1 |
| Bolton Wds. | 6-2 | 2-1 |
| Burnley | 0-3 | 4-3 |
| Bury | 1-1 | 2-0 |
| Derby County | 2-1 | 3-1 |
| Everton | 1-2 | 3-2 |
| Liverpool | 0-0 | 3-3 |
| Nottingham F. | 3-2 | 4-2 |
| PNE | 3-1 | 1-0 |
| Sheffield U. | 2-2 | 0-0 |
| Sheffield W. | 4-0 | 3-1 |
| Stoke | 2-1 | 2-0 |
| Sunderland | 2-1 | 2-4 |
| WBA | 2-0 | 1-3 |
| Wolves | 5-0 | 2-1 |

### Summary:

| Venue | P | W | D | L | F | A | Pts |
|---|---|---|---|---|---|---|---|
| Home | 15 | 10 | 3 | 2 | 36 | 16 | 23 |
| Away | 15 | 11 | 2 | 2 | 37 | 22 | 24 |
| Totals | 30 | 21 | 5 | 4 | 73 | 38 | 47 |

### FA Cup

| Rd 1 | v Newcastle Utd (h) | 5-0 |
|---|---|---|
| Rd 2 | v Notts County (h) | 2-1 |

*Aston Villa - Double winners: 1896-97*
*Back row (l-r): G B Ramsay (secretary), J Grierson (trainer), H Spencer, J Whitehouse, J E Margoschis (Chairman),*
*J Evans, J Crabtree, J T Lees (Director), C Johnstone (Director).*
*Front row (l-r): V Jones (Director), J.A.S Cowan, C Athersmith, J Campbell, J Devey, F Wheldon, John Cowan,*
*J Reynolds, F W Rinder (Director).*

| Rd 3 | v Preston NE (a) | 1-1 |
|------|------------------|-----|
| Rd3R | v Preston NE (h) | 0-0 |
| Rd3 2R | v Preston NE (n) | 3-2 |
| SF | v Liverpool (n) | 3-0 |
| Final | v Everton (n) | 3-2 |

### Facts

Surprisingly the bottom two teams in the Division beat Villa in the League - Burnley 3-0 at Perry Barr and Sunderland 4-2 on Wearside. Three players - Charlie Athersmith, James (Jim) Cowan and Fred Wheldon - were ever-present.

Wheldon top-scored with 22 goals in total (18 League, 4 Cup). Johnny Campbell and Jack Devey each netted 17.

Villa's home League attendance was a creditable 13,200 and remember that their first 13 games were played at Perry Barr, the last two at Villa Park.

Villa won two and drew one of their three games at Bramall Lane this season. They forced a 0-0 draw with Sheffield United in the League and then in the FA Cup defeated PNE and Liverpool in the 2nd replay of the quarter-final and the semi-final respectively.

### DOUGAN, ALEXANDER DEREK

Born: Belfast, 20 January 1938
Career: Distillery, Portsmouth (professional, August 1957), Blackburn Rovers (March 1959), Aston Villa (£15,000, August 1961), Peterborough United (£21,000, June 1963), Leicester City (£25,000, May 1965), Wolverhampton Wanderers (£50,000, March 1967). Retired to become manager of Kettering Town (August 1975-77). Once the PFA Chairman, Dougan became a Sports Presenter on Yorkshire T.V prior to returning to Molineux in August 1982 as Chairman and Chief Executive, a post he held until the arrival of the Bhatti brothers in 1985.

One of the most colourful footballers of his day, centre-forward Derek Dougan shaved his head when he played for Aston Villa! Always a big favourite with the fans, he represented his country at Schoolboy, Youth and Amateur levels as a wing-half or central defender before joining Portsmouth in 1957. Pompey switched him to centre-forward and he went on to score nine goals in 33 League games before moving to Ewood Park in 1959. Dougan hit 25 goals for Rovers and appeared in the 1960 FA Cup Final against Wolves....despite having asked for a transfer on the eve of the big match. Villa then bought him at the start of the 1961-62 season (to replace Gerry Hitchens). Dubbed the 'Clown Prince of Soccer', 'Cheyenne' (when he was bald) and the 'Doog', he was, without doubt, a character, and a fine goalscorer. He hit 26 goals for Villa (in 60 games) up to 1963 when he joined Peterborough. From London Road he switched to Filbert Street in 1965 and in March 1967, Wolves' manager Ronnie Allen enticed him to Molineux.....and what a signing he turned out to be! Dougan quickly scored a hat-trick against Hull City and helped Wolves win promotion from the Second Division that same season. He formed a brilliant partnership with John Richards and in 1974 helped Wolves win the League Cup. He was leading marksman at Molineux in 1967-68, 1968-69 and 1971-72 and went on to net 123 goals for the Wanderers in 323 appearances before leaving Molineux to become manager of Kettering Town (1975-77). Capped 43 times by Northern Ireland, Dougan also gained 'B' caps for his country and held the position of PFA Chairman whilst a player and he later returned to his old hunting ground at Molineux as Chairman and Chief Executive. On leaving Wolves second time round he moved to Codsall, and became involved in raising money for the Duncan Edwards Medical Centre (Dudley).

*'The Doog' in action.*

The 'Doog' suffered a heart attack in 1997 but he made a full recovery after treatment.

Dougan scored more Football League goals than any other Irishman - 222 in 546 appearances - and he is one of only a handful of footballers to have scored a hat-trick in both First and Second Division League games as well as in the FA Cup, League Cup and UEFA Cup competitions.

Dougan's brother was married on the same day as the Queen and Prince Philip; another brother was born on the same day as Prince Charles and the Doog himself became a father of a boy on the day the Queen gave birth to her fourth child.

## DOWDS, PETER

Born: Johnstone, Renfrewshire, December 1867. Died: Scotland, 2 September 1895.

Career: Celtic (1889), Aston Villa (August 1892), Stoke (July 1893), Celtic (August 1894-September 1895).

Peter Dowds was a quality footballer, able to play anywhere. He preferred a wing-half position but also enjoyed a game or two in the forward-line. He was an artist with the ball, always in control of the situation, always displaying a full range of tricks and graces and very creative in the process. Capped once by Scotland v Ireland in 1892, he scored three goals in 21 games for Villa before having a spell with Stoke. He died at the age of 27 following a chest complaint. He was a heavy drinker.

## DRAPER, MARK ANDREW

Born: Long Eaton, 11 November 1970.

Career: Notts County (YTS, June 1986, professional December 1988), Leicester City (£1.25 million, July 1994), Aston Villa (£3.25 million, July 1995), Rayo Vallecano, Spain (on loan, January-May 2000), Southampton (July 2000).

Industrious midfielder Mark Draper had already appeared in almost 320 League and Cup games (54 goals scored) and gained three England Under-21 caps before joining Aston Villa in 1995. Over the next five years he added a further 155 appearances and 11 more goals to his tally as well as helping Villa win the League Cup in 1996. He had only one substitute outing in his last season at Villa Park, failing to fit into manager John Gregory's plans.

## DRAWS

Aston Villa have been involved in two 5-5 draws in League football, both away from home, the first at West Ham United on 31 January 1931 and the second at Tottenham on 19 March 1966.

They have also figured in eight 4-4 scorelines: against Burnley (November 1890), Sunderland (January 1895), Bristol City (October 1907), West Bromwich Albion (April 1934), Manchester United (October 1955), Liverpool (March 1960), Port Vale (November 1971) and Leicester City (February 1995). Villa led 3-0 and 4-1 in this latter game and were 4-0 down v. Liverpool in 1960.

The most games drawn by Villa in a single League campaign has been 16 in 1978-79 (nine at home, seven away). They drew 15 in 1956-57 (Division 1), 1970-71 (Division 3), 1973-74 (Division 2) and 1994-95 (Premiership).

Villa did not draw any of their 26 League matches in season 1891-92.

Villa drew eight League games out of 10 starts between February and April 1976.

Villa's longest sequence of drawn League games is six - from 12 September to 10 October 1981 inclusive.

Up to the end of the 2000-01 season, Villa had drawn most League/Premiership games against Everton (total 41 - 19 at home and 22 away).

## DRINKWATER, CHARLES JOHN

Born: Willesden, 25 June 1914. Died: London, 1998.

Career: Golders Green, Brentford (amateur, June 1934), Walthamstow Avenue (1934-35), Aston Villa (professional, October 1935), Charlton Athletic (July 1938), Walsall (August 1939), Gillingham (1944), Watford (January 1945), Ruislip (player/coach, July 1951. Retired 1953.

Reserve left-winger, only 5ft 4ins tall, but reliable and nippy. Scored once on his debut at home to Chelsea in November 1935 when he deputised for Arthur Cunliffe. He also figured in Villa's next game v Birmingham when he set up one of Dai Astley's goals in the 2-2 draw in front of 60,250 fans at St Andrew's. Drinkwater didn't play first team football for the club again although he remained at Villa Park until the end of the 1937-38 season.

## DUBLIN, DION

Born: Leicester, 22 April 1969.

Career: Oakham United, Norwich City (professional, March 1988), Cambridge United (free transfer, August 1988), Manchester United (£1 million, August 1992), Coventry City (£2 million, September 1994)< Aston Villa (£5.75 million, November 1998).

Released by Norwich without getting a first team game, 6ft 2in striker Dion Dublin then started to score goals aplenty for Third Division Cambridge United (he cracked in a hat-trick on his League debut against Peterborough United). His all-action performances quickly drew scouts and managers from several top clubs to The Abbey Stadium. He went on to net a total of 73 goals in 201 senior appearances for United, ending up as the club's top marksmen three seasons running as well as helping them win the Third Division title in 1991. Just as the 1992-93 campaign was about to kick-off Dublin was swept away to Old Trafford by Alex Ferguson, who splashed out £1 million for his services. Unfortunately Dublin - after scoring on his full debut for the Reds - then suffered a broken leg and ankle ligament damage which effectively ruined the rest of that season. He was actually sidelined for five months without kicking a ball! He came back late on and scored seven goals in 13 Pontins League matches, but following the arrival of Frenchman Eric Cantano, he found himself technically a reserve forward and after claiming three goals in 17 League and Cup appearances for the Reds, moved to Highfield Road.

He slotted in quickly with the Sky Blues and regaining full fitness and his scoring technique, weighing in with 72 more goals (in 171 senior appearances) before transferring to Villa Park. Dublin started off like a house on fire with Villa, grabbing five goals in his first two outings two against Spurs on his debut and a hat-trick at Southampton. Initially there were signs of a tremendous striking partnership with Stan Collymore. That sadly never materialised to its full extent, but he did link up well with Julian Joachim and ended his first term at Villa Park with 11 goals to his name in 24 outings. He put away 12 more goals during the first part of the next season but then in December he suffered a serious injury during the home game with Sheffield Wednesday. Fractured neck vertebrae were diagnosed and surgery was required to repair what could easily have been a life-threatening injury. Dublin was not expected to return that season - but he defied all odds and bounced back to help Villa reach the FA Cup Final, scoring the deciding penalty in the semi-final shoot-out with Bolton Wanderers. A powerful, sometimes awkward looking player, exceptionally strong in the air and no mean performer on the ground, Dublin has now notched 36 goals in close on 100 first XI appearances for Villa - and he's also earned four full England caps.

• Dublin's father was a member of the 1960s pop group, Showaddywaddy which also featured the father of the Luton Town and Leicester City midfielder Scott Oakes.

*Andy Ducat ion the ball against Huddersfield Town in the 1920 F.A. Cup Final.*

## DUCAT, ANDREW
Born: Brixton, Surrey, 16 February 1886. Died: Lord's Cricket ground, Marylebone, London, 23 July 1942 (heart failure).
Career: Brewer Road & Compton House Schools Southend, Westcliff Athletic, Southend Athletic, Woolwich Arsenal (amateur January 1905, professional, February 1905), Aston Villa (£1,000, June 1912), Fulham (May 1921). Retired in May 1924 to become manager at Craven Cottage, a position he held until July 1926 when he was reinstated as an amateur footballer and joined Corinthian Casuals. Ducat ran a sports outfitters' shop during his time with Villa; he also played county cricket for Surrey (1906-31). In those 25 years at The Oval he played as a top-order right-hand batsman and occasional right-arm slow bowler. In a total of 428 first-class matches, he scored 23,373 runs, including 52 centuries, for an average of 38.63, with a best individual score of 306 not out against Oxford University. He also took 21 wickets for 903 runs (av. 43) as well as taking 205 catches (mainly as a close-to-the-wicket fielder). Ducat made one Test match appearance for England v. Australia in 1921, batting twice. He was dismissed in unusual circumstances for a duck in his first innings when a slice of wood flew off his bat and dislodged a bail, but he recorded a fine 50 when he returned to the crease for his second knock. Ducat was later cricketing coach at Eton College, was a part-time journalist and a Surrey publican. He played in various football and cricket matches (mainly for charity) right up until his sudden death which occurred out on the cricket square at Lord's in 1942 when he suffered a heart attack when batting for the Surrey Home Guard against the Sussex Home Guard.

As a footballer Ducat was capped six times by England (1910-12) and skippered Villa to victory in the 1920 FA Cup Final against Huddersfield Town. He was an outstanding right-half of the unflurried, academic type. A great sportsman who was rarely spoken to by the referee, never booked or sent-off, he played every game with passion and total commitment. He was nursing a broken leg (suffered in only his fourth game for the club v Manchester City) and sadly missed the 1913 FA Cup Final win over Sunderland - but he made up for it seven years later when he played one of his best games for Villa.

Signed to replace George Tranter, he didn't return to League action until 5 September 1914 - exactly two years after breaking his leg - but he soon made up for lost time, giving Villa tremendous service right up until 1921 when he moved back to London to sign for Fulham. Ducat made 87 appearances for Aston Villa and scored four goals. Prior to joining Villa he had appeared in 193 games for Arsenal at competitive level (plus another 47 during the War) and afterwards he starred in 69 matches for Fulham.

## DUFFY, DARRELL GERARD
Born: Birmingham 18 January 1971.
Career: Aston Villa (YTS, June 1987, professional, July 1989), Moor Green (August 1992), Scunthorpe United (February 1993-94).
Birmingham-born defender Darrell Duffy made one Football League appearance for Aston Villa - stepping in for right-back Chris Price against Derby County (away) in May 1989 - two months before he became a professional.

## DUGDALE, JAMES ROBERT
Born: Liverpool, 15 January 1932.
Career: Harrowby (Liverpool), West Bromwich Albion (January 1950, professional, January 1951), Aston Villa (£25,000, February 1956), Queen's Park Rangers (October 1962). Retired through injury, May 1963,
Jimmy Dugdale - known by many as the 'laughing cavalier' - was an excellent centre-half who shared the No. 5 shirt at The Hawthorns with Joe Kennedy during the early 1950s before moving to Villa Park. Dugdale had 75 games for Albion, gaining an FA Cup winners medal in 1954, collecting three England 'B' caps and also representing the Football League. With Kennedy taking priority at the heart of defence he was snapped up by Villa boss Eric Houghton early in 1956 as a straight replacement for the versatile Con Martin. The following year Dugdale won his second FA Cup winners medal and then helped Villa

*Jimmy Dugdale.*

capture the Second Division title in 1960. He was brilliant when the team carried off the League Cup twelve months later and went on to amass 255 League and Cup appearances for Villa (three goals scored) before seeing out his career with QPR (he never made a full recovery from a cartilage injury, received in 1962 when playing for Villa in a local derby against Blues). At that point (1963) he left football altogether and became a publican in Witton, later taking over Aston Villa's Lions club and then acting as steward at the Hasbury Conservative club (near Halesowen) and thereafter the Moseley Rugby Union club at the Reddings (Kings Heath). Dugdale, who sadly had a leg amputated in 1990, now lives in Acocks Green, Birmingham and in 1992-93 Villa staged a testimonial match on his behalf (v Blues). In 1957 Dugdale was offered a brand new sports car in exchange for his quota of FA Cup Final tickets. He didn't fall into the trap.

• Jimmy is the uncle of the former Barnsley, Coventry City and Charlton Athletic defender Alan Dugdale.

THE COMPLETE ENCYCLOPAEDIA OF ASTON VILLA F.C.          THE COMPLETE ENCYCLOPAEDIA OF ASTON VILLA F.C.

80

## DUNN, JOHN ALFRED

Born: Barking, 21 June 1944.

Career: Barking & Essex Schools, Chelsea (Schoolboy forms, June 1959, apprentice June 1960, professional February 1962), Torquay United (October 1966), Aston Villa (£8,000, January 1968), Charlton Athletic (free transfer, July 1971), Ramsgate (on loan, December 1974), Tooting & Mitchum (player/coach, February 1975), Woking, Grays Athletic, Craven FC (Essex Business Houses League). Took up refereeing in Essex in 1986 and officiated in the Business Houses' and Sunday Corinthian Leagues for four years.

A competent and courageous goalkeeper, John Dunn was the target of a group of 'supporters' during his last season at Villa Park. Nevertheless, prior to that he had given the club excellent service, appearing in 118 first-class matches including the 1971 League Cup Final at Wembley. He took over the No 1 spot at Villa Park from John Phillips and was eventually replaced by Jim Cumbes from West Bromwich Albion. After

*John Dunn.*

leaving Villa Park, Dunn took over from Charlie Wright at The Valley and went on to appear in 118 games for Charlton. During his career he amassed almost 300 senior appearances (262 in the Football League), as well as making well over 100 at non-League level.

## DUNNING, WILLIAM

Born: Perth, Scotland, August 1866. Died: Southampton, January 1902.

Career: St Johnstone (1886), Celtic (1888), Bootle (1890), Aston Villa (£100, July 1892). Retired in 1895 through ill-health and went to South Africa for a short while before retiring to live in Southampton where he died at the age of 35.

Goalkeeper Bill Dunning stood six feet tall and weighed over 13 stone. He was a daring custodian who replaced Jimmy Warner between the posts, winning a League championship medal in 1894. He appeared in 69 first team games for Villa before handing over his duties to Tom Wilkes.

## DURHAM CITY

There has been no competitive action between Villa and City.

Players with both clubs include: J Hickman, J Hinchcliffe, C Stephenson, G Stephenson, AE Surtees, MS Taylor.

## DUTTON, THOMAS THEODORE

Born: West Bromwich, April 1870. Died: Wednesbury, February 11 1922.

Career: Oak Lane School, Wednesbury Old Athletic (1889), Aston Villa (July 1891), Walsall Town (May 1892-94).

Reserve inside-forward who in his only senior game for Villa (v Blackburn Rovers in March 1892) made two of the three goals scored by Louis Campbell in a 4-3 defeat.

## DYKE, ARCHIBALD SAMUEL

Born: Newcastle-under-Lyme, Staffs, September 1886. Died: c 1955.

Career: Newcastle Congregational, Newcastle PSA, Chesterton, Stoke, Port Vale (August 1912), Stoke (July 1913), Aston Villa (February 1914),

Port Vale (WWI guest, 1916, re-joining Vale in August 1919), Stafford Rangers, Coventry City, Blackpool, Congleton Town, retiring in 1925.

A clever little right-winger with good speed, Archie Dyke made nine first team appearances for Villa as deputy for the more experienced Charlie Wallace.

## DYNAMO BERLIN

Villa's playing record against Dynamo:

European Cup

| Venue | P | W | D | L | F | A |
|---|---|---|---|---|---|---|
| Home | 1 | 0 | 0 | 1 | 0 | 1 |
| Away | 1 | 1 | 0 | 0 | 2 | 1 |
| Totals | 2 | 1 | 0 | 1 | 2 | 2 |

Aston Villa were involved in a tough battle with the German side in the second round of the European Cup in 1981-82. After winning the first leg in Berlin by 2-1 (Tony Morley scoring twice) Villa eventually went through on the away goal after losing the return fixture 0-1 in front of their own supporters.

## DYNAMO KIEV

Villa's playing record against Kiev:

European Cup

| Venue | P | W | D | L | F | A |
|---|---|---|---|---|---|---|
| Home | 1 | 1 | 0 | 0 | 2 | 0 |
| Away | 1 | 0 | 1 | 0 | 0 | 0 |
| Totals | 2 | 1 | 1 | 0 | 2 | 0 |

Aston Villa met the Ukranian club at Simferopol in the 1st leg of a 3rd round European Cup match on 3 March 1982 and in front of 20,000 fans earned a goalless draw. The return fixture at Villa Park a fortnight later attracted an audience of 38,579 and this time goals by Gary Shaw and Ken McNaught gave Villa a 2-0 victory and a passport into the semi-finals.

Kiev had visited Villa Park for a friendly match on 13 November 1961. Villa won 2-1.

## ECCLES, JOSEPH

Born: Stoke, 5 February 1906. Died: c 1970.

Career: Wolseley Motors (1921), Aston Villa (January 1924), West Ham United (August 1926), Northampton Town (July 1928), Coventry City (August 1929). Non-League football from 1932.

Outside-right Joe Eccles walked into Villa Park and asked for a trial. He impressed those watching and was signed as a professional within a fortnight. Owing to the fine form of Dicky York, he found it difficult to get first team action, appearing in only 10 League matches (all in 1924-25) during his two-and-a-half years with the club.

## EDGLEY, HAROLD HORACE

Born: Crewe, January 1892. Died: Nottingham, March 1966.

Career: Whitchurch, Crewe Alexandra, Aston Villa (June 1911 for £50, paid in two instalments), Stourbridge (on loan, September-December 1913), Aston Villa (December 1913), Queen's Park Rangers (August 1921), Stockport

*Harold Edgley.*

THE COMPLETE ENCYCLOPAEDIA OF ASTON VILLA F.C.    THE COMPLETE ENCYCLOPAEDIA OF ASTON VILLA F.C.

81

County (August 1923), Worcester City (1925), then non-League football in the Cheshire League (to 1927). Later became a Notts County Director.

Harold Edgley was a positive outside-left, well-built, quick with a powerful shot. He had cruel luck when he broke his leg in two places during a League game at Chelsea just three weeks before Aston Villa were due at Stamford Bridge to play Huddersfield Town in the FA Cup Final. He was later presented with a specially-designed gold medal, having appeared in all the previous rounds. Edgley scored 17 goals in 86 first team appearances for Villa and later had 75 outings for QPR (6 goals) and 31 (4 goals) for Stockport.

## EDWARDS, ALFRED
Born: Coventry, April 1890.
Career: Stourbridge, Aston Villa (April 1910), Dudley Town (August 1912), Netherton, Cradley St Luke's. Retired 1925.
Compact half-back, small in stature but as keen as mustard, Alf Edwards did exceedingly well in non-League football after making eight first team appearances for Villa, mainly as a replacement for Chris Buckley.

## EDWARDS, GEORGE ROBERT
Born: Norwich, 1 April 1918. Died: Lapworth, 21 January 1993,
Career: Great Yarmouth Priory School, Yarmouth Boys, Yarmouth Caledonians, Norfolk County, Norwich City (amateur, March 1935, professional April 1936), Aston Villa (June 1938). Guested for Birmingham, Chelmsford, Coventry City, Northampton Town, Nottingham Forest, Notts County, Walsall, West Bromwich Albion and Wrexham during Second World War. Joined Bilston United in May 1951, and retired in 1955. Ran a newsagents/sub post-office business in Birmingham and later an Aston Villa shareholder.
George Edwards made only nine appearances for the Canaries before joining Villa just before the Second World War. Then before he could make his debut in the claret and blue strip, he chipped an ankle bone in a tackle with Bob Iverson during a practice session and had to wait another two months before making his bow in the First Division (against Manchester United on 5 November 1938). The injury niggled him throughout his career and he always played carrying a heavy strapping. Nevertheless, Edwards became a huge favourite and great servant at Villa Park, a goalscoring master (certainly during the hostilities), a hard grafting utility forward who could occupy a number of positions, choosing the centre-forward berth as his best. He top-scored for Villa in Wartime football (94 goals in 125 games) and netted a total of 41 in 152 League and FA Cup matches. He helped Villa win the Wartime League Cup in 1944 and scored the fastest goal by a Villa player in the FA Cup - after just 13 seconds against Manchester United in 1948. Indeed, he was top-marksman at Villa Park in 1946-47 and 1947-48, netting no fewer than 43 goals (including two fours) in the transitional season of 1945-46. At the age of 15 he won the Norfolk County Schools' 100 yards sprint title and excelled at both billiards and snooker.

## EDWARDS, RICHARD THOMAS
Born: Kirkby-in-Ashfield, 20 November 1942.
Career: Nottingham Forest (trialist), Notts County (juniors, 1958, professional, October 1959), Mansfield Town (March 1967), Aston Villa (£30,000, March 1968), Torquay United (£8,000, June 1970), Mansfield Town (July 1973), Bath City (player/coach, then manager, 1974-76).
An England Youth international, a long throw expert, and sturdy central defender, Dick Edwards tackled decisively and enjoyed a challenge. A former pit worker, he scored twice in 77 first team appearances for Villa being manager Tommy Cummings' first signing when he took charge at Villa Park. During a fine career Edwards made a total of 469 League appearances (221 for Notts County and 102 for Mansfield). After retiring from soccer, Edwards took up singing on a professional

basis, and with Bruce Stuckey - a former playing colleague at Torquay - they became a very popular Country and Western duo in America with Edwards also going solo.

## EHIOGU, UGOCHUKA 'UGO'
Born: Hackney Marshes, London, 3 November 1972
Career: London Schoolboy football, West Bromwich Albion (YTS, 1988, professional July 1989), Aston Villa (£40,000, July 1991), Middlesbrough (£8 million, October 2000).
Tall, rangy centre-back, determined, reliable, strong in the tackle, quick in recovery, Ugo Ehiogu was another player 'given away' by West Bromwich Albion! He made just two substitute appearances in the League for the Baggies before joining Aston Villa in 1991 for a moderate fee with a sell-on payment clause built in to the transfer (Albion later received £2 million following his big-money switch to Middlesbrough in 2000). Ehiogu became a star performer at Villa Park, winning international honours for England at 'B', Under-21 (15 caps) and senior levels (one cap) as well as helping Villa win the Coca-Cola Cup in 1996. Unfortunately he had a disagreement with manager John Gregory (after being left out of the starting line-up) and subsequently left the club for The Riverside Stadium after making 303 senior appearances for Villa (15 goals scored). He was badly injured on his debut for 'Boro (at Charlton) and was sidelined for almost a month!

*Ugo Ehiogu.*

When he moved to 'Boro Ehiogu became the second costliest defender in British football (behind Manchester United's Jaap Stam). Third in line was Villa's Turkish star, Alpay Ozalan.

## ELLIOTT, JAMES ALEXANDER ERNEST
Born: Middlesbrough, March 1869. Died: Stafford, July 1899.
Career: Middlesbrough Ironopolis, Aston Villa (August 1893). Retired due to ill-health, April 1896.
Tall, beefy defender who weighed over 14 stones, Jim Elliott could occupy both full-back positions and made 25 first team appearances for Villa before he was forced to give up the game through illness. He made his debut for Villa against WBA on 2 September 1893.

## ELLIOTT, PAUL MARCELLUS
Born: Lewisham Hospital, 18 March 1964.
Career: Woodhill Primary School & Blackheath Bluecoat Secondary School, trialist with Luton Town, Millwall and West Ham United, Charlton Athletic (apprentice, July 1980, professional March 1981), Luton Town (£95,000, March 1983), Aston Villa (£400,000, December 1985), Pisa (£400,000, July 1987), Glasgow Celtic (£600,000, June 1989), Chelsea (July 1991). Retired through injury, 1993. Later became a successful summariser on Channel 4's 'Football Italia' covering Italy's Serie 'A' games.
Paul Elliott was a well-proportioned centre-half who gained England Youth international honours while with Charlton (1982) and an

THE COMPLETE ENCYCLOPAEDIA OF ASTON VILLA F.C.

THE COMPLETE ENCYCLOPAEDIA OF ASTON VILLA F.C.

82

England Under-21 caps at Luton (1985 & 1986). In 1990 he picked up Scottish Cup and a Skol Cup runners-up medals with Celtic. After the disappointment of being rejected by three League clubs, Elliott eventually went on to make 70 appearances for Charlton and after 66 League outings for Luton he moved to Villa Park to take over the No 5 shirt from Brendan Ormsby. He made 73 appearances for Villa (5 goals scored) before switching to Italian football with Pisa, later returning to England to have a further 42 League games with Chelsea.

He was badly injured playing against Liverpool in September 1992, following a challenge by future Villa striker Dean Saunders.

On 23 May 1994, a court case began in the High Court Elliott and Saunders, whereby it was alleged that Saunders had put in a supposedly dangerous tackle which effectively ended the playing career of Elliott. The hearing ended on 19 June with Saunders being cleared of making a 'reckless challenge'. Elliott was faced with a legal bill of £500,000.   (See: Court Cases).

*Paul Elliott.*

## ELLIS, H DOUGLAS.

Doug Ellis was born in 1924. A very wealthy businessman, formerly running a highly successful travel agency, he first became Chairman of Aston Villa Football Club in December 1968, and on his appointment quickly engaged Tommy Docherty as the club's new manager.

He was then a Director of Birmingham City (albeit briefly) and also Director/Chairman of Wolverhampton Wanderers (from June-December 1982) but never really severed his connections with Aston Villa football club, returning to the fold (as Chairman) in late 1982. He has retained the position (practically unchallenged) ever since. He is an F.A. International Committee member.

● When he first became a paid Director at Villa Park, Ellis said: "Only women and horses work for nothing."

● And when he handed Tommy Docherty the manager's job at Villa Park, Ellis said to him: "I'm right behind you." The Doc replied: "I'd rather you be in front of me where I can see you!"

## ELSTON, ARTHUR EDWARD
Born: Liverpool, July 1882. Died: 1950.
Career: Crownhills FC, Aston Villa (April 1905), Portsmouth (September 1906). Retired from competitive soccer (basically through injury) in 1909 but continued to play at non-League level until the outbreak of World War One.

Reserve outside-left at Villa Park, Arthur Elston had just one League outing for the club, lining up (after Joe Bache had cried off at the last minute) against Sunderland at Roker Park in February 1906. He went off injured late in the second half as Villa lost 2-0. Elston later made 20 appearances for Pompey in the Southern League.

## ENCKELMAN, PETER
Born: Turku, Finland, 10 March 1977.
Career: Jalkapallo TPS Turku, Aston Villa (£200,000, February 1999).

Signed as cover for David James, talented young goalkeeper Peter Enckelman had already been capped by Finland at Under-21 level before he made his debut (as second-half substitute) for Villa in a Premiership game at Arsenal in September 1999. He retained his place in the side for the next six games and kept five clean sheets! He suffered a knee injury soon afterwards but bounced back and gained his first full international cap (v Wales in Cardiff in March 2000).

Enckelman, who signed an extension to his contract in November 2000, ended the 2000-01 season with 14 first-team appearances under his belt with Villa.

● Enckelman's father, Goran, was a Finnish international who played against England in a World Cup qualifying match in 1976.

## EURO '96
In June 1996, Aston Villa played hosts to four European Championship matches. Villa Park came alight, especially during the first game involving the Dutch against Scotland. The four matches were watched by a combined total of 132,921 spectators.

**The results of the four Euro '96 matches were:**

| | | |
|---|---|---|
| Holland 0 Scotland 0 | Att. | 34,363 |
| Holland 2 Switzerland 0 | Att. | 36,800 |
| Scotland 1 Switzerland 0 | Att. | 34,926 |
| Portugal 0 Czech Republic 1 | Att. | 26,832 |

(See also under Villa Park).

## EUROPEAN COMPETITIONS
Aston Villa's records in the various European club competitions are:

**European Cup**

| Venue | P | W | D | L | F | A |
|---|---|---|---|---|---|---|
| Home | 7 | 5 | 0 | 2 | 16 | 6 |
| Away | 7 | 3 | 3 | 1 | 7 | 4 |
| Neutral | 1* | 1 | 0 | 0 | 1 | 0 |
| Totals | 15 | 9 | 3 | 3 | 24 | 10 |

* 1982 European Cup Final in Rotterdam

**UEFA Cup**

| | P | W | D | L | F | A |
|---|---|---|---|---|---|---|
| Home | 21 | 14 | 2 | 5 | 40 | 20 |
| Away | 21 | 5 | 8 | 8 | 17 | 22 |
| Totals | 42 | 19 | 10 | 13 | 57 | 42 |

**European Super Cup**

| | P | W | D | L | F | A |
|---|---|---|---|---|---|---|
| Home | 1 | 1 | 0 | 0 | 3 | 0 |
| Away | 1 | 0 | 0 | 1 | 0 | 1 |
| Totals | 2 | 1 | 0 | 1 | 3 | 1 |

**Inter Toto Cup**

| | P | W | D | L | F | A |
|---|---|---|---|---|---|---|
| Home | 5* | 4 | 0 | 1 | 11 | 3 |
| Away | 5 | 0 | 2 | 3 | 3 | 6 |
| Totals | 10 | 4 | 2 | 4 | 14 | 10 |

* Two home games staged on a neutral ground (The Hawthorns) at start of the 2000-01 season.

*Doug Ellis.*

THE COMPLETE ENCYCLOPAEDIA OF ASTON VILLA F.C.    THE COMPLETE ENCYCLOPAEDIA OF ASTON VILLA F.C.

83

**Overall Summary:**

| Venue | P | W | D | L | F | A |
|---|---|---|---|---|---|---|
| Home | 34 | 24 | 2 | 8 | 70 | 30 |
| Away | 34 | 8 | 13 | 13 | 27 | 33 |
| Neutral | 1 | 1 | 0 | 0 | 1 | 0 |
| Totals | 69 | 33 | 15 | 21 | 98 | 63 |

Aston Villa's first opponents in a major European Cup game were Antwerp in season 1975-76. And, in fact, the team from Belgium was the first to win a European game at Villa Park, claiming a 1-0 victory in the UEFA Cup on 1 October 1975.

*Skipper Dennis Mortimer, manager Tony Barton and goalscorer Peter Withe celebrate victory in the 1982 European Cup Final.*

Ray Graydon scored Villa's first 'European' goal in the away leg against Antwerp a fortnight earlier, on 17 September 1975. This was also Villa's heaviest defeat in Europe - losing 4-1.

Villa's biggest 'Euro' win is 5-0, achieved twice - against FC Valur (Iceland) in September 1981 (European Cup) and Vitoria Guimaraes (Portugal) in September 1983 (UEFA Cup)....both at home.

Villa played Besiktas of Turkey behind closed doors at Villa Park on 15 September 1982. The official attendance was given as 167.

Villa defeated Inter Milan 5-4 on penalties after the 2nd round UEFA Cup-tie in 1994-95 had finished level at 1-1 over two legs. Full-back Phil King blasted in the winning spot-kick. In the next round Villa were eliminated by the Turkish side Trabzonspor on the 'away goal' rule after the two-legged tie had ended 2-2, Villa having conceded a home goal.

The following season Villa succumbed in the opening round of the UEFA Cup to the part-timers from Helsingborg. After forcing a goalless draw in the away leg, Villa were held 1-1 at home and went out on the 'away goal' ruling for a second time.

Then, it was the turn of Atletico Madrid to knock Villa out of the UEFA Cup - again on the 'away goal' rule - at the quarter-final stage in 1997-98. Villa lost 1-0 in Spain but conceded a goal when winning 2-1 at home.

Villa were trailing Stromsgodset 2-0 in their home UEFA Cup encounter in 1998-99, but scored three times in the last seven minutes to win the contest 3-2 and the tie 6-2 on aggregate.

Villa's biggest aggregate victory in a European contest has been 7-0 over FC Valur in the Champions Cup in 1981-82.

Centre-half Ken McNaught scored five 'European' goals for Villa.

Goalkeeper Nigel Spink's second game for Villa was as an early substitute for the injured Jimmy Rimmer in the 1982 European Cup Final in Rotterdam against Bayern Munich.

Prior to that, Rimmer had been a member of Manchester United's squad against Benfica in the 1968 European Cup Final at Wembley.

Villa entered the InterToto Cup competition at the start of the 2000-01 season, knowing that success would guarantee them a place in the UEFA Cup. But after beating the Czech side Marila Pribram in their

*'Champions of Europe' 1982.*

THE COMPLETE ENCYCLOPAEDIA OF ASTON VILLA F.C.    THE COMPLETE ENCYCLOPAEDIA OF ASTON VILLA F.C.

84

opening round (3-1 on aggregate), they succumbed to the respected Spanish club Celta Vigo in their second, losing 1-0 away and 3-1 at The Hawthorns. Four Villa players were sent-off in this competition: Mark Delaney and Paul Merson, in the away and home legs respectively against the Czech outfit and then Ian Taylor and Alan Thompson, in the final game, the second encounter versus Celta Vigo.

In 2001-02 Villa again entered the InterToto Cup and this time they won through to the UEFA Cup by defeating Slavia Belupo, Stade Rennais and then FC Basel in the Final.

In 1977-78, after being held to a 2-2 home draw by Barcelona in the UEFA Cup, Villa had John Gidman sent-off in the Nou Camp stadium and eventually lost the return leg 2-1 and the tie itself 4-3 on aggregate.

Villa have drawn eight European away games by 0-0.

*Villa return home with the European Cup in 1982.*

### EVANS, ALBERT JAMES

Born: Barnard Castle, 18 March 1874. Died: Warwick, 24 March 1966.
Career: Stortforth & West Auckland Schools, Egglestone Abbey Boys, Barnard Castle (1891), Aston Villa (August 1896), West Bromwich Albion (October 1907). Retired to become trainer at The Hawthorns, June 1909. Briefly coached in Norway before being appointed Coventry City manager in June 1920, remaining in office until November 1924. After this he travelled the world doing many different jobs including gold prospecting in the Yukon and sheep farming in Canada. He returned to England and became Aston Villa's Midland-based scout in the 1950s.

Evans was a very adaptable full-back, a clean, crisp tackler, who was introduced to Aston Villa by former player Bob Chatt who

spotted his talents when he saw him in action in the North-East. Evans gained three League championship winning medals with Aston Villa (1897, 1899 & 1900) as well as an FA Cup winners' medal 1897). He also represented the Football League in 1900. He made 206 first team appearances for the club before switching four miles down the road to neighbouring West Bromwich Albion where he partnered England international left-back Jesse Pennington.

Evans captained Villa several times and had the misfortune to suffer five broken legs during his career, three whilst with Villa (one forced him to miss the 1905 FA Cup Final triumph), a fourth with Albion (on Christmas Day, 1908) and his last in local charity match in 1915. When he took over as Coventry manager he was the Sky Blues' third boss in three months! He inherited a poor side at Highfield Road and although he strengthened it slightly he was always under pressure with regards to gaining results and subsequently lost his job after four years at the helm. Evans died at the ripe old age of 92.

### EVANS, ALLAN JAMES

Born: Polbeath, near Edinburgh, 12 October 1956.
Career: Dunfermline Athletic (apprentice December 1972, professional, October 1973), Aston Villa (£30,000, June 1977), Leicester City (free transfer, August 1989), Brisbane United Australia (1990), Darlington (March 1991-May 1991).

On retiring Evans eventually became assistant-manager to his former Aston Villa colleague Brian Little Leicester City (June 1991), Villa Park (1994), Stoke City (1998) and West Bromwich Albion (1999) before going into management himself with the Scottish side Greenock Morton in June 2000, but was sacked in January 2001 after Morton had lost to Peterhead in the Scottish Cup.

As a teenager Allan Evans spent four years living in Malta and Cyprus before returning to Scotland to join Dunfermline. He had the misfortune to break his right leg when making his League debut for Dunfermline against Glasgow Rangers, but recovered within three months. In his last season with the Scottish club (before moving to Villa Park) he scored 15 goals from the centre-forward position, including two hat-tricks (against Clyde and Stranrear). He then netted a double hat-trick (a sixtimer) for Villa's second XI against Sheffield United - and this performance went a long way in allowing him to make his Football League bow, in March 1978, for Villa against Leicester City when he donned the No 7 shirt. He had two more senior outings before making his mark in the Villa defence where he became a solid performer, initially alongside Ken McNaught and later as partner to Brendan Ormsby, Paul Elliott and Steve Sims plus a few others. Evans was a regular in the side until 1986, going on to amass a superb record of 469 appearances for Villa, scoring 60 goals. He helped the team win the League title in 1981 and both the European Cup and Super Cup in 1982 as well as starring in four international matches for Scotland. Evans was released by Villa in the summer of 1990 after 13 years splendid service with the club.

*Allan Evans.*

### EVANS, ALUN WILLIAM

Born: Stourport, 30 September 1949.
Career: Stourport Junior School, Bewdley Council School, Mid-

THE COMPLETE ENCYCLOPAEDIA OF ASTON VILLA F.C.  THE COMPLETE ENCYCLOPAEDIA OF ASTON VILLA F.C.

85

Worcester Boys, Birmingham & District Schools, Aston Villa (trialist, 1964), Wolverhampton Wanderers (apprentice, July 1965, professional October 1966), Liverpool (£100,000, September 1968), Aston Villa (£72,000, June 1972), Walsall (£30,000, December 1975), South Melbourne Australia (July 1978), Hellas FC (April-July 1979), Melbourne (£10,000, August 1979). Retired 1981.

Alun Evans, the son of the former West Bromwich Albion and Wales Wartime international by the same name, became Britain's costliest teenager when he transferred by Wolves to Liverpool for £100,000 in 1968. After winning England caps at Schoolboy, Youth and Under-23 levels, he was regarded as the 'star of the future' but sadly never reached the heights expected of him. A blond striker with an eye for goal, Evans went on to score 21 times in 79 League games for Liverpool and played in the 1971 FA Cup Final against Arsenal. His stay at Anfield, however, was marred by a much publicised night club incident when he received a badly gashed face which left him scarred for life. He moved to Villa three years later and gained a League Cup winners' medal in 1975 versus Norwich City. Nine months after that Wembley triumph, having scored 17 goals in 72 games for Villa, he moved to Walsall. Whilst at Fellows Park he played more in midfield and amassed over 100 senior appearances for the Saddlers, up to 1978 when, after a trial, he joined the South Melbourne. Evans chose to stay in Australia and now resides with his wife and family in Cheltenham, Victoria.

### EVANS, DAVID GORDON
Born: West Bromwich, 20 May 1958.
Career: Aston Villa (apprentice, June 1974, professional February 1976), Halifax Town (on loan, September 1978, signed permanently for a record £22,500, June 1979), Bradford City (June 1984), Halifax Town (August 1980).
Versatile defender David Evans missed out at Villa Park, having only three senior outings for the club before going on to make over 300 appearances, in three spells, with Halifax Town and more than 230 for Bradford City by which time he had been converted into a defensively-minded midfield player. He helped the Bantams win the Third Division championship in 1985. Evans' debut for Aston Villa was at right-back in the Nou Camp Stadium against Barcelona in a UEFA Cup clash in March 1978 in front of almost 50,000 fans. His League debut followed six months later v. Everton at Villa Park.

### EVANS, OSCAR
Born: Warrington, June 1878. Died: Worcestershire.
Career: Lancaster Town, Aston Villa (July 1901), Broadwell FC (August 1903), Evesham (1905).
Slim-looking reserve inside-forward with Villa, Oscar Evans made just two first team appearances for the club, deputising for Joe Bache against Bolton and Notts County in March and April 1903 respectively.

### EVANS, ROBERT ERNEST
Born: Chester, 21 November 1885. Died: Saltney, 28 November 1965.
Career: Saltney Ferry, Bretton FC (August 1900), Saltney Works FC August 1902), Chester (June 1905), Wrexham (July 1905), Aston Villa (£30, March 1906), Sheffield United (£1,100 plus Peter Kyle, October 1908), Tranmere Rovers (WW2 guest, 1917), Sandycroft FC (WW2 guest, 1918). Retired 1921, Brookhirst FC (manager: 1921-23).
After turning out in friendlies for Saltney Ferry at the age of 14, winger Bob Evans joined Bretton and was 'paid' two turnips a week in lieu of travelling expenses. He won several trophies as a youngster and after a trial with Chester, he scored twice on his debut for Wrexham and was offered a contract worth ten shillings (50p) per week. A splendid all-action display against Villa's reserve side led to his transfer to Villa Park in 1906 and immediately his wages went up to £4-a-week. Unusually tall for a wide player (5 ft 10ins) Evans covered the ground

with long, raking strides and packed a stinging left-foot shot. He went on to score four goals in 17 games for Villa before moving to Sheffield United early in the 1908-09 season. Before arriving at Bramall-Lane Evans had already appeared in 10 full international matches for Wales when the FA discovered, after a tip-off from the Sheffield United secretary John Nicholson, that he had actually been born this side of the English border (in Chester) although his parents had moved to Wales when he was only three weeks old! Consequently, the English FA caused great controversy in Welsh football circles when they selected Evans to represented England....and he went on to win four caps for his 'second' country! In fact, he played for England against Wales at Wrexham in 1910 when four years earlier he had starred for the Principality against England. This led to Evans being described as 'the best winger England and Wales had ever had.'

During the First World War, Evans worked for a petroleum company and guested for Tranmere Rovers and Sandycroft. He played his 225th and last senior match for Sheffield United a few weeks after the end of the Great War and a broken leg the following year brought to an end a fine career. In 1921 Evans took over as team manager of non-League Brookhirst and two months into his new job he came out of retirement in an emergency - and again broke his leg! During the mid to late 1920s Evans worked as a welfare supervising officer for Shell Mex (Ellesmere Port) and acted as trainer to the works soccer team that included a young Joe Mercer.

### EVANS, WILLIAM EMMANUEL
Born: Aston, Birmingham, 5 September 1921. Died: August 1960.
Career: Linread Works FC, Aston Villa (trialist August 1946, professional September 1946), Notts County (June 1949), Gillingham (July 1953), Grimsby Town (June 1955). Retired July 1958 and appointed assistant-trainer at Blundell Park.
Principally an inside-left, Billy Evans was often given a roaming commission which saw him occasionally occupy the right-wing berth but whilst with Notts County he played as an out-and-out centre-forward. He helped the Magpies win the Third Division (S) title in 1950 and the Mariners lift the Third Division (North) crown in 1956. He scored a staggering 57 goals in works soccer for Linread's in 1945-46, a record that set him on the road to a useful League career. He netted three times in seven senior outings for Villa but then struck 14 in 96 League games for County, 12 in 89 for the Gills and 28 in 102 during his time with Grimsby. He died suddenly at the early age of 38.

### EVANS, WALTER GWYNNE
Born: Builth, Radnorshire, 1867. Died: Builth, 10 May 1897.
Career: Builth FC, Bootle (1889-90), Aston Villa (July 1890), Builth FC (August 1893). Retired May 1897.
Full-back Gwynne Evans, the son of a Builth butcher, excelled at rugby, cricket and soccer. The FA of Wales Player Assessment file published in 1891 described him as a 'very good back, tackles unflinchingly and has a safe kick - done himself credit.' He played for Villa against West Bromwich Albion in the 1892 FA Cup Final - one of 68 senior appearances for the club. He won three full caps for Wales, lining up against England each time - twice as a Bootle player in 1890 and 1891 and once as a Villan in 1892. In May 1897 Evans caught a chill while attending a funeral and died within days. His loss was described as 'a calamity for the Builth club.'

### EVER PRESENTS
**Players who were ever-present in League Football for Villa:**

| Season | Games | Players |
|---|---|---|
| 1888-89 | 22 | A Brown, G Cox |
| 1889-90 | 22 | A Brown, Jas Cowan |
| 1890-91 | 22 | J Warner |
| 1892-93 | 30 | J Devey |

THE COMPLETE ENCYCLOPAEDIA OF ASTON VILLA F.C.    THE COMPLETE ENCYCLOPAEDIA OF ASTON VILLA F.C.

86

| | | |
|---|---|---|
| 1893-94 | 30 | Jas Cowan |
| 1894-95 | 30 | WC Athersmith, Jas Cowan |
| 1895-96 | 30 | J Devey |
| 1896-97 | 30 | WC Athersmith, Jas Cowan |
| 1897-98 | 30 | AJ Evans |
| 1898-99 | 34 | T Bowman |
| 1899-00 | 34 | W George, GF Wheldon |
| 1901-02 | 34 | JW Bache |
| 1909-10 | 38 | CW Wallace |
| 1910-11 | 38 | CW Wallace |
| 1921-22 | 42 | AR Dorrell |
| 1922-23 | 42 | T Smart |
| 1926-27 | 42 | RE York |
| 1928-29 | 42 | RE York |
| 1930-31 | 42 | AD Talbot, JT Tate, WH Walker |
| 1931-32 | 42 | AD Talbot |
| 1932-33 | 42 | WE Houghton |
| 1933-34 | 42 | H Morton |
| 1934-35 | 42 | H Morton |
| 1937-38 | 42 | RW Starling |
| 1938-39 | 42 | E Callaghan, RTJ Iverson, A Massie |
| 1946-47 | 42 | LGF Smith |
| 1947-48 | 42 | GR Edwards, LGF Smith |
| 1949-50 | 42 | F Moss, IV Powell |
| 1951-52 | 42 | RD Blanchflower, JT Dixon, HA Parkes |
| 1959-60 | 42 | S Lynn |
| 1961-62 | 42 | VH Crowe |
| 1962-63 | 42 | CA Aitken |
| 1964-65 | 42 | CA Aitken, A Hateley |

| | | |
|---|---|---|
| 1973-74 | 42 | I Ross |
| 1974-75 | 42 | CA Aitken, I Ross |
| 1976-77 | 42 | B Little |
| 1977-78 | 42 | DG Mortimer, JJ Rimmer |
| 1978-79 | 42 | JJ Rimmer |
| 1979-80 | 42 | GS Cowans |
| 1980-81 | 42 | DG Bremner, GS Cowans, DG Mortimer, K McNaught, AW Morley, JJ Rimmer, K Swain |
| 1981-82 | 42 | GS Cowans, JJ Rimmer |
| 1982-83 | 42 | GS Cowans |
| 1987-88 | 44 | K Gage, NP Spink |
| 1988-89 | 38 | DA Platt |
| 1989-90 | 38 | NP Spink |
| 1990-91 | 38 | C Price, GS Cowans |
| 1991-92 | 42 | K Richardson, S Teale |
| 1992-93 | 42 | E Barrett, S Staunton, P McGrath, K Richardson |
| 1995-96 | 38 | M Bosnich, AG Wright |
| 1996-97 | 38 | AG Wright |
| 1998-99 | 38 | AG Wright, G Southgate |
| 2000-01 | 38 | DB James |

### Fact File

Left-back Charlie Aitken (between 1962 and 1975) and midfielder Gordon Cowans (1979-1991) share the Aston Villa club record of being ever-present in the League side five times.

Half-back Jas Cowans (1890s) and goalkeeper Jimmy Rimmer (1977-82) were both ever-present in Villa's League side on four occasions.

Alan Wright had three 'full' seasons in Villa's side in the 1990s.

Arthur Brown was an ever-present in Villa's first two League campaigns (1888-90).

Four Villa players appeared in every Premiership game in the inaugural season of 1992-93 (Barrett, Staunton, McGrath & Richardson).

### EVERTON

Villa's record against the Merseysiders:

Football League/Premiership

| Venue | P | W | D | L | F | A |
|---|---|---|---|---|---|---|
| Home | 86 | 43 | 19 | 24 | 163 | 115 |
| Away | 86 | 23 | 22 | 41 | 104 | 151 |
| Totals | 172 | 66 | 41 | 65 | 267 | 266 |
| FA Cup | | | | | | |
| Home | 1 | 0 | 0 | 1 | 0 | 1 |
| Away | 5 | 2 | 1 | 2 | 10 | 10 |
| Neutral | 2 | 2 | 0 | 0 | 5 | 3 |
| Totals | 8 | 4 | 1 | 3 | 15 | 14 |
| League Cup | | | | | | |
| Home | 3 | 1 | 2 | 0 | 2 | 1 |
| Away | 3 | 1 | 0 | 2 | 4 | 6 |
| Neutral | 3 | 1 | 2 | 0 | 4 | 3 |
| Totals | 9 | 3 | 4 | 2 | 10 | 10 |
| Wartime | | | | | | |
| Home | 1 | 0 | 0 | 1 | 1 | 2 |

Taking out the Great War (1915-19) Villa and Everton played League games against each other for 38 consecutive seasons, from 1888 until 1930 when the Merseysiders were relegated for the first time.

As founder members of the Football League, Villa and Everton first met in this competition on 22 September 1888 at Perry Barr when a crowd of 5,000 saw Villa win 2-1, Denny Hodgetts scoring both goals. Two weeks later Everton gained revenge with a 2-0 win at Anfield, their home at the time.

On 4 January 1890, Villa, who were reduced to 10 men, lost 7-0 at

*Charlie Aitken - five times ever-present.*

| | | |
|---|---|---|
| 1965-66 | 42 | CA Aitken |
| 1966-67 | 42 | JC Slueewenhoek, CC Withers |
| 1967-68 | 42 | WJ Anderson, LC Chatterley |
| 1968-69 | 42 | CA Aitken |
| 1969-70 | 42 | BD Rioch, MJ Wright |
| 1972-73 | 42 | J Cumbes |

THE COMPLETE ENCYCLOPAEDIA OF ASTON VILLA F.C.  THE COMPLETE ENCYCLOPAEDIA OF ASTON VILLA F.C.

87

*Goalmouth action from Villa's F.A. Cup Semi-Final victory over Everton at Nottingham in 1905.*

Everton (their joint heaviest defeat at League level) and twelve months later on a return trip to Anfield they crashed 5-0.

During that 1890 contest Villa's Archie Hunter suffered a heart attack. He was rushed to hospital but never regained his health and sadly died four years later.

Thirteen goals were scored in the two League games between the clubs in 1891-92, Everton completing the double with a 4-3 home win and a 5-1 victory at Perry Barr.

The third goal in Villa's 3-1 home win over Everton on 26 September 1903, was their 1,000th in the Football League.

Villa beat Everton 4-0 at home yet lost 4-2 away in 1905-06.

Everton won 5-1 at Villa Park in February 1915, when there were only 4,500 spectators present.

Len Capewell struck a smart hat-trick when Villa beat Everton 5-3 at home in December 1926.

Fourteen goals were scored in the two League games between the clubs in 1929-30. George Brown hit a hat-trick as Villa won 5-2 at home and Eric Houghton poached a couple when the double was completed with a 4-3 victory at Goodison Park.

A crowd of 61,663 saw the Villa-Everton clash in October 1931 (when the visitors won 3-2) and when the teams drew 3-3 at Goodison Park twelve months later the turnout was almost 39,000.

There were five successive League draws between the clubs in the mid-1930s, with three 2-2s in a row.

The first meeting after the Second World War saw Everton, the reigning League champions, win 1-0 at Villa Park in August 1946 while the following season both teams recorded impressive 3-0 home victories.

Villa put nine goals past Everton in 1956-57. They won 4-0 at Goodison Park in September (all the goals coming in the second-half - two from Jackie Sewell) and 5-1 at Villa Park in January (when Derek Pace scored twice)

When Everton won the League title in 1962-63 they defeated Villa 2-0 in the Midlands and were held 1-1 at Goodison Park. The following season they doubled up over Villa and did likewise again in 1964-65.

Tony Morley scored the 'Goal of the Season' when Villa won 3-1 at Everton in February 1981, but in contrast Villa's first away game in 1982-83 saw them hammered 5-0 at Goodison Park, future Villa player Adrian Heath scoring twice for the Merseysiders.

In front of the 'live' TV cameras, Ian Olney and David Platt both scored twice when Villa beat Everton 6-2 at home in November 1989....their biggest League win over the Liverpool club. Later that season (5 May) six goals were shared at Goodison Park, Villa coming back from 2-0 down to lead 3-2 before succumbing to Kevin Sheedy's 81st minute penalty.

On 19 October 1991 Aston Villa fielded eight black players in their 2-0 away League win at Everton: B Small, P McGrath, D Yorke, C Regis, D Atkinson, M Blake and A Daley while U Ehiogu was on the subs' bench.

Villa's first defeat in the Premiership was 1-0 against Everton at Goodison Park on 25 August 1992.

The first time two Australian-born goalkeepers played against each other in a Premiership match was in February 1993 - Mark Bosnich for Villa and Jason Kearton for Everton. In this same game, the fans also saw in action a Pole, a Yugoslav, a Tobagan, a German, a Welshman, an Irishman, a Scot and a few Englishmen!

John Fashanu and Phil King both made their League debuts for Villa in the 2-2 draw at Everton on 20 August 1994. Fashanu celebrated with a goal.

A late Paul Merson goal gave Villa a 1-0 win at Goodison Park in a 'live TV' Premiership game in November 2000.

Villa won six successive home Premiership games against Everton: 1995-2001. The results were: 1-0, 3-1, 2-1, 3-0, 3-0 and 2-1 in that order. Everton is the club Villa have played most times in League football and scored most League goals against!

Among the players who made the Villa debuts in games against Everton are Frank Moss jnr (1938), Doug Winton (FAC in 1959), Ray

*Walking out to Wembley before the 1977 League Cup Final.*

THE COMPLETE ENCYCLOPAEDIA OF ASTON VILLA F.C.    THE COMPLETE ENCYCLOPAEDIA OF ASTON VILLA F.C.

88

Bloomfield (1964) and Gary Williams (1978).

Villa's first meeting with Everton in the FA Cup was in the 1897 Final at The Crystal Palace. A crowd of 65,891 saw the Merseysiders beaten 3-2 as Villa completed the first part of the double.

Eight years later Villa again beat Everton, this time in a semi-final replay at Nottingham.

Over 60,600 fans saw Villa lose a home quarter-final tie against Everton in February 1953 and there were 60,225 spectators present at Goodison Park when Ron Wylie bagged a hat-trick in Villa's excellent 4-1 win in the 5th round in February 1959.

Andy Gray scored against his future club when Villa lost a 3rd round FA Cup-tie 4-1 at Everton in January 1978 and goals by Steve Stone and Benito Carbone (who was sent-off in the last minute) gave Villa a 2-1 quarter-final victory on Merseyside in February 2000.

On their way to reaching the 1975 League Cup Final, Villa defeated Everton 3-0 at Goodison Park in a 2nd round replay.

Two years later the 1977 League Cup Final between the two clubs went to a third match before Villa won 3-2 at neutral Old Trafford with a last-gasp goal from Brian Little. It was a tension-packed night in front of 54,749 spectators. Everton scored first via former Birmingham City star Bob Latchford. Chris Nicholl (with a left-foot cracker) and Brian Little then edged Villa ahead at 2-1 before the Merseysiders levelled things up through Mick Lyons, only for Little to clinch victory for Villa in the very last minute.

The first encounter at Wembley had finished goalless whilst the replay at Hillsborough had ended 1-1. The total attendance figure for those three League Cup Final encounters was a staggering 205,812 with over 96,000 at Wembley.

Everton gained some revenge by beating Villa 2-1 on aggregate in the 1984 League Cup semi-final.

Villa beat Everton 3-1 in a challenge match in front of 21,000 fans in the national Stadium, Mauritius in May 1993.

Players with both clubs include: W Aspinall, HE Banks, E Barrett, K Bradley (Amateur at Goodison Park), G Farrelly, J Gidman, BC Godfrey, W Groves, AM Gray, TP Griffiths, AP Heath, PT Heard, D Hickson, T Johnson, MR Keown, S McMahon, K McNaught, H Morton, D Mountfield, M Pejic, G Peyton (Villa reserve), K Richardson, P Rideout, BD Rioch, LR Rouse, B Sharp, JS Sharp (also Chairman of Everton), S Teale (Everton apprentice), C Tiler, D Unsworth (no senior games for Villa), S Watson, J Whitley, EML Williams (Villa trialist/reserve, Everton Amateur).

Also: GF Lee (Villa player, Everton manager), J Mercer R Saunders (Everton players, Villa managers), A Hateley (Villa player, Everton FC lottery staff), A Proudler (Villa player, Everton coach), J Barron (coach at both clubs).

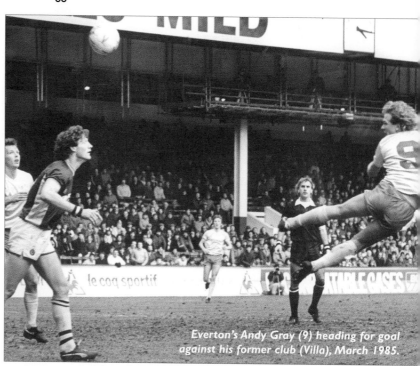

Everton's Andy Gray (9) heading for goal against his former club (Villa), March 1985.

A small, clever winger, able to occupy both flanks but preferring the right, Tommy Ewing actually started his career as a left-back but found marking players far too strenuous! He was unlucky with injuries during his time in Scotland, although he did win two full caps for his country in 1958 and represented the Scottish League, also playing in two losing League Cup Finals with Partick in 1957 and 1959. He netted seven goals in 45 first team appearances for Villa when taking over from fellow Scot Jimmy MacEwan.

## EXETER CITY

Villa's record against the Grecians:

### FA Cup

| Venue | P | W | D | L | F | A |
|---|---|---|---|---|---|---|
| Home | 1 | 1 | 0 | 0 | 2 | 0 |
| Away | 2 | 2 | 0 | 0 | 3 | 1 |
| Totals | 3 | 3 | 0 | 0 | 5 | 1 |

### League Cup

| Venue | P | W | D | L | F | A |
|---|---|---|---|---|---|---|
| Home | 1 | 1 | 0 | 0 | 8 | 1 |
| Away | 2 | 2 | 0 | 0 | 7 | 2 |
| Totals | 3 | 3 | 0 | 0 | 15 | 3 |

A crowd of 10,570 paid record receipts of £80,000 to see Villa beat the Grecians 1-0 in an FA Cup 3rd round tie at St James' Park in January 1994. Dean Saunders' 59th minute penalty decided the issue.

Just before the Great War, Villa had twice knocked Exeter out of the FA Cup, winning 2-1 (away) in 1913-14 and 2-0 (at home) in 1914-15.

Gary Williams, who hadn't scored a single goal in more than 200 senior appearances for Villa, suddenly netted twice when Exeter were defeated 8-1 at home in the second leg of a first round League Cup-tie in October 1985. In the first leg Simon Stainrod, making his debut, scored all Villa's goals in their 4-1 win at St James' Park.

Players with both clubs include: WCW Armfield, P Birch, NG Blake (also Exeter manager), VP Blore (Villa reserve), F Cornan, LA Dennington, DW Gibson, P King, GS Parker, L Phillips, AF Phoenix, CL Roberts (Villa reserve), AJ Scott, PS Varco, RJ Wilson.

Also: FH Broome (Villa player, Exeter manager: 2 spells), BC Godfrey (Villa player, Grecians manager), CH Spiers (Villa player, Exeter manager), M Musgrove (coach at both Exeter & Villa)

## EWING, THOMAS

Born: Swinhill, Lanarkshire, 2 May 1937.

Career: Larkhall Thistle, Partick Thistle (April 1955), Aston Villa (£20,000, February 1962), Partick Thistle (July 1964), Greenock Morton (August 1966), Hamilton Academical (July 1967, then manager for a year from November 1969). Later became a licensee in Scotland.

Tommy Ewing

THE COMPLETE ENCYCLOPAEDIA OF ASTON VILLA F.C.  THE COMPLETE ENCYCLOPAEDIA OF ASTON VILLA F.C.

89

## EYRE, EDMUND

Born: Worksop, 2 December 1882. Died: Worksop, c 1943.
Career: Worksop West End, Worksop, Rotherham Town, Birmingham (March 1907), Aston Villa (December 1908), Middlesbrough (April 1911), Birmingham (April 1914). Retired, May 1919.

Edmund 'Ninty' Eyre was a direct winger who hugged the touchline. He had good pace and the ability to beat a defender and get in a telling cross. He was a prolific goalscorer during the early part of his career (especially with Worksop) when he played through the middle, being converted to a winger whilst at St Andrew's. He and Albert Hall contested the left-wing position at Villa Park and Eyre scored five times in 31 appearances for the club before moving to Middlesbrough. He netted a total of 17 goals in 82 games in his two spells with Blues and 15 in 69 starts for Middlesbrough.

## FAMILY CONNECTIONS

### Brotherly Love

The following sets of brothers have all been associated with Aston Villa Football Club (mainly players): Albert & Arthur Brown (1870s/early '80s), James & John (Jack) Cowan (1890s), John (Jack), Harry & Will Devey (one or all at club between 1887 and 1902), Scots Jimmy & William Gibson (late 1920s), the Hamptons, George & Harry (team-mates in 1914-15), the Hardys (George in the 1930s and Sam Hardy prior to that), the Hunters, Andy & Archie (1879-84), Sammy & Tom Law (1880s), Alan & Brian Little (1970s), Eddie & Reg Lowe (1940s), Alec & James Logan (at Villa Park 1907-09), Albert & John McLachlan (together in 1913-14), George & Harold Matthews (colleagues in the mid-1870s), Amos & Frank Moss (1950s), George & Walter Page (also playing partners in the mid-1870s), Bruce & Neil Rioch (Villans in the 1970s), Bert & Jack Sharp (with Villa, 1897-99), Harry & Joe Simmonds (defenders, early 1880s), Clem, George & Jimmy Stephenson (who all represented the club between 1910-27), the two Vinalls, Albert & Ted (the former a player, the latter a scout) and the two Welsh internationals, Ernie and Mart Watkins (late 1890s/early 1900s).

* The Arce brothers - Hector and Oscar - were both at Villa Park in 1968-69, Oscar being the more prominent player, but neither made the grade in England and they quickly returned home to South America!

### Family Talk

The three Stephenson brothers were together at Villa Park from November 1919 until March 1921. Clem was associated with the club from March 1910 until March 1921, George from November 1919 until November 1927 and Jimmy from April 1914 to May 1921. Between them the three brothers amassed well over 1,100 appearances in competitive club football (1,024 at League level) with Clem totalling 441 in the First Division alone. Clem and George both had spells as team manager of Huddersfield Town. George's son, Bob, played for Derby County, Shrewsbury and Rochdale.

The Buckley brothers, Chris and Franklin (the Major), were born on the same day (9 November)...Chris in 1887 followed Franklin, born in 1883.

Brothers Amos and Frank Moss junior played together in the Aston Villa half-back line more than 50 times during the 1950s.

Brothers Graham and Ron Atkinson were both registered together at Villa Park in the late 1950s. Neither made the first team, but later they did supremely well in the same Oxford United side, with Ron later returning to manage Villa.

Twins Harry Devey and Arthur Devey were both associated with Villa, although Arthur was only a trialist. There were eight brothers and one sister in the Devey family.

Father and son - Frank Moss senior, father to Frank Moss junior - both occupied the centre-half position for Aston Villa and both players skippered the side.

Aston Villa's reserve outside-left of the 1890s, Billy Dorrell, was the father of Arthur Dorrell, who came to the fore after the First Great War.

Danny Blanchflower's brother, Jackie, was seriously injured in the Munich air crash of 1958.

Barrie Hole's father, Will, along with his two bothers, Alan and Colin, all played professional football for Swansea Town, the latter two in 1953-54 and Will in the 1920s.

Villa's 1960s striker Tony Hateley's son, Mark, played in the same position for Portsmouth, QPR, Leeds United, Coventry City, Glasgow Rangers, Hull City and England.

Tom Perry, Villa's right-half at the start of the 20th century, had two other footballing brothers - Walter (the eldest) and Charlie. All three players gave excellent service to West Bromwich Albion. Tom and Charlie also played for England.

Michael Oakes' father, Alan, played in 764 League games for Manchester City, Chester City and Port Vale (1959-84).

Reuben Hazell (Villa reserve: 1997-99) is the cousin of former Wolves and QPR defender, Bob Hazell.

Andy Townsend's father, Don, was a full-back with Charlton Athletic and Crystal Palace. He made 326 League appearances (1954-65).

Between 1979 and 1995 Villa full-back Mike Pejic's brother Mel played for Stoke City, Hereford United and Wrexham and made over 400 League appearances for the Bulls and 100 plus for the Welsh club.

Goalkeeper Peter Enckelman's father, Goran, won full international honours for Finland in the 1970s.

Con Martin's son, Mick, was a midfield player with Manchester United, West Bromwich Albion and Newcastle United during the 1970s/80s and he, like his father, also represented the Republic of Ireland.

Ken McNaught's father, Willie, won full international caps for Scotland.

Syd Howarth's father, Tommy, played League football for Bristol City in 1913-14. He was also registered with Bury.

Fred Wheldon's brother Sam also played professional football with WBA.

Bruce Rioch's son, Gregor, became a professional footballer, playing for Luton Town, Barnet, Hull City, Peterborough United & Macclesfield Town (1993-2001).

Peter Withe's brother, Chris, played for Bradford City and his son Jason was a professional with WBA.

Tom Niblo's son, Alan, was an amateur trialist with Newcastle United while his grandson, Alan junior, captained Wolves' reserve side.

Hugh O'Donnell (ex-Celtic, PNE, Blackpool, Rochdale & Halifax Town) was the younger brother of Frank O'Donnell who played for Aston

*The Stephenson brothers: George, Clem and Jimmy.*

Villa in 1938-39.

Aston Villa hard man Dicky Dorsett was the nephew of the former West Bromwich Albion and Manchester City brothers George and Joe Dorsett.

John Roxborough's brother Andrew also played professional football for Leicester City and they appeared in the same Foxes' side together in 1920-21. A third Roxborough sibling, Walter, had trials with Leicester in 1921.

Ex-Villa midfielder Gary Shelton's son, Andy, played for Chester City in the Nationwide Conference in 2000-01.

Gordon Cowans' father was kit man and steward at Aston Villa's Youth hotel during the 1960s.

1930s Villa winger Tommy Moore was the grandson of Isaac Moore, who was with the club in 1889-90.

Archie 'Aussie' Campbell was the nephew of the 1890s Aston Villa forward John Campbell.

Alec McClure's brother, Sammy, played for Blackburn Rovers while his nephew, Joe, served with Everton.

Alec Leake's cousin, Jimmy Windridge, played for Birmingham, as did Leake himself.

Brothers Albert and Ted Vinall were together at Villa Park in 1939-40 while another brother, Jack, played for Sunderland, Norwich City, Luton Town, Coventry City and Walsall and was appointed as an Aston Villa scout in the 1950s.

Fergus Johnstone, an Aston Villa vice-President in the 1870s, was the father of Villa forward Charlie Johnstone who later joined the Board of Directors and also became a vice-President of the club.

Lee Hendrie's father, Paul, played for Villa's near-neighbours Birmingham City while his Scottish-born cousin, John, starred for Coventry City, Hereford United, Bradford City, Newcastle United, Leeds United, Barnsley and Middlesbrough.

John Fashanu's elder brother, Justinus Soni Fashanu, who committed suicide in 1998, scored over 80 goals in more than 275 League and Cup appearances between 1978-92 when playing for nine different major clubs including Norwich City, Nottingham Forest, Southampton, Manchester City and West Ham.

Villa's 1928-30 full-back John Thomas Brittleton was the son of the former England international Tom Brittleton, who played League football for Stockport County, Sheffield Wednesday and Stoke between 1902-25.

Irish international Archie Goodall's brother, John, also played for Preston North End, Glossop North End and Derby County.

Alan Deakin's brother, Mike, played for Crystal Palace, Aldershot and Northampton Town.

The scorer of Villa's first-ever League goal in 1888, Tommy Green, was the father of the West Bromwich Albion, West Ham United and Coventry City player of the 1930s who had the same name.

Jimmy Dugdale, Villa's centre-half from 1956-62, is the uncle of the former Barnsley, Coventry City and Charlton Athletic defender Alan Dugdale.

Joe Spence, the uncle of Aston Villa's goalscorer from 1929-34, George Brown, had a distinguished playing career with Manchester United and England.

Bert Lyons, younger brother of Aston Villa full-back Tommy Lyons played for Clapton Orient and Tottenham Hotspur during the 1930s.

Billy Fraser, the father of the 1960s Aston Villa full-back Cammie Fraser, played League football for Aldershot and Northampton Town.

Larry Canning was the cousin of the former Scottish international Alex Venters who also played for Blackburn Rovers and Glasgow Rangers.

Roy Chapman (1950s Villa forward) is the father of Lee Chapman, a striker with Stoke City, Arsenal, Sheffield Wednesday, Nottingham Forest, Leeds United, West Ham United etc (1980s/90s).

Terry Morrall's uncle was George 'Lofty' Morrall, who played for Birmingham in the 1931 FA Cup Final v. West Brom.

Cecil Victor Harris (Aston Villa: 1922-26) was Eric Houghton's uncle.

Cyrille Regis and Dave Regis are related to athlete John Regis.

## FANZINES & SUPPORTERS' MAGAZINES

The Aston Villa Supporters' Association monthly magazine 'Villazine' was first launched in 1967.

Aston Villa first published the club's Villa Times in 1971 and then a magazine called The Villa News (issue 1) was first published (by The Daily News) in January 1991....but this soon faded away!

Since then several other official and unofficial club publications have been produced including the one-time best-selling magazine 'Claret & Blue' compiled by Bernard Gallagher and published by Sports Projects (Birmingham).

Nowadays Dave Woodhall produces the Villa Fanzine: Heroes & Villans, while Steve Whitehouse releases Holy Trinity & Holte Enders.

## FARRELL, DAVID WILLIAM
Born: Birmingham, 11 November 1971
Career: Redditch United, Aston Villa (£45,000, January 1992), Scunthorpe United (on loan, January 1993), Wycombe Wanderers (£100,000, September 1995), Peterborough United (free transfer, July 1997).

Dave Farrell is a pacy winger who found it difficult to adjust to League action following his move from Redditch in 1992. He made only eight appearances for Aston Villa (in three-and-a-half years) before moving down the ladder to Adams Park for a Wycombe club record fee of £100,000. Farrell scored the first League hat-trick of his career - in the 2000 Third Division semi-final play-off which helped send Barry Fry's Peterborough through to Wembley and subsequent victory by 1-0 (and promotion) at the expense of Darlington. During the course of the 2000-01 campaign, Farrell passed the personal milestone of 250 senior appearances as a full-time professional.

## FARRELLY, GARETH
Born: Dublin, 28 August 1975.
Career: Aston Villa (YTS, June 1991, professional, January 1992), Rotherham United (on loan, March 1995), Everton (£700,000, July 1997), Bolton Wanderers (on loan, November 1998, signed permanently the following month).

Midfielder Gareth Farrelly made only nine first team appearances for Aston Villa before being sold to Everton in 1997. He developed his game considerably at Goodison Park and after 30 outings for the Merseysiders he went on to establish himself at The Reebok Stadium, scoring on his debut for Bolton with his second touch of the ball against Sheffield United at Bramall Lane.

Farrelly, who helped Bolton win the First Division play-offs final in 2001, has been honoured by the Republic of Ireland at senior (6 caps), 'B' (1), Under-21 (11), Youth and Schoolboy levels.

## FASHANU, JOHN
Born: Kensington, London, 18 September 1962.
Career: Cambridge United (juniors from 1977), Norwich City (October 1979), Crystal Palace (on loan, August 1983), Lincoln City (on loan September-November 1983, signed for £15,000 December 1983), Millwall (£55,000, November 1984), Wimbledon (£125,000, March 1986), Aston Villa (£1,35 million, June 1994). Retired to become a TV personality (featuring on the Gladiators) and also joined a religious sect, becoming an Ambassador for the Third World.

Striker John Fashanu's stay at Villa Park was dogged by ill-luck. He was not quite match-fit when he arrived, struggled with an Achilles injury soon afterwards and then underwent dental work before suffering a career-threatening knee ligament injury in a Premiership game against Manchester United, which saw him stretchered off. Although he didn't know it, Fashanu's playing days ended there - after just 16 games for Villa (3 goals scored).

Capped twice by England (v Chile

THE COMPLETE ENCYCLOPAEDIA OF ASTON VILLA F.C.     THE COMPLETE ENCYCLOPAEDIA OF ASTON VILLA F.C.

91

and Scotland, 1989), Fashanu had an exciting career overall. A robust, all-action, brave and determined striker, he appeared in a total of 463 League and Cup games and scored 162 goals. For Wimbledon alone he netted 132 times in 331 appearances and gained an FA Cup winners medal in 1988 when the Dons beat Liverpool 1-0.

In 1995, goalkeepers Bruce Grobbelaar and Hans Segers along with Fashanu (then of Aston Villa) were charged with alleged match-fixing. (See Court Cases).

● John's elder brother, Justinus Soni (Justin Fashanu) sadly committed suicide in 1998.

## FENCOTT, KENNETH SYDNEY W.

Born: Walsall, 27 December 1943.

Career: Walsall Boys, Staffordshire & Birmingham County FA, Aston Villa (amateur March 1959, professional January 1961), Lincoln City (June 1964), Tamworth (August 1967), Blakenhall (season 1968-69). Later ran a Driving School in Birmingham.

A reserve utiluty forward, Ken Fencott was handed only five first team outings by Villa with his League baptism coming against Bolton Wanderers in November 1961 at outside-left. He scored on his debut for the Imps for whom he played in all five forward-line positions, making 73 appearances and netting 13 goals before drifting into non-League soccer.

## FENERBAHCE

Villa's playing record against the Turkish side:
UEFA Cup

| Venue | P | W | D | L | F | A |
|-------|---|---|---|---|---|---|
| Home | 1 | 1 | 0 | 0 | 4 | 0 |
| Away | 1 | 1 | 0 | 0 | 2 | 0 |
| Totals | 2 | 2 | 0 | 0 | 6 | 0 |

Aston Villa had the pleasure of registering their first-ever victory in a European competition over the Turkish side Fenerbahce, whom they defeated 4-0 at home in a 1st round 1st leg encounter on 14 September 1977. John Deehan (2), Andy Gray and Brian Little scored the goals in front of 30,351 spectators. A fortnight later in-form Villa won 2-0 in Turkey to go through 6-0 on aggregate.

Players with both clubs: D Atkinson, AF Ozalan.

## FENTON, GRAHAM ANTHONY

Born: Wallsend, 22 May 1974.

Career: Aston Villa (YTS, June 1990, professional, February 1992), West Bromwich Albion (on loan, January 1994), Blackburn Rovers (£1.5 million, November 1995), Leicester City (£1.1 million, August 1997), Walsall (free transfer, March 2000), Stoke City (August-September 2000), St Mirren (October 2000), Blackpool (2001).

A decidedly quick, all-purpose, right-sided utility forward, Graham Fenton came on 21 times as a substitute during his 39 games for Aston Villa (three goals scored). Fenton found it hard going at times following his big-money transfer to Ewood Park but battled on before switching to Filbert Street at the start of the 1997-98 season. Fenton twice helped Villa win the League Cup (in 1994 and 1996) and he also gained one England Under-21 cap, later adding a third League Cup Winners' prize to his tally in 2000.

## FERGUSON, MICHAEL KEVIN

Born: Burnley, 9 March 1943.

Career: Burnley Schools, Plymouth Argyle (amateur, March 1959), Accrington Stanley (professional, June 1960), Blackburn Rovers (£1,500, March 1962), Aston Villa (£55,000, May 1968), Queen's Park Rangers (£11,500, November 1969), Cambridge United (July 1973), Rochdale (July 1974), Los Angeles Aztecs, NASL (April-August 1975),

IA Akranes, Iceland (player/coach 1975-76), Halifax Town (December 1976). Retired in May 1977. Rochdale (manager September 1977-November 1978). Thereafter coached around the world, mainly in the Middle East during the 1980s before managing non-League Enfield for a couple of months in 1989.

A well-built, strong-running midfielder, who could also play at right-back and as an orthodox winger, Mike Ferguson's registration papers became the property of the Football League when Accrington Stanley went bankrupt in 1962, Blackburn had to pay the £1,500 transfer fee to the League for his services. He joined Villa for a club record £55,000 in 1968 but made only 40 appearances (two goals scored - one after a quite brilliant 50-yard dribble which took him past six players) before switching to QPR. He played his best football at Ewood Park (36 goals in 248 outings) and later helped IA Akranes win the Icelandic League title in 1976. Ferguson was sacked as manager of Rochdale after a humiliating FA Cup defeat at the hands of non-League Droylsden.

*Mike Ferguson.*

When he joined Blackburn, Ferguson was referred to as a flawed diamond - the flaw, which frustrated fans and management alike, was a suspect temperament (he was sent-off three times during his career - each time for lashing out at an opponent).

## FERRARESI, FABIO

Born: Fano, Italy, 24 May 1979

Career: Cesena, Aston Villa (August 1998-May 2000), Cesena (July 1999).

Capable midfielder, Fabio Ferraresi failed to make an impression during his brief liaison with English football. He made just one substitute appearance for Aston Villa in the away leg of their UEFA Cup-tie clash with Stromsgodset in 1998-99.

## FESTIVAL OF BRITAIN

Aston Villa were scheduled to play two homes games to celebrate the Festival of Britain in 1951....they only played one, the fixture against Sparta being postponed.

The other fixture, played on 19 May against the Danish club Frem of Copenhagen ended in a 1-1 draw in front of 15,000 spectators.

## FIGHT BACKS

Aston Villa trailed Notts County 3-0 in a 5th round FA Cup-tie at Meadow Lane in March 1883. They fought back to 3-3, then had a goal-bound shot handled on the line (no penalties in those days) but then gave away a late goal to lose a seven-goal thriller 4-3.

In February 1900 Villa scored twice in the last four minutes of their League game against Derby County to win 3-2.

Manchester United led Villa 3-0 in a First Division game at Old Trafford on the opening day of the 1930-31 season (31 August). But a brilliant four-goal solo performance by 'Pongo' Waring saw Villa storm back to win the game, Waring's last strike coming in the final minute to stun the 38,000 crowd.

Playing Plymouth Argyle at home in a Second Division game in February 1937 Villa found themselves 3-0 down after half-an-hour's

THE COMPLETE ENCYCLOPAEDIA OF ASTON VILLA F.C.    THE COMPLETE ENCYCLOPAEDIA OF ASTON VILLA F.C.

92

play. They stormed back to win the match 5-4, Eric Houghton scoring a hat-trick.

Villa were 4-0 down to Liverpool in a home Second Division match in March 1960, but they fought back to earn a point from a 4-4 draw. Villa could have won but Peter McParland fired over from four yards with virtually the last kick of the game.

Spurs led Villa 5-1 in a First Division encounter at White Hart Lane in March 1966 but Tony Hateley never gave up trying and his four goals earned Villa point as they fought back to draw 5-5.

Villa have made several comebacks against Spurs!

## FINDLAY, JOHN WILLIAMSON

Born: Blairgowrie, Perth, 13 July 1954

Career: Perth Schools, Aston Villa (apprentice, July 1970, professional June 1972), Luton Town (November 1978), Barnsley (on loan, September 1983), Derby County (on loan, January 1984), Swindon Town (July 1985), Portsmouth (January 1986), Coventry City (August, 1986). Retired through injury, May 1989.

Goalkeeper Jake Findlay joined Villa on leaving school in 1970. A Scottish Youth international trialist, he helped the intermediates win the FA Youth Cup in 1972 but was always 'in reserve' at Villa Park and in 1978 - after 17 outings for the club - he moved to Kenilworth Road. He was eventually forced to retire through injury in 1989. He played 178 League games for Luton, gaining a Second Division championship medal in 1982, but failed to get a single first team outing with either Pompey or the Sky Blues. Findlay - who weighed over 14 stone in his prime - was rewarded with a testimonial match in August 1989 when Coventry City met WBA at Highfield Road.

## FINES

● Goalkeeper Mark Bosnich was fined £1,000 and severely reprimanded by the FA after his 'Hitler style' salute to the fans at White Hart Lane in 1996.

● James Cowan was fined four weeks wages by Aston Villa after travelling up to Scotland to take part in the famous Powderhall Sprint during the 1896-7 season

● Stan Collymore was fined several times for alleged misbehaviour while playing for Liverpool, Aston Villa and Leicester City.

● Aston Villa manager John Gregory has been fined and banned from the touchline after being banished from the bench during a

Premiership game.

● Dean Saunders was once fined for disorderly behaviour in an Essex night club.

● One-time Aston Villa manager Tommy Docherty was fined £100 and suspended after making unkindly remarks to a referee.

● Aston Villa FC was fined £25 by the Football Association for 'losing' the FA Cup in 1895.

● Villa were fined £50 by the FA after they had 'poached' and then 'signed' goalkeeper Billy George out of the Army in 1897.

● Defender Gareth Southgate was fined £5,000 by his manager after being sent-off during Villa's Premiership game at Leicester in 1999.

● Aston Villa FC was fined £9,000 in November 1994, following a pitch invasion by home and away supporters at the end of their UEFA Cup clash with Trabzonspor at Villa Park. Villa had to play their next European home game behind closed doors as a further punishment.

● In 1992-93 Aston Villa (and Notts County) were fined for breaking the 'transfer' regulations when approaching and signing players from Australia.

## FIRSTS

● It is now thought that the first pre-arranged 'football' match played by Aston Villa was against Aston Park Unity in Aston Park on a cold Saturday afternoon in January 1875. There are no clear references as to what the final score might have been, suffice to say Villa seemingly 'lost a closely fought contest.'

● Two months later - on 13 March 1875 - a 15-a-side contest took place between Villa and Aston Brook St Mary's rugby club on a strip of waste ground in Wilson Road, Aston. Around 200 spectators saw Villa record their first victory by 1-0, Jack Hughes scoring the goal in the 70th minute with a ball hired from a Wednesbury shop for just 1s 6d (about 8p). The first half was played under Rugby Union rules, the second half under football rules. With play rather congested at times, Villa fielded this team: W. Scattergood (goalkeeper); W Weiss, WH Price, F Knight, E Lee, G Matthews, H Matthews, C Midgely (defenders) and J Hughes, W Such, H Whateley, G Page, A Robbins, WD Mason and W Sothers (forwards).

● Villa's first officially appointed captain was George Matthews in 1875.

● Villa's first trophy success was the winning of the Birmingham Senior Cup in 1880.

*Villa taking the field before the first all-ticket F.A. Cup Final at Wembley in 1924.*

THE COMPLETE ENCYCLOPAEDIA OF ASTON VILLA F.C.    THE COMPLETE ENCYCLOPAEDIA OF ASTON VILLA F.C.

93

● Villa were the first Midland club to win the FA Cup, doing so in 1887 (beating West Bromwich Albion 2-0 in the Final).

● Tommy Green scored Villa's first League goal against Wolverhampton Wanderers (away) on 8 September 1888.

● Villa's first League hat-trick was scored by Albert Allen against Notts County (won 9-1) on 29 September 1888.

● Aston Villa was the first English professional club to tour Germany (1901).

On 12 March 1892 Villa became the first team to score a dozen goals in a League game - beating Accrington 12-2 at Perry Barr.

● In 1953 Villa and Sunderland became the first two clubs to oppose each other in 100 League matches.

● The first League Cup game to be played on a Saturday was the 1st leg of the semi-final encounter between Sunderland and Aston Villa in January 1963.

● Aston Villa was the first club to reach the milestone of 6,000 League goals when Mark Walters netted against Bournemouth in October 1987 (Division 2).

● The first substitute used by Villa in a League game was Bobby Parker against Tottenham Hotspur (home) in September 1965 (Division 1) and the first substitute to score for Villa was Lew Chatterley against Blackpool in January 1967 (see Substitutes).

● The first African-born footballers to play for Villa were the Zambian duo of Emment Kapengwa and Freddie Mwila in 1969.

● Kapwenge then became the first black footballer to play in a League game for Aston Villa, making his debut for the club against Carlisle United (at home) on 12 November 1969 (Division 2).

● The first hat-trick scored at Villa Park was on 1 September 1897 by Aston Villa's Fred Wheldon against Sheffield Wednesday in a League Division One game.

● The first Villa players to win a full international caps - Howard Vaughton and Albert Brown - both appeared in the same match - for England against Ireland in Belfast in February 1882.

● The first all-ticket game at Wembley was the 1924 FA Cup Final between Aston Villa and Newcastle United.

● Dixie Dean scored the first of his record-breaking 349 League goals for Everton against Aston Villa on 28 March 1925.

● The first 70,000 plus attendance at Villa Park saw the FA Cup-tie against Arsenal in February 1926. It was 71,446.

● In June 1934 Villa appointed their first full-time manager - Jimmy McMullan.

● Villa purchased their first training round in 1952 - from the Aston Unity cricket club in Trinity Road.

● Frank Moss was the first Villa player to captain England at Wembley (v Scotland in 1924).

● The first electric scoreboard was erected at Villa Park in 1981.

● Villa were the first team to play in 100 League Cup matches, reaching that milestone during the 1980-81 season.

● The first international match featuring 22 professionals was staged at Villa Park on 3 May 1902 when England drew 2-2 with Scotland in front of 15,000 spectators. This was, in fact, the replay of the abandoned international played at Ibrox Park a month earlier, on 5 April, when 26 people were killed and some 500 injured after barriers had collapsed.

● The first time two German-born players starred in the same team in a League game in England was on 27 January 1993 when Stefan Beinlich and Matthius Breitkreutz lined-up for Aston Villa against Sheffield United in the Premiership.

● The first time two Australian-born goalkeepers played against each other in a Premiership match was in February 1993 - Mark Bosnich for Villa and Jason Kearton for Everton.

● Aston Villa were the first club to win the championships of the 1st, 2nd and 3rd Divisions of the Football League, the FA Cup, the League Cup, the European Cup, the European Super Cup, the FA Youth Cup, the Southern Junior Floodlit Cup, the Wartime League Cup, the Central League and the Birmingham & District League.

● Floodlights were used at Villa Park for the first time in 1958.

● Tony Cascarino was Villa's first seven-figure signing - a £1.5 million capture from Millwall in 1990.

## FISH, KENNETH HENRY ALBERT
Born: Capetown, South Africa, 20 February 1914.
Ken Fish was a tall, rangy centre-forward who earned international honours with South Africa where he assisted Railway Association FC

*Ken Fish.*

before joining Villa in 1936, soon after his fellow countryman Gordon Hodgson. He did not make Villa's first team and in November 1937 was transferred to Port Vale. Again he struggled to get first team football, making only six senior appearances for the Potteries' club before being sold to the Swiss side, Young Boys of Berne in October 1938. He returned to the Vale as the club's assistant-trainer in July 1939 and re-signed as a player the following month, only for World War Two to disrupt his progress. In September 1939 he joined the forces and guested for Stafford Rangers during the hostilities. In July 1946 he was appointed trainer of Port Vale and temporarily took control of the team for a short time in November/December 1951. In March 1958, he moved to Birmingham City as trainer-coach and later took a similar position with Oxford United for whom he served right up until the late 1980s.

## FISHER, JAMES ALBERT
Born: Glasgow, June 1879. Died: 4 December 1937.
Career: Caledonians, East Stirlingshire, St Bernard's, Glasgow Celtic (1901), Aston Villa (August 1902), Fulham (August 1903), Bristol City (July 1904), Brighton & Hove Albion (August 1905), Manchester City (June 1906), Bradford Park Avenue (June 1907), non-League football in Scotland (1907-12), Merthyr Town (secretary-manager, June 1912-May 1913), Notts County (secretary-manager, July 1913-May 1927). He later went into business.
As a player, Jim Fisher was a finely-built inside-right, clever with a good clean shot and 'plenty of pluck' near goal. He netted five goals in 18 senior appearances and top-scored for the reserves in the Birmingham & District League during his one season at Villa Park. He was Bristol City's leading marksman in 1904-05 with 13 goals in 26 League outings, and was Merthyr's first 'manager' after the Welsh club had become a Limited Company. He was later named as Notts County's first-ever manager and guided the Magpies to two Second Division championships (1914 and 1923) and the FA Cup semi-final in 1922.

## FISHER, JOHN
Born: Scotland, February 1871. Died: Scotland.
Career: St Bernard's FC, Aston Villa (July 1897), Preston North End (August 1898), Edinburgh Emmett.
Aston Villa's gamble on bringing inside-forward Jock Fisher down from Scotland paid off - he scored five goals in 18 appearances in the one season he spent with the club. He was adept at long range shooting. He stayed at Deepdale barely a month before returning to his homeland.

## FLEMING, JAMES JOHN
Born: Leith, Scotland, September 1864. Died: Scotland, August 1934.
Career: Vale of Leven, Army football with the 93rd Argyll & Sutherland Highlanders, Southampton St Mary's (October-December 1891), Aston Villa (May 1892), Lincoln City (October 1892), Larkhall Saints,

94

Strathclyde (May 1903-95).
An aggressive centre-forward, Jock Fleming made just four first team appearances for Aston Villa, scoring twice on his debut against Everton, (won 4-1). He then 'fell out with the club' and joined Lincoln City. He had earlier signed for Southampton after starring against the Saints in an exhibition match whilst in the Army.

*A floodlit Villa Park in 1958.*

## FLOODLIGHTS
The first set of floodlights - erected in 1958 - cost Aston Villa a fraction over £31,280. The system consisted of four tubular steel towers, each standing 179 feet 10 ins tall. Each tower was topped with a bank of 40 powerful 1500 watt lamps linked with some ten miles of cables
The original set were switched on for the first time at half-time (around 8pm) during Villa's home League game against Portsmouth on Monday 25 September 1958. At the time the score stood at 1-1 and it was down to skipper Johnny Dixon to score the first goal under the Villa Park lights to give his side a 2-1 lead. The game eventually finished in a 3-1 win for Villa with Billy Myerscough and Peter McParland netting the other two goals in front of almost 34,800 spectators.
A little over a month later, on 29 October, the first foreign visitors to play under the lights - GAIS (Gothenburg) - were defeated 3-0 and on 19 November, the Scottish League side Heart of Midlothian came south to play Villa in a friendly and forced a 3-3 draw. Incidentally, on this very same day, manager Eric Houghton's contract was terminated by the club.
Over the next ten years three more big-named European club sides came to play under the lights, Rapid Vienna, Dynamo Kiev and FC Twente Enschede.
In December 1989 Villa Park saw the end of its 4-pylon floodlighting system when one was removed from the Witton Lane/North Bank corner of the ground (replaced by a posh 42-seat executive box) and in March 1990, a second pylon on the Trinity Road/North Stand side was taken away.
Soon afterwards the other two disappeared to make way for a brand new set of modern-day floodlights, standing 160 feet tall, ... designed in the shape of 'AV', which are easily spotted when passing Villa Park along the nearby Aston Expressway and M6 motorway. There were also a total of 61 extra powerful lights placed strategically along the front of the newly-erected Holte End stand and on the gantries of the Trinity Road and Witton Lane stand roofs. The lighting was increased from 400 to 800 lux and all this cost the club around £75,000.

## Rays of Light
Aston Villa's old Lower Grounds Meadow staged a floodlit friendly football match as early as 1878 - electric light bulbs being fixed to poles around the playing area! It was rather primitive - but adequate. However, nothing came of the experiment!
Villa's first appearance under floodlights was in the 1957 FA Charity Shield match against Manchester United at Old Trafford on 19 October 1957 (lost 0-4).
Villa officially opened the floodlights at Stark's Park, home of Raith Rovers, in 1960-61.
On 30 September 1980, Villa sent a team to play Willenhall in a game arranged to 'switch on' the non-League club's new floodlighting system.

## FOLLAN, EDWARD HARVEY
Born: 3 Greenock, Scotland, October 1929
Career: Ardeer Recreation (Ayrshire League), Prescot Cables, Army football, Aston Villa (professional, June 1952), Worcester City (May 1956). Retired through injury, April 1961. Signed by Aston Villa while serving in the Army, Eddie Follan underwent a cartilage operation in 1952 and had to wait until October 1954 before making his Football League debut against Manchester City at Maine Road (won 4-2). A talented inside-forward, he scored seven goals in 36 senior appearances for Villa before drifting into non-League football in 1956.

## FA CHARITY SHIELD
Aston Villa have played for the FA Charity Shield on four occasions.
August 1910 at Stamford Bridge - lost 0-1 to Brighton & HA
October 1957 at Old Trafford - lost 0-4 to Manchester United
August 1972 at Villa Park - lost 0-1 to Manchester City
August 1981 at Wembley - drew 2-2* with Tottenham Hotspur
* Each club held the shield for six months.

### Summary of Matches:
| P | W | D | L | F | A |
|---|---|---|---|---|---|
| 4 | 0 | 1 | 3 | 2 | 8 |

### Charity Shield Facts
A crowd of 15,000 saw non-League Brighton & Hove Albion win the trophy in 1910.
Villa's first game under floodlights was when they visited Old Trafford to play Manchester United in the FA Charity Shield in 1957. Under 28,000 fans saw the Reds gain revenge for the FA Cup defeat at the hands of Villa six months earlier with an emphatic 4-0 victory.
Francis Lee's second-half penalty gave Manchester City their win at Villa Park in 1972 when the attendance was almost 35,000.
Against Spurs at Wembley in 1981, Peter Withe scored both Villa's goals in front of 92,445 spectators who paid record receipts of £431,000.
Two FA Charity Shield matches have been staged at Villa

*Action from the 1972 F.A. Charity game between Villa and Manchester City.*

THE COMPLETE ENCYCLOPAEDIA OF ASTON VILLA F.C.     THE COMPLETE ENCYCLOPAEDIA OF ASTON VILLA F.C.

95

Park - in 1931 when Arsenal beat West Bromwich Albion 1-0 and in 1972 when Villa met Manchester City.
Harold Halse scored six goals for Manchester United against Swindon Town in the Charity Shield match of 1911. He joined Villa in July 1912.

## FA CUP

Villa's full record in this competition reads:

| Venue | P | W | D | L | F | A |
|---|---|---|---|---|---|---|
| Home | 164 | 107 | 27 | 29 | 427 | 173 |
| Away | 170 | 71 | 43 | 54 | 285 | 245 |
| Neutral | 41 | 18 | 6 | 17 | 52 | 58 |
| Totals | 375 | 196 | 76 | 100 | 764 | 476 |

Aston Villa scratched from the competition once.
Draws include games that went to a penalty shoot-out.
Ties re-arranged to either home or away venues are as played (i.e. the tie scheduled to take place at Gravesend in January 1996 has been recorded as a Villa Park encounter).

### Details of Villa's seven FA Cup Final victories:

| | | |
|---|---|---|
| 1887 | Villa 2 West Bromwich Albion 0 | Att. 15,534 |
| 1895 | Villa 1 West Bromwich Albion 0 | Att. 42,562 |
| 1897 | Villa 3 Everton 2 | Att. 65,891 |
| 1905 | Villa 2 Newcastle United 0 | Att. 101,117 |
| 1913 | Villa 1 Sunderland 0 | Att. 121,919 |
| 1920 | Villa 1 Huddersfield Town 0 | Att. 50,018 |
| 1957 | Villa 2 Manchester United 1 | Att. 99,225 |

### Winning Reports

●The 1887 Final at The Kennington Oval (home of Surrey CCC) was a tight affair, especially in the first-half. But 10 minutes after the interval Denny Hodgetts who looked yards offside when he collected Arthur Brown's pass, tricked Albion's goalkeeper Bob Roberts to open the scoring. Archie Hunter sewed things up in the 88th minute

by charging the Albion 'keeper to the ground before scrambling the ball over the line from close range.

●The only goal of the 1895 FA Cup Final against West Bromwich Albion at The Crystal Palace was scored after just 39 seconds. Jack Devey kicked-off for Villa. Denny Hodgetts passed to Steve Smith on the left. He quickly switched play with a long ball over to the right to find Charlie Athersmith whose low, hard centre was met by Bob Chatt. His shot struck the legs of the Albion 'keeper Bob Roberts and rebounded back off Chatt and over the line. Some reports say that Devey followed up to get the last touch - but after the game Chatt said it was 'my goal.'
A dead 'throstle' (a thrush) was placed in the window of a shop in Aston prior to the 1895 FA Cup Final!

● When Villa beat Everton 3-2 in the 1897 FA Cup Final, all five goals were scored in the first half between the 18th and 42nd minutes... and there could well have been five more! Villa struck first when Johnny Campbell found the net following excellent work down the right by Charlie Athersmith and Jack Devey. Five minutes later Jack Bell took Abraham Hartley's measured pass in his stride to equalise for Everton, who then edged in front soon afterwards when Dick Boyle smashed home a direct free-kick after John Cowan had been penalised 20 yards from goal. Villa, tough and resilient, bounced back immediately and after two splendid saves by the Everton 'keeper Bob Menham, Jimmy Crabtree found Fred Wheldon with a brilliant pass for the equaliser. Three minutes from the interval Jack Reynolds sent over a looping cross from the right and the alert Crabtree darted forward to plant a downward header past the groping figure of Menham. Everton dominated the second half for long periods but Villa's defence held firm and the League and Cup double was won.

● Over 30,000 Villa supporters travelled to London for the 1905 Final with Newcastle United at The Crystal Palace and they returned home in triumph after their favourites had won a titanic battle 2-0 against the Geordies. Harry Hampton scored the first goal on three minutes, powering home Joe Bache's pin-point cross from the left. Both 'keepers made fine saves either side of half-time before Hampton clinched victory in the 74th minute with his second goal. Albert Hall fired in a cracking drive, United 'keeper Jimmy Lawrence could not hold the ball and the alert Hampton picked up the pieces.

*Villa's F.A. Cup wining team from 1887.*

● A fine headed goal by Tommy Barber from Charlie Wallace's corner late in the game decided the 1913 Final between Sunderland (the subsequent League champions) and Villa (runners-up) again at The Crystal Palace. During the course of the match Harry Hampton, the Villa centre-forward and Sunderland's centre-half Charlie Thomson were often at loggerheads with each other and on a couple of occasions fists and boots were seen to fly. Both players were spoken to frequently by the referee - Arthur Adams of Nottingham - who chose to take no action. After the game the FA suspended both players and the referee for one match. In the 15th minute Villa's Wallace missed a penalty, awarded after Charlie Gladwin and brought down Clem Stephenson. The night before the Final Stephenson had dreamed that Villa won win 1-0 and that Barber would score the goal. A total of 21 minutes added time was played.

● The winning goal in the 1920 Final at Stamford Bridge arrived in the seventh minute of extra-time. After a dogged affair Billy Kirton's header from Arthur Dorrell's precise corner was deflected into the Huddersfield Town net by defender Tommy Wilson.

● Two weeks before the 1957 Final Manchester United had been well on course to win the treble, the League championship, FA Cup and European Cup. Unfortunately they lost to Real Madrid in the European Cup semis but clinched the First Division title before meeting Villa at Wembley. As early as the sixth minute, however, United had suffered a bitter blow when their goalkeeper Ray Wood collided with Villa's Peter McParland. Wood was stretchered off with a fractured cheekbone (returning later on the wing). Jackie Blanchflower was taken out of defence to play in goal and for 20 minutes United dictated the play. They did so again early in the second-half before McParland hit a post from Les Smith's centre. It was McParland who then struck the first goal in the 68th minute, a powerful header from skipper Johnny Dixon's measured cross. Five minutes later it was 2-0, McParland hooking the ball high into the roof of the net after Dixon had hit a post. United, though, battled on. Wood returned to play outfield and from Duncan Edwards' corner Tommy Taylor reduced the deficit with a looping header eight minutes from time. Villa held on and a delighted

THE COMPLETE ENCYCLOPAEDIA OF ASTON VILLA F.C.  THE COMPLETE ENCYCLOPAEDIA OF ASTON VILLA F.C.

96

Dixon duly collected the trophy. Match referee FB Coutlas (Hull) said afterwards:"McParland's challenge was clumsey, not malicious. It was an accidental collision."

## Villa's three FA Cup Final defeats:

| 1892 | Villa 0 West Bromwich Albion 3 | Att. 32,810 |
| 1924 | Villa 0 Newcastle United 2 | Att. 91,645 |
| 2000 | Villa 0 Chelsea 1 | Att. 78,217 |

## Losing Reports

● Left-winger Jasper Geddes scored Albion's opening goal of the 1892 Final at The Crystal Palace after just four minutes play. Dennis Hodgetts then struck the crossbar as Villa hit back but Sammy Nicholls, taking advantage of hesitation by goalkeeper Jimmy Warner, made it 2-0 from close range on the quarter-of-an-hour mark. Ten minutes into the second-half Jack Reynolds, soon to join Villa, fired home from 30 yards - a shot that Warner should have saved!

● A one-sided Final in 1924 - the first game to be made all-ticket at Wembley, - after the fiasco of 1923! should have been won by Villa. They had 20 chances and failed to score; United on the other hand created two openings, both late on, and found the net each time to gain sweet revenge for the defeat they suffered in 1905. In the 83rd minute Neil Harris fired home from 12 yards after a swift three-man move had opened up the Villa defence and then Jimmy Cowan set up Stan Seymour to score a brilliant second goal two minutes from time, the ball zipping high into the net.

● Chelsea's Italian international midfielder Roberto Di Matteo broke Villa's hearts at Wembley in the Wembley Final of 2000 with his 72nd minute winner. In fairness Villa didn't play at all well and the Londoners deserved their victory. Villa created very few scoring chances and the all-important goal followed Gianfranco Zola's free-kick from the left. David James failed to gather the ball which bounced off Gareth Southgate and fell nicely for Di Matteo to belt into the net from two yards.

## Villa's FA Cup Dosier

First FA Cup-tie v Stafford Road (Wolverhampton) (away) on 13 December 1879 (drew 1-1).
First FA Cup victory v Stafford Road, replay, 24 January 1880 (3-2).
Biggest win: 13-0 v Wednesbury Old Athletic (h) 30 October 1886.
Heaviest defeat: 1-8 at Blackburn Rovers, 2 March 1889.
Biggest away win: 9-0 at Shankhouse, 17 December 1887
Heaviest home defeat: 4-6 v Manchester United, 10 January 1948.
Best unbeaten run: 13 matches - from 30 October 1886 to 17 December 1887 inclusive.
Aston Villa have played an FA Cup Final on four different grounds: The Kennington Oval, The Crystal Palace, Stamford Bridge and Wembley. Besides their ten appearances in the Final, Villa have also played in 19 semi-finals.
Villa are the only team to have won all THREE FA Cups...they lifted the 'first' trophy twice (1887 and 1895 when they famously 'lost' it!), the 'second' twice (1897 and 1905) and the 'third' Cup three times (1913, 1920 and 1957).
Villa's Archie Hunter became the first player to score in every round of the FA Cup - doing so in 1886-87. Hunter has scored most FA Cup goals for Villa - total 33.
Harry Hampton equalled Hunter's feat by scoring in every round of the competition in 1904-05.
Aston Villa were disqualified from the FA Cup competition in 1887-88 after crowd trouble had caused several disruptions to their 5th round home tie against Preston North End which had to be abandoned five

minutes from time with the visitors leading 3-1. In fact, both teams wanted to class the game as a friendly and play again at a later date - but the FA would have none of it. They allowed the score to stand, eliminated Villa and severely censured the club for failing to maintain order and control the spectators.
After that Villa went 12 years (February 1889 to March 1901 inclusive) without losing an FA Cup-tie in front of their own supporters. In that time they played 18 games, won 15 and drew three (all 0-0). Their goal-ratio was impressive: 65 for and 14 against.
Harold Halse played in three FA Cup Finals with three different teams: 1909 with Manchester United (winners), 1913 with Villa (winners) and 1915 with Chelsea (losers).
When winning the FA Cup for the first time in 1886-87, Villa used 14 players. In 1894-95 and 1896-97, a total of 15 were on duty throughout the competition. The club utilised only 13 in 1904-05 (nine being ever-present); in 1912-13 they put 14 into the fray and in 1919-20 a total of 16 were called into action, while in 1956-57, only 12 players lined up - a club record. Ten were ever-present with Billy Myerscough and Derek Pace sharing the centre-forward berth.

Villa scratched from the FA Cup competition in 1879-80 after being drawn away against Oxford University. The committee stunned its supporters by announcing that the club had withdrawn from the competition. No-one, to this day, really knows why, although some suggestions indicate that Villa knew realistically they had no chance against one of the strongest teams in the country and didn't want to get a hiding! Another reason is that they wanted to concentrate on winning the Birmingham Senior Cup!
In 1895 Villa offered a reward of £10 for the 'return' of the Cup after it had been stolen from a shop window in Newton Row, Aston. The FA fined Villa £25 for losing it!
The earliest date an FA Cup Final has been staged was on 15 April 1905 when Villa beat Newcastle United. Five days before they met in that Final, Villa and Newcastle played each other in a First Division match - and only one Newcastle player (Billy Gibson) lined up in both matches!
Between 1892 and 1905 Villa appeared in four FA Cup Finals and six semi-finals, winning the trophy on three occasions.
During the period 1906-12 Villa failed to get beyond the 3rd round, losing twice in the opening round, twice in the second and three times in the third. Later, during the 1934-37 years, they fell at the first hurdle each time and made a third round exit in four successive seasons from 1970 to '74.
The longest FA Cup-tie Villa have been involved in went to a fifth game and lasted 510 minutes. It was a 4th round clash with Doncaster Rovers in 1954-55, Rovers finally winning 3-1 at The Hawthorns. A third round tie in 1886-87 with Wolves was decided in the fourth game after 360 minutes play.
On their way to winning the trophy in 1924 Villa registered three 5-0 victories over West Ham United, Bradford (Park Avenue) and Crystal Palace.
Welshman Dai Astley was the last Villa player to score four goals in an FA Cup-tie - doing so against Sunderland in January 1934 . Villa won 7-2.
Frank O'Donnell had scored in every round of the FA Cup for Preston in 1936-37 before joining Villa. Preston then knocked Villa out of the competition in 1937-38 and 1938-39.
Villa lost an FA Cup match in 1945-46 yet still proceeded into the next round! This was the season when ties were played over two legs up to the semi-final stage. Villa lost their third round, first leg encounter 1-2 at Coventry City but won 2-0 at home to go forward 3-2 on aggregate.
The three fifth round FA Cup games between Charlton Athletic and Villa in 1938 attracted over 200,000 spectators (see attendances) and the two clashes with Chelsea in February 1946 attracted a combined total of 121,352 fans - 65,307 at Stamford Bridge and 56,045 at Villa Park.

THE COMPLETE ENCYCLOPAEDIA OF ASTON VILLA F.C.    THE COMPLETE ENCYCLOPAEDIA OF ASTON VILLA F.C.

97

Villa did not play a single FA Cup-tie in the year 1972....the team were knocked out in that season's competition in the first round by Southend United at Roots Hall on 20 November 1971 and their next game in the competition was at Everton in January 1973.

Ipswich Town, playing in the Football League for the first time, drew 1-1 at Villa Park in a third round tie in 1939 but lost the replay 1-2 at Portman Road.

West Bromwich Albion have been Villa's most frequent opponents in the FA Cup, meeting each other on 14 occasions so far, Villa claiming eight victories to Albion's three.

The following teams knocked Villa out of the FA Cup in the year stated and went on to win the trophy (losing in the Final has not been included): Bury 1903, Tottenham Hotspur 1921, Cardiff 1927, Manchester City 1934, Preston North End 1938, Derby County 1946, Manchester United 1948, Newcastle United 1952, Nottingham Forest 1959, Tottenham Hotspur 1961 and 1962, Manchester United 1963, Southampton 1976, Manchester United 1977, West Ham United 1980, Tottenham Hotspur 1982 and Liverpool 1992.

The following players all appeared in an FA Cup Final for Villa in their first season with the club: Howard Spencer and Tom Wilkes 1895, Albert Evans, Fred Wheldon and Jimmy Whitehouse 1897, Harry Hampton 1905. Tommy Barber, Harold Halse, Sam Hardy, Jimmy Harrop, Jimmy Leach 1913, Frank Barson, Arthur Dorrell, Billy Kirton, Tommy Smart and Billy Walker 1920, Stan Crowther and Billy Myerscough 1957, George Boateng, Benito Carbone and David James 2000.

Stan Crowther played for two clubs in the 1957-58 FA Cup competition - Aston Villa first and then Manchester United.

### FA Cup action against the Minnows

Since entering the Football League in 1888, Villa have opposed the following non—League teams in the FA Cup:

| Date | Rd | Opponents | Venue | Score |
|---|---|---|---|---|
| Feb 1889 | 1 | Witton | home | W 3-2 |
| Jan 1890 | 1 | South Shore | away | W 4-2 |
| Jan 1891 | 1 | The Casuals | home | W 13-1 |
| Jan 1891 | 2 | Stoke | away | L 0-3 |
| Jan 1892 | 1 | Heanor Town | home | W 4-1 |
| Feb 1900 | 1 | Bristol City | away | W 5-0 |
| Feb 1900 | 3 | Millwall Ath | away | D 1-1 |
| | R | Millwall Ath | home | D 0-0 |
| | 2R | Millwall Ath. | Reading | L 1-2 |
| Jan 1901 | 1 | Millwall Ath. | Home | W 5-0 |
| Mar 1903 | 3 | Tottenham Hot | Away | W 3-2 |
| Feb 1904 | 2 | Tottenham Hot | home | L 0-1 |
| Mar 1905 | 3 | Fulham | home | W 5-0 |
| Jan 1906 | 1 | Kings Lynn | home | W 11-0 |
| Feb 1906 | 2 | Plymouth Argyle | Home | D 0-0 |
| | R | Plymouth Argyle | Away | W 5-1 |
| Jan 1911 | 1 | Portsmouth | away | W 4-1 |
| Jan 1912 | 1 | Walsall | home | W 6-0 |
| Feb 1912 | 2 | Reading | home | D 1-1 |
| | R | Reading | away | L 0-1 |
| Feb 1913 | 2 | West Ham Utd | home | W 5-0 |
| Feb 1913 | 3 | Crystal Palace | home | W 5-0 |
| Jan 1914 | 1 | Stoke | home | W 4-0 |
| Jan 1914 | 2 | Exeter City | away | W 2-1 |
| Jan 1915 | 1 | Exeter City | home | W 2-0 |
| Jan 1920 | 2 | Queen's P. Rgs | home | W 2-1 |
| Jan 1996 | 3 | Gravesend | home* | W 3-0 |

*This was initially an away game, but the non-League side switched the tie to Villa Park for financial reasons!

### FA YOUTH CUP

Aston Villa's youngsters have won the coveted FA Youth Cup twice and have been beaten in the Final once.

*Villa's youngsters celebrate F.A. Youth Cup success in 1972.*
*Standing (l-r): F Upton, McDonald, George, Betts, Stark, Brown, Little (A).*
*Ground (l-r): Smith, Melling, Gidman, Findlay, Little (B).*

In 1971-72 Villa won the Cup for the first time, beating Liverpool 5-2 on aggregate in the two-legged Final.

The first leg was played at Villa Park on 17 April 1972 and in front of 16,463 fans John Gidman's penalty gave Villa a slender one goal lead.

A crowd of 16,612 attended the second leg at Anfield eight days later when Villa, playing superbly well, won 4-2 with Betts, Brian Little (2) and Kettle (own-goal) the scorers.

Villa's team for both legs was: Findlay; Gidman, McDonald; A Little, Stark, Melling; Brown, George, Betts, B Little and Brady. Smith substituted for Brady in the second leg.

En-route to that 1972 Final, Villa knocked out, in turn, Boldmere St Michael's 8-0, Port Vale 7-0, West Bromwich Albion 3-1, Birmingham City 2-1 (after a 1-1 draw) and Chelsea 3-0 (also after a 1-1 scoreline) all at home before taking care of Arsenal in the semi-final, 1-0 on aggregate. A record crowd of 19,149 saw the replay with Blues while 16,080 had attended St Andrew's for the first game.

Villa's second Youth Cup success followed in season 1979-80 when they defeated Manchester City 3-2 on aggregate after two tightly-fought Final matches.

A crowd of 8,532 saw Villa win the first leg at Maine Road on 21 April 1980 by 3-1 (Trevor Ames was their hero with a hat-trick) and nine days later City came to Villa Park and won 1-0 in front of 13,514 spectators.

Villa's winning line-up (for both matches) was: Kendall; Taylor, Jones; Mail, Blake, Birch; Hopkins, Heath, Ames, Hutchinson, Walters. Sub. Walker.

This time Villa ousted Derby County 3-2, Hereford United 5-0 (away), Hartlepool United 1-0 (also away) and West Bromwich Albion 3-2 (after a 1-1 draw) before accounting for Millwall 2-0 on aggregate in the semi-final.

Villa lost in the 1977-78 Final to Crystal Palace by a goal to nil at Highbury (a one-off game played on a neutral ground). They had earlier defeated Nuneaton Borough 8-0, Tottenham Hotspur 2-0, Southampton 2-1, Grimsby Town 2-0 and Burnley 4-1 on aggregate in the semis.

### Youth Cup Facts & Figures

Villa first entered the competition in season 1954-55, going out in the opening round when losing humiliatingly by 7-0 at home to West

THE COMPLETE ENCYCLOPAEDIA OF ASTON VILLA F.C.　THE COMPLETE ENCYCLOPAEDIA OF ASTON VILLA F.C.

98

Bromwich Albion, who went on to reach the Final only to lose to the up-and-coming Busby Babes!

Villa went out of the competition in the opening round the following season as well, beaten 2-0 at home by Watford.

Villa's first Youth Cup win was 4-0 against Coventry City in a 1st round replay on 6 October 1956 and in the next round they recorded their best-ever FA Youth Cup victory, hammering the hapless amateur side Pegasus Juniors 15-0 at Villa Park. But then Sheffield Wednesday put paid to any Final ambitions with a 3-2 replay win in round four after a thrilling 4-4 draw at Villa Park.

After an 8-0 drubbing of Burton Albion in the first round in 1957-58, Villa then crashed 3-0 at Molineux to a splendid Wolves side in the next round.

In 1958-59, Villa played eight games in the competition before losing a 5th round replay to West Ham by 3-2 at Upton Park. Among Villa's earlier victims were Port Vale (beaten 7-0) and Barnsley (whipped 5-0).

Excellent wins over Leicester (4-1), Derby County (4-1) and Wolves (5-1) all went to waste as Villa lost 3-0 in the 5th round to Chelsea in 1959-60.

The following season Peterborough 4-1, Northampton 5-2 and Derby 1-0 were all defeated before Villa lost in round four at Stoke by 2-0.

A total of 36 goals were scored in Villa's five Youth Cup games in 1961-62. Coventry were crushed 9-1, Leicester slammed 4-1, Port Vale licked 12-1 and Nottingham Forest defeated 4-2 before Villa lost 4-1 to Wolves in round five.

After beating Northampton 8-0 (away) in round two in 1962-63, Villa then gained replay wins over both Watford and Walsall before losing to West Ham 4-2 in London.

Villa failed to proceed beyond the third round during seasons 1963-64 to 1970-71 inclusive. They were knocked out, in turn, by Wolves, Coventry City, Nottingham Forest, Birmingham City, West Bromwich Albion (in 1968 & 1969), Nottingham Forest and Wolves again, gaining only one decent victory in the process - 6-0 at home to Port Vale in November 1969 (1st round).

Then came that 1972 Final triumph, but as holders of the trophy, the youthful Villa side then lost to Swindon Town in a 3rd round replay in 1972-73 and followed up by going out relatively early in each of the next four campaigns, to West Bromwich Albion, Middlesbrough, Crystal Palace and Albion again.

Things bucked up in 1977-78, but Crystal Palace made it a disappointing climax by winning the Final and after losing to Luton Town in a 4th round encounter at Kenilworth Road in 1978-79, Villa gained their second Final success at Manchester City's expense in April 1980.

Unfashionable Shrewsbury Town then caused an upset by knocking Villa, the holders, out of the competition in the 3rd round in December 1980.

Sunderland were Villa's conquerors in round five in 1981-82 (this, after Nottingham Forest, Everton and Cardiff City had all been defeated in earlier rounds).

Disappointingly over the next sixteen seasons - 1982-83 to 1997-98 inclusive - Villa failed to get beyond the 5th round. They went out in the first round on three separate occasions, lost in the second round seven times, had three third round failures, lost once in round four and said farewell twice in round five.

In 1987-88 Villa had three goes at beating Peterborough United in round 2, finally winning 2-0 at London Road after a 1-1 away draw and a 2-2 scoreline at Villa Park. Crewe Alexandra then put Villa out in the next round.

After whipping the Youths of Hednesford Town 9-0 at home in 1989-90 Villa's teenagers went out at the next hurdle, beaten 2-1 by Watford.

In 1993-94 Villa disposed of Cambridge United 4-1, Watford 3-1 and Bristol City 4-1 before crashing out in the 4th round at West Ham United (2-1).

The following season (1994-95) Villa's Youths ousted Derby County 3-0 (after a 1-1 draw at the Bescot Stadium), Leeds United 1-0 (also at Bescot), Leyton Orient 1-0 and Colchester United 4-0, before losing 3-2 at home to Manchester United in round five.

Villa made a massive effort in the FA Youth Cup in 1998-99 when they lost 1-0 to Everton in the 6th round. Earlier Hull City (5-1), Huddersfield Town (4-1) and Watford (2-0) had all been defeated at Villa Park.

In 2000-01 Villa's youngsters squeezed past Gillingham (just - after a penalty shoot-out) in the third round, put out Barnsley in the fourth (2-0 at home) and then beat Leeds United 1-0 before losing to 2-0 to Arsenal.

**Aston Villa's full record in the FA Youth Cup: 1954-2001:**

| Venue | P | W | D | L | F | A |
|---|---|---|---|---|---|---|
| Home | 72 | 41 | 14 | 17 | 208 | 89 |
| Away | 80 | 37 | 15 | 28 | 149 | 110 |
| Neutral | 3 | 1 | 1 | 1 | 2 | 2 |
| Totals | 155 | 79 | 30 | 46 | 359 | 201 |

## FOOTBALL LEAGUE

Aston Villa's full Football League record: 1888-89 to 1991-92:

| Division | P | W | D | L | F | A | Pts |
|---|---|---|---|---|---|---|---|
| 1 | 3146 | 1327 | 693 | 1126 | 5491 | 4891 | 3489 |
| 2 | 422 | 179 | 111 | 132 | 617 | 487 | 491 |
| 3 | 92 | 51 | 21 | 20 | 139 | 78 | 123 |
| Totals | 3660 | 1557 | 825 | 1278 | 6247 | 5456 | 4103 |

**Villa's results in the first season of the competition (1888-89):**

| Opponents | H | A |
|---|---|---|
| Accrington | 4-3 | 1-1 |
| Blackburn R | 6-1 | 1-5 |
| Bolton Wds | 6-2 | 3-2 |
| Burnley | 4-2 | 0-4 |
| Derby County | 4-2 | 2-5 |
| Everton | 2-1 | 0-2 |
| Notts County | 9-1 | 4-2 |
| Preston NE | 0-2 | 1-1 |
| Stoke | 5-1 | 1-1 |
| WBA | 2-0 | 3-3 |
| Wolves | 2-1 | 1-1 |

**Full record in 1888-89:**

| Venue | P | W | D | L | F | A | Pts |
|---|---|---|---|---|---|---|---|
| Home | 11 | 10 | 0 | 1 | 44 | 16 | 20 |
| Away | 11 | 2 | 5 | 4 | 17 | 27 | 9 |
| Totals | 22 | 12 | 5 | 5 | 61 | 43 | 29 |

Villa finished runners-up to PNE, beaten by 11 points.

**Football League Pot Pourri**

On the first day of Football League action - 8 September 1888 - a crowd of 2,500 saw Aston Villa draw 1-1 away at Wolverhampton Wanderers. Gersom Cox, the Villa full-back, conceded an own-goal for the home side but Tommy Green equalised in the 40th minute to earn Villa their first League point and, of course, have the honour of claiming Villa's first-ever League goal.

THE COMPLETE ENCYCLOPAEDIA OF ASTON VILLA F.C.    THE COMPLETE ENCYCLOPAEDIA OF ASTON VILLA F.C.

99

Seven days later, at their Wellington Road ground in Perry Barr, Villa registered their first League victory, beating Stoke 5-1 in front of 2,000 supporters.

Villa's first away win in the League arrived at Bolton on 20 October 1888 (3-2).

Everton inflicted upon Villa their first League defeat, beating them 2-0 on Merseyside on 6 October 1888.

At the end of the end of the 1889-90 season Aston Villa and Bolton Wanderers were both re-elected to the Football League without having to go to a vote. But in 1890-91 Villa had to be re-elected (again) ...and this time they received eight votes, enough to scrape back in!

Villa's first game in the Second Division was against Swansea Town at the Vetch Field on 29 August 1936. They won 2-1, Frank Broome scoring both goals in front of 26,000 spectators.

Villa opened their Second Division home programme on 5 September 1936 with a 4-0 victory over Southampton when Broome again found the net in front of 45,000 spectators.

Villa's first defeat in the Second Division was at Craven Cottage on 19 September 1936 where they lost 3-0 to Fulham.

Their first taste of Third Division football took them to The Recreation Ground, Chesterfield on 15 August 1970 where they won 3-2, Bruce Rioch scoring twice.

Villa's first home game in Division Three followed a week later when they drew 1-1 with Plymouth Argyle.

Villa's first defeat in the Third Division was at home at the hands of Mansfield Town 1-0 on 31 August 1970.

### Fact File

Villa's biggest League win is 12-2 v Accrington (h) 12 March 1892.

Their heaviest defeat has been 0-7 - on four separate occasions: v Blackburn Rovers (a) on 19 October 1889, v West Bromwich Albion (h) on 19 October 1935, v Manchester United (a) on 8 March 1950 and v Manchester United again (a) on 24 October 1964.

The most wins recorded by Villa in a League season has been 32 in Division Three in 1971-72.

The most recorded at home has been 20 out of 23 in 1971-72.

The fewest number of wins has been seven - in 1889-90 and 1890-91. The fewest at home has been five, in 1890-91.

Villa have never gone through a season without losing a game. Their best record to date is four defeats suffered in 1896-97 when they achieved the double. In a League season containing 38 matches or more Villa's best 'loss record' has been seven in 1912-13 (two at home, five away).

They were undefeated at home in seasons 1895-96 (15 games, 14 won), 1898-99 (17 games, 15 won) and 1909-10 (19 games, 17 won).

Villa drew a club record 17 League games in 1975-76 (Division 1).

In contrast, Villa did not draw a single League game in 1891-92.

The record for most home draws in a season was set in 1923-24 with ten and the record for the fewest is nil, in 1888-89 and 1891-92 and one (from 19 or more games) in 1929-30, 1931-32 and 1964-65.

Villa drew a club record nine away games in 1972-73 and equalled it in 1975-76 and again 1979-80. They did not draw a single away game for two complete seasons: 1890-91 and 1891-92. They also had a clean away record for draws in 1902-03 and 1921-22, the latter from 21 games played.

The most defeats suffered by Villa in a League campaign has been 24 (nine at home, 15 away) in 1966-67 when they were relegated to the Second Division.

The most away defeats in a season has been 15 - in 1921-22, 1958-59, 1964-65, 1966-67, 1969-70.

Villa's record for most home defeats is nine in season 1966-67.

The most points gained in a season (2pts for a win) is 70 in 1971-72 (46 matches - Division 3) and (3pts for a win) 78 in 1987-88 (44 matches - Division 2)

The least number of points pocketed in a season (2pts for a win) has been 18 in 1891-92 and (3pts for a win) it is 36 in 1986-87. The fewest

for a 42 match plus programme has been 29 in 1966-67 and 1969-70. Most home wins registered in a season: 20 in 1971-72.

The fewest home wins in a season: 5 from 11 in 1890-91 and with 19 or more games played, it is seven, on seven occasions, the last in 1990-91.

Villa have twice recorded a sequence of nine League wins in succession: (1) from 22 March to 18 September 1897 and (2) from 15 October to 10 December 1910, both inclusive.

Rampant Villa ran up a tremendous run of 14 consecutive home wins in 1903, commencing on 10 January (3-1 over Nottingham Forest) and ending on 28 November (2-1 versus Liverpool).

Villa won 11 consecutive home League games on their way to clinching the Third Division championship in season 1971-72.

Between 6 February and 11 September 1897, Villa ran up a sequence of six successive away wins in the First Division.

Villa suffered 11 straight League defeats (six away, five at home) over a period of five weeks: 23 March to 4 May 1963.

When Villa won the Second Division title in 1937-38 they received a shield and when they won in 1959-60 they collected a cup.

Six players lined up in Villa's last League game of the 1914-15 season and then appeared in the first one at the start of the 1919-20 campaign. They were Sam Hardy, Jimmy Harrop, Harry Hampton, Clem Stephenson, Charlie Wallace and Tom Weston.

In contrast there were five - Frank Broome, 'Mush' Callaghan, George Cummings, George Edwards and Joe Rutherford - who starred in the last League match of 1938-39 and the first in 1946-47.

Villa have registered more home League wins against Sunderland than they have any other club.

Villa have a 100 per-cent League record against Reading, Scunthorpe United and Stockport County while Northampton Town have a 100 per-cent record against Villa.

It cost Aston Villa a premium of two guineas (£2.10p) to play in the Football League in 1888-89.

Villa avoided relegation to the Second Division in 1955-56 on goal-average. Huddersfield Town went down instead!

Villa's best start to a League season was in 1932-33 when they went the first 11 games without defeat (from 27 August to 22 October inclusive).

Aston Villa and Blackburn Rovers, both founder members of the Football League, were relegated to the Second Division for the first time in their histories at the end of the 1935-36 season.

In 1987-88 Villa and Middlesbrough finished with identical playing records in Division Two: 22 wins, 12 draws and 12 defeats from the 46 gams played. But Villa were handed the runners-up spot as they scored more goals (68-63).

Villa played their 4,000th League game (including Premiership matches) on 3 February 2001 and they celebrated the occasion with a 3-0 win at Bradford City in front of 19,591 spectators.

Villa have still to meet the following clubs in League competition: Aldershot, Barnet, Cambridge United, Cheltenham Town, Chester City, Colchester United, Crewe Alexandra, Exeter City, Hartlepool United, Kidderminster Harriers, Peterborough United, Rushden & Diamonds, Southend United, Wigan Athletic and Wycombe Wanderers.

Despite being relegated to the Third Division, during the 1969-70 season Villa made a profit of £35,695 with gate receipts rising by over £50,000.

In 1949-50 Villa's record in the First Division read:
P42 W15 D 12 L15 F61 A61 Pts 42 Position 12th.
On 26 February 1950 Villa's League record that season read:
P30 W10 D10 L10 F40 A40 Pts30.

## FOOTBALL LEAGUE CUP

Aston Villa entered this competition at the outset and this is their full record in the League Cup (1960-2001):

| Venue | P | W | D | L | F | A |
|---|---|---|---|---|---|---|
| Home | 92 | 62 | 18 | 12 | 211 | 82 |
| Away | 86 | 37 | 23 | 26 | 129 | 121 |
| Neutral | 11 | 8 | 2 | 1 | 23 | 10 |
| Totals | 189 | 107 | 43 | 39 | 363 | 213 |

Villa have played more League Cup matches than any other club.

### Football League Cup Fact File

Aston Villa have appeared in seven League Cup Finals, as follows:

| | | | |
|---|---|---|---|
| 1960-61 | v Rotherham Utd | 0-2, 3-0 | (won 3-2 on agg) |
| 1962-63 | v Birmingham City | 0-0, 1-3 | (lost 3-1 on agg) |
| 1970-71 | v Tottenham Hot | 0-2 | (Wembley) |
| 1974-75 | v Norwich City | 1-0 | (Wembley) |
| 1976-77 | v Everton | 0-0*, 1-1+, 3-2 | (Old Trafford) |
| 1993-94 | v Man United | 3-1 | (Wembley) |
| 1995-96 | v Leeds United | 3-0 | (Wembley) |

First game at Wembley; +Replay at Hillsborough.

### Final Reports

● Because of the fixture congestion at the end of the 1960-61 season, the first League Cup Final (Villa against Rotherham United) was carried over to the start of the following campaign. It was played over two legs, the first at Millmoor on 22 August 1961 in front of 12,228 fans. Rotherham played well, Villa huffed and puffed at times (Stan Lynn even missed a penalty) and the outcome was a 2-0 victory for the Millermen (Barry Webster and Alan Kirkman scoring), thus leaving the Claret and Blues an awful lot to do at Villa Park a fortnight later. But Villa showed their mettle and before 30,765 spectators they fought back and eventually overcame stubborn resistance to take the trophy by the narrowest of margins after a 3-0 second leg victory. It was 0-0 at half-time but after the break Villa powered forward, brought the scores level in normal time through Harry Burrows (67 minutes) and Alan O'Neill (70) before Peter McParland swooped to net the extra-time winner and give Villa the honour of being the first winners of the newly-formed competition.

● Two years later Villa met near neighbours Birmingham City in the 1963 Final. A crowd of 31,580 assembled at St Andrew's to witness the first leg on 23 May, but Villa didn't play at all well. Blues looked far more decisive and meaningful and gained a 3-1 lead with goals by Ken Leek (14 and 52 minutes) and Jimmy Bloomfield (66). Scotsman Bobby Thomson had equalised late in the first-half for Villa...and his goal gave them an outside chance of coming back! But it was not to be. Blues defended resolutely when the teams played the second leg at Villa Park four evenings later to hold on for a 0-0 draw and so take the trophy on aggregate - their first victory in a major competition and 37,921 were there to see it happen!

● Villa's third League Cup Final appearance took them to Wembley in 1971 to play Tottenham Hotspur. Third Division Villa were the underdogs but it never showed on the day when 97,204 spectators almost witnessed an upset as Villa matched their top Division opponents kick for kick in an enthralling contest. Andy Lochead knows he should have scored for Villa (to give them the lead) and Pat McMahon clipped the crossbar. Spurs survived and the Londoners struck twice late on (through Martin Chivers) to 'pinch' the trophy from under Villa's noses.

● Four years later - on 1 March 1975 - Villa returned to the Empire Stadium to contest their fourth League Cup Final. This time their opponents were Norwich City who had been beaten in the Final two years earlier by Spurs. This encounter with the Canaries was a dogged affair, played in front of 95,946 spectators. There were few chances created, not too many near misses and the game was settled by Ray Graydon's strike late on when he followed up to net from close range after former Villa 'keeper Kevin Keelan had saved his weakly hit penalty.

● On 12 March 1977 Everton were Villa's opponents when they re-visited Wembley again to compete in their fifth League Cup Final. But unfortunately their display (like Everton's) was well below par and an audience of 96,223 witnessed a predictable goalless draw. And so the replay at Hillsborough four days later when the turnout was 54,840. This was a better contest, both goalkeepers played well but again it ended all square at 1-1 after extra-time. Villa's goal came courtesy of the Everton defender Roger Kenyon (who gave away an 'og') while former Blues' striker Bob Latchford tucked away the Merseysiders' effort. The second replay was staged at Old Trafford on 13 April and this time 54,749 spectators saw the best of three encounters. It was certainly high entertainment on a damp pitch. Villa - without Andy Gray and Frank Carrodus - looked confident from the start and went close early on before Everton threatened with a flurry of raids launched down the centre. Bob Latchford then put his side ahead (perhaps deservedly so) and it took Villa an awful long time to draw level - but when they did Chris Nicholl's left-footer rocket was a beauty on 82 minutes. The game went into extra time before Brian Little, who had been out of sorts, pounced to edge Villa into a 2-1 lead but this was short-lived as back came Everton to level things up through Mick Lyons' scrambled effort. The watch was running down...Villa broke down the right, Everton's defence was caught flat-footed, Little was there: 3-2 - game over, Cup won...what a finish!

● Villa made their sixth appearance in a League Cup Final (now sponsored by Coca-Cola) on 27 March 1994 under Ron Atkinson's management. Their opponents were Manchester United (Big Ron's former club) and in front of 77,231 spectators, Villa pulled out all the stops, played well above their League form, and defeated the Reds 3-1. Former Villa 'keeper Les Sealey replaced the injured Peter Schmeichel in United's goal and he had to pick the ball out of the net on 25 minutes when Dalian Atkinson netted with his right shin after an excellent four-man build-up. It was 50 minutes before Villa struck again, Kevin Richardson's acutely-angled free-kick being converted by the lunging Dean Saunders who was making his 500th League and Cup appearance at club level. United came storming back and Mark Hughes whipped in a heart-stopper to make it 2-1. Then Villa's 'keeper Mark Bosnich pulled off a blinding save to thwart Hughes. With time running out, Andrei Kanchelskis handled Atkinson's shot on the line. The United winger was sent-off and watched in dismay as Saunders stepped up to clinch victory for Villa from the penalty spot with his last kick of the game. It was third time lucky for Villa's skipper and 'Man of the Match' Kevin Richardson, who had lost in two previous Finals with Everton (1984) and Arsenal (1988). And victory meant that Villa joined Liverpool and Nottingham Forest as the only clubs to have won the League Cup four times.

● Villa's seventh League Cup Final outing who was on 24 March 1996 against Leeds United. A crowd of 77,065 attended Wembley Stadium to watch the action and it was, in truth, Villa, who dominated the game for long spells, making Leeds look a poor side to win easing up by 3-0. The Yugoslavian international Savo Milosevic opened the scoring with a brilliant effort on 20 minutes. Ian Taylor darted into the penalty area to fire in number two nine minutes after the interval and Dwight Yorke wrapped things up by putting the icing on the cake with Villa's third goal a minute from time. It could and should have been five or six nil - so well did Villa play. Brian Little was certainly a delighted manager afterwards!

### League Cup Talk-Back

Following the introduction of sponsorship, this competition has also been known as the Milk Cup (1982-86), the Littlewoods Cup (1987-90), the Rumbelows Cup (1991-92), the Coca-Cola Cup (1993-98) and the Worthington Cup (1999-2001).

THE COMPLETE ENCYCLOPAEDIA OF ASTON VILLA F.C.    THE COMPLETE ENCYCLOPAEDIA OF ASTON VILLA F.C.

101

*Jimmy MacEwan gets in a shot during the 1961 League Cup Final, 2nd leg clash with Rotherham United.*

Villa have won the trophy in three different cities - Birmingham (1961), London (1975, 1994 & 1996) and Manchester (1977).

Villa have also lost Finals in two cities - in Birmingham in 1963 and London in 1971.

When they played in the 1971 Final, Villa were heading for promotion from the Third Division while Spurs were lying seventh in Division One.

Villa besides their seven Final appearances, Villa have also played in 10 League Cup semi-finals, losing in three of them, in 1964-65 (to Chelsea), in 1983-84 (to Everton) and in 1985-86 (to Oxford United). Villa entered this competition at the outset 1960-61 and were the first team to reach the milestone of 100 League Cup matches, doing so in season 1980-81.

Villa's first League Cup-tie was played on 12 October 1960 against Huddersfield Town at home in the 2nd round (won 4-1).

Their first away win in the competition was achieved at Plymouth's Home Park ground on 6 February 1961 by 5-3 in a 4th round replay. This is also Villa's biggest away win in terms of goals scored.

Villa suffered their first defeat in the competition when losing 2-0 at Millmoor against Rotherham United in the first leg of the 1961 Final.

Villa's biggest League Cup win to date has been 8-1 at home to Exeter City on 9 October 1985 (2nd round, 2nd leg).

Villa's heaviest League Cup defeat has been 1-6 - away at West Bromwich Albion in a 2nd round tie in September 1966. Their heaviest reverse at home (goals conceded) is 2-3, suffered on two occasions.

Villa's highest scoring draw in the League Cup has been 3-3 - away at Preston in November 1960 and at home to Plymouth the following month.

The most League Cup games played by Villa in a single season has been 12 - in 1960-61 (although the two-legged final was actually carried over to the start of the 1961-62 campaign).

Villa's best unbeaten run in the competition has been 12 matches, completed between 1 September 1976 and 26 October 1977.

Villa's longest League Cup-tie has been the 1977 Final with Everton - three matches, two of which went to extra-time, giving a total of 330 minutes. They also played three games against Plymouth Argyle in 1960-61; three v Burnley in the semi-final, also in 1960-61; three versus Wrexham in August 1971; three against Queen's Park Rangers in the

semi-final in February 1977 and three more v Crystal Palace in October 1978

Villa's Gerry Hitchens top-scored with 11 goals in the League Cup campaign of 1960-61 and Tony Hateley emulated the England international's feat by top-scoring with 10 goals in season 1964-65.

The most goals scored in a two-legged League Cup-tie involving Aston Villa has been 14 (v Exeter City) in season 1985-86. Villa won 4-1 away and 8-1 at home.

Three players have scored four goals in a League Cup game for Villa: Tony Hateley in a 7-1 romp against Bradford City in November 1964, Simon Stainrod on his debut for the club versus Exeter at St James' Park in September 1985 and David Platt against Ipswich Town at Villa Park in November 1988.

The first League Cup match ever to be played on a Saturday was the Sunderland v Aston Villa semi-final 1st leg clash at Roker Park in January 1963. The first 'live' radio broadcast by the BBC was also from this same game.

The 1975 League Cup Final featured two Second Division teams - Villa and Norwich City. Ian Ross skippered Villa to victory in this Final.

The 2nd round League Cup-tie between Villa and Colchester United in August/September 1979 was decided on penalties, Villa eventually winning 9-8 from the spot after the 2-2 aggregate scoreline. It was 2-0 to Villa at Layer Road, but the underdogs then won 2-0 at Villa Park to force a shoot-out.

Villa reached the 1994 Final by beating Tranmere Rovers 5-4 in a penalty shoot-out at Villa Park after the two-legged semi-final had finished level at 4-4.

## FOOTBALL LEAGUE JUBILEE FUND

Aston Villa met rivals West Bromwich Albion twice in this pre-season charity event, each time at Villa Park.

In August 1938 a crowd of 26,640 witnessed a 1-1 draw (Frank Broome scoring for Villa) and a year later, 16,007 spectators witnessed an identical scoreline when Eric Houghton was Villa's marksman.

### Summary

| P | W | D | L | F | A |
|---|---|---|---|---|---|
| 2 | 0 | 2 | 0 | 2 | 2 |

THE COMPLETE ENCYCLOPAEDIA OF ASTON VILLA F.C.          THE COMPLETE ENCYCLOPAEDIA OF ASTON VILLA F.C.

102

*Trevor Ford.*

### FORD, TREFOR (TREVOR)

Born: Swansea, 1 October 1923.
Career: Powys Avenue School, Swansea Boys, Tower United (Swansea), Swansea Town (juniors 1939, professional May 1942), Army football (with Royal Artillery), Leyton Orient (WW2 guest), rejoined Swansea Town (August 1945), Aston Villa (£9,500 plus Tommy Dodds, January 1947), Sunderland (£30,000, October 1950), Cardiff City (£30,000, December 1953), PSV Eindhoven (£5,000, August 1956), Newport County (July 1960), Romford. Retired in May 1962, although he still turned out regularly in charity matches until 1976.

As a youngster Trevor Ford was encouraged to play both cricket and football by his father. He started off on the soccer pitch as a full-back with his School team and took up the centre-forward position during the War. He quickly made up for lost time by scoring 41 goals in the 1945-46 transitional season.

Ford, with his no-nonsense, hard-hitting, bustling style, was capped by Wales in a Victory international against Northern Ireland - the first of many appearances for his country - and he immediately became 'hot property,' with Aston Villa winning the race for his signature early in 1947. He did exceedingly well at Villa Park, scoring 61 goals in 128 League and FA Cup matches, and was leading marksman three seasons running: 1947-50, while also adding 14 full caps to his collection of honours. However, Ford wanted a bigger stage, and after turning down offers from Colombia and Portugal, he joined Sunderland three months into the 1950-51 season (Villa replacing him with Irishman Dave Walsh from neighbours West Bromwich Albion).

He continued to find the net at Roker Park, weighing in with 67 goals in 108 First Division matches alone. He then assisted Cardiff City (signed instead of Tommy Taylor who went to Manchester United) and again he became a firm favourite with the fans as he notched 39 goals in less than 100 games for the Bluebirds. Sadly it all turned sour for Ford in 1956. With Cardiff having a poor run manager Trevor Morris asked Ford to play on the right-wing. The two men had a disagreement and Ford's days at Ninian Park were limited!

His departure from Cardiff was escalated when he was handed a three-year ban from British football after he exposed 'under the counter' payments in his autobiography: 'I Lead The Attack.'

He appealed and was subsequently reinstated only to be banned again after Football League secretary Alan Hardaker uncovered an illegal payment of £100 which had been made by Sunderland to Ford when he was at Roker Park. Undaunted the Welsh goal-ace went abroad and spent three excellent years with the Dutch club PSV Eindhoven. He returned to the UK after his suspension was lifted but a knee injury hastened the end of a very fine career, Ford finishing with a Football League record of 178 goals in 348 appearances. He also notched 23 goals in 38 full internationals for Wales.

People often wonder what sort of contribution Ford would have made in the 1958 World Cup Finals in Sweden? His goalscoring record for his country (shared by Ivor Allchurch) remained in tact for over 30 years (until Ian Rush took over the mantle).

When he was scoring goals for Sunderland, Ford entered the motor trade and pursued a career in this field in South Wales after hanging up his boots.

In August 1968 Trevor Ford was a substitute fielder for Glamorgan at the St Helen's Ground, Swansea, when the West Indian Test cricketer and world's greatest all-rounder, Garfield Sobers (playing for Notts) smashed six sixes on one over off the bowling of Malcolm Nash.

One description summed up Trevor Ford to a tee: 'He was terrorist in the penalty-area in an era when centre-forwards reigned supreme and goalkeepers were cannon-fodder.'

### FOREIGN (OVERSEAS) BORN PLAYERS

Here is an unofficial list of foreign/overseas born players who have been associated with Aston Villa at various levels, whether on trial, as a guest, on loan or as an amateur:

| | |
|---|---|
| Juan Pablo Angel | Colombia |
| Oscar Arce | Argentina |
| Bosko Balaban | Croatia |
| Gustavo Bartelt | Argentina |
| Stefan Beinlich | Germany |
| Gudni Bergsson | Iceland |
| Noel Blake | Jamaica |
| George Boateng | Ghana |
| Mark Bosnich | Australia |
| Matthius Breitkreutz | Germany |
| Alec Bunbury | Canada |
| Nigel Callaghan | Singapore |
| Benito Carbone | Italy |
| Robert Chandler | India |
| Neale Cooper | India |
| Sasa Curcic | Yugoslavia |
| David Curtolo | Sweden |
| Gilles De Bilde | Belgium |
| Tony Dorigo | Australia |
| Peter Enckelman | Finland |
| Fabio Ferraresi | Italy |
| Ken Fish | South Africa |
| Naj Ghrayib | Israel |
| Hans Gilhaus | Holland |
| David Ginola | France |
| Thomas Hitzlsperger | Germany |
| Gordon Hodgson | South Africa |
| George Hunter | India |
| Sergei Kandaurov | Ukraine |
| Emmemt Kapwenge | Zambia |
| Kevin Keelan | India |
| Ronald Koop | Holland |
| Dariusz Kubicki | Poland |
| Theo Kumali | South Africa |
| Nil Lamptey | Ghana |
| Henrik Larsen | Denmark |
| Olof Mellberg | Sweden |
| Savo Milosevic | Yugoslavia |
| Freddie Mwila | Zambia |
| Joe Nagbe | Liberia |
| Fernando Nelson | Portugal |
| Ize Nkubi | Uganda |
| Kent Nielsen | Denmark |
| Luc Nilis | Belgium |
| Alpay Ozalan | Turkey |
| Fernando M de Silva Pelado | Brazil |
| Cyrille Regis | French Guyana |
| Marco Russo | Italy |
| Mikael Sabathier | Germany |
| Loeg Salenko | Russia |
| Peter Schmeichel | Denmark |
| Didier Six | France |
| Giovani Spirenza | Italy |
| Ivo Stats | Czechoslovakia |
| Dwight Yorke | Trinidad & Tobago |
| Charlie Young | Nicosia (Cyprus) |

*Savo Milosevic*

*Fernando Nelson*

*Kent Nielsen*

### Foreign Language

Aston Villa have had four players who were born in India - Robert Chandler, Neale Cooper, born in Darjeeling, goalkeeper Kevin Keelan

THE COMPLETE ENCYCLOPAEDIA OF ASTON VILLA F.C.     THE COMPLETE ENCYCLOPAEDIA OF ASTON VILLA F.C.

103

born Calcutta and George Hunter born in Peshawur, 10 miles from the Khyber Pass.

Two South Africans - Gordon Hodgson and Ken Fish - were on Villa's books in 1935-36. Hodgson became a Football League manager while Fish was a competent trainer for many years, mainly with Oxford United.

The first time two German-born players lined up for an English club side in in a competitive game in England was on 27 January 1993 when Stefan Beinlich and Matthius Breitkreutz starred for Aston Villa against Sheffield United in the Premiership.

## FOREIGN CONNECTION

The following Aston Villa personnel have all been associated with 'foreign' clubs either as a player, manager, coach, trainer, etc.

| | |
|---|---|
| Charlie Aitken | New York Cosmos |
| Peter Aldis | FC Slavia (player-manager), FC Wilhelmina, The Lions Club (all in Australia) |
| Willie Anderson | Portland Timbers |
| Juan Pablo Angel | River Plate (Argentina) |
| Charlie Apperley | South African football |
| Oscar Arce | Argentinian football (Buenos Aires) |
| Alan Ashman | Olympiakos, Greece (coach) |
| Dalian Atkinson | Real Sociedad, Fenerbahce |
| Ron Atkinson | Atletico Madrid (manager) |
| Bosko Balaban | Dinamo Zagreb |
| Joe Bache | Rot Weiss (trainer/coach), FC Mannheim |
| Gustavo Bartelt | AS Roma |
| Stefan Beinlich | PFV Bergmann Borsig |
| Gudni Bergsson | FC Valur (Iceland) |
| Tony Betts | Portland Timbers, Minnesota Kicks |
| Danny Blair | Devonport Albion, Toronto Scottish, Rhode |
| Island, | Willy's Overland Works FC, Providence FC (in Canada & North America) |
| George Boateng | Feyenoord, Excelsior FC (Holland) |
| Mark Bosnich | Sydney Croatia (Australia) |
| Reg Boyne | New Zealand soccer |
| Darren Bradley | Capetown Spurs (SA) |
| Matthius Breitkreutz | PFV Bergmann Borsig |
| Frank Broome | In Australia with Bankstown (coach/manager), Corinthians Sydney (manager) and coach in Middle East |
| Jimmy Brown | Ethnikos (Greece) |
| Mark Burke | Sporting Lisbon, Fortuna Sittard, Rapid Bucharest |
| John Burridge | Coach in China |
| Bobby Campbell | Vancouver Whitecaps (NASL), Brisbane City |
| Benito Carbone | Torino, Napoli, Inter Milan, Ascoli, Casertana, Reggiana |
| Franz Carr | Reggiana |
| Tony Cascarino | Olympique Marseille, Nancy, Red Star FC (France) |
| Gary Charles | Benfica |
| Lew Chatterley | Chicago Sting (coach) |
| Colin Clarke | Los Angeles |
| Gordon Cowans | Bari |
| Arthur Cox | Galatasary (coach) |
| Alex Cropley | Toronto Blizzard |
| Vic Crowe | Atlanta Chiefs (assistant-manager), Portland Timbers (coach/manager) |
| Jim Cumbes | Portland Timbers |
| Sasa Curcic | Partizan Belgrade, New Jersey Metros |
| David Curtolo | FC Vasteras (Sweden) |
| Tony Daley | FC Madeira, Hapoel Haifa |
| Gilles De Bilde | FC Aalst (Belgium), RSC Anderlecht, PSV Eidhoven |

| | |
|---|---|
| Tommy Docherty | Manager of South Melbourne & Sydney Olympic (in Australia) & FC Porto (Portugal). |
| Terry Donovan | Portland Timbers |
| Tony Dorigo | Adelaide Juventus, Adelaide City Giants |
| Mark Draper | Rayo Vallecano (Spain) |
| Paul Elliott | Pisa |
| Peter Enckelman | Jalkapallo TPS Turku (Finland) |
| Albert Evans | Norway (coach) |
| Allan Evans | Brisbane United (Australia) |
| Alun Evans | South Melbourne (Australia) |
| Fabio Ferraresi | Cesena (Italy) |
| Mike Ferguson | IA Akranes, Los Angeles Aztecs, coach in Middle East. |
| Ken Fish | Railway Association FC (South Africa), Young Boys of Berne (Switzerland). |
| Trevor Ford | PSV Eindhoven |
| Naj Ghrayib | Maccabi Paetach, Hapoel Tel Aviv, Hapoel Haifa |
| David Ginola | Toulon, FC Brent, Racing Club de Paris, Paris St Germain |

*Gerry Hitchens (left) with Jimmy Greaves at Inter Milan.*

| | |
|---|---|
| Brian Godfrey | Portland Timbers |
| George Graham | California Surf |
| Ray Graydon | Washington Diplomats |
| Moustapha Hadji | Nancy, Sporting Lisbon, Deportivo la Coruna |
| Ian Hamilton | Minnesota Kicks |
| Willie Hamilton | South African football |
| George Harcus | FC Lyon (France) |
| Steve Harrison | Vancouver Whitecaps |
| Adrian Heath | Espanol (Spain) |
| Gerry Hitchens | Inter Milan, Torino, Atalanta, Cagliari |
| Tom Hitzlsperger | Bayern Munich |
| Steve Hodge | Hong Kong Football |
| Gordon Hodgson | Rustenburg FC, Pretoria FC, Transavaal (all in South Africa) |

THE COMPLETE ENCYCLOPAEDIA OF ASTON VILLA F.C.    THE COMPLETE ENCYCLOPAEDIA OF ASTON VILLA F.C.

104

| | |
|---|---|
| Jimmy Hogan | Coach in Germany, Holland and Hungary, Austria National team coach (2 spells), Young Boys of Berne (manager/coach), |
| Robert Hopkins | South China, Hong Kong |
| Steve Hunt | New York Cosmos |
| George Hunter | Football in Peshawur (India) |
| Lee Jenkins | ROPS (Finland) |
| Hassan Kachloul | Nimes, Dunkerque, Metz, St Etienne |
| Emment Kapwenge | Atlanta Chiefs, Zambian football |
| Kevin Keelan | New England Teamen |
| Mike Kenning | Germiston Callies, Witts University, Durban United (all in South Africa) |
| Dariusz Kubicki | Mielec FC, Zastra FC, Legia Warsaw (all in Poland) |
| Nil Lamptey | Accra union (Ghana), RSC Anderlecht, PSV Eindhoven |

*Gordon Smith*

| | |
|---|---|
| Lanus | Italian football (AS Roma) |
| Henrik Larsen | Pisa |
| Gordon Lee | Reykjavik FC (caretaker-manager) |
| Ivor Linton | Kasko IF & IF Kraft Naipes (Finland) |
| Andy Lochhead | Denver Dynamo (NASL) |
| Barrie Lynch | Atlanta Chiefs, Portland Timbers |
| Alan McInally | Bayern Munich |
| Pat McMahon | Portland Timbers. Atlanta Chiefs (assistant-manager), Caribos Colarado |
| Peter McParland | Atlanta Chiefs, I Club Kuwait (manager), FC Lybia (manager), coach in Cyprus & Hong Kong |
| Jimmy MacEwan | Coaching in South Africa |
| Johnny MacLeod | KV Mechelen (Belgium) |
| Keith Masefield | FC Haarlem (Holland) |

| | |
|---|---|
| Olof Mellberg | Racing Santander |
| Ralph Milne | Sing Tao (Hong Kong) |
| Savo Milosevic | Partizan Belgrade, Real Zaragoza (Spain) |
| Sammy Morgan | Sparta Rotterdam, Groningen & coach in the USA |
| Tony Morley | FC Seiko (Hong Kong), Den Haag (Holland), Tampa Bay Rowdies, Hamrun Spartans (Malta) |
| Terry Morrall | Cyprus & Jordan football |
| Malcolm Musgrove | Coach of Chicago Sting & Connecticut Bi-Centennials (NASL) |
| Freddie Mwila | Atlanta Chiefs, Zambian football |
| Joe Nagbe | AS Monaco |
| Fernando Nelson | SC Salgueiros, FC Porto, Sporting Lisbon |
| Kent Nielsen | FC Brondby, Bronshoj FC, Aarhus |
| Luc Nilis | Winterslag, RSC Anderlecht, PSV Eindhoven |
| Fred Norris | Adelaide FC, French football |
| Alpay Ozalan | Besiktas, Jet-Pa FC, Fenerbahce (Turkey) FM de Silva Pelado Trevisio |
| Mike Pejic | Malazia Celangor & Zimbabwe (manager) |
| Arthur Phoenix | Racing Club de Paris |
| Frank Pimblett | Brisbane City (Australia) |
| David Platt | Sampdoria (player & coach), Juventus, Bari |
| Cyrille Regis | Happy Valley FC (Hong Kong) |
| John Reynolds | New Zealand football |
| Kevin Richardson | Real Sociedad |
| Paul Rideout | Bari, Red Star FC (France), Huang Dong, Shengzhen (both China) |
| Jimmy Rimmer | Hamrun Spartans (Malta) |
| Bruce Rioch | Seattle Sounders |
| Neil Rioch | Atlanta Chiefs, Portland Timbers, Toronto Blizzard |
| Ian Ross | FC Valur (manager), Santa Barbara (NASL), also coach in Middle East, Oman, South Africa, Australia. |
| Marco Russo | Italian football (Serie 'B') |
| Dean Saunders | Galatasaray, Benfica |
| Pat Saward | Nasr Al (manager/coach) |
| Peter Schmeichel | Hvidovre IF, Brondby, Sporting Lisbon |
| Jackie Sewell | Lusaka City, Rhodesia (player/coach), also coach in Zambia and Belgian Congo. |
| Gary Shaw | BK Copenhagen (Denmark), Ernst Borel FC (Hong Kong), FC Klagenfurt (Austria) |
| Geoff Sidebottom | New York Royals, New York Generals, Columbia University (coach) |
| Nigel Sims | Toronto City, Toronto Italia |
| Didier Six | Valencia, Lens, Olympique Marseille, RFC Bruges, Racing Strasbourg, Vfb Stuttgart, Mulhouse, Metz. |
| Gordon Smith | South African football, Pittsburgh Spirit (USA) |
| Giovanni Spirenza | Eintracht Frankfurt |
| Simon Stainrod | Racing Club Strasbourg, FC Rouen |
| Shaun Teale | Happy Valley FC (Hong Kong) |
| Brian Tiler | Atlanta Chiefs, Portland Timbers, Zambia (national coach) |
| Mike Tindall | New York Americans |
| Josef Venglos | Player and manager of Slovan Bratislava, player/coach in Australia, also managed Australian and Czechoslovakian national teams, Sporting Lisbon manager, coach in Malaysia and Indonesia, manager of Fenerbahce (Turkey). |
| Geoff Vowden | Coach in Saudi Arabia |
| Jimmy Warner | Pittsburgh, USA (coach) |
| Peter Withe | Port Elizabeth & Acadia Shepherds (South Africa), Portland Timbers, Thai FA (coach) |
| Colin Withers | Go-Ahead Deventer (Holland) |
| John Woodward | Ostende FC (Belgium) |
| Phil Woosnam | Atlanta Chiefs (manager), USA Soccer Director |
| Ron Wylie | Bulova, Hong Kong (manager/coach), Soccer Advisor in Cyprus |
| Dwight Yorke | Signal Hill FC (Tobago) |

THE COMPLETE ENCYCLOPAEDIA OF ASTON VILLA F.C.  THE COMPLETE ENCYCLOPAEDIA OF ASTON VILLA F.C.

105

## FOREST GREEN ROVERS

Three former Aston Villa stars - winger Tony Daley, defender Dave Norton and veteran goalkeeper Nigel Spink - all played for the Nationwide Conference side Forest Green Rovers during the 2000-01 season (Spink at the age of 42). Norton and Spink were joint-managers but they were disappointed as Rovers went down 1-0 to Canvey Island in the FA Trophy Final at Villa Park at the end of that campaign..

## FORMATION OF CLUB

It is now understood that Aston Villa (Wesleyan) Football Club was formed in the autumn of 1874 (perhaps late October, early November - soon after the cricket season had ended).

There have been so many differing stories relating to the actual forming of the said club that historians from the Church and football (Aston Villa FC in particular) have been unsure as to where or when the club came into being.

For the record books and following information revealed by several supporters over the past decade, it seems more likely than not that the foundation stones were laid under a dimly lit gas lamp on the corner of Heathfield Road and Lozells Road, near to the site of the old Villa Cross public house and opposite the former Wesleyan Chapel (also known as the Aston Villa Church).

The men who gathered there are believed to have been four members of the Wesleyan Chapel cricket team, namely Jack Hughes, Frederick Matthews, Walter Price and William Scattergood.

They agreed, unanimously, to form a football team, calling it Aston Villa (Wesleyan) FC....the title Aston Villa coming from a large mansion-style dwelling of that name in the locality, or possibly the church. The team was to compete against local opposition from neighbouring Aston, Handsworth, Smethwick, West Bromwich, Tipton and Hagley where a style of football had been played for two and three years previously.

It transpired that two Scotsmen - John Campbell Orr and John Carson - the latter a key figure with the famous amateur club, Queen's Park (Glasgow) - introduced the 'Association' game to the area...and soon another Scot, William McGregor, was to make an even bigger impact! Those four 'Villa' men, Hughes, Matthews, Price and Scattergood, immediately assembled a committee. Charles Midgley was introduced as the honorary secretary and he set about collecting one shilling (5p) from each person who wanted to become a playing member of the newly-formed Aston Villa club.

After a couple of months had passed, a full list of would-be players (most of them cricketers or rugby stars) had been drawn up, comprising the following: W Boyle, H Brittain, WW Davies, H Finnemore, T Froggatt, G Greaves, W Griffiths, T Higgs, J Hughes, W Kennedy, FJ Knight, EB Lee, D Lewis, WB Mason, F Matthews, G Matthews, CH Midgley, G Page, W Page, WH Price, W Scattergood, WG Sothers, W Such, F Tye and WW Weiss.

Soon afterwards H Matthews, A Robbins and H Whateley were also registered with the club.

Aston Villa FC was up and running....and soon matches were being arranged, initially part rugby, part soccer, with 14 or 15 players a side. Gradually, though, things were sorted out, the 11-a-side code finally coming into operation in 1876.

## FOSTER, STEPHEN BRIAN

Born: Portsmouth, 24 September 1957.
Career: Hampshire County Schools, Portsmouth (apprentice, June 1973, professional September 1975), Brighton & Hove Albion (£130,000, July 1979), Aston Villa (£150,000 plus Mark Jones, March 1984), Luton Town (£70,000, November 1984), Oxford United (free transfer, July 1989), Brighton & Hove Albion (free transfer, August 1992-May 1996).

A real hard-nut centre-half who was easily recognisable by his head band! He spent 21 years in the game as a professional, giving everything he had. His leadership qualities were second-to-none and at the end of the day was rewarded with well deserved testimonial and benefit

*Steve Foster*

match at Brighton. Foster replaced Brendan Ormsby at the heart of the Villa defence but then became unsettled, allowing Ormsby to regain his place. Foster then went south to Luton.

He played in the 1983 FA Cup Final replay for Brighton against Manchester United at Wembley, having missed the first game through suspension. He later won a League Cup winners medal with Luton (1988), earned three full England caps as well as playing in one Under-21 international. He amassed a total of 804 senior appearances at club and international level and scored 52 goals. His record with Villa was 17 outings and three goals.

## FRASER, JOHN CAMERON

Born: Blackford, Perthshire, 24 May 1941
Career: Dunfermline Athletic, Aston Villa (£24,500, October 1952), Birmingham City (£9,000, May 1964), Falkirk (June, 1966).

A sturdy full-back, strong in the tackle, Cammy Fraser won a Scottish Cup winners medal with Dunfermline a year before manager Joe Mercer signed him for Aston Villa. With Gordon Lee and a youthful Mick Wright challenging him for a first team place, he appeared in only 40 senior games during his time at Villa Park (one goal scored) before transferring to arch rivals Blues. He twice represented his country at Under-23 level (1961-62) and was a League Cup finalist with Villa against Blues in 1963. He skippered Villa's reserve side when they won the Central League championship in 1963-64....his last mission before moving to St Andrew's.

Fraser's father, Billy, played for Aldershot and Northampton Town.

## FRIENDLY MATCHES

Aston Villa's first ever game was a 14-a-side friendly against Aston Hall Unity in January 1875 which they 'lost'. (see FIRSTS).

In their first full season of 1875-76, Villa were beaten 7-0 by Stafford Road (Wolverhampton) but they also ran up some useful victories including those of 5-1 over Grasshoppers and Heart of Oak and 6-0 v Walsall Albion.

Thereafter, until the early 1900s, several friendly matches were arranged and then the numbers gradually lessened, with occasionally only a handful being fulfilled each year.

Listed here are some of Villa's many friendly matches played over the last 125 years: (see also under benefits/testimonials/overseas tours, Scottish opposition etc,)

| 1876-77 | 1879-80 |
|---|---|
| Villa 9 Stafford Road 0 | Villa 4 Small Heath 1 |
| Villa 4 Coventry 0 | Villa 4 Stoke 1 |
| Saltley College 5 Villa 0 | **1880-81** |
| **1877-78** | Villa 5 Nechells 0 |
| Villa 8 Brownhills 0 | Villa 4 Derby County 0 |
| Villa 8 Coventry 0 | Villa 4 Walsall Swifts 0 |
| Villa 8 Burton Robin Hood 0 | Villa 4 Heart of Midlothian 2 |
| Villa 6 St George's Athletic 0 | Villa 4 Blackburn Rovers 3 |
| Villa 9 St George's Athletic 0 | Blackburn Rovers 3 Villa 0 |
| Villa 6 Burton Allsops 0 | **1881-82** |
| **1878-79** | Villa 6 Pollockshields 1 |
| Villa 6 Shrewsbury Engineers 2 | Darwen 4 Villa 4 |
| Villa 8 Arcadians 0 | Blackburn Rovers 7 Villa 2 |

Villa 1 Blackburn Rovers 4
Derby County 0 Villa 3
Glasgow Rangers 7 Villa 1
Villa 6 Hearts 1
1882-83
Villa 6 The Wednesday (Sheffield) 1
Villa 5 Stoke 1
Stoke 0 Villa 9
Blackburn Rovers 3 Villa 4
Villa 6 Wrexham 0
Villa 5 Blackburn Olympic 1
1883-84
Villa 14 Sheffield Town 0
Villa 4 Small Heath 0
Villa 5 Derby Midland 0
Villa 6 Darwen 1
Villa 5 Walsall 1
Villa 1 Wednesbury Town 4
1884-85
Villa 4 Blackburn Olympic 0
Villa 4 Old Carthusians 0
Villa 1 Dumbarton 7
Bolton Wanderers 4 Villa 1
Blackburn Olympic 5 Villa 1
Villa 1 Preston North End 5
Preston North End 7 Villa 2
Northwich Victoria 5 Villa 3
West Bromwich Albion 2 Villa 4
1885-86
Villa 13 Action (London) 0
Villa 11 Gloucester County 0
Villa 6 Halliwell 0
Villa 4 Corinthians 1
Notts County 3 Villa 5
Small Heath 1 Villa 8
Villa 5 Aston Unity 0
West Bromwich Albion 5 Villa 0
Villa 4 West Bromwich Albion 5
West Bromwich Albion 3 Villa 2
West Bromwich Albion 3 Villa 1
1886-87
St Johnstone 1 Villa 11
Arbroath 0 Villa 4
Villa 6 West Bromwich Albion 3
Villa 11 London Caledonians 0
Villa 7 The Wednesday (Sheffield) 0
Villa 7 Notts County 0
Villa 8 Middlesbrough 0
Villa 6 London Casuals 0
Hibernian 3 Villa 8
Villa 3 Hibernian 0
Villa 4 Burlsem Port Vale 0
Villa 7 Small Heath 0
Preston North End 11 Villa 1
Villa 0 West Bromwich Albion 4
Villa 4 West Bromwich Albion 1
Villa 1 West Bromwich Albion 1
Villa 3 West Bromwich Albion 1
1887-88
Villa 8 the Caledonians 0
Villa 6 The Wednesday (Sheffield) 1
Villa 9 Aston Unity 0
Villa 12 Lockwood Bros (Sheffield) 1
Villa 6 London Casuals 0
Notts County 8 Villa 2
Villa 5 Derby County 0
Villa 5 Glasgow Rangers 1

Blackburn Rovers 4 Villa 6
Villa 5 Corinthians 2
Villa 4 Dumbarton 1
Villa 7 The Scottish Crusaders 4
Villa 4 Small Heath 4-1
Villa 4 Preston North End 1
1888-89
Villa 10 Ayr United 0
Villa 4 Canadian Tourists 2
Villa 4 London Casuals 0
Villa 2 Queen's Park (Glasgow) 6
1889-90
Birmingham St George's 2 Villa 7
Villa 11 Welsh Druids 2
West Bromwich Albion 2 Villa 2
West Bromwich Albion 4 Villa 2
Sunderland 7 Villa 2
Shropshire XI 1 Villa 7
Villa 4 West Bromwich Albion 2
Villa 0 West Bromwich Albion 1
Villa 1 West Bromwich Albion 1
1890-91
Villa 6 Kidderminster Harriers 0

Villa 4 Stoke 4
Villa 7 Oxford University 1
Villa 7 Cambridge University 1
Villa 7 London Casuals 2
Villa 11 Derby County 0
Villa 10 Partick Thistle 0
Villa 8 Corinthians 3
Small Heath 4 Villa 5
1891-92
Villa 8 West Bromwich Albion 2
Villa 5 Small Heath 0
Sheffield United 2 Villa 4
West Bromwich Albion 2 Villa 1
1892-93
Villa 6 Wolves 1

Villa 3 Middlesbrough 5
Villa 4 West Bromwich Albion 4
West Bromwich Albion 2 Villa 0
Villa 6 Notts County 2
Corinthians 2 Villa 7
Corinthians 2 Villa 5
Villa 3 West Bromwich Albion 2
West Bromwich Albion 0 Villa 1
1893-94
Villa 3 Celtic 2
Villa 4 Walsall 1
Stoke 4 Villa 1
Wolves 4 Villa 1
Corinthians 4 Villa 6
Woolwich Arsenal 1 Villa 3
1894-95
West Bromwich Albion 5 Villa 4
Villa 1 Football League XI 3
Villa 11 Cambridge University 0
1895-96
Crystal Palace 3 Villa 7
Hibernian 5 Villa 2
Tottenham Hotspur 1 Villa 3

ASTON VILLA v AS MONACO

AT VILLA PARK, MONDAY 8th FEBRUARY 1988 – OFFICIAL PROGRAMME

● Aston Villa's reputation, dating back many years, in terms of attracting top clubs from around the world for prestige friendlies, resumes tonight with the visit of Monaco.

The leaders of the French league, based in the tiny picturesque principality adjacent to Monte Carlo arrive with the added attraction of having two England internationals in their ranks.

Obviously there will be the usual warm Villa Park welcome for the entire party with just the extra 'hello' for Glenn Hoddle and Mark Hateley, whom we are pleased to see back in action in the UK.

When the match was accepted by Manager Graham Taylor at very short notice it was simply because it seemed far too interesting an occasion to turn down.

The French club were due to play Rangers in Glasgow tonight, followed by Newcastle on Wednesday and Spurs, in Hoddle's Testimonial, next Monday. However, the Scottish part of the programme had to be abandoned because Rangers' Scottish Cup third round tie with Raith Rovers was postponed twice because of the weather in the north, thus removing the vacant date.

"We felt that it was something of a compliment while still in the Second Division to be selected in such company" explained the Manager.

"In view of the short notice we accept that we cannot put high expectations on the attendance, but even so, there will be a section of our public who will be interested in seeing us play against attractive foreign opposition.

Basically, I feel that a match of this nature is worth two days training, bearing in mind, that our normal Saturday game at Middlesborough has been put back to Sunday, giving us that extra 24 hours."

Having made that point he quickly dispells any thoughts that it is nearly a training spin. "We would not ever approach a game anything but seriously. It would be unfair both to the on-lookers and to the opposition. The important thing here is that we can abandon the heavy demands of a Second Division fixture in which results are of paramount importance and simply get on with playing football in a relaxed and pleasurable way."

Also there is a good deal of added status in terms of having played the leaders of the Barclays League and the French league within the space of eight days.

"Our supporters who saw how we fared against Liverpool in the limelight of the F.A. Cup and live TV, now have the opportunity to see how we can fare in a lesser atmosphere against another style of League leaders" he added.

He also sees a benefit in terms of the chance to see his players in differing situations. "It's a chance to take a look at individuals and formations" he added.

In some ways tonight is a rare occasion; there aren't any losers!

GLENN HODDLE
Signed from Spurs in the close season, the talented midfielder has 47 England caps. Last played at Villa Park in the 1987 F.A. Cup Semi-Final against Watford.

MARK HATELEY
Son of former Villa centre-forward, Tony, the England striker joined Monaco from AC Milan in the summer. Has 24 full international caps.

1896-97
Corinthians 4 Villa 4
Bristol Rovers 0 Villa 5
Tottenham Hotspur 2 Villa 2
1897-98
Villa 5 Sheffield Wednesday 2
Villa 6 Derby County 2
Villa 9 Halliwell Rangers 1
Tottenham Hotspur 2 Villa 3
1898-99
Villa 6 West Bromwich Albion 1
West Bromwich Albion 4 Villa 0
1899-1900
Villa 7 Kaffirs XI 4
Villa 5 Small Heath 2

Villa 4 Tottenham Hotspur 3
1900-01
Berlin XI 2 Villa 6
Villa 5 Sheffield United 1
1901-02
Villa 6 Portsmouth 0
1902-03
Villa 4 Small Heath 2
West Bromwich Albion 1 Villa 5
1903-04
Villa 4 Wolves 0
1904-05
Villa 1st XI 7 Villa 2nd XI 0
Villa 1st XI 6 Villa 2nd XI 3
1905-06
Corinthians 7 Villa 1
1906-07
Villa 6 Cambridge University 0
Villa 4 George Robey's XI 3
1909-10
Northwich Victoria 1 Villa 4
1911-12
Stourbridge 1 Villa 4
1913-14
Combined Bristol XI 0 Villa 3
1914-15
Villa 8 Hibernian 3
1916-17
West Bromwich Albion 5 Villa 1
1918-19
West Bromwich Albion 3 Villa 4
1921-22
Villa 11 Oxford University 2
1923-24
Army XI 2 Villa 7
1924-25
Villa 0 South African Tourists 3
Villa 5 West Bromwich Albion 5
1925-26
Army XI 5 Villa 1
Villa 6 Birmingham 3
Lyn O.G, Frig 2 Villa 11
1926-27
Army XI 5 Villa 4
Villa 4 Corinthians 2
1927-28
Villa 7 Airdrieonians 2
Army FA XI 2 Villa 7
1928-29
Army FA XI 3 Villa 7
1929-30
Army FA XI 0 Villa 5
Walsall 2 Villa 8
1930-31
Oxford University 0 Villa 8
Villa 7 Army FA XI 1
Oxford University 0 Villa 10
Villa 8 Corinthians 2
1931-32
Army FA XI 1 Villa 7
Army XI 0 Villa 6
Villa 4 Cowdenbeath 2
1932-33
Army FA XI 4 Villa 4
1937-38
Cardiff City 0 Villa 3

THE COMPLETE ENCYCLOPAEDIA OF ASTON VILLA F.C.

THE COMPLETE ENCYCLOPAEDIA OF ASTON VILLA F.C.

107

1939-40
ICI Metal Works 1 Villa 5
(neutral ground)
Leicester City 3 Villa 0
Birmingham 2 Villa 1
Chelmsford City 2 Villa 1
1940-41
Birmingham 0 Villa 3
West Bromwich Albion 4 Villa 3
Villa 6 West Bromwich Albion 1
1941-42
Villa 1 RAF XI 3
Villa 7 Birmingham 0
Birmingham 0 Villa 1
West Bromwich Albion 1 Villa 2
Birmingham 2 Villa 1
Villa 4 Birmingham 1
Walsall 4 Villa 3
Villa 4 Birmingham 0
West Bromwich Albion 3 Villa 4
1942-43
West Bromwich Albion 6 Villa 2
Villa 8 West Bromwich Albion 2
Villa 1 Portsmouth 1
1943-44
West Bromwich Albion 8 Villa 2
Villa 3 Portsmouth 3
Charlton Athletic 1 Villa 1 (neutral)
1944-45
Edinburgh Select XI 3 Villa 4
Portsmouth 3 Villa 4
Villa 4 Wolves 4
1945-46
Wolves 1 Villa 3
Shrewsbury Town 2 Villa 1
Combined West Norway XI 1 Villa 9
Oestfold District (Sarpsborg) 2 Villa 4
South Norway/Oslo XI 2 Villa 2
Edinburgh Select XI 3 Villa 3
1946-47
County of Cornwall XI 0 Villa 5
Villa 1 Celtic 2
1947-48
Brentford 2 Villa 2
The Army 1 Villa 1 (at Aldershot)
Villa v Birmingham City
Villa 4 Northampton Town 2
1948-49
Shamrock Rovers 2 Villa 2
Cheltenham Town 2 Villa 1
Reading 1 Villa 1
Celtic 0 Villa 2
Limerick 1 Villa 8
Munster XI 0 Villa 8
1949-50
Army XI 3 Villa 7
Villa 5 Hibernian 2
Villa XI 4 Merthyr Tydfil 7
Shamrock Rovers 4 Villa 3
1950-51
Villa 4 Shamrock Rovers 1
Shamrock Rovers 1 Villa 5
Luton Town 3 Villa 1
The Army 1 Villa 3 (at Aldershot)
1951-52
The Army 1 Villa 2 (at Aldershot)
Shamrock Rovers 2 Villa 2

International Combination 6 Villa 2
International Combination 0 Villa 3
Gothenburg Alliansen 3 Villa 1
Jydsk Pokalyurnering 1 Villa 2
Villa 3 Birmingham City 2
Villa 1 Shamrock Rovers 1
1952-53
Waterford Select XI 1 Villa 8
Shamrock Rovers 1 Villa 1
Kettering Town 1 Villa 2
The Army 3 Villa 1 (at Aldershot)
Villa 1 Birmingham Cty 1
1953-54
Nottingham Forest 0 Villa 2
The Army 2 Villa 3 (at Aldershot)
F Nuremburg 3 Villa 1
FC St Pauli 2 Villa 3
Preussen 0 Villa 1
1954-55
The Army 0 Villa 1 (at Aldershot)
Villa 5 Aachen University 3
Villa 4 England XI 2
1955-56
Villa 3 Army XI (Royal Tank Regt) 2

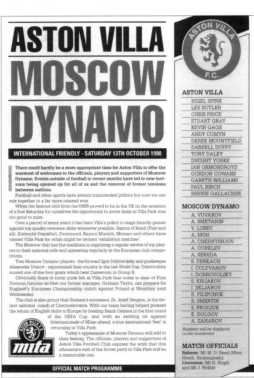

The Army 0 Villa 1 (at Aldershot)
Villa 2 England XI 2
1956-57
Army XI 3 Villa 7 (at Aldershot)
HSV Hamburg 1 Villa 3
FSV Frankfurt 1 Villa 3
Toulouse 2 Villa 1 (in Paris)
1957-58
Villa 6 Army FA XI 3
TSV 1860 Munich 2 Villa 1
Aachen 0 Villa 0
Duisburg 0 Villa 0
1958-59
Villa 3 GAIS 0
Bedford Town 3 Villa 4

Villa 3 Heart of Midlothian 3
1959-60
Villa 2 Rapid Vienna 1
Villa 5 Raith Rovers 1
Villa 4 The Army XI 2
Gothenburg Alliansen XI 2 Villa 1
Helsingborg 2 Villa 3
Raufoos (Norway) 1 Villa 13
Bolnas (Sweden) 0 Villa 6
Trondheim (Norway) 0 Villa 6
Ostersund (Sweden) 1 Villa 7
Swindon Town 3 Villa 4
Bedford Town 3 Villa 4
Heart of Midlothian 2 Villa 2
1960-61
Combined Soviet XI 1 Villa 2
Moscow Combined XI 0 Villa 1
Tblisi Dynamo 2 Villa 0
Moscow Dynamo 2 Villa 0
Raith Rovers 2 Villa 1
1961-62
Villa 2 Dynamo Kiev 1
Inter Milan 2 Villa 4
Swindon Town 1 Villa 2

1962-63
Swansea Town 3 Villa 4
Hereford United 3 Villa 2
WBA 3 Villa 2 (at Stourbridge)
Coventry City 2 Villa 2
(Festival of Sport)
1963-64
Portsmouth 2 Villa 1
Shrewsbury Town 2 Villa 2
Villa 8 Northampton Town 0
1964-65
Bournemouth 1 Villa 1
Southampton 3 Villa 2
Nuneaton Borough 3 Villa XI 3

1965-66
Peterborough United 2 Aston Villa 1
Nuneaton Borough 2 Villa XI 1
Villa 2 FC Twente Enschede 2
DOS Utrecht 3 Villa 3
1966-67
Stdjsk Fodbold AKK 2 Villa 4
FF Malmo 1 Villa 2
Aalborg Boldklub 4 Villa 1
Swindon Town 2 Villa 1
Ajax 2 Villa 0
Schalke 04 2 Villa 3
Nuremburg 1 Villa 2
1968-69
Bedford Town 2 Villa XI 0
Walsall 0 Villa 1
Shrewsbury Town 2 Villa 3
Walsall 3 Villa 0
Kilmarnock 1 Villa 2 (USA)
Tottenham Hotspur 2 Villa 2 (USA)
Dundee 2 Villa 2 (USA)
Dundee 0 Villa 2 (USA)
Wolves 2 Villa 1 (USA)
West Ham United 2 Villa 2 (USA)
Kilmarnock 2 Villa 1 (USA)
Wolves 5 Villa 0 (USA)
West Ham United 2 Villa 0 (USA)
Atlanta Chiefs 0 Villa 2 (USA)
1969-70
Villa 1 Italian Under-21 XI 0
Hibernian 1 Villa 4
Villa 3 Coventry City 3
Villa 3 Dunfermline Athletic 2
Villa 1 Napoli 1
Luton Town 0 Villa 3
SV Jahn 1 Villa 0 (Germany)
Southend United 3 Villa 2
1970-71
Coleraine 0 Villa 4
Glentoran 0 Villa 0
Clydebank 3 Villa 1
Motherwell 2 Villa 1
Villa 1 v WBA 1
1971-72
Villa 1 Gornik Zabrze 1
Villa 2 Birmingham City 1
Villa 2 Santos 1
Kickers Warzburg 2 Villa 4
Alemania Aachen 1 Villa 0
Bayreuth 2 Villa 3
Goppingen 2 Villa 2
EPA (Larnaca) 0 Villa 6
1972-73
Groningen 1 Villa 2
Nijmegen 0 Villa 3
Shrewsbury Town 2 Villa 2
Villa 0 Tottenham Hotspur 0
Villa 1 Bayern Munich 1
St Martin's 0 Villa 5 (in Guernsey)
VBF Ottenburg v Villa
Villa 1 England U-19 XI 3
Hereford United 2 Villa 2
Young Africans 1 Villa 1
Zanzibar XI 0 Villa 3
Young Africans 0 Villa 0
Coventry City 1 Villa 1
Exeter City 2 Villa 2

1973-74
Villa 7 Feyenoord 1
Villa 3 Southampton 0
Villa 0 Leicester City 1
Oldenburg St Paul 2 Villa 3
1974-75
Bury 0 Villa 1
Villa 1 Leeds United 2
Barbados 0 Villa 1
1975-76
Villa 11 SK Brann 0
Vard CF 2 Villa 5
Port Vale 2 Villa 3
Villa 2 Walsall 1
SK Brann 0 Villa 1
1976-77
Villa 2 Rangers 0 (see abandoned matches)
Wellingborough 1 Villa 4
Villa 1 Midland All Stars 6
Villa 3 RSC Antwerp 1
Villa 3 Eintracht Frankfurt 1
Villa 1 Midlands XI 6
1977-78
RSC Anderlecht 4 Villa 3
Aston Villa 0 Swedish National XI 1
Gornik Zabrze 1 Villa 1
1978-79
Villa 1 Nijmegen 1
Hajduk Split 4 Villa 0
Olympia Ljubiyana 3 Villa 5
Villa 6 International XI 6
1979-80
Villa 2 FC Twente Enschede 0
Heart of Midlothian 1 Villa 3
Dundee United 3 Villa 0
1980-81
Vfl Bochum 1 Villa 1
Villa 4 Rapid Vienna 0
Birmingham City 3 Villa 6
FC Valodolid 4 Villa 4
Nantes (Lorient) 4 Villa 0
Villa 2 Vfl Bochum 1
Nuremburg 2 Villa 1
Vfl Bochum 0 Villa 2
FC Buchult 0 Villa 2
1981-82
FC Frauenfeld (Zurich) 0 Villa 4
Villa 4 German Democratic Republic XI 2
Villa 3 England XI 2
Seville 2 Villa 1
1982-83
AEK Athens 2 Villa 2
FC Kaiserslautern 5 Villa 1
FC Schalke '04 4 Villa 2
Werder Bremen 2 Villa 0
Portsmouth 3 Villa 4
Hereford United 1 Villa 2
Villa 1 Dukla Prague 2
1983-84
Plymouth Argyle 0 Villa 3
Torquay United 1 Villa 2
1984-85
Villa 3 West Bromwich Albion 3
Aldershot 4 Villa 1
Villa 1 England XI 4
Leeds United 1 Villa 3

Shrewsbury Town v Villa
Hostels Invitation XI v Villa (Bermuda)
1985-86
Exeter City 2 v Villa 1
Plymouth Argyle 2 Villa 6
Liskeard 1 Villa 3
Shrewsbury Town v Villa
Sutton Coldfield T v Villa XI
Villa v Sunderland
1986-87
Mauritius XI 0 Villa 4
Lamperecchio 0 Villa 8
West Indies Select XI 1 Villa 3
Celtic v Villa
Port Vale v Villa
Leeds United v Villa
Sheffield United 0 v Villa 0
(see abandoned matches)
1987-88
Villa 3 Coventry City 2
Villa 3 AS Monaco 0
Villa 5 Birmingham City 2
(Founders' Day)
Norrtalge (Sweden) 1 Villa 5
Varmbols Golf 0 Villa 8
Villa 2 Wolves 1
1987-88
Gullringen Golf v Villa
NBIS/IAS Eskinunnu v Villa
Norkopping v Villa
Villa 5 Birmingham City 2
1988-89
Hull City 1 Villa 1
St Mirren 1 Villa 0
Morton 2 Villa 3
St Johnstone 1 Villa 2
Villa 4 Walsall 2
Notts County 3 v Villa 2
Barnstaple 0 Villa 6
Bohemians 0 Villa 3
1989-90
FC Servette 1 Villa 0
Echallens 0 Villa 9
Nettleham 1 Villa 5
(see abandoned matches)
Riginal Select 2 Villa 0
FC Solothurn 0 Villa 6
FC Kaufen v Villa
FC Winterthur 4 Villa 4
Villa 1 Hibernian 0
Chester City 0 Villa 5
Halesowen Town 1 Villa 6
Paget Rangers 0 Villa 7
1990-91
Villa 1 Moscow Dynamo 0
Walsall 0 Villa 4
Bohemians 0 Villa 3
Bristol City 2 Villa 0
Ljusbals IF 0 Villa 6
Krybo IF 0 Villa 4
IFK Askersund 1 Villa 11
Sorretalion 1 Villa 5
Assyriska Kurengigem 1 Villa 5
Sollentune Alliansen 0 Villa 1
Real Sociedad 0 Villa 1
1991-92
TUS Ouldeburg 0 Villa 3

Borussia Moenchengladbach 1 Villa 0
Sporting Lisbon 0 Villa 3 (in Paris)
Cheltenham Town 4 Villa 3
Villa 0 Bari 1
Shelbourne 0 v Villa 4
Hibernian 0 Villa 1
Witney Town 0 Villa XI 5

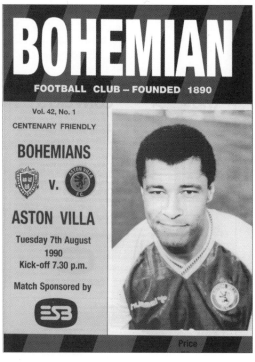

Redditch United v Villa XI
Gloucester City 1 Villa XI 2
Plymouth Argyle v Villa
Villa 2 Wolves 3
Kuala Lumpar 1 Villa 2
Malaysian XI 0 Villa 4
Hannover 0 Villa 2
Gornik Zabrze 1 Villa 0
1992-93
Villa 2 Birmingham City 2
Drogheda v Villa
Bournemouth 2 Villa 2
Wolves 2 Villa 2
Portsmouth 1 Villa 0
Peterborough Utd 1 Villa 1
Shrewsbury Town 1 Villa 2
Fiorentina 2 Villa 1
Dynamo Dresden 1 Villa 3
PFV Bergmann Borsig 0 Villa 5
Witney Town 1 Villa 7
Villa 4 Stoke City 1
Villa 3 Everton 1 (in Mauritius)
Villa 1 Manchester United 1 (in Belfast)
1993-94
Yomrori Nippon 1 Villa 2
(in Japan)
Villa 1 Liverpool 2
(Ellis Park, South Africa)
Manning Rangers 0 Villa 1
(in Durban)
Moroka Swallows 0 Villa 0
Walsall 0 Villa 4
Hull 0 Villa 2
Wigan 0 Villa 1

Port Vale 2 Villa 3
1994-95
Villa 2 Birmingham City 0
Bedford Town v Villa XI
Villa 8 Rapid Bucharest 0
(at Bescot Stadium)
Atletico Madrid 0 Villa 0

(Villa won 3-1 on pens)
Falmouth 1 Villa 3
Torpoint Athletic 1 Villa 9
Drogheda 0 Villa 3
Oxford United 3 Villa 3
Redditch United v Villa XI
Trinidad & Tobago 2 Villa 1
Barbados 3 Villa 1
1995-96
Portsmouth 0 Villa 2
Northampton Town 1 Villa 3
Villa 2 Partizan Belgrade 0
West Bromwich Albion 1 Villa 0
1996-97
Lincoln City 0 Villa 1
Walsall 0 Villa 2
Wrexham 2 Villa 2
Oldham Athletic 0 Villa 3
San Jose Clash 1 Villa 1
Los Angeles Galaxy 1 Villa 1
1997-98
Tamworth 2 Villa XI 2
Birmingham City 0 Villa 0
Wycombe Wanderers 0 Villa 5
West Brom Albion 1 Villa 2
Motherwell 0 Villa 3
Partick Thistle 0 Villa 3
Atherstone United 0 Villa 1
Kidderminster H 1 Villa 5
Moor Green 1 Villa XI 2
Redditch Utd 2 Villa 2
Leicester YMCA XI 0 Villa 5
Fraserburgh 3 Villa 5
Port Vale 3 Villa 5

THE COMPLETE ENCYCLOPAEDIA OF ASTON VILLA F.C.

THE COMPLETE ENCYCLOPAEDIA OF ASTON VILLA F.C.

109

1998-99
Pelsall Villa 0 Villa XI 7
Corby Town 1 Villa XI 2
Blakenall 1 Villa XI 7
Bromsgrove Rovers 0 Villa XI 1
Wycombe Wanderers 0 Villa 3
Hastings United 1 Villa XI 2
Seville 1 Villa 2 (in Spain)
Peterborough United 0 Villa 2
Hednesford Town 0 Villa 4
Hereford United 0 Villa 2
Cardiff City 1 Villa 3
Tamworth 1 Villa XI 6
Total Network Sols 3 Villa XI 2
Nuneaton Borough 1 Villa XI 3

Stratford 1 Villa XI 3
Paget Rangers 0 Villa XI 6
1999-2000
Stevenage Borough 0 Villa 3
Tamworth 3 Villa XI 4
Bromsgrove Rovers 0 Villa 5
Cheltenham Town 1 Villa 6
Swansea City 0 Villa 3
Ajax 2 Villa 2
(in USA Cup)
Fiorentina 4 Villa 0 (in USA Cup)
Feyenoord 0 Villa 0
2000-01
Benfica 2 Villa 2
2001-02
R. Santander 0 Villa 2

## Friendly Talk

To end the season 1887-88 season a crowd of 10,000 saw Villa draw 1-1 at home with West Bromwich Albion on 26 May. Three months later the first Football League game on Villa soil took place when Stoke were beaten 5-1 in front of just 2,000 spectators.

In April 1894 Villa, champions of the Football League, defeated Celtic, the Scottish League champions, 3-2 in a challenge match at Perry Barr in front of 4,000 spectators.

A crowd of 10,000 saw Villa beaten 3-1 by a strong Football League XI on 24 September 1894 in a benefit match for William McGregor.

Ian Dickson scored six goals when Villa defeated Oxford University 11-2 on 1 November 1921.

Tom 'Pongo' Waring scored his first goal for Villa's senior side in a 7-2 friendly win over Airdrieonians on 3 March 1928.

On 5 August 1944 - with World War Two still in progress - Villa travelled to Scotland and played out a 4-4 draw with an Edinburgh Select XI at Tynecastle Park.

Villa beat Portsmouth 4-3 at Fratton Park on 9 May 1945 in a VE Day plus one Charity Match.

Mike Tindall scored 6 goals when Villa beat Raufoos 13-1 in 1959-60.

On 21 February 1972, Villa beat Santos of Brazil (and Pele) 2-1 in a friendly at Villa Park in front of 54,437 fans.

The following year a crowd of almost 22,700 saw Aston Villa held to a 1-1 draw at home by the crack German side Bayern Munich that included 1966 and 1970 World Cup star Franz Beckenbauer.

Villa utilised a total of 20 players when beating Falmouth Town 3-1 in a friendly in July 1994.

As part of the Savo Milosevic deal, Villa agreed to play Partizan Belgrade in home and away friendlies during the first half of the 1995-96 season. After winning 2-0 at Villa Park in August, Villa travelled to Belgrade for the return fixture in November only for the game to be called off through heavy snow!

## FROGGATT, STEPHEN JUNIOR

Born: Lincoln, 9 March 1973.
Career: Aston Villa (YTS June 1989, professional January 1991), Wolverhampton Wanderers (£1 million, July 1994), Coventry City (£1.9 million, October 1998). Retired 2001.

Steve Froggatt completed his transition from outside-left to wing-back during the 1996-97 season when he regained his form and fitness after serious injury and illness problems following his big-money transfer from Villa Park to Molineux in the summer of 1994. He was capped twice by England at Under-21 level during his time with Villa for whom he made 44 appearances and scored three goals as a wide midfielder, occupying the left flank. 'Froggy' went on to earn selection to the PFA's First Division side in 1997 before returning to the Premiership with Coventry City three months into the 1998-99 season. In November 1999, he was named by England boss Kevin Keegan in the squad to play

Scotland in the Euro 2000 play-offs v Scotland. He was out of the Sky Blues side during 2000-01 owing to a series of injuries and retired from competitive football as the season ended.

## FULHAM

Villa's record against the Cottagers:

| Venue | P | W | D | L | F | A |
|---|---|---|---|---|---|---|
| **Football League** | | | | | | |
| Home | 17 | 8 | 5 | 4 | 30 | 22 |
| Away | 17 | 2 | 5 | 10 | 20 | 34 |
| Totals | 34 | 10 | 10 | 14 | 50 | 56 |
| **FA Cup** | | | | | | |
| Home | 2 | 1 | 0 | 1 | 5 | 2 |
| **League Cup** | | | | | | |
| Home | 1 | 1 | 0 | 0 | 2 | 0 |
| Away | 1 | 0 | 1 | 0 | 1 | 1 |
| Totals | 2 | 1 | 1 | 0 | 3 | 2 |
| **Wartime** | | | | | | |
| Home | 1 | 1 | 0 | 0 | 3 | 0 |
| Away | 1 | 1 | 0 | 0 | 4 | 0 |
| Totals | 2 | 2 | 0 | 0 | 7 | 0 |

In the first season they met at League level, Fulham inflicted upon Aston Villa their first-ever defeat in the Second Division, winning 3-0 at Villa Park on 19 September 1936 in front of 49,000 spectators. Later that season they became the first team to complete a Second Division double over Villa with a 3-2 victory at Craven Cottage.

Rodney Marsh scored on his League debut for Fulham in a 1-0 win over Villa at Craven Cottage in March 1963.

A nine-goal thriller at Craven Cottage on 18 September 1965 went in favour of Villa by 6-3. The scoring went: 0-1, 0-2, 1-2. 2-2, 3-2, 3-3 and then upwards to 3-6. Graham Leggatt scored a hat-trick for the Cottagers. Later that season Fulham won 5-2 at Villa Park and then in November 1966 they swamped Villa 5-1 in London, all six goals coming in the second-half.

A crowd of 42,000 saw Villa beat the Cottagers 5-0 in a 3rd round FA Cup-tie in March 1905 (Harry Hampton scored twice). However, Second Division Fulham caused a major shock when they knocked Aston Villa (from the Premiership), out of the same competition in the 4th round in January 1999, winning 2-0 at Villa Park in front of 35,200 fans.

The two League Cup games were played in season 1965-66, Phil Woosnam netting both Villa's goals in their 2-0 replay win at home.

Players with both clubs include: JP Allen (Fulham WW2 guest), DG Bremner, T Bullivant, S Collymore, A Ducat (also Fulham manager), AJ Fisher, W Freeman, AG Gittins, JH Hampton (Fulham WW1 guest), SF Horne, R Houghton, HCL Kingaby, E Lowe, CJH Millington, RB Templeton, A Wilkes.

Also: J Hogan (Fulham player, Villa and Fulham manager, also Villa coach), A Barton (Fulham player, Villa manager), A Cox (Villa coach/assistant & caretaker-manager, Fulham Director of Football), DJ Sexton (coach at both clubs), R Money (Fulham player, Villa coach), JF Easson (Fulham player, Villa trainer).

## FULL MEMBERS CUP

Villa's record in this short-lived competition is:

| Venue | P | W | D | L | F | A |
|---|---|---|---|---|---|---|
| Home | 1 | 1 | 0 | 0 | 4 | 1 |
| Away | 1 | 0 | 0 | 1 | 0 | 1 |
| Totals | 2 | 1 | 0 | 1 | 4 | 2 |

Aston Villa took part in this competition in the 1986-87 season. A crowd of 5,124 saw them beat Derby County 4-1 at home in the first

THE COMPLETE ENCYCLOPAEDIA OF ASTON VILLA F.C.     THE COMPLETE ENCYCLOPAEDIA OF ASTON VILLA F.C.

110

round (Gary Shaw scored twice) but they succumbed to a single goal defeat at Ipswich in the next round when 8,244 fans attended Portman Road.

## GAGE, KEVIN WILLIAM

Born: Chiswick, 21 April 1964.

Career: Wimbledon (apprentice June 1980, professional January 1982), Aston Villa (£100,000, July 1987), Sheffield United (£150,000, November 1991), Preston North End (free transfer, March 1996), Hull City (free transfer, September 1997-May 1999). Retired to concentrate on his pub/restaurant business in the Peak District.

Able to play as a right-back or in midfield, Kevin Gage scored in all four Divisions of the Football League. He did very well with the Dons for whom he accumulated 189 senior appearances before joining Aston Villa. During his four years at Villa Park he starred in 145 first-class matches, scoring 12 goals - after taking over from Gary Williams. He then made over 130 appearances for the Blades prior to winding down his career in the lower Divisions. A compact footballer, aggressive when he had to be, Gage gained England Youth honours as a teenager, helped the Dons win the Fourth Division championship in 1983 and was in Villa's Second Division promotion side in 1988.

*Kevin Gage*

## GAINSBOROUGH TRINITY

Aston Villa and Trinity (a Football League club in the late 1890s/early 1900s) have never played against each other at competitive level.

Players with both clubs include: CV Harris, M Moralee, JG Tooth & JR Williamson (Villa reserves).

## GALLACHER, BERNARD

Born: Johnstone, Perthshire, 22 March 1967

Career: Perthshire County Schools, Aston Villa (apprentice June 1983, professional March 1985), Blackburn Rovers (on loan, November 1990), Doncaster Rovers (non-contract, September 1991), Brighton & Hove Albion (October 1991), Northampton Town (non-contract January-May 1994).

A player who began his career on the left-wing, Bernie Gallacher developed into a very useful full-back who made 69 senior appearances for Villa before joining Doncaster. He later had 50 outings for struggling Brighton alongside another ex-Villa man, Steve Foster.

## GAMES PLAYED

The most senior games played by Aston Villa in one single season has been 60 in 1981-82....42 in the First Division, six in the FA Cup, three in the League Cup and nine in the European Cup. They fulfilled 57 fixtures in 1960-61, 1970-71 and 1982-83; 56 in 1976-77 and 55 in 1974-75

During December/January, halfway through the 1889-90 season Villa played seven competitive games in just over four weeks, five away from home.

In each of three months - April 1920, April 1957 and April 1961 - Villa fulfilled a total of 10 competitive matches.

Villa played 12 matches in 36 days at the end of the 1956-57 season and 13 in 39 at the tailend of the 1960-61 campaign. They completed 16 first-team matches in two months late on in 1976-77 and played out 17 games in two months, five days from 10 March to 15 May 1979. Villa did not play a home League game in 1979 until 3 March.

## GARDNER, THOMAS

Born: Huyton, 28 May 1909. Died: May 1970.

Career: Orrell (1926), Liverpool (amateur July 1928, professional April 1929), Grimsby Town (May 1931), Hull City (May 1932), Aston Villa (£4,500, February 1934), Burnley (April 1938), guested for Blackpool during WW2, Wrexham (December 1945), Wellington Town (August 1947), Oswestry Town (player-manager, 1950, reverting to player-coach, January 1952), Chester (assistant-trainer July 1954-May 1967). Steward at Chester FC for twelve months before becoming a hotelier in Wrexham.

An enthusiastic footballer, the fair-haired Tom Gardner occupied the wing-half position and he had a fine career in the game which spanned more than 40 years. A constructive player, always wanting the ball, he suffered his fair share of injuries but always battled back. He had a decidedly long throw and won a Daily Mail competition in 1932....wind-assisted he could hurl a ball up to a distance of 40 yards! He was capped twice by England in 1934 v Czechoslovakia and 1935 v Holland), he gained a Third Division (N) championship medal with Hull in 1933 and a Wartime League Cup (North) winners medal with Blackpool as a guest in 1943. Gardner made 79 appearances for Villa, scoring one goal, in a 3-2 defeat at Fulham in January 1937.

## GARFIELD, JAMES HENRY

Born: Canterbury, Kent, July 1875. Died: March 1949.

Career: Gravesend United, Aston Villa (April 1899), Northampton Town (June 1900).

A reserve right-winger (initially to Charlie Athersmith), Jim Garfield played in one League game for Aston Villa - deputising for Bobby Templeton against Stoke in November 1899 when he scored in a 2-0 win.

## GARRATT, GEORGE

Born: Byker, County Durham, April 1884. Died: August 1960.

Career: Rowley Regis School, Cradley St Luke's (1899), Brierley Hill Alliance (1902), Crewe Alexandra (1904), Aston Villa (March 1905), Southampton (briefly February 1907), Plymouth Argyle (March 1907),

THE COMPLETE ENCYCLOPAEDIA OF ASTON VILLA F.C.    THE COMPLETE ENCYCLOPAEDIA OF ASTON VILLA F.C.

111

West Bromwich Albion (May 1907), Crystal Palace (May 1908), Millwall (October 1913), Kidderminster Harriers (after WW2 for a season). George Garratt moved to the Black Country with his family in 1892. He played soccer at school and then did well with a handful of local non-League clubs before joining Crewe in 1904. Well built, he was basically an outside-right who was signed by Villa as cover for Billy Brawn. He played in 17 first team games for the club (one goal scored) before leaving for the south coast. Garratt later did very well with Southern League side Crystal Palace for whom he scored eight goals in 185 appearances.

## GARRATY, WILLIAM

Born: Saltley, Birmingham, 6 October 1878. Died: Birmingham 6 May 1931. Career: Church Road and St Saviour's Schools Birmingham, Highfield Villa, Lozells FC, Aston Shakespeare, Aston Villa (professional August 1897), Leicester Fosse (September 1908), West Bromwich Albion (£270, October 1908), Lincoln City (£100, November 1910). Retired May 1911, thereafter a beer-delivery driver for Ansells Brewery until his death in 1931.

An excellent goalscorer throughout his career, Bill Garraty - with his dashing moustache - finished up as top-scorer in the whole country in season 1899-1900 when his 27 goals (in only 33 matches) helped Villa win the League title for the fifth time. He later added an FA Cup winners' medal to his collection (1905) and he also gained one full England cap (v Wales in 1903). A positive forward, always looking to get in a shot on goal, he netted 112 times in 259 first XI outings for Villa. He was part of a brilliant Villa attack in the late 1890s/early 1900s that included Charlie Athersmith, Jack Devey, Fred Wheldon and Steve Smith partnering Jasper McLuckie and Joe Bache, then later still, Harry Hampton, among others. He went on to skipper West Bromwich Albion for whom he netted 22 goals in only 59 appearances. A very fine player.

## GARVEY, BATTY WALTER

Born: Aston, Birmingham 10 February 1894. Died: Birmingham. c 1932. Career: Aston Hall Swifts, Aston Shakespeare, Aston Villa (March 1888-May 1893). Retired through injury.

Signed from a local junior club, 'Bat' Garvey made his debut for Aston Villa in a friendly match against Blackburn Rovers a fortnight later, coming into the side in place of Denny Hodgetts, who was away on international duty, playing for England against Scotland. Villa beat Rovers 6-4 and Garvey scored twice.

At the start of the next season - September 1888 - he lined up at inside-left in Villa's very first Football League game against Wolverhampton Wanderers at Dudley Road. Garvey, who was recognised as a reserve 'utility forward' with the club, went on to appear in just six more first-class games (scoring four goals) before he was forced to retire in 1893, having struggled with injury for three years. He was only 29.

## GATE RECEIPTS

### Gate receipts record at Villa Park since the World War II:

| | | |
|---|---|---|
| £8,651 | Villa v Derby County, FAC | 2.3.1946 |
| £18,012 | Bolton Wanderers v Charlton Ath, FAC sf | 23.3.1946 |
| £18,758 | England v Wales, international | 10.11.1947 |
| £18,817 | Blackpool v Tottenham Hotspur, FAC sf | 13.3.1948 |
| £19,004 | England v Northern Ireland, international | 14.11.1951 |
| £19,995 | Blackpool v Tottenham Hotspur, FAC sf | 21.3.1953 |
| £20,086 | Port Vale v WBA, FAC sf | 27.3.1954 |
| £24,620 | Man City v Tottenham Hot, FAC sf | 17.3.1956 |
| £26,118 | Fulham v Manchester United, FAC sf | 22.3.1958 |
| £27,910 | Burnley v Tottenham Hotspur, FAC sf | 18.3.1961 |
| £30,003 | Man United v Southampton, FAC sf | 27.4.1963 |
| £33,446 | Chelsea v Liverpool, FAC sf | 27.3.1965 |
| £35,200 | Chelsea v Sheffield Wednesday, FAC sf | 23.4.1966 |
| £37,028 | Birmingham City v. WBA, FAC sf | 27.4.1968 |
| £38,929 | Everton v Manchester City, FAC sf | 22.3.1969 |
| £87,978 | Ipswich Town v West Ham, FAC sf | 5.4.1975 |
| £89,995 | Villa v Barcelona, UEFA Cup | 1.3.1978 |
| £167,753 | Everton v West Ham United, FAC sf | 12.4.1980 |
| £211,155 | Arsenal v Manchester Utd, FAC sf | 16.4.1983 |
| £338,051 | Tottenham Hot v Watford, FAC sf | 11.4.1987 |
| £355,372 | Everton v Norwich City, FAC sf | 15.4.1989 |
| £390,035 | Nottingham F. v West Ham, FAC sf | 14.4.1991 |
| £516,607 | Liverpool v Portsmouth, FAC sf | 13.4.1992 |
| £1,005.402 | Crystal Palace v Man Utd, FAC sf | 9.4.1995 |
| £1,067.620 | Chelsea v Manchester Utd, FAC sf | 31.3.1996 |
| £1,196.712 | Czech Republic v Portugal, EC | 23.6.1996 |

### Gate receipts records from games involving Aston Villa (from 1970):

| | | |
|---|---|---|
| £28,499 | Villa v Manchester Utd, L/C sf 2nd leg | 23.12.1970 |
| £35,947 | Villa v Santos, friendly | 21.2.1972 |
| £89,995 | Villa v Barcelona, UEFA Cup | 1.3.1978 |
| £165,481 | Villa v Juventus, European Cup | 2.3.1983 |
| £313,152 | Villa v Liverpool, Premiership | 19.9.1992 |
| £375,000 | Villa v Tottenham Hotspur, Premiership | 25.1.1995 |
| £435,000 | Villa v Liverpool, Premiership | 6.5.1995 |
| £504,958 | Villa v Arsenal League Cup sf 2nd leg | 21.2.1996 |
| £596,657 | Villa v Atletico Madrid, UEFA Cup | 17.3.1998 |

### Money Talk

Record gate receipts were forthcoming from the first eight of Aston Villa's ten FA Cup Finals, thus: 1887 - £656, 1892 - £1,800, 1895 - £1,545, 1897 - £2,162, 1905 - £7,785, 1913 - £9,406, 1920 - £9,722 and 1924 - £14,280. The 1957 Final produced receipts of £48,816 and the Final of 2000 yielded overall takings of around £2.5 million

Gate receipts of £2,801 were taken from the Aston Villa v West Bromwich Albion FA Cup-tie on 21 February 1914 - the highest outside the semi-final or final at that time.

On 12 February 1930, record gate receipts of £4,873.11s.9d were registered at Villa Park when Walsall were the visitors for an FA Cup-tie. The crowd was 74,626. Less than a year later, a new record of £5,137 was set when Arsenal were the visitors to Villa Park for another FA Cup-tie. And then the 1931-32 FA Cup semi-final between Arsenal and Manchester City realised gate receipts of £6,138 from a 50,377 crowd.

In March 1938, £5,511 was taken through the turnstiles when Villa and Manchester City met in yet another FA Cup encounter.

The gate receipts of £18,012 taken from the Bolton-Charlton FA Cup semi-final clash at Villa Park in March 1946 were a record anywhere outside London and Glasgow during the WW2 period.

The 1959 FA Cup semi-final between Villa and Nottingham Forest at Hillsborough realised record gate receipts of £16,200.

The Exeter City-Aston Villa FA Cup-tie at St James' Park on 8 January 1994 revealed record gate receipts for the Devon club of £59,863.

Record gate receipts of £119,799 were banked from the Grimsby Town-Aston Villa FA Cup-tie at Blundell Park on 29 January 1994.

Leicester City's gate receipts record of £377,467 was set when Aston Villa played at Filbert Street in the League Cup semi-final 2nd leg on 2 February 2000.

A then Molineux gate receipts record of £109,655 was achieved when Aston Villa played Wolves in a second round, second leg League Cup game on 4 October 1989.

THE COMPLETE ENCYCLOPAEDIA OF ASTON VILLA F.C.  THE COMPLETE ENCYCLOPAEDIA OF ASTON VILLA F.C.

112

## GAUDIE, RICHARD

Born: Sheffield, July 1874.

Career: Sheffield Saracens, Sheffield United, Aston Villa (August 1898), Dudley Town (September 1899), Darlaston (1900-02). Retired after badly damaging his right ankle.

Dick Gaudie scored on his League debut for Aston Villa against Stoke on 3 September 1898 when he deputised for Fred Wheldon. He was a reserve forward during his time with the club and made a total of five senior appearances.

## GAVAN, JOHN THOMAS

Born: Walsall, 8 December 1939.

Career: Hilary Street Old Boys, Walsall Wood, Aston Villa (professional, November 1962), Doncaster Rovers (July 1967-May 1968), Bilston Town (August 1968-72), Dudley Town.

John Gavan was a centre-forward at school, before developing into a very useful goalkeeper. He made only 33 senior appearances during his career - 12 with Aston Villa - but played in over 150 games at non-League level after leaving Belle Vue.

## GEDDIS, DAVID

Born: Carlisle, 12 March 1958,

Career: Schoolboy football, Ipswich Town (junior, June 1973, professional, August 1975), Luton Town (on loan), Aston Villa (£300,000, September 1979), Luton Town (on loan, December 1982), Barnsley (£50,000, September 1983), Birmingham City (£50,000, December 1984), Brentford (on loan, September 1986), Shrewsbury Town (£25,000, March 1987), Swindon Town (October 1988), Darlington (March-May 1990). In the mid-1990s Geddis was appointed Community Officer at Middlesbrough and later became reserve team coach at The Riverside Stadium (June 2000 to July 2001).

As a raw 20 year-old striker, David Geddis played superbly well for Ipswich Town in the 1978 FA Cup Final against Arsenal, and was immediately marked up as a star of the future. He never quite made it to the top, although he did score plenty of goals at professional level. He went to Portman Road as a 15 year-old and developed quickly. And went on to play League soccer until 1991. Geddis gained caps for England at Youth and 'B' team levels and won both FA Youth Cup and FA Cup winners medals with Ipswich. His record with Villa was 56 first team appearances and 16 goals scored. During his League career he netted a total of 77 goals in 264 games.

*David Geddis - going for goal.*

## GEORGE ROBEY INTERNATIONAL CUP

Aston Villa won this trophy twice: in 1907 and 1910.

## GEORGE, WILLIAM

Born: Shrewsbury, 29 June 1874. Died: Birmingham, 4 December 1933.

Career: Woolwich Ramblers (1894), Army service with Royal Artillery (from February 1895), Trowbridge Town (during Army days, 1895-97), Aston Villa (£50, professional October 1897), Birmingham (player/trainer, July 1911). Retired as a player in 1913 and worked at the Austin Rover plant at Longbridge, Birmingham. George also played cricket for Warwickshire (1901, 1902 and 1907), Wiltshire and Shropshire.

Said by some to have been one of the greatest - if not the greatest - goalkeepers in the history of the club, Billy George was a giant of a man and for many seasons remained at the top of his form after making a splendid debut in the local derby for Villa against West Bromwich Albion on 9 October 1897. He held his position as first choice 'between the posts' right through until 1909 and only injuries, illness and international duties forced him to miss matches. For such a big man (he weighed well over 14 stone at times), he was quick on his feet, had a tremendous reach, was full of resource, punched the ball with great power and could kick like a mule! Described as a rare good man in the side and an ornament to the game, George starred in 401 first-class matches for Villa (358 in the First Division). He won three England caps in 1903 and he was also taking part in the abandoned game against Scotland at Ibrox Park in 1902 when 26 people were killed as terraces collapsed at one end of the ground. As a Villa player he helped them twice win the League championship (1899, 1900) and he also collected an FA Cup winners' medal in 1905.

When George was 'bought' out of the Army in 1897 there was such a hulabaloo surrounding the transaction that two Villa committee members - George Ramsay and Fred Rinder, along with George himself - were suspended by the FA for a month!

## GERMANY

In January 1901, Aston Villa became the first English League club side to play in Germany. They beat a Select XI 6-2 in Berlin when Joe Bache scored on his debut. After retiring, Bache returned to Germany where he became trainer-coach to the Rot Weiss club of Frankfurt in 1921, also assisting FC Mannheim (1924) whilst in Germany.

In May 1938, under manager Jimmy Hogan, Aston Villa went on a nine-day tour of Germany, playing three matches, two of which resulted in victories.

Villa started their programme on 15 May with a hard-fought 3-2 victory in Berlin against a strong 'Austrian international orientated' German Select XI (Deutsche Auswahl-Mannschaft) in front of 110,000 spectators in the sweltering 90 degrees heat of the Olympic Stadium (the Reichsportfield) in Berlin. Frank Broome (2) and Frank Shell scored for Villa. Before the start of this game the Villa had declined to give the Nazi Salute.

THE COMPLETE ENCYCLOPAEDIA OF ASTON VILLA F.C.    THE COMPLETE ENCYCLOPAEDIA OF ASTON VILLA F.C.

113

*Villa in Germany in 1938.*

Three days later, in front of 50,000 fans in Dusseldorf, Villa lost narrowly by 2-1 to a Greater German XI after being persuaded by their Chairman, Fred Normansell to give the Nazi salute prior to kick-off. Some players obeyed the Chairman and did it half-heartedly, incorporating the famous Churchill gesture at the same time, while a few tilted away in the opposite direction of the main stand, looking as if they were signalling semaphore!

The final friendly - on 22 May - was played in the Adolf Hitler Stadium in Stuttgart against a German XI which was attended by 70,000 spectators. Villa won 2-1, Bob Iverson and Houghton the scorers this time.

Villa recorded two wins on tour in Germany in 1956-57; two draws and a defeat in 1957-58; played two games in 1966-67 and lost 1-0 to SV Jahn in 1969-70.

In July 1971, Villa played three friendly tour matches in Germany, winning two and losing one. Villa's Harry Gregory was sent-off in one of these encounters. And in 1982-83 they again trekked over to the Fatherland to play KFC Kaiserslautern and FC Schalke 04.

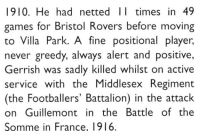

In 1980-81 a pre-season tour to Germany saw Villa win one, draw one and lose one of their three matches.

Villa beat Bayern Munich 1-0 in the 1982 European Cup Final in Rotterdam.

As holders of the trophy, Villa played the German champions Dynamo Berlin in a 2nd round European Cup-tie in 1982-83, eventually going through on the away goal after a 2-2 aggregate score.

A German Democratic Republic XI visited Villa Park for a friendly in 1981-82. Villa won 4-2.

West Germany played two World Cup matches at Villa Park in 1966.

Two German-born players - Stefan Beinlich and Matthias Breitkreutz - played for Aston Villa against Sheffield United in 1993.

### GERRISH, William Webber Walter

Born: Bristol, December 1884. Died: France, 1916.

Career: Bristol Rovers, Aston Villa (£200, April 1909), Preston North End (August 1912), Chesterfield (November 1912).

Able to play at inside-right or centre-forward, Billy Gerrish scored 18 goals in 59 games for Aston Villa whom he served for over three years, gaining a League championship medal in

1910. He had netted 11 times in 49 games for Bristol Rovers before moving to Villa Park. A fine positional player, never greedy, always alert and positive, Gerrish was sadly killed whilst on active service with the Middlesex Regiment (the Footballers' Battalion) in the attack on Guillemont in the Battle of the Somme in France, 1916.

### GHRAYIB, NAJWAN

Born: Israel, 30 January 1974

Career: Maccabi Paetach, Hapoel Tel Aviv, Aston Villa (£1 million, August 1999), Hapoel Haifa (£150,000, February 2001).

When he joined Aston Villa, Naj Ghrayib was already an established Israeli international (16 caps won) but he found it difficult to dislodge Alan Wright from the left wing-back position and, in fact, had to wait until April 2000 before he started his first Premiership match (v Sunderland). He added two more caps to his tally whilst at Villa Park, but then struggled with his fitness during the 2000-01 season after fluid built up on his knee which kept him out of action for some ten weeks. He left the club in the February of 2001 after making just six first team appearances.

### GIBSON, COLIN HAYWARD

Born: Normanby-on-Tees, near Middlesbrough, 16 September 1923. Died: Stourbridge, 27 March 1992.

Career: Penarth Pontoon, Cardiff City (£10, August 1942), Newcastle United (£15,000, July 1948), Aston Villa (£17,500, July 1949), Lincoln City (£6,000, January 1956), Stourbridge (August 1957-May 1958). Retired to become a publican.

An ex-marine engineer on the dockside, Colin Gibson earned his first wage at the age of 15, learning what made the giant eight-and-half thousand ton freight vessels tick! He gradually eased himself into professional football and became a dashing winger with great skill, expert control and a fine shot. Cardiff signed him on the recommendation of ex-Aston Villa goalkeeper Cyril Spiers. A year after helping the Ninian Park club win the Third Division (South) championship, Gibson was transferred to Newcastle and in 1949 he switched to Villa Park where he became a firm favourite with the supporters. He went on to score 26 goals in 167 first team outings for Villa, winning an England 'B' cap against Holland in 1949 and also representing the Football League that same year. Replaced on the right-wing by Tommy Southren (and with Les Smith of Wolves ready to move in) Gibson was transferred to Sincil Bank in 1956, and after a spell with non-League Stourbridge he retired in 1958. He subsequently became licensee of the Spencer's Arms, Hagley. Besides being a very fine footballer, Gibson was also an accomplished pianist.

*Colin Gibson (1950s).*

A 1950 pen-picture desribed Gibson as a 'flank-turning, defence-undermining instrument'.....an out-and-out winger really!

## GIBSON, COLIN JOHN

Born: Bridport, 6 April 1960

Career: Portsmouth Grammar School, West Sussex Schoolboys, Portsmouth (amateur), Aston Villa (YTS, July 1976, professional April 1978), Manchester United (£275,000, November 1985), Port Vale (on loan, September-October 1990), Leicester City (£100,000, December 1990). Blackpool (free transfer, September 1994), Walsall (non-contract, May 1995-96).

Left-back Colin Gibson (who could also occupy a midfield position) had a fine career that spanned some 20 years. He joined Aston Villa as a youngster at the age of 16 and was then capped by England at Youth, Under-21 and 'B' team levels. He gained a First Division championship medal in 1981 and a European Super Cup prize in 1982 and went on to score 17 goals in 238 first team outings for Villa before switching his allegiance to Old Trafford. After a little over five years with United (95 games played) and a loan spell at Vale Park, he linked up with ex-Villa colleague Brian Little at Leicester City before winding down his career with spells at Bloomfield Road and Walsall. Gibson appeared in a total of 364 League games for his six clubs.

*Colin Gibson (1980s).*

## GIBSON, DAVID WEDDERBURN

Born: Winchburgh, Scotland, 23 September 1938.

Career: Livingston United (1953), Hibernian (£1,500, professional, September 1956), Leicester City (£25,000, January 1962), Aston Villa (free transfer, September 1970), Exeter City (£3,500, January 1972)

Davey Gibson spent seven years in Scottish League football before joining Leicester as they prepared to commence their 1962 FA Cup campaign. Eight years later he was transferred to Villa Park - soon after the fans had started to watch Third Division soccer for the first time in the club's history! Gibson made just 24 appearances and scored one goal for Villa before transferring south to Exeter early in 1972, retiring from competitive match action in 1974. He undoubtedly played his best football at Filbert Street (339 appearances and 53 goals for the Foxes). A very fine ball-player, his elegant control and visionary passing skills were a major factor in Leicester reaching two Wembley FA Cup Finals in 1963 and 1969, and winning the League Cup in 1964. He scored three times in seven internationals for Scotland and in fact, he returned to Wembley as Villa's substitute in the 1971 League Cup Final v. Spurs.

## GIBSON, JAMES DAVIDSON

Born: Larkhall, Lanarkshire, 12 June 1901. Died: Erdington, 1 January 1978.

Career: Kirkintillock Rob Roy (1917), Glasgow Ashfield, Partick Thistle (professional, May 1921), Aston Villa (£7,500, April 1927). Retired May 1936.

Scotsman Jimmy Gibson was a wonderfully cultured half-back, able to occupy all three middle-line positions. Standing 6ft 2ins tall and weighing 12 stone, he was a tireless performer with a terrific engine, always surging upfield to assist his forwards and then racing back to help out his defenders. He appeared in almost 200 competitive games for Partick before Aston Villa splashed out a then record fee of £7,500

to bring his talents into the Football League in 1927. Over the next nine years Gibson gave the club sterling service, netting 10 times in 225 senior appearances. He was capped 10 times by his country between 1926-30 and twice represented the Football League. He was part of a brilliant Villa half-back line, comprising himself, Alec Talbot and Joe Tate (perhaps the best in the club's history). Gibson retired in the summer of 1936 and went to work at the ICI factory, Witton (until 1963). He died at the age of 76.

Jimmy's son, Neil Gibson, played for Rangers and Partick Thistle as well as Scotland.

## GIDMAN, JOHN

Born: Liverpool, 10 January 1954.

Career: Merseyside Schoolboy football, Liverpool (apprentice, June 1969), Aston Villa (professional, August 1971), Everton (£650,000, October 1979), Manchester United (£450,000, August 1981), Manchester City (free transfer, October 1986), Stoke City (August 1988), Darlington (player/assistant-manager, February-May 1989), Kings Lynn (manager, early 1990s).

An attack-minded right full-back, John Gidman had an excellent professional career. After playing Schoolboy football in the Garston area of his native Liverpool, he joined the apprentice staff at Anfield but failed to make the breakthrough and subsequently moved to Villa Park at the start of the 1971-72 season, snapped up by eagle-eyed scout Neville Briggs. Gidman took time to establish himself in the first XI with Villa but once in, he stayed and amassed a fine record of 243 senior appearances (nine goals scored). He won England caps at full, 'B' and Under-23 levels, having earlier represented his country as a Youth team player. He helped Villa win the FA Youth Cup in 1972 and the League Cup in 1977, but missed the 1975 League Final win over Norwich after suffering a nasty eye injury when a firework exploded in his face on Bonfire Night, 1974, the year he won the club's Terrace Trophy award. Gidman was unfortunately sent-off in the Nou Camp Stadium when playing for Villa against Barcelona in a UEFA Cup match in 1978. The ten men of Villa failed to hold on and lost 2-1.

Gidman was transferred back to Merseyside (to Goodison Park) in 1979 in a deal that saw Pat Heard move to Villa Park. From Everton he

*John Gidman*

switched his allegiance to Old Trafford in 1981 and four years later collected an FA Cup winners medal when the Reds beat his former club Everton. He then moved across to neighbouring Maine Road on a free transfer in 1986, assisted Stoke for a short while and ended his playing days with his former Villa team-mate Brian Little at Darlington in 1989. He later took charge of Kings Lynn and also ran a café/bar in Spain.

Gidman amassed a total of 432 League appearances during his career.

## GILLAN, JAMES STANLEY

Born: Derby, December 1870. Died: Ilkeston, c 1944.

Career: Burton United, Burton Swifts, Aston Villa (April 1893), Brierley Hill Alliance (September 1894), Cradley Heath (1895-96 season). Retired through injury.

Jim Gillan was reserve to converted left-half Bob Chatt during his brief association with Aston Villa. He made just three senior appearances, lining up against Everton (his debut at home), Nottingham Forest and Darwen in September/October 1893.

THE COMPLETE ENCYCLOPAEDIA OF ASTON VILLA F.C.          THE COMPLETE ENCYCLOPAEDIA OF ASTON VILLA F.C.

115

## GILLINGHAM

Villa's record against the Gills:
Football League

| Venue | P | W | D | L | F | A |
|---|---|---|---|---|---|---|
| Home | 1 | 1 | 0 | 0 | 2 | 1 |
| Away | 1 | 0 | 1 | 0 | 0 | 0 |
| Totals | 2 | 1 | 1 | 0 | 2 | 1 |

The two League encounters took place in season 1970-71 (Division 3). A crowd of 29,383 saw goals by Chico Hamilton and Pat McMahon give Villa a 2-1 home win, while 10,812 assembled at The Priestfield Stadium to watch the return fixture finish all square at 0-0.

Players with both clubs include: WCW Armfield, W Armstrong (Villa reserve), J Boden, MD Buttress, AG Cascarino, SJ Drinkwater, WE Evans, S Grayson, G Leigh, C McElney, W Marriott, J Overton, DF Skea, G Smith, S Smith (player-manager of Gills), JE Travers, H Vallance (Villa reserve), C Wigmore (Villa reserve).
Also: R Saunders (Gills player, Villa manager).

## GILSTON, THOMAS AUBREY

Born: Lichfield, June 1879. Died: Lichfield.
Career: Whittington Royal, Burton United (1898), Aston Villa (July 1900), Brentford (May 1901), Melksham FC (1902-03).
A solid full-back, Tom Gilston was signed as cover for Albert Evans. He was handed just two League outings - both away - at Newcastle and Derby County in April 1901. He was allowed to leave Villa Park at the end of that season.

## GINOLA, DAVID DESIRE MARC

Born: Gossin near Toulon, France, 25 January 1967.
Career: FC Toulon (1985), Racing Club de Paris (1988), Brent (1990), Paris St Germain (1992), Newcastle United (£2.5m, July 1995) Tottenham Hotspur (£2m July 1997), Aston Villa (£3m, August 2000).
When he joined Aston Villa in readiness for the 2000-01 Premiership season, French international David Ginola immediately received £40,000-a-week to become the highest-paid player in the club's history.
Ginola began his career with his hometown club and after brief but interesting spells with two other French teams, he helped PSG win their first French League title in eight years in 1994 when he was also named both France's 'Player of the Year' and the 'Players' Player of the Year.'
After taking his tally of appearances in French football to well over the 200 mark (25 goals scored) and gaining international recognition, Ginola opted to try his luck in England when he signed for Newcastle. He spent two seasons at St James' Park during which time he netted seven times in 76 senior outings for the Geordies as they consolidated their position in the Premiership. In the summer of 1997, Ginola was on the move again, this time travelling 300 miles south to sign for Spurs. He immediately became a star attraction at White Hart Lane and went on to score some stunning goals. He helped the London club win the League Cup at Wembley in 1999 and appeared in exactly 100 Premiership matches (12 goals) and in 27 Cup encounters (9 goals) before leaving for Villa Park in a blaze of publicity!
A player with tremendous on-the-ball skill, he has a splendid body-swerve, stunning right foot shot and a great deal of charisma. He was voted both the Football Writers' and PFA 'Player of the Year' in 1999 and was also selected in the Premiership representative side, being regarded at the time as one of the greatest wingers (left side) in the U.K. A celebrity both on and off the field, he unfortunately fell out with the management of the French national team in the mid-1990s and after attempting to settle his differences, he failed to get a recall and was subsequently missed out on his country's World Cup and European Championship triumphs. His tally of full caps currently stands at 17 with his international debut coming back in 1990 as a 'sub' against

Albania in a European Championship qualifier. His last game for his country was in September 1995 against Azerbaijan, also in a European Championship match. Ginola suffered with injury problems during his first half-season with Villa and when the 2000-01 campaign ended his record with the club was 28 appearances (13 as a sub) and three goals scored.....all with a touch of class!
The Frenchman has also been a male model, drives racing cars and has his own personal websaite (www.ginola14.com).
Ginola's book: 'El Magnifique' was a best-seller in the year 2000.

## GITTINGS, ALFRED G.

Born: Manchester, 3 July 1886. Died: 1949.
Career: Atherton Church House (1902), Adlington FC (1904), Bolton Wanderers (briefly, 1905), Luton Town (August 1906), Queen's Park Rangers (July 1907), Aston Villa (October 1908), Brighton & Hove Albion, Croydon Common (July 1909), Fulham (September 1910), Portsmouth (December 1910), Partick Thistle (1911-14). Retired during the Great War.
A reserve inside-forward at Villa Park, Alf Gittings' only appearance came on Christmas Day 1908 when he deputised for George Reeves in the 1-1 home draw with Liverpool. He did very well in the Southern league after leaving Villa Park.

## GLASGOW RANGERS

Villa's record against the 'Gers:
FA Cup

| Venue | P | W | D | L | F | A |
|---|---|---|---|---|---|---|
| Neutral | 1 | 1 | 0 | 0 | 3 | 1 |

This FA Cup meeting was a semi-final clash at Crewe in March 1887,

*John Deehan (left) getting in a shot on goal during the friendly with Rangers in 1976.*

THE COMPLETE ENCYCLOPAEDIA OF ASTON VILLA F.C. | THE COMPLETE ENCYCLOPAEDIA OF ASTON VILLA F.C.

116

Scottish clubs being eligible at this time. In front of 10,000 fans, Archie Hunter scored twice to help steer Villa into the Final.

In season 1881-82 Rangers beat Villa 7-1 in a friendly in Glasgow but six years later Villa gained sweet revenge with a 5-1 friendly win at Perry Barr.

A riot caused the abandonment of a friendly between Villa and the Scottish club in October 1976. (See under Abandoned matches).

Players with both clubs include: N Cooper, J Cowan, AM Gray, JA Gray, JL Logan, GB Ramsay (Rangers trialist), P Rideout, ME Walters.

## GLOSSOP (NORTH END)

Villa's record against Glossop:

Football League

| Venue | P | W | D | L | F | A |
|---|---|---|---|---|---|---|
| Home | 1 | 1 | 0 | 0 | 9 | 0 |
| Away | 1 | 0 | 0 | 1 | 0 | 1 |
| Totals | 2 | 1 | 0 | 1 | 9 | 1 |

Bill Garraty scored four goals when Villa registered their only League win over Glossop, 9-0 at home in September 1899.

Players with both clubs include: J Boden, S Doncaster, AL Goodall, GH Hampton, AF Phoenix.

## GLOVER, DEAN VICTOR

Born: West Bromwich, 29 December 1963.

Career: Kings Norton Schools, West Midlands Boys, Aston Villa (apprentice, June 1980, professional December 1981), Sheffield United (on loan, October 1986), Middlesbrough (June 1987), Port Vale (£200,000, February 1989). Retired from League football in 1998 and managed local side Newcastle Town for a while before returning to Vale Park as a coach.

Owing to an array of defenders at the club, the hard-tackling, wholehearted commitment of Dean Glover earned him only 39 appearances (one goal scored) during his seven-year stay at Villa Park. He made his debut in the FA Cup-tie against Norwich City in January 1984 and his single goal was tucked away in the 1-1 League Cup draw with Arsenal at Villa Park in January 1986.

After more than 50 outings for Middlesbrough Glover joined Port Vale for a club record fee in 1989 and over the next decade he gave the Potteries' club sterling service, accumulating a magnificent record of 430 League and Cup appearances and 20 goals. He helped Vale win the Sherpa Van Trophy in 1993 and promotion from Division Two the following season.

## GOALKEEPERS

Aston Villa's first prominent goalkeeper was Billy Scattergood who served the club during the 1874-75 season.

In July 1896, Villa paid a then record fee for a goalkeeper of £200 when they recruited Jimmy Whitehouse from Grimsby Town.

In October 1897 Villa infringed the FA Rules by 'buying' goalkeeper Billy George out of the Army for £50. The FA then fined the club that same amount for their misdoing!

Later, in 1930, another 'keeper, Harry Morton, was also 'signed' out of the forces (the Welsh Fusiliers) but by now the rules had been changed to allow this transaction to take place.

In November 1931, Morton was sitting in the stand at Maine Road preparing to watch the League game between Manchester City and Villa, when he was quickly summoned to the dressing room after Fred Biddlestone had injured himself during the pre-match kick-about. It was Morton's debut and he was beaten three times in the 3-3 draw. Morton missed only one League game out of 126 between 1932 and 1935.

Joe Rutherford kept goal for Villa before, during and after the Second

World War. He appeared in 156 League games.

In 1951-52 Irish international defender Con Martin kept goal for Villa in 27 League Division One games and in the 3rd round FA Cup-tie against Newcastle United. He was on the losing side eight times.

Aston Villa had two goalkeepers - Sam Hardy and Ben Olney - capped at full international level by England during the inter-War years.

Billy George (at 14st 2lbs) and Nigel Sims (14st) are said to have been the two heaviest players ever to star for the Villa. George, in fact, appeared in 358 out of a possible 480 League games for Villa during his time at the club.

Only Nigel Spink (361) played in more League games than George Spink also holds the club record for most senior appearances as a 'keeper (460).

Spink never expected to play in the 1982 European Cup Final against Bayern Munich - but he did - replacing the injured Jimmy Rimmer after just 10 minutes in Rotterdam. Prior to that game Spink had only had one other first team outing! He officially retired in May 2000, three months before his 42nd birthday, was elected President of the Aston Villa Cubs in January 1987. He made over 530 appearances during his career.

Nigel Sims

Future Villa goalkeeper Alan Wakeman skippered England at Schoolboy level in seasons 1933-34 and 1934-35.

George Ephgrave, at 6ft. 5in, is the tallest goalkeeper (and indeed player) to be registered with Aston Villa. He was with the club in 1938-39 and was later captured whilst on active service in Crete in 1941.

Mike Pinner won 51 caps for England at amateur level making his League debut for Villa in 1954.

Three former Wolves goalkeepers - Nigel Sims, Geoff Sidebottom and Dennis Parsons - were all at Villa Park during the 1950s.

Sims, shortly after becoming the first recipient of the Villa's Supporters' Terrace Trophy, joined Arsenal as a guest on their Italian tour in the summer of 1958.

Former Villa goalkeeper Kevin Keelan, MBE, who was born in Calcutta, India, amassed 673 senior appearances for Norwich City between 1963 and 1980. He played his last game for the Canaries at the age of 39 years, one month, in February 1980 v Liverpool. He was voted the best goalkeeper in the USA in 1978.

Geoff Crudgington made 250 appearances for Crewe Alexandra and 219 for Plymouth Argyle after leaving Villa Park in 1972.

Once an outfield player, Fred Potter deputised in a Villa Central League game in 1958 when Billy Beaton was injured. He later made the first XI as a goalkeeper and went on to amass a career record of over 150 League and Cup appearances.

Goalkeeper Colin 'Tiny' Withers won the Villa supporters' 'Terrace Trophy' award two years running: 1966 and 1967. Withers, in fact, conceded six goals on his League debut for Birmingham City against Spurs at White Hart Lane in November 1960. Ironically, he then let in four more when playing in his first League game for Villa - against the same opposition on the same ground in November 1964.

Jimmy Rimmer, later to keep goal for Aston Villa, appeared in both legs of the 1970-71 League Cup semi-final for Manchester United against Villa!

Rimmer played in 229 out of a possible 230 League games for Villa over

THE COMPLETE ENCYCLOPAEDIA OF ASTON VILLA F.C.      THE COMPLETE ENCYCLOPAEDIA OF ASTON VILLA F.C.

117

a period of five years (1977-82). He also had a run of 125 consecutive outings during this same period.

Jim Cumbes was a DJ on Radio Birmingham in the 1970s. He also played county cricket.

Jim Herriot, albeit briefly, was on loan to Villa from neighbours Birmingham City in 1971.

Peter Withe was a very capable stand-in goalkeeper but nothing like Irishman Con Martin, who besides playing centre-half for Aston Villa and the Republic of Ireland, also kept goal for club and country!

Goalkeeper Mark Kendall 'scored' when playing for Aston Villa's Youth team against an England Youth XI at Villa Park in December 1978 - his long clearance bounced over the opposing 'keeper and into the unguarded net!

Out of a total of 4,014 League & Premiership games (1888-2001) Villa's goalkeepers, between them, kept 1,057 clean sheets.

## GOALS & GOALSCORERS
List of Aston Villa's leading goalscorers in the various competitions.

### All Senior Games (qualification: 50 goals)

| Billy Walker | 244 | Dicky York | 86 |
|---|---|---|---|
| Harry Hampton | 242 | Charlie Athersmith | 85 |
| Jack Devey | 187 | Ray Graydon | 80 |
| Joe Bache | 185 | Brian Little | 79 |
| Eric Houghton | 170 | Andy M Gray | 78 |
| Tom Waring | 167 | Tommy Thompson | 76 |
| Johnny Dixon | 144 | Joe Beresford | 73 |
| Peter McParland | 120 | Harry Burrows | 73 |
| Billy Garraty | 112 | Bobby Thomson | 70 |

| Eric Houghton | 160 |
|---|---|
| Tom Waring | 159 |
| Johnny Dixon | 132 |
| Peter McParland | 97 |
| Billy Garraty | 96 |
| Dai Astley | 92 |
| Len Capewell | 88 |
| Clem Stephenson | 85 |
| George Brown | 79 |
| Dicky York | 79 |
| Gerry Hitchens | 78 |
| Frank Broome | 77 |
| Charlie Athersmith | 75 |
| Peter Withe | 74 |
| Dwight Yorke | 73 |
| Ray Graydon | 68 |
| Tony Hateley | 68 |
| Fred Wheldon | 68 |
| Joe Beresford | 66 |
| Denny Hodgetts | 62 |
| Arthur Dorrell | 60 |
| Trevor Ford | 60 |
| Brian Little | 60 |
| Andy M Gray | 59 |
| Charlie Wallace | 54 |
| Harry Burrows | 53 |
| Billy Kirton | 53 |
| Allan Evans | 51 |

*'Pongo' Waring*

*Harry Hampton*

*Peter McParland*

| Dai Astley | 100 | Gary Shaw | 69 |
|---|---|---|---|
| Len Capewell | 100 | Arthur Dorrell | 65 |
| Dwight Yorke | 97 | David Platt | 62 |
| Gerry Hitchens | 96 | Trevor Ford | 61 |
| Clem Stephenson | 96 | Albert Hall | 61 |
| Peter Withe | 92 | Allan Evans | 60 |
| Denny Hodgetts | 91 | Billy Kirton | 59 |
| Frank Broome | 90 | Gordon Cowans | 57 |
| George Brown | 89 | Charlie Wallace | 57 |
| Tony Hateley | 86 | Albert Brown | 55 |

### Football League:
(qualification: 50 goals)

| Harry Hampton | 215 | Albert Hall | 51 |
|---|---|---|---|
| Billy Walker | 214 | David Platt | 50 |
| Jack Devey | 169 | | |
| Joe Bache | 168 | | |

### FA Cup: (qualification: 10 goals)

| Archie Hunter | 33 | Billy Garraty | 15 |
|---|---|---|---|
| Billy Walker | 30 | Howard Vaughton | 15 |
| Denny Hodgetts | 29 | Frank Broome | 13 |
| Harry Hampton | 27 | Len Capewell | 12 |
| Peter McParland | 19 | Johnny Dixon | 12 |
| Albert Brown | 18 | Clem Stephenson | 11 |
| Jack Devey | 18 | Charlie Athersmith | 10 |
| Joe Bache | 17 | Eric Houghton | 10 |
| Arthur Brown | 15 | | |

### League Cup: (qualification: 10 goals)

| Harry Burrows | 15 | Tony Hateley | 13 |
|---|---|---|---|
| Brian Little | 15 | Gerry Hitchens | 11 |
| Andy M Gray | 14 | Andy Lochhead | 10 |

### UEFA & European Cups (qualification: 3 goals)

| Peter Withe | 9 | Ken McNaught | 5 |
|---|---|---|---|

*Brian Little (v. QPR).*

THE COMPLETE ENCYCLOPAEDIA OF ASTON VILLA F.C.    THE COMPLETE ENCYCLOPAEDIA OF ASTON VILLA F.C.

118

| Peter Withe | 9 | Ken McNaught | 5 |
| Gary Shaw | 9 | Tony Morley | 5 |
| Stan Collymore | 5 | Brian Little | 3 |
| John Deehan | 5 | Ian Taylor | 3 |

## Wartime (1939-46) (qualification: 25 goals)

| George Edwards | 94 | Billy Goffin | 45 |
| Frank Broome | 91 | Harry Parkes | 41 |
| Eric Houghton | 88 | Freddie Haycock | 25 |
| Dicky Davis | 67 | Albert Kerr | 21 |
| Bob Iverson | 55 | | |

*Ken McNaught*

*Andy Gray*

## Goal-Talk

Eric Houghton scored 258 goals for Villa in Football League, FA Cup and Wartime football. In all matches for the club (at various levels) he netted 345 goals, including 72 penalties!

When winning the Birmingham Senior Cup in 1882-83, Villa's first team scored 53 goals in their six matches, with Arthur Brown claiming 21 of them, including a club record 10 in a 21-0 win over Small Heath Swifts.

Five players have scored five goals in a League game for Aston Villa - Harry Hampton v Sheffield Wednesday, October 1912; Harold Halse v Derby County, October 1912; Len Capewell v Burnley, August 1925; George Brown v Leicester City, January 1932 and Gerry Hitchens v Charlton Athletic, November 1959. Only Hitchens' nap-hand came in Division Two; the others claimed theirs in the top flight.

Harold Halse scored in six successive League games for Villa in September/October/November 1912; Len Capewell netted in eight successive League matches between 7 September and 17 October 1925 and Tom 'Pongo' Waring was also on target in eight successive League games between 3 May and 20 September 1930.

During the first half of the 1945-46 season, George Edwards netted in 11 consecutive Football League (South) matches - from 20 October and 25 December inclusive.....16 goals in total.

Villa conceded a total of 26 goals when losing five successive away games halfway through the 1890-91 season. They lost 7-1 to Notts County, 5-1 at Blackburn, 5-0 at Everton, 5-1 at Sunderland and 4-1 at Preston.

Villa scored in 82 consecutive home Football League games between 14 March 1891 and 19 December 1896.

The fastest-ever League goal scored by a Villa player came after just 9.3 seconds - from the boot of Bob Iverson in the home League game against Charlton Athletic on 3 December 1938.

George Edwards followed up six years later with a goal after 13

seconds in Villa's home FA Cup-tie against Manchester United on 3 January 1948.

Tony Hateley found the Manchester United net after 35 seconds in Villa's home game against the Reds in November 1963.

Cyrille Regis scored for Villa after 22 seconds of the home League game with his former club Coventry City at Villa Park on 2 May 1992....the fastest goal of the season!

The first time Aston Villa scored seven goals in an away League game was on 19 December 1903, when they beat Nottingham Forest 7-3.

Villa conceded seven goals in home League games three times in the space of two months in season 1935-36, losing 7-2 to Middlesbrough, 7-0 to West Bromwich Albion and 7-1 to Arsenal, whose centre-forward Ted Drake scored all his side's goals (from eight shots). Villa also lost 6-2 at home to Grimsby Town during the same period.

Another Arsenal player, Tony Woodcock, netted five goals in the Gunners' 6-2 win on the same ground in October 1983.

Seventeen years earlier, in September 1966, Bobby Tambling of Chelsea netted five times in his side's 6-2 League win on Villa soil.

Villa conceded only 35 goals (in 42 matches) in 1937-38 - the best defensive record in the Football League that season.

Villa's Harry Hampton was the First Division's leading scorer in season 1909-10 with 26 goals (including four hat-tricks, two coming in the space of 24 hours). Hampton also scored a hat-trick in an FA Cup-tie that season and four goals for the Football League side against the Irish League in 1911....to finish with an overall tally of 33.

Harold Halse netted 12 goals in six weeks for Villa during late September/October/early December 1912.

Tom 'Pongo' Waring struck home 15 goals in eight matches for Villa in 1930 (starting 3 May and then from 31 August to 20 September).

Harold Nash v Liverpool in April 1915 and Frank Shell against Stockport County in December 1937 both scored hat-tricks on their home League debuts for Villa.

Despite netting four goals, Villa still managed to incur their only League defeat at home in season 1930-31 (to Derby by 6-4).

In that same season Villa scored four or more goals in a League game on 20 occasions. Tom Waring netted three fourtimers himself.

Waring (50) and Eric Houghton (30) scored 80 senior goals between them for Aston Villa in 1930-31. Waring netted 49 in the League alone - a club record. (See separate entry).

Only four players - Waring and Houghton (above) plus George Brown (36 in 1929-30) and Len Capewell (34 in 1925-26) - have scored 30 or more goals in a season for Villa.

*Tony Hateley*

Gerry Hitchens (23), Peter McParland (22) and Bobby Thomson (20) all scored over '20' goals for Villa in season 1959-60 (a record). And on seven other occasions, two Villa players have netted 20 or more goals in a League season.

Waring finished up as the top marksman in the First Division in 1930-31...Andy Gray was the next Villa player to achieve that feat, 46 years later in 1976-77, when he netted 25 goals.

When they were relegated from the First Division in 1935-36 Villa's 42 League games produced a staggering 191 goals. They scored 81 themselves but conceded 110.

Dai Astley was the last Villa player to score four goals in an FA Cup-tie - against Sunderland in January 1934 (Villa won 7-2).

Three players - Tony Hateley v Bradford City (home) in 1964, Simon Stainrod v Exeter City (away) in 1985 and David Platt v Ipswich Town

THE COMPLETE ENCYCLOPAEDIA OF ASTON VILLA F.C.          THE COMPLETE ENCYCLOPAEDIA OF ASTON VILLA F.C.

119

In season 1988-89 Villa netted 13 goals in 270 minutes of football against their arch rivals Birmingham City - seven in two League Cup encounters and six in a Simod Cup-tie.

Aston Villa scored 18 goals in their last three home League games in 1898-99.

Villa's most successful period for goalscoring came between 25 August 1928 and 6 May 1933. During those five seasons they played 210 First Division matches, scored a total of 512 goals for an average of 102 per season. In 1930-31 they netted 128 goals in their 42 League games, a Division One record, and followed up with 104 in 1931-32.

In 84 League matches, played in 1934-35 and 1935-36, Villa conceded 198 First Division goals. In the latter season alone they gave away 110, with 56 of them going in the net at Villa Park.

Villa players scored only ONE goal in 11 League games between 11 January and 21 March 1992 - a Cyrille Regis effort against Oldham Athletic (won 1-0).

Over that same period in 1992 Villa failed to score a single goal in seven away matches. They ended that barren spell with FIVE at Tottenham on 4 April.

In successive Second Division seasons -1968-69 and 1969-70 - Villa failed to score a single first-half goal in 30 of their 42 matches. In 1959-60, when they won the Second Division title, they did not secure a first-half goal in 23 of their 42 games, a feat they repeated in 1961-62. In 1962-63 they couldn't score a first-half goal in 26 of their 42 First Division encounters; it was 25 blank first-half sheets out of 46 games in 1970-71 (Division 3), likewise in 1973-74 (from 42 matches in Division 2). It was a similar story from their 42 First Division matches in 1975-76, but this time the 'no goal' sequence also included 12 first-half blanks on the trot (from late August to 1 November). In 1971-72, when the Third Division championship was claimed, Villa had 23 incidents of goalless first-half action.

Villa had a club record 20 different goalscorers in 1950-51 (17 of their own players and three opponents). There were 17 different marksman in 1952-53 and 16 in 1894-95, 1903-04, 1935-36 and 1936-37.

Villa have yet to go straight through a season and score in every game!

Sheffield Wednesday have conceded more goals at Villa Park than any other visiting club.

Ronnie Dix became the youngest player at 15 years, 180 days to score a Football League goal when playing for Bristol Rovers against Norwich City (Division 3 South) on 3 March 1928. He was later to play for Aston Villa, who signed him from Blackburn Rovers in May 1933.

Frank Broome scored six goals in his trial game for Aston Villa against Moor Green in 1934. He was quickly taken on as a professional!

In 1938-39, Villa's fourth team scored 28 goals in two Birmingham JOC matches against hapless Handsworth Wood whom they beat 18-0 away and 10-0 at home.

Villa's Tony Morley scored BBC TV's 'Goal of the Season' against Everton at Goodison Park in 1980-81.

### Own-Goals

The highest number of own-goals in Aston Villa's favour in a League season has been four - recorded on several occasions.

Villa centre-half Derek Mountfield conceded an own-goal in both League games against Norwich City in season 1989-90.

Keith Hicks (Oldham Athletic) conceded an own-goal in both home and away League games against Villa in 1974-75.

*Bobby Thomson*

Villa full-back Gersom Cox scored the first 'own-goal' in the Football League - against Wolverhampton Wanderers at Dudley Road on 8 September 1888.

Ted Killean (Blackburn Rovers) conceded the first own-goal at Villa Park - during the opening game there on 17 April 1897.

Len Millard (WBA) conceded an own-goal in both League and Wartime games against Villa.

Andrew Mitchell, the Newton Heath defender, gave away two own-goals when Villa beat the Reds 3-1 in Manchester in December 1893.

Two Sunderland players - Tommy McLain and Arthur Hudgell - scored

*Chris Nicholl going for goal!*

own-goals in Villa's 3-1 victory at Roker Park in September 1951.

Len Chalmers (Leicester) scored an own-goal against Villa in successive seasons: 21 April 1962 and 8 December 1962. And Larry Lloyd (Nottingham Forest) did likewise on 5 April 1980 and 27 December 1980.

Aston Villa's defender Chris Nicholl featured on the scoresheet four times in the 2-2 draw with Leicester City at Filbert Street in March 1976. He netted twice for his own side but also conceded two own-goals!

Three Wolves players - Colin Brazier (1977), Emlyn Hughes (1980) and Geoff Palmer (1981) - all conceded own-goals in League games against Villa and then soon afterwards, two ex-Wolves defenders, Derek Parkin (1982) and George Berry (1985) did the same thing playing for Stoke City against Villa.

Ken McNaught (Everton 1975) and Chris Nicholl (Southampton 1982) both scored an own-goal in a League game against Villa.

Former Villa defender Andy Comyn conceded an own-goal against his club, Derby County, nine seconds after coming off the bench as a substitute!

### GOALS GALORE IN SEASON 1930-31
**Details of Villa's record-breaking 1930-31 season:**

**Football League results (Division 1)**

| Opponents | H | A |
|---|---|---|
| Arsenal | 5-1 | 2-5 |
| Birmingham | 1-1 | 4-0 |
| Blackburn R. | 5-2 | 2-0 |
| Blackpool | 4-1 | 2-2 |
| Bolton Wds | 3-1 | 1-1 |
| Chelsea | 3-3 | 2-0 |
| Derby County | 4-6 | 1-1 |
| Grimsby Town | 2-0 | 2-1 |
| Huddersfield T. | 6-1 | 6-1 |
| Leeds United | 4-3 | 2-0 |
| Leicester City | 4-2 | 1-4 |

| | | |
|---|---|---|
| Leicester City | 4-2 | 1-4 |
| Liverpool | 4-2 | 1-1 |
| Manchester C. | 4-2 | 1-3 |
| Manchester U. | 7-0 | 4-3 |
| Newcastle U. | 4-3 | 0-2 |
| Portsmouth | 2-2 | 0-5 |
| Sheffield U. | 4-0 | 4-3 |
| Sheffield W. | 2-0 | 0-3 |
| Sunderland | 4-2 | 1-1 |
| West Ham U. | 6-1 | 5-5 |

**FA Cup**

| | | |
|---|---|---|
| Arsenal | 1-3 | 2-2 |

### Seasonal Diary
Aston Villa finished runners-up in the First Division, seven points behind the champions Arsenal. This was Villa's overall record:

| Venue | P | W | D | L | F | A | Pts |
|---|---|---|---|---|---|---|---|
| Home | 21 | 17 | 3 | 1 | 86 | 34 | 37 |
| Away | 21 | 8 | 6 | 7 | 42 | 44 | 22 |
| Totals | 42 | 25 | 9 | 8 | 128 | 78 | 59 |

Aston Villa averaged more than three goals a game; netted a goal every 29 minutes of League action; scored in every home game; and failed to find the net on just three occasions.

Tom Waring netted in each of the first seven League matches. He scored in 30 of Villa's 42 matches and grabbed three fourtimers, against Manchester United (away) and v West Ham and Sunderland at home. He also claimed a hat-trick in the home wins over Blackpool and Huddersfield.

Waring's haul of 50 League and FA Cup goals is the best ever recorded by a Villa player in one season. Eric Houghton followed him home with 20, while Billy Walker notched 16 and Joe Beresford 14. Ten different players figured on the scoresheet.

### GODDARD, HENRY
Born: Durham, 1905.
Career: Artwell Royal, Aston Villa (April 1926), Stockton (August 1928). Fourth choice goalkeeper during his stay at Villa Park, Harry Goodard played in just one Football League game - deputising for the injured Tommy Jackson in the 3-1 defeat Bolton in December 1927.

### GODFREY, BRIAN CAMERON
Born: Flint, North Wales, 1 May 1940.
Career: Flint Alexandra (1955-56), Wrexham (trialist), Chester (junior), Tranmere Rovers (junior), Everton (amateur June 1957, professional May 1958), Scunthorpe United (June 1960), Preston North End (October 1963), Aston Villa (in a deal involving Brian Greenhalgh, September 1967), Bristol Rovers (player exchange-deal involving Ray Graydon, May 1971), Newport County (June 1973), Portland Timbers (NASL, March 1975-May 76, under coach Vic Crowe). Retired in 1976 to become manager of Bath City (until December 1978), Exeter City (manager, January 1979-June 1983), Weymouth (manager, 1983-87), Gloucester City (manager, 1987-89 and manager again from February 1992), Cinderford Town (manager 1998-2000). Still played in charity

*Brian Godfrey*

matches until he was 55.

A Welsh international (capped three times at senior level and once by the Under-23s) Brian Godfrey played for Aston Villa in the 1971 League Cup Final - one of 160 senior appearances he made for the club (25 goals scored). He skippered the side more often than not and won the Terrace Trophy award in 1968. He was also qualified as an FA Coach. A gritty, hard-working midfielder, he was given only one outing at Goodison Park and was bitterly disappointed not to make Preston's starting XI in the 1964 FA Cup Final against West Ham. During a lengthy career he starred in well over 600 League and Cup games, netting in excess of 135 goals.

As a manager, Godfrey guided Bath to the Southern League championship in 1978, Exeter to the FA Cup quarter-finals in 1981, saw Weymouth finish fifth in the GM Vauxhall Conference in 1986 and then steered Gloucester City to the Midland League, Southern Division title in 1989 with a massive 92 points.

When he took over as boss of Cinderford Town, one of his first signings was that of the former Aston Villa defender Chris Price.

When Godfrey was manager of Exeter, he saw his side beaten 5-1 at Millwall in 1982. As a punishment to his players he kept them in London overnight and next day arranged for them to play against Millwall's reserve side...and the Lions even won that game 1-0!

### GOFFIN, WILLIAM CHARLES
Born: Amington, Tamworth, 12 December 1920. Died: September, 1987.
Career: Tamworth Schools football, Amington Village FC, Tamworth (August 1935), Aston Villa (amateur August 1937, professional December 1937), Walsall (August 1954), Tamworth (August 1955 - then manager at The Lamb, 1956-58).
Nicknamed 'Cowboy' Billy Goffin could play in any front-line position but preferred to be in the centre-forward berth if possible. A dangerous little player with a powerful right-foot shot, he had the knack of arriving unexpectedly inside the penalty-area and scored some marvellous goals with his quick and decisive reactions. He scored 45 times in Wartime football for Villa and his senior record for the club was impressive: 42 goals in 173 League and FA Cup appearances. He helped Villa win the 1944 League North Cup, playing in the first leg v Blackpool.

### GOODALL, ARCHIBALD LEE
Born: Belfast, 18 June 1864. Died: North London, 29 November 1929.
Career: St Jude's, Liverpool Stanley FC, Preston North End (June 1888), Aston Villa (October 1888), Derby County (May 1889), Plymouth Argyle (May 1903), Glossop North End (January 1904), Wolverhampton Wanderers (October 1905-January 1906). Retired.
Inside-right-cum-centre-half Archie Goodall was well past his 41st birthday when he joined Wolves in 1905. And when he played his last game for the club (v. Everton on 2 December 1905) he was aged 41 years, five months and two days - the oldest player ever to don a Wolves shirt.

Raised in Scotland, Goodall moved south of the border as a teenager and after playing a couple of League games for PNE he scored seven goals in 14 appearances for Villa. He then went on to net 52 times in 423 senior appearances for Derby County, making a club record 151 consecutive League appearances between October 1892 and October 1897. He also helped the Rams twice reach the FA Cup Final (1898 and 1903) and finish runners-up in the League championship. One of the great characters ever to play for Derby, he caused some alarm when, in 1898, he tried to unload his Cup Final tickets on which he had speculated. He also refused to play an extra-half-hour of the United Counties League Cup Final v. West Bromwich Albion in 1894 because he said his contract ended after 90 minutes! Goodall was capped eight times by Northern Ireland between 1898 and 1902, and after ending his playing career he toured Europe and America with a strongman act, walking around with a massive metal hoop. He was a keen sportsman

THE COMPLETE ENCYCLOPAEDIA OF ASTON VILLA F.C.    THE COMPLETE ENCYCLOPAEDIA OF ASTON VILLA F.C.

121

and followed his country avidly at football, cricket and tennis. In later life he worked and lived in North London and died in the capital at the age of 65.

Archie Goodall's brother John also played for Preston North End, Glossop and Derby County.

## GOODE, BERTRAM JOHN

Born: Chester, April 1886. Died: c 1951.

Career: Old St Mary's, Hoole FC, Broughton Combination, Saltney FC, Chester (trialist 1906, signed professional November 1907), Liverpool (1908), Wrexham (August 1910), Aston Villa (£250, July 1911), Hull City (£300, May 1912), Wrexham (May 1913). Retired in 1926, aged 39.

Following his move from Wrexham, Bert Goode scored 46 goals in his only season at Villa Park (1910-11) as the reserve side won the Birmingham & District League championship in style. A good opportunist inside/centre-forward, unfortunately, he was given only three first team appearances, netting three goals, before transferring to Hull City, returning to Wrexham after becoming homesick! He won six Welsh Cup winners' medals between 1908-25, the first with Chester and five with Wrexham, bagging four goals for the latter club in an emphatic 6-0 Final win over Connah's Quay in 1911. Goode played in Wrexham's first-ever Football League game against Hartlepool United in August 1921 and despite missing the whole of the 1922-23 season and most of the 1923-24 and 1925-26 campaigns he went on to establish a quite magnificent record with the club. He secured a total of 136 goals in 276 senior outings in his two spells at the Racecourse Ground, and is regarded as being one of Wrexham's greatest-ever players.

Wrexham played a Liverpool XI for Goode's benefit/testimonial in October 1920.

## GORDON, ROBERT

Born: Leith, 1873. Died: Scotland c 1938.

Career: Edinburgh Thistle (August 1888), Leith Rovers (September 1889), Heart of Midlothian (August 1890), Middlesbrough Ironopolis (September 1891), Heart of Midlothian (July 1893), Aston Villa (May 1894), Leicester Fosse (October 1894), Woolwich Arsenal (June 1895), Reading (August 1896), Forfar Athletic (1897), St Bernard's (1899). Retired 1908.

Aston Villa had high hopes when, in 1894, they signed Bob Gordon, a well-built, bustling centre-forward, who was described perhaps harshly by the Daily Mail as 'cumbrous'. He scored on his League debut against Small Heath but then lost his way! After four outings for Villa (2 goals) plus an appearance and another goal against a strong Football League XI in a benefit match for William McGregor, he moved to Leicester Fosse, having spent just five months with Villa. He reasonably well at Filbert Street (14 goals in 25 games) he took his shooting boots to Plumstead. In February 1897 Gordon played for the Southern League against the London FA and scored twice.

## GORNIK ZABRZE

Villa's record against the Polish side:

UEFA Cup

| Venue | P | W | D | L | F | A |
|---|---|---|---|---|---|---|
| Home | 1 | 1 | 0 | 0 | 2 | 0 |
| Away | 1 | 0 | 1 | 0 | 1 | 1 |
| Totals | 2 | 1 | 1 | 0 | 3 | 2 |

Aston Villa defeated the Polish side 3-1 on aggregate in the second round of the UEFA Cup in 1977-78. After winning 2-0 at Villa Park with two Ken McNaught goals, they held out for a 1-1 draw in Zabrze to ease through comfortably.

*Ken McNaught is mobbed after scoring against Gornik Zabrze.*

## GOSS, FREDERICK CHARLES

Born: Draycott, February 1914. Deceased.

Career: Ilkeston St Clare's. Ilkeston Town, Aston Villa (November 1936), Wrexham (September 1938), Aston Villa (January 1939). Retired through injury during War.

Signed as wing cover for Jackie Maund, Fred Goss never threatened to win a first team place with Villa and made only two League appearances - against Bury and West Ham United, both at home, in April 1937. He returned for a second spell with Villa as reserve to Frank Broome during the second half of the last pre-War campaign.

## GRAHAM, GEORGE

Born: Bargeddle, Lanark, 30 November 1944.

Career: Coatbridge Schools, Swinton FC (West Scotland), Coatbridge Boys, Aston Villa (groundstaff, late 1959, professional December 1961), Chelsea (£5,950, July 1964), Arsenal (£50,000 plus Tommy Baldwin, September 1966), Manchester United (£120,000, December 1972), Portsmouth (November 1974), Crystal Palace (November 1976), California Surf NASL (on loan, March-July 1978). Retired as a player May 1980, appointed Youth team coach/assistant-manager at Selhurst Park; Queen's Park Rangers (coach, 1981), Millwall (manager, December 1982-May 1986), Arsenal (manager, May 1986-May 1995), Leeds United (manager, September 1996-September 1998), Tottenham Hotspur (manager, October 1998-March 2001).

Nicknamed 'Stroller' inside-forward George Graham scored twice in 10 senior games for Aston Villa, figuring in the losing 1963 League Cup Final against Birmingham City. He then went on to greater things - as a player and more so as a manager. He formed a terrific striking partnership at Chelsea with Barry Bridges, netting 46 goals in 102 appearances for the Blues, gaining a League Cup winners' medal in 1965. As a Gunner, he starred in 296 first-class matches and secured a further 77 goals. He gained both League championship and FA Cup winning medals in 1971, earned a runners-up prize in the latter competition in 1972 and also helped Arsenal win the Fairs Cup in 1970 (beating RSC Anderlecht 4-3 on aggregate), as well as collecting two losers' prizes in the League Cup Finals of 1968 and 1969. Graham was

THE COMPLETE ENCYCLOPAEDIA OF ASTON VILLA F.C.   THE COMPLETE ENCYCLOPAEDIA OF ASTON VILLA F.C.

122

the first player Tommy Docherty signed when he took over as boss of Manchester United and for the Reds, he claimed two goals in 46 senior appearances, captaining a struggling side in 1973 and again the following year when they were relegated. He then obtained five goals in 61 League games for Pompey as they dropped into Division Three, and ended his playing days with a couple of strikes in his 44 League outings for Palace, helping the Eagles gain promotion to the Second Division in 1977. During his League career, Graham made 455 appearances and notched 95 goals. Capped as a Schoolboy and Youth player by Scotland, Graham also represented his country twice at under 23 level and then went on to appear in a total of 12 senior internationals.

Moving into management with Millwall in 1982, his first success was to lead the Lions to victory over Lincoln City in the Final of the Football League Trophy in 1983 and then he guided the Londoners to promotion from Division Three two years later. In this same season (1984-85) the Lions reached the sixth round of the FA Cup, only to lose to Luton Town. But after the final whistle at Kenilworth Road there followed some of the worst scenes of violence ever witnessed on an English soccer ground as fans and police fought a raging battle on the pitch, one of the stands being wrecked.

As boss of Arsenal, Graham saw two League titles won - in 1989 and 1991 - victory claimed in the League Cup Final of 1987 with a runners-up prize following in the same competition in 1988, and then the glory of achieving the FA Cup and League Cup double in 1993. He also had a nasty shock when lowly Wrexham dumped Arsenal out of the FA Cup in 1992. Graham, who won all three major domestic competitions with Arsenal (League, FA Cup & League Cup) left Highbury and duly guided Leeds into Europe in 1998, before moving back to North London to take charge of Arsenal's arch rivals Spurs! He guided Spurs to the 2001 FA Cup semi-final (eventually beaten by Arsenal) before losing his job at White Hart Lane - replaced by ex-Spurs favourite Glenn Hoddle.

## GRAHAM, JOHN R

Born: Leyland, Lancashire, 26 April 1926.
Career: Leyland Works FC, Aston Villa (September 1945, professional November 1946), Wrexham (June 1949), Rochdale (February 1953), Bradford City (July 1953).
Utility forward Jackie Graham was 'stand-in' for so many talented players at Villa Park including initially George Edwards, then Trevor Ford and Billy Goffin. He promised so much at first, but sadly never produced the goods. He scored five goals in his 15 first team outings for the club (including Wartime soccer) and had the pleasure of netting on both his League and FA Cup debuts, in a 5-2 home win over Brentford in September 1946 and a 5-1 defeat at Burnley in January 1947. He was transferred to Wrexham in 1949 following the arrival of Colin Gibson and the emergence of Johnny Dixon.

## GRAHAM, JOHN RICHMOND

Born: Smethwick, August 1868. Died: West Bromwich 1932.
Career: Smethwick Centaur, Oldbury Broadwell, Aston Villa (August 1889), Brierley Hill Alliance (August 1893), Dudley Town (1895-97).
An impish footballer, Jack Graham had one very good season with Aston Villa when, as Denny Hodgetts' left-wing partner, he scored seven goals in 18 League and FA Cup games in 1890-91. He ended his Villa days with a total of seven goals to his name in 20 first-team appearances.

## GRAVESEND & NORTHFLEET

Villa's playing record against the non-League side:
FA Cup

| Venue | P | W | D | L | F | A |
|-------|---|---|---|---|---|---|
| Home | 1 | 1 | 0 | 0 | 3 | 0 |

Aston Villa were drawn away against the Beazer Homes League side

Gravesend & Northfleet in the 3rd round of the FA Cup in 1996, but the tie was staged at Villa Park. In fact, this was the first time Villa had been paired against non-League opposition for 76 years - since their clash with Southern League QPR back in January 1920.
Villa's goals in their 3-0 defeat of Northfleet came from Mark Draper, Savo Milosevic and Tommy Johnson. The crowd was 26,021.

Players with both clubs include: JH Garfield, H Johnston (Villa reserve). Also: G Cox (Gravesend coach).

## GRAY, ANDREW ARTHUR

Born: Lambeth, London, 22 February 1964.
Career: Lambeth & London Borough Schools, Corinthian Casuals, Dulwich Hamlet, Crystal Palace (£2,000, professional November 1984), Aston Villa (£150,000, November 1987), Queen's Park Rangers (£425,000, February 1989), Crystal Palace (£500,000, August 1989), Tottenham Hotspur (£900,000, February 1992), Swindon Town (on loan, December 1992-January 1993). Quit League football in 1994.
Andy Gray was a forceful midfield player, able to turn his hand to any request. Unfortunately he failed to fit in with manager Graham Taylor's style or system and after scoring six goals in 46 senior appearances, he was transferred to QPR following the arrival of Messrs Callaghan and Ormondroyd. Capped twice by England at Under-21 level, Gray also gained one full cap and in 1991 helped Palace win the Zenith Data Systems Cup (v Everton). Gray went on to amass a fine record of 335 club appearances and 61 goals.

*Andy Gray (with manager Graham Taylor) in 1987.*

## GRAY, ANDREW MULLEN

Born: Gorbals, Glasgow, 30 November 1955.
Career: Clydebank Strollers, Dundee United (Amateur, 1970, professional May 1973), Aston Villa (£110,000, September 1975), Wolverhampton Wanderers (£1,15 million, September 1979), Everton (£250,000, November 1983), Aston Villa (£150,000, July 1985), Notts County (on loan, August 1987), West Bromwich Albion (£25,000, September 1987), Glasgow Rangers (September 1988), Cheltenham Town (August 1989), Aston Villa (assistant-manager/coach, July 1991-June 1992).

THE COMPLETE ENCYCLOPAEDIA OF ASTON VILLA F.C.  THE COMPLETE ENCYCLOPAEDIA OF ASTON VILLA F.C.

123

*Andy Gray (left) and ex-Villa centre-half Chris Nicholl.*

Park to pursue a career in television and became a familiar face as an analyst with Sky TV. He also contributed a column to the Daily Express. In June 1997 he was linked with the vacant manager's job at his former club Everton but declined the offer, choosing to stay with Sky TV instead. Capped 20 times by Scotland, Gray also won Under-23, Youth and Schoolboy honours for his country and all told netted over 200 goals in more than 600 senior club matches, with his Villa record reading 212 appearances and 78 goals (two spells).
• Gray scored in three competitive Finals - the FA Cup (with Everton, 1984), the League Cup (with Wolves, 1980) and the European Cup winners Cup (with Everton, 1985). He actually appeared in a major Final with five of his clubs: Dundee United (Scottish Cup), Villa and Wolves (League Cup), Everton (FAC and ECWC) and Rangers (Skol Cup).

### GRAY, FRANKLIN JAMES SAMUEL
Born: Oldbury, September 1868. Died: Birmingham.
Career: Oldbury Richmond, Hockley Belmont, West Bromwich United, Aston Villa (July 1889), Wednesbury Town (May 1890), Darlaston (1891-92 season).
A reserve forward with Aston Villa, Sammy Gray's two appearances for the club were both in the Football League, versus Preston North End and neighbours WBA in September 1889.

### GRAY, JAMES A.
Born: Bristol, c 1878. Died: London.
Career: Bristol Rovers, Aston Villa (August 1904), Glasgow Rangers (April 1905), Tottenham Hotspur, Leyton (1908-May 1912). Retired.
A very useful wing-half, Jimmy Gray did well with Bristol Rovers before making seven first tam appearances for Aston Villa, all at the start of the 1904-05 season. He was then a regular choice for Rangers for two years before having 24 games for Spurs, his debut coming against his old club, Bristol Rovers! He was suspended by Spurs after a 'breach of club discipline' in February 1907. A further breach whilst suspended led to an indefinite ban and Gray made no further appearances for the London club who released him at the end of the 1907-08 campaign.

### GRAY, STUART
Born: Withernsea, 19 April 1960.
Career: Withernsea Youth Club, Nottingham Forest (apprentice, June 1976, professional December 1980), Bolton Wanderers (on loan, March-May 1983), Barnsley (£40,000, August 1983), Aston Villa (£150,000, November 1987), Southampton (£200,000, September 1991). Retired as a player in 1993, later on the coaching staff at The Dell. Was appointed caretaker-manager of Saints in March 2001 following the departure (to Spurs) of Glenn Hoddle, became Manager in July 2001. In October, however, Gray was 'relieved of his duties'.
A versatile defender, able to play as a centre-half or left-back (as well as in midfield) Stuart Gray made over 50 appearances for Nottingham Forest and more than 125 for Barnsley before joining Aston Villa. He spent four years at Villa Park and amassed a further 132 appearances (15 goals scored), skippering the side on several occasions and helping the team gain promotion from the Second Division in 1988 when he battled in centre-field alongside Paul Birch and Andy Gray. He was forced to quit first-class soccer in 1992 through injury.

### GRAYDON, RAYMOND JACK
Born: Bristol, 21 July 1947.
Career: Bristol Rovers (apprentice, July 1963, professional September 1965), Aston Villa (£50,000 plus Brian Godfrey, June 1971), Coventry City (£50,000, July 1977), Washington Diplomats NASL (summer, 1978), Oxford United (£35,000, November 1978). Retired as a player in May 1981 and was appointed coach at The Manor Ground, later

Striker Andy Gray became the most expensive footballer in Britain when Wolves paid Aston Villa £1,150,000 for his services in 1979, Gray actually completed the move by signing the appropriate forms on the pitch at Molineux before Wolves' League game with Crystal Palace. Gray was certainly a colourful figure wherever he played. Brave, determined, totally committed, he was a tremendous header of the ball and as well as netting a considerable number of goals, he helped set up scores more for his colleagues. He made almost 80 appearances for the Tannadice club, gaining a runners-up medal in the 1974 Scottish Cup Final. Villa signed him for a club record fee of £110,000 in 1975 and two years later he played in the two drawn games of the 1977 League Cup Final v Everton and was voted 'Player of the Year' and 'Young Player of the Year' by the P.F.A.

After leaving Villa Park for the first time, Gray scored 45 goals in 162 appearances for Wolves, notching the all-important winner v Nottingham Forest in the 1980 League Cup Final. He then did the business with Everton, hitting 23 goals in 71 games. During his time at Goodison Park he collected winners' medals in three competitions - the FA Cup, Football League championship and European Cup-winners Cup. As a stop-gap, Villa re-signed Gray in 1985 and after a loan spell with Notts County he was signed by his former boss Ron Saunders for West Bromwich Albion. Still his career was not over and early in the 1988-89 season Gray joined Glasgow Rangers, whom he helped win the Skol-sponsored League Cup and Premier League title. At the end of that season, his job done, he was released from Ibrox Park and went off to play for Cheltenham Town before rejoining Villa in the summer of 1991 as assistant manager to Ron Atkinson. He eventually left Villa

*Ray Graydon*

holding the same appointment with Watford (1988-90), Southampton (Youth team coach, early 1990s), Queen's Park Rangers coach (1997) and Port Vale (coach, March 1998) before becoming Walsall's manager in May 1998.

Coach Ray Graydon loved to hug the right-hand touchline. A speedy winger with good, close control, he could cross a ball with great precision and power, and possessed a strong right-foot shot. He won England caps at both Amateur and Youth team levels as a youngster and netted 38 goals in 157 appearances for Bristol Rovers before moving to Villa Park..... just in time to help his side win the Third Division championship in 1971-72 when he missed only one League game and netted 14 important goals.

At Wembley in March 1975 he was given the responsibility of taking a late penalty against Norwich City in the League Cup Final. Former Villa 'keeper Kevin Keelan saved Graydon's spot-kick but was left helpless as the winger reacted quickest to put away the rebound and so earn his side a 1-0 victory.

After netting 82 times in 231 first-team outings for Villa, Graydon moved to Coventry City and ended his playing days with Oxford after a stint in the NASL. Graydon appeared in a total of 476 League and Cup matches (for all his clubs) and notched more than 140 goals.

After a series of coaching appointments Graydon guided the Saddlers to promotion from Division Two at the end of his first season as manager at The Bescot Stadium and then, after relegation, he duly repeated the act in 2001 when the Saddlers defeated Reading 3-2 in the Second Division Play-off Final at Cardiff's Millennium Stadium in front of a 50,000 plus crowd. Ex-Villa man Darren Byfield scored the winning goal in extra-time.

### GRAYSON, SIMON NICHOLAS
Born: 16 December 1969.
Career: Leeds United (YTS, June 1986, professional June 1988), Leicester City (£50,000, March 1992), Aston Villa (£1.35 million, July 1997), Blackburn Rovers (£750,000+ July 1999), Sheffield Wednesday (on loan, September-October 2000), Gillingham (on loan, Februaary 2001), Stockport County (March 2001), Notts County (September 2001).
After making 229 appearances for Leicester, whom he also helped win the League Cup in 1997, full-back-cum-midfielder Simon Grayson moved to Villa Park, manager Brian Little (who had been his boss at Filbert Street) paying out a massive fee for the 27 year-old.
Grayson had failed to establish himself at Elland Road but was a sterling performer for the Foxes. He struggled at times with Villa and indeed for a fair proportion of the 1998-99 season had to contend with a place on the subs' bench. Extremely versatile, able to link effectively when going forward, and intervene at crucial times, he made 64 appearances for Villa (2 goals scored) before moving to the Nationwide Division One side Blackburn Rovers at the start of the 1999-2000 campaign. He quickly found himself in the first XI at Ewood Park following an injury to full-back Jeff Kenna but when the Irish international regained full-fitness Grayson went into the reserves and even had a loan spell with Sheffield Wednesday.

### GREEN, THOMAS WALTER
Born: Worcester, August 1863. Died: 2 October 1923.
Career: Dreadnought FC (Worcester), Mitchell St George's, Small Heath, Wolverhampton Wanderers (guest), Church Villa (guest), Mitchell St George's, Aston Unity, Great Lever FC (Bolton), Mitchell St George's (for a third time), West Bromwich Albion (June 1885), Aston Villa (June 1887), , Kidderminster Harriers (August 1889), Worcester Rovers (September 1901). Retired 1905.
Father of the West Bromwich Albion, West Ham United and Coventry City player from the 1930s, Tommy Green was an enthusiastic inside or centre-forward who had the pleasure of notching Villa's first-ever goal in the Football League against Wolverhampton Wanderers at Dudley Road on 8 September 1888. He had earlier appeared in both the 1886 and 1887 FA Cup Finals for Albion, the latter against Villa. He claimed 19 goals in his 29 senior outings for Villa before drifting out of League soccer in 1889.

### GREENHALGH, BRIAN ARTHUR
Born: Chesterfield, 20 February 1947.
Career: Chesterfield & District Schools, Preston North End (apprentice, June 1963, professional February 1965), Aston Villa (£35,000, September 1967), Leicester City (£15,000, February 1969), Huddersfield Town (June 1969), Cambridge United (July 1971),

*Brian Greenhalgh*

Bournemouth (February 1974), Torquay United (on loan, July-October 1974), Watford (March 1975), Dartford (August 1976), Staines Town (1977-78), Carshalton Athletic (player-manager), Maidenhead United (coach), Chesham United (coach).
Brian Greenhalgh was a youthful striking partner alongside Brian Godfrey at both Deepdale and Villa Park before helping Leicester fight off the threat of relegation in 1969. He netted nine goals in his 19 League games for PNE and added 12 in 42 first-class appearances with Villa. He did very little at Leicester and after leaving Filbert Street played in the same forward-line as Frank Worthington at Huddersfield. He scored over 50 times for Cambridge - his best effort for any of eight major clubs - and when he drifted out of top-class soccer in 1976, his overall League record stood at 77 goals in 245 outings.

### GREENHALGH, SAMUEL
Born: Eagley, Lancashire, 1882. Died: Bolton, 1955.
Career: Eagley FC, Turton, Bolton Wanderers (June 1902), Aston Villa (October 1905), Bolton Wanderers (September 1907), Chorley (August 1914). Later became licensee of The Cheetham Arms, Dunscar, Bolton.
Fair-haired Sam Greenhalgh and already made over 100 appearances and played in the 1904 FA Cup Final for Bolton before moving to Villa Park. A powerfully built defender, occupying the right-half position in the Villa side, he continued to perform positively, adding a further 48 appearances to his tally (2 goals scored) before returning to Burnden Park for a second spell. He went on to serve Bolton until 1914 when he moved into non-League soccer with Chorley, having drawn up a fine record with the Wanderers of 278 appearances and 20 goals. He skippered the Lancashire side to the Second Division championship in 1909 and led them to promotion again two years later after a swift

THE COMPLETE ENCYCLOPAEDIA OF ASTON VILLA F.C.  THE COMPLETE ENCYCLOPAEDIA OF ASTON VILLA F.C.

125

relegation. Unfortunately in March 1912 he fell foul of the club after refusing to play on the wing in an emergency. He apologised to the Board and resumed in the half-back line after serving his suspension.

## GREGORY, GORDON
Born: Hackney, London, 24 October 1943.
Career: Daubeney Road School (Homerton) & Lea Marsh Schools, Hackney Boys, Leyton Orient (juniors, June 1959, professional October 1961), Charlton Athletic (in exchange for John Sneddon & Cliff Holton, July 1966), Aston Villa (£7,777, October 1970), Hereford United (August 1972), Villa Old Stars (1975-80), Chelmsford United (September 1975), Maldon Town (player-manager), also played for Bollingbroke & Wenley FC on Sundays. Retired 1982.
'Harry' Gregory won England Youth honours as a teenager and scored on his League debut for Orient against Ipswich Town in the First Division in 1962.
A versatile player with plenty of ability and effort, Gregory netted 15 goals in 87 games for the 'O's' and followed up with 26 in 160 appearances during his four years at The Valley. Having skippered the 'Addicks', he did likewise at Villa Park (and later Hereford). Playing mainly as an inside-forward, he netted twice in his 29 outings in the claret and blue strip and all told appeared in 325 League matches for his four clubs (44 goals).
Because of a poor disciplinary record (he was sent-off five times in major competitions) Gregory landed himself in trouble with the Essex FA after being dismissed playing for his Sunday team, Bollingbroke & Wenley. He was given a 56-day ban, fined £15 and received a final warning!

## GREGORY, JOHN CHARLES
Born: Scunthorpe, 11 May 1954.
Career: Schoolboy football, Watford (trialist), Northampton Town (apprentice, June 1969, professional May 1973), Aston Villa (£40,000, June 1977), Brighton & Hove Albion (£250,000, July 1979), Queen's Park Rangers (£300,000, June 1981), Derby County (£100,000, November 1985), Portsmouth (player/coach, August 1988 - then manager from January 1989 until January 1990, transferring his playing registration from Derby to Pompey in August 1989), Plymouth Argyle (non-contract player/caretaker-manager, January 1990), Bolton Wanderers (non-contract, March 1990), Leicester City (coach, June 1991), football analyst on Sky TV during 1991-92, Aston Villa (coach, 1994-96), Wycombe Wanderers (manager, October 1996), Aston Villa (manager, February 1998).
Having played with Brian Little at Villa in the late 1970s and then been a coach under his managership at Filbert Street, Gregory then took over as team boss at Villa Park (from Little) in February 1998 - and quickly bedded in to 'old' surroundings.
As a player Gregory grafted hard and long in midfield (he actually fulfilled nine different outfield positions whilst with Villa). He made 202 senior appearances for his first club, Northampton. He added 76 outings (and 10 goals) to his tally with Villa and afterwards starred in 82 matches for Brighton, 191 for QPR, 125 for the Rams, three for Plymouth and seven for Bolton. He was capped six times by England at senior international level, collected an FA Cup losers' medal with QPR (v Spurs) in 1982, won the Second Division championship twice in

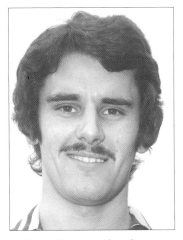
*John Gregory...the player.*

1983 and 1987 with Derby and gained promotion from the Third Division, also with the Rams, in 1986.
At the end of the 2000-01 season Gregory's record in the Premiership as manager of Aston Villa was: played 125, won 52, drawn 38, lost 35.

## GRIFFIN, HARRY G.
Born: Dudley, September 1879. Died: Wolverhampton, April 1946.
Career: Lye Town, Aston Villa (July 1902), Dudley Town (October 1903), Cradley Heath St Luke's (1905-06).
A reserve inside-forward at Villa Park, Harry Griffin made just one appearance for the club, lining up against Sunderland in October 1902 after a pre-match injury to George Johnson.

## GRIFFITHS, JEREMIAH ALBERT
Born: Birmingham, September 1872. Died: Wednesbury.
Career: Birmingham St George's, Aston Villa (April 1895), Bilston Town (November 1897), Bloxwich Strollers (1899-1901).
Tough-tackling wing-half, reserve to Jack Burton, Bob Chatt and Jimmy Crabtree during his brief stay at the club during which time he made just three senior appearances (two League, one FA Cup).

## GRIFFITHS, JOHN
Born: Oldbury, 16 June 1951.
Career: Oldbury & West Smethwick Schools, Aston Villa (apprentice, October 1966, professional November 1968), Stockport County (May 1970), Kidderminster Harriers (August 1975).
John Griffiths was a useful centre-forward who was never given a chance at Villa Park, making just four senior appearances. However, he did tremendously well at Edgeley Park, scoring 31 goals in 182 League games before switching to Aggborough in 1975.

## GRIFFITHS, THOMAS PERCIVAL
Born: Moss, near Wrexham, 21 February 1906. Died: Moss, 25 December 1981.
Career: Ffrith Valley FC, Wrexham & District Schools, Wrexham Boys Club, Wrexham (amateur, December 1922), Everton (£2,000, December 1926), Bolton Wanderers (December 1931), Middlesbrough (£6,500, March 1933), Aston Villa (£5,000, November 1935), Wrexham (player/coach August 1938-February 1939). Retired after battling against rheumatism for some considerable time. He had two further spells as coach at The Racecourse Ground and in the early 1950s acted as trainer to Wales. He then became a Director at Wrexham, and was also a successful landlord of the Turf Hotel, the Hand Hotel and finally the Red Lion in Marchwiel.
Outside football Griffiths was an excellent cello player and performed in several local concerts.
Tom Griffiths began his soccer life as a centre-forward but much to his indignation he was thrown in at centre-half when chosen to represent Wrexham & District Schools. He did well but reverted back to leading his junior club's attack within a week! The former Wrexham and Wales full-back Tom Matthias saw Griffiths net eight goals in a match and immediately introduced him to Wrexham. He played as an amateur for a

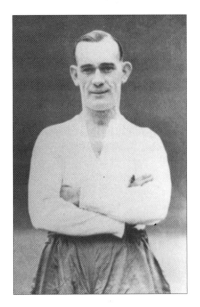

THE COMPLETE ENCYCLOPAEDIA OF ASTON VILLA F.C.    THE COMPLETE ENCYCLOPAEDIA OF ASTON VILLA F.C.

126

while and when he reached the age of 17 he was offered professionalism by a number of clubs - but refused. He was asked to play at right-half in a reserve game for Wrexham but halfway through he switched to centre-half. He enjoyed it and almost at once won both inter-League and junior international caps for Wales. He joined Everton after scoring twice in 36 League games for Wrexham and played his first game for the Merseysiders behind the great Dixie Dean....the following Saturday he lined up for Wales in his first full international, his opponent Dean of England! A stylish defender, Griffiths, who was a cabinet-maker by trade, was a fine header of the ball and wasted very little time in clearing his lines. He took over the centre-half spot in the national side from Fred Keenor, the famous Cardiff City skipper, and went on to lead his country, attaining a total of 231 full caps (his last coming in 1937 against Northern Ireland). He made 76 League appearances for Everton and followed up with 48 for Bolton before moving to Villa Park on the transfer deadline in 1933. Unfortunately he struggled with rheumatics over the next few years and after 67 appearances and one goal for Villa he went back to Wrexham. Griffiths was at centre-half when Arsenal's centre-forward Ted Drake slammed seven goals past Villa in a First Division League game in 1935.

## GRIMSBY TOWN

Villa's record against the Mariners:
Football League

| Venue | P | W | D | L | F | A |
|---|---|---|---|---|---|---|
| Home | 10 | 5 | 3 | 2 | 29 | 19 |
| Away | 10 | 5 | 1 | 4 | 16 | 20 |
| Totals | 20 | 10 | 4 | 6 | 45 | 39 |
| FA Cup | | | | | | |
| Away | 1 | 1 | 0 | 0 | 2 | 1 |
| League Cup | | | | | | |
| Home | 1 | 0 | 1 | 0 | 1 | 1 |
| Away | 1 | 0 | 1 | 0 | 0 | 0 |
| Totals | 2 | 0 | 2 | 0 | 1 | 1 |

Aston Villa and Grimsby first met in season 1900-01 (Division 1). Jasper McLuckie (3) led the goal-chase when the Mariners lost 4-1 at Villa Park in the December, but it was a different story in the return fixture when Grimsby won by exactly the same score!
Villa completed the double over the Mariners in 1929-30, winning 4-1 at home and 2-0 in Cleethorpes.
Villa ran up their best-ever win over Grimsby in September 1931, whipping then 7-1 at home in a First Division match.
The Mariners took three years before gaining ample revenge, beating Villa 5-1 at Blundell Park in October 1934.
Thirteen goals were scored in the two League games between the clubs in 1935-36, and it was the Mariners who took the honours, winning 6-2 at Villa Park and 4-1 at Blundell Park.
Villa's first game back in the top flight (after two seasons in Division 2) was against Grimsby at Blundell Park on 27 August 1938, which they won 2-1 (Frank Broome scoring both goals).
In December 1946 Villa won 3-0 at Blundell Park and then in the return fixture they repeated that scoreline at Villa Park - but only in the first-half, allowing the Mariners to storm back after the break and earn a point from a 3-3 draw.
The following season the Mariners were relegated from the First Division after beating Villa 3-0 at home and drawing 2-2 away, Dicky Dorsett's penalty saving a point for Villa in the latter contest.
Shaun Teale was sent-off when Villa beat the Mariners 2-1 in a 4th round FA Cup-tie at Blundell

Park in January 1994. Dwight Yorke netted the 76th minute winner. The two League Cup matches took place in 1991-92 when the Mariners went through on the away goal rule.

Players with both clubs include: JW Bache (also coach at Grimsby), H Brain (Villa reserve, Town WW2 guest), L Canning (Town WW2 guest), FA Carr (Mariners' trialist), LC Chatterley, P Crichton (Villa on loan), TC Donovan, R Dorsett (Mariners WW2 guest), WE Evans, T Gardner, RSM Gray, JE Griffiths, G Harper, CV Harris, G Harris, H Johnston (Villa reserve), W Leigh, JB Lynch, M Moralee, C Nicholl (player/coach & assistant-manager at Grimsby), A Rees, AE Watkins, J Whitehouse, C Wilson (Villa reserve).

Also: G Taylor (Town player, Villa manager), H Hadley & IH Price (Villa senior & reserve players respectively, Town managers), K Swain (Villa player, Mariners coach & manager), J Ward (Grimsby player, Villa assistant-manager & coach), WC Athersmith & J Bache (Villa players, Grimsby trainer/coaches), WE Evans (Villa player, Town assistant-trainer).

## GROUNDS

Aston Villa have so had five official home grounds, as follows:

| | |
|---|---|
| Aston Park | 1875 |
| Wilson Road (Birchfields) | 1875-76 |
| Aston Lower Grounds Meadow | 1875-78 |
| Wellington Road, Perry Barr | 1878-97 |
| Villa Park, Aston | 1897 to date |

During the early part of 1875 (January-March) Aston Villa certainly played inside Aston Park and also on a strip of land in Wilson Road, Perry Barr.
In the 1875-76 season they utilised both Aston Park and the Lower Grounds Meadow for first team matches.

### Ground Facts

In July 2000 Villa played two 'home' InterToto Cup games at the Hawthorns, the ground of neighbours West Bromwich Albion.
Villa used Solihull Town's ground during the early part of World War Two.
In the 1960s Villa's third team utilised a sports ground in Handsworth Wood that belonged to the Raleigh Cycle Company.
In season 1950-51 (prior to the purchase of the Trinity Road training ground from Aston Unity Cricket Club) Villa's fourth team played its home games on the ground belonging to the HP Sauce company in Erdington.
Trinity Road was used throughout the 1950s and 1960s and thereafter Bodymoor Heath came along and was used frequently with Villa's first, second, third, fourth and even fifth teams playing matches there!
Villa utilised the Bescot Stadium, Walsall for certain pre-season matches in July/August 1994. They beat Rapid Bucharest 8-0 in a friendly there on 15 August in front of 5,081 spectators.

## GROUNDSMEN

Mr. R (Dick) Leeson was Aston Villa's groundsman for a total of 27 years - from 1894 until 1921.
Tony Eden, a former Villa reserve, was groundsman at Villa Park during the 1980s and '90s. In 1992 he resorted to throwing buckets of sand over the pitch to cover up bare patches. The state of Villa Park's surface at the time almost cost the club an F.A. Cup Semi-Final - Liverpool against Portsmouth.

*Graham Taylor (Grimsby player, Villa manager).*

THE COMPLETE ENCYCLOPAEDIA OF ASTON VILLA F.C.          THE COMPLETE ENCYCLOPAEDIA OF ASTON VILLA F.C.

127

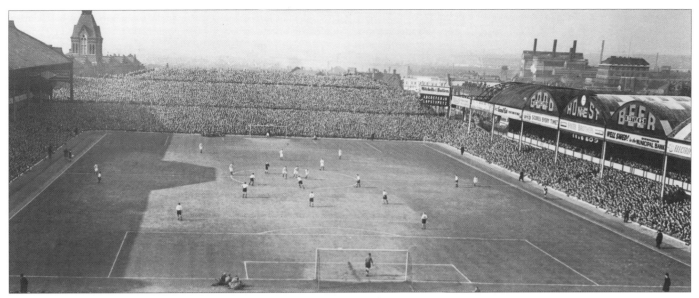

*Villa Park: March 1954 (WBA v. Port Vale, F.A. Cup Semi-Final).*

### GROVES, WILLIAM

Born: Leith, 9 November 1869. Died: Glasgow, February 1908.

Career: Thistle Club (Edinburgh), Hibernian (1887), Celtic (1888), Everton (early 1889), Celtic (mid-1889), West Bromwich Albion (October 1890), Aston Villa (£100, September 1893), Hibernian (August 1894), Celtic (1896), Rushden (1898). Retired 1902.

Initially Willie Groves was a dashing centre-forward who developed into a stylish left-half. A player with masterly distribution qualities, he gained three full caps for Scotland (1888-89), represented the Football League and Edinburgh (in an Inter-City match), won a Scottish Cup winners' medal with Hibs in 1887 and collected runners-up prizes in the same competition with Celtic in 1889 and Hibs 1896. He was an FA Cup winner with WBA (v Villa) in 1892 and the after leaving Albion he won a League championship with Aston Villa in 1894. He did not play a senior game for Everton, leaving the club after a dispute arose regarding his registration.

### GUEST PLAYERS

Eight Aston Villa players guested for rivals Birmingham (City) during the Second World War. They were Jimmy Allen, Jack Bate, Frank Broome, George Cummings, George Edwards, Bob Iverson, Jack Martin and Frank Moss.

Tom 'Pongo' Waring made a guest appearance for Aston Villa in a Wartime friendly against West Bromwich Albion in February 1944 and over 4,000 fans turned out to see their old favourite in action.

Dicky Davis, guesting for Aston Villa from Sunderland, scored six times (a double hat-trick) in a Wartime game against Worcester City (away) in November 1941. Davis netted 67 goals (in only 53 games) for Villa during the WW2 hostilities.

Frank Barson (aged 49) guested for Villa in a local charity match against Sutton Town in October 1940 - 21 years after he had made his League debut for the club following his record transfer from Barnsley.

For further information re guest players, see under Wartime Football.

### GUTTRIDGE, RONALD

Born: Widnes, 28 April 1916.

Career: St Helens Schools, Liverpool (amateur), Stockport County (trialist), Prescot Cables FC, Aston Villa (March 1937), Liverpool (WW2 guest), Brighton & Hove Albion (June 1948)

Known as 'Roy', full-back Guttridge acted as reserve to Vic Potts and George Cummings during his time at Villa Park. He made 15 senior appearances before moving south to Brighton.

### HADJI, MOUSTAPHA

Born: Ifrane, Morocco, 16 November 1971.

Career: Nancy, Sporting Lisbon, Deportivo La Coruna, Coventry City (August 1999), Aston Villa (player-exchange, June 2001).

Powerfully built, hard-working, hard-running attacking midfielder and Africa's 'Footballer of the Year' Moustapha Hadji had been capped 65 times by Morocco prior to his transfer to Villa Park in June 2001.

After turning down the chance to play for France at Under-21 level, he starred in both the 1994 and 1998 World Cup Finals for Morocco and when the Sky Blues were relegated to the Nationwide League at the end of the 2000-01 season, Hadji had no second thoughts when John Gregory asked him to sign for Villa in exchange for Julian Joachim - thus remaining in the Premiership. He made his debut for Villa in the InterToto Cup competition a month after leaving Highfield Road.

### HADLEY, GEORGE ANGUS

Born: Glasgow, 5 June 1893. Died: Birmingham, April 1963.

Career: Scottish Schoolboy football, West Bromwich Victoria (1909) Willenhall Swifts (1911), Southampton (July 1913), Aston Villa (May 1919), Coventry City (August 1920-23).

A stocky versatile half-back, George Hadley lived in Scotland until he was 16 and played in a junior international north of the border. He came to England with his parents after his father took a job in West Bromwich. He made 62 appearances for Southampton before the Great War put a dent in his career. After the hostilities he was given four outings by Villa and then starred in over 70 games during his time at Highfield Road. He was forced to retire through injury in 1923.

### HADLEY, HARRY

Born: Barrow-in-Furness, Lancashire, April 1878. Died: West Bromwich, September 1942.

Career: Cradley Heath & District Schools, Colley Gate United, Halesowen (1893-96), West Bromwich Albion (£100, February 1897), Aston Villa (£250, February 1905), Nottingham Forest (April 1906), Southampton (April 1907), Croydon Common (August 1908), Halesowen (February 1910), Merthyr Town (manager, May 1919-April 1922), Chesterfield (manager April-August 1922), Merthyr Town (three more spells as manager between 1923-27), Aberdare Athletic (manager, November 1927-November 1928), Gillingham (manager, briefly in 1929-30), Aberdare Athletic (manager April 1930-September 1931), Bangor City (manager, July 1935-April 1936).

Harry Hadley was an industrious half-back who also displayed a lot of composure when required. He was capped once by England (v Ireland

THE COMPLETE ENCYCLOPAEDIA OF ASTON VILLA F.C.    THE COMPLETE ENCYCLOPAEDIA OF ASTON VILLA F.C.

128

at Wolverhampton in 1905) and helped WBA win the Second Division title before joining Aston Villa in 1905. He made over 180 appearances for the Baggies but managed only 11 for Villa before embarking on a very successful managerial career, leading Merthyr into the Football League in 1920. Harry's brother, Ben, also played at The Hawthorns.

## HAGGART, WILLIAM R.
Born: Edinburgh, August 1874. Died: Scotland c 1934.
Career: Dairy Primrose FC (Edinburgh), Edinburgh Royal, Aston Villa (£40, April 1897), Edinburgh Thistle (1898-98).
Highly rated 'North of the Border' and nicknamed 'Cock', left-back Billy Haggart won Junior international honours for Scotland as a teenager before coming down to Birmingham to play twice for Villa. He never lived up to his reputation despite being paid a seemingly massive wage of £6-a-week for first team games and £4 in the reserves!

## HALE, ALFRED
Born: Waterford, 28 August 1939.
Career: Waterford (August 1957), Aston Villa (£4,000, June 1960), Doncaster Rovers (July 1962), Newport County (August 1965), Waterford (July 1966-70).
Alfie Hale was a clever, scheming inside-forward who represented the Republic of Ireland at both amateur and professional levels, winning a total of 13 full caps. He scored twice in his seven senior outings fior Villa but then netted 42 goals in 119 League games during his three seasons with Doncaster.

## HALIFAX TOWN
Villa's record against the Shaymen:
Football League

| Venue | P | W | D | L | F | A |
|-------|---|---|---|---|---|---|
| Home | 2 | 1 | 1 | 0 | 2 | 1 |
| Away | 2 | 1 | 0 | 1 | 2 | 2 |
| Totals | 4 | 2 | 1 | 1 | 4 | 3 |

In their first-ever Third Division campaign of 1970-71, Aston Villa drew 1-1 at home and lost 1-0 away to Halifax, but the following season things were completely different as Villa doubled up with two 1-0 victories, Ray Graydon scoring in both matches...to set them up for the championship!

Players with both clubs include: L Butler, RM Campbell, DG Evans, MK Ferguson, A Little, CJ Nicholl, J Overton, F Turnbull.
Also: MA Lillis (Villa player, Town manager), A Cox (coach at both clubs, also Villa assistant & caretaker-manager).

## HALL, ALBERT EDWARD
Born: Wordsley, Stourbridge, February 1882. Died: Stourbridge, 17 October 1957.
Career: Amblecote Council School, Stourbridge (August 1900), Aston Villa, (July 1903), Millwall (December 1913). Retired August 1916 when he returned to Stourbridge where he went into business as an enamelware manufacturer. Albert Hall was an exceptionally talented footballer, a goalscoring outside-left, a real box-of-tricks, who was lightning quick over 20-30 yards and possessed a cracking shot. He won an FA Cup winners' medal with Villa in 1905 and a League Championship medal five years

later when he also earned his only England cap, partnering his clubmate Joe Bache on the left-wing v Ireland in Belfast. Hall scored 62 goals in 215 first-team appearances for Villa before moving to London to sign for Millwall. Besides being very useful at soccer, Hall was also a very talented cricketer and billiards player, representing Stourbridge CC (in the Birmingham League) and Amblecote Institute respectively.

## HALSE, HAROLD JAMES
Born: Stratford, East London, 1 January 1886. Died: Colchester, 25 March 1949.
Career: Park Road School (Wanstead), Newportians FC (Leyton),

Wanstead FC, Barking Town (1904), Clapton Orient (Amateur, August 1905), Southend United (June 1906), Manchester United (£350, March 1908), Aston Villa (£1,200, July 1912), Chelsea (May 1913), Clapton Orient (guest during WW1), Charlton Athletic (July 1921-May 1923 when he retired to become scout at The Valley, a position he held until 1925.

Harold Halse scored over 200 goals in just two seasons for Southend United before joining Manchester United in 1908...and then he netted just 45 seconds into his debut for United - the first of 56 goals in 125 appearances for the Lancashire club.

When United beat Swindon Town 8-4 in the 1911 FA Charity Shield game, Halse netted a double hat-trick (6 goals). He gained an FA Cup winners' medal with both United and Villa and collected a runners-up medal in the same competition with Chelsea (a feat later equalled by another United player, Ernie Taylor who did it with Newcastle, Blackpool and Manchester United in the 1950s). Not a player to catch the eye, Halse was, nevertheless, one of the finest marksmen of his day. Small, rather slight in build, he had the knack of snapping up the half-chance - a real top-class opportunist. Capped once by England, he also played for the Football League XI and won both First Division championship and runners-up medals with United and Villa respectively in 1912 and 1913. Halse's record with Villa was tremendous - 28 goals in only 37 games in his one season with the club - and that haul included a five-goal salvo against Derby County on 19 October 1912. He captained Charlton in their first season in the Football League (1921-22).

## HAMILTON, IAN MICHAEL
Born: Streatham, 31 October 1950
Career: Streatham & London Schools, Chelsea (juniors 1965, professional January 1968), Southend United (£5,000, September 1968), Aston Villa (£40,000, June 1969), Sheffield United (July 1976), Minnesota Kicks (summer of 1979-80). Returned to England and later was appointed Community Officer at Rotherham United.
'Chico' Hamilton won England Youth caps as a teenager. He had a terrific left foot and did some sterling work in the midfield engine-rooms at each of his four English clubs. He netted 65 goals in a career total of 308 League games, his Villa record reading 48 goals in

*Ian 'Chico' Hamilton in action against West Bromwich Albion in 1974.*

THE COMPLETE ENCYCLOPAEDIA OF ASTON VILLA F.C.    THE COMPLETE ENCYCLOPAEDIA OF ASTON VILLA F.C.

129

252 outings. He played in two League Cup Finals (1971 and 1975) and, in fact, was the youngest player ever to appear in a League game for Chelsea - aged 16 years, 4 months, 18 days v Tottenham Hotspur in March 1967.

## HAMILTON, WILLIAM MURDOCH
Born: Airdrie, 16 February 1938. Died; Canada, April 1976.
Career: Drumpellier Amateurs (Coatbridge), Sheffield United (February 1956), Middlesbrough (£12,000, February 1961), Heart of Midlothian (£5,000, June 1962), Aston Villa (£25,000, August 1965), Hibernian (free transfer, August 1967), South African football (August 1969-April 1970), Ross County (July 1970), Hamilton Academical (October 1970). Retired 1972.
In a career marred by illness and injury, ball-playing inside-forward Willie Hamilton still performed exceedingly well at both club and international level. He was capped by Scotland against Finland in 1965, played twice for the Scottish League and won a League Cup winners' medal with Hearts in 1963. He scored nine goals in 54 senior games for Villa after netting 21 times in 79 League outings for Sheffield United and once in 10 starts for 'Boro.

## HAMPSON, JOHN
Born: Oswestry, 28 December 1887.
Died: Burslem, December 1960.
Career: Oswestry Town, Northampton Town, Leeds City, Aston Villa (£1,000, October 1919), Port Vale (£1,000, June 1921), Hanley Social Club (August 1924).
An efficient, hard-working half-back, Jack Hampson occupied six different positions during his time at Villa Park, including all five in defence. He appeared in only 15 first-class games for the club (following his move from the defunct Leeds City) but later made well over 100 for Port Vale before he suffered a serious leg injury which required two major operations.

## HAMPTON, GEORGE H
Born: Wellington, 1889. Died: Wellington, July 1956.
Career: Wellington Council Schools, Wellington St George's, Glossop North End (August 1909), Aston Villa (August 1914), Shrewsbury Town (May 1915). Did not figure after 1919.
Wholehearted full-back, signed as reserve to Bill Littlewood and Tom Lyons prior to the last season before the Great War, George Hampson made only three first-team appearances for Villa - having starred in 110 League games for Glossop.

## HAMPTON, JOSEPH HARRY
Born: Wellington, Shropshire, 21 April 1885. Died: Wrexham, 15 March 1963.
Career: Wellington Council Schools, Shifnal Juniors, Wellington Town, Aston Villa (April 1904), Birmingham (February 1920), Newport County (September 1922-May 1923), prematurely retired, but returned to the game with Wellington Town (January 1924) and then served Preston North End (as coach, June 1925-January 1926), Birmingham (colts' coach, October 1934-April 1936). Guested for Derby County, Fulham and Nottingham Forest during the Great War. Quit football in 1937 and later ran a successful catering business in Rhyl.
Elder brother of George, centre-forward 'Appy Arry Ampton' as he was so-called, was a real terror to opposing goalkeepers and defenders alike. During the decade leading up to the outbreak of the First World

War he was one of the finest all-action goalscorers in Britain (perhaps Europe). He was afraid of no-one and his strong, forceful, determined style was admired and appreciated by plenty! The idol of the Villa Park faithful, Hampton was robust in the extreme. He often barged the goalkeeper, including the hefty 22 stone body-weight of Billy 'Fatty' Foulke of Sheffield United and Chelsea fame, and the ball (if he had it in his possession) into the back of the net, sometimes taking a co-defender along for good measure with one almighty shoulder-charge! With a devil-may-care attitude his record as a marksman speaks for itself - it was quite brilliant. He rattled in no fewer than 242 goals for Aston Villa in 376 first-team appearances - and after leaving Villa Park he still continued to blast bullets into the net, firing home 31 goals in 59 outings for neighbours Blues and then he notched a few more for Newport County.
Capped by England on four occasions (2 goals scored), Hampton also represented the Football League side three times. He gained a League Championship medal with Aston Villa in 1901 and added two FA Cup winners' medals to his collection in 1905 and 1913, scoring both goals in the 2-0 win over Newcastle in the former final. He also featured in the losing Final of 1920 and a year later helped Blues win the Second Division title. He was badly gassed during the Great War - but recovered full fitness and health within two months.
Hampton only discovered that his first name was Joseph late in life when there was a query about his date of birth. He went along to Somerset House in London and unearthed his own birth certificate which revealed that he was and had been christened 'Joseph Harry Hampton'.

## HANDLEY, BRIAN
Born: Wakefield, 21 June 1936. Died: 1982.
Career: Goole Town, Aston Villa (September 1957), Torquay United (September 1960), Bridgwater Town (August 1964), Rochdale (February-May 1966). Captained Paignton cricket club between 1961 and 1966.
Centre-forward Brian Handley never got an opportunity to show his worth at Villa Park, making only three first team appearances owing to the presence of Gerry Hitchens. He did however, come good with Torquay, scoring 33 goals in 80 League games for the Plainmoor club.

## HARDY, GEORGE C.
Born: Newbold Verdun, Derbyshire, 18 January 1912. Deceased.
Career: Newbold Victoria, Nuneaton Town (1932), Aston Villa (February 1934), Blackburn Rovers (August 1938). Did not play League football after the War.
Younger brother of Sam (below) George Hardy was an attacking half-back, deputy to Messrs Gardner, Iverson and Massie at Villa Park, making only six first team appearances and scored one goal - in the 2-1 home defeat by Nottingham Forest in March 1938.

## HARDY, SAMUEL
Born: Newbold Verdun, Derbyshire, 25 August 1883. Died: Chesterfield, 24 October 1966.
Career: Newbold White Star (July 1901), Chesterfield (profesional, April 1903), Liverpool (£500, October 1905), Aston Villa (May 1912), Nottingham Forest (August 1921-May 1925). Retired and became a hotelier in Chesterfield.

THE COMPLETE ENCYCLOPAEDIA OF ASTON VILLA F.C.    THE COMPLETE ENCYCLOPAEDIA OF ASTON VILLA F.C.

130

"One of the greatest goalkeepers I ever played in front of" said Jesse Pennington, the West Bromwich Albion and England full-back of the pre-First World War era. Sam Hardy was quite a player and during a splendid career amassed in excess of 600 appearances at club and international level.

His anticipation was so masterly, he made the art of goalkeeping look easy and would have been considered a classic player in any era. He won 21 full caps for England over a period of 14 years: 1907-21. He also starred in three Victory internationals and represented the Football League. He won a First Division championship medal with Liverpool in 1906 and a Second Division championship medal with Forest in 1922. In between times he collected two FA Cup winners' medals with Aston Villa: 1913 and 1920.

He joined Liverpool soon after playing tremendously well (despite conceding six goals) for Chesterfield against the Merseysiders. He made 239 League and Cup appearances for the Anfield club and starred in 183 competitive matches for Villa before going on to play 109 times for Forest, having made over 70 for Chesterfield at the start of his career.

During the Great War he served in the Royal Navy and escaped serious injury on two occasions. He also guested for Nottingham Forest in the 1919 championship play-off against Everton at Goodison Park. Forest won 1-0 after a 0-0 draw at The City Ground. Hardy was permitted to play under Wartime regulations which allowed him to guest for the club closest to his billet!

### HARE, CHARLES BOYD

Born: Yardley, Birmingham, June 1871. Died: February 1934.
Career: Warwick County, Birmingham United, Aston Villa (April 1891), Woolwich Arsenal (August 1895), Small Heath (November 1896), Watford (July 1898) Plymouth Argyle (season 1903-04). Retired 1904 and served with the Warwickshire Yeomanry in the Boer War. On his return from South Africa he attempted to pick up his career in Devon non-League football but without success.

One of a host of fine players produced by Warwick County, Charlie Hare was a talented inside-forward who scored 13 goals in 26 games for Aston Villa whom he helped with the League title in 1893-94. He later netted 14 times in 45 outings for Blues where he was a great favourite with the fans.

### HARKUS, GEORGE CECIL, MBE

Born: Newcastle-upon-Tyne, 25 September 1898. Died: Southampton, 28 September 1950.
Career: Scotswood FC, Aston Villa (May 1921), Southampton (£250, May 1923), Lyon, France (1930), Oldham Athletic (trialist, December 1930), New Milton FC (August 1931 - after taking over the Wheatsheaf pub in that village), Southampton (£250, February 1932), Southport (reserve team player-coach, September 1932-May 1933). Retired as a player in October 1932 after suffering a serious injury during a game against Barrow's second XI. He served in the Air Force during the Second World War when he became a Flight Lieutenant and was afterwards awarded the MBE in the King's Honours List in 1949 'for keeping up morale in the forces while stationed in the Middle East.' He was a member of the RAF's soccer team and served on the selection

committee after the War, holding office until his death in 1950, after a short illness.

An enthusuiastic wing-half, George Harkus was reserve to George Blackburn and Frank Moss at Villa Park and made only four first-team appearances for the club before joining Southampton. He became an inspirational captain of the Saints for whom he amassed 220 appearances during his two spells at The Dell. In 1926 Harkus toured Canada with the FA party, participating in 13 matches.

### HARLEY, CHARLES CEDRIC

Born: Wednesday, March 1871. Died: Wolverhampton, c 1940.
Career: Bloxwich Strollers, Aston Villa (April 1890), Notts County (September 1891).
Small, compact outside-right, reserve to Albert Brown during his brief stay with Aston Villa, Charlie Harley made just one first team appearance for the club, against Bolton Wanderers (a) in October 1890 (lost 4-0).

### HARPER, ROWLAND RICHARD G.

Born: Lichfield, April 1881. Died: Birmingham, August 1949.
Career: Walsall Wood, Small Heath (April 1904), Burton United (September 1906), Aston Villa (August 1907), Notts County (March 1908), Mansfield Invicta (1910-11 season).
Temporary signing by Aston Villa as cover for Charlie Wallace, Roly Harper made just two first team appearances for the club before transferring to Notts County. He scored on his debut for Blues for whom he made 29 appearances during a two-year stay.

### HARRIS, CECIL VERNON

Born: Grantham, 1 October 1896. Died: 16 August 1976.
Career: Grantham, Llandrindod Wells (briefly), Aston Villa (September 1922), Grimsby Town (May 1926), Gainsborough Trinity (May 1929). Retired through injury in 1930.
Eric Houghton's uncle, Cec Harris was a sound, two-footed defender who made 26 first-team appearances for Aston Villa and followed up with 47 in the League for Grimsby.

### HARRIS, EDWARD JAMES

Born: Willenhall, July 1872. Died: Birmingham, 1940.
Career: Willenhall Pickwick, Bilston Town, Aston Villa (May 1895), Wolverhampton Wanderers (August 1896), Darlaston (1898).
Reserve to goalkeeper Tom Wilkes, Ted Harris made just one League appearance for Aston Villa - in the 2-2 home draw with Sheffield United in November 1895. He failed to make the first XI at Molineux.

### HARRIS, GEORGE ABNER

Born: Halesowen 1 January 1878. Died: June 1923.
Career: Gorsty Hill Council School, Haden Hill Rose, Halesowen, Coombs Wood, Halesowen (1898), Aston Villa (June 1901), West Bromwich Albion (£400, January 1909), Coventry City (June 1910). Retired through injury in 1913 and became licensee of the Sportsman, Old Hill. He was tragically killed in a shipyard accident.

Selected as a Junior international in 1905 and again in 1906, George Harris had an outstanding

*George Harris*

THE COMPLETE ENCYCLOPAEDIA OF ASTON VILLA F.C.    THE COMPLETE ENCYCLOPAEDIA OF ASTON VILLA F.C.

131

physique, a solidly built player possessing great drive and a keen eye. He scored once in 21 first team outings for Villa, acting initially as reserve defender to the likes of Albert Leake, Joe Pearson and Joey Windmill. After Harris had moved from Villa Park to The Hawthorns it was to be another 70 years before another player was transferred in the same direction (John Deehan in 1979).

## HARRIS, WALTER H.
Born: Plymouth, 7 July 1904. Deceased.
Career: Plymouth Ivanhoe, Torquay United (1920), Aston Villa (August 1922), Bristol City (July 1929), Loughborough Corinthians (May 1930), Bath City (September 1931). Retired 1934.
A tiny inside-forward with a good technique, Wally Harris netted four times in his 20 senior outings for Aston Villa. He later scored 15 goals in 26 games for Bristol City and weighed in with over 30 goals for non-League Bath before injury began to cause him some concern.

## HARRISON, JAMES CHARLES
Born: Leicester, 12 February 1921.
Career: Wellington Victoria, Leicester City (December 1940), Aston Villa (£12,000, July 1949), Coventry City (July 1951), Corby Town (July 1953). Served in the RAF in India and Burma and guested for Reading during the Second World War. He became a successful haulage businessman based at Wigmore (nr Leicester).
Jim Harrison made his senior debut for Leicester as a centre-forward but developed into a fine full-back. He played 81 games for the Foxes including an appearance in the 1949 FA Cup Final against Wolves. He scored once in his eight outings for Aston Villa (covering four different positions) before ending his League career at Highfield Road in a side with an average age of 31.

## HARRISON, THOMAS
Born: Birmingham, April 1867. Died: c 1943.
Career: Aston Manor Council School, Coombs Wood, Aston Villa (August 1888), Halesowen (September 1889), Handsworth Richmond (1890-92).
Reserve outside-left with a good turn of speed, Tom Harrison made one League appearance for Aston Villa, deputising for Denny Hodgetts in a 4-2 win at Notts County in December 1888.

## HARROP, JAMES
Born: Heeley, Sheffield, 1884. Died: 1958.
Career: Heeley County School, Sheffield Wednesday (Amateur, 1904), Denaby United (1906), Rotherham Town (1907), Liverpool (January 1908), Aston Villa (£600, June 1912), Sheffield United (March 1921-May 1922).
The son of a Yorkshire farmer, centre-half Jimmy Harrop moved to Villa Park from Liverpool a month after goalkeeper Sam Hardy had also left Anfield to join Villa. A cool, methodical defender, crafty at times with a clever brain, Harrop's presence at the heart of the Villa defence went a long way to winning the FA Cup in 1913. He scored four times in 171 senior appearances for the club before moving back his roots to sign for Sheffield United. He twice represented the Football League side, appeared in two international trials for England but had the misfortune (as team captain) to miss Villa's 1920 FA Cup Final triumph through injury. During the First World War Harrop worked as an agricultural implement manufacturer.

## HARTLEPOOL UNITED
Villa's record against the 'Pool:
League Cup

| Venue | P | W | D | L | F | A |
|---|---|---|---|---|---|---|
| Home | 1 | 1 | 0 | 0 | 6 | 1 |
| Away | 1 | 0 | 1 | 0 | 1 | 1 |
| Totals | 2 | 1 | 1 | 0 | 7 | 2 |

Aston Villa defeated Hartlepool United in a 4th round replay on their way to reaching the 1975 League Cup Final. That emphatic 6-1 home win was witnessed by 17,686 spectators. Brian Little, Ray Graydon and Ian Hamilton all scored twice, the latter two both netting penalties.

Players with both clubs include: F Barson, J Beresford ('Pool WW2 guest in 1943), G Hodgson ('Pool WW2 guest), J Hickman, J Hinchcliffe, A Little (also coach at Hartlepool), RC Park, F Pimblett, K Poole.
Also: A McAndrew ('Pool player, Villa coach).

## HARVEY, HOWARD
Born: Wednesbury, April 1875. Died: Birmingham, c 1938.
Career: Wolverhampton Road Council School (Wednesbury), Walsall Town Swifts (reserves), Small Heath (briefly), Aston Villa (September 1896), Burslem Port Vale (£50, June 1898), Manchester City (January 1900), Burton United, West Bromwich United (1900), Darlaston (1902). Retired in the summer of 1905.
Inside-right Howard Harvey scored three goals in 11 senior games for Villa before going on to net 30 times in 65 first team matches for Port Vale, top-scoring for the Potteries' club in season 1899-1900. He was sold to Manchester City because of Vale's increasing financial problems.

## HARVEY, RICHARD ARNOLD
Born: Nottingham, January 1860. Died: Nottingham, December 1932.
Career: Sandiacre Lime Firms, Notts Rangers, Aston Villa (April 1882), Normanton (October 1883), Repton School (1885). Retired cs 1892 (broken leg).
Dick Harvey was a full-back who scored once in four FA Cup games for Villa - his goal coming from 'long distance' in the 4-1 home win over Wednesbury Old Athletic in November 1882.

## HARVEY, WALTER ALFRED
Born: Derby, November 1861. Died: Nottingham, c 1940.
Career: Derby St Luke's, Derby Midland, Aston Villa (April 1884), Chester (November 1885). Retired through injury circa 1888.
Walter Harvey began as a full-back but developed into s very competent goalkeeper who played in four FA Cup-ties for Aston Villa.

## HATELEY, ANTHONY
Born: Derby, 13 June 1941.
Career: Derby Schoolboy football, Normanton Sports Club, Derby County (Schoolboy forms 1955-56), Notts County (May 1956, professional June 1958), Aston Villa (£20,000, August 1963), Chelsea (£100,000, October 1966), Liverpool (£100,000, July 1967), Coventry City (£80,000, September 1968), Birmingham City (£72,000, August 1969), Notts County (£20,000, November 1970), Oldham Athletic (£5,000, July 1972), Bromsgrove Rovers (May 1974), Prescot Town (July 1975), Keyworth United (December 1978), retiring in August 1979. He later worked in the Everton lottery office and thereafter was employed by a brewery in Nottinghamshire.
Tony Hateley was a real soccer nomad whose League record was exceptional - 211 goals scored in 434 League and Cup appearances. An out-and-out centre-forward and father of Mark, Hateley senior was tall and muscular, exceptionally strong in the air. He helped Notts County win both the Third and Fourth Division championships in 1960 and

THE COMPLETE ENCYCLOPAEDIA OF ASTON VILLA F.C.                    THE COMPLETE ENCYCLOPAEDIA OF ASTON VILLA F.C.

132

1971 respectively and was an FA Cup finalist with Chelsea in 1967. His record with Aston Villa was marvellous - 86 goals in 148 appearances - and he was the club's top-marksman three season's running: 1963-66. Hateley is one of only three players to score four goals in a League Cup game for Villa - doing so in the 7-1 home win over Bradford City in November 1964.

*Tony Hateley*

## HAT-TRICKS
Details of all hat-tricks scored by Villa players at competitive level (including Wartime):

### Football League

| | |
|---|---|
| A Allen (3) v Notts County (h) | 29.9.1888 |
| A Allen (3) v Burnley (a) | 5.10.1889 |
| B Garvey (3) v Stoke (h) | 7.12.1889 |
| WC Athersmith (3) v Wolves (h) | 14.3.1891 |
| J Devey (3) v Burnley (h) | 5.12.1891 |
| J Devey (4) v Accrington (h) | 12.3.1892 |
| L Campbell (4) v Accrington (h) | 12.3.1892 |
| WC Athersmith (3) v Nottm For (a) | 12.11.1892 |
| CB Hare (3) v Sheffield United (h) | 30.10.1893 |
| J Devey (3) v Newton Heath (h) | 3.2.1894 |
| S Smith (3) v Blackburn Rovers (a) | 1.12.1894 |
| CW Athersmith (3) Stoke (h) | 26.12.1894 |
| J Campbell (4) v Small Heath (h) | 7.9.1895 |
| CW Athersmith (3) v Burnley (h) | 2.11.1895 |
| J Campbell (3) v Stoke (h) | 22.2.1896 |
| GF Wheldon (3) v Blackburn Rov (a) | 28.11.1896 |
| J Devey (3) v Burnley (a) | 8.2.1897 |
| GF Wheldon (3) v Sheffield Wed (h) | 1.9.1897 |
| GF Wheldon (3) v West Brom A (h) | 4.9.1897 |
| J Devey (3) v Notts County (h) | 22.4.1899 |
| W Garraty (3) v West Brom A (h) | 24.4.1899 |
| W Garraty (4) v Glossop (h) | 4.9.1899 |
| G Johnson (3) v Notts County (a) | 18.10.1899 |
| S Smith (3) v Preston North End (a) | 2.12.1899 |
| W Garraty (3) v Sunderland (h) | 30.12.1899 |
| W Garraty (3) v Notts County (h) | 17.2.1900 |
| J Devey (3) v Preston North End (h) | 4.9.1900 |
| G Johnson (4) v Manchester City (h) | 1.12.1900 |
| J McLuckie (3) v Grimsby Town (h) | 14.12.1901 |
| J McLuckie (3) v Sheffield United (h) | 18.8.1903 |

| | |
|---|---|
| JW Bache (3) v Newcastle United (h) | 7.11.1903 |
| JW Bache (3) v Nottingham Forest (h) | 19.12.1903 |
| J Nibloe (3) v Nottingham Forest (a) | 19.12.1903 |
| H Hampton (3) v Liverpool (h) | 11.9.1905 |
| J Cantrell (3) v Wolves (h) | 25.11.1905 |
| J Cantrell (3) v Sheffield United (h) | 15.12.1906 |
| H Hampton (3) v Sheffield Wed (h) | 9.2.1907 |
| H Hampton (3) v Bristol City (a) | 6.4.1907 |
| JW Bache (4) v Nottingham For (h) | 25.12.1907 |
| JW Bache (3) v Sheffield Wed (h) | 15.2.1908 |
| JW Bache (3) v Notts County (h) | 2.3.1908 |
| JW Bache (3) v Liverpool (h) | 4.4.1908 |
| JE Travers (3) v Bury (h) | 26.12.1908 |
| WW Gerrish (3) v Chelsea (h) | 11.9.1909 |
| H Hampton (3) v Nottingham For (a) | 1.1.1910 |
| H Hampton (3) v Blackburn Rov (h) | 29.1.1910 |
| J Walters (3) v Manchester United (h) | 26.2.1910 |
| H Hampton (3) v Middlesbrough (h) | 25.3.1910 |
| H Hampton (3) v Bury (h) | 26.3.1910 |
| JW Bache (3) v Middlesbrough (h) | 26.11.1910 |
| JW Bache (3) v Manchester City (a) | 16.9.1911 |
| H Hampton (4) v Oldham Athletic (h) | 26.12.1911 |
| H Hampton (4) v Bury (h) | 2.3.1912 |
| C Stephenson (3) v Manchester U (h) | 30.3.1912 |
| H Hampton (5) v Sheffield Wed (h) | 5.10.1912 |
| HJ Halse (5) v Derby County (h) | 19.10.1912 |
| H Hampton (3) v Oldham Athletic (h) | 26.12.1912 |
| JW Bache (3) Manchester United (a) | 14.3.1914 |
| H Hampton (3) v Liverpool (h) | 3.4.1915 |
| HE Nash (3) v Liverpool (h) | 3.4.1915 |
| W Boyman (3) v Middlesbrough (a) | 25.10.1919 |
| C Stephenson (3) v Middlesbrough (h) | 1.11.1919 |
| C Stephenson (4) v Sheffield Utd (h) | 29.11.1919 |
| WH Walker (3) v Newcastle United (h) | 5.4.1920 |
| WH Walker (4) v Arsenal (h) | 28.8.1920 |
| WH Walker (3*) v Bradford City (h) | 12.11.1921 |
| RE York (3) v Burnley (h) | 26.12.1922 |
| W Dickson (3) v Stoke (h) | 17.2.1923 |
| WH Walker (3) v Huddersfield T (a) | 10.3.1923 |
| WH Walker (3) v Preston NE (h) | 29.9.1923 |

*Bill Garraty (two hat-tricks in 1899)*

| | |
|---|---|
| WH Walker (3) West Bromwich A (h) | 23.10.1923 |
| LK Capewell (3) v Tottenham Hot (a) | 20.3.1924 |
| WH Walker (3) v Newcastle U (h) | 21.4.1924 |
| LK Capewell (5) v Burnley (h) | 29.8.1925 |
| WH Walker (3) v Burnley (h) | 29.8.1925 |

| RE York (3) Bury (a) | 24.10.1925 |
|---|---|
| LK Capewell (3) v Huddersfield T (h) | 14.11.1925 |
| LK Capewell (3) Everton (h) | 4.12.1926 |
| J Beresford (3) v Portsmouth (h) | 5.9.1927 |
| GW Cook (3) v Middlesbrough (h) | 8.10.1927 |
| J Beresford (3) v Sheffield Wed (h) | 24.12.1927 |
| RE York (3) v Bury (h) | 13.10.1928 |
| T Waring (3) v Arsenal (a) | 24.11.1928 |
| T Waring (3) v Burnley (h) | 2.2.1929 |
| RA Chester (3) v Huddersfield T (h) | 20.4.1929 |
| G Brown (3) v Arsenal (h) | 25.9.1929 |
| G Brown (3) v Everton (h) | 12.10.1929 |
| WH Walker (4) v Sheffield United (h) | 14.12.1929 |
| T Waring (4) v Manchester United (a) | 31.8.1930 |
| T Waring (4) v West Ham United (h) | 6.9.1930 |
| T Waring (4) v Sunderland (h) | 18.2.1931 |
| J Beresford (3) v Leicester City (h) | 28.9.1931 |
| T Waring (3) v Blackpool (h) | 28.3.1931 |
| T Waring (4) v Chelsea (a) | 19.9.1931 |
| T Waring (4) v West Ham United (h) | 26.9.1931 |
| T Waring (3) v Blackpool (h) | 7.11.1931 |
| WE Houghton (3) v Middlesbrough (h) | 25.12.1931 |

*'Pongo' Waring*

| J Beresford (3) v Middlesbrough (h) | 25.12.1931 |
|---|---|
| G Brown (5) v Leicester City (a) | 2.1.1932 |
| G Brown (4) v Liverpool (h) | 16.1.1932 |
| G Brown (4) v Bolton Wanderers (h) | 3.9.1932 |
| G Brown (4) v Blackburn Rovers (a) | 29.4.1932 |
| DJ Astley (3) v Leeds United (h) | 30.4.1934 |
| DJ Astley (3) v Preston North End (h) | 29.9.1934 |
| DJ Astley (3) v Leicester City (h) | 29.1.1935 |
| DJ Astley (3) v Stoke City (h) | 2.3.1935 |
| DJ Astley (3) v Huddersfield Town (h) | 25.12.1935 |
| G Hodgson (3) v Bradford City (h) | 14.9.1935 |
| RW Dix (3) v Swansea Town (h) | 26.12.1936 |
| WE Houghton (3) v Plymouth A (h) | 13.2.1937 |
| FH Broome (3) v Blackpool (h) | 20.3.1937 |
| FH Broome (3) v Blackburn Rovers (a) | 27.3.1937 |
| FH Shell (3) v Stockport County (h) | 11.12.1937 |
| JR Martin (3) Birmingham (h) | 4.3.1939 |
| T Ford (4) v Wolverhampton W (h) | 27.12.1948 |
| JT Dixon (3) v Stoke City (a) | 1.11.1952 |
| T Thompson (3) v Middlesbrough (h) | 14.11.1953 |
| T Thompson (3) v Manchester C (a) | 16.10.1954 |
| T Thompson (3) v Wolverhampton Wds (h) | 12.4.1955 |
| D Pace (3) v Sheffield United (h) | 14.4.1956 |
| S Lynn (3) v Sunderland (h) | 11.1.1958 |

| GA Hitchens (3) v Bolton Wanderers (a) | 15.3.1959 |
|---|---|
| GA Hitchens (5) v Charlton Athletic (h) | 14.11.1959 |
| GA Hitchens (3) v Bristol City (a) | 21.11.1959 |
| RGM Thomson (3) v Huddersfield Town (h) | 6.2.1960 |

*Gerry Hitchens*

| GA Hitchens (3) v Birmingham City (h) | 22.10.1960 |
|---|---|
| PJ McParland (3) v Blackpool (h) | 23.9.1961 |
| RGM Thomson (3) v Leicester City (h) | 21.4.1962 |
| H Burrows (3) v Blackpool (a) | 7.9.1963 |
| A Hateley (4) v Tottenham Hotspur (a) | 19.3.1966 |
| A Lochhead (3) v Oldham Athletic (a) | 27.11.1971 |
| SJ Morgan (3) v Hull City (h) | 28.8.1974 |
| R Graydon (3) v Millwall (h) | 21.9.1974 |
| B Little (3) v Oldham Athletic (h) | 12.4.1975 |
| AM Gray (3) v West Ham United (h) | 21.8.1976 |
| AM Gray (3) v Ipswich Town (h) | 4.9.1976 |
| AM Gray (3) v West Bromwich Albion (h) | 23.5.1977 |
| G Shelton (3) v Arsenal (h) | 25.4.1979 |
| GR Shaw (3) v Bristol City (a) | 29.12.1979 |
| P Rideout (3) v Newcastle United (h) | 22.12.1984 |
| ME Walters (3) v Crystal Palace (h) | 21.10.1987 |
| D Platt (3) v Tottenham Hotspur (h) | 16.3.1991 |

*Hat-trick of penalties

**Premiership**

| D Saunders (3) v Swindon Town (h) | 12.2.1994 |
|---|---|
| T Johnson (3) v Wimbledon (h) | 11.2.1995 |
| S Milosevic (3) v Coventry City (h) | 16.12.1995 |
| D Yorke (3) v Newcastle United (a) | 30.9.1996 |
| D Dublin (3) v Southampton (a) | 14.11.1998 |

**FA Cup**

| H Vaughton (3) v Wednesbury Old Athletic (a) | 29.12.1883 |
|---|---|
| D Hodgetts (3) v Wednesbury Old Athletic (h) | 30.10.1886 |

*Dennis Hodgetts*

*Ron Wylie*

| | | |
|---|---|---|
| A Brown (3) v Wednesbury Old Athletic (h) | | 30.10.1886 |
| A Brown (3) v Horncastle (h) | | 5.2.1887 |
| D Hodgetts (4) v The Casuals (h) | | 17.1.1891 |
| L Campbell (3) v The Casuals (h) | | 17.1.1891 |
| D Hodgetts (3) v Heanor Town (h) | | 16.1.1892 |
| J Devey (4) v Bristol City (a) | | 10.2.1900 |
| G Johnson (3) v Millwall (h) | | 26.1.1901 |
| J McLuckie (3) v Barnsley (h) | | 21.2.1903 |
| AE Hall (3) v Kings Lynn (h) | | 13.1.1906 |
| CJH Millington (4) v Kings Lynn (h) | | 13.1.1906 |
| H Hampton (3) v Derby County (h) | | 5.2.1910 |
| H Hampton (3) v Bradford Park Avenue (a) | | 8.3.1913 |
| WH Walker (3) v Derby County (h) | | 7.1.1922 |
| WA Dickson (3) v Stoke (h) | | 22.2.1922 |
| WH Walker (3) v Port Vale (h) | | 10.1.1925 |

*One of Tony Hateley's 4 goals v. Spurs in 1966.*

| | |
|---|---|
| LK Capewell (4) v Port Vale (h) | 10.1.1925 |
| CW Cook (3) v Crewe Alexandra (h) | 28.1.1928 |
| T Waring (3) v Clapton Orient (a) | 30.1.1929 |
| G Brown (3) v Blackburn Rovers (h) | 15.2.1930 |
| DJ Astley (4) v Sunderland (h) | 27.1.1934 |
| WE Houghton (3) v Sunderland (h) | 27.1.1934 |
| FH Broome (3) v Millwall (h) | 28.1.1946 |
| RM Wylie (3) v Everton (a) | 14.2.1959 |
| D Geddis (3) v Notts County (a) | 5.1.1982 |
| D Yorke (3) v Derby County (a) | 5.2.1992 |
| B Carbone (3) v Leeds United (h) | 30.1.2000 |

**Football League Cup**

| | |
|---|---|
| GA Hitchens (3) v Plymouth Argyle (a) | 6.2.1961 |
| AD Dougan (3) v Peterborough United (h) | 24.9.1962 |
| A Hateley (4) v Bradford City (h) | 23.11.1964 |
| B Little (3) v Queen's Park Rangers S/F (n) | 22.2.1977 |

| | |
|---|---|
| AM Gray (3) v Exeter City (a) | 31.8.1977 |
| S Stainrod (4) v Exeter City (a) | 25.9.1985 |
| D Platt (4) v Ipswich Town (h) | 30.11.1988 |

**European Cup**

| | |
|---|---|
| GR Shaw (3) v Dinamo Bucharest (h) | 3.11.1982 |

**UEFA Cup**

| | |
|---|---|
| P Withe (3) v Victoria Guimaraes (h) | 29.8.1983 |
| SV Collymore (3) v Stromsgodset (a) | 29.9.1998 |

**Wartime**

| | |
|---|---|
| R Davis (3) v Revo Electric (a) | 21.9.1940 |
| R Davis (3) v RAF Bridgnorth (h) | 15.2.1941 |
| R Davis (3) Revo Electric (a) | 22.2.194 |
| FH Broome (3) v RAF Bridgnorth (h) | 5.4.1941 |
| R Davis (3) v West Bromwich Albion (h) | 26.4.1941 |
| R Davis (3) v Hednesford Town (a) | 6.9.1941 |
| R Davis (3) v Wellington Town (h) | 27.9.1941 |
| R Davis (6) v Worcester City (a) | 1.11.1941 |
| R Davis (4) v Worcester City (h) | 6.12.1941 |
| AW Kerr (3) v RAF Hednesford (h) | 14.2.1942 |
| FH Broome (3) Revo Electric (3) v | 21.2.1942 |
| FH Broome (4) v RAF Lichfield (h) | 24.3.1942 |
| HA Parkes (4) v RAF Lichfield (h) | 24.3.1942 |
| WC Goffin (4) v RAF Lichfield (h) | 24.3.1942 |
| L Canning (3) v RAF Hednesford (h) | 17.1.1942 |
| A Massie (5) v RAF Hednesford (h) | 17.1.1942 |
| FH Broome (4) v RAF Hednesford (h) | 17.1.1942 |
| AW Kerr (3) v Hednesford Town (h) | 23.5.1942 |
| WE Houghton (3) v West Bromwich Albion (h) | 17.10.1942 |
| WE Houghton (3) v Leicester City (h) | 19.12.1942 |
| FH Broome (3) v Wolverhampton Wanderers (a) | 2.1.1943 |
| R Davis (3) v Walsall (a) | 27.2.1943 |
| WE Houghton (3) v Wolverhampton Wds (h) | 6.3.1943 |
| R Davis (3) v Wolverhampton Wanderers (a) | 13.3.1943 |

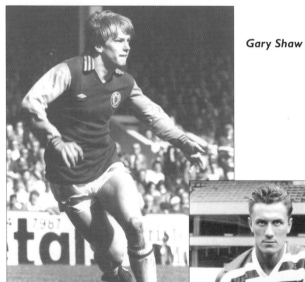

*Gary Shaw*

*Simon Stainrod*

THE COMPLETE ENCYCLOPAEDIA OF ASTON VILLA F.C.        THE COMPLETE ENCYCLOPAEDIA OF ASTON VILLA F.C.

135

| | |
|---|---|
| FH Broome (3) v West Bromwich Albion (h) | 10.4.1944 |
| FJ Haycock (3) v Leicester City (h) | 9.12.1944 |
| GR Edwards (3) v West Bromwich Albion (a) | 2.4.1945 |
| WE Houghton (3) v Leicester City (h) | 14.4.1945 |
| GR Edwards (4) v Coventry City (h) | 5.5.1945 |
| GR Edwards (4) v Luton Town (h) | 1.9.45 |
| GR Edwards (4) v Arsenal (h) | 29.9.1945 |
| GR Edwards (3) v Plymouth Argyle (a) | 3.11.1945 |

## Hat-trick Facts

Harry Hampton scored most senior hat-tricks for Aston Villa: total 12 (10 in the First Division and two in the FA Cup). Billy Walker netted 11 (nine in the Football League) whilst Dicky Davis notched 10 (all during World War Two, although 'two' came in one match when he grabbed a sixtimer) likewise 'Pongo' Waring, nine of his 10 trebles coming in the First Division. Frank Broome netted nine hat-tricks (two League, one FAC, six Wartime), George Brown, Jack Devey and Eric Houghton each weighed in with seven, Dai Astley notched six and George Edwards and Gerry Hitchens netted five apiece.

Aston Villa's first Football League hat-trick was scored by England international Albert Allen in a 9-1 home win over Notts County on 29 September 1888.

The first hat-trick at Villa Park was claimed by England international Fred Wheldon, for Villa against Sheffield Wednesday on 1 September 1897 (Division One).

Harry Hampton scored five hat-tricks (including two in 24 hours) in season 1909-10 (four League, one FA Cup).

Harold Nash scored a hat-trick on his League debut for Aston Villa in a 6-3 win over Liverpool on 3 April 1915.

Frank Shell netted a hat-trick on his home League debut for Villa against Stockport County in December 1937.

Derek Pace for Sheffield United (February 1961), Derek Dougan for Leicester City (September 1966) and Harry Burrows for Stoke City (December 1966) all scored hat-tricks against their previous club - Aston Villa.

Future Aston Villa manager Ron Saunders scored two hat-tricks against the same side in the same season - for Portsmouth v Leyton Orient in 1963-64.

Billy Walker scored a hat-trick of penalties for Villa against Bradford City in a First Division match in 1921 and ex-Villa star Andy Blair did likewise for Sheffield Wednesday against Luton in a League Cup-tie in 1984 whilst Charlie Mitten (Manchester United) hit 3 penalties v Villa in 1950 (see Penalty Kick).

## HAYCOCK, FREDERICK JAMES

Born: Bootle, April 1911. Died: Birmingham April 1989.
Career: Bootle Schoolboys (June 1925), Liverpool & District Schools, Waterford (1928), Prescot Cables FC (1932), Aston Villa (February 1934), Wrexham (September 1945), Stourbridge (season 1947-48). Retired and later managed two local junior teams in Birmingham minor football. He also worked at ICI (Witton) for over 30 years. Haycock guested for Nottingham Forest, Northampton Town, Notts County, Plymouth Argyle and Wolves during the Second World War.

As a youngster, soccer-mad Freddie Haycock played for the Bootle Schools team on a Saturday morning and worked in his father's butchers shop in the afternoon. After a very useful spell in Ireland with Waterford, he returned to England to play non-League football with Prescot Cables before becoming a full-time professional with Aston

Villa in 1934. He spent 11 years at Villa Park, appearing in 110 first-class games (99 in the League), scoring 33 goals. He was even chosen to play for Ireland in a representative match in 1934 - despite being a scouser! (The Irish clearly remembered his skills when he was with Waterford some years earlier). Nicknamed 'Schneider' he was a grafter more than a goalscorer and was a key member of Villa's Second Division championship-winning side in 1937-38. He was a dedicated dahlia grower.

## HAYNES, ARTHUR EDWIN

Born: Birmingham, 23 May 1924. Died: 1990.
Career: Birmingham Schoolboy football, Aston Villa (amateur, August 1945, professional January 1946), Walsall (June 1948), Weymouth (August 1950), Worcester City (season 1952-53). Later appointed scout for Leeds United.

A well-built second-string utility forward (who preferred the right-wing position), Arthur Haynes made just four first team appearances for Aston Villa before moving to Fellows Park.

## HAZELDEN, WALTER

Born: Ashton-in-Makerfield, 13 February 1941.
Career: Wigan Schoolboy football, Aston Villa (junior, June 1956, professional February 1958), Wigan Athletic (July 1960), Rugby Town (August 1961), Ashton FC (July 1964). Retired in May 1968.

An England Youth international (1957-58) inside-forward, Wally Hazelden became the youngest player ever to appear in a Football League game for Aston Villa when he scored on his debut against West Bromwich Albion in November 1957, at the age of 16 years, 257 days......15 year-old Jimmy Brown took over the mantle in 1969. A skilful player he fared a lot better in non-League circles after netting five times in his 19 first XI appearances for Villa.

## HEANOR TOWN

Villa's record against the non-League club:

FA Cup

| Venue | P | W | D | L | F | A |
|---|---|---|---|---|---|---|
| Home | 1 | 1 | 0 | 0 | 4 | 1 |

This 4th round cup-tie was played in front of 2,000 fans at Villa's Perry Barr ground in January 1892. Denny Hodgetts hit a hat-trick.

## HEARD, TIMOTHY PATRICK

Born: Hull, 17 March 1960.
Career: Hull & Humberside District Schools, Everton (apprentice June 1976, professional, March 1978), Aston Villa (£150,000 plus John Gidman, October 1979), Sheffield Wednesday (£60,000, January 1983), Newcastle United (September 1984), Middlesbrough (August 1985), Hull City (March 1986), Rotherham United (July 1988), Cardiff City (August 1999), Hull City (non-contract, August-October 1992).

An England Youth international, Pat Heard was a good 'stand-in' during Villa's League Championship-winning season of 1980-81. A defender with the 'right attitude' he scored twice in 26 outings for Villa, having earlier collected an FA Youth Cup-winners' medal with Everton (1977). During his career Heard made well over 300 senior appearances at club level (293 in the Football League).

## HEATH, ADRIAN PAUL

Born: Stoke-on-Trent, 17 January 1961.
Career: Stoke City (apprentice, June 1977, professional January 1979), Everton (£700,000, January 1982), Espanyol, Spain (August 1988-July 1989) Aston Villa (£360,000, August 1989), Manchester City (February 1990), Stoke City (March 1992), Burnley (August 1992), Sheffield United (December 1995), Burnley (non-contract, March 1996). Later

THE COMPLETE ENCYCLOPAEDIA OF ASTON VILLA F.C.          THE COMPLETE ENCYCLOPAEDIA OF ASTON VILLA F.C.

136

manager of Burnley (March 1996-97); also Sheffield United (assistant-manager/coach), Sunderland (coach from 2000-01).

Capped eight times by England at Under-21 level and once by the 'B' team. Adrian Heath was - for most of the time - a sharp-shooting, nippy, all-action striker, with good close control who pounced on the half-chance in front of goal. He had a fine career, netting 120 goals in 525 Football League games in England alone. Unfortunately he never settled at Villa Park and failed to hit the target in his 12 senior outings for the club. Heath won two League Championship medals with Everton (1985 & 1987), an FA Cup winners' medal in 1984 and a European Cup Winners Cup medal, also in 1985, plus four FA Charity Shield triumphs at Wembley. He starred in over 300 games for the Merseysiders (110 goals) but unfortunately failed in his efforts as manager at Turf Moor.

## HEDNESFORD TOWN
Villa's playing record against the Pitmen:
Birmingham League

| Venue | P | W | D | L | F | A |
|---|---|---|---|---|---|---|
| Home | 1 | 1 | 0 | 0 | 8 | 0 |
| Away | 3 | 1 | 0 | 2 | 4 | 8 |
| Totals | 4 | 2 | 0 | 2 | 12 | 8 |
| Birmingham League Cup | | | | | | |
| Home | 1 | 1 | 0 | 0 | 3 | 2 |
| Keys Cup | | | | | | |
| Home | 1 | 1 | 0 | 0 | 5 | 0 |

All six matches were played during the early part of the Second World War when Villa fielded their first team in these respective competitions.

Villa's biggest 'League' win was 8-0 - at home (Solihull Town's ground) in January 1942 when three players - Billy Goffin, Bob Iverson and Eric Houghton - each scored twice.

The 'League Cup' victory came in the semi-final of that competition in January 1942 when Frank Broome netted twice while the 5-0 Keys Cup success was claimed in the Final in May 1942 when Albert Kerr (3) and Goffin (2) found the net in front of 1,200 spectators.

Players with both clubs: SE Bowen, DM Bradley, A Comyn, JD Cordell, S Crowther, DL Jackson, GF Lee, AT Lyons, JR Martin (also Town manager), JH Maund, JH Morby, PJ Robinson, S Smith, AD Talbot, WH Walker.

Also: G Cummings (Villa player, Hednesford manager).

## HEIGHT
### Tallest
Reserve goalkeepers George Ephgrave (1938-39) and Percy Maggs (1928-32) were both 6ft. 5in tall and are believed to be the tallest players ever registered with Aston Villa as professionals.

Lanky striker Ian 'Legs' Ormondroyd was 6ft 4ins tall when he was at Villa Park during the 1989-91 period. Full-back Tom Riddell (1880s) was also 6ft 4ins tall (and 14st 10lbs in weight) as was goalkeeper Bob Roberts (1892-93) while Charlie Hobson from the 1880s was also believed to be around 6ft 4ins in height, so too was 1990's defender David Hughes.

### Shortest
Herbie Smith at 5ft 3ins is believed to have been Villa's shortest League player (1947-54). At 5ft 4ins tall we have Villa's 1930s left-winger Charlie Drinkwater and present-day left-back Alan Wright whilst several players have measured 5ft 5ins, including Welsh international Jackie Williams from the 1930s and Wally Harris (1920's).

## HELSINBORG
Villa's playing record against the Swedish side:
UEFA Cup

| Venue | P | W | D | L | F | A |
|---|---|---|---|---|---|---|
| Home | 1 | 0 | 1 | 0 | 1 | 1 |
| Away | 1 | 0 | 1 | 0 | 0 | 0 |
| Totals | 2 | 0 | 2 | 0 | 1 | 1 |

Aston Villa were eliminated from the 1996-97 UEFA Cup tournament in the opening round, beaten by the Swedish part-timers of Helsingborg who claimed a dramatic 1-1 draw at Villa Park to go through on the away goal rule.

## HENDRIE, LEE ANDREW
Born: Birmingham 18 May 1977.
Career: Aston Villa (YTS, June 1993, professional May 1994).
Honoured by England at Youth, Under-21 (13 times) and 'B' team levels, midfielder Lee Hendrie has also added one senior cap to his collection when he represented his country against Czechoslovakia in November 1998. He shared the Midland Football Writers' 'Young Player of the Year' award with Robbie Keane of Wolves in 1998-99 after playing in his 50th League game for the club. A purposeful competitor with a powerful right-foot shot, Hendrie, who has suffered his fair share of injury problems over the last three years, can be a little hot-headed at times and has already received a couple of red-cards (he was sent-off on his Premiership debut for Villa against QPR in December 1995).
He ended the 2000-01 campaign with an Aston Villa record of 145 appearances and 16 goals.
Lee Hendrie's father, Paul, played for rivals Birmingham City and his cousin, John, starred for Coventry City, Hereford United, Bradford City, Newcastle United, Leeds United, Barnsley and Middlesbrough.

## HENSHALL, HORACE VINCENT
Born: Hednesford, 14 June 1889. Died: Nottingham, 7 December 1951.
Career: Bridgetown Amateurs (Walsall League), Aston Villa (Amateur May 1905, professional May 1906), Notts County (November 1912), Barnsley (WWI guest), Sheffield Wednesday (player & reserve team coach, June 1922), Chesterfield (August 1923-May 1924), Lincoln City (manager, May 1924-June 1927), Notts County (manager June 1927-May 1934, then secretary at Meadow Lane until April 1935). Retired from football to become licensee of the Navigation Inn, Nottingham (1935 onwards).
During his playing days Horace Henshall - an England Junior international v Scotland in April 1908 - was a hard-running, enthusiastic inside-forward with a powerful right-foot shot. He scored 11 goals in 50 first team appearances for Aston Villa and followed up with 27 in 164 League outings for Notts County before winding down his career at Hillsborough and Chesterfield. He was a very popular figure at Meadow Lane and when he returned there as manager the fans again took to him deeply as he guided the Magpies to the Third Division (South) title in 1931 when they finished eight points clear of their nearest rivals.

## HEREFORD UNITED
Villa's record against the Bulls:
League Cup

| Venue | P | W | D | L | F | A |
|---|---|---|---|---|---|---|
| Home | 1 | 1 | 0 | 0 | 4 | 1 |

THE COMPLETE ENCYCLOPAEDIA OF ASTON VILLA F.C.     THE COMPLETE ENCYCLOPAEDIA OF ASTON VILLA F.C.

137

Hereford United were elected to the Football League on 2 July 1972. Three weeks later they were drawn out of the hat to play Aston Villa the first round of the League Cup. A crowd of 32,324 saw the Bulls beaten 4-1 at Villa Park on 16 August.

Players with both clubs include: WJ Carey, LM Craddock, G (H) Gregory, T Hughes (also Hereford manager), MAW Jones, D Norton, DR Parsons, F Potter, C Price, I Ross, D Rudge, B Sharp, JS Sharp, FH Shell, HF Trentham (Villa trialist). Villa sold Gregory and Rudge to the Bulls in a joint deal in August 1972.
Also: A Massie & G Turner (manager of both clubs, Massie also Villa player), A Ashman (Hereford assistant-manager, Villa scout).

## HIBERNIAN

Aston Villa (the English FA Cup winners) met Hibernian (the Scottish Cup holders) in two challenge matches in 1887-88. Villa won them both - 8-3 in Scotland and 3-0 at Wellington Road. Around 10,000 spectators cheered Villa to victory in the latter contest which confirmed them as ' best football team in Great Britain'.
In 1914-15, that 8-3 scoreline over Hibs was repeated in a friendly at Villa Park and in another friendly encounter at Easter Road in 1969-70, Villa won comfortably by 4-1.
Aston Villa played Hibs in a Testimonial match in Edinburgh for the Scottish club's long-serving defender Alan Sneddon in 1991-92.

Players with both clubs include: DG Bremner, J Burridge, JK Brown, L Campbell, TB Craig (Hibs' player/coach), AJ Cropley, DW Gibson, W Groves, WH Hamilton, A Logan, JM MacLeod, N Mackay, RB Templeton, J Ward.

## HICKMAN, JOSEPH

Born: County Durham, August 1901. Deceased.
Career: Lintz Colliery, Hartlepools United, Aston Villa (December 1927), Spennymoor United (August 1928), Durham City (briefly), Connah's Quay, Hartlepools United, Scarborough. Retired 1936.
Goalkeeper Joe Hickman was reserve to Tommy Jackson and Ben Olney during his nine-month stay at Villa Park. During that time he played in just two League games, conceding a total of nine goals - in a 5-4 home win over Sheffield Wednesday and a 5-0 defeat at Derby in the space of two days, on the 24 & 26 December 1927.

## HICKSON, DAVID

Born: Ellesmere Port, Cheshire, 30 October 1929.
Career: Ellesmere Port FC (1944), Everton (amateur 1947, professional May 1949), Aston Villa (£17,500, September 1955), Huddersfield Town (£16,000, November 1955), Everton (£6,500, July 1957), Liverpool (£10,500, November 1959), Cambridge City (July 1961), Bury (£1,000 paid to Liverpool, January 1962), Tranmere Rovers (July 1962, two-month trial, signed permanently, September 1962), Ballymena (player/manager July 1964), Ellesmere Port (February 1965, player/manager, March 1965), Northwich Victoria (1966), Winsford United (September 1967), Fleetwood Town, Ellesmere Port Town

(manager again, 1973-74). Later became a bookmaker in Liverpool.
Dave Hickson was a colourful, dashing centre-forward who excelled in the air. Often in the headlines (more often than not due to brushes with authority) he was a quiet, unassuming man off the field, even shy! He had scored 71 goals in almost 150 games for Everton before moving to Villa Park as a replacement (or so it seemed) for the departed Dave Walsh. However, he failed to settle down in Birmingham and after netting once in 12 games he was transferred to Huddersfield, Villa losing £1,500 in the process! Hickson later returned to Goodison Park where he took his goal-tally up to 111 in 243 games. He then claimed another 37 goals in 60 outings for Liverpool and when he quit League soccer in 1964, he had amassed a terrific record of 182 goals in 404 in that competition (over 200 scored in all matches).
Hickson actually scored the Everton goal that knocked Villa out of the FA Cup in 1953.

## HICKTON, ARTHUR JOSEPH

Born: Birmingham, June 1867. Died: Warwick c 1940.
Career: Birmingham Waterworks FC (1886), Aston Villa (July 1889), Rugby Wanderers (Novemnber 1890), Coventry Standard, Nuneaton Welfare. Retired 1902.
Tall, strong, versatile player, able to occupy the centre-half or centre-forward positions, Arthur Hickton was a reserve at Villa and made just one League appearance, taking over from Archie Hunter for the League game against Accrington (away) in September 1889.

## HINCHCLIFFE, JOHN

Born: Tillicoultry, Scotland, 4 June 1938.
Career: L. Pieter's Boys Club (Glasgow), Aston Villa (junior, July 1954, professional, September 1956), Workington (June 1958), Hartlepools United (October 1961), Durham City (August 1964). Retired 1968-69.
A Scottish Schoolboy international, right-winger Jack Hinchcliffe spent two years as a professional at Villa Park, playing in two League games, both in 1957-58, away at Manchester United and Chelsea. He was unfortunate to have Les Smith and Tommy Southren to contest a first team place with, but later did very well in the lower Divisions, making over 120 senior appearances for Workington and 88 in the League for Hartlepools United.

## HINCHLEY, ALBERT AUDLEY

Born: Warwick, August 1869. Died: Birmingham, June 1922.
Career: Warwick County, Aston Villa (September 1890), Cape Hill (August 1892).
Albert Hinchley provided adequate cover for goalkeeper Jack Warner during Aston Villa's FA Cup Final season of 1891-92, making all of his 11 League appearances in succession in the middle of that campaign.

## HINDLE, JOHN R.

Born: Preston, 10 November 1921. Died: 1987.
Career: Clifton Boys' Club, Preston North End (professional November 1946), Barrow (May 1948), Aston Villa ((June 1950), Barrow (August 1951).
Goalkeeper Jack Hindle made only one League appearance for PNE before establishing himself between the posts at Barrow. He performed with confidence and diligence at Holker Street, attracting the attention of several big-named clubs with Villa stepping in with a £6,000 bid to bring him down to the Midlands in 1950, basically as cover for Joe Rutherford and Keith Jones. Hindle appeared in 15 first team games for Villa before returning to Barrow after just a season in the First Division. He later took his League appearance tally with the Cumbrian club up to 266 before retiring through injury in 1955.

THE COMPLETE ENCYCLOPAEDIA OF ASTON VILLA F.C.        THE COMPLETE ENCYCLOPAEDIA OF ASTON VILLA F.C.

138

## HISBENT, JOSEPH S

Born: Plymouth, May 1884. Died: Devon, c 1949.
Career: Green Waves FC (1903), Aston Villa (August 1905), Portsmouth (September 1906), Brentford (August 1908).
Strongly-built, very alert defender, reserve to Albert Evans, Harry Hadley and Joey Windmill at Villa Park, Joe Hisbent had just two League outings for the club, his debut coming at left-back against Sunderland at Roker Park in February 1906. He later made 30 appearances for the Bees in the Southern League.

## HISLOP, PERCY DAVID

Born: Glasgow, September 1870. Died: Scotland 1929.
Career: Glasgow Royal (season 1888-89), Aston Villa (May 1891), Forfar Athletic (September 1892), Perth (1894-95).
Squarely-built inside-forward with good skills, Percy Hislop never settled down in Birmingham despite doing well in the handful of games he played. He scored three goals in seven League appearances for Villa, opening his account on his debut in a 5-1 home win over Blackburn Rovers on 5 Septemnber 1891 when he partnered Denny Hodgetts on the left-wing.

## HITZLSPERGER, THOMAS

Born: Germany, 5 April 1982
Career: Bayern Munich, Aston Villa (August 2000).
Reserve and talented young midfielder who made one substitute appearence for Villa v Liverpool at Villa Park during the 2000-01 season.

## HITCHENS, GERALD ARCHIBALD

Born: Rawnsley, Staffs 8 October 1934. Died: North Wales, April 1983
Career: Highley Council School, Highley Youth Club, Highley Village Boys, Highley Miners' Welfare FC, Kidderminster Harriers (August 1953), Cardiff City (£1,500, January 1955), Aston Villa (£22,500, December 1957), Inter Milan (£60,000, June 1961), Torino (£50,000, November 1962), Atalanta of Bergamo (£25,000, June 1965), Cagliari of Sardinia (£5,000, June 1967), Worcester City (November 1969), Merthyr Tydfil (September 1971). Retired May 1972 and went into business in Pontypridd.

Gerry Hitchens, the blond-bomber, was spotted by Kidderminster playing in a local Cup Final. Within eighteen months - after some sensational performances for the Harriers - he was on his way to fame and stardom after joining Cardiff City. He scored on his League debut for the Bluebirds against Wolves, his goal setting up a crucial win as the Welsh club escaped relegation from the First Division by the skin of their teeth. Forming a tremendous partnership with ex-Villa star Trevor Ford, he top-scored for Cardiff in two successive seasons, going on to net 40 goals in 95 League appearances for the Ninian Park club. He also fired in another 18 goals in 12 Test Match appearances whilst on tour to South Africa with the FA in 1956. After moving to Villa Park just before Christmas, 1957, Hitchens continued his magnificent strike-record and was Villa's leading marksman three seasons running (1958-61), going on to claim a total of 96 goals in 160 League and Cup outings for the club. He bagged a five-timer when Charlton were hammered 11-1 in November 1959, helping Villa win the Second Division championship that season, and then he did superbly well as the team raced through to reach the League Cup Final the following year. A swash-buckling, all-action centre-forward, fearsome and deadly, Hitchens starred for England at Under-23 level and won the first of his seven full England caps in an 8-0 win over Mexico at Wembley in 1961 before leaving Villa Park for the sun and lire of Italy . Hitchens then spent six years playing Serie 'A' and 'B' soccer and netted a further 75 goals in that time before returning to England to wind down his career in non-League football. He died suddenly while playing in a Charity match in North Wales.
This is how author John Crooks described Hitchens in his book, A Who's Who of Cardiff City.....'Ninian Park fans saw Gerry as an uncut diamond before being polished into a precious jewel.'

## H.M.S. ASTON VILLA

The Royal Navy minesweeper HMS Aston Villa was built in 1937 and requisitioned and converted in 1939. It was subsequently attacked by enemy aircraft off the coast of Norway on 3 May 1940 and scuttled several hours later.

## HOBSON, CHARLES SIDNEY HERBERT

Born: Walsall, November 1861. Died: c 1927.
Career: Walsall Miners' Welfare, Walsall Swifts, Aston Villa (August 1884), Bilston (September 1887), Darlaston (1888).
Charlie Hobson was a very lean, wiry goalkeeper, 6ft 4ins tall, who was first-choice between the posts for Aston Villa in the 1885-86 season, playing in two FA Cup-ties.

## HOCKEY, TREVOR

Born: Keighley, Yorkshire, 1 May 1943. Died: Keighley, 1 April 1987.
Career: Yorkshire Schools, West Riding Under-19s, Keighley Central Youth Club, Bradford City (amateur, June 1958, professional May 1960), Nottingham Forest (£15,000, November 1961), Newcastle United (£25,000, November 1963), Birmingham City (£22,500, November 1965 - making over 230 appearances for Blues), Sheffield United (£35,000, January 1971), Norwich City (£30,000 plus Jim Bone, February 1973), Aston Villa (£38,000, June 1973), Bradford City (June 1974), Athlone Town (player/manager, March 1976), San Diego Jaws (NASL, April-August 1976), San Jose Earthquakes (April-May 1977), Los Angeles Quicksilvers (June-July 1977), Stalybridge Celtic (manager, August 1977). Later coached the British Army soldiers' children's soccer team on the Rhine and attempted to start a soccer School at Keighley Rugby Club (1980).
One of football's great journeymen, Trevor Hockey's professional career spanned almost 16 years during which time he amassed well over 600 senior appearances (24 for Aston Villa, one goal scored) and played on all the major League grounds which were being used when he was in action. Hockey played both Rugby League and Rugby Union

THE COMPLETE ENCYCLOPAEDIA OF ASTON VILLA F.C.    THE COMPLETE ENCYCLOPAEDIA OF ASTON VILLA F.C.

139

as well as soccer at school and after doing well for the West Riding Under-19s and his local Youth club, he joined Bradford City at the age of 15, turning professional two years later. After that, midfielder Hockey toured the country, literally! He won nine full caps for Wales (via parentage qualification), his first in 1972 v Finland when he was based at Bramall Lane, thus becoming the first 'Anglo' to play for Wales. His last international outing came as a Villa player against Poland in Katowice in 1974 when he suffered the indignity of being sent-off! He gained a Second Division championship medal with Newcastle in 1965 and also helped Sheffield United win promotion to the First Division in 1971. A real gritty performer, full of drive and endeavour, Hockey sadly died of a heart attack whilst taking part in a 5-a-side tournament in Keighley in 1987.

In 1976, at the age of 25, Hockey - nicknamed 'Dai Fungus' because of a bushy beard he once grew - became the youngest player to have appeared in a competitive game on every Football League ground.

*Trevor Hockey - with his footballing memorabilia.*

### HODGE, STEPHEN BRIAN

Born: Nottingham 25 October 1962

Career: Notts Schools, Nottinghamshire Boys, Nottingham Forest (apprentice May 1978, professional October 1980), Aston Villa (£450,000, August 1985), Tottenham Hotspur (£650,000, December 1986), Nottingham Forest (£575,000, August 1988), Leeds United (£900,000 July 1991), Derby County (on loan, August 1994), Queen's Park Rangers (£300,000, October 1994), Watford (free transfer, February 1995), Hong Kong football (January 1996), Leyton Orient (August 1997-May 1998). Retired and became Notts County Academy Coach (2000-01).

An exceptionally skilful, hard-working left-sided midfield player, Steve Hodge had a fine career which spanned 20 years from his apprenticeship with Nottingham Forest until his retirement in 1998.

During that time he amassed well over 500 club and international appearances and scored in excess of 100 goals. Capped 24 times by England (the first against USSR in March 1986) he also represented his country in two 'B' and eight Under-21 matches. He was twice a League Cup winner during his second spell with Forest, in 1989 and 1990, gained a Simod Cup winners prize as well (1989) and played in the 1991 FA Cup Final defeat against his old club Spurs, having appeared in the Final for Spurs against Coventry City four years earlier. In 1992 he helped Leeds United win the last Football League championship before the Premiership was introduced.

Accompanying Paul Birch and Mark Walters across the Villa midfield, Hodge had a very good 1985-86 season, making 48 appearances, but then along came Spurs' boss David Pleat with a big-money offer and off he went to White Hart Lane. He netted 16 times in 70 senior appearances for Villa. Unfortunately he was sent-off in new manager Terry Venables' opening match in charge of the London club and from that point Hodge's career with Spurs was on the line! He suffered with injuries after that but still came up with a handful of useful performances and some important goals.

### HODGETTS, DENNIS

Born: Birmingham, 28 November 1863. Died: Birmingham, 26 March 1945.

Career: Birmingham St George's (1878), Great Lever (August 1879), Birmingham St George's (1882), Aston Villa (February 1886), Small Heath (August 1896). Retired in August 1898 when he returned to Aston Villa as coach to the younger players. Became a publican in Birmingham in June 1910, taking over the Salutation Inn on Summer Lane, Aston. He was elected as Vice-President of Aston Villa FC in June 1930, a position he held until his death in 1945 at the age of 81.

Denny Hodgetts was a born footballer, a very powerful outside-left who could also play inside. With his immaculately waxed moustache and parted hair, he was a star performer, adored by the fans. Strong, decisive, clever with many original ideas, he could use both feet, was difficult to dispossess and could unleash a terrific shot. His ball distribution was exceptional and altogether he was an uncommonly fine goalscoring forward who became an admirably fine coach, helping develop several future players for the club.

During his twelve-and-a-half years with Villa, Hodgetts scored 91 goals in 215 first-class matches. He won two League Division One championship medals (1894 and 1896), appeared in three FA Cup Finals, gaining winners' medals in two, 1887 and 1895, and a loser's prize in 1892. He also starred in six international matches for England (1888-94). He was a very fine billiards player, winning a major national tournament in 1899.

THE COMPLETE ENCYCLOPAEDIA OF ASTON VILLA F.C.     THE COMPLETE ENCYCLOPAEDIA OF ASTON VILLA F.C.

140

## HODGSON, GORDON

Born: Johnannesburg, 16 April 1904. Died: Stoke-on-Trent, 15 June 1951.

Career: (in South Africa) Rustenberg FC (1921), Pretoria (1922-23) and Transvaal (1924-25); then Liverpool (December 1925), Aston Villa (£3,000, January 1936), Leeds United (£1,500, March 1937), Youth team coach at Elland Road (August 1942-October 1946); Hartlepools United (WW2 guest). Retired as player in 1945. Appointed manager of Port Vale, October 1946. Died whilst still at club. Played cricket for Transvaal, Lancashire (56 matches between 1928-32) and Forfarshire (1934-36) and he also excelled at baseball.

Inside-forward Gordon Hodgson scored 240 goals for Liverpool in 378 appearances before joining Aston Villa in 1936. He won three England

caps (after qualification) and also played twice for the Football League side.

He is the only player to have scored five goals in a League game for Leeds United, doing so against Leicester City on 1 October 1938.

He first came to England with the South African touring party in 1924 - and impressed all and sundry, hence his 'move' to Anfield. He actually held the aggregate scoring record for the Merseyside club, which was eventually bettered by Roger Hunt. He bagged 32 goals in 1928-29 and 36 in 1930-31. He claimed 11 goals in 28 outings for Villa, partnering Eric Houghton on the left-wing most of the time in between tedious injury problems.

Taking in all types of games, Hodgson scored 304 goals during his career.

He was in charge of Port Vale when they moved to their present ground in 1950 and his death came as a great shock to everyone associated with the Potteries' club.

## HOGAN, JAMES

Born: Nelson, 16 October 1882. Died: Burnley, 30 January 1974.

Career: Burnley Belvedere FC (1897), Nelson (1900), Rochdale (1902), Burnley (August 1902), Fulham (£100, July 1905), Swindon Town (£100, July 1908), Bolton Wanderers (£150, October 1908-May 1910), Holland (coach, for a year), Bolton Wanderers (August 1911-April 1913), Austria national team coach (1913-15), Young Boys of Berne (coach, 1921-24), held major coaching positions in both Hungary and Germany (1924-34), Fulham (manager, May 1934-February 1935), Austria national coach (June 1935-October 1936), Aston Villa (manager, November 1936-September 1939). After the Second World War coached at Celtic and Brentford, Aston Villa (Youth team manager: July 1953-July 1959). Retired out of football when approaching his 77th birthday.

As a player Jimmy Hogan occupied the outside-right and inside-right berths and made close on 100 first-class appearances. He was in the Fulham side that reached the 1908 FA Cup semi-final and gained two Southern League championship medals with the Cottagers before helping Bolton win the Second Division crown in 1909, going on to become one of the greatest coaches in the history of the game.

When he took over as coach to the Austrian national team in 1914, Hogan formed a tremendous partnership with Hugo Meisl and these two men were certainly responsible for the development of the game in Europe to the point whereby it certainly equalled, if not surpassed, the British game! Interned in Budapest during the First World War, he spent 20 years on the European coaching circuit and was highly respected everywhere he went.

Hogan did not have too much success at Fulham (his training methods were not appreciated to the full - simply because he deplored the stifling tactics employed by the Arsenal boss Herbert Chapman). In

fact, very little credit is attached to the Fulham board for the way they handled his dismissal - he learned his fate while recuperating in hospital after undergoing an operation.

At that point Hogan returned to Austria and almost immediately guided that country to the 1936 Olympic Games soccer Final. He returned to England and guided Aston Villa back into the First Division as champions in his second season with the club. He returned to Villa Park in the 1950s (under Eric Houghton's management) and helped develop some exceptionally fine players. He was given a great deal of credit for the rise of Hungarian football - especially after they had whipped England twice with 6-3 and 7-1 victories at Wembley in 1953 and Budapest in 1954.

During Hogan's time as manager, Villa played 126 League games of which 57 were won, 28 drawn and 41 lost.

Hogan was 91 when he died in his native Lancashire.

*Hogan (extreme right, standing) with his Villa team in 1938.*

## HOGG, ANTHONY RAYMOND

Born: Lowick, Northumberland, 11 December 1929.

Career: Lowick WMC (1945), Berwick Rangers (1950), Aston Villa (March 1955), Mansfield Town (July 1958), Peterborough United (August 1960). Retired through injury, June 1961. Later became a bookmaker, based in Lozells and Handsworth, Birmingham.

One-time shoe manufacturer in the North of the England, Ray Hogg skippered Berwick Rangers for three seasons before moving to Villa Park. A useful full-back or wing-half, as hard as nails, quick in recovery, he made 21 appearances for Villa as cover for Vic Crowe and Stan Lynn.

## HOLE, BARRINGTON GERARD

Born: Swansea, 16 September 1942.

Career: Swansea & District Schools, Swansea Town (trialist), Cardiff City (juniors June 1958, professional February 1960), Blackburn Rovers (£45,000, June 1966), Aston Villa (£60,000, September 1968), Swansea Town (£20,000, July 1970). Retired as

a 'pro' in 1972 but contiunued to play non-League and intermediate Sunday League football until 1978.

A frail-looking player, Barrie Hole was a superbly confident 'artiste on the ball', a wing-half or inside-forward who made over 300 League and Cup appearances for Cardiff City and Blackburn Rovers before moving to Villa Park. A Welsh Schoolboy international he joined Cardiff in preference to his home-town club on

THE COMPLETE ENCYCLOPAEDIA OF ASTON VILLA F.C.    THE COMPLETE ENCYCLOPAEDIA OF ASTON VILLA F.C.

141

the recommendation of his father, Billy Hole, a former Swans' player. He made his Football League debut at the age of 17 and became a permanent fixture in the Bluebirds' first team in 1960-61, showing great maturity way beyond his years. Whilst at Ninian Park he won five Welsh Under-23 caps and made the first of his 30 full international appearances.

He had scored nine goals in 53 first-team games for Villa when he caused a sensation by walking out on the club after a disagreement with caretaker-manager Arthur Cox in 1970 - a year after being voted the supporters' Terrace Trophy winner.

On quitting football Hole became a greengrocer, like his father before him, his shop being based in Swansea.

His brothers Alan and Colin also played for Swansea Town in 1953-54.

## HONOURS & AWARDS

Listed here are certain honours won/received/presented by/to Aston Villa players and managers, along with other awards and decorations gained by personnel either before, with or after serving the club. (Listed in no specific order of merit).....

Andy Gray (1977), David Platt (1990) and Paul McGrath (1993) all won the PFA 'Player of the Year' award when registered with Aston Villa. Gray was also voted 'Young Player of the Year' in 1977.

Aston Villa's striking duo of Peter Withe and Gary Shaw received the Midland 'Player of the Year' and 'Young Player of the Year' awards respectively in 1981, while future Villa star Cyrille Regis won the same honour as Shaw in 1979 with West Bromwich Albion.

The 'Midland Footballer of the Year' accolade went to Ron Wylie 1965), Andy Lochhead (1972), Charlie Aitken (1975), Steve Hodge (1988),

Paul McGrath was voted Aston Villa's 'Player of the Year' four seasons in a row: 1990 to 1993 inclusive. He also took the Midland 'Player of the Year' title in the latter season (1992-93).

Mark Bosnich received the Midland Soccer Writers' 'Player of the Year' award in 1993.

*Peter Aldis*

Future Villa star David Ginola was voted both the FWA and the PFA 'Footballer of the Year' in 1998-99 (having won similar awards in France) and Dwight Yorke (Manchester United), Ginola (Spurs) and Dion Dublin (Coventry City) all gained Player of the Month awards midway through the 1998-99 season.

George Harkus, MBE and Kevin Keelan, MBE, both played for Aston Villa and received their honours after leaving the club, Keelan whilst still a player with Norwich City.

Peter Aldis, ex-Villa left-back, won the Australian 'Player of the Year' award in 1966.

George Curtis (Coventry City, later Aston Villa) was chosen as the 'Midland Footballer of the Year' in 1963-64 while future Villa goalkeeper Mervyn Day was voted 'Young Footballer of the Year' in 1975 (aged 19).

Danny Blanchflower, after leaving Villa Park, twice won the FWA 'Player of the Year' award as Spurs' skipper, in 1958 and 1961.

Joe Mercer, Aston Villa's manager for six years from 1958 to 1964, was awarded the OBE in 1976 for services to football. Mercer was also voted 'Footballer of the Year' after skippering Arsenal to FA Cup glory in 1949-50.

Future Villa manager Billy McNeill received the MBE in 1974, nine years after being voted Scotland's 'Player of the Year' for 1965 when Celtic's dominant centre-half was rated as the best defender in Europe!

Brian McClair, released by Aston Villa, also collected the SFWA 'Player of the Year' prize in 1987 after scoring 36 goals for Celtic whilst

defender Paul Elliott followed him with the same honour in 1991, when he was also a Celtic player.

Ex-Villa star Alan Curbishley twice won the Carling Manager of the Month award in 1998-99 with Charlton Athletic.

Frank McAvennie (St Mirren), later to play for Villa, was the SPFA 'Young Player of the Year' in 1982.

Sir William Dugdale was Chairman and President of Aston Villa in the mid-1970s; Sir Partick Hannon MP (1924-63) and Sir Theodore Pritchett (1963-69) were both Presidents of Aston Villa and Sir Percival Bowler, MBE, JP was a club Vice-President in the 1940s.

Several personnel associated with Aston Villa down the years have held the title JP (Justice of the Peace), likewise MP (Members of Parliament), with second team player David Hughes being included in the latter category.

### Manager of the Month

The following men all received individual 'Manager of the Month' awards during their respective reigns in office at Villa Park: Ron Saunders, Josef Venglos, Ron Atkinson, Brian Little and John Gregory (first award in September 1998).

### Other Awards

Ex-player, Secretary and Director George Ramsay received two Football League Long Service medals in 1909 and 1927.

Fred Rinder was made a Life Member of the Football League in May 1938.

In 1950 Villa's secretary Billy Smith was presented with the Football League 21 years long service medal and in 1961 Fred Archer received the same award followed by secretary Alan Bennett in 1983.

During the Great War (1914-18) goalkeeper Leigh Richmond Roose was awarded the Military Medal whilst Joe Windmill received both the DCM and MC.

The British Empire Medal was awarded to Aston Villa defender Ernie Callaghan for showing 'conspicuous bravery' during an air raid on Birmingham during World War Two.

Bernie Gallagher received the Barclays 'Young Eagle of The Month' Award in October 1987.

Peter Broadbent won the Professional Footballers' golf title in 1968.

Derek Dougan became Chairman of the PFA in 1970-71.

Eric Houghton assumed the role of senior Vice-President of Aston Villa. Houghton also received the Bell's Whisky Supreme Services to Soccer award in 1986.

Phil Woosnam gained a Bachelor of Science degree at Bangor University in the 1950s.

Albert Wilkes, a Villa wing-half from 1898 to 1907, was awarded the Royal Humane Society's Vellum during the early part of the twentieth century for rescuing a boy who had fallen through the ice in the pool at Dartmouth Park, West Bromwich. His daughter received a similar medal some years later for saving the life of a child in Aberdovey.

Villa's Joey Windmill won a Distinguished Conduct Medal and the Military Cross during the Great War of 1914-18.

Villa winger Dicky York served as an officer in the Royal Flying Corps in World War One whilst Frank Buckley attained the rank of Major (1918) while serving with the Middlesex Regiment.

Aston Villa football club won the Bassetts Liquorice All Sorts award in 1985 - in recognition of the Villa Park family enclosure and other excellent crowd behaviour.

## HOPKINS, ROBERT ARTHUR

Born: Hall Green, Birmingham, 25 October 1961,

Career: South Birmingham Schools, West Midland County Boys, Aston Villa (apprentice, June 1977, professional July 1979), Birmingham City (in a deal involving Alan Curbishley, March 1983), Manchester City (£130,000, September 1986), West Bromwich Albion (£60,000 plus Imre Varadi, October 1986), Birmingham City (£25,000, March 1989), Shrewsbury Town (July 1991), South China FC & Instant Dictionary FC

THE COMPLETE ENCYCLOPAEDIA OF ASTON VILLA F.C.          THE COMPLETE ENCYCLOPAEDIA OF ASTON VILLA F.C.

142

in Hong Kong (May-December 1992), Solihull Borough (January 1993), Colchester United (non-contract, February 1993), Solihull Borough (July 1993).

Robert Hopkins' early career was littered with disciplinary problems, but he always gave total commitment whether playing wide on the right of midfield, as a central midfield position or even as a full-back. After three games and having the pleasure of scoring with his first kick in League football, as a substitute for Aston Villa against Norwich City on 26 March 1980, he switched across the city to St Andrew's. In 1986 he was transferred to Manchester City and in 1989 after a decent spell with the Baggies, he returned to Blues for a second time. Hopkins won an FA Youth Cup winners medal with Villa and helped Blues win promotion to Division One in 1985 being a non-playing 'sub' for Blues when they lifted the Leyland DAF Trophy in 1991. He appeared in a total of 307 Football League games for his six major clubs in Britain (46 goals scored).

## HORNCASTLE

Villa's record against Horncastle:

FA Cup

| Venue | P | W | D | L | F | A |
|-------|---|---|---|---|---|---|
| Home  | 1 | 1 | 0 | 0 | 5 | 0 |

Aston Villa easily beat the Lincolnshire market town team of Horncastle in a one-sided 5th round tie at Perry Barr in February 1887. Arthur Brown scored a hat-trick in the 5-0 win before a crowd of 3,000.

## HORNE, STANLEY FREDERICK

Born: Clanfield near Witney, Oxfordshire, 17 December 1944.

Career: Bampton Youth Club (1959), Aston Villa (amateur, August 1960), professional, December 1961), Manchester City (September 1965), Fulham (£18,000, February 1969), Chester City (£2,000, August 1973), Rochdale (December 1973-May 1975).

The versatile, hard-working Stan Horne was advised to give up playing football whilst at Villa Park. After just six first-team outings (in a variety of positions) he chose to defy his doctor's orders and went on to amass in excess of 200 appearances in major competitions for the next four clubs he served! A hard-working player, he was basically a reserve at Villa Park before settling in at left-back with Manchester City. He later starred in 80 games as Fulham's right-half, skippering the Cottagers on several occasions.

## HORTON, THOMAS ALBERT

Born: Dudley Port, Tipton, April 1859. Died: West Bromwich c 1921.

Career: Tipton BCT, Aston Villa (September 1880), Walsall Town Swifts (August 1882), Dudley Royal Exchange, Swan Village.

A lively utility forward, reserve to Ollie Whateley and Howard Vaughton, Tommy Horton made one FA Cup appearance for Villa, in a 4-2 defeat by Wednesbury Old Athletic in the 4th round in January 1882.

## HOUGHTON, RAYMOND JAMES

Born: Glasgow, 9 January 1962.

Career: Junior football in London, West Ham United (junior June 1977, professional July 1979), Fulham (free transfer, July 1982), Oxford United (£147,000, September 1985), Liverpool (£825,000, October 1987), Aston Villa (£900,000, July 1992), Crystal Palace (£300,000, March 1995), Reading (free transfer, July 1997-June 1999, retired), Crystal Palace (assistant-manager/coach, season 2000-01).

After a hesitant start at Upton Park (he made just one substitute appearance for the Hammers) midfielder Ray Houghton's career blossomed at Fulham. He played in 145 competitive matches for the Cottagers before transferring to The Manor Ground. The son of an

Irish farmer, he added a further 105 first-team appearances to his tally with the 'Us', helping them win the League Cup in 1986. He then did exceedingly well at Anfield where he fitted in nicely behind his former Oxford colleague John Aldridge. More prizes came along, Houghton collecting two League Championship winning medals in 1988 and 1990, plus Charity Shield successes in the same two years, as well as gaining two FA Cup winners' medals in 1989 and 1992. He netted 38 goals in 202 outings for the Merseyside club and whilst at Anfield his total of Republic of Ireland caps also grew steadily. He eventually took his total to 73, doing splendidly in both the European Championships and World Cup competitions under Jack Charlton's management.

A player able to unlock the tightest of defences, he had played 121 times and scored 11 goals for Aston Villa and collected a second League Cup winners' medal in 1994 before losing his place in the side following the arrival of new boss Brian Little. In fact, Houghton was the last player to be transferred on deadline day, 1995. He was too late to save Palace from relegation but was then instrumental in getting the London club into the 1997 First Division Play-off Final at Wembley, where joy turned to despair as the Eagles were gobbled up by the Foxes of Leicester City! That disappointment was quickly forgotten though as Palace went one better the following year and beat Sheffield United 1-0 in an identical Play-off Final to regain their Premiership status.

Houghton ended his playing days with Reading in 2000, having clocked up a quite outstanding record of 716 League and Cup appearances and 93 goals.

*Eric Houghton in action.*

## HOUGHTON, WILLIAM ERIC

Born: Billingborough, Lincolnshire, 29 June 1910. Died: Sutton Coldfield, 1 May 1996.

Career: Donington School, Boston Town (1925), Billingborough FC (1926), Aston Villa (trialist then professional, August 1927), guested for Coventry City, Leicester City, Nottingham Forest & Notts County during WW2, Notts County (player, December 1946, then manager April 1949-August 1953), Aston Villa (manager August 1953-November 1958), Nottingham Forest (chief scout, November 1958-November 1960), Rugby Town (manager, February 1961-March 1964), Walsall (scout late 1965, then Director at Fellows Park), Aston Villa (1970 as coach/assistant to club's Youth Development Department, then Director from September 1972-December 1979 and thereafter senior vice-President from January 1983 until his death in 1996). Also played cricket for Lincolnshire and Warwickshire.

Eric 'Coog' Houghton played soccer as a pupil at Donington School, which in itself, holds a unique place in football history, being one of the

THE COMPLETE ENCYCLOPAEDIA OF ASTON VILLA F.C.        THE COMPLETE ENCYCLOPAEDIA OF ASTON VILLA F.C.

143

15 entries for the very first FA Cup competition of 1871-72. After assisting two local teams, he was all set to join Boston United before his uncle and former Villa player, Cec Harris, persuaded him to have trails at Villa Park. Houghton came through with flying colours, gave up his baker's job and signed professional forms, to earn £3-a-week in wages with a further 50 shillings (£2.50) coming his way when he got into the reserve side. As a direct left-winger, he developed quickly in the Central League side before making his bow in the First Division in January 1930 against Leeds United. Villa lost the game 4-3 and Houghton missed a penalty! But he never let that affect his progress and was a regular in the side within twelve months (after Arthur Dorrell had moved to Port Vale). He starred in the attack-minded forward-line of 1930-31 when Villa netted a total of 128 goals in 42 League matches, Houghton scoring 30 himself. Two-footed, fast, strong, stylish in full stride and totally committed, he was a highly consistent performer who possessed a cracking shot, often

*Eric Houghton*

sending free-kicks and spot-kicks towards goal with tremendous force. He went on to score 170 goals in 392 League and FA Cup matches for Aston Villa. He also notched a further 88 goals in 157 Wartime appearances and during his playing days at the club (in the first team, reserves and other competitions) Houghton cracked in no fewer than 345 goals, 79 of them penalties (he missed only seven times from 12 yards) in more than 700 outings. He is the fifth highest scorer in the club's history. He belted home one of the greatest goals ever seen at Villa Park - a thundrous 40 yard free-kick against Derby County in December 1931. He later helped Villa regain their First Division status in 1938 and then celebrated with his colleagues when the Wartime League (North) Cup was won in 1944. Capped seven times by England at full international level, Houghton also represented the Football League XI on four occasions and was an English trialist.

Houghton scored a penalty in his last appearance for Villa against Huddersfield reserves at home on Boxing Day 1946 (won 4-1) before he was transferred to Notts County shortly after the start of the 1946-47 season. After retiring as a player, he took over as boss of the Magpies and guided them to the Third Division (South) championship and ultimate promotion in 1950. Then, seven years later he proudly led Aston Villa out at Wembley to contest the FA Cup Final against Manchester United....and was obviously delighted as anyone when Irish international Peter McParland struck home a couple of crackers to enable Villa to beat the Busby Babes 2-1.

After five years in charge of Villa, Houghton was dismissed as the team began to struggle. He quickly teamed up (as scout) with his former playing colleague Billy Walker, who was manager of Nottingham Forest and then in 1972 Houghton returned to Villa Park as a member of the Board of Directors. When he died in 1996 at the age of 86, he had been associated with Aston Villa Football Club for a total of 46 years. Houghton made his first-class cricket debut for Warwickshire against

India at Edgbaston in August 1946 - just as he began his 18th season as an Aston Villa professional.

As manager of Villa, Eric Houghton led his team in 223 League games....78 ended in wins, 54 were drawn and 91 lost.

## HOWARTH, SYDNEY
Born: Bristol, 28 June 1923
Career: Bristol Schoolboy football, Bury (Amateur), Bristol City (trialist), Notts County (trialist), Arsenal (trialist), Barry Town (1939-40), Aberaman (1945). Merthyr Tydfil (1946), Aston Villa (June 1948), Swansea Town (September 1950), Walsall (September 1952), Merthyr Tydfil (August 1954-May 1957). Retired.
Son of a former Bristol City player, Syd Howarth was a tough character, a forward with power and terrific right-foot shot. He was reliable cover for George Edwards and Trevor Ford, but was given just nine first team outings (2 goals scored). He netted seven times in 39 League games for the Swans.

## HUDDERSFIELD TOWN
Villa's record against the Terriers:
Football League

| Venue | P | W | D | L | F | A |
|---|---|---|---|---|---|---|
| Home | 32 | 20 | 9 | 3 | 74 | 31 |
| Away | 32 | 7 | 10 | 15 | 32 | 51 |
| Totals | 64 | 27 | 19 | 18 | 106 | 82 |

FA Cup

| | | | | | | |
|---|---|---|---|---|---|---|
| Home | 4 | 2 | 0 | 2 | 5 | 4 |
| Neutral | 1 | 1 | 0 | 0 | 1 | 0 |
| Totals | 5 | 3 | 0 | 2 | 6 | 4 |

League Cup

| | | | | | | |
|---|---|---|---|---|---|---|
| Home | 1 | 1 | 0 | 0 | 4 | 1 |

Aston Villa first met Huddersfield Town in a League game on 12 March 1921 - eleven months after they had beaten them 1-0 in the FA Cup Final. The League clash at Villa Park ended goalless in front of 20,000 fans and a week later the Terriers won 1-0 at Leeds Road.

On 3 March 1923 Villa beat Huddersfield 2-1 at home. Then seven days after, thanks to Billy Walker's hat-trick, Villa doubled-up with an impressive 5-3 win at Leeds Road.

After a Len Capewell hat-trick had set up a 3-0 win over Huddersfield at Villa Park in November 1925, the return fixture in March ended in a resounding 5-1 victory for the Terriers.

Not very often - very rarely in fact - does a team register precisely the same high-scoring victory in both League games against the same team in the same season. But in 1930-31, Villa did just that, slamming the Terriers 6-1 at home and away. Billy Walker netted a hat-trick in the win at Villa Park.

Over the Christmas period of 1935 Villa won 4-1 at home yet lost 4-1 at Huddersfield.

Only 5,287 spectators saw Villa beat Huddersfield 2-1 in a League game at Leeds Road in February 1955 - the lowest crowd anywhere in the First Division that season.

Bobby Thomson cracked in a hat-trick as Villa beat Huddersfield 4-0 at home in a Second Division match in February 1960. And when the teams met again at League level on the same ground in December 1967 the scoresheet remained blank, as it did in the return fixture at Leeds Road four months later.

The 1920 FA Cup Final between Villa and Huddersfield at Stamford Bridge went to extra-time before a 97th minute corner was deflected into the Terriers' net seemingly off Billy Kirton's head to give Villa a 1-0 victory.

The following season two goals by Billy Walker saw Villa win a 3rd round tie 2-0 in front of 50,627 spectators at Villa Park.

THE COMPLETE ENCYCLOPAEDIA OF ASTON VILLA F.C.  THE COMPLETE ENCYCLOPAEDIA OF ASTON VILLA F.C.

144

A crowd of 65,732 witnessed Town's 2-1 win at Villa Park in a quarter-final tie in March 1930 and six years later there an audience of 62,620 saw Huddersfield again win at Villa Park, this time by 1-0 in the 3rd round.

Villa's first-ever League Cup-tie was against Huddersfield Town, at home, on 12 October 1960. A crowd of 17,057 saw the Terriers beaten 4-1, Ron Wylie (2), Gerry Hitchens and Harry Burrows the Villa scorers.

*The captain's meet before the 1920 F.A. Cup Final. Andy Ducat is the Villa skipper.*

Players with both clubs include: J Barker (Town WW2 guest), S Beaton (Villa reserve), G Brown, NI Callaghan, RM Campbell, RA Chester, GW Cook, BA Greenhalgh, D Hickson, MA Lillis, FD Mann, PJ Robinson, CH Slade, C Stephenson (also Town manager), JJ Williams, P Withe (also assistant-manager & coach at Huddersfield).
Also: I Ross (Villa player, Terriers' manager), GT Stephenson (Villa player, assistant-manager & manager at Leeds Road), C Dobson (Town player, Villa coach), PD Doherty (Town player, Villa chief scout).

### HUGHES, DAVID THOMAS
Born: Birmingham 19 March 1958.
Career: Birmingham Parks football, Aston Villa (apprentice June 1974, professional February 1976), Lincoln City (£20,000, April 1977), Scunthorpe United (June 1981), Lincoln City (March-April 1982), Worcester City (January 1983).
An very useful schoolboy footballer, midfielder David Hughes did very well at Sincil Bank after leaving Villa Park where he was reserve to Des Bremner, Gordon Cowans, Dennis Mortimer & Co. He made over 60 appearances for the Imps and more than 20 for Scunthorpe before entering non-League football in 1983.

### HUGHES, ROBERT DAVID
Born: Wrexham, 1 February 1978
Career: Aston Villa (YTS June 1994, professional July 1996), Carlisle United (on loan March-May 1998), Shrewsbury Town (September

1999), Cardiff City (February 2001).
An efficient central defender, Robert Hughes was handed seven first team outings by Villa before moving to Shrewsbury.
He has won Welsh caps at Youth, Under-21 and 'B' team levels.

### HUGHES, THOMAS ALEXANDER
Born: Dalmuir, Scotland, 11 July 1947.
Career: Clydebank (juniors, 1963), Chelsea (July 1965), Aston Villa (£12,500, June 1971), Brighton & Hove Albion (on loan, February-March 1973), Hereford United (£15,000, August 1973). After retiring in October 1982 was appointed manager at Edgar Street, a position he retained until March 1983.
Tommy Hughes was the unfortunate understudy to Peter Bonetti at Stamford Bridge and made only 11 appearances for the London club despite winning two Scottish Under-23 caps. After breaking a leg, he was subsequently replaced at Stamford Bridge by Villa's John Phillips and ironically after recovering from that set-back he was then transferred to Villa Park! Unfortunately he found himself struggling to hold down a first team place and made just 23 senior appearances (plus enduring a loan spell at Brighton) before moving to Edgar Street. He went on to amass a fine record of more than 250 League and Cup games for Hereford, helping the Bulls win the Third Division championship in 1976.

### HULL CITY
Villa's playing record against the Tigers:
Football League

| Venue | P | W | D | L | F | A |
|---|---|---|---|---|---|---|
| Home | 8 | 4 | 3 | 1 | 21 | 8 |
| Away | 8 | 2 | 2 | 4 | 7 | 12 |
| Totals | 16 | 6 | 5 | 5 | 28 | 20 |

FA Cup

| | P | W | D | L | F | A |
|---|---|---|---|---|---|---|
| Home | 3 | 2 | 1 | 0 | 7 | 1 |
| Away | 1 | 1 | 0 | 0 | 3 | 0 |
| Totals | 4 | 3 | 1 | 0 | 10 | 1 |

Zenith Data Systems Cup

| | P | W | D | L | F | A |
|---|---|---|---|---|---|---|
| Away | 1 | 1 | 0 | 0 | 2 | 1 |

Aston Villa and Hull City first met at League Division Two level in 1959-60. A Peter McParland goal gave Villa a 1-0 win at Boothferry Park on Boxing Day but 48 hours later Stan Lynn's penalty denied the Tigers their revenge in a 1-1 draw.
Sammy Morgan scored a hat-trick when Villa beat the Tigers 6-0 in a home League game on 28 August 1974 (Villa scored five goals in the second-half). Eight days earlier at Boothferry Park, Charlie Aitken had made his 500th League appearance for the club, and the return fixture was, in fact, his 500th League 'start' for Villa, having previously come on twice as a substitute.
On New Year's Day 1988 Villa whipped the Tigers 5-0 at home, Warren Aspinall netting twice.

Len Capewell scored twice when Villa beat the Tigers 3-0 at Hull in a 3rd round FA Cup-tie in January 1926. That scoreline was repeated 73 years later when almost a full house of 39,217 saw the Tigers knocked out of the competition at the same stage in January 1999.

Only 2,888 fans saw Villa win 2-1 at Boothferry Park in the ZDSC in November 1989.

Players with both clubs include: L Butler, M Carruthers, A Cunliffe, JT Dixon (City WW2 guest), K Gage, T Gardner, HJ Goode, PT Heard, J Neal, D Norton, I Ormondroyd, G Parker, B Petty, J Sewell, RW Starling, TE Tebb (Villa & City reserve), J Whitehouse, GJ Williams.

THE COMPLETE ENCYCLOPAEDIA OF ASTON VILLA F.C.          THE COMPLETE ENCYCLOPAEDIA OF ASTON VILLA F.C.

145

Also: T Docherty (manager of both clubs), R Brocklebank & B Little (Villa players, City managers, Little was also a Villa player), E Blackburn, FC Buckley & H Green (Villa players, City managers), GS Martin (City player, Villa manager).

## HUMPHRIES, HOWARD

Born: Aston, Birmingham, February 1894. Died: 1955.
Career: Handsworth County School, Handsworth Amateurs (1911). Aston Villa (professional, July 1913), Southend United (December 1921), Rotherham County (March 1922-April 1924).
Nurtured initially as cover for inside-forward Clem Stephenson, Howard Humphries developed into a very useful utility player who occupied four different positions during his time at Villa

*Howard Humphries*

Park. He scored twice in 21 senior outings and six times in 10 games during the First World War before moving to Southend.

## HUNT, DAVID

Born: Leicester, 17 April 1959.
Career: Derby County (apprentice June 1975, professional February 1977), Notts County (March 1978), Aston Villa (June 1987), Mansfield Town (June 1989-May 1990).
When 28 year-old David Hunt arrived to bolster up the Villa midfield in the summer of 1987, he had already appeared in more than 350 League and Cup games for his previous two clubs (the majority with the Magpies). However, owing to some frustrating injuries, a couple of suspensions and a lack of form, he never really settled down with any authority at Villa Park and despite a handful of very competitive displays he was given just 15 outings in two seasons before moving to Field Mill.

*Steve Hunt*

## HUNT, STEPHEN KENNETH

Born: Perry Barr, Birmingham, 4 August 1956.
Career: Yew Tree Infants & Junior Schools, Aston & Witton Boys, Warwickshire Schoolboys, Stanley Star, Aston Villa (apprentice July 1972, professional January 1974), New York Cosmos (£50,000, February 1977, Coventry City (£40,000, August 1978), New York Cosmos (on loan, May 1982), West Bromwich Albion (£80,000, March 1984), Aston Villa (£90,000 plus Darren Bradley, March 1986). Forced to retire with a knee injury in May 1988. Appointed manager of Willenhall Town (summer of 1988), Port Vale (Youth team coach, July 1989, Community Officer at Vale Park June 1990), Leicester City (Youth coach 1991-92) later manager of both VS Rugby Town and AP Leamington (1990s).
An energetic, hard-working, purposeful midfielder with a fine left foot, Steve Hunt gave his three Midland clubs excellent service. After scoring once in eight first XI outings for Aston Villa he moved into the NASL with New York Cosmos, returning to England to sign for Coventry City

in 1979. A further spell in the NASL with the Cosmos preceded his transfer to WBA and after winning two full England caps, he returned to Villa Park for what what to be his last season in League football. He made a total of 79 senior appearances for Villa (nine goals scored) and had the misfortune to play in successive relegation teams (WBA in 1986, Villa in 1987). In his first spell in the NASL, Hunt, playing alongside Pele and Franz Beckenbauer, helped Cosmos win two Super Bowl titles (1977 & 1978) and was voted 'The Most Valuable Player' in the former competition. He made 216 appearances for Coventry (34 goals) and certain supporters believe that he would have become one of the Sky Blues' all-time greats if he had decided to stay at Highfield Road!

## HUNTER, ANDREW

Born: Joppa, Ayrshire, Scotland, August 1864. Died: Australia, June 1888.
Career: Ayr Thistle, Third Lanark, Vale of Leven, Aston Villa (August 1879). Retired in May 1884 with a thigh injury and emigrated to Australia late that year.
Brother of Archie (below) Andy Hunter had tremendous all-round ability, a strong, well-built inside-forward he could take out three players with one hefty challenge. He scored five goals in 10 FA Cup games for Villa before his career was brought to an abrupt end. He later died suddenly of a heart attack in Australia, still only 23.

## HUNTER, ARCHIBALD

Born: Joppa, Ayrshire, 23 September 1859.
Died: Birmingham, 29 November 1894
Career: Third Lanark, Ayr Thistle (1877), Aston Villa (August 1878).
There is no doubt that the auburn-haired Archie Hunter was a truly great player - one of the best footballers of the 1880/90s. He was an individualist with a commanding personality; he was robust yet decidedly fair and never committed a foul in anger.
Known as 'The Old Warhorse' he was a mixture of toughness and cleverness, a centre-forward who often ran the touchline, pulling defenders all over the field.
He was such an important member of the Villa side that in 1889 he was transported to an away game against Notts County in a specially chartered train!
A business engagement brought him down to Birmingham in 1878 and he was enquiring as to the whereabouts of the Calthorpe Football Club which had earlier toured Scotland and played a game in Ayr near to where he lived. Fate led him to Aston Villa....a missguided direction....he never looked back.
It was Villa's George Ramsay who took Hunter under his wing. He looked after the Scot during his early days in Birmingham and initially played Hunter under a different name to hide his true identity - so that other clubs (mainly from Scotland) didn't get to know of his whereabouts!
Hunter appeared in 73 first-class matches for Villa, scoring 42 goals, 33 coming in the

*Archie Hunter*

FA Cup - a club record that still stands today. Hunter, in fact, was the first player to score in every round of the FA Cup competition - for Villa in 1886-87 when he skippered the side to a 2-0 victory at West

THE COMPLETE ENCYCLOPAEDIA OF ASTON VILLA F.C.     THE COMPLETE ENCYCLOPAEDIA OF ASTON VILLA F.C.

146

Bromwich Albion's expense in the Final at The Kennington Oval Cricket Ground. Hunter also played in about 250 friendlies for the Villa, scoring at least 100 goals.

A real Scottish gentleman and a throroughbred amongst sportsmen, Hunter collapsed of a heart attack while playing for Villa against Everton on Merseyside on 4 January 1890. Medical advice stated that he should never play again. Sadly he didn't....and after struggling with his health, he died peacefully in a Birmingham hospital four years later at the age of 35.

The headstone on Hunter's grave reads: 'This monument is erected in loving memory of Archie Hunter (the famous captain of Aston Villa) by his football comrades and the club, as a lasting tribute to his ability on the field and his sterling worth as a man.'

So much was written about Archie Hunter that it would take another book to reveal all. But here are some snippits to sum up a wonderful 'Aston Villa' footballer and team captain.

'Hunter was rather a severe critic - on the field. He knew how to play football so well - he had a natural adaptability for the game - that he thought everybody else should be as proficient. And sometimes the 'boys' under his charge would feel that he was almost harsh in his strong desire to see the match carried through in his own way.'

'.....everybody who knew him, thoroughly loved him with a real affection for his manly qualities and the kindly way in which he treated every one who came in touch with him.'

'Archie was a Scottish gentleman. He never talked about himself, he let other people do that for him, out of his hearing, for he waxed impatience if people prattled of his prowess in his presence. But he always had a kind word and very honest praise for a comrade who did good things on the field or who had been trying hard for his side.'

'He absolutely trusted the strong men on his side and this confidence by their skipper made them stronger still.

'He was an autocrat when the mimic strife was on and a gentle and approachable comrade off the field.'

'He set an example that has been, in many respects, most admirably copied by the men who came after him.' In 1998 as part of the Football League's 100th season celebrations, a Football League 'All Time greats' Committee included Archie Hunter as one of the League's 100 greats.

## HUNTER, GEORGE C.
Born: Peshawar, India, 16 August 1886. Died: London, February 1934.
Career: Junior football in Peshawar (arranged by his father), Maidstone, Croydon Common, Aston Villa (February 1908), Oldham Athletic (£1,200, January 1912), Chelsea (£1,000, March 1913), Manchester United (£1,300, March 1914-May 1915), guested for Croydon Common, Birmingham and Brentford during WW1, Portsmouth (August 1919-May 1922). Retired.

A well-built, powerful half-back, noted for his tough and vigorous tackling, George 'Cocky' Hunter - a comedian in the dressing room - was rather reckless at times and often conceded free-kicks in dangerous positions while also giving away his fair share of penalties! Nevertheless, he was always a very competitive footballer with a fiery temper, who scored once in 98 first-class appearances for Villa, with whom he won a League championship medal in 1909-10 and twice represented the Football League in 1911. He made only two appearances for Chelsea before being released - the manager and his colleagues being unable to control him.

Hunter went on to skipper Manchester United and played behind the great Billy Meredith during his time at Old Trafford. He was in trouble with the United directorate in January 1915 and was suspended sine-die for failing to comply with training regulations and as the club captain it was thought he should have set a better example. Hailing from a military background (he was born within 10 miles of the Khyber Pass) Hunter saw active service in France and Gallipoli during World War One in which he served as a CSM.

## INGLIS, JOHN FRANCIS
Born: Leven, Fife, Scotland, 19 May 1947.
Career: Leven Schools, Glenrothes FC, Aston Villa (professional, September 1965), Crewe Alexandra (July 1968-May 1970).
A reserve centre-forward who scored once in two League outings for Villa before going on to do reasonably well at Gresty Road, netting 10 goals in 47 lower Division appearances for the 'Alex.'

## INJURIES & ILLNESS
In 1907, Aston Villa goalkeeper Harold Cooch had his left index finger amputated after breaking it in three places. He retired in May 1908.

Andy Ducat missed the 1913 FA Cup Final victory over Sunderland with a broken leg, suffered in the fourth game of the season against Manchester City (14 September 1912). Ducat, in fact, as out of action for over two years, making his comeback on 26 September 1914.

Harold Edgley broke his leg at Chelsea three weeks before the 1920 FA Cup Final with Huddersfield Town. He had scored the clinching goal in the semi-final against Chelsea just days before the teams met in the League.

Villa full-back John Robson was forced to quit the game in 1978 with multiple sclerosis.

Luc Nilis suffered a double fracture of the right leg (breaking his tibia and fibia) in the Premiership game against Ipswich Town at Portman Road in September 2000.

Archie Hunter suffered a heart attack while starring in a League game at Everton in 1890. He never played again for Aston Villa and died four years later (see Deaths).

## INTER MILAN
Villa's record against the Italian club:

UEFA Cup

| Venue | P | W | D | L | F | A |
|-------|---|---|---|---|---|---|
| Home | 2 | 2 | 0 | 0 | 3 | 0 |
| Away | 2 | 0 | 0 | 2 | 0 | 4 |
| Totals | 4 | 2 | 0 | 2 | 3 | 4 |

The second round, first leg UEFA Cup home encounter on 24 October 1990 against Inter Milan deservedly went Villa's by 2-0, Kent Nielsen and David Platt the scorers in front of 36,461 spectators. But inside the San Siro Stadium, the return clash a fortnight later played on a difficult pitch, ended in a 3-0 victory for the Italian club before a near 76,000 crowd.

On a terrible playing surface, Dutchman Dennis Bergkamp converted a 75th minute 'disputed' penalty to give Inter a 1-0 first leg lead over Villa in a first round UEFA Cup-tie in front of 22,639 fans at the San Siro Stadium on 15 September 1994. But a fortnight later, 30,533 spectators witnessed a 41st minute 'equalising' goal by Ray Houghton as Villa fought back. The tie subsequently went to a penalty shoot-out. Garry Parker, Steve Staunton and Andy Townsend all netted for Villa, while Giovanni Bia, Bergkamp and Andrea Seno did likewise for Inter to leave it level at 3-3. Then Davide Fontolan (Inter), Guy Whittingham (Villa) and Ruben Sosa (Inter) all missed in that order, leaving left-back Phil King with the last kick to win the tie for Villa. He made no mistake, Villa through 4-3.....what a night! The game ended at 10.37pm - having kicked-off at 8.05pm.

Villa sold Gerry Hitchens to Inter Milan for £60,000 in June 1961 and he was immediately dubbed 'Champion the Wonder Horse'.

Players with both clubs: B Carbone, GA Hitchens.
Also: Dai Astley (Villa player, Inter coach).

THE COMPLETE ENCYCLOPAEDIA OF ASTON VILLA F.C.    THE COMPLETE ENCYCLOPAEDIA OF ASTON VILLA F.C.

147

## INTERMEDIATE CUP COMPETITIONS

In the seasons leading up to the outbreak of the Second World War, Aston Villa ran at least eight teams and those featuring junior players entered many local Cup/Shield competitions.

**Here are details of Villa's triumphs:**

| | |
|---|---|
| Leamington Hospital Cup: | 1934, 1937 |
| Ipswich Hospital Cup: | 1939 |
| Worcestershire Senior Cup: | 1939 |
| Hinckley Hospital Cup: | 1939 |
| Norman Chamberlain Shield: | 1938, 1939 |

Villa won the Worcestershire Cup again in 1954. Centre-forward Roy Chapman scored twice and also missed a penalty as Atherstone were defeated 5-2 in the Final.

## INTERNATIONAL SECTION

Details of Villa players who won representative honours at various levels whilst serving with the club:

**Full Caps:**
**Australia**
M Bosnich (3 caps: 1995-98)
**Colombia**
JP Angel (4 caps: 2000-01)
**Denmark**
K Nielsen (11 caps: 1989-92)
**England**
A Allen (1 cap) 1887-88, WC Athersmith (12) 1891-1900, JW Bache (7) 1902-11, G Barry (4) 1999-2001, F Barson (1) 1919-20, J Beresford (1), 1933-34, GF Blackburn (1) 1923-24, WF Brawn (2) 1903-04, FH Broome (7) 1937-39, A Brown (3) 1881-82, G Brown (1) 1932-33, GS Cowans (8) 1982-91, JW Crabtree (11) 1895-1902, AM Daley (4) 1991-92, JHG Devey (2) 1891-94, AR Dorrell (4) 1924-26, D Dublin (4) 1999-2000, A Ducat (3) 1919-21, U Ehiogu (1) 1999-2000, T Gardner (2) 1933-35, W Garraty (1) 1902-03, W George (3) 1901-02, J Gidman (1) 1976-77, AE Hall (1) 1909-10, H Hampton (4) 1912-14, S Hardy (7) 1912-20, LA Hendrie (1) 1998-99, GA Hitchens (3) 1960-61, SB Hodge (8) 1985-86, D Hodgetts (6) 1887-94, WE Houghton (7) 1930-33, DB James (3) 2000-01, WJ Kirton (1) 1921-22, A Leake (5) 1903-05, B Little (1) 1974-75, E Lowe (3) 1946-47, AW Morley (6) 1981-83, T Mort (3) 1923-26, F Moss snr (5) 1921-24, B Olney (2) 1927-28, D Platt (22) 1989-91, J Reynolds (5) 1893-97, K Richardson (1) 1993-94, T Smart (5) 1920-27, S Smith (1) 1894-95, G Southgate (41) 1996-2000, H Spencer (6) 1896-1905, NP Spink (1) 1982-83, R Starling (1) 1936-37, JT Tate (3) 1931-33, T Thompson (1) 1951-52, HA Vaughton (5) 1881-84, WH Walker (18) 1920-33, CW Wallace (3) 1912-20, O Whateley (1) 1882-83, GF Wheldon (4) 1896-98, A Wilkes (5) 1900-02, P Withe (11) 1980-85, RE York (2) 1921-26.
**Finland**
P Enckelman (1 cap) 1999-2000
**France**
D Six (2 caps) 1984-85
**Ghana**
N Lamptey (1 cap) 1994-95
**Israel**
N Ghrayib (2 caps) 1999-2000
**Northern Ireland**
RD Blanchflower (8 caps) 1951-54, AD Dougan (3) 1962-63, N Lockhart (4) 1953-56, PJ McParland (33) 1953-61, CJ Martin (2) 1948-50, SJ Morgan (8) 1973-76, CJ Nicholl (12) 1974-77, WT Renneville (1) 1910-11.
**Poland**
D Kubicki (2 caps) 1991-92
**Portugal**
F Nelson (5 caps) 1997-99

**Republic of Ireland**
AG Cascarino (15 caps) 1989-91, ES Deacy (4) 1981-82, T Donovan (2) 1979-80, G Farrelly (3) 1996-97, A Hale (1) 1961-62, P McGrath (51) 1990-97, CJ Martin (24) 1948-56, T Muldoon (1) 1926-27, P Saward (13) 1956-61, S Staunton (52+) 1991-1998/2001-02, AD Townsend (28) 1994-98, DJ Walsh (6) 1950-54.
**Scotland**
D Blair (1 cap) 1932-33, Jas Cowan (3) 1895-98, G Cummings (6) 1935-39, A Evans (4) 1981-82, J Gibson (4) 1927-30, AM Gray (6) 1975-79, A McInally (2) 1988-89, A Massie (7) 1935-38, TB Niblo (1) 1903-04, RB Templeton (1) 1901-02.
**Sweden**
O Mellberg (2 caps 2001-02)
**Trinidad & Tobago**
D Yorke (16 caps) 1991-98
**Turkey**
Alpay Ozalan (5 caps: 2000-01)
**Wales**
DJ Astley (9 caps) 1931-36, VH Crowe (16) 1958-63, M Delaney (4) 1999-2001, RE Evans (4) 1905-08, WG Evans (1) 1891-92, T Ford (14) 1946-51, AW Green (1) 1900-01, TP Griffiths (4) 1935-37, T Hockey (1) 1973-74, B Hole (4) 1968-70, K Jones (1) 1949-50, C Phillips (3) 1935-38, L Phillips (26) 1974-79, IV Powell (4) 1948-51, H Price (1) 1906-07, AE Watkins (2) 1899-1900, WM Watkins (3) 1903-04, AP Woosnam (2) 1962-63.
**Yugoslavia**
S Curcic (2 caps) 1996-97, S Milosevic (7 caps) 1995-99

### 'B' Internationals
**England**
E Barrett (1 cap) 1991-92, GS Cowans (2) 1980-90, AM Daley (1) 1995-96, CH Gibson (1) 1949-50, U Ehiogu (1) 1997-98, J Gidman (2) 1977-79, LA Hendrie (1) 1997-98, S McMahon (1) 1984-85, AW Morley (2) 1980-81, D Mortimer (1) 1980-81, D Platt (1) 1988-89, R Scimeca (1) 1997-98.
**Republic of Ireland**
T Donovan (1 cap) 1980-81.

**Wales**
RD Hughes (2) 1996-99.

**Unofficial Internationals (including Victory/Wartime):**
**England**
FH Broome (2 caps) 1939-40, S Hardy (3) 1918-20, JR Martin (2) 1939-40, B Olney (2) 1928-29, LGF Smith (1) 1945-46

**Scotland**
GW Cummings (1 cap) 1944-45

**Scotland XI**
A Massie (1 cap) 1943-44

**Malta Island Select XI**
AW Kerr (1 cap) 1945-46

*Bill Renneville*

*Tom Mort*

*Pat Saward*

**Under 23 Internationals:**
**England**
H Burrows (1 cap) 1962-63, S Crowther (3) 1957-58, A Deakin (6) 1961-64, J Gidman (4) 1974-76, JD Robson (1) 1972-73, J Slueewenhoek (2) 1962-63.

**Scotland**
C Aitken (3 caps) 1961-62, C Fraser (1) 1962-63, AM Gray (1) 1975-76

**Under 21 Internationals:**
**England**
G Barry (7 caps+) 1997-2000, M Blake (8 caps) 1989-92, GS Cowans (5) 1978-80, JM Deehan (7) 1976-80, A Dorigo (7) 1986-87, U Ehiogu (15) 1991-97, C Gibson (1) 1981-82, AA Gray (2) 1987-88, LA Hendrie (13) 1998-2000, SB Hodge (2) 1985-86, M Keown (8) 1986-88, S McMahon (1) 1983-84, M Oakes (6) 1996-98, I Olney (9) 1989-91, D Platt (3) 1988-89, P Rideout (4) 1984-85, R Scimeca (9) 1996-99, G Shaw (7) 1980-83, B Small (12) 1996-98, D Vassell (7+) 1999-2001, ME Walters (9) 1983-86,

**Republic of Ireland**
G Farrelly (1) 1997-98, AD Lee (1) 1997-98, JM McGrath (2) 1999-2001.

**Scotland**
A Blair (3) 1981-82, A McInally (1) 1988-89, N Tarrant (5) 1999-2000

**Wales**
RD Hughes (12) 1996-99.

**England XI:**
CW Athersmith (2 apps) 1890-92, F Broome (1) 1939-40, R Chatt (2) 1894-95, JW Crabtree (3) 1896-99, A Dorrell (2) 1924 & 1925, JR Martin (1) 1939-40, AW Morley (1) 1981-82, WH Walker (2) 1924-25, GF Wheldon (4) 1897-1900, P Withe (1) 1981-82.

**Ireland XI**
F Haycock (1 app) 1934-35

**Scotland XI**
C Aitken (1 app) 1961-62, A Massie (2) 1943-46

**Wales/Ireland XI**
DJ Astley (1 app) 1934-35

**Anglo-Scots (v Home Scots)**
D Blair (1 app) 1934-35, Jas Cowan (4) 1896-98, IW Dickson (1) 1921-22, JL Logan (1) 1908-09, J McLachlan (1) 1912-13, TB Niblo (1) 1903-04, RB Templeton (2) 1900-02.

**FA XI**
F Broome (5) 1939-45, JE Crabtree (1) 1896-97, AR Deakin (1) 1961-62, JR Dugdale (1) 1957-58, W George (1) 1901-02, CH Gibson (1) 1949-50, JR Martin (6) D Pace (1) 1950-51, 1939-45, LGF Smith (3) 1945-48.

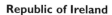
*John Reynolds*

**Scottish FA (tour to USA & Canada)**
GW Cummings (5) 1934-35

**Irish FA (tour to Canada)**
RD Blanchflower (8) 1952-53, N Lockhart (7) 1952-53.

**Birmingham County FA**
N Ashe (2 games) 1959-60, R Brown (2) 1959-60, R Cairns (2) 1959-60, A Dorrell (1), 1925-26, K Fencott (2) 1959-60, D Pratt (2) 1959-60, A Talbot (1), 1925-26, OE Tidman (1) 1933-34, WH Walker (1) 1925-26.

**England trials**
CW Athersmith (1891-1900), JW Bache (1904-12), F Barson (1919-20), J Beresford (1933-34), WF Brawn (1903-04), Albert Brown (1887-91), Arthur Brown (1881-82), CS Buckley (1910-11), GF Burton (1892-95), JW Crabtree (1899-1900), JHG Devey (1891-94), A Dorrell (1924-26), A Ducat (1920-21), GR Edwards (1945-46), T Gardner (1934-35), W Garraty (1902-03), W George (1901-02), AE Hall (1909-10), H Hampton (1911-13), S Hardy (1913-19), J Harrop (1913-14), D Hodgetts (1889-94), WE Houghton (1931-32), GH Johnson (1898-99), WJ Kirton (1921-22), A Leake (1904-05), T Mort (1924-26), H Morton (1933-34), F Moss, snr (1922-24), J Reynolds (1894-96), T Smart (1921-29), LGF Smith (1945-46), S Smith (1985-97), H Spencer (1896-1903), C Stephenson (1911-19), A Talbot (1930-31), JT Tate (1930-31), WH Walker (1921-19), CW Wallace (1910-15), J Walters (1910-11), T Waring (1931-32), A Wilkes (1901-02), RE York (1925-26).

**Junior Internationals (England)**
W Garraty (2 caps) 1896-97, GA Harris (2) 1905-06, HV Henshall (1) 1907-08, GJ Jakeman (1) 1916-17, WIG Kingdon (1) 1925-26, A Mitchell (1) 1907-08, HA Parkes (1) 1938-39, RE York (1) 1919-20.

**Birmingham & District Juniors**
WS Corbett (5 caps) 1904-07

**United Kingdom**
WS Corbett (3 caps) Olympic Games of 1908

**Amateur/Professional XI**
WS Corbett (1 cap) 1905-06

**Malta Select XI**
AW Kerr (1 app) 1943-44

*John Deehan*

*Alan Deakin*

**Football League (Inter League)**
CW Athersmith (9 apps) 1891-1901, JW Bache (7) 1905-11, T Barber (2) 1914-18, GW Beeson (1) 1934-35, J Beresford (2) 1931-34, G Brown (2) 1932-33, CS Buckley (2) 1909-10, R Chatt (1) 1894-95, JW Crabtree (6) 1896-1901, JHG Devey (4) 1894-97, W Dorrell (1) 1894-95, AR Dorrell (2) 1922-25, AJ Evans (1) 1899-1900, W George (1) 1900-01, CH Gibson (1) 1948-49, AE Hall (2) 1907-08, HJ Halse (1) 1912-13, H

THE COMPLETE ENCYCLOPAEDIA OF ASTON VILLA F.C.

THE COMPLETE ENCYCLOPAEDIA OF ASTON VILLA F.C.

149

Hampton (3) 1905-11, S Hardy (7) 1913-20, J Harrop (2) 1913-14, HV Henshall (1) 1910-11, G Hitchens (1) 1960-61, D Hodgetts (1) 1894-95, WE Houghton (4) 1930-32, GH Hunter (2) 1910-11, A Leake (1) 1904-05, A Lockett (1) 1902-03, PJ McParland (1) 1959-60, F Moss snr (2) 1923-24, J Reynolds (2) 1894-95, Nigel Sims (2) 1957 & 1960, J Slueewenhoek (1) 1961-62, T Smart (1) 1927-28, S Smith (2) 1895 & 1898, H Spencer (9) 1896-1906, C Stephenson (3) 1914-19, AD Talbot (1) 1931-32, JT Tate (1) 1930-31, T Thompson (1) 1950-51, WH Walker (6) 1921-30, CW Wallace (5) 1908-14, GF Wheldon (2) 1897-98, RE York (2) 1925-26.

*Con Martin*

*Jimmy Rimmer*

*Tommy Thompson*

### Football League XI
GW Cummings (1 app) 1939-40, F Haycock (1) 1941-42, JR Martin (1) 1939-40.

### Young England
Nigel Sims (1 app) 1953-54

### All-British XI XI
F Broome (1 app) 1939-40, GW Cummings (1) 1939-40, F O'Donnell (1) 1939-40.

### Grand Military Internaational
H Hampton (1 app) 1915-16

### Eastern Command
JR Martin (1 app) 1941-42

### London Command
G Thompson (1 app) 1941-42

### Northern Command
J Rutherford (3 apps) 1943-45

### Combined Services
JR Martin (1 app) 1943-44

### Civil Defence
E Callaghan (1 app) 1943-44
### London District
JR Martin (1 app) 1943-44

### National Police XI (v RAF)
E Callaghan (1 app) 1942-43

### Police Reserve XI
E Callaghan (2 apps) 1942-44, AW Kerr (2) 1944-45

### Police & Civil Defence XI
E Callaghan (1 app) 1943-44

### Army
K Jones (3 apps) 1946-49, D Pace (1) 1949-50

### Army FA XI
K Jones (1 app) 1946-47

### Royal Navy
L Latham (1 app) 1944-45, AW Kerr (3) 1943-45

### Birmingham Association
T Bryan (3 apps) 1881-82

### Staffordshire
AR Dorrell (1 app) 1927-28, WH Walker (1) 1927-28

### FOR AMATEUR & YOUTH INTERNATIONALS SEE UNDER SEPARATE CATEGORIES (i.e. Amateur & Youth).

### Capped Before & After Playing For Villa
Here is an unofficial list of players who represented their country at senior level either (a) before joining Aston Villa or (b) after leaving Villa. Wartime guests have not been included, neither have players who were released by the club, having had trials or had been registered on Schoolboy forms:

**Australia** - M Bosnich
**Belgium** - G De Bilde, L Nilis
**Colombia** - JP Angel
**Croatia** - B Balaban
**Denmark** - K Nielsen, P Schmeichel
**England** - AJ Aldridge, ED Barrett, JT Brittleton, PF Broadbent, G Brown, FC Buckley, GA Charles, SV Collymore, WS Corbett, GS Cowans, JW Crabtree, A Cunliffe, RW Dix, AR Dorigo, D Dublin, RE Evans, J Fashanu, SB Foster, AA Gray, JC Gregory, H Hadley, HJ Halse, S Hardy, GA Hitchens, SB Hodge, G Hodgson, S Hunt, DB James, MR Keown, AH Lockett, S McMahon, PC Merson, FJ O'Donnell, M Pejic, T Perry, DA Platt, C Regis, J Reynolds, K Richardson, JJ Rimmer, RJ Roberts, J Sharp, J Sewell, LGF Smith, R Starling, C Stephenson, GT Stephenson, SB Stone, T Thompson, D Unsworth, ME Walters.
**France** - DDM Ginola, D Six
**Ghana** - N Lamptey
**Iceland** - G Bergsson
**Israel** - N Ghrayib
**Morocco** - M Hadji, H Kachloul
**Northern Ireland** - RD Blanchflower, RM Campbell, AD Dougan, AL Goodall, NH Lockhart, PJ McParland, CJ Martin, SJ Morgan, CJ Nicholl, WTJ Renneville, J Reynolds, DJ Walsh
**Republic of Ireland** - AG Cascarino, P Daly, G Farrelly, A Hale, RJ Houghton, P McGrath, AF McLoughlin, CJ Martin, P Saward, S Staunton, AD

*Frank McAvennie*

THE COMPLETE ENCYCLOPAEDIA OF ASTON VILLA F.C. | THE COMPLETE ENCYCLOPAEDIA OF ASTON VILLA F.C.

150

Townsend, DJ Walsh.
**Portugal** - F Nelson
**Scotland** - D Blair, DG Bremner, C Calderwood, J Campbell, TB Craig, AJ Cropley, GW Cummings, P Dowds, T Ewing, DW Gibson, JD Gibson, G Graham, AM Gray, W Groves, WM Hamilton, J Herriot, J Logan, F McAvennie, B McClair, A McInally, JM MacLeod, JS McLuckie, A Massie, J Nibloe, BD Rioch, RB Templeton.
**South Africa** - K H A Fish
**Sweden** - O Mellberg
**Trinidad & Tobago** - D Yorke
**Turkey** - AF Ozalan (Alpay)
**Wales** - M Allen, DJ Astley, WWG Evans, RE Evans, T Ford, AW Green, TP Griffiths, T Hockey, BG Hole, C Phillips, JTS Phillips, L Phillips, IV Powell, I H Price, A Rees, D Richards, LR Roose, D Saunders, M Thomas, AE Watkins, WM Watkins, JJ Williams, AP Woosnam.
**Yugoslavia** - S Curcic, S Milosevic
**Zambia** - E Kapengwe, F Mwila

## Representative Honours
The following future or ex-Villa players/personnel all gained representative honours at various levels during the Second World War: DJ Astley, RAJ Brown, A Cunliffe, CJ Martin, J Mercer, LGF Smith, DJ Walsh.

*Tommy Docherty*

## Capped Managers
These nine Villa managers, namely Vic Crowe (Wales), Tommy Docherty (Scotland), John Gregory (England), Eric Houghton (England), Brian Little (England), Jimmy McMullan (Scotland), Billy McNeill, MBE (Scotland), Alex Massie (Scotland) and Joe Mercer, OBE (England) all won full international caps as players. Villa bosses, Tommy Docherty (Scotland), Joe Mercer (England), Graham Taylor (England) and Josef Venglos (Czechoslovakia) all managed their respective national teams while Venglos (Australia) and Jimmy Hogan (Austria) were both in charge of other countries for a short time.

Former Aston Villa players Peter McParland and Brian Tiler were coach/manager of Lybia and Zambia respectively.
Dave Sexton (Villa scout) acted as England assistant-manager/coach for a number of years.
David Platt was named as Englnd Under-21 coach in July 2001.

## International Talk back
Almost 120 different players had won full international honours whilst associated with Aston Villa - 59 for England up to 2001.
The first time two Aston Villa players appeared in the same international match - Howard Vaughton and Arthur Brown for England against Ireland in Belfast in February 1882. They both scored - Vaughton five times and Brown four - in England's 13-0 win.
Albert Allen scored a hat-trick on his England debut against Ireland in Belfast in March 1888 and never received another cap!
Likewise Villa's inside-forward Billy Dickson...he scored four times on his international debut for Scotland against Ireland in the same year and was never chosen to play for his country again!
The first international to take place at Villa's Perry Barr ground was between England and Ireland in February 1893. England won 6-1 without a Villa player in the side!
Villa's utility defender Jimmy Crabtree played for England in both full-back berths and all three half-back positions.
Wing-half John 'Baldy' Reynolds was capped by both Ireland and England in the 1890s whilst Robert E Evans won caps for both England and Wales in the 1900s.
The Villa trio of goalkeeper Billy George and Albert Wilkes (England)

and Bobby Templeton (Scotland) all played in the international match at Ibrox Park on 5 April 1902 when 26 fans were killed and a further 517 injured (192 seriously) after barriers had collapsed on the terracing.
Former Villa defender Alec Leake was chosen as a reserve for England at the age of 41.
Sam Hardy (Villa) was England's first-choice goalkeeper for 13 years (1907-20). His international career spanned 13 years, 54 days, while another Villa player, Billy Walker, was in international football for 12 years, 45 days. Andy Ducat won his first England cap in February 1910 and his last 10 years eight months later, in October 1920.
The Aston Villa trio of Hardy, Andy Ducat and Charlie Wallace helped England beat Scotland 5-4 at Hampden Park in 1920 in front of 136,000 spectators. Three Villa players - Frank Moss, Billy Walker and Dicky York - played for England against Scotland at Villa Park in April 1922. The Scots won 1-0, and in November 2000 three Villa players - goalkeeper David James, left-back Gareth Barry and centre-half Gareth Southgate - were in England's team that lost 1-0 to Italy in Turin.
Villa's two Tommys - Mort and Smart - were England's full-backs against Wales at Blackburn in March 1924.
Villa wing-half Jimmy Gibson starred for Scotland (the Wembley Wizards) in the famous 5-1 win over England in 1928.
Bruce Rioch was the first English-born player to captain Scotland.
Villa left-half Eddie Lowe played for England in their 10-0 win over Portugal in Lisbon in 1947 and had a hand in three of the goals.
Sammy Morgan is Port Vale's most-capped player - gaining a total of seven for Northern Ireland during his time in the Potteries.
Steve Staunton holds the record for gaining most senior caps for the Republic of Ireland - total 92+. Tony Cascarino won 88 and Paul McGrath won 83 ....and all three players served with Aston Villa with Staunton winning 52+ whilst at Villa Park - a club record.
In season 2000-01, striker Dean Saunders became Wales' most capped outfield player when appearing in his 74th international.
Frank Moss senior was the first Villa player to captain England at Wembley, doing so against Scotland in 1924.
Villa's Billy Walker scored nine goals for England in 18 appearances spread over a period of 12 years (October 1920 to December 1932).
The Villa duo of Danny Blair (Scotland) and Dai Astley (Wales) played against each other in the home international match in October 1932.
And in 1937 Alex Massie (Scotland) and Ronnie Starling (England) battled against each other in front of 134,000 fans at Hampden Park.
Brian Little's England career amounted to just 10 minutes! He came on as an 80th minute substitute for Mick Channon against Wales at Wembley in May 1975.
Villa's George Brown scored a hat-trick for the Football League against the Irish League in 1932.
Gordon Cowans' two England 'B' caps were won almost 10 years apart.
Villa's double-winning team of 1896-97 contained eight full internationals. And in season

1933-34 Villa had no fewer than 14 full internationals on their books: Joe Beresford, George Brown, Arthur Cunliffe, Tom Gardner, Eric Houghton, Tommy Mort, Tommy Smart, Joe Tate, Billy Walker and 'Pongo' Waring (England), Danny Blair, Jimmy Gibson and Joe Nibloe (Scotland and Dai Astley (Wales).
Frank Broome was capped in four different positions by England: outside-right (7), inside-right (8), centre-forward (9) and inside-left (10).

THE COMPLETE ENCYCLOPAEDIA OF ASTON VILLA F.C.            THE COMPLETE ENCYCLOPAEDIA OF ASTON VILLA F.C.

151

By 1936 Villa had supplied more players than any other professional club for England at senior level - total 39.

When Arsenal visited Villa Park for in a League game in November 1932, there were 17 full internationals on view.

Jack Martin, Frank Broome and Leslie Smith all played for England in Wartime/victory internationals.

'Sailor' Brown and Les Smith played at Villa Park for England against Wales in February 1945. They both later joined Villa.

Albert Allen and Denny Hodgetts (1888), Albert Hall and Joe Bache (1910), Billy Walker and Arthur Dorrell (1925) and Billy Walker and Eric Houghton (1932) all played for England as left-wing partners in the years given.

Villa's Charlie Athersmith played in the first ever Inter League game on 20 April 1891 for the Football League XI against the Football Alliance at Olive Grove (Sheffield).

Jack Sharp represented England at both football and cricket....a dual international!

'Watty' Corbett and Les (LGF) Smith both played for England at amateur and senior levels, likewise Leigh Richmond Roose for Wales. Corbett also played for the Great Britain side in the 1908 Olympic Games.

A crowd of 67,770 saw England play Scotland at Villa Park in November 1947.

Gareth Barry scored a hat-trick in England Under-18's 9-0 win over San Marino in October 1999. (See also Youth Football).

John Martin (2) and Frank Broome scored for an England XI in a 4-3 win over the Army at Selhurst Park in January 1940.

Broome scored twice in the FA XI's 7-2 defeat by the RAF at Bristol in November 1941.

## IPSWICH TOWN

Villa's playing record against Town:
Football League/Premiership

| Venue | P | W | D | L | F | A |
|---|---|---|---|---|---|---|
| Home | 21 | 12 | 6 | 3 | 42 | 18 |
| Away | 21 | 6 | 4 | 11 | 22 | 31 |
| Totals | 42 | 17 | 10 | 14 | 64 | 49 |

FA Cup

| | P | W | D | L | F | A |
|---|---|---|---|---|---|---|
| Home | 1 | 0 | 1 | 0 | 1 | 1 |
| Away | 4 | 2 | 0 | 2 | 7 | 6 |
| Totals | 5 | 2 | 1 | 2 | 8 | 7 |

League Cup

| | P | W | D | L | F | A |
|---|---|---|---|---|---|---|
| Home | 3 | 1 | 1 | 1 | 10 | 7 |
| Away | 1 | 0 | 0 | 1 | 0 | 1 |
| Totals | 4 | 1 | 1 | 2 | 10 | 8 |

Full Members Cup

| | P | W | D | L | F | A |
|---|---|---|---|---|---|---|
| Away | 1 | 0 | 0 | 1 | 0 | 1 |

Aston Villa and Ipswich Town first met each other at League level in September 1959 (Division 2). A crowd of 36,608 saw Peter McParland (2) and Ron Wylie score the goals to give Villa a 3-1 home victory.

The return fixture that season ended in a 2-1 defeat for Villa, Jimmy Dugdale scoring for both sides!

The first meeting in the top flight of English football followed on 9 December 1961 when Villa won 3-0 at home, McParland again netting twice. Ipswich went on to clinch the championship after beating Villa 2-0 at home in the penultimate game of the season.

Ipswich won a seven-goal thriller at Portman Road by 4-3 in April 1964 - but only 11,658 fans saw the action. Dave Pountney scored twice for Villa while Joe Broadfoot did likewise for Town.

Andy Gray scored a hat-trick in Villa's 5-2 home win over Ipswich in September 1976 and in April 1978 the Scotsman was on target again

as the subsequent FA Cup winners were slammed 6-1, also at Villa Park. It was 4-0 at half-time.

Villa recorded their first League win at Ipswich in September 1978 by 2-0 - John Gregory and Andy Gray (penalty) the scorers.

Villa and Ipswich battled it out for the League championship in 1980-81....and after a long, hard season it went right down to the wire. Villa's last match was at Arsenal while Ipswich had two to play, Middlesbrough away and Southampton at home.

Villa needed a draw at Highbury...but only if Ipswich won at Middlesbrough and then defeated Saints at Portman Road.

As it happened, Ipswich lost at Ayresome Park, so despite Villa going down to the Gunners, the title went to Villa Park for the first time in 71 years.

*Villa's goalkeeper Jim Cumbes tussles with Ipswich midfielder Brian Talbot during a League game at Portman Road.*

Ironically in 1980-81 Ipswich won both League games against Villa - 1-0 at home and 2-1 away - the latter being their first victory at Villa Park in 11 attempts.

Villa's first game in the Premiership saw them draw 1-1 with Ipswich at Portman Road on 15 August 1992, Dalian Atkinson having the pleasure of scoring the Villa goal - against his former club!

Luc Nilis suffered a career-ending double fracture of the right leg when Villa beat newly-promoted Ipswich 2-1 at Portman Road in September 2000. Lee Hendrie and Dion Dublin scored the goals. That scoreline was repeated later in the campaign as Villa completed the double of over European-chasing Ipswich.

John Deehan (1975), Lee Jenkins (1978) and Kevin Gage, David Hunt and Steve Sims (1987) all made their debuts for Villa against Ipswich Town.

Villa met Ipswich for the first time at competitive level in a 3rd round FA Cup-tie at Portman Road in January 1939, Villa forcing a 1-1 draw before winning the replay 2-1. In the first encounter, left-winger Charlie Fletcher of Ipswich missed a penalty 10 minutes into the second-half after Villa's George Cummings had dislodged the ball from the spot with a snowball just as the player was about to take the kick! Jimmy Allen's smart header gave Villa the lead on 83 minutes but justice was done when Jock Hutcheson, on his debut, equalised for Town two minutes from time.

THE COMPLETE ENCYCLOPAEDIA OF ASTON VILLA F.C.

THE COMPLETE ENCYCLOPAEDIA OF ASTON VILLA F.C.

152

When Villa won the League championship in 1980-81 they lost 1-0 to Ipswich (runners-up in the First Division) in the 3rd round of the FA Cup at Portman Road in front of more than 27,700 fans.

Dwight Yorke and Mark Draper scored early goals to set Villa up for a 3-1 win at Ipswich in a 5th round FA Cup-tie in 1996.

Villa suffered their first home defeat in the League Cup on 21 November 1961 when Ipswich Town won a 3rd round tie 3-2 despite two Harry Burrows goals (one a penalty). The crowd was 22,704.

When Villa beat Ipswich 6-2 at home in the same competition in November 1988, David Platt netted four times.

The Full Members Cup clash at Portman Road took place in 1986-87 (round 3).

Players with both clubs include: D Atkinson, JM Deehan, D Geddis, JS McLuckie, A Mulraney, JJ Wiliams.

## IRISH CONNECTIONS

List of Aston Villa personnel, including players (at various levels), managers, coaches who have been associated with clubs in Ireland (Northern Ireland and The Republic of Ireland):

| | |
|---|---|
| RD Blanchflower | Glentoran |
| FH Broome | Shelbourne |
| P Daly | Shamrock Rovers |
| E Deacy | Galway Rovers, Galway United |
| PD Doherty | Coleraine, Glentoran |
| AD Dougan | Distillery |
| A Hale | Waterford |
| D Hickson | Ballymena (manager) |
| T Hockey | Athlone Town (manager) |
| NH Lockhart | Distillery, Linfield |
| P McGrath | St Patrick's (Dublin) |
| PJ McParland | Dundalk, Glentoran (manager) |
| JC Martin | Drumcondra, Glentoran, Waterford (player-manager) |
| A Massie | Dublin Dolphin |
| TP Muldoon | Athlone Town |
| A Mulraney | Sligo Rovers (trialist) |
| B Ormsby | Waterford |
| AF Phoenix | Shelbourne (Dublin) |
| MJ Pinner | Belfast Distillery |
| J Reynolds | Distillery, Ulster |
| S Staunton | Dundalk |
| N Tarrant | Shamrock Rovers |
| DJ Walsh | Corinthians (Ireland), Shelbourne, Waterford, Linfield, Limerick, Shelbourne |
| J Welford | Belfast Celtic |
| L Williams | Shamrock Rovers |

### Irish Blarney

Billy Renneville was the first Villa player to win an Irish international cap, doing so on 28 January 1911 against Wales.

The first player to gain a Republic of Ireland cap whilst at Villa Park was Tommy Muldoon, in season 1926-27.

Derek Dougan scored 222 goals in a total of 546 Football Leagues games during his professional career (a record for an Irishman)- and in all competitions (at club level and international soccer) he netted close on 300 goals in more than 700 matches. After leaving Villa Park in 1963 Dougan went on to score a further 168 goals in League football.

Peter McParland scored five goals for Northern Ireland in the 1958 World Cup Finals in Sweden.

Pat Saward played for Villa against Manchester United in the 1957 FA Cup Final and four days later he returned to Wembley to star for the Republic of Ireland against England in a World Cup qualifying match.

Danny Blanchflower skippered both Villa and Spurs as well as Northern Ireland.

Con Martin played at centre-half and in goal for both Aston Villa and the Republic of Ireland - and he also scored a vital penalty for Eire in their historic 2-0 win over England at Goodison Park in 1949.

Paul McGrath won 83 caps for the Republic of Ireland before his tally was bettered by another former Villa player, Tony Cascarino with 88. In 2001 Steve Staunton then took his total of Eire caps to over 90. Staunton is the most capped Villa player with 52+ international appearances, beating the previous record-holder, another Irishman, Paul McGrath (with 51).

*Bob Iverson*

## IVERSON, ROBERT THOMAS JAMES

Born: Folkestone, 17 October 1910.
Died: Birmingham, 20 April, 1953.
Career: Folkestone County School, Folkestone FC (August 1926), Tottenham Hotspur (August 1932), Northfleet (Spurs' nursery side, season 1932-33), Ramsgate Press Wanderers (June 1933), Lincoln City (September 1933), Wolverhampton Wanderers (February 1935), Aston Villa (December 1936-May 1948). Retired to become reserve team coach at Villa Park. Guested for Birmingham, Bournemouth, Leicester City, Northampton Town, Notts County and Nottingham Forest during WW2.

Bob Iverson was a honest competitor, big and strong, with receding hairline (he was almost bald when he retired). Able to play as a wing-half or inside-forward, he wasn't given much of a chance at Molineux to show off his skills but after joining Aston Villa he became a firm favourite with the home fans and made 326 first team appearances in the claret and blue strip. He netted 12 times in 153 in League and FA Cup encounters and weighed in with a further 55 goals in 173 Second World War matches. He helped Villa win the Second Division championship in 1938 and the Wartime Cup in 1944. He also netted the fastest-ever goal by a Villa player, finding the back of the net after just 9.3 seconds from the start of a League game against Charlton in December 1938. Amazingly he repeated that feat on Christmas Day 1947 when he scored just as quickly in a reserve team game against Everton. A keen angler and self-taught pianist, Iverson revelled in jazz

## JACKSON, DENNIS LEONARD WILLIAM

Born: Birmingham, 8 March 1932
Career: Birmingham & District Schools, West Bromwich Albion (Amateur, August 1949-52), Hednesford Town (July 1954), Aston Villa (professional, October 1954), Millwall (May 1959), Rugby Town (August 1961). Retired in May 1966 to go into the bookmakers' business. Later worked in a bakery (late 1970s).

Dennis Jackson spent three years playing as an amateur with WBA before going into the Army. Had a cartilage operation in 1953 and joined Hednesford Town on his demob, signing professional forms at Villa Park after a trial. A competitive defender he was handed

THE COMPLETE ENCYCLOPAEDIA OF ASTON VILLA F.C.    THE COMPLETE ENCYCLOPAEDIA OF ASTON VILLA F.C.

153

just eight first team outings by Villa manager Eric Houghton before going on to make over 80 appearances for Millwall.

## JACKSON, THOMAS

Born: Benwell Village, Newcastle-upon-Tyne, 16 March 1898. Died: Sheldon, Birmingham, 1975.
Career: Rutherford College (Newcastle), Rutherford College Old Boys, Benwell Colliery FC, Northumberland Fusiliers in WWI (serving in Belgium & France), Durham University (1918), Aston Villa (amateur, August 1919, professional July 1920), Kidderminster Harriers (May 1930-May 1931). Retired.
Tommy Jackson qualified to become a teacher at Durham University before embarking on a successful footballing career. A very useful weekend goalkeeper, he was approached one evening during an after-match tea at Newcastle's Station Hotel by Aston Villa's North-East scout Billy Wright, who had been chatting with Norman Anderson, one of the best goalkeepers in the League. He asked Jackson if he would like to play for the Villa! At first Jackson thought it was Bolden Villa (a town side)..."No" said Wright, "Aston Villa in Birmingham".
After first discussing it with his family (and friends) Jackson duly accepted the offer and moved to Villa Park, initially as an amateur before signing as a professional in 1920. As cover along with Cyril Spiers, for the great Sam Hardy, he made his Football League debut against a strong Sunderland side that included Charlie Buchan, in February 1921 - and he did well. Then, following Hardy's departure in August 1921, Jackson established himself in the first team at Villa Park (although he was under pressure at times from Spiers). He went on to amass 186 senior appearances for the club and played in the 1924 FA Cup Final defeat by Newcastle United at Wembley. Jackson retired from the game in May 1931 and got a job as a part-time teacher while also working in a Birmingham factory as well as covering Central League matches for the Sports Argus at weekends.
Jackson was one of four 'Tommys' on Villa's books in the 1920-21, the others being Smart, Boyman and Weston. Another Tommy, Mort, then replaced Boyman for the following season.

*Tommy Jackson shaking hands with the Duke of York prior to the start of the 1924 F.A. Cup Final.*

## JAKEMAN, GEORGE JOHN WILLIAM

Born: Small Heath, Birmingham, 19 May 1899. Died: Hall Green, Birmingham, 1970.
Career: Yardley Road School, Wolseley Motor Works FC, Small Heath Boys Club (1913), Metropolitan Carriage Works FC (Smethwick), Aston Villa (Amateur 1916, professional May 1922), Notts County (August 1929), Kidderminster Harriers (August 1933). Retired 1935. Also played second XI cricket for Worcestershire and later coached both cricket and football at Rugby Public School.
An England Junior international (1917), resolute defender George Jakeman played as an amateur for Aston Villa during the Great War but had to wait until February 1925 before making his debut in the Football League at West Bromwich Albion (lost 4-1).
With far too many other quality defenders at the club, Jakeman found it difficult to make headway and played in only seven more senior games before moving to Meadow Lane. He went on to appear in 75 League and FA Cup games for the Magpies.

## JAMES, DAVID BENJAMIN

Born: Welwyn Garden City, 1 August 1970
Career: Watford (YTS June 1986, professional July 1988), Liverpool (£1 million, July 1992), Aston Villa (£1.8 million, June 1999), West Ham United (£4 million, July 2001).

David James was recruited to replace Mark Bosnich (transferred to Old Trafford). He had already established himself as one of the country's leading goalkeepers with 98 senior appearances for Watford and 277 for Liverpool. He had also earned the first of his three full England caps after representing his country at Youth, Under-21 (10 games) and 'B' team levels. An FA Youth Cup winner at Vicarage Road in 1989, he added a League Cup winners' medal to his collection in 1995 and during his first season at Villa Park (when he suffered briefly with a knee injury) his form got him into Kevin Keegan's squad (behind David Seaman and Nigel Martyn) for Euro 2000. He helped Villa reach the 2000 FA Cup Final after making some brilliant penalty saves during the shoot-out in the semi-final with Bolton Wanderers. A big, powerful fella, who dominates his area well, James is likely to have the odd momentary lapse in concentration - and that has led to goals being conceded!
He had made 85 senior appearances for Villa before moving to West Ham.

*David James*

## JASZCZUN, ANTONY JOHN

Born: Kettering, 16 September 1977
Career: Aston Villa (YTS, June 1994, professional July 1996), Blackpool (£30,000, January 2000).
After making just one substitute appearance for Aston Villa in a Worthington Cup-tie against Chelsea at Stamford Bridge in October 1998, left-sided defender 'Tommy' Jaszczun was transferred to Blackpool halfway through the 1999-2000 season. He quickly established himself in the Seasiders' side, scoring on his debut for the Bloomfield Road club against Stoke City in the Auto Windscreen Shield.

## JEFFRIES, RONALD JOHN

Born: Hall Green, Birmingham, 24 March 1930. Died: 1981.
Career: Moor Green, Birmingham City (trialist), Aston Villa (professional, December 1950), Walsall (November 1953-May 1954). Non-League football.
On 17 February 1951 - just two months after joining Aston Villa and a week after playing in a first team friendly against Luton Town - Ron Jeffries made his Football League debut in place of Dave Walsh against

THE COMPLETE ENCYCLOPAEDIA OF ASTON VILLA F.C.    THE COMPLETE ENCYCLOPAEDIA OF ASTON VILLA F.C.

154

Tottenham Hotspur in front of 48,000 fans at White Hart Lane. A big, strong, thrustful centre-forward, he did quite well in a 3-2 defeat and was called on to deputise for the Irishman a fortnight later at Arsenal when the turnout was 43,747. Those were Jeffries' only senior appearances for the club - but what memories! He was then a reserve for the next two years before being sold to Walsall for whom he had three outings at League level. Jefferies later ran an ironmonger's shop near to St Andrew's.

### JENKINS, LEE ROBERT
Born: West Bromwich, 17 March 1961.
Career: Barr Beacon School, Villa Boys, Aston Villa (apprentice, June 1977, professional January 1979), Port Vale (November 1980), Rovenaniemi Palloseura (ROPS, Finland, August 1981), Birmingham City (October 1985), Finnainin Palloilijat, FinnPa (1986-88).
An attacking midfielder, England Youth international Lee Jenkins helped Aston Villa's youngsters win the FA Youth Cup before leaving the club for Port Vale on a free transfer after just three substitute appearances for the first team. He did very well during his two spells in Finland, but struggled at Vale Park and failed to finish his only game for Blues (injured against WBA).

### JOACHIM, JULIAN KEVIN
Born: Boston, Lincs. 20 September 1974.
Career: Leicester City (YTS, June 1990, professional, September 1992), Aston Villa (£1.5 million, February 1996), Coventry City (player-exchange deal, June 2001).
Striker Julian Joachim, who has represented England at Youth team level and won nine Under-21 caps, scored 31 goals in 119 first team outings for Leicester City before his former manager Brian Little signed him for Aston Villa in 1996.
After a slow start when he had Tommy Johnson, Savo Milosevic and Dwight Yorke to contest with for a first team place, he had a much better 1997-98 season at Villa Park and became a hit with the fans. He

manfully strove on, scored some excellent goals and generally gave a good account of himself, despite suffering a few niggling injuries and losing his form and appetite at times.
A dashing player with plenty of speed, Joachim unfortunately lost his place in the side following an abortive attempt to play for St Vincent in the World Cup qualifying competition during the 1999-2000 campaign. He flew to the Caribbean only to be told that the games he had played for England at Under-21 level some years earlier ruled him out of contention.
Transferred to Coventry in an exchange-deal involving Moustapaha Hadji, Joachim made 173 appearances (59 as a substitute) and scored 46 goals duriing his time at Villa Park.

### JOHNSON, GEORGE EDWARD
Born: West Bromwich, April 1871. Died: Walsall, 1934.
Career: West Bromwich Baptist & Beeches Road Schools, West Bromwich Sandwell, West Bromwich Baptist FC, Wrockwardine Wood (1892), West Bromwich Albion (professional, May 1895), Walsall (September 1896), Aston Villa (April 1898). Retired through injury, December 1904, but made a brief comeback in 1906 with Plymouth Argyle, finishing again in 1907.
George Johnson was a thoughtful and aggressive inside or centre-forward. He was restricted to just two games with WBA but struck 26 goals in 59 outings for Walsall before moving to Villa Park. He spent over six years with Villa, scoring 47 goals in 110 first XI appearances, first as 'strike' partner to Jack Devey and Fred Wheldon, then Devey and Bill Garraty and finally to Garraty and Joe Bache (among others). Johnson won a League championship medal in 1898-99 and then helped Villa retain the trophy the following season when he made only nine appearances.

### JOHNSON, THOMAS

Born: Newcastle, 15 January 1971
Career: Notts County (apprentice, June 1987, professional January 1989), Derby County (£1.3 million, March 1992), Aston Villa (£1.45 million, January 1995), Celtic (£2.4 million, March 1997), Everton (on loan, September-October 1999), Sheffield Wednesday (September 2001).
Positive striker Tommy Johnson scored 57 goals in 149 games during his time at Meadow Lane and followed up with 41 in 129 outings for the Rams. He continued to fire in some cracking goals with Villa, notching a further 17 in 71

*Tommy Johnson*

appearances before losing his way under Brian Little, eventually moving north of the border to join Celtic for big money! Capped seven times by England at Under-21 level, Johnson suffered an apalling knee injury at Parkhead which sidelined him for six months in 1999. He regained match fitness at Goodison Park and then returned to have a very useful season with Celtic under new manager Martin O'Neill, winning League and Cup medals.

### JOHNSON, WILLIAM FREDERICK
Born: Bradeley, Smallthorne, Staffs, 29 August 1902. Died: c 1967.
Career: Bradeley Juniors, Ravensdale Mission, Leek Alexandra, West Bromwich Albion (Amateur, 1924), Buxton, Aston Villa (January 1926), Charlton Athletic (May 1928), Yeovil Town (May 1929).
Goalkeeper Bill Johnson, the son of a coal miner, played only four games for Aston Villa during his two seasons with the club when he

*Julian Joachim*

acted as reserve to Tommy Jackson. Those games produced 24 goals, Villa winning three of them by 5-3, 5-1 and 7-2. A six-footer, weighing almost 13 stone, Johnson was signed by a former Villa player, then manager of Charlton, Albert Lindon, when he moved to The Valley in 1928. He helped the Addicks win the Third Division (South) championship in his only season with the club (making 10 appearances).

### JOHNSTONE, CHARLES SAMUEL
Born: Aston, Birmingham 8 January 1858. Died: Birmingham c 1946.
Career: Saltley College, Aston Villa (August 1878), Lozells British Constitutionals (May 1881). Retired in 1882 to concentrate on teaching and later became headmaster of both Jenkins Street (1883) and Burbury Street Schools in Lozells, Birmingham. Joined the Aston Villa Board of Directors in 1896. Later became an enthusiastic vice-President of the club in the 1920s (with another former player, Tom Pank).
The son of Fergus Johnstone, vice-President of Aston Villa in the late 1870s, Charlie Johnstone was a fast-raiding inside-forward who always wore a red skull cap - thus distinguishing him from all the other players on the field! A grand little footballer, he only made two FA Cup appearances for Villa but played in scores of friendly matches and other local competitions.

### JOHNSTONE, JOHN CHARLES
Born: Dundee, 7 April 1896. Died: Erdington, Birmingham, 1952.
Career: Dundee Schoolboy football, Dundee Harp, Dundee, Aston Villa (February 1922), Reading (August 1928-May 1929). Retired through injury and subsequently returned to Birmingham where he became the licensee of the Red Lion in Erdington. He remained in the licensing trade until his death.
'Jock' Johnstone was a cheerful, solidly built half-back whose speed in recovery was second to none. Injuries prevented him from being one of the great Villa stars of the 1920s, his best season coming in 1925-26 when he appeared in 38 matches. His overall record for the club was 115 appearances and one goal scored - in the League at home to Leicester City in April 1927 (won 2-0).

### JONES, ALLAN RAYMOND
Born: Winshall, near Burton-on-Trent, 3 November 1941
Career: Schoolboy football, Bilston Boys, Aston Villa (amateur, August 1957, professional November 1958), Nuneaton Borough (on loan, January 1962, signed February 1962). Retired through injury, May 1963.
Founder member of the Bilston Table Tennis Association, outside-left Allan Jones' career was plagued by injuries. He made only one appearance for Villa, deputising for Harry Burrows on the wing in a 3-1 defeat at Fulham in October 1961.

### JONES, KEITH
Born: Nantyglo, Monmouthshire, 23 October 1928.
Career: Stourport Swifts (1943-44), West Bromwich Albion (amateur, 194-45), Kidderminster Harriers (August 1945-April 1946), Aston Villa (professional May 1946), Port Vale (July 1957), Crewe Alexandra (April 1959), Southport (July 1960-May 1961).
After doing exceedingly well at Aggborough with the Harriers, Keith Jones took over between the posts at Villa Park during the second half of the 1947-48 season when regular goalkeeper Joe Rutherford was injured. His debut came against Wolves at Molineux on Christmas Eve in front of 50,000 spectators.
Two years later, in November 1949, Jones was capped by Wales against Scotland and although he was on the losing side (2-0) the selectors were satisfied with his performance and called him in for the next game against Belgium. Unfortunately 72 hours before he could collect

his second cap, Jones was injured - and there his international career ended! Jones fought his way back to full fitness and went on to make 199 senior appearances for Villa during his 11 years with the club. He was replaced by Nigel Sims and after leaving played 64 League games for Port Vale and 46 for Crewe. He was a reserve at Southport.

### JONES, LESLIE CLIFFORD
Born: Mountain Ash, mid-Wales, 1 January 1930
Career: West Park School, Craigath Juniors, Bedfordshire Boys, Luton Town (professional, October 1950), Aston Villa (January 1958), Worcester City (July 1959-May 1960). Served and played in the Army: 1948-50.
A well-built full-back, Les Jones made over 100 first-team appearances for the Hatters before moving to Villa Park, primarily as cover for Stan Lynn and Peter Aldis. He was given just five first team outings during his stay at the club - the first in February 1958 against Blackpool when he marked Stanley Matthews.

### JONES. MARK ANTHONY WALDRON
Born: Warley, West Midlands, 22 October 1961
Career: Warley Schools, Aston Villa (apprentice June 1977, professional July 1979), Brighton & Hove Albion (£50,000, March 1984), Birmingham City (player/deal involving Mick Ferguson, October 1984), Shrewsbury Town (on loan, February 1987, signed March 1987), Hereford United (June 1987), Worcester City (July 1991-92).
A tidy, efficient full-back, never overawed, Mark Jones made only 33 appearances during his five professional years at Villa Park. An FA Youth Cup and Southern Floodlit Cup winner in 1980, Jones later added a European Super Cup winners' medal to his collection and also played in the World Club Championship game for Villa against Penarol in Japan in 1982. His career at St Andrew's was hampered by injury and he made 40 first-class appearances for Blues, having starred in only nine matches for 'Albion of Hove.'

### JONES, PERCY OSWALD
Born: Aston, Birmingham, 1899. Died: Birmingham, c 1960.
Career: Elisons Works FC, Birmingham University Old Boys, Aston Villa (October 1921). Retired through injury in the summer of 1924.
Tough-nut defender, deputy to George Blackburn, Tommy Smart and Tommy Weston, Percy Jones made 15 senior appearances for Aston Villa before a knee injury curtailed a promising career.

### JONES, THOMAS WILLIAM
Born: Edgbaston, Birmingham, June 1905. Deceased.
Career: Birmingham St George's, Oakengates Town (August 1921), Aston Villa (professional, July 1922), Burnley (August-December 1926).
Tom Jones spent almost three seasons in Villa's reserve team before making the first of five senior appearances for the club against Arsenal in April 1925. An attacking half-back who enthused over taking long shots at goal, he once netted from 45 yards with a hefty toe-ender in a second team fixture at Villa Park.

### JONES, JAMES WALTER EDMUND
Born: Wellington, Salop, April 1890. Died: Bristol, September 1951.
Career: Wellington Schools, Wellington Ravenhurst FC, Shrewsbury Town (August 1909), Aston Villa (July 1910), Bristol Rovers (May 1919). Retired in April 1924.
Jimmy Jones was a 'galloping' centre-forward who scored once (against Bradford City) in his two First Division games for Aston Villa before going on to net 12 times in 38 Southern League matches for Bristol Rovers.

THE COMPLETE ENCYCLOPAEDIA OF ASTON VILLA F.C.  THE COMPLETE ENCYCLOPAEDIA OF ASTON VILLA F.C.

156

## JONES, WALTER ARCHIBALD

Born: Wednesfield, 25 January 1861. Died: Wolverhampton, c 1940.
Career: Walsall Young Baptists, Walsall Town Swifts, Aston Villa (April 1885). Retired through injury (broken leg) in May 1886.
A slightly built centre-forward, awkward looking in style, Wally Jones appeared in two FA Cup encounters for Villa before suffering a fractured leg in a Birmingham Senior match.

## JUVENTUS

Villa's record against the Italian giants:
European Cup

| Venue | P | W | D | L | F | A |
|---|---|---|---|---|---|---|
| Home | 1 | 0 | 0 | 1 | 1 | 2 |
| Away | 1 | 0 | 0 | 1 | 1 | 3 |
| Totals | 2 | 0 | 0 | 2 | 2 | 5 |

Italian giants Juventus knocked Villa out of the European Cup at the quarter-final stage in season in 1982-83. Over 45,500 fans saw the Serie 'A' champions win 2-1 at Villa Park and 66,000 attended the return leg in Turin which Juventus eased through by 3-1 to take the tie in style by 5-2 on aggregate. European Footballer of the Year, Paolo Rossi, was in the Juventus side.
Ex-Villa player David Platt joined Juventus from Bari for £6.5 million in June 1992.

## KACHLOUL, HASSAN

Born: Agadir, Morocco,
19 February 1973.
Career: Nimes (France), FC Dunkerque (1995-96), Metz (1996-97), St Etienne (1998), Southampton (1999), Aston Villa (June 2001).
Moroccan international midfielder, 6ft 1in tall, strong and mobile with a solid frame, Hassan Kachloul enjoys a left-sided position and prior to his transfer to Villa Park he had been capped seven times by his country. He made his Villa debut during the InterToto Cup competition at the start of the 2001-02 season.

## KAPENGWE, EMMENT

Born: Zambia, 27 March 1943.
Career: Zambia national football, Atlanta Chiefs (NASL), Aston Villa (September 1969), Atlanta Chiefs (May 1970-72).
Zambian international utility forward Emment Kapwenge was recommended to Aston Villa, along with his colleague Freddie Mwila, by former player Phil Woosnam. Unfortunately he failed to live up to expectations and after just three senior outings returned to the NASL. Kapwenge was the first black footballer to appear in a League game for Villa - versus Carlisle United (h) on 12 November 1969.

## KEARNS, JOHN H.

Born: Chasetown, 21 January 1883. Died: Chasetown, 5 April 1928.
Career: Brownhills Albion (1898), Coventry City (1903), Birmingham (£100, April 1906), Aston Villa (player/exchange, February 1909), Bristol City (April 1912). Retired in May 1915.
Jack Kearns was a wonderful positional player, a composed left-back whose attitude and biting tackle were allied to a clean-kicking technique. He gave nothing away, was very positive and had a useful career, appearing in 40 senior games (as stand-in for Tommy Smart and Alf Miles) for Aston Villa, 64 for Blues and 93 for Bristol City. He failed to make the first XI at Coventry.

## KEELAN, KEVIN DAMIEN, MBE

Born: Calcutta, India, 5 January 1941.
Career: Worcestershire County Schools, Carpet Traders FC (Kidderminster & District League), Kidderminster Harriers (trialist, 1956), Aston Villa (junior, July 1957, professional, July 1958), Stockport County (April 1961), Kidderrminster Harriers (August 1961), Wrexham (November 1961), Norwich City (£7,000, July 1963-February 1980). Had three separate spells in the NASL with the New England Teamen whilst at Carrow Road (late 1970s). He was voted 'top goalkeeper' in the NASL in 1978 and later became a Director of the New England Teamen.
Given just five first team outings by the club, Kevin Keelan left Villa Park in 1961 after failing to displace Nigel Sims. At this point his career took off. He had three games for Stockport, played in over 70 League and Cup matches for Wrexham and amassed a club record 673 first-class appearances for Norwich City - after his boss at Carrow Road, Ron Ashman, had called his signing the 'bargain of the century'. Keelan was an ever-present for the Canaries in five seasons, including three in succession: 1971-74. He starred as the last line of the Norwich defence when the Second Division championship was won in 1972 (ahead of Birmingham City) and he helped guide the Canaries back into the top flight for a second time in 1975. He also played in two losing League Cup Final sides: 1973 against Spurs and 1975 against his old club, Aston Villa. A flawless 'keeper, with a massive pair of hands, Keelan was a spectacular, extrovert showman who overcame early hotheadedness and rashness to continually turn in 'blinding displays' for City. He was acrobatic when he had to be, shrewd in judgement and a tremendous clubman to Norwich City....although he did become the first goalkeeper in the Norfolk club's history to be sent-off in a major game! He also saw the framework of the goal fall on top of him during one game, and faced four penalties, in normal time, in another.
Awarded the MBE for services to Football (and Norwich City in partticular) Keelan now runs a successful construction company in Florida, USA with another ex-League goalkeeper, Peter Mellor.

## KENNING, MICHAEL JOHN

Born: Erdington, Birmingham, 18 August 1940.
Career: Slade Road School (Erdington), Erdington Boys, Birmingham & District Schools, Brookhill (Sunday League), Aston Villa (amateur, June 1957, part-time professional while working as an apprentice-welder, full-time professional October 1959), Shrewsbury Town (£2,000, May 1961), Charlton Athletic (£10,500, November 1962), Norwich City (£27,000, December 1966), Wolverhampton Wanderers (£35,000, January 1968), Charlton Athletic (£20,000, March 1969), Queen's Park Rangers (guest, May 1971), Watford (£9,000, December 1971), Germiston Callies in South Africa (1973-74), Atherstone United (briefly in 1974-5), Germiston Callies (player-manager 1975-79), Durban United (manager 1979-80), Witts University (part-time manager 1980-81). He now works in South Africa for a safety equipment company.
Mike Kenning's professional career in England spanned 14 years. He started off by playing in three senior games for Aston Villa before moving to Shrewsbury Town. An out-and-out right-winger, with good pace and strong shot, he then went on to appear in 515 competitive matches, scoring well over 100 goals, before switching his allegiance to South Africa where he later became a well-respected manager.
Kenning netted 59 of his goals in 238 outings during two excellent spells at The Valley and whilst with Charlton, Kenning had a lucky escape in August 1970 when his car was involved in a head-on collision on the M1. He received eight stitches to a deep wound to his right leg, but far more serious was the damage done to his right knee (described initially as a slight chip). The injury restricted the movement in the joint so badly that later in the season he was admitted to hospital for a major operation.

MEMORY LANE

JULES RIMET CUP
WORLD CHAMPIONSHIP
ENGLAND 1966 JULY 11-30
WEMBLEY·EVERTON·SHEFFIELD·SUNDERLAND·ASTON VILLA·MANCHESTER·MIDDLESBROUGH·WHITE CITY

ASTON VILLA
PREPARED

THE VILLA NEWS
AND RECORD

THE ASTON HOTEL,
Opposite Tram Terminus and Witton Railway Station.
Adjoining the Villa Ground, WITTON ROAD. Adjoining the Villa Ground.
The most complete and up-to-date Hotel in Aston.

Wines and Spirits of highest quality.    All noted brands in stock.
Every Accommodation on the Spot.    Motor Garage and Stabling.
ANSELLS ASTON ALES.

FOREWORD BY
RON SAUNDERS
IAN JOHNSON

CHAMPIONS

THE VILLA NEWS
AND RE...

The
OFFICIAL
Souvenir
PROGRAMME

ASTON VILLA

Aston Villa
Blackburn Olympic
Blackburn Rovers
Bury
Barnsley
Bradford City
Clapham Rovers
Everton
Manchester Utd
Manchester City
Notts County
Notts Forest
Newcastle Utd
Old Carthusians
Old Etonians
Oxford Univ.

HUDDERSFIELD
TOWN

Preston N.E.
Royal Engineers
Sheffield Wed
Sheffield Utd
Tottenham H'r
Wanderers
West Bromwich
Albion
Wolverhampton
Wanderers

cyclist
e have
penny

1919-20

STAMFORD
BRIDGE
S.W.

of the
FINAL TIE
FOOTBALL ASSOCIATION
CHALLENGE CUP
COMPETITION

APRIL
24
1920

BERNARD HUGH

VICTORIA SQUARE

10s.,

ASTON VILLA F.C.

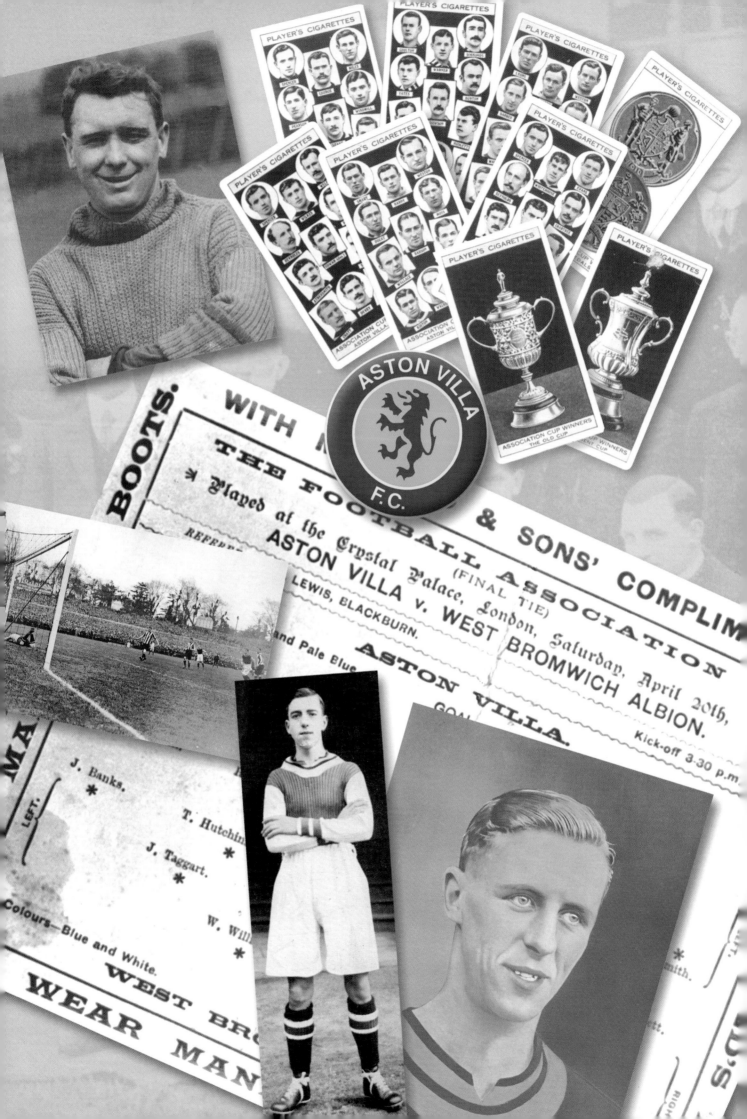

PLAYER'S CIGARETTES

ASTON VILLA
F.C.

ASSOCIATION CUP WINNERS
THE OLD CUP

BOOTS.

WITH

& SONS' COMPLIM

THE FOOTBALL ASSOCIATION

Played at the Crystal Palace, London, Saturday, April 20th,
(FINAL TIE)
ASTON VILLA v. WEST BROMWICH ALBION.

LEWIS, BLACKBURN.

and Pale Blue

ASTON VILLA.

Kick-off 3-30 p.m.

GOAL

MA

LEFT.

J. Banks.
*
T. Hutchin
*
J. Taggart.
*
W. Will
*

Colours—Blue and White.

WEST BR

WEAR MAN

FC BAYERN — ASTON VILLA

# CHAMPIONS C
THE 1982 EUROPEAN CUP

**Stadion Sportnieuws**

EXTRA EDITIE

EUROPACUP-FINALE

BAYERN
MÜNCHEN

ASTON
VILLA

emeen Dagbla
ELKE OCHTEND. OVERAL!

АСТОН ВИЛЛА
Бирмингем, Англия

СТАДИОН

ОРД N.V. - ROTTERDAM

CONTROLE N. 020562
STADION FEIJENOORD

pacup v. Landskampioenen
AG 26 MEI 1982 - 20.15 UUR

ADION FEIJENOORD N.V. - ROTTERDAM

Finale Europacup v. Landskampioenen
WOENSDAG 26 MEI 1982 - 20.15 UUR

CONTROLE N. 020562
STADION FEIJENOORD

E    ZIJVAK-TRIBUNE

ZITPLAATS 1e RING

KONINKLIJKE
NEDERLANDSCHE
VOETBALBOND

26 MEI 1982
ROTTERDAM
UEFA

PRIJS f 40.--

EUROPE

ASTON VILLA v BAYERN MUNICH

**COLIN
GIBSON**
ASTON VILLA

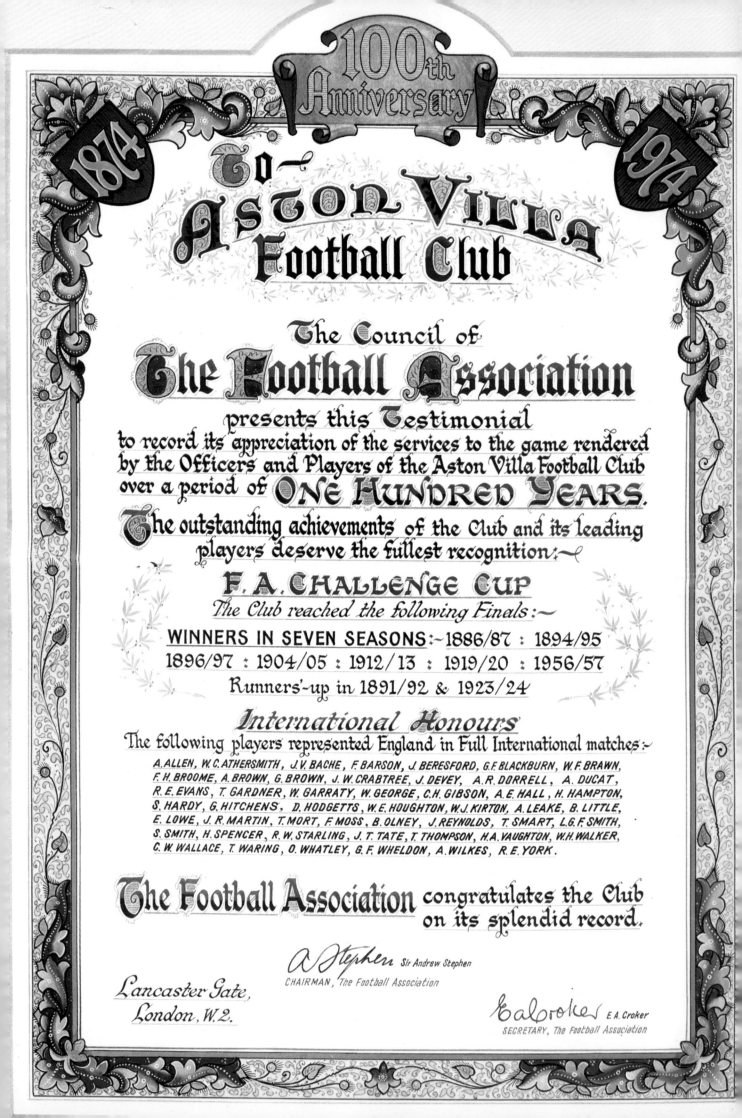

**100th Anniversary**

1874 — 1974

To

# ASTON VILLA
## Football Club

The Council of
## The Football Association
presents this Testimonial
to record its appreciation of the services to the game rendered
by the Officers and Players of the Aston Villa Football Club
over a period of ONE HUNDRED YEARS.
The outstanding achievements of the Club and its leading
players deserve the fullest recognition:—

### F.A. CHALLENGE CUP
The Club reached the following Finals:—

**WINNERS IN SEVEN SEASONS:—1886/87 : 1894/95
1896/97 : 1904/05 : 1912/13 : 1919/20 : 1956/57**
Runners'-up in 1891/92 & 1923/24

### International Honours
The following players represented England in Full International matches:—

A. ALLEN, W. C. ATHERSMITH, J. V. BACHE, F. BARSON, J. BERESFORD, G. F. BLACKBURN, W. F. BRAWN,
F. H. BROOME, A. BROWN, G. BROWN, J. W. CRABTREE, J. DEVEY, A. R. DORRELL, A. DUCAT,
R. E. EVANS, T. GARDNER, W. GARRATY, W. GEORGE, C. H. GIBSON, A. E. HALL, H. HAMPTON,
S. HARDY, G. HITCHENS, D. HODGETTS, W. E. HOUGHTON, W. J. KIRTON, A. LEAKE, B. LITTLE,
E. LOWE, J. R. MARTIN, T. MORT, F. MOSS, B. OLNEY, J. REYNOLDS, T. SMART, L. G. F. SMITH,
S. SMITH, H. SPENCER, R. W. STARLING, J. T. TATE, T. THOMPSON, H. A. VAUGHTON, W. H. WALKER,
C. W. WALLACE, T. WARING, O. WHATLEY, G. F. WHELDON, A. WILKES, R. E. YORK.

## The Football Association congratulates the Club
on its splendid record.

*A. Stephen* — Sir Andrew Stephen
CHAIRMAN, The Football Association

Lancaster Gate,
London, W.2.

*E. A. Croker* — E. A. Croker
SECRETARY, The Football Association

THE COMPLETE ENCYCLOPAEDIA OF ASTON VILLA F.C.       THE COMPLETE ENCYCLOPAEDIA OF ASTON VILLA F.C.

157

## KEOWN, MARTIN RAYMOND

Born: Oxford, 24 July 1966

Career: Arsenal (apprentice, June 1982, professional February 1984), Brighton & Hove Albion (on loan, February 1985), Aston Villa (£200,000, June 1986), Everton (£750,000, August 1989), Arsenal (£2 million, February 1993).

Aston Villa did good business in the transfer market when they sold central defender Martin Keown to Everton in 1989, making a profit of more than half-a-million pounds.... but should they have let him go?

When he joined the club from Arsenal in 1986, he had already made over 50 first-class appearances as a professional. He added 133 more to his tally (plus three goals) during his time at Villa Park, where he played alongside Paul Elliott, Steve Sims and Allan Evans, plus a few others.

Strong in the tackle, dominant in the air, a defender of the highest quality, he went on to greater things.

He starred in 126 senior games for Everton and after returning to Highbury he became an established England defender, going on to collect almost 40 senior caps (at 2001)....to go with those he had won earlier at Youth (4 games), Under-21 (8) and 'B' team levels.

With fellow 'Gunner' Tony Adams (and occasionally Steve Bould) he developed a fine club (and international) partnership in defence. He gained both Premiership and FA Cup winners' medals when Arsenal completed the double in 1998 and he has also collected two FA Charity Shield prizes. When the 2000-01 season ended, his record with Arsenal stood at 364 appearances and 8 goals.

## KERR, ALBERT WIGHAM

Born: Lancaster, County Durham, 11 August 1917. Died: Birmingham, May 1979.

Career: Lanchester RFC, Gateshead Colts, Medomsley Juniors (1935), Aston Villa (professional, July 1936). Retired in 1947 after having a steel plate inserted in his hip following a footballing injury. Guested for Charlton Athletic, Luton Town, Northampton Town, Plymouth Argyle, Portsmouth and Solihull Town during the Second World War when he also served with the Police

*Albert Kerr.*

Reserve, as well as playing for the Royal Navy in Inter-services matches and a Malta Select XI. He later ran a grocer's shop in Aston and attended as many games at Villa Park as he could.

An inspirational player at times, always willing, unfortunately outside-right Albert Kerr's footballing career was dogged by injury and illness. He scored four goals in his 29 senior games for Aston Villa, helping them win the Second Division title in 1938. As a guest he appeared in several Wartime fixtures with other teams.

## KERR, PAUL ANDREW

Born: Portsmouth, 9 June 1964.

Career: Aston Villa (apprentice June 1980, professional May 1982), Middlesbrough (January 1987), Millwall (March 1991), Port Vale (£140,000, July 1992), Leicester City (on loan, March 1994), Portsmouth (on trial, August 1994), Port Vale (September 1994), West Bromwich Albion (trialist), Wycombe Wanderers (non-contract, October 1995), Waterlooville, Whitby Town (player-coach).

A consistent marksman in Aston Villa's intermediate and reserve sides, Paul Kerr won a Birmingham Senior Cup winners' medal before transferring to Ayresome Park in 1987. He netted six times for Villa in 34 appearances. He went on to score 13 goals in 125 League games for 'Boro, notched 14 in 44 for Millwall, grabbed 20 in 84 first-team games for Port Vale, whom he helped win promotion from Division Two in 1994. He ended his career with a fine set of statistics: 62 goals in 339 club matches. A loss by Villa?

## KEYS CUP

Aston Villa won the Keys Cup in the Second World War season of 1941-42. They beat Worcester City 10-1 on aggregate (6-0 & 4-1) in the opening round before ousting Revo Electric (away) in the semi-final by 2-1. Hednesford Town were their opponents in the Final and Villa easily took the prize with a competent 5-0 victory at Solihull's ground in front of 1,200 spectators. Albert Kerr (3) and Billy Goffin (2) scored the goals.

## KIDDERMINSTER HARRIERS

No major competitive match action as yet between Aston Villa and the Harriers, who gained entry into the Football League in 2000.

Villa did, however, defeat the Harriers 10-1 in a Birmingham Senior Cup-tie on their way to winning throphy in 1891.

Players with both clubs include: J Baird, A Blair, M Blake, S Brock (Villa reserve), H Chapman, J Cumbes, AG Davies, G Garratt, TW Green, J Griffiths, L Hines (Villa reserve), GA Hitchens, T Jackson, GJW Jakeman, K Jones, KD Keelan, P King, WIG Kingdon, WJ Kirton, WH Maiden, E Malpass (Villa reserve), A Moss (Harriers player/coach), A Mulraney, DR Parsons, GA Shaw (Harriers trialist), H Vallance (Villa reserve), C Wilson (Villa reserve), J Woodward.

Also: JF Chambers & LGF Smith (Villa players, Harriers managers, Smith also a Harriers player)

## KIMBERLEY, WALTER JOHN

Born: Aston, Birmingham, May 1886. Died: France, May 1918.

Career: Gravelly Hill Schools, Tower Unity, Selly Oak St Mary's, Coldstream Guards, Aston Manor, Aston Villa (professional, July 1907), Coventry City (August 1912).

A hard-tackling defender, reserve to Alf Miles and George Tranter, Walter Kimberley had just seven senior games with Aston Villa and over 20 with Coventry City before losing his life after being wounded during the Battle of Marne. He died of TB due to ill-treatment in hospital.

## KING, PHILIP GEOFFREY

Born: Bristol, 28 December 1967.

Career: Exeter City (apprentice, January 1984, professional, January 1985), Torquay United (£3,000, July 1986), Swindon Town (£155,000, February 1987), Sheffield Wednesday (£400,000, November 1989), Notts County (on loan, October 1993), Aston Villa (£250,000, August 1994), West Bromwich Albion (on loan, November 1995), Swindon Town (free transfer, March 1997, later appointed player/coach), Brighton & Hove Albion (1998), Kidderminster Harriers (May 1999).

A competent, attacking left-back, Phil King accumulated almost 150 senior appearances for Swindon Town during his first spell at the club. He spent two-and-a-half years with Aston Villa and it was his vital spot-kick in the penalty shoot-out against Inter Milan that took Villa through to the second round of the UEFA Cup in September 1994. He became a 'forgotten player' at Villa Park and left after making only 23 appearances for the club. Capped once by England 'B', King gained a League Cup winners' medal with Wednesday in 1991.

THE COMPLETE ENCYCLOPAEDIA OF ASTON VILLA F.C.    THE COMPLETE ENCYCLOPAEDIA OF ASTON VILLA F.C.

158

## KINGABY, HERBERT CHARLES LAWRENCE JAMES

Born: London, August 1880. Died: London, 1957.

Career: West Hampstead FC, Clapton Orient (1903), Aston Villa (£400, March 1906), Fulham (May 1906), Leyton (July 1907-September 1910), Peterborough City (October 1910), Croydon Common (1914-15).

Nicknamed 'Rabbit' because of his speed, outside-right Charlie Kingaby scored Clapton Orient's first-ever League goal in September 1905. He stayed with Aston Villa for barely two months and made just four League appearances (all away from home in place of George Garratt) before leaving seemingly under a cloud regarding a transfer fee! He made almost 200 competitive appearances during his chequered career.

In 1912, a legal test case was heard in the King's Bench Division: Aston Villa v H.C.L.J. Kingaby. Kingaby stated that six years earlier (in 1906) he believed he was entitled to a percentage of a transfer fee. The hearing lasted half-a-day, the judgement went against the player, Villa won the case and were awarded costs as well!

## KINGDON, WILLIAM ISSACHER GARFIELD

Born: Worcester, 25 June 1905. Died: Weymouth, 18 March 1977.

Career: Kepex FC (Worcester Junior League), Kidderminster Harriers (1924), Aston Villa (amateur, August 1925, professional March 1926), Southampton (June 1936), Yeovil & Petters United (player/manager January 1938-May 1939), Weymouth (manager, 1950-60 and was also a hotelier in the Dorset town).

An England Junior International, capped v Scotland in April 1926, Billy Kingdon was a small, compact wing-half who wore his heart on his sleeve! A really forceful player, he displayed a neat line in distribution and was a great asset to the team after taking over from Charlie Johnstone on a regular basis during the 1926-27 campaign. He made 241 appearances for Aston Villa and scored five goals before going on to appear in 49 games for Saints. A carpenter by trade, Kingdon did very well as manager of non-League Weymouth whilst also running the Fountain Hotel in the town.

*Billy Kingdon*

## KING'S LYNN

Villa's record against the non-League side:

FA Cup

| Venue | P | W | D | L | F | A |
|-------|---|---|---|---|---|---|
| Home | 1 | 1 | 0 | 0 | 11 | 0 |

In a 1st round FA Cup-tie in January 1905, in front of 23,000 spectators, Villa easily accounted for the minnows of King's Lynn to the tune of 11-0. Charlie Millington (4), Albert Hall (3) and Bill Garraty (2) were the principal scorers. This is Villa's biggest victory in a competitive match at Villa Park.

## KINSEY, GEORGE

Born: Burton-on-Trent, 20 June 1866. Died: 10 January 1911.

Career: Burton Crusaders (1883), Burton Swifts (1885), Mitchell St George's (1888), Wolverhampton Wanderers (professional, July 1891), Aston Villa (£500, June 1894), Derby County (May 1895), Notts County (March 1897), Eastville (Bristol) Rovers (July 1897), Burton Swifts (seasons 1902-04), Burton Early Closing FC (1904-06, after being reinstated as an amateur). Retired to become a publican in Burton.

Left-half George Kinsey had his best playing days with Wolverhampton

Wanderers, gaining an FA Cup winners' medal and playing twice for England. He had spent eight years in non-League football before becoming a professional at Molineux in 1891. He was a dominating figure on the field, and had a magnificent game for Wolves in the 1893 FA Cup Final against Everton before being transferred to Aston Villa the following year. Unfortunately and perhaps surprisingly, the move to Villa did not work out for Kinsey and after making just three first team appearances (in place of George Russell) he was off again, this time to Derby. He was an ever-present in his first season with the Rams who were spending their first campaign at the Baseball Ground, and at the end of 1895-96 he gained a League championship runners-up medal, having also appeared in another FA Cup semi-final against his old club, Wolves. Kinsey played twice more for England and after a short spell with Notts County, he helped establish Bristol Rovers (who were then Eastville Rovers of the Bristol & District League) in the Southern League.

## KIRTON, WILLIAM JOHN

Born: Newcastle, 2 December 1896. Died: Hartopp Nursing Home, Sutton Coldfield, 27 September 1970.

Career: Todd's Nook School (North Shields), Pandon Temperance FC (1917), Leeds City (May 1919), Aston Villa (£500, October 1919), Coventry City (September 1928), Kidderminster Harriers (September-October 1930), Leamington Town (November 1930). Retired in July 1931 and later ran a tobacconist/newsagents shop in Kingstanding, Birmingham. A teetotaller and non-smoker, Billy Kirton was also a very fine golfer and got down to a handicap of eight.

*Billy Kirton*

As a footballer, he was a strongly built, gifted inside-forward who was at his best when going full tilt at defenders, running with the ball close to his feet. It took an awful lot to disposses him when in sight of goal. He teamed up superbly well with Clem Stephenson and Billy Walker and then with Billy Dickson and Walker, later with Len Capewell and Dicky York. He lost his place in the team in 1927 after scoring 59 times in 261 first-class appearances for Villa over a period of nine years. Kirton gained an FA Cup winners' medal in 1920 and a losers' prize in 1924, and three years earlier he had scored in his only international match for England against Ireland in October 1921.

## KUBICKI, DARIUSZ

Born: Warsaw, Poland, 6 June 1963

Career: Mielec FC, Zastra FC, Legia Warsaw (August 1988), Aston Villa (£200,000, August 1991), Sunderland £100,000, March 1994), Wolverhampton Wanderers (August 1997-May 1998), Tranmere Rovers (on loan, March 1998), Carlisle United (free transfer, July 1998), Darlington (October 1998). Returned home to Poland in December 1999 after ending his studies at Sunderland University.

Full-back Dariusz Kubicki was one of Ron Atkinson's first signings after taking over as manager of Aston Villa in July 1991. Already an established and experienced Polish international, Kubicki was fast approaching the personal milestone of 50 full caps for his country and was relishing the thought of performing in the top flight of British football. He had an excellent first season with Villa, appearing in 31 senior games before losing his place in the side (late on) to Earl Barrett. After failing to regain the right-back berth, Kubicki switched his allegiance to Roker Park, leaving Villa on the transfer deadline of 1994.

He did very well with Sunderland, amassing over 150 senior

THE COMPLETE ENCYCLOPAEDIA OF ASTON VILLA F.C.          THE COMPLETE ENCYCLOPAEDIA OF ASTON VILLA F.C.

159

appearances and helping them climb into the Premiership. He was then released after relegation was suffered in 1997. He quickly found his way to Molineux but never really settled with Wolves and after a loan spell with Tranmere Rovers in March 1998 he was released at the end of that season. He terminated his Football League career at Darlington having appeared in a total of 218 competitive matches (34 with Villa) during his nine years in England .

### KYLE, PETER
Born: Rutherglen, Glasgow, September 1878. Died: c 1961.
Career: Glasgow & District Schools, Glasgow Parkhead (1896), Partick Thistle, Clyde (trialist), Liverpool (July 1899), Leicester Fosse (May 1900), Wellingborough, West Ham United (November 1902), Kettering Town, Heart of Midlothian (trialist), Larkhall Thistle (February 1904), Port Glasgow Athletic (July 1904), Tottenham Hotspur (July 1905), Woolwich Arsenal (April 1906), Aston Villa (March 1908), Sheffield United (October 1908), Royal Albert (July 1909), Watford (November 1909-May 1910). Returned to Scotland before the Great War.
Peter Kyle was a dangerous centre-forward with an eye for goal. He had a nomadic career in the game, travelling all over Britain. He participated at various levels with 17 different clubs and made well over 200 League and Cup appearances, scoring more than 40 goals.

*Peter Kyle*

Kyle could be somewhat temperamental at times and was suspended by Spurs for a breach of club rules in March 1906 (he never played for the London club again). A Scottish international trialist, his last game for Arsenal was against Aston Villa - next month he moved from the Gunners to Villa Park! He scored 19 goals in 41 games for Spurs, 22 in 60 for Arsenal but only played five times for Villa after failing to settle in Birmingham.
• There is no firm evidence that this Peter Kyle did assist all the clubs listed above as there was another Scottish-born player bearing the same name and desription around at the same time (possibly related). However, I have listed all the clubs who did have a Peter Kyle (forward) registered with them between 1896 and 1910.

### LAIDLAW, JOHN WALLACE
Born: Muirkirk, Kilmarnock, December 1891. Died: Scotland, July 1954.
Career: Muirkirk Athletic, Kilmarniock (briefly), South Shields (October 1913), Aston Villa (December 1913), Kilmarnock (June 1914-May 1915).
A nippy little player, able to perform in all three inner forward positions but he only made two appearances for Aston Villa after failing to settle in the industrial city of Birmingham!

### LAMPTEY, NIL ODARTEY
Born: Accra, Ghana, 10 December 1974.
Career: Accra Union FC (Ghana), PSV Eindhoven (Netherlands), RSC Anderlecht, Aston Villa (£1 million, August 1994), Coventry City (August 1995). Left Highfield Road in the summer of 1997 after failing to obtain a work permit (due to insufficient games at competitive level).
A striker, rarely given a chance by Aston Villa, Nil Lamptey scored three goals (all in the League Cup) in nine first team appearances for the club.

When he left British football in 1998 Lamptey had won 21 full international caps for his country. He was a member of Ghanaian team that competed in the African Nations Cup in 1996 but suffered in the indignity of being sent-off in the semi-final.
Before he had reached the age of 16, Lamptey had already made a sensational start to his League career in Belgium, scoring in each of his four games. Then, in a UEFA Cup-tie on 20 March 1991, his 82nd minute goal for Anderlecht against AS Roma made him the youngest marksman ever in any major European Cup competition.

### LAW, SAMUEL RICHARD
Born: Handsworth, Birmingham, January 1850. Died: Birmingham, August 1920.
Career: Aston Hall School, Aston Unity (1873), Aston Villa (August 1878). Retired through injury, summer of 1882.
Brother of Tom (a Villa reserve) and nephew of Alfred Law, the 1890s Warwickshire cricketer, Sammy Law was nicknamed 'Mutton Chops' by his collagues, because of his heavy, drooping moustache and long side-burns. A tough-tackling half-back, he scored once in 10 FA Cup games for Villa and he also played cricket for the Warwickshire Club & Ground.

### LAWRENCE, JAMES
Born: Earlstown, June 1892. Died: Nuneaton, April 1937.
Career: Earlstown Boys Club, Earlstown FC, served in the Army during World War One (from 1914), Aston Villa (WWI guest, then professional, May 1918), Coventry City (June 1920). Retired through injury, June 1925.
A hardy defender, Jimmy Lawrence deputised in 14 first-class matches for Tommy Weston at full-back during the 1919-20 season and was named among the reserves for the FA Cup Final before his departure to Highfield Road. He made 136 senior appearances for the Sky Blues (2 goals scored).

### LAYTON, ARTHUR EDMUND
Born: Durham, February 1885. Died: Durham, 1959.
Career: Durham & District Schhols, Royston United, Sheffield United (trialist), South Kirby, Rotherham Town (trialist), Aston Villa (January 1908), Middlesbrough (September 1911), Cardiff City (September 1914), Stockport County (December 1920-April 1923). Retired.
A former Durham miner, right or left-back Arthur Layton made 17 first team appearances for Aston Villa. A worthy competitor, he possessed a hefty challenge and acted as a diligent deputy for Tommy Lyons. Became surplus to requirements when Tom Weston joined Lyons and Alf Miles to contest the full-back position.
Layton was with Cardiff when the Welsh club gained entry into the Football League in 1919. He made almost 70 appearances for the Bluebirds and had 61 first team games for Stockport, gaining a Third Division (North) championship medal in 1922.

*Jim Leach*

### LEACH, JAMES M.
Born: Spennymoor, County Durham, July 1890.
Career: Durham & District Schools, Newcastle St Wilfred's (1908), Spennymoor United (1910), Black & White FC in the Tyneside League (1911), Aston Villa (August 1912), Queen's Park Rangers (July 1922).
An elegant wing-half, Jim Leach was also brainy, witty and confident on the ball, always having plenty of time to assess the situation before him. After

THE COMPLETE ENCYCLOPAEDIA OF ASTON VILLA F.C.   THE COMPLETE ENCYCLOPAEDIA OF ASTON VILLA F.C.

160

gaining a winners' medal in the FA Cup Final and a runners-up prize in the Football League championship with Aston Villa in 1913, injury forced Leach to miss the whole of the first season after the Great War. Consequently he had to sit and watch Villa record another FA Cup Final victory over Huddersfield Town in 1920. He went on to appear in 78 first-class games for the club and scored three goals before ending his career in London with QPR.

## LEAKE, ALEXANDER

*Alex Leake*

Born: Small Heath, Birmingham, 11 July 1871. Died: Birmingham 29 March 1938.
Career: Jenkins Street & Green Lane Schools (Bordesley Green), Hoskins & Sewell FC, Kings Heath Albion, Saltley Gas Works FC, Singers, Hoskins & Sewell (again), Old Hill Wanderers, Small Heath Alliance (now Birmingham City, July 1894), Aston Villa (June 1902), Burnley (December 1907-May 1910), Wednesbury Old Athletic (July 1910). Retired as a player in May 1912. Crystal Palace (trainer/coach, July 1912-May 1915), Merthyr Town (trainer/coach, October 1919-July 1920). Later Walsall trainer (from September 1932-May 1933).
Football to Alex Leake was a pleasure! He often cracked a joke with an opponent while robbing him of the ball and regularly burst out laughing just before a corner kick was being taken. He was a genuine 'Brummagem Button', a good humoured, easy-going defender whose temperament was second to none. A determined, honest worker, tireless to the extreme, his stamina was unsurpassed. He never played to the gallery, always battling for his team; he never shirked a tackle and gave 110 per-cent effort every time he took the field. He was as safe as houses, never dallied on the ball and often came out best in the 50-50 challenges.
He went on to score 23 goals in 221 games in eight years with Blues (the last six as captain) before leaving Muntz Street for Villa Park in the summer of 1902. Three years later he starred for Villa when they won the FA Cup and during his five seasons with the club he netted nine times in 140 senior games. During his two-and-a-half years with Burnley, he played in 90 League and Cup matches (most of them as skipper). He quit League soccer in May 1910, having scored 34 goals in 464 senior appearances at club level. He returned to the Midlands at that point and assisted Wednesbury Old Athletic (briefly) before taking up a coaching position with Crystal Palace, holding a similar post at Merthyr Town before the upheaval of the First World War. After the hostilities Leake attempted to pass on some of his vast knowledge of football by coaching at several Council Schools and colleges in the Birmingham area.
With his dapper moustache and well-groomed hair, Leake won five full caps for England and also represented the Football League XI. He was actually chosen as a 'stand-by' reserve for his country in 1912 when coaching at Palace. He was fast-approaching his 41st birthday at the time.
Besides being a fine footballer, Leake was also a very good swimmer and often dived to the bottom of the brine baths at Droitwich to retrieve a coin!
He was very useful on the athletics track as well, specialising in the 400 yards and hurdles events, and was a keen gardener despite being a blacksmith by trade! The original 'Clown Prince of Soccer' Alec Leake was the humorist in the dressing room, the comedian in the pack, a real joker.
His cousin, Jimmy Windridge, also played for Birmingham. Ex-Villa

player Charlie Johnstone was headmaster of Jenkins Street School when Leake was a pupil there in 1880.

## LEE, EDWARD BOTTERILL
Born: Harborne, Birmingham, April 1857. Died: South Africa, August 1903.
Career: Lordswood Council & Aston Manor Schools, Aston Villa (1874-75 season, founder-member). Retired due to ill-health, April 1883. Emigrated to South Africa.
Ted Lee was a smart player, hard but fair, who lined up as a half-back in 11 FA Cup matches for Aston Villa during the club's early years.

## LEE, GORDON FRANCIS
Born: Pye Green near Hednesford, 13 July 1934.
Career: Littleworth School, Girton Road Gasworks FC, Hednesford Town (1951), National Servcie in the RAF, Aston Villa (professional, October 1955), Shrewsbury Town (player-coach, July 1966), Port Vale (manager, May 1968-January 1974), Blackburn Rovers (manager, January 1974-June 1975), Newcastle United (manager, June 1975-February 1977), Everton (manager, February 1977-May 1981), Preston North End (manager, December 1981-December 1983), KR Reykjavik, Iceland (manager/coach, mid-1980s). Coached briefly in the Middle East, Saudi Arabia (1985-87), Leicester City (coach, January 1988, then assistant-manager at Filbert Street and later caretaker-manager, January-May 1991). Thereafter acted as a Scout for several League clubs.
Gordon Lee scored two goals in 142 senior games for Aston Villa. A resourceful defender, able to play in a variety of positions, he was recommended to the club by Hednesford manager, Jackie Martin who in fact had been Lee's schoolteacher some years earlier and had himself starred for Villa as a forward. Lee played in both the 1961 and 1963 League Cup Finals, collecting a winners' prize in the former.
After surveying the scene as coach under Arthur Rowley at Shrewsbury, Lee hit the rocky road of club management in the Potteries. He won a hard-earned reputation as a soccer troubleshooter at Vale Park and Ewood Park before being enticed by bigger clubs in the First Division.
He never paid more than £5,000 for a player before guiding Vale to the Fourth Division championship in 1970. He then led Blackburn to Third Division glory in 1975 and over the next two years saw both Newcastle and Everton lose League Cup Finals, the latter to his former club Villa in 1977. He was on £20,000 per-annum at Goodison Park (big money for a boss in those days) but he found it difficult to handle certain players on Merseyside and with the Board of Directors continually at his throat he was sacked at the end of the 1980-81 season. He had some success as a coach in Iceland and the Middle East before spending some time with Leicester. He kept them out of the Second Division as caretaker-boss in 1991 but lost his job for his efforts! Such is football. Lee now resides in Lytham St Anne's.

## LEE, JAMES THOMAS
Born: Brierley Hill, 12 April 1892. Died: Dudley, c 1955.
Career: Cradley Heath St Luke's, Wulfurians (1915), wartime service, Aston Villa (March 1919), Stoke (£750, August 1921), Macclesfield Town (1923). Retired cs 1924.
Sam Hardy's deputy during his short stay at Villa Park, goalkeeper Jim Lee often relied on his long legs stopping the ball rather than using his hands! He was nevertheless a good positional 'keeper who made 18 senior appearances for Villa and followed up with 24 for the Potters before having a season with Macclesfield Town

## LEEDS CITY
No match action between the clubs.
Aston Villa signed two players - John Hampson for £1,000 and Billy

THE COMPLETE ENCYCLOPAEDIA OF ASTON VILLA F.C.        THE COMPLETE ENCYCLOPAEDIA OF ASTON VILLA F.C.

161

Kirton for £500 - from Leeds City in October 1919 and soon after George Stephenson was acquired.

The Yorkshire club was expelled from the Football League after playing just eight Second Division matches at the start of the 1919-20 season. Other players with both clubs include: FD Mann, IH Price, J Whitley, TC Wilson.

## LEEDS UNITED
Villa's playing record against United:

Football League/Premiership

| Venue | P | W | D | L | F | A |
|---|---|---|---|---|---|---|
| Home | 37 | 18 | 10 | 9 | 61 | 44 |
| Away | 37 | 8 | 13 | 16 | 36 | 59 |
| Totals | 74 | 26 | 23 | 25 | 97 | 103 |

FA Cup

| | P | W | D | L | F | A |
|---|---|---|---|---|---|---|
| Home | 3 | 3 | 0 | 0 | 8 | 3 |
| Away | 1 | 1 | 0 | 0 | 2 | 1 |
| Totals | 4 | 4 | 0 | 0 | 10 | 4 |

League Cup

| | P | W | D | L | F | A |
|---|---|---|---|---|---|---|
| Home | 2 | 1 | 1 | 0 | 2 | 1 |
| Away | 6 | 4 | 0 | 2 | 12 | 10 |
| Neutral | 1 | 1 | 0 | 0 | 3 | 0 |
| Totals | 9 | 6 | 1 | 2 | 17 | 11 |

Zenith Data Systems Cup

| | P | W | D | L | F | A |
|---|---|---|---|---|---|---|
| Home | 1 | 1 | 0 | 0 | 2 | 0 |

Aston Villa lost 6-0 in their first League game against Leeds at Elland Road on Christmas Day 1924, but 24 hours later they won the return fixture 2-1 at Villa Park.

It was honours even in 1926-27 as Villa won 5-1 at home only to lose 3-1 at Leeds.

Eric Houghton, making his League debut, missed a penalty for Villa against Leeds at home on 4 January 1930 (saved by goalkeeper Jimmy Potts). Villa lost the game 4-3!

Earlier that season Villa had crashed 4-1 at Elland Road.

Villa doubled up over Leeds in 1933-34, winning 4-2 (away) and 3-0 (home). Dai Astley netted a hat-trick in the latter match which was attended by under 10,000 spectators.

There were six goals scored in each of the two League games between Villa and Leeds in 1935-36. United won 4-2 at Elland Road whilst the clash at Villa Park ended all square at 3-3.

Villa started their charge towards winning the League championship in 1980-81 with a 2-1 opening day home victory over Leeds (Tony Morley and Gary Shaw the scorers).

Villa were well beaten to the tune of 4-1 at home by relegation-threatened Leeds in April 1982 and after joining the Elland Road side in the Second Division, the next time they met United again was on 10 October 1987, Villa winning 3-1 in Yorkshire.

Leeds pulverised Villa to the tune of 5-2 at Elland Road in May 1991 as they claimed fourth place in the League championship. When United captured the title the following season they won 4-1 at Villa Park (Lee Chapman scored his 50th goal for Leeds in this game whilst Nigel Spink saved Gordon Strachan's penalty) but were held 0-0 at Elland Road.

Villa's first home game in the Premiership saw them draw 1-1 with Leeds on 19 August 1992.

Mark Bosnich was sent-off at Leeds on 29 April 1995 as Villa lost 1-0 to remain in relegation trouble.

Gareth Southgate scored in successive away Premiership games at Elland Road, helping Villa defeat United on their own patch by identical scores of 2-1 in January and December 2000.

A Villa Park crowd of 51,000 saw Len Capewell strike twice as Villa

*Leeds' goalkeeper David Harvey collects a high ball during the League Cup-tie at Villa Park in October 1972.*

knocked Leeds out of the FA Cup in a 3rd round tie in January 1924. Andy Gray and Alan McInally were on target in Villa's excellent 2-1 win at Elland Road in the 3rd in January 1988 and the Italian Benito Carbone grabbed a superb hat-trick as Villa won a televised 5th round encounter in January 2000.

In January 1991, Leeds eliminated Villa from the League Cup with a 4-1 home win, Lee Chapman (son of a former Villa player) leading from the front with a couple of goals.

Villa defeated Leeds 3-0 in the 1996 League Cup Final at Wembley where the Yugoslav Savo Milosevic scored a quite stunning goal. The following season Villa rubbed salt into the Elland Road club's wounds by knocking them out of the same competition in the 3rd round (2-1).

The ZDSC tie at Villa Park in 1989-90 attracted over 11,500 fans.

Villa celebrated their Centenary with a home friendly game against Leeds in August 1974 when almost 29,500 fans saw the visitors win 2-1. Ray Graydon missed two penalties for Villa.

Players with both clubs include: NGL Blake, G Brown, MR Day, AR Dorigo, S Grayson, SB Hodge, G Hodgson, B Little (United trialist), RW McDonald, CJ Martin, FJ O'Donnell (United WW2 guest), B Ormsby, G Sellars, GT Stephenson (Leeds reserve), J Whitley, G Williams.

Also: FC Buckley and G Graham (Villa players, United managers), AET Haynes (Villa player, United scout), IV Powell (Villa player, United trainer-coach), J Burridge (Villa 'keeper, United part-time coach).

## LEICESTER CITY (FOSSE)
Villa's playing record against Leicester:

Football League/Premiership

| Venue | P | W | D | L | F | A |
|---|---|---|---|---|---|---|
| Home | 39 | 18 | 9 | 12 | 80 | 60 |
| Away | 39 | 6 | 11 | 22 | 51 | 94 |
| Totals | 78 | 24 | 20 | 34 | 131 | 154 |

FA Cup

| | P | W | D | L | F | A |
|---|---|---|---|---|---|---|
| Home | 3 | 1 | 0 | 2 | 7 | 5 |
| Away | 1 | 1 | 0 | 0 | 1 | 0 |
| Totals | 4 | 2 | 0 | 2 | 8 | 5 |

| League Cup | | | | | | |
|---|---|---|---|---|---|---|
| Home | 2 | 1 | 1 | 0 | 2 | 0 |
| Away | 2 | 0 | 1 | 1 | 0 | 1 |
| Totals | 4 | 1 | 2 | 1 | 2 | 1 |
| | | | | | | |
| Wartime | | | | | | |
| Home | 5 | 5 | 0 | 0 | 22 | 5 |
| Away | 5 | 4 | 0 | 1 | 12 | 5 |
| Totals | 10 | 9 | 0 | 1 | 34 | 10 |

*Leicester 'keeper Mark Wallington beats Frank Carrodus to a cross - September 1976.*

Season 1908-09 saw Aston Villa and Leicester (Fosse) meet for the first time at League level. It was all-square at 1-1 on Villa soil, while the Foxes (battling unsuccessfully to avoid relegation) raced to a convincing 4-2 victory in Leicester, despite two spanking goals by Villa's Joey Walters.

It wasn't until 1925-26 that the teams faced each other again. Villa won 2-1 at Filbert Street, but were held to a 2-2 draw on home ground.

Arthur Chandler scored the first of his three hat-tricks for the Foxes against Villa in November 1926 (5-1). He followed up with trebles in February 1930 (4-3) and September 1934 (5-0).

Eleven goals were scored in the two League games between Villa and City in 1928-29. It was 4-1 to the Foxes at Filbert Street and 4-2 to Villa on their own patch.

Villa have defeated Leicester City 8-3 in a League game twice - at Filbert Street in January 1932 and at Villa Park in April 1962. George Brown scored five times in the 1932 game whilst Bobby Thomson netted a hat-trick at Villa Park 30 years later when a certain Gordon Banks was between the posts for the Foxes.

It was tit-for-tat in season 1934-35 when both Villa and City won their respective home game against each other with a 5-0 scoreline. Dai Astley notched a hat-trick in Villa's victory, whilst Chandler (see earlier) did likewise for City.

In 1954-55, after Leicester had won promotion, their two League games with Villa produced 13 goals, City winning 5-2 (away) and 4-2 (home). Then, by coincidence in 1957-58, the two First Division tussles

provided the fans with another 13 goals - Villa winning 5-1 at home but losing 6-1 at Filbert Street.

City's Derek Hines scored four goals as Villa crashed 6-3 at Filbert Street in November 1958 (at half-time Villa led 3-1).

City crushed Villa 5-0 at Filbert Street in September 1966 and duly completed the double with a 1-0 win at Villa Park early in February.

In the League game at Filbert Street in April 1970, Villa had a goal ruled out although the ball went over the line...it actually struck the stanchion holding up the netting, but the referee and linesman both agreed (at the time) that it had struck the woodwork. Villa lost the game 0-1.

Villa were 4-1 up on Leicester in a Premiership game in February 1995 but were clawed back to 4-4 after the Foxes scored three times in the last 13 minutes, David Lowe bagging their equaliser deep into stoppage time. This was Villa's eighth 4-4 draw in League football and the attendance was almost 31,000.

When Villa beat City 2-1 in a home Premiership match in April 2001, it was their first major victory over the Filbert Street club since 1988.

Joe Bache scored twice in Villa's convincing 5-1 FA Cup win over the Foxes in February 1905 whilst Andy Gray's effort was enough to see Villa come through a difficult 3rd round tie at Filbert Street in January 1977. Leicester won 2-1 at Villa Park in a 4th Round tie in 2001.

Leicester beat Villa 1-0 on aggregate in the League Cup semi-final of 1999-2000. After a 0-0 draw at Villa Park, the Foxes went through to Wembley with a goal by Matt Elliott in the second leg at Filbert Street.

Villa beat Leicester 5-0 and 7-2 in successive home Wartime games in December 1944 and April 1945. Eric Houghton scored a hat-trick in both matches.

On 17 November 1994 Leicester City Chairman Martin George announced that it would cost Aston Villa £1.5m in compensation should they wish to take Brian Little and his two assistants from Filbert Street to Villa Park. Little became Villa manager a week later!

Players with both clubs include: B Anstey, J Baird, M Blake, R Boyne (City WW1), J Brown, RAJ Brown (City WW2 guest), JH Browne (Villa reserve), F Carr, GA Charles, WA Cobley (City WW2 guest), SV Collymore, W Dorrell, AD Dougan, M Draper, H Edgley & GR Edwards (City WW2 guests), A Evans (also City assistant-manager/coach), G Fenton, W Garraty, CJ Gibson, DW Gibson, WC Goffin (City WW2 guest), R Gordon, S Grayson, JC Harrison, the trio of F Haycock, WE Houghton & RJ Iverson (all City WW2 guests), J Joachim, JH Joyce (Leicester WW1 guest), P Kerr, P Kyle, A Lochhead, C Millington (Leicester WW1 guest), M Moralee, JH Morby (City WW2 guest), R Noble (Villa reserve), I Ormondroyd, GS Parker, K Poole, J Roxborough, S Sims, DF Skea, LGF Smith (City WW2 guest), JE Travers, AE Watkins

Also: B Little (Villa player & manager, City manager), JC Gregory (Villa player & manager, City coach), GF Lee (Villa player, City coach/assistant-manager & caretaker-manager), K Macdonald (City player, Villa coach), CH Spiers (Villa player, City scout), SK Hunt (Villa player, Leicester coach), R Shaw (Villa trainer/physio, City scout), M Musgrove (coach at both clubs), Alan Bennett (secretary of both clubs).

## LEIGH, WALTER HERBERT

Born: Yardley, Birmingham, November 1874. Died: 1938.

Career: Hall Green School, Calishead amateurs, Aston Villa (August 1898-April 1899), Altrincham (July 1899), Runcorn (1901).

Well-built amateur centre-forward who appeared in one League game for Aston Villa, in the 1-1 draw at Everton on 15 April 1899, when he deputised for Jack Devey. He was a seasonal trialist with the club at the time. He failed to make the grade and retained his Amateur status when moving north to work in a laboratory.

## LEONARD, KEITH ANDREW

Born: Birmingham, 10 November 1950

Career: West Bromwich Albion (trialist, 1965), Kidderminster Harriers (1966), Darlaston (1967), Highgate United (1968), Aston Villa (trialist, March 1972, professional April 1972), Port Vale (on loan, November 1979-February 1974). Forced to retire at the age of 24 through injury, suffered while playing for Villa against Arsenal in September 1975. Later became coach at Villa Park (1975-77), Birmingham City (1982-86) and West Bromwich Albion (1986-87), while also acting as assistant-manager to Ron Saunders at both St Andrew's and The Hawthorns. Was rewarded with a Testimonial Match (by Villa) and after his footballing days were over he ran a post office at Shirley. He now lives in Solihull.

Keith Leonard was a burly striker who acted as the perfect foil to Brian Little after taking over from Sammy Morgan as leader of the attack. An uncompromising player, he helped Villa win the League Cup and promotion from the Second Division in 1975, and prior to his career-ending injury against the Gunners, he had suffered a double fracture of the same leg in a road accident in December 1972. Leonard scored 17 goals in 46 outings for Villa.

## LEYTON ORIENT (CLAPTON ORIENT & ORIENT)

Villa's playing record against Orient:

Football League

| Venue | P | W | D | L | F | A |
|---|---|---|---|---|---|---|
| Home | 5 | 4 | 1 | 0 | 8 | 3 |
| Away | 5 | 1 | 2 | 2 | 3 | 6 |
| Totals | 10 | 5 | 3 | 2 | 11 | 9 |

FA Cup

| Venue | P | W | D | L | F | A |
|---|---|---|---|---|---|---|
| Home | 1 | 0 | 1 | 0 | 0 | 0 |
| Away | 1 | 1 | 0 | 0 | 8 | 0 |
| Totals | 2 | 1 | 1 | 0 | 8 | 0 |

Aston Villa and Orient first met at League level in 1962-63 (Division 1). Harry Burrows' goal gave Villa a 1-0 home victory whilst Phil Woosnam and Ron Wylie netted at Brisbane Road as Villa doubled up with a 2-0 win.

In February 1973 Villa returned to Orient and crashed 4-0 in a Second Division game.

On 26 January 1929, Villa (lying third in Division 1) were held to a 0-0 draw by Clapton Orient (rock bottom of Division 2) in a 4th round FA Cup-tie at Villa Park in front of 53,086 fans. Four days later at Orient's Millfields ground, a crowd of over 27,500 saw Villa win the replay 8-0 with 'Pongo' Waring netting his first Cup hat-trick for the club.

Players with Orient/Clapton include: J Boden, G Charles (Orient trialist), RJ Codling, MR Day, T Ford (Orient WW2 guest), G ('H') Gregory, AJ Halse (Orient Amateur and WW1 guest), SB Hodge, W Leigh, A Mulraney (Orient WW2 guest), JR Nicholson, MJ Pinner, L Sealey, AE Surtees, OE Tidman, FC Tully, PA Woosnam.

Also: M Musgrove & DJ Sexton (Orient players, Villa coaches, Sexton also managed the 'Os'), B Whitehouse (Orient player, Villa scout).

The following all played for Villa and Leyton FC: CL Aston, JA Gray, HCL Kingaby, WT Renneville, LF Skiller, JT Wootten

## LESCOTT, AARON ANTHONY

Born: Birmingham, 2 December 1978.

Career: Aston Villa (YTS, June 1995, professional, July 1996), Lincoln City (on loan, March-April 2000), Sheffield Wednesday (£100,000, October 2000).

The versatile Aaron Lescott was unable to gain a first team place at Villa Park, making just one substitute appearance, in the FA Cup-tie against Hull City (h) in January 1999. However, he quickly made his mark with the Owls after his transfer to Hillsborough three months into the 2000-01 season.

## LILLIS, MARK ANTHONY

Born: Manchester, 17 January 1960

Career: Manchester & District Schools football, Lancashire County Youths, Manchester City (juniors, 1976-77), Huddersfield Town (professional July 1978), Manchester City (£150,000, June 1985), Derby County (£100,000 plus player, August 1986), Aston Villa (£130,000, September 1987), Scunthorpe United (£40,000, September 1989), Stockport County (September 1991-May 1992), various coaching positions (1993-98), Halifax Town (manager, June 1999-September 2000).

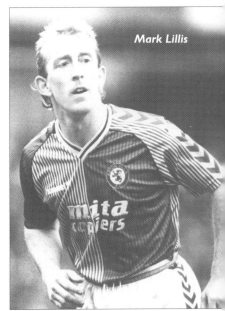

*Mark Lillis*

An attacking midfielder, strong and willing, Mark Lillis was a prolific marksman from centre-field with Huddersfield, scoring 62 goals in 142 outings before going on to net 15 times in 51 appearances for Manchester City. He failed to impress at Derby and notched four goals in his 39 games for Aston Villa as they gained promotion from the Second Division in 1988. Lillis had earlier helped Huddersfield climb out of the Fourth and Third Divisions in 1980 and 1983 respectively. He didn't have much success as manager at The Shay.

## LIMITED COMPANY

Aston Villa Football Club first became a Limited Company in January 1896. Over the next 25 years interest within the club gained rapidly and in 1921 the registered share capital of the club stood at £10,000. Villa became a Public Limited Company in 1969.

• Percy Harper, President of the Aston Villa Shareholders' Association in the 1960s, was the referee who allowed the controversial 'ball over the line' goal to stand when Newcastle United defeated Arsenal 2-1 in the 1932 FA Cup Final.

## LINCOLN CITY

Villa's playing record against the Imps

Football League

| Venue | P | W | D | L | F | A |
|---|---|---|---|---|---|---|
| Home | 1 | 0 | 1 | 0 | 1 | 1 |
| Away | 1 | 0 | 1 | 0 | 0 | 0 |
| Totals | 2 | 0 | 2 | 0 | 1 | 1 |

The two Football League games were played in season 1959-60 (Division 2). Almost 14,000 fans saw the goalless draw at Sincil Bank and there were 33,868 present to see the Imps battle to gain a point in the return fixture, Bobby Thomson netting for Villa.

Players with both clubs include: KB Barrett, J Burridge, L Butler, RC Chapman (Imps player-manager), A Campbell, WA Dinsdale, J Fashanu, K Fencott, J Fleming, W Garraty, CH Gibson, DT Hughes, RTJ Iverson, GH Lawrence (Villa trialist), AA Lescott, FJ O'Donnell (Imps WW2 guest), GS Parker, SF Sims (Imps trialist), CC Withers.

THE COMPLETE ENCYCLOPAEDIA OF ASTON VILLA F.C.

THE COMPLETE ENCYCLOPAEDIA OF ASTON VILLA F.C.

164

Also: G Taylor (Imps player, coach and manager & Villa manager), HV Henshall (Villa player, Imps manager), H Green (Villa player, City assistant-manager), J Ward (City player, Villa coach).

## LINDON, ALBERT EDWARD

Born: Aston, 24 January 1891. Died: Dowlais, Wales, 1 October 1976.
Career: Aston Hall Schools, Birmingham Fruiterers FC (1905-06), Delta Metals Works FC (1907), Birmingham (June 1910), Aston Villa (£750, August 1911), Barnsley (briefly 1912-13 season), Coventry City (£1,000, March 1918), Merthyr Town (August 1920, then player/manager August 1924-January 1928), Charlton Athletic (as a player in December 1927, player/manager January-May 1928, player/coach & assistant-manager June 1928-December 1932, retired as a player in 1931, caretaker-manager December 1932-May 1933, assistant-manager again, May 1933-March 1934), Arsenal scout September 1947-December 1949), Cardiff City (scout, January 1950, later assistant-manager), Merthyr Tydfil (manager June 1957-May 1959 & August-November 1959), Swindon Town (scout July 1960), Newport County (scout, October 1961 until his death in 1976).

Albert Lindon's career in major competitive football spanned 66 years (1910-76) during which time he was a player, coach assistant-manager, caretaker-manager, manager and scout. A competent goalkeeper, he gained a Welsh Cup runners-up medal with Merthyr in 1924, a Third Division (South) championship medal with Charlton in 1929, Birmingham Senior Cup and League medals while at Villa Park and was selected for the Welsh League XI v the Irish League in 1927, but his club (Merthyr) would not release him! He made just one first team appearance for Villa (v Tottenham Hotspur in March 1912) and before retiring as a player he appeared in a further 325 League and Cup games for his other main clubs (234 for Merthyr). A much respected man by his fellow professionals, club managers and directors (even supporters) alike, Lindon was an excellent judge of a player and it was he who 'found' Dai Astley (for Charlton). He was manager of Merthyr when they twice had to seek re-election to the Football League and was in charge of Charlton when they were relegated from the Second Division in 1933. Lindon also goes into the record books as being one of the heaviest players to serve Aston Villa (16 stone).

## LINTON, IVOR

Born: West Bromwich, 20 November 1959.
Career: West Bromwich & District Schools, Staffordshire Boys, Aston Villa (trialist, then apprentice June 1976, professional September 1977), Peterborough United (August 1982), Birmingham City (December 1983-February 1984), Bilston Town, Kasko IF & then IF Kraft Naipes in Finland (1984-89).
Midfielder Ivor Linton was rated very highly as a teenager at Villa Park, gaining an FA Youth Cup runners-up medal in 1978, but he failed to make the necessary breakthrough. He had 30 senior outings with the club (13 as a substitute) before moving to London Road. Later he did much better in Finland after being converted into a striker.

## LITTLE, ALAN

Born: Horden, County Durham, 5 February 1955.
Career: Horden & District Schools, Durham County Boys, Aston Villa (apprentice, June 1971, professional Janaury 1973), Southend United (£10,000, December 1974), Barnsley (£6,000, August 1977), Doncaster Rovers (£30,000, December 1979), Torquay United (October 1982),

Halifax Town (November 1983), Hartlepool United (July 1985....retired as a player in 1986 to become coach at the club in May 1986), York City (assistant-manager/coach, then manager March 1993-February 1999), Southend United (manager, March 1999), Halifax Town (manager, October 2001).

Inside-forward Alan Little (brother of Brian) had just six first team outings for Aston Villa before leaving the club to join Southend in 1974. Then, over the next 12 years, he amassed more than 450 League and Cup appearances before hanging up his boots to become a coach and later manager. As a player he won both FA Youth Cup and Southern Junior Cup winners' medals with Villa and helped Doncaster win promotion from Division Four in 1981. Then as a manager he successfully guided York to promotion from Division Three in 1993.

In November 1998, for the first time since 1974, two brothers, namely Alan of York City and Brian of Stoke City, were in charge of their respective League clubs when they met at The Britannia Stadium in a Nationwide Division Two game.

## LITTLE, BRIAN

Born: Peterlee, County Durham, 25 November 1953.
Career: County Durham Schools, East Durham Boys, East Durrham Senior Schools, Durham County Youths, trialist with Burnley, Leeds United, Manchester City, Newcastle United, Stoke City, Sunderland & West Bromwich Albion (between August 1968 and May 1969), Aston Villa (trialist, then apprentice, July 1969, professional June 1971).

Retired in 1982 after working briefly in the offices of the club's Development Association Department. Appointed coach at Villa Park (for season 1985-86), Wolverhampton Wanderers (coach, January 1986, caretaker-manager August-October 1986), Middlesbrough (coach), Darlington (manager, February 1989-May 1991), Leicester City (manager May 1991-November 1994), Aston Villa (manager November 1994-February 1998), Stoke City (manager, February 1998-August 1999), West Bromwich Albion (manager September 1999-March 2000), Hull City (manager August 2000).

*Brian Little - captain of Aston Villa!*

Brian Little was a star performer with Aston Villa during the 1970s. He won just one England cap, coming on as a substitute against Wales at Wembley in May 1975 in place of Mick Channon late in the game. He deserved more. He was an inspirational, all-action, goal-seeking (and scoring) utility forward with pace, skill and splendid shot. With his long hair (and good looks) he was a huge favourite with the fans and top-scored for Villa in their successful 1976-77 League Cup campaign with 10 goals, including two in the second replay of the Final against Everton at Old Trafford. He played exceptionally well off Andy Gray and John Deehan and went on to claim 82 goals in 301 first-class appearances for the club (his best season coming in 1976-77 when he netted 26 times in 56 outings).

He also won an FA Youth Cup winners' medal with Villa in 1972 (versus Liverpool) and helped the team win promotion from Division Two in

THE COMPLETE ENCYCLOPAEDIA OF ASTON VILLA F.C.      THE COMPLETE ENCYCLOPAEDIA OF ASTON VILLA F.C.

165

1975. During the 1979-80 season, a proposed £600,000 transfer from Villa Park to neighbouring St Andrew's broke down on medical grounds.

After guiding Darlington back into the Football League as GM Vauxhall Conference champions in 1990, he then lifted the Quakers out of the Fourth Division the following season before taking over at Filbert Street. Little returned to Villa Park as team manager in place of Ron Atkinson, but in 1998, almost two years after Villa had recorded an excellent 3-0 League Cup Final victory over Leeds United at Wembley, he was replaced by another ex-Villa player, John Gregory. Little later managed two more Midland clubs and was sacked seven months into his two-year contract at The Hawthorns.

His Football League record as Villa's manager was moderate: 130 games played, 51 won, 36 drawn and 43 lost.

• Brian's mother is a relative of Malcolm Musgrove, Villa's assistant-manager in 1968-69 and it was Malcolm who got Brian a trial at Villa Park!

## LITTLEWOOD, WILLIAM A

Born: Aston, Birmingham, December 1892. Died: Shrewsbury, 1949
Career: Verity's FC, Worcester City (1908), Aston Villa (June 1910), Wellington Town (August 1920), GKN Sankeys (1923-25). Retired.
Bill Littlewood was a useful defender able to play at full-back or centre-half. A strong, clean striker of the ball, he gained a regular place in the side in 1914 before the War disrupted his progress. Littlewood left the club after making 51 senior appearances.

## LIVERPOOL

Villa's playing record against Reds:
Football League/Premiership

| Venue | P | W | D | L | F | A |
|---|---|---|---|---|---|---|
| Home | 76 | 37 | 17 | 22 | 152 | 100 |
| Away | 76 | 13 | 15 | 48 | 80 | 172 |
| Totals | 152 | 50 | 32 | 70 | 232 | 272 |

FA Cup

| Venue | P | W | D | L | F | A |
|---|---|---|---|---|---|---|
| Home | 1 | 0 | 0 | 1 | 0 | 2 |
| Away | 3 | 0 | 0 | 3 | 0 | 5 |
| Neutral | 3 | 1 | 0 | 2 | 3 | 5 |
| Total | 7 | 1 | 0 | 6 | 3 | 12 |

Aston Villa first met Liverpool in the Football League in September 1894 - and they won 2-1 on Merseyside. A month later Villa doubled up with a 5-0 home victory when John 'Baldy' Reynolds scored twice including a penalty.

At half-time of their final First Division League game of the 1898-99 season against Liverpool, Villa were 5-0 up, three goals (two by Fred Wheldon) having been scored between the 34th and 39th minutes. There was no further scoring in the second-half.

Liverpool, though, quickly gained revenge with a 5-1 home win in November 1900.

There was another 5-0 Villa win in September 1905 when Harry Hampton hit a hat-trick and Villa won 4-0 at home in November 1906 only to lose 5-2 at Liverpool in the same season.

In December 1907, during the away game at Liverpool ten players were cautioned by the referee, six of them from Villa. Liverpool won 5-0.

But Villa turned things round later on with a 5-1 revenge victory at home when Joe Bache scored a hat-trick.

Villa doubled up over the Reds in 1911-12, winning 5-0 at home (Billy Walker and Herbert Goode both scoring twice) and 2-1 away.

Another double was achieved in 1914-15 when Villa scored twelve goals against Liverpool. They won 6-3 at Anfield on 28 November (when six different players found the net) and 6-1 at Villa Park on 3 April when both Harry Hampton and League debutant Harold Nash netted hat-tricks.

Villa beat Liverpool 4-2 at Anfield in August 1924 but lost 4-1 in the return game five months later.

George Brown was a four-goal hero in Villa's superb 6-1 home win over Liverpool in January 1932 and in season 1933-34 Eric Houghton scored twice in Villa's 4-2 home win whilst 'Pongo' Waring did likewise in a 3-2 victory at Anfield.

Villa came out best in both League games again in 1952-53, winning 4-0 at home and 2-0 away - but it was to be another 40 years before they claimed their next double over the Reds.

Liverpool were relegated at the end of the 1953-54 season - but not before they had thrashed Villa 6-1 at Anfield in October.

*Jimmy Rimmer punches clear during a Villa League game with Liverpool at Anfield in November 1977.*

Liverpool were leading Villa 4-0 after an hour's play in a Second Division game at Villa Park on 30 March 1960. But cheered on by their fans Villa pulled out all the stops to gain a point from a 4-4 draw. In truth, they should have won - but Peter McParland fired over the top from four yards with time running out fast.

It was Liverpool 4 Villa 0 and Villa 2 Liverpool 0 in 1962-63 before the Reds romped to a 5-2 win at Anfield in October 1963.

The following season Liverpool won 5-1 on Merseyside and 1-0 at Villa Park.

One of the finest performances by an Aston Villa side for some time came at Villa Park in December 1976 when Liverpool, the reigning League champions and UEFA Cup holders, fielding nine full internationals, were thumped 5-1 in front of almost 43,000 fans. Andy Gray and John Deehan both scored twice, all six goals coming in the first-half. Earlier that season Liverpool had won 3-0 at Anfield!

The only time Liverpool conceded three goals in a game in season 1978-79 was when they lost 3-1 at Villa Park on 16 April.

Liverpool went into their final game of the 1979-80 season knowing that victory over Villa would see them clinch their 12th League championship. They won 4-1 with a grand second-half performance after being held 1-1 at half-time.

When Villa lost 2-1 at Liverpool on 22 November 1980, their 12-match unbeaten League run came to an end.

A six-goal thriller at Anfield in September 1986 ended all square at 3-3 and Villa claimed their first League double over the Reds for 40 years when winning 4-2 (h) and 2-1 (a) in 1992-93.

Dwight Yorke had the honour of scoring the last goal in front of the Holte End terracing at Villa Park in a 2-1 win over Liverpool on 7 May 1994. A crowd of 45,347 turned out - the biggest in the Premiership for two years.

Over 40,000 fans saw Villa beat Liverpool 2-0 a year later (May 1995) as they battled to retain their Premiership status. Yorke scored both goals this time but it took a streaker to show him - and Villa - the way to goal!

John Gregory's first game in charge of Aston Villa was against Liverpool at home on 28 February 1998. Villa won 2-1.

Villa's 12-match unbeaten run in the Premiership, which began at the start of the season, ended when they lost 4-2 at home to Liverpool on 21 November 1998. No doubt it was Robbie Fowler's hat-trick that destroyed Villa - but Stan Collymore's dismissal (against his former club) didn't help matters either! (He was red-carded after a clash with Steve Harkness).

Steve Staunton (Liverpool) was sent-off against his past and future club (Villa) in October 1999.

Liverpool completed the 'Premiership' double over Villa in 2000-01, winning 3-1 at Anfield and 3-0 at Villa Park when the crowd was a best-of-season 41,366. Danny Murphy's second goal brought up the century for the Reds on Villa soil. Villa have met Liverpool three times in FA Cup semi-finals. They beat they Merseysiders 3-0 at Bramall Lane in 1897, lost 2-0 at White Hart lane in 1914 and succumbed to a 3-0 defeat at Old Trafford in 1996.

In between times, Villa lost four other FA Cup matches, including a 2-0 home reverse in the 4th round in January 1988 in front of 46,324 spectators. Liverpool was the first club Villa played twice on live TV.

Liverpool have scored more goals at Anfield against Aston Villa than they have past any other club.

Since World War Two the average attendance for an Aston Villa v Liverpool League game at Anfield and Villa Park is over 35,000.

Players with both clubs include: M Bosnich (Liverpool trialist), SV Collymore, RW Dix (Liverpool WW2 guest), R Dorsett (Villa player, 'Pool WW2 guest and later assistant-trainer at Anfield), A Evans, T Gardner, J Gidman (Liverpool Amateur), HJ Goode, R Guttridge ('Pool WW2 guest & Amateur), S Hardy, J Harrop, A Hateley, D Hickson, G Hodgson, R Houghton, DB James, P Kyle, S McMahon, FJ O'Donnell (Liverpool WW2 guest), I Ross, W Roberts, D Saunders, S Staunton, ME Walters.

Also: K Macdonald & R Money (Liverpool players, Villa coaches).

## LLOYD, FRANK

Born: West Bromwich, September 1881. Died: c 1945.
Career: Wednesbury Old Athletic, Woolwich Arsenal (May 1899), Aston Villa (May 1900), Dundee (July 1902-03).

An outside-right of no mean skill, Frank Lloyd was being watched by several Midland clubs before Woolwich Arsenal swooped to take him to London in 1899. He scored three goals in 19 League and FA Cup games for the Gunners and then added one goal in seven senior outings to his tally with Aston Villa when acting as reserve to Charlie Athersmith.

## LOACH, ARTHUR ALBERT

Born: West Bromwich, November 1863. Died: Rhyl, February 1958.
Career: Christ Church School, George Salter Works FC (1878), West Bromwich Albion (August 1882), Aston Villa (May 1886), Rhyl (1888). Retired 1890 (injured).

Speedy player and a useful goalscorer, Arthur Loach played for Albion against Aston Villa in the 1886 FA Cup Final. The following season he hit four goals in his three senior outings for Villa (including a brace on his debut against Wednesbury Old Athletic in a 13-0 FA Cup win).

## LOCHHEAD, ANDREW LORIMAR

Born: Lenzie near Milngavie, Scotland, 9 March 1941.
Career: Renfrew Juniors, Burnley (December 1958), Leicester City (£80,000, October 1968), Aston Villa (£30,000, February 1970), Oldham Athletic (August 1973), Denver Dynamo, NASL (on loan, April-June 1974), Oldham Athletic (coach, 1974-75), Padiham (manager, 1975-76). Scouted for several Lancashire clubs (including Burnley) during the 1980s when he also ran a pub. Later became steward of the Ightenmount Bowling Club in Burnley.

*Andy Lochhead*

Described in Paul Taylor's book 'Fossils & Foxes' as a 'six-foot, bullet-domed central striker', Andy Lochhead won one Under-23 cap for Scotland and scored 128 goals in 266 games for Burnley before going on to net 19 times in 63 outings for Leicester City, collecting an FA Cup runners-up medal in 1969. Powerful in the air, he was brave and determined and could take the heftiest of challenges without batting an eye-lid. He was leading marksman with 25 goals when Villa won the Third Division championship in 1971-72, and was also voted 'Midland Footballer of the Year' and the supporters' Terrace Trophy winner that same season. It is said that he was the player who got Villa going and formed a fine striking partnership with Geoff Vowden. He left Villa Park for Boundary Park after assembling a fine record of 44 goals in 153 appearances.

## LOCKETT, ARTHUR H.

Born: Alsagers Bank, near Stoke-on-Trent, August 1875. Died: Crewe, 1957.
Career: Crewe Alexandra, Stoke (May 1900), Aston Villa (April 1903), Preston North End (September 1905), Watford (July 1908-May 1912). Returned to North Staffordshire, played non-League football and retired in 1915.

A very swift and talented left-winger, Arthur Lockett's only fault was that he held onto the ball a fraction too long at times. Nevertheless he had an excellent career, accumulating more than 350 senior appearances and scoring over 25 goals for his five professional clubs. Capped by England in February 1903 in a 4-0 win over Ireland at Molineux, he also represented the Football League and claimed five goals in his 41 outings for Aston Villa.

## LOCKHART, NORMAN

Born: Belfast, 4 March 1924.
Career: Springfield Road School, Windsor Star, Distillery (1940), Linfield (£225, August 1942), Swansea Town (£2,500, October 1946), Coventry City (£7,000, October 1947), Aston Villa (£15,500, September 1952), Bury (£2,000, November 1956).

A fast-raiding outside-left, Norman Lockhart could cross a ball splendidly on the run. He played in the same Linfield forward-line as another future Aston Villa player, Dave Walsh, when they helped that club win two Irish Cup Finals (1945 & 1946) as well as a runners-up

THE COMPLETE ENCYCLOPAEDIA OF ASTON VILLA F.C.    THE COMPLETE ENCYCLOPAEDIA OF ASTON VILLA F.C.

167

medal in the same competition in 1944. Lockhart then did exceptionally well during his five years at Highfield Road, netting 44 goals in 189 appearances for the Sky Blues, despite suffering with injuries, including a broken ankle. He replaced Billy Goffin on the left-wing at Villa Park and after fellow Irishman Peter McParland had taken over the number 11 shirt, Lockhart had a few outings on the opposite flank. He scored 12 times in 85 first team outings for Villa before moving north to Gigg Lane. Lockhart, who made in excess of 500 club appearances during his career (in Ireland and the Football League) gained eight senior caps for Northern Ireland (four coming as an Aston Villa player). He also toured Canada with the Irish FA in 1953 (appearing in seven of the 10 games played).

## LOGAN, ALEC

Born: Barrhead, Glasgow, February 1880.
Died: Scotland.
Career: Barrhead Veronese, Hibernian (1901), Arthurlie (1905), Falkirk (1906), Aston Villa (March 1907), Falkirk (July 1909-10).
Old-fashioned centre-forward, rough and ready, who deputised several times for Harry Hampton in Aston Villa's attack. He scored 12 goals in his 25 appearances for Villa and earlier had gained a Scottish Cup winners' medal with Hibs (1902). Brother of James Logan (below).

*Alec Logan*

## LOGAN, JAMES

Born: Troon, 24 June 1870. Died: Loughborough, 25 May 1896.
Career: Ayr United, Sunderland (August 1891), Aston Villa (July 1892), Notts County (October 1893), Dundee, Newcastle United (August 1895), Loughborough (March 1896). Taken ill and died at the age of 25. Capped by Scotland in 1891, Jimmy Logan won an FA Cup winners' medal with Notts County three years later when he netted a superlative hat-trick against Bolton Wanderers in the Final at The Crystal Palace (a joint record to this day). A stocky, weighty centre-forward he was a prolific and cunning marksman who was always a danger in front of goal. He made 200 appearances in League and Cup football north and south of the border and claimed over 60 goals. His Villa record was eight goals in 15 outings.

*Jock Logan*

## LOGAN, JAMES L

Born: Glasgow, August 1885. Died: Scotland.
Career: Barrhead Ferense (1900), Queen's Park (August 1903), Aston Villa (July 1905), Glasgow Rangers (September 1912-15).
Jock Logan was a magnificent all-round defender, strong-shouldered, beefy at the thighs and a player who was both fearless and resolute. During his career he amassed in excess of 250 League and Cup games in the Scottish and Football Leagues. He scored four goals in 157 senior appearances for Aston Villa when he partnered Alf Miles at full-back before taking over the centre-half berth from Chris Buckley, later switching to wing-half on Buckley's return to the side.

## LONG SERVICE

George Ramsay spent some 55 years with Aston Villa Football Club. He was a player from 1876 to 1882; committee member 1882-84; then secretary (and initially committee member) for the next 40 years: 1884

to 1926; he afterwards acted as honorary advisor and vice-President. Charlie Wallace was an 'Aston Villa Man' for a total of 50 years. He initially served as a player from May 1907 until May 1921, returned to the club in May 1924 and thereafter worked as a boot-room attendant, kitman, scout, steward, occasional ground-assistant and odd job man until June 1960. Even after that he was an avid supporter until his death in 1970.
Fred Rinder was associated with Aston Villa for a total of 46 years (two spells): 1881-1925/1936-38. He was a committee member, director & chairman during that time.
Eric Houghton also spent a total of 46 years with Aston Villa FC. He was a star player from 1927-46, then manager 1953-58, coach/Youth assistant 1970-72, Director from 1972-79 and vice-President 1983-96.
Secretary Billy Smith was a member of the staff at Villa Park for 45 years. He was clerk/assistant-secretary from 1910 to 1926 and then acted as secretary from 1926 until his retirement in 1955.
Jack Devey was associated with the club for 43 years - first as a player (1891 to 1902) and thereafter as a Director (1902-34).
A colleague of Devey's, Howard Spencer, served Aston Villa for 42 years, first as a full-back (1892-1907), then as a Director (1909-36).
Chris Buckley was a player with Aston Villa from 1906 to 1914 and then a Director (also Chairman) from 1936-67. A total of 39 years with the club.
William McGregor - the man who 'founded' the Football League - was part of the Aston Villa club for 35 years: 1876-1911.
Sir Patrick Hannon was Villa's Club President from 1924 to 1963 (some 39 years in total).

*Eric Houghton*

Doug Ellis first became a Director of Aston Villa in 1968 and except for an odd year or two in between times, he has been at the club for over 30 years; Chairman since 1982.
Steve Stride joined the staff at Villa Park in June 1972 and was appointed secretary in May 1979. He later become a Director of Aston Villa (summer of 1995) and is now approaching the milestone of 30 years association with AVFC.
In 2001, Ron Wylie completed 23 years service with Aston Villa - as a player (1958-63), assistant-manager, community officer and coach.
Fred Archer was employed by Aston Villa for more than 21 years - initially as a clerk, then assistant-secretary and finally club secretary (1955-69).
Bert Bond was a groundsman for 30 years (1941-71) - initially at Villa Park and later at the club's Bodymoor Heath training ground. Bond died in January 1973.
Dick Leeson was Villa's groundsman for 27 years (1894-1921).
Hubert Bourne served Aston Villa FC for 34 years (1919-53): first as a player, then as a coach and finally as a trainer.
Joe Grierson was on Aston Villa's training staff for some 30 years (1886 -1916) and during the period from 1894-1915 he looked after the first team and saw Villa win the Football League Championship five times and the FA Cup on four occasions. And they completed the double in 1897.
An Aston Villa employee for over 25 years, Abdul Rashid first joined the staff on a permanent basis in 1977, having previously been a supporter, ball-boy and club shop assistant. He has been Villa's Commercial Manager since July 1988.
Howard Vaughton spent some 22 years with Aston Villa - first as a

THE COMPLETE ENCYCLOPAEDIA OF ASTON VILLA F.C.  THE COMPLETE ENCYCLOPAEDIA OF ASTON VILLA F.C.

168

player (1880-88), then as a Vice-President (1923), club President (1924), Director (1924-32) and Life Member (1932-37).

Dr David Targett served Villa as the club doctor and also as a Director for more than over 25 years until his sudden death in 1999. Dr H J Jessop was Villa's club doctor from 1903-28.

Chief Scout Neville Briggs joined Villa's staff in the early 1960s and went on to serve the club for over 25 years.

Ernie 'Mush' Callaghan spent 17 years as a player with Aston Villa (1930-47) and then acted as the club's odd-job for many years after that, serving the club for a quarter of a century.

## LONGEST SEASONS

Villa's longest season in terms of competitive match action was in 1962-63, which, due to the atrocious weather, lasted for nine months and nine days - from 18 August to 27 May.

The 1978-79 campaign started on 19 August and ended on 15 May (almost nine months).

The 1944-45 Wartime season also lasted nine months - commencing on 26 August and ending on 26 May.

Two other lengthy campaigns have been: 1946-47 (31 August-26 May) and 1981-82 (29 August to 26 May).

The latest date Villa have finished a competitive season was on 27 May 1963 and the earliest they have started one is July 2000 and July 2001 (IntetrToto Cup).

The two-legged League Cup Final of 1961 was actually carried over until the start of the following campaign.

## LORD MAYOR OF BIRMINGHAM CHARITY CUP

This competition was played for between 1880 and 1939 by the first teams of all the top-line Midland clubs, and Aston Villa reached the Final no fewer than 46 times, achieving an excellent record of 28 outright victories as well as taking a part share of the trophy on six other occasions. They suffered only 10 defeats in the Final, plus one default (1887) whilst the 1926 Final was postponed.

Here are the results of the Lord Mayor of Birmingham Charity Cup Finals involving Aston Villa:

| Season | Opponents & Result |
|--------|--------------------|
| 1881-82 | Villa 4 Walsall Swifts 1 |
| 1882-83 | Villa 8 Walsall Town 0 |
| 1883-84 | Villa 3 Wednesbury Old Athletic 2 |
| 1884-85 | Villa 1 Walsall Swifts 1 (after 1-1)* |
| 1885-86 | Villa 4 Wednesbury Old Athletic 1 |
| 1886-87 | Villa v Wolverhampton Wds+ |
| 1887-88 | Villa 2 Walsall Town Swifts 2* |
| 1888-89 | Villa 2 Wolverhampton Wanderers 0 |
| 1889-90 | Villa 2 Wolverhampton Wanderers 1 |
| 1890-91 | Villa 3 Wolverhampton Wanderers 0 |
| 1892-93 | Villa 3 Small Heath 2 |
| 1893-94 | Villa 3 Wolverhampton Wanderers 1 |
| 1894-95 | Villa 5 Small Heath 3 |
| 1896-97 | Villa 1 Walsall 2 (after 1-1 draw) |
| 1897-98 | Villa 2 Walsall 4 |
| 1897-99 | Villa 1 Walsall 0 |
| 1900-01 | Villa 2 West Brom Albion 0 (after 1-1) |
| 1901-02 | Villa 1 West Brom Albion 0 |
| 1903-04 | Villa 4 Small Heath 2 |
| 1904-05 | Villa 1 Small Heath 0** |
| 1905-06 | Villa 4 West Bromwich Albion 3 |

| | |
|--------|--------------------|
| 1906-07 | Villa 1 Birmingham 1* |
| 1907-08 | Villa 0 Birmingham 4 |
| 1908-09 | Villa 2 Birmingham 5 |
| 1909-10 | Villa 2 Birmingham 1 |
| 1910-11 | Villa 2 West Brom Albion 1 |
| 1911-12 | Villa 4 West Brom Albion 0 |
| 1912-13 | Villa 5 West Brom Albion 1 |
| 1913-14 | Villa 0 West Brom Albion 1 |
| 1914-15 | Villa 2 West Brom Albion 3 |
| 1919-20 | Villa 1 Birmingham 4 |
| 1922-23 | Villa 2 West Brom Albion 0 |
| 1923-24 | Villa 3 Birmingham 3* |
| 1925-26 | Villa v West Bromwich Albion *** |
| 1926-27 | Villa 4 Birmingham 2 |
| 1927-28 | Villa 3 Birmingham 2 |
| 1928-29 | Villa 2 Birmingham 1 |
| 1929-30 | Villa 5 Wolverhampton Wds 1 |
| 1930-31 | Villa 3 West Brom Albion 2 |
| 1931-32 | Villa 2 Wolverhampton Wds 1 |
| 1932-33 | Villa 4 West Brom Albion 0 |
| 1933-34 | Villa 0 Birmingham 2 |
| 1934-35 | Villa 1 Birmingham 2 |
| 1935-36 | Villa 2 Birmingham 4 |
| 1936-37 | Villa 2 Birmingham 2* |
| 1938-39 | Villa 1 Coventry City 0 |

+ Aston Villa withdrew from Final, Wolves won by default.

\* Walsall 'retired' from competition, Villa handed trophy.

\** Game abandoned in the 50th minute (trophy held jointly for six months).

\*** The 1926 Final between Villa and Albion was not played due to the General Strike.

NB - The two-legged LMBCC Final in April 1964 finished all-square between the Youth teams of Aston Villa and Birmingham City. The first leg at St Andrew's ended in a 3-3 draw and then the return fixture at Villa Park finished level at 1-1. Each club held the trophy for six months.

### Charity Cup Talk

Aston Villa first entered the Lord Mayor's Charity Cup in 1881-82, beating Wednesbury Old Athletic 2-0 in the semi-final before defeating Walsall Swifts 4-1 in the Final, both matches taking place at the Lower Grounds Meadow.

The following year Walsall Town were beaten in the Final (this time emphatically by 8-0) and the Villans made it a hat-trick of victories in 1884 at the expense of Wednesbury Old Athletic. WOA were beaten again in the Final two years later, three weeks after Villa had slammed Aston Unity 7-0 in the semis.

Aston Villa (the FA Cup winners) scratched from the 1886-87 Lord Mayor's Cup after beating Birmingham St George's 3-1 in the semi-final.

The 1889 Final victory over Wolves was achieved at the Warwickshire CCC ground (Edgbaston)...and the side from Molineux was then defeated in each of the next two Finals as Villa completed the 'hat-trick' over their Black Country challengers.

Before beating Small Heath in the 1893 Final, Villa accounted for West Bromwich Albion 6-0 in the semis.

Although they completed the League and FA Cup double in 1896-97, Villa lost in the second round of the Birmingham Senior Cup and in the Final of the Lord Mayor's Charity Cup. This ended a run of

*1897 BCC Cup Final programme.*

THE COMPLETE ENCYCLOPAEDIA OF ASTON VILLA F.C.    THE COMPLETE ENCYCLOPAEDIA OF ASTON VILLA F.C.

169

six successive Final victories in the Lord Mayor's Charity Cup competition.

Villa beat Wolves 6-0 in the semi-final of the Charity Cup in 1901 and then ran up a 4-3 scoreline at the same stage in 1904.

Villa played in 16 consecutive LMBCC Finals (1903-04 to 1919-20 inclusive). They won four on the trot (1909-10 to 1912-13).

They were defeated in the semi-final in 1924-25; the 1925-26 Final was postponed (General Strike) and thereafter did not lose again in the competition until until May 1934 when neighbours Blues defeated them in the Final. Villa won seven successive Finals in that time.

Aston Villa met Birmingham (Small Heath) no fewer than 17 times in the LMBC Cup Final; they played Albion on eleven occasions, Walsall Town Swifts/Walsall in seven encounters and Wolves six.

The statuette on the lid of the Lord Mayor of Birmingham Charity Cup is the model of Tom Pank, who played as a half-back for Aston Villa from 1875 to 1883.

The Lord Mayor of Birmingham Charity Cup was renamed the Birmingham Senior Amateur Cup in 1974.

## LOWE, EDMUND

Born: Halesowen, 11 July 1925.
Career: Napier Aircraft Compnay (Finchley), Kynoch Works FC, Aston Villa (May 1945), Fulham (£15,000, with his brother Reg, May 1950), Notts County (September 1963-April 1965). Retired to become a purchasing manager for a boiler & central heating company in Nottingham. He worked down the pits as a 'Bevin Boy' during the second half of the War (1942-45)
Eddie (or 'Sticks') Lowe was a player who thrived on hard work, being first on the training pitch no matter what the weather! He was a solid defender, able to occupy several positions. He was tenacious in the tackle and could mark the best inside-forwards out of a game. His leggy stride and balding head were prominent all over the country as he amassed a splendid career record of more than 600 club appearances for Villa, Fulham and Notts County over a period of 21 years. He scored three goals in 117 games during his five seasons at Villa Park, made 511 first team appearances for Fulham (10 goals) and added another nine to his tally whilst at Meadow Lane. Lowe, under the tuition of manager Alex Massie, became Villa's first post-War international, capped by England against France, Switzerland and Portugal in 1947, starting in a 10-0 win over the latter country in Lisbon. He was placed fourth in the Footballer of The Year awards in 1963.

Eddie and his brother Reg played in more than 50 games together in Fulham's League side (1950-53).

## LUTON TOWN

Villa's playing record against Hatters:

Football League

| Venue | P | W | D | L | F | A |
|---|---|---|---|---|---|---|
| Home | 16 | 10 | 1 | 5 | 29 | 15 |
| Away | 16 | 1 | 3 | 12 | 8 | 24 |
| Totals | 32 | 11 | 4 | 17 | 37 | 39 |

FA Cup

| | P | W | D | L | F | A |
|---|---|---|---|---|---|---|
| Home | 2 | 2 | 0 | 0 | 3 | 0 |
| Away | 1 | 0 | 1 | 0 | 2 | 2 |
| Totals | 3 | 2 | 1 | 0 | 5 | 2 |

League Cup

| | P | W | D | L | F | A |
|---|---|---|---|---|---|---|
| Home | 1 | 0 | 0 | 1 | 0 | 2 |
| Away | 1 | 1 | 0 | 0 | 1 | 0 |
| Totals | 2 | 1 | 0 | 1 | 1 | 2 |

*David Platt attempting to barge through the Hatters' defence at Villa Park.*

| Wartime | | | | | | |
|---|---|---|---|---|---|---|
| Home | 1 | 1 | 0 | 0 | 7 | 1 |
| Away | 1 | 0 | 1 | 0 | 1 | 1 |
| Totals | 2 | 1 | 1 | 0 | 8 | 2 |

Aston Villa first met Luton at League level in season 1955-56. Johnny Dixon's goal gave Villa a 1-0 home win whilst the Hatters gained revenge with a 2-1 victory at Kenilworth Road.

In October 1991 Villa registered their best win over Luton, beating the 4-0 at home with Kevin Richardson, Dwight Yorke, Cyrille Regis and Paul Mortimer the scorers in front of 18,722 fans.

Almost 54,000 fans saw Villa beat the Hatters 1-0 at home in a 2nd round FA Cup-tie in January 1922. Then in contrast just under 23,400 spectators attended the 3rd round replay at Villa Park in January 1957 when Johnny Dixon's two goals gave Villa a comfortable victory.

Villa opened their 1964-65 League Cup programme with a 1-0 win at Kenilworth Road, Bobby Park on target in front of 9,011 fans.

In November 1984 Villa sold centre-half Steve Foster to Luton Town and in December 1985 they signed another centre-half Paul Elliott....from the Hatters.

George Edwards scored four times when Villa beat the Hatters in a Football League South Wartime game in September 1945.

When Villa beat Luton 2-1 in a friendly at Kenilworth Road in February 1951 (both goals scored by Tommy Thompson) the Oxford Blue, AR Smith, played for Villa.

Players with both clubs include: J Adam, JP Allen (Hatters WW2 guest), MS Burke, MR Day, PM Elliott, J Findlay, SB Foster, D Geddis, AG Gittins, RSM Gray, LC Jones, AW Kerr (Hatters WW2 guest), CJ Nicholl, GS Parker, BD Rioch, DG Rioch, HJ Reece (Villa reserve), L Sealey, B Small, GH Stephenson,
Also: GS Martin (Luton player, Villa assistant-manager & manager, coach & scout), R Money & DJ Sexton (Luton players, Villa coaches), EJ Vinall & B Whitehouse (Luton players, Villa scouts).

THE COMPLETE ENCYCLOPAEDIA OF ASTON VILLA F.C.     THE COMPLETE ENCYCLOPAEDIA OF ASTON VILLA F.C.

170

## LYNCH, BARRIE JOHN

Born: Northfield, Birmingham, 8 June 1951

Career: Rubery Schools, Cross Castle FC, Aston Villa (apprentice, June 1967, professional January 1969), Oldham Athletic (on loan, September 1969), Atlanta Chiefs, NASL (June 1971), Grimsby Town (September 1972), Scunthorpe United (July 1973), Portland Timbers, NASL (May 1975), Torquay United (September 1975-May 1977). Later managed Halesowen Town (early 1980s), Stratford Town (1986-87) and Redditch United (November     1988-89).

A busy, biting player, who occupied the full-back berth, Barrie Lynch made over 150 League appearances after leaving Aston Villa in 1972, having failed to dislodge a certain Charlie Aitken! He was given just three senior outings during his time at Villa Park.

## LYNN, STANLEY

Born: Bolton, 18 June 1928

Career: Devonshire Road School, Accrington Stanley (professional, 1947), Aston Villa (£10,000, March 1950), Birmingham City (October 1961), Stourbridge (August 1966)

A solidly built full-back with a kick like a mule, Stan Lynn - nicknamed 'Stan the Wham' and 'Lynn the Lash' - was a terrific defender who was always totally committed. He was recruited as cover for Harry Parkes and Peter Aldis (and eventually became a terrific partner to the latter). But surprisingly during his early days at Villa Park, Lynn played as an emergency centre-forward, scoring from that position against Derby in December 1950 and Fulham in November 1951.

In his own words Lynn said: 'I wasn't worth £10,000' but during his eleven years with Aston Villa he repaid that money three or four times over by appearing in 324 games and netting 38 goals, including a host of penalties. He bagged a hat-trick in a League game against Sunderland in January 1958 to become the first full-back to achieve this feat in a Division One game. Lynn won an FA Cup winners' medal in 1957 and collected a Second Division championship medal in 1960. He left Villa Park for neighbouring St. Andrew's in 1961. Two years later he gained his second League Cup winners' prize when Blues defeated his former club Villa in the two-legged final of 1963. Lynn, who quit League football in 1966 after almost 150 games for Blues, was a keen golfer who later worked in the stores at Lucas. He now resides in Shirley.

## LYONS, ALFRED THOMAS

Born: Littleworth, Hednesford, 5 July 1885.
Died: Hednesford, October 1938.
Career: Hazelslade School (Hednesford), Heath Hayes Boys, Hednesford Town, Hednesford Victoria, Bridgtown Amateurs, Aston Villa (trialist, January 1907, professional April 1907), Port Vale (WWI guest January 1917, signed August 1919), Walsall (player/coach July 1922-May 23).

Tommy Lyons (left) was a fearless tackler, a defender with an astute footballing brain who invariably played with his head bowed forward. In his younger days he was a determined centre-half but was groomed into a classy full-back at Villa Park, teaming up splendidly with Alf Miles. Lyons gained a League championship medal in 1910 and an FA Cup

winners' medal in 1913. He appeared in 238 first-class games for Villa and later added a further 66 to his tally with Port Vale.

Tommy's younger brother, Bert Lyons, played as a full-back for Clapton Orient and Tottenham Hotspur in the 1930s.

## MacEWAN, JAMES

Born: Dundee, 22 March 1929

Career: Arbroath (amateur 1945, professional April 1946), Raith Rovers (June 1950), Aston Villa (£8,000, July 1959), Walsall (player, August 1966-May 1968, then trainer, 1968-75), South Africa (coach, 1975-77)

A fragile-looking right-winger but nevertheless a very competent one, Jimmy MacEwan had been a regular marksman in Scottish football during the late fifties, being Raith Rovers' top scorer in 1956-57, 1957-58 and 1958-59 when he totalled 54 goals in 209 appearances, also gaining a Scottish 'B' cap. During his seven seasons at Villa Park he did sterling work in the claret and blue strip. He helped the team win the Second Division title in 1960 and the Football League Cup the following year while accumulating a fine personal record of 181 appearances and 31 goals.

*Jimmy MacEwan*

After retiring in 1968 he held the position of trainer at Fellows Park for seven years. He then coached in South Africa for a time before returning to Birmingham to work firstly at Ansells Brewery and then for the Social Services Department in Handsworth. He later took up residence in Castle Bromwich.

## MacLEOD, JOHN MURDOCK

Born: Edinburgh, 23 November 1938

Career: Edinburgh Junior football, Edinburgh Thistle, Armadale (1955), Hibernian (August 1957), Arsenal (£40,000, July 1961), Aston Villa (£35,000, September 1964), KV Mechelen, Belgium (July 1968), Raith Rovers (1971), Newtonrange Star (1972). Retired 1975.

Darting little winger, able to occupy both flanks, Johnny MacLeod was capped by Scotland at Under-23 level before going on to play in four full internationals as well as representing the Scottish League. He scored 28 goals in 112 senior games for the Gunners (an excellent record for a player in his position) and then netted 18 times in 139 appearances during his spell with Villa, where he linked up with a variety of inside partners including Ron Wylie, Willie Hamilton, Phil Woosnam and Peter Broadbent. MacLeod was eventually replaced at Villa Park by Mike Ferguson.

## MACKAY, NORMAN

Born: Edinburgh, 26 May 1902. Deceased.

Career: Edinburgh Royal, Broxburn, Blackburn Rovers (trialist), Hibernian (August 1923), Aston Villa (December 1923), Lovells Athletic (April 1925), Clydebank (trialist, 1926), Yoker Athletic, Plymouth Argyle (£200, January 1928), Southend United (July 1934), Clydebank (July 1935). Retired 1938.

Inside or centre-forward Norman Mackay made only two League appearances for Aston Villa, against Sheffield United and Huddersfield Town, both away, in 1923-24. With so much competition for places he

THE COMPLETE ENCYCLOPAEDIA OF ASTON VILLA F.C.    THE COMPLETE ENCYCLOPAEDIA OF ASTON VILLA F.C.

171

drifted into the Welsh League with Lovells and was combining playing football with a job as a rep selling toffees to shops when Plymouth moved in and enticed him back into League action. He did splendidly at Home Park, netting a hat-trick against Coventry City on his debut for the Pilgrims. He was eventually switched to wing-half and went on to claim 14 goals in 241 first-class matches before joining Southend United, later signing for Clydebank in 1935, nine years after the Scottish club had rejected him following a fortnight's trial! Described as a 'hard nut, small but tough' Mackay was certainly a player 'missed' by Aston Villa.

Mackay was a marvellous musician who could play the banjo, ukulele, violin, mandoline and the bagpipes. He also loved boxing and possessed a tremendous collection of football photographs.

## MAGGS, PERCY

Born: Clutton near Bristol, February 1905. Died: Griffithstown, 19 December 1985.

Career: Bath City (1925), Aston Villa (May 1928), Blackpool (August 1931), Torquay United (June 1932-September 1939).

Giant reserve goalkeeper, initially understudy to Tommy Jackson, Percy Maggs' best season with Villa was in 1930-31 when, fighting for a place with Fred Biddlestone and Reg Miles, he made 12 appearances out of a total of 14 for the club. After leaving Villa Park Maggs went on to star in 24 League games for Blackpool and 206 for Torquay. He did not feature after the Second World War.

## MAIDEN, WALTER HENRY

Born: Kidderminster, 1896.

Career: Worcester Road Council School, Kidderminster Harriers (August 1914), Aston Villa (March 1915), to War, but re-joined Villa (August 1919), Stourbridge (September 1920).

A steady, safe-kicking reserve right or left full-back, Wally Maiden made only one League appearrance for Aston Villa, partnering Jimmy Lawrence in a 6-1 defeat at Bradford in September 1919.

## MAJOR, JOHN, MP

Just prior to his appointment as Prime Minister, John Major was forced to postpone his family holiday so that his son, James, could have a trial with Aston Villa. Nothing came of the trial.

## MAKITA TOURNAMENT

In August 1990 Aston Villa competed in the Makita (International) Tournament at Wembley. On the 10th of the month they were defeated 2-0 by Arsenal in front of 20,083 spectators and 24 hours later succumbed to a 1-0 defeat at the hands of the Spanish club Real Sociedad when the attendance was 18,000.

## MANAGERS

(For career details of managers, see under individual entries).
**List of Aston Villa's managers down the years:**

| Name | Term in Office | |
| --- | --- | --- |
| Jimmy McMullan | June 1934 | October 1936 |
| Jimmy Hogan | November 1936 | September 1939 |
| Alex Massie | September 1945 | August 1950 |
| George Martin | December 1950 | August 1953 |
| Eric Houghton | September 1953 | November 1958 |
| Joe Mercer | December 1958 | July 1964 |
| Dick Taylor | July 1964 | May 1967 |
| Tommy Cummings | July 1967 | November 1968 |
| Arthur Cox* | November 1968 | December 1968 |
| Tommy Docherty | December 1968 | January 1970 |
| Vic Crowe | January 1970 | May 1974 |
| Ron Saunders | June 1974 | February 1982 |
| Tony Barton | February 1982 | May 1984 |
| Graham Turner | July 1984 | September 1986 |
| Billy McNeill | September 1986 | May 1987 |
| Graham Taylor | July 1987 | July 1990 |
| Josef Venglos | July 1990 | May 1991 |
| Ron Atkinson | July 1991 | November 1994 |
| Brian Little | November 1994 | February 1998 |
| John Gregory | February 1998 | To date |

* Cox was appointed caretaker-manager until Docherty arrived.

### Boss Talk

Prior to Aston Villa appointing Jimmy McMullan as manager, the club's

*Ron Saunders*

team affairs were run indirectly by the club secretary and a chosen committee that included the captain. As far back as late 1874 when Aston Villa came into being, a group of elected club personnel selected the team (not a manager) and this was the case right up until 1934.

Indeed, from 1884 to 1926, under the aegis of secretary George Ramsay, many honours were won, including six First Division titles and five FA Cup Finals. And then Billy J. Smith (also the Villa secretary) took over the reins for the next eight years, but unfortunately he did not have any success at all in terms of winning trophies!

### Assistant-Managers

Bill Moore was assistant-manager/trainer (under Eric Houghton) when Villa won the FA Cup in 1957.

Manager Joe Mercer's assistant at both Sheffield United and Aston Villa was Dick Taylor.

Malcolm Musgrove was assistant-boss to Tommy Cummings and Arthur Cox was Villa's assistant under manager Tommy Docherty.

John Ward, assistant to Graham Taylor, scored over 100 League goals while playing for Grimsby Town, Lincoln City and Watford.

Steve Harrison also acted as assistant-manager to Graham Taylor.

Andy Gray was Ron Atkinson's right-hand man at Villa Park.

Ex-Villa midfielder Tommy Craig became assistant-manager of Celtic.

Former defender Allan Evans was understudy to Brian Little when he was in charge at Villa Park and both Ron Wyle and Peter Withe haave also acted as assistant-managers at Villa Park.*

**Villa players who went on to become managers with League clubs (various countries):**

| | |
| --- | --- |
| Peter Aldis | Slavia FC (Australia) |
| Jimmy Allen | Colchester United |
| Ron Atkinson | Cambridge United, West Bromwich Albion (two spells), Manchester United, Atletico Madrid, Sheffield Wednesday, Coventry City, Nottingham Forest |
| Ernie Blackburn | Accrington Stanley, Wrexham, Hull City, Tranmere Rovers |
| Noel Blake | Exeter City |
| Danny Blanchflower | Chelsea |
| Bob Brocklebank | Chesterfield, Birmingham City, Hull City, Bradford City |
| Frank Broome | Notts County, Exeter City (twice), Southend United, Bankstown (NSW), Corinthians (Sydney) |

THE COMPLETE ENCYCLOPAEDIA OF ASTON VILLA F.C.        THE COMPLETE ENCYCLOPAEDIA OF ASTON VILLA F.C.

172

| | |
|---|---|
| George Brown | Darlington |
| Mjr Frank Buckley | Norwich City, Blackpool, Wolverhampton Wanderers, Hull City, Leeds United, Walsall |
| Terry Bullivant | Reading, Barnet |
| Roy Chapman | Lincoln City, Stockport County |
| Neale Cooper | Ross County |
| James Cowan | Queen's Park Rangers |
| Vic Crowe | Portland Timbers (manager/coach), Aston Villa |
| Alan Curbishley | Charlton Athletic |
| George Curtis | Coventry City |
| Mervyn Day | Carlisle United |
| John Deehan | Norwich City, Wigan Athletic |
| Andy Ducat | Fulham |
| Albert Evans | Coventry City |
| Allan Evans | Greenock Morton |
| Tommy Ewing | Hamilton Academical |
| Mike Ferguson | Rochdale |
| James A Fisher | Merthyr Town, Notts County |
| Brian Godfrey | Exeter City |
| Edmund Goodman | Crystal Palace |
| George Graham | Millwall, Arsenal, Leeds United, Tottenham Hotspur |
| Stuart Gray | Southampton |
| Ray Graydon | Walsall |
| Haydn Green | Hull City, Swansea Town, Watford |
| John Gregory | Portsmouth, Plymouth Argyle*, Wycombe Wanderers, Aston Villa |

| | |
|---|---|
| Steve McMahon | Swindon Town, Blackpool |
| Ken McNaught | Swansea City* |
| Peter McParland | Glentoran, 1 Club of Kuwait, FC Lybia |
| Con Martin | Waterford |
| Alex Massie | Aston Villa, Torquay United |
| Archie Mitchell | QPR, Brentford |
| Derek Mountfield | Scarborough* |
| John Neal | Wrexham, Middlesbrough, Chelsea |
| Chris Nicholl | Southampton, Walsall |
| Mike Pejic | Malazia Celangor & Zimbabwe (manager) |
| David Platt | Sampdoria (coach & player-manager), Nottingham Forest |
| Ivor Powell | Port Vale, Bradford City, Carlisle United |
| Jimmy Rimmer | Swansea City* |
| Bruce Rioch | Torquay United, Middlesbrough, Millwall, Bolton Wanderers, Arsenal, Norwich City, Wigan Athletic |
| Ken O Roberts | Chester |
| Ian Ross | FC Valur (Iceland), Huddersfield Town |
| Pat Saward | Brighton & Hove Albion, Al Nasr |
| Steve Smith | New Brompton (Gillingham) |
| Cyril Spiers | Cardiff City (twice), Norwich City, Crystal Palace, Exeter City |
| Simon Stainrod | Falkirk*, Dundee*, Ayr United |
| Clem Stephenson | Huddersfield Town |
| George Stephenson | Huddersfield Town |
| Kenny Swain | Grimsby Town |

*Kenny Swain*

*John Gidman*

*Brian Godfrey*

| | |
|---|---|
| Harry Hadley | Merthyr Town (twice), Gillingham, Chesterfield, Aberdare Athletic |
| Adrian Heath | Burnley, Sheffield United |
| Horace Henshall | Lincoln City, Notts County |
| Dave Hickson | Ballymena |
| Trevor Hockey | Athlone Town |
| Gordon Hodgson | Port Vale |
| Eric Houghton | Notts County, Aston Villa |
| Tommy Hughes | Hereford United |
| Mick Kenning | Durban United |
| Gordon Lee | Port Vale, Blackburn Rovers, Newcastle United, Everton, Preston North End, KR Reykjavik (Iceland), Leicester City* |
| Mark Lillis | Halifax Town |
| Albert Lindon | Charlton Athletic |
| Alan Little | York City, Southend United, Halifax Town |
| Brian Little | Wolverhampton Wanderers, Darlington, Leicester City, Aston Villa, Stoke City, West Bromwich Albion, Hull City |
| Eddie Lowe | Notts County |

| | |
|---|---|
| Shaun Teale | Motherwell (player-manager) |
| Garry Thompson | Bristol Rovers (carertaker-manager) |
| Brian Tiler | Portland Timbers, Miami Americans, San Diego Sockers |
| Billy Walker | Sheffield Wednesday, Nottingham Forest |
| Tommy Wilson | Rochdale |
| Peter Withe | Wimbledon |
| Phil Woosnam | Atlanta Chiefs |
| Ron Wylie | West Bromwich Albion |
| * Caretaker-manager | |

**Villa personnel who also managed at non-League level:**

| | |
|---|---|
| Peter Aldis | Alvechurch |
| Alan Ashman | Penrith |
| Ron Atkinson | Kettering Town |
| Frank Barson | Rhyl |
| George Blackburn | Cheltenham Town |
| John Burridge | Blyth Spartans |
| John Chambers | Kidderminster H, Stourbridge, Halesowen Town |

THE COMPLETE ENCYCLOPAEDIA OF ASTON VILLA F.C.    THE COMPLETE ENCYCLOPAEDIA OF ASTON VILLA F.C.

173

| | |
|---|---|
| Roy Chapman | Stafford Rangers (twice), Walsall SportsCo, Stourbridge |
| Lew Chatterley | Poole Town |
| Vic Crowe | Bilston Town (advisory-manager) |
| George Cummings | Hednesford Town |
| Tommy Docherty | Altrincham |
| Derek Dougan | Kettering Town |
| Dick Edwards | Bath City |
| Bob Evans | Brookhirst (Wales) |
| Mike Ferguson | Enfield |
| Tom Gardner | Oswestry Town |
| John Gidman | King's Lynn |
| Dean Glover | Newcastle Town |
| Brian Godfrey | Bath City, Weymouth, Gloucester City, Cinderford Town |
| Billy Goffin | Tamworth |
| Haydn Green | Ebbw Vale, Guildford City |
| Brian Greenhalgh | Carshalton Athletic |
| 'Harry' Gregory | Maldon Town |
| Harry Hadley | Bangor City |
| Dave Hickson | Ellesmere Port Town (twice) |
| Eric Houghton | Rugby Town |
| Steve Hunt | Willenhall Town, AP Leamington, VS Rugby |
| Mike Kenning | Germiston Callies, Durban United, Witts University (all in South Africa) |
| Billy Kingdon | Yeovil & Petters United, Weymouth |
| Albert Lindon | Merthyr Tydfil |
| Andy Lochhead | Padiham (Lancashire) |
| Barrie Lynch | Halesowen Town, Stratford Town, Redditch United |
| Jimmy McLuckie | Clacton Town |
| John R Martin | Hednesford Town |
| Alex Massie | Hereford United (S.L) |
| Archie Mitchell | Dartford |
| Sammy Morgan | Gorleston |
| Terry Morrall | Stourbridge, Warley Borough |
| Dennis Mortimer | Redditch United |
| Frank Moss snr. | Bromsgrove Rovers |
| Jock Mulraney | Cradley Heath, Brierley Hill Alliance |
| Tom Niblo | Hebburn Argyle |
| David Norton | Forest Green Rovers (joint-manager) |
| Frank O'Donnell | Buxton |
| Ben Olney | Bilston United |
| Derek Pace | Walsall Wood |
| Bobby Park | Peterlee Newtown FC (Northern League) |
| Mike Pejic | Leek Town, Northwich Victoria |
| Leighton Phillips | Llanelli |
| Dave Pountney | Oswestry Town |
| Ivor Powell | Bath City |
| Arthur Proudler | Dorchester Town |
| Neil Rioch | Aston Villa Old Stars |
| Leslie (GF) Smith | Kidderminster Harriers, Aston Villa Old Stars |
| Nigel Spink | Forest Green Rovers (joint-manager) |
| Barry Stobart | Willenhall, Dudley Town |
| Joe Tate | Brierley Hill Alliance |
| Brian Tiler | Wigan Athletic |
| Alan Wakeman | Bloxwich Strollers, Walsall Wood, Stratford Town, Bilston Town, Armitage FC. |
| Billy Walker | Chelmsford City |
| Ray Walker | Newcastle Town |
| Tommy Wilson | Chorley |

### Managerial Chit-Chat

Jimmy McMullan was Villa's first official and full-time team manager, appointed in June 1934.

Joe Mercer was the first man to manage a League Cup-winning side (Aston Villa in 1961).

Vic Crowe became only the third Division Three manager to take his team to Wembley - leading Villa to the 1971 League Cup Final.

Tony Barton had been manager of Aston Villa for just four months when they won the European Cup in 1982.

Ron Saunders went to Wembley three years running as a manager of a League Cup Final side: 1973 Norwich City (lost to Spurs), 1974 Manchester City (lost to Wolves) and 1975 Aston Villa (beat Norwich).

Tommy Docherty was sacked as boss of Manchester United only six weeks after leading the Reds to victory in the 1977 FA Cup Final ...because of tabloid revelations about his love-affair with the wife of Laurie Brown, the Old Trafford club's physiotherapist. The 'Doc' who, in his own words, said that he'd had more clubs than Jack Nicklaus, managed Rotherham United, QPR and Aston Villa in a six-week period: 6 November to 18 December 1968.

Brian Little spent just 49 days in charge at Molineux and Ron Atkinson three months (94 days) as boss of Atletico Madrid.

Ex-Villa star Billy Walker was the first manager to lead two different clubs to FA Cup glory at Wembley: Sheffield Wednesday in 1935 (v WBA) and Nottingham Forest in 1959 (v Luton Town).

Ex-Villa right-half Danny Blanchflower managed the Northern Ireland national team; two former Villa bosses have also managed England: Joe Mercer and Graham Taylor; Tommy Docherty managed Villa and Scotland, Josef Venglos managed both the Australian and Czechoslovakian national teams and Brian Tiler was in charge of the Zambian national team that qualified for the 1980 Olympic Games.

Alex Massie and Bruce Rioch both managed Torquay United.

Noel Blake, Frank Broome and Brian Godfrey all had spells in charge of Exeter City.

Brian Little, Graham Turner and Graham Taylor managed both Villa and Wolves.

Ex-Villa players Bob Brocklebank and Ivor Powell both managed Bradford City, while Gordon Hodgson and Gordon Lee were once in charge of Port Vale.

Ron Atkinson, Brian Little and Ron Saunders all managed both Aston Villa and West Bromwich Albion.

Future Aston Villa managers Tony Barton and Ron Saunders were in the Portsmouth forward-line together when Pompey won the Third Division championship in 1961-62.

Brian Little and John Gidman were appointed manager and assistant-manager respectively at Darlington in February 1989.

Allan Evans was Brian Little's assistant at Villa Park, Leicester City, Stoke City and West Bromwich Albion.

Eric Houghton, later to return as Villa manager, signed Ron Wylie on professional forms when he was boss of Notts County in 1950.

Ex-Villa player Ken O. Roberts was manager of Chester when they played Aston Villa in the semi-final of the League Cup in 1975.

During their respective careers the following ex-Aston Villa players and/or managers all received various 'Manager of the Month' or 'Manager of the Year' awards: Ron Atkinson, Vic Crowe, John Gregory, Brian Little, Chris Nicholl, Bruce Rioch, Ron Saunders, Graham Taylor, Graham Turner and Josef Venglos.

David Platt is currently in charge of the England U21 team.

### MANCHESTER CITY (ARDWICK)

Villa's playing record against City:
Football League/Premiership

| Venue | P | W | D | L | F | A |
|---|---|---|---|---|---|---|
| Home | 63 | 32 | 20 | 11 | 116 | 69 |
| Away | 63 | 15 | 15 | 33 | 82 | 119 |
| Totals | 126 | 46 | 35 | 44 | 198 | 188 |

| FA Cup | | | | | | |
|---|---|---|---|---|---|---|
| Home | 3 | 2 | 0 | 1 | 7 | 5 |
| Away | 3 | 0 | 1 | 2 | 1 | 3 |
| Neutral | 1 | 0 | 0 | 1 | 1 | 6 |
| Totals | 7 | 2 | 1 | 4 | 9 | 14 |

THE COMPLETE ENCYCLOPAEDIA OF ASTON VILLA F.C.          THE COMPLETE ENCYCLOPAEDIA OF ASTON VILLA F.C.

174

League Cup
Home    3      2      0      1      6      1

FA Charity Shield
Home    1      0      0      1      0      1

Aston Villa and Manchester City first met at League level in season 1899-1900. Villa won both matches: 2-1 at home and 2-0 away.
In December 1900 Villa whipped City 7-1 at home, George Johnson scoring four times. However, on the last day of that season the boot was on the other foot when just 7,000 fans saw City beat Villa 4-0!

*Goal - for Dean Saunders against Manchester City at Villa Park in April 1993.*

City completed their first double over Villa in 1903-04; it would be over 70 years before they claimed their second (in 1977-78).
Joe Bache scored a hat-trick when Villa won 6-2 at City in September 1911 and four months later Charlie Wallace netted twice (one from the penalty spot) as Villa doubled up with a 3-1 home victory.
Villa's last League win before the Great War was a 4-1 home success over City on 21 April 1915.
In December 1928 Villa licked City 5-1 at home but four months later they went down 3-0 at Maine Road!
In December 1929 a crowd of 70,000 saw Villa win 2-1 at Maine Road but when Villa returned to that venue and lost 3-1 twelve months later the attendance had dropped to 30,000.
In 1934-35, FA Cup holders City lost 4-2 at Villa Park but triumphed 4-1 at Maine Road. And it was City 5 Villa 0 in Manchester in December 1935. This latter defeat dropped Villa to the foot of the First Division where they stayed until the season ended!
Almost twenty years later, in October 1954, Tommy Thompson scored a hat-trick as Villa won 4-2 at Maine Road and then Stan Lynn netted twice in a 2-0 home win to earn Villa the double.
City and Villa were involved in a First Division relegation battle at the end of the 1958-59 season. City survived with a 3-1 last match win over Leicester while Villa went down after drawing 1-1 at West Brom.
In 1960-61 Villa, after returning to the top flight, beat City 5-1 at home, but then lost the return League game 4-1 at Maine Road. Gerry Hitchens netted a rare penalty in the home win and Vic Crowe scored in the away game.
Villa ended a club record run of 11 successive League defeats by beating City 3-1 at home in a First Division game on 8 May 1963. Harry Burrows netted two penalties in this fixture....but he hit the bar with a third spot-kick which could have equalled the record of three penalties in a game claimed by former Villa favourite Billy Walker.

Villa lost 4-1 at home to City in August 1977; they gained revenge with a 3-2 victory at Maine Road on the last day of the 1978-79 campaign and then took three points off City when winning the championship in 1980-81, drawing 2-2 away (Peter Withe netting both goals) and gaining a 1-0 success at home courtesy of a Gary Shaw effort.
David Platt's penalty was no consolation at all as Villa were crushed 5-1 at home by City in April 1991 but this was quickly forgotten when the corresponding fixture eight months later saw Villa win 3-1 with three black players, Tony Daley, Cyrille Regis and Dwight Yorke all on target.
David Ginola's wicked 20-yard drive (his first goal for the club) earned Villa a point from a 2-2 home draw with City in December 2000.
In the return fixture at Maine Road that season, City's 'keeper Nicky Weaver gifted Dion Dublin the simplest of goals in Villa's 3-1 win - a result that helped send the Mancunians back to the First Division!
Villa and City both won 20 out of 30 home League games against each other up to World War Two.
Villa had one excellent run of seven successive home victories during the 1920s.
Gordon Cowans (1976) and Vic Crowe (1954) both made their Football League debuts for Villa in games against City at Maine Road.

Villa suffered their heaviest defeat in the FA Cup in March 1934, beaten 6-1 in the semi-final at Leeds Road, Huddersfield by Manchester City in front of 45,473 spectators. Fred Tilson scored four times for City in a one-sided contest.
Four years later (in March 1938) Villa gained some revenge with a 3-2 quarter-final home win over City in front of 75,540 fans - a record at the time and now registered as the second biggest ever attendance at Villa Park.

Villa's two League Cup wins over City were both 3-0 - in the opening round of the 1976-77 competition and in the third round in 1983-84. City knocked Villa out of the competition in 2000-01, winning 1-0 at Villa Park.
Francis Lee scored the only goal of the Charity Shield game at Villa Park in August 1972.

Players with both clubs include: D Atkinson, E Barrett, RAJ Brown (City WW2 guest), CS Buckley (City reserve), FC Buckley (Villa reserve), J Burridge, F Carrodus, JM Deehan, AJ Fisher, J Gidman, H Harvey, JH Harvey (City reserve, Villa trialist), AP Heath, R Hopkins, SF Horne, MA Lillis, B Little (City trialist), RW McDonald, JS McLuckie, S McMahon, K McNaught, W Myerscough (City junior trialist), CL Roberts (Villa reserve), LGF Smith (City WW2 guest), B Stobart, J Whitehouse (City reserve), PA Woosnam (City Amateur).
Also: W McNeill, J Mercer & R Saunders (managers of both clubs), J McMullan (City player, Villa manager), Arthur Cox (Villa assistant-manager/caretaker-manager, City Chief Scout), RS Chatt (Villa player, City trainer), AJE Scott (Villa player, City coach), PD Doherty (City player, Villa chief scout).

## MANCHESTER UNITED (NEWTON HEATH)

Villa's playing record against United:
Football League/Premiership

| Venue | P | W | D | L | F | A |
|---|---|---|---|---|---|---|
| Home | 68 | 32 | 17 | 19 | 135 | 98 |
| Away | 68 | 10 | 15 | 43 | 62 | 140 |
| Totals | 136 | 42 | 32 | 62 | 197 | 238 |

FA Cup

| | | | | | | |
|---|---|---|---|---|---|---|
| Home | 2 | 0 | 0 | 2 | 4 | 8 |
| Away | 5 | 1 | 0 | 4 | 5 | 11 |
| Neutral | 1 | 1 | 0 | 0 | 2 | 1 |
| Totals | 8 | 2 | 0 | 6 | 11 | 20 |

THE COMPLETE ENCYCLOPAEDIA OF ASTON VILLA F.C.  THE COMPLETE ENCYCLOPAEDIA OF ASTON VILLA F.C.

175

League Cup

| | | | | | | |
|---|---|---|---|---|---|---|
| Home | 4 | 3 | 0 | 1 | 7 | 3 |
| Away | 1 | 0 | 1 | 0 | 1 | 1 |
| Neutral | 1 | 1 | 0 | 0 | 3 | 1 |
| Totals | 6 | 4 | 1 | 1 | 11 | 5 |

FA Charity Shield

| | | | | | | |
|---|---|---|---|---|---|---|
| Away | 1 | 0 | 0 | 1 | 0 | 4 |

The first ever League encounter between the clubs was on 19 November 1892 when Newton Heath beat Villa 2-0 at North Road.

Welsh international wing-wizard Billy Meredith made his Football League debut for Manchester United against Villa in January 1907, helping the Reds to a 1-0 victory.

Villa were 4-0 up at half-time against United in a League game in February 1910. They eventually triumphed 7-1 with Joey Walters scoring a hat-trick.

Ten months later - on 17 December 1910 - United won 2-0 at home and so ended Villa's record-equalling run of nine successive League victories. This was Villa's first visit to Old Trafford.

A total of 28 goals were scored in the five League games against United at Villa Park leading up the Great War.

In April 1911, Villa won 4-2 after United forward Enoch West had been sent-off; they romped to a 6-0 win in March 1912 (when Clem Stephenson scored a hat-trick); recorded another 4-2 victory in November 1912; won 3-1 in November 1913 and were held at 3-3 in the final match in December 1914. Nine months earlier, on 14 March, Villa had raced to an emphatic 6-0 win at Old Trafford, Joe Bache netting a hat-trick in front of 30,000 fans.

A record League crowd at Old Trafford of 70,504 saw Villa beat United 3-1 on 27 December 1920 - just 48 hours after United had won 4-3 at Villa Park! Goalkeeper Ed Wright made his League debut for Villa in the clash at Old Trafford and he played a blinder! Billy Walker and Clem Stephenson shared the six Villa goals between them.

In 1927-28, the two League encounters produced another 10 goals as Villa lost 5-1 at Old Trafford, but won 3-1 at Villa Park.

United's inside-right Jimmy Hanson was sent-off when Villa were held to a 0-0 home draw in September 1928.

Villa lost 2-1 to United in the second League game between the two clubs after World War Two....at Maine Road on 8 March 1947. Earlier in the season the teams had drawn 0-0 at Villa Park.

The following season Villa played TWO League matches at Maine Road v Manchester City and United. They lost 2-0 to the Reds.

United hit top form by running in eleven goals without reply against Villa in the two League matches in 1949-50. They won 4-0 at Villa Park and 7-0 at Old Trafford (this second scoreline was repeated 14 years later). In this 'first' seven-goal romp, United netted six times after half-time as Villa's defence crumbled under pressure. Charlie Mitten hit a hat-trick of penalties for the Reds.

In October 1951 it was Villa 2 United 5 (after Villa had led 2-1 at the break); it was all-square at 3-3 on Villa soil in September 1952 and an eight-goal thriller ended level at 4-4 at Villa Park in October 1955. Villa were 4-2 up after 60 minutes in the latter game

In season 1957-58, besides United's big Charity Shield win, the Reds also whipped Villa 4-1 at Old Trafford in the League.

Villa then beat United, the FA Cup holders, 4-0 at Villa Park in November 1963 (Tony Hateley opening the scoring after 35 seconds while Denis Law of United was later sent-off). But a year or so later United slammed the 10 men of Villa 7-0 at Old Trafford for the second time. Hateley was the player who went off as Law made up for his early bath by whipping in four goals for the Reds. In May 1966 Villa slumped to another heavy defeat in Manchester, losing 6-1 on this occasion in front of just 23,034 spectators!

Twelve goals were scored in the two First Division matches between Villa and United in 1980-81. Both ended in 3-3 draws.

The following season United beat Villa 4-1 at Old Trafford and took the

points with a 3-1 victory on the same ground in January 1983.

A week after losing 6-2 at home to Arsenal, Villa went to Old Trafford in November 1983 and beat United 2-1 with a brace of goals from Peter Withe.

United twice beat Villa 4-0 at Old Trafford in 1985 - first in March and then in August (on the opening day of the season).

In December 1986 there was another 3-3 draw at Villa Park while three years later (on Boxing Day 1989) a best-of-season crowd of 41,247 saw Villa beat United 3-0 at home.

Villa began their 1995-96 Premiership programme with a 3-1 home win over United. They led 3-0 at half-time.

United doubled up over Villa in the Premiership in 1999-2000 and again in 2000-01. They were victorious by 3-0 at Old Trafford and 1-0 at Villa Park in the former and won 1-0 away and 2-0 at home in the latter. There was an attendance of 67,533 for the game at Old Trafford in January 2001 ....the first 60,000 plus crowd Villa had played in front of at League level since August 1962 when 64,751 fans saw the home game with Spurs.

As holders of the FA Cup, Villa were brushed aside in the 3rd round of the competition in 1906, beaten 5-1 by United at the Reds' Bank Street ground.

After scoring first after just 13 seconds through George Edwards (the second-fastest goal at Villa Park) Villa then found themselves 5-1 down

*Johnny Dixon's shot hits the Manchester United bar in the 1957 F.A. Cup Final - but Peter McParland pounced to crack home the rebound.*

to Manchester United at half-time in a third round FA Cup-tie in January 1948. Villa fought back gallantly and reduced the deficit to 5-4 before United clinched the game to win 6-4.

Harold Halse and Stan Crowther both appeared in FA Cup Finals for Villa and United.

Crowther lined up for Villa against United in the 1957 showdown when 99,225 spectators inside the stadium saw Villa win 2-1 and so deny United the double. Peter McParland netted both goals that day while Tommy Taylor headed a late consolation for the Reds whose 'keeper Ray Wood was injured in a collision with McParland early in the game when the sheet was blank. This injury upset United's game and with Jackie Blanchflower in goal, Villa capitalised on the obvious advantage to lift the trophy for the seventh time.

The last two FA Cup meetings have gone United's way, Villa losing 1-0 in the 4th round in 1963 and 2-1 in the quarter-final in 1977, each time at Old Trafford, the latter tie attracting a crowd of over 57,000.

Underdogs Aston Villa from the Third Division met mighty Manchester United over two legs in the semi-final of the League Cup in 1970-71. After a terrific performance at Old Trafford where they gained a 1-1 draw, Villa were pegged back by a fourteenth minute Brian Kidd goal in the return leg. But Andy Lochhead equalised on 37 minutes and then Pat McMahon brought Villa Park to its feet with a dramatic 72nd minute winner to send Villa to Wembley for the first time in 14 years. Dean Saunders' 75th goal was enough to see Villa knock the holders United out of the League Cup in October 1992

In March 1994 a crowd of 77,231 saw Villa defeat United 3-1 in the League Cup Final at Wembley. Dalian Atkinson (25 minutes) gave Villa a deserved lead and Dean Saunders, appearing in his 500th League and Cup game of his career, scored twice late on (in the 75th and 89th minutes). His second came from the penalty spot after the Ukranian

*Gary Shaw with Gordon McQueen in close attention: Villa Park.*

Andrei Kanchelskis had handled on the line and was subsequently sent-off. Mark Hughes had brought United briefly back into the game with an 83rd minute strike.

With this victory Villa joined Liverpool and Nottingham Forest as the only clubs to win the League Cup four times, each having played in six Finals. For skipper Kevin Richardson, who was voted 'Man of the Match' it was third time lucky, having been a loser in 1984 with Everton and 1988 with Arsenal. Former Villa goalkeeper Les Sealey played for United as a late replacement for the injured Peter Schmeichel.

The FA Charity Shield game between the two clubs was at Old Trafford five months after the 1957 FA Cup Final. A crowd of almost 28,000 saw United gain revenge for the Wembley defeat by winning 4-0. This was the first time Villa had, in fact, played a full first-class game under floodlights!

Players with both clubs include: WJ Anderson, F Barson, M Bosnich, HE Bourne (United reserve), FB Brett (Villa reserve), FC Buckley, RA

Chester, A Comyn (United 'A' team), S Cooke (United School of Excellence, Villa junior), S Crowther, D Dublin, CJ Gibson, J Gidman, HJ Halse, P McGrath, AF McLoughlin (United reserve), FD Mann, R Milne (Villa trialist), MJ Pinner, DA Platt (United reserve), JJ Rimmer, L Sealey, W Thompson (Villa reserve), JE Travers, J Warner, J Whitehouse, TC Wilson, W Yates (Villa reserve).

Also: R Atkinson & T Docherty (managers of both clubs), DJ Sexton (United manager, Villa coach), M Musgrove (assistant-manager/coach at United & Villa coach), B Whitehouse (scout of both clubs, also coach at United).

### MANDLEY, JOHN

Born: Hanley, Stoke-on-Trent, 12 February 1909. Died: Bucknall, Stoke-on-Trent, December 1988.

Career: Hanley Council School, North Staffs Sunday League football, Port Vale (Amateur, August 1926, professional February 1928), Aston Villa (£7,000, March 1930), Retired May 1934.

A tricky, elusive winger with good pace and strong shot, Jack Mandley could deliver the perfect cross (given the chance). He worked as a haulage hand at the Cobridge coalpit before joining Port Vale. After 51 outings for the Valiants (six goals scored) he took over the right-wing berth at Villa Park from Dicky York, but then lost his place following the arrival of Arthur Cuniffe as Eric Houghton switched wings. Nicknamed 'Potter', Mandley netted 26 times in 112 senior outings for Villa.

### MANN, CHRISTOPHER JAMES

Born: West Smethwick, January 1877. Died: Birmingham, July 1934.

Career: Smethwick Hall, West Bromwich Albion (Amateur), Aston Villa (March 1899), Burton United (September 1901), Mickleover FRD (September 1905).

A strong, positive defender, Chris Mann replaced James Cowan in each of his 11 senior games for the club. After leaving Villa Park, Mann went on to appear in more than 120 League and Cup games for Burton Utd.

### MANN, FRANK DRURY

Born: Newark, 17 March 1891. Died: Nottingham, February 1959

Career: Newark Castle United, Newark Castle Rovers, Newark Town, Leeds City (amateur, February 1909), Lincoln City (amateur, March 1909), Aston Villa (amateur December 1909, professional May 1911, Huddersfield Town (£1,000, July 1912), Manchester United (£1,750, March 1923), Mossley (August 1930), Meltham Mills FC (re-instated as an amateur, October 1931). Retired in 1932, aged 41.

Signed as an orthodox right-winger, Frank Mann made just one appearance for Aston Villa versus Blackburn Rovers (home) in March 1912, as a replacement for Charlie Wallace.

He headed Huddersfield's scoring charts in his first two seasons at Leeds Road. He retained his goal touch after the hostilities and netted 18 times in 43 games in 1919-20 when the Terriers came so close to completing the double, finishing runners-up in both the First Division championship and FA Cup Final (the latter against his old club, Villa).

Mann collected his FA Cup winners' medal in 1922 and a year later, after netting 75 goals in 226 outings for Huddersfield, he was transferred to Manchester United at the age of 32. Amazingly after his departure the Yorkshire club went on to record three successive League championship triumphs! Mann continued to play superbly well for the Reds who successfully converted him a wing-half. He starred in the Old Trafford club's Second Division promotion-winning side in 1924-25, being the important link between defence and attack. Nimble, fleet of foot, quick-thinking and remarkably consistent, Mann made 197 first-class appearances for United (five goals scored) before drifing into non-League football at the ripe old age of 39.

After leaving Villa Park, Mann went on to make a total of 423 League and FA Cup appearances and notched 80 goals. Certainly 'one that got away' as far as Aston Villa were concerned!

## MANSFIELD TOWN

Villa's playing record against the Stags:
Football League

| Venue | P | W | D | L | F | A |
|-------|---|---|---|---|---|---|
| Home | 2 | 0 | 0 | 2 | 0 | 2 |
| Away | 2 | 0 | 1 | 1 | 1 | 3 |
| Totals | 4 | 0 | 1 | 3 | 1 | 5 |

The first time the teams met at competitive level was in season 1970-71 (Division 3) and, in fact, it was the Stags who inflicted upon Villa their first ever defeat in this section, winning 1-0 at Villa Park on 31 August, Malcolm Partridge the scorer.

The following April, Mansfield duly completed the double with a 2-0 win at Field Mill.

The very next season over 28,000 fans saw Villa once more suffer their first home defeat of the season at the hands of the Stags, who again won 1-0 on 22 September 1971 with a goal by Davey Jones on 79 minutes.

However, the point gained by Villa from the 1-1 draw at Field Mill on 24 April 1972 was enough to clinch promotion from the Third Division.

Players with both clubs include: J Beresford, F Biddlestone (Stags reserve), GF Blackburn, M Blake, C Calderwood, RC Chapman, RA Chester (Stags trialist), GB Clarke, J Depledge (Villa reserve), RT Edwards, RA Hogg, D Hunt, T Mitchinson, W Moore (Villa reserve), AF Phoenix, MJ Pinner, LP Price, RT Pritchard (Stags' WW2 guest), FH Shell, T Ward & L Williams (Villa reserves).

Also: T Cummings (Mansfield player & manager of both clubs), J Barron (assistant-manager of Stags, coach and assistant-boss of Villa).

## MARILA PRIBRAM

Villa's playing record against the Czech club:

InterToto Cup

| Venue | P | W | D | L | F | A |
|-------|---|---|---|---|---|---|
| Home | 1 | 1 | 0 | 0 | 3 | 1 |
| Away | 1 | 0 | 1 | 0 | 0 | 0 |
| Totals | 2 | 1 | 1 | 0 | 3 | 1 |

Aston Villa played the Czechoslovakian side in a two-legged InterToto Cup-tie in July 2000....and had a player sent-off in each game - Mark Delaney in the away leg and Paul Merson in the return fixture. After forcing a 0-0 draw in the Stadion Na Litavce in Prague in front of 7,852 spectators, Villa progressed into the next round with a 3-1 win at The Hawthorns, the ground they used while redevelopment work was being carried out at Villa Park. On target on Baggies' territory were Dion Dublin, Ian Taylor and Luc Nilis (on his Villa debut). Lee Hendrie missed a penalty and the attendance was 8,205.

## MARRIOTT, WILLIAM W.

Born: Northampton, April 1880. Died: Cambridge, January 1944.
Career: Wellingborough, Aston Villa (April 1901), Bristol Rovers (September 1902), Northampton Town (August 1904), New Brompton (July 1905-May 1908).

An energetic winger, Bill Marriott had a brief run in Villa's first team when injuries were causing a problem during the 1901-02 season. He made eight senior appearances before moving to Bristol Rovers for whom he netted six times in 56 outings. He later did well with the Cobblers (34 games) and also with New Brompton, scoring 14 goals in 80 Southern League encounters for the latter club.

## MARSHALL, FREDERICK ARNOLD

Born: Walsall, 1870. Died: Wednesbury
Career: Broadway Council School (Walsall), Wednesbury Old Athletic, Aston Villa (April 1890), Nechells (September 1891), Walsall Town Swifts season 1892-93), Bordesley Green Victoria (1893-96).

A determined winger, able to play on both flanks, Fred Marshall made just three League appearances for Aston Villa and followed up with six in Division Two with the Swifts.

## MARTIN, CORNELIUS JOSEPH

Born: Dublin, 20 March 1923
Career: Drumcondra, Glentoran, Leeds United (December 1946), Aston Villa (September 1948), Waterford (player-manager, July 1956-May 1964). Retired to live and work Ireland.

'A broth of a Bhoy from Dublin's fair city' Con Martin, 6ft 1in tall and weighing 13 stone, was a wonderful, versatile footballer who could play anywhere and often did!

Under manager Major Frank Buckley (once a Villa reserve team player), he had appeared in 49 League and FA Cup games for Leeds United as a left-back, centre-half, left-half and inside-forward, before moving to Villa Park to become the only Irishman at the club.

He was immediately installed in the centre-half position but during his first season played a few games at right-back. He missed only two games in 1949-50 and was a permanent fixture in defence for two-thirds of the following campaign before injury sidelined him for two months.

Then, having shown what his capabilities were, he became Villa's first-choice goalkeeper at the start of the 1951-52 campaign, taking over between the posts from Joe Rutherford. Martin had started the campaign at left-back with Rutherford in goal, but thereafter he took on the green jersey and played exceptionally well, making 27 appearances (26 League, one FA Cup) as the last line of defence in two spells that were split when John Cordell stepped in for three games and Rutherford returned for his last outing for the club in October. Martin eventually reverted back to the centre-half position following the emergence of Keith Jones and he remained in Villa's defence (injuries and international duties apart) until December 1955 when Jimmy Dugdale was recruited as pivot from neighbouring West Bromwich Albion.

Martin left Villa Park after making 213 senior appearances and scoring one goal - a penalty in a 4-1 League win at Charlton in April 1950.

He represented both Northern Ireland and the Republic of Ireland at senior international level, winning a total of 36 caps between 1946 and 1956 (30 for the FAI and six for IFA). He was rated as one of the best three centre-halves in European football in 1949-50 after helping Eire to that historic and record-breaking 2-0 win over England at Goodison Park.

So keen and determined to play football, Con Martin was Villa's centre-half against Stoke City on 10 April 1948 and 24 hours later he lined up for the Republic of Ireland against Belgium in Dublin.

One interesting statistical fact is that more than one million spectators attended the 27 League games Con Martin kept goal in for Aston Villa - and 56,177 were present for the Cup-tie at St James' Park.

Con's son, Mick Martin, was a professional with Manchester United, West Bromwich Albion and Newcastle United during the 1970s/80s and he too played for the Republic of Ireland.

## MARTIN, GEORGE SCOTT

Born: Bothwell, Lanarkshire, 14 August 1899. Died: Luton, 1972.
Career: Cadzow St Anne's FC (Motherwell), Bo'ness, Hamilton Academical (season 1920-21), Bathgate FC (on loan), Hull City (October 1922), Everton (March 1928), Middlesbrough (May 1932), Luton Town (August 1933, retired 1937, appointed coach at Kenilworth Road and then manager, August 1939-May 1947), Newcastle United (manager, May 1947-December 1950)), Aston Villa (manager, December 1950-August 1953), Luton Town (chief scout, 1960, caretaker-manager, February 1965-November 1966).

As a player, George Martin was a fast, powerful versatile footballer who occupied five different outfield positions. He appeared in more than

THE COMPLETE ENCYCLOPAEDIA OF ASTON VILLA F.C.   ASTON VILLA   THE COMPLETE ENCYCLOPAEDIA OF ASTON VILLA F.C.

178

*George Martin*

425 League and FA Cup games and scored in excess of 120 goals, and performing alongside the great Dixie Dean, he helped Everton win the Second Division championship in 1931. In his first spell in charge of Luton, Martin introduced several quality players and successfully built the club up again after the War. A smart, elegant man, he then guided Newcastle back to the First Division in 1948 before managing Aston Villa for almost three years, during which time the team competed in a total of 104 League games, winning 41, drawing 28 and losing 35. His first major signing for the club was centre-forward Dave Walsh and he also secured the services of three more Irish internationals, Danny Blanchflower, Norman Lockhart and Peter McParland ...

...plus a few others.

Martin was a talented sculptor and fine singer who made several records during the 1940s.

## MARTIN, JOHN

Born: Ashington, 4 December 1946
Career: Ashington & County Durham Schools, Aston Villa (apprentice July 1962, professional July 1964), Colchester United (May 1966), Workington (July 1969), Southport (August 1974-May 1976), Torquay United (briefly, August-September 1976).
John Martin was a useful winger, neat and tidy who was given just one first-team outing by Villa, against Blackpool at Bloomfiueld Road in September 1964, when he occupied the left-wing berth, allowing Harry Burrows to move inside. After leaving Villa Park, Martin scored 11 goals in 78 League appearances for Colchester, netted 32 in 207 games for Workington and notched another seven in 63 matches for Southport.

## MARTIN, JOHN ROWLAND

Born: Hamstead, Birmingham 5 August 1914. Died: 1996.
Career: Rugeley High School, St Mark's & St John's College (London), London Combined Colleges (1932-33), Hednesford Town (October 1934), Aston Villa (January 1935). Retired May 1949 to concentrate on teaching, later becoming headmaster of Lilleworth Secondary Modern School, Hednesford. He also managed Hednesford Town and guested for Tottenham Hotpur during WW2.
Jackie Martin was a 'Corinthian-type' forward, big and strong who won international honours during the Second World War when assisting England aginst Wales and Scotland. He also represented the Football League, the FA XI and an All-British side between 1939 and 1943. The hostilities certainly disrupted Martin's career but nevertheless he still netted 22 goals in 53 League and FA Cup appearances for Aston Villa as well as playing for the club in 48 Wartime games (14 goals scored).

## MARTIN, LIONEL JOHN

Born: Ludlow, 15 May 1947
Career: Cleobury Mortimer & Clee Hill Schools, Shropshire Boys, Clee Hill Boys, Aston Villa (apprentice, July 1962, professional July 1964), Doncaster Rovers (on loan, March-April 1971), Worcester City (£2,500, July 1972-80). Later assistant-manager of both Dudley Town and Tamworth. Earned a living after football as a stores manager for the Birmingham Parks Department (Erdington) and also as a garage manager.
A clever, hard-working inside-forward, Lionel Martin scored nine goals in 58 first-team outings for Aston Villa, but made only one appearance, as a substitute, in the 1971-72 Third Division championship-winning season. He later helped Worcester City win the Southern League Premier title in 1979.

*Lionel Martin*

## MASEFIELD, KEITH LEONARD

Born: Birmingham, 26 February 1957
Career: Warwickshire & District Schools, Aston Villa (apprentice, June 1972, professional October 1974-August 1977), Haarlem in Holland (September 1977-79).
Having done very well at intermediate and reserve team levels, full-back Keith Masefield made the first of his three senior appearances for Aston Villa as a substitute (for Ray Graydon) in a 2-0 home League win over Manchester United in February 1975. His contract was cancelled by mutual consent in August 1977. Later did reasonably well in Dutch football.

## MASON, THOMAS WALTER

Born: Burton-on-Trent, April 1861. Died: Derby.
Career: Burton Alsopp's FC (1890), Aston Villa (July 1882), Burton (August 1883), Derby St Luke's (season 1885-86).
A reliable and safe goalkeeper who weighed in excess of 14 stones, Tommy Mason made three FA Cup appearances for Aston Villa during his one season at the club.

## MASON, WILLIAM BERNARD

Born: Birmingham, February 1885. Died: Birmingham, September 1922.
Career: Moseley Grasshoppers (1872), Aston Villa (player, late 1874, the player/secretary of club from season 1874-75), Wednesbury Town (August 1880).
Founder member of Aston Villa Football Club and its first honorary secretary, Bill Mason was a well-built forward who enjoyed dribbling with the ball, to the annoyance of his colleagues! He played in the club's first two FA Cup games against Stafford Road (Wolverhampton), scoring twice in the 3-2 replay victory.

## MASSIE, ALEXANDER C.

Born: Possilpark, Glasgow, 13 March 1906. Died: Welwyn Garden City, 20 September 1977.
Career: Shawfield Juniors, Partick Thistle, Petershill, Glasgow Benburb, Glasgow Ashfield, Ayr United, Bury (£1,000, January 1927), Bethlehem Steel Corporation FC, USA (August 1928), Dolphin FC, Dublin (August 1930), Heart of Midlothian (October 1930), Aston Villa (£6,000, December 1935-May 1945, retired, appointed manager, August 1945-

THE COMPLETE ENCYCLOPAEDIA OF ASTON VILLA F.C.                    THE COMPLETE ENCYCLOPAEDIA OF ASTON VILLA F.C.

179

August 1950), Torquay United (manager, November 1950-September 1951), Hereford United (manager, October 1951-November 1952); thereafter coached local amateur sides in Welwyn Garden City. Guested for Birmingham, Hearts, Nottingham Forest, Notts County, Portsmouth and Solihull Town during WW2.

A Scottish international wing-half (18 caps won) Alex Massie also played for the Scottish League representative side on six occasions and helped Villa win the Second Division championship in 1938 and the Wartime League North Cup in 1944. After failing to impress at Gigg Lane as a 21 year-old he went to America to work and play football, returning with an appetite for the game which he never lost. A player who always wore an odd-sized pair of boots, Massie was successfully converted from an inside-forward into a wing-half at Tynecastle. He was a methodical footballer with poise, skill and commitment. He had remarkable positional sense and drove his team-mates on with unstinting determination. He made well over 350 League and Cup appearances either side of the border before the outbreak of the Second World War. His record with Aston Villa in peacetime football was 152 appearances and five goals scored and during the hostilities he added a further 131 games to his tally before retiring to take over as manager. Massie was subsequently barracked by the supporters after failing to bring success on the field. During his time in charge, Villa played 168 League matches, recorded 68 victories, played out 40 draws and suffered 60 defeats.

## MATTHEWS, WILLIAM
Born: Mansfield, July 1880. Died: Nottinghamshire.
Career: Ripley FC, Aston Villa (August 1903), Notts County (December 1906), Derby County, Newport County. Retired through injury, summer of 1914.
Bill Matthews was an aggressive, dynamic centre-forward, full of enterprise who scored a goal every two games for Aston Villa - 12 in 25 senior appearances. He went on to net 36 times in 177 League games for Notts County and, in fact, is one of only a handful of footballers, who have served with three League clubs, each possessing the name of County.

## MAUND, JOHN HENRY
Born: Hednesford, 5 January 1914. Died: Stafford 19 August 1995.
Career: Hednesford Town (1932), Aston Villa (October 1934), Nottingham Forest (July 1939), Walsall (October 1946), non-League football 1947-50.
Short. Stocky wing-forward (5ft 4in in height and weighing barely 11 stone), Jackie Maund (right) scored eight times in 48 first team appearances for Aston Villa. The War disrupted his time with Forest but after the hostilities he netted seven times in 32 Third Division (South) games for the Saddlers.

## MAYOR
Former 1920s Aston Villa centre-forward Percy Seymour Varco had two separate spells as Lord Mayor of Fowey, Cornwall.
Villa's 1905 FA Cup winning right-half Joe Pearson held the position of Mayor of Stourbridge for two years: 1941-42.
Alderman Sir T. Pritchett, a former Aston Villa President, was also the Lord Mayor of Birmingham. And in 1960 he was made a Honorary Freeman of the City of Birmingham.

## McAULEY, WILLIAM
Born: Glasgow, September 1879. Died: Scotland.
Career: Glasgow & District Schools, Celtic (trialist), Walsall, Sheffield Wednesday (trialist), Celtic (1898-99), Aston Villa (August 1900), Portsmouth (May 1901), Middlesbrough (July 1902-May 1903).
An orthodox inside-forward who replaced Jack Devey on six occasions during his season at Villa Park. He made 28 senior appearances for Walsall and 21 for Middlesbrough plus 11 in the Southern League with Pompey.

## McAVENNIE, FRANK
Born: Glasgow, 22 November 1959.
Career: St Johnstone Boys' club (1978), St Mirren (March 1980), West Ham United (£340,000, June 1985), Glasgow Celtic (£800,000, October 1987), West Ham United (£1.25 million, March 1989), Aston Villa (on trial, August-September 1992), Glasgow Celtic (January 1993), Swindon Town (on loan, February 1994). Left Celtic summer of 1994.
After doing well north of the border with St Mirren (50 goals in 135 League games), striker Frank McAvennie then made a massive impact in the Football League with West Ham. Teaming up with Tony Cottee, he netted 39 times in less than 100 appearances for the Hammers in his first two seasons at Upton Park. He then returned to Scotland where he notched 35 goals in 70 appearances for Celtic before returning to West Ham for a second spell in 1989. Manager Ron Atkinson enticed him to Villa Park on trial early in the 1992-93 season but he failed to meet the required standard and left after just three substitute appearances. An international Youth team player, McAvennie was voted Scotland's 'Young Player of the Year' in 1982. He won five Scotland Under-21 caps with St Mirren and later added five full caps to his collection whilst with West Ham and Celtic, also helping the Parkhead side clinch the League and Cup double in Scotland in 1988.

## McCLURE, ALEXANDER
Born: Workington, 3 April 1892. Died: Birmingham, August 1973.
Career: Grangemouth Juniors (Cumbria), Birmingham (January 1912), Aston Villa (December 1923), Stoke (October 1924), Coventry City (1926), Walsall (March-May 1928), Bromsgrove Rovers (coach), Market Harborough (coach), Birmingham (assistant-trainer 1928-32, then assistant-manager 1932-34).
Alec McClure was a solid defender with superb positional sense who served with five different Midland clubs between 1911 and 1928. He became the fulcrum of the defence at St Andrew's and for almost twelve seasons was like a rock, accumulating a fine record of 198 senior appearances and scoring four goals. He spent just 10 months at Villa Park, playing in only seven first-class games, deputising for George Blackburn and Vic Milne.
A sailor during World War One, McClure participated in the Zebrugge Affair (one of the great military actions) and after the hostilities had ended, returned to St Andrew's and helped Blues win the Second Division championship (1921). In May 1923 while on tour with Blues in Spain, he was sent-off against Real Madrid for telling his goalkeeper Dan Tremelling where to stand (right by an upright) when facing a penalty kick!
In 1924 McClure was transferred to Stoke and after serving with Coventry and Walsall, ending his playing days in 1928. He later returned to St Andrew's as assistant-trainer, looking after the junior team (the third XI). In 1932 he was upgraded to assistant-manager, a position he until 1934 when he went to work for Rudge Motor Cycles. McClure later ran a very successful haulage business in Small Heath.
There was a strong link with football within the McClure family. Alec's brother Sammy played for Blackburn Rovers and his nephew Joe for Everton. His daughter now lives in Droitwich.

THE COMPLETE ENCYCLOPAEDIA OF ASTON VILLA F.C.  THE COMPLETE ENCYCLOPAEDIA OF ASTON VILLA F.C.

180

## McDONALD, ROBERT WOOD

Born: Aberdeen, 13 April 1955

Career: Aberdeen Schoolboy football, King Street Sports Club (Aberdeen), Aston Villa (apprentice, June 1971, professional September 1972), Coventry City (£45,000, August 1976), Manchester City (October 1980), Oxford United (September 1983), Leeds United (£25,000, February 1987), Wolverhampton Wanderers (on loan, February-March 1988), VS Rugby (July 1988), Burton Albion (1990), Redditch United (1991), Armitage (1991-92), Burton Albion again (1992-93).

An efficient midfielder or left-back, Bobby McDonald had a fine career in professional football, amassing well over 500 senior appearances for six different clubs with his best set of statistics coming at Highfield Road: 15 goals in 180 outings. He had 45 games for Aston Villa and claimed five goals. He won Scottish Schoolboy caps as a 15 year-old and afterwards served his country at Youth team level. McDonald gained both Junior Floodlit League Cup and FA Youth Cup winners' medals in 1971-72, received a League Cup winners tankard in 1975 and helped Villa win promotion from the Second Division that same year. He was one of John Bond's first signings for Manchester City in 1980.

## McELENY, CHARLES RICHARD

Born: Scotland, June 1876. Died: Scotland.

Career: Celtic (1894-95), Burnley (November 1895), New Brighton (August 1896), Aston Villa (May 1899), Swindon Town (September 1900), Brentford (August 1901), Edinburgh Thistle (1902).

Charlie McEleny was a hard-working, forceful right-half who made well over 100 League and Cup appearances during his career. He was given just one first team outing by Aston Villa, taking over from Tommy Bowman in a 5-0 win at Preston in December 1899. He had a hand in two of the goals.

## McGRATH, JOHN

Born: Limerick, Ireland 27 March 1980.

Career: Irish junior football, Belvedere FC, Aston Villa (professional, March 1998).

An aggressive midfielder, John McGrath made his Premiership debut for Aston Villa as a second-half substitute (for Steve Staunton) in the away game at Chelsea on New Year's Day 2001. He has already won under 21 caps for Republic of Ireland and has had three senior outings for Villa....all as a substitute.

## McGRATH, PAUL

Born: Ealing, London, 4 December 1959.

Career: St Patrick's Athletic (Dublin), Manchester United (£30,000, April 1982), Aston Villa (£450,000, August 1989), Derby County (£100,000, October 1996), Sheffield United (free transfer, August 1997). Retired May 1998.

Born in London, Paul McGrath moved to Ireland with his parents as a youngster and he was 22 years of age when Ron Atkinson signed him for Manchester United. A tall, commanding central defender, well built, he was cool, controlled and steady under pressure and went on to play in 203 first-class games during his seven years at Old Trafford (16 goals scored), gaining an FA Cup winners medal in 1985. Despite his dodgy knees, McGrath continued to do the business for Aston Villa and he certainly paid back the near half-a-million pound transfer fee (with interest!)

He helped Villa beat his old club United in the 1994 League Cup Final and added a second League Cup medal to his collection in 1996 (v Leeds United). As his career continued, so his performances got better and better! He went on win 83 full international caps for the Republic of Eire and starred in 323 senior games for Villa before moving to Derby County in 1996. He ended his career in 1998 with a magnificent club and international record of 648 appearances.

McGrath had his testimonial match in May 1995 when Villa beat Birmingham City 2-0 in front of 12,014 fans at Villa Park (recs. £98,900).

*Paul McGrath in action.*

## McGREGOR, WILLIAM

(Founder of the Football League)

A Scotsman, born in the picturesque village of Braco, Perthshire in 1846, William McGregor saw his first football match 'north of the border' in 1854 (by a group of stonemasons, but in what form is a question unanswered). He was never really interested in playing the game (he tried it once but didn't like it) and moved to Birmingham in 1870. He quickly purchased a drapery business on the corner of Brearley Street and Summer Lane, Aston - a rough area run by the notorious 'Harding Street Gang' where often police were pelted with stones and rocks and indeed ocassionally 'severely manhandled' as they patrolled the streets during the hours of darkness. The infamous Aston riots were instigated by the 'Harding Street Gang' after a Tory Party meeting had been held at the Lower Grounds.

McGregor, a dedicated Methodist and member of the local Liberal Association, a lifelong teetotaller and dour evangelist, renown for his sense of mirth, was lucky enough to get involved with Aston Villa Football Club, initially in 1876 as an organiser and administrator.

By 1880 he was the club's vice-President and soon afterwards became a Director, later taking the position of vice-Chairman, then Chairman and also becoming President of the Football League (1892-94), having earlier acted as Chairman of the both the Football League (1888-92) and the Football Association. He was eventually made a Life Member of the Football League (1895-1911).

One winter's evening in 1886, while chatting with a good friend, Joe Tillotson, the forthcoming friendly match between Aston Villa and Walsall Town crept into the conversation and it was thought that not much of a crowd would turn up. The likes of Blackburn Rovers and

THE COMPLETE ENCYCLOPAEDIA OF ASTON VILLA F.C.        THE COMPLETE ENCYCLOPAEDIA OF ASTON VILLA F.C.

181

Preston North End from Lancashire rarely ventured south and therefore it was commonplace for non-competitive matches to be regularly arranged between local clubs. The chit-chat continued and Tillotson stated that he had heard rumours that a number of clubs in the north were contemplating forming a soccer League modelled on the American baseball system. This left McGregor thinking as he went about putting up the shutters on his shop. A few days later McGregor mentioned the matter to two of his Aston Villa colleagues, Fergus Johnstone and Josuah Margoschis, both of whom were enthusiastic about the idea. Things developed quickly and after a handful of meetings with various members of other clubs, by early March 1888 McGregor knew he had gained enough support to set the ball rolling and form a competition whereby teams would form a League and play against each other at home and away on a seasonal basis.

On 22 March 1888, McGregor called a meeting at Anderton's Hotel in London. The clubs represented were Aston Villa, Derby County, Notts County, Stoke, Wolverhampton Wanderers and West Bromwich Albion from the Midlands, but only Blackburn Rovers and Burnley from the north. No clubs from the south attended.

A month later, however, on 17 April 1888 at the Royal Hotel in Manchester, representatives from fifteen clubs were present, the others being Accrington, Bolton Wanderers, Everton, Halliwell (Sheffield), Nottingham Forest, Preston North End and Sheffield Wednesday. Halliwell, Forest and Wednesday were not accepted because of the difficulty in arranging fixtures - but the others were....and on that very day the Football League was formed, the original 12 members agreeing to an annual subscription of £2. 2s (£2.10).

*William McGregor*

McGregor had done a wonderful job and soccer lovers throughout the world can be proud of what the Scotsman, who came to Birmingham to be readily associated with Aston Villa Football Club, started all those many years ago....a great new competition, which would become the bedrock of the English game.

McGregor (who had been ill since May 1910) died at Miss Storer's Nursing Home in Newhall Street, Birmingham just before Christmas 1911, aged 65. Soon afterwards Villa endowed a bed in his name in the children's Ward of the Birmingham General Hospital.

Two years later, a drinking fountain, set in the wall of the Midland Bank on Lozells Road (the remains of which are now preserved at Villa Park) was unveiled by the Birmingham County FA in memory of William McGregor. And in 1938, an oil painting of the great man was loaned out by Aston Villa to the Football League to celebrate its jubilee year.

### McINALLY, ALAN BRUCE

Born: Ayr, 10 February 1963
Career: Ayrshire & District Schools, Ayr United (season 1979-80), Glasgow Celtic (£110,000, August 1985), Aston Villa (£225,000, July 1987), Bayern Munich (£1 million, July 1989 to 1992).
Striker Alan McInally had a rather disappointing first season in English football, scoring just six goals in 31 games for Aston Villa. But then he

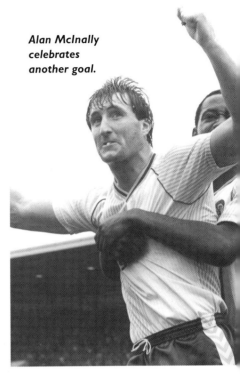

*Alan McInally celebrates another goal.*

netted in each of his first four League matches at the start of the 1988-89 campaign and went on to finish with an excellent record of 28 goals in his 72 appearances for the club before his big-money move to the German Bundesliga.

A member of the Scottish 1990 World Cup squad, McInally, strong and powerful, went on to gain eight full caps for his country. He helped Celtic win the Scottish Premiership in 1985 and 1986 and was a member of Villa's Second Division promotion-winning side in 1988. He hit 35 goals in exactly 200 games for Ayr, notched 22 in 86 outings for Celtic and went on to average a goal every three games with Bayern.

After retiring from football, McInally became a journalist, working amongst others, for the Sunday Mercury newspaper, also acting as a soccer analyst on various TV programmes.

### McKENZIE, JOHN WILSON

Born: Montrose, September 1875. Died: Scotland.
Career: Montrose (1902-04), Dundee (August 1904), Aston Villa (April 1908), Bristol Rovers (July 1909). Retired through injury 1914.
A well built, strong-kicking right-back, Jock McKenzie made well over 100 League and Cup appearances for Dundee before moving to Villa Park where he spent just the one season, having five outings in place of the injured Tommy Lyons.

### McKNIGHT, THOMAS VICTOR

Born: Lichfield, April 1868. Died: Birmingham.
Career: Lichfield St Paul's, Burton Swifts (1889), Aston Villa (May 1890), Leek Alexandra (September 1891-May 1893).
Of medium height but weighty, inside-forward Tom McKnight was a plucky competitor who struggled with injuries throughout his career. He was sent-off along with his Welsh international opponent Caesar Jenkyns, for fighting in a 'friendly' encounter against Small Heath (Birmingham) in February 1891. McKnight scored three times in his 10 outings for Villa before being released.

### McLACHLAN, ALBERT

Born: Kirkcudbright, February 1892. Died: Edinburgh.
Career: St Cuthbert Wanderers, Aston Villa (September 1913), Aberdeen (July 1914), Served in the Military (1916-19), re-engaged by Aberdeen (August 1919), Heart of Midlothian (September 1927). Retired with a persistent groin injury in May 1928.
Younger brother of John (below) Bert McLachlan was a tigerish left-half who tackled strongly, possessing good positional know-how. He never settled in Birmingham however, making just three senior appearances for Aston Villa before going on to amass a grand total of 358 for Aberdeen (16 goals scored). He was the first player to receive two benefits from the Dons. McLachlan represented the Scottish League in 1920.

THE COMPLETE ENCYCLOPAEDIA OF ASTON VILLA F.C.  THE COMPLETE ENCYCLOPAEDIA OF ASTON VILLA F.C.

182

## McLACHLAN, JOHN ANDREW

Born: Dumfries, July 1888. Died: Glasgow, January 1944.
Career: St Catherine's Boys Club, Dundee (1909), Aston Villa (August 1912), Dundee (August 1915). Did not figure after World War One.
A player with boundless energy, Andy McLachlan was an inside-forward who had done well with Dundee before trying his luck at Villa Park. He scored three goals in 17 first-XI games in English football before returning to Dens Park where he ended his career.

## McLAVERTY, JOHN G.

Born: South Shields, October 1892.
Died: Durham
Career: Chester Moor, Sacriston United, Birtley Colliery, Aston Villa (February 1913), South Shields (on loan, August-September 1914), Aston Villa (October 1914-May 1915). Served in the Great War and later played with West Stanley (July 1922-April 1923).
A well-built centre-half, Jack McLaverty was reserve to Jimmy Harrop at Villa Park and consequently found it difficult to gain a place in the side, making just two first team appearances, his League debut coming on Christmas Day 1913 (in a 2-0 away win at Derby).

## McLOUGHLIN, ALAN FRANCIS

Born: Manchester, 20 April 1967
Career: Manchester United (YTS, June 1983, professional April 1985), Swindon Town (free transfer, August 1986), Torquay United (on loan, March 1987), Southampton (£1 million, December 1990), Aston Villa (on loan, September 1991), Portsmouth (£400,000, February 1992), Wigan Athletic (£250,000, December 1999).
Republic of Ireland international midfielder, Alan McLoughlin had one game for Aston Villa whilst on loan at the club from The Dell. Capped 42 times by his country, he has also played for Eire's 'B' team and when the 2000-01 season ended he had appeared in well over 550 League and Cup games as a professional, having failed to make the first team at Old Trafford!

## McLUCKIE, JAMES SIME

Born: Stonehouse, Lanarkshire, 2 April 1908. Died: Edinburgh, November 1986.
Career: Hamilton Accies, Tranent Juniors, Hamilton Academical (July 1928), Manchester City (February 1933), Aston Villa (£6,500, December 1934), Ipswich Town (June 1936), Clacton Town (player-manager, 1946, retired as a player June 1949).
A brilliant ball-artist and inspiring captain, Jimmy McLuckie was capped by Scotland against Wales in 1934. He made over 50 appearances for the Accies, had 37 games for Manchester City and scored once in 15 outings for Aston Villa. He then served Ipswich Town superbly well for three years and was the first player to sign professional forms for the East Anglian club. He later skippered the Portman Road side during its first League season of 1938-39.

## McLUCKIE, JASPER

Born: Lancashire, 1877. Died: 1941.
Career: Accrington Fereday, Pine Villa Colts, Darwen (trialist), Jordanhill FC, Bury (1898), Aston Villa (August 1901), Plymouth Argyle (May 1904-April 1905).

Described as being a 'grand goalscoring forward' Jasper McLuckie was sharp and incisive inside the penalty area, a real terrier whose career record was outstanding. He struck 30 League goals in 95 outings for Bury, netted 45 times in only 62 first-class games for Aston Villa and scored six goals in 20 Southern League matches for Plymouth. Unfortunately a knee injury cut short an exciting career.

## McMAHON, PATRICK

Born: Croy near Kilsyth, Scotland, 19 September 1945.
Career: Glasgow & Kilsyth District Schools, Inverness Colts, Kilsyth Rangers (1965-67), Dumbarton (trialist), Chelsea (trainee trialist), Glasgow Celtic (August 1967), Aston Villa (free transfer, June 1969), Portland Timbers (March 1976), Caribous of Colorado (1977), Atlanta Chiefs (assistant-manager/coach, 1978). Retired to live in America where he formed his own company, supplying aluminium to the industry. He later became a copywriter for an agency in Portland, Oregon.

*Pat McMahon celebrates his goal v. Notts County in 1972.*

Nicknamed 'Mahogany,' Pat McMahon was a skilful ball player, fast, alert with good heading ability and powerful right-foot shot. He scored Villa's winning goal in the 1970-71 League Cup semi-final second leg victory over Manchester United but then received a loser's medal when Tottenham lifted the tophy at Wembley. He helped Villa win the Third Division championship the following season, having been a Scottish Junior Cup winner with Kilsyth Rangers back in 1967. McMahon netted 30 goals in 150 League and Cup appearances during his seven-year stay at Villa Park.

## McMAHON, STEPHEN

Born: Liverpool, 20 August 1961.
Career: Everton (apprentice, June 1977, professional August 1979), Aston Villa (£300,000, May 1983), Liverpool (£350,000, September 1985), Manchester City (December 1991), Swindon Town (player-manager, November 1994-October 1999), Blackpool (manager, January 2000).
An aggressive, hard-tackling, totally committed central midfielder, Steve McMahon gained medals galore at Anfield - three League championships (1986, 1988 & 1990), two for winning the FA Cup (1988 & 1989), a European Super Cup winning trophy (1989) and three FA Charity Shield prizes (1986, 1988 & 1989). He earned 17 full caps for England and he also represented his country in six Under-21 and two 'B' internationals in the process. He was in his country's 1990 World Cup squad. McMahon made 120 first team appearances for Everton (14 goals scored), had 91 outings for Villa (7 goals), starred in 277 matches for Liverpool (50 goals), played 90 times (one goal) for Manchester City and ended up with 51 appearances for Swindon. He battled on well (as always) during his time at Villa Park, manning midfield with Dennis Mortimer and Alan Curbishley and then Gordon Cowans.
McMahon led Blackpool to promotion from Division Three in May 2001 via the Millennium Stadium Final v., Leyton Orient (won 4-2).
* McMahon was once a ball-boy at Goodison Park for a Merseyside derby.

THE COMPLETE ENCYCLOPAEDIA OF ASTON VILLA F.C.          THE COMPLETE ENCYCLOPAEDIA OF ASTON VILLA F.C.

183

## McMORRAN, JAMES WILSON

Born: Muirkirk, Ayrshire, 29 October 1942.

Career: Aston Villa (junior, July 1958, professional October 1959), Falkirk (trialist, January 1963), Third Lanark (February 1963), Walsall (£6,000, November 1964), Swansea City (June 1968), Walsall (November 1968), Notts County (July 1969), Halifax Town (August 1970), Worcester City (July 1971), Redditch United (August 1974-May 1977).

Jimmy McMorran won Scottish Schoolboy honours as a teenager before signing for Aston Villa. He never really made an impact at Villa Park and in 1963 - after just 12 senior outings for the club - he was transferred to Third Lanark (after a brief trial with Falkirk). Eighteen months later he returned to the Football League with Walsall and played in well over 100 games for the Saddlers as a central midfielder. In 1968 he moved to the Vetch Field, but returned to Fellows Park for a second spell with five months. McMorran retired in 1977, but continued to participate in various local charity matches for the next 10 years.

## McMULLAN, JAMES

Born: Denny, Stirlingshire, 26 March 1895. Died: Sheffield, 28 November 1964.

Career: Denny Hibernians, Third Lanark (1911-12), Partick Thistle (November 1913), Maidstone United (player-manager, July 1921), Partick Thistle (August 1923), Manchester City (£4,700, February 1926 - retired May 1933), Oldham Athletic (manager, May 1933-May 1934), Aston Villa (manager, May 1934-October 1936), Notts County (manager, November 1936-December 1937), Sheffield Wednesday (manager, December 1937-April 1942).

A Scottish international half-back (16 caps won) Jimmy McMullan also appeared in four Victory internationals and represented the Scottish League on four occasions. He helped Manchester City win the Second Division title in 1928 and reach the 1926 and 1933 FA Cup Finals, receiving a runners-up medal each time. He missed the Scottish Cup Final with Partick in 1921 through injury. A fine captain for both club and country, McMullan led the famous Wembley Wizards to that emphatic 5-1 victory over England in 1928. In the early 1920s he turned down a £5,000 transfer to Newcastle United, preferring to stay in Scottish football but later came south and played in 242 first-class matches during his five years at Maine Road. He didn't have much success as a manager, taking Villa down into the Second Division after spending well over £30,000 on new players! He did though drag Sheffield Wednesday clear of relegation to Division Three but then missed out on promotion to the First Division by just a point in 1938-39. When he was manager at Villa Park, McMullan saw the team play 53 League games - 17 were won, 15 drawn and 21 lost.

## McNAUGHT, KENNETH

Born: Kirkcaldy, Fife, 17 January 1955.

Career: Everton (junior, July 1970, professional, May 1972), Aston Villa (£200,000, July 1977), West Bromwich Albion (£125,000, August 1983), Manchester City (on loan, December 1984-January 1985), Sheffield United (£10,000, July 1985, retired in May 1986), Dunfermline Athletic (coach), Swansea City (assistant-manager).

Ken McNaught gained both Youth and Amateur honours for Scotland as a teenager. After more than 65 outings for Everton, with Villa he developed into an excellent centre-half, commanding in the air, positive and sure in the tackle. He was the back-bone of Villa's defence during his time at the club, scoring 13 goals in 260 senior appearances while collecting a League championship, European Cup and Super Cup winners medals under the managership of Ron Saunders and then Tony Barton.

He made his Baggies' debut in their 4-3 defeat at Villa Park and played over 100 games for The Hawthorns club before switching to Bramall Lane after a loan spell at Maine Road. On his retirement in the summer of 1986 McNaught was appointed coach at Dunfermline Athletic, later holding the position of assistant-boss at Swansea.

Ken McNaught's father, Willie, was a full Scottish international.

## McNEILL, WILLIAM, MBE

Born: Bellshill, Lanarkshire, 2 March 1940.

Career: Blantyre Victoria, Glasgow Celtic (£250, August 1957, retired May 1975), Clyde (manager, April-June 1977), Aberdeen (manager, June 1977-May 1978), Celtic (manager, May 1978-June 1983), Manchester City (manager, June 1983-September 1986), Aston Villa (manager, September 1986-May 1987), Celtic (manager, May 1987-May 1991).

Billy McNeill signed a four-year contract worth £70,000-a-year when he was appointed manager of Aston Villa on 22 September 1986.

Villa won seven and drew 12 of the 34 League games played under McNeill before he was sacked at the end of the 1986-87 season.

As a player, McNeill occupied the centre-half position. He played in 831 games for Celtic and gained a League championship medal in each of nine successive seasons (1966-74) as well as collecting many more winners and runners-up prizes, including seven Scottish FA Cup triumphs, seven League Cup successes and a European Cup victory in 1967. As a manager he again tasted League championship glory north of the border in 1979, 1981, 1982 and 1989, later leading Manchester City to promotion from the Second Duivision (in 1985) and to the Full Members Cup Final (in 1986). He could do nothing wrong in Scottish football - but he did have a torrid time when making his international debut....England thrashing Scotland 9-3 at Wembley in 1961.

He went on to win 29 full caps for his country, played in five Under-23 internationals and had nine games for the Scottish League side. He was awarded the MBE for services to Scottish football - and well deserved too.

(See under Medal Winners).

## McPARLAND, PETER JAMES

Born: Newry, County Down, Northern Ireland, 25 April 1934,

Career: Newry Schoolboy football, Dundalk (1950), Aston Villa (£3,880, August 1952), Wolverhampton Wanderers (£35,000, January 1962), Plymouth Argyle (£30,000, January 1963), Atlanta Chiefs (summer of 1964), Peterborough United (briefly in 1965-66, with Vic Crowe), Worcester City (1966-67), Glentoran (player-manager and later manager, 1968-71). Coached in Kuwait, Lybia and Hong Kong and was briefly in charge of the No.1 Club of Kuwait (up to 1980).

*Peter McParland*

Peter 'Packy' McParland was a brilliant goalscoring outside-left, fast, direct, with a terrific left foot shot. In 1952, while serving his apprenticeship as a coppersmith and having been watched several times, George Martin, the Aston Villa manager, signed him for less than

THE COMPLETE ENCYCLOPAEDIA OF ASTON VILLA F.C.     THE COMPLETE ENCYCLOPAEDIA OF ASTON VILLA F.C.

184

£4,000. What a buy....over the next ten years McParland gave his all for the club, scoring 120 goals in 341 senior appearances. He netted twice when Villa beat Manchester United 2-1 in the 1957 FA Cup Final; he gained a Second Division championship medal in 1960 and then collected a League Cup winners' tankard in 1961. In between times McParland represented the Football League XI and won a then club record 33 full caps for Northern Ireland, later adding another cap to his collection as a Wolves player. He played for his country in the 1958 World Cup Finals.

After returning from a spell in the Far East, McParland ran a successful property business with his son in Bournemouth for many years. He now lives in Dorset from where he still keeps in touch with the fortunes of Aston Villa.

## MEDAL WINNERS

Charlie Athersmith won five League championships medals with Aston Villa: 1894, 1896, 1897, 1899 and 1900. He also two FA Cup winners' medals (1895 and 1897) and one runners-up medal in 1892. After leaving Villa Park he collected a Second Division runners-up medal with Birmingham City (Small Heath)        in 1903.

Both Steve Smith and Jack Devey also won five League championship medals with Villa, all in the same seasons as Athersmith, but Smith only collected one FA Cup winners' medal (in 1895) while Devey won two (in 1895 and 1897) as well as a runners-up prize (1892).

Howard Spencer gained three FA Cup winners' medals with Villa: 1895, 1897 and 1905. He also collected League championship winning medals in 1896, 1897 and 1900. He only played in 10 matches when Villa won the title in 1899 (two short of the required number).

Andy Gray won a Scottish League Cup runners-up medal with Dundee United in 1974. He followed up by gaining two Football League Cup winners' medals with Aston Villa 1977 and Wolves 1980 and added FA Cup and European Cup Winners Cup winners medals to his tally with Everton in 1984 and 1985 respectively. He also collected a First Division championship medal with the Merseysiders in 1985 and four years later he received winners' medals for both the Skol Cup and Premier League championship in Scotland with Rangers in 1989.

Villa's early 1930s full-back Joe Nibloe (with Kilmarnock 1929 and Sheffield Wednesday 1935) and Jim Welford (with Celtic 1899 and Villa 1895) gained both English FA Cup and Scottish FA Cup winners' medals during their respective careers.

Welford was also the first footballer to win English, Scottish and Irish League championship medals, doing so in 1894 and 1896 with Villa, 1898 with Celtic and 1900 with Belfast Celtic.

Neale Cooper won a total of 11 medals during his playing career - all in the 1980s - three Scottish League titles, four Scottish Cup wins, a League Cup triumph, European Cup Winners Cup success and Super Cup glory with Aberdeen and then a League championship victory with Rangers to round off with (1988-89).

Peter Withe (Nottingham Forest and Villa) and Kevin Richardson (Arsenal and Everton) won League championship medals with two different clubs. Withe also won European Cup and Super Cup winners' medals with Villa, whilst Richardson collected both FA Cup and European Cup Winners Cup prizes with Everton (1984 and 1985) and later added a League Cup winners medal to his tally with Villa in 1994.

Clem Stephenson won two FA Cup winners medals with Villa (1913 and 1920) and a third with Huddersfield Town in 1922. He then gained three successive League championship medals with Huddersfield (mid 1920s) and an FA Cup runners-up medal in 1928.

Ronnie Starling won an FA Cup winners medal with Sheffield Wednesday in 1935 and a Second Division championship and League Wartime Cup medal with Villa in 1938 and 1944 respectively. He also appeared in four FA Cup semi-finals with four different clubs: Hull City (1930), Newcastle United (1932), Sheffield Wednesday (1935) and Villa (1938).

Harold Halse played in three FA Cup Finals with three different clubs: Manchester United, Chelsea and Villa. He gained winners' medals with

United (1909) and Villa (1913) but was a loser with Chelsea (1915). Halse also gained a League championship medal with United in 1911.

Bob Chatt won an FA Cup winners medal with Villa in 1895 and four years later gained an FA Amateur Cup winners medal with Stockton. Jimmy Dugdale won FA Cup winners medals with WBA in 1954 and Aston Villa in 1957. He also gained a Second Division championship medal and a League Cup winners tankard with Villa in 1960 and 1961. John 'Baldy' Reynolds won an FA Cup winners medal with WBA against Villa in the 1892 Final and then collected two more winners medals in the same competition - three years later with Villa (against WBA) and

*Andy Gray - multi medal winner and goalscorer!*

in 1897 (v Everton). Reynolds also gained an Irish Cup winners medal in 1891 and three League championship medals with Villa: 1894, 1896 and 1897.

Harry Hampton won FA Cup winners' medals with Villa eight years apart - in 1905 and 1913. Sam Hardy played in the winning Final of 1913 and the losing Final of 1920.

Stan Crowther won an FA Cup winners medal with Villa (versus Manchester United) in 1957 and a losers medal with United (v Bolton Wanderers) in 1958.

Stan Lynn won an FA Cup winners medal and a Second Division championship medal with Villa (1957 and 1960) and then he collected a League Cup winners prize with Birmingham City (versus Villa) in 1963.

Nigel Sims was a winner with Villa in the FA Cup (1957), Second Division championship (1960) and League Cup (1961).

After leaving Villa, Danny Blanchflower won two League Championship medals with Spurs (1960 and 1961) as well as an FA Cup winners medal (1961) and a European Cup Winners Cup medal (1963).

Before joining Villa, centre-forward George Brown won three League championship medals with Huddersfield Town in successive seasons (1924-25-26) and an FA Cup runners-up medal in 1928.

David Platt helped Arsenal win the Premiership and FA Cup double in 1998.

Jimmy Rimmer was a European Cup winner with Villa (in 1982). He also gained a League championship medal and a European Super Cup winners' medal with Villa in 1981 and 1982 respectively.

Derek Dougan gained an FA Cup runners-up medal in 1960 with

THE COMPLETE ENCYCLOPAEDIA OF ASTON VILLA F.C.    THE COMPLETE ENCYCLOPAEDIA OF ASTON VILLA F.C.

185

Blackburn Rovers and later gained both UEFA Cup and a Second Division runners-up medals plus a League Cup winners medal with Wolves (in 1967, 1972 and 1974 respectively).

Manager Ron Atkinson won medals as player with Oxford United (twice as Southern League champions in 1961 and 1962 and as Third Division champions in 1968). Then, as a manager, he collected medals galore with Cambridge United (Fourth Division champions 1977, Third Division runners-up 1978 - half-a-season's work), Manchester United (FA Cup winners twice in 1983 and 1985 and League Cup runners-up in 1983), Sheffield Wednesday (League Cup victors in 1991) and Aston Villa (Premier League runners-up in 1993 and League Cup winners in 1994).

Billy McNeill won medals aplenty as a player and manager before taking the reins at Villa Park in 1986. As Celtic's centre half, he helped the Bhoys win one European Cup Final, nine Scottish League championships, seven Scottish Cups and seven Scottish League Cups (1965 and 1975). He also picked up five Scottish Cup runners-up prizes and a European Cup runners-up medal. As manager of Aberdeen (1977-78) and Celtic (1978-83) he won four Scottish Premiership titles, three Scottish Cup Finals and one Scottish League Cup Final as well as earning two Scottish Cup runners-up medals and a League Cup runners-up prize. Then with Manchester City he guided them to promotion to the First Division and led them to the runners-up spot in the Full Members Cup at Wembley.

As a football club manager, Ron Saunders won the Second Division title with Norwich City in 1972 and the League championship with Villa in 1981. In between times he guided both Norwich City and Manchester City to runners-up positions in the 1973 and 1974 League Cup Finals and then guided Villa to success in the same competition in 1977. He also saw Villa finish runners-up in the Second Division in 1975 and later guided Birmingham City back into the First Division as runners-up in 1985.

Josef Venglos, before managing Villa, won a European Championship medal with Czechoslovakia in 1976, two Czech League championships (1974 and 1975) and one Czech Cup (1974).

As a player, goal-ace Billy Walker won the FA Cup with Villa in 1920 and a runners-up medal in 1924. Thereafter as a manager, he collected two more Cup winners' medals, with Sheffield Wednesday (1935) and Nottingham Forest (1959). He also guided Forest to the Third Division (North) title in 1951 and to runners-up spot in Division Two in 1957. Joe Mercer won plenty of medals as well (see following).

## MELLBERG, OLOF

Born: Amncharad, Sweden, 3 September 1977.
Career: Racing Santander, Aston Villa (£5.7 million, July 2001).
Hard-tackling central defender, signed as a straight replacement for the departing Gareth Southgate in the summer of 2001, highly-rated Swedish International defender Olof Mellberg played almost 100 games in Spain's Primera Liga with Real Santander.

Secured on a five-year deal, he was John Gregory's fourth signing in rapid succession following the arrivals of Hadji, Kachloul and Schmeichel...all full internationals. Mellberg turned down a lucrative move to Inter Milan in preference of Premiership football with Villa.

Mellberg, on moving to Villa Park said: "This is a dream come true for me."

## MERCANTILE CREDIT FOOTBALL FESTIVAL

On 16 and 17 April 1988, Aston Villa - under manager Graham Taylor - participated in the celebration Mercantile Credit Centenary Festival at Wembley. They were drawn in phase one and defeated Blackburn Rovers 2-1 on penalties (after a 0-0 draw) in their opening game. The second (a phase one quarter-final match) was against Nottingham

Forest and after another goalless draw, this time Villa succumbed 1-0 on penalties.

Each game lasted just 40 minutes and therefore the appearances made by the respective players have not been registered in the club's official records. The attendance at Villa's two fixtures was estimated at 20,000. Forest went on to win the championship, beating Sheffield Wednesday - again after a penalty shoot-out (3-2).

## MERCER, JOSEPH, OBE

Born: Ellesmere Port, Cheshire, 9 August 1914. Died: Merseyside, August 1990.
Career: Ellesmere Port & Cheshire Schools (with Frank Soo), Elton Green FC, Shell Mex FC, Runcorn, Ellesmere Port Town, Everton (amateur, August 1931, professional September 1932), Arsenal (£7,000, November 1946). Guested for Aldershot during WW2. Retired as a player twice, in May 1953 and again in June 1954, the second time after

Joe Mercer

suffering a double fractire of his leg in a League game against Liverpool at Highbury. He guested for Aldershot during WW2. Sheffield United (manager, August 1955-December 1958), Aston Villa (manager, December 1958-July 1964), Manchester City (manager, July 1965-October 1971, then general manager until June 1972), Coventry City (general manager, June 1972-June 1975; was appointed director at Highfield Road in April 1975, a position he retained until July 1981). Acted as England caretaker-manager in May 1974.

Genial Joe Mercer, with his bandy legs, was an outstanding wing-half with a biting tackle and a never-say-die attitude. Over a period of 21 years, from April 1933 to April 1954, he starred in more than 450 competitive games for Everton and Arsenal and won six full and 27 Wartime caps for England as well as representing the Football League.

He was part of a tremendous international half-back line which also comprised tough-nut Cliff Brittan and the redoubtable Stan Cullis. Mercer gained three League championship medals, the first with Everton in 1939 and then two with the Gunners in 1948 and 1953. He also skippered the London club to victory in the 1950 FA Cup v Liverpool and then collected a runners-up prize in the same competition two years later. He was voted 'Footballer of the Year' in 1950.

After retiring as a player in 1954, shortly before his 40th birthday, Mercer then spent a year or so out of the game, running a grocery shop in the Wirral. He moved back into football as manager at Bramall Lane before taking over the hot-seat at Villa Park on 23 December 1958, bringing with him his assistant Dick Taylor. Mercer introduced several youngsters into League and Cup action, calling them 'Mercer's Minnows'. After further developing striker Gerry Hitchens, he then sold the England star to Inter Milan, replacing him with Derek Dougan. Later he signed Tony Hateley. He guided Aston Villa to the Second Division championship and League Cup success in successive seasons (1960 & 1961) and saw them finish runners-up in the latter competition in 1963. But after a humiliating FA Cup defeat at the hands of Fourth Division Aldershot in 1964 he lost his job (some say he was sacked, a doctor said it was through ill-heath: hypertension). His assistant Dick Taylor took over the reins. As manager of Villa, Mercer saw his team compete in 229 League games - 91 were won, 50 drawn and 88 lost.

Mercer stayed out of the game for a short while (his wife and friends thought the pressure would kill him). But he re-appeared as manager of Manchester City in 1965 and with Malcolm Allison alongside, he revitalised the Maine Road club, subsequently guiding the Blues to the Second Division championship in 1967, First Division glory in 1968, to an FA Cup win over Leicester City in 1969, a League Cup Final triumph two years later and victory in the European Cup winners Cup Final in 1971 as well as lifting the Charity Shield.

He later spent two years as boss of Coventry City and managed England for a handful of games in 1974, between the respective reigns of Sir Alf Ramsey and Don Revie. And he brought a smile back to the players' and indeed the fans' faces with some positive results. He lived in retirement in Birkenhead and watched Tranmere Rovers quite regularly until his death in 1990 at the age of 76.
• These were 'Mercers Minnows': Charlie Aitken, Norman Ashe, Alan Baker, Harry Burrows, Alan Deakin, John Slueewenhoek and Mike Tindall.

## MERTHYR TOWN (AND TYDFIL)

No competitive match action between Aston Villa and the Welsh former-League club, but several players have had a foot in both camps, including: T Barber, DJ Astley, S Howarth, HE Nash, D Richards (Villa trialist), CL Roberts (Villa reserve).
Also: JA Fisher, H Hadley & AE Lindon (Villa players, Merthyr managers).

## MERSON, PAUL CHARLES

Born: Harlesden, 20 March 1968
Career: Harlesden junior football, Brent & Ealing District Boys, Middlesex Schools, Forest United, trialist with Chelsea, QPR & Watford (1981-82), Arsenal (Schoolboy forms, April 1982, apprentice, July 1984, professional December 1965), Brentford (on loan, January-February 1987), Middlesbrough (£4.5 million, July 1997), Aston Villa (£6.75 million, September 1998).
By the time he joined Aston Villa shortly after the start of the 1998-99 season, the versatile Paul Merson had already appeared in more than 500 first-class matches for clubs and country, and had scored almost 120 goals. A powerfully built player, able to adapt to whatever his manager/coach required whether it be as a creative midfielder or all-out attacker, he had also gained 21 full caps for England, plus four with the 'B' team, four at Under-21 level and a handful as a Youth team player. In fact, he had been a surprise choice for the France '98 World Cup Finals after successfully overcoming a well-publicised personal drug-addiction problem that required lengthy hospital treatment. He returned to action a far leaner, more positive player and consequently again became a top-line performer, hence his big-money (and surprise) transfer to Middlesbrough whom he helped reach the Premiership in his first season at the Riverside Stadium.

The former PFA 'Young Player of the Year' (1989), Merson helped Arsenal win two League championships in 1989 & 1991, the FA Cup and League Cup in 1993 and the European Cup Winners Cup in 1994. He actually scored for the Gunners in their 1993 League Cup Final win over Sheffield Wednesday.

Granted a testimonial (at Highbury) in 1996, he is a big crowd pleaser, and his talent, work-rate, endeavour and undoubted ability is certainly recognised by his fellow professionals.

He has had a few problems at Villa Park (both on and off the field) and was bitterly disappointed when Chelsea won the 2000 and last FA Cup Final at Wembley. He has always given 100 per-cent out on the field and when the curtain came down on the 2000-01 season, his record with Aston Villa read 117 appearances and 16 goals.

**Paul Merson**

## MID-RHONDDA

Two Villa players - B Anstey and JW Bache - were also associated with Mid-Rhondda FC during their respective careers.
IH Price was a Villa reserve who later managed the Welsh club

## MIDDLESBROUGH

Villa's playing record against 'Boro:
Football League/Premiership

| Venue | P | W | D | L | F | A |
|---|---|---|---|---|---|---|
| Home | 56 | 32 | 11 | 13 | 126 | 61 |
| Away | 56 | 19 | 16 | 21 | 75 | 82 |
| Totals | 112 | 51 | 27 | 34 | 201 | 143 |

THE COMPLETE ENCYCLOPAEDIA OF ASTON VILLA F.C.    THE COMPLETE ENCYCLOPAEDIA OF ASTON VILLA F.C.

187

FA Cup

| | | | | | | |
|---|---|---|---|---|---|---|
| Home | 2 | 1 | 1 | 0 | 5 | 3 |
| Away | 2 | 1 | 1 | 0 | 3 | 2 |
| Neutral | 1 | 0 | 0 | 1 | 0 | 3 |
| Totals | 5 | 2 | 2 | 1 | 8 | 8 |

League Cup

| | | | | | | |
|---|---|---|---|---|---|---|
| Home | 3 | 3 | 0 | 0 | 5 | 2 |
| Away | 1 | 1 | 0 | 0 | 1 | 0 |
| Totals | 4 | 4 | 0 | 0 | 6 | 2 |

Zenith Data Systems Cup

| | | | | | | |
|---|---|---|---|---|---|---|
| Home | 1 | 0 | 0 | 1 | 1 | 2 |
| Away | 1 | 0 | 0 | 1 | 1 | 2 |
| Totals | 2 | 0 | 0 | 2 | 2 | 4 |

Wartime

| | | | | | | |
|---|---|---|---|---|---|---|
| Home | 1 | 1 | 0 | 0 | 2 | 0 |

Aston Villa completed their first League double over 'Boro in 1902-03, winning 5-0 at home and 2-1 away.

Villa whipped 'Boro 6-0 at home in December 1907 and then doubled up with a 1-0 away win the following April.

When Villa lost 3-2 at Middlesbrough on 28 March 1910, it ended their record-equalling 15-match unbeaten run in League football.

Later that year - in November - in-form Joe Bache scored a hat-trick when Villa beat 'Boro 5-0 at home.

'Boro had the better of things in 1913-14, beating Villa 5-2 at home and 3-1 away.

The following season Villa won 5-0 at home (in mid-March) after Harry Hampton and Clem Stephenson had caused havoc inside the 'Boro penalty-area.

Villa beat 'Boro 4-1 (a) and 5-3 (h) in the space of eight days in October/November 1919. Dick Boyman and Stephenson scored hat-tricks in that order.

On 22 October 1921 Villa lost 5-0 at Ayresome Park. Seven days later it was Villa 6 'Boro 2 in Aston!

In October 1927, George Cook scored three times as Villa beat 'Boro 5-1 and four years later, when the Teesiders again travelled to Villa Park, they succumbed to an 8-1 defeat with three players, 'Pongo' Waring, Billy Walker and Eric Houghton, all scoring twice.

Houghton scored a first-half hat-trick when Middlesbrough were defeated 7-1 at Villa Park in a League game in December 1931. In the second-half Houghton was switched to full-back in place of the injured Tommy Mort.

It was 'Boro's turn to slam in the goals at Villa Park in September 1935, winning 7-2 - just five days after having lost 2-1 to Villa at Ayresome Park!

Villa's last 'valid' League game before World War Two saw them draw 1-1 at home with 'Boro on 6 May 1939, Freddie Haycock scoring their goal in front of 17,793 spectators.

Then, as it so happened, Villa's first League fixture when peacetime football resumed on 31 August 1946 was also against Middlesbrough at home. But on this occasion a crowd of 50,572 saw the Teeside club win 1-0, Wilf Mannion the goalscorer.

This is the only time Villa have played successive League matches against the same club at the same venue, albeit, seven years apart!

And by coincidence Villa ended the 1938-39, 1947-48 and 1948-49 seasons with League games against 'Boro.

There was a big League win for 'Boro at Ayresome Park in December 1948 when they triumphed 6-0 with Mick Fenton notching a hat-trick.

Billy Goffin scored twice in each game when Villa doubled up over 'Boro in 1949-50, winning 4-0 at home and 2-0 at Ayresome Park. Then three goals by Tommy Thompson helped see off relegation-threatened 'Boro to the tune of 5-3 at Villa Park in November 1953 (it was 4-2 at half-time).

'Boro lost their First Division status in April 1954 and they didn't meet

Villa at League level again until 1959-60 (Division 2) when they were defeated 1-0 in both matches.

The next time the teams met in the League was 1967-68 and they resumed activities in the top flight in 1975-76.

On 25 April 1981 Villa beat 'Boro 3-0 at home to virtually clinch the First Division title.

Six goals were shared at Middlesbrough later that year (November 1981) before Allan Evans' goal gave Villa a 1-0 home win in the return fixture to severely hinder 'Boro's relegation fight.

When Villa lost 2-1 at 'Boro on St Valentine's Day 1988, it brought to an end their 12-match unbeaten League run. And on the same ground eight months later Villa earned a point from a 3-3 draw (Alan McInally scoring twice).

After beating Middlesbrough 5-1 at home in January 1993, Villa went to the top of the Premiership table. All six goals in this game were scored by different players, including both Villa's centre-backs, Paul McGrath and Shaun Teale.

Julian Joachim's goal at The Riverside Stadium in September 2000 earned Villa a draw in a Premiership game - and it was also the 200th goal Villa had scored at League level against 'Boro. Ugo Ehiogu returned to haunt his old team mates by heading his side's equaliser in the 1-1 draw at Villa Park later in the season.

Villa's 3rd round FA Cup-tie with Middlesbrough in 1949-50 went to a second replay before the Teesiders won 3-0 at neutral Elland Road.

Over 42,000 fans saw Villa beat 'Boro 3-2 in a 4th round encounter at Ayresome Park in January 1957, Derek Pace, skipper Johnny Dixon and Les Smith the Villa scorers.

Villa's League Cup victories over 'Boro were recorded in 1987 (1-0 at home and away), 1990 (3-2) and 1994 (1-0).

Villa were beaten in the two-legged Northern Area Final of the ZDSC by 'Boro in season 1989-90.

*Action from the Villa v. Boro League game in April 1935.*

Players with both clubs include: S Beaton (Villa reserve), WF Brawn, MS Burke, NJ Cox, A Cunliffe, IW Dickson, JT Dixon ('Boro WW2 guest), U Ehiogu, E Eyre, D Glover, RSM Gray, TP Griffiths, WM Hamilton, PT Heard, P Kerr, AE Layton, C Liddle (Villa reserve), W McAuley, PC Merson, TBD Niblo, RC Park ('Boro Amateur), K Poole, D Richards (Villa trialist), CH Slade, G Southgate, J Suddick ('Boro reserve), N Swales, MR Thomas (Villa on loan), AD Townsend.

Also: GS Martin ('Boro player, Villa manager), J Neal (Villa player, 'Boro manager), BD Rioch (Villa player, 'Boro assistant-manager & manager), B Little (Villa player, 'Boro coach & assistant-manager), D Geddis (Villa player, 'Boro coach), A McAndrew ('Boro player, Villa coach), S Harrison & P Barron (coaches at both clubs).

## MIDDLESBROUGH IRONOPOLIS

A Football League club for a short time, Ironopolis did not play Villa at any level, but two players who served with both clubs were JAE Elliott and R Gordon.

THE COMPLETE ENCYCLOPAEDIA OF ASTON VILLA F.C.     THE COMPLETE ENCYCLOPAEDIA OF ASTON VILLA F.C.

188

## MIDLAND YOUTH CUP

Aston Villa first entered a junior team in the highly-competitive Midland Youth Cup in season 1983-84. They defeated Notts County 6-1 at home in their opening match, played on 11 October 1983. Leicester were ousted in the second round before Coventry City won the two-legged semi-final 2-1 on aggregate.

The following season Villa reached the Final after beating Stoke City, Shrewsbury Town and Coventry City. But after a resilient performance they unfortunately lost 5-3 on aggregate over two legs (2-2 at home, 1-4 at St Andrew's) to Blues. The Final, in fact, was carried over until the start of the next campaign.

Villa were eliminated from the competition in the opening round in each of the next five seasons, losing in turn to Coventry City, Birmingham City (twice in succession), Derby County and Wolves. They succumbed to Birmingham City (again) in the second round in 1990-91 before powering through to the Final in 1991-92. En-route Villa put out Port Vale 3-1, Wolves 1-0 and Oxford United on penalties in the semi-finals (after a 1-1 aggregate score). Walsall were then defeated in the Final by 5-4, Villa coming back from a 3-2 first leg deficit.

As holders, Villa lost to Stoke City in the preliminary round in 1992-93 and it was the Potters who went through to Round Three in 1993-94 (after Villa had earlier dismissed Hereford United and Leicester City). Knocked down by Derby County at the first hurdle in 1994-95, Villa's youngsters quickly made amends by winning the trophy for a second time the very next season. They accounted for Nottingham Forest, Grimsby Town and Wolves before registering an excellent 4-2 win at Leicester in the Final on 25 April 1996.

Proud and powerful Villa then retained the trophy in 1997 and made it a hat-trick of successes the following season.

In 1996-97, Derby County, Port Vale and Grimsby Town were all tossed aside before Stoke City were defeated 3-1 in the two-legged Final, and twelve months later, after ousting Lincoln City, Port Vale (again), Hereford United (8-0) and Leicester City (4-2 on aggregate), Villa's teenagers gleefully made it hat-trick of triumphs by beating Nottingham Forest 3-1 at home in the Final.

Villa have not entered the competition since.

## MIDLAND PURITY YOUTH LEAGUE CUP

Aston Villa beat neighbours Birmingham City 2-1 in the Final of the Midland Purity Youth Cup in 1995. In earlier rounds they had eliminated Northampton Town (8-0), Wolverhampton Wanderers (3-2) and Derby County (2-0). A young and purposeful midfielder by the name of Lee Hendrie was one of the star performers, scoring in every round.

*Alf Miles*

## MILES, ALFRED

Born: Aston, January 1884. Died: Wylde Green, Sutton Coldfield, 8 February 1926.
Career: Heath Villa, Aston St Mary's (1900), Aston Villa (July 1902). Retired in May 1914 and became first team trainer at Villa Park immediately after the War (1919), retaining the position until August 1925.

Full-back Alf Miles, the doyen in the side, acted as team skipper several times, especially in seasons 1910-12. A sportsman through and through, and admired the fans, he made 270 first-class appearances for Aston Villa, gaining an FA Cup winners' medal in 1905 but missed the 1913 Final after being dislodged by Tom Weston. A great volleyer (left-footed) he was the embodiment of pluck and determination, possessing a never-say-die attitude but was not too strong constitutionally. Miles was Villa's spongeman at Wembley for the 1924 FA Cup Final.

## MILES, REGINALD

Born: Enfield, Middlesex, 8 July 1905. Died: Enfield, 1978.
Career: Enfield Schools, Enfield Town (August 1921), Dulwich Hamlet, British Army, Aston Villa (November 1930), Millwall (August 1931), Dulwich Hamlet.

Reg Miles was a stock-broker and amateur goalkeeper who caught Villa's eye while playing Army football. Sound rather than spectacular, he was first-choice between the posts at Villa Park (ahead of Fred Biddlestone and Percy Maggs) during the second-half of the 1930-31 season, making 16 senior appearances. He left the club following the emergence of Harry Morton.

*Reg Miles*

## MILLER, ARTHUR THEODORE

Born: Cardiff, January 1876. Died: Shrewsbury.
Career: Aberdare (1894), Millwall Athletic (August 1896), Aston Villa (£200, April 1900), Wellington (July 1902).

Wing-half Arthur Miller made well over 100 Southern League appearances for Millwall before joining Aston Villa for a small fee in 1900. For a brief period he suggested that he had the capabilities of competing at the highest level but failed to establish himself in the side, playing in just 10 first team games before moving to Wellington.

*Charlie Millington*

## MILLINGTON, CHARLES JOHN HENRY

Born: Lincoln, 25 April 1884. Died: Lincoln, 13 June 1955.
Career: Grantham, Ripley Athletic (January 1905), Aston Villa (September 1905), Fulham (£400, October 1907), Birmingham (August 1909), Wellington Town (August 1912), Brierley Hill Alliance (March 1913), Stourbridge (April 1914). Leicester Fosse (WWI guest), Retired in May 1920, returned to Lincoln to work in the iron industry. Also a prominent all-rounder with Lincolnshire cricket club.

Charlie Millington was a strong, purposeful outside-right, quick and cunning with plenty of willpower. He scored 14 goals in 38 games for Aston Villa, netted 21 times in 63 outings for Fulham and claimed 13 goals in his 87 appearances for Blues.

## MILLWALL

Villa's playing record against the Lions:

Football League

| Venue | P | W | D | L | F | A |
|---|---|---|---|---|---|---|
| Home | 9 | 4 | 4 | 1 | 14 | 8 |
| Away | 9 | 3 | 2 | 4 | 9 | 12 |
| Totals | 18 | 7 | 6 | 5 | 23 | 20 |

FA Cup

| Venue | P | W | D | L | F | A |
|---|---|---|---|---|---|---|
| Home | 5 | 3 | 2 | 0 | 18 | 2 |
| Away | 3 | 1 | 1 | 1 | 5 | 4 |
| Neutral | 1 | 0 | 0 | 1 | 1 | 2 |
| Totals | 9 | 4 | 3 | 2 | 24 | 8 |

League Cup

| Venue | P | W | D | L | F | A |
|---|---|---|---|---|---|---|
| Home | 3 | 3 | 0 | 0 | 7 | 1 |

THE COMPLETE ENCYCLOPAEDIA OF ASTON VILLA F.C.      THE COMPLETE ENCYCLOPAEDIA OF ASTON VILLA F.C.

189

| Wartime | | | | | | |
|---|---|---|---|---|---|---|
| Home | 1 | 1 | 0 | 0 | 2 | 0 |
| Away | 1 | 0 | 1 | 0 | 2 | 2 |
| Totals | 2 | 1 | 1 | 0 | 4 | 2 |

Aston Villa and Millwall first met at League level in season 1967-68 (Division 2). Villa won 2-1 at The Den and 3-1 at Villa Park, Willie Anderson scoring twice in the latter game.

After Villa had won 1-0 at Millwall in a Second Division game in April 1969, it was to be another 22 matches before they claimed another away victory in the League - at Birmingham City!

Ray Graydon netted a hat-trick (including a penalty) in Villa's 3-0 home win over the Lions in September 1974 and when the teams met at The Den later that season Villa doubled up by winning 3-1, 'Chico' Hamilton scoring from the spot on this occasion.

When Villa lost 2-1 at home to the Lions in November 1987, it ended a run of 12 League games without defeat.

Villa's 3rd round FA Cup-tie with non-League Millwall in 1899-1900 went to a second replay before the Lions won 2-1 at neutral Reading. The following season George Johnson scored a hat-trick as Villa knocked the Lions out of the same competition in this opening round. All 22 players wore black arm-bands in this Cup-tie on 26 January 1901 because of the death of HRH Queen Victoria.

In a two-legged 4th round FA Cup-tie with Millwall in 1945-46, Villa scored a total of 13 goals, conceding three. They won 9-1 at home and 4-2 away. This tally of 16 goals is the most ever scored in a competitive game involving Aston Villa.

Villa's last FA Cup defeat at the hands of the Lions came in a 4th round replay in 1986 when they went down 1-0 at The Den.

Villa's three League Cup victories, all at home, came in 1976 (1-0), 1988 (3-1) and 1990 (2-0).

Players with both clubs include: M Allen, HE Banks, RAJ Brown (Millwall WW2 guest), AG Cascarino, PM Elliott (Lions' trialist), G Garratt, AA Gray, AE Hall, DL Jackson, P Kerr, E Lowe (Millwall Amateur), R Miles, AT Millar, R Noble (Villa reserve), P Saward, H Shutt, JE Travers. J Tyrrell, J Walters, AE Watkins, TC Wilson.

Also: G Graham & BD Rioch (Villa players, Millwall managers).


## MILNE, DR. VICTOR EDWARD

Born: Aberdeen, 22 June 1897. Died: Little Aston, nr Birmingham, 6 September 1971.

Career: Boys Brigade football, Aberdeen City Boys, Aberdeen University (1915), Royal Engineers (1916-18), Aberdeen (August 1919), Aston Villa (August 1923). Retired in May 1929 to concentrate on his profession as a doctor. He was the Aston Villa club doctor from 1930-33 and was also General Practioner and Medical of Health Officer for Aldridge for 40 years (1939-68 inclusive).

Vic Milne gained both soccer and cricket blues and competed on the athletics track whilst studying to become a doctor at Aberdeen University. He served in France during the Great War (called up by the Royal Engineers because of his chemistry experience and was transferred 500 miles south to Plymouth before crossing the English Channel). He graduated as a Doctor in 1921, gaining a Diploma in Health two years later.

An 'Apollo-sized' defender, Milne took over the centre-half mantle from murder-victim Tommy Ball in 1923 and was Villa's first-choice pivot for six years (medical duties permitting). Powerfully built, he gained an FA Cup winners' medal in 1924, when he also became the first Doctor to play at Wembley and, indeed, was the first Scotsman to appear in a Final for Villa since 1897.

Dr Milne, who took over the duties from Dr Jessop at Villa Park in 1930, made 175 League and Cup appearances for Villa, scoring one goal, the winner against Notts County (2-1) in September 1925.


## MILOSEVIC, SAVO

Born: Bijelina, Yugoslavia, 2 September 1973.

Career: Partizan Belgrade (1990), Aston Villa (£3.5 million, July 1995), Real Zaragoza (£3.7 million June 1999), Parma (£16 million, July 2000).

*Savo Milosevic*

Many eyebrows were raised when the 6ft 2in, 13st 4lb striker was signed by Villa manager Brian Little in the summer of 1995 - after he had been watched and assessed on video!

Such scepticism seemed well founded after he was substituted on his Premiership debut against Manchester United, but he soon got going and hit five goals in two games against Coventry City to silence his critics! A strong, powerful player with heaps of talent, he tended to drift in and out of the game - but he did score some cracking goals, including a real gem in Villa's 3-0 win over Leeds United in the 1996 League Cup Final at Wembley. A proposed move to the Italian club Perugia fell through before he got back to business in the Premiership. He eventually took his goal-tally to 32 (in 117 appearances) before quitting the British soccer scene to join the Spanish club Real Zaragoza, later switching to Italy's Serie 'A' with Parma after a very successful European championship campaign, when he finished up as the tournament's joint-top scorer with five goals. When the 2000-01 season ended Milosevic had been capped 40 times by Yugoalavia.


## MITCHINSON, THOMAS WILLIAM

Born: Sunderland, 24 February 1943.

Career: Sunderland & Wearside Schoolboy football, Sunderland (apprentice, July 1958, professional December 1960), Mansfield Town (January 1966), Aston Villa (£18,000, August 1967), Torquay United (£8,000, May 1969), Bournemouth (£2,000, December 1971). Retired through injury, May 1973.

*Tommy Mitchinson*

A steady, probing inside-forward with a good eye, Tommy Mitchinson was the first of two players (his Mansfield colleague Dick Edwards was the other) signed by Tommy Cummings when he took over as Aston Villa manager in 1967. During his career Mitchinson amassed more than 300 senior appearances and scored almost 50 goals; his Villa record was nine goals in 52 outings.


## MOORE, ISAAC GEORGE

Born: Tipton, December 1867. Died: West Bromwich, September 1948.

Career: St Stephen's FC, Aston Villa (July 1889), Dudley Town (August 1890), Netherton Saints (1892-94).

Muscular inside-forward, hardy and mobile, Ike Moore made six competitive first-team appearances for Aston Villa, plus more than 20 in 'other' matches during his one and only season at the club.

THE COMPLETE ENCYCLOPAEDIA OF ASTON VILLA F.C.  THE COMPLETE ENCYCLOPAEDIA OF ASTON VILLA F.C.

190

## MOORE, THOMAS D.
Born: Dudley Port, Tipton, April 1910. Deceased.
Career: Dudley Welfare, Tipton All Saints, Stourbridge, Aston Villa (February 1932), Bournemouth (August 1934), Dudley Town (1935-36).
A smart, tricky left-winger, Tommy Moore was out of the game for eight months after breaking his right leg during a reserve team game on 27 December 1932. He never recovered from that set-back and left the club after making just one League appearance v Huddersfield Town on the last day of the 1931-32 season when he scored the winning goal in a 2-1 scoreline.
He was the grandson of Isaac (above).

## MORALEE, MATTHEW
Born: Mexborough, 21 February 1912. Died: Doncaster, September 1991.
Career: Ormsby United, Denaby United (April 1929), Gainsborough Trinity (May 1930), Grimsby Town (February 1931), Aston Villa (October 1936), Leicester City (November 1937), Shrewsbury Town (July 1939), then WW2 guest with Grimsby Town, Doncaster Rovers, Rotherham United and Denaby United. Retired 1944.
An intelligent, prompting inside-forward, Matt Moralee never quite bore out his early promise. He scored once in his 12 first-team outings for Aston Villa, grabbed five goals in 27 outings for Grimsby and netted six times in his 43 games for Leicester.

## MORBY, JOHN H.
Born: Wednesfield, August 1920.
Career: Hednesford Town (1938), Aston Villa (December 1943), Worcester City (July 1948).
A Wartime signing, Jack Morby was a strapping defender able to occupy a variety of positions but preferred the centre-half berth. He played in three FA Cup games for Aston Villa in the 1945-46 season, two versus Chelsea which pulled in a combined total of 116,000 fans. Later in life he resided in Essington near Wolverhampton.

## MORGAN, SAMUEL JOHN
Born: Belfast, 3 December 1946
Career: Gorleston & Norfolk Schools, Gorleston (amateur), Port Vale (trialist January 1970, professional, July 1970), Aston Villa (August 1973 for £22,222 with an extra £5,400 following later), Brighton & Hove Albion (£10,000, December 1975), Cambridge United (August 1977), in Holland with Sparta Rotterdam (1978) & Groningen (1979), Gorleston (player 1980, later manager). Also manager, secretary and chairman in that order of the Great Yarmouth Schools FA. He was also a Schoolboy coach in the USA and was later junior coach of Norwich City, becoming Director of the Football Academy at Carrow Road in 2000-01.
A tall, aggressive striker, capped 18 times by Northern Ireland (1972-78), Sammy Morgan was Port Vale's 'Player of the Year' in 1971-72 and top-scorer for the Potteries club the following season. He ended up with 27 goals in 126 first-team outings for the Valiants before moving to Villa Park on a stayed payment scheme. He battled hard and long during his time with Villa, netting 15 times in 51 outings before moving to Brighton. During his entire playing career (in the Football League and Holland) Morgan claimed a total of 65 goals in more than 300 competitive appearances.

## MORLEY, WILLIAM ANTHONY
Born: Ormskirk, 26 August 1954.
Career: Ormskirk & District Schools, Preston North End (apprentice, July 19769, professional August 1972), Burnley (£100,000, February 1976), Aston Villa (£200,000, June 1979), West Bromwich Albion (£75,000, December 1983), Birmingham City (on loan, November-December 1984), FC Seiko, Japan (August 1985), FC Den Haag, Holland (July 1986), trialist with Walsall & Notts County (early 1987), West Bromwich Albion (August 1987), Burnley (on loan, October-November 1988), Tampa Bay Rowdies (NASL), Hamrun Spartans, Malta (1989), New Zealand (1990-91), Sutton Coldfield Town (1992-93). Assisted both Aston Villa and West Bromwich Albion Old Stars in charity matches.
A fast-raiding left-winger, Tony Morley could deliver pin-point crosses on the run, drive in some powerful shots, with both feet, and score some stunning goals - his effort at Goodison Park in a League game against Everton in February 1981, was voted 'Goal of the Season.'

*Tony Morley*

Morley became a vital cog in the Aston Villa machine, helping them win the Football League title, the European Cup and European Super Cup in double-quick time in the early 1980s. Halfway through the 1983-84 season - after scoring 34 goals in 180 games - he left Villa Park for neighbours West Bromwich Albion. He did well at The Hawthorns before trying his luck in Japan, having had a loan spell at St Andrews late in 1984. Thereafter Morley visited Holland, had trials with Walsall and Notts County, returned briefly to both The Hawthorns and Burnley, played in the NASL, Malta and New Zealand before returning home to enter non-League football with Sutton. Capped six times by England at senior level, Morley played for his country's Youth team on seven occasions and also won one 'B' and one Under-23 cap.
During his career in 'England' he amassed in excess of 450 League and Cup appearances and scored over 65 goals. He helped Den Haag win promotion to the Dutch First Division and also gained a Cup runners-up medal in his only season in Holland (1986-87).

*Terry Morrall in action against Spurs.*

## MORRALL, TERENCE STEPHEN
Born: Smethwick, 24 November 1938.
Career: Smethwick Schools, Birmingham County Boys, Church Rovers, Aston Villa (juniors 1953-54, professional November 1955), Shrewsbury Town (May 1961), Wrexham (July 1963), Southport (July 1965), Stourbridge (player-manager, 1966-68), Warley Borough (manager (1970s). Played football in Cyprus and Jordan during his National Service years (1958-59).
Like his uncle, George 'Lofty' Morrall, ex-Birmingham player, Terry Morrall was also a stern, rugged defender, whose chances at Villa Park were restricted owing to the presence of so many other fine full-backs and centre-halves. He made just nine first-team appearances before moving to Gay Meadow. He added 74 more League games to his tally before moving down the ladder in 1966. Morrall now lives in Wall Heath near Dudley.

THE COMPLETE ENCYCLOPAEDIA OF ASTON VILLA F.C.     THE COMPLETE ENCYCLOPAEDIA OF ASTON VILLA F.C.

191

## MORRIS, WILLIAM

Born: Danesmoor, February 1888. Died: Birmingham
Career: Clay Cross, Derby County (September 1907), Clay Cross (December 1907), Alfreton (August 1910), Chesterfield (July 1911), Aston Villa (March 1912-May 1915), Alfreton (after WW2).

A tall defender, mainly a centre-half, Bill Morris was a regular in Aston Villa's League side during the first-half of the 1912-13 season before losing his place following the arrival of Tommy Barber and the emergence of Jimmy Leach. He was never a regular after that and ended his days at Villa Park with 53 senior appearaces under his belt, one goal scored (in a 5-0 FA Cup win over West Ham United in February 1913).

## MORT, THOMAS

Born: Kearsley, Bolton, 1 December 1897. Died: Wigan 6 June 1967
Career: Farnworth Council School, Kearsley St Stephen's FC (Sunday School team), Newton Lads' Club, Lancashire Fusiliers, Altrincham (December 1918), Rochdale (June 1921), Aston Villa (April 1922-May 1935). Retired to go into business in Wigan.

Tommy Mort was a marvellous full-back partner to Tommy Smart, the pair being known affectionately as 'Death and Glory' as they defended magnificently week after week. Mort, who took over from another Tommy - Weston - was a great exponent of the sliding tackle, especially on the heavy grounds. He won three England caps in the mid-1920s, appeared in the 1924 FA Cup Final and scored twice in his 368 senior matches for Aston Villa, accumulated over a period of 13 years.

## MORTIMER, DENNIS GEORGE

Born: Liverpool, 5 April 1952
Career: Kirkby Boys, Coventry City (apprentice, july 1967, professional September 1969), Aston Villa (£175,000, December 1975), Sheffield United (on loan, December 1984), Brighton & Hove Albion (August 1985), Birmingham City (August 1986), Kettering Town (July 1987), Redditch United (player-manager, November 1987-October 1988), West Bromwich Albion (August 1989 as Football in the Community Officer, later reserve team coach and player at The Hawthorns), Aston Villa (junior coach/assistant).

An excellent midfield player with drive, determination, loads of skill and the will to win, Dennis Mortimer first shot to prominence with Coventry City when his hair was so long that the fans called him Doris! He went to Highfield Road as a 15 year-old and turned professional in 1969. 'Morty' made 215 appearances and scored 10 goals for the Sky Blues before transferring to Villa Park halfway through the 1975-76 season (signed by Ron Saunders). He became a vital cog in the midfield engine-room as Villa stormed to victory in the League Cup Final of 1977, won the Football League championship in 1981 and carried off both the European and Super Cups in 1982. 'Morty'

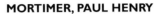
Dennis Mortimer

skippered Villa in each of the last three triumphs.

After a loan spell at Bramall Lane, he switched to the south coast to assist Brighton, having scored 36 goals in 406 outings in a Villa shirt. He perhaps surprisingly joined rivals Birmingham in 1986 before entering non-League soccer a year later. In 1989 'Morty' took up a position with another West Midlands club, WBA.

Capped by England six times as a Youth team player, the quiet-speaking Mortimer also starred in three 'B' and six Under-23 internationals for his country, and in 1971 he toured Australia with the FA. As a teenager with Kirby Boys, Mortimer played alongside his future Villa colleague Kenny Swain.

## MORTIMER, PAUL HENRY

Born: Kensington, London, 8 May 1968
Career: Henry Compton Secondary School team, West London Schools, Fulham (junior, 1984 for two years), Farnborough Town, Charlton Athletic (trialist, July 1987, professional, September 1987), Aston Villa (£350,000, July 1991), Crystal Palace (£500,000, October 1991), Brentford (on loan, January-February 1993), Charlton Athletic (£200,000, July 1994), Bristol City (free transfer, August 1999-May 2000).

Able to play as a full-back, central-defender or midfield (even as a stand-in striker) Paul Mortimer - a former bookshop assistant in Fleet Street - spent barely three months with Aston Villa, appearing in only 14 first-class games and scoring one goal. Seemingly destined to play his football in London, he had already starred in more than 120 League and Cup games for Charlton before moving to Villa Park, and after returning to the capital he went on to appear in a further 160 competitive matches for Palace, Brentford, Charlton (again) and Bristol City. Capped twice as a left-sided midfielder by England at Under-21 level, he was troubled with a hamstring injury during the late 1990s which eventually led to him quitting League football at the age of 32.

## MORTON, HAROLD

Born: Oldham, 7 January 1908. Deceased.
Career: Chadderton School, Middleton Road Primitives, Oldham Boys, Bury (trialist), Bolton Wanderers (trialist), Royal Welsh Fusiliers (Army service, 1928-30), Aston Villa (trialist, professional September 1930), Everton (March 1937), Burnley (May 1939). Retired during the War.

Goalkeeper Harry Morton, a former fireman and Rugby League full-back, was spotted by Aston Villa playing Army football and as soon as humanly possible, after his demob, he was invited down to Birmingham for a trial. He impressed the gallery and was offered a professional contract within a week. He made his senior debut in unusual circumstances against Manchester City at Maine Road in November 1930. He was, in fact, sitting in the stand awaiting the kick-off when

he was called down to the dressing after Fred Biddlestone had been injured during the pre-match warm-up. He never looked back and went on to make a total of 207 appearances for the club before leaving for Everton on the transfer deadline of 1937. One of the smallest 'keepers in the game, he commanded his area well, being both brave and daring. Unfortunately Morton was between the posts at Villa Park when Ted Drake of Arsenal put seven goals past him in a First Division League game in 1935. He played in one game (as Ted Sagar's deputy) when the Merseysiders won the First Division championship in 1938-39.

THE COMPLETE ENCYCLOPAEDIA OF ASTON VILLA F.C.　　THE COMPLETE ENCYCLOPAEDIA OF ASTON VILLA F.C.

192

## MOSELEY, GRAHAM

Born: Manchester, 16 November 1953

Career: Blackburn Rovers (apprentice, July 1969, professional September 1971), Derby County (September 1972), Aston Villa (on loan, August-September 1974), Walsall (on loan, October 1977), Brighton & Hove Albion (November 1977), Ipswich Town (on loan, 1983-84), Cardiff City (August 1986-May 1988). Goalkeeper Graham Moseley was the second player who was signed on loan by Aston Villa. He was brought over from Derby County for three games at the start of the 1974-75 Second Division season after Jim Cumbes had been injured.

An England Youth international, Moseley played for the Rams in the 1976 FA Cup semi-final. He then helped Brighton twice win promotion, from Division Three in 1977 and into the First Division in 1979. He also played in the 1983 FA Cup Final defeat by Manchester United. An agile six-footer, he amassed a total of 265 League appearances during his career (189 with Brighton).

## MOSS, AMOS

Born: Aston, Birmingham, 28 August 1921

Career: Birmingham CBC, Aston Villa (amateur May 1937, professional May 1939), Kettering Town (June 1956), Wisbech Town, Kidderminster Harriers (player-coach, August 1961), Rugby Town (player-coach, 1962-May 1963, when he retired fron the game).

The blond-haired Amos Moss, standing an inch over six feet, was a tough-teak half-back, younger brother of Frank (Junior) who did artful work in Villa's reserve side before making headway in the first XI. Also able to fill in as an inside-forward, he went on to appear in 110 League and FA Cup games for the club (scoring five goals) before ending his nine-year association at Villa Park in 1956.

## MOSS, ARTHUR JAMES

Born: Crewe, April 1888

Career: Crewe Central, Willeston White Star, Alexandra, Whitchurch FC, Aston Villa (£250, September 1908), Bristol City (July 1912 - May 1915), Runcorn. Retired shortly after the Great War.

Initially introduced to first team action in place of the injured Chris Buckley in 1908, wing-half Arthur Moss went on to appear in five first team games for Villa, but starred resolutely in well over 100 second and third team matches. He went on to make 85 League appearances for Bristol City up to the outbreak of War.

## MOSS, FRANK (SENIOR)

Born: Aston, Birmingham, 17 April 1895. Died: Worcester, 15 September 1965.

Career: Burlington Street School (Aston), Aston Manor, Walsall (August 1912), Aston Villa (February 1914), Cardiff City (£2,500, January 1929), Oldham Athletic (August 1929), Bromsgrove Rovers (player-manager 1930), Worcester City (1932). Retired in 1934 to continue as the licensee of the Grosvenor

*Frank Moss (Senior)*

Arms, Worcester (1930-65).

Father of Amos and Frank junior, Frank Moss senior was, like his two sons, a blond-haired half-back, strong and resilient. Nicknamed 'Snowy' he captained both his club (Aston Villa in the FA Cup Final v Newcastle United) and his country (England v Scotland) on successive Saturdays at Wembley in April 1924. Earlier he had made a fairytale debut for Villa in the 1920 FA Cup Final victory over Huddersfield Town when he replaced the injured Jimmy Harrop at the eleventh hour and played a 'blinder.'

Moss was the athlete in the Villa defence, strong, dominant, quick in recovery and excellent in the air. He won five full caps, represented the Football League twice and scored nine goals in 283 senior appearances for the club before moving to Cardiff in 1929 after the Welsh club had been hammered 6-1 by Villa in an FA Cup-tie!

Moss was seriously injured during the First World War while serving as a corporal with the 4th Lincolnshire Regiment at Bouchezvenes (France). He was sent back to England as a PTI.

## MOSS, FRANK (JUNIOR)

Born: Aston, Birmingham, September 1917. Died: Looe, Cornwall, 5 May 1997.

Career: Cowper Street & Ryland Road Schools (Birmingham), St Clement's School (Worcester), Worcester Nonedescripts FC (1930), Worcester City (August 1933), Sheffield Wednesday (trialist, 1934), Wolverhampton Wanderers (professional, August 1937), Aston Villa (£2,000, May 1938). Guested for Birmingham, Northampton Town and Southampton during the War when he served in the Royal Navy, operating on gun-boats and destroyers in the Middle East. Retired through injury in June 1955. Coached the younger players at Villa Park for a season (1955-56) and then ran a newsagent's business in Kingstanding, Birmingham, which he started in 1940. Later (1969) he moved to the Cornwall seaside resort of Looe where he died at the age of 79.

Elder brother of Amos, Frank Moss junior was a born fighter for club (at football) and country (at war). A resourceful defender who had the habit of subduing the best centre-forwards and inside men in the game. He established himself in the Villa side in 1946-47 and was a regular in the side over the next eight years, accumulating an excellent record of 313 League and Cup appearances (three goals scored).

## MOUNTFIELD, DEREK

Born: Liverpool, 2 November 1962

Career: Tranmere Rovers (juniors, June 1978, professional November 1980), Everton (£30,000, June 1982), Aston Villa (£450,000, June 1988), Wolverhampton Wanderers (£150,000, November 1991), Carlisle United (free transfer, May 1994), Northampton Town (on loan, October 1995), Walsall (November 1995, player-coach July 1997), Bromsgrove Rovers (September 1998), Scarborough (caretaker-manager, January-April 1999), Workington (player/coach, May 1999-2000).

*Derek Mountfield*

Full-back or centre-half Derek Mountfield had made only 29 appearances for Tranmere when Everton brought him into the First Division. It was a good move for player and club as Mountfield went on to make 154 appearances for the Merseysiders, scoring 25 goals and helping them twice win the Football League championship (in 1985 & 1987), capture the FA Cup (in 1984) and the European Cup-winners' Cup (in 1985). He also played in the losing FA Cup Finals of 1985 and 1986 and represented England once at both under 21 and 'B' team levels.

THE COMPLETE ENCYCLOPAEDIA OF ASTON VILLA F.C.  THE COMPLETE ENCYCLOPAEDIA OF ASTON VILLA F.C.

193

Mountfield scored 17 goals in 120 first team games for Aston Villa (partnering first Allan Evans and then Paul McGrath at the heart of the defence on many occasions). After spells with Wolves (almost 100 outings), Carlisle and Northampton, he returned to the West Midlands in 1995 to assist Walsall and two years later was appointed player-coach at The Bescot Stadium. He took his tally of first-class appearances at club level to well past the 600 mark before joining Bromsgrove Rovers. In 1999 Mountfield tasted management for the first time with Scarborough.

## MULDOON, THOMAS PATRICK
Born: Athlone, Ireland, February 1901. Deceased.
Career: Athlone Town (1919-20), Aston Villa (October 1924), Tottenham Hotspur (September 1927), Walsall (July 1929-May 1931).
A chunky Irishman, Tommy Muldoon mainly occupied the left-half position and made 34 senior appearances during his three-year stay with Aston Villa. He failed to make the first XI at White Hart Lane but went on to play in over 50 League games for the Saddlers.

## MULRANEY, AMBROSE
Born: Wishaw, near Motherwell, 18 May 1916,
Career: Wishaw White Rose (1929), Carluke Rovers (1930), trials with Heart of Midlothian, Celtic, Hamilton Academical, Blackpool, Sligo Rovers, and Clapton Orient; joined Dartford (August 1935), Ipswich Town (1938-39); guested for Birmingham, Blackburn Rovers, Brentford, Charlton Athletic, Chelsea, Hibernian, Leicester City, Manchester City, Millwall, Third Lanark & Wolverhampton Wanderers during the War (1939-45), Birmingham City (£3,750, October 1945), Shrewsbury Town (July 1947), Kidderminster Harriers (July 1948), Aston Villa (September 1948), Cradley Heath (player-manager, August 1949), Brierley Hill Alliance (manager, 1952-53). Retired from football 1954.
Jock Mulraney was a fast-raiding winger who could occupy both flanks. A Scottish Schoolboy international trialist, represented the Scottish Alliance XI before joing Dartford. He had the pleasure of scoring Ipswich Town's first-ever hat-trick in the Football League (against Bristol City in April 1939).
He hit 57 goals in 159 games for Blues during and immediately after the hostilities. He helped them win the Football League (South) championship and reach the FA Cup semi-finals in 1946. After a season with Shrewsbury he switched his allegiance to Kidderminster Harriers only to return to the Football League with Aston Villa in double-quick time. He spent the remainder of that season at Villa Park before leaving competitive soccer to become player-manager of Cradley Heath. He hung up his boots in 1954 to concentrate on his carpentry work in Kinver where he still resides, having overcome a major heart attack in 1968.
During the Second World War Mulraney served in the RAF where he attained the rank of Flight Sergeant, PT Instructor.

## MURRAY, JAMES ARTHUR
Born: Benwhat, Scotland, February 1879. Died: Glasgow, June 1933
Career: St Augustione's FC, Ayr United (1897), Aston Villa (March 1901), Small Heath (July 1901), Watford (1902-03), Kettering Town (1903-04), Kings Heath Albion (December 1904-05).
Stocky reserve utility forward whose capabilities were somewhat limited. He played in just two games for Aston Villa, but scored in his only game for Blues and notched five goals in 24 Southern League outings for Watford.

## MURRAY, SCOTT GEORGE
Born: Aberdeen, 26 May 1974
Career: Fraserburgh FC, Aston Villa (£35,000, professional March 1994), Bristol City (£150,000, December 1997).
Right-sided midfield player Scott Murray made only four Premiership

appearances for Aston Villa but then became something of a folk hero at Ashton Gate, making 170 appearances for the Bristol club up to the end of the 2000-01 season.

## MUSIC
Several records appertaining to Aston Villa FC have been cut over the last 20 years or so.
A double 'A' sided disc was struck in 1979, comprising 'A.S.T.O.N.V.I.L.L.A' on one side and 'We're The Holte End' on the other. The lyrics for both songs were written by Jeremy Cash and Larry Rushton.
Others include: 'We're On The Holte End' by Dave Ismay & The Holte End with We're Going Up, an instrumental on the 'B' side; Hey! Aston Villa (by Ricki Disoni with Trevor Anthony's Brass Foundation); Aston Villa 'Claret & Blue' (with David James & the Villa squad).
In 1982, Radio WM released an album ('Villa, Champions In Europe') to celebrate the winning of the European Cup.
'Villa, The Musical' was released in 1999.
Former Villa players Dick Edwards (1960s) and Mark Draper were exceptionally talented musicians. The former in fact, took up a career in country and western music to the accompaniment of his own guitar in America after retiring from the game while Draper likes to think he's another Jimi Hendrix!
...And we can't forget Ron Atkinson's singing - or can we?
Former Villa goalkeeper Jim Cumbes and his counterpart from WBA, John Osborne, acted as DJs on a local Birmingham Radio station in the early 1970s.

## MWILA, FREDERICK
Born: Zambia, 6 July 1946
Career: Zambian football, Atlanta Chiefs (NASL), Aston Villa (June 1969), Atlanta Chiefs (May 1970 to summer of 1977).
A utility forward, Freddie Mwila came across from the States with fellow countryman Emment Kapwenge but failed to make any impression in English football. He had just one game for Villa - in the 0-0 home draw with Blackpool in November 1969. In his first season back with the Chiefs he scored 12 goals and continued to be a star performer over a period of seven years, netting 25 goals with seven assists in 1975 (his best return).

## MYERSCOUGH, WILLIAM HENRY
Born: Farnworth, Bolton, 22 June 1930. Died: Manchester, March 1977.
Career: Ashfield FC, Walsall (professional June 1954), Aston Villa (player-exchange deal, July 1955), Rotherham United (July 1959), Coventry City (July 1960), Chester (March 1962), Wrexham (July 1963). Retired through injury in May 1964.

*Billy Myerscough in action.*

Billy Myerscough was a whole-hearted centre-forward who could also occupy an inside or wing position. A Lancastrian, he played junior football in the Manchester area before signing as a professional for Walsall. After a year at Fellows Park he moved to Aston Villa in exchange for Dave Walsh and he did well at a higher level despite having to contest the No.9 shirt with Derek Pace. Myerscough netted 17 goals in 74 appearances for Villa, including the winner against West Bromwich Albion in the 1957 FA Cup semi-final replay at St Andrew's. He then starred at Wembley as Villa lifted the trophy at Manchester United's expense. After decent spells with Rotherham and Coventry, Myerscough played out his career with Chester and Wrexham, retiring in 1964 through injury. He died suddenly in Manchester, aged only 39.

## NAMES
### Shortest
The player with the shortest name ever to play professional football for Aston Villa (Christian and surname added together) has been Ian Ross (seven letters).
Other short-named players include: Gersom Cox, John Neal and Didier Six, while among the players with three-lettered surnames but with two (or more) Christian names, we have Mervyn R. Day, Neil J. Cox, Ronald W. Dix, Samuel R. Law, Edward B. Lee, Gordon F. Lee and James T. Lee.

Ian Ross

### Longest
The player with the longest surname ever to appear at first team level for Aston Villa (double-barrel surname) has been William Ewart Barnie-Adshead (25 letters in total, 13 in his surname).
Sleeuwenhoek (surname of 12 letters) also has two Christian names, John Cornelius, giving him an overall total of 25 letters.
The Villa player, however, with the most letters in his entire name is Herbert Charles Lawrence James Kingaby with a grand total 33.
Other long-named players include: William Charles Wassell Armfield (29 letters), William Charles Athersmith (23), Robert Dennis Blanchflower (24), Robert Edward Brocklebank (23), Robert Thomas James Iverson (24), William Arthur Littlewood (23), Charles John Henry Millington (26), Thomas William Mitchinson (23), Thomas John Seymour Phillips (25), William Thomas James Renneville (28), Joseph Henry Hamilton Rutherford (29), George Ternent Stephenson (23), Kenneth Charles Tewkesbury (23), Robert Gillies Mckenzie Thomson (28), Oliver Howard Vaughton (20), Arthur Wilbert Wollaston (22) and Philip Abraham Woosnam (20), among others.

### Name Game
Aston Villa probably took its name after a house called 'Aston Villa' that stood on the corner of Lozells Road and Heathfield Road, Handsworth, Birmingham.
Three players on Aston Villa's books in the mid-1920s had surnames representing towns/cities - George Blackburn, Reg Chester and Dicky York.
Aston Villa had four Tommys in their senior squad in the 1920s - goalkeeper Tommy Jackson and full-backs Tommy Smart, Tommy Mort and Tommy Weston.
Ten players with the surname of Brown have represented Aston Villa in League football. There have been eight players named Evans, eight Jones', six Smiths, five Campbells, five Grays, five Roberts' and five Williams'.
Smith is the commonest name regarding members of staff at the club (playing side, secretary, administration, directors etc).

## NASH, HAROLD E.
Born: Troedyrhiw, near Cardiff, South Wales, 10 April 1893. Died: Fishponds, Avon.
Career: Brislington United, Mardy, Aberdare, Abertillery, Pontypridd (1913), Aston Villa (February 1915), Coventry City (June 1920), Cardiff City (December 1920), Merthyr Town (May 1923), Aberbargoed (1925), Ystrad Mynach (1927) Retired 1930.
Deputising for Joe Bache, inside-left Harry Nash made a terrific start to his Football League career - scoring a hat-trick on his debut for Aston Villa against Liverpool (h) in April 1915 (won 6-3). He netted twice more before the end of that season and then came back after the hostilities to take his overall total of appearances for the club up to 12 before moving to Coventry City. He spent just half a season at Highfield Road but did a useful job at Cardiff, playing mostly in the reserves but always reliable when called into the first XI.

## NEAL, JOHN
Born: Silksworth, County Durham, 3 April 1932.
Career: Seaham Harbour Schools, Silksworth Colliery Welfare Juniors, RAF (clerk), Hull City (professional, August 1949), King's Lynn (July 1956), Swindon Town (July 1957), Aston Villa (£6,000, July 1959), Southend United (November 1962). Retired June 1967, worked at Fords of Dagenham (1967-68), Wrexham (coach, then manager September 1968-May 1977), Middlesbrough (manager, May 1977-May 1981), Chelsea (manager, May 1981-June 1985, then advisor at Stamford Bridge until 1987).
A keen tackling full-back, quick in recovery, John Neal made 60 League appearances for Hull City (under Raich Carter's management) and 91 as captain for Swindon Town before joining Aston Villa in 1959 to replace Doug Winton and so accompany Stan Lynn. He helped Villa win the Second Division championship and League Cup in successive seasons and went on to appear in 114 senior games for the club before transferring to Roots Hall in 1962. He made over 100 appearances for the Shrimpers and quit League football with 416 competitive games under his belt at club level, having also represented the League South v the North as a Swindon player
He enjoyed success as boss of Wrexham, leading them to promotion from the Fourth to the Third Division in 1970 and to victory in the 1972 and 1975 Welsh Cup Finals gaining entry into the European Cup Winners Cup, reaching the quarter-finals in 1976. He left a strong side at The Racecourse Ground when he took charge of Middlesbrough, but whilst on Teeside he sold some star players, Graeme Souness to Liverpool and David Mills to WBA among them. He quit Ayresome Park after a dispute regarding another sale - that of Craig Johnston to the Anfield club. Neal led Chelsea to the Second Division championship in 1984 before being replaced by John Hollins. Neal was a sprint champion as a teenager.

## NELSON
A Football League club in the late 1920s/early 30s, Nelson never met Villa at competitive level.

Players with both clubs include: F Cornan, H Shutt, TE Tebb (Villa reserve).
Also: J Hogan (Nelson player, Villa manager and coach).

## NELSON, FERNANDO
Born: Portugal, 5 November 1971.
Career: SC Salgueiros (professional, November 1988), Sporting Lisbon (£240,000, August 1991), Aston Villa (£1.75 million, July 1996), FC Porto (May 2000).
As a junior right-back Fernando Nelson represented Portugal in the under-14 championships before signing professional forms for the Salgueiros club with whom he won a Portuguese Second Division

THE COMPLETE ENCYCLOPAEDIA OF ASTON VILLA F.C.  THE COMPLETE ENCYCLOPAEDIA OF ASTON VILLA F.C.

195

championship medal. Following his big-money transfer to Sporting Lisbon, he appeared in four domestic Cup Finals, being on the winning side twice, including the Super Cup. On the international front, he added four Under-21 caps to his tally and collected a runners-up medal in the European Under-21 championships. He went on to play in no fewer than 23 Under-23 matches and also made his full international debut before moving to Villa Park.

Nelson was the only member of Portugal's Euro '96 squad to star in the English Premiership. Playing initially at right-back, then as a wing-back and finally in midfield (after Gary Charles had arrived) he made 73 appearances for Aston Villa - 39 in his first season and 34 in his second - and he also upped his total of international caps to six before returning to Portugal in the summer of 2000.

## NIELSEN, KENT

Born: Brondby, Denmark, 28 December 1961
Career: Bronshoj FC (affiliated member 1976, part-time professional, August 1978), IF Brondby (professional, August 1986), Aston Villa (£500,000, July 1989), Aarhus FC (February 1992).

Kent Nielsen played a lot of football as a youngster but surprisingly on leaving school he became a laboratory assistant. However, at weekends he starred for his junior team and gradually developed into a solid, uncompromising defender who was signed by Villa boss Graham Taylor as a straight replacement for Martin Keown.

Neilsen had already won 29 full caps for Denmark prior to moving to Villa Park and during his time in the Football League he added another 11 to that total as well as appearing in 92 games for Villa (4 goals scored).

## NEUTRAL GROUNDS

Aston Villa have played major domestic, European and foreign matches on the following neutral grounds:

**Baseball Ground, Derby**
1900-01 v Sheffield United     lost 0-3 FA Cup sf replay

**Bramall Lane, Sheffield**
1891-92 v Sunderland          won 4-1 FA Cup sf
1896-97 v Preston North End   won 3-2 FA Cup 3rd 2nd replay
1896-97 v Liverpool           won 3-0 FA Cup sf
1919-20 v Chelsea             won 3-1 FA Cup sf
1923-24 v Burnley             won 3-0 FA Cup sf
1937-38 v Preston North End   lost 1-2 FA Cup sf

**City Ground (The), Nottingham**
1900-01 v Sheffield United    drew 2-2 FA Cup sf
1904-05 v Everton             won 2-1 FA Cup sf replay

**Crystal Palace (The)**
1894-95 v West Bromwich A     won 1-0 FA Cup Final
1896-97 v Everton             won 3-2 FA Cup Final
1898-99 v Queen's Park (Scot) drew 0-0 Sheriff of London CS
1899-00 v Corinthians         lost 1-2 Sheriff of London CS
1900-01 v Corinthians         won 1-0 Sheriff of London CS
1904-05 v Newcastle United    won 2-0 FA Cup Final

**Elland Road, Leeds**
1949-50 v Middlesbrough       lost 0-3 FA Cup 3rd rd 2nd replay

**Elm Park, Reading**
1899-1900 v Millwall          lost 1-2 FA Cup 3rd rd 2nd replay

**Ewood Park, Blackburn**
1894-95 v Sunderland          won 2-1 FA Cup sf
1912-13 v Oldham Athletic     won 1-0 FA Cup sf

**Feyenoord Stadium, Rotterdam**
1981-82 v Bayern Munich    won 1-0 European Cup Final

**Goodison Park, Liverpool**
1902-03 v Bury             lost 0-3 FA Cup sf

**Hawthorns (The), West Bromwich**
1954-55 v Doncaster Rovers lost 1-3 FA Cup 4th rd 4th replay
1959-60 v Wolverhampton W  lost 0-1 FA Cup sf
1964-65 v Wolverhampton W  lost 1-3 FA Cup 5th rd 2nd replay
1971-72 v Wrexham          won 4-3 League Cup 2nd rd replay
2000-01 v Marila Pribram   won 3-1 Inter Toto Cup
2000-01 v Celta Vigo       lost 1-2 Inter Toto Cup

**Highbury, London**
1928-29 v Portsmouth          lost 0-1 FA Cup sf
1937-38 v Charlton Athletic   won 4-1 FA Cup sf replay
1976-77 v Queen's Park Rangers won 3-0 League Cup sf replay

**Highfield Road, Coventry**
1978-79 v Crystal Palace      won 3-0 League Cup 3rd rd 2nd replay

**Hillsborough, Sheffield**
1954-55 v Doncaster Rovers    drew 0-0 FA Cup 4th rd 3rd replay
1958-59 v Nottingham Forest   lost 0-1 FA Cup sf
1976-77 v Everton             drew 1-1 League Cup sf replay

**Kennington Oval (The), London**
1886-87 v West Bromwich A.    won 2-0 FA Cup Final
1891-92 v West Bromwich A     lost 0-3 FA Cup Final

**Leeds Road, Huddersfield**
1933-34 v Manchester City     lost 1-6 FA Cup sf

**Maine Road, Manchester**
1954-55 v Doncaster Rovers    drew 1-1* FA Cup 4th rd 2nd replay
* Match abandoned, failing light

**Molineux, Wolverhampton**
1956-57 v West Bromwich A     drew 2-2 FA Cup sf
1957-58 v Stoke City          lost 0-2 FA Cup 3rd rd 2nd replay

**Old Trafford, Manchester**
1960-61 v Burnley             won 2-1 League Cup sf replay
1976-77 v Everton             won 3-2 League Cup Final 2nd replay

*Andy Gray (9) in action for Villa against Everton in the League Cup Final, 2nd replay at Old Trafford in 1977.*

THE COMPLETE ENCYCLOPAEDIA OF ASTON VILLA F.C.          THE COMPLETE ENCYCLOPAEDIA OF ASTON VILLA F.C.

196

*Goal for Villa against Newcastle United in the 1905 FA Cup Final at Crystal Palace.*

**St Andrew's, Birmingham**
1956-57 v West Bromwich A won 1-0 FA Cup sf replay

**Stamford Bridge, London**
1910-11 v Brighton & Hove A  lost 0-1 FA Charity Shield
1912-13 v Sunderland    won 1-0 FA Cup Final
1919-20 v Huddersfield Town  won 1-0 FA Cup Final

**Tokyo (National Stadium), Japan**
1982-83 v Penarol    lost 0-2 World Club Championship

**Victoria Ground (The), Stoke**
1904-05 v Everton    drew 1-1 FA Cup sf

**Wembley Stadium, London**
1923-24 v Newcastle United lost 0-2 FA Cup Final
1956-57 v Manchester United won 2-1 FA Cup Final
1970-71 v Tottenham Hotspur lost 0-2 League Cup Final
1974-75 v Norwich City   won 1-0 League Cup Final
1976-77 v Everton    drew 0-0 League Cup Final
1981-82 v Tottenham Hotspur drew 2-2 FA Charity Shield
1993-94 v Manchester United won 3-1 League Cup Final
1995-96 v Leeds United   won 3-0 League Cup Final
1999-00 v Bolton Wanderers drew 0-0* FA Cup sf
1999-00 v Chelsea    lost 0-1 FA Cup Final
*Villa won on penalties.

**White Hart Lane, Tottenham**
1913-14 v Liverpool    lost 0-2 FA Cup sf

• Villa have also played various matches abroad on a neutral ground and among the big-named venues we have Ellis Park in South Africa, And during the period 1947-49 Villa played League games v Manchester United at Maine Road after Old Trafford had been closed for repair following wartime bomb damage,

## NEWCASTLE UNITED
Villa's playing record against United:
Football League/Premiership

| Venue | P | W | D | L | F | A |
|---|---|---|---|---|---|---|
| Home | 63 | 32 | 15 | 16 | 119 | 68 |
| Away | 63 | 13 | 9 | 41 | 80 | 139 |
| Totals | 126 | 45 | 24 | 57 | 199 | 207 |

FA Cup

| | | | | | | |
|---|---|---|---|---|---|---|
| Home | 3 | 3 | 0 | 0 | 13 | 1 |
| Away | 2 | 0 | 1 | 1 | 3 | 5 |
| Neutral | 2 | 1 | 0 | 1 | 2 | 2 |
| Totals | 5 | 3 | 0 | 2 | 16 | 7 |

Aston Villa recorded their joint-biggest League win when hammering United 7-0 at home in November 1902.

Howard Spencer played his last game for Villa in the 3-3 home draw with Newcastle in November 1907. Later that season Villa won 5-2 in the North East!

The gate receipts from the home League game with Newcastle United in April 1910 (which Villa won 4-0) went towards the Harry Hampton benefit fund. The attendance was 25,000.

United swamped Villa 6-2 on Tyneside in December 1911, but on the final day of that season Villa gained revenge with a 2-0 win at Aston.

Villa's last League game before the Great War saw them lose 3-0 at Newcastle on 28 April 1915.

Villa's first win over United after the hostilities came at home in April 1920 - to the tune of 4-1 as Billy Walker notched his first hat-trick for the club.

The opening League game in 1926-27 saw Villa lose 4-0 at St James' Park and in March 1928 a crowd of 25,000 witnessed a 12-goal thriller on the same ground when United won 7-5. The game started in a snowstorm and United led 4-0 after 30 minutes. As the sun came out Villa hit back and reduced the deficit by half-time. After the break United went into overdrive as the floodgates re-opened. By the 76th minute it was 7-2 to United, Jonathan Wilkinson having scored a hat-trick. But Villa, despite losing goalkeeper Ben Olney, came again and scored three times in eight minutes before running out of steam and time.

On 30 March 1937, just four days after winning 2-0 at St James' Park in front of 46,000 fans, a crowd of 65,437 - the biggest in the Second Division during the course of the season - saw United gain revenge with a 2-0 victory at Villa Park.

United 5 Villa 3 was the result of a terrific First Division game at St James' Park in September 1954 when the crowd was close to 40,000. A seven-goal thriller ended in Villa's favour by 4-3 in October 1957 and then in the return fixture at St James' Park in March 1958 a rare goal by Jimmy Dugdale helped Villa complete the double with an excellent 4-2 victory.

After a spell in the Second Division, United returned to the top flight for the 1965-66 season and promptly beat Villa 1-0 at St James' Park before losing the return fixture 4-2 at Villa Park, Phil Woosnam netting twice. Paul Rideout netted a hat-trick when Villa beat the Geordies 4-0 at home in December 1984

When Villa crashed 5-1 at Newcastle on 27 April 1994, United's Peter Beardsley celebrated his 600th senior appearances with two goals. This was manager Ron Atkinson's biggest defeat as Villa's boss, after he had seen his side take a 10th minute lead through Stefan Beinlich!

Despite Dwight Yorke's smartly-taken hat-trick, Villa still lost 4-3 to United at St James' Park in September 1996.

Referee Uriah Rennie sent-off Alan Shearer (United) against Villa on the opening day of the 1999-2000 Premiership season

Arthur Dorrell, Charlie Athersmith and Jack Devey all scored twice in Villa's 7-1 FA Cup win over United in February 1895 and when the Magpies were clipped 5-1 in the same competition in 1897, Fred Wheldon netted twice and Athersmith once.

Harry Hampton scored twice when Villa beat United 2-0 in the 1905 FA Cup Final in front of 101,117 spectators.

Nineteen years later the first all-ticket game at Wembley featured Villa against Newcastle in the 1924 Final and this time United gained revenge with a 2-0 victory in front of 91,645 fans. In fact, five days before that showdown Newcastle played a First Division match at Villa Park. Villa fielded virtually their strongest side but only one Newcastle player (Billy Gibson) was a first team regular at that time. The visitors lined up with ten reserves as Villa won 6-1. Only Gibson played in both the League game and the Cup Final for the Geordies.

That 1924 Final was heading for extra-time but as Villa's defenders lost concentration so United struck twice in the last five minutes.

Villa's skipper Frank Moss said: "We had 20 chances and missed 'em all. They had two and scored them both."

Johnny Dixon, a former United player, scored both Villa's goal in their 4-2 FA Cup defeat at St James' Park in January 1952 when the crowd topped 52,000.

Steve Stone scored a rare goal to earn Villa a replay from a 1-1 third round draw at Newcastle in January 2001 and then a 'flukey' effort by Darius Vassell earned his side a 1-0 replay victory to set up a 4th round home clash with Leicester City.

Players with both clubs include: M Allen, TE Ball (United reserve), S Beaton (Villa reserve), RAJ Brown (United WW2 guest), J Burridge (also United goalkeeping coach), F Carr, TB Craig (also United coach), AJ Cropley, JT Dixon (United Amateur & WW2 guest), CH Gibson, DDM Ginola, PT Heard, T Hockey, B Little (United trialist), J Logan, TBD Niblo, RW Starling, RB Templeton, MR Thomas (Villa on loan), A Thompson, T Thompson, S Watson, P Withe.

Also: GF Lee (Villa player, United manager), A Cox (United manager, Villa coach/assistant & caretaker-manager).

## NEW BRIGHTON

No Football League or FA Cup action between Villa and the Wirral club.

Players with both clubs include: CR McElney, CL Roberts (Villa reserve), T Waring (New Brighton WW2 guest), JE Worrall (Villa trialist).

## NEWPORT COUNTY

Villa's playing record against County:

Wartime

| Venue | P | W | D | L | F | A |
|-------|---|---|---|---|---|---|
| Home | 1 | 1 | 0 | 0 | 5 | 2 |
| Away | 1 | 1 | 0 | 0 | 4 | 0 |
| Totals | 2 | 2 | 0 | 0 | 9 | 2 |

These two Wartime games took place over a period of three days in December 1945 (League South competition). Frank Broome scored twice in Villa's 5-2 home win

Players with both clubs include: LM Craddock, T Ford, BC Godfrey, A Hale, H Hampton, JH Harvey (Villa trialist), W Matthews, F Pimblett, G Pritty, D Richards (Villa trialist).

Also: AE Lindon (Villa player, County scout).

## NIBLO, THOMAS BRUCE D

Born: Dunfermline, 24 September 1877. Died: Newcastle, December 1929.

*Tom Niblo*

Career: Dunfermline Schools football, Hamilton Academical (amateur), Linthouse FC (Glasgow), Newcastle United (£90, April 1898), Middlesbrough (on loan, April 1899-March 1900), Aston Villa (January 1902), Nottingham Forest (July 1904), Watford (June 1906), Newcastle United (August 1907), Hebburn Argyle (manager, July 1908), Aberdeen (December 1908), Blyth Spartans (April 1911-May 1913). Was also a publican on Tyneside (initially in 1907 - during his second spell at Newcastle).

Tall, well-built Scottish international utility forward (one cap gained v England in 1904), Tom Niblo was a 'capital' player, full of dash from start to finish, a real forceful footballer who was described as being '...a trier of the first water and with more care in avoiding the backs or in passing, would have doubled his value. He was also prone to be a rather greedy dribbler, much to the annoyance of his colleagues.' He scored nine goals in 52 appearances for Aston Villa, partnering Joe Bache on the left-wing most of the time, although he did appear at regular intervals in the centre-forward position. Niblo made over 250 appearances at club level.

Tom Niblo's son, Alan, was on Newcastle's books for a time and his grandson, Alan junior, captained Wolves' reserve side.

## NIBLOE, JOSEPH

Born: Corkerhill, Renfrewshire, 23 November 1903. Died: Doncaster, October 1976.

Career: Kirkdonald School, Shawfield Juniors (Glasgow), Rutherglen Glencairn, Glencairn Green, Kilmarnock (professional, August 1924), Aston Villa (£1,875 September 1932), Sheffield Wednesday (August 1934 in exchange for George Beeson). Retired in May 1938, but returned to Hillsborough after the War as a part-time coach to the younger players while also working at the Sheffield steelworks of Samuel Fox, although he was a brass moulder by trade!

Joe Nibloe started out as a centre-forward; he then had a few games as a wing-half before establishing himself as a commanding full-back, strong and resilient, who cleared his lines with alacrity. He gained 11 full caps for Scotland (1929-32) and also represented the Scottish League on two occasions. He won a Cup winners' medal with Kilmarnock in 1929, followed by a runners-up prize three years later and in 1935 he was an FA Cup winner with Wednesday (over WBA) when former Villa star Billy Walker was the Owls' manager. Nibloe played in 52 games for Villa as full-back partner to fellow countryman Danny Blair and amassed 128 senior appearances during his five years with Wednesday. A fine player.

## NICHOLL, CHRISTOPHER JOHN

Born: Wilmslow, Cheshire, 12 October 1946.

Career: Macclesfield Schools, Burnley (apprentice, June 1963, professional April 1965), Witton Albion (August 1966), Halifax Town £1,000, June 1968), Luton Town (£30,000, August 1969), Aston Villa (£90,000, March 1972), Southampton (£90,000, June 1977), Grimsby Town (player/assistant-manager, August 1983; retired as a player July

*Chris Nicholl introducing Gordon Cowans to HRH Princess Anne before the 1977 League Cup Final at Wembley.*

1985), Southampton (manager, July 1985-May 1991), Wigan Athletic (scout 1991-93), Walsall (manager, September 1994-June 1997). Nicholl is now resident in Southampton and plays tennis in his leisure time.

A natural central defender, capped 51 time by Northern Ireland, Chris Nicholl made over 800 senior appearances during his 22-year playing career (647 in the Football League alone, none as a substitute). Rejected by Burnley as 19 year-old he spent two years in non-League football before returning with lowly Halifax Town in 1968. He never looked back again! He joined Luton for a record fee and quickly became the cornerstone of the Hatters' defence. Honest, efficient, strong in the air, he was sold to Aston Villa to help balance the books at Kenilworth Road and he became a star in the claret and blue, especially when he cracked in a stunning goal in the 1977 League Cup Final second replay against Everton which set Villa up for a tremendous 3-2 victory at Old Trafford. He had earlier helped Villa win the Third Division title and then gain promotion and carry off the League Cup as a Second Division side in 1975. He netted 20 goals in 252 League and Cup outings for Villa before moving to The Dell. He continued to perform superbly well for the Saints and was in their 1979 League Cup Final side that lost to Nottingham Forest.

As Southampton's manager, he took them into second spot in the First Division - the highest placing in the club's history - but after a flourish in the UEFA Cup and a poor 1990-91 season, he was sacked with a year of his contract still to run.

As Walsall's 25th boss, replacing Kenny Hibbitt, Nicholl did reasonably well without achieving a great deal of success and having passed the age of 50, he called it a day, handing over his duties to the Dane, Jan Sorensen.

Statistically unique, Nicholl is the only player (so far) who, in the same match, has scored two goals (all from open play) for both sides. The dubious and unlikely feat occurred when he was playing for Aston Villa in a First Division encounter against Leicester City at Filbert Street in March 1976 (2-2 draw).

## NICHOLSON, JOSEPH ROBINSON

Born: Ryhope, near Sunderland, 4 June 1898. Died: Durham, 1974.
Career: Ryhope FC, Clapton Orient (July 1919), Cardiff City (August 1924), Aston Villa (June 1926 - in exchange for George Blackburn),

Spennymoor United, (August 1927), Bangor City (1930). Retired 1932. Able to play at wing-half or centre-forward, Joe Nicholson was a regular in the Orient side for four years, making 147 appearances for the London club before moving to Wales. He battled on with Cardiff and netted 12 goals in 46 outings prior to his exchange-deal involving George Blackburn. Unfortunately Nicholson never fitted in with Villa's plans and made just one League appearance - at centre-forward in a 4-0 defeat at Newcastle on the opening day of the 1926-27 season.

## NICKNAMES

Every player to a certain degree has had a nickname attached to him...here are a few of those associated with Aston Villa stars: Derek 'Paleface' Ashton, Jeffrey 'Ginger' Barker, Fred 'The Councillor' Biddlestone, Robert 'Danny' Blanchflower, Mark 'Bozzie' Bosnich, Bob 'The Toff' Brocklebank, Albert 'Sailor' Brown, Arthur 'The Tamworth Sprinter' Brown, George 'Bomber' Brown, Harry 'The Blast' Burrows, Ernie 'Mush' Callaghan, Archie 'Aussie' Campbell, George 'Monkey Brand' Campbell, Gary 'Fluff' Charles, Norman 'Nobby' Clarke, Walter 'Watty' Corbett, John 'Lemon Squash' Cordell, Gordon 'Sid' Cowans, Neil 'Billy' Cox, Vic 'Spike' Crowe, George 'Icicle' Cummings, Tony 'TD' Daley, John 'Dixie' Deehan, Dicky 'The Brownhills Bomber' Dorsett (also 'Iron Man' & 'Brick Wall'), Derek 'The Doog' Dougan (also 'Cheyenne', Lovable Irish Scamp' & 'Jolly Play Boy'), Jimmy 'The Laughing Cavalier' Dugdale, John 'Jake' Findlay, Steve 'Fozzie' Foster, Steve 'Froggy' Froggatt, Billy 'Cowboy' Goffin, George 'Stroller' Graham, Gordon 'Harry' Gregory, Ronald 'Roy' Guttridge, Billy 'Cock' Haggart, Ian 'Chico' Hamilton, 'Appy 'Arry Hampton (also 'The Wellington Whirlwind'), Freddie 'Schneider' Haycock, JB 'Ossie' Higgins, Trevor 'Dai Fungus' Hockey, Eric 'Coog' Houghton, Ray 'Razor' Houghton, Archie 'The Old Warhorse' Hunter, George 'Cocky' Hunter, Antony 'Tommy' Jaszczun, John 'Jocky' Johnstone, Herbert 'Rabbit' Kingaby, Alec 'The

*Villa's half-back line: Gibson, Talbot & Tate (Wind, Sleet & Rain).*

Clown Prince of Soccer' Leake, Andy 'Bald Eagle' Lochhead, Eddie 'Sticks' Lowe, Stan Lynn was 'Stan The Wham' and ' Lynn the Lash', Jack 'Potter' Mandley, Alan 'Rambo' McInally, Paul 'God' McGrath, Pat 'Mahogony' McMahon, Peter 'Packy' McParland, JC 'Con' Martin, Dennis 'Doris','Morty' Mortimer, Frank 'Snowy' Moss (senior), Ambrose (Jock) 'Mull' Mulraney, Ian 'Legs' Ormondroyd, Derek 'Doc' Pace, Jack 'S.O.S' Palethorpe, Garry 'Barry Manilow/Gail Tyldesley' Parker, Graham 'Fezz' Parker, Leighton 'Brodwen' Phillips, Kevin 'Mr Reliable' Richardson, Daniel 'Neil' Rioch, Ken 'Shunter' Roberts, Ian 'Roscoe' Ross, Joey 'Red Cap' Simmonds, John 'Tulip' Slueewenhoek, Tommy 'Tic' Smart, 'Gentleman Howard' Spencer (also 'Prince of full-backs'), Ronnie

THE COMPLETE ENCYCLOPAEDIA OF ASTON VILLA F.C.    THE COMPLETE ENCYCLOPAEDIA OF ASTON VILLA F.C.

199

'Flutterfoot' Starling, Steve 'Stan' Staunton, Shaun 'Ceefax' Teale, Alan 'Thommo' Thompson, Garry 'Bruno' Thompson, Tommy 'Toucher' Thompson, Percy 'Saccho' Varco, Tom 'Pongo' Waring, Oliver 'Daisy-Cutter' Whateley, Fred 'Diamond' Wheldon, Jim 'Ripper' Whitehouse, Guy 'The Count' Whittingham, Jackie 'Josh' Williams, Tom 'Smokey' Wood, John 'Woodie' Woodward, Harry 'Tubby' Yates, Dwight 'Yorkie' Yorke.

Aston Villa's famous half-back trio of the 1930s, Jimmy Gibson, Alec Talbot and Joe Tate, were referred to as 'Wind, Sleet and Rain' while the club's 1920 full-back duo of Tommy Mort and Tommy Smart were known as 'Death and Glory'.

It was 'Big Ron' Atkinson....and it's 'Deadly Doug' Ellis.

And when Aston Villa played at their Wellington Road ground the team was known as the 'Perry Barr Pets'. The current nickname of the team is basically the 'Villa' or the 'Villans'.

## NILIS, LUC

Born: Hasselt, Belgium, 25 May 1967,
Career: Winterslag, RSC Anderlecht (1988), PSV Eindhoven (1993), Aston Villa (July 2000). Retired through injury (double fracture of right leg) in 2001.

Experienced Belgian international striker Luc Nilis (56 caps won) joined Aston Villa in the summer of 2000 and scored on his debut in English football - in the second leg of the InterToto Cup clash with Marila Pribram. But then soon afterwards, in a Premiership game at Portman Road against Ipswich Town, he suffered a horrific double fracture of the right leg in a clash with home 'keeper Richard Wright. The injury was so severe he was forced to give up competive football having played in just five games for Villa (2 goals scored).

Nilis was a prolific marksman in both Belgian and Dutch football as well as on the international scene and had scored 67 goals in 109 first-class matches for PSV and Anderlecht before arriving at Villa Park.

Nilis admitted in a local Birmingham newspaper in November 2000, that he came mighty close to having part of his right leg amputated. The limb became infected and doctors considered that the only way to stop the disease from spreading was to amputate. "I cried when I was told about it" said Nilis. "It has been a nightmare struggling on....I didn't know how I got through some of the days. The injury has affected me very badly mentally." Thankfully the disease cleared up but it was to be a long hard slog for Nilis to regain full fitness, even to walk properly.

## NOON, MICHAEL T.

Born: Burton-on-Trent, June 1876.
Died: Leicester, 4 February 1939.
Career: Burton Schools, Burton Swifts, Aston Villa (March 1899), Plymouth Argyle (June 1906). Retired in May 1907 to become trainer at Home Park until 1908 when he took over the Rose and Crown public house at Whitwick, Leicestershire.

A stylish defender who could occupy most positions satisfactorily, Michael Noon was never a first team regular at Villa Park but still managed 82 League and Cup appearances during his seven years with the club (one goal scored against Everton, won 2-1, in October 1902). His best season was in 1902-03 when he helped Villa take the runners-up spot in the First Division (appearing in 16 matches). At the start of his career he played in 35 League matches for Burton Swifts and ended up by having 30 for Argyle.

*Michael Noon*

## NORRIS, FREDERICK HAROLD

Born: Aston, Birmingham 14 August 1902. Deceased.
Career: Adelaide FC, Birmingham Victorian League (1920-22), Halesowen Town (August 1922), Aston Villa (February 1925), West Ham United (June 1928), Crystal Palace (June 1933-December 1934), French League football (1935-36). Retired and returned to England before WW2.

A sprightly footballer, a man of many parts, the versatile Fred Norris scored twice in nine games during his two years at Villa Park - but had to wait until April 1926 before making his debut (v Arsenal). He later did well (mainly as a right-half) with the Hammers, netting six times in 65 first team appearances (including a hat-trick as a stand-in centre-forward against Oldham Athletic in October 1932). He had a short spell with Palace before trying his luck in France!

## NORTHAMPTON TOWN

Villa's playing record against the Cobblers:

| Football League | | | | | | |
|---|---|---|---|---|---|---|
| Venue | P | W | D | L | F | A |
| Home | 1 | 0 | 0 | 1 | 1 | 2 |
| Away | 1 | 0 | 0 | 1 | 1 | 2 |
| Totals | 2 | 0 | 0 | 2 | 2 | 4 |
| | | | | | | |
| FA Cup | | | | | | |
| Away | 1 | 1 | 0 | 0 | 1 | 0 |
| | | | | | | |
| League Cup | | | | | | |
| Home | 1 | 1 | 0 | 0 | 3 | 0 |
| Away | 2 | 0 | 1 | 1 | 2 | 4 |
| Totals | 3 | 1 | 1 | 1 | 5 | 4 |
| | | | | | | |
| Wartime | | | | | | |
| Home | 6 | 5 | 1 | 0 | 19 | 7 |
| Away | 6 | 3 | 0 | 3 | 11 | 15 |
| Totals | 12 | 8 | 1 | 3 | 30 | 22 |

Aston Villa's two League tussles with the Cobblers took place in 1965-66 (Division One). Bobby Park scored to no avail in the 2-1 defeat at The County Ground whilst Ian Hamilton did likewise in the return fixture at Villa Park! The Cobblers were relegated at the end of the season.

Mark Walters scored Villa's goal at The County Ground when the Cobblers were knocked out of the FA Cup in the 3rd round in January 1983 in front of 14,529 fans.

Villa's only League Cup win over the Cobblers was registered in a 3rd round replay in October 1970, Andy Lochhead scoring two of the three goals in front of almost 26,000 fans.

Players with both clubs include: A Blair, WF Brawn, FB Brett (Villa reserve), FH Broome (Cobblers WW2 guest), D Byfield, L Canning, LC Chatterley, RJ Codling, L Davies (Villa trialist/reserve), GR Edwards (Cobblers WW2 guest), B Gallacher, JH Garfield, JC Gregory (also Villa manager), JE Griffiths, J Hampson, the trio of FJ Haycock, RTJ Iverson & AW Kerr (all Cobblers WW2 guests), W Marriott, F Moss jnr (Cobblers WW2 guest), D Mountfield, D Norton, RC Park, HA Parkes (Cobblers WW2 guest), K Poole, N Rioch, PJ Robinson, I Ross, both JHH Rutherford & FH Shell (Cobblers WW2 guests), WS Simpson, RW Starling (Cobblers WW2 guest), GL Thompson (also Cobblers' coach), WJ Thompson (Villa reserve), A Wakeman (Cobblers WW2 guest), AM Watkins, GJ Williams.

Also: A Barton (manager of both clubs), NP Spink (Villa player, Cobblers' goalkeeping coach), F Upton (Cobblers' player, Villa coach).

## NORTON, DAVID WAYNE

Born: Cannock, 3 March 1965

Career: Aston Villa (apprentice, June 1981, professional March 1983), Notts County (August 1988), Rochdale (on loan, October 1990), Hull City (on loan, January 1991, signed August 1991), Northampton Town (August 1994), Hereford United (August 1996), Cheltenham Town (August 1998), Forest Green Rovers (2000-01 - joint manager with Nigel Spink in the latter year).

England Youth international Dave Norton graduated through the ranks at Villa Park and developed into a very competent defender. He appeared in 57 first team games for Villa (two goals scored) before transferring to Notts County in 1988. Over the decade he accumulated a fine playing record in major League and Cup football by appearing in more than 350 matches before dropping into the Nationwide Football Conference with Hereford United, managed by former Villa boss Graham Turner. Norton himself was joint-manager of Forest Green Rovers when they lost the 2001 FA Trophy Final at Villa Park to Canvey Island by a goal to nil.

## NORWICH CITY

Villa's playing record against the Canaries:

Football League/Premiership

| Venue | P | W | D | L | F | A |
|---|---|---|---|---|---|---|
| Home | 23 | 14 | 6 | 3 | 42 | 25 |
| Away | 23 | 4 | 7 | 12 | 28 | 41 |
| Totals | 46 | 18 | 13 | 15 | 70 | 66 |

FA Cup

| Venue | P | W | D | L | F | A |
|---|---|---|---|---|---|---|
| Home | 1 | 0 | 1 | 0 | 1 | 1 |
| Away | 2 | 1 | 0 | 1 | 3 | 5 |
| Totals | 3 | 1 | 1 | 1 | 4 | 6 |

League Cup

| Venue | P | W | D | L | F | A |
|---|---|---|---|---|---|---|
| Home | 2 | 2 | 0 | 0 | 6 | 2 |
| Away | 1 | 1 | 0 | 0 | 2 | 0 |
| Neutral | 1 | 1 | 0 | 0 | 1 | 0 |
| Totals | 4 | 4 | 0 | 0 | 9 | 2 |

Aston Villa won 11 and drew three of their first 15 home League games against Norwich (1936-84).

Villa first met the Canaries at League level in December 1936 (Division 2). They won 3-0, but then crashed 5-1 at Carrow Road four months later!

On 7 May 1938, a crowd of 42,337 saw Norwich beaten 2-0 as the Second Division trophy was presented to Villa's skipper Alex Massie.

When Villa went to Norwich on the last day of the 1974-75 season, promotion to the First Division (along with the Canaries) had already been achieved and they celebrated in style, winning 4-1 in front of 36,000 fans. Goals by Keith Leonard, John Gidman, Bobby McDonald and Frank Carrodus destroyed the home side, who had been defeated in the League Cup Final just eight weeks earlier!

Amazingly Villa travelled back to Norwich soon after the start of the next season - and this time they were beaten 5-3 despite Charlie Aitken scoring a fine goal.

Allan Evans scored two penalties as Villa drew 2-2 at Norwich in March 1985. And a year-and-a-half later the Canaries won 4-1 at Villa Park.....only their second victory on Villa soil (the first had been registered on 9 August 1969 by 1-0).

Villa let a 3-1 lead disappear when they were held to a 3-3 draw at home by Norwich in April 1990.

It was 'D Day' for Villa at Carrow Road on 14 May 1995. Battling for their Premiership lives (with Crystal Palace) they needed a point against Norwich City to stay up. Steve Staunton scored on seven minutes to give them the lead but Jeremy Goss equalised 10 minutes after half-time to set up a tense finish. Villa held on, got the point and retained their top-flight status.

A crowd of 33,346 saw Villa beat the Canaries 3-2 in a 3rd round FA Cup-tie at Carrow Road in January 1938, but when Villa returned to East Anglia for a 3rd round replay in January 1984 it was a different story as the Canaries called the tune to win 3-0.

Villa's first League Cup win over the Canaries was a 4-1 success at home in the 5th round of the 1962-63 tournament. Bobby Thomson scored twice in front of almost 14,000 fans.

Ray Graydon's follow-up to his penalty 'miss' (saved by ex-Villa 'keeper Kevin Keelan) at Wembley, earned Villa victory over the Canaries by a goal to nil in the 1975 League Cup Final which was attended by 95,946 spectators (paying record receipts at the time of £196,000).

Norwich City's manager in 1992 was Mike Walker who, 13 years earlier, had missed from the spot in a penalty shoot-out at Villa Park while playing in goal for Colchester United in a League Cup game against Villa.

Seven players who lined up in the 1975 League Cup Final later became League club managers: Villa's Ray Graydon, Brian Little, Chris Nicholl and Ian Ross and Mel Machin, Peter Morris and Dave Stringer of Norwich.

Players with both clubs include: M Allen, LW Askew, SE Bowen, FC Buckley (Villa reserve, also Norwich manager), P Crichton, JM Deehan (also Villa coach and City manager), D Dublin (Canaries junior), GR Edwards, GA Ephgrave (Villa reserve), J Fashanu, T Hockey, KD Keelan, M Kenning, AD Townsend, JE Travers, PS Varco, A Vinall (City Amateur). Also: R Saunders (manager of both clubs), BD Rioch & CH Spiers (Villa players, Canaries' managers), EJ Vinall & B Whitehouse (City players, Villa scouts), SJ Morgan (Villa player, Norwich junior coach/Director of Football Academy).

## NOTTINGHAM FOREST

Villa's playing record against Forest:

Football League/Premiership

| Venue | P | W | D | L | F | A |
|---|---|---|---|---|---|---|
| Home | 54 | 34 | 10 | 10 | 110 | 53 |
| Away | 54 | 16 | 17 | 21 | 76 | 99 |
| Totals | 108 | 50 | 27 | 31 | 186 | 152 |

FA Cup

| Venue | P | W | D | L | F | A |
|---|---|---|---|---|---|---|
| Home | 3 | 2 | 1 | 0 | 10 | 3 |
| Away | 6 | 3 | 0 | 3 | 7 | 8 |
| Neutral | 1 | 0 | 0 | 1 | 0 | 1 |
| Totals | 10 | 5 | 1 | 4 | 17 | 12 |

League Cup

| Venue | P | W | D | L | F | A |
|---|---|---|---|---|---|---|
| Away | 2 | 1 | 0 | 1 | 3 | 4 |

Zenith Data Systems Cup

| Venue | P | W | D | L | F | A |
|---|---|---|---|---|---|---|
| Home | 2 | 1 | 0 | 1 | 2 | 3 |

Wartime

| Venue | P | W | D | L | F | A |
|---|---|---|---|---|---|---|
| Home | 1 | 1 | 0 | 0 | 3 | 1 |
| Away | 1 | 1 | 0 | 0 | 3 | 1 |
| Totals | 2 | 2 | 0 | 0 | 6 | 2 |

The first League game between the clubs resulted in a 1-0 win for Villa on 15 October 1892 (Albert Brown the scorer) at Perry Barr.

Then, in a classic nine-goal League encounter at Nottingham a month later, Charlie Athersmith scored a hat-trick for Villa who recorded an excellent 5-4 victory to complete their first double over Forest.

Freddie Miles and Albert Hall both made their debuts for Villa and Joe Bache and Tommy Niblo scored hat-tricks in the 7-3 win away at Forest in December 1903 - this being the first time Villa had scored

THE COMPLETE ENCYCLOPAEDIA OF ASTON VILLA F.C.        THE COMPLETE ENCYCLOPAEDIA OF ASTON VILLA F.C.

201

seven times in away League match. In fact, this is Villa's second biggest League win on the road in terms of goals scored.

Joe Bache celebrated the festive season in style by scoring all his side's goals when Villa beat Forest 4-0 at home on Christmas Day 1907. Later, Harry Hampton followed him with a treble when Forest were whipped 4-1 by the River Trent on New Year's Day, 1910.

After a long period of relatively rare encounters (Forest were out of the top flight for 32 years from 1925) Villa crashed 4-1 at The City Ground in November 1957 and then suffered two League defeats and an FA Cup semi-final set-back the following season!

Three years later, in April 1962, Villa gained some revenge by beating Forest 5-1 at Villa Park.

In November 1964, Frank Wignall became the first Forest player to score a League hat-trick against Villa, doing so in a 4-2 win at The City Ground.

The following season Villa doubled up over Forest, winning 2-1 away and 3-0 at home, Phil Woosnam scoring twice in the latter game in front of 14,846 spectators.

Forest equalled Leeds United's League record of 34 games without defeat when they won 2-1 at Villa Park in September 1978. Then towards the end of that season Forest doubled up by beating Villa 4-0 at The City Ground!

Nigel Spink made his League debut for Villa against Forest on Boxing Day 1979 (but he ended up on the losing side, 2-1).

Forest came to Villa Park and won hands down by 5-0 in September 1984; in September 1986 Villa travelled to The City Ground and were walloped 6-0 and they also lost 4-0 at Forest in January 1989.

Shaun Teale conceded an own-goal in just 12 seconds before Villa stormed back to beat Forest 3-1 at home in September 1991. This is one of the fastest own-goals in Football League history.

The 100th League game between Villa and Forest took place on 4 April 1993 at The City Ground. Villa won 1-0 with a Paul McGrath goal on 63 minutes.

A record crowd of 6,000 packed into Villa's Perry Barr ground to watch the FA Cup-tie against Forest on 5 November 1881. Villa won 4-1, Oliver Whateley and Arthur Brown both scoring twice.

Bob Chatt and Steve Smith each netted twice when Forest were bounced out of the FA Cup 6-2 at Perry Barr in a 3rd round clash in March 1895, and it took two extra-time goals to see Villa overcome Forest 3-1 in a 2nd round replay in February 1901.

A crowd of 64,882 (recs. £16,200) saw Villa beaten 1-0 by Forest in the 1959 FA Cup semi-final at Hillsborough, John Quigley knocking in the deciding goal on 65 minutes.

John Deehan was sent-off when Villa lost 2-0 in a 3rd round tie at Forest in January 1979 and the last time the teams met in this competition was in the 1996 quarter-finals when former Forest winger Franz Carr's goal gave Villa a hard-fought 1-0 victory down by the River Trent.

Villa, the holders, were knocked out of the League Cup by Forest to the tune of 4-2 at The City Ground in the 4th round in November 1977 in front of 29,333 fans.

The two ZDSC encounters took place in seasons 1989-90 and 1991-92. Villa won the first (2-1) in front of 6,530 fans and Forest the second (2-0) before 7,859 spectators.

Players with both clubs include: WR Boyman, FH Broome (Forest WW2 guest), RAJ 'Sailor' Brown, C Calderwood, L Canning (Forest WW2 guest), F Carr, GA Charles, S Collymore, P Crichton (Forest reserve, Villa loanee), GR Edwards (Forest WW2), RT Edwards (Forest trialist), WC Goffin (Forest WW2 guest), S Gray, AW Green, H Hadley, JH Hampton (Forest WW1 guest), S Hardy, FJ Haycock (Forest WW2 guest), T Hockey, WE Houghton (Forest WW2 guest, also Forest scout & Villa manager), SB Hodge, both JR Martin & A Massie (Forest WW2 guests), JH Maund, TBD Niblo, FJ O'Donnell, GS Parker, D Platt (also

Forest manager), G Pritty, JHH Rutherford (Forest WW2 guest), D Saunders, R Scimeca, CH Slade (Forest trialist), RW Starling (Forest WW2 guest, also Forest coach), SB Stone, J Suddick, K Swain, C Tiler, G Vowden, A Wakeman (Forest WW2 guest), P Withe

Also: R Atkinson (manager of both clubs), A Barton (Forest player, Villa manager), WH Walker (Villa player, Forest manager), WE Houghton (Villa player & manager, Forest scout), J Barron (Forest player, Villa coach and assistant-manager), A Ashman (Forest player, Villa scout).

## NOTTS COUNTY

Villa's playing record against the Magpies:

Football League

| Venue | P | W | D | L | F | A |
|---|---|---|---|---|---|---|
| Home | 33 | 23 | 7 | 3 | 83 | 29 |
| Away | 33 | 12 | 8 | 13 | 49 | 52 |
| Totals | 66 | 35 | 15 | 16 | 132 | 81 |

FA Cup

| | | | | | | |
|---|---|---|---|---|---|---|
| Home | 6 | 4 | 1 | 1 | 15 | 8 |
| Away | 8 | 2 | 4 | 2 | 17 | 13 |
| Totals | 14 | 6 | 5 | 3 | 32 | 21 |

League Cup

| | | | | | | |
|---|---|---|---|---|---|---|
| Home | 2 | 1 | 0 | 1 | 5 | 2 |
| Away | 1 | 0 | 0 | 1 | 0 | 1 |
| Totals | 3 | 1 | 0 | 2 | 5 | 3 |

Aston Villa won 12 of their first 14 home League games against County and recorded 18 victories out of the first 23.

The Magpies crashed to a 9-1 defeat on Villa soil in September 1888 - the first League meeting between the two teams. Albert Allen grabbed a hat-trick in this game - and the defeat still stands as County's joint heaviest in the competition. John Holland was the unfortunate keeper in the County goal!

Villa lost 7-1 at Trent Bridge in November 1890 and 5-2 on the same ground in January 1892, but in return the Magpies were defeated 5-1 at Perry Barr in November 1891 and then Jack Devey's hat-trick gave Villa a 6-1 home victory in April 1899.

In season 1899-1900 two Villa players scored hat-tricks against County - Bill Garraty in the 6-2 home win and George Johnson in a 4-1 success at Trent Bridge.

Another hat-trick hero for Villa was Joe Bache who bagged three goals when County were defeated 5-1 at Villa Park in March 1908.

After bouncing back from 2-0 down to beat County 3-2 in the last game played at Trent Bridge on 16 April 1910, Villa duly clinched their sixth Football League championship.

Three days after losing 2-0 at Nottingham, Villa bounced back to hammer County 5-1 in the return fixture in March 1912.

En-route to winning the Third Division title in 1971-72, Villa won 3-0 at Meadow Lane in front of 34,208 spectators, County's biggest home crowd for 25 years.

Villa's 14-match unbeaten League run came to an end when they lost 2-0 at Notts County in September 1973.

As reigning champions, Villa commenced their 1981-82 League programme by losing at home 1-0 to the Magpies.

Villa crashed 5-2 at Meadow Lane in November 1983 but won the return fixture 3-1 to help send the Magpies back to the Second Division!

It took Villa three attempts to eliminate County from the FA Cup in 1881-82. A 2-2 home draw in front of a record 7,000 crowd at Perry Barr was followed by a 2-2 scoreline in the replay. Villa finally went through to the fourth round with a 4-1 victory, again at Perry Barr, which attracted a new record crowd, this time of 12,000.

In March 1883 a 5th round FA Cup-tie between County and Villa at

THE COMPLETE ENCYCLOPAEDIA OF ASTON VILLA F.C.    THE COMPLETE ENCYCLOPAEDIA OF ASTON VILLA F.C.

202

*Goal...for Pat McMahon against Notts County at Meadow Lane in March 1972.*

Nottingham was evenly balanced at 3-3, Villa having come back from 3-0 down. But with time running out a County defender used his hand to keep out a goal-bound shot from Archie Hunter. A free-kick was awarded inside the 'area' (no penalties in those days) but the ball was cleared downfield for County to snatch a dramatic winner!

Villa lost 4-3 again to County in a 4th round replay in 1922, whilst in a 3rd round contest at Meadow Lane in January 1982, David Geddis grabbed a hat-trick as County were battered 6-0.

The last FA Cup encounter was in 1997 when Villa won a 3rd round replay 3-0 at home.

Villa beat County 4-0 at home in the 1st round of the 1970-71 League Cup competition, Willie Anderson, Pat McMahon, Bruce Rioch and Ian Hamilton the scorers in front of 17,843 spectators.

Players with both clubs include: FH Broome (also County caretaker-manager), R Brown, C Caldwerwood, J Cantrell, H Chapman, RA Chester (County trialist), P Crichton (Villa loanee), RD Davis (WW2 guest for both clubs), W Devey, M Draper, GR Edwards (County WW2 guest), RT Edwards, WE Evans, AM Gray, S Grayson, AW Green, C Harley, R Harper, A Hateley, FJ Haycock (County WW2 guest), HV Henshall (also County secretary/manager), S Howarth (County trialist), D Hunt, RT Iverson (County WW2 guest), GJW Jakeman, T Johnson, P King, G Kinsey, J Logan, E Lowe (also County manager), JW McMorran, W Matthews, D Norton, D Pace, D Pearce (Villa reserve), MJ Pinner, LP Price, RT Pritchard, P Rideout, PJ Robinson, I Ross, J Sewell, G Shelton, S Sims, JW Smith (Villa reserve), KC Tewksbury, A Wakeman (County guest), RM Wylie,

Also: WE Houghton (Villa player & manager, County manager), FC Buckley (Villa reserve, County manager), JA Fisher (Villa player, County secretary-manager), H Edgley (Villa player, County Director), Steve Hodge (Villa player, County Academy coach), F Upton (County player, Villa coach), W Moore (Villa reserve and trainer at both clubs), PD Doherty (Villa chief scout, County Joint Soccer Advisor).

## NUMBERING OF PLAYERS

Aston Villa players first wore numbers on the back of their shirts in the Football League Jubilee Fund game against West Bromwich Albion on 20 August 1938. The first time numbers were seen in a League game

was when Villa met Grimsby Town at Blundell Park a week later, on 27 August.

The first time supporters saw the numbers 1-11 on the backs of the claret and blue jerseys at Villa Park was on Saturday 3 September 1938 when Derby County were the visitors.

Squad numbers were first introduced to the Premiership for the 1993-94 season.

## OAKES, MICHAEL CHRISTIAN

Born: Northfield, Birmingham, 30 October 1973
Career: Aston Villa (apprentice July 1989, professional July 1991), Scarborough (on loan, September 1993), Bromsgrove Rovers (on loan), Gloucester City (on loan), Wolverhampton Wanderers (£400,000, October 1999).

After becoming third-choice goalkeeper at Villa Park (behind David James and Peter Enckleman) Michael Oakes had no hestitation in moving across the Midlands to Molineux when Wolves boss Colin Lee came in with a substantial bid for his services. He had made 61 first-team appearances during his time at Villa Park and had also played twice for Scarborough. Capped six times by England at Under-21 level, Oakes is an excellent shot-stopper who was rated as one of the best goalkeepers in the First Division in the 2000-01 season.

Oakes' father, Alan, appeared in 669 games for Manchester City.

## O'DONNELL, FRANK JOSEPH

Born: Buckhaven, Fife, 31 August 1911. Died: Macclesfield 4 September 1952.
Career: Scottish Schoolboy football, Wellesley Juniors, Celtic (1929), Preston North End (£5,000 plus his brother Hugh, May 1935), Blackpool (£8,000, plus two players, November 1937), Aston Villa (£10,500, November 1938); guested for Blackpool, Crystal Palace, Heart of Midlothian, Leeds United, Lincoln City, Liverpool and Tottenham Hotspur during WW2; Nottingham Forest (January 1946), Buxton (player-manager, 1948-52).

Big, strong, thrustful inside or centre-forward Frank O'Donnell was on target for PNE in every round of their 1936-37 FA Cup run including his side's only goal in the Final defeat by Sunderland - one of 42 he

THE COMPLETE ENCYCLOPAEDIA OF ASTON VILLA F.C.   THE COMPLETE ENCYCLOPAEDIA OF ASTON VILLA F.C.

203

scored in his 100 appearances for the Deepdale club. Capped six times by Scotland (1936-38) he went on to net 17 times in his 30 League outings for Blackpool before fellow Scot and international colleague Alex Massie lured him to Villa Park.

He did very well with Villa, playing in between Freddie Haycock and Ronnie Starling, and netted 14 times in 31 outings before the Second World War hostilities severely disrupted his perfomances.

## OFFSIDE LAW

The current offside law was introduced for the 1925-26 season and Aston Villa started off with a bang, thrashing luckless Burnley 10-0 at home in their opening League match on 29 August.

## OLD CROWN & CUSHION

The Old Crown & Cushion public house, situated on the corner of Birchfield Road and Wellington Road was Villa's headquarters when they played at their Perry Barr ground.

## OLDBURY TOWN

Villa's playing record against Town:
FA Cup

| Venue | P | W | D | L | F | A |
|---|---|---|---|---|---|---|
| Away | 1 | 1 | 0 | 0 | 4 | 0 |

Aston Villa easily accounted for the Black Country side in a 1st round FA Cup-tie in October 1887, Albert Brown scoring twice in front of 3,000 spectators.

## OLDHAM ATHLETIC

Villa's playing record against the Latics:
Football League/Premiership

| Venue | P | W | D | L | F | A |
|---|---|---|---|---|---|---|
| Home | 15 | 9 | 3 | 3 | 34 | 8 |
| Away | 15 | 7 | 6 | 2 | 29 | 17 |
| Totals | 30 | 16 | 9 | 5 | 63 | 25 |
| FA Cup | | | | | | |
| Away | 3 | 2 | 0 | 1 | 5 | 4 |
| Neutral | 1 | 1 | 0 | 0 | 1 | 0 |
| Totals | 4 | 3 | 0 | 1 | 6 | 4 |
| | | | | | | |
| League Cup | | | | | | |
| Home | 1 | 1 | 0 | 0 | 2 | 0 |

*The captains meet: Davey Wilson (Oldham) and Joe Bache (Villa) before the 1913 F.A. Cup Semi-Final at Ewood Park, Blackburn.*

Harry Hampton (4) and Clem Stephenson (2) netted the goals when Villa beat the Latics 6-1 at home in December 1911 and both players figured on the scoresheet again when Villa doubled up by winning 2-1 at Boundary Park the following April.

Hot-shot Hampton was a hat-trick hero again when Villa beat Oldham 7-1 at home in December 1912.

Many years later, in November 1971, Andy Lochhead, later to play for the Latics, scored a hat-trick when Villa won 6-0 at Oldham in a Third Division game. Brian Little claimed a treble as Villa won 5-0 at home in April 1975.

Villa's 1-0 victory at Oldham in November 1987 started a run of 12 League matches without defeat.

When the Latics won 1-0 at Villa Park on 2 May 1993, the Premiership trophy went to Manchester United!

Only 21,114 spectators saw Villa lose 2-1 at home to the Latics in the Premiership on 19 March 1994. Eight days later 35,000 fans went to Wembley to cheer Villa to a 3-1 League Cup Final victory over Manchester United. Villa have so far recorded five League doubles over the Latics.

Clem Stephenson's goal gave Villa a 1-0 FA Cup semi-final victory over the Latics at Ewood Park, Blackburn in March 1913.

Villa won a 3rd round FA Cup-tie 3-0 at Oldham in January 1975 but lost by the same score in a quarter-final clash in March 1990.

Villa's League Cup victory was achieved in the 2nd round in September 1975, Keith Leonard and Chris Nicholl the scorers.

Players with both clubs: E Barrett, GC Harkus (Latics' trialist), A Hateley, GH Hunter, A Lochhead, BJ Lynch, E Malpass (Villa reserve), F Moss snr, I Olney, I Ormondroyd, JC Slueewenhoek, S Stainrod, CW Wallace, J Walters, J West (Villa reserve).
Also: J McMullan (Manager of both clubs).

## OLNEY, BENJAMIN ALBERT

Born: Holborn, London, 15 March 1899. Died: Derby, 23 September 1943.

Career: Fairleys Athletic, Aston Park Rangers, Stourbridge (August 1919), Derby County (April 1921), Aston Villa (December 1927), Bilston United (player-manager, July 1930), Walsall (August 1931), Shrewsbury Town (August 1932), Moor Green (1933-35).

England international goalkeeper Ben Olney was capped twice by his country - lining up against France and Belgium in 1928. He also played in two unofficial Test Matches against South Africa in 1929 as well as winning a Junior cap as a teenager. He made 240 League and FA Cup appearances for Derby County before moving to Villa Park in 1927 - a week or so after the Rams had completed the double over Villa in the First Division! Olney missed only 11 games (through injury and illness) during his five years at The Baseball Ground and his impressive appearance record stood for over 40 years until beaten by Reg Matthews in 1968. He helped the Rams win promotion from Division Two in 1926. He quickly bedded himself at Villa Park, going on to make 97 first-class appearances as an efficient 'last line of defence.' He replaced Tommy Jackson in the Villa side before giving way to Fred Biddlestone in 1930. He was working at the Rolls Royce factory in Derby when he died suddenly at the age of 44.

## OLNEY, IAN DOUGLAS

Born: Luton, 17 December 1969.

Career: Gloucestershire Schools, Ebley FC, Aston Villa (YTS, June 1986, professional, July 1988), Oldham Athletic (£700,000, July 1992). Forced to retire in the summer of 1998 but later returned to the game with Halesowen Town in January 2000.

A very useful 6ft 1in striker, strong and mobile, Ian Olney made the breakthrough at Villa Park during the 1988-89 season after two

THE COMPLETE ENCYCLOPAEDIA OF ASTON VILLA F.C.     THE COMPLETE ENCYCLOPAEDIA OF ASTON VILLA F.C.

204

excellent scoring campaigns with the reserve & intermediate sides. He netted on his senior debut against Birmingham City in the League Cup in October 1988 and went on to register 19 goals in a total of 104 first team appearances before transferring to Boundary Park in 1992. He was capped 10 times by England at Under-21 level during his time at Villa Park. Olney had a good first season with the Latics (13 goals in 39 games) but then ran into injury problems which eventually made him quit the top-class arena.

*Ian Olney*

## O'NEILL, ALAN

Born: Sunderland, 13 November 1937

Career: Sunderland (juniors, July 1953, professional February 1956), Aston Villa (£9,000, October 1960), Plymouth Argyle (November 1962), Bournemouth (February 1964).

Five days after his transfer from Roker Park, Alan O'Neill scored with his first kick (after 25 seconds) for Aston Villa in the local derby against Birmingham City on 22 October 1960, and later added a second goal in a 6-2 win. He went on to net 14 times in his 36 senior outings for the club before moving to Plymouth in 1962.

A workmanlike inside-forward, he did well at Sunderland (27 goals in 74 League games). He followed up with 14 strikes in 40 appearances for the Pilgrims and eight in 37 starts for the Cherries. Christened Alan Hope, he changed his name to O'Neill in 1956 after his mother had remarried. He now lives in Bournemouth.

## ONES THAT GOT AWAY!

Here are some of the many players released, sold or given away by Aston Villa who went on to achieve excellent records with other clubs (listed in no specific order of preference or seniority):

Full-back Jesse Pennington released by Villa after trials (no first team appearances) went on to play in almost 500 games for West Bromwich Albion (1903-22). And he won 25 England caps.

Charlie L Roberts was given a free transfer by Villa in 1922 without having made the first XI. Over the next 16 years he served with 17 different clubs, amassed 350 senior appearances and netted more than 100 goals. His record in League football was excellent: 304 appearances and 96 goals.

After retiring as a player, Major Frank Buckley became one of the finest managers in the country, doing especially well with Wolverhampton Wanderers for a number of years. After failing to make a single first team appearance for Villa, he later amassed almost 200 in League and Cup competitions while serving with seven other clubs including Brighton, Manchester City, Manchester United, Birmingham and Derby County.

Les Askew had just two outings for Villa (1910-12), before making over 100 for West Ham in last three pre-First World War seasons.

Martin Carruthers made six first-team appearances for Villa and after leaving the club in 1993 he went on to star in over 300 games as a professional and scored 75 goals for other League teams

Youth international Trevor Berry, signed from Bournemouth for £50,000 in 1992, failed to make a first team appearance for Villa, but after leaving the club in 1995 he went on to play in more than 200 first-class games for Rotherham United.

Striker Steve Cowe, an Aston Villa reserve who did not break into the first XI, went on to make over 100 senior appearances for Swindon Town (1996-2001).

Gareth Williams, signed for £30,000 from Gosport Borough in 1988,

left Villa Park in 1991 with just 16 appearances under his belt. Over the next ten years he made over 325 more at senior level (123 for Scarborough).

Jimmy Birch scored twice in three games for Villa before going on to net 144 goals in 363 games for QPR (1912-26).

Noel Blake played in just four senior games for Villa at the start of his career. He left Villa Park in 1982 and over the next 18 years amassed more than 700 appearances for seven other clubs including 173 for Portsmouth and 159 for Exeter City.

Reg Butcher, released by Villa in 1936 having failed to make the first XI, went on to play 18 League games for Reading and 173 for Chester before the Second World War.

Sid Chandler, a Villa reserve in 1925-26, was released without playing in the first team. He went on to amass 65 League appearances for Preston and 83 for Reading before 1932.

David Farrell made only eight senior appearances for Villa (early 1990s) but made over 200 for Peterborough United after leaving the club.

Gareth Farrelly made nine appearances for Villa (1992-97). Later he became an Irish international and in 2001 was well on his way to totting up a record of 100 senior appearances (with Villa, Rotherham, Everton and Bolton). He helped Bolton reach the Premiership in 2001 by scoring the opening goal in the Play-off Final v Preston.

Centre-forward Norman Mackay made just two appearances for Villa in 1923-24. After leaving the club he went on to star in 241 League and Cup games for Plymouth Argyle (14 goals scored).

Forward Tommy Mooney never got a first team game in Villa's colours but after leaving the club in 1990 he went on to appear in over 400 competitive games for Scarborough, Southend United and Watford (up to 2001), starring in the Premiership with the Hornets. He joined Birmingham City from Watford.

Midfielder Ray Walker played in 27 games for Villa (18 plus nine as a sub) before going on to amass in excess of 420 first-class appearances for Port Vale (up to 1996).

Dennis Pearce did not play in Villa's first team but after leaving the club made 11 appearances for Wolves and almost 150 for Notts County (1997-2001).

Goalkeeper Kevin Poole made 32 first team appearances for Villa at the start of his career. Come 2001 he had made almost a further 300 with other clubs at senior level.

Another goalkeeper, Bob Wilson, played in nine games for Villa up to 1964 and afterwards amassed over 350 appearances while serving with Cardiff City, Bristol City and Exeter City.

Charlie Aston made 24 first team appearances for Villa (1898-1901) and went on to accumulate well over 200 during his playing career.

Fred Chapple scored three goals in eight matches for Villa (1906-08) but afterwards made over 100 appearances for other clubs, including Birmingham.

Scott Murray, with just four Premiership games under his belt with Villa, later appeared in more than 170 League and Cup games for Bristol City (1997-2001).

Lee Williams, capped by England at Youth team level whilst at Villa Park but who failed to appear in the first team, later made over 100 appearances for Peterborough and almost 150 for Mansfield Town as well as playing for Shamrock Rovers.

Arthur Davis played in five League games for Villa (1919-21) and after leaving the club he went on to amass over 200 appearances while serving with QPR, Notts County and Crystal Palace.

Dual England and Welsh international Robert Evans netted four times in 17 games for Villa before going on to make over 200 League appearances for Sheffield United (1900-08).

Mid-1920s centre-forward Percy Varco scored twice in 10 games for Villa and after leaving the club netted 82 goals in 164 League games for three other clubs.

Dean Spink (no relation to Nigel) was a junior with Villa (no first team games) before being sold to Shrewsbury for £75,000 in 1990. Over the next decade he amassed more than 450 League and Cup appearances for the Shrews and Wrexham, and netted over 70 goals.

THE COMPLETE ENCYCLOPAEDIA OF ASTON VILLA F.C.   THE COMPLETE ENCYCLOPAEDIA OF ASTON VILLA F.C.

205

Villa 'sold' Walter Freeman to Fulham in 1905 without giving him an opportunity in the first XI. He went on to score 33 goals in over 100 League and Cup games while playing for the Cottagers and Birmingham.

Winger George Garratt made 227 League appearances for other clubs after leaving Villa Park in 1906.

Irish international Archie Goodall spent one season with Aston Villa (1888-89) before going on to score 49 goals in 379 League games in 15 years with Derby County.

After just seven outings for Villa in 1911-12, Herbert Goode left the club and went on to appear in over 100 matches for Hull City and Wrexham.

Arriving from Bristol Rovers in 1904, James Gray made only seven appearances for Villa, but after leaving the club he went on to amass a further 180 plus with other teams.

Goalkeeper Fred Potter was given just seven first team outings by Villa before moving to Northampton and later Hereford. He ended his career with 136 League appearances to his name.

Dave Roberts had just 19 first-team games for Villa (1963-68) and then went on to score 20 goals in 230 League games for Shrewsbury Town plus one in 37 for Swansea.

George Stephenson made only four senior appearances and scored one goal for Aston Villa before going on to net 58 times in almost 200 League games for Luton 1934-39.

Robert Gray was released by Aston Villa in 1895 with no first team games to his credit. He went on to score over 40 goals in more than 100 appearances with four other clubs.

Arthur Green was transferred from Villa Park in 1901 after failing to make a single first team appearance. Later he starred in a total of 172 League games with the two Nottingham clubs, County and Forest.

John Griffiths did not play in a single game for Aston Villa (1895-98) but afterwards he made over 120 appearances during his spells at Grimsby Town and Northampton.

Another John Griffiths (born in 1951) played four times for Aston Villa before being released - he later scored 31 goals in 182 League games for Stockport County (1970-75).

Left-back Jimmy Lawrence was a Wartime signing by Villa in 1918. He made only two first team appearances before going on to amass 136 for Coventry City (1920-25).

Billy Kellock, an apprentice at Villa Park, was released in 1972 without making the first XI. He went on to score 77 goals in 298 League games for nine other clubs up to 1986.

George Harper failed to make Aston Villa's first XI (early 1890s) but in later years he amassed well over 100 League and Cup appearances when serving with Wolves, Grimsby and Sunderland.

Arthur Layton had only 17 outings for Aston Villa between 1908-11 and then starred in over 140 games for three other clubs.

Goalkeeper Albert Lindon made just one first team appearance for Aston Villa, in March 1912, before moving to Barnsley. He later assisted Coventry City, Merthyr Town and Charlton before retiring in 1931 having appeared in a further 325 League and Cup games.

Walter Leigh had one game for Aston Villa (in the late 1890s) and afterwards he appeared in a further 156 League matches whilst serving with four other clubs.

Paul Kerr scored 62 goals in 339 appearances at senior level, the majority after leaving Villa Park for Middlesbrough in 1987.

*Ian Ormondroyd jumps highest against WBA.*

John Martin made just one League appearance for Villa in 1964 - afterwards he amassed 348 with his next three clubs: Colchester United, Workington & Southport.

Defender David Evans made only two senior appearances for Aston Villa (1978-79) before going on to appear in over 300 first-class games (in two spells with Halifax Town) and more than 230 for Bradford City.

Brian McClair, released by Aston Villa in 1981 without having a senior outing, went on to score goals 20 goals in 52 games for Motherwell, 122 in almost 200 appearances for Celtic (1983-87) and 128 in 474 matches for Manchester United. He won medals galore both north and south of the border and represented Scotland on 30 occasions at senior level as well as playing in Youth, 'B' and Under-21 internationals.

Albert McLachlan played in three League games for Villa (1913-14). He then went back to Aberdeen and made 315 appearances for the Scottish club (up to 1927).

Chris Mann, after 11 League and Cup games for Villa (1899-1901) went on to appear in over 120 for Burton United.

Frank Mann had one League outing with Villa in 1912 before leaving the club. He later starred in 226 games for Huddersfield Town (75 goals) and 197 for Manchester United (5 goals).

Billy Marriott netted once in five League starts for Villa (1901-02). He went on to appear in a further 181 League games for Bristol Rovers, Northampton and New Brompton (Gillingham).

Between 1903 and 1906 Bill Matthews scored 12 goals in 25 games for Villa. After that he netted 36 times in 178 League outings for Notts County.

After netting five times in 12 games for Villa, Harold Nash left for Coventry City in 1920, later assisting Cardiff City and Merthyr Town. He scored a further 13 goals in 104 League games.

John Sharp scored 15 goals in 24 first team appearances for Villa before leaving the club to join Everton in 1899. Over the next 11 years he played in almost 300 games for the Merseysiders.

After 54 League appearances for Leyton and just one for Villa (in January 1909) Leon Skiller went on to play in more than 300 League and Cup games for Swindon Town.

Charlie H. Slade had three first team outings for Villa (1913-14). He then left to join Huddersfield Town and went on to appear in over 200 games for the Terriers, Middlesbrough and Darlington.

James Stephenson scored once in 32 outings for Villa (1914-21). He later appeared in 234 League games for Sunderland, Watford and QPR.

David Stokes, released by Villa in 1901 having failed to make the first team, went on to amass 420 senior appearances for Bolton Wanderers, scoring 46 goals.

Bobby Templeton was perhaps 'sold' by Villa far too early. After 71 appearances for the club (1899-1903) he went on to play in another 350 League and Cup games for Newcastle United, Arsenal, Celtic, Kilmarnock and Fulham.

Villa reserve Jack Tooth failed to get into the first XI and left the club in 1905. He later appeared in over 80 games as a 'pro' for Burton United, Coventry City and Gainsborough Trinity.

James E. Travers scored four goals in four games for Villa in 1908-09. After that he went on to serve with eight other League clubs and starred in a further 250 senior matches up to 1921.

Bought from Leicester in 1899, Alf Watkins made one appearance for Villa before joining Grimsby. He later played for Millwall and Southend and added over 150 more appearances to his tally.

Goalkeeper Jack Whitley made nine appearances for Villa at the start of the 20th century. He then left the club and went on to tot up over

200 at League and Cup level with four other teams.

Bill Yates was released from Villa in 1905 without playing first team football. By the time he retired in 1914 he had totted up some 275 senior appearances (258 in the Football League) while serving with Brighton, Manchester United, Hearts, Portsmouth and Coventry City.

John Overton had three senior games for Aston Villa in the early 1970s. He later played in 178 League matches for Gillingham (1976-81).

George Graham was sold by Aston Villa to Chelsea in 1964 after just 10 first team appearances. He went on to make over 500 more during the remainder of his career - 455 coming in the Football League (95 goals).

Goalkeeper Kevin Keelan MBE, made only five first team appearances for Aston Villa right at the start of his professional career. He left the club in 1961 and thereafter amassed a truly magnificent record by playing in more than 800 club games - including a record 673 for Norwich City (1963-80).

## OPEN DAY

In the summer of 1988, Villa Park staged an open day to allow supporters, young and old, to have a look behind the scenes at the club. Over 6,000 turned up.

In September 1995, another open day was arranged and this time the turnout was huge - just over 20,000 - double the number that was first anticipated. Nevertheless, all went off smoothly - as always at Villa Park!

## ORMONDROYD, IAN

Born: Bradford, 22 September 1964

Career: Thackley FC, Bradford City (professional, September 1985), Oldham Athletic (on loan, March 1987), Aston Villa (£650,000, February 1989), Derby County (£350,000, September 1991), Leicester City (March 1992), Hull City (on loan, January 1995), Bradford City (£75,000, July 1995), Oldham Athletic (free transfer, September 1996), Scunthorpe United (£25,000, September 1997-May 1998).

A record signing in February 1989, Ian 'Sticks' or 'Legs' Ormondroyd was a tall, lanky striker, 6ft 4ins tall and 13st 6lbs in weight, who spent two-and-a-half years at Villa Park during which time he scored 10 goals in 74 first team appearances. Good in the air, able and generally useful on the ground, he had 13 years in competitive football and overall drew up a pretty good record of 451 senior appearances and 83 goals. A niggling ankle injury eventually resulted in him leaving the League stage.

## ORMSBY, BRENDAN THOMAS CHRISTOPHER

Born: Edgbaston, Birmingham, 1 October 1960

Career: Ladywood Comprehensive School, Aston Villa (apprentice, March 1976, professional October 1978), Leeds United (£65,000, February 1986), Shrewsbury Town (on loan, January 1990), Doncaster Rovers (July 1990), Scarborough (August 1992), Waterford United (1993-94 season), Wigan Athletic (non-contract, August-September 1994).

Ginger-haired centre-half, strong and reliable, totally committed, Brendan Ormsby came through the junior ranks at Villa Park to earn England Youth honours. He scored seven goals in 140 first-team appearances for the club before transferring to Elland Road in 1986 after being injured and then losing his place in the side to Paul Elliott. He went on to have a further 150 plus outings at club level.

*Brendan Ormsby*

## OVERSEAS OPPOSITION

The Canadian tourists were the first overseas team to come to England and play against Aston Villa, contesting a friendly match at the Aston Lower Grounds Meadow in October 1888.

A strong South African side visited Villa Park in October 1924 and defeated Aston Villa's first XI 3-0 in a friendly encounter in front of 5,000 spectators.

In December 1945, Villa Park was set to stage a prestigious friendly between the famous Russia touring side Moscow Dynamo and an FA Select XI (all internationals). Arrangements for match were already in place. Around 70,000 tickets had been printed and a bumper crowd was expected. But sadly the event never took place...the Russians were called home (although no-one really knew why) and Villa officials were left scratching their heads.

Frem (Copenhagen) played Aston Villa in a Festival of Britain game in 1951.

(See also under friendlies and European Competitions).

## OVERSEAS TOURS & MATCHES

In 1901, Aston Villa became the first English professional League club side to play in Germany. They beat a German Select XI 6-2 in Berlin, a game that saw Joe Bache make an impressive debut in the claret and blue strip.

In May-June 1926, Aston Villa underwent their first major European tour, playing six games in Scandinavia. They won four and lost 2, the results being as follows: Orgryte Idrott lost 2-5, Kombineral Goteburgslag lost 1-2, Lyn O.G. Frig won 11-2, Stockholm XI won 5-4, Copenhagen XI won 4-1 and Copenhagen XI won 5-2.

In May 1938, Villa returned to Germany where they played three matches, winning two and losing one....in the heat of Hitler's Nazi saluting supporters! (See under Germany).

Villa played three games in Norway in the summer of 1946, winning two and drawing one. They beat Norway/Combined Stavanger XI 9-1.

In 1951-52 Villa toured Sweden and Denmark winning two and losing two of their four fixtures.

Villa toured Germany in 1953-54, winning all three games and in 1959-60 a visit to Scandinavia saw the team play six matches, five of which were won and the other lost (goal ratio: 36-6).

In May 1961, Villa played three matches behind the 'Iron Curtain'. They were defeated 2-0 by Moscow Dynamo in the Lenin Stadium, lost 2-0 to Dynamo Tblisi in Georgia and then returned to the Lenin Stadium to defeat a Combined Soviet XI 1-0 (Jimmy MacEwan the scorer).

In 1966-67, Villa toured Sweden to play three matches, winning two. In the same year they also toured Germany and Holland.

In 1969-70, Villa embarked on a pre-season tour of Germany then took part in an international club tournament in Atlanta, USA. The other participating clubs in this well-prepared, well-organised and well-supported tourney were Dundee United and Kilmarnock from Scotland and West Ham United and Wolverhampton Wanderers from England. Each team played against each other twice. Wolves came out on top with 57 points overall (including 21 bonus points). West Ham amassed 52 (19), Dundee United 31 (13), Villa 28 (10) and Kilmarnock 26 (11). These were Villa's results: Dundee United - drew 2-2, won 2-0; Kilmarnock - won 2-1, lost 1-2; West Ham - drew 2-2, lost 0-2; Wolves - lost 1-2, lost 0-5. Also on this trip to the States, Villa drew 2-2 with Tottenham Hotspur in a friendly match and beat the host club, Atlanta Chiefs 2-0 in an exhibition game.

In July 1971, Villa visited Germany once more. This time they played three matches: against

THE COMPLETE ENCYCLOPAEDIA OF ASTON VILLA F.C.          THE COMPLETE ENCYCLOPAEDIA OF ASTON VILLA F.C.

207

Alemania Aachen (lost 1-0), Kickers Wurzburg (won 4-2) and FC Bayreuth (won 3-2).

In 1972-73 Villa took part in a pre-season tour of Holland, winning all of their three games.

While Villa's first team toured Tanzania in the summer of 1973, the Youth squad visited Zambia. The seniors played four games, winning one (3-0 against a Zanzibar XI) and drawing three while the youngsters won three, drew two and lost two of their seven matches.

In 1974-75 Villa travelled to Germany; the following year they played in Martinique and Guadeloupe.

A pre-season tour of France and Portugal in 1976-77 saw Villa beat St. Etienne 2-1, draw 0-0 with Rheims and 1-1 with Porto and on trips to Yuglosavia in 1978-79 and Germany in 1980/81 three games were played in each country.

As reigning League champions, Villa toured Greece and Morocco in 1981-82 before revisiting Germany for another interesting tour in 1982-83.

A trip to Italy in 1986-87 saw Villa participate in two games; then a visit was made to Jamaica in June 1987 before the team played five matches during a pre-season tour to Scandinavia.

The Israeli national team was taken on in the Middle East in December 1988 and in March 1989, Villa took in the sun when visiting Trinidad and Tobago.

An overseas tournament in 1989-90 saw Villa beat Nantes 3-2, lose and draw against Porto 1-2 and 2-2 respectively and lose also against Partizan Belgrade in a ten goal thriller by 4-6.

In July 1989, Aston Villa played a series of matches in Switzerland; then in 1991-92 they participated in the Hanover tournament in Germany (playing one game against Borussia Moenchengladbach).

In 1990-91 Villa took part in a pre-season tour of Hong Kong, Malaysia, Kuala Lumpar and Scandanavia.

Also in 1991-92 Villa played Shelbourne (twice) in Ireland as well as travelling to Paris to take on Sporting Lisbon; then to Edinburgh to play Hibernian.

In 1992-93 Villa went on tour to the island of Mauritius; they also played two games in Germany (v Dynamo Dresden and PFV Bergmann Borsig) and travelled to Ireland to play Manchester United and Drogheda.

At the end of the 1993-94 season Villa toured South Africa (where once again they met Liverpool, among others). They also played against Yomrori Nippon and entered a Cup competition in Japan.

Twelve months later - during 1994-95 - Villa again visited Ireland and they also played in Spain (versus Atletico Madrid).

In May 1995, Villa lost to a Trinidad & Tobagan side 2-1 and a Barbadian XI 3-1 on an end-of-season tour to the West Indies.

A tour of America in 1996-97 saw Villa play Los Angeles Galaxy and San Jose Clash.

On their pre-season tour to Scotland in the summer of 1997 Villa played Partick Thistle and Motherwell and in 1999-2000 they took part in the USA Gotham Cup, competing against Ajax Amsterdam and Fiorentina of Italy. Villa also played Feyenoord in Holland.

For their 2000-01 build-up Villa played a friendly in Portugal against Benfica (drew 2-2).

(See also under the category of Friendly Matches where several of these tour games are mentioned).

## OVERTON, JOHN

Born: Rotherham, 2 May 1956

Career: Yorkshire Schools, Aston Villa (apprentice, June 1972, professional January 1974), Halifax Town (on loan, March 1976), Gillingham (June 1976-81). Non-League football (1981-88).

Overton was a reserve defender at Villa Park, getting very few opportunities (all three outings came in February 1976). Later he spent five seasons at The Priestfield Stadium, starring in 178 League games for the Gills (10 goals scored).

## OXFORD UNITED

Villa's playing record against United:

Football League

| Venue | P | W | D | L | F | A |
|---|---|---|---|---|---|---|
| Home | 7 | 4 | 2 | 1 | 9 | 3 |
| Away | 7 | 1 | 3 | 3 | 8 | 11 |
| Totals | 14 | 5 | 5 | 4 | 17 | 14 |

League Cup

| Venue | P | W | D | L | F | A |
|---|---|---|---|---|---|---|
| Home | 2 | 1 | 1 | 0 | 4 | 3 |
| Away | 2 | 1 | 0 | 1 | 3 | 3 |
| Totals | 4 | 2 | 1 | 1 | 7 | 6 |

The first time Villa and Oxford met each other in the Football League was in season 1968-69 (Division 2). Villa won 2-0 at home but lost 1-0 at The Manor Ground. The following season both matches ended in draws.

The teams met four times in the top flight between 1985 and 87, Oxford recording their only win at Villa Park in that time (2-1 in September 1986).

Oxford United beat Aston Villa 4-3 on aggregate in the semi-final of the 1985-86 League Cup competition. After a 2-2 draw at Villa Park they won the return leg 2-1 at The Manor Ground and then went on to beat QPR in the Final.

Players with both clubs include: Brothers GJ and RF Atkinson (Villa juniors, later players together at Oxford; Ron also Villa manager), NA Cutler, TC Donovan, SB Foster, R Graydon (also Oxford coach), R Houghton, RW McDonald, D Saunders, G Shelton, G Whittingham. Also: R Saunders (manager of both clubs), KHA Fish (Villa reserve & trainer at both clubs), J Barron (Oxford player, Villa coach & assistant-manager), C Clarke (Oxford player, Villa coach).

## OXFORD UNIVERSITY

Aston Villa were scheduled to play Oxford University in the 2nd round of the FA Cup in February 1880, but 24 hours before the away tie the Villa committee decided to scratch from the competition, anticipating a heavy and perhaps embarrassing defeat at the hands of the much-respected amateur side.

## OZALAN, ALPAY FEHMI

Born: Karsiyaka, Turkey, 29 May 1973

Career: Karsiyaka schoolboy football, Besiktas, Jet-Pa FC, Fenerbahce, Aston Villa (£5.5 million, July 2000)

Turkish international defender Alpay Ozalan was signed on a four-year contract by Aston Villa boss John Gregory in readiness for the start of the 2000-01 season. He had previously been registered with Fenerbahce on a long-term loan period and when Villa secured his services there was uproar in Turkey - because everyone thought he was going to sign permanently for Fenerbahce! Vastly experienced with over 50 caps under his belt, Alpay, whose agreement meant that he would earn £22,000-a-week, is married to an ex-model and played in all of Turkey's 14 Euro 2000 matches (including 10 qualifying games). He was sent-off for elbowing Nuno Gomes of Portugal in the quarter-final clash. A well built, hard-tackling centre-back he played in the European Champions League with Besiktas and helped Fenerbahce finish fourth in the Turkish First Division in 1999-2000. In his first season in English football, Alpay amassed 35 appearances for Aston Villa and added considerably to his tally of full caps for Turkey. He scored a hat-trick for his country in a World Cup qualifying game v. Macedonia in June 2001.

THE COMPLETE ENCYCLOPAEDIA OF ASTON VILLA F.C.     THE COMPLETE ENCYCLOPAEDIA OF ASTON VILLA F.C.

208

## PACE, DEREK JOHN

Born: Essington near Wolverhampton, 17 March 1932. Died: 1989.

Career: Bloxwich Strollers, Aston Villa (professional, September 1949), Sheffield United (December 1957), Notts County (December 1964), Walsall (July 1966). Retired May 1967; Walsall Wood (manager, 1968-70).

Centre-forward 'Doc' Pace scored over 40 goals for Bloxwich Strollers before becoming a professional with Aston Villa. 'Discovered' by the club's former defender George Cummings, he went on to amass a fine scoring record during his time at Villa Park, notching 42 goals in 107

*Derek Pace*

appearances before transferring to Bramall Lane on Boxing Day, 1957 (signed by future Villa manager Joe Mercer). He spent seven years with the Blades, adding 140 more goals to his tally (in 253 games). After assisting Notts County, he spent just under a year at Fellows Park (injuries annoying him considerably) before announcing his retirement in May 1967. Pace represented the Army v Ireland during his National Service in the RAMC. He also played in the 1960-61 FA Cup semi-final for Sheffield United (v Luton) and helped the Yorkshire club gain promotion to the First Division in that same season.

## PALETHORPE, JOHN THOMAS

Born: Leicester, 23 November 1909. Died: May 1984.

Career: Maidenhead United (Spartan League, 1927-28), Crystal Palace (professional, August 1929), Reading (March 1931), Stoke City (March, 1933), Preston North End (December 1933), Sheffield Wednesday (December 1934), Aston Villa (November 1935), Crystal Palace (October 1936), Chelmsford City (August 1938-May 1939). Retired during the Second World War.

Jack Palethorpe was a big, bustling centre-forward, known as 'SOS' because of his ability to rise to the occasion! He won promotion from the Second Division in successive seasons with Stoke City in 1933 and Preston North End in 1934 and gained an FA Cup winners' medal with Sheffield Wednesday (v WBA) in 1935. But then he went down from the First Division with Aston Villa in 1936 after he had been unable to hold down his place in the side. In fact he scored only twice in six first team outings for the club before moving to Palace. The dressing room comic, Palethorpe gave up his job as a shoe-manufactuer to become a professional footballer in 1929. He had a fine career, netting a total of 107 goals in only League appearances over a period of eight years: 1930-38.

## PANK, THOMAS

Born: Aston, Birmingham, January 1853. Died: Oxford, August 1929.

Career: Birmingham Excelsior FC, Aston Villa (August 1875),. Retired through injury, May 1883, and went into business in Oxford where he lived until his death. He was made a vice-President of Aston Villa in the 1920s (with Charlie Johnstone).

With his heavy moustache and long stride, defender Tom Pank was a true Victorian footballer, hard as iron, rough and ready but very competitive. He would play anywhere in defence as long as he could

get a game! He was a member of Aston Villa's first-ever FA Cup side v Stafford Road FC in December 1879 and in all he appeared in 10 senior matches for the club as well as many friendlies and local Cup games.

Pank was an outstanding athlete and founder member of the Birchfield Harriers Athletic club before he took up football. His manly physique was considered to be so well nigh perfect that the statue on the lid of the Lord Mayor of Birmingham Charity Cup was a model of Pank in action.

## PARK, ROBERT CLYDESDALE

Born: Edinburgh, 3 July 1946.

Career: Peterlee Schools, East Durham Boys, Middlesbrough (Amateur, summer 1961), Darlington Wool Firms FC (Sunday side), Aston Villa (apprentice, September 1961, professional July 1963), Wrexham (May 1969), Peterborough United (June 1972), Northampton Town (February 1973), Hartlepool United (July 1974-May 1975), Peterlee Newtown, (player/manager, retired as a player in 1977).

A ball-playing wing-half or inside-forward, Bobby Park, who lined up in the same Durham Boys team as Colin Bell, later of Manchester City & England, signed apprentice forms for Villa after he had scored a hat-trick playing for Darlington Wool Firms FC in a Sunday morning fixture. He quickly made an impression at Villa Park with some useful Central League displays and after becoming a professional, had to fight for a first team place with the likes of Alan Deakin, Brian Godfrey, Willie Hamilton, Dave Pountney, Mike Tindall and Ron Wylie, among others during his eight years at Villa Park. nevertheless he persevered and made 86 appearances scoring 10 goals before he became a casualty of Tommy Docherty's axe! Then, under former Villa full-back John Neal's managerial guidance he went on to star in 125 senior matches for Wrexham (8 goals), collecting a Welsh Cup runners-up medal in 1971.

## PARKER, GARRY STUART

Born: Oxford, 7 September 1965.

Career: Luton Town (apprentice, June 1981, professional May 1983), Hull City (£72,000, February 1986), Nottingham Forest (£260,000, March 1988), Aston Villa (£650,000, November 1991), Leicester City (£300,000, February 1995). Retired as a player in June 1999 to take on a coaching post at Filbert Street.

Regarded as one of the finest right-sided midfielders in League football during the early 1990s, Garry Parker had already established himself firmly in the game by the time he joined Aston Villa in 1991. He had made 54 first-team appearances for the Hatters, 95 for Hull and 151 for Forest, whom he helped win the European Super Cup in 1989 and register two successive League Cup Final victories (in 1989 & 1990). Capped by England at Youth, 'B' and Under-21 levels (six caps gained for the latter) he went on to star in 119 senior matches for Villa, scoring 14 goals before transferring to Leicester City. With the Foxes he added another League Cup triumph to his collection in 1997 and was in the side that gained promotion back to the Premiership that same year. Parker made close on 150 appearances for Leicester before taking up coaching duties at Filbert Street.

## PARKER, GRAHAM SYDNEY

Born: Coventry, 23 May 1946

Career: Coventry & Warwickshire Schools, Aston Villa (apprentice, July 1961, professional May 1963), Rotherham United (£6,000, December 1967), Lincoln City (£2,500, July 1968), Exeter City (March 1969), Torquay United (May 1974-May 1975). Retired 1977 after playing in various charity matches for two years.

Perhaps a player allowed to slip away by Aston Villa, for midfielder Graham Parker - nicknamed 'Fezz' - went on to amass a further 250 senior appearances after leaving the club 1967. He had just 21 outings for Villa (one goal scored) before manager Tommy Cummings trimmed his squad! Parker, a neat, compact player, won six caps for England at Schoolboy level.

## PARKES, HENRY ARTHUR

Born: Erdington, Birmingham, 4 January 1920.
Career: Slade Road School (Erdington), GEC works team (Witton), Boldmere St Michael's (1937), Aston Villa (Amateur April 1939, professional August 1939). Guested for Northampton Town and West Bromwich Albion during WW2. Retired in June 1955 to concentrate on his flourishing sports-outfitters' shop in Corporation Street, Birmingham, which ran with pride for some 40 years. He later served on the Board of Directors at both Villa Park and neighbouring Birmingham City.

*Harry Parkes in action against Chelsea.*

Harry Parkes was selected to play for Aston Villa in 10 different positions. A tremendously versatile footballer, he was a 'hard-boiled' Brummie, the dressing room comic who possessed a biting tackle, was quick in recovery, cleared his lines diligently without any fuss or bother, was utterly reliable and never complained! A wonderful professional he preferred the right-back position where he partnered the likes of George Cummings, Dicky Dorsett and Peter Aldis to great effect before handing over his duties to Stan Lynn. Parkes scored four goals in 345 League and FA Cup games for Aston Villa as well as appearing in a further 134 wartime fixtures (41 goals), gaining a Wartime League North Cup Medal in 1944.
He was in line for an England cap in 1946, but had the misfortune to suffer a severe arm injury in a League game at Derby which cost him his place in the Villa side as well as his international baptism! He never got another chance with England!

## PARSONS, DENNIS RONALD

Born: Birmingham, 29 May 1925. Died: 1980.
Career: BSA Cycle Works, Wolverhampton Wanderers (February 1944), Hereford United (1951), Aston Villa (September 1952), Kidderminster Harriers (September 1956). Retired through May 1960. Dennis Parsons - a sound and safe goalkeeper - was reserve to England's Bert Williams at Molineux and then understudy to Welsh international Keith Jones at Villa Park. He was playing for the BSA

Cycles team when Wolves spotted his talent and brought him to Molineux in February 1944. Unfortunately the War was still on and the luckless Parsons had to wait three years before making his League debut, ironically against the team he was to join later in his career, Aston Villa. In the summer of 1951 Parsons left Molineux to assist Hereford United (of the Southern League) and he rejoined the bigtime when signing for Villa in 1952. Four years and 41 games later he moved back into non-League football with Kidderminster Harriers.

## PARTNERSHIPS

Every club has its great partnerships - at full-back, half-back, in midfield and in attack. And over the years Aston Villa have been blessed with their fair share of talented 'double and treble acts' some of which are listed here (in date order as they appeared for the club).

**Full-back** - H Spencer/J Welford; H Spencer/A Evans; T Lyons/A Miles; T Smart/S Bowen; T Smart/T Mort; D Blair/T Mort; G Beeston/D Blair; E Callaghan/G Cummings; H Parkes/P Aldis; S Lynn/P Aldis; M Wright/C Aitken; J Robson/C Aitken; K Swain/C Gibson; E Barrett/S Staunton.

**Central defence (centre-halves)** - J Cowan/H Devey; AE Wood/A Leake; C Buckley/G Hunter; J Harrop/J Leach; F Barson/F Moss; A Talbot/J Tate (also J Gibson/Talbot/Tate); J Allen/R Iverson; F Moss/C Martin; F Moss/R Dorsett; J Dugdale/P Saward; C Nicholl/I Ross; A Evans/K McNaught; P McGrath/D Mountfield; G Southgate/U Ehiougu (& G Barry).

**Right-wing** - C Athersmith/R Chatt; C Wallace/W Gerrish; C Wallace/J Walters; C Wallace/H Halse; C Wallace/W Kirton; R York/W Kirton; R York/C Stephenson; F Broome/F Haycock; F Broome/D Astley; L Smith/J Sewell;

**Left-wing** - D Hodgetts/A Woolley; D Hodgetts/S Smith; F Wheldon/S Smith; W Garraty/F Wheldon; J Bache/R Templeton; W Garraty/S Smith; J Bache/A Hall; C Stephenson/J Bache; J Bache/H Edgley; C Stephenson/A Dorrell; W Walker/A Dorrell; L Capewell/A Dorrell; W Walker/E Houghton; R Dix/A Cunliffe; R Dorsett/L Smith; J Dixon/P McParland; R Wylie/P McParland; R Wylie/H Burrows; B Godfrey/W Anderson; I Hamilton/W Anderson; G Cowans/A Cropley; G Shaw/A Morley; P Birch or S Hodge/M Walters.

**Midfield** - A Massie / R Starling; R Wylie / A Deakin; P Woosnam / A Deakin; A Baker / A Deakin; B Rioch / B Tiler; F Carrodus / B Rioch; D Bremner / G Cowans / D Mortimer; S McMahon / G Cowans; S Hodge / P Birch; GS Parker / K Richardson / R Houghton / AD Townsend and / or M Draper; I Taylor / G Boateng / L Hendrie.

**Strike-force** - J Devey/D Hodgetts/J Campbell; J Devey/W Garraty/F Wheldon; J Bcahe/H Hampton/W Garraty; C Stephenson/H Hampton;

*Ernie Callaghan (left) and George Cummings (right) either side of goalkeeper Fred Biddlestone.*

THE COMPLETE ENCYCLOPAEDIA OF ASTON VILLA F.C.  THE COMPLETE ENCYCLOPAEDIA OF ASTON VILLA F.C.

210

W Walker/W Kirton/C Stephenson; W Dickson/W Walker; W Walker/L Capewell; G Brown/W Walker; T Waring/W Walker/G Brown; D Astley/T Waring; R Dorsett/G Edwards; A Brown/T Ford; C Gibson/T Ford; J Dixon/T Thompson/D Walsh; G Hitchens/R Thomson; A Lochhead/G Vowden; A Gray/B Little (J Deehan); P Withe/G Shaw; D Atkinson/D Saunders.

**Defensive formations** - Three Tommys, Jackson / Smart / Morton (1920s); Sims / Lynn / Aldis (1950s); J Rimmer / Swain / Gibson / Evans / McNaught (1980-82).

## PATON, DANIEL THOMAS
Born: Birmingham, 1870.
Career: Bordesley Green Baptists, Aston Royal, Aston Villa (September 1892), Birmingham Excelsior (December 1892).
Inside-right Dan Paton was an amateur who spent barely four months with Aston Villa, appearing in the home League game v Sunderland two weeks after joining the club. He was out of his depth as Villa lost 6-1.

## PATON, JAMES JABEZ
Born: Glasgow, July 1855. Died: Scotland.
Career: Vale of Leven (1884), Aston Villa (July 1889), Dundee Harp (September 1891-May 1893).
Centre-forward Jim Paton was 34 years of age when he joined Villa as a reserve to Archie Hunter and Albert Allen. He failed to impress and returned to Scotland after scoring once in three senior outings for the club.

## PEARSON, JOSEPH FRANK
Born: Brierley Hill, September 1877. Died: Birmingham, 1946.
Career: Saltley College FC (1895), Aston Villa (August 1900). Retired in

*Joe Pearson*

May 1908 to concentrate on his teaching, eventually becoming headmaster at both Pensnett Junior and Wollaston Church of England Schools. He also qualified as a 'professional' linesman and carried the flag during the England-Scotland international at Villa Park in 1922, when three home players, Frank Moss, Billy Walker and Dicky York all starred for England.

As a player, Joe Pearson was a grand, orthodox wing-half, sharp and incisive in everything he did. He was an FA Cup winner in 1905 and went on to score seven goals in 118 senior games for Villa before giving up the sport after failing to overcame a niggling knee injury that had troubled him for two years.

## PEJIC, MICHAEL
Born: Chesterton, Staffs, 25 January 1950.
Career: Chesterton & North Staffs Schols, Stoke City (apprentice, June 1966, professional January 1968), Everton (£135,000, February 1977), Aston Villa (£225,000, September 1979). Retired in the summer of 1980 after failing to recover from a serious groin injury suffered against Liverpool in December 1979. He then tried his luck with farming (unsuccessfully) before returning to football in 1981 as coach/manager of Leek Town. He then took on a similar position with Northwich Victoria before teaming up as assistant-manager/coach to John Rudge at Port Vale. He returned to Stoke City as the club's Youth team coach in 1996 under Lou Macari's management. Thereafter Pejic was manager in Zimbabwe, of Malazia Celangor and he was also the England Under-

18 coach for a short time before becoming involved in coaching in the NE, Yorkshire & Humberside areas.
He had worked for Corona Drinks before signing 'pro' forms at The Victoria Ground.
Son of a Yugoslav miner, full-back Mike Pejic was a thoughtful player who covered well, tackled decisively and cleared his lines with determination and commitment. During a fine career he won four full England caps and appeared in eight Under-23 internationals as well as helping Stoke win the League Cup in 1972. He made 89 appearances for Everton, over 300 for the Potters but only 12 for Villa.
His brother Mel Pejic also played for Stoke and made over 400 League appearances for Hereford and 100 plus for Wrexham (1979-95).

## PENALTY KICK
The penalty kick was introduced to League and Cup football in England in September 1891; the first to be awarded in a Villa game went to West Bromwich Albion in a friendly match in January 1892, but Tom Pearson fired over the top!
Villa received their first competitive spot-kick in the opening game of the 1893-94 League season, also against Albion, and this time former Baggies' star John Reynolds scored in a 3-2 home win.
Eric Houghton scored 79 penalties in his total of 345 goals for Villa (first team League & Cup, reserves, intermediates friendlies, tour games, Wartime). He missed from the 'spot' on his senior debut v Leeds United in 1930, but scored a penalty in his last outing for the club, in a Central League encounter against Huddersfield Town on Boxing Day 1946. Houghton missed only seven spot-kicks during his time as a Villa player.
On 21 November 1891, Villa were leading Stoke 2-1 in a League game at Perry Barr, when in the very last minute, the referee awarded the visitors a penalty. But before the spot-kick could be taken Villa's fuming goalkeeper Bill Dunning picked the ball up and hoofed it clean out of the ground. Before it was retrieved the final whistle sounded and Villa won the match! This resulted in the law being changed to allow time for such a kick to be taken at the end of a game or indeed at the end of the first-half.
Villa goalkeeper Arthur Cartlidge saved penalties in successive League games in September 1909 - in a 4-3 home win over Chelsea and a 3-2 defeat at Blackburn.
Charlie Wallace missed a penalty at Blackburn in the penultimate League game of the 1910-11 season. The result was a 0-0 draw, whereas a win for Villa would have given them the championship. The point dropped meant that they finished runners-up to Manchester United.
Two years later Wallace became the first player to miss a penalty in an FA Cup Final - firing two yards wide against Sunderland at The Crystal Palace in April 1913. In the fifteenth minute Charlie Gladwin fouled Clem Stephenson inside the area and Nottingham referee Arthur Adams had no hesitation in pointing to the spot.
A penalty (given for handball by Teddy Bowen) decided the 1929 FA Cup semi-final between Villa and Portsmouth at Highbury, Pompey winning 1-0.
Billy Walker, the England international, scored a hat-trick of penalties when Villa beat Bradford City 7-1 at Villa Park in a First Division game on 12 November 1921 and he struck home two spot-kicks in Villa's 3-0 home League win over Blues in March 1923.
Charlie Mitten scored a hat-trick of penalties in his tally of four goals for Manchester United in their 7-0 First Division League win over Villa in March 1950.
Harry Burrows could have equalled Billy Walker's feat of three penalties in a League game for Villa when he missed a third spot-kick in the home match with Manchester City in May 1963, having scored with two earlier efforts.
Villa knocked Colchester United out of the League Cup in 1979-80 thanks to a penalty shoot-out, 'keeper Mark Bosnich saving two penalties when Villa defeated Tranmere Rovers in a semi-final shoot-

THE COMPLETE ENCYCLOPAEDIA OF ASTON VILLA F.C.    THE COMPLETE ENCYCLOPAEDIA OF ASTON VILLA F.C.

211

*Tony Hateley scores from the 'spot' for Villa v. Sheffield United in April 1965.*

out to reach the League Cup Final in February 1994. The Aussie then saved two more spot-kicks four days later when Villa drew 1-1 in a Premiership game at Tottenham in March 1994. In all Bosnich made eight penalty saves during that 1993-94 season.

Villa qualified for the 2000 FA Cup Final (the last at Wembley) by beating Bolton Wanderers in a penalty shoot-out.

Villa goalkeeper Alan Wakeman saved three penalties out of four in Wartime football during April 1943. His saves came against Bristol City, Blackpool and Birmingham.

On 11 January 1958, Villa's Stan Lynn became the first full-back to score a hat-trick in a League Division One game, doing so against Sunderland at Villa Park, two of his goals coming from the penalty spot.

Lynn, on the other hand, was the first player to miss a penalty in a League Cup Final, doing so when Villa met Rotherham United in the first leg of the 1961 Final at Millmoor.

Hot-shot Lynn - nicknamed 'Stan the Wham' - scored a penalty in both local derby League games for Blues against his former club (Villa) in the 1963-64 season.

Ray Graydon missed two penalties when Villa met Leeds United in the club's Centenary Match at Villa Park in August 1974.

Seven months later, in the 1975 League Cup Final at Wembley, Graydon had his late penalty kick saved by the former Villa goalkeeper Kevin Keelan but he reacted quickest and netted the rebound to earn his side a 1-0 victory over Norwich City.

When Villa lost 5-2 to Blues in the Lord Mayor of Birmingham Charity Cup at St Andrew's in September 1908 they were awarded a second-half penalty. Harry Hampton took it but fired straight at Blues' 'keeper Jack Dorrington. The ball rebounded to Joe Bache, but as he was about to shoot at goal, he was fouled by Frank Womack. A second spot-kick was awarded and again Hampton fired directly at Dorrington, who this time held the ball to his chest.

In April 1988, Aston Villa played in the Mercantile Credit Centenary Festival at Wembley Stadium. They defeated Blackburn Rovers 2-1 on penalties (after a 0-0 draw) in phase one, but were then beaten themselves 1-0 on spot-kicks by Nottingham Forest (after a 0-0 draw) in phase two.

Ex-Aston Villa midfielder Andy Blair netted a hat-trick of penalties for Sheffield Wednesday against Luton Town in a League Cup-tie at Hillsborough in November 1984.

Gordon Cowans scored seven League penalties for Villa in season 1982-83, including two in the 4-1 home win over Luton Town.

Villa's Jimmy Crabtree missed a penalty for England v Ireland in 1899. David Platt scored from the spot for his country in World Cup semi-final 'shoot-out' against Germany in 1990.

Villa goalkeepers Billy George and Sam Hardy both saved penalties playing for England, against Ireland in 1902 and Scotland in 1909 respectively.

A total of 17 penalties were awarded in various Aston Villa matches during the 1993-94 campaign....only eleven were successfully converted.

## PENAROL

After winning the European Cup the previous season, Aston Villa were officially asked by UEFA Cup to play in the World Club Championship against the South American Copa Libertadores winners Penarol from Uruguay. The game took place on 12 December 1982 in Tokyo and in front of 61,445 spectators Penarol won 2-0.

## PENDLETON, JOHN JAMES

Born: Liverpool, August 1896. Died: Lancaster, 1955.

Career: South Liverpool (1915), Aston Villa (January 1920), Wigan Borough (August 1921), Walsall (July 1924-April 1925).

Right-half or centre-half Jack Pendleton was signed by Aston Villa as cover for Frank Barson (on Barson's say so) halfway through the first post-war season of 1919-20. He was a strong, well-built defender who was perhaps a shade out of his depth in the First Division. He made just six senior appearacnes for Villa.

## PENRICE, GARY KENNETH

Born: Bristol, 23 March 1964

Career: Mangotsfield (1982), Bristol Rovers (professional, November 1984), Watford (£500,000, November 1989), Aston Villa (£1 million, March 1991), Queen's Park Rangers (£625,000, October 1991), Watford (£300,000, November 1995), Bristol Rovers (free transfer as player/coach, September 1997). Retired as a player in 2000.

An exceptionally fine attacking player, able to perform as an out-and-out striker if required, Gary Penrice did far better in the lower Divisions than he did at a higher grade. Good on the ball, he was able to hold play up and bring his fellow attackers into the game with a

THE COMPLETE ENCYCLOPAEDIA OF ASTON VILLA F.C.    ASTON VILLA    THE COMPLETE ENCYCLOPAEDIA OF ASTON VILLA F.C.

212

positive pass or movement. He failed to hit it off at Villa Park, scoring just once in 20 outings for the club. But overall his career in League and Cup competitions was superb - 119 goals in 518 appearances with 74 of his goals coming in 311 outings for Bristol Rovers.

## PERRY, THOMAS

Born: West Bromwich, August 1871. Died: West Bromwich, July 1927.
Career: Christ Church School (West Bromwich), Christ Church FC, West Bromwich Baptists, Stourbridge (1889), West Bromwich Albion (July 1890), Aston Villa (October 1901). Retired in January 1903 through injury. Later worked with one of his three brothers in West Bromwich.

Although only 30 years of age, England international wing-half Tom Perry was well past his best when he joined Aston Villa from West Bromwich Albion in 1901. He remained at Villa Park for twelve months, appearing in 29 first-class games and scoring one goal - in a 3-2 home win over Derby County in February 1902.

Earlier he had been a stalwart performer for Albion, amassing a fine record of 277 League and FA Cup appearances during his eleven-year stay with the Baggies. He won one England cap (in 1898), played three times for the Football League XI (mid-1890s) and also starred in a representative game for a League Division One select XI v Villa in 1894. He lined up for Albion against Villa in the 1895 FA Cup Final and played regularly for the Throstles' during their first season at The Hawthorns (1900-01).

Tom Perry had two other footballing brothers - Walter (the eldest) and Charlie, and they too played for the Albion. Tom died two weeks after Charlie, whilst Walter died a year later in 1928.

## PETERBOROUGH UNITED

Villa's playing record against Posh:

FA Cup
| Venue | P | W | D | L | F | A |
|---|---|---|---|---|---|---|
| Home | 1 | 1 | 0 | 0 | 2 | 1 |
| Away | 1 | 0 | 1 | 0 | 1 | 1 |
| Totals | 2 | 1 | 1 | 0 | 3 | 2 |
| League Cup | | | | | | |
| Home | 2 | 2 | 0 | 0 | 12 | 1 |
| Away | 1 | 0 | 1 | 0 | 1 | 1 |
| Totals | 3 | 2 | 1 | 0 | 13 | 2 |

Fourth Division Posh, in their first season of League football, held Villa to a 1-1 draw in a 3rd round FA Cup-tie at London Road in January 1961 in front of 28,266 spectators. There were over 64,500 fans present to see the replay, which went Villa's way 2-1, Peter McParland netting both goals.

Derek Dougan scored a hat-trick (against his future club) when Villa beat Posh 6-1 in a 2nd round League Cup-tie in September 1962 (Villa led 4-0 at half-time). When Villa won 7-1 on aggregate in a two-legged 2nd round League Cup encounter in September 1995, Dwight Yorke put away two penalties in the 6-0 home victory, which was seen by almost 20,000 fans.

Players with both clubs include: K Bradley, M Carruthers, RA Chester, P Crichton (Villa loanee), VH Crowe, AD Dougan, D Farrell, RA Hogg, HCL Kingaby, I Linton, PJ McParland, RC Park, I Ross, ND Sims, G Whittingham, L Williams (Villa reserve), C Wilson (Villa reserve).
Also: J Barron & R Downes (Posh players, Villa coaches, Barron also Villa assistant-manager).

## PHILLIPS, CUTHBERT

Born: Victoria, Monmouthshire, 23 June 1910. Died: Lichfield, 21 October 1969.
Career: Ebbw Vale (August 1924), Wolverhampton Wanderers

(professional, August 1929), Aston Villa (£9,000, January 1936), Birmingham (March 1938), Chelmsford City (August 1939). Retired 1945.

Cuthbert Phillips, who was always known as 'Charlie', won Welsh Schoolboy honours, later working as a boilerman and playing Welsh League football for Ebbw Vale in the 1924-25 season. Several clubs wanted to sign him and he had offers from Plymouth Argyle, Torquay United and Cardiff City before signing professional forms for Wolves in 1929. He was a speedy forward, mostly at home on the right wing, and that is where he played the majority of his 202 senior games in his time at Molineux (65 goals scored). As a 'Wolf' he was capped ten times by Wales and gained a Second Division championship in 1931-32, netting 18 important goals that season. He also scored on his international debut against Northern Ireland at Wrexham in 1931. He went on to captain his country on six occasions. At Christmas 1935 he was sent off whilst skippering Wolves against Bolton and a month later, he was transferred to Aston Villa. He was capped three more times as a Villa player, but made only 25 appearances for the club, scoring the first of five goals on his debut in a 3-1 win at Derby. Unfortunately he could not save Villa from relegation and when they returned as Second Division champions in 1937-38 he managed only a handful of games. After a little over a season at St Andrew's Phillips went into non-League football and, during the War guesting for several clubs until retiring in 1945. Phillips was a fine all-round sportsman who also excelled at cricket, golf, tennis, rugby union and various athletics events. He was later a licensee in Bushbury and Lichfield.

## PHILLIPS, LEIGHTON

Born: Briton Ferry, near Swansea, 25 September 1949.
Career: Bryn Hyfred Junior & Cort Sart Secondary Schools (Briton Ferry), also Neath Area Schools (aged 8), Neath Under-12s (aged 9), Cardiff City (apprentice, June 1965, professional April 1967), Aston Villa (£100,000, September 1974), Swansea City (£70,000, November 1978), Charlton Athletic (£25,000, August 1981 - appointed player/coach, June 1982), Exeter City (free transfer, March-May 1983), Llanelli (player-manager, August 1984). Retired as player 1985.

Represented Wales at Schoolboy, Under-21, Under-23 and senior levels (58 full caps - record haul for a defender in over a century of Welsh football), Leighton Phillips was a fine player, not the flashy type, just a good, honest performer who gave nothing away. He scored on his senior debut as a midfielder for Cardiff, then after being successfully converted into a defender he went on to appear in 180 League games for the Ninian Park club before moving to Villa Park. Having been cup-tied with Cardiff, he missed Villa's 1975 League Cup victory over Norwich but did help steer the side to promotion from Division Two that same season and then he duly made up for that earlier disappointment by gaining a League Cup winners' medal himself in 1977 (v Everton). After 176 outings for Villa (4 goals scored) Phillips moved to Swansea and

THE COMPLETE ENCYCLOPAEDIA OF ASTON VILLA F.C.    THE COMPLETE ENCYCLOPAEDIA OF ASTON VILLA F.C.

213

quickly starred in two more promotion campaigns (in 1979 and 1981). A superb 'reader' of the game, he was nicknamed 'Brodwen' and made a total of 472 League appearances during a fine career.

## PHILLIPS, THOMAS JOHN SEYMOUR

Born: Shrewsbury, 7 July 1951

Career: Shropshire County Boys, Shrewsbury Town (apprentice, July 1966, professional November 1968), Aston Villa (£35,000, October 1969), Chelsea (£30,000, June 1970), Swansea City (on loan, March 1979), Crewe Alexandra (on loan, August-September 1979), Brighton & Hove Albion (£15,000, March 1980), Charlton Athletic (free transfer, July 1981), Crystal Palace (free transfer, January-May 1983).

On his day John Phillips was a fine, agile goalkeeper but also suffered from inconsistency. Nevertheless, he won four caps at both Under-23 and senior levels for Wales and had 17 outings between the posts for Villa. Earlier he had made over 50 appearances for the Shrews and despite understudying Peter Bonetti during his long association with Chelsea, he still had almost 150 games for the London club, helping them reach the 1971 European Cup Winners' Cup Final. He was signed by Chelsea after future Villa 'keeper Tommy Hughes had broken his leg and was then Alan Mullery's first capture when he took over as manager of Charlton.

## PHOENIX, ARTHUR FREDERICK

Born: Patricroft, Lancashire, 5 July 1897.

Career: Urmston Council School, Hadfield, Glossop North End (1922), Birmingham (May 1923), Aston Villa (May 1924), Barnsley (September 1925), Exeter City (July 1926), Wigan Borough (July 1929), Bath City (briefly in 1930), Torquay United (November 1930), Mansfield Town (July 1931), Racing Club de Paris (August 1932), Sandbach Ramblers (October 1933), Dublin Shelbourne (January 1934), Colwyn Bay United (August 1934), Brierley Hill Alliance (January 1935-April 1937). Retired.

Arthur Phoenix was almost 40 years of age when he kicked his last football in 1937. A very efficient, hard-working centre-forward, he was certainly a soccer nomad who served with no fewer than 15 clubs after leaving School. He never really settled down anywhere and scored three goals in his four games for Villa. His best days were spent at St James' Park Exeter, where he netted nine times in 52 League outings.

## PHYSIOTHERAPISTS

(See under trainers/coaches etc)

## PIMBLETT, FRANCIS ROY

Born: Liverpool, 12 March 1957

Career: Liverpool & Merseyside District Scools, Aston Villa (apprentice June 1973, professional October 1974), Newport County (on loan, March 1976), Stockport County (July 1976), Brisbane City (Australia, May 1979), Hartlepool United (March-April 1980).

An efficient midfield player, Frank Pimblett won eight Schoolboy caps for England and was also a Youth international trialist. He struggled for three years at Villa Park during which time he made only 11 first team appearances before having his contract cancelled by mutual consent. He only made 20 League appearances during his career in England.

## PINNER, MICHAEL JOHN

Born: Boston, Lincolnshire, 16 February 1934

Career: Boston Grammar School, Wyberton Rangers (Boston), Notts County (October 1945), Cambridge University, Pegasus, Aston Villa (May 1954), Sheffield Wednesday (December 1957), Queen's Park Rangers (July 1959), Manchester United (February 1961), Middlesex

Wanderers, Hendon, Chelsea Casuals, Chelsea (October 1961), Arsenal (briefly 1961), Swansea Town (May 1962), Leyton Orient, October 1962, professional October 1963), Belfast Distillery (July 1965-May 1967). Retired to continue his work as a solicitor.

Goalkeeper Mike Pinner decided to turn professional at the age of 29 in 1963, after having appeared in more than 250 competitive games as an amateur with a number of clubs as well as winning more than 50 caps for his country at the same level. He played in the Olympic Games soccer tournaments in Melbourne (1956) and Rome (1960), represented the RAF (he was an officer in the forces) and played in four Varsity matches against Oxford University.

A fine 'keeper, daring, agile and a fine shot-stopper, Pinner made 110 League appearances in all, 77 with Orient but only four with Villa.

## PLASTIC PITCHES

Aston Villa played their first League game on a plastic pitch on 3 September 1983 when they travelled to Loftus Road to meet Queen's Park Rangers (Division 1). Villa lost 2-1 despite a Peter Withe goal.

Villa recorded their first win on plastic when they visited the same London club on 17 December 1985. Paul Birch was on target this time in a 1-0 victory over QPR in front of 11,237 fans.

Villa's other two 'wins' were claimed against Oldham Athletic on 14 November 1987 (1-0) and versus Luton Town (1-0) on 14 October 1989.

Villa's two draws were against the Hatters at Kenilworth Road (1-1) on 17 December 1988 and QPR on 20 March 1990 (also 1-1)

The League Cup defeat was suffered at QPR on 30 October 1984 while the FA Cup reverse came at Boundary Park v Oldham Athletic on 14 March 1990.

This is Villa's League record on artificial surfaces (all games away):

| Comp. | P | W | D | L | F | A |
|---|---|---|---|---|---|---|
| F/League | 12 | 3 | 2 | 7 | 7 | 14 |
| FA Cup | 1 | 0 | 0 | 1 | 0 | 3 |
| L/Cup | 1 | 0 | 0 | 1 | 0 | 1 |
| Totals | 14 | 3 | 2 | 9 | 7 | 18 |

NB - Villa have also played on artificial surfaces in America.

## PLATT, DAVID ANDREW

Born: Oldham, 10 June 1966

Career: Chadderton, Manchester United (apprentice, June 1982, professional July 1984), Crewe Alexandra (free transfer, February 1985), Aston Villa (£200,000, February 1988), Bari (£5.5 million, July 1991), Juventus (£6.5 million, June 1992), Sampdoria (£5.25 million, August 1993), Arsenal (£4.75 million, July 1995), Sampdoria (free-transfer, player/coach/manager, August-November 1998), Nottingham (player-manager, August 1999). Appointed England Under-21 coach in July 2001.

David Platt became Britain's most 'expensive' footballer of all time in terms of total transfer fees (£22.2 million) when he joined Arsenal from Sampdoria in 1995. He had earlier moved from Villa Park to Bari to Juventus to Sampdoria for a combined total of £17.25 million).

An attacking midfielder with flair, drive and an excellent scoring record Platt was 'given away' by Manchester United in 1985 without ever appearing in a first-team game for the Reds. He was steadily nurtured at Gresty Road, and claimed 60 goals in 152 games for the 'Alex' before making a name for himself in a big way, first with Aston Villa, next in Italy and then with Arsenal.

Platt then returned to Sampdoria for a brief but unsuccessful spell as coach, rejoining the Football League in 1998 to take charge of relegated Nottingham Forest (in succession to Ron Atkinson).

He helped Villa win promotion to the First Division in his first season with the club and, aided and abetted by Messrs Spink, Price, McGrath, Mountfield, Nielsen, Gray, Olney, Cowans, Daley and Ormondroyd among others, he did his bit in ensuring Villa maintained their position

THE COMPLETE ENCYCLOPAEDIA OF ASTON VILLA F.C.     THE COMPLETE ENCYCLOPAEDIA OF ASTON VILLA F.C.

214

in the top flight. But the lure of the Italian lira meant that he was a 'dead cert' to play in Italy's Serie 'A' and he spent four excellent seasons over there during which time he played in more than 100 matches (at various levels) and scored 30 times.

With 27 goals in 62 international appearances for England, Platt is now in eighth position in the list of his country's top 10 marksmen of all-time. He scored his country's only goal in Euro' 92. He also represented England in three 'B' and three Under-21 matches and gained both a Premiership and FA Cup winners' medal with the Gunners in 1997-98. When the curtain came down on the 2000-01 season Platt's overall record as a professional footballer (for clubs and country) was superb - 585 appearances, 201 goals. His record with Villa was 68 goals in 145 outings,

Platt was appointed England U21 coach in July 2001; he is also these days a racehorse owner.

*David Platt scoring for Villa against Inter Milan in the UEFA Cup, October 1990. (Villa won 2-0).*

## PLAYERS

Thirty players were on the field throughout the ninety minutes of Villa's 15-a-side friendly contest against Aston Brook St Mary's Rugby Club on 13 March 1875. A total of 28 had bravely battled through a game between Aston Park Unity and Villa two months earlier.

Villa used only 12 players during their successful FA Cup run in 1957 and when the First Division championship was won in 1980-81, manager Ron Saunders utilised only 14 players. Seven were ever-present.

A total of 30 players were used in Villa's relegation season of 1935-36.

## PLYMOUTH ARGYLE

Villa's playing record against the Pilgrims:

Football League

| Venue | P | W | D | L | F | A |
|---|---|---|---|---|---|---|
| Home | 7 | 5 | 1 | 1 | 19 | 9 |
| Away | 7 | 2 | 2 | 3 | 12 | 12 |
| Totals | 14 | 7 | 3 | 4 | 31 | 21 |

FA Cup

| | | | | | | |
|---|---|---|---|---|---|---|
| Home | 1 | 0 | 1 | 0 | 0 | 0 |
| Away | 1 | 1 | 0 | 0 | 5 | 1 |
| Totals | 2 | 1 | 1 | 0 | 5 | 1 |

League Cup

| | | | | | | |
|---|---|---|---|---|---|---|
| Home | 1 | 0 | 1 | 0 | 3 | 3 |
| Away | 2 | 1 | 1* | 0 | 5 | 3 |
| Totals | 3 | 1 | 2 | 0 | 8 | 6 |

* Game abandoned after 90 minutes bur result was allowed to stand.

Wartime

| | | | | | | |
|---|---|---|---|---|---|---|
| Home | 1 | 1 | 0 | 0 | 4 | 2 |
| Away | 1 | 1 | 0 | 0 | 3 | 0 |
| Totals | 2 | 2 | 0 | 0 | 7 | 2 |

A record crowd of 43,686 saw Plymouth Argyle held to a 2-2 draw by Aston Villa in a Second Division game at Home Park in October 1936.

The return fixture at Villa Park in February 1937 ended in a 5-4 win for Villa, Eric Houghton scoring a hat-trick.

Villa's first home game in Division Three saw them held to a 1-1 draw by Argyle on 22 August 1970. Then exactly twelve months later Pat McMahon broke an ankle in a 3-1 home win over the same opponents as Villa opened their 1971-72 League campaign in style in front of more than 26,000 fans.

Paul Birch scored twice when Villa beat Argyle 5-2 at home in February 1988 - the last time the teams met in the League.

As holders of the trophy, Villa knocked Argyle out of the FA Cup in a 2nd round replay in February 1906, winning 5-1 at Home Park - after the underdogs from Devon had forced a goalless draw in the initial game. Bill Garraty scored twice in the victory.

After being held to a 3-3 draw at Villa Park in a 4th round League Cup-tie in December 1960, Villa travelled to Plymouth for the replay but the game, standing at 0-0, was abandoned at the end of 90 minutes. The 2nd replay followed almost seven weeks later (in February) and this time Villa triumphed 5-3, Gerry Hitchens scoring a hat-trick. In this second game at Home Park, Argyle were awarded a penalty. Carter ran up and touched the ball forward, thus allowing Newman to come from behind and score with ease from less than 12 yards!

Villa were the first team to play Argyle at their Home Park ground, doing so in a friendly in 1902.

Players with both clubs include: J Boden, H Burrows, A Comyn, JW Crabtree, G Crudgington (also Argyle Community Officer), MK Ferguson (Argyle Amateur), G Garratt, AL Goodall, JC Gregory (also Argyle caretaker-manager & coach), CB Hare, GE Johnson, AW Kerr (Argyle WW2 guest), J McLuckie, PJ McParland, N Mackay, M Noon, A O'Neill, DG Rioch, L Sealey, G Smith,

Also: P Barron & C Clarke (Argyle players, Villa coaches), M Musgrove (Argyle coach & physio, Villa coach).

## PODMORE, WILLIAM HORACE

Born: Derby, July 1872. Died: Nottingham, 1940.

Career: Derby Council Schools, Burton United, Aston Villa (August 1894), Derby Midland (April 1896), Great Lever (August 1896).

Billy Podmore was a long striding inside-right who spent just a season with Villa, appearing in an one FA Cup-tie against his home town club, Derby County, on 2 February 1895 (won 2-1).

THE COMPLETE ENCYCLOPAEDIA OF ASTON VILLA F.C.    THE COMPLETE ENCYCLOPAEDIA OF ASTON VILLA F.C.

215

## POLICE FORCE (POLICE RESERVE)
The following - all of whom played for Aston Villa - served in the Police Force (in various capacities): Danny Blair, Albert 'Sailor' Brown, Mike Buttress, Ernie Callaghan, Gersom Cox (special constable), Albert Kerr and Ivor Powell.

## POOLE, KEVIN
Born: Bromsgrove, 21 July 1963.
Career: Aston Villa (apprentice, June 1979, professional June 1981), Northampton Town (on loan, November 1984), Middlesbrough (August 1987), Hartlepool United (on loan, March 1991), Leicester City (£40,000, July 1991), Birmingham City (free transfer, August 1997). Owing to the presence - and form - of Jimmy Rimmer, Nigel Spink and to a certain extent Mervyn Day, goalkeeper Kevin Poole made only 32 first-class appearances for Aston Villa plus three on loan with the Cobblers before going on to star in a further 247 games at senior level with Middlesbrough (deputy to Stephen Pears), Hartlepool and Leicester. He then returned 'home' to the Midlands to sign for Blues (as cover for Ian Bennett). He gained a League Cup winners' medal in 1997 with the Foxes. Sound on crosses and a specialist penalty-saver, it is thought Poole has stopped a dozen spot kicks in open play.

## PORT VALE
Villa's playing record against the Valiants:
Football League

| Venue | P | W | D | L | F | A |
|---|---|---|---|---|---|---|
| Home | 2 | 2 | 0 | 0 | 3 | 0 |
| Away | 2 | 0 | 1 | 1 | 4 | 6 |
| Totals | 4 | 2 | 1 | 1 | 7 | 6 |

FA Cup

| Home | 3 | 3 | 0 | 0 | 16 | 2 |
|---|---|---|---|---|---|---|
| Away | 1 | 1 | 0 | 0 | 2 | 1 |
| Totals | 4 | 4 | 0 | 0 | 18 | 3 |

Wartime

| Home | 1 | 1 | 0 | 0 | 4 | 0 |
|---|---|---|---|---|---|---|
| Away | 1 | 0 | 0 | 1 | 1 | 2 |
| Totals | 2 | 1 | 0 | 1 | 5 | 2 |

Aston Villa first met Port Vale at League level in season 1970-71 (Division 3). Over 11,000 fans saw the Valiants win their home game 2-0 and there were almost 29,000 present when Bruce Rioch scored the only goal to bring Villa victory in the return fixture.
The following season, the League game in the Potteries ended all square at 4-4, Villa having led 4-2 before two late goals by future Villa star Sammy Morgan robbed them of victory. In the return game Andy Lochhead and Pat McMahon netted to give Villa 2-0 home win in front of 32,806 spectators.

Villa's three home FA Cup wins over Vale have been 7-2 (in the 1st round in 1925), 3-0 (in the 5th round in 1977) and 6-0 (in the 4th round in 1990).
A record crowd of 48,749 saw the Port Vale v Aston Villa 5th round FA Cup-tie in the Potteries in January 1960. Gerry Hitchens and Bobby Thomson netted for Villa.
Port Vale lost 2-1 to West Bromwich Albion in the 1954 FA Cup semi-final at Villa Park in front of more than 68,000 spectators.

Players with both clubs include: A Betts, MS Burke, L Campbell, RC Chapman, J Connor (Vale trialist), AR Dorrell, AS Dyke, KHA Fish (Villa reserve, also Vale coach & trainer & caretaker-manager), CJ Gibson, D Glover, J Hampson, JH Harvey (Villa trialist), K Jones, P Kerr, A Lee, K Leonard, AT Lyons, J Mandley, SJ Morgan, IV Powell (also Vale manager),

RT Pritchard, I Taylor, R Walker, AE Wood, J Woodward, RE York.
Also: G Hodgson & GF Lee (Villa players & Vale managers), R Graydon, SK Hunt & M Pejic (Villa players & Vale coaches with Hunt also Vale's Community Officer).

## PORTSMOUTH
Villa's playing record against Pompey:
Football League

| Venue | P | W | D | L | F | A |
|---|---|---|---|---|---|---|
| Home | 30 | 19 | 7 | 4 | 73 | 39 |
| Away | 30 | 8 | 7 | 15 | 42 | 65 |
| Totals | 60 | 27 | 14 | 19 | 115 | 104 |

FA Cup

| Home | 3 | 2 | 0 | 1 | 4 | 3 |
|---|---|---|---|---|---|---|
| Away | 4 | 1 | 3 | 0 | 9 | 6 |
| Neutral | 1 | 0 | 0 | 1 | 0 | 1 |
| Totals | 8 | 3 | 3 | 2 | 13 | 10 |

League Cup

| Home | 1 | 1 | 0 | 0 | 3 | 2 |
|---|---|---|---|---|---|---|
| Away | 1 | 0 | 1 | 0 | 2 | 2 |
| Totals | 2 | 1 | 1 | 0 | 5 | 4 |

Wartime

| Home | 1 | 1 | 0 | 0 | 3 | 2 |
|---|---|---|---|---|---|---|
| Away | 1 | 1 | 0 | 0 | 3 | 2 |
| Totals | 2 | 2 | 0 | 0 | 6 | 4 |

Joe Beresford scored a hat-trick (including a penalty) when Aston Villa beat Pompey 7-2 at home in September 1927. Five days earlier the first meeting between the clubs at Fratton Park had resulted in a 3-1 win for Pompey.

When Villa won 4-2 at Fratton Park in September 1932, both George Brown and Dai Astley netted twice and two years later a thrilling League encounter at Villa Park in November 1934 ended Villa 5 Pompey 4. Frank Chester and Eric Houghton both scored twice on this occasion.
The hymn 'O God Our Help In Ages Past' was sung manfully before kick-off at the Villa v Portsmouth League game in October 1938 - in appreciation of Neville Chamberlain's noble efforts to gain peace at Munich.
'Sailor' Brown scored in both games for Villa when they doubled up over Portsmouth in 1947-48, winning 2-1 (h) and 4-2 (a).
Pompey had to beat Villa on the last day of the 1949-50 season to win the First Division championship...they did just that in some style, to the tune of 5-1 at Fratton Park in front of 42,295 fans. The following season Villa played out two 3-3 draws against the reigning League champions. Johnny Dixon scoring in each match. In February 1953 Villa romped to a 6-0 home League win but three years later it was a different story as Pompey won 5-1 at Fratton Park in October 1956.

**Plymouth Argyle 3** (Carter, Newman, Williams)   **Aston Villa 5** (Burrows, O'Neill, Hitchens 3)
We visited Plymouth, for the second time, last Monday, for on the first occasion the match was abandoned at ninety minutes with the score 0-0 and the ground declared unfit for extra time to be played. The composition of our side showed several changes from the team that had played at Manchester last Saturday. Despite bad ground conditions it was a well played game between two hard fighting sides but, in a high-scoring game, it was won by the side possessing the greater stamina and power. Plymouth opened the scoring when in the 11th minute Carter beat Sims and, shortly afterwards, they increased their lead by a curiously taken penalty, Newman netting from a tap from the spot by Carter. Right on half-time, Burrows scored for Villa. Fifteen minutes after the re-start, O'Neill equalised. Then Hitchens got busy and with two quick goals put Villa on the winning way. Argyle, not disheartened, fought back and Williams, from thirty yards out, beat Sims to make the score 4-3. With but two minutes to go Hitchens, by scoring his third goal in the space of eleven minutes, made the game safe for his side.
Aston Villa : Sims ; Lynn, Winton ; Crowe, Dugdale, Thomson ; MacEwan, O'Neill, Hitchens, Deakin, Burrows.

*Match report from League Cup game v. Plymouth in 1961.*

THE COMPLETE ENCYCLOPAEDIA OF ASTON VILLA F.C.    THE COMPLETE ENCYCLOPAEDIA OF ASTON VILLA F.C.

216

Villa and Pompey were relegated together at the end of the 1958-59 season allowing Villa to claim their first Second Division double for almost 20 years as they beat Pompey 5-2 at home and 2-1 away in September 1959.
In January 1970, Pompey came to Villa Park and won 5-3 in a ding-dong Second Division encounter. It was 2-2 at half-time.

Harry Hampton's two goals helped Villa to a 4-1 win at Southern League Portsmouth in a 1st round FA Cup-tie in 1911, but it wasn't such a happy day in March 1929 as Villa succumbed to Pompey by a goal to nil in the FA Cup semi-final at Highbury.
The other three FA Cup-ties between the clubs all went to replays. Portsmouth won 1-0 at Villa Park in the 4th round in 1932, Villa triumphed 3-2 at home in a 3rd round contest in 1986 and succeeded again also at home by 1-0, in another 3rd round tussle in 1998, Savo Milosevic the marksman in the latter game.

Villa beat Pompey 5-4 on aggregate in a 2nd round League Cup-tie in October 1983. Defender Allan Evans scored in both legs.

*Villa and Portsmouth players obey a minute's silence prior to the League game at Villa Park in February 1952.*

Players with both clubs include: JP Allen, W Aspinall, M Blake, NLG Blake, T Bowman, JK Brown, AJ Cropley, S Dearn (Villa reserve), AD Dougan, AE Elston, J Findlay, SB Foster, CJ Gibson (Pompey Amateur), AG Gittins, G Graham, JC Gregory (Pompey reserve & coach, also manager of both clubs), G Harris, JS Hisbent, GH Hunter, AW Kerr (Pompey WW2 guest), PA Kerr (Pompey trialist), W McAuley, A McLoughlin, C Price, R Salmond (Villa reserve), S Smith, K Swain, GF Wheldon, G Whittingham, W Yates (Villa reserve).
Also: A Barton & R Saunders (Pompey players, Villa managers - Barton also coach/assistant & caretaker-manager at Fratton Park and assistant-manager at Villa Park), JF Easson (Pompey player, Villa trainer), R Money (Pompey player, Villa coach), J. Tinn (Pompey manager, Villa scout).

## POSTPONED MATCHES

During the arctic winter of 1946-47, Aston Villa played only seven League games between New Year's Day and 8 March. The season was extended, some matches being played in June. During the course of the 'winter' eight scheduled games were postponed due to snow and ice.
In the freezing winter of 1962-63, Aston Villa had almost 20 League and Cup games called off due to the adverse weather conditions between mid-December and early March. In fact, the team played just two First Division matches over that prolonged period of 13 weeks - drawing 0-0 at home with Blackburn Rovers and losing 4-0 at Liverpool. The season was extended until the end of May.

## POTTER, FREDERICK

Born: Cradley Heath, 29 November 1940
Career: Homer Street School (Cradley), Cradley Heath Juniors, Aston Villa (Amateur, June 1956, professional July 1959), Doncaster Rovers (July 1962), Burton Albion (1966-70), Hereford United (July 1970-May 1974). Retired after failing to recover from a cartilage operation.
As a youngster Fred Potter was an outfield player occupying four or five different positions before becoming a goalkeeper with Cradley Heath Juniors. He was in line as a possible replacement for Nigel Sims but made only seven senior appearances. He left Villa Park to join Northampton for whom he appeared in more than 125 competitive games, once at inside-forward. He helped Hereford gain entry into the Football League in 1972.

## POTTS, VICTOR ERNEST

Born: Aston, Birmingham, 20 August 1915. Died: Sutton Coldfield, 22 October 1996.
Career: Birchfield Road Schools, Metro Welfare FC, Tottenham Hotspur (amateur, August 1933, part-time professional August 1936 after three seasons playing for Spurs' nursery side, Northfleet), Doncaster Rovers (£3,000, August 1938), Aston Villa (WW2 guest, joining club permanently, August 1945). Retired in May 1949. Notts County (reserve team trainer, June 1949), Wolseley Athletic FC (part-time player, 1951-52), Walsall (trainer, May 1957-1963), Tottenham Hotspur (scout).
A member of the successful Birchfields Road Schools football team, right-back Vic Potts slipped the eye of Aston Villa by joining Spurs at the age of 18. He played in the London club's nursery side (Northfleet) and then became acquainted with some of the finest players in the game who later became managers, namely Bill Nicholson, Vic Buckingham and Freddie Cox. Cartilage trouble, however, affected his progress and he underwent surgery twice inside three years. Having lost so much playing time he was eventually given a free transfer from White Hart Lane and with both Barnsley and Doncaster Rovers seeking his

services, he chose the latter club, moving to Belle Vue in 1938. The outbreak of the Second World War brought Potts back to his native Birmingham to work on aircraft generators. One day he bumped into Norman Smith, who had been closely associated with the Birchfield Road School side and after a brief chat, Potts agreed to guest for Villa during the hostilities. He actually played over 200 games for the club between 1941 and 1946, and was signed on a permanent basis at the start of the 1945-46 transitional campaign by his Wartime playing colleague Alex Massie. Potts was an exceptionally fine player, very consistent and seemingly always at ease, never flustered. He went on to star in 72 League and FA Cup games for Villa after the War before

THE COMPLETE ENCYCLOPAEDIA OF ASTON VILLA F.C.    THE COMPLETE ENCYCLOPAEDIA OF ASTON VILLA F.C.

217

announcing his retirement with knee trouble in 1949. At that juncture he left Villa Park to join up with his old buddy Eric Houghton at Meadow Lane as the Magpies' second team trainer. He later came out of retirement to briefly assist Wolseley Athletic before taking over as trainer of Walsall under Bill Moore's managership (1957-63). Potts later scouted for several clubs (including Spurs) as well as working for British Leyland. He spent his latter years living in Sutton Coldfield.

## POUNTNEY, DAVID HAROLD

Born: Baschurch, Salop, 12 October 1939
Career: Baschurch County School, Shropshire & District Boys, Myddle Youth Club, Shrewsbury Town (professional, September 1957), Aston Villa (£20,000, October 1963), Shrewsbury Town (£10,000, February 1968), Chester City (June 1970), Oswestry Town (player-manager, July 1973). Retired in 1976 and thereafter ran a sports shop in Church Stretton, Shropshire.

Dave Pountney was a powerfully built wing-half or inside-forward, happy to play on either side of the pitch. He made over 500 League and Cup appearances during his career - 128 for Villa (seven goals scored). He performed in 'midfield' alongside the likes of Alan Deakin, Ron Wylie, Mike Tindall, Phil Woosnam and others and also defended resolutely alongside John Sleeuwenhoek.

## POWELL, IVOR VERDUN

Born: Gillach, near Bargoed, Glamorgan, 5 July 1916.
Career: Bargoed, Queen's Park Rangers (trialist), Barnet, Queen's Park Rangers (professional, September 1937), Bradford City and Blackpool as a WW2 guest, Aston Villa (£17,500, December 1948), Port Vale (player-manager, July-November 1951), Barry Town (December 1951), Bradford City (May 1952, player-manager, May-November 1954, then manager until February 1955), Leeds United (trainer/coach July 1956), Carlisle United (manager, May 1960-May 1963), Bath City (manager, June 1964-65), PAOK Salonika (coach), Head Football Coach at the University of Bath (late 1960s/70s).

Welsh international Ivor Powell was an attacking half-back, solid, industrious, totally committed with an exceptionally long-throw, who gained eight full caps between 1946-51 (four as a Villa player). He also starred in four Wartime/Victory internationals. In 1943 he was playing against England at Wembley when he suffered a broken collar-bone and was substituted by an Englishman, Stan Mortensen (Blackpool).

*Ivor Powell*

A chance conversation on a bowling green between a South Wales football enthusiast and a director of QPR led to Powell being invited along to Loftus Road for a trial. His performances were not fully appreciated at first and he went off to assist Barnet before Rangers took another look at him and this time offered him a contract! The Second World War, however, interrupted his progress and after serving in the War Police Reserve and in the RAF in India, he became a PT instructor, based in Blackpool. Whilst there Powell struck up a great friendship with Stanley Matthews who subsequently became his best man at his wedding. When he joined Aston Villa in 1948 - after having gained a Third Division South championship medal with QPR - the fee was a record for both clubs and also a record for a half-back at that time. During his association with Villa he underwent two cartilage operations from which he never really recovered. He formed a fine middle-line at Villa Park (along with Frank Moss and Con Martin) and scored five goals in

86 senior games before moving to Port Vale.
Unfortunately he was not well-liked by the players at Vale Park whom he tried 'to rule by fear' and as a result, with the club bottom of the Third Division (South) his contract was cancelled after he had been in charge for only four months. His contract was also cancelled by Carlisle, following relegation in 1963...twelve months after winning promotion from Division Four!
In between his service at Bradford City and his appointment at Elland Road, Powell was a publican in Manningham.

## PREMIER LEAGUE

Aston Villa played in the inaugural FA Premiership (Premier League) season of 1992-93 when they finished as distant runners-up to Manchester United (84 points to 74), despite leading the table through February and March, only to fall away in April.

This is Villa's full record in the Premier League: 1992 to 2001......

| Venue | P | W | D | L | F | A | Pts |
|---|---|---|---|---|---|---|---|
| Home | 177 | 84 | 51 | 42 | 254 | 170 | 303 |
| Away | 177 | 58 | 50 | 69 | 191 | 217 | 224 |
| Totals | 354 | 142 | 101 | 111 | 445 | 387 | 527 |

**Premiership Facts:**
Aston Villa were one of the 22 clubs which played in the first Premiership season of 1992-93.
That inaugural season saw Villa record their best performance so far: 21 wins and 11 draws from 42 matches played. They scored 57 goals and conceded 40 in finishing runners-up.
Their worst season so far came in 1994-95 when Villa won only 11 of their 42 matches, They finished 18th with 48 points (their lowest tally to date).
Aston Villa's first-ever Premiership game was against Ipswich Town at Portman Road on 15 August 1992. The result was a 1-1 draw and Dalian Atkinson (against his old club) scored Villa's first goal in this 'Division' before a crowd of 16,818.
Villa's first Premiership home match followed four days later versus Leeds United. Again the outcome was a 1-1 draw, in front of 29,151 spectators.
Villa's first Premiership victory was achieved at Bramall Lane, 2-0 over Sheffield United, on 29 August 1992.
Villa escaped relegation from the top flight by just three points in 1994-95. They collected four points from their last two matches to stay up!
Villa's 50th Premiership away draw was a 0-0 scoreline at Tottenham on 28 April 2001. This followed their 100th Premiership draw at home to Southampton (also 0-0) the previous week.
Only three teams - Aston Villa, Blackburn Rovers and Everton - played in the very first Football League season of 1888-89 and in the first Premiership campaign of 1992-93.

## PRESIDENTS

List of Aston Villa's Presidents down the years:

| 1877 | Rev. CS Beechcroft |
|---|---|
| 1877-1886 | WM Ellis |
| 1886-1887 | George Kynock, MP |
| 1887-1895 | George Hinks |
| 1895-1923 | Joseph Ansell, JP |
| 1924 | Howard Vaughan (briefly) |
| 1924-1963 | Sir Patrick Hannon |
| 1963-1969 | Sir Theodore Pritchett |
| 1969-1975 | Pat Matthews |

| 1975-1976 | Sir William Dugdale |
| 1976-1986 | Trevor Gill |
| 1986-1996 | Harold Musgrove |
| 1996 to date | John Alderson |

### Presidential Chit-Chat

Aston Villa's first President was the Reverend Charles S. Beechroft of Handsworth, Birmingham.

The club's President in the 1880s, Mr George Kynock was the MP for Aston and a local industrialist of some esteem.

Sir Patrick H Hannon held the position of President for 39 years

Alderman Sir T. Pritchett, a former Aston Villa President, was also the Lord Mayor of Birmingham, and in 1960, he was made a Honorary Freeman of the City.

### PRESTON NORTH END

Villa's playing record against the Lilywhites:

Football League

| Venue | P | W | D | L | F | A |
|---|---|---|---|---|---|---|
| Home | 49 | 37 | 3 | 9 | 108 | 44 |
| Away | 49 | 13 | 11 | 25 | 64 | 90 |
| Totals | 98 | 50 | 14 | 34 | 172 | 134 |

FA Cup

| | P | W | D | L | F | A |
|---|---|---|---|---|---|---|
| Home | 3 | 1 | 1 | 1 | 3 | 3 |
| Away | 3 | 1 | 1 | 1 | 2 | 3 |
| Neutral | 2 | 1 | 0 | 1 | 4 | 4 |
| Totals | 8 | 3 | 2 | 3 | 9 | 10 |

League Cup

| | P | W | D | L | F | A |
|---|---|---|---|---|---|---|
| Home | 2 | 2 | 0 | 0 | 9 | 3 |
| Away | 1 | 0 | 1 | 0 | 3 | 3 |
| Totals | 3 | 2 | 1 | 0 | 12 | 6 |

*Action from Villa's home League game v. Preston North End in 1956-57. Left to right: Peter Aldis (Villa), Tommy Thompson (ex-Villa), Nigel Sims and Pat Saward.*

In the first season of League football (1888-89) Preston North End were the only side to win on Aston Villa soil (2-0 on 9 February) whilst Villa were the only team to gain a point at Preston (1-1 on 10 November). The following season - on 21 September 1889 - Villa became the first team to beat double-winners Preston in the Football League, registering a 5-3 home victory in front of 11,500 spectators. Villa lost 3-2 at Preston on Christmas Day 1890 - after home centre-

forward Jimmy Ross had scored two second-half goals from seemingly offside positions, the winner from two yards out!

After losing 5-1 at Preston in January 1891, Villa achieved the double over the 'Invincibles' in 1893-94 - winning 2-0 at home and 5-2 at Deepdale where James Cowan and Jack Devey both scored twice

In December 1899 Steve Smith scored a hat-trick when Villa won 5-0 at Preston and Jack Devey followed up with three goals in Villa's 4-0 home win in September 1900.

Villa beat Preston 1-0 at home on 9 October 1920. Seven days later, fielding the same team, they crashed 6-1 at Deepdale!

In 1935-36 both teams cancelled each other out - Villa winning 5-1 at home but losing 3-0 at Deepdale.

Just before playing West Brom in the 1954 FA Cup Final, Preston were defeated 1-0 at Villa Park in front of 32,000 spectators.

Villa completed a double over North End in 1955-56; drew 3-3 at Deepdale in a thrilling League game in November 1956, but then lost 4-2 at Preston in April 1959 as they battled in vain to avoid relegation! Villa and Preston were relegated to the Third Division together at the end of the 1969-70 season. It was the first time the two founder members of the League had slumped to this level.

After a spell in the Third Division, Villa celebrated their return to the Second with a 1-0 win at Preston on 12 August 1972, Willie Anderson the scorer in front of 17,371 fans.

The biggest-ever crowd at Villa's Wellington Road ground in Perry Barr - 26,849 - assembled there to watch a 5th round FA Cup-tie on 7 January 1888. With Preston leading 3-1, the tie was abandoned late on through crowd trouble but the result was allowed to stand and Preston went on to reach the Final.

In March 1897, Villa defeated North End in a second replay in the 3rd of the FA Cup, winning 3-2 at Bramall Lane after draws of 1-1 (home) and 0-0 (away).

Over 55,000 fans saw Villa lose to North End, again at Bramall Lane, in the FA Cup semi-final of 1938 and there were almost 70,000 spectators present to see Villa reach the 1960 semi-final with a 2-0 home victory, Gerry Hitchens and Peter McParland the scorers.

Villa's last FA Cup success over the Lilywhites was 1-0 at Deepdale in the 3rd round in 1967.

Villa's first away game in the League Cup took them to Deepdale for a 3rd round clash in November 1960. They drew 3-3 in front of 7,677 fans and then won the replay by 3-1. Gerry Hitchens scored in both matches.

Two years later (in November 1962) Villa crushed North End 6-2 at home in a 4th round League Cup-tie when three players - Alan Baker, Harry Burrows and Alan O'Neill - all scored twice.

Players with both clubs include: J Beresford, P Birch, AF Brown, JK Brown, D Byfield, SE Chandler (Villa reserve), JA Fisher, K Gage, WW Gerrish, BC Godfrey, AL Goodall, BA Greenhalgh, JJ Hindle, AH Lockett, AW Morley, FJ O'Donnell, JT Palethorpe, G Smith, GT Stephenson, S Teale, T Thompson.

Also: T Docherty (PNE player & manager of both clubs), GF Lee (Villa player, PNE manager), A Cox (Villa coach/assistant & caretaker-manager, PNE coach), PD Doherty (PNE assistant-manager, Villa chief scout), S Harrison (coach at both Villa Park & Deepdale).

### PRICE, CHRISTOPHER JOHN

Born: Hereford, 30 March 1960.

Career: Hereford Schoolboy football, Hereford Schools Select, Hereford United (junior, June 1976, professional January 1978), Blackburn Rovers (£25,000, July 1986), Aston Villa £125,000, May 1988), Blackburn Rovers (£150,000, February 1992), Portsmouth (£50,000,

THE COMPLETE ENCYCLOPAEDIA OF ASTON VILLA F.C.     THE COMPLETE ENCYCLOPAEDIA OF ASTON VILLA F.C.

219

January 1993), Hereford United (1995), Cinderford Town (1998-2000).

Right-back Chris Price had already appeared in 373 games for Hereford and over 90 for Blackburn before joining Aston Villa in 1988.

A 1977 England Youth international trialist, he gained a Full Members Cup winners' medal with Blackburn in 1987 and two years later helped Villa reach second spot in the First Division. Price was a fine, determined defender, quick in responding to a fast, direct winger. An exceptionally good overlapper, possessing natural ability and a strong kick, he partnered Derek Mountfield, Kevin Gage and Stuart Gray (among others) at full-back and made 132 appearances for Villa (two goals scored) before returning to Ewood Park in 1992. Price later joined former Aston Villa manager Graham Turner at his old club, Hereford, and then teamed up with ex-Villa midfielder Brian Godfrey at non-League Cinderford Town in 1998.

Price held the appearance record for Hereford until it was bettered by Mel Pejic in 1991.

## PRICE, IOAN HAYDN
Born: Mardy, Glamorgan, 1883. Died: Portsmouth, 7 March 1964.
Career: Mardy Corinthians, Aberdare (1902-04), Aston Villa (December 1904), Burton United (September 1906), Wrexham (July 1908), Leeds City (May 1909), Shrewsbury Town (November 1909), Walsall (July 1910, then player/secretary-manager, July 1912-May 1915), Tottenham Hotspur (WWI guest), Mid-Rhondda United (manager, season 1919-20), Grimsby Town (manager, July-November 1920), Walsall (secretary, November 1920-May 1921), Mid-Rhondda United (secretary / manager, 1921-22).

A schoolmaster by profession, Hadyn Price was a semi-professional throughout his career whist he pursued his full-time employment as a teacher. An outside-left, he was capped by Wales against Scotland in March 1907 while playing in Villa's third team and, in fact, never made the first XI during his time at Villa Park. He was a Welsh Cup runner-up with Aberdare in 1904 but missed Wrexham's success in the same competition in 1909 through injury having played in all the previous rounds. When he took over as boss of Grimsby he recruited five Mid-Rhondda players, but failed in his efforts to bring success to the Blundell Park club. He was blamed for poor results; Price himself blamed the board for not allowing him to go on scouting missions and announcing his resignation in the Grimsby Evening Telegraph and promptly returned to Walsall.

## PRICE, LLEWELLYN PERCY
Born: Caersws on 12 August 1896. Died: 1969.
Career: Barmouth, Hampstead Town, Mansfield Town, Aston Villa (March 1921), Notts County (June 1922), Queen's Park Rangers (August 1928), Grantham Town (1929-30 season).

Winger, able to play on both flanks, Percy Price was signed to deputise for the injured Arthur Dorrell at the end of the 1920-21 season. After Dorrell had regained full fitness, Price became surplus to requirements and was allowed to leave the club in the summer of 1922.

## PRICE, ROBERT OSCAR
Born: Hereford, February 1860. Died: Worcester, c 1921.
Career: Hereford Thistle, Worcester Rovers, Aston Villa (April 1884). Retired in June 1887 after dislocating his hip.
A muscular, rugged defender Bob Price played in eight FA Cup games for Villa during his three years with the club.

## PRITCHARD, ROY THOMAS
Born: Dawley, Shropshire, 9 May 1925. Died: Willenhall, January 1993
Career: Dawley Council School, Dawley & District Schools, Wolverhampton Wanderers (junior, 1941, professional, August 1945), guested for Mansfield Town, Notts County, Swindon Town and Walsall in WW2, Aston Villa (February 1956), Notts County (November 1957), Port Vale (August 1958) Wellington Town (August 1960-June 1964).

Former 'Bevin Boy', Roy Pritchard was a tough tackling full-back who gained experience by guesting for established League clubs during the War. He made his League debut in the first post-war season with Wolves before establishing himself in the team the following season. In 1949 he gained an FA Cup winners' medal and five years later added a League championship medal to his collection. After more than 220 senior appearances for Wolves he moved to Villa Park but had the

misfortune to break his jaw in his first outing in the claret and blue against Arsenal. That proved to be his only appearance of the season and he appeared just once in 1956-57 and once again the following term before joining Notts County, later assisting Port Vale and Wellington Town. Pritchard continued to appear in charity games right up until 1990.

* In the 1990s Wolves introduced the Roy Pritchard Trophy for their 'Young Player of the Year'.

## PRITTY, GEORGE
Born: Birmingham, 4 March 1915.
Career: Metro Old Boys, Newport County (May 1933), Aston Villa (May 1935), Nottingham Forest (December 1938). Retired in May 1948.

Hardy, resolute wing-half, George Pritty made only four first team appearances during his three-and-a-half years at Villa Park, deputising for Bob Iverson in the main. He went on to appear in 54 games for Forest.

## PROFESSIONALISM
Professionalism in football was first seen as long ago as 1879 when Blackburn Rovers and Darwen recruited players from Scotland and paid them wages. Over the next year or so Bolton, Preston North End and several other Lancashire clubs covertly followed suit.

But it wasn't until 20 July 1885 that professionalism was officially accepted into English soccer...an important step in the history of the game.

Immediately it meant that the teams attracting fair attendances, Aston Villa amongst them, could sign star players and reward them overtly with payment for their efforts! However, there were restrictions initially...which stated that no professional player could play in an FA Cup game before he had resided in the local area for at least two years!

## PROGRAMMES (VILLA NEWS & RECORD)
In the early days of League football there were no programmes as such. Most clubs (including Aston Villa) produced a single card (which included the season's fixtures) and stated the date of the match, the names of the two clubs and the 22 players taking part, plus the referee for the day's action. One the oldest of these 'match cards' now currently in existence is for a game between Aston Villa and West Bromwich Albion at Perry Barr on 24 May 1890, staged for the Benefit of Albert Allen and Jack Burton. Villa won 1-0.

In the late-1890s, a Birmingham-based company called Sport & Play Ltd

THE COMPLETE ENCYCLOPAEDIA OF ASTON VILLA F.C.          THE COMPLETE ENCYCLOPAEDIA OF ASTON VILLA F.C.

220

(later Colmore Press) began publishing 8-page programmes for a number of Midland clubs, including Aston Villa. The programmes printed for Villa's matches were entitled: 'The Villa News, incorporating the official card'. They were certainly in existence, via this company, late in the 1896-97 season (after the club had moved to Villa Park) and there is one of those early programmes around today - issue no.46, dated

*An Aston Villa programme from 1922.*

Saturday 23 April 1898, when Villa's reserve side met Eastville Rovers (the seniors were away playing a friendly at Leicester Fosse).

Aston Villa Football Club itself began producing its own matchday programme 'The Villa News' in 1906 and the first issue was for the home League game with Blackburn Rovers on 1 September of that year. It comprised 16 pages in total (including the claret and blue cover). There was also a separate photograph of Howard Spencer, the team captain slipped inside. Mr EW Cox, a well-known and respected journalist, was engaged by the club to edit the programme. On the first text page it stated....'For the first time in its history, the Aston Villa Football Club to-day has its own official journal. The idea has been in contemplation for some time, and in thus carrying it out the Directors are falling into line with other important clubs'. It is believed that around 5,000 programmes were printed for that game against Blackburn which saw Villa win 4-2 in front of 40,000 spectators.

Ever since then - except for a brief period after the Second World War and perhaps during the 1960s - the Villa News has been regarded as one of the best programmes in the country.

The British Programme Collectors' Club began its annual awards in 1965-66 whereby its members voted for the best club programme in the country. Eleven years later the BPCC handed over its duties to the Commercial Managers' Association who set up a panel comprising printers, journalists, Football League Commercial Managers and serious collectors of programmes to make their selections for each season.

The Villa News was voted the best programme out of all the 92 Football League club publications on five occasions and finished runners-up three times between 1970 and 1978. It has continually received awards ever since, mainly under the production and guidance of Bernard Gallagher at Sports Projects, based in Broad Street, Birmingham. The Villa News was voted into second spot no fewer seven times during the 1980s (five years in succession) before returning to winning ways in 1990, chalking up 170 points (20 more than second-placed Everton).

### Programme Notes

A total of 50,166 programmes were sold for the Birmingham City v West Bromwich Albion FA Cup semi-final at Villa Park in 1968.

For seasons 1977-78, 1978-79 and 1979-80 - Aston Villa produced a large A4 format programme.

### PROMOTION

Following relegation from a higher Division, Aston Villa subsequently gained promotion as follows:

From Division 2 in 1937-38, 1959-60, 1974-75, 1987-88.

From Division 3 in 1971-72

Transferred from Division 1 into Premiers League in 1992.

Villa duly gained promotion in 1960 and again in 1988, immediately after suffering relegation the previous season.

As a player Chris Nicholl gained promotion with four different League clubs: Halifax Town, Luton Town, Aston Villa and Southampton.

### PROUDLER, ARTHUR

Born: Kingswinford near Dudley, 3 October 1929.

Career: Brierley Hill Schools, Halesowen Town (1945), Aston Villa (professional, December 1947), Crystal Palace (June 1956), Dorchester Town (player-manager, 1959), Stourbridge (August 1961), Bristol City (coach, 1964-65), Everton Youth team coach, 1966-70), Blackburn Rovers (coach, 1971-72). Later ran a mail order firm in Liverpool.

Half-back Arthur Proudler played just 20 minutes of first team football for Aston Villa before going off with a nasty gash above his eye on his debut against Leicester City in November 1953. An expert with penalty kicks, he did very well in reserve and intermediate competitions with Villa before going on to make 26 appearances for Palace. Later Proudler became a very fine and respected coach.

### PUBLIC LIMITED COMPANY

Aston Villa officially became a Public Limited Company in 1969.

### PURSLOW, THOMAS

Born: Perry Barr, Birmingham, June 1870. Died: Birmingham, November 1937.

Career: Nechells Old Boys, Aston Villa (August 1894), Walsall Town Swifts (September 1895), Darlaston (1897), Willenhall Pickwick (1899). Retired cs 1903.

Reserve to forward Denny Hodgetts during his time with Aston Villa, Tom Pursell scored in his only first team game against West Bromwich Albion in November 1894. He hit three hat-tricks for the reserves in season 1894-95.

### QUEEN'S PARK

Villa's playing record against the Scottish amateur club:

FA Cup

| Venue | P | W | D | L | F | A |
|-------|---|---|---|---|---|---|
| Away | 1 | 0 | 0 | 1 | 1 | 6 |

Sheriff of London Charity Shield

| | | | | | | |
|-------|---|---|---|---|---|---|
| Neutral | 1 | 0 | 1 | 0 | 0 | 0 |

THE COMPLETE ENCYCLOPAEDIA OF ASTON VILLA F.C.     THE COMPLETE ENCYCLOPAEDIA OF ASTON VILLA F.C.

221

Scottish amateur side Queen's Park knocked Villa out of the FA Cup on 19 January 1884, beating them 6-1 in a fourth round tie in Glasgow in front of 10,000 spectators.

A few years earlier Villa had played Queen's Park in a friendly at Titwood Park.

The Charity Shield game was played at The Crystal Palace on 11 March 1899 in front of 14,000 spectators. The game went into extra-time before it was agreed that each club should hold the shield for six months.

## QUEEN'S PARK RANGERS

Villa's playing record against Rangers:
Football League/Premiership

| Venue | P | W | D | L | F | A |
|---|---|---|---|---|---|---|
| Home | 19 | 8 | 4 | 7 | 32 | 26 |
| Away | 19 | 3 | 3 | 13 | 14 | 29 |
| Totals | 38 | 11 | 7 | 20 | 46 | 53 |

FA Cup

| Venue | P | W | D | L | F | A |
|---|---|---|---|---|---|---|
| Home | 2 | 2 | 0 | 0 | 4 | 2 |

League Cup

| Venue | P | W | D | L | F | A |
|---|---|---|---|---|---|---|
| Home | 3 | 2 | 1 | 0 | 4 | 2 |
| Away | 2 | 0 | 1 | 1 | 0 | 1 |
| Neutral | 1 | 1 | 0 | 0 | 3 | 0 |

Aston Villa first met Rangers in a Football League game at Loftus Road in September 1967. They lost 3-0 - and were beaten in the return fixture as well, 2-1!

Villa's first League win of the 11 so far recorded against Rangers arrived in August 1977 - a 2-1 success at home on the opening day of the season when the crowd was 34,750.

Villa first played a League game on a plastic surface on 3 September 1983 when they lost 2-1 at Loftus Road. Peter Withe had the 'pleasure' of scoring Villa's first synthectic-assisted goal!

In April 1985, Villa ran up their best-ever League win over the Londoners, 5-2 at home, Peter Withe and Paul Rideout both scoring twice.

When Rangers won 3-1 at Villa Park, former Birmingham City striker Trevor Francis (then player-manager at Loftus Road) scored a hat-trick before being substituted.

Andy Townsend made his debut for Villa in the 4-1 home League win over Rangers on the opening day of the 1993-94 season. For this game the players wore squad numbers and names on their shirts for the first time.

Villa's two home wins over Rangers in the FA Cup have both been by 2-1 .....in the 1st round in 1920 and the 3rd round in 1969. Billy Walker scored twice on his debut in the earlier clash.

Rangers spent £12,000 on hot-air balloons to dry their Loftus Road pitch prior to the League Cup semi-final first-leg encounter with Villa on 1 February 1977. The game ended in a draw (0-0) as did the return leg at Villa Park (2-2 after extra-time) before Villa triumphed 3-0 in the replay at neutral Highbury where Brian Little scored a splendid hat-trick to take his side back to Wembley. In the drawn game at Villa Park, Villa's 'keeper John Burridge saved a penalty before Peter Eastoe scored the Rangers second equaliser in the 115th minute. Over 117,500 spectators attended those three League Cup encounters in space of 21 days.

Players with both clubs include: CL Aston, E Beats (Villa reserve), J Birch, AF Brown, J Burridge, GB Clarke, WS Corbett, AG Davies, R Dorsett (QPR WW2 guest), JR Dugdale, HH Edgley, MK Ferguson, AG Gittins, AA Gray, JC Gregory, R Hitchcock (Villa reserve), SB Hodge, MJ Kenning (QPR guest), JM Leach, AP Mitchell (Villa reserve, also QPR

*Goal for Keith Leonard against QPR in August 1975.*

coach & manager), R Noble (Villa reserve), GK Penrice, MJ Pinner, IV Powell, LP Price, D Rogers (Villa reserve), S Stainrod, J Stephenson, GL Thompson, JE Travers, H Vallance (Villa reserve), PS Varco, G F Wheldon, TC Wilson, J Yates.

Also: T Docherty (manager of both clubs), Jas Cowan (Villa player, QPR manager), DJ Sexton (QPR manager, Villa coach), G Graham & R Graydon (Villa players, QPR coaches), P Barron (QPR player, Villa coach).

## RACHEL, ADAM

Born: Birmingham, 10 December 1976.
Career: Aston Villa (trainee, June 1993, professional May 1995), Blackpool (free transfer, September 1999).

An agile shot-stopper, goalkeeper Adam Rachel made just one substitute appearance for Aston Villa, in a Premiership game at Blackburn on Boxing Day, 1998 (taking the place of red card victim Michael Oakes). Although Mark Bosnich was out injured, he found himself third in line to Oakes and Peter Enckelman and subsequently joined Blackpool on a two-year contract.

## RAF BRIDGNORTH

Villa's playing record against the 'RAF' is:
Birmingham League

| Venue | P | W | D | L | F | A |
|---|---|---|---|---|---|---|
| Home | 2 | 2 | 0 | 0 | 11 | 2 |

Aston Villa's first team completed the double over RAF Bridgnorth in these two Birmingham League in 1940-41 - winning 3-1 at home and 8-1 away. Dicky Davis (a guest from Sunderland) scored a hat-trick in the first game while Frank Broome did likewise in the second.

## RAF COSFORD

Villa's playing record against RAF Cosford is:
Birmingham League

| Venue | P | W | D | L | F | A |
|---|---|---|---|---|---|---|
| Home | 3 | 1 | 1 | 1 | 3 | 1 |
| Away | 1 | 0 | 0 | 1 | 1 | 3 |
| Totals | 4 | 1 | 1 | 2 | 4 | 4 |

These four matches took place in seasons 1940-41 and 1941-42 when Villa chose to field their first XI. Villa's only win came in October 1941 to the tune of 3-0, guest player Dicky Davis (2) and Billy Goffin the scorers.

THE COMPLETE ENCYCLOPAEDIA OF ASTON VILLA F.C.

THE COMPLETE ENCYCLOPAEDIA OF ASTON VILLA F.C.

222

## RAF HEDNESFORD

Villa's playing record against the 'RAF'
Birmingham League

| Venue | P | W | D | L | F | A |
|---|---|---|---|---|---|---|
| Home | 4 | 3 | 0 | 1 | 17 | 6 |

Birmingham League Cup

| Home | 1 | 1 | 0 | 0 | 14 | 1 |
|---|---|---|---|---|---|---|

## RAF LICHFIELD

Villa's playing record against RAF Lichfield is:
Birmingham League

| Venue | P | W | D | L | F | A |
|---|---|---|---|---|---|---|
| Home | 2 | 2 | 0 | 0 | 28 | 2 |

## RALPHS, ALBERT

Born: Nantwich, Cheshire, 10 February 1892. Died: Chester, November 1964.
Career: Nantwich FC (1907), Burnell's Ironworks FC (1908), Whitchurch (1909), Aston Villa (November 1911), Chester (June 1912), Mold FC (season 1914-15). Did not figure after WWI.
Short, stocky right-winger who stood in for Charlie Wallace v Notts County (away) in March 1912 - his only game for Aston Villa.

## RAMSAY, GEORGE BURRELL

Born: Glasgow, 3 March 1855. Died: Llandrindod Wells, 7 October 1935.
Career: Cathcart Schoolboy football (Glasgow), Glasgow Rangers (trialist, 1875), Aston Villa (August 1876). Retired as a player (through injury) in June 1882 but reamained at club. Appointed Villa club secretary in 1884, serving in that capacity until 1926. Later appointed honorary advisor and vice-President at Villa Park.
George Ramsay must go down as one of the giants of English Football, a man with a brilliant brain who supervised Aston Villa's amazing advance from an obscure Birmingham club to their becoming the leading team of their day, within a period of about ten years. Alongside William McGregor and Fred Rinder, Ramsay emerged as the central figure of a trio of pioneers who were responsible for this meteoric rise.

George Ramsay

A brilliant footballer in his own right, Ramsay, nattily turned out in polo cap and long white pants, captained Villa for four seasons before injury forced his retirement. Undeterred, he now turned his wonderful brain to administration as Villa's secretary from 1884 to1926. His extraordinary football knowledge enabled him to supervise Villa's advancement on and off the field, his reputation attracting star players. As secretary he ran the team, (there would be no 'manager' until 1934) achieving unprecedented success with six League titles and six FA Cup triumphs, including one 'double!'
He was quick to appreciate the limitations of the cramped Perry Barr ground, brilliantly masterminding the club's move back to Aston where

Villa Park would materialise under Fred Rinder's expert supervision. Ramsay received two Football League Service award medals in 1909 and 1927.

## RAMSEY, JOHN

Born: Bordesley Green, Birmingham, 11 September 1870. Died: Birmingham, December 1942.
Career: Church FC (Birmingham), Aston Unity (August 1892), Ward End (June 1893-94).
A big, brave, brawny left-back, Jack Ramsey's temper let him down on many occasions and this resulted in him leaving the club! He made just four senior appearanes for Villa.

## RANDLE, WALTER WILLIAM

Born: Aston, Birmingham, August 1870. Died: January 1931.
Career: Aston Hall School, Aston Unity, Aston Villa (May 1893), Leek (September 1894), Aston Victoria (1896). Retired 1903 and returned to Aston to work in the licensing trade.
Bill Randle was a determined outside-right who had very little chance of regular first-team football owing to the prolonged form of Charlie Wallace. He made just one senior appearance (v Sunderland in November 1893) before leaving the club.

## READING

Villa's playing record against the Royals:
Football League

| Venue | P | W | D | L | F | A |
|---|---|---|---|---|---|---|
| Home | 2 | 2 | 0 | 0 | 4 | 2 |
| Away | 2 | 2 | 0 | 0 | 7 | 3 |
| Totals | 4 | 4 | 0 | 0 | 11 | 5 |

FA Cup

| Home | 2 | 1 | 1 | 0 | 6 | 2 |
|---|---|---|---|---|---|---|
| Away | 2 | 1 | 0 | 1 | 3 | 2 |
| Totals | 4 | 2 | 1 | 1 | 9 | 4 |

League Cup

| Home | 2 | 2 | 0 | 0 | 7 | 2 |
|---|---|---|---|---|---|---|
| Away | 1 | 0 | 1 | 0 | 1 | 1 |
| Totals | 3 | 2 | 1 | 0 | 8 | 3 |

The first time Villa netted five goals in a Third Division fixture was at Elm Park in October 1970 when they beat Reading 5-3 in front of 13,312 fans. On the last day of that season Villa won 2-1 at home to complete the double.
Southern League Reading knocked Villa out of the FA Cup in a 2nd round replay in 1912, winning 1-0 at home after a 1-1 draw in the Midlands.
'Pongo' Waring scored twice in Villa's 2-0 FA Cup 5th round victory at Reading in 1929 and the following year, in a 3rd round tie, a crowd of 39,000 saw the Royals hammered 5-0 at Villa Park when Eric Houghton scored twice and Billy Walker crashed in an unstoppable penalty!
Villa lost to non-League side Millwall in an FA Cup-tie at Reading's Elm Park ground in 1900.
Villa defeated Reading 5-2 on aggregate in a two-legged 2nd round League Cup-tie in September/October 1986. Midfielder Steve Hodge scored in both games for Villa.

Players with both clubs: J Boden, NJ Cooper, R Gordon, the trio of R Butcher, SE Chandler & CG Dean (Villa reserves), LA Dennington, RW Dix, JC Harrison (Reading WW2 guest), R Houghton, JC Johnstone, JT Palethorpe, AD Watkins.
Also: LC Chatterley (Villa player, Reading coach), P Barron (Reading player, Villa coach).

THE COMPLETE ENCYCLOPAEDIA OF ASTON VILLA F.C.    THE COMPLETE ENCYCLOPAEDIA OF ASTON VILLA F.C.

223

## REEVES, GEORGE

Born: Huthwaite, Hucknall, July 1884. Died: Yorkshire, September 1954.
Career: Sutton-in-Ashfield FC, Ripley Athletic, Sutton Town, Barnsley (December 1906), Aston Villa (November 1907), Bradford Park Avenue (November 1909), Blackpool (1912). Did not figure after WW1.

Described as a 'strong, nifty forward' George Reeves had good technique and a big heart. He netted 15 goals in only 30 League games for Barnsley, scored 11 times in his 36 senior outings for Aston Villa and added 17 goals to his tally in 59 League appearances for Park Avenue. He helped Villa to runners-up spot in the First Division in 1908 when deputising for Charlie Wallace on the wing. Unfortunately, Reeves suffered a serious knee injury in March 1909 and thereafter was always 'in reserve'

## REGIS, CYRILLE

Born: Maripiasoula, French Guyana, 9 February 1958.
Career: Hayes, West Bromwich Albion (£5,000, May 1977), Coventry City (£250,000, October 1984), Aston Villa (July 1991), Wolverhampton Wanderers (free transfer, August 1993), Wycombe Wanderers (free transfer, August 1994), Chester City (August 1995). Retired May 1996,

*Cyrille Regis (left) with Dave Regis.*

West Bromwich Albion (reserve team coach, summer 1997- February 2000). Played as a guest for Happy Valley FC (Hong Kong in 1978-79. Later became a football agent (2000-01 season).

One of the great goalscorers of the late 1970s & '80s, 'Smokin' Joe' Regis made a rapid rise from non-League football with Hayes to reach the FA Cup semi-final with WBA in just eight months. He cost Albion 'peanuts' in 1977, having been spotted by the club's former centre-forward Ronnie Allen. He scored on his Central League, Football League, FA Cup and League Cup debuts for Albion and went on to net 112 goals in more than 300 appearances for the Baggies, playing in three Cup semi-final matches and in the UEFA Cup quarter-final.

Capped four times at full international level by England with Albion - he later added a fifth cap to his tally with Coventry - Regis also appeared in three 'B' and six Under-21 matches. And as a 'Baggie' was voted PFA 'Young Footballer of the Year' in 1979 and took the runners-up behind Spurs skipper Steve Perryman in the 1982 'Footballer of the Year' poll.

Two years later he left The Hawthorns for Highfield Road (to the dismay of the fans) and three years later helped the Sky Blues win the FA Cup. After netting 62 goals in more than 280 outings for Coventry, Regis moved to Villa Park in the summer of 1991. He scored 12 times in his 63 outings in the claret and blue strip before switching to nearby Wolves on a free transfer in 1993 (mainly as a squad

player). He went from Molineux to Wycombe, also on a 'free' and ended his playing career in the summer of 1996 after a brief spell with Chester. Regis scored in excess of 200 goals in top-class football and he became the first professional player at senior level to represent these four West Midlands clubs - Albion, Coventry, Villa and Wolves. He returned to his first club, Albion as reserve team coach in the summer of 1997.

## RENNEVILLE, WILLIAM THOMAS JAMES

Born: Mullinar, near Dublin, 16 April 1884. Died: Birmingham, 19 April 1943.
Career: Irish Schoolboy football, London Colleges, Leyton (1908), Aston Villa (May 1910). Retired due to injury, May 1912.
A positive centre-forward, with dash and determination, Bill Renneville was only 5ft 6ins tall but could battle it out fairly and squarely with the toughest defenders around. Capped four times by Ireland (1910-12) he scored once in his two outings for Villa before badly injuring himself in a reserve team game.

## RESERVES

Aston Villa Football Club has fielded a reserve team (a second XI) ever since season 1884-85.

Originally, like their senior counterparts, they participated in quite a lot of friendly matches until membership was gained to the Birmingham & District League in 1889.

During the first two seasons of that competition - 1889-90 & 1890-91 - Villa's second string fulfilled well over 30 fixtures each time. But unfortunately match details were not fully registered by the organising committee and consequently both competitions were declared null and void, although some references indicate that Villa may well have won the title in one of those campaigns!

Villa continued to play in the B&D League until the outbreak of the First World War.

They won the title fourteen times in 18 seasons between 1894 and 1912, including an impressive sequence of ten consecutive triumphs during the early 1900s - from 1902-03 to 1911-12 inclusive.

In season 1894-95 Villa scored 133 goals in their 30 second team matches, then in 1898-99 ran up an impressive and record tally of 142 in 34 games. The team, in fact, netted over a century of goals in each season between 1903-04 and 1906-07 and totalled an amazing 449 in all.

The Central League came into being just before the Great War and Villa entered it for the 1919-20 season, placing their third/fourth teams in the B&D League.

Having finished runners-up in 1919-20 and 1928-29, Villa's second XI finally won the Central League title for the first time in season 1929-30 with a very impressive record of 27 wins and six draws from their 42 games. Their goal-ratio was impressive enough - 127 for and 72 against - as they totalled 60 points. As reigning champions, Villa again took the runners-up spot in 1930-31 and repeated that performance in 1932-33 and 1933-34, finishing behind neighbours West Bromwich Albion both times.

Villa went on to win the Central League championship (Division 1) twice more - in 1963-64 and 1992-93 - and they also finished runners-up on four other occasions, once to their rivals, the Albion and lastly to Manchester United in 1993-94.

In 1963-64, Villa's second string recorded 25 wins and nine draws, scored 76 goals 'for' and conceded 36 for a total of 59 points.

THE COMPLETE ENCYCLOPAEDIA OF ASTON VILLA F.C.    THE COMPLETE ENCYCLOPAEDIA OF ASTON VILLA F.C.

224

Their record in 1992-93 was: P34 W21 D8 L5 F64 A32 Pts 71.

They finished three points ahead of Nottingham Forest with their best win was 5-0 at home to Manchester City. The title was clinched with a penultimate game 1-0 victory over Newcastle United at the Bescot Stadium (Walsall), Ugo Ehiogu scoring the crucial goal.

First and Second Divisions were introduced to Pontins (Central) League football in the early 1990s, but Villa were relegated from the top flight at the end of the 1994-95 season after finishing third from bottom.

Thankfully, they quickly gained promotion to the newly-formed Premier Division as runners-up in Division One in season 1996-97, finishing just two points behind Preston North End reserves (54-52). For the 1999-2000 season the FA Premier Reserve League was introduced....Villa taking 10th spot (out of 13) in that inaugural campaign.

Cammie Fraser led Villa's second string to the title in 1963-64 while Ugo Ehiogu skippered the side to victory in 1992-93.

During the Second World War Villa's first team (combined at times with a handful of reserves) played two seasons - 1940-41 and 1941-42 - in the Birmingham & District League, using Solihull Town's ground at Shirley for their home matches.

**Reserve XI Facts:**

Aston Villa was the first club in the country to run three teams, doing so in season 1906-07.

When Villa first entered the Central League in 1919-20 they netted a total of 104 goals in their 42 matches to claim the runners-up spot.

Villa's first opponents in the Central League were Port Vale in August 1919, but despite fielding a strong side Villa lost 2-0.

After beating Leeds United 7-3 at home on the opening day of the 1926-27 season, Villa's second string went another 21 games before registering their second victory!

In season 1927-28, Villa scored 107 goals and conceded 91 in their 42 Central League games.

Tom 'Pongo' Waring made his debut in a Villa shirt in February 1928 against Birmingham in a Central League match at Villa Park and 23,667 fans turned out to give him a hearty welcome to 'Brummagem' by scoring a hat-trick in a 6-2 victory.

Two seasons later (in 1929-30) Villa captured their first Central League title. Among some high-scoring victories were those of 8-4 v Sheffield Wednesday, 8-2 v PNE, 7-1 v Stoke City, 7-3 v Liverpool, 8-1 v Manchester United and 5-3 v Sheffield United. Villa netted a total of 127 goals in their 42 matches but only managed to pip Derby County on goal-average to clinch the title.

Dai Astley scored 28 Central League goals for Villa in 1931-32 and England international George Brown netted 30 in 1933-34.

The Central League derby at The Hawthorns in March 1934, between West Bromwich Albion and Villa, who at the time were both chasing the championship, a crowd of 22,372 witnessed the 2-2 draw. Over 14,000 watched the corresponding game the following season.

Villa went into their final Central League game of the 1963-64 season requiring at least a point off Newcastle United at home to secure the championship...they won 7-0 to make sure!

Villa suffered their heaviest Central League defeat of all-time when they crashed 9-1 at Liverpool in season 1965-66.

Allan Evans scored six goals when Villa's reserve side beat Sheffield United 10-0 in February 1978.

Villa's second string took the wooden spoon in seasons 1970-71 and 1985-86.

Ian Olney top-scored in the Central League side in 1988-89 with 22 goals in only 20 games.

In November 1999 Villa's second XI played Dr Martens Eastern side Raunds Town in a friendly and manager John Gregory named a squad that was valued at around £30 million! It was Enckelman, Wright, Watson, Jaszczun, Stone, Draper, Collymore, Merson, Ghrayib, Lescott, Myhill, Cooke, Bewers, Melaugh and Jackman.

## REVO ELECTRIC

Villa's playing record against Revo is:

Birmingham League

| Venue | P | W | D | L | F | A |
|---|---|---|---|---|---|---|
| Home | 1 | 1 | 0 | 0 | 3 | 0 |
| Away | 3 | 2 | 0 | 1 | 13 | 10 |
| Totals | 4 | 3 | 0 | 1 | 16 | 10 |

Worcester Cup

| | | | | | | |
|---|---|---|---|---|---|---|
| Home | 1 | 0 | 0 | 1 | 1 | 2 |
| Away | 1 | 0 | 0 | 1 | 1 | 2 |
| Totals | 2 | 0 | 0 | 2 | 2 | 4 |

Keys Cup

| | | | | | | |
|---|---|---|---|---|---|---|
| Away | 1 | 1 | 0 | 0 | 2 | 1 |

These seven matches were played in seasons 1940-41 and 1941-42, Villa fielding their first team each time after the club had been forced to use Solihull Town's ground after Villa Park had been shut temporarily.

Villa's best win of the four achieved over Revo was 5-1 (away) in a 'League' match in September 1941 when Dicky Davis scored twice.

Revo's biggest victory was an 8-4 scoreline at home in the 'League' in September 1940, Davis scoring a hat-trick this time.

Revo beat Villa 2-1 and then 2-0 to win and retain the Worcester Cup in December 1940 and December 1941 respectively.

Villa went through to the Final of the 1942 Keys Cup at Revo's expense (2-1 in February).

## REYNOLDS, JOHN

Born: Blackburn, 21 February 1869. Died: Sheffield, 12 March 1917.

Career: Park Road School (Blackburn), Witton FC, Blackburn Rovers, Park Road FC, East Lancashire Regiment (1886), Distillery (August 1890), Ulster (December 1890), West Bromwich Albion (March 1891),

Droitwich Town (guest, 1891-92), Aston Villa (April 1893), Celtic (August 1897), Southampton (February 1898), Bristol St George's (July 1898), New Zealand (as coach, 1902-03), Stockport County (July 1903), Willesden Town (1904), Cardiff City (coach, season 1907-08). Moved to Sheffield on leaving Ninian Park and worked as a collier until his death in 1917. Right-half Jack 'Baldy' Reynolds had played five times for Ireland before his Lancashire birth was discovered. He went on to win a further eight English caps as well as three League Championship medals and two more FA Cup winners medals with Aston Villa in 1895 and 1897, having gained his first with WBA (versus Villa) in 1892, when he scored in a 3-0 victory.

He also represented the Football League XI on three occasions and featured in an England trial match in 1894.

A marvellously competitive player, Reynolds mastered every trick in the book and aided by some remarkable ball skills, his footwork was, at times, exceptionally brilliant. He left Villa Park with 17 goals and 117 appearances under his belt, plus a lot of happy memories. In 1898 he won a Scottish League championship medal with Celtic and that completed a hat-trick of Cup triumphs, having collected an Irish winners' prize with Ulster in 1891. He left Albion after falling out with the committee!

THE COMPLETE ENCYCLOPAEDIA OF ASTON VILLA F.C.    THE COMPLETE ENCYCLOPAEDIA OF ASTON VILLA F.C.

225

## RHYL

The seaside resort of Rhyl on the North Wales coast was where Aston Villa retreated to for their big-match training sessions during the period 1887 to 1912, and occasionally afterwards as well.

## RICHARDS, LEONARD JOSEPH

Born: Bilston, October 1892. Died: Wednesbury, c 1954.
Career: Hurst Hill Wesleyans, Stourbridge, Aston Villa (March 1911), Bilston (April 1915). Retired during the War.
Amateur goalkeeper who quit playing football to concentrate on his teaching profession. Len Richards made seven appearances for Aston Villa during his four seasons with the club, six at the end of the 1911-12 campaign as deputy for the injured Brendel Anstey. A good handler of the ball, he saved two penalties in those initial games against Preston and Oldham.

## RICHARDSON, KEVIN

Born: Newcastle-upon-Tyne, 4 December 1962
Career: Everton (apprentice, June 1978, professional December 1980), Watford (£225,000, September 1986), Arsenal (£200,000, August 1987), Real Sociedad (£750,000, July 1990), Aston Villa (£450,000, August 1991), Coventry City (£300,000, February 1995), Southampton (£150,000, September 1997), Barnsley (£300,000, July 1998), Blackpool (on loan, January-February 1999).
Kevin Richardson was a very consistent performer over the years, working tirelessly in midfield for every club he served. He began his career as an apprentice at Goodison Park and went on to play in over 140 games for the Merseysiders before transferring to Watford. The following August he moved to Highbury and had over 120 outings for the Gunners who then transferred him to Real Sociedad. He returned to the British scene with Aston Villa in 1991 and went on to make 180 appearances for the claret and blues (16 goals scored) in his three-and-a-half years with the club, skippering the side to victory over Manchester United in the 1994 League Cup Final at Wembley. His next port of call was Highfield Road and after that he assisted Blackpool and Barnsley before calling it a day in 2001.
Capped once by England, Richardson gained winners' medals in the FA Cup (1984), European Cup winners Cup (1985) and League championship (1985) with Everton and followed up by collecting a second League championship title prize with Arsenal in 1989. He also played in Everton's Charity Shield winning side of 1984.

*Kevin Richardson*

## RIDDELL, THOMAS CYRIL

Born: Handsworth, Birmingham, 20 March 1858. Died: Birmingham, c 1934.
Career: Excelsior FC, Aston Villa (August 1882). Retired with a knee injury, May 1887.
Tom Riddell was 6ft 4ins tall, well built and an extremely strong full-back, who weighed almost 15 stone at one stage during his career. He could kick a ball up to 100 yards from a standing positon but was described as a 'bit of a plodder'. He appeared in 10 early FA Cup games for Villa.

## RIDEOUT, PAUL DAVID

Born: Bournemouth, 14 August 1964.
Career: Priestlands School, Southampton & Hampshire Schools, Lawrence Boys Club, Lymington, Southampton (Schoolboy forms, season 1979-80), Swindon Town (apprentice, June 1980, professional August 1961), Aston Villa (£250,000, June 1983), Bari, Italy (£400,000, July 1985), Southampton (£430,000, July 1988), Swindon Town (on loan, March-April 1991), Notts County (£250,000, September 1991), Glasgow Rangers (£500,000, January 1992), Everton (£500,000, August 1992), Red Star, France (August 1998), Huang Dong, Shengzhen, China (1999), Tranmere Rovers (free transfer, August 2000).
Paul Rideout achieved footballing fame as a youngster playing for England Schoolboys when he netted a stunning goal in the televised game against Scotland at Wembley. He was on Southampton's books at the time, but was allowed to join Swindon as a 17 year-old. He returned to The Dell (signed by ex-Villa defender Chris Nicholl) in 1988, aged 24, having by then scored 75 goals in some 250 competitive matches, including 22 in 63 outings for Aston Villa. He had also added eight England Youth caps and five more at Under-21 level to those he had earned as a Schoolboy.
Rideout was a record 'sale' by Swindon to Aston Villa in 1983 and during his two seasons in the claret and blue strip he played very well alongside Peter Withe and Gary Shaw.
In a fine career Rideout has claimed more than 150 goals in almost 550 first-class appearances.
When he made his Football League debut in November against Hull City, Rideout became Swindon's youngest-ever player at the age of 16 years, 107 days.

## RILEY, THOMAS

Born: Blackburn, March 1882. Died: Southampton.
Career: Lancaster Council School, Chorley, Blackburn Rovers, Brentford (August 1905), Aston Villa (April 1906), Brentwood (June 1908), Southampton (season 1909-10). Retired through injury.
Tom Riley was a lightweight full-back who could use both feet to good effect but was said to be 'slow in recovery.' He made 16 senior appearances for Aston Villa during his two years with the club. Earlier he had played 29 games for Brentford in the Southern League and 25 for Blackburn in the Football League. He did not make a first team appearance for Saints.

## RIMMER, JOHN JAMES

Born: Southport, 10 February 1948.
Career: Southport & Merseyside Schoolboys, Manchester United (amateur May 1963, apprentice September 1963, professional May 1965), Swansea City (on loan, October 1973-February 1974), Arsenal (£40,000, February 1974), Aston Villa (£65,000, August 1977), Swansea City (August 1983), Hamrun Spartans, Malta (August 1986), Swansea City (coach, July 1987-May 1988). Quit football to run a golf centre in Swansea.
After making his League debut for Manchester United in April 1968, the following month goalkeeper Jimmy Rimmer was in the squad for the Reds against Benfica in the European Cup Final at Wembley. The

following season he appeared in both legs of the semi-final in the same competition against AC Milan. He went on to make 46 senior appearances during his time at Old Trafford (plus 17 on loan with the Swans) before transferring to Highbury for a bargain price of just £40,000. Agile and positive, he did not command his area with the sort of authority a manager would have liked - that finally arrived with

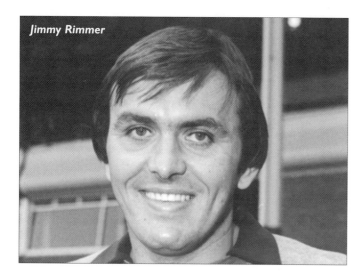

Jimmy Rimmer

experience some ten years after his United debut! And as a result - after gaining a full England cap against Italy in Milan in 1976 to go with the two he had already won at Under-23 level - he went on to give Villa excellent service during his six years at the club.

Rimmer amassed a fine record of 287 first team appearances, helping Villa win the League title in 1981, the European Cup (although he was only on the field for a few minutes before going off with a back injury) and the Super Cup in 1982. He was an ever-present on four occasions between the posts.

A real fitness fanatic, always on the bounce, he was voted Villa's Jubilee Club's 'Player of the Year' in 1977-78. In his professional career (1965-87) he accumulated in excess of 550 appearances at club and international level (470 in the Football League).

## RINDER, FREDERICK W.

Fred Rinder was born in Liverpool in 1857 and first became associated with Aston Villa football club in the late 1870s (as a supporter), in 1881 joining the committee. As a disciplinairian and tireless worker, he made steady progress and after serving as a senior Director (from 24 February 1893) he rose to the position of Chairman in 1898, holding office for 27 years. He was not an easy man to get on with, although it was said he mellowed with age!

Before the outbreak of the First World War he drew up plans to turn Villa Park into a 120,000 capacity stadium - but this never materialised as it was scuppered by the fighting in Europe!

In the summer of 1925, he resigned as Chairman after a confrontation with various people (including Directors) after he had agreed a large overspend on the building costs of the Trinity Road Stand.

Having been appointed Villa vice-President in 1930, he returned to the

fold (back on the Board) in 1936 and quickly put the club's finances into order. He remained in office this time for only two years, until ill-health caused him to hand over his duties again.

An FA Committee member for 13 years (from 1917 to 1930 .....he finally got elected after nine attempts), Rinder was also a much-respected international selector, who toured Scandinavia with the England team at the age of 80.

He sadly died - after a long innings - on Christmas Day morning 1938, seven months after being made a Life Member of the Football League. He was 81 and had attended a mid-week League game at Leicester where he was taken ill and rushed to hospital. A truly wonderful gentleman.

## RIOCH, BRUCE DAVID

Born: Aldershot, 6 September 1947

Career: Luton Town (apprentice, September 1962, professional September 1964), Aston Villa (£100,000, with brother Neil, July 1969), Derby County (£200,000, February 1974), Everton (£180,000, December 1976), Derby County (£150,000, November 1977), Birmingham City (on loan, December 1978), Sheffield United (on loan, March 1979), Torquay United (player/coach, October 1980), Seattle Sounders (on loan in the NASL, March-June 1981), Torquay United (player-manager, July 1982-January 1984), Seattle Sounders (coach, July 1985-January 1986), Middlesbrough (assistant-manager, January 1986, then manager from March 1986-March 1990), Millwall (manager, April 1990-March 1992), Bolton Wanderers (manager, May 1992-May 1995), Arsenal (manager, June 1995-August 1996), Norwich City (manager, June 1998-April 2000), Wigan Athletic (manager, July 2000 to February 2001).

Bruce Rioch had the distinction of being the first English-born player ever to captain Scotland. Born in Aldershot, the son of a Scottish sergeant major, he joined Luton on leaving school and after becoming a full-time professional his career took off! As a dynamic, all-action, hard-shooting midfielder, Rioch

went on to win 24 full caps for Scotland and he accumulated in excess of 600 League and Cup appearances at club level. He moved with his brother Neil to Villa Park in 1969 and over the next five years or so scored 37 goals in 176 appearances for Aston Villa, helping them win the Third Division championship in style in 1972. He piled up his appearances with Derby, Everton and Derby (again) and after loan spells at St Andrew's and Bramall Lane he became player/coach of Torquay and also played in the NASL. Rioch then took his first steps to becoming a successful manager at Plainmoor and he paid a return visit to Seattle to coach the Sounders. His next appointment saw him given the assistant-manager's post at Middlesbrough, taking over as boss at Ayresome Park in 1986 and holding office for four years. He left the hot-seat at Highbury after 61 weeks (with Arsene Wenger preparing to move in) and managed Norwich for just over two years before taking the reins at Wigan for the 2000-01 season.

As a player - and a good one at that - Rioch helped Derby win the First Division title in 1975, then as a manager he guided Middlesbrough to promotion from Division Three to Division One in successive seasons: 1987-88. He steered Bolton to promotion from Division Two in 1993 and into the Premiership two years later.

THE COMPLETE ENCYCLOPAEDIA OF ASTON VILLA F.C.    THE COMPLETE ENCYCLOPAEDIA OF ASTON VILLA F.C.

227

## RIOCH, DANIEL ('NEIL')GORDON
Born: Paddington, 13 April 1951.
Career: Paddington & Central London Schools, Luton Town (apprentice, June 1966, professional July 1968), Aston Villa (with brother Bruce, September 1969), Portland Timbers (1971), York City (on loan, February 1972), Northampton Town (on loan March 1972), Plymouth Argyle (May 1975), Atlanta Chiefs (1976-77), Toronto Blizzard (1978), Southend United (briefly in 1978-79), then Midlands non-League football: 1979-90. Aston Villa Old Stars manager (1990s). Neil Rioch was overshadowed throughout his career by big brother Bruce, but he defended well when given the opportunity at his respective clubs. He appeared in 25 senior games for Villa (three goals) but made more of an impact in the NASL than he did in the Football League. Rioch is also a fine club cricketer, capable of competing with the best!

## RITCHIE, STUART ARTHUR
Born: Southampton, 20 May 1968.
Career: Hampshire County Schools, Aston Villa (apprentice, June 1984, professional May 1986), Crewe Alexandra (June 1987-May 1988). Midfielder Stuart Ritchie had the briefest of professional careers with Aston Villa, making just one substitute appearance against Manchester United in May 1987, when he replaced Andy Gray in front of 35,000 fans. He played in 18 League games for the 'Alex.'

## ROBERTS, DAVID
Born: Erdington, Birmingham, 21 December 1946.
Career: Marsh Hill School, Birmingham Works Under-12s, Lucas Eagle FC, Aston Villa (junior, 1962, professional December 1963), Shrewsbury Town (£5,000, March 1968), Swansea Town (May 1974-June 1975). A honest worker as a wing-forward, Dave Roberts made just 19 first-team apperrarances for Aston Villa (two goals scored) before going on to net 21 times in 230 League outings for the Shrews.

## ROBERTS, KENNETH
Born: Crewe, 10 March 1931.
Career: Crewe Villa, Cardiff City (amateur), Aston Villa (June 1951, professional August 1951). Non-League football 1955-58 with Kynoch's Works FC. Good-class cricketer with Kynoch's CC, Dunlop CC and Lea Marston.
A former driver in the RASC and one-time railway porter at Crewe station, (so you know where his nickname came from!) Ken 'Shunter' Roberts was recommended to Villa Park while on military service. He was a tough, thoughtful utility forward possessing strength and mobility. He scored seven goals in 46 senior apperrarances for Aston Villa before injury cut-shot a promising career. He once scored a century in less than an hour for Kynoch's CC.

## ROBERTS, KENNETH OWEN
Born: Rhosmedre Cefn near Wrexham, 27 March 1936.
Career: Wrexham (amateur 1950, juniors May 1951), Aston Villa (professional May 1953). Retired in May 1958 due to a knee injury. Oswestry (trainer/coach 1958-61), Wrexham (coach 1961, later assistant-manager), Bradford Park Avenue (assistant-manager), scout for various clubs (1964-67), Chester (manager March 1968-September 1976). Moved into administration at Sealand Road, 1979-80, also acting as assistant-manager for a short time.
Outside-right Ken Roberts shares the record with Everton's Albert Geldard, of being the youngest-ever Football League debutant, aged 15 years, 158 days old when appearing for Wrexham against Bradford Park Avenue in September 1951. Capped by Wales at Youth team level, Roberts had pace, ample skill and penchant for hard-work when injury forced him into an early retirement. He scored three goals in 38 appearances for Villa.

He was only 32 years of age when appointed manager of Chester and in 1974-75 guided the Sealand Road club to promotion from Division Four. In that same season he came within a whisker of taking Chester to Wembley but his dream was shattered when they lost 5-4 on aggregate to his former club Aston Villa in semi-final of the League Cup. He did gain some consolation though with a Welsh Cup Final triumph.

## ROBERTS, ROBERT JOHN
Born: West Bromwich, April 1859. Died: Byker, Newcastle, 26 October 1929.
Career: Christ Church School, Salter's Works, West Bromwich Albion (amateur 1879, professional August 1885), Sunderland Albion (May 1890), West Browmcih Albion (May 1891), Aston Villa (May 1892). Retired June 1893.
Goalkeeper Bob Roberts was the first West Bromwich Albion player to be capped - for England against Scotland in 1887. A fine figure of a man, 6ft 4ins tall and weighing over 13 stones, he wore a size 13 boot and actually started out as a forward before establishing himself as the 'last line of defence.' He appeared in more than 400 games for Albion (at various levels, League, FA Cup, friendlies) and won a total of three full caps. He played for the Football Alliance (when at Sunderland Albion), starred in three international trials and in three successive FA Cup Finals - for the Throstles v Blackburn Rovers in 1886, v Aston Villa in 1887 and v Preston in 1888 - gaining a winners' medal in the latter. He also played in Albion's first-ever FA Cup-tie v Wednesbury Town in November 1883 and the club's first Football League game v. Stoke in September 1888. He was well past his best when he joined Villa (as cover for Bill Dunning) and made just four appearances before retiring.

## ROBERTS, WALTER DAVID
Born: Stourbridge, July 1859. Died: 1914.
Career: Norton FC (Stourbridge), Aston Villa (May 1882), Church FC (September 1884), Stourbridge (September 1886).
An ambling-type of forward with strong right-foot shot, Wally Roberts scored once in five FA Cup games for Villa.

## ROBERTSON, RICHARD REX
Born: Hockley, Birmingham, December 1860. Died: Birmingham, 1921.
Career: Excelsior, Aston Villa (August 1884), Stourbridge (September 1887), Halesowen, Coombs Wood, Netherton St Luke's. Retired 1895 after injury.
Centre-half Dick Robertson was a tough competitor who made three FA Cup appearances for Aston Villa, the first against Wednesday Town in 1884.

## ROBEY, JAMES HENRY
Born: Ratcliffe, January 1911.
Career: Stalybridge Celtic, Aston Villa (May 1935), Aberdeen (February 1938). Retired during the War.
Another tough defender able to take the strongest of challenges, Jim Robey played in just three League games for Aston Villa and four for the Dons.

## ROBINSON, PHILIP JOHN
Born: Stafford, 6 January 1967
Career: Stafford & District Schools, Aston Villa (groundstaff aged 14, apprentice, June 1983, professional January 1985), Wolverhampton Wanderers (£5,000, June 1987), Notts County (£67,500, August 1989), Birmingham City (on loan, March 1991), Huddersfield Town (£50,000, September 1992), Northampton Town (on loan September 1994), Chesterfield (£15,000, December 1994), Notts County (£80,000,

THE COMPLETE ENCYCLOPAEDIA OF ASTON VILLA F.C.  THE COMPLETE ENCYCLOPAEDIA OF ASTON VILLA F.C.

228

August 1996), Stoke City (free transfer, June 1998), Hednesford Town (August 2000).

Equally adept in defence or midfield, the red-headed Phil Robinson always gave a good account of himself. After scoring once in three senior games for Aston Villa, he joined Wolves and went on to play in 90 first team games for the Molineux club (nine goals) helping the Wanderers win both the Fourth and Third Division championships as well as the Sherpa Van Trophy. He was a key member of Notts County's Third Division promotion winning side in 1990 and whilst at Meadow Lane was loaned out to Blues, whom he helped carry off the Leyland DAF Cup at Wembley in 1991.

After giving Chesterfield, Notts County (again) and Stoke City more excellent service, Robinson ventured into physiotherapy while playing for Conference side Hednesford. He appeared in 534 games at competitive level and scored 51 goals.

### ROBSON, JOHN DIXON

Born: Consett, 15 July 1950.
Career: Durham Schools, Birtley Youth Club, Derby County (junior, July 1966, professional, October 1967), Aston Villa (£90,000, October 1972). Contract cancelled in November 1978 after he was forced to quit football with Multiple Sclerosis. Awarded a testimonial match in October 1978.

Full-back John Robson collected both First and Second Division championship medals and made 211 first-class appearances (five goals scored) for Derby before moving to Villa Park. Capped seven times by England at Under-23 level, he starred in Villa's promotion-winning side of 1975 and gained two League Cup winners' medals as well - in 1975 v Norwich City and 1977 v Everton. He played in 176 first class matches for Villa (one goal). The sure-footed Robson was a valuable member of the defence and occasionally filled in as an extra centre-half. He teamed up superbly well with Charlie Aitken and John Gidman. Now lives in Sutton Coldfield.

### ROCHDALE

Villa's playing record against the 'Dale:
Football League

| Venue | P | W | D | L | F | A |
|-------|---|---|---|---|---|---|
| Home | 2 | 2 | 0 | 0 | 3 | 0 |
| Away | 2 | 0 | 1 | 1 | 1 | 2 |
| Totals | 4 | 2 | 1 | 1 | 4 | 2 |

Villa played the 'Dale four times in two seasons of Third Division football in the early 1970s. In 1970-71 Villa won 1-0 at home (Geoff Vowden the scorer) and drew 1-1 at Spotland and twelve months later they triumphed 2-0 at Villa Park (Andy Lochhead and Ray Graydon on target) but lost 1-0 at Rochdale.

Players with both clubs include: W Armstrong (Villa reserve), JD Cordell, A Cunliffe (also 'Dale trainer), RD Davis (WW2 guest for both clubs), J Graham, B Handley, SF Horne, AT Mort, D Norton, CL Roberts (Villa reserve), G Shelton, J Walters, DJ Winton.
Also: MK Ferguson, A Little & TC Wilson (all Villa players & 'Dale managers, Wilson also 'Dale chairman), J Hogan ('Dale' player, Villa manager & coach), R Downes ('Dale player, Villa coach).

### ROOSE, LEIGH RICHMOND

Born: Holt, near Wrexham, 27 November 1877. Died: France, 7 October 1916 (killed in action).
Career: UCW Aberystwyth, Aberystwyth Town (1898), Druids (August 1900), London Welsh (soccer), Stoke (amateur, October 1901), Everton (November 1904), Sunderland (January 1908), Huddersfield Town (April 1911), Aston Villa (August 1911), Woolwich Arsenal (December 1911), Llandudno Town (1912-13). Joined the 9th Battalion Royal Fusiliers immediately the War broke out in 1914 but Lance Corporal Roose was sadly killed in action two years later, aged 38.

The son of a Presbyterian minister, 'Dicky' Roose obtained his early education at the Holt Academy where he was taught for a short time by HG Wells.

He took a science degree at University College of Wales in Aberystwyth and learnt his goalkeeping skills with the town's football team, gaining a Welsh Cup winners' medal almost immediately (1900). He was a sporting hero when playing for Druids before moving to King's College Hospital in London to train as a doctor, but despite his keen interest in bacteriology, he never qualified and remained a perpetual student. On joining Stoke he thought nothing of travelling by train to the Victoria Ground, charging the cost to the club! He once took a horse and carriage to get to a game and on another occasion used someone's bicycle.

H Catton ('Tityrus' of the Athletic News) described Roose as "...dextrous though daring, valiant though volatile." Another writer was more expansive, stating: "Few men exhibit their personality so vividly in their play as LR Roose. You cannot spend five minutes in his company without being impressed by his vivacity, his boldness, his knowledge of men and things - a clever man undoubtedly, but one entirely unrestrained in word or action. On the field his whole attention is centred on the game, he rarely stands listlessly by the goalpost even when the ball is at the other end of the enclosure, but is ever following the game keenly and closely"

He was certainly a character, also a very wealthy man as well as being a marvellously-gifted 'keeper, who thought nothing of charging some 15-20 yards away from his goal to clear the ball if he thought his defenders were under pressure. He was unorthodox in style when dealing with shots hit straight at him, often double-punching the ball away or even heading it! After Stoke he went to Everton where he replaced the Irish international Billy Scott and played his part as the Merseysiders reached the semi-final of the FA Cup and runners-up spot in the First Division in 1905. He certainly saved Sunderland from relegation during his time on Wearside and the club wanted to award him a Testimonial match for his efforts, but the FA stepped in and scotched the idea because of Roose's amateur status. He had to settle instead for an illuminated address, presented to him by the Mayor.

An inveterate practical joker, Roose once turned up for a match in Belfast with his hand heavily bandaged, moaning and groaning. With everyone in suspense, wondering whether he was fit or not, minutes before kick-off, to the disbelief of the press, he shouted out "I'm okay", quickly stripped off the dressing and went out and played a blinder!

An erratic genuis, he never took the field wearing a clean pair of shorts, his boots used to last him for years and generally he had a scruffy appearance about him - but what a star!

He won 24 caps 'senior' for Wales plus a handful at amateur level (it could and should have been far more in both instances). And quite often he would ask if he could stand down to allow eight times reserve Alf Edwards an opportunity to show his worth. But the FAW would have none of it! Roose was recruited by Villa to fill in for Brendel Anstey. He played in only 10 League games before joining Arsenal. He made over 300 appearances in club and international football during a splendid career and one suspects that he would have carried on longer had he lived!

Roose was the brother-in-law of JC Jenkins, the famous Welsh Rugby Union international of 1911.

THE COMPLETE ENCYCLOPAEDIA OF ASTON VILLA F.C.    THE COMPLETE ENCYCLOPAEDIA OF ASTON VILLA F.C.

229

## ROSS, IAN

Born: Glasgow, 26 January 1947

Career: Glasgow & District Schools, Liverpool (apprentice, June 1963, professional August 1965), Aston Villa (£70,000, February 1972), Notts County (on loan, October 1976), Northampton Town (on loan, November 1976), Peterborough United (December 1976), Santa Barbara FC (USA), Wolverhampton Wanderers (player/coach, August 1979), Hereford United (non-contract player/coach, October 1982), Wolverhampton Wanderers (coach), coached in Oman (1983), Birmingham City (reserve team coach), FC Valur (manager/coach, August 1984-June 1988), coached in South Africa & Australia (1988 to late 1991), Huddersfield Town (manager March 1992-93). Later entered the licensing trade, taking over the Gardners' Arms in Timperley near Altrincham. He now resides in Wolverhampton.

*Ian Ross holds aloft the League Cup in 1975.*

Defender Ian Ross was a fine professional, a trier to the last, a player who simply loved football, battling every inch of the way in every game whatever the circumstances. He was mainly a reserve at Anfield, being considered an exceptionally useful squad player by manager Bill Shankly. After leaving Liverpool for Villa Park he became a firm favourite with the fans and went on to appear in 204 senior games for the club (three goals scored).

Nicknamed 'Roscoe' he helped Villa tie up the Third Division championship in 1972 and then led the side to victory in the 1975 League Cup Final at Wembley, as well as to promotion from Division Two that same season. He played in over 100 games for Peterborough and by the time he went into management in Iceland he was already an experienced coach. He guided FC Valur to their domestic League championship in 1985 and after four successful years coaching in South Africa and Australia he took his first and only managerial post in England with Huddersfield, steering the Terriers into the promotion play-offs in 1992 and then pulling them clear of relegation the following season only to be replaced by Neil Warnock.

As a player Ross appeared in more than 400 club matches (356 in the Football League) and late in 1976 he had the 'distinction' of playing for four different clubs in four months!

## ROTHERHAM UNITED (ALSO COUNTY, TOWN)

Villa's playing record against the Millermen:

Football League

| Venue | P | W | D | L | F | A |
|---|---|---|---|---|---|---|
| Home | 4 | 3 | 0 | 1 | 8 | 3 |
| Away | 4 | 2 | 1 | 1 | 6 | 3 |
| Totals | 8 | 5 | 1 | 2 | 14 | 6 |

FA Cup

| | | | | | | |
|---|---|---|---|---|---|---|
| Home | 2 | 1 | 0 | 1 | 2 | 2 |
| Away | 1 | 1 | 0 | 0 | 3 | 1 |
| Totals | 3 | 2 | 0 | 1 | 5 | 3 |

League Cup

| | | | | | | |
|---|---|---|---|---|---|---|
| Home | 1 | 1 | 0 | 0 | 3 | 0 |
| Away | 1 | 0 | 0 | 1 | 0 | 2 |
| Totals | 2 | 1 | 0 | 1 | 3 | 2 |

The normally subdued Jimmy MacEwan was sent-off during Villa's 2-1 defeat at Rotherham in a Second Division game in December 1959. He was suspended for seven days. This was the first meeting between the two clubs.

The return fixture on 23 April 1960 drew a crowd of almost 32,000 to Villa Park as Bobby Thomson (2) and Ron Wylie netted to give Villa a 3-0 victory as they celebrated the Second Division championship in style after their nearest challengers, Cardiff, could only draw 1-1 at Sunderland.

Villa won 3-1 at home to Rotherham on 26 August 1967 to end a run of 11 League games without a victory.

Dave Walsh scored twice when Villa beat United 3-1 in a 5th round FA Cup-tie at Millmoor in 1953 and there was a mini upset as Villa crashed out of the competition to United in 1968, beaten 1-0 at home in the 4th round.

Villa's full-back Stan Lynn was the first player to miss a penalty in a League Cup Final when he fluffed his spot-kick in the first leg of the 1961 Final against Rotherham at Millmoor. Villa lost the game 2-0, but won the return fixture 3-0 (after extra-time) to clinch the trophy in the first season of the newly-formed competition.

The final was actually held over until the start of the next season and was played in August/September 1961. A crowd of 12,226 saw the game at Rotherham and 30,765 were present at Villa Park to see Harry Burrows (67 minutes), Alan O'Neill (70) and Peter McParland (with the vital third goal in extra-time) find the net as Villa stormed back from two down to take the trophy.

*Johnny MacLeod had this F.A. Cup "goal" disallowed v. Rotherham United at Villa Park in February 1968.*

Players with both clubs include: N Ashe, T Berry (Villa reserve), GW Cook, P Crichton (Villa loanee), J Depledge (Villa reserve), TC Donovan, E Eyre, G Farrelly, J Harrop, TP Heard, H Humphries, B Jones, AE Layton, AD Lee (Villa reserve), M Moralee (United WW2 guest), W Myerscough, GS Parker, CL Roberts (Villa reserve), B Tiler, W Watson. Also: T Docherty (manager of both clubs), I Hamilton (Villa player, United Community Officer), HC Slade (Villa player, Rotherham coach).

THE COMPLETE ENCYCLOPAEDIA OF ASTON VILLA F.C.

## ROWAN, BRIAN
Born: Glasgow, 28 June 1948
Career: Glasgow Schools, Ballieston Juniors, Aston Villa (Amateur April 1969, professional May 1969), Watford (October 1971-May 1972).
Left-back Brian Rowan, one-time heating engineer in Glasgow, was almost 21 years of age when he arrived at Villa Park. It was hoped he might follow in the footsteps of fellow Scot Charlie Aitken but he failed to make the grade and made only one senior appearance for the club, in September 1969 versus Watford, whom he joined two years later! As a 16 year-old, Rowan was forced to pull out of a Scottish Junior international v Wales through injury.
Brian Rowan's father was a Scottish professional.

## ROXBOROUGH, JOHN A.
Born: Granton, Edinburgh, 10 November 1901. Deceased.
Career: Edinburgh Emmett, Rugby Town, Leicester City (June 1920), Aston Villa (October 1922), Stoke (February 1924), Sheffield United (August 1925), Sheffield FC (1927-28).
John Roxborough was selected for an England Amateur international before his birthplace was confirmed! A jinky outside-left, full of vim and vigour, he made his League debut for Leicester City at the age of 18 (v West Ham United) and went on to score three goals in 50 senior games for the Foxes before moving to Villa Park. He had a useful 'half-season' with Villa, replacing Billy Kirton in the main and scored twice on his debut against his future club Stoke. He ended up with three strikes to his credit in 12 outings before going on to play in 14 League games for the Potters and five for the Blades.
John's brother Andrew also played for Leicester City and they appeared in the same side together during their time at Filbert Street (1920-21). A third Roxborough sibling, Walter, had trials with Leicester in 1921.

## ROYALTY
When Queen Victoria celebrated her golden and diamond jubilees, Villa also celebrated in those same years, winning the FA Cup in 1887 and completing the double in 1897.
HRH The Duke of York (later King George VI) attended Villa Park in January 1924.
In June 1951 HRH Princess Elizabeth (soon to be crowned Queen) visited Villa Park during her trip to Birmingham.
HRH Queen Elizabeth II handed the FA Cup to Johnny Dixon in 1957.
HRH Prince William is an avid Villa supporter.

## RUDGE, DAVID HARRY
Born: Wolverhampton, 21 January 1948
Career: Wolverhampton & District Boys, Aston Villa (apprentice, June 1964, professional May 1965), Hereford United (£5,000, August 1972), Torquay United (December 1975-May 1978), Kingsbury United (Midland Combination/Sutton League).
A go-ahead winger, good on the ball, Dave Rudge was voted Villa's 'Terrace Trophy Player of the Year' in 1969-70. He made an impressive debut for the club against Arsenal at Highbury in August 1966 - the first of 60 appearances (10 goals scored). He went on to play in 82 League games for Hereford and 64 for Torquay.

## RUGBY UNION
In 1908, Villa Park was chosen as the venue for the Rugby Union international between England and the touring Australians. A crowd of 5,000 attended the contest.
Sixteen years later, on 8 October 1924, Austin Woodward of Moseley RUFC, captained the North Midlands XV against the famous All Blacks touring side at Villa Park. Moseley supplied seven players and in front of a 17,000 crowd (recs. £1,620) the New Zealanders won by seven points.
A try was scored after just seven seconds of the Midland Counties XV

versus the Australia tourists in another Rugby Union international at Villa Park on 17 September 1947.
In April 1951, a fourth Rugby Union contest was staged at Villa Park when R.I. Scorer's International XV beat the North Midlands Select side 21-16 in front of 12,000 spectators.

## RUSHDEN & DIAMONDS
Elected to the Nationwide Football League for the 2001-02 season, 'Diamonds' have yet to play Villa in a competitive match.

## RUSSELL, GEORGE QUENTIN
Born: Ayrshire, August 1869. Died: Glasgow
Career: Ayr FC, Aston Villa (April 1892), Glasgow United (May 1895).
A player with boundless energy, George Russell was a left-half who was always eager to get forward and assist the front men - thus his positional sense left a lot to be desired. He scored three goals in 37 senior games for Villa during his three seasons with the club.

## RUTHERFORD, JOSEPH HENRY HAMILTON
Born: Fatfield, near Chester-le-Street, County Durham, 20 September 1914. Died: Sutton Coldfield, 27 December 1994.
Career: Chester-le-Street Schools, Chester-le-Street Juniors, West Ham United (trialist, 1928), Fatfield Juniors, Chester Moor Temperance FC, Ferryhill, Blyth Spartans, Chester-le-Street FC, Birtley Colliery, Southport (amateur, August 1931, professional August 1936), Aston Villa (£2,500, February 1939). Served in the Army during WW2, attaining the rank of Sargeant Major and guested for Nottingham Forest when stationed at Mansfield. After retiring in October 1951, aged 37, he ran a road haulage company and was clerk for Bryant's Builders as well as working behind the scenes at Villa Park, including a spell in the pools office. Later he became ground-assistant at the club's Bodymoor Heath complex.
Joe Rutherford started to keep goal at the age of eight and by the time he joined Southport as an amateur in 1931 he had already been playing intermediate and junior football for almost nine years. He made almost 100 first-class appearances during his time at Haig Avenue before moving to Villa Park.

*Joe Rutherford (Villa) dives at the feet of Johnny Berry (Blues) in the local derby at St. Andrews in 1950.*

THE COMPLETE ENCYCLOPAEDIA OF ASTON VILLA F.C.    THE COMPLETE ENCYCLOPAEDIA OF ASTON VILLA F.C.

231

A brave and fearless 'keeper, he slowly bedded himself and eventually took over the green jersey from Fred Biddlestone towards the end of the 1938-39 season. He played quite a few games for Villa during the hostilities and was an ever-present in the League side in 1946-47, one of his best performances coming at Everton when he twice saved a re-taken penalty. He was between the posts when Charlie Mitten fired a hat-trick of spot-kicks past him in Manchester United's emphatic 7-0 League victory at Old Trafford in March 1950. After 156 League and FA Cup appearances for Villa, Rutherford handed over his duties indirectly to Con Martin, the centre-half he had played behind in more than 75 matches prior to 1951.

## SABIN, ARTHUR HENRY

Born: Kingstanding, Birmingham, 25 January 1939. Died: Birmingham, March, 1958
Career: Kingstanding Schools, Aston Boys, Birmingham County FA, Aston Villa (juniors, June 1955, professional January 1957).
Arthur Sabin was a promising goalkeeper who had appeared in two League games, chipping a bone in his neck during his second outing in a home draw with Spurs in November 1957. Sadly that injury caused problems and four months later he died. He was only 19.

## SAMUEL, JLLOYD

Born: Trinidad, 29 March 1981.
Career: Aston Villa (trainee, June 1997, professional February 1999).
Capped four times by England at Under-18 level, defender JLloyd Samuel made his anticipated breakthrough at Villa Park during the 1999-2000 season when he played in 10 first-class matches (five as a substitute). He also sat on the bench for the last FA Cup Final at Wembley but was not called into action. A talented footballer with a lot to offer, Samuel had appeared in 17 matches when the 2000-01 season came to an end.

## SANTOS

When the South American giants, Santos, came to Villa Park to play a friendly match under floodlights in 1972, they had the World's greatest footballer in their side - Pele, the Brazilian international.
A crowd of 54,437 was present to see Third Division Aston Villa register a famous 2-1 victory.

## SAUNDERS, DEAN

Born: Swansea, 21 June 1964
Career: Swansea City (apprentice, professional June 1982), Cardiff City (on loan, March 1985), Brighton & Hove Albion (free transfer, August 1985), Oxford United (£60,000, March 1987), Derby County (£1 million, October 1988), Liverpool (£2.9 million, July 1991), Aston Villa (£2.3 million, September 1992), Galatasary (£2.35 million, July 1995), Nottingham Forest (£1.5 million, July 1996), Sheffield United (free transfer, December 1997), Benfica (£500,000, December 1998), Bradford City (free transfer, August 1999).
One of the game's most prolific marksmen, Dean Saunders struck his first goal in League football for Swansea against Oldham Athletic in March 1984. Seventeen years later he was still finding the back of the net! A positive, all-action, unselfish 'centre-forward' who simply knows where the 'goal' is, he has scored in each and every season since making his debut at competitive level in 1983-84 - and when the 2000-01 campaign ended his record in club and international football was very impressive indeed - 805 appearances and 276 goals....with more

to come! Saunders also holds the Welsh international record for being the most capped outfield player (75).
Surprisingly Saunders has only won two club medals, the first with Liverpool in the FA Cup in 1992 and his second with Villa in the League Cup in 1994 when he scored twice in the 3-1 win over Manchester United.
His best performances on the whole have come with Derby (131 senior appearances and 57 goals) and Villa (144 outings and 49 goals)...but wherever he's played he has given his all and during his three years at Villa Park the fans certainly enjoyed what they saw from a top-class striker.
In May 1994, a case commenced in the High Court (London) involving former Villa defender Paul Elliott (Chelsea) and Saunders (then with Villa). It revolved round an alleged tackle by Saunders (playing for Liverpool) on Elliott which effectively ended his playing career. (See Court Cases) Saunders was also arrested for disorderly behaviour in April 1993 after an incident in an Essex night club.

## SAUNDERS, RONALD

Born: Birkenhead, 6 November 1932
Career: Birkenhead & Liverpool Schools, Everton (junior, 1948, professional, February 1951), Tonbridge (July 1956), Gillingham (£800, May 1957), Portsmouth (£8,000, September 1958), Watford (£10,000, September 1964) and Charlton Athletic (August 1965), Yeovil Town (manager, May 1967-late 1968), Oxford United (manager, March-June 1969), Norwich City (manager, July 1969-November 1973), Manchester City (manager, November 1973-April 1974), Aston Villa (manager, June 1974-February 1982), Birmingham City (manager, February 1982-January 1986) and West Bromwich Albion (manager, February 1986-September 1987). Quit football to concentrate on playing golf, although he did do some scouting.
A hard-shooting 1950s centre-forward, Ron Saunders then became a positive, award-winning and very successful manager. As a striker - and England Youth international - he scored well over 200 League goals in almost 400 appearances, his best set of figures coming with Portsmouth (145 goals in 236 games). He kicked his last ball in earnest in 1967 with Charlton.
As a manager he won plenty of prizes, and taking them in order they were, with Norwich: Second Division champions 1972, League Cup runners-up 1973; with Manchester City: League Cup runners-up 1974; with Villa: League Cup winners 1975 and 1977, League champions 1981, Second Division runners-up 1975; with Blues: Second Division runners-up 1985. Unyielding at times, possibly blunt and certainly a strict disciplinarian, Saunders was strong in his approach but without doubt he gained the respect of the players under his charge. He knew the game inside out and although at times he was never the fans' favourite manager with his seemingly dull and occasionally negative approach on the field and his dour image off it, he did the business, perhaps not with West Brom though, especially as he sold striker Steve Bull to Wolves saying that his first touch wasn't good enough....Bull went on to score over 300 goals for Wolves!

He did an excellent job initially at non-League Yeovil; worked wonders in a short time at money-scarce Oxford; did very well for a while at Norwich before resigning after a bitter row with the Board; did a fine job in five months at Maine Road; bought in and introduced some tremendous players to Villa Park, including Des Bremner, John Burridge, Frank Carrodus, Gordon Cowans, Alex Cropley, John Deehan, Allan Evans, Colin Gibson, Andy Gray, Ray Graydon, John Gregory, Ken McNaught, Tony Morley, Dennis Mortimer, Brendon Ormsby, Jimmy Rimmer, Gary Shaw, Gordon Smith, Kenny Swain and Peter Withe. He celebrated - with thousands of others - when the League Championship was won in 1981 but before he could rejoice again (with the European and Super Cups) he had left to be replaced by his assistant Tony Barton

Villa played a total of 317 League matches while Saunders was manager. They won 139, drew 87 and lost 91, scoring 470 goals and conceding 353.

## SAWARD, PATRICK
Born: Cork, 17 August 1928
Career: Cork & Cobh County Schools, Beckenham (1945), Crystal Palace (amateur), Millwall (professional, July 1951), Aston Villa (£7,000, August 1955), Huddersfield Town (March 1961), Coventry City (October 1963, then player/coach and later assistant-manager, July 1967), Brighton & Hove Albion (manager, July 1970-October 1973); went into café/bar business in Menorca; NASR AI of Saudi Arabia (General manager/coach: 1973-75).

Pat Saward was a tough competitor, best seen as a wing-half although he did occasionally occupy an inside-forward berth. He was badly missed by Millwall after his departure to Villa Park where

he became a solid and valuable member of the team that won the FA Cup in 1957 and Second Division championship three years later. He made 170 first-team appearances and scored two goals during his five-and-a-half years at Villa Park. He won 18 caps for the Republic of Ireland.

As a manager, Saward was an extrovert, his good humour creating a happy feeling in the dressing room. He had a good eye for a player (he 'found' Willie Carr and Dennis Mortimer) and was very successful as a coach at Coventry, leading the youngsters to the FA Youth Cup Final. The Sky Blues also enjoyed European experience when he was right-hand man to boss Noel Cantwell. Saward guided Brighton to promotion from Division Three in 1972 but was sacked from the Goldstone Ground after a poor start to the 1973-74 season.

## SCARBOROUGH
There has been no competitive match action as yet involving Villa and Scarborough.
Players with both clubs include: J Burridge, TJ Mooney (Villa reserve), MC Oakes, B Ormsby, DP Spink (Villa reserve), N Swales, WJ Thompson (Villa reserve), GJ Williams.

## SCHMIECHEL, PETER BOLESLAW
Born: Gladsaxe, Denmark, 18 November 1963
Career: Hvidore (1984), Brondby IF (1987), Manchester United (£550,000, August 1991), Sporting Lisbon (June 1999), Aston Villa (free transfer, July 2001).
Signed on a free transfer from the Portuguese giants, Sporting Lisbon (to replace the departed David James) Peter Schmeichel made almost 400 senior appearances for Manchester United (one goal scored) during his eight years at Old Trafford. He helped Alex Ferguson's side win five Premiership titles, three FA Cup Finals, the League Cup, the European Cup, the European Super Cup and four FA Charity Shields - and that haul of prizes including the treble and double! He left the Reds after skippering the side to European Championship glory (and the treble) in 1999, signing a £580,000-a-year deal with Sporting Lisbon.
A highly-influential figure between the posts, he is a goalkeeper with great presence, a terrific shot-stopper exceptional aerial skills and supremely confident.
Capped 128 times by Denmark, he helped Brondby win the Danish League title, was a European Championship winner with his country in 1992, was voted Danish 'Footballer of the Year' in 1990 and was crowned best goalkeeper in Europe in 1998.
Schmiechel made his Villa debut in the home leg of the InterToto Cup-tie against the Croatian side Slavia Belupo in July 2001. In the Premier League match at Everton in October 2001, Schmeichel scored the TENTH goal of his goalkeeping career!

## SCIMECA, RICCARDO
Born: Leamington Spa, 13 June 1975
Career: Aston Villa (YTS June 1971, professional July 1993), Nottingham Forest (£3 million, July 1999).
After making 97 appearances and scoring two goals for Aston Villa, the versatile Riccardo Scimeca became David Platt's first signing when he took over as manager of Nottingham Forest in 1999. He was appointed captain and had a fine first season at The City Ground, missing only a handful of matches. Honoured by England at 'B' and Under-21 levels (nine caps won for the latter) he had a couple of agonising periods of injuries during his time at Villa Park and never really commanded a regular place in the side. But when fit and in the team he displayed excellent skills, good control and had an appetite for hard work. He was a League Cup winner in 1996.

## SCOTT, ANTHONY JAMES ERNEST

Born: St Neots, Cambridgeshire, 1 April 1941.

Career: Huntingdon Boys, St Neots Town, West Ham United (juniors June 1957, professional May 1958), Aston Villa (£25,000, October 1965), Torquay United (£5,000, September 1967), Bournemouth (July 1970), Exeter City (June 1972-May 1974). Retired through injury, later a Youth team coach at Manchester City.

After winning twelve England Youth caps, appearing in an FA Youth Cup Final and making a scoring League debut against Chelsea, orthodox winger Tony Scott went on to net a total of 19 goals in 97 senior appearances for the West Ham United before moving to Villa Park. There he lined up on the left-flank with Phil Woosnam who had been a colleague of his at Upton Park. In his two years wearing the 'other' claret and blue strip, Scott who had pace, used both feet and delivered excellent crosses, starred in 57 first-class games for Aston Villa and netted four goals. He then did very well on the south coast, adding a further 199 League appearances to his tally (12 goals).

## SCOTTISH CONNECTION

Here is a list of Aston Villa personnel who were also associated with Scottish football either as a player (at various levels), manager, assistant-manager, scout, coach etc.

| | |
|---|---|
| J Adam | Falkirk, Blantyre Celtic |
| C Aitken | Edinburgh Thistle |
| J Baird | Vale of Leven |
| HE Banks | Third Lanark |
| W Baxter | East Fife (manager) |
| W Beaton | Dunfermline Athletic, Airdrieonians |
| L Benwell | Berwick Rangers |
| D Blair | Clyde, Parkhead Juniors |
| NGL Blake | Dundee |
| DG Bremner | Deverondale, Hibernian |
| WW Briggs | Musselburgh Windsor, East Fife, Falkirk |
| J Brown | Renton |
| JK Brown | Heart of Midlothian, Hibernian |
| RAJ Brown | East Fife (WW2 guest) |
| J Burridge | Hibernian, Aberdeen, Falkirk, Hibernian, Queen of the South |
| L Butler | Dunfermline Athletic |
| G Campbell | Renton, Dundee |
| J Campbell | Celtic, Third Lanark |
| L Campbell | Dumbarton & Helensburgh, Glasgow United, Hibernian, Dumbarton |
| AG Cascarino | Celtic |
| WG Clarke | Third Lanark |
| N Cooper | Aberdeen, Glasgow Rangers, Ross County (manager) |
| Jas Cowan | Vale of Leven |
| TB Craig | Aberdeen, Hibernian (player/coach), Celtic (assistant-manager) |
| AJ Cropley | Hibernian |
| VH Crowe | Stirling Albion (trialist) |
| GW Cummings | Falkirk (WW2) & Partick Thistle |
| IW Dickson | Queen of the South |
| WA Dickson | Dundee Strathmore |
| T Docherty | Celtic |
| TC Donovan | Louth United |
| P Dowds | Celtic |
| W Dunning | Celtic, St Johnstone |
| P Elliott | Celtic |
| A Evans | Dunfermline Athletic, Greenock Morton (manager) |
| T Ewing | Hamilton Academical (player & manager), Partick Thistle, Greenock Morton |
| G Fenton | St Mirren |

| | |
|---|---|
| AJ Fisher | Celtic |
| J Fisher | St Bernard's |
| J Fleming | Vale of Leven, Larkhall Saints |
| JC Fraser | Dunfermline Athletic |
| DW Gibson | Hibernian, Livingston United |
| JD Gibson | Partick Thistle |
| W Gibson | Partick Thistle |
| RG Gittins | Partick Thistle |
| R Gordon | St Bernard's, Edinburgh Thistle, Leith Rovers, Heart of Midlothian, Forfar Athletic |
| AA Gray | Falkirk |
| AM Gray | Dundee United, Glasgow Rangers |
| JA Gray | Glasgow Rangers |

*Alex Cropley (Villa & Hibernian).*

| | |
|---|---|
| W Groves | Hibernian, Celtic |
| W Haggart | Edinburgh Royal, Edinburgh Thistle |
| WM Hamilton | Hibernian, Ross County, Hamilton Academical |
| GC Harkus | Edinburgh Emmett |
| PD Hislop | Glasgow Royal, Forfar Athletic, Perth |
| J Hogan | Celtic (coach) |
| RA Hogg | Berwick Rangers |
| TA Hughes | Clydebank |
| Andy Hunter | Third Lanark, Vale of Leven |
| Archie Hunter | Third Lanark, Ayr United |
| JF Inglis | Glenrothes |
| H Johnson | Airdrieonians, Clyde, Third Lanark |
| T Johnson | Celtic |
| JC Johnstone | Dundee, Dundee Harp |
| P Kyle | Clyde (trialist), Partick Thistle, Glasgow Parkhead, Heart of Midlothian, Port Glasgow Athletic |
| JW Laidlaw | Kilmarnock, Muirkirk |
| F Lloyd | Dundee |
| A Logan | Falkirk, Hibernian, Arthurlie |
| J Logan | Ayr United, Dundee |
| JL Logan | Queen's Park, Glasgow Rangers |
| W McAuley | Celtic |

THE COMPLETE ENCYCLOPAEDIA OF ASTON VILLA F.C.

THE COMPLETE ENCYCLOPAEDIA OF ASTON VILLA F.C.

234

| | |
|---|---|
| F McAvennie | Celtic, St Mirren |
| K Macdonald | Inverness Caledonian (T), Villa (coach) |
| B McClair | Celtic, Motherwell |
| C McElney | Celtic, Edinburgh Thistle |
| J MacEwan | Raith Rovers, Arbroath |
| A McInally | Ayr United, Celtic |
| JW McKenzie | Montrose, Dundee |
| A McLachlan | Aberdeen, Heart of Midlothian |
| JA McLachlan | Dundee |
| JM MacLeod | Edinburgh Thistle, Armadale, Hibernian, Raith Rovers |
| JS McLucklie | Hamilton Academical |
| P McMahon | Celtic, Dumbarton (trialist), Kilsyth Rangers |
| J McMorran | Falkirk (trialist), Third Lanark |
| J McMullan | Partick Thistle, Third Lanark |
| K McNaught | Dunfermline Athletic (coach) |

*Ken McNaught (Villa & Dunfermline Athletic).*

| | |
|---|---|
| W McNeill, MBE | Celtic (player & manager), Clyde (manager), Aberdeen (manager) |
| N Mackay | Edinburgh Royal, Broxburn, Hibernian, Clydebank |
| GS Martin | Bo'ness, Hamilton Academical, Bathgate |
| A Massie | Peterhill, Glasgow Benburb, Ayr United, Heart of Midlothian |
| Ralph Milne | Dundee United |
| Dr VE Milne | Aberdeen |
| A Mulraney | Celtic reserves, Heart of Midlothian (trialist), Hamilton Academical (trialist) |
| JA Murray | Ayr United |
| J Nibloe | Kilmarnock, Rutherglen Glencairn |
| TBD Niblo | Aberdeen, Hamilton Academical |
| FJ O'Donnell | Celtic, Hearts (WW2 guest) |
| JJ Paton | Vale of Leven, Dundee Harp |
| GB Ramsay | Glasgow Rangers (trialist) |
| J Reynolds | Celtic |
| P Rideout | Glasgow Rangers |
| JH Robey | Aberdeen |
| B Rowan | Ballieston Rovers |
| G Russell | Ayr United, Glasgow United |
| R Salmond | Dundee North End |

| | |
|---|---|
| GR Shaw | Kilmarnock |
| WS Simpson | Dunbar, Clyde, Cowdenbeath |
| DF Skea | Arbroath, Dundee Thistle |
| GM Smith | St Johnstone |
| S Stainrod | Falkirk (player & player/caretaker-manager), Dundee (player/caretaker-manager), Ayr United (manager) |
| N Tarrant | Ross County, Ayr United, Motherwell |
| S Teale | Motherwell (player-manager) |
| RB Templeton | Hibernian, Celtic, Kilmarnock |
| A Thompson | Celtic |
| W Thompson | Dumbarton |
| RGM Thomson | Albion Rovers, Airdrieonians |
| J Venglos | Celtic (manager) |
| ME Walters | Glasgow Rangers |
| J Ward | Clyde, Hibernian, Dundee United |
| J Welford | Celtic |
| J Whitehouse | Third Lanark |
| ES Williams | Third Lanark, Celtic |
| DJ Winton | St Johnstone (trialist) |
| W Yates | Heart of Midlothian |
| WJ Young | Clyde (trialist), Arthurlie |

**Tartan Talk Back**

In 1924 Dr Vic Milne became the first Scotsman to play in an FA Cup Final for Aston Villa since 1897. He was also the first Doctor to appear in a competitive game at Wembley.

The first Villa player to win a Scottish international cap was James Cowan in 1886.

Billy Dickson scored four goals on his international debut for Scotland against Ireland in 1888 and was never capped again!

Villa signed Jimmy Gibson from Partick Thistle in 1927 for a club record fee of £7,500. The following year he starred for Scotland (the Wembley Wizards) in their famous 5-1 win over England.

Bruce Rioch was the first English-born player to captain Scotland.

When Aston Villa won the Southern Junior Floodlit Cup in 1981, their star striker was future Scottish international and Manchester United star Brian McClair.

Alan McInally scored 16 goals for Ayr United in season 1983-84 and then netted a hat-trick on his debut for Celtic against Hibernian in 1986. He moved to Villa Park from Parkhead for £225,000 in 1987.

**SCOTTISH OPPOSITION**

The first Scottish side Villa met was the Queen's Park second XI in a home friendly on 20 January 1879. The Scots won 2-1.

Villa's initial senior game was against Heart of Midlothian at Perry Barr on 1 January 1881 (won 4-2).

On 1 October 1881 Villa beat Pollockshield 6-1 at Perry Barr and three weeks later they were defeated 4-0 at home by Queen's Park (Glasgow).

On 25 March 1882, Villa first came up against Glasgow Rangers whom they defeated 3-2 at Perry Barr in front of 4,000 spectators and the following month Villa travelled to Edinburgh where they lost 6-1 to Heart of Midlothian.

Queen's Park won again on Villa soil in October 1882 before Rangers claimed their revenge with a 4-1 drubbing of Villa in Glasgow on 24 March 1883, only for Villa to win a return fixture 2-1 seven days later! Knocked out of the FA Cup in the 4th round by Queen's Park in January 1884 by 4-1, Villa finally beat the amateur side 2-1 at Perry Barr ten months later before a 5,000 crowd.

Villa first toured Scotland in August 1886. They fulfilled seven matches in 11 days, beating Falkirk 3-2, East Stirlingshire 5-2, St Johnstone 11-1 and Arbroath 4-0, and losing to Renton 2-6, Dundee Harp 2-3 and Airdrieonians 1-3.

Glasgow Rangers were dumped out of the FA Cup by Villa 3-1 in a semi-final at Crewe on 5 March 1887 and soon afterwards, Hibernian

THE COMPLETE ENCYCLOPAEDIA OF ASTON VILLA F.C.     THE COMPLETE ENCYCLOPAEDIA OF ASTON VILLA F.C.

235

*Villa's Leighton Phillips and Rangers' skipper John Greig exchange pennants before the friendly 'battle' in 1976.*

With World War Two still in progress Villa lost 4-3 to an Edinburgh Select XI in Scotland in August 1944 and on 1 March 1947 Celtic were the first Scottish team to visit Villa Park after the hostilities, winning 2-1.

A 2-0 Villa win at Parkhead in February 1949 was followed a year later by a 5-2 home victory over Hibernian. On 13 November 1958, Heart of Midlothian came down to officially 'switch on' the Villa Park floodlights, drawing 3-3 after a cracking game. The following year, however, Raith Rovers failed to match their Scottish neighbours and lost 5-1 - but they did claim something back in return when they beat Villa 2-1 on 27 September 1960, in a game arranged to turn on the new floodlights at Stark's Park.

Competing in a club tournament in Atlanta, USA in May/June 1969, Villa played against both Kilmarnock and Dundee United (see under USA Tournament).

A pre-season trip to Scotland in August 1970 resulted in defeats at Motherwell (1-2) and Clydebank (1-3) and in October 1976 a friendly against Glasgow Rangers at Villa Park was abandoned in the 53rd minute after crowd violence (see under Crowd Disturbances).

In August 1979 Villa beat Hearts 3-1 at Tynecastle but lost 3-0 to Dundee United at Tannadice, and on a trip to Glasgow on 2 August 1986 they went down 1-0 at Celtic.

Since then several mini tours (pre-season) have taken place in Scotland (some involving the first team, some the reserves) and among the teams Villa have played against are St Johnstone, St Mirren and Montrose.

• In the 1880s Glasgow Rangers used to have an identical badge to that of Villa.

were walloped 8-3 by Villa in a friendly in Edinburgh. Ironically 28 years later Hibs travelled to Villa Park and received the same sort of hiding, Villa again winning 8-3 in May 1915.

A 4-2 win at Ayr on New Year's Eve 1887 was followed by a 1-1 draw on Glasgow Rangers' territory two days later and when Rangers visited Perry Barr in February of that same year Villa beat them 5-1.

Dumbarton were beaten 4-1 by Villa in April 1888, Rangers gained some revenge with a 3-1 home win the following month and in September, Ayr United succumbed to a 10-1 mauling at Perry Barr as Villa turned the screw on the travelling Scots!

Another team to suffer a heavy defeat was Partick Thistle, crushed 10-0 by Villa in March 1891 and in September 1893 a crowd of 5,000 witnessed a thrilling 3-3 draw between Villa and Queen's Park at Perry Barr.

Both Rangers 3-1 and Celtic 3-2 were defeated in friendly matches on Villa soil during a fortnight in late March and early April 1894 but on their next visit to Birmingham, Rangers won 3-1 in April 1895.

Hibernian completed a 'friendly' double over Villa in April 1896, winning 2-1 at Perry Barr and 5-2 in Scotland when, during a short tour, Villa also lost 3-2 at Celtic but won 3-1 at Ayr.

The first Scottish club side to visit Villa Park were Celtic, on 3 September 1900, when Villa won 2-1. Later that year (on 21 December) they again came south to play Villa in Albert Evans' benefit match. Again Villa won, this time by 3-1.

Since then, perhaps surprisingly, there has been very little friendly action involving Aston Villa and Scottish clubs at the ground.

Villa did play two games in Scotland in April 1912, beating Third Lanark 1-0 and drawing 1-1 with Celtic.

On 3 March 1928 'Pongo' Waring, making his first team debut, scored two goals as Villa beat Airdrieonians 7-2 and four years later he was again on target when Cowdenbeath lost 4-2, also at Villa Park.

## SCOUTS

Aston Villa Football Club has had a scouting system in operation since the early 1920s and over the years some great players have been spotted by eagle-eyed scouts who have covered every part of the country and, indeed, Europe!

### Scout's Note-pad

Among the many scouts who have been employed by Aston Villa we have ex-players: Malcolm Beard, Albert Evans (1950s), 'Sailor' Brown, Charlie Wallace, Peter Withe and Ron Wylie.

As manager Jack Tinn guided Portsmouth to victory in the 1939 FA Cup Final over the red-hot favourites Wolves. Eight years later he was appointed Chief Scout at Villa Park.

Peter Doherty, the Irish international inside-forward, who played for Huddersfield Town, Derby County and Manchester City among others, was Aston Villa's chief scout in season 1968-69.

In 1984 the former Coventry City, Blues and Walsall player Don Dorman was appointed Chief Scout at Villa Park.

Brian Whitehouse, who played for WBA, Charlton, Leyton Orient, Crystal Palace and others, was coach/scout at Arsenal and Manchester United before acting as chief scout at Villa Park for three-and-a-half years up to January 1995.

Between them Peter Downes, Neville Briggs and Dave Manship all brought excellent quality players to the club during the 1950s/60s/70s, likewise Billy Wright who covered the North-East of England.

Ex-Villa players who took up scouting positions elsewhere include: Bob Brocklebank (WBA), John Deehan (Sheffield United), Eric Houghton (Nottingham Forest) Vic Potts (Doncaster Rovers, Spurs and other London clubs), Cyril Spiers (Leicester City) and Kenny Swain.

Former Aston Villa managers Tony Barton and Ron Saunders both held scouting positions with other clubs after leaving Villa Park.

Jack Vinall, brother of the Aston Villa defender Albert Vinall (1939-54) was scout at Villa Park during the 1950s.

Ross MacLaren was Villa's Chief Scout in 2000-01.

## SCUNTHORPE UNITED

Villa's playing record against the Iron:

Football League

| Venue | P | W | D | L | F | A |
|-------|---|---|---|---|---|---|
| Home | 1 | 1 | 0 | 0 | 5 | 0 |
| Away | 1 | 1 | 0 | 0 | 2 | 1 |
| Totals | 2 | 2 | 0 | 0 | 7 | 1 |

League Cup

| Venue | P | W | D | L | F | A |
|-------|---|---|---|---|---|---|
| Home | 1 | 1 | 0 | 0 | 3 | 1 |
| Away | 1 | 1 | 0 | 0 | 3 | 2 |
| Totals | 2 | 2 | 0 | 0 | 6 | 3 |

Aston Villa doubled up over Scunthorpe in season 1959-60 when they claimed the Second Division championship at the first attempt. They romped to an emphatic 5-0 victory at home (two goals apiece for Peter McParland and Gerry Hitchens) and won 2-1 away (Hitchens again scoring twice).

Villa were involved in two League Cup games with United in 1984-85. They eventually won through to the 3rd round 6-3 on aggregate with Colin Gibson scoring in both legs.

Players with both clubs include: J Barker, L Butler, M Carruthers, NJ Cox, D Duffy, D Farrell, BC Godfrey, DT Hughes, MA Lillis, JB Lynch, I Ormondroyd, CL Roberts (Villa reserve), G Sidebottom, J Woodward. Also: Richard Money (Villa & United coach, also United caretaker-manager & manager), G Taylor (Villa manager, United Amateur).

## SEALEY, LESLIE JESSE

Born: Bethnal Green, London, 29 September 1959. Died: London, August 2001.

Career: Coventry City (apprentice, July 1975, professional May 1977), Luton Town (£120,000, August 1983), Plymouth Argyle (on loan, October 1984), Manchester United (on loan, March 1990, free transfer permanently to Old Trafford, June 1990), Aston Villa (free transfer, July 1991), Coventry City (on loan, March 1992), Birmingham City (on loan, October 1992), Manchester United (free transfer, January 1993), Blackpool (free transfer, July 1994), West Ham United (free transfer, November 1994), Leyton Orient (non-contract, July 1996), West Ham United (non-contract, November 1996).

Goalkeeper Les Sealey's eventful career spanned 21 years. During that time he served with nine different clubs and made a grand total of 568 League and Cup appearances. His last senior outing came as a West Ham substitute in an emotional farewell Premiership game against one of his former clubs, Manchester United, at Old Trafford in front of 55,249 spectators on 11 May 1997.

A real character, strong-willed, confident, aggressive, boisterous at times, even annoying and rather too vocal, Sealey was, without doubt, a very competent 'keeper. He was brought in for the 1990 FA Cup Final replay against Crystal Palace after a poor first game showing by Jim Leighton and duly collected a winners' medal as Manchester United won 4-0. A year later he was on the losing side in the 1991 League Cup Final defeat by Sheffield Wednesday but soon afterwards gained a winners' medal when United won the European Cup Winners' Cup Final in Barcelona.

Sealey suffered another League Cup disappointment when Aston Villa beat United to lift the trophy in 1994. Earlier, as a Luton player, he had missed the 1988 League Cup Final through injury, but was then a loser as Forest beat the Hatters in the Final of the same competition twelve months later.

No international caps for Sealey but plenty of memories - and 24 games between the posts for Aston Villa, when he took over from the injured Nigel Spink during the course of the 1991-92 season. He died from a heart attack in 2001.

## SECRETARIES

The following have all held the position of 'secretary' of Aston Villa Football Club: William B. Mason, H Jefferies, Philip Clamp, George Ramsay, Billy Smith, Fred Archer, Alan Bennett and Steve Stride.

J Dunkley was honorary financial secretary of the club in the mid 1890s. He was a Football League Committee member for three years (1895-98). **Secretary's Minutes**

*Villa secretary Fred Archer (1959-69).*

Aston Villa's first honorary secretary was William B. Mason (1874-75) Philip Clamp (later a Director of the club) was honorary secretary of Aston Villa for four years: 1880-84.

Ex-player George Ramsay was secretary of the club for 42 years - from 1884 to 1926. During that time he also controlled the selection of the team (sitting with a chosen committee).

WJ (Billy) Smith held office for 29 years - from 1926 until 1955. He was presented with the Football League's 21 years long service medal in 1950. Smith retired in May 1955 after serving Villa for 45 years in total.

Fred Archer, who took over the reins from Smith, was also presented with the Football League's long service medal in 1961. He held office for fourteen years, until 1969.

Alan Bennett had been assistant-secretary at Chelsea since 1961 when he left Stamford Bridge to take over as secretary at Villa Park on 1 July 1969, a position he held for a further ten years, until 31 March 1979, when he moved to Leicester City.

Steve Stride then took over the mantle from Bennett on 1 April 1979. At the time he was the youngest club secretary in the First Division and he was still in office in season 2001-02, having also been opted onto the Board of Directors at Villa Park.

*George Ramsay*

*Secretary/Director Steve Stride.*

THE COMPLETE ENCYCLOPAEDIA OF ASTON VILLA F.C.　　ASTON VILLA　　THE COMPLETE ENCYCLOPAEDIA OF ASTON VILLA F.C.

237

Former Villa player Edmund Strange (from the 1890s) was assistant-secretary at Villa Park from 1899-1925. Edmund Goodman (born in Birmingham on 8 October 1873) lost a leg after being injured playing for Villa's reserve side in 1893. He later became the club's joint assistant-secretary, holding office until 1905 when he left to take over as the Crystal Palace secretary. He moved up to secretary-manager in April 1907 and remained until November 1925. He then took the secretarial seat again, staying until May 1933. After leaving football Goodman ran a successful grocery shop in Annerley.

## SELLARS, GEOFFREY

Born: Stockport, 20 May 1930
Career: Stockport & District/Cheshire Schools, Altrincham (amateur, 1947), Leeds United (professional, April 1950), Aston Villa (August 1950), Altrincham (August 1951). Out of football 1954 onwards.

An orthodox outside-right, Geoff Sellars failed to make the first XI at Elland Road and only appeared in two Football League games for Aston Villa - against Arsenal and Derby County, both at home, during the first half of the 1950-51 season. He was hardly a first-class competitor and returned to non-League football after spending just a year at Villa Park.

*Allan Evans - sent off v. Coventry City in 1979.*

## SENDINGS-OFF

The first player to be sent-off in a Football League match was Aston Villa's Dennis Hodgetts, dismissed for punching the Everton defender Alec Dick in the last minute of the home League game against the Merseysiders on 22 September 1888. Two months later, a distraught Hodgetts was suspended for two games by the Birmingham County FA.

In a home friendly against local rivals Small Heath on St Valentine's Day 1891 Tom McKnight (Villa's reserve forward) and opposing defender Caesar Jenkyns were both dismissed in the second-half for fighting! Villa won the game 3-0.

Mark Delaney, Villa's enterprising right-wing back, was sent-off three times in ten matches - twice while playing for his club and once for his country, Wales. He suffered the indignity of receiving a red card at Wembley during Villa's FA Cup semi-final with Bolton Wanderers in April 2000 and saw red in an international match against Portugal soon afterwards. Then, in July, he was dismissed in Villa's InterToto Cup game in Prague, Czechoslovakia against FC Marila Pribram. Manager John Gregory read the riot act in no uncertain terms - having just agreed a new four-year contract with Delaney, worth £6,000-a-week!

Three players - Villa midfielders Ian Taylor and Alan Thompson and Spanish defender Velasco of Vigo - were all sent-off during the second leg of the InterToto encounter between Aston Villa and Celta Vigo at The Hawthorns in August 2000.

In the World Cup Group 2 match between Argentina and West Germany at Villa Park in July 1966, the Argentinian midfielder Jorge Albrecht was sent-off for 'repeated dangerous play.'

Trevor Hockey - winning his last full cap - became the first Welsh player to be sent-off in a full international when he was dismissed in a 3-0 defeat by Poland in Katowice in a World Cup qualifier on 2 September 1973.

Ex-Villa winger Mark Walters was one of four players sent-off during the Rangers v Celtic Scottish Cup quarter-final tie in 1991.

Future Villa player, Cyrille Regis (WBA), was sent-off for throwing a punch at Allan Evans during the local derby between the Baggies and Aston Villa at The Hawthorns in May 1982.

## Early Baths

Here is an unofficial/incomplete list of other players (not mentioned above) who, during their respective careers with Aston Villa, were sent-off in a first team match (named in A-Z order): Frank Barson (twice), Mark Bosnich (v Leeds United, April 1995, also sent-off in reserve team game v. Nottingham Forest in 1992), Harry Burrows (v West Bromwich Albion, October 1962), Benito Carbone (v. Everton, away, FA Cup, 1999-2000), Stan Collymore (v Bolton Wanderers, October 1997, v Liverpool 1998-99), Eamonn Deacy, John Deehan (v Nottingham Forest, January 1979, FA Cup), Derek Dougan (v Nottingham Forest, September 1962), Mark Draper (v. Newcastle United, 1996-97), Ugo Ehiogu (v Crystal Palace, November 1994 League Cup and v Arsenal, May 1998), Allan Evans (v Coventry City, March 1979 and v Barcelona S/Cup 1983), Bernie Gallagher, Colin Gibson, John Gidman (v Barcelona, SC January 1983), Ray Graydon (in Holland, 1972), Harry Gregory (in Germany, 1971), Lee Hendrie (v QPR, December 1995 and v Arsenal, Manchester City, December 2000), Steve Hunt (v Barnsley, September 1987), George Hunter (v Manchester United, April 1911), Martin Keown (v Southampton, 1986, League Cup), Jimmy MacEwan (v Rotherham United, December 1959), Alan McInally (v Middlesbrough, September 1987, League Cup), Jimmy McLuckie, Steve McMahon (v Liverpool, September 1983), Paul Merson (v Marila Pribram, ITC, 2001), Sammy Morgan (v Arsenal, January 1974, FA Cup), Tony Morley (v West Bromwich Albion, January 1982, League Cup), Frank Moss senior (v Manchester United, August 1928), Michael Oakes (v Blackburn Rovers, December 1998 - red card later rescinded), Paul Rideout (v Polytechnia of Romania, August 1983), Leslie Smith (v Everton, November 1948), Gareth Southgate (v Leicester City, 1999-2000), goalkeeper Cyril Spiers (v Sheffield United, November 1925), Nigel Spink (v Southampton, April 1994), Steve Staunton (v. Middlesbrough, 1996-97), Ian Taylor* (v Newcastle United, May 2001), Shaun Teale (v Grimsby Town, January 1994, FA Cup), Andy Townsend (v Wimbledon, November 1994, v Arsenal, December 1994, v. Nottingham Forest away September 1995), Mark Walters, Tom 'Pongo' Waring (v Tottenham Hotspur, January 1934), Steve Watson (v. Charlton Athletic, 1998-99), and Gary Williams (v Southampton, 1986 League Cup).

* Changed to Yellow Card on appeal.

*John Gidman, dismissed in Spain.*

THE COMPLETE ENCYCLOPAEDIA OF ASTON VILLA F.C.        THE COMPLETE ENCYCLOPAEDIA OF ASTON VILLA F.C.

238

## SEQUENCES

Aston Villa ran up a club record 14 successive home League wins between 10 January and 25 November 1903 and repeated that feat between 27 December 1930 and 10 October 1931.

They won nine League games (home & away) in a row between 22 March and 18 September 1897 and again between 15 October and 10 December 1910.

Villa went 13 away League games without defeat between 5 September 1987 and 23 January 1988.

Villa suffered 11 successive League defeats between 23 March and 4 May 1963.

From 12 September to 10 October 1981 Villa played out six successive League draws.

Villa have gone a record 15 home and away League games without defeat on three occasions: (1) from 16 January to 18 September 1897, (2) between 18 December 1909 and 26 March 1910 and (3) from 12 March to 27 August 1949.

Villa were undefeated at home in 37 League matches between 24 April 1909 and 22 April 1911 (two years). Prior to that their previous 'best' was 30 matches - 13 October 1894 to 12 September 1896 inclusive.

Villa's best away sequence is 13 games without defeat from 5 September 1987 to 23 January 1988.

Villa won six successive away League games between 6 February and 11 September 1897.

Villa recorded 16 successive home League victories over Sheffield United between September 1901 and December 1922.

Villa went 27 away games without a League win between 21 September 1963 and 26 December 1964.

On two occasions (1) between 10 November 1973 and February 1974 and (2) between 27 December 1986 and 25 March 1987, Villa went 12 League games without a win.

Villa had a run of eight home League games without registering a single victory between 11 December 1920 and 28 March 1921.

Villa's best start to a League season saw them go 11 games without defeat in 1932-33.

Their worst start to a campaign was in 1969-70 when they recorded their first League win in the 10th match.

Villa scored at least one goal in 35 successive League games between 10 November 1894 and 14 December 1895.

Villa went 13 FA Cup games without defeat from 30 October 1886 to 17 December 1887 inclusive.

Villa's longest unbroken run in the First Division of the Football League is 44 seasons - 1888-89 to 1935-36 inclusive.

## SEWELL, JOHN

Born: Kells Village, near Whitehaven, 24 January 1927

Career: Kells Centre FC, Whitehaven Town, Notts County (October 1944, professional August 1945), Sheffield Wednesday (£34,500, March 1951), Aston Villa (£20,000, December 1955), Hull City (October 1959), Lusaka City, Rhodesia (player/coach, September 1961-May 1964). Later coached in Zambia (1968-71) and the Belgian Congo (1972). Guested for Carlisle United and Workington during WW2. Later a car salesman for Bristol Street Motors in West Bridgeford, Nottingham (1973-87).

Inside-forward Jackie Sewell gained championship medals with Notts County (Division 3 South, 1950) and Sheffield Wednesday (Division 2 in 1952 and 1956); was the subject of a record transfer from Meadow Lane to Hillsborough in 1951 and helped Villa win the FA Cup in 1957. He was also with a relegated League club on four occasions: Wednesday twice, Villa (in 1959) and Hull City,

and he played for England in those two heavy defeats against Hungary, 3-6 at Wembley and 1-7 in Budapest in the 1953-54 season. He won a total of six full caps overall, represented the Football League XI and toured Canada/North America with the FA in June 1950 (scoring six goals in seven games including a hat-trick in a 9-0 win over Alberta). A very talented inside-forward, Sewell scored 92 goals in 175 senior games for Sheffield Wednesday to pay back double the amount of money the Owls had spent on him in 1951. He had earlier responded brilliantly to the promptings of Tommy Lawton at Notts County and did likewise in a Villa forward-line that also comprised Les Smith, Billy Myerscough/Derek Pace/Gerry Hitchens, Johnny Dixon/Ron Wylie and Peter McParland. In a fine career he netted almost 250 goals in 550 competitive matches (228 in 510 League games)...and all this despite (at times) suffering a baffling loss of form!

## SHANKHOUSE

Villa's playing record against Shankhouse:

| FA Cup | | | | | | |
|---|---|---|---|---|---|---|
| Venue | P | W | D | L | F | A |
| Away | 1 | 1 | 0 | 0 | 9 | 0 |

Aston Villa completely overwhelmed the semi-professionals in a 4th round encounter in December 1887. Archie Hunter, Albert Allen, Tommy Green and Albert Brown all scored twice and Denny Hodgetts once in front of 3,000 spectators.

## SHARP, BERTRAM A.

Born: Hereford, January 1876. Died: Liverpool, c 1941.

Career: Hereford Comrades (1893), Hereford Thistle (1894), Hereford Town (1895), Hereford Thistle (1986), Aston Villa (April 1897), Everton (August 1899), Southampton (May 1900), Everton (May 1901), Kirkdale (August 1904 after being re-instated as an amateur), Southport Central (January 1905). Retired 1907. Later appointed a Director of Everton Football Club (with his brother Jack, below).

Younger brother of the more famous Jack Sharp (below), Bert was never in the same class as his brother. An honest, hard-working defender nevertheless, he was versatile and a good athlete who performed consistently well for each club he served, making 23 appearances for Villa, 22 for Saints and 10 for Everton at top-class level. He was also a useful cricketer, and in 1900 averaged 40 with the bat for his county, Herefordshire.

## SHARP, JOHN S

Born: Hereford, 15 February 1878. Died: Wavertree, Liverpool, 27 January 1938.

Career: Hereford Thistle (1985), Aston Villa (April, 1987), Everton (August 1899). Retired in May 1910. Opened a sports shop in Liverpool, became a wealthy businessman and joined the Board of Directors at Goodison Park (with his brother Bert). He was later chairman of Everton FC.

Jack Sharp represented England at both football and Test Match Cricket. On the soccer pitch, he was a short, thick-set outside-right, a 'Pocket Hercules' who made only 24 senior appearances for Aston Villa (15 goals scored) before transferring to Everton. With the Merseysiders he developed into an international quality player, gaining two full caps and representing the Football League. He was a regular in the side for 11 years, and during that time netted 80 goals in 342 senior appearances and played in two FA Cup Finals (1906 and 1907). The famous referee Jack Howcroft, in the game for 30 years, rated Sharp as the best outside-right he ever

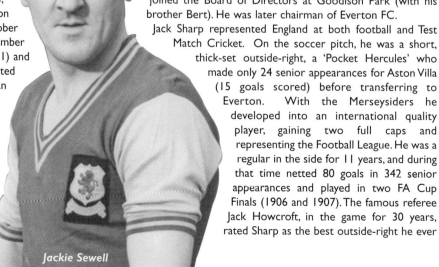

*Jackie Sewell*

*Gary Shaw, 80 goals for Villa in 205 outings.*

saw play.

On the cricket field, Sharp played in three Test Matches and recorded a century against the Aussies at The Oval in 1909. He spent 26 years with Lancashire (1899-1925), scored over 22,700 runs (38 centuries), took 440 wickets and held 223 catches. (See Cricketing-Footballers).


## SHARPLES, JOHN

Born: Wolverhampton, 8 August 1934.

Career: Heathtown FC, Walsall (amateur, 1951-52), Aston Villa (amateur, 1953, professional, October 1955), Walsall (August 1959), non-League football with Darlaston (1964-68).

Strongly-built defender, John Sharples understudied Peter Aldis at Villa Park and made 13 senior appearances for the club in four years (two of which were spent in the Army) before transferring to Walsall in 1959. He went on to star in 130 games for the Saddlers, occupying both the full-back and centre-half positions, helping the Fellows Park club twice win promotion.

He signed 'pro' forms for Villa 24 hours before joining the Army, a deferment until he had completed his engineering apprenticeship.


## SHAW, GARY ROBERT

Born: Castle Bromwich, Birmingham, 21 January 1961

Career: Kingshurst Comprehensive School, North Warwickshire Boys, Erdington & Saltley Boys, Colehill Town Colts, Coleshill Town, Warwickshire & District Schools, Aston Villa (apprentice July 1977, professional January 1979), Blackpool (on loan, February 1988), BK Copenhagen, Denmark (May 1988), FC Klagenfurt, Austria (March-May 1989), Sheffield Wednesday (on loan, August-September 1989), Walsall (February 1990), Kilmarnock (briefly), Shrewsbury Town (September 1990), Ernst Borel FC (Hong Kong, 1991). Retired on his return to England. Later became a football summariser on local radio.

After doing so well, scoring goals aplenty and winning medals, Gary Shaw's career was ruined over a period of four years (1983-87) when he underwent six knee operations! Although he tried a comeback by playing abroad he was never able to totally commit himself to the action and decided to quit soccer in 1991 at the age of 30.

Forming a brilliant partnership with Peter Withe, he netted 20 goals in 1980-81 (when the League championship was won), 14 the following year and 24 in 1982-83. He appeared in a total of 205 senior games for Villa and netted 80 goals, adding both European Cup and European Cup prizes to his League medal. He had made his senior debut at Bristol City in August 1978 and a year later grabbed his first hat-trick for the club on the same ground in an FA Cup-tie.

Shaw was voted PFA 'Young Player of the Year' 1981 and took the European Cup 'Player of the Year' award in 1982. Earlier in his career he had collected nine Youth and seven Under-21 caps for England and came so close to earning a full cap in 1981 when he was the only Birmingham-born player in Villa's First Division championship-winning side.


## SHEFFIELD UNITED

Villa's playing record against the Blades:

Football League/Premiership

| Venue | P | W | D | L | F | A |
|---|---|---|---|---|---|---|
| Home | 60 | 40 | 12 | 8 | 145 | 55 |
| Away | 60 | 17 | 16 | 27 | 85 | 111 |
| Totals | 120 | 57 | 28 | 35 | 230 | 166 |

FA Cup

| | | | | | | |
|---|---|---|---|---|---|---|
| Home | 1 | 1 | 0 | 0 | 4 | 1 |
| Away | 2 | 2 | 0 | 0 | 3 | 0 |
| Neutral | 2 | 0 | 1 | 1 | 0 | 3 |
| Totals | 5 | 3 | 1 | 1 | 7 | 4 |

Wartime

| | | | | | | |
|---|---|---|---|---|---|---|
| Home | 1 | 1 | 0 | 0 | 3 | 2 |
| Away | 1 | 0 | 1 | 0 | 2 | 2 |
| Totals | 2 | 1 | 1 | 0 | 5 | 4 |

The first time Villa met the Blades at League level was in season 1893-94 (Division 1). United won 3-0 at Bramall Lane while Villa triumphed 4-0 at Perry Barr, Charlie Hare scoring a hat-trick.

Villa didn't start the year 1902 off too well, losing 6-0 at Bramall Lane on New Year's Day. But they made up for that disaster by winning both League games by 4-2 the following season, with Jasper McLuckie claiming a hat-trick in the triumph at Villa Park.

Villa doubled up again in 1903-04, winning 6-1 at home and 2-1 in Sheffield.

Jimmy Cantrell weighed in with three goals in Villa's 5-1 home success in mid-December 1906 and soon after winning the FA Cup in April 1913, Villa returned to League duty with a 4-2 home win over United. Charlie Wallace scored twice, but only 4,850 fans turned up to see this end-of-season encounter - the lowest attendance for a League game between the two clubs.

On 29 November 1919, having won 2-1 at Bramall Lane a week earlier, Clem Stephenson netted all Villa's goals as they eased to a 4-0 home victory to complete the double over the Blades.

Just after Christmas 1921, the two League games between Villa and United produced 13 goals. Villa won both encounters: 3-2 (away) and 5-3 (home). Villa's centre-half Frank Barson headed a goal from 30 yards in the first game whilst Billy Dickson netted a hat-trick in the second.

That 5-3 victory gave Villa a run of 16 successive home League wins over the Blades (commencing September 1901).

Billy Walker netted four times when Villa blunted the Blades 5-1 at home in December 1929 and Eric Houghton scored twice in the 3-3 draw at Bramall Lane four months later.

Fourteen goals were forthcoming from the two League encounters in 1931-32 - United winning a pulsating tussle by 5-4 at Bramall Lane while Villa won 5-0 in Birmingham. Crowds of 20,000 attended both matches.

In October 1949, Villa held a 3-0 half-time lead over the Blades at home, but struggled in the end to gain a 4-3 victory. Trevor Ford and George Edwards both scored twice.

Derek Pace scored a hat-trick (against his future club) when Villa beat the Blades 3-0 at home in April 1956.

When Aston Villa captured the Second Division championship in 1959-60, only one team came to Villa Park and collected both points, Sheffield United winning 3-1 on 27 February.

In November 1975 Villa sliced through the Blades to win a First Division match 5-1, Chico Hamilton scoring twice.

Ian Olney was booked after just 15 seconds of Villa's home League game with United in March 1992 - one of the fastest yellow cards on record.

When Villa beat the Blades 2-0 in August 1992, it was their first League success at Bramall Lane for 31 years (since September 1961 - won 2-0).

Villa became the first English club to field two German-born players in a League game v. Sheffield United (h) on 27 January 1993 (won 3-1). The players were: Stefan Beinlich and Matthias Breitkreutz. This season Villa completed the League double over the Blades for the first time since 1954-55.

Villa's first victory in the Premiership was a 2-1 success over the Blades at Bramall Lane on 29 August 1992.

*Ian 'Chico' Hamilton played for both clubs, Villa and United.*

Garry Parker scored both goals.

When Kevin Richardson netted the opening goal in a 2-1 win at Bramall Lane on 16 April 1994, it was Villa's first goal in 415 minutes of football - since the 'og' conceded by Oldham's Steve Redmond four weeks earlier.....and in fact it was the first by a Villa player for 724 minutes of Premiership action since Tony Daley's winner at Coventry in early March.

Villa were knocked out of the FA Cup by the Blades in a semi-final replay at Derby in 1901, losing 3-0 after a goalless draw at Nottingham. Keith Leonard netted twice when Villa beat United 4-1 at home in a 4th round FA Cup-tie in 1975 and Dwight Yorke's penalty at Bramall Lane saw Villa through to the 5th round in 1996.

Players with both clubs include: E Barrett, WF Brawn, J Burridge, RM Campbell, F Carr, GS Cowans, MR Day, RE Evans, K Gage, R Gaudie, D Glover, IM Hamilton, WM Hamilton, J Harrop, T Hockey, P Kyle, A Layton, P McGrath, K McNaught, DG Mortimer, D Pace, BD Rioch, JH Roxborough, D Saunders, S Stainrod, C Tiler, C Wilson (Villa reserve, United trialist), P Withe.

Also: J Mercer (manager of both clubs), AP Heath (Villa player, United manager), RE Blackburn (Villa player, United assistant-manager), GA Vowden (Villa player, United coach), J Barron (assistant-manager at both clubs), A Hodgkinson (United player, Villa goalkeeping coach), A Ashman (United Amateur, Villa scout).

## SHEFFIELD WEDNESDAY

Villa's playing record against the Owls:
Football League/Premiership

| Venue | P | W | D | L | F | A |
|---|---|---|---|---|---|---|
| Home | 64 | 45 | 9 | 10 | 159 | 67 |
| Away | 64 | 18 | 8 | 38 | 89 | 132 |
| Totals | 128 | 63 | 17 | 48 | 248 | 199 |

| FA Cup | | | | | | |
|---|---|---|---|---|---|---|
| Away | 2 | 1 | 0 | 1 | 3 | 3 |

| League Cup | | | | | | |
|---|---|---|---|---|---|---|
| Home | 2 | 1 | 0 | 1 | 2 | 2 |

Fourteen goals were scored in the two League encounters between the teams in 1892-93 - Aston Villa won 5-1 at home but lost 5-3 away. Fred Wheldon scored a hat-trick when the Owls were beaten 5-2 at Villa Park on the opening day of the 1897-98 League season.

The Wednesday-Villa League game at Olive Grove, Sheffield on 26 November 1898 was abandoned due to fading light with almost 11 minutes still left to play. The match had been delayed by half-an-hour owing to the non-arrival of the referee, Aaron Scragg, a Crewe fuel agent and FA Councillor. He eventually turned up at the ground during the half-time interval and consequently it was far too dark for him to complete the full 90 minutes. The Owls were 3-1 up at the time, but a request from both sides for the result to stand was rejected by the Football League committee who ordered Villa to travel back to Sheffield on 13 March 1899 to play out the remaining 630 seconds. In that time Wednesday added a fourth goal to win the contest 4-1. Villa made one change from the 'first game' (Bill Garraty for goalscorer Fred Bedingfield) while the Owls made five. Villa went on to win the League title that season.

When Villa beat Wednesday 8-1 at home in February 1907, Harry Hampton scored a hat-trick and the following season Villa rattled in another eight goals past the Owls, winning 5-0 at home and 3-2 in Yorkshire.

It was goalless at half-time in the Villa v Wednesday League game on 12 March 1910. The final score was 5-0 to Villa, Joe Bache scoring twice and making two others.

Sheffield Wednesday's heaviest League defeat is 10-0 at the hands of Aston Villa (away) on 5 October 1912. In this game hot-shot Harry

Hampton created a club record by scoring five times (equalled later by four other players). The desperate Owls' goalkeeper was Teddy Davison.

A nine-goal thriller (including a hat-trick from Joe Beresford) ended in Villa's favour by 5-4 in December 1927, but Wednesday then beat Villa 2-0 on the last day of that season to retain their First Division status. Both Villa and Wednesday won their respective home League games over each other by 4-1 in 1928-29, and in December 1932 the Owls raced to a 6-3 win at Villa Park, only to lose 2-0 at Hillsborough later in the season!

Only 9,604 fans saw Villa beat Wednesday 2-1 at home on 31 March 1954 - the lowest attendance in the First Division that season.

The Owls won 6-3 at Hillsborough in August 1954 (Jackie Sewell, a future Villa player scoring twice) but crashed 5-0 at Villa Park in April 1957. The Owls also lost 5-2 at Hillsborough eight months later (Villa were 3-0 up at half-time) and at the end of that season Wednesday ' were relegated to the Second Division...again!

Johnny Dixon played his last League game for Villa and Charlie Aitken his first when Sheffield Wednesday visited Villa

*Ronnie Starling after retiring.*

Park in April 1961.

Villa completed the double over the Owls on their way to promotion from Division Two in 1974-75. They won 3-1 at home and 4-0 at Hillsborough, Brian Little netting twice in the latter contest which clinched Villa's place in the top flight.

Dalian Atkinson, Cyrille Regis and Steve Staunton all scored on their League debuts for Villa in the 3-2 win at Hillsborough on the opening day of the 1991-92 season....as manager Ron Atkinson returned to haunt his former club!

Andy Townsend's run of 128 consecutive appearances ended when a back injury prevented him from playing in the 2-2 home draw with the Owls in December 1993.

Bob Chatt scored both Villa's goals when they lost to Wednesday in a 3rd round FA Cup-tie in Sheffield in 1894 and there were 57,000 fans present to see Villa beat the Owls 1-0, also in Yorkshire, in a 4th round tie in March 1914.

Despite a goal by Garry Thompson (against his former club) Villa went out of the League Cup to Wednesday in the 4th round in November 1987.

Players with both clubs include: D Atkinson, E Barrett, GW Beeson, A Blair, B Carbone, F Carr, TB Craig, G De Bilde, S Grayson, J Harrop (Owls reserve), PT Heard, HV Henshall, T Johnson, P King, A Lescott (Villa reserve), W McAuley, J Nibloe (also Owls coach), JT Palethorpe, MJ Pinner, CL Roberts (Villa & Owls reserve), J Sewell, GR Shaw, G Shelton, S Stainrod, RW Starling, GT Stephenson, I Taylor, GL Thompson, G Whittingham, C Wilson (Villa reserve), JE Worrall (Villa reserve).

Also: Ron Atkinson & J McMullan (managers of both clubs), WH Walker (Villa player, Owls manager), E Davison (Villa reserve, Owls player-manager & manager), C Dobson (Owls player, Villa coach).

## SHELL, FRANCIS HARRY

Born: Hackney, London, 2 December 1912. Died: Axminster, July 1988.

Career: Ilford & District Schools, Barking (April 1930-May 1936), Ford Sports, Dagenham (August 1936), Aston Villa (professional, May 1937), guested for Northampton and Walsall during WW2, Birmingham City (September 1946), Hereford United (June 1947), Mansfield Town (August 1947). Retired in May 1948.

Frank Shell, a big, strapping inside or centre-forward, entered the professional arena at the rather late age of 24. He quickly adapted to League soccer and formed a fine understanding with Frank Broome in the Villa side in 1937-38. He scored 13 goals in 31 games for Villa before moving to neighbours Birmingham City with whom he failed to get a first team outing!

## SHELTON, GARY

Born: Nottingham, 21 March 1958.

Career: St Bernadette's School (Nottingham), Notts County Schools, Parkhead FC, Walsall (apprentice, June 1972, professional, March 1976), Aston Villa (£60,000, January 1978), Notts County (on loan, March 1980), Sheffield Wednesday (£50,000, March 1982), Oxford United (£150,000, July 1987), Bristol City (August 1989), Rochdale (on loan, February 1994), Chester City (July

1994, as player/assistant manager and coach under Kevin Ratcliffe). Soon after Chester had been relegated from the Football League, Shelton was appointed reserve team coach (under Gary Megson) at West Bromwich Albion (July 2000).

Capped once by England at Under-21 level earlier in his career, creative and hard-working midfielder Gary Shelton drew up an exceptionally fine record as a professional footballer, appearing in well over 550 competitive matches and scoring 62 goals.

After 27 games and eight goals for Villa, he helped Sheffield Wednesday win promotion to the First Division in 1984.

## SHERIFF OF LONDON CHARITY SHIELD

Aston Villa played for this prestigious Sheriff of London Charity Shield on three occasions:

| | | |
|---|---|---|
| 11 March 1899 | v Queen's Park (Glasgow), drew 0-0 (aet) | Att. 14,000 |
| 8 November 1899 | v Corinthians, lost 2-1 (Garraty) | Att. 8,000 |
| 2 March 1901 | v Corinthians, won 1-0 (Athersmith) | Att. 10,000 |

All three games were staged at The Crystal Palace.

## SHREWSBURY TOWN

Villa's playing record against the Shrews:

Football League

| Venue | P | W | D | L | F | A |
|---|---|---|---|---|---|---|
| Home | 3 | 3 | 0 | 0 | 6 | 0 |
| Away | 3 | 1 | 1 | 1 | 4 | 4 |
| Totals | 6 | 4 | 1 | 1 | 10 | 4 |

THE COMPLETE ENCYCLOPAEDIA OF ASTON VILLA F.C.    THE COMPLETE ENCYCLOPAEDIA OF ASTON VILLA F.C.

242

Aston Villa first met the Shrews in a Third Division game at Villa Park on Boxing Day 1970. A crowd of 31,186 saw Pat McMahon and Bruce Rioch find the net in Villa's 2-0 victory. Later that season despite Fred Turnbull's goal, Villa lost 2-1 at Gay Meadow.

The following season, on their way to winning the Third Division title, Villa took three points off Shrewsbury, winning 3-0 at home and drawing 1-1 away, Chris Nicholl's goal earning a point in the latter contest.

The other two encounters took place in 1987-88 (Division 2). Villa won them both - 2-1 at home and 1-0 away - Warren Aspinall scoring in each match.

Players with both clubs include: NLG Blake, C Boden, PF Broadbent, R Butcher (Villa reserve), D Geddis, GH Hampton, R Hopkins, RD Hughes, JWE Jones, MAW Jones, M Kenning, GF Lee, E Malpass (Villa reserve), M Moralee, TS Morrall, A Mulraney, BA Olney, B Ormsby, JTS Phillips, D Pountney, IH Price, D Roberts, GR Shaw, DP Spink (Villa reserve), B Stobart, A Wakeman, T Wood.
Also: G Turner (Shrews player-manager, Villa manager).

### SHUTT, HARTLEY GEORGE
Born: Burnley, 1874. Died: Nottingham
Career: Brierfield FC, Nelson, Bolton Wanderers, Swindon Town, Millwall Athletic, Aston Villa (September 1900), Hucknall Town (1904), Beasley RCA (1906).
An effective, hard-tackling full-back with a tremendous right-foot, Hartley Shutt was a fine partner to Jimmy Crabtree in 1901-02, making 26 senior appearances after taking over from Howard Spencer. He lost his place when Spencer returned the following season and subsequently drifted down the scale. Before moving to Villa Park, Shutt had made 83 Southern League appearances for Swindon and 28 for Millwall.

### SIDEBOTTOM, GEOFFREY
Born: Mapplewell, Yorkshire, 29 December 1936
Career: Mapplewell Village Youths, Wath Wanderers, Wolverhampton Wanderers (professional, January 1954), Aston Villa (February 1961), Scunthorpe United (January 1965), New York Royals/Generals (1968) and then coached the Columbia University side in the USA before signing for Brighton & Hove Albion (January 1969). Retired through injury, May 1971.
Despite being told by his doctor not to play football because of a chest complaint, goalkeeper Geoff Sidebottom developed into a fine understudy to Bert Williams at Molineux before moving to Villa Park. There he became reserve to another ex-Molineux man, Nigel Sims, but managed 88 appearances for Villa whom he served four years, having gained a League Cup winners tankard in 1961. He retired in 1971 after failing to recover from a serious head injury, suffered in a reserve game in October 1970. He was rewarded by Brighton with a Testimonial in 1971.

### SIMMONDS, HENRY RICHMOND
Born: Birmingham, June 1858. Died: Birmingham, 1914
Career: Hockley St John's Athletic, Aston Waverley, Aston Villa (July 1878). Retired through injury (broken ankle) May 1890.
Brother of Joe, Harry Simmonds was an ever-present in Villa's defence during

the 1880-81 season. A quality footballer, strong and resilient, always urging his team on, he played in 10 FA Cup games for the club before injury ended his career.

### SIMMONDS, JOSEPH OSCAR
Born: Birmingham, May 1861. Died: Birmingham, 1931.
Career: Hockley Hill Council School, Key Hill Methodists, Hockley St John's Athletic, Aston Villa (August 1882). Retired through injury (damaged shoulder), May 1887.
Slim-looking defender, nothing like his elder brother, Joe Simmonds was fast, aggressive when required, always driving forward. He wore a tight-fitting red polo cap and consequently was dubbed 'Red Cap' by his team-mates. He lacked height but not pluck and woe-betide an opponent if his cap fell off! Simmonds made 22 FA Cup appearances for Villa, gaining an FA Cup winners' medal in 1887.

### SIMMONS, DAVID JOHN
Born: Ryde, Isle-of-Wight, 24 October 1948.
Career: Gosport Borough Schools, Gosport Boys, Arsenal (amateur June 1963, professional, November 1965), Bournemouth (on loan, November 1968), Aston Villa (£15,000, February 1969), Walsall (on loan, October 1970), Colchester United (December 1970), Cambridge United (March 1973), Brentford (March 1974), Cambridge United (November 1975-May 1976).
As a youngster Dave Simmons was almost killed when he fell

through a plate glass window, receiving multiple cuts and lacerations. He survived, thankfully going on to have a very useful career as an out-and-out striker in the lower Divisions, scoring over 50 goals in almost 200 competitive appearances (48 coming in 179 League matches). He didn't do much at Highbury, Bournemouth or Villa Park (seven goals in 19 outings for the claret & blues including a strike on his debut against Charlton in February 1969) but thereafter he became a star, helping Colchester knock mighty Leeds out of the FA Cup in 1971.

### SIMOD CUP
Villa's record in this competition reads:

| Venue | P | W | D | L | F | A |
|---|---|---|---|---|---|---|
| Home | 2 | 1 | 0 | 1 | 6 | 5 |
| Away | 1 | 0 | 0 | 1 | 1 | 2 |
| Totals | 3 | 1 | 0 | 2 | 7 | 7 |

Aston Villa first entered this sponsored competition in season 1987-88, but they crashed out in the opening round, beaten 5-0 at home by Bradford City in front of 4,217 spectators.
The following season Birmingham City were hammered 6-0 at Villa Park in the first round before a crowd of 8,324, Alan McInally netting twice but at the next hurdle, away to Derby County, a crowd of 10,086 saw Villa eliminated 2-1, McInally again their scorer.

### SIMPSON, WILLIAM SWAN
Born: Cowdenbeath, 1 May 1907. Deceased.
Career: Cowdenbeath & District School, Donibristle Colliery, Cowdenbeath YMCA, Foulford White Rose, Musselburgh Bruntonians, Dunbar, Clyde (April 1928), Aston Villa November 1931), Cowdenbeath (July 1935), Northampton Town (August 1936), Walsall (July 1937-May 1939). Did not figure after WW2.

THE COMPLETE ENCYCLOPAEDIA OF ASTON VILLA F.C.     THE COMPLETE ENCYCLOPAEDIA OF ASTON VILLA F.C.

243

Tall, slender wing-half who loved to attack, Billy Simpson won a Junior International cap for Scotland v Ireland in March 1928 and at the time looked a useful prospect, but he failed to do the business in the First Division with Aston Villa and after scoring once in 29 games, he returned to Scotland. He later came back to England and did surprisngly well with Northampton (42 appearances) and Walsall (67 League outings, four goals).

## SIMS, NIGEL DAVID

Born: Coton-in-the-Elms, Burton-on-Trent, 9 August 1931.
Career: Coton Swifts, Stapenhill, Wolverhampton Wanderers (amateur, August 1948, professional September 1948), Aston Villa (March 1956), Arsenal (guest, May 1959), Peterborough United (September 1964), Toronto City (1965), Toronto Italia (1966). Retired on his return to England.

For his size and build Nigel Sims was a very agile goalkeeper. With Bert Williams bedded in as first-choice 'keeper at Molineux, he bided his time in the reserves, having less than 40 senior outings, although he did win a 'Young' England cap v England in 1954 before transferring Villa Park in 1956. He performed superbly well over the next eight years, amassing 309 senior appearances, gaining an FA Cup winners medal (1957), a Second Division championship medal (1960) and a League Cup winners' tankard (1961). He also played for the Football League XI against the League of Ireland at Leeds in October 1957, was voted Villa's 'Terrace Trophy' winner in 1958 and even guested for Arsenal! Sims left Villa for Peterborough in 1964 and over the next two years played his football in Canada. On his return to England he worked for an Insurance Company in Wolverhampton and now lives in Swansea.

*Nigel Sims in action against Chelsea.*

## SIMS, STEPHEN FRANK

Born: Lincoln, 2 July 1957
Career: Lincoln County Schools, Lincoln City (trialist), Leicester City (apprentice, August 1973, professional July 1974), Watford (£175,000, December 1978), Notts County (£50,000, September 1984), Watford (£50,000, October 1986), Aston Villa (£50,000, June 1987-).

A centre-half with a footballing father (Frank, a Lincoln City club man in the 1950s) Steve Sims made a rapid rise through the ranks at Filbert Street. He appeared in 87 first-class games for the Foxes, gained 10 England Under-21 caps and played in one 'B' international, having

earlier represented his country as a Youth team player. He switched to Vicarage Road in 1978 for a then record outlay for a Third Division club of £175,000 and made over 150 League appearances for the Hornets in his first spell. He also did well at Meadow Lane (85 League games) before going back to Watford from where he joined Villa in 1987 - signed by his old boss Graham Taylor! Partnering Martin Keown at the heart of the defence Sims duly helped Villa win promotion from Division Two in his first season at the club, but after that he struggled with injuries and was eventually released in the summer of 1989, having made 47 senior appearances in the claret and blue colours.

## SINGLETON, HERBERT

Born: Manchester, June 1900. Died: c 1958
Career: Manchester Central, Aston Villa (trialist, November 1923, professional December 1923). Retired after fracturing his skull in a reserve team game on 28 November 1926.

A very capable goalkeeper, Bert Singleton was signed as cover for Tommy Jackson and made two first team appearances before receiving his injury.

## SIX, DIDIER

Born: France, 21 August 1954
Career: Lens, Olympique Marseille, Valencia (Spain), RFC Bruges (Belgium), Strasbourg, Vfb Stuttgart (Germany), Mulhouse FC (France), Aston Villa (September 1984), Metz (June 1985).

Didier Six had already scored 163 goals in 421 games in European League football (including 72 in 152 games for Spanish giants Valencia and 30 in one season for Stuttgart) before moving to Villa Park in 1984. Unfortunately he never settled in England, was always struggling to find his form and after netting twice in his 18 outings for Villa he returned 'home' to France at the end of the 1984-85 season. Six, the first Frenchman to play in the Football League, won 52 caps for his country (13 goals scored). He also played in two World Cups and ran his own TV programme in Lille.

## SIX-A-SIDE TOURNAMENTS

During the 1980s and early '90s, Aston Villa entered several six-a-side tournaments (including those sponsored by Guinness and Atari) ....and they did very well.

In January 1990, they took part in a prestigious one organised by the French club, Paris St Germain, and after beating Nantes 3-2, they lost 2-1 to FC Porto, then drew 2-2 with the same Portuguese side before succumbing to a 6-4 defeat at the hands of the Yugoslavian outfit Partizan Belgrade.

## SKEA, DAVID FREDERICK

Born: Scotland, February 1869. Died: Scotland.
Career: Arbroath (1888-92), Aston Villa (July 1892), Darwen (July 1893), Bury (November 1893), Leicester Fosse (August 1894), Swindon Town (May 1896), New Brompton (£10, June 1897-1899).

As he got older David Skea became more of an inside-forward 'hot-shot' who scored Leicester's first-ever goal in the Football League, recorded the Foxes' first hat-trick at the same level and netted the club's first penalty!

He went on to hit 37 goals in only 52 outings for Leicester - having earlier struggled with all his previous clubs, popping in just one goal in one game for Villa (v Notts County in December 1892). He later did well in the Southern League with Swindon and New Brompton (Gillingham).

Skea's spell with Swindon was cut short following disciplinary measures taken by the club after he had arrived late for training 'in an intoxicated condition.' He was transfer-listed at £25 and actually spent six months out of the game before joining New Brompton for just a tenner!

## SKILLER, LEON FERDINAND

Born: Penzance, Cornwall, 1885. Died: Devon, July 1936
Career: Leytonstone, Leyton (1906), Aston Villa (September 1908), Swindon Town (July 1909-May 1922). Retired.
After 54 games for Leyton, long-legged goalkeeper Leon Skiller, active on his line with a safe pair of hands, made just one senior appearance for Aston Villa, deputising for Billy George against Nottingham Forest in January 1909. After leaving Villa Park he did exceedingly well between the posts for Swindon, starring in more than 300 League and Cup encounters for the Wiltshire club.

## SLADE, HOWARD CHARLES

Born: Bath, 20 January 1891. Died: Doncaster, April 1971.
Career: Bath City (1910), Stourbridge (1911), Nottingham Forest (trialist, 1912), Aston Villa (June 1913), Huddersfield Town (March 1914), Middlesbrough (October 1922), Darlington (September 1925-May 1927), Folkestone (season 1927-28). Thereafter coached Rotherham United and Aldershot before being engaged as an instructor by the Middlesex Schools Authority in October 1934. He also played cricket for Lockwood during his time with Huddersfield.
Durable inside-forward Charlie Slade had just three first-team outings for Villa in season 1913-14. He then left to join Huddersfield Town where he was converted into a half-back, going on to appear in 129 games for the Terriers before assisting Middlesbrough and finally Darlington. He lined up in two FA Cup Finals for Huddersfield, gaining a loser's medal in 1920 (versus Villa) and a winners' prize two years later (v PNE). He also helped the Yorkshire club gain promotion to the First Division in the initial post-war campaign. He broke his leg in November 1916 against Notts County and battled hard to regain full fitness.

## SLAVEN BELUPO (Minos)

Villa's playing record against the Croatian side:
InterToto Cup

| Venue | P | W | D | L | F | A |
|---|---|---|---|---|---|---|
| Home | 1 | 1 | 0 | 0 | 2 | 0 |
| Away | 1 | 0 | 0 | 1 | 1 | 2 |
| Totals | 2 | 1 | 0 | 1 | 3 | 2 |

Villa qualified for the semi-final of the 2001-02 InterToto Cup with a hard-earned aggregate victory over a tough Croatian side.

After David Ginola's vital 'away' goal in front of barely 3,000 spectators, Lee Hendrie struck twice to earn Villa a 2-0 home victory in front of 21,412 spectators to set them up with a semi-final showdown with the French side Stade Rennias.

## SLOLEY, Richard

Born: London, 1895. Died: 1964.
Career: Corinthians, Cambridge University, Brentford (season 1913-14), Corinthians (1917-18), Ason Villa (on loan for three weeks, October 1919), Corinthians (October 1919-22).
An amateur inside-forward throughout his career, Dick Sloley won England international caps at this level and was taken 'on loan' by Aston Villa for two games when senior players were absent through illness and injury.

## SLOVAN BRATISLAVA

Villa's playing record against the Slovakians:
UEFA Cup

| Venue | P | W | D | L | F | A |
|---|---|---|---|---|---|---|
| Home | 1 | 1 | 0 | 0 | 2 | 1 |
| Away | 1 | 0 | 1 | 0 | 0 | 0 |
| Totals | 2 | 1 | 1 | 0 | 2 | 1 |

Aston Villa made progress into the 2nd round of the 1993-94 UEFA Cup competition after a hard-fought 2-1 aggregate victory over Slovan Bratislava. Just under 11,000 fans saw the first leg end goalless in Tehelne Pole on 15 September and then a fortnight later 24,461 fans saw Villa squeeze through with goals by Dalian Atkinson and Andy Townsend.
Associated with both clubs: J Venglos.

## SLUEEWENHOEK, JOHN CORNELIUS

Born: Wednesfield, 26 February 1944. Died: Birmingham, July 1989.
Career: Aston Villa (junior, June 1959, professional February 1961), Birmingham City (£45,000, November 1967), Torquay United (on loan, March-May 1971), Oldham Athletic (July 1971). Retired from League competition in 1972.
Son of a Dutch parachute instructor, John 'Tulip' Slueewenhoek was a fine centre-half, strong in the air, dominant on the ground. He was born in the Black Country and as a youngster was brought up on cheese and stout! He went on to amass 260 appearances for Villa (one goal

scored) winning England honours at Schoolboy, Youth and Under-23 levels. He also represented the Football League and collected the supporters' 'Terrace Trophy' award in 1963-64. He was sidelined with a troublesome knee at St Andrew's which resulted in him moving to Boundary Park in 1971 after he had been with Torquay on loan. He served the Latics for just a season before a weight problem caused him to quit League soccer. He did play occasionally in the Cheshire League and for the Aston Villa All Stars, as well as working in the lottery office at Villa Park. Slueewenhoek died of a heart attack in 1989, aged 45.
His son, Kris, was a junior footballer with Wolverhampton Wanderers and Derby County.

*John Slueewenhoek*

THE COMPLETE ENCYCLOPAEDIA OF ASTON VILLA F.C.    THE COMPLETE ENCYCLOPAEDIA OF ASTON VILLA F.C.

245

## SMALL, BRYAN
Born: Birmingham, 15 November 1971.
Career: Aston Villa (April 1988, professional July 1990), Birmingham City (on loan, September 1994), Bolton Wanderers (free transfer, March 1996), Luton Town (on loan, September 1997), Bradford City (on loan, December 1997), Bury (free transfer, January 1998), Stoke City (free transfer, July 1998-May 2000), Carlisle and Brentford (trials), Walsall (January 2001).
Tenacious left wing-back Bryan Small, an England Youth and Under-21 international (12 caps won at the latter level), played in a total of 45 games for Aston Villa before leaving the club in 1996 (after a loan spell at neighbouring St Andrew's). He made over 100 senior appearances during the next four years prior to his release by the Icelandic-run Stoke City club!

## SMART, HERBERT HORACE
Born: Smethwick, April 1892. Died: Birmingham, 1951
Career: Bilston United (1910), Aston Villa (January 1914), Wolverhampton Wanderers (December 1919), Willenhall (August 1920), Dudley Town (1924). Retired in 1929.
Inside-left Herby Smart was restricted in what he could do. He was given just one League outing by Villa - replacing Joe Bache in an away game at Newcastle in April 1914. He failed to make the grade at Wolves either!

## SMART, THOMAS
Born: Blackheath, 20 September 1896. Died: 10 June 1968.
Career: Rowley Regis Schools, Blackheath Town, Army football (1915-18) Halesowen (July 1919), Aston Villa (January 1920), Brierley Hill Alliance (May 1934). Retired in 1936.
Aston Villa signed full-back Tommy Smart from non-League football in January 1920. Three months later he was clutching an FA Cup winners medal after Huddersfield Town had been beaten 1-0 in that year's Final.
He made great strides in top-class soccer in double-quick time and went on to become a real quality defender, amassing 452 senior appearances for Villa and scoring eight goals. The barrel-chested Smart - nicknamed 'Tic' - was a fierce tackler, and his sheer size used to place a certain amount of apprehension in the eyes of the opposing forwards! One report stated that he was built like a 'buffalo and kicked like a mule'. In fact, he had a war-cry 'Thik Hai' (Hindustani language) which he yelled out quite often when clearing his lines. He had picked this up during his Army service in India.
Forming a formidable partnership in the Villa rearguard with Tommy Mort, Smart won five full caps for England and in 1924 added a Cup runners-up medal to the one he won four years earlier. Smart, who would often turn up for morning training on his bike wearing a flat cap, eventually handed over his position in the Villa side to Danny Blair.

## SMITH
In season 1949-50 there were no fewer than SEVEN Smiths associated with Aston Villa football club. Antony, Herbert, Jeff and Leslie were all players; Billy Smith was the club secretary and Edward Smith and Norman Smith were both Directors.

## SMITH, GEORGE
Born: Preston, 12 July 1879. Died: Southampton, 3 July 1908.
Career: Leyland FC, Preston North End (July 1899), Aston Villa (July 1901), Blackburn Rovers (October 1901), New Brompton (December 1901), Plymouth Argyle (August 1906), Southampton (August 1907-April 1908).
Originally a half-back, George Smith ended his career as a utility forward able to occupy three different positions. A direct player,

nothing flashy about his game, he was a good, old fashioned footballer who made over 125 appearances at competitive level, but managed only five with Villa.
He collapsed and died suddenly at his home in Southampton just before his 29th birthday.

## SMITH, GORDON MELVILLE
Born: Glasgow, 3 July 1954.
Career: Schoolboy football, St Johnstone (amateur June 1969, professional July 1971), Aston Villa (August 1976), Tottenham Hotspur (£150,000, February 1979), Wolverhampton Wanderers (August 1982). Quit Britain for South African football in June 1984 and later (January 1985) he switched to the United States of America where he spent four years playing indoor soccer for Pittsburgh Spirit before injury forced him into an early retirement at the end of the 1989 season. He now works for an advertising company based in Glasgow.
After representing his country at Youth team level, industrious full-back Gordon Smith went on to gain four Scottish Under-23 caps. He did well North of the Border before appearing in 92 senior games for Aston Villa (four goals scored), the majority coming in his first two seasons at the club when he partnered John Gidman. He gained a League Cup winners' medal in 1977, albeit as a substitute, but then dropped out of favour, hence his transfer to White Hart Lane. He played in 67 first-class games for Spurs, helping the London club re-establish itself in the First Division. Upset by injuries he moved to Molineux in 1982 and was a member of the Wolves side that won promotion from Division Two. He then lost his place in the defence, and that led him to making the big decision to go overseas where he did well for a number of years.

*Gordon M. Smith*

## SMITH, HERBERT HENRY
Born: Birmingham, 17 December 1922. Died: Birmingham, 11 January 1996.
Career: Moor Green (1945), Aston Villa (professional, May 1947), Southend United (June 1954-April 1955), Moor Green (August 1955-May 1957). Retired.
A small, pencil-slim winger with good pace and ability, 'Little Herbie' Smith was only 5ft 3ins tall and weighed barely nine stone, but he could battle it out with the meanest and toughest defenders in the game. During his seven years at Villa Park, despite there being an abundance of wingers, he managed to appear in 51 senior games for the club, scoring eight goals, his best season coming in 1951-52 (26 games). He made his debut for Villa in the FA Cup 2nd replay against Bolton in January 1949 and scored the winner in extra-time. However, he performed very well and consistently in Villa's Central League side before transferring to Southend in 1954. Smith ended his career back at Moor Green and was later keenly associated with the Mackadown Sports & Social Club near Lea Village, Birmingham.

## SMITH, LESLIE GEORGE FREDERICK
Born: Ealing, London, 23 March 1918. Died: Lichfield, 20 May 1995.
Career: St John's Grammar School (Brentford), Petersham FC, Brentford (junior, 1933), Wimbledon (August 1934), Hayes (July 1935), Brentford (professional, March 1936), Aston Villa (£7,500, October

*Les Smith (1945-52).*

1945), Brentford (June 1952), Kidderminster Harriers (player-manager, August 1953), Wolverhampton Wanderers (scout, 1954-55). Managed Aston Villa Old Stars (1960-65) and also ran a successful electrical business in Aston for a number of years.

'Cockney' Leslie Smith was Aston Villa's 'Will-o'-the'Wisp' outside-left who thrilled the crowds with his precocious confidence, exquisite ball-control, wing wizardry, dash and a goalscoring and goal-making technique that earned him England recognition.

After playing in Wimbledon's losing 1935 FA Amateur Cup Final side, Smith won 13 Wartime and Victory international caps as well as one at senior level (1939). He also played for the FA (in Romania, Italy and Yugoslavia) and the RAF, during the War guesting for Chelsea (winning a League South Cup winners' medal in 1945), Leicester City, Manchester City and WBA. He scored 37 goals in 197 League and FA Cup appearances for Aston Villa and also had 22 outings (three goals) in the transitional campaign of 1945-46. He made his Villa debut at Plymouth on 3 November 1945 (League South) and his 'senior' bow followed on 5 January 1946 when he celebrated with a goal in a 2-1 FA Cup defeat at Coventry. His Football League baptism in a Villa shirt arrived on the opening day of 1946-47 (31 August) when Middlesbrough won 1-0 in the Midlands!

Smith held on to his place on the left-wing until the 1951-52 season when he was replaced by Billy Goffin. Besides his 181 League outings for Villa he also starred in 76 games for the Bees (nine goals).

Smith spent his later years living in Lichfield where he died in 1995, aged 77.

## SMITH, LESLIE JOSEPH
Born: Halesowen, 24 December 1927.
Career: Wolverhampton Wanderers (amateur, June 1945, professional April 1946), Aston Villa (£25,000, February 1956-January 1960). Retired through injury.
Leslie Smith was a fast, clever and direct winger, who made his Football League debut for Wolves in 1947-48. Owing to the form of Johnny Hancocks and Jimmy Mullen, he was mainly a reserve at Molineux and played in only four games in the 1953-54 championship-winning season. He finally broke through on a regular basis the following year, starring in 34 games as Wolves finished runners-up to Chelsea in the First

*Leslie Smith (1956-60)*

Division. After scoring over 20 goals in just under 100 appearances for the Wanderers, Smith moved to Villa Park in 1956. There he found less competition and with Jackie Sewell initially his main partner on the right, he went on to net 25 goals in 130 outings, collecting an FA Cup winners' medal at the end of his first season at the club. An Achilles tendon injury forced Smith into an early retirement on 23 January 1960. He now lives in Halesowen.

## SMITH, NORMAN
Born in Birmingham in 1900, Norman Smith was a former Handsworth Grammar School pupil, who became an Aston Villa Director in 1939, holding office until 1968, and spending the last two years with the club as its Chairman (October 1966 to December 1968).

Earlier, in 1922, Smith was appointed secretary of the Birmingham Boys' Association, which later became the Birmingham Youth Committee. On the change of name, Smith moved with the Committee to the Birmingham Education Department where he continued to work for many years, even when he was Chairman of Aston Villa.

Smith had taken up refereeing at the age of 20 and after graduating through the various local and intermediate competitions, he went on to officiate in Football League and FA Cup matches. He later became treasurer of the Association of the Football League Referees & Linesmen. He was also a member of the Council of the Birmingham County FA (elected in 1925) and was its Honorary Treasurer for several years. Smith, who also served on the FA Disciplinary Committee, died in 1980.

## SMITH, STEPHEN
Born: Hazelslade, Halesowen 7 January 1874. Died: Benson, Oxon, 19 May 1935.
Career: Cannock & Rugeley Colliery, Cannock Town, Rugeley Ceal, Hednesford Town (September 1891), Aston Villa (August 1893), Portsmouth (May 1901), New Brompton (July 1906, then player-manager December 1906-May 1908). Lived in Portsmouth until 1932 when he took over a business, Roke Stores, in Benson, Oxfordshire, where he remained until his death at the age of 61.

Steve Smith was an accomplished outside-left, very tricky, who could pass a ball with pin-point accuracy,

*Steve Smith*

whip in a stunning shot and was a player who seemed to rise to the big occasion! Signed by Fred Rinder directly after working a 10-hour shift as a haulage machine operator at the coalface, Smith shared the left-wing berth with Albert Woolley in Villa's League championship-winning season of 1893-94. He then figured prominently himself in the sides that captured the same title four times in five years: 1896-97-99-1900. He also gained two FA Cup winners' medals (in 1895 and 1897) and was capped by England against Scotland at Everton in 1895. He made 194 senior appearances for Villa and netted 42 goals, making scores of others! After leaving Villa Park he helped Pompey with the Southern League crown in 1902.

## SOUTH SHIELDS (GATESHEAD)
Aston Villa have never met the North-east club at any level of competitive football.
Players with both clubs include: J Burridge, RS Chatt, AW Kerr (Gateshead colts), JW Laidlaw, JG McLaverty, AE Surtees.

THE COMPLETE ENCYCLOPAEDIA OF ASTON VILLA F.C.    THE COMPLETE ENCYCLOPAEDIA OF ASTON VILLA F.C.

247

## SOUTHAMPTON (ST MARY'S)

Villa's playing record against the Saints:
Football League/Premiership

| Venue | P | W | D | L | F | A |
|---|---|---|---|---|---|---|
| Home | 26 | 13 | 9 | 4 | 41 | 18 |
| Away | 26 | 6 | 7 | 13 | 25 | 44 |
| Totals | 52 | 19 | 16 | 17 | 66 | 62 |

FA Cup

| | | | | | | |
|---|---|---|---|---|---|---|
| Home | 3 | 2 | 0 | 1 | 4 | 3 |
| Away | 2 | 0 | 2 | 0 | 3 | 3 |
| Totals | 5 | 2 | 2 | 1 | 7 | 6 |

League Cup

| | | | | | | |
|---|---|---|---|---|---|---|
| Home | 1 | 1 | 0 | 0 | 4 | 0 |
| Away | 1 | 0 | 0 | 1 | 1 | 2 |
| Totals | 2 | 1 | 0 | 1 | 5 | 2 |

Wartime

| | | | | | | |
|---|---|---|---|---|---|---|
| Home | 1 | 1 | 0 | 0 | 2 | 0 |
| Away | 1 | 1 | 0 | 0 | 5 | 3 |
| Totals | 2 | 2 | 0 | 0 | 7 | 3 |

Aston Villa first met Southampton at League level on 5 September 1936 - and they celebrated with a 4-0 win - their first at Villa Park in the Second Division. A crowd of 45,000 saw the action.

There was no League action between the clubs from 16 January 1938 until 5 September 1966 when Saints re-opened with a 1-0 win at Villa Park. The return fixture that season saw Villa officially relegated to the Second Division after they had crashed 6-2 at The Dell on 13 May 1967.

In February 1986, a crowd of 8,456 saw Villa draw 0-0 with Southampton. This was the lowest League attendance at Villa Park for 29 years, since April 1957, when 8,252 attended the First Division clash with Sunderland.

Goalkeeper Nigel Spink was sent-off when Villa crashed 4-1 at The Dell in a Premiership match in April 1994. Neil Cox took over for the last 12 minutes, conceding one goal.

Dion Dublin scored a hat-trick when Villa beat the Saints 4-1 away in November 1998. It was only Dublin's second outing for the club

*Tony Barton - Manager of Villa, assistant-manager of Saints.*

following his move from Coventry City.

After producing one of their worst performances of the season, Villa lost 2-0 at Southampton in November 2000.

Over 59,000 fans saw Second Division Villa knock First Division Saints out of the FA Cup by 2-1 in a 4th round replay in January 1969 (after a 2-2 draw at The Dell). Seven years later, again at Villa Park, a crowd of 44,623 looked on as Southampton, on their way to a Wembley triumph, knocked Villa out of the competition, also with a 2-1 replay victory. The sides had drawn 1-1 in the first game.

Gareth Southgate's goal was enough to send Villa through to the 5th round of the FA Cup in January 1994.

In December 1999 Villa cruised through to the 5th round of the League Cup with an emphatic 4-0 home win over Saints, Dion Dublin scoring twice. Players with both clubs include: JP Allen (Saints WW2 guest), T Bowman, AF Brown, J Burridge, LC Chatterley (also Saints coach and Youth Development Officer), R Dorsett (Saints WW2 guest), M Draper, GA Ephgrave (Villa reserve), G Garratt, S Gray (later Saints coach & manager), G Hadley, H Hadley, GC Harkus, WIG Kingdon, AF McLoughlin, F Moss jnr (Saints WW2 guest), CJ Nicholl (also Saints manager), J Reynolds, K Richardson, P Rideout, T Riley (Sainst reserve), B Sharp, FC Tully, A Vinall (Saints Amateur), ME Walters, JM Wilcox, AE Wood (no games for Saints).

Also: A Barton (Villa manager, Saints assistant-manager), R Graydon (Villa player, Saints coach).

## SOUTHEND UNITED

Villa's playing record against the Shrimpers:
FA Cup

| Venue | P | W | D | L | F | A |
|---|---|---|---|---|---|---|
| Away | 1 | 0 | 0 | 1 | 0 | 1 |

A crowd of almost 17,000 saw Villa embarrassingly knocked out of the FA Cup by the Shrimpers at Roots Hall in the 1st round in November 1971.

Players with both clubs include: H Barnes (Villa reserve), J Burridge, M Carruthers, JF Chambers, S Collymore, A Ducat, HJ Halse, IM Hamilton, H Humphries, JA Humphreys & VA Jones (Villa reserves), A Little, N Mackay, TJ Mooney (Villa reserve), J Neal, D Reid (Villa reserve), DG Rioch, HH Smith, AE Surtees, MR Thomas (Villa loanee), J Walters, AE Watkins, J Whitehouse.

Also: FH Broome (Villa player, United manager).

## SOUTHERN JUNIOR FLOODLIT CUP

Aston Villa entered this competition for the first time in 1969-70 and since then had a lot of success, including Final triumphs in 1973, 1975, 1976, 1979, 1980, 1981 and 1994

The SJFC was initially introduced in 1965 with only a limited number of clubs (mainly from the London area and the south of England) taking part.

West Ham United were finalists five times in seven years up to 1970 when Villa came in with all guns blazing. Nowadays between 50 and 60 clubs enter the competition annually which is second in status only to the FA Youth Cup in English soccer at intermediate level, although Villa haven't participated since February 1998 when they lost in that season's semi-final to Arsenal.

Villa's first-ever SJFC game was against Oxford United at home on 16 September 1970 which they won 4-0. They defeated Crystal Palace (after a replay) in the next round before going out to West Ham in London (0-2).

After knocking out Arsenal and gaining revenge over the Hammers in 1971-72, Villa were beaten 1-0 by Chelsea in the semi-final and en-route to their first Final victory the following season, Villa beat Oxford United (2-0), Cambridge United (5-0), neighbours West Bromwich Albion (2-1) and Bristol City (4-0 after two drawn games). Ipswich were then eclipsed 2-1 on aggregate in an evenly-contested Final.

As holders of the trophy, Villa were beaten in the first round by WBA in March 1974 but the competition was subsequently suspended and

THE COMPLETE ENCYCLOPAEDIA OF ASTON VILLA F.C.     THE COMPLETE ENCYCLOPAEDIA OF ASTON VILLA F.C.

248

as holders, Villa surprisingly were allowed to keep the trophy!

It was all systems go once more in season 1974-75 - and again Villa went on to defeat Ipswich Town in the Final, this time by 5-3 on aggregate (3-1 at home, 2-2 away). On their way through the rounds, Villa put out Colchester United 1-0, Plymouth Argyle 2-0, Bristol City 2-0 and Southampton 1-0 on aggregate in the semis. The Final was once more held over until the next season due to a build-up of fixtures.

Twelve months on, in 1975-76, in-form Aston Villa made it a hat-trick of triumphs when once again they overcame the Portman Road club in the Final, beating them 3-1 on aggregate (2-0 at home, 1-1 away). Orient 4-3, Coventry City 2-1, Bristol City 3-2 and Portsmouth 2-1 were eliminated in the earlier rounds.

Villa didn't do too well in 1976-77 (beaten in the first round proper by QPR) or in 1977-78 (when they crashed out to Orient in a second round replay).

But it was back to business in 1978-79 and another successful campaign for Villa as first Tottenham Hotspur 2-1, then Hereford United 3-0 (in a replay at Bodymoor Heath), Crystal Palace 4-0 and Coventry City 2-1, all fell by the wayside before Leicester City were defeated 1-0 in the two-legged Final.

The following season Villa retained the trophy again. In the earlier rounds they successfully knocked out Watford 4-0 (after a replay), Chelsea 2-1, Aldershot 6-1, Leicester City 2-1 and Bristol Rovers 2-1 in the semis, before taking on Queen's Park Rangers in the Final. They gained a 3-1 lead in the first leg and then held out for a narrow but deserved 5-4 triumph overall after a tightly-fought second leg at Craven Cottage.

Villa made it a 'double' hat-trick of victories in 1980-81, conquering the favourites West Ham United in the Final 2-1 on aggregate (2-0 away, 1-1 at home).

Oxford United were Villa's first round victims, beaten 2-0. Colchester United came next, 3-0, followed by Fulham 3-2 (after a replay) and then Arsenal 2-1 in the semis.

But the Hammers gained sweet revenge twelve months later when they took the trophy from Villa with a 2-0 aggregate victory in the Final of May 1982.

Villa had progressed win wins over Plymouth Argyle 4-1, Bournemouth 6-0, Southend United 1-0, Chelsea 2-1 and Birmingham City 3-2 the two-legged semi-final. But after a goalless first leg draw at Upton Park Villa were defeated in the return leg of the Final 2-0.

In season 1982-83, Villa lost in round two to Watford; they were defeated by Norwich City in the third round twelve months later and succumbed in another third round tie to Portsmouth (after three matches) in 1984-85.

After losing respectively in 1985-86 and 1986-87 to first Southend United in a second round replay and then to Arsenal in a first round, second replay by 5-2 (following 3-3 and 1-1 draws) Villa reached the semi-final stage of the SJFC competition in 1987-88 but missed out on another Final appearance by losing to Luton Town 4-2 at home, having looked in great shape after earlier round wins over Bristol City 5-1, Reading 6-1 and Charlton Athletic 3-0.

It was even more disappointing in 1988-89 when Villa lost in the Final to Southampton, going down 3-1 on aggregate (the score of the first leg at Villa Park). On their way through the rounds Villa put out Northampton Town 1-0, Bristol City 4-0, Gillingham 2-0 and Brentford 1-0.

Dumped out in the opening round of both the 1989-90 and 1990-91 tournaments by Luton Town 1-0 and Arsenal 2-0 respectively, Villa

powered through to another semi-final in 1991-92. They took out Portsmouth 4-2, West Ham 4-1 and Chelsea 3-1 before losing 1-0 to Arsenal in a replay at Villa Park (after forcing a 2-2 draw at Highbury). In 1992-93 Villa went out in round two to Leyton Orient (2-3) but bounced back in style with another Final victory twelve months later, Tottenham Hotspur the victims on this occasion.

Starting off with a 2-1 win over Fulham, Villa then accounted for Bournemouth 2-1, Bristol City 2-0 and Brighton 2-1 in a semi-final replay before beating Spurs 1-0 at home and drawing 2-2 away in the two-legged Final.

As holders (again) Villa lost to Wimbledon 5-2 in the third round in 1994-95 (after beating Oxford 4-0 and Northampton Town 6-3); went out to Norwich City in a second round replay by 1-0 in 1995-96 and they lost in the opening round 4-2 at home to Millwall in 1996-97.

Villa's last escapades in the Southern Junior Cup came in season 1997-98 and they did very well, reaching their thirteenth (and seemingly unlucky) semi-final. In the first round they beat Wolves 4-2, then defeated Charlton 3-1 and Wimbledon 3-0 all at home before losing a five-goal thriller by 3-2 to Arsenal at Highbury on 10 February 1998.

This is Villa's full record in the Southern Junior Floodlit Cup

| Venue | P | W | D | L | F | A |
|---|---|---|---|---|---|---|
| Home | 67 | 43 | 11 | 13 | 151 | 76 |
| Away | 52 | 27 | 15 | 10 | 98 | 61 |
| Neutral | 1 | 0 | 0 | 1 | 2 | 3 |
| Totals | 120 | 70 | 26 | 24 | 251 | 140 |

*Gareth Southgate*

## SOUTHGATE, GARETH

Born: Watford, 3 September 1970

Career: Crystal Palace (YTS, January 1987, professional January 1989), Aston Villa (£2.5 million, July 1995), Middlesborough (£6.5 million, July 2001).

A classy central defender, calm under pressure, confident in possession, a sound header of the ball, clean tackler and a fine reader of situations, the unflappable Gareth Southgate made 191 senior appearances for Palace before transferring to Villa Park in a record deal in the summer of 1995, twelve months after helping the Eagles win the First Division championship. He immediately slotted into the Villa defence, alongside Paul McGrath and later had as his partner(s) Ugo Ehiogu, Colin Calderwood, Gareth Barry and Alpay Ozalan (among others). Now a regular member of the England international squad, he unfortunately missed a crucial spot-kick in the nail-biting penalty shoot-out against Germany in the Euro '96 semi-final at Wembley, but thankfully he quickly put that disappointment behind him and went on to play in the World Cup Finals of 1998 and Euro 2000, while taking his tally of full caps past the 40 mark.

Southgate who was fined £5,000 by the club after being sent-off at Leicester in 1999, made 242 appearances for Villa (nine goals scored) before moving to Middlesborough.

## SOUTHPORT

No competitive action between the two clubs as yet.

Players with both clubs include: A Betts, J Cumbes, GC Harkus (Southport reserve team player/coach), K Jones, J Martin, TS Morrall, JHH Rutherford, B Sharp, S Teale, P Withe (Southport amateur), JE Worrall (Villa trialist).

THE COMPLETE ENCYCLOPAEDIA OF ASTON VILLA F.C.    THE COMPLETE ENCYCLOPAEDIA OF ASTON VILLA F.C.

249

## SOUTHREN, THOMAS CANSFIELD

Born: Southwick, near Sunderland, 1 August 1927.

Career: Peartree Old Boys, Arsenal (amateur), West Ham United (professional, December 1949), Aston Villa (£12,000, December 1954), Bournemouth (October 1958). Retired in 1961.

Although born in the North-East of England, speedy right-winger Tommy Southren played most of his early football in Hertfordshire junior competitions after his parents had moved to Welwyn. He gained a first team place at Upton Park in 1950 and was a member of the Hammers' side that won the Combination League and Cup double in 1953-54, also representing the London FA against the Berlin FA in that same season.

After making 66 appearances and scoring two goals for the London club he joined Aston Villa on Christmas Eve, 1954, sitting in the waiting room on platform six of Euston Station to sign the appropriate forms! Southren was quick, especially over 30-40 yards, and always tried to get to the bye-line before delivering a telling cross, high or low. Replacing Irishman Norman Lockhart in the front-line, he had an excellent debut at Old Trafford three days after signing, helping Villa to a 1-0 win over Manchester United in front of almost 50,000 fans. He went on to net seven goals in 72 League and Cup encounters for Villa before transferring to Dean Court. He played in 64 Third Division games for the Cherries before announcing his retirement in 1961.

## SPARTAK MOSCOW

Villa's playing record against the Russian side:

UEFA Cup

| Venue | P | W | D | L | F | A |
|---|---|---|---|---|---|---|
| Home | 1 | 0 | 0 | 1 | 1 | 2 |
| Away | 1 | 0 | 1 | 0 | 2 | 2 |
| Totals | 2 | 0 | 1 | 1 | 3 | 4 |

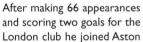

Having beaten the Portuguese side Vitoria Setubal 5-1 on aggregate in the 1st round of the 1983-84 UEFA Cup competition, Aston Villa found the Russian outfit a totally different kettle of fish and were beaten 4-3 on aggregate, losing at home, after a well deserved 2-2 draw behind the Iron Curtain in front of almost 50,000 fans.

## SPENCER, HOWARD

Born: Edgbaston, Birmingham, 23 August 1875.
Died: Four Oaks, Sutton Coldfield, 14 January 1940.
Career: Albert Road School, Handsworth (Birmingham), Stamford FC (1890), Birchfield All Saints (August 1891), Birchfield Trinity (January 1892), Aston Villa (amateur, April 1892, professional June 1894). Retired in November 1907, and two years later was elected to the Board of Dirctors at Villla Park, remaining in office until May 1936, thus ending a 42-year association with the club.

Full-back 'Gentle' Howard Spencer was scrupulously fair (he was never known to commit a ruthless foul). His anticipation was his forte and he became one of the biggest names in football, referred to continuously as the 'Prince of Full-backs' during the pinnacle of his career: 1895-1907. When he first got into the Villa team he partnered Jim Welford and then became an excellent aide to Albert Evans - both pairings were quite brilliant at times.

Spencer captained both club and country, winning six full England caps after appearing in a Junior international in 1894. Many thought that to have been scant reward for his many superb and sterling displays in the full-back position. He gained four

League championship-winning medals and starred in two FA Cup Final winning sides, skippering Villa to victory in 1905. He received two benefits (1900 and 1906) and appeared in 295 first-team games for Villa, scoring just two goals. After hanging up his boots at the relatively young age of 32 (following a knee injury) he continued to prosper as a partner in a firm of fuel merchants (Spencer & Abbot) and he was also a very active and key member on the Board at Villa Park!

## SPIERS, CYRIL HENRY

Born: Witton, Birmingham 4 April 1902. Died: 21 May 1967

Career: Brookvale United, Handsworth Central, Halesowen (1919), Aston Villa (December 1920), Tottenham Hotspur (trialist November 1927, signed December 1927), Wolverhampton Wanderers (September 1933, retired as a player in May 1935 and was appointed coach/assistant-manager, August 1935), Cardiff City (assistant-manager, March 1939, manager April 1939), Norwich City (manager, June 1946), Cardiff City (manager, December 1947-April 1954), Crystal Palace (manager, October 1954-June 1958), Leicester City (chief scout, September 1958-April 1962), Exeter City (manager, May 1962-February 1963), Leicester City (chief scout, February 1963-May 1965). Goalkeeper Cyril Spiers worked his way judiciously through the various levels of local football before joining Aston Villa in 1920. He bided his time, playing in the intermediate and reserve sides at Villa Park before gaining a regular first team place in 1922-23 (taking over from Tommy Jackson). However, Jackson bounced back to form the following season and Spiers again found himself acting as a reserve before re-establishing himself between the posts in 1924-25. Consistent and reliable, Spiers was injured early in the 1926-27 campaign when he regained full fitness, but was surprisingly released, eventually teaming up with Spurs. He made 112 appearances for Villa and added a further 186 to his tally during his six-year stay at White Hart Lane. He didn't miss a single game for almost three years (November 1928 to October 1931) having a run of 124 consecutive outings in that time. He was called up to represent the Football League against the Scottish League in 1930 and played in an international trial for England in March 1931, but lost out to Birmingham's 'keeper Harry Hibbs.

Given a free transfer in May 1933 he joined Wolves where he became assistant-manager to Major Frank Buckley (a former Villa reserve some years earlier). In April 1939 he received his first managerial appointment at Cardiff and thereafter did very well as a team boss, taking the Ninian Park club into the First Division in 1952 during his second spell in charge, later discovering Johnny Byrne when he was in charge at Crystal Palace.

## SPINK, NIGEL PHILIP

Born: Chelmsford, 8 August 1958.

Career: Chelmsford City Schools/Boys, West Ham United (on Schoolboy forms), Chelmsford City, Aston Villa (£4,000, January 1977), West Bromwich Albion (free transfer, January 1996), Millwall (£50,000, September 1997). Also employed by Birmingham City (early 1999), Swindon Town (late 1999) & Northampton Town (2000) as a goalkeeping coach before becoming player and joint-manager (with another ex-Villa man, David Norton) of the Nationwide Conference side, Forest Green Rovers for season 2000-01. Currently lives in Sutton Coldfield.

Nigel Spink was an apprentice plasterer before becoming a goalkeeper! Quite a few clubs had been seeking his services when Villa stepped in with an offer in 1977, but when he arrived at the club he found himself third choice behind John Burridge and Jake Findlay, being knocked

down to fourth when Jimmy Rimmer arrived. Unperturbed, 'Spinky' slowly applied himself, playing in Villa's intermediate and reserve sides before finally establishing himself as the club's number one 'keeper in 1982, having only made two senior appearances in the previous five years....his League debut on 21 December 1979 against Nottingham Forest followed by an unexpected early appearance in the 1982 European Cup Final against Bayern Munich in Rotterdam after Rimmer had left the field injured.

Spink developed into a tremendously effective 'keeper. Powerfully built (6ft 2ins tall and weighing 14st 10lbs) he could withstand the severest of challenges, handled the ball well, was a smart shot-stopper, had great anticipation and was courageous as well as confident. He gleefully collected his European Cup winners' medal in 1982 and then added one full England cap to his collection (as a substitute) versus Australia in June 1983 plus two 'B' caps. Five years later he helped Villa win promotion to the First Division, the season he was granted a

testimonial. Unfortunately he lost his place in the team for a while (to Les Sealey) but regained it and went on to accumulate an exceptionally fine record of 460 senior appearances (361 in the League). In fact, he has played in more League, League Cup and competitive games all told, than any other Villa 'keeper - and he was in goal for Villa's first Premiership game against Ipswich Town in August 1992.

He played his last competitive game for Millwall away at Wigan (League Division Two) in January 2000 at the age of 41 years, five months, seven days - and that was his 540th appearance in major League, Cup and international action before he stepped into 'Conference' soccer with Forest Green Rovers. Spink is also a very competent cricketer, especially with the ball!

Spink is the oldest goalkeeper and the second oldest player ever to appear for West Bromwich Albion. He was 39 years, 19 days old when he starred for the Baggies v Cambridge United in a League Cup-tie in August 1997, having earlier made his Albion debut aged 37 years, 179 days v Ipswich Town (a) in February 1996. He is also the second oldest player to serve Millwall.

As joint-manager of Forest Green Rovers, Spink returned to Villa Park for the 2001 FA Trophy Final which his side lost 1-0 to Canvey Island.

## SPONSORSHIP

Most football clubs in the UK took on sponsorship in a big way in the mid-to-late 1970s as advertising gradually developed more significantly at certain grounds, especially with live TV transmissions flowing all over the world.

As time went by so ground/shirt/club advertising came to the forefront in a big way, more so since Premiership football came into being in 1992.

### Sponsorship Data

These have been Aston Villa's main club sponsors (since 1982):

| | |
|---|---|
| 1982-1983 | Davenport's |
| 1983-1992 | Mita Copiers |
| 1992-1993 | Mita Copiers (UK) Ltd |
| 1993-1995 | Muller |
| 1995-1998 | AST Computers |
| 1998-2000 | LDV Vans |
| 2000-2001 | NTL |

* Panini Stickers sponsored the clubs' family enclosure at Villa Park in the late 1980s.

## STADE RENNAIS

Villa's playing record against the French side:

Inter Toto Cup

| Venue | P | W | D | L | F | A |
|---|---|---|---|---|---|---|
| Home | 1 | 1 | 0 | 0 | 1 | 0 |
| Away | 1 | 0 | 0 | 1 | 1 | 2 |
| Totals | 2 | 1 | 0 | 1 | 2 | 2 |

Villa met Stade Rennais in the semi-final of the 2001-02 Inter Toto Cup Competition. A crowd of 15,753 saw the first leg in France where Villa went down 2-1, Darrius Vassell scoring a 'crucial' away goal.

The return leg attracted an audience of 30,782 and Dion Dublin's early strike was enough to send Villa through on the away-goal rule.

## STAFFORD ROAD (RAILWAY WORKS)

Villa's playing record against the Wolverhampton side:

FA Cup

| Venue | P | W | D | L | F | A |
|---|---|---|---|---|---|---|
| Home | 2 | 1 | 0 | 1 | 5 | 5 |
| Away | 2 | 1 | 1 | 0 | 6 | 2 |
| Totals | 4 | 2 | 1 | 1 | 11 | 7 |

THE COMPLETE ENCYCLOPAEDIA OF ASTON VILLA F.C.    THE COMPLETE ENCYCLOPAEDIA OF ASTON VILLA F.C.

251

These four FA Cup matches all took place between December 1879 and December 1883. Villa won 3-2 at home in a 1st round replay in January 1880 and 5-1 away in a 2nd round encounter when the teams last met.

## STAFFORDSHIRE CUP

This keenly contested competition featured the first teams of several clubs (senior and non-League) from 1877 until the First World War. Thereafter mainly the reserve sides of League clubs entered but occasionally Villa did field a mixed XI comprising first team players, reserves and intermediates.

Here are details of Aston Villa's 22 Staffordshire Cup Final appearances, 16 of which ended in triumph.

1880 lost to Wednesbury Old Athletic 2-1
1881 beat Walsall Swifts 4-1
1891 beat Stoke 4-1
1892 lost to Burton Swifts 2-1
1893 beat Walsall Town Swifts 3-0
1894 beat Wolverhampton Wanderers 2-1
1896 beat Stoke 5-0 (after 1-1)
1899 beat Walsall 2-0
1906 beat Burton United 2-0
1907 beat West Bromwich Albion 5-0
1909 beat Birmingham 5-0
1910 beat West Bromwich Albion 3-1
1911 beat Walsall 3-0
1913 beat Birmingham 2-0 (after 1-1)
1915 lost to Birmingham 1-0
1925 beat West Bromwich Albion 1-0
1928 beat Port Vale 2-0
1929 lost to Walsall 1-0
1931 beat Walsall 6-0
1933 lost to West Bromwich Albion 3-0
1934 lost to Stoke City 1-0
1954 beat Stafford Rangers 4-0

### Staffordshire Cup Chit-Chat

Aston Villa played the 1880 Final at Stoke and to get there they knocked out Walsall Swifts (a) 7-1, Stoke (h) 6-2, Wednesbury Strollers (h) 3-2 and Goldenhill (neutral) 9-1 in the semis.

Villa's team for their first Staffs Cup Final was: J Ball; H Simmonds, S Law; T Pank, E Lee, Andy Hunter; Archie Hunter, G Ramsay, WB Mason, C Johnstone, E Davis. Davis and Mason were the goalscorers and the attendance was 4,000.

In a second round tie on 15 January 1881, Villa beat Fenton (Stoke) 14-0 at home with Eli Davis scoring six goals and William Mason four.

Villa whipped Stoke in a semi-final in March 1894 and then defeated West Bromwich Albion 3-1 and 2-0 at the same stage over the next two seasons.

Albion were then defeated 6-1 at Villa Park in a 1st round tie in October 1898 and lost 4-0 at Villa Park in the semi-final in October 1905.

Villa's second biggest win in the Staffordshire Cup is 11-0 against Burton Wanderers (home) on 22 October 1900.

The Villa side that won the trophy in 1954 comprised 1st, 2nd and 3rd team players. The actual line-up was: Parsons; Lynn, Ashfield; Canning, Martin, A Moss; Slattery, Tyrrell, Pace, Folland, Lockhart. Derek Pace scored twice and Eddie Follan and Joe Tyrrell once apiece.

### STAINROD, SIMON ALLAN

Born: Sheffield, 1 February 1959
Career: Sheffield & South Yorkshire Boys, Sheffield United (apprentice, June 1974, professional, July 1976), Oldham Athletic (£60,000, March 1979), Queen's Park Rangers (£275,000, November 1980), Sheffield Wednesday (£250,000, February 1985), Aston Villa ((£250,000,

September 1985), Stoke City (£90,000, December 1987-May 1988), Racing Club Strasbourg (1988-89), FC Rouen, France (1989-90), Falkirk (player, June 1990, later player / caretaker-manager), Dundee (player/ caretaker-manager), Ayr United (manager).

When he joined Aston Villa from Hillsborough in 1985, Yorkshireman Simon Stainrod had already established himself as a quality marksman, having netted 97 goals in 336 first-class matches. And what a terrific start he made with Villa, bagging all four goals on his debut in a crushing 4-1 League Cup win at Exeter on 25 September 1985.

Capped by England at Youth team level, Stainrod - bought essentially to replace Gary Shaw - was an aggressive striker, easily losing his temper, but he had a knack of being in the right place at the right time to snap up the half-chances that came his way. He scored 27 goals in 82 first-team outings for Villa before moving to The Victoria Ground, Stoke. He later did well on the European scene before returning to the UK to round off his career in Scotland prior to taking up management. He helped QPR win the Second Division title in 1983

### STARK, ROY HOWARD

Born: Stapleford, Nottingham, 28 November 1953
Career: Stapleford & Nottinghamshire Boys, Aston Villa (apprentice June 1967, professional, June 1969), non-League football 1975-80 (after receiving a free transfer from Villa Park).

Central defender, who could also play at full-back, Roy Stark made just two senior appearances for Aston Villa, his debut coming against Sheffield Wednesday in April 1974. Two years earlier he had skippered the youngsters to victory in the 1972 FA Youth Cup Final. He suffered with injuries during his eight years at Villa Park, undergoing two major cartilage operations.

### STARLING, RONALD WILLIAM

Born: Pelaw-on-Tyne, near Gateshead, 11 October 1909. Died: Sheffield Hospital, 17 December 1991.
Career: Durham County Schools/ Boys, Newcastle United (trialist, November 1923), Usworth Colliery (January 1924), Washington Colliery (September 1924), Hull City (amateur, June 1925, professional August 1927), Newcastle United (£3,750, May 1930), Sheffield Wednesday (£3,250, June 1932), Aston Villa (£7,500, January 1937). Retired in July 1948 after guesting for Northampton Town, Nottingham Forest & Walsall during WW2. He became coach at Nottingham Forest (1949-50) under former Villa player Billy Walker. He later ran a successful newsagents/tobacconists shop within walking distance of the Hillsborough ground.

Ronnie Starling's playing career spanned well over 20 years. A great strategist, whose tactics could completely turn the flow of a game, he possessed all the tricks in the trade and often produced them to the full on the field of play. At his peak he was rated better than the great Alex James!

Nicknamed 'Flutterfoot', he was discovered by the long-serving Newcastle United defender Billy McCracken and, in fact, had trials at St James' Park but was not accepted and

went to work down the pit. He did very well playing intermediate football for his colliery teams and once scored eight goals in one game and 45 in a season. Hull City jumped in and Starling joined the Tigers to start his journey to the top! He netted 16 goals in 89 League and Cup outings for Hull before joining, ironically, Newcastle seven years after being rejected! He spent two seasons with the Geordies, claiming eight goals in 53 appearances and then followed up with a haul of 31 in 193 games for Sheffield Wednesday, whom he skippered to victory in the 1935 FA Cup Final over West Brom. He joined Villa at the age of 27 - with perhaps six, seven even eight years left in his legs. But after helping the club climb back into the top flight as Second Division champions in 1938, twelve months later World War Two arrived.

He continued to play during the hostilities (sometimes as a wing-half) and made one more League appearance for Villa in April 1947 before hanging up his kit with a magnificent record under his belt - 431 club appearancs (393 in the Football League) and 65 goals. His senior statistics with Villa were 12 goals in 99 League and FA Cup encounters plus 141 outings in wartime (four goals). He was capped twice by England - against Scotland in 1933 and again in 1937 - and was on the losing side both times.

Starling appeared in four FA Cup semi-finals with four different clubs in nine seasons: Hull (1930), Newcastle (1932), Sheffield Wednesday (1935) and Villa (1938).

He could also preach a sermon as good as any vicar.

## STAUNTON, STEPHEN

Born: Drogheda, Ireland, 19 January 1969
Career: Dundalk (1985), Liverpool (£20,000, September 1986), Bradford City (on loan, November 1987), Aston Villa (£1.1 million, August 1991), Liverpool (free transfer, July 1998), Crystal Palace (on loan, August-September 2000), Aston Villa (free transfer, December 2000).

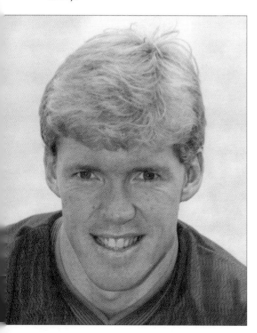

Honoured on the international front by the Republic of Ireland at Youth, Under-21 (four caps) and senior level (over 90 outings), the versatile Steve Staunton is able to play as an orthodox left-back, central defender or in midfield. He was a snip-of-a-signing by Liverpool in 1986 and over the next five years starred in 90 first-class games for the Anfield club (plus 11 on loan with Bradford). He gained an FA Cup winners medal in 1989 and a League championship medal twelve months later before newly-appointed manager Ron Atkinson moved in to bring him to Villa Park in 1991. Immediately the 22 year-old red-head made his mark with a string of splendid defensive displays, using his sweet left-foot to good effect, to the appreciation of the diehard supporters! Staunton scored some cracking goals in amassing over 260 competitive games in his 'first' seven years with Villa. He also added two League Cup winners' medals to his collection before rejoining Liverpool on a free transfer in the summer of 1996. After an excellent first season 'back home' he had to fight for his place in the Merseysiders' first XI with Dominic Matteo in 1999-2000 and it was no surprise when he joined Crystal Palace on loan at the start of

the next campaign, only to be recalled to Anfield when injuries and suspensions intervened. Surprisingly, however, he was brought back to Villa Park for a second spell halfway through the season and has now taken his total number of senior appearances for the club to over 280 (18 goals) and he is Villa's most capped player to date.

## STEAUA BUCHAREST
Villa's playing record against the Romanian side:
UEFA Cup

| Venue | P | W | D | L | F | A |
|---|---|---|---|---|---|---|
| Home | 1 | 1 | 0 | 0 | 2 | 0 |
| Away | 1 | 0 | 0 | 1 | 1 | 2 |
| Totals | 2 | 1 | 0 | 1 | 3 | 2 |

Aston Villa made progress into the fourth round of the 1997-98 UEFA Cup competition by ousting the Romanian side 3-2 on aggregate. Dwight Yorke's goal in Bucharest set things up and in front of 35,102 fans Villa won a tight return leg 2-0 with second-half goals from Savo Milosevic (71 minutes) and Ian Taylor (85).

## STEPHENSON, CLEMENT
Born: New Delaval, County Durham, 6 January 1890. Died: Huddersfield, 24 October 1961.
Career: New Delaval Villa, West Stanley, Blyth Spartans, Durham City, Aston Villa, (£165, March 1910), Stourbridge (on loan, August 1910-February 1911), Leeds City (WW1 guest), Huddersfield Town (£3,000, March 1921). Retired in May 1929 to become manager at Leeds Road, a position he held until May 1942.

Inside-forward Clem Stephenson played in four FA Cup Finals at three different venues and was then a manager in two other Finals. As a player, he gained winners' medals with Aston Villa in 1913 versus Sunderland at the Crystal Palace and in 1920 over his future club Huddersfield at Stamford Bridge. With Huddersfield he was a winner versus Preston in 1922, also at Chelsea, and a loser at the hands of Blackburn Rovers in 1928 at Wembley. Then as a manager he guided Huddersfield to Wembley for the 1930 and 1938 Finals but lost on both occasions to Arsenal and Preston respectively.

Stephenson actually dreamed that Villa would win the 1913 Final 1-0 and that Tommy Barber would score the goal with a header. That's what precisely happened! Villa even missed a penalty in that game - Charlie Wallace shooting wide after Stephenson had been brought down!

Elder brother of George T and Jimmy, Clem Stephenson was loaned out to Stourbridge 'to gain experience' against exiled professionals shortly after joining Aston Villa in 1910. He made rapid progress and on his return scored on his League debut in a 4-0 win over Tottenham Hotspur. He went from strength to strength after that....and won one England cap v Wales in 1924 (there should have been more). A fine schemer, he passed the ball precisely with fine judgment, was no mean goalscorer, he could shoot powerfully with both feet, had reasonable pace (not lightning quick) and was never

THE COMPLETE ENCYCLOPAEDIA OF ASTON VILLA F.C.    THE COMPLETE ENCYCLOPAEDIA OF ASTON VILLA F.C.

253

afraid to 'rough it' with the burly defenders who tried to mark him! With Joe Bache his wing partner initially, then Harold Edgeley and Arthur Dorrell after that Stephenson went on to net 96 goals in 216 League and Cup games for Villa before embarking on a 21-year association with Huddersfield Town, first as a player, then as a manager. When he arrived at Leeds Road, Herbert Chapman was in the process of assembling a useful side that was soon to embark on a hat-trick of League championship triumphs. Stephenson was a vital ingredient in the mixture and he starred in all three campaigns. He rattled in 50 goals in 275 outings for the Yorkshire club up to 1929 when he decided, after serious consideration, to hang up his boots and take over as team manager from Jack Chaplin. He did well at Leeds Road, acquired several fine footballers - George McLean and David Mangnall among them - and guided the Terriers to fourth spot in the First Division in 1932, saw them take second spot in 1934 and finish third in 1936....as well as leading his players out in those two Cup Finals (1930 & 1938). In fact, he saw the trophy snatched away from him in the dying seconds of extra time in the latter contest as Preston's George Mutch hammered in a dubious penalty! When he resigned from the manager's seat in 1942 Stephenson left football for good.

## STEPHENSON, GEORGE HENRY

Born: Billingborough, 29 September 1908. Died: 1964
Career: Stockton Schools, Carlton Iron Works FC, Stillington, Durham City (professional, September 1927), Aston Villa (April 1931), Luton Town (July 1934), Leeds United (August 1939). Did not feature after WW2.
No relation to the other Stephensons, George H was an outside-left, clever on the ball, who struggled to make an impact during his three years at Villa Park. He made only four senior appearances and scored one goal before leaving to join Luton for whom he netted 58 times in almost 200 League outings up to the end of the 1938-39 season.

## STEPHENSON, GEORGE TERNENT

Born: New Delaval, 3 September 1900. Died: Derby, 18 August 1971.
Career: County Durham County Schools, New Delaval Villa, Leeds City (August 1919), Aston Villa (signed for £250 in November 1919 at an auction held at the Metropole Hotel, Leeds after the Yorkshire club had folded and its players were put up for sale), Stourbridge (on loan, August 1920-March 1921), Derby County (£2,000, November 1927), Sheffield

Wednesday (£2,500, February 1931), Preston North End (£1,500, July 1933), Charlton Athletic (£660, May 1934). Retired through injury, May 1937 and joined the coaching staff at The Valley, before becoming assistant-manager to brother, Clem, at Huddersfield Town. Appointed manager at Leeds Road in August 1947, holding office until March 1952 when he quit football to work as a blacksmith. Was licensee of the Sportsman's Inn near Huddersfield from 1954-56; a Rolls Royce factory worker (Derby) in 1957-58 and later coached Derby County's 'A' team (1961-63).
A former grocer, smithy and pit-worker, George Stephenson - like brother Clem - also became an England international, winning three full caps, the first versus France in Paris in May 1928 when he netted twice in a 5-1 win, and against Belgium that same month then France again in Paris in May 1931. He had already starred in a Junior match - England v Scotland in April 1920. A brainy, cultured inside-forward, Stephenson

scored 120 goals in 319 League games during his career. He netted fourtimers in two separate First Division matches for Derby, whom he helped guide into second spot in the League championship in 1930. Small in stature, with a big heart, he was a key member of the Preston side which finished runners-up in Division Two in 1934. A year later he helped Charlton clinch the Third Division (South) title.
Stephenson, after following the same format as Clem (a loan spell with Stourbridge) returned to score 22 goals in 95 games for Aston Villa, his best season coming in 1926-27 when he netted 13 times in 36 First Division outings when partnering Dicky York on the right-wing.
As a manager Stephenson, stern and respected, found it hard going at times as Huddersfield continually battled against relegation. He finally quit the 'hot seat' in 1952 with the club heading towards the Second Division.
• His son, Bob, played professional football for Derby County, Shrewsbury Town and Rochdale and cricket (as a wicket-keeper) for Derbyshire and Hampshire.

## STEPHENSON, JAMES

Born: New Delaval, 10 February 1895. Died: Co. Durham, April 1960.
Career: New Delaval, Aston Villa (April 1914), Sunderland (May 1921), Watford (July 1922), Queen's Park Rangers (July 1927), Boston Town, New Delaval Villa, Ashington, New Delaval Villa.
Midget winger (5ft 5ins tall) Jimmy Stephenson was a useful

acquisition to the Villa ranks and deputisied (most of the time) for Charlie Wallace in 32 senior games (one goal scored). He made his League debut in fact, at centre-forward in the 0-0 draw away at Everton in September 1914 and his single goal was a decisive one, earning Villa a point from a 2-2 draw at Bradford City in April 1915. After leaving Villa Park, Stephenson played in 22 games for Sunderland before netting 18 times in 213 League appearances for Watford. He was still playing intermediate soccer in County Durham when WW2 broke out.

## STOBART, BARRY HENRY

Born: Dodsworth, near Doncaster, 6 June 1938,
Career: Dodsworth County School, Wath Wanderers, Wolverhampton Wanderers (amateur, June 1953, professional, December 1955), Manchester City (£20,000, August 1964), Aston Villa (£22,000, November 1964), Shrewsbury Town (£10,000, October 1967), Willenhall Town (August 1970-72). He later returned to Willenhall as manager (1979-81) and also managed Dudley Town (1984-90) while running his own greengrocer's business.
After making only five first team appearances, inside-forward Stobart was called into Wolves' 1960 FA Cup Final team v Blackburn in place of Bobby Mason, manager Stan Cullis having no second thoughts about playing the 21 year-old in front of almost 100,000 fans at Wembley. Stobart did a good job and duly claimed a winners' medal after helping his team-mates beat Rovers 3-0. He found it hard to get a regular game in the first XI at Molineux with so many talented forwards in the squad, but he stuck to his guns and remained with Wolves until 1964, scoring 22 goals in just over 50 games. Unfortunately Stobart failed to settle down at Maine Road and was quickly sold to Aston Villa. He attained a similar strike record with Villa as he did at Wolves, netting 20 times in his 53 first team appearances. Struggling at times (owing to injury) to hold down a first team place, he eventually transferred to Shrewsbury in 1967 and three years later Stobart left the League scene to join Willenhall.

THE COMPLETE ENCYCLOPAEDIA OF ASTON VILLA F.C.

THE COMPLETE ENCYCLOPAEDIA OF ASTON VILLA F.C.

254

## STOCKPORT COUNTY

Villa's playing record against the Hatters:

Football League

| Venue | P | W | D | L | F | A |
|---|---|---|---|---|---|---|
| Home | 1 | 1 | 0 | 0 | 7 | 1 |
| Away | 1 | 1 | 0 | 0 | 3 | 1 |
| Totals | 2 | 2 | 0 | 0 | 10 | 2 |

FA Cup

| | | | | | | |
|---|---|---|---|---|---|---|
| Home | 1 | 1 | 0 | 0 | 3 | 0 |

League Cup

| | | | | | | |
|---|---|---|---|---|---|---|
| Home | 1 | 1 | 0 | 0 | 2 | 0 |

Aston Villa's centre-forward Frank Shell - on his home debut - grabbed a hat-trick as County were thrashed 7-1 at Villa Park in a Second Division game in December 1937. Frank Broome then netted twice in the return fixture which Villa won 3-1 in April.

Villa's FA Cup win over the Hatters came in the 1st round in January 1908 in front of 16,000 fans.

Players with both clubs include: GO Ashfield, T Bennett, T Birch, PF Broadbent, RJ Codling, GS Cowans, HH Edgley, S Grayson, J Griffiths, KD Keelan, AE Layton, MA Lillis, F Pimblett, J Reynolds, RGM Thomson, OE Tidman.
Also: RC Chapman (Villa player, County manager)

## STOKE CITY

Villa's playing record against the Potters:

Football League

| Venue | P | W | D | L | F | A |
|---|---|---|---|---|---|---|
| Home | 44 | 31 | 7 | 6 | 108 | 36 |
| Away | 44 | 13 | 13 | 18 | 54 | 66 |
| Totals | 88 | 44 | 20 | 24 | 162 | 102 |

FA Cup

| | | | | | | |
|---|---|---|---|---|---|---|
| Home | 4 | 2 | 1 | 1 | 12 | 5 |
| Away | 5 | 1 | 3 | 1 | 6 | 8 |
| Neutral | 1 | 0 | 0 | 1 | 0 | 2 |
| Totals | 10 | 3 | 4 | 3 | 18 | 15 |

League Cup

| | | | | | | |
|---|---|---|---|---|---|---|
| Home | 1 | 1 | 0 | 0 | 3 | 1 |

Wartime

| | | | | | | |
|---|---|---|---|---|---|---|
| Home | 8 | 7 | 0 | 1 | 20 | 3 |
| Away | 8 | 3 | 0 | 5 | 14 | 17 |
| Totals | 16 | 10 | 0 | 6 | 34 | 20 |

As founder members of the Football League, Villa registered their first victory in the competition when they beat the Potters 5-1 at home on 15 September 1888. Just over a year later Stoke returned to Perry Barr and this time lost 6-1, Walter Garvey scoring a hat-trick. Then, in September 1893 Stoke crashed 5-1 again on Villa soil before being held to a 3-3 draw at The Victoria Ground.

Charlie Athersmith's hat-trick helped Villa hammer the Potters 6-0 at home on Boxing Day and in February 1896 Johnny Campbell claimed a treble as Villa won 5-1 at Perry Barr

With the Potters having been out of the League for quite some time, Villa's first League game with them after World War One took place on 17 February 1923 and ended in a 6-0 victory, Billy Dickson scoring a hat-trick.

In 1934-35 it was 4-1 to Stoke City at The Victoria Ground and 4-1 to Villa on their own patch. Dai Astley netted a hat-trick in the latter game.

Villa rounded off their 1950-51 League campaign with a handsome 6-2 home win over Stoke - sweet revenge for the 1-0 defeat suffered at The Victoria Ground earlier in the season. Villa led 4-1 at half-time and both Tommy Thompson (a future Potter) and Dave Walsh scored twice.

On 16 February 1952, when Stoke won 3-2 at Villa Park, one of their goals was scored by 'keeper Dennis Herod who was injured and went to play on the left-wing.

The following season the Potters doubled up over Villa - winning 4-1 (home) and 3-2 (away). But then Johnny Dixon netted three goals as Villa hammered a few nails into the Potters' relegation coffin with a 4-1 at Stoke in November 1952.

Stoke caned Villa 6-1 at The Victoria Ground in December 1966 and the man who did most of the damage was Harry Burrows, an ex-Villan, who scored a hat-trick for the Potters.

When Villa beat Stoke 1-0 at home on Boxing Day 1980 (Peter Withe the scorer) it started a 10-match unbeaten run that continued until late March.

Only 10,874 fans saw Villa beat Stoke 2-0 at home in March 1985 - the lowest League crowd at Villa Park since April 1966 when just over 10,400 saw the Northampton Town game.

The first of the ten FA Cup encounters went Stoke's way to the tune of 3-0 in a 2nd round clash in the Potteries in January 1891.

Villa won 3-2 on Stoke soil in the opening round of the 1903-04 competition and succeeded 4-0 at home in the 1st round in January 1914 when 18,000 fans saw Clem Stephenson and Harry Hampton both score twice. Villa repeated that scoreline in a 3rd round replay in January 1922 when Billy Dickson notched a hat-trick in front of 53,385 spectators.

The 3rd round meeting between the clubs in January 1958 went to a second replay before Stoke won 2-0 at Molineux after draws of 3-3 at Villa Park and 1-1 at The Victoria Ground.

Villa's only League Cup game against the Potters was in the 3rd round in October 1962 when a crowd of almost 25,000 saw Villa triumph 3-1 with goals by Bobby Thomson, Tommy Ewing and Harry Burrows (penalty).

In March 1944, a Wartime game at Stoke ended in a 5-4 win for Villa, Frank Broome and Eric Houghton both scoring twice. Four months later Harry Parkes netted twice in Villa's 4-0 home win over the Potters.

Players with both clubs include: J Adam, NLG Blake, R Burgess (reserves at both clubs), H Burrows, M Carruthers, A Cartlidge, AD Collins & L Collins (Villa & Stoke reserves), N Cutler, L Davies (Villa trialist/reserve), WA Dickson, A Dixon (Stoke reserve), AR Dorigo, P Dowds, AS Dyke, G Fenton, J Gidman, JH Harvey (trialist with Villa & Stoke), AP Heath, I King (Villa junior, Stoke reserve), JT Lee, H Leigh, AH Lockett, A McClure, W Moore (Stoke trialist), JT Palethorpe, L Palin (Villa reserve), M Pejic, B Petty, PJ Robinson, LR Roose, JH Roxborough, G Scott (Villa and Stoke junior), B Small, S Stainrod, E

*Harry Morton saves on his knees during Villa's 1-1 draw at Stoke in 1933-34.*

THE COMPLETE ENCYCLOPAEDIA OF ASTON VILLA F.C.    THE COMPLETE ENCYCLOPAEDIA OF ASTON VILLA F.C.

255

Stevenson, T Thompson, ME Walters, MW Watkins, T Weston, J Whitley, TH Wilkes, AE Wood, J Woodward.
Also: B Little (Villa player & manager, Potters trialist & manager), A Evans (Villa player, Stoke assistant-manager/coach), P Barron (Stoke player, Villa coach)

## STOKES, ARTHUR WILBERFORCE
Born: West Bromwich, April 1867. Died: Smethwick, June 1939.
Career: Bratt Street School (West Bromwich), White Hill FC, Wednesbury Old Athletic, Aston Villa (April 1892), Burton Swifts (March 1893), Walsall Town Swifts (August 1894). Retired through injury 1895.
A strong-looking defender, Archie Stokes was an efficient tackler whose thoughtfulness was not always in evidence. He scored once in 13 senior games for Villa.

## STONE, STEPHEN BRIAN
Born: Gateshead, 20 August 1971.
Career: Nottingham Forest (YTS, June 1987, professional, May 1989), Aston Villa ((£5.5 million, March 1999).
First spotted by Nottingham Forest as a 13-year-old, midfielder Steve Stone signed as an apprentice at The City Ground in 1987. He turned 'pro' before his 18th birthday and went on to appear in 229 first-class games (27 goals scored) for Forest as well as winning nine England caps and a First Division championship medal (1998) before transferring to Villa Park in 1999....having recovered full fitness after a serious knee injury.
Unfortunately his first full season with Villa was a disappointing one, Stone failing to fully establish himself in the team and suffering a back injury in the process. He did, however, come on as a 'sub' to play in the last 15 minutes of the 2000 FA Cup Final v Chelsea. He did much better during the next campaign although he did have to battle for his

place on the right side of the Villa midfield. Stone has now appeared in 88 senior games and scored six goals during his time at Villa Park.

## STOURBRIDGE
Aston Villa and Stourbridge have never played against each other at competitive level, but several players who wore the claret and blue strip have been associated with the Glassboys, including: F Barson (Stourbridge manager), J Beresford, J Birch, WR Boyman, JR Brown, JF Chambers (Stourbridge player & manager), J Corbett, HH Edgley, A Edwards, CH Gibson, AE Hall, FJ Haycock, J Jeffries, S Lynn, WH Maiden, CJH Millington, TD Moore, TS Morrall (Stourbridge player-manager), BA Olney, T Perry, LJ Richards, WD Roberts, RR Robertson, CH Slade, H Slater (Villa reserve), C Stephenson, GT Stephenson, A Talbot, GH Tranter, J Walters, S Webb & JR Williamson (both Villa reserves), JE Worrell, J Yates.

## STRANGE, EDMUND WALLACE
Born: Bordesley Green, March 1871.
Died: Birmingham, December 1925.
Career: Small Heath Ravenshurst, Hoskins & Sewell FC, Small Heath, Langley Mill, Unity Gas, Aston Villa (August 1895), Langley St Michael's (September 1898). Retired in April 1899 with a serious knee injury and immediately returned to Villa Park as assistant-secretary (under George Ramsay: 1899-1925). Also managed Villa's second XI when they won the Birmingham & District League title eight seasons running: 1903-10 inclusive.
Edmund Strange was a beautifully balanced footballer who occupied the left-half berth, but unfortunatelty his career was dogged by injury. One of the game's gentlemen, he made just two senior appearances for Villa, assisting in the goal that earned a point on his debut v Stoke (home) in April 1898.

## STROMSGODSET IF
Villa's playing record against the Norwegian side
UEFA Cup

| Venue | P | W | D | L | F | A |
|-------|---|---|---|---|---|---|
| Home | 1 | 1 | 0 | 0 | 3 | 2 |
| Away | 1 | 1 | 0 | 0 | 3 | 0 |
| Totals | 2 | 2 | 0 | 0 | 6 | 2 |

Aston Villa scored three goals in the last seven minutes of their home second leg UEFA Cup encounter with Stromsgodset on 15 September 1998 to win the contest 3-2..
Almost 29,000 fans were present for this clash and they saw Stromsgodset take a 2-0 half-time lead through Michelsen and George. But after Gary Charles' goal had reduced the deficit on 83 minutes, substitute Darius Vassell struck twice in the last 90 seconds to give Villa a slender and perhaps undeserved lead.
A confident Villa side, however, then went away and won 3-0 in front of just 4,835 fans in Norway, courtesy of a Stan Collymore hat-trick to take the tie 6-2 on aggregate

## SUBSTITUTES
The first substitute used by Aston Villa was Bobby Parker who replaced centre-forward Tony Hateley during the home League game against Tottenham Hotspur on 25 September 1965. Jimmy MacEwan was the first 'sub' to come on in away game - at Burnley ion 20 November 1965.
Villa used only five substitutes during that first 'sub' season of 1965-66.

THE COMPLETE ENCYCLOPAEDIA OF ASTON VILLA F.C.          THE COMPLETE ENCYCLOPAEDIA OF ASTON VILLA F.C.

256

The first 'sub' to score for Villa was Lew Chatterley against Blackpool at home on 14 January 1967. He replaced Mike Tindall and helped Villa win 3-2.

The first substitute to come off the bench and score a hat-trick in a Football League game was Geoff Vowden - for Birmingham City against Huddersfield Town in September 1968. Three years later Vowden moved from St Andrew's to Villa Park.

Brian Little came off the substitute's bench in the 80th minute to replace Mick Channon for his only England appearance v Wales at Wembley in 1975.

Paul Birch

Stuart A Ritchie made ONE appearance for Aston Villa - as a late second half substitute against Manchester United at Old Trafford in a First Division game in May 1987. He may well hold the record of having the shortest 'League' career as a Villa player!

Goalkeeper Adam Rachel also made one "sub" appearance for Villa.

Paul Kerr came on as substitute for Villa against Luton Town in September 1986 and scored twice to earn a 2-1 victory.

Robert Hopkins scored with his first touch on his Villa debut, coming on as a substitute against Norwich City in March 1980.

Nigel Spink came off the bench in the 10th minute of the 1982 European Cup Final to replace the injured Jimmy Rimmer - and played a blinder in Villa's 1-0 win. This was only Spink's second senior game for the club. Villa's four unused substitutes for this Final were Andy Blair, David Geddis, Colin Gibson and Pat Heard.

Villa's three substitutes for the away Premiership game at Old Trafford on 19 October 1993 - Nigel Spink, Tony Daley and Gordon Cowans - had amassed 1,232 League appearances between them.

'Watty' Corbett (Aston Villa) came on as a substitute against his own club for George Robey's XI in a friendly match in 1906.

### Sub Appearances

Here is a list giving Villa's top substitute appearance-makers:

| Player | League | Cups | Total |
|---|---|---|---|
| Julian Joachim | 51 | 8 | 59 |
| Darius Vassell | 34 | 15 | 49 |
| Dwight Yorke | 36 | 4 | 40 |
| Tony Daley | 31 | 7 | 38 |
| Lee Hendrie | 24 | 14 | 38 |
| Ian Olney | 26 | 3 | 29 |
| Paul Birch | 20 | 5 | 25 |
| Steve Stone | 16 | 7 | 23 |
| Ian Taylor | 18 | 5 | 23 |

NB - Julian Joachim also made 27 substitute appearances for Leicester City (22 in the League)

### SUDDICK, JAMES

Born: Middlesbrough, August 1875. Died: c 1932.

Career: Middlesbrough junior football, Aston Villa (July 1897), Nottingham Forest (August 1898-April 1900), Middlesbrough (1902), Thornaby (1904-05).

Reserve inside-forward, Jimmy Suddick's only goal (in his two senior outings for Aston Villa) was scored in the 4-0 home win over Preston North End in February 1899. He hit four goals in 14 outings for Forest and netted once in his only senior outing for Middlesbrough (at Sunderland in January 1904).

• There were two James Suddicks playing football around the same time and it has not been possible to clarify whether the details above are all correct.

### SUNDAY FOOTBALL

Aston Villa's first competitive game played on a Sunday was against Wolverhampton Wanderers at Molineux (League Division One) on 23 October 1983. A crowd of just 13,202 witnessed the 1-1 draw when Peter Withe netted against his former club to earn Villa a point.

Villa Park staged its first Sunday game on 12 March 1989 when Manchester United were the visitors (Division One). A crowd of 28,332 saw the 0-0 draw.

### SUNDERLAND

Villa's playing record against the Wearsiders:

Football League/Premiership

| Venue | P | W | D | L | F | A |
|---|---|---|---|---|---|---|
| Home | 72 | 46 | 13 | 13 | 145 | 89 |
| Away | 72 | 14 | 22 | 36 | 90 | 138 |
| Totals | 144 | 60 | 35 | 49 | 235 | 227 |

FA Cup

| Venue | P | W | D | L | F | A |
|---|---|---|---|---|---|---|
| Home | 5 | 4 | 0 | 1 | 15 | 7 |
| Away | 1 | 0 | 1 | 0 | 2 | 2 |
| Neutral | 3 | 3 | 0 | 0 | 7 | 2 |
| Totals | 9 | 7 | 1 | 1 | 24 | 11 |

League Cup

| Venue | P | W | D | L | F | A |
|---|---|---|---|---|---|---|
| Home | 1 | 0 | 1 | 0 | 0 | 0 |
| Away | 3 | 3 | 0 | 0 | 9 | 3 |
| Totals | 4 | 3 | 1 | 0 | 9 | 3 |

Aston Villa met Sunderland for the first time on 26 December 1890 (Division One). A little over 62 years later, the two teams became the first in England to play against each other in 100 Football League matches when they fought out a 2-2 draw at Roker Park in January 1953 (Division One).

Those first two encounters in 1890-91 ended 0-0 at Perry Barr and a 5-1 victory for Sunderland at Newcastle Road.

Villa gained revenge with a 5-3 home win in September 1891 but lost the return 2-1 before Sunderland hit 12 past Villa in 1892-93, winning 6-1 at Perry Barr and 6-0 win at Newcastle Road.

Villa's first 4-4 away draw in League football was against Sunderland in January 1895.

Billy Garraty scored a hat-trick in Villa's 4-2 home win over Sunderland in December 1899. This earned the Villans the double following a 1-0 victory at Roker Park earlier in the season.

Sunderland beat Villa 6-1 at home in September 1903 but later that season they lost 2-0 at Villa Park.

Sunderland and Villa were both going for the League and Cup double in 1912-13. In the end Villa beat the Wearsiders in the FA Cup and finished runners-up in the First Division. A crucial League game, played just four days after the Cup Final, saw Sunderland force a 1-1 draw at Villa Park in front of almost 60,000 fans. In the end the title went to Roker Park by four points (54-50).

The following January, Villa won the corresponding League game 5-0 when Joe Bache and Harold Edgeley both scored twice.

Villa crashed 5-1 at Sunderland in February 1921....nine days later Sunderland lost 1-0 at Villa Park!

The only team to win a League game at Villa Park in 1923-24 was Sunderland (1-0 on 9 February).

Villa recorded a terrific 5-1 win at Roker Park in December 1938 when Frank Broome scored a superb goal.

Over Easter 1947, Villa lost 4-1 at Roker Park but won the return fixture 4-0 with Trevor Ford scoring twice against his future club!

One of Villa's goals in their 3-0 defeat of Sunderland at home on 1 September 1952 was scored by full-back Peter Aldis whose header went into the net from 35 yards!

Sunderland pulled all the strings in 1955-56, beating Villa 5-1 at Roker Park and 4-1 in Birmingham.

THE COMPLETE ENCYCLOPAEDIA OF ASTON VILLA F.C.      THE COMPLETE ENCYCLOPAEDIA OF ASTON VILLA F.C.

257

Stan Lynn created Football League history in January 1958 when he became the first full-back to score a hat-trick in a League Division One game as Villa beat Sunderland 5-2 at Villa Park. Two of Lynn's goals-came from the penalty spot. Jimmy Dugdale went off in the 25th minute with two fractured ribs. The score at the time was 2-2, Lynn having netted his first spot-kick after just four minutes. The ten men of Villa though tore into Sunderland and before half-time had raced into a commanding 5-2 lead, Lynn burying his second penalty after George Aitken had handled in the 26th minute. Lynn could have had a fourth goal in the second-half but his 20 yard free-kick flew two inches wide! When Villa beat Sunderland 2-1 at home in September 1964 it ended a run of 10 League games without a victory.

On 26 April 1975 a crowd of 57,266 packed inside Villa Park to see Sunderland defeated 2-0 as Villa surged toward promotion to the First Division.

*Action from the Aston Villa v. Sunderland F.A. Cup tie at Villa Park in 1903. (Villa won 4-1).*

Ten years later, in May 1985, Villa won 4-0 at Roker Park.

As European Cup winners, Villa started their 1982-83 League programme by losing 3-1 at home to Sunderland, who later completed the double with a 2-0 victory at Roker Park.

Dalian Atkinson scored twice in Villa's splendid 4-1 win at Roker Park in October 1993

Villa have registered more home League wins (46) against Sunderland than they have any other club.

Villa went through to the 1892 FA Cup Final after beating Sunderland 4-1 at Bramall Lane in the semis. Two seasons later Villa won a 2nd round replay 3-1 at Perry Barr and the following year qualified for another Final after accounting for the Wearsiders 2-1 at Blackburn.

Over 47,000 fans saw Villa beat Sunderland 4-1 in a 1st round tie in January 1903 and ten years after that came Charlie Wallace's penalty miss in the 15th minute of the 1913 Final at The Crystal Palace. His blushes were spared however when Tommy Barber headed a second-half match-winner. The night before the Final Clem Stephenson had dreamed that Villa would win 1-0 and that Barber who head the all-important goal!

Jimmy Harrop produced heroics between the posts for seven minutes soon after half-time when Sam Hardy had to leave the field for treatment. He made three superb saves in quick succession.

Villa walloped hapless Sunderland 7-2 in a 4th round FA Cup game at Villa Park in January 1934. A crowd of 57,268 saw Dai Astley (4) and Eric Houghton (3) blaze happily away on the goal trail.

Villa defeated Sunderland 3-1 on aggregate in the semi-final of the 1962-63 League Cup competition (0-0 at home, 3-1 at Roker Park).

In fact, Villa have a 100 per-cent League Cup record at Sunderland - three wins from three starts, including an emphatic 4-1 scoreline in October 1993, Dalian Atkinson scoring twice.

Players with both clubs include: RD Davis (Villa WW2 guest), WA Dickson, JT Dixon (Sunderland WW2 guest), F Farrell (Villa reserve), T Ford, G Harper, H Johnston (Villa reserve), D Kubicki, B Little (Sunderland trialist), J Logan, T Mitchinson, A O'Neill, J Stephenson, WM Watkins, JR Williamson (Villa reserve).

Also: T Cummings (Villa manager, Sunderland scout), A Cox (Sunderland assistant-manager, Villa coach/assistant and caretaker-manager), LC Chatterley & AP Heath (Villa players, Sunderland coaches), PD Doherty (Sunderland assistant-manager, Villa chief scout).

## SUPPORTERS' CLUBS

Aston Villa have 61 registered branches of their supporters' club all over the world......35 are based in the UK alone with 26 abroad,

## SURTEES, ALBERT E.

Born: Willington Quay, 1902. Deceased.

Career: Durham City (1920), Aston Villa (July 1922), Southend United (August 1926), Clapton Orient (August 1927), Wellington Town (season 1928-29).

A tall, strong, forceful inside or centre-forward, Albert Surtees made eleven first-team appearacnes for Aston Villa, scoring one goal - in a 3-0 home win over Burnley in December 1924 when he replaced Billy Walker.

## SUSPENSIONS

Aston Villa's Dennis Hodgetts was suspended for two games by the Birmingham County FA after becoming the first player to be sent-off in a Football League game - dismissed against Everton on 22 September 1888 for punching an opponent (see Sendings-off).

George Cummings, Villa's tough-tackling Scottish full-back, was handed a sine-die ban from football following incidents during a Wartime match against Leicester City on 18 January 1943. Cummings lodged an appeal and the ban was lifted on 20 August of that same year.

Under the totting up (of points) system, the Villa midfielder Bruce Rioch was suspended for four weeks by an FA Disciplinary Committee in October 1971.

Andy Townsend set a new discipline record in 1994 when he was suspended for six Premiership matches. He received a three-match ban for reaching 21 points and a further three-match ban for a sending-off. Villa manager John Gregory received a 28-day touchline ban from the FA for comments made about a referee (November 1999).

During his professional career, striker Stan Collymore has received suspensions totalling four months after various disciplinary offences (including a handful of sendings-off).

Derek Dougan, ex-Villa, was suspended for eight weeks in October 1969 after receiving three bookings and a sending-off whilst playing for Wolves

## SWAIN, KENNETH

Born: Birkenhead, 28 January 1952.

Career: Liverpool/Birkenhead & Merseyside District Schools, Kirkby Boys, Bolton Wanderers (Schoolboy forms, 1967), Peckham Comprehensive & Streatham Schools, Shoreditch Teachers' Training College (Surrey), South East Counties Colleges (after moving south), Wycombe Wanderers (amateur April 1973), Chelsea (professional August 1973), West Bromwich Albion (on loan, November 1978), Aston Villa (£100,000, December 1978 to October 1982), Nottingham Forest (October 1982), Portsmouth (July 1985), West Bromwich Albion (on loan, February-March 1988), Crewe Alexandra (August 1988-May 1989, then player/coach & assistant-manager under Dario Gradi), Wigan Athletic (manager, season 1993-94), Grimsby Town (reserve team coach/assistant-manager, 1995, then caretaker-manager October 1996-May 1997). Scouted for several clubs after that. He

THE COMPLETE ENCYCLOPAEDIA OF ASTON VILLA F.C.  THE COMPLETE ENCYCLOPAEDIA OF ASTON VILLA F.C.

258

qualified in handicrafts and PE at college and played alongside Dennis Mortimer for Kirkby Boys.

Although a striker during his early days, Kenny Swain developed into a fine right full-back, sound in the tackle with splendid positional sense, a steady nerve and excellent technique. He was a valuable member of Aston Villa's League Championship, European Cup and Super Cup winning sides of 1981 and 1982, in his four years with the club making 179 senior appearances and scored five goals. He replaced John Gidman in the No.2 slot and when he left the club Mark Jones took over the role before Gary Williams moved over from the left. He helped Pompey win promotion from Division Two in 1987 and Crewe from Division Four two years later. During his playing days Swain amassed in excess of 500 League and Cup appearances.

*Kenny Swain*

## SWALES, NORMAN
Born: New Marske, October 1898. Deceased.
Career: Irton FC, Scarborough, Middlesbrough (August 1925), Aston Villa (November 1928), Scarborough (May 1932), Whitley Bay (1934-35).
No mean ball player, wing-half Norman Swales appeared in eight League games for Aston Villa, making his League debut against Burnley in February 1929 when he stood in for Joe Tate.

## SWANSEA CITY (TOWN)
Villa's playing record against the Swans:
Football League

| Venue | P | W | D | L | F | A |
|---|---|---|---|---|---|---|
| Home | 7 | 7 | 0 | 0 | 19 | 0 |
| Away | 7 | 4 | 0 | 3 | 12 | 10 |
| Totals | 14 | 11 | 0 | 3 | 31 | 10 |

FA Cup

| | | | | | | |
|---|---|---|---|---|---|---|
| Away | 2 | 2 | 0 | 0 | 5 | 1 |

League Cup

| | | | | | | |
|---|---|---|---|---|---|---|
| Away | 1 | 0 | 0 | 1 | 3 | 2 |

Wartime

| | | | | | | |
|---|---|---|---|---|---|---|
| Home | 1 | 1 | 0 | 0 | 6 | 3 |
| Away | 1 | 0 | 0 | 1 | 4 | 5 |
| Totals | 2 | 1 | 0 | 1 | 10 | 8 |

Aston Villa's first-ever game in the Second Division was against Swansea Town at the Vetch Field on 29 August 1936. A crowd of 26,000 saw them register a 2-1 victory, Frank Broome scoring both goals, one a real beauty! Later in the season Villa won 4-0 at home with the help of a Ronnie Dix hat-trick.

After Villa had been relegated at the end of the previous season, their first Second Division home victory for 21 years came at the expense of the Swans who lost 1-0 at Villa Park on 29 August 1959. Peter McParland netted the all-important goal in front of 34,666 spectators. The following season Villa repeated their 4-0 home victory over the Swans, Frank Shell netting twice in front of 50,387 fans.

Five days before playing in the 1982 European Cup Final, Villa beat Swansea City 3-0 at home - but only 18,294 fans turned up, the lowest crowd of the season!

As you can see the Swans have never gained a point or scored a League goal at Villa Park.

Villa knocked the Swans out of the FA Cup in successive seasons: 2-0 in 1924 and 3-1 in 1925, each time in the 2nd round.

Swansea lost an FA Cup semi-final to Preston North End at rain-swept Villa Park in 1964.

Appropriately Welshman Phil Woosnam scored twice when Villa beat Swansea 3-2 at The Vetch Field in a 2nd round League Cup-tie in September 1965.

Eighteen goals were scored in the two League South Wartime games between the two clubs in September 1945. Bob Iverson netted four of Villa's ten, two in each match.

Players with both clubs include: W Aspinall, J Beresford, TB Craig, G Crudgington, TB Dodds, T Ford, BG Hole, S Howarth, N Lockhart, J McMorran, L Phillips, MJ Pinner, JJ Rimmer (also Swans' coach & caretaker-manager), D Roberts, D Saunders.
Also: F Barson (Villa player, Swans' trainer, K McNaught (Villa player, Swans' coach/assistant-manager).

## SWINDON TOWN
Villa's playing record against the Robins:
Football League/Premiership

| Venue | P | W | D | L | F | A |
|---|---|---|---|---|---|---|
| Home | 5 | 3 | 1 | 1 | 10 | 5 |
| Away | 5 | 2 | 2 | 1 | 6 | 4 |
| Totals | 10 | 5 | 3 | 2 | 16 | 9 |

FA Cup

| | | | | | | |
|---|---|---|---|---|---|---|
| Away | 1 | 1 | 0 | 0 | 2 | 1 |

Aston Villa first met the Robins at League level in Division Two in August 1969 when they were beaten 2-0 at home. Villa's burly centre-half George Curtis scored the goal in the 1-1 draw at Swindon later that season before Villa finally conjured up their first win (2-1) in September 1972 doubling up later that season with a 3-1 victory at The County Ground.

When Villa drew 0-0 at Swindon on the last day of the 1987-88 campaign, clinching promotion to the First Division as runners-up.

Dean Saunders netted two penalties when claiming his first hat-trick for Villa as they beat Swindon 5-0 at home in a Premiership game February 1994.

Dwight Yorke and Steve Froggatt were on target when Villa beat Swindon 2-1 in a 5th round FA Cup-tie in front of 16,402 fans at The County Ground in 1992.

THE COMPLETE ENCYCLOPAEDIA OF ASTON VILLA F.C.  THE COMPLETE ENCYCLOPAEDIA OF ASTON VILLA F.C.

259

Players with both clubs: W Armstrong (Villa reserve), RD Blanchflower (Swindon WW2 guest), FW Butcher (Villa reserve), C Calderwood, S Cowe (Villa reserve), P Crichton (Villa loanee), L Davies (Villa trialist/reserve), GF Ephgrave (Villa reserve), J Findlay, D Geddis, AA Gray, P King, F McAvennie, C McElney, AF McLoughlin, J Neal, RT Pritchard (Town WW2 guest), P Rideout, CL Roberts (Villa reserve), HG Shutt, DF Skea, LF Skiller, C Tiler, JE Travers, ME Walters, TC Wilson, Also: J Hogan (Villa manager, Swindon player), S McMahon (Villa player, Town manager), J Barron (Swindon player, Villa coach, assistant-manager), AE Lindon (Villa player, Swindon scout).

## TAINTON, WALTER
Born: Smethwick, August 1882. Died: Birmingham, December 1937.
Career: Smethwick Centaur, Aston Villa (April 1906), Birmingham Welfare FC (1908), Hockley Hill Methodists (1910).
Walter Tainton was a reserve right-half with Aston Villa and made one League appearance against Notts County (home) in April 1907 when he replaced Sam Greenhalgh. He later worked for the Birmingham Health Department.

## TALBOT, ALEXANDER DOUGLAS
Born: Cannock, 13 July 1902. Died: Stourbridge, 13 August 1975
Career: West Cannock Colliery, Cannock Church & Chapel League, Hednesford Town (1918), Aston Villa (professional April 1923), Bradford Park Avenue (June 1936), Stourbridge (August 1939). Retired in 1940 and went to work for the Austin Motor Compnay at Longbridge after the War prior to starting his own dairy business in Stourbridge which flourished during the 1950s.

A mixture of courage and culture, finesse and skilfully applied force made Alex 'Tiny' Talbot what he was, a fine centre-half, who was first-choice at the heart of the Aston Villa defence for a decade. He was signed after completing a ten-hour shift down the mine and became part and parcel of what has been described as the greatest Villa middle line of all-time, Alex Gibson and Joe Tate playing either side of him in the two wing-half positions. A reliable 'stopper; when he had to be, Talbot was a confident footballer who represented the Football League v the Scottish League in 1933 but alas never won an England cap. He was rewarded with a benefit by Aston Villa for his loyal and dedicated service to the club for whom he appeared in 263 League and FA Cup games and scored seven goals. He was given his nickname because he was the shortest of that brilliant half-back line!

## TATE, JOSEPH THOMAS
Born: Old Hill, 4 August 1904. Died: Cradley Heath, 18 May 1973.
Career: Stourbridge Council School, Birch Coppice Primitives, Grainger's Lane Primitives, Round Oak Steel Works FC (Brierley Hill), Cradley Heath (April 1923), Aston Villa (£400, April 1925), Brierley Hill Alliance (player-manager, May 1935-May 1937). Retired after breaking his right leg playing against Moor Green in a Birmingham & District League game. He became a successful businessman, running his own tobacconist shop for a number of years in Brierley Hill (which he had started in 1936). He was also a very useful cricketer, playing for the Warwickshire Club & Ground.
Joe Tate was an outstanding tactician who preferred to play the ball on the ground rather than giving it the big heave-oh! Described as being 'strong in attack and quick in recovery' he loved to participate in a triangular movement involving his inside-forward and winger or perhaps his full-back. He was, of course, a member of that great half-back trio that served Villa for a decade and made 193 senior appearances for the club, scoring four goals. The youngest of five brothers, he was capped three times by England against France, Belgium and Wales (1931 & 1932) but suffered with niggling injuries during the latter stages of his Villa career, having only one first team game during his last two seasons before becoming player-manager of Brierley Hill.

## TAYLOR, GRAHAM
Born: Worksop, 15 September 1944
Career: Scunthorpe United (amateur 1959-60), Grimsby Town (apprentice, August 1961, professional July 1962), Lincoln City (player/coach, July 1969, retired as player in December 1972 due to hip injury; then manager until June 1977), Watford (manager, June 1977-July 1987), Aston Villa (manager, July 1987-July 1990), England Youth, Under-21 and 'B' team manager, between November 1982-June 1990, then national manager July 1990-November 1993), Wolverhampton Wanderers (manager, March 1994-December 1995) Watford (General manager, February 1996, team manager May 1997-May 2001). Returned to Villa Park in mid-May 2001 as a non-Executive member of the Board of Directors.
As a player, Graham Taylor served as a full-back, making 215

*Graham Taylor (left) with his back-room staff: Bobby Downes, Steve Harrison and Jim Walker.*

appearances for Grimsby and well over 150 for Lincoln before moving into management at Sincil Bank in 1972. He was Imps' boss for five years, during which time he saw the team win the Fourth Division championship in 1976 with a record total of 74 points and 100 goals. He rejected an offer from West Bromwich Albion to take over the reins at Elton John's Watford and whilst at Vicarage Road did a superb job. He guided the Hornets into Europe and to the 1984 FA Cup Final after earlier seeing the club rise from the Fourth to the First Division in double-quick time, win the Fourth Division title in 1979 and finish a creditable runners-up in the Football League in 1983.

After ten years excellent service with Watford, Taylor took charge of Aston Villa and to a certain extent he did well, steering them back to the top flight in 1989 along with Millwall before leading the Villans to runners-up spot in the First Division (behind Liverpool) in 1989.

After seeing Villa fulfil a total of 120 League games, of which 52 were won, 32 drawn and 36 lost, in 1990 Taylor was given the highest honour in English football, that of team manager of the national side - after he had graduated through the ranks as boss of the Youth, Under-21 and 'B' teams.

Although he strove manfully to get things going he didn't quite fit the bill and despite qualifying for the 1992 European Championships, England missed out on a World Cup place and as a result Taylor lost his job. After a short spell out of the game he was brought back into League football by Wolves, who appointed him manager towards the end of the 1993-94 season. Taylor, like a handful of managers before him, failed to bring eagerly awaited Premiership football to Molineux and was subsequently dismissed after less than eighteen months in office. Soon afterwards he returned to his former club Watford, as General Manager and guided them to promotion from Division Two. In November 1998 Taylor was rushed to hospital with a throat infection. He made a full recovery and against all the odds - took the Hornets into the Premier League of English football after a 2-0 victory over Bolton Wanderers in the First Division Play-off Final at Wembley in May 1999. Relegated in 2000, Taylor then worked earnestly to get the Hornets back into the top flight - without success!

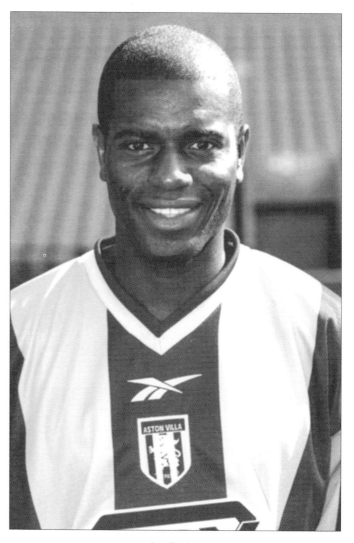

*Ian Taylor*

### TAYLOR, IAN KENNETH
Born: Birmingham, 4 June 1968
Career: Moor Green, Port Vale (£15,000, professional, July 1992), Sheffield Wednesday (£1 million, July 1994), Aston Villa (£1 million, December 1994).

The versatile Ian Taylor is the first player marked down on the team sheet by Villa boss John Gregory. A workaholic in the midfield, whether playing as an anchorman or acting as the main driving force, he covers every blade of grass during the course of a game, has a tremendous engine and although he's had to battle against ankle, knee and hamstring injuries, he has always bounced back in style, giving nothing less than 110 per-cent every time he takes the field. Strong in the tackle, his workrate is phenomenal and when the 2000-01 season ended Taylor's record in a Villa shirt was 254 appearances and 37 goals....with more to come.

He had supported Villa as a youngster, attending home games whenever possible. After doing well in non-League circles with Moor Green he went on to make 106 appearances for Port Vale (35 goals), helping the Potteries' club win the Asuto Windscreen Shield at Wembley in 1993. He netted twice in 18 games for the Owls before making his second £1 million move, this time to Villa Park. In 1996 he gained a League Cup winners medal and collected a runners-up prize in the FA Cup Final of 2000.

### TAYLOR, MARTIN SEYMOUR
Born: Annfield, May 1899. Deceased.
Career: Annfield, Aston Villa (June 1920), Durham City (August 1922).
A relatively unknown reserve centre-forward, Martin Taylor played in

one League game for Villa against Preston (at home) in September 1921 when he deputsied for Billy Dickson. He helped set up both goals in Villa's 2-1 win.

### TAYLOR, RICHARD ERIC
Born: Wednesfield, near Wolverhampton, 9 April 1918. Died: Birmingham, 28 January 1995.
Career: Junior football, Grimsby Town (professional, May 1935), Scunthorpe United (April 1948-May 1954), then reserve team manager & trainer/coach at the Old Showground until summer of 1956), Sheffield United (coach/assistant-manager, August 1956), Aston Villa (coach/assistant-manager, December 1958, then manager, July 1964-May 1967).

An old-fashioned centre-half, rough and ready, Dick Taylor was a tremendously hard worker, the sheet-anchor at the back who made 35 senior appearances for the Mariners and well over 150 for Scunthorpe during the Iron's Midland League and Third Division (North) days.

He worked with Joe Mercer at Bramall Lane before moving to Villa Park with Mercer in 1958, eventually taking over as manager after the former Arsenal, Everton and England international departed company with the club in 1964. He sold Tony Hateley to Chelsea for £100,000 and then spent all that money plus another £40,000 on new players in an effort to bring success to Villa Park. Nothing materialsed and after being in charge for 125 League games, of which 42 were won and 66 lost, Taylor was sacked along with his assistant Jimmy Easson, the former Portsmouth player. Taylor later ran a sports shop some 600 yards away from Villa Park in Witton Lane.

THE COMPLETE ENCYCLOPAEDIA OF ASTON VILLA F.C.  THE COMPLETE ENCYCLOPAEDIA OF ASTON VILLA F.C.

261

## TEALE, SHAUN

Born: Southport, 10 March 1964.

Career: Weymouth (August 1985), Bournemouth (£50,000, February 1989), Aston Villa (£300,000, July 1991), Tranmere Rovers (£450,000, August 1995), Preston North End (on loan, February-March 1997), Motherwell (player-manager), Southport (non-contract, 2000-01).

Rugged, combative defender, able to occupy a variety of positions including that of sweeper, Shaun Teale won a semi-professional cap for England as a Weymouth player before joining the Football League with Bournemouth. A fearless competitor, he appeared in 116 first-class games for the Cherries and then added a further 181 outings to his tally (five goals scored) during four seasons at Villa Park. Did very well initially in Villa's colours, then lost his way before re-establshing himself in the side under Brian Little as the relegation battle hotted up. He was an ever-present at Prenton Park before losing his place half-way through the 1996-97 season.

haun Teale

## TELEVISION

The first time Villa were seen 'live' on TV was when they played Manchester United in the 1957 FA Cup Final at Wembley.

Villa's first appearance on BBC's 'Match of the Day' was on 19 December 1964 when they defeated Arsenal 3-1 at home in front of just 11,780 spectators. Two Bakers scored that day - Alan twice for Villa and Joe for the Gunners.

The first Second Division League match to be screened 'live' on TV featured Middlesbrough against Aston Villa in February 1988.

## TEMPLETON, ROBERT BRYSON

Born: Coylton, 22 June 1879. Died: Scotland, 2 November 1919.

Career: Kilmarnock (juniors, August 1894), Hibernian (July 1897), Aston Villa (£250, March 1899), Newcastle United (£400, January 1903), Woolwich Arsenal (£250, May 1906), Celtic (£250, June 1906), Kilmarnock (October 1907), Fulham (June 1913-May 1914). Kilmarnock (August 1914-May 1915). Did not figure after the Great War.

A tremendously gifted footballer. Bobby Templeton was one of the characters of pre-First World War football. Tall and thin, selfish but brilliant, he was able to play as a direct right or left-winger, even as an inside-forward (he preferred the left flank). He tended to be

inconsistent at times but on his day was an exceptionally fine footballer who produced the goods on the big occasion! It was often claimed that Templeton was the cause of the Ibrox Park disaster in 1902 when several fans were killed. He was waltzing his way down the wing when the vast crowd swayed to see his dribbling skills - hence the collapse of a retaining wall and crush barriers. A real showman, Templeton was capped eleven times by Scotland, won both League championship and Scottish Cup winners' medals with Celtic and of course appeared in that ill-fated international against England in 1902. He starred in well over 400 club games and scored 40 goals, his Villa record being

seven strikes in 71 outings. He helped Villa win the First Division title in 1900 (four goals in 11 games) and formed a fine partnership with Fred Wheldon and then Joe Bache before leaving to join Newcastle. Templeton was also the fooballers' billiards champion whilst at St James' Park.

## TERRACE TROPHY
## (SUPPORTERS PLAYER OF THE YEAR TROPHY)

Aston Villa fans launched their own award in the late 1950s - the AV Supporters Terrace Trophy - presented to the best player, in their opinion, during any one season.

Among the many winners of the star prize we have:

Nigel Sims (first in 1958) plus Charlie Aitken, Jimmy Brown, Gordon Cowans, Vic Crowe, Johnny Dixon, Tony Dorigo, Jimmy Dugdale, John Gidman, Brian Godfrey, Andy Gray, Barrie Hole, Andy Lochhead, Paul Merson, Paul McGrath, David Rudge, John Slueenwenhoek, Colin Withers and Ron Wylie

## TEWKESBURY, KENNETH CYRIL

Born: Hove, Sussex, 10 April 1909. Died: Brighton, 20 November 1970.

Career: Birmingham University, Birmingham (October 1929), Aston Villa (December 1931), Notts County (September 1932), Aston Villa (January 1933), Bradford Park Avenue (July 1935), Walsall (May 1937). Retired in May 1939 and worked for many years in Birmingham's jewellery quarter. Gained a Bachelor of Science Degree at Birmingham University.

An England amateur international goalkeeper (six caps won), Ken Tewkesbury was well over six feet tall and was reserve to Fred Biddlestone and Harry Morton during his time at Villa Park. He made only one first team appearance, against Newcastle United (home) in April 1933 (won 3-0). After leaving Villa (second time) he 14 League appearances for Bradford and 75 for the Saddlers.

## THOMAS, ROBERT SAMUEL

Born: Newtown, Birmingham, April 1867. Died: Edgbaston, Birmingham, March 1936.

Career: Cocknage FC, Aston Villa (April 1888), Walsall Town (August 1889) Bilston (1891).

Squarely built full-back whose career was plagued by injury, Bob Thomas made one first team appearance for Villa, away at Blackburn Rovers in a 3rd round FA Cup-tie in March 1889.

## THOMPSON, ALAN

Born: Newcastle, 22 December 1973

Career: Newcastle United (YTS, June 1980, professional, March 1991), Bolton Wanderers (£250,000, July 1993), Aston Villa (£4.5 million, June 1998), Celtic (£3.25 million, August 2000).

THE COMPLETE ENCYCLOPAEDIA OF ASTON VILLA F.C.

THE COMPLETE ENCYCLOPAEDIA OF ASTON VILLA F.C.

262

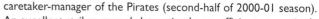

*Alan Thompson*

Capped by England at both Youth and Under-21 levels earlier in his career, midfielder Alan Thompson was John Gregory's first signing after he had taken over as manager at Villa Park. He was introduced to give the left hand-side of midfield a more solid and combative look to it, but unfortunately 'Thommo' struggled with ankle and hamstring injuries after a useful start to his Villa career. A dead-ball specialist, he packs a tremendous shot in his left foot but after being unable to hold down a regular place in the side during the 1999-2000 campaign, he was transferred to Celtic and what a magnificent first season he had in Scotland, helping the Bhoys complete a treble, namely the winning of the Premiership title, the League Cup and the Scottish Cup. Thompson's record as a Villa player was 60 appearances and five goals.

### THOMPSON, GARRY LINDSEY

Born: Kings Heath, Birmingham, 7 October 1959.
Career: Brandwood & Maypole Schools, Coventry City (apprentice, July 1975, professional, June 1977), West Bromwich Albion (£225,000, February 1983), Sheffield Wednesday (£450,000, August 1985), Aston Villa (£400,000, July 1986), Watford (£150,000, October 1988), Crystal Palace (£200,000, March 1990), Queen's Park Rangers (£125,000, August 1991), Cardiff City (free transfer, July 1993), Northampton Town (free transfer, February 1995). Retired in the summer of 1997 to become reserve team manager/coach at Sixfields Stadium. He was appointed coach at Bristol Rovers at the commencement of the 1999-2000 season, later taking over as

*Garry Thompson*

caretaker-manager of the Pirates (second-half of 2000-01 season).
An excellent striker, rugged, determined, very efficient, strong in the air and on the ground, Garry Thompson had a fine career that spanned 20 years during which time he played in all four Divisions of the Football League. During his six years of first team football with the Sky Blues, he scored 49 goals in 158 appearances and also gained six England Under-21 caps. Nicknamed 'Thommo', he then spent two-and-a-half years at The Hawthorns, initially teaming up with Cyrille Regis, who, ironically, was sold to Coventry! He netted 45 times in 105 outings for the Baggies. Recruited from Hillsborough by Villa boss Graham Turner, seemingly to replace Andy Gray, he went on to score 19 goals in 73 appearances during his two years with the club. He formed a very useful striking partnership with first Simon Stainrod, then Warren Aspinall and to a certain extent with David Platt when promotion was gained from Division Two in 1988.
Thompson continued in competitive football until 1997, calling it a day with a fine record of 614 League and Cup appearances and 164 goals safely under his belt.

### THOMPSON, JAMES GILBERT

Born: Crewe, July 1900. Deceased.
Career: Nantwich Victoria (1918), Aston Villa (September 1919), Brighton & Hove Albion (August 1921), Chesterton (August 1924-May 1926).
Right-back Jim Thompson was a burly player, fearsome in the tackle who did well for Aston Villa when appearing in 28 competitiive matches during his two seasons with the club. He struggled to gain regular first team football after the arrival of Tommy Smart but went on to play in 100 first-class games for Brighton.

### THOMPSON, THOMAS

Born: Fencehouses, near Houghton-le-Spring, County Durham, 10 November 1929.
Career: Lumley YMCA (1944), Newcastle United (£15, August 1946), Aston Villa (£12,000, September 1950), Preston North End (£28,500, June 1955), Stoke City (£10,000, July 1961), Barrow (£5,000, March 1963). Retired in May 1965 when he returned to Preston where he became a carpenter.
Inside-forward Tommy Thompson had a fine career, appearing in almost 450 League games and scoring 224 goals for his five clubs. He was one of the finest players in the game during the 1950s, his delicate touches, speed off the mark and expert finishing being his hallmarks. Small and stocky, he combined well with Colin Gibson, Johnny Dixon, Trevor Ford and Les Smith at Villa Park and was always looking for an opening, often trying his luck with long range shots. Replaced by Jackie Sewell in the Villa forward-line, Thompson was capped twice by England (v Wales in 1952 and Scotland five years later); he also represented the Football League side and England 'B'. Nicknamed 'Toucher' he played exceedingly well alongside Tom Finney at Preston and then Stan Matthews at Stoke. Thompson netted 76 goals in 165 first-class matches for Villa.

### THOMSON, ROBERT GILLIES McKENZIE

Born: Dundee, 21 May 1937
Career: Dundee & Dunblane Schools, Albion Rovers (amateur, 1951), Airdrieonians (amateur, August 1952), Wolverhampton Wanderers (amateur July 1953, professional, August 1954), Aston Villa (£8,000, June 1959), Birmingham City (September 1963), Stockport County (December 1967-May 1968), Bromsgrove Rovers (August 1968-May 1970)
Scottish inside-forward Bobby Thomson went on to have a splendid career after leaving Molineux in 1959. Unable to gain a first team place, he left Wolves for Villa Park and quickly settled into his stride, going on to net 70 goals in 171 appearances in four seasons with Aston Villa. He

*Bobby Thomson*

help them win the Second Division title in 1960 and the League Cup in 1961, as well as gaining a runners-up medal in the latter competition in 1963 when his future club Blues won the trophy. As hard as nails, the chunky, wavy-haired Thomson stayed four years at St Andrew's, hitting another 25 goals in less than 130 games before ending his Football League duties at Edgeley Park in the late 1960s. Keeping himself fit by playing squash and tennis, Thomson now lives in Birmingham.

## TIDMAN, OLIVER EUSTACE
Born: Margate, Kent, May 1911.
Career: Tufnell Park FC (1928), Aston Villa (May 1932), Stockport County (July 1935-August 1936), Bristol Rovers (August 1936), Clapton Orient (July 1937), Chelmsford City (1938-39). Did not figure after World War Two.
Ollie Tidman was a nimble outside-left, who was brought in by Aston Villa to cover for Eric Houghton and Frank Chester. He made just one senior appearance - in a First Division game against Chelsea at Stamford Bridge in February 1933, figuring on the winning side (1-0) in front of 30,000 spectators. In April 1934, Tidman played for the Birmingham County FA against the Scottish Juniors in a snowstorm at Dundee - his only representative honour. After leaving Villa Park in 1935 he went on to score four times in 25 outings for Stockport and once in 16 League games for Bristol Rovers before slowly winding down and entering non-League soccer in August 1938. Tidman retired to live in Bromley and is believed to be the oldest former Villa player alive today (at 2001).

## TILER, BRIAN
Born: Whiston, Rotherham, 15 March 1943. Died: Italy, 30 June 1990
Career: Rotherham United (juniors July 1958, professional July 1962), Aston Villa (£50,000, December 1968), Atlanta Chiefs (1971), Portland Timbers (mid-1972), Carlisle United (October 1972-May 1974), Wigan Athletic (coach/player-manager, July 1974-May 1976), Portland Timbers (manager/coach, 1976-77), Zambian national coach/manager (1977-79), Miami Americans (coach/manager, 1979-81), San Diego Sockers (coach/manager, 1982), Bournemouth (managing-director/secretary, January 1984, holding office at Dean Court until his death in 1990).
Brian Tiler was the first player signed by Aston Villa manager Tommy Docherty, who had been his boss at Millmoor, albeit for only a year. Originally an inside or centre-forward with Rotherham, for whom he made 212 League appearances Tiler developed into a solid and consistent wing-half. At one time whilst at Millmoor he was all set to join QPR (when the 'Doc' was manager there) but the London club couldn't raise enough cash and the deal fell through! With Villa, Tiler took over the captaincy and went on to appear in 127 League and Cup games for the club, scoring four goals. He played in the 1971 League Cup Final against Spurs and the following season gained a Third Division championship medal. After a decent spell in the NASL, he left

Villa Park for Carlisle and quickly helped the Cumbrians reach the First Division (1974). But with top-class football ready and waiting, the impatient streak in Tiler's nature saw him forego that dream as he moved into management with non-League Wigan Athletic, whom he guided to the Northern Premier League title in his first season at Springfield Park (1975). He then returned to the States to take charge of Portland Timbers, learning a bit about the marketing side of football while in America. He was then appointed coach/manager of the Zambian national team and successfully guided them through the qualification stages for the 1980 Olympic Games as well as organising a national coaching scheme in that African country. After failing in an effort to become manager of Rotherham he then had a spell as coach

*Brian Tiler*

of the Miami Americans and later had a twelve-month appointment as coach with the San Diego Sockers. In 1982 he returned to his native Yorkshire (to live in Rotherham) where he formed his own company: Brian Tiler (Management), also acting as an agent for the Zambia FA. He then did superbly well in his capacity as managing-director of Bournemouth.
Tiler was tragically killed in car crash in Italy. His Bournemouth colleague at the time, Harry Redknapp, was in the vehicle as well, but only received minor injuries.

## TILER, CARL
Born: Sheffield, 11 February 1970.
Career: Barnsley (YTS June 1986, professional February 1988), Nottingham Forest (£1.4 million, May 1991), Swindon Town (on loan, November 1994), Aston Villa (£750,000, October 1995), Sheffield United (£650,000, March 1997), Everton (£500,000, November 1997), Charlton Athletic (£700,000, September 1998), Birmingham City (on loan February 2001), Portsmouth (£250,000, March 2001).
A strong, tall, dominant defender, Carl Tiler had already gained 13 England Under-21 caps and made over 170 senior appearances as well as spending three years in the shadows at Nottingham Forest before joining Aston Villa for a big fee. Unfortunately he suffered a hamstring injury on his debut against Everton and missed the remainder of that 1995-96 season. He was out of action for a year before returning to score his only Villa goal against his old club, Forest. However, more injury problems and the good form of Ugo Ehiogu and Gareth Southgate eventually led to Tiler moving to his home city of Sheffield on transfer deadline day in 1997 when he teamed up with the Blades of Bramall Lane. He had 15 outings for Villa - and afterwards went on to appear in 100 games for the Blades, Everton and Charlton, helping the latter club reach the Premiership in 2000.

## TINDALL, MICHAEL CHADWICK
Born: Acocks Green, Birmingham, 5 April 1941
Career: South Birmingham Boys, Aston Villa (amateur, April 1956, professional April 1958), New York Americans (on loan, 1961), Walsall (June 1968). Non-League football from August 1969; assisted Aston Villa Old Stars (1975-88). Later became licensee of the Coach & Horses at Bromsgrove.
Capped eight times by England at Youth international level, midfielder Mike Tindall played in the Final of the FIFA Youth Tournament in Luxembourg in 1958. He made his Villa debut in December 1959 against Hull City at home (Division 2). This was the first of 136 senior appearances for the club (nine goals scored). Fighting for a place in the

THE COMPLETE ENCYCLOPAEDIA OF ASTON VILLA F.C.        THE COMPLETE ENCYCLOPAEDIA OF ASTON VILLA F.C.

264

team initially with Alan Deakin, Jimmy McMorran and Ron Wylie and then with Alan Baker and Phil Woosnam, he had the misfortune to suffer a broken leg against Tottenham in November 1964. But this did not curb his enthusiasm and although he took quite some time to recover full fitness, Tindall battled on to re-establish himself in the League side in 1965-66. After 12 years on Villa's books he left the club in 1968 for neighbouring Walsall but quit League soccer after just twelve months at Fellows Park.

## TORQUAY UNITED

Villa's playing record against the Gulls:

Football League

| Venue | P | W | D | L | F | A |
|---|---|---|---|---|---|---|
| Home | 2 | 1 | 0 | 1 | 5 | 2 |
| Away | 2 | 0 | 1 | 1 | 2 | 3 |
| Totals | 4 | 1 | 1 | 2 | 7 | 5 |

FA Cup

| | P | W | D | L | F | A |
|---|---|---|---|---|---|---|
| Away | 1 | 0 | 0 | 1 | 1 | 3 |

Aston Villa clinched the Third Division championship with an emphatic 5-1 home win over the Gulls in front of 37,582 fans on 29 April 1972. Earlier in the season Villa had lost 2-1 at Plainmoor!
Over 9,000 fans saw Villa knocked out of the FA Cup by United in a 1st round tie at Plainmoor in November 1970.

Players with both clubs include: LC Chatterley (player/coach at Plainmoor), NF Clarke, P Crichton (Villa loanee), JA Dunn, RT Edwards, BA Greenhalgh, B Handley, WH Harris, P King, A Lee, A Little, JB Lynch, AF McLoughlin, P Maggs, T Mitchinson, GS Parker, AF Phoenix, BD Rioch (also United manager), D Rudge, AJ Scott, JC Slueewenhoek, PS Varco (Torquay reserve), WJ Young.
Also: A Massie (Villa player & manager, Torquay manager).

## TOKYO

Aston Villa lost 2-0 in Tokyo to the South American champions Penarol from Uruguay, in the World Club championship in December 1982 in front of 61,445 fans.
Almost eleven years later, on 19 July 1993, Villa returned to Tokyo (the Big Egg Stadium) to play Yomiuri of Japan in the country's Coca-Cola Cup. A crowd of 20,000 saw Villa win 2-1 with Dalian Atkinson netting both goals.

## TOTTENHAM HOTSPUR

Villa's playing record against Spurs:

Football League/Premiership

| Venue | P | W | D | L | F | A |
|---|---|---|---|---|---|---|
| Home | 58 | 26 | 15 | 17 | 93 | 79 |
| Away | 58 | 19 | 10 | 29 | 92 | 115 |
| Totals | 116 | 45 | 25 | 46 | 185 | 194 |

FA Cup

| Venue | P | W | D | L | F | A |
|---|---|---|---|---|---|---|
| Home | 3 | 0 | 1 | 2 | 0 | 3 |
| Away | 8 | 4 | 0 | 4 | 8 | 9 |
| Totals | 11 | 4 | 1 | 6 | 8 | 12 |

League Cup

| Venue | P | W | D | L | F | A |
|---|---|---|---|---|---|---|
| Home | 1 | 1 | 0 | 0 | 2 | 1 |
| Away | 2 | 1 | 0 | 1 | 3 | 5 |
| Neutral | 1 | 0 | 0 | 1 | 0 | 2 |
| Totals | 4 | 2 | 0 | 2 | 5 | 8 |

FA Charity Shield

| Venue | P | W | D | L | F | A |
|---|---|---|---|---|---|---|
| Neutral | 1 | 0 | 1 | 0 | 2 | 2 |

Wartime

| Venue | P | W | D | L | F | A |
|---|---|---|---|---|---|---|
| Home | 1 | 1 | 0 | 0 | 5 | 1 |
| Away | 1 | 0 | 0 | 1 | 0 | 3 |
| Totals | 2 | 1 | 0 | 1 | 5 | 4 |

The first meeting in the Football League took place on 20 November 1909 at Villa Park when a crowd of 20,000 saw Spurs defeated 3-2, Billy Gerrish, Harry Hampton and Joe Bache the Villa scorers. The return game ended all square at 1-1.
Villa completed the League double over Spurs in 1910-11, winning 4-0 at home and 2-1 in London.
The last season before the Great War (1914-15) saw Villa win 2-0 at Tottenham and 3-1 at Villa Park, but only 13,000 supporters witnessed the latter game - the lowest on record for a game between the two clubs.
In 1920-21, Villa doubled up over Spurs (the subsequent FA Cup winners) with victories of 4-2 at home and 2-1 away, and in 1922-23 Villa repeated the act with a 2-0 triumph at Villa Park followed by a 2-1 win in London.
Spurs won a thrilling contest by 3-2 at Villa Park in November 1927 and after a spell in the Second Division they returned to complete the double over Villa in 1933-34 - winning 5-1 at Villa Park and 3-2 at White Hart Lane. Another Spurs double followed 22 years later (in 1955-56) when they gained a 4-3 victory at home and a 2-0 success at Villa Park. The first League meeting after the Second World War did not take place until September 1950 when almost 50,000 fans at Villa Park saw Spurs scrape a 3-2 win. Later that season Spurs repeated that scoreline to take the points at White Hart Lane
In March 1958, Villa crashed 6-2 win at White Hart Lane. Internationals Bobby Smith (4) and Terry Medwin (2) claiming the London club's goals!
When Spurs completed the League and Cup double in

*Villa drew 1-1 at Torquay in March 1971.... here Harry Gregory watches Geoff Vowden's header hit the net for his first goal for the club.*

THE COMPLETE ENCYCLOPAEDIA OF ASTON VILLA F.C.          THE COMPLETE ENCYCLOPAEDIA OF ASTON VILLA F.C.

265

*This header by Villa's John Gregory struck the Spurs' crossbar!*

season 1960-61 they met Villa three times, beating them 6-2 at home (they led 4-0 at the break) and 2-1 away in the First Division and 2-0 in the 5th round of the FA Cup.

Almost 182,000 fans witnessed those three matches - 61,356 in London and 50,810 in Aston for the respective League clashes and 69,672 at Villa Park for the cup-tie.

On 20 August 1962, a crowd of 64,751 saw Spurs beaten 2-1 at Villa Park and nine days later over 55,600 fans assembled at White Hart Lane to see Spurs gain revenge with a 4-2 victory.

Ten goals were scored in the two League games between the clubs in 1963-64. Spurs won 4-0 at White Hart Lane whilst it was all square at 3-3 at Villa Park.

Villa midfielder Mike Tindall broke his leg in the 4-0 defeat by Spurs at White Hart Lane in November 1964.

Tony Hateley scored four goals in Villa's exciting 5-5 draw with Spurs at White Hart Lane in March 1966. Villa were trailing 5-1 soon after half-time, but driven on by the two Alans, Baker and Deakin, they fought back to earn a point with Hateley's fourth goal coming late on. It was a pity that only 28,290 fans turned out to see such an exciting contest.

Villa's 1-0 triumph at Spurs in October 1966 ended a run of 17 visits to White Hart Lane without a League success.

When Villa returned to the First Division in 1975 (after a break of eight years) they drew 1-1 at home with Spurs but then crashed 5-2 at White Hart Lane.

Villa's first away game of the 1978-79 season took them to White Hart Lane where they beat a star-studded Spurs side that included the Argentinian World Cup duo of Ossie Ardiles and Ricky Villa, 4-1 in front of 48,000 spectators.

Gordon Cowans scored twice (once from the spot) in Villa's 4-0 home win over Spurs in October 1982.

The lowest-ever crowd for a Spurs-Villa League game in London - just 14,854 - saw Spurs win 4-2 in May 1986. Earlier that season 14,099

spectators had witnessed a 2-1 win for the London club at Villa Park. Villa, in fact, ended both their 1985-86 and 1986-87 League programmes with matches against Spurs.

When Villa held Spurs 0-0 at White Hart Lane in November 1992 it was the first-ever goalless draw on Spurs soil and the first draw of any kind since 1954.

Four months later at Villa Park (on 10 March 1993) a crowd of 37,727 witnessed another 0-0 draw in what was the 100th League meeting between the two clubs.

In between times Villa came back from 2-0 down to win 5-2 at Spurs in April 1992.

Goalkeeper Mark Bosnich saved two penalties - one from Darren Anderton, the other from Nick Barmby - in Villa's 1-1 Premiership draw with Spurs in London in March 1994.

In November 1994 Villa, with Jim Barron acting as caretaker-boss following the departure of Ron Atkinson, were 3-0 up after 26 minutes at White Hart Lane in their Premiership game against Spurs, Graham Fenton having netted twice. The Londoners clawed back to 3-3 but Dean Saunders scored a 90th minute winner to earn Villa a 4-3 victory. On Boxing Day 1997, Villa beat Spurs 4-1 at home with Mark Draper and Stan Collymore both scoring twice.

Twelve months later Dion Dublin netted twice on his Aston Villa debut as Spurs (having led 2-0) lost 3-2 at Villa Park. And in April 2000, Spurs were 2-0 up again, this time at White Hart Lane only to see Villa storm back and register a famous 4-2 victory by scoring three times in seven minutes halfway through the second-half.

Another two-goal hero against Spurs was Ian Taylor when the London club lost 2-0 at Villa Park in November 2000.

Aston Villa have yet to score a 'home' FA Cup goal against Spurs, having lost two of their three encounters at Villa Park. But at White Hart Lane Villa's record is good, claiming four victories - in 1903 (3-2), 1920 (1-0 with a Clay own-goal in front of 52,179 fans), in 1934 (1-0, Dai Astley on target) and 1-0 again (in 1992) when Dwight Yorke found the net. On their way to FA Cup glory in 1921, Spurs beat Villa 1-0 at home in front of a then record 56,991 White Hart Lane crowd.

Then, as holders of the same trophy, Spurs again knocked Villa out of the competition by 2-0 at the quarter-final stage in 1962 in front of another bumper crowd of 63,879, also at White Hart Lane.

The eleven FA Cup matches between the two teams have attracted almost 480,000 spectators, revealing an average of 43,620.

Two Martin Chivers goals (late on) sank Third Division challengers Aston Villa in the 1971 League Cup Final at Wembley where Spurs won 2-0 in front of 97,024 spectators.

On their way to winning the League Cup in 1994, Villa ousted Spurs in the 5th round, winning 2-1 at White Hart Lane with goals by Ray Houghton and Earl Barrett. This took Villa into their ninth semi-final - a record.

The FA Charity Shield game was played at Wembley in August 1981 before a crowd of 92,445. Peter Withe scored twice for Villa, Mark Falco doing likewise for Spurs.

When Villa beat Spurs 5-1 at home in a League South Wartime game in February 1946, George Edwards and Frank Broome both netted twice.

Players with both clubs include: S Beaton (Villa reserve, Spurs WW1 guest), G Bergsson (Villa trialist), RD Blanchflower, WF Brawn (Spurs WW1 guest), MS Burke (Spurs trialist), C Calderwood, J Cantrell, GW Cook, RW Dix, DDM Ginola, AA Gray, JA Gray, SB Hodge, RTJ Iverson (Spurs junior), P Kyle, JR Martin (Spurs WW2 guest), TP Muldoon (Spurs junior), FJ O'Donnell (Spurs WW2 guest), J Parsons (Villa reserve, Spurs WW1 guest), E Phypers (Villa reserve), V Potts (also Spurs scout), IH Price (Villa reserve, Spurs WW1 guest), A Ralston (Villa junior, Spurs WW1), GM Smith, CH Spiers, TE Tebb (Villa & Spurs reserve), JE Travers (Spurs WW1 guest), J Walters (Spurs WW1 guest), F Wilson (Villa reserve).

Also: G Graham (Villa player, Spurs manager), J Tresadern (Spurs manager, Villa scout).

## TOWNSEND, ANDREW DAVID

Born: Maidstone, Kent, 27 July 1963

Career: Welling United (August 1980), Weymouth (March 1984), Southampton (£35,000, January 1985), Norwich City (£300,000, August 1988), Chelsea (£1.2 million, July 1990), Aston Villa (£2.1 million, July 1993), Middlesbrough (£500,000, August 1997), West Bromwich Albion (£50,000, September 1999). Retired as first-team player in January 2000 to take over as reserve-coach at The Hawthorns, a position he held until for six months before being replaced by another ex-Villa player, Gary Shelton. Now a soccer summariser on ITV.

Capped 70 times by the Republic of Ireland at senior level and once by the 'B' team, midfielder Andy Townsend had an excellent career in top-class football. On his day he was an effective, hard-working performer, on par with most of the leading professionals manning the same position. Before joining Villa he had made over 100 appearances for Saints, 88 for the Canaries and 138 for Chelsea. He was already established in the Eire side and quickly made his mark at Villa Park. His inspirational displays from centre-field sparked off many attacks, and his experience and, indeed, his presence on the field, was appreciated to the full by the younger players. Townsend gained two League Cup winners' medals with Villa (1994 & 1996), skippering the side in the latter final, and he scored 11 goals in 176 first team outings for the club before transferring to Middlesbrough at the start of the 1997-98 season. He helped 'Boro regain their Premiership status at the end of his first season on Teeside and went on to play in 88 matches under Bryan Robson before moving to The Hawthorns where he ended his career in the year 2000.

• Townsend's father, Don, was a full-back with Charlton Athletic and Crystal Palace.

*Andy Townsend*

## TRABZONSPOR

Villa's playing record against the Turkish side:

UEFA Cup

| Venue | P | W | D | L | F | A |
|---|---|---|---|---|---|---|
| Home | 1 | 1 | 0 | 0 | 2 | 1 |
| Away | 1 | 0 | 0 | 1 | 0 | 1 |
| Totals | 2 | 1 | 0 | 1 | 2 | 2 |

The Turkish side went through to the 3rd round of the UEFA Cup in 1994-95 by virtue of an away goal. After beating Villa 1-0 at the Avni Aker Stadium on the edge of the Black Sea, the Turks came to Birmingham for the return leg and scored a dramatic 90th minute goal, despite having had a player (Termizkanoglu Ogun) sent-off and losing the contest 2-1. Dalian Atkinson made his 100th appearance for Villa in the second leg.

Soon after that second leg - on 11 November 1994 - Villa were fined £9,000 following the pitch invasion by supporters at the end of that clash with Trabzonspor. The Turkish club was fined £6,000.

## TRAINERS (MASSEURS & PHYSIOTHERAPISTS)

*Fred Pedley*

Aston Villa's first senior trainer was R (Dick) Oxenbould who was employed by the club from 1886 to 1894. He saw Villa reach the FA Cup Finals of 1887 and 1892 and win the League in 1894,

Joe Grierson took over from Oxenbould, remaining as Villa's first team trainer for 22 years, up to the summer of 1916. During that time the team won five League titles, the FA Cup four times and completed the double.

Former full-back Freddie Miles returned to Villa Park as first team trainer in 1919 and was spongeman at both the 1920 and 1924 FA Cup Finals.

Hubert Bourne, an ex-player, was Villa's first team trainer for some 20 years: 1932-52.

Harry Cooch (ex-goalkeeper) was also a trainer at Villa Park.

Ex-players Frank Barson and Charlie Wallace were trainers together at Villa Park in 1938-39, looking after the third and fourth teams respectively. Scotsman Bill Baxter was trainer in 1964-68.

Fred Pedley had a good spell as Villa's physio in the 1970's after earlier serving WBA.

Jim Williams was physiotherapist at Villa Park when the League championship was won in 1980-81 - the season when Villa used only 14 players, emphasising the fitness level within the club.

Jim Walker was physio at Blackburn Rovers when they won the Simod Cup at Wembley in 1987. He is now Villa's physio.

## TRANMERE ROVERS

Villa's playing record against Rovers:

Football League

| Venue | P | W | D | L | F | A |
|---|---|---|---|---|---|---|
| Home | 2 | 2 | 0 | 0 | 3 | 0 |
| Away | 2 | 1 | 1 | 0 | 2 | 1 |
| Totals | 4 | 3 | 1 | 0 | 5 | 1 |
| League Cup | | | | | | |
| Home | 1* | 1 | 0 | 0 | 3 | 1 |
| Away | 1 | 0 | 0 | 1 | 1 | 3 |
| Totals | 2 | 1 | 0 | 1 | 4 | 4 |

*Villa won the tie 5-4 on penalties.

THE COMPLETE ENCYCLOPAEDIA OF ASTON VILLA F.C.          THE COMPLETE ENCYCLOPAEDIA OF ASTON VILLA F.C.

267

*An Aston Villa training session by the seaside in 1960.*

The first League games between the two clubs took place in season 1970-71 (Division 3). Ian Hamilton's goal gave Aston Villa a 1-0 home win, scoring again in the 1-1 draw at Prenton Park. The following season when Villa won the Third Division championship, they doubled up over Rovers, winning 2-0 at home and 1-0, Charlie Aitken netting the all-important goal in the latter fixture in front of 12,054 fans.

After the 1994 two-legged League Cup semi-final between Villa and Rovers had ended level at 4-4, the tie went to a penalty shoot-out. Both sides took their allocated five spot-kicks and as a result the scores were again level at 4-4, Ugo Ehiogu having struck the bar for Villa whilst Mark Bosnich had saved from Rovers' Ged Brannan. Villa's skipper Kevin Richardson then fired over giving Liam O'Brien the chance to send Rovers through to the Final, but Bosnich saved his effort. Up stepped Tony Daley to edge Villa 5-4 in front and it was down to Bosnich again, the Aussie pulling off his third save to take Villa through to Wembley.

By drawing level with Tranmere at 4-4, Villa created League Cup history, for no other team had previously overturned a two-goal deficit from the first leg of a semi-final.

Players with both clubs include: J Cumbes, S Curcic (Rovers trialist), RE Evans (WW1 guest), BC Godfrey (Rovers trialist), R Hazell (Villa reserve), D Hickson, D Kubicki, D Mountfield, EW Spencer (Villa reserve), S Teale, T Waring.
Also: E Blackburn (Villa player, Rovers trainer).

## TRANSFER TRAIL
Details of how and when Aston Villa's 'in and out' transfer records have been broken (or equalled) down the years:

### Players signed......

| | | |
|---|---|---|
| £100 | Archie Goodall from Preston NE | October 1888 |
| £100 | Willie Groves from West Brom A | September 1893 |
| £250 | Jimmy Crabtree from Burnley | August 1895 |
| £350 | Fred Wheldon from Small Heath | June 1896 |
| £400 | Martin Watkins from Stoke | January 1904 |
| £500 | Charlie Wallace from Crystal Palace | May 1907 |
| £1,000 | Andy Ducat from Woolwich Arsenal | June 1912 |
| £1,000 | John Hampson from Leeds City | October 1919 |
| £2,850 | Frank Barson from Barnsley | October 1919 |
| £7,500 | Jimmy Gibson from Partick Thistle | April 1927 |
| £10,775 | Jimmy Allen from Portsmouth | June 1934 |
| £12,000 | Trevor Ford from Cardiff City | January 1947 |
| £17,500 | Ivor Powell from QPR | December 1948 |
| £17,500 | Colin Gibson from Newcastle Utd | February 1949 |
| £25,000 | Dave Walsh from West Brom A | December 1950 |
| £25,000 | Jimmy Dugdale from West Brom A | February 1956 |
| £25,000 | Les Smith from Wolverhampton Wds | February 1956 |
| £30,000 | Bill Beaton from Dunfermline Ath | October 1958 |
| £35,000 | Brian Greenhalgh from Preston NE | September 1967 |
| £35,000 | Dick Edwards from Mansfield Town | March 1968 |
| £55,000 | Mike Ferguson from Blackburn Rov | May 1968 |
| £60,000 | Barrie Hole from Blackburn Rovers | September 1968 |
| £60,000 | Andy Lochhead from Leicester City | October 1968 |
| £100,000* | Bruce Rioch/Neil Rioch from Luton | July 1969 |
| £100,000 | John Burridge from Blackpool | September 1975 |
| £110,000 | Andy Gray from Dundee United | October 1975 |
| £175,000 | Dennis Mortimer from Coventry C | December 1975 |
| £200,000 | Ken McNaught from Everton | August 1977 |
| £275,000 | Tommy Craig from Sheffield Wed | January 1978 |
| £300,000 | David Geddis from Ipswich Town | September 1979 |
| £500,000 | Peter Withe from Nottingham Forest | May 1980 |
| £650,000 | Ian Ormondroyd from Bradford City | February 1989 |
| £1.5m | Tony Cascarino from Millwall | March 1990 |
| £1.7m | Dalian Atkinson from Real Sociedad | July 1991 |
| £2.3m | Dean Saunders from Liverpool | September 1992 |
| £2.5m | Gareth Southgate from Crystal Pal | July 1995 |
| £3.5m | Savo Milosevic from Partizan Belg | July 1995 |
| £4m | Sasa Curcic from Bolton Wanderers | August 1996 |
| £7m | Stan Collymore from Liverpool | May 1997 |
| £9.5m | Juan Pablo Angel from River Plate | January 2001 |

* Joint deal involving two players.

*Villa doing their training in 1936.*

THE COMPLETE ENCYCLOPAEDIA OF ASTON VILLA F.C.     THE COMPLETE ENCYCLOPAEDIA OF ASTON VILLA F.C.

268

*Tommy Craig - a £275,000 buy from Sheffield Wednesday in 1978.*

*Dean Saunders - signed from Liverpool for £2.3 million in 1992.*

## Players transferred......

| £100 | Fred Wheldon to West Bromwich A | August 1900 |
|---|---|---|
| £400 | Bobby Templeton to Newcastle Utd | January 1903 |
| £400 | George Harris to West Brom Albion | January 1909 |
| £1,200 | George Hunter to Oldham Athletic | January 1912 |
| £5,000 | Frank Barson to Manchester United | August 1922 |
| £10,000 | Eddie Lowe to Fulham | May 1950 |
| £30,000 | Trevor Ford to Sunderland | October 1950 |
| £30,000 | Danny Blanchflower to Tottenham H | October 1954 |
| £60,000 | Gerry Hitchens to Inter Milan | June 1961 |
| £100,000 | Tony Hateley to Chelsea | October 1966 |
| £200,000 | Bruce Rioch to Derby County | February 1974 |
| £1.15m | Andy Gray to Wolves | September 1979 |
| £5.5m | David Platt to Bari | July 1991 |
| £12.6m | Dwight Yorke to Manchester United | August 1998 |

## Other 'big' money signings made by Aston Villa (£500,000+)

| £6.75m | Paul Merson from Middlesbrough | September 1998 |
|---|---|---|
| £5.75m | Dion Dublin from Coventry City | November 1998 |
| £5.7m | Olof Mellberg from Racing Santander | July 2001 |
| £5.5m | Alpay Ozalan from Fenerbahce | July 2000 |
| £5.5m | Steve Stone from Nottingham Forest | March 1999 |
| £4.5m | George Boateng from Coventry City | July 1999 |
| £4.5m | Alan Thompson from Bolton Wds | June 1998 |
| £4m | Steve Watson from Newcastle U | October 1998 |
| £4m | Moustapha Hadji from Coventry City | June 2001 |
| £3.25m | Mark Draper from Leicester City | August 1995 |
| £3m | David Ginola from Tottenham Hot | August 2000 |
| £3m | David Unsworth from West Ham U | July 1998 |
| £2.35m | Dean Saunders to Galatasary | July 1995 |
| £2.1m | Andy Townsend from Chelsea | July 1993 |
| £1.75m | David James from Liverpool | June 1999 |
| £1.75m | Fernando Nelson from Sport. Lisbon | July 1996 |
| £1.7m | Earl Barrett from Oldham Athletic | February 1992 |
| £1.5m | Julian Joachim from Leicester City | February 1996 |
| £1.45m | Gary Charles from Derby County | January 1995 |
| £1.45m | Tommy Johnson from Derby Co | January 1995 |
| £1.35m | John Fashanu from Wimbledon | August 1994 |

| £1.35m | Simon Grayson from Leicester City | July 1997 |
|---|---|---|
| £1.3m | Guy Whittingham from Portsmouth | August 1993 |
| £1.1m | Steve Staunton from Liverpool | August 1991 |
| £1m | Gary Penrice from Watford | March 1991 |
| £1m | Naj Ghrayib from Hapoel Haifa | August 1999 |
| £1m | Alan Wright from Blackburn Rov | April 1995 |
| £1m | Ian Taylor from Sheffield Wed | December 1994 |
| £900,000 | Ray Houghton from Liverpool | July 1992 |
| £750,000 | Carl Tiler from Nottingham Forest | October 1995 |
| £650,000 | Ian Ormondroyd from Bradford City | February 1989 |
| £650,000 | Nigel Callaghan from Derby County | February 1989 |
| £500,000* | Mark Delaney from Cardiff City | March 1999 |
| £500,000 | Kent Nielsen from Brondby | July 1989 |

\* Initial payment made, rising to £500,000 after appearances etc.
+ Joint transfer, with Cowans @ £450,000 & Rideout @ £400,000.

## Other big-money departures from Villa Park (£500,000+)

| £8m | Ugo Ehiogu to Middlesbrough | October 2000 |
|---|---|---|
| £6.5m | Gareth Southgate to Middlesbrough | July 2001 |
| £4m | David James to West Ham Utd. | July 2001 |
| £3.7m | Savo Milosevic to Real Zaragoza | June 1998 |
| £3m | Riccardo Scimeca to Nottingham F | July 1999 |
| £3m | David Unsworth to Everton | August 1998 |
| £3.25m | Alan Thompson to Celtic | August 2000 |
| £2.5m | Steve Watson to Everton | June 2000 |
| £2.4m | Tommy Johnson to Celtic | March 1997 |
| £2.35m | Dean Saunders to Galatasaray | July 1995 |
| £1.6m | Earl Barrett to Everton | January 1995 |
| £1.5m | Gary Charles to Benfica | January 1999 |
| £1.5m | Graham Fenton to Blackburn Rovers | November 1995 |
| £1.25m | Tony Daley to Wolves | June 1994 |
| £1.1m | Tony Cascarino to Celtic | July 1991 |
| £1.1m | Neil Cox to Middlesbrough | July 1994 |

*Earl Barrett*

| £1m | Sasa Curcic to Crystal Palace | March 1997 |
|---|---|---|
| £1m | Steve Froggatt to Wolves | July 1994 |
| £1m | Alan McInally to Bayern Munich | July 1989 |
| £850,000+ | Gordon Cowans/Paul Rideout to Bari | July 1985 |
| £750,000 | Martin Keown to Everton | July 1989 |
| £750,000 | Simon Grayson to Blackburn Rovers | July 1999 |
| £700,000 | Ian Olney to Oldham Athletic | July 1992 |
| £700,000 | Guy Whittingham to Sheffield Wed | December 1994 |
| £700,000 | Gareth Farrelly to Everton | July 1997 |
| £650,000* | John Gidman to Everton | October 1979 |
| £650,000 | Steve Hodge to Tottenham Hotspur | December 1986 |
| £650,000 | Carl Tiler to Sheffield United | March 1997 |
| £625,000 | Gary Penrice to QPR | October 1991 |
| £600,000 | Mark Walters to Glasgow Rangers | December 1987 |

THE COMPLETE ENCYCLOPAEDIA OF ASTON VILLA F.C.  THE COMPLETE ENCYCLOPAEDIA OF ASTON VILLA F.C.

269

£500,000 Paul Mortimer to Crystal Palace          October 1991
£500,000 Andy Townsend to Middlesbrough          August 1997
£400,000+ Michael Oakes to Wolverhampton W       October 1999
* Deal brought Pat Heard to Villa Park
+ Fee reached £500,000 after appearances.

## Transfer Talk

Dwight Yorke became the most expensive overseas footballer to be transferred within English soccer when he moved from Villa Park to Old Trafford in 1998. He was also Manchester United's record signing.

In contrast Stan Collymore's £7 million move from Anfield to Villa Park was Liverpool's record 'sale'. Collymore was sold by Villa to Leicester for £250,000 - the most money Villa have ever lost on one player in terms of transferring him to another club.

When David Platt moved from Villa Park to Bari for £5.5 million in 1991 the fee involved was a record for the sale of a British player abroad.

*Trevor Ford*

Also in 1991, when Dean Saunders (a future Villa player) switched from Derby County to Liverpool, the fee involved (£2.9 million) was a record involving two British (English) clubs. His £2.3 million move from Anfield in 1992 was a record 'buy' for Villa.

Jimmy Gibson became Britain's most expensive player when he joined Villa from Partick Thistle for £7,500 in 1927.

Trevor Ford's £30,000 transfer from Villa to Sunderland in October 1950 was also a British record which was bettered six months later when future Villa star Jackie Sewell switched from Notts County to Sheffield Wednesday for £34,500.

In September 1979 Andy Gray became Britain's costliest footballer following his move from Villa Park to Wolves for £1.15 million (£1.47m with levy & Vat added).

Aston Villa signed the Yugoslav Sasa Curcic from Bolton for £4 million in August 1996, then sold him to Crystal Palace for just one quarter of that amount of money in March 1998 - a loss of £3 million!

Striker Dion Dublin moved from Coventry City to Aston Villa (in effect to replace Yorke) for a Highfield Road record fee of £5.75m in November 1998.

The present-day (and authorised) transfer loan system was introduced in 1967; at the outset two players were allowed to be 'signed' on loan by each club in any one season.

Aston Villa's first loan signing was goalkeeper Evan Williams (from Wolves) in August/September/October 1969. Prior to Williams, Villa had signed the amateur inside-right Dick Sloley on a two-match 'loan' deal in October 1919, when illness and injuries made it necessary.

Villa 'loaned' goalkeeper Tom Wilkes to Stoke in March/April 1898 and midfielder Mike Tindall to the NASL club New York Americans in 1961.

Archie Goodall's transfer from Preston North End to Aston Villa in October 1888 was the first to be approved by the Football League.

Villa paid Fred Wheldon's transfer fee to Blues (Small Heath) in 1896 in two instalments: £100 and £250.

The first time Villa paid a four-figure fee for a player was in 1912 when they secured the services of Andy Ducat from Woolwich Arsenal.

Frank Barson, signed by Villa for £2,850, was sold to Manchester United for £5,000 in August 1922.

Villa made their first five-figure signing when they bought Jimmy Allen from Portsmouth in 1934.

Alun Evans became the first £100,000 teenager when he moved from Wolves to Liverpool in September 1968. He was signed by Villa in June 1972.

Brothers Bruce and Neil Rioch joined Villa from Luton Town together in July 1969 for an overall fee of £110,000.

When West Bromwich Albion paid £424,000 for Villa striker John Deehan in 1979 he became the first player to move to the Baggies from Villa since 1909.

In June 1983, Swindon Town set a club record by selling Paul Rideout to Aston Villa for £250,000.

Rideout and Gordon Cowans, were then transferred to the Italian club Bari in a joint deal worth £850,000 in June 1985.

Villa signed seven experienced players in a vain attempt to avoid relegation to the Second Division in 1935-36. They were George Cummings, Tom Griffiths, Gordon Hodgson, Alex Massie, Jack Palethorpe, Charlie Phillips and Jimmy Williams.

In the early 1920s Frank Barson, Sam Hardy, Jimmy Harrop and Clem Stephenson all refused to move house and live in Birmingham when requested by the Villa board. They were subsequently transferred - Barson to Manchester United, Hardy to Nottingham Forest, Harrop to Sheffield United and Stephenson to Huddersfield Town.

Lee Turnbull joined Villa from Middlesbrough in August 1987. Inside four months he was transferred to Doncaster Rovers for £20,000 having failed to get a game for Villa. He went on to amass well over 350 League and Cup appearances before moving into non-League football in 1998.

When Villa signed Lee Butler from Lincoln City in August 1987 he became the first goalkeeper to leave a non-League club for a fee of £100,000!

Villa spent £9.25 million in double-quick time in 1994 when signing Gareth Southgate, Savo Milosevic and Mark Draper for £2.5m, £3.5m and £3.25m respectively.

Aston Villa manager Brian Little signed Yugoslavian striker Savo Milosevic from Partizan Belgrade on video evidence - sent to him by Savo's agent. He was impressed with what he saw! In July 2000, two years after leaving Villa Park, striker Milosevic was sold by Spanish club Real Zaragoza to the Italian giants Parma for £16m.

David Platt, who cost Villa £200,000 and was sold for £5.5m to Bari, later moved to Juventus for £6.5 million in June 1992. He went from Juve' to Sampdoria for £4.5m before returning to England to sign for Arsenal for £4.5m in July 1995. In all, Platt's transfer fees amounted to over £20 million.

Between August 1985 and August 1999 Dean Saunders was involved in a total of ten transfer deals that amounted to well over £10.6 million.

Villa made over £12million profit on the sale of Dwight Yorke, having signed him for just £120,000!

Stan Collymore moved from Stafford Rangers to Crystal Palace for £100,000 in 1991, He switched to Southend United for the same fee in 1992, joined Nottingham Forest for £2m in 1993, found his way to Liverpool for £8.5m in 1995 and was secured by Aston Villa for £7m in 1997. He next move (after a loan spell with Fulham) took him to Leicester City for £250,000 in 1999 and in October 2000 he went on a 'free' to Bradford City.

Brian Little agreed a £160,000 transfer from Villa Park to rivals Birmingham City in July 1979 but the deal fell through after the striker had failed a medical.

And one of Villa's bargain buys was the £400,000 purchase of Paul McGrath from Manchester United in August 1989.

Villa and Notts County were both fined after breaking rules when signing players from Australia in 1993.

Colin Calderwood (later to play for Villa) moved from Mansfield Town to Tottenham Hotspur in July 1993 for £655,000 - a record transfer sale for the Stags.

Earl Barrett's move from Oldham Athletic to Villa Park in February 1992 was a record 'sale' for the Latics.

Scunthorpe United's biggest transfer deal came in February 1991 when they sold Neil Cox to Aston Villa for £350,000.

Sean Teale became Tranmere Rovers' record buy when he joined the Birkenhead side from Villa Park for £450,000 in August 1995.

David Unsworth joined Villa on 28 July 1998 for £3 million and left the club 25 days later for the same amount of money having failed to make a first team appearance!

THE COMPLETE ENCYCLOPAEDIA OF ASTON VILLA F.C.  THE COMPLETE ENCYCLOPAEDIA OF ASTON VILLA F.C.

270

## Return Transfers

Here is a list of players who had two spells with Aston Villa:

| | |
|---|---|
| Andy Blair | 1981-84/1986-89 |
| Gordon Cowans | 1974-76/1988-89* |
| Andy Gray | 1975-79/1985-87* |
| Steve Hunt | 1972-77/1986-87 |
| John McLaverty | 1913-14/1914-22 |
| Steve Staunton | 1991-98/2000-01 |

*Also returned for a third time as coach/assistant-manager.

## The following had two (or more) spells with Aston Villa Football Club in different capacities.

| | |
|---|---|
| Joe Bache | player/coach |
| Frank Barson | player/coach/trainer |
| Malcolm Beard | player/coach/scout |
| Des Bremner | player/Sch of Exc. Coach |
| Chris Buckley | player/director |
| 'Sailor' Brown | player/coach |
| Larry Canning | player/director |
| Bob Chatt | player/scout |
| Vic Crowe | player/manager |
| John Deehan | player/coach |
| Jack Devey | player/director |
| Arthur Dorrell | player/coach |
| Doug Ellis | Chairman/director/Chairman |
| Albert Evans | player/coach |
| John Gregory | player/coach/manager |
| Dennis Hodgetts | player/vice-president |
| Eric Houghton | player/manager/president |
| Charlie Johnstone | player/director |
| John Johnstone | player/vice-president |
| Keith Leonard | player/coach/assistant-manager |
| Brian Little | player/manager |
| Harry Parkes | player/director |
| Dennis Mortimer | player/junior coach |
| George Ramsay | player/secretary |
| Howard Spencer | player/director |
| Edmund Strange | player/Villa ass-secretary |
| Graham Taylor | Manager/non-Executive Director |
| Howard Vaughton | player/director/president |
| Alan Wakeman | player/office clerk |
| Charlie Wallace | player/coach |
| Peter Withe | player/assistant-manager |
| Ron Wylie | player/coach/2nd XI coach / community officer |

• Several players were later in life given the title of vice-president of Aston Villa FC, among them Dennis Hodgetts, Eric Houghton, Joe Johnstone and Howard Vaughton.

## TRANTER, GEORGE HENRY

Born: Quarry Bank, Brierley Hill, April 1887. Died: Dudley, September 1940.

Career: Netherton Recreation, Brierley Hill Alliance, Stourbridge, Aston Villa (January 1905). Retired through injury, June 1915.

Right-half George Tranter was a real tough defender, as hard as nails. A player who never shirked a tackle, he was totally committed and had an infallibly cool temperament as well as a good distribution. He very rarely hoofed the ball downfield....if he did it was simply for safety purposes!

He established himself in the Villa side in 1907-08 and held his place for five years making 175 League and Cup appearances, scoring one goal - a well struck effort against Notts County in the 1-1 home draw in November 1908. He suffered a knee injury in January 1914 and never played for the first XI again. He was replaced in the middle-line by Tommy Barber.

## TRAVELLING MEN

Goalkeeper John Burridge had links with no fewer than 28 football clubs in Britain during a splendid career. He actually played for 22 different League clubs (17 in England, five in Scotland). He also assisted Leeds United as a goalkeeping coach, did a similar coaching job in China and kept goal at non-League level for Enfield, Barrow, Witton Albion, Blyth Spartans and Gateshead (in the Spalding Challenge Cup)

Les Roberts was registered with 17 different clubs between 1922 and 1938 although he never actually made a League appearance with all of them! He began at Villa Park and then served, in turn, with Chesterfield, Sheffield Wednesday, Bristol Rovers, Merthyr Town, Bournemouth, Bolton Wanderers, Swindon Town, Brentford, Manchester City, Exeter City, Crystal Palace, Chester, Rochdale, Rotherham United, Scunthorpe United (Midland League), and New Brighton. He made around 300 League appearances in all.

Arthur Phoenix was a footballer with 15 clubs (1912-37) including Glossop NE, Birmingham, Aston Villa, Exeter City, Racing Club de Paris, Torquay United and Mansfield Town.

Peter Withe, too, served with 15 football teams as a player. He was also a manager and community officer at two other clubs as well as taking charge of the Thai national team.

During his soccer days, Tony Hateley was linked with eleven different clubs (eight in the Football League).

Other players who 'did the rounds' include goalkeeper Les Sealey and George Travers (below).

## TRAVERS, JAMES EDWARD (GEORGE)

Born: Newtown, Birmingham, 11 November 1888. Died: Smethwick, 31 August 1946.

Career: Bilston United (1904), Rowley United (1905), Wolverhampton Wanderers (July 1906), Birmingham (August 1907), Aston Villa (December 1908), Queen's Park Rangers (May 1909), Leicester Fosse (August 1910), Barnsley (January 1911), Manchester United (February 1914), Swindon Town (July 1919), Millwall Athletic (June 1920), Norwich City (October 1920), Gillingham (June 1921), Nuneaton Town (September 1921), Cradley St Luke's (November 1922), Bilston United (August 1929-May 1931, retired aged 42). Guested for Tottenham Hotspur in WWI when on leave from the Army (in Salonika).

A well-built, hard-shooting inside or centre-forward with good ability, George Travers was something of a soccer nomad and never really settled down in one place, or indeed, with any one club, except Barnsley where he spent three years. He made over 80 appearances for the Tykes and gained an FA Cup winners medal v WBA in 1912. For the Villa, he scored four goals in four outings including a hat-trick against Bury on Boxing Day 1908 when deputising for his personal idol, Harry Hampton. He helped Manchester United avoid relegation to the Second Division, appeared in Millwall's first League game v Bristol Rovers in August 1920 and scored for Norwich when they recorded their first-ever League win a few months later. His career in the Football League, Southern League and in the FA Cup spanned 250 matches and he netted 75 goals.

## TULLY, FREDERICK ARTHUR

Born: St Pancras, London, July 1907. Deceased.

Career: Priory School, Tynemouth Schools, Rosehill Villa, Preston Colliery, Chaddleton FC, Aston Villa (October 1926), Southampton (June 1933), Clapton Orient (June 1937-May 1939). Did not figure after WW2, choosing to work for his father in the carpentry trade in East London. He was later employed as an attendent at the Cheddeston Manor Mental Hospital, North Staffs.

Described in the press as a 'winger with thrust and enterprise' Fred Tully was a short, stocky, busy footballer who, in fact, could turn up anywhere in the forward-line! He spent seven years at Villa Park, mainly as a reserve to the likes of Armfield, Chester, Dorrell, Houghton, Mandley and York. He made only seven first team

THE COMPLETE ENCYCLOPAEDIA OF ASTON VILLA F.C.     THE COMPLETE ENCYCLOPAEDIA OF ASTON VILLA F.C.

271

appearances in that time, but later scored nine goals in 109 appearances for Saints and netted 18 times in 57 League games for Orient. An excellent club man, he did very well in Villa's second XI.

## TURNBULL, FREDERICK

Born: Wallsend, 28 August 1946.
Career: Centre 64 FC (Blyth), Aston Villa (trialist August 1966, professional September 1966), Halifax Town (on loan, October-November 1969). Retired in May 1975 through injury. Awarded a testimonial match (Aston Villa v WBA) in April 1976. Later returned to the North-east where he became self-employed at 'home' in Blyth, Northumberland.

Despite being rather thin-looking, quiet and somewhat withdrawn in his ways, Fred Turnbull was a fine, resolute, hard-tackling defender who made 183 senior appearances for Aston Villa and scored three goals during his nine years with the club. He gained a League Cup runners-up medal in 1971, collected a Third Division championship medal twelve months later and helped Villa consolidate themselves in the Second Division before injury forced him into early retiremenet at the age of 28.

## TURNER, GRAHAM JOHN

Born: Ellesmere Port, Cheshire, 5 October 1947
Career: Cheshire Schoolboy football, Wrexham (professional, July 1965), Chester (January 1968), Shrewsbury Town (£30,000, January 1973, then player-manager at Gay Meadow November 1978 to July 1984, retired as a player in the latter year), Aston Villa (manager, July 1984-September 1986), Wolverhampton Wanderers (manager, October 1986-November 1995), Hereford United (manager, July 1996).
Graham Turner was a no-nonsense, reliable defender who won an England Youth cap during his time at the Racecourse Ground. He went on to appear in more than 75 games for Wrexham and over 225 for Chester before transferring to Shrewsbury Town in 1973. He remained at Gay Meadow for thirteen years, until the summer of 1984 when he became manager of Aston Villa. All told he chalked up in excess of 400 first team appearances for the Shropshire club (355 in the Football League). Indeed, Turner appeared in his 600th League game as player-manager of Shrewsbury Town on 28 March 1981. He struggled to come to terms with the situation at Villa Park and after seeing Villa compete

*Graham Turner*

in 90 League games...26 which were won, 25 drawn and 39 lost....he left to take charge of Wolves just three months into the 1986-87 season. He quickly snapped up Steve Bull and Andy Thompson from neighbours West Bromwich Albion and slowly built a team which proved good enough to win promotion from the Fourth and then Third Divisions in successive seasons, as well as capturing the Sherpa Van Trophy at Wembley. But once into the reconstructed First Division, Turner's Wolves failed to produce the goods and this led to him being axed. Into his place at Molineux stepped another Graham - Taylor - the former England and Watford manager and also the ex-Aston Villa boss. Turner himself was out of football for a while, but returned in the summer of 1996 to take over the reins at Hereford United, who sadly under his control, lost their Football League status in May 1997 after failing to win their last game of the season at home to Brighton & Hove Albion. In 1999 Turner was appointed Chairman & Director of Football at Edgar Street.

## TURNER, GILBERT HORACE HUGO

Born: Hall Green, Birmingham, March 1886. Died: Wolverhampton, July 1957.
Career: Linton Boys Club, Birmingham St Mark's, Aston Villa (January 1907), Willenhall (May 1912), Wolverhampton United (1913-15). Did not figure after WWI.
Reserve goalkeeper, tall and agile, Bert Turner covered for England international Billy George. He left the club unwillingly after five years service during which time he made just 14 first team appearances, his best run coming in September/October 1907 when he had seven consecutive League outings.

## TYRRELL, JOSEPH JAMES

Born: Stepney, London, 27 January 1932.
Career: Littleton Council School (Evesham), Bretforton Old Boys, Aston Villa (amateur, June 1948, professional May 1950), Millwall (March 1956), Bournemouth (June 1957).
A utility forward who developed through Villa's nursery system, Joe Tyrrell scored twice on his League debut against West Bromwich Albion in April 1954. A purposeful player, he underwent a cartilage operation in 1955 and never really made an impression after that. Tyrrell netted once more for Villa in a further six League outings before going on to claim 18 goals in 37 Third Division (South) matches for Millwall.

## UNITED BANK INTERNATIONAL FESTIVAL

As Football League Cup holders, Aston Villa went over to South Africa in May 1994 to play in the United Bank International Soccer festival.
In their first match at Ellis Park, Johannesburg, a crowd of 25,000 saw Villa lose 2-1 to Liverpool, Neil Cox their scorer. Forty-eight hours later at Kings Park, Durban, some 6,500 spectators saw Villa beat Manning Rangers by a goal to nil (Guy Whittingham on target) and the festival ended when Villa fought out a goalless draw with Moroka Swallows, again at Ellis Park, on 29 May in front of 45,000 fans.

## UNITED COUNTIES LEAGUE

Aston Villa withdrew from the United Counties League in 1893-94 without playing a single game.

## UPSETS

A crowd of just 200 saw Aston Villa's first team lose 2-1 at home to works side Revo Electric in a Worcestershire Senior Cup-tie in December 1941. The Villa side was: Wakeman; Potts, Cummings; Massie, Callaghan, Iverson; Kerr, Houghton, Davis, Bate, Goffin.
Aston Villa have been ousted from the FA Cup by non-League opposition as follows: Stoke 1891, Millwall 1900, Tottenham Hotspur 1904 and Reading 1912. (See under FA Cup).

## VALE, ARCHIBALD FOSTER

Born: Kings Heath, Birmingham, July 1861. Died: Walsall, August 1937.
Career: Edwardians FC (Birmingham), Aston Villa (August 1883), Erdington Lads' Club (September 1884), Walsall Royal Star (1888-90). A big, sturdy goalkeeper, Archie Vale was safe and sure when the occasion demanded it. He appeared in three FA Cup games for Aston Villa (two 5-1 wins v. Walsall Town Swifts and Stafford Road FC in November and December 1883 and a 6-1 defeat at the hands of the Scottish club Glasgow Rangers in January 1884).

## VALUR (FC)

Villa's record against the Icelandic part-timers:
European Cup

| Venue | P | W | D | L | F | A |
|---|---|---|---|---|---|---|
| Home | 1 | 1 | 0 | 0 | 5 | 0 |
| Away | 1 | 1 | 0 | 0 | 2 | 0 |
| Totals | 2 | 2 | 0 | 0 | 7 | 0 |

Aston Villa's first-ever European Cup game ended in a goal-feast as the part-timers from Iceland were hammered 5-0 at Villa Park on 16 September 1981. A crowd of 20,841 saw Peter Withe (2), Terry Donovan (2) and Tony Morley find the net. Gary Shaw scored twice in the return fixture to sew things up 7-0 on aggregate.
Associated with both clubs: Ian Ross played for Villa and managed FC Valur., G Bergsson (Villa trialst, FC Valur player).

## VARCO, PERCY SEYMOUR

Born: Fowey, Cornwall, 17 April 1904.
Died: Fowey, 29 January 1982.
Career: Fowey Council School, Torquay United (1920), Aston Villa (£200, December 1923), Queen's Park Rangers (August 1926), Norwich City (July 1927), Exeter City (February 1930), Brighton & Hove Albion (August 1932), St Austell (August 1933). Retired through injury, 1936. Later became a fish merchant, running two aquariums. He also had two spells as Lord Mayor of Fowey.
Powerfully built and difficult to knock off the ball, a pen-picture in the 1920s described centre-forward Percy 'Saccho' Varco as a player who 'loses no time with the ball, fearless in attack and has a kick that sometimes makes one gasp. He goes for goal like a bull at a gatepost.' He netted twice in 10 first team outings for Villa and after leaving the club went on to score over 90 goals in more than 175 competitive games, including three hat-tricks and one fourtimer. He had a tremendous first season with Norwich (29 goals in 41 League outings) and later scored 23 times in 39 Division Three (South) encounters for Exeter in 1930-31.

## VARTEKS NK

Villa were eliminated from the 2001-02 UEFA Cup competition by the Croatian side, NK Varteks. The 1st round, 1st leg encounter at Villa Park ended in a 3-2 win for the Croatians, and although Villa won 1-0 in the return fixture (Hadji scoring a super goal) they went out on the away goal rule, making Juan Pablo Angel's brace at Villa Park worthless.

## VASSELL, DARIUS

Born: Birmingham, 13 June 1980
Career: Birmingham & District Schools, Aston Villa (YTS, June 1996, professional April 1998).

Strong-running, hard-working striker with pace and abilty to match, Darius Vassell graduated through the ranks at Villa Park and after representing England at Youth team level he went on to become a key member of his country's Under-21 squad, gaining a total of (7 caps). Was used as a regularly as a substitute during his first three seasons as a professional and when the 2000-01 campaign ended his record for the club was 58 appearances (made up of nine starts and 49 substitute call-ups) and seven goals scored with more to come!

## VAUGHTON, OLIVER HOWARD

Born: Aston, Birmingham, January 1861. Died: Birmingham, January 1937.
Career: Waterloo FC, Birmingham FC (no connection with the current day Blues), Wednesbury Strollers, Aston Villa (August 1880). Retired in May 1888 with a serious thigh injury. A year later he began his own silversmith's business in the jewellery quarter (Hockley, Birmingham) which still exists today. After the FA Cup had been stolen from a shop window on Newtown Row in 1895 (after Villa had won it by beating West Bromwich Albion 1-0 in the Final) Vaughton's firm was asked to make a new one at a cost of £25. Vaughton returned to Villa Park as vice-President in 1923, taking over the Presidency in June 1924. In September of that same year he joined the Board of Directors and held his position until ill-heath caused him to retire from office in December 1932. He was later made a Life Member of the club (February 1933).
Howard Vaughton was Aston Villa's inside-left in the 1887 FA Cup Final. He was regarded as one of the club's finest-forwards during the 1880s and scored 15 goals in 26 FA Cup appearances before injury forced him into an early retirement at the age of 27. He (with Arthur Brown) was Villa's first international, capped by England against Ireland in February 1882 when he scored five goals in a 13-0 win. He went on to add another further four caps to his tally (up to March 1884). Described as a 'roamer on the field of play' Vaughton was inclined to be somewhat erratic with his shooting but he made up for that with his superb ball skills. He 'dribbled like an angel' wrote one reporter! He and Eli Davis formed a fine left-wing partnership in Villa's forward-line. Besides being an accomplished footballer (the people's favourite and one of Archie Hunter's pet pupils!) Vaughton was also a competent ice-skater (he won the all-England title); he played cricket for Warwickshire and Staffordshire; was a County hockey player; a racing cyclist and a first-class swimmer, competing regularly over distances of between 50 and 200 yards.

## VENGLOS, JOSEF Ph.D

Born: Czechoslovakia, 18 February 1936.
Josef Venglos graduated as a Ph. D from the University of Bratislava. He speaks four languages - English, Portuguese, Russian and Slovak. As a player he occupied a midfield position with FC Ruzomberok for two seasons 1953-55 and Slovan Bratislava for 11 years, from 1955 to 1966 when he retired. He gained one League Championship and three Cup winners medals in Czechoslovakian football

THE COMPLETE ENCYCLOPAEDIA OF ASTON VILLA F.C.    THE COMPLETE ENCYCLOPAEDIA OF ASTON VILLA F.C.

273

and also represented his country 25 times in the junior Olympic 'B' team.

At the age of 40 he became an advisor to FIFA and a FIFA instructor, claiming that two of his students were Don Howe and Bobby Robson! And in 1967 he took his first job in management with Prague Sydney, later taking charge of the Australian national team. He returned to Czechoslovakia in 1970 as boss of USS Kosice and in two seasons guided them to second and third positions in the top Division. He also became coach of the Czech Under-23 team, winning the European title. In 1973 Venglos returned to Slovan Bratislava as boss and in three years they twice won the League championship and also the domestic Cup.

For his efforts he was appointed assistant-manager of the Czech national team which went on to win the European championship in 1976. After this triumph he was upgraded to full team manager in 1978 and two years later saw the Czechs finish third in Euro '80 as well as qualifying for the Finals of the World Cup in Spain. In 1981 he was assistant-manager of a European XI that beat the then reigning World Champions, Italy, 3-0 in Rome. He has also managed a European XI v the Rest of the World XI in New York.

Venglos returned to club management in 1982 with Sporting Lisbon and during his two years in office with the Portuguese club they reached third spot in the League and were beaten Cup finalists.

Between 1985 and 1987 Venglos managed the Kuala Lumpur team and was also the Malaysian national coach. He returned again as the Czech national team coach in 1988 and led them in the World Cup Finals (Italia '90) where they lost in the quarter-finals to the eventual winners, West Germany. On joining Villa as team manager in July 1990, Venglos had already won several cups as boss of the Czech national 'A' team. He remained at Villa Park until June 1991 having 'tried his best' in difficult circumstances (Villa finished 17th in Division One, went out of the FA Cup in the 3rd round and reached the 5th round of the League Cup). From 1991-93 Venglos was with the Turkish side Fenerbahce. He then became the Slovan national coach and guided them into the World Cup Finals in the USA in 1994. He later became co-ordinator and technical-Director of Slovan Bratislava and was also appointed President of the European Coaches Union. In 1997 he had a brief spell as manager of Celtic.

Venglos's managerial career at Villa Park at League level was: played 38, won 9, drawn 14 and lost 15.

## VICTORY LEAGUE (MIDLAND)

Aston Villa, along with Derby County, West Bromwich Albion and Wolverhampton Wanderers, took part in the Midland Victory League in March/April 1919 (arranged to help clubs get re-established after the Great War).

Villa played six games as follows:

| | | | |
|---|---|---|---|
| 22 March | v Derby County (h) 3-1 | Att. 10,000 |
| 29 March | v Derby County (a) 2-3 | Att. 12,000 |
| 5 April | v Wolves (a) 1-1 | Att. 10,000 |
| 12 April | v Wolves (h) 2-5 | Att. 20,767 |
| 19 April | v West B Albion (a) 1-5 | Att. 8,218 |
| 26 April | v West B Albion (h) 0-3 | Att. 10,000 |

As a result of these matches, Villa finished bottom of the mini-League table with a record of one win, one draw and four defeats plus a goal-ratio of 9 'for' and 18 'against'.

Harry Hampton top-scored with five goals including one penalty (v. Derby).

## VILLA PARK

Aston Villa FC has been playing at Villa Park since 17 April 1897. The first game staged there was a League Division One encounter against Blackburn Rovers. Villa won 3-0, John Campbell, John Cowan and Ted Killean (own-goal) the scorers in front of 15,000 spectators.

*Villa Park in the early days.*

### Villa Park Fact File

The Holte End was named after Sir Thomas Holte who built Aston Hall.

The Villa Park pitch initially measured 115 yards long by 72 yards wide. For the 1966 World Cup it was increased to 75 yards wide but in the 1990s, following ground work/improvements it reverted back to being 115 yards by 72.

When Villa Park was 'opened' in 1897, Aston Villa paid an annual rent of £250 (for the land). The freehold was owned by Flowers & Co (Brewers) of Stratford-upon-Avon.

Villa Park was built around an existing cycle track; this was not removed until 1914 enabling the attendence to increase from 40,000 to 60,000.

Villa eventually purchased the freehold in 1911 for the princely sum of £11.750...and this figure included land, buildings, carriage drive and bowling green (now the banqueting suite).

Johnny Campbell (Villa) scored the first goal at Villa Park - against Blackburn Rovers on 17 April 1897 (Division One).

The first opponent to score for his team on the ground was Bill Dryburgh of Sheffield Wednesday on 1 September 1897 (Division 1).

Villa suffered their first defeat at Villa Park on 15 January 1898 when Sheffield United won 1-0.

The Trinity Road stand (with seating) was built at a cost of £90,000. It was opened in 1923 and knocked down in the year 2000.

HRH The Duke of York (later King George VI) attended Villa Park in January 1924.

A South Africa XI beat Villa 3-0 in an 'international' friendly at Villa Park on 15 October 1924...soon after a beer, wines and spirits licence was obtained to sell liquor inside the ground.

The first of two FA Charity Shield matches was staged at Villa Park in 1931 when Arsenal beat West Bromwich Albion 1-0. The second was in 1972 when Villa met Manchester City. This time Francis Lee's second-half penalty gave City a 1-0 victory.

Part of the roof of the Witton Lane stand was blown off by German bombers in World War Two.

Villa Park was the only football stadium in the country where ground improvements were carried out during the Second World War - the Holte End embankment and terracing was completed.

The stand roof at the Holte End was erected in 1962 and seats were put in front of the Trinity Road Stand nine years later.

A helicopter was used to dry out the Villa Park pitch prior to the home game with Southampton in March 1975.

Double segregation fencing was installed at the Holte End in 1978. Prior to seating being put in it could house 19,210 spectators...making it one of the biggest spion kops in the country.

The North Stand at Villa Park was erected by Fairclough Building Ltd.

The top deck of the new Witton Lane stand was opened on 1 January 1994 when Villa met Blackburn Rovers in the Premiership. Almost 41,000 fans turned up - the biggest crowd at Villa Park for four years.

Undersoil heating was installed at Villa Park in 1997.

In 1980 Villa Park staged an FA Cup semi-final and two semi-final replays in the same month.

THE COMPLETE ENCYCLOPAEDIA OF ASTON VILLA F.C.          THE COMPLETE ENCYCLOPAEDIA OF ASTON VILLA F.C.

274

Villa Park has staged more FA Cup semi-finals than any other ground - 50 to end of the 2000-01 season. Tommy Docherty (later to be boss of Villa) was Chelsea manager when they played in three successive FA Cup semi-finals at Villa Park: 1965, 1966 and 1967.

The curtain was brought down on Villa Park's famous Holte End terracing in on 7 May 1994. The last game prior to alteration before it was made into an-all seater stand was against Liverpool in the Premiership, when a crowd of 45,347 (19,210 packed into the Holte End) saw Villa win 2-1. Dwight Yorke had the pleasure of scoring the last goal at the Holte End before the terracing disappeared.

The upper tier of the 'new' Holte End stand was officially opened on 28 December 1994 when Villa beat Chelsea 3-0 in the Premiership in front of almost 33,000 spectators (the biggest gate of the season at that time).

In 2001 work was completed on a new stand at Villa Park.

The Holte End is now capable of housing 13,462 fans all seated.

Between August 1975 and April 1987 Aston Villa received a total of £335,202 in grants for safety purposes from the Football Grounds Improvements Trust.

14 September 1986 saw the official opening of the Aston Villa Sports & Leisure Centre near to the ground.

HRH The Princess Elizabeth (later the Queen) visited Birmingham in June 1951 and called in at Villa Park as part of the tour.

Douglas Hurd. M.P. (the Home Secretary) was present at the Villa-Manchester United League game in March 1989.

On average a football match at Villa Park produces 85 throw-ins, five corner-kicks are awarded, the commonest scoreline is 2-1 (either way) and at least 14 shots are put in on goal (between the two teams).

For the use of Villa Park for the 1966 World Cup, Aston Villa received £46,000 and a loan of £9,900.

## International matches at Villa Park

| 8.4.1899 | England 2 Scotland 1 | Att. 25,590 |
| 3.5.1902 | England 2 Scotland 2 | Att. 15,000 |
| 8.4.1922 | England 0 v Scotland 1 | Att. 33,646 |
| 3.2.1945 | England 3 Scotland 2 | Att. 65,780 |
| 10.11.1948 | England 1 Wales 0 | Att. 67,770 |
| 14.11.1951 | England 2 Northern Ireland 0 | Att. 57,889 |
| 26.11.1958 | England 2 Wales 2 | Att. 41,581 |
| 4.6.1995 | Brazil 1 Sweden 0 | Att. 20,131 |
| 28.2 2001 | England 3 Spain 0 | Att. 42,129 |

## World Cup matches

| 13.7.1966 | Argentina 2 Spain 1 | Att. 42,738 |
| 16.7.1966 | Argentina 0 W. Germany 0 | Att. 46,487 |
| 20.7.1966 | W. Germany 2 Spain 1 | Att. 45,187 |

## European Championships

| 10.6.1996 | Holland 0 Scotland 0 | Att. 34,363 |
| 13.6.1996 | Holland 2 Switzerland 0 | Att. 36,800 |
| 18.6.1996 | Scotland 1 Switzerland 0 | Att. 34,926 |
| 23.6.1996 | Portugal 0 Czech Republic 1 | Att. 26,832 |

## European Cup Winners Cup Final

| 19.5.1999 | Lazio 2 Real Mallorca 1 | Att. 33,021 |

## Under-23 International

| 7.3.1973 | England 1 Czechoslovakia 0 | Att. 8,003 |

## Inter League games

| 9.4.1898 | Football League 1 Scottish League 2 | Att. 22,200 |
| 29.2.1908 | Football League 2 Scottish League 0 | Att. 11,054 |
| 7.11.1928 | Football League 2 Scottish League 1 | Att. 25,115 |
| 21.3.1962 | Football League 3 Scottish League 4 | Att. 18,459 |

## FA Cup semi-finals

| 8.4.1901 | Tottenham Hotspur 4 W.B.A. 0 | Att. 34,979 |
| 21.3.1903 | Derby County 3 Millwall 0 | Att. 40,500 |
| 31.3.1906 | Everton 2 Liverpool 0 | Att. 37,000 |
| 27.3.1915 | Chelsea 2 Everton 0 | Att. 22,000 |
| 26.3.1930 | Arsenal 1 Hull City 0 (replay) | Att. 46,200 |
| 12.3.1932 | Arsenal 1 Manchester City 0 | Att. 50,377 |
| 16.3.1935 | Burnley 0 Sheffield Wednesday 3 | Att. 56,625 |
| 23.3.1946 | Bolton Wanderers 0 Charlton 2 | Att. 70,819 |
| 13.3.1948 | Blackpool 3 Tottenham Hotspur 1 | Att. 70,687 |
| 21.3.1953 | Blackpool 2 Tottenham Hotspur 1 | Att. 68,221 |
| 27.3.1954 | Port Vale 1 West Bromwich A. 2 | Att. 68,221 |
| 26.3.1955 | Manchester City 1 Sunderland 0 | Att. 58,498 |
| 17.3.1956 | Manchester City 1 Tottenham H. 0 | Att. 69,788 |
| 22.3.1958 | Fulham 2 Manchester United 2 | Att. 69,745 |
| 18.3.1961 | Burnley 0 Tottenham Hotspur 3 | Att. 69,968 |
| 31.3.1962 | Burnley 1 Fulham 1 | Att. 59,989 |
| 27.4.1963 | Manchester United 1 Southampton 0 | Att. 68,312 |
| 14.3.1964 | Preston North End 2 Swansea T 1 | Att. 45,354 |
| 27.3.1965 | Chelsea 0 Liverpool 2 | Att. 67,686 |
| 23.4.1966 | Chelsea 0 Sheffield Wednesday 2 | Att. 61,321 |
| 29.4.1967 | Chelsea 1 Leeds United 0 | Att. 62,378 |
| 27.4.1968 | Birmingham City 0 WBA 1 | Att. 60,831 |
| 22.3.1969 | Everton 0 Manchester City 1 | Att. 63,025 |
| 23.3.1970 | Leeds United 0 Manch. U 0 (replay) | Att. 62,492 |
| 31.3.1971 | Arsenal 2 Stoke City 0 (replay) | Att. 62,388 |
| 15.4.1972 | Arsenal 1 Stoke City 1 | Att. 56,576 |
| 3.4.1974 | Leicester City 1 Liverpool 3 (replay) | Att. 55,619 |
| 5.4.1975 | Ipswich Town 0 West Ham United 0 | Att. 57,835 |
| 31.3.1979 | Arsenal 2 Wolverhampton Wds. 0 | Att. 46,244 |
| 12.4.1980 | Everton 0 West Ham United 1 | Att. 47,685 |
| 16.4.1980 | Arsenal 1 Liverpool 1 (replay) | Att. 40,679 |
| 28.4.1980 | Arsenal 1 Liverpool 1 (2nd replay) | Att. 42,975 |
| 11.4.1981 | Ipswich Town 0 Manchester City 1 | Att. 46,537 |
| 3.4.1982 | Leicester City 0 Tottenham Hot 2 | Att. 46,606 |

*Villa Park, pictured in 1907.*

THE COMPLETE ENCYCLOPAEDIA OF ASTON VILLA F.C.  THE COMPLETE ENCYCLOPAEDIA OF ASTON VILLA F.C.

275

| | | |
|---|---|---|
| 16.4.1983 | Arsenal 1 Manchester United 2 | Att. 46,535 |
| 14.4.1984 | Plymouth Argyle 0 Watford 1 | Att. 43,858 |
| 13.4.1985 | Everton 2 Luton Town 1 | Att. 45,289 |
| 5.4.1986 | Everton 2 Sheffield Wednesday 1 | Att. 47,711 |
| 11.4.1987 | Tottenham Hotspur 4 Watford 1 | Att. 46,161 |
| 15.4.1989 | Everton 1 Norwich City 0 | Att. 46,553 |
| 8.4.1990 | Crystal Palace 4 Liverpool 3 | Att. 38,389 |
| 14.4.1991 | Nottingham Forest 4 West Ham U. 0 | Att. 40,041 |
| 13.4.1992 | Liverpool 0 Portsmouth 0 (replay)* | Att. 40,077 |
| 9.4.1995 | Crystal Palace 2 Manchester U 2 | Att. 38,256 |
| 12.4.1995 | Crystal P 0 Manchester U. 1 (replay) | Att. 17,987 |
| 31.3.1996 | Chelsea 1 Manchester United 2 | Att. 38,421 |
| 5.4.1998 | Arsenal 1 Wolverhampton Wds. 0 | Att. 39,372 |
| 11.4.1999 | Arsenal 0 Manchester United 0 | Att. 39,217 |
| 14.4.1999 | Arsenal 1 Manchester U 2 (replay) | Att. 30,223 |
| 8.4.2001 | Liverpool 2 Wycombe Wanderers 1 | Att. 40,037 |

\* Liverpool won 3-1 on penalties

## Football League Cup Final
| | | |
|---|---|---|
| 6.4.1981 | Liverpool 2 West Ham U 1 (replay) | Att. 36.693 |

## FA Charity Shield
| | | |
|---|---|---|
| 7.10.1931 | Arsenal 1 West Bromwich Albion 0 | Att. 21,276 |
| 5.8.1972 | Aston Villa 0 Manchester City 1 | Att. 34,890 |

## Mercantile Credit Trophy Final
| | | |
|---|---|---|
| 9.10.1988 | Arsenal 2 Manchester United 1 | Att. 22,182 |

## FA Cup replays & 2nd replays
| | | |
|---|---|---|
| 1899-00 | Blackburn Rovers 5 Portsmouth 0 | Att. 10,000 |
| 1903-04 | Derby County 1 Wolverhampton 0 | Att. 10,000 |
| 1904-05 | Fulham 1 Manchester United 0 | Att. 6,000 |
| 1905-06 | Blackpool 1 Crystal Palace 0 | Att. 12,000 |
| 1906-07 | Stoke 1 West Brom Albion 3 | Att. 32,500 |
| 1908-09 | Norwich City 3 Reading 2 | Att. 6,087 |
| 1913-14 | Manchester City 0 Sheffield Utd 1 | Att. 23,147 |
| 1922-23 | Southampton 0 West Ham United 1 | Att. 22,184 |
| 1923-24 | Crystal Palace 0 Notts County 0 | Att. 16,440 |
| 1923-24 | Crystal Palace 2 Notts County 1 | Att. 10,259 |
| 1926-27 | Manchester United 1 Reading 2 | Att. 16,486 |
| 1926-27 | Everton 2 Hull City 3 | Att. 14,000 |
| 1930-31 | Charlton Ath 1 West Brom Albion 3 | Att. 27,764 |
| 1934-35 | Bolton Wanderers 2 Tottenham H 2 | Att. 26,692 |
| 1946-47 | Brentford 1 Leicester City 4 | Att. 7,506 |
| 1949-50 | Cheltenham Town 2 Hereford Utd 4 | Att: 1,000 |
| 1951-52 | Reading 1 Southport 0 | Att. 6,000 |
| 1951-52 | Chelsea 5 Leeds United 1 | Att. 30,504 |
| 1952-53 | Chelsea 1 West Bromwich Albion 1 | Att. 33,534 |
| 1952-53 | Queen's Park R 1 Shrewsbury 4 | Att. 12,590 |
| 1953-54 | Blackpool 1 Luton Town 1 | Att. 15,665 |
| 1960-61 | Aldershot 2 Shrewsbury Town 0 | Att. 6,014 |
| 1966-67 | Nottingham Forest 3 Swindon T 0 | Att. 52,596 |
| 1971-72 | Alvechurch 1 Oxford City 0 | Att. 1,952 |
| 1972-73 | Leeds United 5 Norwich City 0 | Att. 33,275 |
| 1972-73 | Crystal Palace 2 Sheffield Wed. 3 | Att. 19,151 |
| 1975-76 | Mansfield Town 2 Wrexham 1 | Att. 1,470 |
| 1976-77 | Bristol Rovers 0 Nottingham For 6 | Att. 5,736 |

## Football League Cup replays
| | | |
|---|---|---|
| 1963-64 | Huddersfield T 2 Plymouth Argyle 1 | Att. 2,997 |
| 1970-71 | Northampton Town 2 York City 1 | Att. 2,561 |
| 1972-73 | Blackpool 2 AFC Bournemouth 1 | Att. 2,337 |

## FA Amateur Cup 4th rd
| | | |
|---|---|---|
| 1966-67 | Enfield 6 Highgate United 0 | Att. 31,570 |

## FA Trophy Final
| | | |
|---|---|---|
| 2000-01 | Canvey Island 1 Forest Green Rov 0 | Att, 10,007 |

## FA Vase Final
| | | |
|---|---|---|
| 2000-01 | Berkhamstead 1 Taunton Town 2 | Att, 8,439 |

## Youth Championship
| | | |
|---|---|---|
| 1982-83 | England 0 USSR 0 | Att. 1,700 |

## County FA Match
| | | |
|---|---|---|
| 1954-55 | B'ham County FA 4 FA of Ireland 2 | Att. 1,000 |

A packed Holte End.

## Junior Internationals
| | | |
|---|---|---|
| April 1902 | Birmingham 3 Scotland 3 | Att. 4,000 |
| April 1909 | Birmingham 2 Scotland 2 | Att. 4,000 |
| April 1921 | Birmingham 1 Scotland 2 | Att. 6,000 |
| April 1931 | Birmingham 5 Scotland 2 | Att. 5,545 |

## Inter Association Matches
| | | |
|---|---|---|
| 1910-11 | Birmingham 1 London 3 | Att. 4,500 |
| 1912-13 | Birmingham 5 London 1 | Att. 6,000 |

## Birmingham Junior FA Cup
| | | |
|---|---|---|
| 1948-49 | Castle Rovers 1 Walsall Trinity 2 | Att. 2,500 |

## Warwicks/Birmingham WATC 50th Anv Squadron Cup Final
1990-91 84/2nd City of Coventry v 479 Rubery Att 600

NB. There have also been Schoolboy, Youth and international trial matches held at Villa Park, along with several minor fixtures including works end-of-season Cup Finals and various charity matches.

## Other Events at Villa Park
In season 1908-09, Villa Park was chosen as the venue for the Rugby Union international between England and the touring Australians. A crowd of 5,000 attended.

In October 1924, some 17,000 fans saw a North Midlands XV rugby side take on the famous New Zealand All Blacks.

In 1947, the Australians came over again and played a Midlands Counties XV, then in April 1951, in yet another Rugby Union contest, R.I. Scorer's XV took on the North Midlands Select side in front of 12,000 spectators.

Two British & Empire Boxing championship contests have been staged at Villa Park: the first featuring Randolph Turpin (June 1948) and in June 1972 when Danny McAlinden defeated Jack Bodell in the second round of a light-heavyweight bout. Over 40,000 fans saw the Turpin fight.

Further bouts have since taken place at the nearby Villa Leisure Centre including the British Heavyweight fight between Irishman Gordon Ferris (the winner) and Billy Aird.

Three years later, in May 1975, American singer 'Big' Barry White and the Love Unlimited Orchestra came to Villa Park for an open air concert.

THE COMPLETE ENCYCLOPAEDIA OF ASTON VILLA F.C.     THE COMPLETE ENCYCLOPAEDIA OF ASTON VILLA F.C.

276

In July 1982, an estimated 18,000 fans attended a Villa Park concert featuring local band, Duran Duran.

On a week's tour in during late June/early July 1984, the American Evangelist, Billy Graham attracted over 257,000 supporters to his organised rallies inside Villa Park.

In August 1985 the British Superbowl (American Football) contest saw the much stronger London Ravens beat the Streatham Olympians 45-7 in front of a 7,800 crowd.

In June 1987 there were some 16,000 Jehovah's Witnesses inside Villa Park for a two-day convention.

The 'Boss' - Bruce Springstein - drew over 40,000 fans to each of his two four-hour concerts at Villa Park in June 1988.

Archbishop Desmond Tutu selected Villa Park as his venue for a religious gathering in April 1989.

In the summer of 1995, a concert featuring superstars Rod Stewart and Belinda Carlisle was seen by 35,000 fans at Villa Park.

## VINALL, ALBERT

Born: Hockley, Birmingham 6 March 1922. Died: 2000.

Career: Hockley Brook School, Norwich City (amateur), Southampton (amateur), Aston Villa (amateur, August 1939), professional August 1946), Walsall (August 1954). Retired in July 1957.

Albert Vinall was a solid full-back who rendered yeoman service to Aston Villa's Central League side but only managed 11 first-team appearances owing to the Second World War.

His brother Jack played for Sunderland, Norwich City, Luton Town, Coventry City and Walsall and also managed Worcester City (1948-50) before becoming a scout at Villa Park (mid 1950s). Albert's son, Micky, was a Police Contable, based in Handsworth, Birmingham (1966-76).

## VITORIA GUIMARAES

Villa's playing record against the Portuguese club:

UEFA Cup

| Venue | P | W | D | L | F | A |
|---|---|---|---|---|---|---|
| Home | 1 | 1 | 0 | 0 | 5 | 0 |
| Away | 1 | 0 | 0 | 1 | 0 | 1 |
| Totals | 2 | 1 | 1 | 1 | 5 | 1 |

**Geoff Vowden**

Aston Villa eased through their 1st round 1983-84 UEFA Cup tie against the Portuguese side with a competent second leg performance after struggling in the away match. Peter Withe scored a hat-trick in the 5-0 demolition job at Villa Park which was seen by 23,732 spectators.

## VOWDEN, GEOFFREY ALAN

Born: Barnsley, 27 April 1941.

Career: Jersey football, Nottingham Forest (amateur, 1958, professional January 1960), Birmingham City (£25,000, October 1964), Aston Villa (£12,500, March 1971), Kettering Town (player/assistant-manager, July 1974), New York Cosmos (1975). Coached in Saudi Arabia (1976-78) and also at Schools and Youth clubs in the Nottingham area. Between 1980 and 1981 he was second XI coach at Sheffield United.

Geoff Vowden started his playing career in the Channel Islands before joining Nottingham Forest. He developed quickly and became a fine marksman who scored over 150 goals in under 500 competitive matches over the next 14 years. After hitting 40 goals in 90 League games for Forest he moved to St Andrew's in 1964 and duly paid that money back with huge dividends by netting another 95 goals in 253 appearances for Blues. On transfer deadline day, 1971, he switched his loyalties to Villa Park and a little over a year later helped Villa win the Third Division championship. A beautifully balanced player, he formed a fine strike-force in the claret and blue strip with Andy Lochhead. Vowden scored 25 goals in 114 first-class games for Villa before joining non-League Kettering Town in 1974. He later became a succesful coach.

Vowden was the first Football League substitute to come off the bench and score a hat-trick, achieving the feat for Blues against Huddersfield Town in September 1968.

## WAKEMAN, ALAN

Born: Walsall, 20 November 1920.

Career: Elmore Green School (Walsall), Leamore FC (Walsall), Leamore Boys, Walsall & District Schools (aged 12-14), Bloxwich Strollers (amateur: 1935-36), Aston Villa (amateur, August 1937, professional August 1938), Doncaster Rovers (July 1950), Shrewsbury Town (February 1953-May 1954), Bloxwich Strollers (manager 1954-59), Shrewsbury Town (player, briefly in late 1959), Walsall Wood (manager, August 1960-May 1967), Stratford Town (manager, 1968-69), Bilston Town (manager, 1969-70). Retired to work for the NCB (manager at the Bridgetown Colliery). He also assisted in the Villa Park offices on a part-time basis before taking over as manager of Armitage Town (West Midlands League) in 1982. Guested for Northampton Town, Nottingham Forest and Notts County during the Second World War.

An out-and-out centre-forward at school, Alan Wakeman gained six England Schoolboy caps in 1934 and 1935 (two as team captain). He was converted into a goalkeeper when serving with Bloxwich Strollers and joined Aston Villa as deputy to Fred Biddlestone, having Joe Rutherford also challenging for a first team place. A brave 'keeper, his career was severely interrupted by the hostilities of WW2, but he still managed to play in 20 competitive games for the club as well as starring in 183 regional matches during the War, helping Villa win the Football League North Cup in 1944 (v Blackpool). He saved three penalties in the month of April 1943.

## WALKER, RAYMOND

Born: North Shields, 28 September 1963

Career: Mansfield & District Schools, Nottinghamshire Boys, Aston Villa (apprentice, July 1979, professional September 1981), Port Vale (on loan, September-November 1984, signed permanently for £12,000, plus fifty per-cent of any future sale price above that figure, July 1986), Cambridge United (on loan, September 1994). Retired in 1996 to take over as manager of Newcastle Town (Staffs).

THE COMPLETE ENCYCLOPAEDIA OF ASTON VILLA F.C.     THE COMPLETE ENCYCLOPAEDIA OF ASTON VILLA F.C.

277

A skilful midfielder, Ray Walker gained England Youth honours as a teenager with Aston Villa and collected an FA Youth Cup winners' medal in 1980. Unfortunately with so many other talented midfield players at the club he found it hard to establish himself in the senior side at Villa Park and made only 27 appearances (nine as a substitute) before leaving for Vale Park. He developed into a fine player with the Potteries' club and went on to make 427 appearances (scoring 43 goals) for Vale before hanging up his boots in 1996. He was Vale's 'Player of the Year' in 1988 and was chosen in the respective PFA Third Division sides in 1987-88 and 1988-89 and the Second Division side in 1992-93 when Vale won the Auto Windscreen Shield at Wembley, but lost to WBA in the Second Division Play-off Final.

Walker was fined £150 by Vale in February 1988 after being sent-off for stamping on the head of the 20 year-old Grimsby Town left-half Ian Toale.

## WALKER, RICHARD MARTIN

Born: Birmingham, 8 November 1977
Career: Aston Villa (YTS, July 1994, professional December 1995), Cambridge United (on loan, December 1998), Blackpool (on loan February 2001).
Pacy striker Richard Walker took full advantage of injuries to Dion Dublin and Darius Vassell to make his mark in Villa's first XI in 1999-2000. A very useful player both on the ground and in the air, he was loaned out to Cambridge to gain 'experience' and scored four times in 24 outings for the Abbey Stadium club before returning to Villa Park. Walker ended the 2000-01 season with 10 first XI appearances under his belt for Villa (two goals scored).

## WALKER, WILLIAM HENRY

Born: Wednesbury, 29 October 1897. Died: Sheffield, 28 November 1964.
Career: King's Hill School (Wednesbury), Walsall Boys, Hednesford Town, Darlaston, Wednesbury Old Park, Wednesbury Old Athletic, Aston Villa, (March 1915, professional June 1920-November 1933 when he retired), Sheffield Wednesday (manager, December 1933-November 1937), Chelmsford City (manager, January-October 1938),

Nottingham Forest (manager, March 1939-July 1960). Retired at the end of the 1959-60 season owing to illness, but he remained on the Forest committee until his death in 1964. He played eight games for Forest during the War (1940-44) including three outings as a goalkeeper! He had guested for Birmingham in 1916-17. He also represented Warwickshire Club & Ground on the cricket square.

Inside or centre-forward Billy Walker scored an amazing total of 80 goals in the Walsall Boys League in season 1910-11. This sort of marksmanship quickly brought scouts/managers and indeed interested spectators flocking to watch the Wednesbury-born striker in action. He slowly but surely gained experience in non-League circles before being snapped up by Aston Villa towards the end of the last season before the Great War - and what a star he turned out to be!

Walker became an institution at Villa Park! An all-round sportsman of the highest calibre, he had tremendous ability on the ball. He skippered Villa for six seasons (1926-32), scored nine goals in 18 full international matches for England, leading his country in a famous 3-2 victory over Austria in 1932 which is regarded as one of the greatest internationals ever seen in England! He netted twice on his senior debut for Villa in the home 3rd round FA Cup-tie against Queen's Park Rangers in January 1920 and at the end of that season collected an FA Cup

winners' medal after Huddersfield Town had been beaten 1-0 in the Final. Unfortunately he wasn't so lucky four years later when Villa lost 2-0 to Newcastle United in the 1924 Final.

Walker, who often chose to shoot on sight, possessed a cracking right or left foot shot and he was also a fine header of the ball. Besides being a champion marksman, he was also a superb tactician who went on to claim a record 244 goals in 531 League and FA Cup appearances for Aston Villa during his eighteen-and-a-half years with the club. He cracked home 11 hat-tricks (nine in the First Division, two in the FA Cup), weighed in with a fourtimer against Arsenal in August 1920, and is one of only a dozen or so players worldwide to score a hat-trick of penalties, doing so for Villa against Bradford City in a home League game in November 1921. His heroic feats were not confined to his goalscoring, but also to keeping out goals as well for he was an exceptionally talented custodian acting as Villa's deputy 'keeper on many occasions. He also donned the yellow jersey for England against France in Paris in 1925 taking over from the injured Fred Fox (Millwall) in the second-half and helping his side win 3-2.

With Arthur Dorrell as his left-wing partner in the Villa front-line Walker was irresistible at times. He reached double-figures in the scoring charts every season from 1919-20 to 1930-31, his best campaign coming in 1920-21 when he netted 31 times in 42 appearances.

After retiring as a player in 1933 Walker took over as boss at Hillsborough and two years later (after keeping the Yorkshire club in the First Division) he guided the Owls to FA Cup glory over West Bromwich Albion at Wembley. Twenty-six years later he repeated that feat with Nottingham Forest (2-1 winners over Luton Town) having earlier helped the Reds win promotion from the Third Division (S) in 1951 and the Second Division in 1957. He quit football management in 1960, three years later suffering a stroke from which he never fully recovered.

## WALLACE, CHARLES WILLIAM

Born: Southwick near Sunderland, 20 January 1885. Died: 7 January 1970.
Career: Sunderland & District Schools, Southwick FC (1903), Crystal Palace (July 1905), Aston Villa (£500, May 1907), Oldham Athletic (£1,000, May 1921). Retired 1923 to become a painter and decorator, assisting at Villa Park on a part-time basis in various departments etc. He was mentor to Aston Villa's J.O.C. team in the late 1930s, leading them to the runners-up spot behind WBA in their respective League in 1938-39. In fact, Wallace spent over 50 years with Aston Villa football club, serving as a player, boot-room attendant, kit-man, scout, steward and odd-job man.

A speedy, direct winger, he helped Villa win the League championship in 1910 and the FA Cup in 1913 and 1920. He had the misfortune to miss a penalty in the 1913 Final against Sunderland but made amends by taking the corner from which Harold Edgley headed the winning goal. He won three England caps (against Ireland, Scotland and Wales) and also represented the Football League on five occasions and appeared in three international trial matches. He amassed a fine record with Villa - 350 appearances and 57 goals. He stayed two seasons with the Latics before retiring from football in 1923. A Villa man through and through, he spent practically the whole of his career wearing claret and blue - the colours of Southwick, Palace and the Villa! Wallace died shortly before his 85th birthday.

## WALSALL

Villa's playing record against the Saddlers:
Football League

| Venue | P | W | D | L | F | A |
|---|---|---|---|---|---|---|
| Home | 2 | 0 | 2 | 0 | 0 | 0 |
| Away | 2 | 0 | 1 | 1 | 1 | 4 |
| Totals | 2 | 0 | 3 | 1 | 1 | 4 |

THE COMPLETE ENCYCLOPAEDIA OF ASTON VILLA F.C.          THE COMPLETE ENCYCLOPAEDIA OF ASTON VILLA F.C.

278

1929-30 SEASON WILL BE REMEMBERED FOR ONE OR TWO OUTSTANDING EPISODES. T'WAS ON 25 JAN. 1930 VILLA BEAT WALSALL 3-1 IN THE F.A. CUP... 74,600 SPECTATORS GATHERED AT VILLA PARK FOR THAT EPIC ENCOUNTER!

VENUE WAS CHANGED FROM WALSALL TO VILLA PARK

Excuse me!

FRED BIDDLESTONE, WALSALL'S GOALKEEPER, SO IMPRESSED IN THAT CUP-TIE HE WAS TRANSFERRED TO VILLA WITHIN A MONTH!

McAuley, J MacEwan, A McClure, J McMorran, JH Maund, G Moseley, F Moss snr, D Mountfield, TP Muldoon, W Myerscough, BA Olney, D Pace, L Pember (Villa reserve), JJ Pendleton, RT Pritchard (Saddlers' WW2 guest), J Sharples, FH Shell (Walsall WW2 guest), G Shelton, D Simmonds, WS Simpson, B Small, RW Starling (Walsall WW2 guest), KC Tewkesbury, R Thomas, MC Tindall, A Vinall, DJ Walsh, SS Whittaker, A Wilkes, G Williams, TE Wood (Walsall WW2 guest), J Woodward,

Also: R Graydon & CJ Nicholl (Villa players, Walsall managers), A Ashman (Walsall manager, Villa scout), FC Buckley (Villa reserve, Walsall manager), A Leake & VE Potts (Villa players, Walsall trainers), W Moore (Villa trainer, Walsall trainer & manager), R Shaw (Villa trainer, physio & Walsall Amateur, trainer & manager), A Cox (Villa coach/assistant & caretaker-manager, Walsall coach), IH Price (Villa reserve, Walsall secretary), WE Houghton (Villa player, manager & Director etc, Walsall Director), D Dorman & EJ Vinall (Walsall players, Villa scouts), K Macdonald (Walsall player, Villa coach).

| FA Cup | | | | | | |
|---|---|---|---|---|---|---|
| Home | 2 | 2 | 0 | 0 | 9 | 1 |

| Wartime | | | | | | |
|---|---|---|---|---|---|---|
| Home | 5 | 2 | 3 | 0 | 15 | 9 |
| Away | 5 | 4 | 0 | 1 | 10 | 4 |
| Totals | 10 | 6 | 3 | 1 | 25 | 13 |

The first time Aston Villa met Walsall in a League game was at Fellows Park on 2 January 1971 (Division 3). The bumper crowd of 19,203 saw the Saddlers win 3-0 (Colin Taylor almost ripping a hole in the net with his penalty-kick). The return fixture that season finished goalless in March when two ex-Villa players were in the Saddlers' side - Alan Deakin and John Woodward.

The two League games the following season both ended in draws: 0-0 again at Villa Park (in front of almost 46,000 fans) and 1-1 at Walsall.

A crowd of 18,000 saw the Saddlers beaten 6-0 by Villa in a 1st round FA Cup-tie in January 1912, Harry Hampton and Horace Henshall both scoring twice.

Eighteen years later, Walsall were drawn at home to Villa in the 4th round of the competition but elected to switch the game to Villa Park. They would have only packed in around 15,000 fans at their Fellows Park ground but there was a record attendance of 74,626 present at Villa Park to to see the Saddlers beaten 3-1.

Eric Houghton scored two goals for Villa in their exciting 4-4 home draw with the Saddlers in a Wartime game in October 1943. Villa, in fact, were leading 4-0 in this game before the Saddlers, for whom Gilbert Alsop also netted twice, stormed back to salvage a point. In February 1945 he netted two more when Villa won 6-1.

Players associated with both clubs: CL Aston, AR Baker, T Barber, GW Beeson, T Bennett, F Biddlestone, MA Blake, D M Bradley, DG Bremner, D Byfield, LK Capewell, SV Collymore (Saddlers, YTS), AM Daley, AR Deakin, W Devey, CJ Drinkwater (Walsall reserve), GR Edwards (Walsall WW2 guest), A Evans, G Fenton, W Freeman, B Gallagher (Saddlers trialist), CJ Gibson, WC Goffin, AW Green, AE Haynes, T Horton, S Howarth, R Jeffries, JL Jenkins, G Johnson, AT Lyons, W

## WALSALL SWIFTS

Villa's playing record against Swifts:

| FA Cup | | | | | | |
|---|---|---|---|---|---|---|
| Venue | P | W | D | L | F | A |
| Home | 1 | 1 | 0 | 0 | 4 | 1 |
| Away | 1 | 1 | 0 | 0 | 5 | 1 |
| Totals | 2 | 2 | 0 | 0 | 9 | 2 |

Andy Hunter scored a brilliant goal when Villa beat the Swifts 4-1 in a 1st round FA Cup-tie in October 1882 when the Swifts were crushed 5-1 in the opening round of the following season's competition his brother Archie Hunter scored twice.

Players with both clubs: AJ Aldridge, AL Benwell, GF Burton, R Davis, W Devey, CHS Hobson, WA Jones, FA Marshall, T Purslow, AW Stokes, J Warner, HR Yates.

## WALSALL TOWN

Villa's playing record against the Town:

| FA Cup | | | | | | |
|---|---|---|---|---|---|---|
| Venue | P | W | D | L | F | A |
| Home | 1 | 1 | 0 | 0 | 2 | 1 |
| Away | 2 | 2 | 0 | 0 | 7 | 0 |
| Totals | 3 | 3 | 0 | 0 | 9 | 1 |

All five forwards scored when Villa beat Town 5-0 in a 1st round FA Cup-tie at the Chuckery in October 1885.

Players with both clubs include: AJ Aldridge, L Campbell, TT Dutton, NB - Walsall Swifts and Walsall Town joined forces in 1888 to become Walsall (Town Swifts). Therefore, several players who served with both Walsall Town and Walsall Swifts also played for Walsall Town Swifts and subsequently for Walsall FC, the club's title since 1895.

## WALSH, DAVID JOHN

Born: Waterford, 28 April 1923.
Career: St. Joseph's, Corinthians, Shelbourne (Waterford), Glen Rovers, Limerick, Shelbourne (Dublin), Linfield (1943), West Bromwich Albion (£3,500, May 1946), Aston Villa (£25,000, December 1950), Walsall (July 1955-May 1956), Worcester City (August 1956-May 1957). Retired to

THE COMPLETE ENCYCLOPAEDIA OF ASTON VILLA F.C.    THE COMPLETE ENCYCLOPAEDIA OF ASTON VILLA F.C.

279

concentrate on running his sports-shop/general store in Droitwich, Worcs. In 1984 he moved to South Devon where he ran a string of holiday homes at Thurlestone near Kingsbridge. Walsh still lives in Thurlestone today and is a life member of the golf club there.

Sharp-shooting Irish international centre-forward Dave Walsh made a terrific start to his Football League career by scoring in each of the first six games in the First Division for WBA at the start of the 1946-47 Second Division season. A player with an eye for goal, he continued to net regularly for the Baggies and was a key figure when promotion was gained in 1948-49. He went on to score a century of goals for The Hawthorns club before signing for Aston Villa in a record transfer deal in 1950 as a replacement for Trevor Ford. He did just as well at Villa Park, notching a further 40 goals in 114

*Dave Walsh*

League and Cup games before rounding off his League career with Walsall in the mid-1950s. After a brief spell with Worcester, he retired to concentrate on his business in Droitwich.

Walsh, nimble, decisive in front of goal, had the knack of being in the right spot at the right time. He netted no fewer than 122 goals while playing in Ireland, including 73 in season 1945-46 (61 in League and Cup games) for Linfield when they won the Irish League championship and the Irish Cup, having earlier lifted the Irish Cup in 1945. Capped 29 times at full international level (playing in 20 games for the Republic of Ireland and nine occasions for Northern Ireland) his record in English League football was excellent - 137 goals in 293 appearances.

## WALTERS, JOSEPH

Born: Stourbridge, December 1886. Died: New Moston, Manchester, 24 December 1923 (from pneumonia).

Career: Wordesley Athletic (1900), Stourbridge (August 1902), Aston Villa, (June 1905), Oldham Athletic (£900, June 1912), Accrington Stanley (August 1920), Southend United (£200, September 1920), Millwall Athletic (May 1921), Rochdale (October 1922), Crewe Alexandra (November 1923). Guested for Tottenham Hotspur during WWI when available from the Royal Flying Corps

Joey Walters was a fine, consistent inside or outside-left who scored 48 goals in 225 first-team appearances during his seven years with Aston Villa. An England Junior international trialist in 1911, he was clever on the ball, creative in style, had good

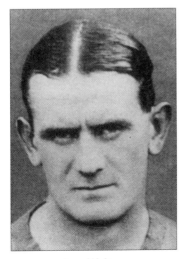

*Joey Walters*

pace, packed a fine shot in either foot and had a first-rate temperament. He helped Villa clinch the League title in 1910, the season when he whipped in a terrific hat-trick in a 7-1 home win over Manchester United. He scored 36 goals in 110 senior outings for Oldham and during his professional career he claimed over 100 goals in more than 425 League and FA Cup games. Walters died before he could make his debut for Crewe.

## WALTERS, MARK EVERTON

Born: Aston, Birmingham, 2 June 1964,

Career: Hampton Junior and Holte Grammar Schools (Lozells, Birmingham), Aston & District Boys, Birmingham Schools, Aston Villa (juniors, June 1980, professional May 1982), Glasgow Rangers (£600,000, December 1987), Liverpool (£1.25 million, August 1981), Stoke City (on loan, March/April 1994), Wolverhampton Wanderers (on loan, September/October 1994), Southampton (free transfer, January 1996 Swindon Town (free transfer, July 1996), Bristol Rovers (November 1999).

Wing-forward Mark Walters could occupy either flank. A tricky player with excellent pace, clever tricks and telling shot, he crossed a ball with great precision (on the run or otherwise) and had one marvellous feature whereby he used to drag his foot over the ball before gliding past a defender. He joined Aston Villa as a teenager and remained with the Midlands club until moving to Scotland in 1987. He scored 48 goals in 224 League and Cup games for Villa. After representing England at both Schoolboy and Youth team levels, Walters went on to add one full, one 'B' and nine Under-21 caps to his collection. He gained an FA Youth Cup winners medal (1980) and a European Super Cup winners medal (1982) with Villa and then added three Scottish Premier Division and two Skol League Cup winners medals to his tally whilst at Ibrox Park before collecting winner's prizes in both the FA Cup and League Cup competitions with Liverpool in 1992 and 1995 respectively.

When the 2000-01 season came to an end and having been relegated to the Third Division with Bristol Rovers, Walters' career record in competitive football was outstanding: over 700 appearances and more than 170 goals (at club and international levels).

## WARD, JOSEPH

Born: Glasgow, 25 November 1954

Career: Glasgow & District Schools, St Roch's FC (Glasgow), Clyde (Amateur, 1970, professional November 1972), Aston Villa (£80,000, December 1978), Hibernian (£80,000 plus Des Bremner, September 1979), Dundee United (July 1980-82).

Before joining Aston Villa, well built inside or centre-forward Joe Ward won both Amateur and Youth caps north of the border as well as collecting a Second Division championship medal with Clyde in 1978. Unfortunately he never settled in Birmingham and after just three outings for Villa he returned to Scotland as part of the deal that saw Des Bremner move from Easter Road to Villa Park.

## WARING, THOMAS

Born: Birkenhead, 12 October 1906. Died: 20 December 1980.

Career: Birkenhead & District Schools, Tranmere Celtic (August 1922), Tranmere Rovers (professional February 1926), Aston Villa (£4,700, February 1928), Wolverhampton Wanderers (July 1936), Tranmere Rovers (October 1936), Accrington Stanley (November 1939-July 1939), Bath City (August-September 1939) and after the hostilities assisted Ellesmere Port, Graysons FC, Birkenhead Dockers and Harrowby FC whilst working in the Merseyside docklands. He also guested for New Brighton in season 1939-40 and Aston Villa in February 1944.

Tall, long striding, six feet of sinew, muscle and bone, Tom 'Pongo'

THE COMPLETE ENCYCLOPAEDIA OF ASTON VILLA F.C.          THE COMPLETE ENCYCLOPAEDIA OF ASTON VILLA F.C.

280

Waring was a free-scoring centre-forward, supremely confident in his own ability. A colourful character, the stories about him apocryphal or otherwise, are legion. Some 23,667 fans saw him net a hat-trick on his debut for Aston Villa in a comprehensive 6-2 Central League victory over rivals Birmingham in February 1928 - shortly after he had scored six goals for Tranmere Rovers in an 11-0 win over Durham City in a Third Division (North) game.

Waring attended school in his native town and was a chocolate seller at Prenton Park while playing at weekends for Tranmere Celtic. He then joined Tranmere Rovers in 1926, succeeding the great Dixie Dean in their attack. Two years later he moved to Villa Park and over the next

*Pongo Waring takes on the Spurs defence at White Hart Lane in 1933.*

ten years netted 167 goals in 226 first team appearances (10 hat-tricks, nine in the First Division).

An England international (five caps won between 1931 and 1932) Waring claimed a record 49 League goals (plus one in the FA Cup) for Villa in 1930-31 when he was dubbed the 'Gay Cavalier' as he streaked past defenders time and again to smash the ball into the net! Indeed, every kid around Villa Park wanted to be 'Pongo' Waring - for he was more popular than the Prime Minister at that time! He was sensationally sent-off while playing against Spurs in January 1934, and as he walked, head bowed, from the field he received a bigger cheer than the whole team would have got if they'd won the FA Cup!

In July 1936 Waring moved to Molineux, but he failed to settle down to Wolves' style of play (under Major Frank Buckley's management) and after barely three months at Molineux he returned to his first club, Tranmere Rovers. In a sparkling career Waring, who was also referred to as the 'Birkenhead Bombadier' and the 'Claret and Blue Torpedo', scored 245 goals in 362 League games. He only won one medal at club level - helping Tranmere take the Third Division (North) championship in 1937-38.

• In the mid-1990s, Kidderminster-based Villa supporter John Peutherer (60) bought his wife, Janina, a racehorse for £20,000 and named it Pongo Waring - after the great Villa goalscorer. The horse (ridden mostly by Jamie Osborne) did well and won a few races for its owner while being backed by several Villa supporters as well!

## WARNER, JAMES

Born: Lozells, Birmingham, April 1865. Died: 1929.

Career: Hampton Road School, Milton FC, Aston Villa (May 1886), Newton Heath/Manchester United (July 1892), Walsall Town Swifts (September 1893-May 1894). Retired with a back injury. Later went to the USA to coach in Pittsburgh (September 1907-1909).

A supple and shrewd goalkeeper, agile enough to reach the most difficult of shots (or headers), Jimmy Warner played in two FA Cup Finals for Aston Villa, both against West Bromwich Albion. He gained a winners' medal in the first (1887 when Villa won 2-0) but rumours abounded he 'sold' the 1892 Final which Villa lost 3-0. As a result, his pub in Aston came in for a bit of a battering from irate supporters! He later sold it under pressure. His 101st and last competitive game for Villa was, in fact, that 1892 Cup Final against the Baggies!

A 'keeper who preferred to punch the ball rather than catch it, he joined Newton Heath prior to their first season in League football and went on to make 22 appearances for the Reds before ending his playing days with Walsall. He had infuriated the Manchester club's committee by failing to turn up for a game against Stoke which ended in a 7-1 defeat! He was suspended for 'carelessness' and played in only two more games afterwards.

Warner went over to the USA to coach in Pittsburgh in 1907.

## WARTIME FOOTBALL

This is Aston Villa's competitive playing record (first team level) during the two World War periods (friendlies are not included in the figures):

**1918-19 (Midland Victory League)**

| P | W | D | L | F | A |
|---|---|---|---|---|---|
| 6 | 1 | 1 | 4 | 9 | 18 |

**1939-40 (Division 1)**

| P | W | D | L | F | A |
|---|---|---|---|---|---|
| 3 | 1 | 0 | 2 | 3 | 3 |

**1940-41 (Birmingham & District League, Birmingham League Cup, Worcester Cup, Worcester Infirmary Cup)**

| P | W | D | L | F | A |
|---|---|---|---|---|---|
| 20 | 5 | 1 | 14 | 50 | 57 |

**1941-42 (Birmingham & District League, Worcester Cup, Worcester Infirmary Cup, Birmingham League Cup, Keys Cup)**

| P | W | D | L | F | A |
|---|---|---|---|---|---|
| 29 | 24 | 1 | 4 | 135 | 27 |

**1942-43 (Football League North 1st & 2nd Championships, Football League War Cup)**

| P | W | D | L | F | A |
|---|---|---|---|---|---|
| 38 | 23 | 3 | 12 | 91 | 63 |

**1943-44 (Football League North 1st & 2nd championships, Football League North Cup, South v North Challenge)**

| P | W | D | L | F | A |
|---|---|---|---|---|---|
| 40 | 24 | 7 | 9 | 94 | 62 |

**1944-45 (Football League North 1st & 2nd championships)**

| P | W | D | L | F | A |
|---|---|---|---|---|---|
| 43 | 26 | 5 | 12 | 124 | 64 |

**1945-46 (Football League South)**

| P | W | D | L | F | A |
|---|---|---|---|---|---|
| 42 | 25 | 11 | 6 | 106 | 57 |

**Villa's full record in World War Two (not including FA Cup):**

| P | W | D | L | F | A |
|---|---|---|---|---|---|
| 215 | 128 | 28 | 59 | 603 | 333 |

• Villa also played eight FA Cup matches in season 1945-46 (listed under FA Cup).

THE COMPLETE ENCYCLOPAEDIA OF ASTON VILLA F.C.    THE COMPLETE ENCYCLOPAEDIA OF ASTON VILLA F.C.

281

## War Cry

Aston Villa played very little football during the Great War (1915-19) owing to having so many players away on duty with the armed forces. The greatest disappointment during that period, however, was that the hostilities in Europe prevented Frederick Rinder's plans to make Villa Park into a 120,000 capacity stadium.

Villa met neighbours West Bromwich Albion six times in various local Wartime fund matches: two games in each of the 1915-16, 1916-17 and 1917-18 seasons, one home, one away. Their record against the Baggies was one victory (2-1 away), one draw and four defeats, with a goal-ratio 6-14.

In May 1919, Villa lost 2-1 at home to rivals Birmingham in another Charity Fund match.

Villa presented the British Red Cross with a motor ambulance during the First World War.

On 26 September 1939, Villa held an emergency meeting to decide if the club should continue playing competitive football. Villa Park itself was not available and, in fact, 16 senior Villa players were all tied up with Police and/or Reserve duties. In any case all football matches had to be played 'away' from home as the Chief Constable of Birmingham (AA Moriarty) had banned football in the City.

On 14 October 1939, four Villa players - Frank Broome, George Edwards, Bob Iverson and Alex Massie - guested for neighbours Birmingham in a friendly match.

On 18 March 1940, Chief Constable Moriarty at long last lifted the ban on football in the City of Birmingham. Villa utilised Solihull Town's ground at Shirley for first team matches during the 1940-41 season and Birmingham played their home games at Villa Park during the 1942-43 campaign.

Villa played their first war game at Villa Park on 13 September 1941 against RAF Hednesford in the Birmingham & District League (won 2-1).

Later that season (on 24 March 1942) in another Birmingham & District League fixture, Villa beat RAF Lichfield 19-2 at Villa Park (their best Wartime victory). Three players - Frank Broome, Billy Goffin and Harry Parkes - all scored four goals apiece.

Villa won the Birmingham & District League title in season 1941-42. They fulfilled 18 fixtures, won 15, drew one and lost two. They netted 87 goals and conceded only 16 for a total of 31 points (out of 36). Davis (19) and Broome (12) top-scored.

They also lifted the Keys Cup on 23 May 1942, beating Hednesford Town 5-0 in the Final with Albert Kerr netting a hat-trick. Only 1,200 spectators saw this Villa team in action: Wakeman; Potts, Cummings; Massie, Callaghan, Iverson; Kerr, Canning, Davis, Goffin, Edwards.

Villa reached the semi-final of the Football League North Cup in 1942-43 (beaten by Blackpool). But the following season, after eliminating Bath City (4-3 on aggregate) and Sheffield United (5-4 over two legs), they met the Seasiders again, this time in the Final. And after losing 2-1 at Bloomfield Road in front of 28,000 fans, Villa overturned the deficit to win the return leg 4-2 to take the trophy 5-4 on aggregate. A crowd of 54,824 watched the second game at Villa Park when Frank Broome (2), George Edwards and Bob Iverson scored the goals. Villa's team against the Seasiders (second leg) was: Wakeman; Potts, Cummings; Massie, Callaghan, Starling; Broome, Edwards, Parkes, Iverson, Houghton. Goffin had played on the left-wing at Bloomfield Road. Stanley Matthews lined up for Blackpool in both matches.

Vic Potts (on loan from Doncaster Rovers from October 1940 until May 1946) made most competitive League and Cup appearances for Villa during the Second World War - 203 (including eight in the FA Cup).

George Edwards netted most goals between 1939-46, totalling 98 (four in the FA Cup). In season 1945-46, Edwards scored 43 times

altogether whilst in 1941-42, Dicky Davis netted 30.

Davis in fact, scored a total of 11 hat-tricks for Villa between 1940 and 1943.

Villa netted 135 goals in season 1941-42 and 128 in 1945-46 (when they played 42 League South and eight FA Cup games).

In January 1942, Villa beat RAF Hednesford 14-1 in a Birmingham League Cup-tie. Alex Massie (5) and Frank Broome (4) led the goal-rush with Eric Houghton (2), Harry Parkes (2) and Albert Kerr rounding things off.

Villa's best away win during their Second World War exploits was an 8-1 triumph over Worcester City in November 1941 (Birmingham & District League), Dicky Davis scoring six goals.

Villa defender George Cummings was suspended 'sine die' on 18 January 1943 following incidents 'of a serious nature' during the game with Leicester City on Christmas Day 1942. The ban was lifted on 20 August 1943.

On 21 October 1944 Villa held a mock auction for the Wartime Cup they won the previous season and raised £450 for the Red Cross funds. The Cup itself remained at Villa Park.

Villa suffered their heaviest Wartime defeat when they lost 8-4 to Revo Electric in September 1940 (Birmingham & District League).

Villa missed out on winning the Football League South championship in 1945-46 by just 0.273 of a goal, pipped by rivals Birmingham City. Blues' goal-ratio was 96-45 to Villa's 106-57.

Villa had to win both their remaining two matches to overtake Blues. Sadly they couldn't manage it - drawing 2-2 at Coventry City before defeating Millwall 2-0.

Villa played two 'first team' matches on 19 February 1944 and repeated the act five weeks later on 25 March. Each time the 'best' XI participated in the Football League Wartime Cup qualifying competition and the other side met West Bromwich Albion in friendlies, Tom Waring guesting for Villa in the February home encounter which the Baggies won 4-2 in front of more than 4,000 spectators.

George Edwards scored in 11 consecutive matches for Villa during the 1945-46 season.

Alex Massie played his last game for Villa on 1 September 1945 - in a 7-1 home win over Luton Town (League South). Between 20 October and 25 December 1945 Villa ran up 11 successive home wins in the Football League South.

Trevor Ford (Swansea Town) was the Football League South's top scorer in 1945-46. He joined Villa in January 1947. Villa's Albert Kerr was a Royal Navy wireless telegraph operator during World War Two.

In September 1942 George Edwards played for hard-up Villa against Walsall with his arm encased in plaster.

On 26 September 1942, the British Empire Medal was awarded to Aston Villa defender Ernie 'Mush' Callaghan for showing 'conspicuous bravery' during an air raid on Birmingham. He was serving with the Police Reserve Force at the time.

The 9th Battalion of the Royal Warwickshire Regiment took over the dressing rooms at Villa Park during World War Two.

*Alex Massie*

Bloomfield Road Ground
WAR CUP—FINAL.
SATURDAY, 29th APRIL, 1944.

BLACKPOOL
versus
ASTON VILLA
KICK-OFF 3-0.
Official Programme - One Penny
Ground has been loaned by kind permission of
Air-Commodore J. H. Simpson.

**Wartime Guests:**
Only three players guested for Villa (from other clubs) during the Second World War. They were Dicky Davis (Sunderland), Vic Potts (Doncaster Rovers) & goalkeeper Bob Scott (Wolves).

In contrast several Villa players guested for other clubs and here are details of some of their exploits: Jimmy Allen (Birmingham, Chelsea, Crystal Palace, Fulham, Luton Town, Portsmouth, Southampton); Frank Broome (Birmingham, Northampton Town, Nottingham Forest, Notts County); Ernie Callaghan (Solihull); Larry Canning (Grimsby Town, Nottingham Forest); Bill Cobley (Leicester City); George Cummings (Birmingham, Falkirk, Northampton Town, Nottingham Forest); George Edwards (Birmingham, Chelmsford City, Coventry City, Northampton Town, Nottingham Forest, Notts County, Walsall, West Bromwich Albion, Wrexham); Billy Goffin (Leicester City, Nottingham Forest); Freddie Haycock (Leicester City, Northampton Town, Nottingham Forest, Notts County, Wolverhampton Wanderers, Wrexham); Eric Houghton (Coventry City, Leicester City, Nottingham Forest, Notts County); Bob Iverson (Birmingham, Leicester City, Northampton Town, Nottingham Forest, Notts County); Albert Kerr (Charlton Athletic, Luton Town, Northampton Town, Plymouth Argyle, Portsmouth, Solihull Town); John Martin (Aldershot, Birmingham, Nottingham Forest, Tottenham Hotspur); Alex Massie (Birmingham, Nottingham Forest, Notts County); Frank Moss (Birmingham, Northampton Town); Harry Parkes (Northampton Town, West Bromwich Albion); Joe Rutherford (Northampton Town, Nottingham Forest), Frank Shell (Leicester City, Northampton Town, Notts County, Walsall); Ronnie Starling (Northampton Town, Nottingham Forest, Walsall); Alan Wakeman (Northampton Town, Nottingham Forest, Notts County); Tommy Wood (Walsall).

During the Great War (1915-19) Villa's Ioan Price and Dicky York guested for Tottenham Hotspur and Chelsea respectively, while Lloyd Davies (Northampton Town), Charlie Millington (Stourbridge), Teddy Davison and Jack Worrall (Sheffield Wednesday) and George Lawrence (Derby County) all guested for Villa.

## WATFORD
Villa's playing record against the Hornets:
Football League/Premiership

| Venue | P | W | D | L | F | A |
|---|---|---|---|---|---|---|
| Home | 7 | 4 | 2 | 1 | 15 | 6 |
| Away | 7 | 1 | 2 | 4 | 10 | 16 |
| Totals | 14 | 5 | 4 | 5 | 25 | 22 |

| FA Cup | | | | | | |
|---|---|---|---|---|---|---|
| Home | 1 | 1 | 0 | 0 | 4 | 1 |

The first time Aston Villa met the Hornets at League level was in season 1969-70 (Division 2). After losing 3-0 at Vicarage Road in mid-September, Villa then slumped to a 2-0 home defeat in December.
Tony Morley scored twice when Villa stung the Hornets 3-0 in a home League game in October 1982 and at Vicarage Road in September 1984, Villa were 2-0 down before fighting back to earn a 3-3 draw.
When drawing 1-1 at home with Watford on 25 March 1987, Villa equalled a club record run of 12 League matches without a win.
Villa slammed the Hornets 4-0 at home in a Premiership game in February 2000, Paul Merson scoring twice.
Villa's comfortable 5th round FA Cup victory over the Hornets was recorded in February 1983 in front of 34,330 fans. Gary Shaw, Tony Morley, Colin Gibson and Gordon Cowans were the scorers.

Players with both clubs include: M Allen, CL Aston, HE Banks, F Barson, NI Callaghan, NJ Cox, AM Daley, CJ Drinkwater (Watford reserve), GA Ephgrave (Villa reserve), BA Greenhalgh, JC Gregory (Watford trialist), CB Hare, SB Hodge, DB James, M Kenning, AH Lockett, TJ Mooney (Villa reserve), JA Murray, TBD Niblo, GK Penrice, B Rowan, Kevin

*Steve Harrison - coach at both clubs.*

Richardson, S Sims, J Stephenson, GL Thompson, G Whittingham, G Williams, JE Worrall (Villa trialist).
Also: Graham Taylor (manager of both clubs, also Villa non-Executive Director), R Saunders (Watford player, Villa manager), H Green (Villa reserve player, Watford manager), S Harrison (coach at both clubs), J Ward (Watford player, Villa assistant-manager), R Downes (Watford player, Villa coach).

## WATKINS, ALFRED ERNEST
Born: Llanwnnog, Montgomeryshire, 1878. Died: Barking, Essex, 7 December 1957
Career: Caersws (1893), Oswestry (1895-97), Leicester Fosse (October 1897), Aston Villa (April 1899), Grimsby Town (February 1901), Millwall (May 1901), Southend United (August 1906-May 1907). Later became an assistant station-master, then cemetery caretaker. He sadly died in an accidental fire at his Barking home in 1957.
The eldest of six brothers, Ernie Watkins relied on skill rather than graft and had an almost languid approach to the game. A difficult player to knock off the ball, he was a natural inside-forward who could also occupy either the left-wing or left-half berths. He won five caps for Wales (his first with Leicester in 1898 and his last with Millwall in 1904). He represented his country twice as a Villa player in 1900 but only played in one Football League game during his time at Villa Park - a 2-1 win at Burnley in March 1900. He made well over 130 appearances for Millwall in the old Southern League.

## WATKINS, ARTHUR DENNIS
Born: Stapleford, Notts, November 1911. Deceased.
Career: Stapleford FC (1927), Aston Villa (November 1932), Reading (July 1936). Did not feature after World War Two.
A cheeky but clever little winger, Archie Watkins scored five goals in 21 first team appearances for Aston Villa during his four years with the club. He often roughed it with the burly defenders who challenged him but always had a smile on his face! He went on to net 22 goals in 88 League games for Reading.

## WATKINS, WALTER MARTIN
Born: Llanwnnog, Montgomeryshire, 1880. Died: Stoke-on-Trent, 14 May 1942.
Career: Caersws (1894), Oswestry United (1896), Stoke (1900), Aston Villa (£400, January 1904), Sunderland (October 1904), Crystal Palace (June 1905), Northampton Town (May 1906), Stoke (May 1907), Crewe Alexandra (July 1908), Stafford Rangers (1909-10), Tunstall (player/coach, 1910-11), Stoke (August 1911-May 1914). Retired.
Martin and his elder brother, Ernie (q.v), were brought up on a farm in mid-Wales and both graduated to Oswestry United, one of the nearest football clubs. Mart made the quickest progress and joined Stoke in 1900. Thereafter his career hardly ever faltered. He went on to win 10 full caps for Wales (three as a Villa player) and appeared in more than 200 games at club and international level, scoring more than 70 goals, netting just once in his six outings for Villa.
In 1901 inside-forward Watkins was described as a 'smart player who marshals his forces splendidly in midfield, keeps the game open and the wing men supplied with opportunities.' However, a more critical

THE COMPLETE ENCYCLOPAEDIA OF ASTON VILLA F.C.    THE COMPLETE ENCYCLOPAEDIA OF ASTON VILLA F.C.

283

comment about him said that he was 'inclined to get too much under the ball when shooting at goal.' Watkins was the subject of an approach by Manchester City in January 1904. A big pal of Billy Meredith, he was keen to join him at the Lancashire club who couldn't find the £450 fee required. Watkins subsequently joined Villa instead - for £400.

## WATSON, STEPHEN CRAIG
Born: North Shields, 1 April 1974
Career: Schoolboy football, Newcastle United (apprentice, June 1990, professional April 1991), Aston Villa (£4 million, October 1998), Everton (£2.5 million, July 2000).
Calm under pressure and a player who always gives 100 per-cent every time he takes the field, strong-running right-back Steve Watson made 54 appearances for Aston Villa during his time at Villa Park. Before his big-money move to the Midlands he played in 263 first-class matches for Newcastle, as well as gaining England honours at Youth, Under-21 (12 caps won) and 'B' team levels whilst at St James' Park. He had a disappointing 1999-2000 season with Villa, hence his transfer to Goodison Park - £1.5 million less than he had cost!

## WATSON, WALTER
Born: Sheffield, November 1890. Deceased.
Career: Worksop Town (December 1911), Aston Villa (March 1912), Rotherham Town (July 1913), Worksop Town (1915).
Outside-left, signed as cover for Horace Henshall, Walter Watson was given three first team outings by Aston Villa, his debut coming in a 6-0 home win over Manchester United on 30 March 1912, just 48 hours after he had joined the club. He had a hand in three of the goals that afternoon.

## WATTS, WILLIAM HENRY
Born: Yardley, Birmingham, April 1859. Died: September 1913.
Career: Cocknage FC, Aston Villa (August 1880). Retired in 1882 with a serious knee injury.
A versatile footballer, Bill Watts played in two FA Cup games for Villa in the 1880-81 season. He was a strapping footballer whose career ended prematurely with a leg injury.

## WEDNESBURY OLD ATHLETIC
Villa's playing record against Old Athletic:
FA Cup

| Venue | P | W | D | L | F | A |
|---|---|---|---|---|---|---|
| Home | 2 | 2 | 0 | 0 | 17 | 1 |
| Away | 2 | 1 | 0 | 1 | 9 | 8 |
| Totals | 4 | 4 | 0 | 0 | 26 | 9 |

These four FA Cup matches all took place over a period of five years. Villa lost 4-2 (away) in January 1882, won 4-1 (home) nine months later, triumphed 7-4 (away) in December 1883 and romped to a 13-0 home victory in October 1886.
That 11-goal encounter in 1883 was played on a quagmire of a pitch in failing light at the Elwells sports ground, Wednesbury. One report stated: '....it was like a sort of Walpurgis night with just enough light to follow the game nearly to the end - then the mist rolled in.' Villa were 2-0 up after 10 minutes but then found themselves 3-2 behind halfway through the first-half as the 'Old Uns', inspired by England international George Holden suddenly found their form. It was 3-3 at the interval and then the home side popped in another, prompting the reporter to state. "It made the spectators blink with jollification and consternation (as the case might be)."
Villa though, quickly levelled things up and then took control of the game as the Athletic players began to tire. Howard Vaughton was the star of the show with a hat-trick.

Players with both clubs include: AW Clarke, TT Dutton, AE Leake, F Lloyd, FA Marshall, AW Stokes, S Webb (Villa reserve), WH Walker.

## WEDNESBURY TOWN
Villa's playing record against Town:
FA Cup

| Venue | P | W | D | L | F | A |
|---|---|---|---|---|---|---|
| Home | 1 | 1 | 0 | 0 | 4 | 1 |

This Cup win was claimed in the 1st round of the 1884-85 tournament. Arthur Brown scored twice for Villa in front of 4,000 spectators at The Wednesbury Oval.
Wednesbury Town were the visitors for the opening game at Villa's Wellington Road ground (Perry Barr) on 30 September 1876 when just 21 spectators attended to witness Villa's 1-0 victory.

Players with both clubs include: J Birch, FJS Gray, WB Mason.

## WEIGHT
Goalkeeper Billy George is believed to have been the heaviest player ever to appear in a League or Cup game for Aston Villa.
At one stage during his career at Villa Park (1897-1911) he tipped the scales at 16 st. 2 lbs and averaged between 14st 2lbs and 15st during the rest of his playing days.
Another Villa goalkeeper - Albert Lindon - weighed 16 st (maximum). Tom Riddell, a Villa full-back in the 1880s, tipped the scales at 14st 10lbs.
Three more Villa goalkeepers, Tommy Mason (1880s), Nigel Sims (1956-64) and Jake Findlay (1980s) all touched the 14 stone mark when registered with the club. Another 14 stone heavyweight was 1890s full-back Jim Elliott.

## WELFORD, JAMES WILLIAM
Born: Glasgow, September 1872. Died: Scotland, 1940
Career: Glasgow Schoolboy football, Stockton (1886), Bishop Auckland (1890), Mitchell St George's (1892), Aston Villa (August 1893), Celtic (November 1896), Belfast Celtic (August 1898). Retired through injury in May 1905. Played cricket for the Warwickshire club and ground whilst assisting Villa (1894-96).
Full-back Jim Welford was the first Englishman to win both FA Cup and Scottish Cup winners medals - doing so with Villa in 1895 and Celtic in 1899.
A sturdy defender, strong in the tackle, he partnered Howard Spencer before Albert Evans entered the fray in 1896.
He scored one goal (in a 2-0 home League win over Bolton in December 1895) in 83 first-class appearances during his three years with Villa, gaining respect from all the players he opposed!

*Jim Welford*

## WELLINGTON ROAD GROUND
Aston Villa used the Wellington Road ground in Perry Barr from September 1876 until April 1897 (when they moved to Villa Park).
The rental for the first year of occupation was £5 but this rose to £8 for the 1877-78 campaign and within a matter of years the annual rent had risen to £200.
Villa's first game there was a friendly against Wednesbury Town (on 30 September 1876) which attracted only 21 spectators. The receipts

THE COMPLETE ENCYCLOPAEDIA OF ASTON VILLA F.C.

THE COMPLETE ENCYCLOPAEDIA OF ASTON VILLA F.C.

284

amounted to 5s 3d (approx. 27p). The game resulted in a narrow win for Villa (1-0).

Initially the adult admission price was 3d. There was no stand, just a field marked out for play. Players changed in a nearby blacksmith's shed. In January 1888 for the FA Cup-tie with mighty Preston North End, a record crowd of 26,849 packed into the ground - but nine months later, Villa's lowest-ever home League crowd, just 600, attended the game with Accrington (October 1888).

George Ramsay, the Villa secretary, introduced turnstiles to the ground in 1892.

The last first team game staged at Wellington Road was on 22 March 1897 when a crowd of 8,000 saw Villa beat Bolton Wanderers 6-2 in a First Division game. The last match of any nature featured Villa's reserve side against Shrewsbury Town on Good Friday 1897, when 500 fans turned up.

This ground sadly soon disappeared, engulfed by houses, shops, factories and cafés which now make up part of the busy shopping precinct on Birchfield Road, Perry Barr.

In 1974 there was talk of Villa moving to a new ground, the Birchfield Harriers Athletics' Stadium on Aldridge Road in Perry Barr, but this was quickly nipped in the bud - even before plans had been drawn up!

## Other games played at Wellington Road

### International Match
| | | |
|---|---|---|
| 1892-93 | England 6 Ireland 1 | Att. 10,000 |

### FA Cup semi-finals
| | | |
|---|---|---|
| 1889-90 | Bolton Wds. 1 Sheffield Wed 2 | Att. 12,000 |
| 1895-96 | Derby Co 1 Wolverhampton Wds 3 | Att. 20,000 |

### Inter Association matches
| | | |
|---|---|---|
| 1877-78 | Birmingham 1 London 0 | Att. 2,000 |
| 1878-79 | Birmingham 1 London 7 | Att. 2,000 |
| 1879-80 | Birmingham 5 London 2 | Att. 3,000 |
| 1880-81 | Birmingham 0 London 2 | Att. 3,000 |
| 1882-83 | Birmingham 3 London 1 | Att. 2,500 |
| 1884-85 | Birmingham 4 London 2 | Att. 2,000 |
| 1886-87 | Birmingham 3 London 0 | Att. 3,000 |
| 1889-90 | Birmingham 6 London 1 | Att. 3,000 |

### Junior International
| | | |
|---|---|---|
| April 1896 | England 0 Scotland 4 | Att. 5,000 |

## WELLINGTON TOWN (OAKENGATES, TELFORD UNITED)

Villa's playing record against Town is:

Birmingham League
| Venue | P | W | D | L | F | A |
|---|---|---|---|---|---|---|
| Home | 2 | 1 | 0 | 1 | 6 | 5 |
| Away | 2 | 0 | 0 | 2 | 2 | 9 |
| Totals | 4 | 1 | 0 | 3 | 8 | 14 |

Birmingham League Cup
| | | | | | | |
|---|---|---|---|---|---|---|
| Home | 1 | 1 | 0 | 0 | 5 | 0 |
| Away | 1 | 0 | 0 | 1 | 1 | 2 |
| Totals | 2 | 1 | 0 | 1 | 6 | 2 |

Aston Villa's first XI played Wellington four times in two seasons of Birmingham League competition in 1940-41 and 1941-42.

Villa's best win was 5-1 at home on 27 September 1941 when Dicky Davis (from Sunderland) scored a hat-trick. In contrast Wellington won 5-1 in Shropshire a week later to gain sweet revenge.

Villa's ousted Town from the 'League Cup' in the first round in November 1941, winning 6-2 on aggregate, Eric Houghton and Davis both netting twice in the 5-0 home win.

Players with both clubs: DO Ashton, LK Capewell, WS Corbett, T Gardner, H Hampton, TW Jones, WA Littlewood, AT Miller, CJH Millington, RT Pritchard, AE Surtees, JM Wilcox.

## WELSH CONNECTION

Here is a list of Aston Villa personnel (players at various levels, managers, coaches etc) who have been associated with Welsh League clubs (not including Football League clubs):

| | |
|---|---|
| B Anstey | Mid-Rhondda |
| DJ Astley | Merthyr Town |
| JW Bache | Mid-Rhondda |
| T Barber | Pontypridd, Merthyr Town |
| F Barson | Rhyl Athletic (player-manager) |
| GW Cook | Colwyn Bay United |
| L Davies | Druids |
| M Delaney | Carmarthen |
| AW Green | Ebbw Vale, Aberystwyth |

*Len Capewell (3rd from left on front row) in the Wellington Town team of 1919.*

| H Green | Bangor City (manager), Ebbw Vale (manager) |
| H Hadley | Aberdare (manager), Merthyr Town (manager), Bangor City (manager) |
| GA Hitchens | Merthyr Tydfil |
| S Howarth | Barry Town, Aberaman, Merthyr Tydfil |
| AE Leake | Merthyr Town (trainer) |
| AE Lindon | Merthyr Town |
| AA Loach | Rhyl |
| AT Miller | Aberdare |
| HE Nash | Aberdare, Abertillery, Mardy, Pontypridd, Merthyr Town, Aberbargoed |
| JR Nicholson | Bangor City |
| C Phillips | Ebbw Vale |
| L Phillips | Llanelli (player-manager) |
| AF Phoenix | Colwyn Bay United |
| IV Powell | Bargoed, Barry Town, Bath City (manager) |
| IH Price | Aberdare, Mardy Corinthians, Mid-Rhondda (manager) |
| LP Price | Barmouth |
| D Richards | Merthyr Town, Pentrebach |
| CL Roberts | Merthyr Town |
| LR Roose | Ruabon Druids, Aberystwyth, Llandudno Town |
| AE Watkins | Caersws |
| MW Watkins | Caersws |
| JJ Williams | Aberaman, Llanelli |
| WH Williams | Chirk, Mold, St Asaph |
| AW Wollaston | Chirk |
| PA Woosnam | Bangor City |
| JE Worrall | Aberdare |

## Dragon Talk

The first Villa player to win a Welsh cap was Billy Evans against England in March 1892 at Wrexham.

Haydn Price was capped by Wales v Scotland in 1907 while a Villa reserve, yet he never made a senior appearance for the club.

Bob Evans won 10 caps for Wales (1906-10) but after it was discovered he had been born the 'other side' of the border he went on to gain four caps for England (1911-12).

Three Villa players - Dai Astley, Tom Griffiths and Charlie Phillips - lined up for Wales against England in February 1936

And three more - Trevor Ford, Keith Jones and Ivor Powell - played against England in November 1947.

Trevor Ford scored 67 goals for Sunderland and 39 for Cardiff City after leaving Villa Park in 1950. He won 49 Welsh caps during his playing career.

Leighton Phillips made over 200 appearances for Cardiff City before joining Villa in 1974.

Villa wing-half Barrie Hole emulated his father by playing for Wales at full international level.

## WEMBLEY STADIUM

### Villa's playing record at the Empire Stadium:

| Comp | P | W | D | L | F | A |
| --- | --- | --- | --- | --- | --- | --- |
| FA Cup | 4 | 1 | 1* | 2 | 2 | 4 |
| L/Cup | 5 | 3 | 1 | 1 | 7 | 3 |
| FACS | 1 | 0 | 1 | 0 | 2 | 2 |
| Festival | 2 | 0 | 2+ | 0 | 0 | 0 |
| Makita | 2 | 0 | 0 | 2 | 0 | 3 |
| Totals | 14 | 4 | 5 | 5 | 11 | 12 |

*This was the 0-0 semi-final draw with Bolton Wanderers which Villa eventually won on penalties (4-1) to become the first team to reach the Final via a shoot-out!
+ These fixtures both went to penalty shoot-outs, Villa winning one and losing one.

### Wembley Fact File

Aston Villa's first trip to Wembley was to contest the 1924 FA Cup Final with Newcastle United. This was the Villa team that lost 2-0 to the Magpies in what was the first all-ticket Final at the Empire Stadium: Jackson; Smart, Mort; Milne, Moss (snr), Blackburn; York, Kirton, Capewell, Walker, Dorrell. The official attendance was 91,645.
Vic Milne was the first Doctor to play at Wembley - doing so for Aston Villa in that 1924 Final.

A fortnight earlier - 12 April 1924 - Billy Walker had become the first Villa player to score a goal at Wembley - for England against Scotland in the home international. Two other Villa players appeared in this match - right-back Tommy Smart and centre-half Frank Moss, who skippered his country as he did Villa in the Cup Final.
Jimmy Dugdale won FA Cup winners' medals at Wembley with West Bromwich Albion in 1954 and Aston Villa in 1957.
Stan Crowther played for Villa v. Manchester United in the 1957 FA Cup Final and for Manchester United v Bolton in the following season's Final.

Ray Graydon scored Villa's dramatic late winner v Norwich City in the 1975 League Cup Final - following up to net from close range after his penalty kick had been saved by former Villa goalkeeper Kevin Keelan.
Mark Delaney was sent-off in the FA Cup semi-final clash with Bolton at Wembley on 2 April 2000.
Villa met Chelsea in the very last FA Cup Final staged at Wembley - on 20 May 2000 in front of 78,217 spectators. Villa's team that afternoon was: James; Delaney, Wright (Hendrie); Southgate, Ehiogu, Barry; Taylor (Stone), Boateng, Dublin, Carbone (Joachim), Merson.

On 16-17 April 1988, Aston Villa participated in the celebration Mercantile Credit Centenary Festival at Wembley. They defeated Blackburn Rovers 2-1 on penalties (after a 0-0 draw) in their opening phase one game, but then lost 1-0 on penalties (after another 0-0 draw) to Nottingham Forest in their first phase quarter-final encounter. Each game lasted just 40 minutes and the attendance for both fixtures was estimated at 20.000. Forest went on to win the championship.

Ron Saunders took three different teams to Wembley for League Cup Finals - Manchester City (1974), Norwich City (1975) and Aston Villa (1977).

Manager Ron Atkinson guided Manchester United to FA Cup victories in 1983 and 1985, Sheffield Wednesday to League Cup glory (over Manchester United) in 1991 and Aston Villa to League Cup success in 1994 (v United) all at Wembley.

THE COMPLETE ENCYCLOPAEDIA OF ASTON VILLA F.C.    THE COMPLETE ENCYCLOPAEDIA OF ASTON VILLA F.C.

286

## WEST BROMWICH ALBION

Villa's playing record against the Baggies:

Football League

| Venue | P | W | D | L | F | A |
|---|---|---|---|---|---|---|
| Home | 62 | 39 | 8 | 15 | 118 | 74 |
| Away | 62 | 19 | 15 | 28 | 86 | 99 |
| Totals | 124 | 58 | 23 | 43 | 204 | 173 |

FA Cup

| | P | W | D | L | F | A |
|---|---|---|---|---|---|---|
| Home | 5 | 3 | 1 | 1 | 9 | 3 |
| Away | 5 | 3 | 1 | 1 | 7 | 6 |
| Neutral | 5 | 3 | 1 | 1 | 6 | 5 |
| Totals | 15 | 9 | 3 | 3 | 22 | 14 |

League Cup

| | P | W | D | L | F | A |
|---|---|---|---|---|---|---|
| Home | 3 | 0 | 1 | 2 | 3 | 5 |
| Away | 4 | 2 | 0 | 2 | 6 | 11 |
| Totals | 7 | 2 | 1 | 4 | 9 | 16 |

Football League Jubilee

| | P | W | D | L | F | A |
|---|---|---|---|---|---|---|
| Home | 2 | 0 | 2 | 0 | 2 | 2 |

Wartime

| | P | W | D | L | F | A |
|---|---|---|---|---|---|---|
| Home | 12 | 5 | 2 | 5 | 42 | 33 |
| Away | 10 | 4 | 0 | 6 | 25 | 27 |
| Totals | 22 | 9 | 2 | 11 | 67 | 60 |

As founder members of the Football League, the first encounter between the teams at this level was on 19 January 1889 when Aston Villa won 2-0 at Perry Barr. A week later six goals were shared at Albion's Stoney Lane ground.

Villa were beaten 4-0 at home by Albion in September 1890, but then won 3-0 in West Bromwich three weeks later.

On the opening day of the 1893-94 season, Albion were defeated 3-2 at Perry Barr when Jack Reynolds scored Villa's first League penalty against his former club. Soon afterwards Villa doubled up with an

*John Deehan scoring with this header against Albion in April 1978 (Won 3-0).*

excellent 6-3 win in the Black Country, Jack Devey netting twice on this occasion.

Villa spoilt Billy Bassett's farewell party when they whipped Albion 7-1 at Villa Park in the penultimate League game of the 1898-99 season. Billy Garraty (hat-trick) and Fred Wheldon (2), who both became Albion players, led the goal-rush.

Villa were the first team to register a League win at The Hawthorns, beating Albion there 1-0 in September 1900 in front of a record 35,417 spectators. Former 'Throstle' George Johnson scored the vital goal.

Albion ended Villa's record-breaking run of 37 home League games without defeat when they won 3-0 at Villa Park in a First Division match on 4 September 1911.

Over 55,000 fans saw Albion win 4-2 at Villa Park in September 1912, the Baggies repeating that scoreline on the same ground in November 1919 when the turnout was 58,273.

A Villa Park attendance record of 66,694 saw a goalless draw with the Baggies in November 1920, a Billy Walker hat-trick helping Villa to an exciting 4-0 home win over their near neighbours in October 1923.

Albion restored some pride with a 4-1 home victory over Villa in February 1925, before an eight-goal thriller ended all-square at 4-4 when Albion visited Villa Park in April 1934.

'W.G' Richardson scored four times as Albion won 7-0 on Villa territory in October 1935, the Baggies' best-ever victory over Villa who at the same time suffered their joint heaviest League defeat! But Villa gained revenge with a 3-0 triumph at The Hawthorns on April Fool's Day 1936.

Over 65,000 fans saw Villa open their 1950-51 League programme with a 2-0 home win over Albion.

Villa walloped the Baggies 6-1 at home in April 1954 - just as their rivals were lining up a last-ditch effort to win the League title, having already qualified for the FA Cup Final. Villa led 5-1 at half-time in this Easter encounter which was attended by 45,557 spectators, 400 fewer than had watched the 1-1 draw at The Hawthorns 24 hours earlier.

A goal right at the death by West Brom's Ronnie Allen sent Villa into the Second Division in April 1959. Villa had to win at The Hawthorns to stay up but could only draw 1-1 in front of 48,281 spectators. Manchester City remained up instead! Earlier that season Albion had come back from a goal down to win 4-1 at Villa Park.

Albion pipped Villa 4-3 in a seven-goal thriller at The Hawthorns in October 1963 (Villa had been 2-1 ahead at half-time) and when Villa were fighting to pull clear of the relegation zone in November 1966, they beat the Baggies 3-2 at home in pouring rain, Johnny MacLeod having a brilliant game.

Andy Gray snapped in an evening hat-trick as Villa rounded off the 1976-77 season with an excellent 4-0 home win over Albion for whom Johnny Giles was making his farewell appearance as a player.

A sun-drenched crowd of almost 30,000 saw Villa open their 1983-84 League programme with a 4-3 home win over Albion, Brendan Ormsby heading in the second-half winner. But in the return clash at The Hawthorns Villa allowed the Baggies to score three times in the last 10 minutes after Gary Shaw had given them the lead.

Charlie Aitken and Johnny Dixon both made 15 League appearances for Villa in local derbies against West Bromwich Albion. Dixon also scored five goals.

In the space of eight years Villa and Albion met in three FA Cup Finals. Villa won the first in 1887 by 2-0 at The Oval. Albion gained revenge with a 3-0 victory at The Crystal Palace in 1892 before Villa, with one of the fastest goals on record for a Final (39 seconds from Bob Chatt), took the 1895 Final 1-0, also at The Crystal Palace. (See FA Cup).

Villa also defeated the Baggies in the 1957 FA Cup semi-final, winning the replay 1-0 at St Andrew's after a 2-2 draw at Molineux where Peter McParland scored his second equaliser two minutes from time. Billy Myerscough was the hero in the win on Birmingham City soil.

Earlier, there had been massive crowds for the two 3rd round Cup clashes in 1924-25.....a record attendance of 64,612 at The Hawthorns witnessed a 1-1 draw and then 60,015 fans flocked to the mid-week replay at Villa Park which Albion won 2-1.

Villa registered 2-1 away wins over the Baggies in the 1925-26 and 1931-32 FA Cup competitions. Derek Mountfield's first-half effort and a superb individual goal by Tony Daley gave Villa a 2-0 win at the Hawthorns in the 5th round in 1990. Dwight Yorke netted twice as Villa waltzed through a 4th round home tie in January 1998, winning 4-0, easing up!

Villa's heaviest defeat in the League Cup has been 6-1 - at The Hawthorns against Albion in a 2nd round tie in September 1966. The previous season Albion had beaten Villa 3-1 on the same ground (in round 5).

Tony Morley (later to play for Albion) was sent-off at half-time when Villa lost 1-0 to the Baggies in a home League Cup-tie in January 1982. Villa's first League Cup victory over Albion came in November 1983 when they won a 4th round encounter 2-1 in front of 31,114 fans. Two

THE COMPLETE ENCYCLOPAEDIA OF ASTON VILLA F.C.      THE COMPLETE ENCYCLOPAEDIA OF ASTON VILLA F.C.

287

*Keith Leonard (9) scores Villa's equaliser against Albion in March 1975. (Won 3-1).*

## WEST HAM UNITED
Villa's playing record against the Hammers:
Football League/Premiership

| Venue | P | W | D | L | F | A |
|---|---|---|---|---|---|---|
| Home | 38 | 19 | 9 | 10 | 75 | 49 |
| Away | 38 | 6 | 13 | 19 | 47 | 81 |
| Totals | 76 | 25 | 22 | 29 | 122 | 130 |
| FA Cup | | | | | | |
| Home | 2 | 2 | 0 | 0 | 8 | 0 |
| Away | 1 | 0 | 0 | 1 | 0 | 1 |
| Totals | 3 | 2 | 0 | 1 | 8 | 1 |
| League Cup | | | | | | |
| Home | 2 | 0 | 1 | 1 | 0 | 2 |
| Away | 6 | 2 | 1 | 3 | 9 | 10 |
| Totals | 8 | 2 | 2* | 4 | 9 | 12 |

*Villa lost 5-4 on penalties (see below)

Wartime

| | | | | | | |
|---|---|---|---|---|---|---|
| Home | 1 | 0 | 1 | 0 | 2 | 2 |
| Away | 1 | 1 | 0 | 0 | 2 | 1 |
| Totals | 2 | 1 | 1 | 0 | 4 | 3 |

seasons later Villa repeated that victory on the same ground in a 4th round replay (after a 2-2 draw at Villa Park).

The 22 competitive games played between Albion in the First and Second World Wars produced no fewer than 127 goals (average almost six per game).

There was not a single goalless draw, whilst Villa's best win of the 10 gained over the Baggies was an 8-2 triumph at home in October 1942 when Eric Houghton scored a hat-trick. Villa also registered home wins of 6-1 and 6-2 in April 1941 and January 1945 respectively whilst the Baggies won 6-2 at home and away in October 1942 and May 1943. The Boxing Day fixture between the clubs in 1944 was abandoned through fog with nine minutes left. Albion were leading 4-3 at the time and the result was allowed to stand.

Players with both clubs include: AJ Aldridge, DM Bradley, CS Buckley (WBA trialist), RM Campbell (Albion reserve), FA Carr, A Comyn, P Crichton (Villa on loan), J Crisp (Villa trialist), VH Crowe (Albion amateur), S Crowther (Albion amateur), J Cumbes, NA Cutler (Albion reserve), JM Deehan (also Villa coach), D Dudley (reserve goalkeeper at both clubs), JR Dugdale, GR Edwards (WBA WW2 guest), U Ehiogu, AJ Evans, G Fenton, G Garratt, W Garraty, AM Gray, TW Green snr, W Groves, H Hadley, GA Harris, T Haywood, R Hopkins, SK Hunt, DLW Jackson (Albion amateur), G Johnson, WF Johnson (WBA amatuer), K Jones (Albion junior), P Kerr (Albion trialist), P King, AA Loach, K McNaught, CJ Mann (Albion amateur), AW Morley, HA Parkes (Albion WW2 guest), J Pennington (Villa trialist), T Perry, A Rees (Villa trialist), C Regis, J Reynolds, RJ Roberts, LGF Smith (WBA WW2 guest), JL Spencer (Villa reserve), NP Spink, K Swain, GL Thompson, AD Townsend, HF Trentham (Villa trialist), DJ Walsh, GF Wheldon, JJ Williams (Albion reserve), C Wilson (Villa reserve), CC Withers (Albion junior).

Also: R Atkinson, B Little & R Saunders (managers of both clubs - Atkinson also a Villa junior and Little a senior Villa player), RM Wylie (Villa player & coach, Albion manager), VH Crowe (Albion Amateur, Villa player & manager), A Evans & G Shelton (Villa players, Albion coaches), R Brocklebank (Villa player, WBA coach/scout), DG Mortimer (Villa player, Albion assistant-manager/coach), R Downes (Albion reserve, Villa coach), A Newman (reserve both clubs), P Barron (Albion player, Villa coach), P Hunt (Albion reserve, Villa trainer), F Pedley (physio/trainer with both clubs), SG Williams (Albion player & trainer, Villa trainer), R Downes (Albion reserve, Villa coach), K Leonard (Villa player, Albion assistant-manager/coach), A Ashman (Albion manager, Villa scout), RA Ryan & B Whitehouse (Albion players, Villa scouts), PD Doherty (Albion WW2 guest, Villa chief scout), K Smith (Albion player, Villa lottery staff), R Fairfax (Albion player, Villa ticket office clerk), T Cardall (Commercial Manager with both clubs).

Aston Villa first met the Hammers at League level in 1923-24, but it wasn't until Boxing Day 1925 that Villa recorded their first win over the Londoners - a 2-0 victory in front of 50,000 fans at Villa Park, following a 5-2 defeat at Upton Park 24 hours earlier!

In 1926-27 it was the Hammers who took all four points as they fired ten goals past Villa with 5-1 victories at home and away to claim their first double.

Twelve goals were scored in the two Villa-West Ham League matches in 1928-29. After losing 4-1 in London, Villa gained revenge by winning the return match 5-2.

In January 1931 Villa played out the first of two 5-5 draws in League football when they shared 10 goals with the Hammers at Upton Park. A crowd of 16,000 saw Joe Beresford score twice for Villa and Vivian Gibbins do likewise for the Hammers.

Vic Watson scored two hat-tricks for the Hammers against Villa in season 1929-30 - the first in a 5-2 win at Upton Park and the second in a 3-2 victiory at Villa Park.

On 26 September 1931, a week after scoring four goals against Chelsea, 'Pongo' Waring rattled in four more against another London club as West Ham were defeated 5-2 at Villa Park.

Villa played the Hammers three times (all in the League) in the space of four matches....home and away in April 1937 and at home in August 1937 to start a new season.

Just after gaining promotion to the First Division, the Hammers slammed Villa 7-2 at Upton Park in August 1958 when future Villa coach Malcolm Musgrove scored twice in front of 30,506 spectators. The Hammers were 4-0 up at half-time. Later that season Villa lost the return game 2-1.

A total of 18 goals were scored in the four League games between Villa and the Hammers during 1960-61 and 1961-62. In the former campaign Villa lost 5-2 at Upton Park but won 2-1 at home and a year later the Hammers won 4-2 on Villa soil and 2-0 in London.

After West Ham had registered a 2-0 win at Villa Park in March 1967 it was to be another 22 years before they won on the same ground again (1-0 in March 1989).

Villa began their 1976-77 League programme with a 4-0 home win over West Ham. Later they completed their first double over the Londoners with a 1-0 victory at Upton Park.

Warren Aspinall scored twice when Villa beat the Hammers 4-0 at home in April 1987.

Savo Milosevic scored twice as Villa ran up one of their best away wins in the Premiership by beating the Hammers 4-0 at Upton Park in November 1995.

David Ginola netted with a tremendous free-kick in the 2-2 draw between the two clubs at Villa Park in April 2001.

THE COMPLETE ENCYCLOPAEDIA OF ASTON VILLA F.C.    THE COMPLETE ENCYCLOPAEDIA OF ASTON VILLA F.C.

288

Harold Halse scored twice in Villa's 5-0, second round home FA Cup win over the Hammers (then in the Southern League) in 1913. Then in their second meeting in this competition - 64 years later in January 1977 - John Deehan netted twice as Villa won through to the 5th round with a comfortable 3-0 home victory in front of almost 47,000 spectators.

*Malcolm Musgrove (right) gets in a cross v. Villa in 1958-59. John Slueewenhock is the Villa defender.*

A late, late penalty by West Ham's Ray Stewart stunned Villa as they crashed out of the FA Cup 1-0 at Upton Park in a quarter-final tie in March 1980. The Hammers went on to win the Final.

After losing to the Hammers 5-4 on penalties in a 5th round League Cup-tie at Upton Park in December 1999, the Football League committee ordered that the game should be replayed because the Hammers fielded an ineligible player. This time Villa came out on top, winning 3-1 to enter the semi-finals.

Goalkeeper Mervyn Day and midfielder Phil Woosnam both made over 100 appearances for the Hammers before joining Villa.

Dennis Mortimer made his debut for Villa against the Hammers on Boxing Day 1975, starring in a 4-1 win.

Players with both clubs include: L Askew, VP Blore (Villa reserve), RAJ Brown (Hammers' WW2 guest), F Carr, GA Charles, LC Curbishley, MR Day, J Eccles, LC Curbishley, PM Elliott (WHU trialist), R Houghton, DB James, Kyle, F McAvennie, R Milne (Villa trialist), FH Norris, L Ridgewell (Villa reserve), JHH Rutherford (Hammers' WW2 guest), AJ Scott, L Sealey, TC Southren, NP Spink (West Ham on Schoolboy forms), D Unsworth (no games for Villa), PA Woosnam.

Also: M Musgrove & DJ Sexton (Hammers players, Villa coaches etc).

## WEST MIDLANDS REGIONAL LEAGUE

Aston Villa's reserve/intermediate teams played in the West Midlands League from 1889 until 1915 (23 full seasons).

Their complete record was:

| P | W | D | L | F | A | Pts |
|---|---|---|---|---|---|-----|
| 738 | 480 | 118 | 140 | 2262 | 945 | 1078 |

For nine seasons from 1946-47 to 1954-55 and for three more 1956-57 to 1958-59, Villa's 'A' team played in the same competition, acquiring this overall record:

| P | W | D | L | F | A | Pts |
|---|---|---|---|---|---|-----|
| 414 | 141 | 72 | 201 | 734 | 883 | 354 |

## WESTON, THOMAS

Born: Halesowen, August 1890. Died: Stourbridge, 1952

Career: Red Hill School, Quarry Bank (1907), Old Hill Comrades (1908), Coombs Wood (1909), Aston Villa (professional, July 1911), Stoke (August 1921-November 1922), Stourbridge until announcing his retirement in May 1924. Afterwards he coached at various schools in the Stourbridge, Old Hill and Cradley Heath areas.

Some supporters considered full-back Tommy Weston to be rather impetuous at times, wanting him to show more caution in his play, but he was undoubtedly a very fine footballer, dedicated, strong-willed, competitive and solid. He introduced a strong element of dash into Villa's defence where he formed an excellent partnership at full-back with first Tommy Lyons (before the Great War), then with Tommy Smart during the early 1920s. He appeared in 179 first-class games for Villa, gaining an FA Cup winners' medal in 1920. During the War he was badly wounded at Ervilliers (France) in March 1918.

## WHATELEY, OLIVER

Born: Coventry, 8 August 1861. Died: Birmingham, October 1926

Career: Gladstone Unity, Coventry FC (1878), Aston Villa (July 1880). Retired with cancer of the face, May 1888. Underwent a severe but successful operation in 1911 and between 1914-18 (after declaring himself fit to join the forces although over military age) he worked in the YMCA hut in Rouen (France). He was in very poor health for many years prior to his death at the age of 65.

Variable in performance, at his best, Olly Whateley was a formidable amateur inside-forward who had an aggressive spirit in his general play. He possessed an excellent shot (reputed to be one of the hardest of his day) and often had a crack at goal from anywhere within reason! Nicknamed 'daisy-cutter' because a lot of his efforts skimmed along the ground, Whateley scored nine goals in 19 FA Cup appearances for Aston Villa and helped build up the club during the early 1880s. He gained two full England caps in 1883, against Ireland (when he scored twice in a 7-0 win at Liverpool) and Scotland. An artist and designer by profession, he was the son of the Birmingham councillor, James Whateley.

## WHELDON, GEORGE FREDERICK

Born: Langley Green, Oldbury, 1 November 1869. Died: Worcester, 13 January 1924.

Career: Chance's Infants and Langley St Michael's senior Schools, Rood End White Star, Langley Green Victoria, West Bromwich Albion (trialist, summer 1898), Small Heath, now Birmingham City (February 1890), Aston Villa (£350, June, 1896), West Bromwich Albion (£100, August 1900), Queen's Park Rangers (£400, December 1901), Portsmouth (£150, August 1902), Worcester City (July 1904), Coventry City (May 1905-January 1907).

An inside-forward, the youngest in a family of ten children, Fred 'Diamond' Wheldon was a brilliant footballer, an exceptional talent, a tremendous goalscorer who went on to great things with club and country.

Often seen wearing a pair of golfing stockings (instead of the footballing type), he scored 84 goals in 134 games for Blues, helping them win the Second Division championship and promotion in successive years (1893, 1894). In fact, Wheldon notched Blues' first-ever Football League goal against Burslem Port Vale in a 5-1 win on 3 September 1892 and he scored the club's first penalty in the 2-2 home draw with Aston Villa at Muntz Street in October 1894. But he wanted a bigger stage and in the summer of 1896 he moved to Aston Villa for

THE COMPLETE ENCYCLOPAEDIA OF ASTON VILLA F.C.　　　THE COMPLETE ENCYCLOPAEDIA OF ASTON VILLA F.C.

289

a club record fee of £350 (around £3.5 million on today's price-scale!). He impressed all and sundry with his performances with Villa, being instrumental in three League championship triumphs (1897, 1898 & 1900) and in the 1897 FA Cup Final which was the year, of course, the double was achieved. Wheldon played in four international matches for England (it should have been far more) and he also starred in four Inter League games. He participated in 138 League and Cup games for Villa, scoring 74 goals. That gave him an overall record of 156 goals in 267 first-class outings for the two second City clubs. He then played in the first League game at The Hawthorns (for WBA against Derby County on 3 September 1900) and thus became the first professional to appear at competitive level for the three central West Midland clubs. However, he struggled to find his form with Albion and eight months after they had been relegated to the Second Division he moved to London to join QPR. He switched to Portsmouth in 1902 before finally calling it a day in 1907 after brief spells with Worcester City and Coventry City. Besides being a splendid footballer, Wheldon was also a very useful cricketer and scored almost 5,000 runs in 138 matches for Worcestershire between 1899 and 1906. He averaged over 22.50 at

the crease and hit three centuries into the bargain as well as claiming 95 catches, some as a wicketkeeper. He also played cricket for Carmarthenshire and later became a publican in Worcester where he died in 1924. Wheldon's brother Sam also played for West Brom. An unusual incident occurred early in Wheldon's playing career with Blues whereby one of his booming shots struck the referee on the pocket of his jacket. The pocket contained a box of matches, used to light the official's pipe! The box burst into flames and the ref's jacket was ruined!

## WHITEHOUSE, JAMES

Born: Birmingham, 9 April 1873. Died: Birmingham, 7 February 1934.
Career: Albion Swifts, Mitchell St George's (1890), Grimsby Town (June 1892), Aston Villa (£200, July 1896), Bedminster (May 1898), Grimsby Town (May 1899), Newton Heath (September 1900), Manchester City (February 1903), Third Lanark (September 1993), Hull City (July 1904), Southend United (July 1905-May 1907).
Well built goalkeeper Jimmy Whitehouse was described as being 'a clean handler and reliable last line of defence' - a 'ripper' between the sticks (which to present day ears sounds like dated slang from of a PG Woodhouse novel)....and in an emergency he also proved to be an above average inside-forward! A League and FA Cup double winner with Aston Villa in 1897, he made 43 first-class appearances during his two seasons with the club. In his two separate spells with Grimsby he amassed over 160 appearances.

## WHITLEY, JOHN

Born: Seacombe, Cornwall, April 1880. Died: London, c 1955.
Career: Liskeard YMCA (1897), Darwen (1898-99 season), Aston Villa (May 1900) Everton (August 1902), Stoke (September 1904), Leeds City (April 1906), Lincoln City (September 1906), Chelsea (September 1907). Retired in May 1914 to become trainer at Stamford Bridge, a position he held until May 1939, spending in total 32 years with the London club.
Goalkeeper Jack Whitley was sound and competent deputising for Billy George in 11 first team games during his time with Aston Villa. He helped Chelsea win promotion to the First Division in 1912 and made 138 senior appearances for the Londoners. During his days as a trainer, he was a father figure to generations of young players at Stamford Bridge and as he dashed onto the field (to treat the injured) his bald

head and flapping coat-tails were very much part of the Chelsea scene during the inter-war years.

## WHITTAKER, SAMUEL SAMSON

Born: Shelfield, Walsall, August 1888. Died: Wednesfield, September 1952.
Career: Shelfield Methodists, Rushall Red Cross (1906), Aston Villa (April 1908), Walsall (May 1915). Did not figure after the Great War.
A hard-working inside-forward, with poise and penetration, Sammy Whittaker scored six goals in 68 League and Cup games for Villa during his seven seasons with the club. His best was in 1911-12 when he starred in 27 matches. He had the knack of keeping his shorts clean after playing on the muddiest of pitches!

## WHITTINGHAM, GUY

Born: Evesham, 10 November 1964
Career: Yeovil Town, Army football, Portsmouth (June 1989), Aston Villa (£1.2 million, Augfust 1993), Wolverhampton Wanderers (on loan, February 1994), Sheffield Wednesday (£700,000, December 1994), Wolverhampton Wanderers (on loan, November 1998), Portsmouth (on loan, January 1999), Watford (on loan, March 1999), Portsmouth (free transfer, July 1999), Peterborough United (August 2000), Oxford United (on loan, September 2000), Portsmouth (player/coach & assistant-manager, October 2000), Wycombe Wanderers (March 2001).
Centre-forward Guy Whittingham, strong and willing, spent just sixteen months at Villa Park during which time he scored six goals in 33 senior appearances. He never really settled in Birmingham but during his career on the whole, the former soldier (who was bought out of the Army by Portsmouth in 1989) has had an excellent career, netting more than 150 goals in just over 400 competitive matches.

## WIGAN ATHLETIC

Villa's playing record against the Latics:
League Cup

| Venue | P | W | D | L | F | A |
|---|---|---|---|---|---|---|
| Home | 1 | 1 | 0 | 0 | 5 | 0 |
| Away | 2 | 2 | 0 | 0 | 5 | 1 |
| Totals | 3 | 3 | 0 | 0 | 10 | 1 |

Aston Villa defeated Wigan 8-0 on aggregate in a 2nd round League Cup in September/October 1994. Dalian Atkinson scored twice in the 5-0, 1st leg victory whilst debutant Nil Lamptey netted twice in the return fixture at Springfield Park when goalkeeper Michael Oakes also made his Villa debut.

Players with both clubs include: W Aspinall, L Butler, RM Campbell, W Hazelden, B Ormsby, AF McLoughlin.
Also: JM Deehan & BD Rioch (Villa players, Wigan managers), B Tiler (Villa player, Wigan assistant-manager), CJ Nicholl (Villa player, Wigan scout).
NB - The following players were all associated with Villa and Wigan Borough: F Barson, JJ Pendleton, AF Phoenix, TE Tebb (Villa reserve).

## WILCOX, JAMES MITCHELL

Born: Stourbridge, January 1887. Died: Lichfield, August 1940
Career: Stourbridge Standard, Cradley Heath, Dudley Town, Aston Villa (amateur, March 1906, professional April 1906), Birmingham (November 1908), Southampton (£250, May 1911), Wellington (July 1912-13).
A quick and decisive outside-right, sometimes erratic with his crosses, Jim Wilcox, who could 'manoeuvre astutely past his full-back' made only six appearances for Aston Villa before going on to play in almost 50 games for Blues and 28 for Saints.

THE COMPLETE ENCYCLOPAEDIA OF ASTON VILLA F.C.

THE COMPLETE ENCYCLOPAEDIA OF ASTON VILLA F.C.

290

## WILKES, ALBERT

Born: West Bromwich, October 1875. Died: Bromsgrove, 9 December 1936.

Career: Walsall Street School (West Bromwich), Oldbury Town, Walsall (1896), Aston Villa (May 1898), Fulham (June 1907), Chesterfield (February-May 1909). Retired after a fire had badly damaged his photographic studio in West Bromwich. He had it all remodernised and flourished in the trade, specialising in team groups as well as individual players' profiles and action shots. After he died the business remained in the family for many years (run by his son, Albert junior) until the whole collection of Wilkes' pictures were sold to the London-based company, Colorpost (late 1970s).

Wilkes also took up refereeing (initially as a hobby) and in September 1934 was appointed to the Board of Directors at Villa Park.

Albert Wilkes himself was a 'straight-as-a-die, no-nonsense' wing-half renowned for his competitiveness and hard-work. He possessed a formidable tackle, and was a fine helpmeet to his full-back, being scrupulously fair. He won five full England caps (1901-02) and gained two League championship medals (1899 & 1900). He scored eight goals in 159 senior apearances for Aston Villa before transferring to Fulham in 1907, having been all set to join West Bromwich Albion in December 1906, the deal falling through at the eleventh hour.

As well as being a fine footballer, Wilkes was also a marvellous singer and delighted thousands round the Midlands music halls in the 1920s. He also enjoyed swimming and he received the Royal Humane Society's award for life-saving when he dived fully clothed into a West Bromwich park pool to save a young boy from drowning. His daughter received a similiar prize when she saved a child from drowning in the sea off Aberdovey in Wales.

## WILKES, THOMAS HENRY

Born: Alcester, 19 June 1874. Died: Stoke-on-Trent, 9 February 1921

Career: Congregational Unity FC (Redditch), Redditch Town (1891-93), Aston Villa (April 1893), Stoke (on loan, March/April 1898), Aston Villa (April 1898), Stoke (August 1899-May 1903). Retired to become landlord of the Wharf Tavern in Stoke city centre. In April 1913 a benefit match was arranged for Wilkes when it was learnt that he had fallen on hard times and was suffering with his health.

An agile and brave goalkeeper, Tom Wilkes was 6ft 1in tall and was 13st in weight. He spent six years with Aston Villa during which time he appeared in 57 first-team games, collecting an FA Cup winners medal in 1895 (v WBA) and a League championship medal the following season. He was replaced between the posts by Jimmy Whitehouse. Wilkes had 89 outings in total for the Potters.

## WILLIAMS, EVAN SAMUEL

Born: Dumbarton, Scotland, 15 July 1943

Career: Third Lanark (amateur, August 1958, professional July 1960), Wolverhampton Wanderers (£5,000, March 1966), Aston Villa (on loan, August/September 1969), Celtic (May 1970-May 1972).

Despite his Welsh-sounding surname, goalkeeper Evan Williams was born north of the border. He was a capable 'keeper with good technique who acted as reserve to both Phil Parkes and Fred Davies at Molineux. He began his playing career with Third Lanark who signed him straight from school in 1958, making him a professional on his 17th birthday. He had 26 games for the now defunct Scottish League club before joining Wolves in 1966. Williams became the first loan signing made by Aston Villa in August 1969 (following an injury to John Dunn) and after 13 games for Villa he duly returned to Molineux and eventually went back to his homeland to sign for Celtic, retiring from first-class football in 1972.

## WILLIAMS, GARETH JAMES

Born: Cowes, Isle of Wight, 12 March 1967

Career: Gosport Borough, Aston Villa (£30,000 as a full-time professional, January 1988), Barnsley (£200,000, August 1991), Hull City (on loan, September 1992 and again, January 1994), Bournemouth (non-contract, September 1994), Northampton Town (transfer, September 1994), Scarborough (August 1996), Hull City (free transfer, November 1998), Scarborough (December 1999).

A left wing-back or left-sided midfielder, Gareth Williams was highly-rated when he moved to Villa Park in 1988. Unfortunatelty he never settled or indeed established himself at the club and after just 16 first-team appearances (half as a substitute) he was sold to Barnsley for a profit of £170,000! Over the next decade Williams went on to amass over 325 senior appearances at club level and duly enters the category 'Ones That Got Away'.

## WILLIAMS, GARY

Born: Wolverhampton, 17 June 1960

Career: St Alban's & Coppice High Schools, Wolverhampton & South Staffs District Boys, Aston Villa (apprentice, July 1976, professional, June 1978), Walsall (on loan, March 1980), Leeds United (July 1987), Watford (January 1990), Bradford City (December 1991-May 1994).

Gary Williams made 303 appearances for Aston Villa and scored two goals. A versatile player, he skippered Villa's youngsters from the centre-half position in 1977-78 when they reached the FA Youth Cup Final. After that he developed into a fine left-back who could also do a good job in midfield. He performed with consummate ease and authority and helped Villa win the League title in 1981, both the European Champions Cup and Super Cup in 1982 and was also in the Walsall team that gained promotion from Division Four in 1980 when on loan at Fellows Park. He lost his chance of an England Under-21 cap v the Republic of Ireland in 1981 through injury and sadly never got another opportunity on the international circuit. Williams quit top-class football in 1994 having accumulated over 500 League and Cup appearances at club level.

## WILLIAMS, JOHN JAMES

Born: Aberdare, Glamorgan, 29 March 1912. Died: Wrexham, 12 October 1987.

Career: Aberaman, Llanelli (amateur August 1931, professional, October 1932), Huddersfield Town (November 1932), Aston Villa (£2,000, November 1935), Ipswich Town (July 1936), Wrexham (November 1938-September 1939). He continued to play throughout the War for the Welsh club, but did not play after 1946.

A short, dark haired winger, Jackie Williams was only 5ft 5ins tall and like so many other flank players, more than made up for his build with guile and trickery. An amateur with Aberaman and Llanelli, he turned 'pro' a fortnight before joining Huddersfield in 1932. After scoring 14 goals in 50 League games for the Terriers he joined Villa where he occupied the right-wing berth, allowing Eric Houghton to switch to the left. He netted five times in just 17 senior outings during his brief stay at Villa Park and then did well with Ipswich Town, helping them win the Southern League title in 1937 and gain entry into the Football League, appearing in their first-ever Third Division (South) match versus Southend United in August 1938 prior to moving to Wrexham with whom he won his only Welsh cap against France in 1939. He was employed as a storekeeper for Hunt's capacitators in Wrexham for many years after giving up soccer.

## WILLIAMS, WILLIAM HUGH

Born: Wrexham, September 1886. Died: Chester, November 1957
Career: Chirk (1904) Wrexham (May 1909), Aston Villa (April 1912), Chirk (1915), Mold (1919), St Asaph (1920), Chester Lymphets (1921). Reserve left-back, strong and upright, Bill Williams made one League appearance for Aston Villa, standing in for Tommy Weston against Derby County (home) in April 1914 (won 3-2).

## WILLIS, JOHN JOHNSON

Born: East Boldon, Durham, 28 May 1934
Career: Boldon Colliery, Blackburn Rovers (amateur, July 1953, professional, August 1954), Accrington Stanley (briefly), Mossley FC (December 1957), Aston Villa (August 1958), Bolden FC (August 1960). Reserve outside-left Jack Willis played one League game for Blackburn and one for Villa, the latter against Wolves at Molineux in September 1958 when although wearing No.9, Willis played on the left wing with McParland switching to the centre.

## WILSON, ROBERT JOHN

Born: Small Heath, Birmingham, 23 May 1943
Career: Bordesley Green Rovers, St Andrew's Boys Club, Aston Villa (juniors, July 1958, professional September 1961), Cardiff City (£2,000, August 1964), Bristol City (on loan, October 1969), Exeter City (January 1970). Retired in 1976 and latter settled in Devon.
Lanky goalkeeper Bob Wilson had nine games for Villa between 1959 and 1964. After leaving Villa Park he went on to appear in more than 350 League and Cup matches for his three City clubs Cardiff, Bristol and Exeter, retiring in 1976.

## WILSON, THOMAS CARTER

Born: Preston, 20 October 1877. Died: Blackpool, 30 August 1940.
Career: Fishwick Ramblers (Preston), Ashton-in-Makerfield, West Manchester, Ashton North, Ashton North End, Oldham County (August 1896), Swindon Town (May 1897), Blackburn Rovers (May 1898), Swindon Town (May 1899), Millwall Athletic (May 1900), Aston Villa (April 1901), Queen's Park Rangers (August 1902), Bolton Wanderers (May 1904), Leeds City (December 1906), Manchester United (February 1908), Chorley (manager, August 1912), Rochdale (chairman, October 1919, manager at Spotland until February 1923). Married the daughter of an Oldham publican.
A well built wing or inside-forward, Tommy Carter was very popular during his two spells with Swindon. He never got a chance at Villa Park, making just two senior appearances before moving to London and QPR. He made close on 200 appearances during his career.

## WILSON ROAD

Villa used a piece of wasteland in Wilson Road, Perry Barr (near to the present-day Birchfield Road roundabout) for practice purposes soon after the club was formed. They played very few first team matches there.

## WIMBLEDON

Villa's playing record against the Dons:
Football League/Premiership

| Venue | P | W | D | L | F | A |
|---|---|---|---|---|---|---|
| Home | 13 | 6 | 2 | 5 | 22 | 12 |
| Away | 13 | 3 | 5 | 5 | 20 | 21 |
| Totals | 26 | 9 | 7 | 10 | 42 | 33 |
| FA Cup | | | | | | |
| Home | 3 | 0 | 2 | 1 | 2 | 3 |
| Away | 2 | 0 | 1* | 1 | 0 | 1 |
| Totals | 5 | 0 | 3 | 2 | 2 | 4 |

* Dons won 6-5 on penalties (see below).

League Cup

| | | | | | | |
|---|---|---|---|---|---|---|
| Away | 1 | 0 | 0 | 1 | 0 | 1 |

Aston Villa's first League meeting with the Dons was in August 1986 at Plough Lane. Only 6,366 fans turned out - the lowest for a League game involving Villa since 1973.
Dalian Atkinson's stunning strike in Villa's 3-2 win at Wimbledon in October 1992 was voted 'Goal of the Season' on BBC TV.
With 25 minutes remaining, Villa were leading the Dons 3-1 in a League game at Selhurst Park in November 1994. But suddenly Villa's defence started to creek, the Dons began to buzz and in the end the Londoners ran out winners by 4-3, having scored twice in the last seven minutes. The 40th minute dismissal of Andy Townsend, who was later banned for six matches, didn't help matters!
When Villa beat the Dons 7-1 at home in a Premiership game on 11 February 1995, it was their biggest League victory for 33 years, since Leicester City had crashed 8-3 in April 1962. This seven-goal romp equalled the best Premiership win at that time and star of the show was Tommy Johnson with a hat-trick. Villa led 4-1 at half-time.
Dwight Yorke (2), Savo Milosevic (2) and Ian Taylor scored in Villa's 5-0 romp over the Dons in December 1996. Villa won 2-0 at Selhurst Park to complete the double that season.
Over 25,000 fans saw Villa knocked out of the FA Cup in the 4th round by the holders, Wimbledon, in January 1989. Four years later, the Dons again shot Villa out of competition at the same stage by winning a penalty shoot-out 6-5 at Selhurst Park after draws of 1-1 (at Villa Park) and 0-0. Kevin Richardson missed the last kick to leave Villa frustrated. Neil Cox had fluffed an earlier effort.

Players with both clubs include: J Fashanu, K Gage, LGF Smith.
Also: P Withe (Villa player & assistant-manager coach, Dons manager).

## WINDMILL, JOSEPH WALTER

Born: Halesowen, June 1881. Died: October 1927.
Career: Saltley College (Birmingham), Halesowen, Aston Villa (April 1902-May 1910). Retired to concentrate on his teaching profession. He later became headmaster of Brook Street School, Wordesley, Sourbridge.
Joe Windmill was part of a fine half-back line at Villa Park during the period 1904-06 when he lined up alongside Joe Pearson and Alec Leake. A fine player, Windmill let the ball do the work and created many openings for his forwards with sweetly struck passes. He won an FA Cup winners' medal in 1905 and scored once in 50 first-class appearances for Aston Villa. He was awarded the DCM and MC during the First World War.

## WINS

The most League wins recorded by Aston Villa in a single League season has been 32 in 1971-72, when they won the Third Division title. They claimed 26 victories when winning the First Division championship in 1980-81. And totals of 25 were recorded in 1930-31, 1937-38, 1959-60 and 1974-75 (the last three all in Division 2).
The most home League wins in one campaign has been 20 in 1971-72 (Division 3).
Villa have twice recorded a sequence of 14 successive home League victories: between 10 January and 28 November 1903; also between 27 December 1930 and 10 October 1931.
In contrast, Villa's longest sequence of League games without a win is 12 - between 10 November 1973 and 2 February 1974; also from 27 December 1986 to 25 March 1987.
Villa's biggest League win so far (in terms of goals scored) has been 12-2 at home against Accrington on 12 March 1892. Both Jack Devey and Louis Campbell scored four goals apiece.
Charlton Athletic were hammered 11-1 at Villa Park in a Second Division match in November 1959 when Gerry Hitchens struck a fivetimer. Sheffield Wednesday were beaten 10-0 in October 1912 with

THE COMPLETE ENCYCLOPAEDIA OF ASTON VILLA F.C.        THE COMPLETE ENCYCLOPAEDIA OF ASTON VILLA F.C.

292

five of the goals coming from Harry Hampton. Burnley were also eclipsed 10-0, again at Villa Park, in another First Division encounter on the opening day of the 1925-26 season, when Len Capewell registered a nap-hand.

Other big Villa League victories include, at home: 9-0 over Glossop in September 1899, 9-1 v Notts County in September 1888, 7-0 and 9-0 v Darwen in December 1891 and December 1893 respectively, then 7-1 v Wimbledon in February 1995 (their biggest in Premiership). Villa have twice beaten Leicester 8-3 (at home in 1932 and 1962).

And away: 6-2 at Burnley in October 1889, 6-3 at West Bromwich Albion in October 1893 and 6-3 at Burnley in April 1894.

The most League/Premiership victories Villa have achieved over one club is 66 v Everton (43 at home, 23 away). A total of 63 have been recorded against Sheffield Wednesday, 60 v Sunderland and 58 over neighbours West Bromwich Albion.

In the FA Cup, Villa's best win has been 13-0 at home to Wednesbury Old Athletic in October 1886. They whipped Casuals (London) 13-1 in January 1891 and crushed Kings Lynn 11-0 in January 1906. Villa have also accounted for Millwall 9-1 in January 1946, powered past Newcastle United 7-1 in February 1895, beat Port Vale 7-2 in January 1925, and knocked out Sunderland, also by 7-2 in January 1934.

Also in the FA Cup, Villa defeated Shankhouse 9-0 away in December 1887 and Wednesbury Old Athletic 7-4, also away in December 1883.

Villa's biggest League Cup win has been 8-1 v Exeter City in October 1985 and their best in Europe has been 5-0, achieved twice, against Vitoria Guimaraes in September 1983 (UEFA Cup) and FC Valur in September 1981 (European Cup).

During World War Two, Villa beat RAF Lichfield 19-2 in a in March 1942, thrashed RAF Hednesford 14-1 two months earlier and demolished Coventry City 9-2 in May 1945.

The biggest win ever recorded by an Aston Villa side (at first team level) has been that of 21-0 over Small Heath Swifts in a Birmingham senior Cup-tie in 1882-83.

Aston Villa won their first three home League games in 1891-92 by scores of 5-1, 5-1 and 5-3. Then right at the end of the 1898-99 campaign they cracked in 18 goals when recording three consecutive home wins of 6-1, 7-1 and 5-0.

*Peter Withe - waiting for a slip.*

Wolverhampton Wanderers (on loan October 1973, signed for £13,500, November 1973), Portland Timbers, NASL (May 1975), Birmingham City (£50,000, August 1975), Nottingham Forest (£42,000, September 1976), Newcastle United (£200,000, August 1978), Aston Villa (£500,000, May 1980), Sheffield United (free transfer, July 1985), Birmingham City (again, on loan September-November 1987), Huddersfield Town (player/coach, July 1988), Aston Villa (assistant-manager/coach, January-October 1991), Wimbledon (manager, October 1991-January 1992), Port Vale (Football in the Community officer, 1992-95), Aston Villa (chief scout, 1998), Thailand (national team coach/soccer advisor, 2000-01).

Peter Withe was a goalscoring soccer nomad whose playing career spanned almost 20 years during which time he netted over 200 goals in more than 600 appearances while serving with 15 different clubs at various levels in three countries.

Withe gained a First Division Championship medal with Nottingham Forest in 1978 and then added a second winners medal to his tally with Villa in 1981. He also scored the winning goal in the 1982 European Cup Final - a moment he, nor the Villa fans, will never forget. He was also capped 11 times by England (1981-85) winning his first against Brazil. A big favourite with the fans at Villa Park Withe, who was the perfect foil and aide to Gary Shaw and who relished the crosses sent over by winger Tony Morley, scored 92 goals in 233 senior outings for Villa. He was tremendous in the air, competent on the ground and could hold the ball up with neat, close control - acting as the perfect target man!

He returned to Villa Park as assistant to manager Josef Venglos, spent three hellish months at Plough Lane as boss of the Dons and later had a third spell as chief scout with Villa before embarking on a new and prosperous venture with the Thai FA.

Peter Withe's brother Chris played for Bradford City and his son was a professional with WBA.

## WINTON, DOUGLAS GEORGE
Born: Perth, Scotland, October 1929

Career: Jeanfield Swifts, St Johnstone (trialist), Perth Youth Club, Burnley (Amateur July 1945, professional September 1947), Aston Villa (January 1959), Rochdale (June 1961). Retired through injury, May 1965.

Capped by Scotland 'B' in 1957, full-back Doug Winton made almost 200 appearances for Burnley before transferring to Villa Park in 1959. He had been first choice at Turf Moor for 12 years. He took over the left-back slot in the Villa ranks, allowing John Neal to switch flanks following the departure of Stan Lynn to Blues. He went on to play 50 times in Villa's senior side and then gave way to Charlie Aitken in 1961.

## WITHE, PETER
Born: Liverpool, 30 August 1951.

Career: All Hallow's School (Speke), Smith Coggins FC of Liverpool (1966), Skelmersdale (amateur, 1968-69), Smith Coggins FC (1969-70), Southport (amateur July 1970, professional, August 1971), Preston North End (briefly in mid-1971), Barrow (trialist, December 1971), Port Elizabeth & Arcadia Shepherds in South Africa (during 1972-73),

## WITHERS, COLIN CHARLES
Born: Erdington, Birmingham, 21 March 1940

Career: West Bromwich Albion (amateur, 1956-57), Birmingham City (professional, May 1957), Aston Villa (£18,000, November 1964), Lincoln City (June 1969), Go-Ahead Eagles of Deventer in Holland (summer, 1970), Atherstone Town (season 1973-74). Retired to take over a hotel on Osborne Road, Blackpool before becoming a licensee in Bridgnorth.

Colin 'Tiny' Withers - 6ft 3ins tall - conceded six goals on his Football League debut for Birmingham City against Tottenham Hotspur (away) in November 1960 and on the same ground against the same team he let in four goals when appearing in his first game for Aston Villa in 1964. However, after that initial crushing

THE COMPLETE ENCYCLOPAEDIA OF ASTON VILLA F.C.    THE COMPLETE ENCYCLOPAEDIA OF ASTON VILLA F.C.

293

experience his form improved greatly and throughout his career he put in some supreme performances for both Blues and Aston Villa. After gaining an England Schoolboy cap at the age of 15, he played for West Bromwich Albion's third team and signed professional forms with Blues in 1957. After seven-and-a-half seasons at St. Andrew's he was transferred to Aston Villa and did very well there, amassing a further 163 senior appearances, after taking over the green jersey from Geoff Sidebottom and then handing it over to John Dunn.

## WITTON
Playing Record against Witton;
FA Cup

| Venue | P | W | D | L | F | A |
|---|---|---|---|---|---|---|
| Home | 1 | 1 | 0 | 0 | 3 | 2 |

Aston Villa met close neighbours Witton in a 1st round FA Cup-tie at Perry Barr on 2 February 1889 and in front of just 1,500 hardy spectators, they scraped through by the odd goal in five with Albert Allen, Archie Hunter and Tommy Green breaching the visitors defence to score for Villa.

## WOLVERHAMPTON WANDERERS
Villa's playing record against the Wolves:
Football League

| Venue | P | W | D | L | F | A |
|---|---|---|---|---|---|---|
| Home | 48 | 26 | 10 | 12 | 109 | 64 |
| Away | 48 | 15 | 12 | 21 | 67 | 86 |
| Totals | 96 | 41 | 22 | 33 | 176 | 144 |

FA Cup

| | P | W | D | L | F | A |
|---|---|---|---|---|---|---|
| Home | 6 | 4 | 2 | 0 | 13 | 7 |
| Away | 5 | 1 | 3 | 1 | 8 | 8 |
| Neutral | 2 | 0 | 0 | 2 | 1 | 4 |
| Totals | 13 | 5 | 5 | 3 | 22 | 19 |

League Cup

| | P | W | D | L | F | A |
|---|---|---|---|---|---|---|
| Home | 3 | 3 | 0 | 0 | 6 | 3 |
| Away | 2 | 1 | 1 | 0 | 3 | 2 |
| Totals | 5 | 4 | 1 | 0 | 9 | 5 |

Wartime

| | P | W | D | L | F | A |
|---|---|---|---|---|---|---|
| Home | 11 | 7 | 2 | 2 | 32 | 18 |
| Away | 10 | 8 | 1 | 1 | 27 | 11 |
| Totals | 21 | 15 | 3 | 3 | 59 | 29 |

Tommy Green scored Villa's first League goal in the 40th minute of the opening game in the competition away to Wolves on 8 September 1888. Gersom Cox, the Villa full-back, had conceded an own-goal to put Wolves in front.
In March 1891 Villa whipped Wolves 6-2 at home when Charlie Athersmith scored a hat-trick but it was a different story in April 1892 when Villa crashed 6-3 at Molineux!
A 4-1 home win for Villa in April 1896 was quickly followed by a 5-0 triumph when Wolves first visited Villa Park on 19 April 1897. A crowd of 35,000 saw this game in which John Cowan and Johnny Campbell both scored twice.
Jimmy Cantrell scored a hat-trick when Villa beat Wolves 6-1 at home in November 1905, but Wolves gained revenge four months later with a 4-1 victory at Molineux.
Fifteen goals were scored in the two League games between Villa and Wolves over the Christmas period of 1933 - just after the Molineux team had returned to the First Division. Villa won 6-2 at home but lost 4-3 away. Almost 100,000 fans witnessed both matches.
The following season the respective fans again saw plenty of goals as Wolves won 5-2 at Molineux but lost 2-1 at Villa Park. This time the

*The goal that beat Villa in the 1960 F.A. Cup Semi-Final at The Hawthorns!*

aggregate attendance figure was less than 60,000.
In contrast, the two League games between Villa and Wolves in 1947-48 were witnessed by an aggregate total of 118,099 spectators - and this time Wolves came out on top, winning 2-1 at Villa Park and 4-1 at Molineux. In the former game Villa used three goalkeepers - Joe Rutherford (broken finger), Harry Parkes and 'Sailor' Brown.
The following season - when Wolves won the FA Cup - they whipped Villa 4-0 at Molineux on Christmas Day in front of 40,000 fans, but lost 5-1 at Villa Park some 48 hours later when the turnout was 63,572. Trevor Ford scored four goals for Villa....after Welshman Sid Howarth had opened the scoring in his first local derby.
In March 1951, Villa narrowly beat Wolves 3-2 on a quagmire of a pitch. They led 2-0 at half-time and then 3-1 before Johnny Hancocks fired in a penalty to make a match of it.
Villa visited Molineux twice in four weeks in March/April 1957. First they drew 2-2 with WBA in the FA Cup semi-final and then lost to the hosts Wolves 3-0 in a League game just 24 hours after beating the Wanderers 4-0 at Villa Park when Les Smith scored twice against his former colleagues.
Wolves doubled up over Villa in their championship-winning season of 1958-59. They won 3-1 at Villa Park and 4-0 at Molineux in the space of nine days in September.
Villa's 1-0 victory at Molineux on Boxing Day 1964, ended a club record run of 27 away League games without a win.
Villa completed the double over Wolves in 1978-79, Andy Gray scored in the 1-0 win at home whilst Ken McNaught and Gary Shelton figured on the scoresheet when Villa triumphed 4-0 at Molineux.
By coincidence, Villa met Wolves on the last day of both the 1977-78 and 1978-79 League seasons.
When Villa beat Wolves 2-1 at home on 20 September 1980 it started a run of 12 matches without defeat - as they drove on towards the League championship.
When Villa beat Wolves 4-0 at home in February 1984, the goals came from ex-Wanderers' striker Peter Withe (2) and future Wolves players Paul Birch and Mark Walters.
Villa's first-ever FA Cup-tie against Wolves went to a fourth game. The 3rd round clash started on 11 December 1886 and finished on 29 January 1887. The initial contest on Villa soil ended 2-2; the replay at Dudley Road finished level at 1-1, whilst the second replay, also on Wolves' territory, produced six goals and resulted in a 3-3 draw. Villa then won the third replay 2-0 at Perry Barr after 360 minutes of action.
On their way to the 1892 FA Cup Final Villa put Wolves out in the 3rd round (winning 3-1 at home). Two years later Villa registered their best FA Cup win over Wolves with a 4-2 victory in the 1st round, Jack Devey scoring twice while John Reynolds also missed a penalty!
A crowd of 55,596 saw Villa beaten 1-0 by Wolves in the FA Cup semi-final at The Hawthorns in March 1960 (Norman Deeley the goalscorer). Five years later Villa again succumbed to Wanderers on West Brom's pitch, losing a 5th round, second replay 3-1 on a snowbound surface, having drawn 1-1 at Villa Park and 0-0 at Molineux.

*Barry Stobart (left) in action for Villa against his former club (Wolves) in 1964-65.*

Peter Withe, ex-Wolves, scored the only goal of a 4th round FA Cup-tie at Villa Park in January 1983 when over 41,000 fans saw Villa record their last FA Cup win over the Molineux men

A 2nd round League Cup-tie went Villa's way 5-3 on aggregate in October 1981. Gordon Cowans scored twice (one a penalty) in a vital 2-1 win at Molineux after Villa had won 3-2 on home soil.

Villa again defeated Wolves 3-2 in another 2nd round League Cup-tie in September/October 1989, Derek Mountfield scoring a vital goal against his future club in the second leg encounter at Molineux.

Villa won 14 successive Wartime games against Wolves during the period January 1942 to September 1944. The biggest single victory was that of 6-1 at home in May 1942 (Birmingham & District League) when Eric Houghton netted twice.

Peter McParland made 15 appearances for Villa in derby games against Wolves, his future club!

Players with both clubs include: DO Ashton, W Baxter, T Bennett, P Birch, A Blair, M Blake, PF Broadbent, FH Broome (Wolves WW2 guest), RAJ Brown (Wolves WW2 guest), MS Burke, J Burridge, JGT Clayton, S Collymore (Wolves junior), AJ Conway (Villa reserve), GS Cowans, G Crudgington (Wolves Amateur), AM Daley, W Devey, R Dorsett, AD Dougan, A Evans, M Forman (Villa reserve), S Froggatt, C Gibson (Wolves WW2 guest), AM Gray, G Harper, GA Harris (Wolves reserve), FJ Haycock (Wolves WW2 guest), M Hellin (Villa reserve), HV Henshall (Wolves reserve), RJT Iverson, M Jones (Villa Schoolboy), W Kellock (Villa junior), M Kenning, G Kinsey, D Kubicki, RW McDonald, PJ McParland, HD Middleton (Villa reserve), D Mountfield, F Moss jnr (Wolves reserve), A Mulraney & F O'Donnell (Wolves WW2 guests), MC Oakes, D Parsons, D Pearce (Villa reserve), C Phillips, RT Pritchard, C Regis, PJ Robinson, I Ross (Wolves reserve & caretaker manager), AR Scott (Villa WW2 guest), G Sidebottom, ND Sims, B Smart (Wolves reserves), HH Smart (Wolves reserve), GM Smith, LJ Smith, CH Spiers, B Stobart, D Stokes (Villa reserve), A Thomas (trialist both clubs), RGM Thomson, JE Travers (Wolves reserve), ME Walters, T Waring, R Westwood (Villa trialist, Wolves reserve), G Whittingham, ES Williams, G Williams (Wolves reserve), P Withe , T Wood (Wolves WW2 guest).

Also associated: T Docherty, B Little, G Taylor & G Turner (managers of both clubs - Little also Villa player), Major FC Buckley (Villa reserve, Wolves manager), J Barron (Wolves player, Villa coach/assistant-manager. J Ward (assistant-manager at both clubs). R Atkinson (Wolves

junior, Villa reserve and later Villa manager), W Shorthouse (Wolves player, Villa coach), Steve Harrison (Wolves coach, Villa assistant-manager/coach), R Downes (coach at both clubs), GW Cummings (Villa player/coach, Wolves scout), HD Ellis (Villa Chairman & Director of both clubs), LGF Smith (Villa player, Wolves scout).

## WOOD, ALFRED EDWARD

Born: Smallthorne, Stoke-on-Trent, June 1876. Died: April 1919.
Career: Stoke-on-Trent Council School, Smallthorne Albion, Burlsem Port Vale (December 1892), Southampton (summer, 1895), Stoke (October 1895), Aston Villa (March 1901), Derby County (May 1905), Bradford Park Avenue (May 1907). Retired in May 1908 through injury.
The versatile Alf Wood who could play at outside-left, inside-forward and in all three half-back positions, had starred in 65 League and Cup games for Port Vale and more than 100 for Stoke before joining Aston Villa as a replacement for Jas Cowan. He was, however, handed the left-half position during his first full season at the club (1901-02) and performed exceedingly well alongside Tom Perry and Albert Wilkes. He later reverted to the pivotal role and went on to score seven goals in 111 first-class matches before transferring to Derby County in 1905. He helped Villa take the runners-up spot in the First Division in 1903. He made 58 League appearances for the Rams and four for BPA before hanging up his boots in 1908.
When Wood signed for Southampton in 1895, there was a dispute about his transfer from Vale. A special commision was set up and the deal was cancelled in Vale's favour without Wood ever having played in a single game for Saints.

## WOOD, THOMAS

Born: Wednesbury, April 1908. Deceased.
Career: White Hill School (Wednesbury), Wednesbury United, Shrewsbury Town (August 1925), Aston Villa (February 1929), Newport County (December 1936). Guested for Walsall during WW2. Retired 1945. He was also a champion crown green bowler, winning the Farcroft Floodlit tournament in Handsworth, Birmingham in September 1933, beating 500 other contestants.
Nicknamed 'Smokey', Tommy Wood was an efficient, serviceable wing-half and the dressing room comedian who was initially 'first' reserve to Jimmy Gibson at Villa Park but later turned out in various other positions, making in total 71 appearances for the club and scoring two goals. He went on to appear in over 100 first-class games for Newport (27 goals).

## WOODWARD, JOHN

Born: Tunstall, Stoke-on-Trent, 16 January 1947.
Career: Tunstall Park, Stoke City (apprentice, June 1962, professional October 1964), Aston Villa (£27,500, October 1966), Walsall (free transfer, May 1969), Port Vale (£2,250, February 1973), Scunthorpe United (July 1975), Ostende FC (Belgium), Kidderminster Harriers (1978-79).
After just 11 outings for Stoke, swashbuckling striker John 'Woodie' Woodward looked like being a terrific marksman in the first Division with Aston Villa until he suffered a severe ankle injury during a League game at The Hawthorns (v WBA) in October 1966. This knocked him back considerably and although he recovered full fitness he was never able to establish himself in the Villa side again. He scored eight goals in 27 first-team appearances for the club before tranferring to Walsall in 1969. In his four years with the Saddlers he notched 29 goals in 145 League and Cup appearances and top-scored for Port Vale in his first season with the Potteries' club for whom he netted 32 times in his tally of 95 senior outings.
He did reasonably well for a while in Belgium before rounding off his career in non-League soccer with Kidderminster Harriers.

## WOLLASTON, ARTHUR WILBERT

Born: Shrewsbury, March 1865. Died: Chirk, October 1933.
Career: Layton Road Council School, Stafford Road FC (1886), Aston Villa (April 1888), Chirk (August 1890).
A well-built wing-half, Archie Wollaston appeared in four League games and one FA Cup-tie for Aston Villa in season 1888-89.

## WOOLLEY, ALBERT

Born: Hockley, Birmingham, June 1870. Died: Manchester, 3 February 1896.
Career: Park Mills, Aston Villa (March 1892), Derby County (January 1895). Retired through ill-heath, January 1896.
A whole-hearted, enthusiastic outside-left, quick off the mark with a strong shot, Albert Woolley scored twice on his League debut for Aston Villa against Accrington in March 1893 and went on to net a total of 13 goals in 24 first-team appearances for the club before transferring to Derby County for whom he scored three times in only six outings.
Unfortunately injury and then illness ruined a promising career and he was forced to quit the game at the age of 25, tragically dying a couple of weeks later.

## WOOSNAM, PHILIP ABRAHAM BSc.

Born: Caersws, Montgomeryshire, 22 December 1932
Career: Montgomeryshire Schools, Wrexham (Amateur, 1947), UCNW, Bangor University (from January 1951), Peritus FC (February-April 1951), Manchester City (amateur, July 1951, professional June 1952), Army XI, Sutton United (Athenian League, 1953-54) Middlesex Wanderers, Leyton Orient (amatuer, March 1955, professional December 1955), West Ham United (£30,000, November 1958), Aston Villa (£27,000, November 1962), Atlanta Chiefs, NASL (player for season 1967-68). He was then appointed commisioner of the North American Soccer League in 1969 and held that position for 14 years until 1983, being mainly responsible for bringing the likes of Franz Beckenbauer, Pele, George Best and others stateside to display their footballing talents.
Phil Woosnam's own footballing skills were recognised at an early age and after making rapid progress via Montgomersyhire junior football, he gained Welsh Schoolboy caps at the age of 15 and represented his country at Youth team level before entering Bangor University in 1951. He then captained the varsity side to the Welsh Universities championship in 1952. Although Woosnam signed for Manchester City and played a handful of Central League games for the Maine Road club,

it came as a big surprise when he was released - but he continued to play soccer whenever he could and after graduating with a BSc degree from university, he joined the Royal Artillery as a 2nd Lieutenant to complete his National Service.
On demob Woosnam became a physics teacher in Leyton (London) and subsequently signed for Orient as an Amateur, moving onto West Ham as a professional. With the Hammers (where he linked up with Bobby Moore among others) his intelligent footballing skills came to the fore.
An elegant and constructive inside-forward, sleek and slender-looking, with a crew-cut hair-style, Woosnam possessed craft rather than graft and used his brain rather than brawn. He played for the London select side versus Lausanne Sports in the semi-final of the Inter Cities Fairs Cup in 1957 and proceeded to score 27 goals in 147 League and Cup appearances for the Upton Park club whom he helped establish itself in the First Division.
Always one move ahead of his colleagues - and indeed, his opponents - Woosnam joined Aston Villa three months into the 1962-63 season and went straight into the first XI as Harry Burrows' left-wing partner. He did superbly well during his time at Villa Park, teaming up in midfield with Alan Deakin, Mike Tindall and Ron Wylie. He netted 30 goals in 125 senior outings for Villa and took his total of full caps for Wales up to 17 (gaining one with Orient, 14 with West Ham and two during his time with Aston Villa). Earlier, in 1955, he was voted 'Amateur Footballer of the Year'. He also represented the Football League side on one occasion and helped Orient win the Third Division (South) title in 1956.
When Woosnam joined West Ham for £30,000 in 1958, only three other players in British football had cost more money when switching clubs!

## WORCESTER CITY

Villa's playing record against Worcester is:

Birmingham League

| Venue | P | W | D | L | F | A |
|-------|---|---|---|---|---|---|
| Home | 1 | 1 | 0 | 0 | 2 | 0 |
| Away | 3 | 1 | 0 | 2 | 13 | 9 |
| Totals | 4 | 2 | 0 | 2 | 15 | 9 |

Birmingham League Cup

| | | | | | | |
|-------|---|---|---|---|---|---|
| Home | 2 | 1 | 1 | 0 | 6 | 4 |
| Away | 1 | 0 | 0 | 1 | 0 | 2 |
| Totals | 3 | 1 | 1 | 1 | 6 | 6 |

Worcester Infirmary Cup

| | | | | | | |
|-------|---|---|---|---|---|---|
| Away | 2 | 1 | 0 | 1 | 4 | 2 |

Birmingham League Cup
Keys Cup

| | | | | | | |
|-------|---|---|---|---|---|---|
| Home | 1 | 1 | 0 | 0 | 6 | 0 |
| Away | 1 | 1 | 0 | 0 | 4 | 1 |
| Totals | 2 | 2 | 0 | 0 | 10 | 1 |

All these eleven fixtures between Villa and Worcester City took place during the second and third Wartime seasons of 1940-41 and 1941-42. In 1940-41, City ousted Villa from the Birmingham League Cup and also beat them 2-1 in the Final of the Worcester Infirmary Cup.
The following season Villa gained revenge with a 3-0 Infirmary Cup Final victory and also a 4-2 triumph in the Birmingham League Cup Final.
In a two-legged 1st round Keys Cup contest in December 1941 Villa caned Worcester with a 10-1 aggregate victory (winning 6-0 at home and 4-1 away). Dicky Davis scored four goals in the first game and two in the second.
Villa's biggest Birmingham League victory arrived in November 1941 when they won 8-1 at St George's - hot-shot Davis scoring a double

*Phil Woosnam getting an ear-full!*

THE COMPLETE ENCYCLOPAEDIA OF ASTON VILLA F.C.  THE COMPLETE ENCYCLOPAEDIA OF ASTON VILLA F.C.

296

hat-trick this time round in front of 3,000 spectators.
Players with both clubs include: C Aitken, J Brown, J Cumbes, E Follan, AET Haynes, GA Hitchens, TD Hughes, L Jones, F Moss jnr, F Moss snr, WA Littlewood, JW McMorran, PJ McParland, LJ Martin, JH Morby, the foursome of HJ Reece, H Vallance, S Webb & C Wilson (all Villa reserves), GF Wheldon.
Also: F Upton (City player, Villa coach), EJ Vinall (Worcester manger, Villa scout).

## WORKINGTON
Villa never met the former Football League club at competitive level.

Players with both clubs include: J Burridge, J Hinchcliffe, J Martin, D Mountfield, J Sewell (Workington WW2 guest).
Also: F Upton (Workington player, Villa coach), J Ward (Workington player, Villa assistant-manager/coach), A Ashman (Workington manager, Villa scout).

## WORLD CLUB CHAMPIONSHIP
As winners of the European Cup in 1981, Villa were invited by UEFA to play Penarol of Uruguay (the South American Copa Libertadores winners). The game took place in Tokyo in December 1982 and in front of almost 61,500 fans Villa were defeated 2-0.

## WORLD CUP
Villa Park staged three World Cup matches in July 1966. They were:
Argentina 2 Spain 1
Argentina 0 West Germany 0
West Germany 2 Spain 1
(See under Villa Park).

## WORRELL, JOSEPH ERIC
Born: Stourbridge, July 1886.
Career: Wordesley Council School, Stourbridge Swifts (1906) Stourbridge (1912), Aston Villa (May 1919), Cradley St Luke's (May 1921), Netherton (seasons 1922-23-24), Dudley Town (1924-26), Old Hill Wanderers (1926-27), Brierley Hill Alliance (1927-28).
A tough-looking defender, best suited to the hurly-burly of local Black Country soccer! He appeared in just four League games for Aston Villa (early in 1919-20) following an injury to Frank Moss. He was almost 44 years of age when he played his last game for Brierley Hill.

## WREXHAM
Villa's playing record against the Welsh club
Football League

| Venue | P | W | D | L | F | A |
|---|---|---|---|---|---|---|
| Home | 2 | 1 | 0 | 1 | 5 | 4 |
| Away | 2 | 2 | 0 | 0 | 5 | 2 |
| Totals | 4 | 3 | 0 | 1 | 10 | 6 |
| League Cup | | | | | | |
| Home | 3 | 2 | 1 | 0 | 10 | 3 |
| Away | 1 | 0 | 1 | 0 | 1 | 1 |
| Neutral | 1 | 1 | 0 | 0 | 4 | 3 |
| Totals | 5 | 3 | 2 | 0 | 15 | 7 |

Aston Villa's first League meeting with Wrexham was at The Racecourse Ground on 26 September 1970 (Division 3). A crowd of 18,335 saw Villa win 3-2 - but later on in the season - on May Day - the Welsh side came to Villa Park and recorded an excellent 4-3 victory to balance the books.

The following season Villa completed the double by winning both matches 2-0.
After two draws (2-2 at home and 1-1 away), the League Cup 2nd round replay between Villa and Wrexham on 31 August 1971 was played at The Hawthorns. A crowd of 20,697 saw Villa win 4-3 with Andy Lochhead scoring twice.
On their way to winning the League Cup in 1977, Villa beat Wrexham 5-1 at home in the 4th round, Brian Little scoring twice in front of 42,428 spectators.

Players with both clubs include: M Blackwood (Villa reserve), F Carrodus, RW Dix (Wrexham WW2 guest), GR Edwards (Wrexham WW2 guest), RE Evans, T Gardner, BC Godfrey (Wrexham trialist), HJ Goode, FC Goss, J Graham, TP Griffiths, FJ Haycock (also Wrexham WW2 guest), KD Keelan, TS Morrall, W Myerscough, RC Park, IH Price, D Richards (Villa trialist), KO Roberts (also Wrexham assistant-manager), DP Spink (Villa reserve), EML Williams (Villa reserve), JJ Williams, WH Williams.
Also: G Turner (Wrexham player, Villa manager), E Blackburn (Villa player, Wrexham manager), J Neal (Villa player, Wrexham trainer/coach & manager).

## WRIGHT, ALAN GEOFFREY
Born: Ashton-under-Lyne, 28 September 1971
Career: Blackpool (YTS, June 1987, professional April 1989), Blackburn Rovers (£400,000, October 1991), Aston Villa (£1 million, March 1995). At 5ft 4in tall, Alan Wright is one of the smallest defenders in the Premiership - but what he loses in height, he certainly makes up for in commitment, giving nothing less than 110 per-cent effort each and every time he takes the field.
A very consistent performer, he made 131 appearances for Blackpool and 91 for Blackburn before transferring to Villa Park in March 1995. He has hardly missed a match in the six years he has been with the club (seemingly absent only through injury) and when the 2000-01 season ended, Wright's appearance record stood at 286 (five goals scored).

He helped Villa win the League Cup in 1996 and on the international front, after gaining Schoolboy and Youth caps, he starred in two Under-21 matches for England versus Spain and Denmark in 1993 as a Blackburn player. He, in fact, holds the Villa record of 79 consecutive Premiership appearances (from August 1997-September 1999).
For a brief period - all of 15 months - left-back Alan Wright also held the record of being the youngest player ever to appear in a League game for Blackpool - aged 16 years, 217 days v Chesterfield in May 1988. Trevor Sinclair surpassed it in August 1989.

THE COMPLETE ENCYCLOPAEDIA OF ASTON VILLA F.C.    THE COMPLETE ENCYCLOPAEDIA OF ASTON VILLA F.C.

297

## WRIGHT, EDMUND
Born: Leytonstone, London, March 1902. Deceased.
Career: High Wycombe (season 1918-19), Aston Villa (May 1919) Brentford (September 1921).
A rather shortish goalkeeper, Ed Wright was reserve to Sam Hardy, Jim Lee and Cyril Spiers during his two seasons at Villa Park and made just two senior appearances, his debut coming in front of more than 70,500 spectators at Old Trafford in December 1920 when Villa won 3-1.

## WRIGHT, JOHN MICHAEL
Born: Ellesmere Port, Cheshire, 25 September 1946
Career: Ellesmere Port Grammar School, Ellesmere Port FC, Aston Villa (apprentice July 1962, professional September 1963). Retired through injury in May 1973 and became an auction director/officer working briefly in engineering. He was granted a testimonial match in the 1973-74 season.
After amassing almost 150 senior appearances for Aston Villa, England Youth international full-back Mick Wright broke a bone in his leg at Middlesbrough in October 1967. Obviously there was concern at the time but he made an excellent recovery, regained his place in the side by mid-December and went on to take his overall tally of League and Cup games for the club to an impressive 315 before retiring at the end of the 1972-73 season. He netted just one goal - in a 3-0 home win over Manchester City in September 1966 (Division 1).
Wright played both rugby and soccer at School and was recommended to Villa by Bill Roberts, the man who had many years earlier 'coached' Joe Mercer! Capped by England at Youth team level, Wright took over the right-back position from Cammie Fraser and had the challenge of Keith Bradley to hold off as he battled to retain his first-team spot. He did it splendidly and gained a Third Division Championship medal in 1972. He eventually handed over his duties to John Gidman.

## WYCOMBE WANDERERS
There has been no competitive match action between Villa and Wanderers as yet, although the Wanderers did play their 2001 FA Cup semi-final with Liverpool at Villa Park which the Merseysiders won 2-1 in front of moe than 40,000 spectators.

Players with both clubs include: N Davis, D Farrell, PA Kerr, C Regis, K Swain, G Whittingham.
Also: JC Gregory (Villa player & manager, Wanderers manager).

## WYLIE, RONALD MAURICE
Born: Glasgow, 6 August 1933
Career: Clydesdale Juniors (August 1947-March 1949), Notts County (amateur April 1949, professional September 1950), Aston Villa (£9,250, November 1958), Birmingham City (July 1965). Retired in May 1970 to become PRO at St Andrew's, Aston Villa (coach, June 1970-72), Coventry City (coach, 1975, then assistant-manager, 1978-81), Cyprus (coach), Bulova, Hong Kong (coach, 1982), West Bromwich Albion (manager, July 1982-February 1984), Aston Villa (reserve-team coach, February 1984-May 1987), then scouted for several clubs before returning to Villa Park as Community Officer, August 1990 (later Community Liaison Officer from August 1995).
Barrel-chested midfielder Ron Wylie appeared in more than 700 senior games during an excellent professional career that spanned some 20 years. A broad-speaking Glaswegian, he won two Scottish international caps at Schoolboy level before joining Notts County in 1948 when former Villa star Eric Houghton was a player at Meadow Lane. He did

very well with County, making over 200 senior appearances and playing alongside Tommy Lawton for a short while. Houghton eventually took over as manager of the Magpies before taking charge at Villa Park, making Wylie his last signing before being sacked in November 1958. Two years later, after Villa had suffered relegation, Wylie helped the team regain its First Division status with some excellent performances. The following year he was a League Cup winner and after 244 outings in the claret and blue strip (28 goals scored) he was surprisingly transferred to neighbours Birmingham City in 1965 - after having been voted 'Midland Footballer of the Year.' Thought to be well past his best at the time of his move, Wylie surprised even himself by going on to play in almost 150 games for Blues, skippering the team in the 1967 League Cup and 1968 FA Cup semi-finals. He announced his retirement in May 1970 to become Public Relations Officer at St Andrew's. However, after just three weeks in the job he quit and returned to Villa Park as a coach, later taking up a similar position with Coventry City, where he also acted as assistant-manager. After working in Cyprus and Hong Kong, Wylie then became manager of West Bromwich Albion (July 1982) in succession to Ronnie Allen. He had mixed fortunes at The Hawthorns and in February 1984 returned to Villa Park to look after the second team (holding office until May 1987). He then scouted for several Midlands clubs up and down the country before his appointment as Community Officer at Villa Park in 1990, thus having his fourth spell with the club. Wylie assumed the title Community Liaison Officer in 1995 and completed 23 years service with Aston Villa FC in 2001.

## XXXVI TRPHEO CONCEPCION ARENAL
Aston Villa played Atletico Madrid in this pre-season tournament at the Compo Municipal De A Malata in Ferrol, Spain on 5 August 1994 and in front of 5,000 spectators drawing 0-0 before winning the penalty shoot-out 3-1.

## YATES, HARRY RICHARD
Born: Walsall, August 1861. Died: Birmingham, c 1932
Career: Walsall Swifts (April 1883), Aston Villa (July 1885). Retired in May 1891 with a hip injury.
Harry 'Tubby' Yates was a solid right-half, who weighed 14 stones and possessed immense power. A strong, forceful tackler, he gained an FA Cup winners medal with Aston Villa in 1887 - one of 29 senior appearances he made for the club before his career ended prematurely after suffering a serious hip injury.

## YATES, JOHN
Born: Manchester, 26 September 1903. Deceased.
Career: Manchester Central, Boston Town, Coventry City (trialist 1923), Chesterfield (1924), Aston Villa (May 1925), Queen's Park Rangers (May 1929), Stourbridge (August 1930-May 1932).
Left-half Jack Yates had boundless energy, a very competitive footballer, who was described as being 'an India rubber man.' Very mobile, full of vim and vigour, he played 14 times in Villa's first XI, deputising for Frank Moss in the main. He had failed to make the senior side at Chesterfield.

## YORK CITY
Villa's playing record against the Minstermen:
Football League
| Venue | P | W | D | L | F | A |
|---|---|---|---|---|---|---|
| Home | 2 | 2 | 0 | 0 | 5 | 0 |
| Away | 2 | 1 | 1 | 0 | 2 | 1 |
| Totals | 4 | 3 | 1 | 0 | 7 | 1 |

League Cup
| Away | 1 | 0 | 0 | 1 | 0 | 1 |
|---|---|---|---|---|---|---|

Aston Villa's first League game against the Minstermen was at home on 5 February 1972 - and in front of almost 27,000 fans Willie Anderson's penalty decided the Third Division contest in Villa's favour. Later in the season, Bruce Rioch's goal won the game for Villa at Bootham Crescent.

In mid-December 1974, a crowd of 15,840 saw Villa beat York 4-0 at home in a Second Division match.

Villa's League Cup defeat at Bootham Crescent came in round 2 in October 1973 in front of almost 8,000 spectators.

Players with both clubs include: RAJ Brown (City WW2 guest), RW Dix (York WW2 guest), M Carruthers, G Livingstone (Villa reserve), DG Rioch, C Stuart (Villa reserve), N Tarrant (Villa reserve).
Also: A Little (Villa player, City assistant-manager/coach & manager), J Ward (Villa coach, assistant-manager, York manager).

## YORK, RICHARD ERNEST

Born: Handsworth, Birmingham, 25 April 1899. Died: Handsworth, Birmingham, 9 December 1969
Career: Icknield Street Council School (Hockley), King Edward Grammar School, Birmingham Boys (captain), Handsworth Royal, Birchfield Rangers, RAF, Chelsea (WWI guest), Aston Villa (professional, May 1919), Port Vale (June 1931), Brierley Hill Alliance (August 1932-May 1934). Later became manager of a plumbing, building and decorating company based in Coventry.

*Dicky York*

Right-winger Dicky York was capped by England on two occasions as a Schoolboy and later represented his country twice at senior level (in 1922 and 1926). He had a tremendous turn of speed, developed as a successful sprinter on the athletics track with Birchfield Harriers for whom he ran and competed from the age of eight. An FA Cup winner with Villa in 1924 he actually made the first of his 390 senior appearances for the club at right-half versus Sunderland on the opening Saturday of the 1919-20 season. In fact, he played a handful more games in that same position before taking over on the right-wing from Charlie Wallace on a regular basis during the second half of the 1920-21 campaign. He remained first choice in the side for the next decade until Jack Mandley appeared in the scene in 1931. An ever-present in 1926-27 and 1928-29, he amassed a total of 324 League appearances in nine seasons (1921-30) after establishing himself in the first XI. He scored 86 goals
After leaving Villa Park he played in 26 competitive games for Port Vale before entering non-League soccer in 1932.

## YORKE, DWIGHT

Born: Canaan, Tobago, 3 November 1971
Career: Signal FC (Tobago), Aston Villa (£120,000, December 1989), Manchester United (£12.6 million, August 1998).
When Dwight Yorke joined Manchester United, he became the 12th costliest footballer in the game's history and the second highest-priced player involved in a transfer between two British clubs.
A buddy of the great West Indies Test cricketer Brian Lara, Yorke took time to establish himself in Villa's League side, eventually making one of the striking positions his own in 1991-92 when he made 39 senior appearances and scored 16 goals, while donning in the main the number 11 shirt! A positive footballer, good on the ball with neat skills and penetrative approach, a natural athlete with great balance and a

positive attitude, he went on to net 97 goals in 287 League and Cup appearances for Villa, coming on as a substitute no fewer than 40 times - 36 in the League - a club record. Now a regular performer in the Trinidad & Tobago national team (he already has over 30 caps under his belt) Yorke gained a League Cup winners medal with Villa in 1996 and since then has helped United win three Premiership titles (1999, 2000 and 2001), the FA Cup in 1999 and the European Cup, also in 1999 when, of course, he was part of the famous Old Trafford treble-winning side. When the curtain came down on the 2000-01 season, despite having to battle for a first team place with Andy Cole (for a while), Teddy Sheringham and Ole Gunnar Solskjaer, Yorke had already netted 65 goals in 136 appearances for United - with more to come (at both club and international level).

## YOUNG, ANDREW

Born: Darlington, 17 September 1896. Died: c 1964.
Career: Darlington junior football, Blyth Spartans (1914), Aston Villa (November 1919), Arsenal (March 1922), Bournemouth (June 1927), Kidderminster Harriers (July 1928-30).
With Aston Villa Andy Young proved to be a very useful inside or centre-forward, a player who loved a challenge and one who was totally committed. He scored 11 goals in 26 senior games for during his three years with the club during which time he had to battle for a place in the forward-line along with Billy Kirton, Harry Hampton and Billy Walker. After leaving Villa Park he did very well at Highbury where he was converted into a half-back in 1923, remaining in that position for the remainder of his career. He notched nine goals in his 71 outings for the Gunners. He helped Arsenal's reserve side win two London Combination championships (in 1923 and 1927) and also the London FA Challenge Cup (in 1924).

## YOUNG, CHARLES FREDERICK

Born: Nicosia, Cyprus, 14 February 1958
Career: Chester Schoolboys, Aston Villa (apprentice, June 1974, professional November 1975), Gillingham (£30,000, March 1978). Forced to quit League football through injury in May 1983.
The son of an English-born serviceman and a Welsh mother, both based in Cyprus, Charlie Young stood over six feet tall and was a strong, reliable defender who deputised at the 'back' for Chris Nicholl and Leighton Phillips during his time at Villa Park, making 11 appearances. Later he was handed 28 League outings by Gillingham.

## YOUNG, NORMAN JAMES

Born: Kings Heath, Birmingham, March 1907. Deceased.
Career: Cobden Works FC (1922), Redditch Town (1923), Aston Villa (June 1926), Barnsley (July 1936-May 1937). Retired through injury.
Unyielding and efficient full-back Norman Young appeared in just nine first team fixtures during his ten years' association with the club. In fact, he had to wait until 14 September 1935 (nine years and more than 170 second team appearances after first joining the club) before he made his Football League debut in a 5-1 home win over Preston North End. He played in 22 League matches for the Tykes during his only season at Oakwell.

## YOUNG, WILLIAM JOHN

Born: Glasgow, 24 February 1956
Career: Clyde (triallist, 1975), Arthurlie (1976-77 season), Aston Villa (professional, July 1978), Torquay United (October 1981-May 1983). Returned to Scotland to play in non-League football.
Inside or outside-left Willie Young played in three League games for Aston Villa, the first in the number 10 shirt in front of 36,000 fans against Manchester United (home) in October 1978. He went on to appear in 38 League matches during his time at Plainmoor.

THE COMPLETE ENCYCLOPAEDIA OF ASTON VILLA F.C.          THE COMPLETE ENCYCLOPAEDIA OF ASTON VILLA F.C.

299

## YOUTH FOOTBALL

Aston Villa teenagers who have represented their country at Youth team level whilst registered with the club include:

England - N Ashe, AR Baker, G Barry, T Berry, A Betts, J Bewers, LC Chatterley, P Child, NF Clarke, GS Cowans, AM Daley, JM Deehan, D Duffy, M Ghent, J Gidman, W Hazelden, LA Hendrie, JR Hylton, GJ Jakeman, LR Jenkins, MA Jones, M Kendall, B Little, S Moore, DW Norton, B Ormsby, JL Samuel, G. Shaw, B Small, M Standing, MC Tindall, D Vassell, R Walker, ME Walters, L Williams.

Northern Ireland - RM Campbell

Republic of Ireland - G Farrelly, A Kirby

Scotland - RW McDonald

Wales - RD Hughes, KO Roberts

Also: England U-18 XI (v Israel Olympic team) - DW Norton

### Youth Banter

The FA Academy Under-17 and Under-19 Leagues were introduced in 1999-2000. Villa's youngsters did exceedingly well at Under-17 level, winning Group 'C' with 14 victories from their 22 matches. This took them into the competition proper but after eliminating Bolton Wanderers (h) 6-2, Sunderland (h) 2-0 and Newcastle United (a) 3-1, they lost in the semi-final to Crewe Alexandra (a) 1-0.

Nine 'promising' and 'highly-rated' Aston Villa teenagers won England Youth caps during the early 1970s, among them: John Gidman, Gordon Cowans, Brian Little, Brendan Ormsby and Gary Shaw, all of whom went on to establish themselves as prominent League footballers, with Gidman, Cowans and Little winning full caps.

Villa's Gareth Barry scored a hat-trick in England Youth's emphatic 9-0 win over San Marino in 1999.

Villa teenager Stefan Moore was capped by England at under 16, 17 and 18 levels in 1999-2000 and he also scored 20 goals for Villa's Academy under-17 side in this same season.

David Richardson was Director of Youth at Villa Park in the late 1990s/early 2000s.

## ZENITH DATA SYSTEMS CUP

Villa's record in the ZDSC is:

| Venue | P | W | D | L | F | A |
|---|---|---|---|---|---|---|
| Home | 4 | 2 | 0 | 2 | 5 | 5 |
| Away | 3 | 2 | 0 | 1 | 5 | 3 |
| Totals | 7 | 4 | 0 | 3 | 10 | 8 |

Aston Villa had two seasons in this short-lived competition. In 1989-90 they defeated Hull City 2-1 at Boothferry Park in front of 2,888 fans in their opening game before accounting for Nottingham Forest by the same score at Villa Park, a victory that took them into the Northern Area semi-final. Here they met Leeds United, also at home, and won 2-0 before an appreciative and surprisingly large crowd of 17,543 to earn a place against Middlesbrough in the Area Final. This was played over two legs, 'Boro winning both encounters by the same score of 2-1 with 20,806 fans being present for the game at Villa Park.

In 1990-91 after a 2-0 win at Coventry in front of 6,447 supporters, Villa were ousted from the competition in the next round by Nottingham Forest who won 2-0 at Villa Park before a crowd of under 7,900.

David Platt (with three goals) top-scored for Villa in this competition. Derek Mountfield netted twice.

## VILLA A-Z - LATE NEWS

In the run-up to the first Premier game at Spurs, Villa beat Racing Santander 2-0 in Spain, both goals came from Juan Pablo Angel.

Details of Villa's matches in their 2001-02 Premiership programme:

| | | | |
|---|---|---|---|
| 18 Aug | v. Tottenham Hotspur (a) | 0-0 | 36,059 |
| 26 Aug | v. Manchester United (h) | 1-1 | 42,632 |
| 8 Sept | v. Liverpool (a) | 3-1 | 44,102 |
| 15 Sep | v. Sunderland (h) | 0-0 | 31,688 |
| 24 Sept | v. Southampton (a) | 3-1 | 26,794 |
| 30 Sept | v. Blackburn Rovers (h) | 2-0 | 28,623 |
| 14 Oct | v. Fulham (h) | 2-0 | 28,579 |
| 20 Oct | v. Everton (a) | 2-3 | 33,352 |
| 24 Oct | v. Charlton Athletic (h) | 1-0 | 27,701 |
| 27 Oct | v. Bolton Wanderers (h) | 3-2 | 33,599 |

### UEFA Cup

| | | | |
|---|---|---|---|
| 20 Sept | v. Vartecks (h) | 2-3 | 27,132 |
| 27 Sept | v. Vartecks (a) | 1-0 | 12,100 |

### Worthington Cup

| | | | |
|---|---|---|---|
| 10 Oct | v. Reading (h) | 1-0 | 23,431 |

• An own-goal in the last minute by Alpay Ozalon handed Manchester United a point. Darius Vassell scored early for Villa.

• Liverpool had Steven Gerrard sent-off (for a rash tackle on George Boateng) in Villa's splendid win at Anfield in early September.

• Rory Delap and Dion Dublin were sent-off (separately) in Villa's win v. Southampton. Dublin's red card was later changed to yellow.

• Peter Schmeichel scored for Villa in their 3-2 defeat at Everton - his NINTH League goal of his career - and his TENTH overall.

### UEFA CUP EXIT

By beating FC Basel 5-2 on aggregate to win the InterToto Cup, Villa qualified for the 2001-02 UEFA Cup, from which they suffered an early exit, losing in the first round to FK Varteks on the away goal rule (Villa lost 3-2 at home and won 1-0 away). For the leg in Croatia, Villa fielded nine players from different countries, a tenth (Angel) came on later while another two (Enckelman & Staunton) were on the subs bench.

### CAPTAINS

Paul Merson started the 2001-02 season as Villa's first team captain; Lee Hendrie took over the role in September and then goalkeeper Peter Schmeichel was handed the job.

### WHEREABOUTS OF EX-VILLA PLAYERS/PERSONNEL...

Graham Fenton joined Blackpool in August 2001...Tommy Craig is on the coaching staff at Newcastle United...Richard Walker signed on loan for Wycombe Wanderers in September 2001....Mark Blake has signed for Kidderminster Harriers....former Villa star David Platt is the new England Under-21 national coach...Steve Harrison and Paul Barron have both taken coaching positions with Middlesbrough...Tommy Mooney (one-time Villa reserve) from Watford to Birmingham City...Ben Petty has joined Hull City (managed by Brian Little) from Stoke City...Brian's brother, Alan Little is manager of Halifax Town...Stuart gray was sacked as manager of Southampton in October 2001...Garry Parker briefly took over the managerial seat at Filbert street after Peter Taylor's abrupt sacking...then, on the arrival of Dave ('Harry') Bassett at Filbert Street, Garry Parker decided to move on...Peter J Ross (Belbroughton)

THE COMPLETE ENCYCLOPAEDIA OF ASTON VILLA F.C.    THE COMPLETE ENCYCLOPAEDIA OF ASTON VILLA F.C.

300

# SUBSCRIBERS ROLE OF HONOUR

**Presentation copies:**

Mr H D Ellis, Chairman, Aston Villa FC
Mr P D Ellis, Non-Executive Director, Aston Villa FC
Mr G Taylor, Non-Executive Director, Aston Villa FC
Mr S M Stride, Operations Director & Secretary, Aston Villa FC
Mr M J Ansell, Deputy Chief Executive/ Financial Director, Aston Villa FC
Mr T Hales, Non-Executive Director, Aston Villa FC
Mr D M Owen, Non-Executive Director, Aston Villa FC
John Gregory, Manager, Aston Villa FC
Mr J A Alderson, President, Aston Villa FC
Margaret Matthews, Wife of author
Roger Marshall, Managing Director, Britespot Publishing Solutions
HRH Prince William c/o Buckingham Palace

Reg Thacker
David Goodyear
Dave & Pam Bridgwater
Paul Delaney
Paul Yeomans
John Russell
Paul & Rachel Burns
Darren Cartwright
Kenneth David Taylor
Luke Hobbs
Malcolm Taylor
John Kibble
Mark Pearce
John S Brown
Anthony Woolley
David Hodges
Tony Spraggon
Nathan David Stevens
Adam Gary Hackett
Roy James Hackett
Denise Dann
Lewis Carswell
Andrew Collins
Vic Collins
Paul John Knowles
Mr Derek T Hough
Vera Ellen Ragsdale
Gareth C Jones (Bones)
Keith Blackmore
Peter Lockett
Ryan James Fordy
Andrew Mason
Ann-Marie Bass
Stuart T Swann
Stuart Merchant
Jodie Horton

J T O'Brien
Sheree Whatley
Martin Ellacott
Alexander Keble
F W Rose
Steve Ashford
Frank Antram
James H Dawes
Peter Howard
Guy Edward Foster
Frank Macdonald
Matthew Lingard
Mark Ford
David Baker
Dr Stephen Tovey
Mr Ian W. Thomas
Philip Gray
Edwin Smith
John Dennis Croft
Yvonne A Graves
Tony C Dacey
Jacob Williams
Robert Graham Hinken
Wendy Jordan
Philip D. Brown
Mr Kevin Smith
Master Benjamin Smith
Derek Day
Neil Kavanagh
The Matthews Family,Spain
John Lockley
Bernard Dain
David John Edward Clayton
Stephen J Evans
David, Susan And Oliver Eagle
Jonathan Haynes
Harry Suter
David England
Adrian Thorne Horsham
Bolin Jorgen
Debbie Thorne
Kevin Dolman
Adam John Dolman
Jack Cameron Dolman
Gareth Lewis
Dirk Unschuld
Mr Ian Rourke
Antonio Durante
Joan Taylor
Robert Gough
Johan Nilsson
David M Clayton
James Parkes
Jodie Ellis
Paul J Edwards
Martin Greenslade
Nicola Royles
Alison Royles
A.J. Pettifer
Gregory Upton
Malcolm Cooper
Kevin Larkin
Todd Palmer
Peter Tuite
Susan Pudge
Luke Gresty
Andrew Nielsen
John Douglas Dunning
Keith Morris
Keith Feaver
Anthony Meacham
Barry Harrison
Peter & Michael Wells
David Smith

Mr B.J. Geddis
Brad Hennessy
Nigel and Simon Renshaw
Dan (The Villa Man) Renshaw
Steve Renshaw
Mr Ken Noon
Kevin Lennon
Francis Johnson
David Barron
Colin Brown
Lloyd Ball
Matthew Silcock
Mr Curt Hall
Michael John Griffin
Captain and Daz Slater
Shane O'Hara
Dominic Banner
Gerard Masterson
Luke Humphreys
Goran Bylund
Robin Madders
Gary Roy Hackett
Rodney Vassallo
Christopher Davis
Lynburn (Bunny) Lamey
Ian Caughtry
Wayne Roy Edwards
Adam Walshe
Steve Thorne
Kevin, Ethan and Aidan Fox
Rob Vincent
Rick Vincent
Jamie Smith
Richard Love
George Hill
Steve Smith
Matthew Bonner
Geoff Roberts
Sheila and Alan Roberts
Kim Sykes
Sheila Berridge
Mr Chris Ballantine
Arthur Bent
Martin Wells
Paul Garner
Roger Wilcox
Adam Whitehouse
Neil Witcomb
Rob Goodby
Alan Wood
Christopher Smith
Mark Davies
Satoshi Okayasu
Mr John Parker
Kevin Rollason
Espen Skotterud
Storebror Are A Kjaer
Warren McDivitt
Steven Roberts
Mr Robert Jones
Glyn Penrice
Liam Foley
Diarmuid Foley
Miss Jennie Taylor
Mr Andrew Lester
Mr Spencer Claye
Brendan Gallagher
Lee Pockett
Paul O'Brien
Mr Stephen Kell
Clint Hughes
Daniel Deakin
Louis Bailey
Brian Hemphill

Steven Mobberley
David Skidmore
Mark Tamburro
David W Bindley
Leo Domaingue
Alan Gee
Peter Jesse Hewins
Andrew John Minshull
E Southall
Barry William Sutton
Juliet Elizabeth Reynolds
Ross Aston Weake
Michael J. Ramsdale
Mr Jason Webb
Steve Chappell
Neil Brewer
Gerard Murphy
Kevin John Williams
Simon 'Wilf' Wheeler (Tamworth)
Mr John A Gould (1934)
Richard Garrigan
Lars Nilsson
Thomas Johansson
Pamela Harris
Graham Weaver
Colin Burgess
Mr Lyn Powell
Michael Arthur
Brendan Glynn
Greg Dollery
Desmond Nevin
Adrian Nevin
Damion Barrow
Marcus Knight
David Knight
Steven Knight
Mr N.M Fenton
Christopher Thomas
William Hanmer
Jason Dingley
Brian Norbury
Mr Joseph K. Smith
Paul Williams
Mr Mark Brew
Mr James Lines
Martin & Andrew Maguire
Keith Rickett
Sophie A Balfe
Mr Paul Howard
Daniel Perrett
William Perrett
Mr Guy Cooke
Patrick Sean McCabe
Michel Emilsson
Rick Morris
Grahame Vincent Hall
Douglas Talbot
Anthony Paul Heath
John (Villa) Power
Robin D Wilkes
Ben Harkcom
Sue & Mick Tilt
Mr Colton Field
Glenn Douglas
Mr John Ward
Terry Hanks
The Tomkinson Family
Kimberley Shuter
Phil Shuter
David Shaw
Bill Parker
James Marshall
Robert Marshall
Phil Plumber